HoW

Art Class

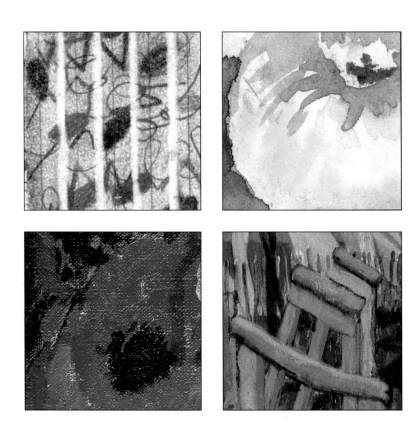

Art Class

*A beginner's complete guide
to painting and drawing*

Edited by

KEN HOWARD

BLOOMSBURY

First published in 1990 by
Bloomsbury Publishing Limited,
2 Soho Square, London W1V 5DE

First paperback edition 1993

Copyright © Swallow Publishing Ltd 1988, 1989, 1990, 1993

ISBN: 0–7475–1521–2

British Library Cataloguing in Publication Data
A CIP record for this book is available
from the British Library

Printed in Singapore by Imago

Contents

Foreword by Ken Howard

'I wish I could do that.'
This is probably the most common exclamation by anyone watching an artist at work. Wishing will not achieve it but practice might. It is my belief that most people can paint and draw if they really want to and if they receive some form of guidance. When we are at school it is taken for granted that everyone can be taught to write but not necessarily that they will write great poetry or prose. I believe that everyone can be taught to paint and draw for their own pleasure, but that does not mean that they will produce masterpieces. Great artists are born, but how can we know whether we are an artist or not until we have learned to paint?

Ken Howard 'Spring Light Mousehole' 1200 × 1000mm (48 × 40in.). Oil.

7

Ken Howard 'Summer Evening '89'
200 × 300mm (8 × 12in.).
Watercolour.

In the past, artists learned by going to work in a master's studio. There they would start by cleaning the artist's palette and doing odd jobs around the studio, then begin to learn about materials and methods, and eventually be trusted to lay in the foundation of the master's work. Finally, they would set out on their own towards excellence and individuality.

At the end of the nineteenth century, with the advent of the photograph and decline in commissioned works, the artist's studio was replaced by the art schools. Through foundation and degree courses, students again learned the basics of materials and methods and were encouraged to develop their imaginations so that when they graduated they could start on the long road to achieving excellence in their chosen field.

Today, through the social reforms that have cut working hours and given people the time and money to pursue their passions, there are many thousands of amateur artists who are looking for an equivalent of the master's studio or the art school in order to learn the basic skills of their avocation. In the past, amateurs – the 'lovers of art' – pursued excellence with as much dedication as professionals; the only difference was that they did not earn their living from art. Just as in sport and other fields, this did not mean that the amateur did not strive for perfection in what he or she was practising.

Art Class is a book geared specifically to the requirements of the amateur artist. Its aim is to give the would-be painter training equal to what might be learned as an artist's apprentice or in an art school foundation course. The first three sections, covering drawing, working in watercolour and working in oils, are technique-based to help you to acquire first the basic, then the more advanced, skills you need to start working in a particular medium; the final section deals with composition and perspective, outlining the theory and principles which you should understand and then apply in order to produce pleasing and technically adept works of art. The book is full of sound practical advice, and suggests exercises and projects like those the students on foundation courses are given to ensure their clear understanding of a subject. All the contributing writers, as well as being highly regarded professional artists, have at some time in their careers been involved in teaching in art schools; indeed I have had the pleasure of teaching with them on one of the most prestigious foundation courses at a leading London art school.

Drawing and painting involve the heart, the hand and the head. The heart moves us to paint. The hand we can only develop through practice, and this book at all times stresses the importance of practice. The head involves understanding what goes into the process of making a painting and this book covers these main elements: drawing, tone, and colour, as well as composition, which is the most important of all.

Drawing I consider to be the basis of all painting. There have been many draughtsmen who could not paint, but I have never discovered a painter who could not draw. Drawing, like writing, has a grammar. Just as writing is made up of letters, words, sentences and paragraphs, drawing is made up of marks, lines, shapes and tones. When we are young, we learn to write through practice and thus we develop our own handwriting. Drawing too demands practice, and through that we develop our own style.

Jason Bowyer's contribution to this book is a coherent introduction to the elements of drawing. Starting with advice on materials and organizing a work space, he considers the most basic questions such as whether you should stand or sit to work and how to make marks with pencils, ink and charcoal. He then takes us step by step through projects in various media and opens our eyes to ideas for subjects to draw. His advice is equally appropriate whether you want to draw for its own sake, using the techniques described to produce finished works, or improve your drawing skills in order to make more successful paintings.

Charles Bartlett, who contributes the section on Starting in Watercolour, is a man of great experience in both the practice and teaching of watercolour painting, and is President of the Royal Society of Painters in Water-Colours. His own watercolours are full of experiment and verve and in this book he encourages the same lively approach. He describes a whole variety of materials, based on his experience over many years. He explores watercolour techniques, beginning with the most traditional methods of working with transparent washes and working wet into wet, followed by more varied and adventurous approaches. Although he cannot actually have you sit and watch him work, he does the next best thing and takes you step by step through projects, explaining the development of a painting clearly and concisely.

Jason Bowyer 'Jimmy's Boat'
175 × 228mm (6¾ × 9in.).
Charcoal.

Charles Bartlett 'Reeds'
426 × 575mm (17 × 23in.).
Watercolour.

Roy Rodgers' contribution, Starting in Oils, is full of helpful instruction and knowledge about the process of oil painting of which he has a wide experience as an exhibiting painter, as a designer for film and television, and as a teacher of many years' experience. He shows oil paint to be a liberating medium, full of varied possibilities and not in the least hidebound by tradition or technique.

The most important element of learning to paint is that you must love to do it. That does not mean that it will not be difficult and that you may want to give up, but once you have been bitten, you will always try again. As you practise you will get better, and as you get better you will want to practise more, and as you practise more you will get even better.

A very common mistake among people who are beginning to paint is to believe that having done a subject once, that is enough. This of course is quite wrong. If you look at works by Masters, you will see that they sometimes pursued the same idea for years. When using a book like *Art Class* there is the danger that having worked through a project once, you may feel it is done or, worse still, that you have failed to achieve a result that satisfies you. In order to achieve a good result it is necessary to do the projects many times, and each time you will find you get nearer to the desired aim.

The most difficult, but very necessary, element to grasp in drawing and painting is composition, or the arranging of the parts into a whole. In painting a landscape, for example, it is relatively easy to draw a building, a tree or a fence, but fitting them together coherently is the hard part, and it is here of

Roy Rodgers 'Grass in Sunlight'
1010 × 760mm (40 × 30½in.).
Oil.

course that the element of perspective clearly enters into the problem. In the last section of the book, Bill Ward, an experienced painter, etcher and illustrator, offers a thorough explanation of the principles of composition and perspective to give anyone who is interested in a serious understanding of picture making a solid base on which to practise and build.

At one time, every art student had to learn the fundamentals of perspective. It was never an easy process and yet it was a discipline which every student came to understand. The fundamentals of composition were also taught, as was an understanding of the principles of the golden section or divine proportion. What we learned with time was that through practice these disciplines could eventually become intuitive.

By understanding the golden section it becomes part of our sensibility; by understanding perspective it is eventually part of our way of seeing, which we can use, discard, or bend according to our needs.

I have enjoyed editing the contributions of these four gifted artists and teachers to *Art Class* enormously. For me, the experience was one of rediscovery. We learn things consciously when we begin to draw and paint and eventually they become part of our subconscious, and we use them intuitively. To have these lessons brought back to the surface by this book has indeed been an exciting revelation, sometimes a re-evaluation.

Read this book, enter into its enthusiasms, practise what is given and, basing your efforts on its sound foundation, enjoy drawing and painting as they are meant to be enjoyed.

T. W. Ward 'Hauled Out for a Polish' 624 × 477mm (25 × 19in.). Gouache.

PART ONE

Starting
Drawing

Introduction

Drawing is the simplest and oldest art form. Drawn images are created by adults and children of all ages, in order to express feelings, communicate ideas to others, or simply for pleasure and the exhilaration of the act. Drawing is practised using different methods and materials, and in various forms in every culture and society throughout the world. Whatever the tools, whether pencil, charcoal, ink or pastel, all drawings are executed either in line or tone (or both). Line drawings are made purely in lines, whereas tone involves shading and degrees of light and dark.

The ability to draw and communicate through drawn marks is not a talent possessed by only a few people, but can be embraced by everyone with a little effort. This section will provide you with only a fraction of the enormous vocabulary of techniques and materials used in drawing. It is not intended to be definitive, but will show you one way to approach your first steps in drawing. At the heart of the information lies the belief that the person starting to draw must begin by observing the world around them before embarking on problems of expression.

". . . and every day I am more convinced that people who do not first wrestle with nature never succeed."
Van Gogh, Nuenan, January 1885

This is how I started to draw myself. Seated at the kitchen table, working in pencil from observation, I learned the rudiments of measurement and simply got on with it. One of my earliest subject matters was a mound of potato peelings. It became an exciting wriggling pattern once I started to draw and observe.

". . . Now hardly a day passes that I do not make something. As practice makes perfect, I cannot but make progress; each drawing one makes, each study one paints, is a step forward."
Van Gogh, Denthe, October 1883

For this reason, this section is built around exercises which are designed to develop your visual vocabulary of marks, lines and tone. I hope you will gain confidence through them and be unafraid to make mistakes as you progress. The simple exercises will begin to develop your awareness of space around you and the scale of objects; you will then be able to learn how to work from observation and to produce drawings exploring measurement and proportion.

Vincent van Gogh 'La Crau from Mont Majour' (detail) 480 × 608mm (19¼ × 24⅓in.). Van Gogh achieves a unified and peaceful composition using short, staccato lines and dots in ink. He creates a vast panorama with varying tonal marks that recede from the denser marks of the foreground to the vague suggestion of the horizon line.

Peter Paul Rubens 'Cows' (detail) 340 × 522mm (13⅜ × 20½in.). This drawing uses a combination of brown sepia ink and dip pen. The delicate, flowing lines of the dip pen capture the movement of the cows. The small sketches around the main study emphasize Rubens' interest in analysing the changing forms of the cow.

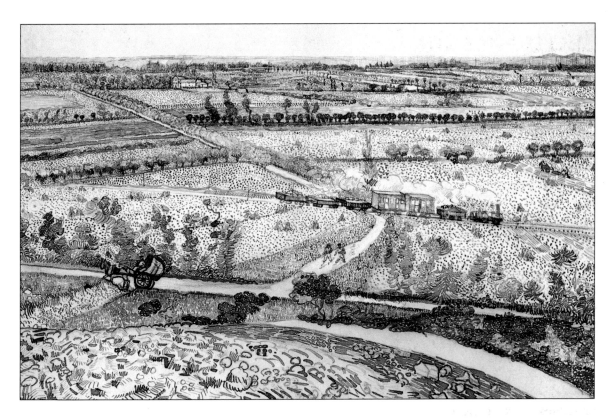

Materials, equipment and the workspace

You need only spend a little money to buy the simple materials needed to start drawing. There is, in fact, a wide variety of materials and equipment available, all of them with their uses, but only a selection of them is necessary for the beginner. To enable you to acquire equipment gradually, a list of materials is given wherever specific drawing projects are prescribed in this section, and you can just buy what you need for that type of drawing if you do not already have it.

The marks produced by different drawing media that are illustrated here are not to be taken as being definitive; they are merely examples of how to achieve various effects. It is important to develop your own way of working.

A selection of equipment from the kit recommended for the drawing exercises and projects.

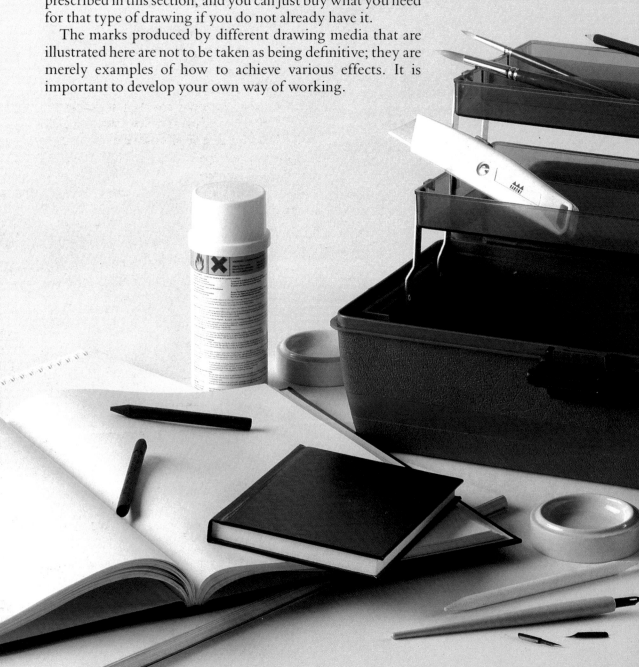

Recommended kit

The following pieces of equipment are easily available from art shops and hardware stores. The materials can be bought fairly inexpensively, especially if you shop around. With these you will be able to do the exercises and projects given in this section.

a plywood drawing board measuring 55 × 50cm (22 × 20in.)
white cartridge (drawing) paper in different sizes
an A3 (18 × 12in.) sketchpad of cartridge paper
a hardback sketchbook
2B, 4B and 6B pencils
a box of thick charcoal sticks, a few pieces of compressed charcoal and a soft charcoal pencil
a metal dip pen with a variety of nibs
a reed or bamboo pen
three nylon brushes
a plastic eraser
a bottle of Indian (India) ink (waterproof)
a white oil crayon
a tube of white gouache
a plastic or ceramic stacking palette (cabinet nest)
a sharp craft knife such as a Stanley knife
a roll of masking tape or adhesive tape
a roll of gummed tape
rubber-based adhesive
a can of spray fixative
a metal ruler
a storage box

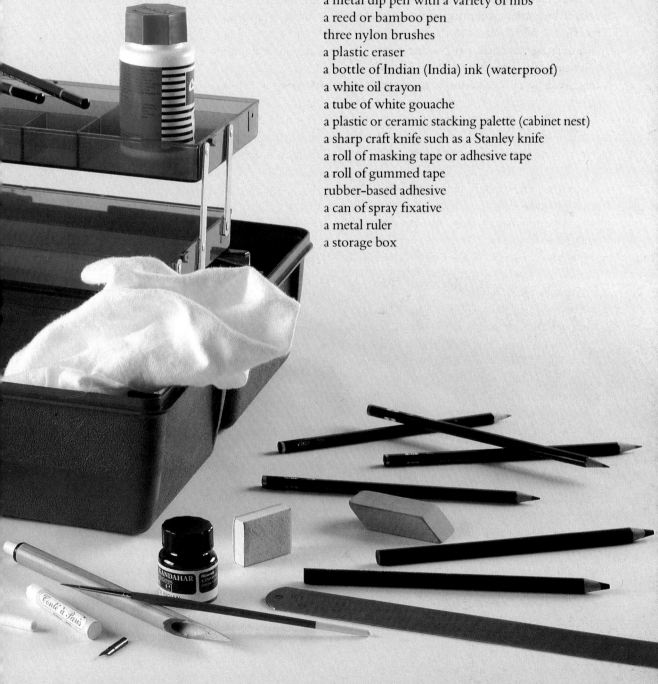

Basic equipment

Pencils

Pencil is a very popular medium due to its wide variety of uses in line drawing and tonal work, and its portability, which makes it ideal for impromptu sketching. It is probably also the tool that most readily comes to mind when people think of drawing. In artistic terms, however, the pencil is a relative newcomer, being invented by a Frenchman, Nicolas Jacques Conté, in 1795.

The central part of the pencil is made from carbon and clay. This part varies from hard to soft, and all pencils are graded accordingly. The harder ones range from H to 8H; the higher the number, the harder they are. Likewise with the soft ones, which start at B and go up to 8B. HB pencils are of intermediate hardness.

Hard pencils make a fine, sharp line, soft ones a dark line that can be sharp or soft, and are therefore more versatile in their use. Sharpened they make fine lines, rounded they produce soft, thick ones, and they are also useful in producing areas of tone. A good basic group to have is a range from soft to very soft, say a 2B, 4B and 6B.

Charcoal

Charcoal is the oldest drawing medium, and its origins probably go back to when the first cave-dweller picked a piece of burnt wood from the fire and started to make marks with it. When used for drawing it is shaped into sticks, or is in the form of a pencil. Like pencil, it can vary in hardness. Charcoal is often used to create tonal drawings because of the ease with which it can cover large areas.

Three types of charcoal are available:

Stick charcoal   This comes in a variety of thicknesses and lengths. Sometimes the sticks are sold separately but generally they are in a box containing 10 or 20. The thinnest sticks are usually used for line drawing. The thicker sticks are suitable for making tonal areas but can also be used for making a variety of lines.

Compressed charcoal   This comes in short sticks, and has a darker tone than stick charcoal. It is difficult to make a thin line with a piece of compressed charcoal unless it is sharpened but is very useful when you need a deep black tone to heighten the contrast in a stick charcoal drawing.

Charcoal pencils   These are graded extra soft, soft, medium and hard. They are used for line drawings and work well in quick sketchbook drawings. They are valuable when you need a sharp line to define the shape in a tonal stick charcoal drawing.

Paper

Paper is available in a range of sizes and surfaces. It is made from various combinations of wood fibre, flax, hemp and cotton. Sizes are identified by a coding system. The largest size ordinarily available is A1, measuring 841 × 594mm (or about 36 × 24in.), the smallest A5, measuring 210 × 148mm (about 8½ × 5½in.).

The surface of paper can vary. Hand-made paper may have a textured surface or a smooth finish. A mass-produced paper will have a smooth finish. Papers made with a rag content make by far the most stable surface for your drawings, but can be prohibitively expensive. A simple A3 sketchpad of mass-produced cartridge (drawing) paper, measuring 420 × 297mm (18 × 12in.), will be adequate for the beginner.

Pens

Pens have been used for drawing since the early Middle Ages. They are commonly used by designers and draughtsmen, as well as by fine artists. Ink gives a darker, firmer line than pencil, the thickness of the line being determined by the fineness of the nib.

Reed and bamboo pens   Soft-wooded pens do not have any kind of canal or storage chamber to hold ink in, and therefore have to be dipped into ink frequently. The line that they create is usually rich and thick, varying according to the way the nib is cut.

Quill pens   The quill feathers of birds, sharpened to a point, are often used for drawing with. Only naturally discarded feathers are suitable as they have to have attained sufficient maturity. The line created is elegant, and this makes them popular for calligraphy.

Metal dip pens   The metal nibs which you insert into wooden or plastic pen holders come in varying thicknesses. These nibs retain a certain amount of ink, and so they do not have to be dipped too often.

Reservoir and fountain pens   The reservoir pen has interchangeable nibs and is used by graphic and commercial artists. The ordinary fountain pen does not produce the versatility of line that is useful for the beginner to explore, and so is not generally recommended.

Initially you need only a wooden pen holder and a range of different thicknesses of nib. It would be useful, however, to have either a reed or bamboo pen.

Brushes

A pen and brushes that can be used together can create exciting marks and are especially valuable in doing tone work. Your basic drawing equipment should include brushes made from nylon fibre or nylon with a mix of sable. A size 2 round-ended, a size 7 round-ended and a size 8 flat-ended are a good basic set to begin with. With these brushes you will be able to work in line as well as create tonal washes for your drawings.

Ink

The first inks were made from candle soot and gum water in ancient China; they came in a solid form and were mixed with water. The Chinese used them for writing and drawing. Modern drawing inks like Indian ink (more often known as India ink in the USA) are made from gas black in aqueous adhesive; the addition of shellac soap makes them waterproof. Indian ink is excellent for drawing with, particularly for beginners because it is readily available and easy to manipulate.

Drawing board

It is essential to have a drawing board as this gives you a firm surface to work on. The best type of drawing board for the beginner is one made of light plywood measuring approximately 55 × 50cm (22 × 20in.). Your local timber merchant can cut you a board to size.

Erasers

The first erasers were made of either soft leather or freshly baked bread, but the discovery of rubber and the development of plastic have resulted in these crude forms of erasers dying out. Plastic erasers are excellent for pencil and charcoal. However, erasing ink is difficult, and commercial erasers cannot cope. The best way is to scrape the surface of the paper lightly with a sharp craft knife or a scalpel (X-acto knife). To get a sharp edge to a plastic eraser, cut with a sharp knife periodically.

Fibrous paper sticks commonly known as paper stumps (stomps) and properly called tortillon, are useful for spreading charcoal.

Other equipment

Charcoal and soft pencil will smudge quite easily if not treated, so fixatives are available which make dry mediums more permanent on paper. They come in the form of spray-on liquid. Instructions for use are always given on the side of the container and should be followed carefully.

Artists' oil crayons are impervious to water and are used when working in mixed media.

Cutting tools are essential for sharpening pencils and for cutting paper or card. A sharp craft knife is ideal for both of these tasks.

Drawing pins and masking tape are needed to attach paper to a drawing board or to put newly made drawings on the wall.

A metal ruler at least 30cm (12in.) in length is helpful both for cutting card and for marking out areas to draw in.

Finally, a storage box such as an old tool box or a plastic art bin is useful for organizing your equipment and keeping it together.

Recommended furniture (from left to right): a table, drawing board, chair, box easel, sketching easel, and radial easel.

Furniture

Table   You are going to need a table both to work at and to rest your drawing board against. It should be at a comfortable height.

Chair   A good kitchen chair without arms and giving your back support is essential for drawing in a seated position. A stool placed beside you is often useful for materials.

Easel   An easel is not essential when you are starting to learn to draw providing that you have a drawing board. If, however, you do have one it will give you a vertical surface to work on. You can either sit comfortably at arm's length from your board or stand to draw if your subject matter is on a shelf. The benefit of standing is that you can view your work from a varying distance more easily. This gives the eye a chance to scan the whole of the drawing. The proportions will become clearer to you: the size and scale of objects in relation to one another can be understood and altered.

There are three varieties of easel:

Radial easel   Commonly used in art schools, it is a large piece of equipment and hence not suitable for the average home.

Sketching easel   A collapsible easel that can easily be stored in a cupboard.

Box easel   A collapsible easel that folds down into and around the main box support. A useful, more stable version of the sketching easel.

Setting up

A little effort given to setting up will give you the chance to use your precious time more profitably. Looking for a missing pencil or eraser is frustrating and destroys your creative urge, leaving you exasperated and in no frame of mind to concentrate. It is best, therefore, to have everything you will need to hand when you start.

If you don't have anywhere you can use as a small permanent workspace, store all your materials in an art bin or tool box. Keep them in separate compartments so that you can find them without having to rummage around.

Organizing a small space

If possible, use part of a room permanently as your art area. An hour or two spent initially in arranging furniture, obtaining materials and organizing lighting will ultimately give you more time to draw. In deciding upon a desirable space, consider these points:

Light   It's important to choose somewhere with good, constant light – a space near a window, not a badly lit corner. You may want to work at night, so also make sure that you have sufficient artificial light to avoid straining your eyes.

Noise   Obviously, it's difficult to concentrate with constant noise and people moving around. Try to find a place where you will not be continually disturbed.

Heat   You may need to use your space in the winter for drawing. Find a place that has adequate heating. It's not advisable to have your space right next to a radiator as the heat would adversely affect the paper and art materials.

Sitting and standing to draw

Standing   Work at arm's length; it is impossible to get the proportions right if you work too close to the paper. It is a good idea to have a stool close by so that you can sit down occasionally to rest your legs, while you contemplate your work from a different position.

The author standing to draw.

Sitting   Most people find that sitting is more comfortable for drawing than standing, and certainly with most drawings there is no reason why you should not sit down. The important thing is that you have a good view of both your subject matter and your drawing board.

Choose a chair that gives your back support, then lean your drawing board on the edge of the table at an angle of 45 degrees so that it can rest easily on your lap. Try not to slouch or lean on your board as you draw. It is important to move away from your board at intervals of about 30 minutes so as to view your work from a distance. This enables you to check that the proportions are correct and that the tones work together as a whole. But do not move your chair or your subject, as when you sit down again you need to see what you are drawing from the same angle and position.

The author sitting to draw.

Stretching paper

When you come to draw with washes (pen and ink), you will need to be able to stretch the paper first. This is a way of wetting the paper and letting it dry so as to prevent it from wrinkling as the ink dries. The procedure is not as difficult as you might think and can be learned quickly.

If you are going to use your actual drawing board, keep to one side only, so you can preserve the other as a clean drawing surface. If you prefer, keep a separate board just for stretching paper. This will enable you to prepare paper and continue with other drawings at the same time.

First, place the paper in the centre of the board. Measure four lengths of gummed tape for the sides of the paper, making them slightly longer so they will overlap at the corners. Put these aside.

Then, gently dampen the surface of the paper with a sponge, turn the paper over, and repeat the process. Make sure the sponge is not too saturated with water – squeeze it out lightly before you start. Take care not to rub too hard as you could damage the surface of the paper.

Now fix the paper to the board. Run a strip of gummed tape under the tap (or through a dish of water) and lightly pull it through your fingers and thumb to get rid of the excess water (but do not remove the gum from the surface). Place the strip of tape along one edge of the paper so that half the width is over the paper and half is over the board. Repeat with the remaining strips of tape.

As you fix the tape, wipe along its edges with the sponge to absorb any excess water, and to make sure it is flat and has stuck all the way round. Do the same over the surface of the paper but just dabbing gently.

Allow the paper to dry at room temperature. Keep the board flat so the paper can dry evenly. Do not attempt to speed up the process by using a fan heater or by putting it beside a radiator as this would probably make the paper tear or buckle. When the paper is dry, it should be completely flat and ready to use.

HOW TO STRETCH PAPER

After placing your paper in the centre of the board, measure the four lengths of gummed tape to be slightly longer than each side of the paper (in order to overlap at the corners).

Using a sponge that is wet but not saturated, dampen the surface of the paper evenly to relax the fibres in the paper. Then turn the paper over and dampen the other side.

Wet the gummed tape by either running it under a tap or through a dish of water, gently taking off the excess water with your fingers and thumb.

Having fixed the gummed tape along the four edges of the paper in such a way that half of the tape width is over the board, wipe off any excess water with the sponge.

Basic line techniques

Line drawing is simply the drawing of shapes with lines only, without any shading or tone. It is the most basic form of drawing, and as such is the foundation for every other technique. However, this does not mean that it is somehow inferior to other forms of art, for line on its own provides enormous scope. Look at the different types of line that are all around you: the sharp, straight line of a window, the curved lines of a cup, or the crinkly edge of a fern, for example.

The initial step when approaching drawing for the first time is to investigate the varieties of line made by the different media so as to become familiar with them before working from observation.

You will need
- ☐ a drawing board
- ☐ A3 (18 × 12in.) paper
- ☐ 2B, 4B and 6B pencils
- ☐ a dip pen, nibs and ink
- ☐ brushes
- ☐ a plastic eraser
- ☐ a ruler
- ☐ masking tape
- ☐ a sharp craft knife
- ☐ a stacking palette (cabinet nest)
- ☐ a container of water

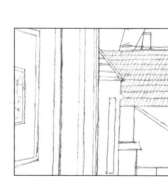

Far left: The sharp, straight lines of the window frame make a stark contrast to the zig-zagging, curling plant leaves.
Left: View through a window showing the different weights of line in the architecture of the buildings and the various angles that they make.

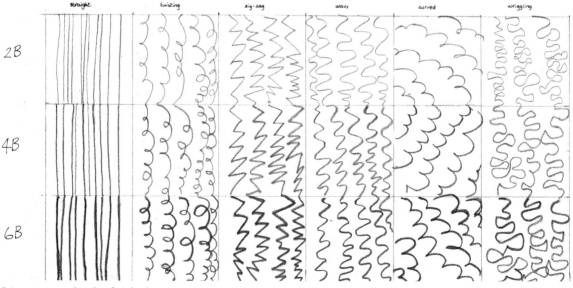

Lines in pencil – the finished exercise.

Lines in pencil

Always sharpen your pencils with a sharp craft knife or scalpel (X-acto knife). This gives you a much stronger point and is less wasteful of the pencil than using a pencil sharpener.

Attach the sheet of paper to the drawing board horizontally, and mark out a box measuring 15 × 30cm (6 × 12in.). Divide the box into 50mm (2in.) squares. Write the number of each of the different grades of pencil you are using down the left-hand side, next to the first three squares. Below each vertical line of boxes, write a different word to describe a type of line: for example, straight, twisting, zig-zag, wavy, curved, wriggling.

Start in the top left-hand corner box and fill it with lines according to the type you have chosen, using a 2B pencil. When you reach the bottom edge of that box, change to a 4B pencil and continue down, connecting the lines. Change to a 6B pencil for the bottom box. As you use the various grades of pencil, try different pressures on the point to see the different density of line. The greater the pressure, the darker the line will be.

Lines in dip pen and brush

On an A3 sheet of paper, attached vertically to the drawing board, mark out a box measuring 30 × 15cm (12 × 6in.) with a pencil and ruler. Mark out two lines at 50mm (2in.) intervals, running from top to bottom. Measure 50mm (2in.) down from the top of the box and mark out two lines 12mm (½in.) apart running horizontally across the paper. Measure another 50mm (2in.) from the lower line, and then draw another two horizontal lines 12mm (½in.) apart. Proceed in this way down the paper until you reach the bottom of the box.

In each of the 12mm (½in.) wide spaces beneath the boxes, write a word describing the type of line that you are trying to create. Write underneath the box for the bottom three squares. Then draw these lines in the boxes with Indian (India) ink, using both different nib widths and

brushes. You should try to make each line or group of lines within each box contrast with the next one. One way of achieving this contrast is to experiment with different nibs and brushes.

When you are making lines inside the boxes, try not to use a ruler; it is better to work freehand. Be patient about your ability to manoeuvre the pen or brush and don't worry about smudges.

Lines in dip pen and brush – the finished exercise.

Working from observation

By practising drawing different lines in pencil, dip pen and brush, you will begin to have an understanding of materials and their effects. Next is to learn how to look. The first exercise to develop the skill of co-ordinating your eye and your hand is to make a series of small line drawings in pencil and dip pen from observation. At this stage the question of proportion need not worry you. Just respond to what you see in front of you, the shape and movement of the line. These are your first tentative steps in observational drawing, so the results might seem rather limited but don't be discouraged.

Looking at straight lines

New students often complain of not being able to draw a straight line. Indeed, drawing straight lines freehand does take practice, but the following exercise will help. It will also start you looking properly at angles.

Attach an A3 sheet of paper horizontally to the drawing board. Draw a line down the middle of the paper in pencil. Work on either side of this line, alternating your drawings in dip pen with your drawings in pencil. If your pen seems to be clogging up with ink and not making a steady line, clean it in water.

Look at the top right-hand corner of the drawing board; you are now going to draw that angle. Make a dot on the paper (on the right-hand side) to represent the point where the two edges of the board meet. Look along the top line of your board and place another dot on the paper, about 75mm (3in.) to the left of the first. Now look down the right-hand side of the board and place a dot on the paper, about 75mm (3in.) below the original dot. Join the three dots, and you should have an angle of approximately 90 degrees.

This method of line construction gives points of reference as you plot angles and create straight lines. It is a good basis for building up an image on paper from observation.

Look around you in the room and draw different angles, either using the dot-line method to plot angles or just trying to draw straight lines from observation. It is difficult to draw a straight line longer than 15cm (6in.). If, however, you first make a series of dots at 75mm (3in.) intervals, it becomes easier. Fill the two halves of the A3 sheet with studies of angles and straight lines.

When you are working from observation, you should always glance from the subject to the drawing repeatedly and quickly.

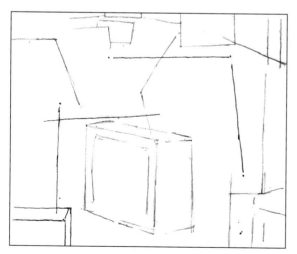

Drawing straight lines.

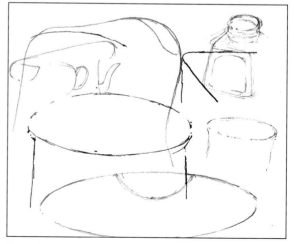

Drawing curves.

Looking at curves

Attach an A3 sheet of paper horizontally to the drawing board. Arrange an assortment of cups, saucepans, and other items that have simple curves, in front of you.

Using a dip pen and pencil alternately, create a series of curves based on those in the objects in front of you. As in the previous exercise, remember to keep glancing at the object and back to the paper. Try to draw each curve in an unbroken line without removing your pen or pencil from the paper, varying the shapes and sizes of the curves according to the objects in front of you. At first your curves may not flow smoothly, but you should soon be able to draw a curve with a single stroke of the pen or pencil.

After a number of attempts, when you feel more satisfied with your efforts, look around you in the room for any other curves such as the side of a fruit bowl or a lamp base and stand.

In the case of a more complex or larger curve, try drawing it by the dot-line method that you used to draw straight lines. Mark three dots, the middle one at the highest point of the curve and the others at either end. Join them together, again glancing at the object and back to the paper to help you get the right shape.

Looking at crumpled paper

The edge of a piece of crumpled paper has a combination of different lines. In some places it is straight; in others it can be crinkly. Drawing the outline of the paper, with these different lines is a good test of the skills you have started to develop.

Divide an A3 sheet of paper with a pencil line down the middle and attach it horizontally to the board. Then crumple an A4 piece of paper, so you have a shape that has a series of different contours. Place it on the table in front of you, preferably on a darker background.

Attempt to follow the line of the contours of the crumpled paper by observation and convey this on one half of the A3 paper in pencil or ink. You should try to make the density of line delicate, by varying the pressure on the point of the pencil or pen.

Change the shape or position of the crumpled piece of paper to get a different edge for each drawing on the two halves of the paper.

Drawing crumpled paper is a demanding exercise, so you will need to persevere. You could also try drawing other crumpled objects like cushions or a pile of washing. The line of your non-drawing hand is another interesting subject as it can take so many different positions.

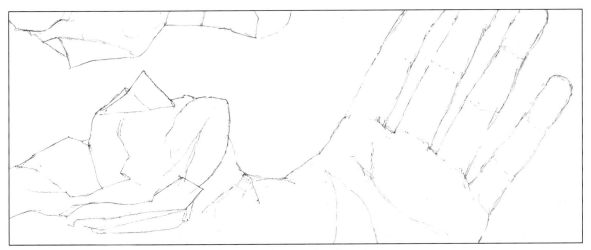

A drawing of crumpled paper and the author's non-drawing hand.

Measurement and proportion

Perspective is a means of representing three-dimensional forms on a two-dimensional surface. The theory is the most difficult prospect for people starting to draw from observation, but it is essential to grasp in order to do representational drawings. The basic rules were developed during the early Italian Renaissance, and are still used today.

Right: Interior of the Kew Bridge Steam Museum. Using sight-size measurement as a framework, I worked in Indian (India) ink to create a tonal perspective of the architecture and machinery.

Measurement techniques

The practical process of sight-size measurement is the simplest way to teach yourself how to understand perspective. Sight-size means that the object should be the same size as it would appear to be if the paper were transparent and you simply traced the object on it at arm's length.

Look around your room and try this little experiment. Place a bottle 2 metres (6ft) away from you, at eye level; hold a pencil at arm's length and measure the bottle's height against the length of the pencil with one eye closed. Now place the bottle 4 metres (12ft) away and measure it again in the same way. The bottle should be considerably smaller against the length of the pencil.

The main principle of perspective is that the further away objects are, the smaller they appear to the eye. This is immediately discernible by sight-size measurement.

Before you start to measure an object, you should consider the following important points:

Position   Keep the same position in relationship to the object. While measuring, hold your head at the angle you wish to draw at.

Eyes   Look at an object in front of you with your left eye closed, then open your left eye and close your right. Repeat this procedure a few times in quick succession. The object jumps from side to side.

Arm   When you measure, keep your arm fully extended and straight.

Pencil   Keep your pencil vertical while measuring. Imagine that there is a pane of glass at arm's length and hold your pencil against it.

Accuracy   Try to be correct, but bear in mind that total precision is not possible. The sight-size system will help give your observational drawing a simple structural base, but is not meant to produce mathematical accuracy.

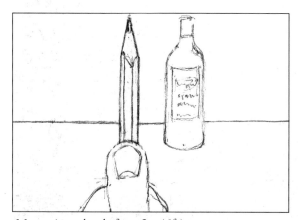

Measuring a bottle from 2m (6ft).

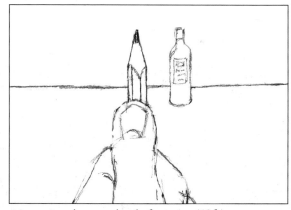

Measuring the same bottle from 4m (12ft).

Drawing an object sight-size

Place a cup 15cm (6in.) beyond arm's length on a table. Measure the cup's height with your arm extended, one eye closed and your pencil vertical.

Mark the top point of the rim of the cup on the paper; do the same with the bottom point of the cup to the distance indicated by your pencil.

Next, measure the distance from the mark you have made for the top of the rim to the lowest point of the rim, and mark it. You should now have three marks directly in line with one another. Draw a straight line through these marks.

To work out the width of the cup, measure horizontally across it from rim to rim. Place two marks to represent these points on the drawing. Draw a straight line extending horizontally through these marks.

Join the marks with curves to create the rim of the cup. When drawing curves, remember to move your eyes from drawing to object quickly – look and draw. The rim is now complete.

To draw the sides of the cup, measure them by sight, make two marks and connect. Draw the bottom of the cup in the same way.

Next draw the handle of the cup by measuring the top, bottom and side points of the handle, make three marks and then connect them, using the scanning process described above.

Look at the inside of the handle and draw its shape in relationship to the outside edge.

Finally, draw the table edge behind the cup, measuring the distance from the top of the rim.

Now repeat the drawing, this time placing it 45cm (18in.) beyond arm's length. Compare the size of the cup in your first and second drawings. This will demonstrate clearly how objects appear smaller as they move further away from you.

When connecting your marks, try to use them only as general reference. You should look from the object to your drawing, scanning the images swiftly rather than pondering. In this way, comparisons of the marks and actuality can be made more efficiently.

Joining the first three marks that indicate the rim.

Drawing a straight line across the cup's width.

Drawing the rim of the cup with curves.

The sides and bottom edge of the cup drawn in.

Putting in the cup handle, after measuring it.

After measuring the distance from the top point of the rim to the table edge, the line of the table edge is drawn.

Drawing a group of objects

When you draw a combination of objects, the spaces between them are just as important as the outline of each item and its proportions. You should treat each object as part of the group. In this way you are better able to involve the relationship between each item, which is very important in terms of creating a cohesive scale drawing. In the early stages of such a drawing, you should try to get used to leaving the objects in an unfinished form.

In this exercise you should measure both the objects and the spaces between them to sight-size.

Place a group of four objects on a table in front of you. The objects should include a cylinder (for example, a tall glass, an aerosol can, or a tube container of talcum powder), a sphere (a tennis ball, a softball, or an orange), an angular or curved shape (a pepper mill, a large perfume bottle, or a sauce bottle), and an irregular sphere (a large potato, stones or large pebbles). The objects should not be higher than 20cm (8in.) and not

smaller than 75mm (3in.) Arrange them as shown, with the cylinder in the centre.

Make a mark with a 2B pencil for the top left-hand point of the cylinder in the top centre of the paper (point A). Measure the distance using sight-size to the irregular sphere below. Make a mark (point B), then draw a line between the two marks. From point B, measure across to the far right-hand side of the regular sphere, make a mark and draw part of its curve. This is point C.

Now, work out the horizontal dimension, from point B to the far left-hand side of the angular shape. This is point D, mark and draw part of its edge. If the table edge crosses the AB line, measure from point A and draw it in.

Again, measure horizontally from point B across to the other side of the cylinder. As this is obscured by the sphere, you will have to judge its position and make a mark. Draw the line of the cylinder. Measure diagonally downwards from point C to the far left-hand edge of the irregular sphere. Mark this point E and draw part of its edge on your drawing.

The objects arranged on a table.

The first lines emerging.

Drawing in the line for the table edge as it crosses the AB line.

Measure diagonally upwards from point E to the top left-hand point of the angular shape (point F). Mark and draw part of its edge. From point F, measure to the highest point of the cylinder and draw its top curve.

Now that you have drawn the basic framework of the objects, start to measure and look at them individually. Draw their outlines. Measure the distances between shapes that are next to each other and mark them. Keep the drawing simple, concentrating on the outlines of the objects.

Finally, draw the contour lines on the objects. At this stage, stick to lines and do not worry

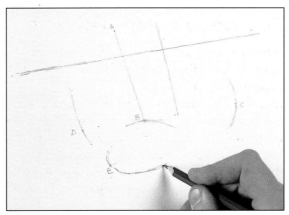

Putting in the irregular curves of the potato.

Drawing the top curve of the cylinder.

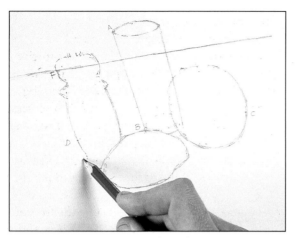

Giving the objects their simple outlines.

about tone. Make marks, shapes and lines that suggest the objects' form. Use an eraser to clarify your drawing where necessary, and to remove the lines that run through the objects.

If you have to leave the drawing unfinished for a few days, mark the positions of the objects on the table with masking tape (alternatively, you could place a sheet of paper under the objects when setting the group up, and draw round them to mark their position on this). Try to leave your chair in the same position, or make a note of exactly where you placed it, so that when you come back you will be in the same position in relation to the objects.

Finally, making marks, shapes and lines that suggest the objects' forms.

Further ideas

Enlarging and reducing

The process of sight-size measurement creates a framework and guidelines for you to work within. If you want to make a drawing that is larger than sight-size, start by measuring the objects sight-size, but then double the measurements. The same process can be used to reduce the image: measure the objects to sight-size, but then halve the measurements. These techniques of enlarging and reducing a scene are useful when you need to work on a small scale or want to cover a larger area.

Format

A simple method of extending your understanding of measurement and proportion is to change the format and size of your paper. Cut an A3 (18 × 12in.) sheet of cartridge (drawing) paper into different-sized squares, rectangles and circles. Make drawings in outline that cover the whole of each piece of paper. On a thin, horizontal rectangular shape, for instance, you could draw a slice or section only of a scene, such as the shopping arcade (mall) I drew. On the round piece I chose a flower to echo the format. You could also use different measurements: sight-size, half sight-size or twice sight-size.

As an exercise in understanding format and measurement I drew a series of different subjects on different shaped pieces of paper. The study of a figure in a landscape was done sight-size; the scene of the shops and the doorway drawings were made to half sight-size; the flower and the figure were twice sight-size.

Tonal techniques

Line is a very beautiful medium to work in on its own, but its representational range can be enhanced by combination with tone. Tone is the world of colour represented in black and white. To show mass, tonal areas have to be drawn, and the graduations of light and dark need to be realized.

Before you start to work on a tonal drawing, make this simple comparison. Switch on your television set, and if it is colour turn down the brightness and turn up the contrast. You should see a limited image that seems to be essentially only light and dark. As you look at the image, increase the brightness. The greys should start to appear, creating more definition and more intricate forms.

Now go and sit a few paces away from a window. Slowly close your eyes until you are squinting. You should see a limited image with great contrast, like the television screen without the brightness. As you slowly open your eyes, the forms will become more defined, and the variety of tones between light and dark will become greater. The eye can pick out many more tones than the television image.

As with the television, the materials used when drawing cannot define the range of tones that the eye perceives. The subtlety has to be simplified.

You will need
☐ a drawing board
☐ A3 (18 × 12in.) cartridge (drawing) paper
☐ 2B, 4B and 6B pencils
☐ a dip pen and nibs
☐ Indian (India) ink
☐ brushes
☐ charcoal sticks
☐ a plastic eraser
☐ a ruler
☐ masking tape
☐ a sharp craft knife
☐ a paper stump (stomp)
☐ a stacking palette (cabinet nest)
☐ a container of water

The tonal range picked out by the human eye.

Definition is reduced when squinting.

Dark to light and light to dark

As in line, the first step is to get accustomed to perceiving and representing linear shapes, so with tone, the first step is to become familiar with basic tonal techniques.

Attach an A3 sheet of paper to the board vertically. Mark a pencil line horizontally across the centre of the paper.

Mark 22 straight lines at 12mm (½in.) intervals, 25mm (1in.) above the central line. Write the letter D (for 'dark') underneath the first vertical channel. Mark the next channels, from left to right, 1 to 9. Mark the tenth channel L (for 'light'), the next channels 9 to 1 and the last D.

Using a pencil create a deep tone with heavy, merged marks in the first channel. Go on to the next channel, making the marks slightly less black. Continue until the middle channel which should be left clear. Then continue, making each channel to the right gradually darker again. The art is to judge it so as to achieve an evenness to the increasing lightness and darkness.

Using a pencil alone is very unlikely to produce accurate results. Work into the graduated channels with an eraser, lightening areas, or use a paper stump (stomp) to spread the carbon and create subtle tones. You can also use your fingers.

You may have to work up and down the series of channels, lightening or darkening as you go; this is quite acceptable, do not expect to get it right the first time.

Pencil

Pencil can be used to produce shading, and often is in a sketchbook. However, when you begin to look at tone, pencil gets you involved with drawing only small areas and detail, whereas one should first master overall tonal scale. Charcoal and ink are much better for this. When using pencil for tone you can use the edge of the lead as well as the point.

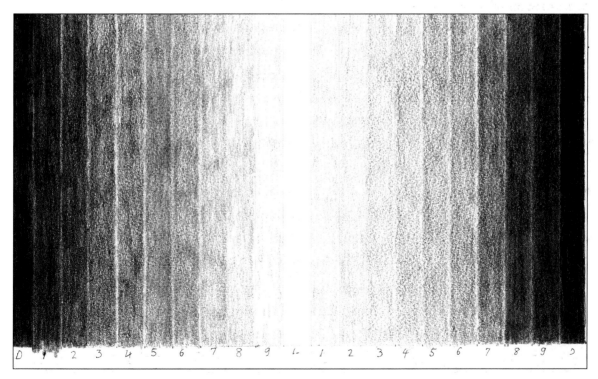

Graduated tones from dark to light and light to dark.

Using charcoal

Underneath your first tonal exercise in pencil, mark eleven 25mm (1in.) vertical straight lines, about 160 mm (6½ in.) high. Mark a straight diagonal line from the top left-hand corner to the bottom right-hand corner.

At the top left-hand corner above your first channel write the letter L, then write from 1 to 8 above the next eight channels and the letter D above the last channel. Write in the same letter and numerals, but in reverse order, at the bottom of the channels. The letter D denotes the darkest tone, the letter L the lightest tone.

This time build a series of tones in the top section above the diagonal line, working from light to dark in gradual steps with a stick of charcoal. In the section below the diagonal line, work from dark to light in gradual steps.

Although charcoal can be messy and difficult to preserve due to its powdery quality, its subtlety in tonal gradations is such that it is well worth persevering to learn how to use it. You may well need to use a paper stump or your fingers to spread the charcoal. A plastic eraser is useful to take away built-up tones of charcoal.

Using a paper stump to spread charcoal.

Tonal steps – the finished exercise.

Working with ink

Tone can be achieved with different intensities of ink. Pencil out a 25cm (10in.) square on an A3 sheet of paper. Draw a diagonal line from the top left-hand corner to the bottom right-hand corner, then draw another line from the top right-hand corner to the bottom left.

Mark six points at 25mm (1in.) intervals on each diagonal line starting from the central point. Connect the points with straight lines, creating a series of squares. You should be left with a border of 6mm (¼in.) on the outside.

Mark the central square D, denoting darkest. Number the outside squares from 1 to 5. Leave the remaining border completely clear.

Now take a plastic palette. To obtain the gradation of tones you need, put pure ink in one section. Put pure ink in the next section, but add a small quantity of water, progressively adding more water to each section until you have a series of different washes that become lighter.

Working flat on the table to prevent the ink running, use a brush to make the central square of your tonal square completely black with pure ink. As you work towards the outside of the subsequent squares, make each one slightly lighter by using a more diluted wash.

Use a flat-ended brush to make the washes. Work as swiftly as you can but try to keep the tones created by the brush even and straight. After each different square is completed, wash your brush in clean water and remove the excess water from the bristles with a tissue.

It takes time to learn how to make even washes. Initially, the effect of gradation from the black square in the centre to the white of the border is more important than an exact, smooth wash.

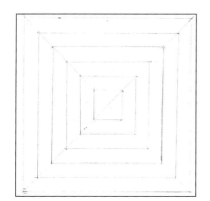

Above left: The tonal square drawn out; with some washes (below left); and completed (right).

Cutting the square notches in the top section.

Cutting the slits in the back section.

Making notches in one of the side sections.

Tonal theatre

A good way of learning to see how objects are made up of light and dark tone areas, is to use a tonal theatre or light modulator. The tonal theatre or light modulator is quite easy and quick to make and will help your appreciation of tone by confining your vision.

Making the tonal theatre

When cutting out card, always use a drawing board to protect the surface of the table. It is also helpful to have an extra strip of card under the area you are going to cut; this stops the knife embedding itself in the drawing board and prevents the surface from getting too many gouges. Always use a craft knife and a sturdy ruler to keep the cuts straight. Make sure the blade is sharp, but keep your fingers at a safe distance.

Place the card on the drawing board on a firm surface. Mark and cut out two rectangles measuring 32.5 × 25cm (13 × 10in.) and two rectangles measuring 27.5 × 25cm (11 × 10in.).

Place one of the larger rectangles on the drawing board. This will be the top section. Mark a 25mm (1in.) square in pencil in each corner. Cut these squares out with a craft knife.

Place the other larger rectangle on the drawing board vertically. This will be the back section. Draw lines horizontally right across the card with the ruler 25mm (1in.) in from both ends. Measure 40mm (1½in.) in at each of the four ends of the two horizontal lines and mark these points. The middle section of these lines should measure 17.5cm (7in.). Cut slits horizontally between these points with a craft knife as shown.

The sides of the tonal theatre are identical. Place one of the smaller rectangles on the board so that the 27.5cm (11in.) edges are at the top and bottom. On the right-hand side of the rectangle, mark and cut out two corner pieces 50mm (2in.) deep and 25mm (1in.) wide. Measure 50mm (2in.) down from the top of the card. Mark a line horizontally across the board. Measure 18mm

(¾in.) in to the left of the top corner point and to the right of the left-hand end, and cut slits along the horizontal line with a craft knife for the back section to slot into. Repeat the process with the other smaller rectangle to make the second side.

Assemble the tonal theatre by pushing the sides through the back slits. Then push the top through the side slits. Widen the slits if they are too tight to take the card.

Using the tonal theatre

When you have assembled your card theatre, place it on a table and put different objects inside. These should vary in their surface, shape and material. Try to imagine them as small sculptures. Look out for interesting things you could use: small artifacts, little boxes or anything that you may have collected on country walks or when beachcombing. You should choose a contrasting selection of objects; you can also try various combinations of articles in different positions. You could even make some objects yourself, or wrap some of the items in paper or material to disguise or soften the shapes.

Move the theatre around on the table so that you can see the variety of light and the way it falls inside the theatre.

You will find that by putting objects in this box you cut out distractions and can concentrate on their tonal features. Draw them in ink or charcoal.

Further ideas

When you have become familiar with the tonal theatre, you can experiment with different effects. To get different lighting on the objects inside it, cut shapes or slots in the top. Experiment with dramatic lighting effects at night by placing an angled desk lamp or a bedside lamp above the box. Make studies of different objects in charcoal; try to achieve a strong contrast of tone to match what you see. Also draw something in pencil, concentrating on just a section of the theatre rather than showing the whole thing.

Try also putting a mirror in the tonal theatre, either a piece of mirror specially cut to fit in, or a hand mirror. Place this mirror under a single object and do a drawing of it looking at the shape of both the object itself and its mirror image.

You can also create several small studies across one sheet of cartridge paper, changing the object every time you finish a drawing. Work on each drawing for no more than 15 minutes. You can achieve different effects by moving your theatre around to change the direction of the light.

Slotting the side piece into the back section.

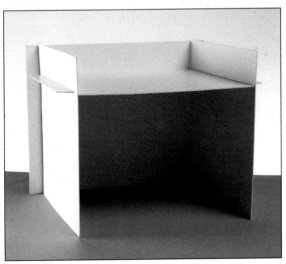

The completed tonal theatre.

Projects: Tonal drawings

This drawing will take you step-by-step through the process of working in charcoal from dark to light. Charcoal is often worked this way; it involves first covering the paper with a layer of charcoal, and then removing it in parts. The commentary is merely a guideline for you to follow, not the definitive method. Try to develop your own techniques for looking and working from my approach. As charcoal is difficult to manipulate on a small scale, it is often advisable to work larger than sight-size, as in this project.

You will need
- a drawing board
- A2 (24 × 18in.) paper
- grey paper or card
- stick charcoal
- a charcoal pencil
- compressed charcoal
- a dip pen and nibs
- Indian (India) ink
- brushes
- a paper stump (stomp)
- a plastic eraser
- masking tape
- spray fixative
- a ruler
- a soft rag
- a container of water

A charcoal drawing

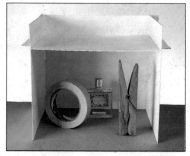

Above: I selected three objects for my arrangement that had a combination of contrasting lines. Left: The finished drawing.

Setting up the tonal theatre
The tonal theatre was set in front of me on a table. Underneath it I placed a piece of grey paper, allowing a distance of about 60cm (2ft) from the edge of my drawing board (when sitting in my drawing position) to where I placed the theatre. I then selected three objects from my collection of articles that I found interesting, and arranged them so that I would use the back, middle and front sections of the theatre.

Basic outline
After attaching to my drawing board a single A2 sheet of cartridge (drawing) paper cut down to fit the board, I positioned myself directly in front of the theatre. The first job was to make a basic outline drawing using charcoal pencil of the frame of the theatre to twice sight-size. It was important to be as accurate as possible (within reason, of course) with the measurements, as this was the structure from which the tonal

44

arrangement would emerge. The twice sight-size scale meant that I had to use a ruler as well as my pencil, to take the measurements with. I made a couple of small charcoal marks on the outside edges of my theatre drawing to indicate the main lines. These would be obliterated by the thick charcoal layer I was about to apply.

Establishing the lightest point

In order to get a clear idea of the strongest tones I looked at the objects inside the theatre with my eyes half closed, as if squinting in sunlight. The very lightest section, which was the crescendo of light in the theatre, was to be left completely free of charcoal in my drawing. Within the rest of the framework I applied a thick layer of stick charcoal, which I worked into the paper with bold strokes, creating a deep tonal layer of charcoal covering almost the entire frame of the theatre.

Creating mid-tone

I looked at the tonal theatre again with my eyes half closed. The back wall of the theatre seemed to be a mid-tone; certainly it was lighter than the floor of the theatre. Using a soft rag, I very lightly erased a layer of charcoal from the back wall of the theatre to create a mid-tone layer.

Starting on the objects

Taking a piece of compressed charcoal, which is darker than stick charcoal, I started to measure with a ruler and pencil and draw the outline of the objects inside the theatre to twice sight-size. I could quite easily see the shapes emerging from the stick charcoal layer. It is important that the measurements of the objects relate to each other and the frame of the theatre.

Light sections

With the lightest section of my drawing free from charcoal, I wanted to bring out the other light areas inside the tonal theatre. Again, I squinted, looking at the theatre to check the relative tonal values. Using a soft rag, I lightly erased a section

Drawing out the basic outline of the tonal theatre.

Covering almost the whole surface in charcoal.

Creating the mid-tones.

of the foreground of the theatre to indicate the light entering it. With an eraser I highlighted those parts of the roll of tape caught by the light (the sharp edge of a plastic eraser allows you to be more controlled and remove more charcoal).

Dark sections

I then had to put in the darkest lines and sections. The darkest areas seemed to be at the back edges of the theatre, around and in between the objects. I again used compressed charcoal to draw in these darkest sections. At this point in the drawing I knew the lightest and darkest parts of the drawing and had drawn them in. All the other tones had to be between these values.

Increasing definition

I stepped back and looked at the drawing from a distance. The drawing needed more mid-tones, so I worked these using a plastic eraser, a soft rag and sometimes my fingers. I also used the compressed charcoal to emphasize some lines and shadows. I

assessed the tone by frequently glancing at the subject, then working on my drawing. The definition of the shadows around the objects became more obvious by the removal of a layer of charcoal from the objects themselves, and by application of the compressed charcoal. The process of removal of charcoal and adding to and slightly changing the lines using the charcoal pencil to create more exacting shapes was completed at this stage.

Finishing off

In this last step I used the plastic eraser to create sharp, light lines at the front corner of the theatre. Then with the stump (stomp) I merged and spread the mid-tones in the foreground and midground. I then decided that the drawing was finished, so I used a spray fixative (always follow the instructions carefully) to protect the drawing and prevent it smudging. You can use a soft rag gently to remove thin lines of charcoal if necessary before spraying a drawing with fixative.

Drawing the outline of the shapes against the charcoal background.

Removing a charcoal layer with an eraser.

Merging the mid-tones with a paper stump.

A drawing in pen and wash

Having worked from dark to light in the last drawing, this one uses mid-tones with washes and lines, working more from light to dark. Although one can work from light to dark with charcoal, it is the only way of working with ink washes as the ink, once applied, cannot be removed like unfixed charcoal. The method one uses will depend a little on the darkness desired for the end result, but is mainly determined by taste. Only towards the end of the drawing is the darkest tone established. The process of slowly creating a series of transparent tonal washes is an excellent starting point for anyone who wishes to paint in watercolour.

Do not forget the principles you have learned in measurement and proportion drawings; try to use them in conjunction with these new methods.

Arranging the composition

I set up the tonal theatre in the same position as for the charcoal drawing. The objects were arranged so that they overlapped but still filled the entire space of the theatre.

I then positioned myself directly in front of the theatre, resting the drawing board with stretched paper on my lap and against the edge of the table. I made a sight-size outline drawing of the frame of the theatre in soft charcoal pencil.

The arrangement of objects inside the tonal theatre.

The finished drawing in pen and wash.

Drawing the basic outlines of the objects.

Basic outline

Using charcoal pencil, I started to measure and draw the outline of the objects within the theatre. As I drew, I observed carefully the shapes between the objects as well as the objects themselves. I kept the lines faint as in the first step.

Drawing the mid-tones

Judging that this would be the number needed, I mixed four different washes in my stacking palette. They represented an even progression across the tonal scale; the last wash had just a touch of water added. It is important to test the strength of each wash in a corner of the stretched paper before applying it to the drawing. You can then lighten or darken the wash if it does not seem right. This testing is especially important in the later stages of a drawing when the scope for correction is less.

I looked at the darker and medium areas of the theatre and the objects using the technique of screwing up my eyes to determine their exact location. Then with a flat-ended brush I drew them all in a mid-tone wash. As I applied the washes, I kept looking at the subtle changes in the shapes of the objects in relation to the theatre, changing them as I wished. This was not just a matter of filling in the drawn-out spaces, but was crucial to the whole drawing. I then went over the darkest areas in a slightly darker wash.

The shapes emerge

Using a slightly lighter wash, I applied another layer of tone to the areas in the tonal theatre that appeared to use the next lightest once I had established a range of mid-tones in the drawing. I then felt ready to tackle the darker edges of the theatre and the objects, and drew them in with a dip pen. At this point in the drawing I was looking at the general shapes, and not getting involved with the patterns on the objects or with any detail.

Achieving contrast

Some of the areas I had drawn in with mid-tone washes now seemed too light in contrast with the darker areas I had just drawn in, so I went over these in darker washes.

The darkest tones

In this final step, I washed in the darkest tones using my round-ended brushes. The washes very often overlapped and started to provide detail. The shadows became more defined; the feeling was that of looking at an entrance to an enclosure which was the effect I had been hoping to create. The final washes were added to create a strong contrast and I was now satisfied with the drawing.

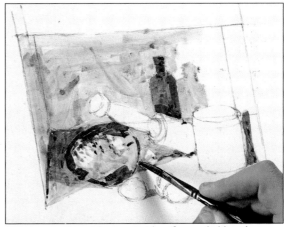
Putting in the mid-tones with a flat-ended brush.

Drawing the darker edges in dip pen.

Creating a contrast with the final, darkest washes.

Mixed media techniques

Drawing in mixed media might sound like a contemporary invention, but the process has in fact been around for centuries. Mixed media means using combinations of different materials together, such as pencil and ink. Exciting patterns and textures can be created as you experiment with different combinations of materials. These exercises will help you to explore the richness and variety of marks, lines and tone. You should try to make each one have an individual quality; you aren't just doodling, you are exploring a vocabulary for future drawings.

Guidelines are given in each of the different exercises as to how to create the marks, but they are only suggestions and you should follow them loosely. It is important to create your own qualities and to be prepared to combine the unexpected and the accidental in these exercises.

Degas 'Ballet Dancers' (detail) 473 × 625mm (19 × 25in.). A quick study in line on toned paper captures the dancers' momentary movement.

You will need
- ☐ a drawing board
- ☐ A3 (18 × 12in.) paper
- ☐ 2B, 4B and 6B pencils
- ☐ a dip pen, nibs and ink
- ☐ a bamboo pen
- ☐ brushes
- ☐ white oil crayon
- ☐ white gouache
- ☐ charcoal
- ☐ a charcoal pencil
- ☐ a plastic eraser
- ☐ a ruler
- ☐ a sharp craft knife
- ☐ a stacking palette (cabinet nest)
- ☐ rubber-based glue
- ☐ a container of water

Mixed media line techniques

On an A3 sheet of paper mark out a rectangle measuring 37.5 × 15cm (15 × 6in.) with a pencil and ruler. Divide the rectangle into five rectangles measuring 15 × 7.5cm (6 × 3in.). Mark these boxes 1 to 5 from left to right.

1 Draw a series of lines the length of the box alternating between pen and brush. Make the lines of different widths and draw them in one movement; do not worry about how straight they are. Using your waxed crayon, zig-zag a line across the width of the box, dragging the still-wet ink as you go.

2 Starting at the top of the box make a looped line in 4B pencil that runs to the bottom. Using charcoal pencil, start to create a spiral effect by overlapping the pencil lines as you loop to the bottom of the page. Do the same with stick charcoal and brush and ink.

3 Draw an oval in charcoal pencil that is approximately the length of the box. Draw a continuous pencil line in a random manner looping and zig-zagging through the oval. With the dip pen, draw a series of tight, thin lines in your pencil loops. Using a brush, splatter or flick

ink on to the central part of the oval, first covering the other boxes with spare paper to prevent their getting spotted with ink. Finally make a few random spotted marks with your brush and bamboo pen to add contrast to the line.

4 Gently draw a series of thick lines in stick charcoal across the box. You should vary the width of line, leaving some gaps of plain white paper. Draw a series of random charcoal pencil lines with a finely sharpened charcoal pencil over the stick charcoal. Vary the width of the charcoal pencil line by changing the pressure on the point as you move across the box. Using the sharp edge of a plastic eraser, rub out a series of sharp lines across the surface of the box.

5 Using charcoal pencil, draw sharp lines all across the box with different tonal gradations. Smudge these lines together in places with your fingers. When you feel that you have a sufficient tonal range, draw over the top in dip pen. Try to make as many varied lines in dip pen as you can.

Write under each box the combination of materials you have used. This will help you later if you wish to research more line or tone mixed media techniques and experiment further with the effects you can create.

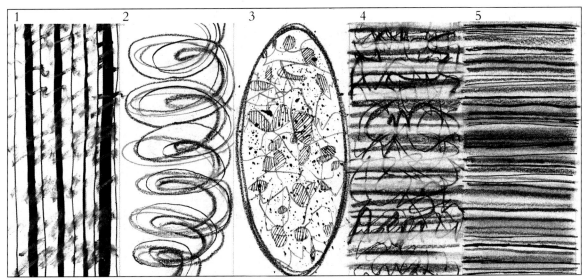

The finished exercise.

Mixed media tonal techniques

The materials for this exercise are the same as those used for the techniques in line except that a jar of water is also needed. Draw out the boxes using the same measurements as in the line techniques exercise.

With the tonal techniques a certain amount of physical pressure is needed, both in erasing vigorously and in scratching the surface of the drawing to create the slightly raised textures that appear as subtle patterns.

1 Pour a tiny amount of ink into a stacking palette, press your fingers into the ink and apply the resulting finger-prints at different strengths across the whole of the box. Then place a small object with a textured or raised surface, such as a metal food grater or a coin, under your dry finger-prints and make a series of small rubbings. Contrast the patterns created by the finger-prints with the rubbings.

2 Draw a variety of diagonal lines in oil crayon from the bottom left-hand corner to the top right-hand corner of the box. Mix Indian (India) ink with an equal quantity of water in your palette. Apply this mid-tone wash across the whole of the box. You will see that the wax of the crayon resists the water, and that the white lines will appear against the grey of the background.

3 Starting with a stick of charcoal, and then going on to a charcoal pencil, compressed charcoal, and finally a 4B pencil, make a series of horizontal lines across the box to create a tonal sandwich. Apply each material in turn across the entire width of the box, making the width of each line the same as your drawing instrument. Leave occasional glimpses of paper beneath your lines to add contrast.

4 Make a thin layer of charcoal across the box. With a 6B pencil and a charcoal pencil draw looping pencil lines and zig-zagging charcoal lines over your charcoal layer. In oil crayon, draw a series of dense lines together at random parts of the box. On top of this mixture of line and tone, make a series of small tonal ovals in charcoal pencil and pencil.

Using a ruler make a series of sharp vertical lines 6 mm (¼in.) apart across your box. Erase every other line as much as you can, to create a contrast of tone and line.

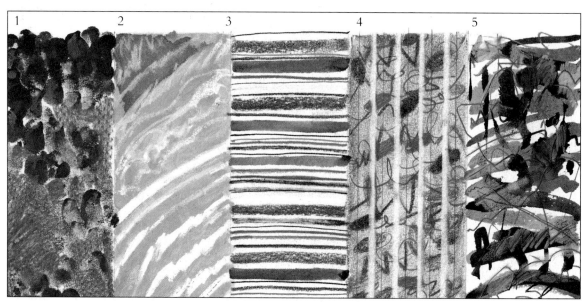

The finished exercise.

5 Draw a series of large ink lines in brush across your box. Then draw over the top of these lines in pencil even if they are still wet; be sure to press hard with your pencil. Draw another series of large ink lines across your box. Using oil crayon, try to bring out the line of the pencil against the ink, varying the pressure of the oil crayon as you rub. Finally rub out different sections of your box with an eraser to create subtle changes of pattern and texture.

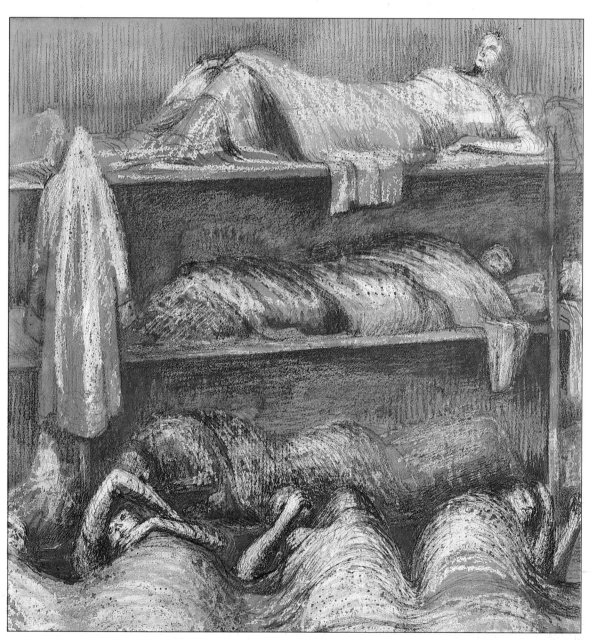

Henry Moore 'Shelter Scene – Bunks and Sleepers' (detail) 480 × 426mm (19 × 17in.). Henry Moore uses a combination of varied media to create character and a sense of environment through tone.

Further ideas

To try out these techniques, you should choose different still-life subjects to draw. A section or detail of a leafy plant, a bowl of fruit, or a vase of flowers would be ideal.

Gouache resist

Divide an A3 sheet of paper into four rectangles and cut these out using a ruler and a knife. Mark out a 10cm (4in.) square in pencil in the centre of one of the rectangular sheets.

Using the white gouache, start to paint, working from the still-life subject that you have chosen. Try to vary the thickness of the lines and marks, and concentrate on the patterns within the objects and their linear quality.

When the gouache has dried completely, paint an even coat of undiluted Indian ink over the whole square. Allow that to dry.

Place the paper under a running tap, and let the gouache wash away, taking out the ink in those areas too. Rub gently with your fingers or use a soft brush until the whole image you have painted has reappeared. Place the wet paper on your drawing board to dry. You can at this stage stretch the paper (see pages 24–5) to ensure that it stays flat when it is completely dry.

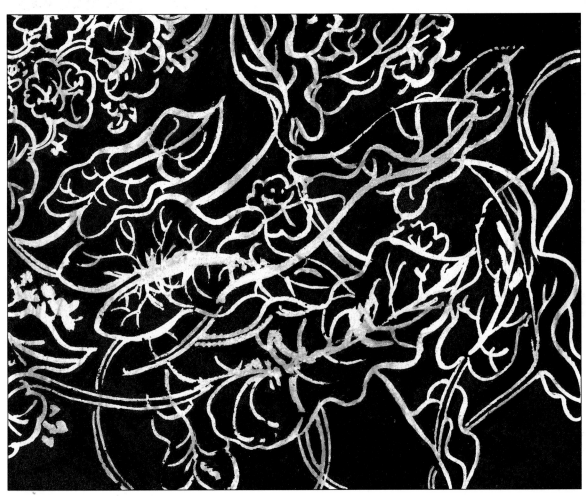

Gouache resist – a finished exercise.

Scratch technique – a finished exercise.

Glue resist – a finished exercise.

Scratch technique

Mark out a 10cm (4in.) square in the centre of one of the prepared rectangles as described above in the gouache resist technique. To prevent the paper from buckling, you may wish to stretch the paper now (see pages 24-5). If so, allow the paper to dry before continuing with the exercise.

Paint a dense, even coat of undiluted ink over the whole square. Allow the ink to dry thoroughly.

Cover the whole square again, this time with a thick layer of white oil crayon. Go over the square several times so that it becomes completely white, and you cannot see the ink underneath. Make sure that you build up a thick layer of oil crayon as this will ensure you get very dark lines when you scratch into the surface.

Using a sharp craft knife, start to scratch away at the surface you have created. You will find that this will reveal the dark lines of the ink, in contrast to the white background. Using this scratching method, draw the image you have chosen and try to achieve the same qualities as in the gouache resist exercise, but using a very different technique.

Glue resist

Once again, mark out a 10cm (4in.) square in the centre of a prepared rectangle. Paint the image, this time with the glue, and allow it to dry thoroughly. Pots of glue are often supplied with a brush, but you may need a thin brush to vary the thickness of the marks. It need only be a cheap brush or an old one as the glue may ruin it for other use.

When the glue has hardened, paint the square completely with an even coat of Indian ink. Once the ink has dried, rub at the surface gently with your fingers and you will find that the glue will start to peel away from the paper, revealing a clean white image.

Project: A window in mixed media

In this project I decided to do two drawings of the same window from close to and from further away, using the mixed media techniques developed in the last section. Whereas each of these could have been executed in simple tone, the interplay of line, tone and light that one gets from a window lent itself better to the more complex medium.

The first drawing was a partial view of the window. By moving my chair back a couple of metres, but still positioning it in the same relationship to the window, I could then change the focus and include the window. Both drawings started with some simple measurements, made to sight-size, of the objects in the composition. When I was satisfied with these, I then drew them in quickly. This is often a good way to start a drawing, but you have to watch out for it becoming too loose when you are drawing quickly, and be ready to make more measurements in order to reassert the structure. Measurement is a useful tool, but I find that it must not be allowed to begin to dominate the spirit of an image.

You will need
- ☐ a drawing board
- ☐ A3 (18 × 12in.) cartridge (drawing) paper
- ☐ a 2B pencil
- ☐ a charcoal pencil
- ☐ stick charcoal
- ☐ a bamboo pen and ink
- ☐ brushes
- ☐ a white oil crayon
- ☐ a plastic eraser
- ☐ a paper stump (stomp)
- ☐ a stacking palette (cabinet nest)
- ☐ tissues
- ☐ a container of water

The finished drawing of the window (partial view).

Window – partial view

A partial view of the window set up.

Setting up

First, I stretched the sheet of cartridge paper on to my drawing board and set myself up close to the window. With the board balanced on my lap and my materials all within easy reach I focused on a small section of the window, the table, net curtains and plants.

Establishing the basic structure

Working in pencil, I made some basic sight-size measurements of the composition. To make the drawing manageable with the details clear and at the same time show most of the plant, I decided it needed to be sight-size.

I marked the section of the window frame in pencil and drew it in lightly, and then drew in the position of the plants in pencil and the lines of the net curtain in white oil crayon.

This initial stage has to be done very carefully, as a drawing whose basic structure is not properly established is difficult to get into proportion. While doing this drawing I glanced frequently from the drawing to the subject.

Filling in detail

In a light wash, and using a round-ended brush, I set about starting to fill in the shapes of the plants, window frames and net curtains. I did not

measure these lines but used the basic framework of my composition in pencil as a guide. The wash was made up as I went along, which gave me the opportunity to create some varieties in tone. I made very basic, thin washed lines to represent the net curtains.

Light tones

The lightest area in my composition was to the left of the plants where the light came in. I decided to leave this blank using the tone of the paper. The next lightest areas were the table top and net curtains where the light played on them. With an oil crayon I made bold lines and spotted marks on the areas that reflected this sensation, in the first stage of a resist technique.

Drawing the basic composition sight-size.

Laying a wash with a round-ended brush.

Using the oil crayon to create the resist surface.

Applying the wash over the oil crayon.

Applying a wash to the resist

Before applying a wash to the resist it was necessary to establish the contrasts in the composition, so I went over the darker leaves with a dark wash. When this was done I could then go over the table and curtains with a light wash, trying to make the wash reflect what I could see: light playing against the texture of the net curtain. The oil crayon repels the water of the wash, keeping these areas even lighter.

Supplying darker tones

I now felt ready to start on the darker tones. I went over the darkest areas of the side of the table and the earth in the pots with a dark wash. Using a charcoal pencil, I drew the outlines of the leaves and table edge in line, as they seemed to need emphasizing.

Final light touches

Finally, I scanned the whole of the small scene at arm's length to see what else needed doing. I decided that areas of the table top, curtains, stems and leaves were still too faint so I went over them again with a dark wash. I also felt that the curtains looked rather flat so I drew in gestural lines with the white oil crayon to give the sensation of the light shimmering against the darker shapes of the ferns.

Using a charcoal pencil to emphasize the edges.

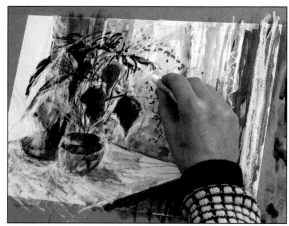

Making gestural lines with oil crayon.

Window – full view

I moved back from my original position to give myself a good overall view of the window. This meant that I was now going to be working against the light. It was therefore even more important to establish the lightest and darkest tones in the drawing, so that the tonal proportions would be easier to attain as they fell between these extremes.

The drawing board was positioned in the same way as for the partial view drawing. When I had got this right I measured the window to sight-size as this scale seemed to fit the vertical format that I had chosen.

The framework

Using a 2B pencil for a soft line, I drew the frame of the window in lightly, making basic sight-size measurements to get the scale correct. Constantly glancing from the drawing to the subject I then scanned the plants and drew them in too. The lines of the plants are loose and flowing and had to be drawn so as not to appear rigid.

Applying darker tones

This time I elected to handle the darker areas first. The dark-toned sections of the window frame were drawn in thick charcoal, leaving the edges around it that catch the light free from charcoal.

The finished drawing.

A full view of the window set up.

Drawing the lines of the plants.

When I had finished making the tonal layer of charcoal I worked it into the paper using a paper stump (stomp) which let me achieve subtle gradations of the charcoal. I then used the plastic eraser to remove any unwanted charcoal. Next, the stump was ideal for making the lines for the plants in front of the window, providing a gentle spread of the layer of charcoal.

I created a light tonal layer of charcoal on the wall and drew in the shadow of the window frame by spreading the charcoal with the stump and erasing with the edge of a plastic eraser.

Establishing the darkest areas

At this point in the drawing I wanted to find the darkest areas. Squinting, I could see that the edges that catch the light on the window frame had the darkest lines next to them. Using brush and ink for the blackness I drew them in. The edges of the plant pot were the darkest section of the subject so I made these black using a bamboo pen.

Emphasizing light

Having done the dark areas, I then turned to the lighter ones. The net curtains were not to be shown in great detail so I drew them in a wash of ink mixed with a little water and applied with a round-ended brush. I then looked at the pots and plants and drew them in short lines using two washes, one darker than that used on the curtains.

Conveying light

Around the outside of the window the bright edges that caught the light needed sharpening, so I used a plastic eraser to make sharp lines along them. Details that did not look dark enough were filled in with charcoal. The table top was rightly the brightest part of the drawing, but the corner in reality was less bright than the rest, so I rubbed in a light layer of charcoal with the residue on a used paper stump. This also had the effect of having a crescent of light to the left of the drawing. At this point I considered the drawing finished as I had created the feeling of light entering a room.

Working the first charcoal layer.

Drawing in the darkest sections with a bamboo pen.

The net curtains put in using a round-ended brush.

Highlighting the edges with a sharpened eraser.

Further ideas

Window scenes like this make good subjects. They do not involve going outside and being exposed to the elements; you can set yourself up comfortably; there are usually several suitable objects around the window for you to draw; and you always have varied light effects. Try similar drawings, say at night or showing the view through the windows.

Window at night

Set yourself up in the same position as you used for the full view of the window. Make sure that the curtains are drawn back so that you can see the reflections in the window. If there is a reflection of yourself there, don't be modest but put it in the drawing! This time you should aim to create a drawing using mixed media that shows the relationship between the window's reflection and the window frame.

First, get the basic framework of your drawing correct by measurement, then build the major tonal relationship before you become involved with the smaller details. By combining wet and dry materials you will be able to achieve different textures and depths.

Near and far

You can also make a drawing through the window into the distance. If you would like to try the idea, you should take up the position you were in for the partial view of the window, except that you may have to be slightly higher so as to have a clear view out of the window.

A variety of mixed media materials will be necessary to do justice to the variety of the subject matter. Accurate measurement is essential to create a recession of scale and size into the background. Try using a different format of paper; for example, a thin rectangular piece. Focus on the smaller shapes in the background and show them with clarity. The objects within the room should be drawn in simple line and tone.

Project: Using a sketchbook

You will need
- a sketchbook
- 2B, 4B and 6B pencils
- a plastic eraser
- a sharp craft knife or Stanley knife

A sketchbook is your portable studio; use it whenever you do not have the time for a formal session of drawing. A sketchbook is essential for all visual artists. When you are on holiday, take it with you so that you can make studies wherever you go. The opportunities for using a sketchbook are limitless: draw out of the window of a train; draw while you are waiting in an airport lounge; draw the people you see in your local park. This will give you some practice and you will also teach yourself to observe intuitively.

Sketchbooks are available in a variety of sizes and formats; some are only pocket-sized, while others can be 60cm (2ft) wide or more. It is important to buy a sketchbook with a hardback and strong bindings that make it durable. The paper used in most sketchbooks is light cartridge (drawing), try to find one with at least this quality of paper. A sketchbook measuring about 20 × 15cm (8 × 6in.) is a convenient size.

The length of time you spend on drawings in your sketchbook should be varied. Try to make as many short studies, taking up to two minutes, as long ones.

You should occasionally use odd materials – ballpoint pens, fibre tips or stubby pencils; even draw with a stick dipped in ink or anything else that comes to hand. A change of materials can very often release inhibitions that have blocked your artistic development. The sketchbook is your secret world, and there is no such thing as a mistake in it.

J.M.W. Turner, detail from the sketchbook 'Hesperides I'.

Producing a study

This exercise and the following may lead you to question your own ideas on perception. They may also instinctively become a part of the way you draw. Equally, you should never be afraid to develop existing methods in creating your own drawings.

However, before embarking on more complex drawings in your sketchbook, try some experimental exercises using intuitive observation. Keep an open mind; this is a chance to be rash, to make instinctive marks, and to exaggerate the methods and techniques that you have learned.

Working from observation, make a continuous line drawing of a figure or object, keeping your

The completed study of a figure in pencil.

The basic framework.

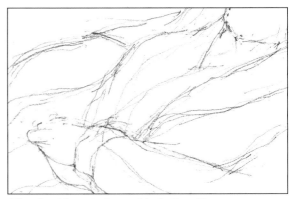

The shoulders, jacket and bed. Detail.

hand moving constantly as you look at the subject. This will help you to ensure the line is unbroken. You should try to get the proportions of the composition correct. You can use any materials you like to make the studies and vary the length of time you take.

Another good exercise is to make a series of line drawings of figures or objects. Do not look at your drawing after you have started – just look at the object and try to create the shape and line by intuition. Again you can use any materials you like, but make these studies in under a minute.

Study of a figure
A typical subject that I would want to sketch is a figure relaxing at home. People usually stay fairly still for between 15 and 30 minutes while watching television or reading. If they do make slight movements, I draw over my original lines; I frequently find this enhances the drawing, creating an animated quality. If the figure changes

position, be patient. I often have a series of positions drawn on different pages in my sketchbook. We are all creatures of habit, so a position or postures may well be repeated. If so, I can simply continue with the drawing.

I always try to look at the whole figure and in relation to its surrounding. I draw intuitively in lines of different strengths as I move around and across the shapes, constantly scanning the figure. I never measure – my sketchbook is a place for exploring instinctive marks. For this reason do not use an eraser to make changes.

Head, shoulders and pillows
The model was lying down on some pillows, watching television. I started from where the forehead and edge of the pillow met. I drew the outline of the pillow looking constantly at the subject, not at the paper. I observed the space between the pillow and the head. At first I used tentative light marks; then I worked round and across the forms. As I became more confident about the correctly plotted positions and crucial angles, I made darker marks and lines.

Shoulders, jacket and bed
I jumped from the point of the chin and marked an angle for the collar of the jacket; drawing with flowing lines the creases and folds of the jacket. I looked at the space between the figure and the outside of the bed, and drew it in outline.

A detail of the figure's head.

The head

Then I went back to drawing the head. I looked at the proportions of the nose and cheekbones, and worked from mark to mark: lips to chin, lips to eyes, cheekbone to neck. I made tentative, light marks to indicate these points in space. As I grew more confident of the positions, I made lines and angles. As I was drawing these marks, the model changed position. The drawing was unfinished but it had been excellent practice and I could always continue with a study of a different position.

A walk with my sketchbook

Whenever I go out with my sketchbook, it is a visual adventure. One of my favourite walks takes me to the River Thames, about a mile from my home in Chiswick, London. You too may have a walk that you particularly enjoy, so you can combine this with a sketchbook project. You will be surprised what ordinary things you may have taken for granted, and how much you can enjoy drawing on your way. I decided to make six 10-minute studies on my way to the river and one of 30 minutes, when I reached my destination. I would draw objects in the local environment en route and finally a landscape. I wrote a commentary on the sketches I made as I went along; I described the last drawing – the landscape sketch – in a step-by-step sequence.

A terraced house.

Terraced house

Outside my house I made a quick drawing of my front door and balcony window. I drew the door frame and columns in pencil carefully. The decorative ironwork of the balcony made an intricate pattern against the window. I suggested the brickwork with horizontal lines at regular intervals. I drew the dustbins (trash cans) at odd angles to contrast with the rectangular doorway.

Bicycles against a stand.

Bicycles

I walked to the end of my road, where there was a group of bicycles propped against their stands. Standing a few paces away, I started to draw a single bicycle in relation to its stand.

I drew the frame first. Working instinctively, not using measurement, I kept the pencil on the page almost continuously. The wheels were a series of circular lines. The shape of the stand helped to give the feeling of a bicycle leaning against a stand. The essence of all sketchbook work is spontaneity, so work quickly!

Shop window

Turning off the main road and down a side street towards the river was a row of small shops. The display of fresh fish and shellfish arranged in a window was tempting. I looked at the patterns created by the different seafood and decided to draw a lobster. Flowing pencil lines seemed right for the curvaceous subject, varying the intensity and width of line. I tried to contrast the simple shape of the lobster against the rest of the fish on display around it.

Tree

At the end of the street there was a large roundabout. Struggling amidst the mass of road and cars was a number of trees. I chose one with a simple shape and drew it from the trunk towards its tapering branches, trying hard to follow the exact direction of the shape of the trunk. This was so as to capture the sense of energy rising up the tree from the ground that attracted me to it in the first place. I used light lines and marks, redrawing in heavier lines if I thought that the width or direction of the branches was wrong.

Trees are excellent linear subject matter, because their complex shape and often constant movement are difficult to draw. If you persevere and draw many of them in your sketchbook, it will enhance your skill with line.

Roof top

Then I turned down another side street and looked up at the architectural features of the houses. A chimney and part of the roof stood out against the sky. The rectangular shape of the chimney was drawn first, with the angle of the roof. I drew the chimney pots in line, trying to get their shape and convoluted outline, then quickly toned in the shape of the pots to create contrast.

Churchyard

Walking down the small, winding road I came to a churchyard and noticed a large decorative tomb. It bore an inscription: 'William Hogarth, a painter of moral tales'. Above the inscription was a charming, small stone relief. For an artist, this was irresistible. I drew it in outline, paying special attention to the overlapping features of the relief. The short study took less than 10 minutes to do.

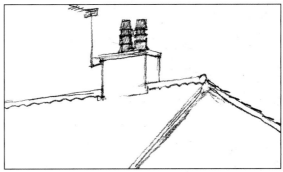

A roof top.

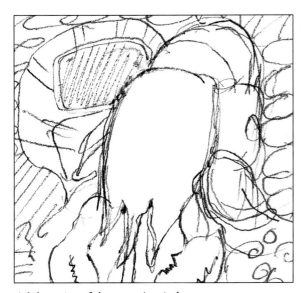

A lobster in a fishmonger's window.

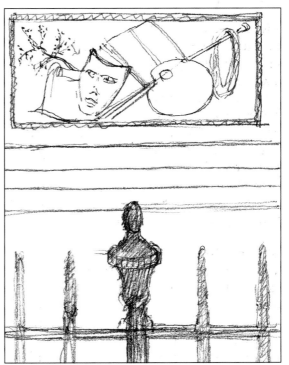

A tree against an urban landscape.

Hogarth's tomb and railings.

The river

Basic structure

Now I was at the river, I chose a subject for the longer, 30-minute sketch. Riversides are never short of interesting subject matter, so the only difficulty in selecting this barge and roadside view was the variety of choice.

Working quickly in pencil, I drew a line bisecting the page in my sketchbook for the edge of the road, in front of the river. Drawing the line of the quay with the moored barge came next. The pencil moved constantly, with my eyes flicking from paper to scene rapidly.

The author drawing the river.

Fence, barge, signs and trees

Next I decided to draw the fence-posts, starting with the farthest one, as all the others would get larger as they came closer to me. Not wanting to make decisions about the tonal balance of the sketch yet, I just drew them in. The signs came next. I was trying to guess distances without measuring, jumping from point to point making marks and lines, so as to maintain the spontaneity. I varied the strength of marks when an object or angle seemed important. Lastly, I drew in the straight line for the height of the river and the edge of the boat, which meant that the basic shapes were established.

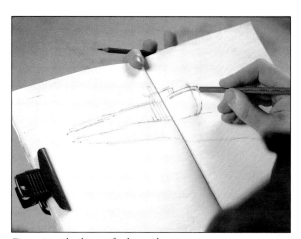

Drawing the bow of a houseboat.

The river

The afternoon light created rippled flowing lines on the surface of the river. I echoed this flow, making my pencil glide across the surface of the paper. Twisting and curling the pencil lines, I tried to create the impression of the slowly receding tide before me.

Contrast

I decided the fence-posts needed contrast against the surface of the river so I made them dark in tone. I also conveyed their haphazard placement by drawing the poles between them which were at odd angles. The surface of the road had random

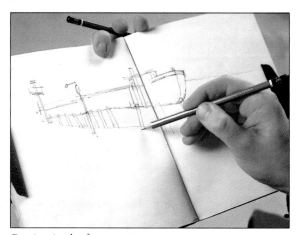

Putting in the fence-posts.

patterns; I drew these in short strokes and curved lines. I also drew in the shore and pavement.

Human scale

While I was drawing, a bearded, bohemian painter set up an easel near me and started to paint vigorously. I added his rotund outline and the line of his portable easel. The figure gave the drawing a human scale. Never be afraid to add animals or people to your pencil studies, if they appear while you are drawing; they add a spontaneous touch. One of the great problems of drawing outdoors affected me then: it began to rain so I stopped the drawing and began to walk home.

Using pencil to create contrast.

Adding another artist painting to give human scale to the drawing.

PART TWO

Starting in Watercolour

Introduction

Watercolour painting has a long and living tradition. There are paintings in watercolour in the caves at Altamira and at Lascaux, making it likely that this is the earliest method used by man to record his existence. From that time, people from almost all cultures – including the ancient Egyptians, the Chinese, and the European and English masters of the eighteenth century – have taken the tradition, added to it and developed it. Today, the popularity of watercolour, even in the face of more modern alternatives, seems undiminished, and certainly it is a medium which still attracts many beginners to painting every year.

Watercolour is often called the 'English' medium, although English landscape art really developed from the Dutch school of painting – the two countries are, after all, very close to one another. The topographical artists in England – who were trying to make accurate records of what they saw, usually landscapes, and architectural and botanical drawings – drew their subjects, and then stained them lightly in watercolour, normally pale brown or green. The Dutch influence encouraged a more painterly approach. The French, and through them, the Italian landscape schools also played a part in the development of English watercolour art.

There are many reasons why watercolour painting flourished in Britain around 1800. The Industrial Revolution meant that more people had more money, but it was also a time when people of culture started to travel widely – the 'grand tour' became an essential part of a gentleman's education – and they began to collect works of art. Thomas Gainsborough and Paul Sandby were just two of the great artists who started the Royal Academy and who were instrumental in encouraging collecting, and the vogue for amateur painting. At about this time, there was a large number of gifted and enthusiastic artists using watercolour as a creative medium. The Royal Society of Painters in Water-Colours was formed in London in 1804. Watercolour painting in America owed a great deal to European art in the nineteenth century. In this century, however, a strong national style has developed. As well as producing some brilliant professional artists, the American interest in watercolour painting has encouraged amateur artists and the number of amateur painters in watercolour has increased enormously over the last twenty or thirty years.

Paul Sandby 'Windsor Castle: the Round Tower' 290 × 510mm (11½ × 20½in.). Some of Sandby's most interesting works are his numerous drawings of Windsor Castle. This example is one of his best; it is transparent watercolour over pencil and is a good example of topographical painting in which the drawing predominates.

Charles Bartlett 'Fishing Boats' 350 × 425mm (14 × 17in.). An example of the use of transparent watercolour where the drawing is established by shapes of colour.

This section of *Art Class* is designed to help those people who want to know how to paint in watercolour. It illustrates basic principles and techniques from which you can develop your own approach to the subject and your own personal style. Equipment and materials are listed with advice as to what is necessary and most suitable for the beginner, and through practical instruction you are encouraged to carry out specific projects and exercises. If you follow the guidelines and advice given and work systematically through the projects, by the time you reach the end, you should be able to produce satisfying and technically adept paintings.

For me one of the great charms of watercolour painting is its fluidity and transparency, which can produce a beauty which is unique. I find the spontaneous quality, the simplicity and ability to express mood and light suits my expression as an artist. But one has to be careful that the medium and technique don't become all important; first and foremost one is an artist with something to express.

I believe that the beginner in watercolour is best advised not to spend years learning the academics of drawing first, but rather to start painting and let the drawing develop alongside. They should run hand in hand. Drawing and observation are fundamental to painting and will improve with practice. Enjoy your painting, paint what you know and love best and don't worry too much about what other people say or think.

There are three main styles of watercolour painting. The watercolour drawing (below left) is the traditional use of the medium (as used by the great topographical artists). The drawing in pen or pencil tends to predominate, and the colour is applied in light transparent washes simply to tint the drawing. Watercolour painting (which is the method of painting mostly dealt with here) relies on transparent washes of colour laid over white or pale paper. Some drawing is indicated but the painting is largely colour against colour (right). Gouache (or body colour, below) is the use of opaque watercolour. Its consistency, opacity and visible texture make it different from the more traditional use of watercolours.

Materials and equipment

There are three basic essentials for painting in watercolours – paper (usually called the support), paints and brushes. However, as you will see from the descriptions below (and as a visit to a reputable art supplier will show you), there is a wide range of choice in each of these items. In this section, all the materials and equipment you are likely to come across are considered and the major differences between them discussed.

Paper

Paper is available in a large variety of sizes, weights, qualities and colours, but white or lightly toned papers are the most useful for watercolour. The best papers are hand made from pure linen rags. Mould-made papers are cheaper and quite satisfactory as long as they are made from linen or cotton rags.

Paper comes in three different finishes: Hot-pressed, Cold-pressed (or 'Not', meaning simply not Hot-pressed) and Rough. The surface of

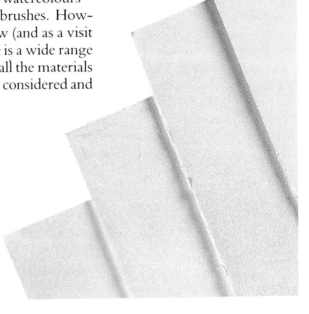

Left to right: Not, Rough, Rough and Hot-pressed.

PAPER TEXTURE

Smooth Hot-Pressed 140lb (295gsm) paper. This paper is the most delicate and sensitive, it is lovely to draw on and probably the most useful for watercolour drawing. It is, however, difficult to control large washes on it and dark colours often go patchy.

Medium Not 140lb (295gsm) paper. This surface has enough texture to produce a delicate painting but also the ability to break up the paint and give crispness in handling. This paper takes washes well and is probably the paper most often used by watercolour artists.

Hot-pressed paper is the smoothest and most absorbent, so this type of paper is less suitable for the transparent watercolour technique than either Not or Rough, both of which take a wash more easily. Not is a textured semi-rough paper which is good for large smooth washes, yet it will also take fine brush detailing. Rough paper is rough textured, and a wash will not always fill the crevices in the surface, presenting a slightly speckled effect. It lends itself to dry-brush techniques (see pages 104–5), but it is difficult to paint fine details on this type of paper. For these reasons Not and Rough are the two most favoured surfaces for watercolour painting; Hot-pressed is more suitable for, and used more often for, drawing or pen work.

Paper is graded by weight, either by pounds per ream (500 sheets) or grams per square metre (gsm). The most common weights available are 72lb (150gsm), 90lb (185gsm) and 140lb (295gsm). Generally, the larger the painting you intend to do, the heavier the paper you use should be, so 72lb (150gsm) is suitable for small paintings and

Paper sizes		
Double Elephant	686 × 1001mm	(27 × 40in.)
A1	594 × 840mm	(24 × 36in.)
A2	420 × 594mm	(18 × 24in.)
Imperial	559 × 762mm	(22 × 30in.)
½ Imperial	381 × 559mm	(22 × 15in.)
Royal	490 × 610mm	(19½ × 25in.)

sketches, 90lb (185gsm) for moderate sized works, and 140lb (295gsm) is necessary for larger works. Traditional Imperial sizes are retained in Britain and the United States for better quality hand- and mould-made papers. For other papers, including cartridge (drawing), the international 'A' sizes (see page 20) are more common.

I use 90lb (185gsm) and 140lb (295gsm) paper, usually Not surface, although occasionally for larger works I use Rough surface. I buy Imperial sheets and cut them down if necessary to the size I require. I find I usually have to stretch the paper (see page 78). This is because once you put a wash on a sheet of paper, the water will make the fibres stretch so the paper will wrinkle and become bumpy. You cannot get a smooth wash on a wavy surface. The heavier grades of paper do show less tendency to wrinkle, particularly in fairly small sizes, so if you are going to do a small painting and not get the sheet too wet, the paper will not need stretching. Certainly anything less than 140lb (295gsm) should always be stretched.

Always be careful to use the right side of the paper; the watermark if held up to the light reads correctly on the side to paint on. Stretch a larger piece of paper than you think you will need, as this will give you some room to manoeuvre over your composition. Sometimes you may want to add a bit on one side or the other to make a better arrangement.

Blocks and pads of watercolour paper are useful, particularly if you are travelling light, but wherever possible I do prefer to buy my paper in sheets and stretch it myself.

Rough 140lb (295gsm) paper. The surface is very coarse and this gives a broken effect to the paint, often making it rather 'jumping' and lively. This surface is not suitable for delicate subjects and lends itself to large paintings.

STRETCHING PAPER

Trim the paper to size. It should be at least 50mm (2in.) smaller all round than the board you intend to stretch it on to. Make sure you use stout board – not one made from thin plywood or hardboard (Masonite). Check the paper for the watermark, when it reads correctly you have the paper right side up. Cut four pieces of 40mm (1½in.) gummed paper strip, one for each side.

Sponge both sides of the paper – wrong side first – with lukewarm water. Warm water softens the size in the paper faster than cold, but don't have the water too hot or you could break down the fibres in the paper. Apply the water gently in case you damage the surface of the paper. Use a full sponge but don't over-saturate the paper. Lay out the damp paper in the correct position on the board.

Press out any air bubbles that form gently from the middle to the edge of the paper with a clean rag. Allow the paper to relax for about five minutes (for 90lb/185gsm – allow up to ten for 140lb/295gsm). Wet the lengths of gumstrip, and lay them around the edges of the paper, allowing approximately equal overlap between the paper and board. Rub the gumstrip well down.

Place drawing pins through the gumstrip and paper at each corner to ensure that the paper lies flat. Allow the paper to dry naturally in a horizontal position (this will take a few hours or overnight). The stretching will be spoiled if you use artificial heat. Once it is completely dry, the paper is ready to use.

Brushes

Brushes are the most personal tool an artist uses. For this reason, buy the best you can afford – it is better to have one or two good-quality brushes than several indifferent ones. The best watercolour brushes are, unfortunately (but not surprisingly), the most expensive. They are made from red sable hair, and are soft, springy and very well set in the ferrule. They also hold a lot of water (which makes them ideal for washes) and the hairs always go to a good point. Less expensive natural-hair brushes are made from either ox hair or camel hair. Ox hair is more springy than sable and tougher, but it does not hold so much water or produce such a fine point. Camel hair (actually usually squirrel) is relatively cheap, but it does not have the spring or life of either sable or ox hair, and the hairs often tend to come out of the ferrule. There is also a range of watercolour brushes on the market that combine synthetic fibre with a proportion of sable. These are superior to camel hair and cheaper than natural hair and can be recommended if you cannot afford pure sable.

Watercolour brushes range in size from the tiny 000 to a size 14. The size is directly related to the number of hairs in the ferrule – a No. 10, for instance, has approximately ten times as many hairs as a No. 1. To begin with, I would suggest you buy one each of Nos 2, 5, 7 and 10.

Good brushes are expensive, but will last a long time if they are properly cared for. Always wash out your brushes in clean water before you finish for the day. If the brush is stained, and clean water alone does not remove the paint, wash it gently with lukewarm water and soap but make sure the brush is well rinsed with clean water afterwards. Shape the brush naturally either between your lips, or by gently shaking the hairs to a point. Do not store brushes until they are completely dry. If a brush is in constant use, store it with its bristles upright in a jam (jelly)-jar or similar container. For longer term storage, they can be kept in a brush container or box with some mothballs.

The marks made by watercolour brushes of different sizes: (left to right) Nos 00, 2, 5, and 10.

79

Paints

The standard of paint manufacture, on the whole, is extremely high and a wide range of colours is now produced. Watercolours are made up of transparent pigments ground extremely finely and mixed with gum. Gouache or designers' colour differs from watercolour in that the colour has precipitated chalk, as well as gum, mixed with it.

Pure watercolour is available in several forms, as dry cakes, semi-moist pans, tubes and bottles of concentrated colour. Dry cakes contain pigment in its purest form; semi-moist pans and tubes usually have glycerine added to keep them moist.

Dry cakes

These are the traditional form of watercolour. The colour in these hard round cakes is pure and is still preferred by some watercolourists. These cakes need more water than pans or tubes to release the colour, and unless they are used regularly, they get very hard and need a lot of scrubbing up.

Pans and half pans

These are small blocks of semi-moist watercolour, which are designed to fit into watercolour boxes which can be purchased separately. You can, therefore, buy the colours individually, making your own selection. Whole pans are slightly more economical, but both offer a strong yield of colour that can be easily worked and diluted. They are very convenient for use out of doors.

Tubes

The colour in tubes is more loosely ground and does not dry out provided the tubes are re-sealed after use. Tubed watercolour is convenient for squeezing out large amounts and is instantly workable, it doesn't need 'scrubbing up'. For this reason, it is probably more suitable for use in the studio or on a large-scale painting. A special box or container is not necessary to hold the tubes – a plastic bag will suffice – and a white plate makes a good palette.

Tubes and pans of watercolour are available in Artists' quality or Students' quality, Students' quality generally being about one-quarter of the price of Artists' quality. All reputable paint manufacturers grade their products according to durability and permanence. Winsor and Newton, for example, classify their Artists' watercolours in four grades of permanence: Class AA Extremely durable; Class A Durable; Class B Moderately durable; and Class C Fugitive. The durability and permanence of Artists' colours should be checked against the manufacturer's colour list – do not select colours which are fugitive.

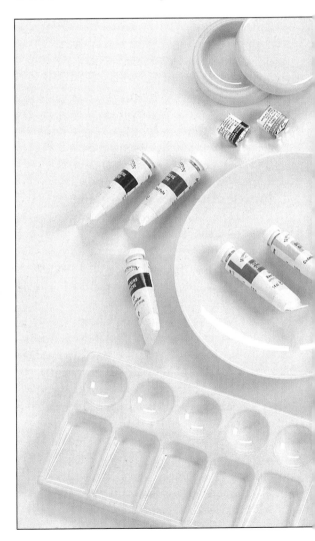

Some of the pigments used in Artists' quality paints are expensive and this is reflected in the price. However, I would recommend you buy the best available materials; in this case, Artists' quality paints. It is a mistake to think anything will do – you will only add to any problems.

Palettes and paintboxes

The watercolour box usually has white enamelled recesses for mixing colour, this is the most convenient form of carrying and using semi-moist watercolours, particularly for outdoor work.

If you are using tube colours you will need well palettes or pots. A conventional kidney-shaped palette is very useful but it must be white and have recesses for mixing colour.

If you are buying a paintbox (or having one for a gift) it is better to choose one that is not too small, say with spaces for about 12 or 14 pans. It should have large mixing pans and clips for holding the pans so that they can be changed. A box with a thumb-hole or ring is easier to hold. Also, buy the paints separately from the paintbox. In this way, you can select colours to suit you and your style of working.

A selection from the range of available watercolour equipment: paints – in pans, half pans, bottles, tubes and cakes, and palettes.

Artists' furniture

Stools

If you are working out of doors a good folding stool is very useful but make sure it is strong and reasonably comfortable. A stool which is too small or too low can mean you get terrible cramp, often just when you have reached a critical point in your watercolour. There are some good light aluminium (aluminum) stools on the market.

Folding table

If you are working at home and have to pack your gear away after use, a folding table is necessary, unless of course you are fortunate enough to have a studio. There are drawing tables (some of which are used in schools) with adjustable angled boards and drawers but the better quality ones do not fold away. An ordinary 1.25m (4ft) wooden folding table is adequate.

Easels

Although an easel is not essential, it is very useful, if for no other reason than it leaves both your hands free. It needs to be the folding type for outdoor work and must be stable and light. There is a three-legged easel on the market which has a pivoting main shaft that can be swung either vertically or horizontally. This makes it useful for standing or sitting to work. Easels are made from wood or aluminium, both of which are reasonably light and satisfactory.

Drawing boards

These really fall into two categories, the one to be used at home or in the studio and the one used for sketching and outdoor work. In the former case weight doesn't matter too much so a good solid ½ Imperial board is what is required (or full Imperial if you have room). For outdoor work it is probably best to make a drawing board out of exterior plywood, in fact make several of different sizes: 38 × 56cm (15 × 22in.), 28 × 38cm (11 × 15in.) and 38 × 45cm (15 × 18in.). You can use

An easel with a pivoting main shaft enables you to stand or sit to work so is probably the most versatile buy, though table top ones are also available.

them to stretch paper on both sides if you get the ply thick enough (otherwise it will bow under the strain of the stretched paper). Use plywood that is at least 7mm (⅜in.) thick for a board 38 × 56cm (15 × 22in.) – it can be thinner for smaller sizes.

Other useful equipment

Sponges of all sizes are useful for dampening a small area, washing off a small area of paint, or painting or creating a texture. You will also need one large one for sponging and stretching paper. Natural sponge is better than synthetic.

Soft cotton rags are useful for wiping your brushes on.

Absorbent paper tissues of any kind can be used for mopping out colour, or correcting a watercolour. It is also possible to create texture with them (see page 104).

A toothbrush is useful for splatter work. The toothbrush is dipped in paint and then a knife is drawn across the bristles; this causes fine splatter or mottling (see page 92).

Cottonwool buds (cotton swabs) are used for mopping out tiny areas of colour, and correcting.

Erasers are necessary for rubbing out pencil or charcoal marks. You will need a vinyl eraser for charcoal, and a soft eraser for pencil. An ink or typewriter eraser can also be useful for taking out small areas of colour.

Pencils are ideal for sketching in lines before painting and planning your paintings, also for making studies and notes. Initially, softer grades are the most useful.

Gummed paper is necessary when you are stretching paper (see page 78) and for sealing the back of frames.

You may find some (or all) of these items useful in your work. Apart from household items like rags, sponges and a toothbrush, you may need a bottle of masking fluid or gum arabic for a particular effect.

Blades, either single-sided razor blades or sharp craft knife blades, are useful for scraping and correcting small areas of paint (see pages 102 and 112). A sharp craft knife is a useful tool for cutting paper and mounts (mats).

Masking fluid protects areas of work when applying washes (see pages 106-7).

Masking tape is necessary in order to fasten paper to boards (although not for stretching paper) and to mask straight lines, for example, the borders of a painting.

Gum arabic is used in the manufacture of watercolour, and is useful to have in the studio for thickening paint and to create a texture.

A palette knife (metal spatula) is a useful implement for spreading paint, particularly gouache, on to paper. It can also be used for moving colour around or for putting small touches of colour into a painting.

Water containers are vital. Plastic bottles with screw tops are the simplest to get hold of, but specially made containers for watercolour painting are available on the market. These have a top which can be clipped on to your paintbox as a water pot. In the home or studio, jam-jars or plastic bowls are alternatives.

Recommended kit

The items detailed and illustrated here are ones that I consider suitable for a beginner in watercolour. All are readily available and reasonably priced, and with them you should be able to produce good-quality paintings.

Paper Either Arches mould-made Not 90 lb (185 gsm) or T.H. Saunders Waterford Not 90 lb (185 gsm). Both of these papers are ideal for a beginner since they take washes well, yet are sufficiently robust to allow you to sponge out areas you don't like. You should stretch either of these papers before you use it unless you are simply carrying out a small exercise. Both of these papers are readily available from artists' suppliers.

Paints You should have a watercolour box containing the following colours in semi-moist whole or half pans of Artists' quality colours: cadmium yellow, yellow ochre, raw sienna, raw umber, burnt umber, light red, cadmium red, viridian, cobalt blue, prussian blue, alizarin crimson, and neutral tint. Chinese white may also be useful. With these colours you can mix almost any shade for still-life or landscape painting.

Brushes Nos 2, 5, 7 and 10. The No. 10 could be either ox hair or synthetic as a sable brush this size would be very expensive.

Additional items A ½ Imperial (22 × 15in.) drawing board, either bought or home made; pencils (grades B and 2B); some sticks of vine charcoal; a soft pencil eraser and a vinyl eraser; an easel and stool; water containers – jam-jars or plastic bowls will do; a sponge; some cotton rags; and a sketching bag (to keep all your equipment in – this is more important for work outdoors).

You don't need a vast array of materials and equipment to start painting in watercolour. The main items you are likely to need to carry out the exercises and projects in this section are illustrated here.

Colour mixing

To mix a colour, first put some clean water into your palette or container, then take a clean brush, moisten it and dip just the point into your selected colour and mix this with the brush into the prepared water on the palette. To vary this colour, make sure your brush is clean, then dip it into the second colour and mix with the original wash.

Make marks on a sheet of paper of all the colours you use and mix. Write against these colour splurges the correct name of the colour you are using, and the colour you make; for example,

cobalt blue + cadmium yellow = green, or cadmium yellow + cadmium red = orange. Cover a sheet of paper with these little exercises and you will begin to learn more about how colours look when mixed with one another.

The more colours you mix together, the greater your chances of producing a muddy brown, so initially at least limit yourself to mixing two or three colours. Also, always make sure that you have plenty of clean water available, at least one container for cleaning your brush and one for use in making your colour.

Starting to paint

Watercolour painting relies on transparent washes of colour laid over a reflecting light-toned paper (unlike gouache which has white mixed with the colour and so can be painted on any coloured paper). This means that to paint successfully in watercolour you must master the basic technique of laying a wash. For any area you wish to paint which is too large for a simple brush stroke a wash is necessary.

In all successful paintings a satisfactory composition depends upon simple flat areas (washes) being played against complex areas. One only has to study a watercolour by John Sell Cotman or David Hockney to realize the importance of a flat wash. If you start by mastering this technique it will give confidence and lead you into both the fun and the mystery of watercolour painting. It is a bit like learning scales if you want to play the piano, both need a lot of practice. After you have bought the equipment suggested on page 84, take and stretch several pieces of watercolour paper – for these experiments they do not have to be very big, about 25 × 30cm/10 × 12in. should be large enough – and practise laying washes as described opposite.

You will need
☐ a drawing board with stretched paper
☐ two jars of clean water
☐ paints
☐ brushes
☐ a white plate or palette
☐ a stick of charcoal
☐ a soft pencil and eraser
☐ masking fluid
☐ razor or craft knife blades

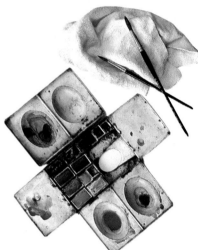

This paintbox is well designed: it has a thumbhole for ease of holding, there are four deep mixing pans, spaces for ten whole pans of paint, and it is robust, yet not too heavy.

The author in his studio, showing details of worktop and watercolour equipment. Normally, work is done on the workbench but it is useful when putting finishing touches to a painting to use an easel; it enables you to stand back from the work.

Flat washes

A flat wash is an even distribution of transparent watercolour, and laying one is the basic technique of all pure watercolour painting. There is something very seductive and beautiful about a lovely watercolour wash.

To mix the colour for the wash, first put a quantity of water into your container (for large washes separate porcelain stacking palettes/cabinet nests are very useful). The quantity will vary according to the area you wish to cover but on an average start with about a small egg cup (4 tablespoons) of water. Add the colour by moistening your brush and with the point lifting the paint from the pan. The more paint you add to the water, the more intense the colour will be but remember that the watercolour will always dry lighter than it looks when it is applied. It is easier to lay a flat wash on a Rough or Not surfaced paper and if the area you wish to cover is fairly large and simple it will help your wash if you dampen the paper first. (If you were painting around small shapes, this would not be possible.)

Use as large a brush as possible, depending upon the complexity of the area. Keep the board tilted at about a 30 degree angle and start at the top of the sheet with a well-loaded brush. Continue backwards and forwards horizontally, working left to right and right to left down your paper.

Work systematically at the speed the wash runs, so that you always pick up the band of colour that is forming at the bottom of the stroke. This means that if you are working with a very watery wash you will have to work faster than if you are using a wash with a higher proportion of colour in it.

When you arrive at the bottom of your paper you will find a surplus pool of colour gathering. Mop this up with a squeezed out brush or sponge. If you don't, you will find the colour running back on itself as it dries and spoiling the flatness of your wash. If the wash does go blotchy, let it dry completely, then with a clean sponge and water gently sponge it down.

LAYING A FLAT WASH

Mix plenty of colour, more than you think you'll need.

Lay strokes alternately left to right and right to left.

Pick up the pool of colour from the previous brush stroke.

Graduated washes

A graduated (or graded) wash is one that starts with intense saturated colour at the top, then progresses through carefully controlled tonal gradations to a colour so pale that it merges with the colour of the paper at the bottom.

Dampen the paper. Start by mixing plenty of colour, remembering that the paint will dry several shades lighter than it appears when wet. When you are satisfied with the colour, load a brush with full strength paint and lay a stroke of colour across the top of the paper, working quickly. Your board should be tilted so that a stream of wash gathers along the bottom of the band of colour. Next dip the brush into the container of clean water, and without adding more paint to the brush lay another stroke of colour under the first, making sure that you pick up the fluid paint along the base of the previous stroke. Repeat this process until you reach the bottom of the sheet of paper. The wash will gradually get weaker until it merges with the colour of the paper.

Mop up any excess paint which has accumulated at the bottom of the paper, then allow the paint to dry, leaving the board tilted at about a 30 degree angle so that the wet colour does not flow back over the dry colour.

LAYING A GRADUATED WASH

Start at the top with full strength colour.

Add increasing amounts of water as you progress.

This simple painting relies on graduated and variegated washes. The sky is a graded wash of blue and the strokes of yellow and mauve make a variegated wash at the horizon.

Variegated washes

The term variegated wash usually means two or three colours, rather than tones of a single colour, being merged together. Dampen your paper first using either a sponge or a large brush and clean water, as this will help the colours to merge. Mix your three colours in separate containers. They do not all have to be of the same consistency; you could, for example, make one more intense by using more colour and less water.

Starting at the top of the sheet of paper, paint a strip of your first colour (as if you were laying a flat wash). Quickly, while this is still wet, lay a strip of your second colour, then repeat this with your third. The edges of the colour will spread out and melt into one another. Whatever you think of the initial result, leave the wash well alone until it is completely dry. Additions or corrections can be made then.

Only experience will tell you how much colour you may need and the result will always be rather unpredictable, but practice will help. Changing the tilt of the board can also help you control the merging of the colours. If the board is kept flat, the colours will spread out into each other; as you increase the tilt of the board, the upper layers of wash will run down and melt and merge into the lower ones.

LAYING A VARIEGATED WASH

The first colour merges into the second.

The second colour will then merge into the third.

The sea is a graded wash in reverse; that is, it starts at the horizon with a pale wash, and increasing amounts of colour are added as it reaches the bottom.

Wet into wet

'Wet into wet' implies laying wet paint on a wet surface; in this way, the technique is very similar to laying variegated washes in that the second colour you add spreads and merges into the first.

Watercolour relies for its charm upon its transparency and freshness and a lot of this effect can best be achieved by a wet-into-wet technique, particularly in the early stages of painting. While the wash is still wet, areas can be lifted out with blotting paper or a squeezed out sponge or brush, and edges can also be softened. Artists usually work a stiffer, more intense colour into the wet surface of a pale colour. Try to create some of the effects in the exercises on these two pages yourself – they were all achieved by adding wet paint to wet paint. Wet into wet involves a good degree of the unknown, and hence leaves room for the happy accident – perhaps that is the gambling instinct coming out in the artist! Having said that, experimenting with these techniques will give you the familiarity with what watercolour will do to enable you to control the paint. Do not be worried by mistakes but be prepared to learn by them.

Right: A pale flat wash of prussian blue was put over the whole surface, and while this was still wet I dropped a darker blob of the same colour into the centre and allowed it to spread. I then dabbed another blob of darker thicker colour into the middle and before it could be allowed to spread too much, I lifted out some of the colour with a squeezed out brush.

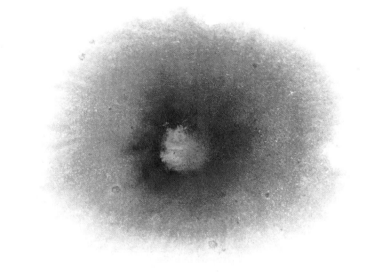

Below right: A pale wash of raw sienna was put over the whole surface, and before it was completely dry random brush strokes of prussian blue were added. Unless the surface is dried off fairly rapidly, the whole will merge together and the effect will be lost. This technique can be useful for cloud effects or foliage.

Far right: A wash of raw sienna was put over the whole surface, and before it was completely dry I applied a squiggle of drier light red very rapidly. This merged in places. This technique is unpredictable but can achieve unexpectedly interesting results.

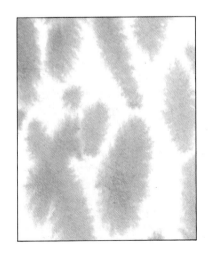
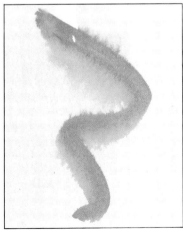

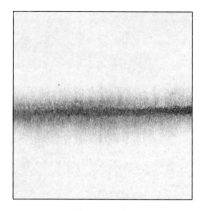

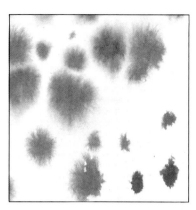

Far left: A wash of cadmium yellow was put over the whole surface, and while this was still wet, I drew a single brush stroke across the middle using a rather thick mixture of indigo. If you don't want the second colour to spread too widely, dry off the paint in front of a fire or radiator, or use a hairdryer, but keep the dryer well away from the paint surface or it will move the colour (see page 102).

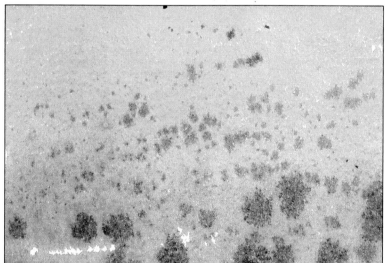

Left above: A thin wash of cadmium yellow was put over the whole surface and because the board was kept at an angle, the top started to dry first. I then touched the surface in spots with just the tip of a brush loaded with prussian blue. Where the paper was damper the spots spread wider; the ones near the bottom right hardly spread at all.

Left: This is a graduated wash of raw sienna to which increasing quantities of light red were gradually added. Before this was completely dry, prussian blue was splattered (see page 92) from the bottom upwards. The dots tend to be bigger the nearer they are to the toothbrush, and again the wash is wetter at the lower edge.

Left: This technique is not easy to control but it is used a lot by artists. A horizontal stripe of cadmium yellow was brushed into the top and while this was still wet a similar stripe of prussian blue laid next to it. The two merged together. The third colour (burnt sienna, with a little light red added) was added while the other two colours were still wet; this then also merged with the prussian blue.

Wet into dry

Working 'wet into dry' – that is, putting wet paint on a layer of paint that has dried, or on dry paper – gives you the greatest control over the application of paint. The paint can be applied direct to the white paper or over another colour. Always be sure that one colour is completely dry before putting on a second. To cover an area, apply the paint in the same way as for a wet surface wash, starting at the top and working down the paper from side to side. Make sure that you have mixed enough colour before you start.

When you work wet into dry, the paint does not run as freely as it does when you work wet into wet because of the resistance of the paper to the paint. This can be useful, however, as it gives the colour a sparkling effect which you don't get when you work wet into wet, because the colours blur. Wet-into-dry techniques should always be used for painting round intricate shapes, and for painting details.

It is sometimes useful to drag the paint across the paper using a fairly dry colour, or to paint with a quick brush stroke which will often produce a broken effect at the end of the stroke. This effect, which is very typical of the medium, is easier to achieve on a Rough or Not paper.

Splatter

Splatter relies on dots of paint of various sizes for its effect. It is fairly random since you have little control over where the spots of colour will go but it is a useful technique to master.

Dip an old toothbrush or hog hair brush into paint until it is well coated but give it a shake to get rid of surplus liquid. Hold it over the surface of your paper and gently draw a craft knife blade towards you through the bristles. This will create a spray of paint, with larger dots of colour the nearer they are to the brush. When this is completely dry, a second colour can be splattered over the first. Masking tape can be combined with the splattering to create shapes and patterns.

SPLATTERING

Build up colour gradually to avoid blots.

Stippling

This wet-into-dry technique is useful as it is easily controlled and gives a vigorous effect. Modelling of light and shade can be achieved by varying the size of the dots, how closely they are packed together and, of course, by the use of different coloured dots. It is possible to get brighter secondary colours such as green by mixing blue and yellow spots. In this way the colours mix in the spectator's eye at a certain distance to give a brighter and clearer green than one can get by mixing on the palette. This is the basic theory of the Pointillists.

A brush that has lost its point can sometimes be an ideal tool for this technique. Don't get the brush too overloaded with colour or you will find your dots are in danger of running together. Hold the brush nearly vertical and dab the colour on.

If this technique is executed with very fine dots, the painting can come to look like a photograph and in Victorian times artists used it for this very reason. But the science of colour theory as evolved by the Impressionists and Post-Impressionists has given this technique a modern application. Comparing it with splatter, you have more control both on where it goes and over the size of the dots.

I selected this subject for this exercise because it was simple and lent itself well to stippling. The dots on the near foliage and in the foreground are larger and further apart than those behind the house to create a feeling of distance, and a sense of light and shade. For this painting, I used the point of a number 4 sable-haired brush. Do not overload the brush with colour if you intend to try this technique, as the dots may run together.

Project: Painting a still life

A still life is simply an arrangement of inanimate objects. Usually these objects are brought together by the artist, but a still life could also be a collection of items from the corner of a room or on a shelf, or a completely random group of objects or plants. A still life is a good choice of subject for a beginner, since the objects are easily available and tend to be familiar, and because of this, you know their basic structures. When you are arranging a still life for a painting at this stage, don't make it too complicated or include too many colours. Instead, as I have here, select a few objects that have differing textures and whose tones contrast.

You will need
- ☐ a drawing board with stretched paper
- ☐ two jars of clean water
- ☐ paints
- ☐ brushes
- ☐ a white plate or palette
- ☐ a stick of charcoal
- ☐ a soft pencil and eraser
- ☐ a cotton rag
- ☐ a sponge

Preliminary sketches

Set out your work space and start with everything clean. You will need a table on which to lay out your materials and work. Prop your board at about a 30 degree angle to the left-hand side of your table (if you are right-handed) – this will leave space on your right for materials. Work in a good light; it is usually better to have the light source slightly from the left (again, if you are right-handed) although this, of course, is dictated to a certain extent by where you arrange your still-life group. You will need to stretch your paper beforehand (see page 78) so that it is dry by the time you want to start work. For this project, I have used a ½ Imperial sheet of Not 90lb (185gsm) watercolour paper. I would recommend at this stage that you have two stretched pieces of paper ready. You'll find you worry much less about making a mistake and therefore paint in a more relaxed way if you have the freedom to discard a sheet if something goes wrong. Arrange your materials on the right of your board so that you can easily reach your paintbox and the water.

Don't try to produce a painting exactly the same as mine, but use this as a guide to method. I chose the objects for my painting partly for their contrasting textures and tones. The smooth, polished enamel jug and plain flat background are played against the texture of the pears and orange and the movement in the leaves. In choosing and arranging your group of objects you may consider some of the following factors, but don't let these suggestions confuse or intimidate you – skill in composition will grow with experience:

1 the size of the objects – try to vary them;
2 the dominant colour – decide whether you want the finished picture to be warm or cool;
3 try to include some straight lines, and some curved or wriggling shapes;
4 try to have one object that attracts the eye first – this can be achieved by colour, size or definition.

Try several arrangements of your objects and perhaps make several small pencil sketches. These

The preliminary sketch to establish composition and tones.

The drawing is sketched in on the stretched paper.

are probably more use if the tones are scribbled in, rather than being in line only. These preliminary sketches are a great help in clarifying the picture in the artist's mind.

Once you have decided on your still-life arrangement, sketch the main lines of your composition on to your sheet of paper with a soft pencil or stick of charcoal.

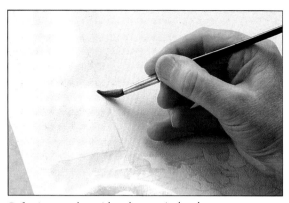

Softening an edge with a clean moist brush.

The first two washes on the painting.

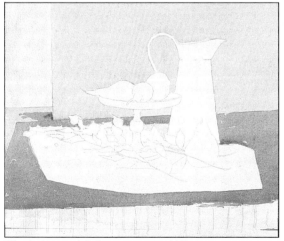

The darker wash helps to create a middle tone.

The initial washes

Once you have established the drawing, you are ready to paint. Initially, I laid a flat wash of raw sienna over the whole surface of the paper, apart from the jug, which will be the lightest area of the finished painting. An initial wash of one colour over a large area of the painting like this unifies it and will hold the later colours together. It also gives an overall warmth to the painting, which, because watercolour is a transparent medium, will come through all the later colours to the finished painting.

While the raw sienna wash was still wet, a thin wash of cadmium yellow was flooded into the upper left of the picture and on to the table top. After allowing this to dry completely, I added the warm pink/brown over the table area and the background; this was made up with a mixture of raw sienna and light red with a very little alizarin crimson added. Again this was put on as a flat wash, starting at the top and working down. Before this was dry, to avoid a hard edge between the colours in this part of the painting, I softened the edge of the upright on the left-hand side with a clean moist brush.

At this stage, there are really only two washes on the paper and, with drying time, it probably took me about 15 minutes.

Adding the darker washes

The previous washes had obscured some of the drawing so I strengthened this slightly, although still keeping the lines light – you don't want the drawing to dominate the finished painting. The single darker wash on the table top was added next. This was made up with burnt sienna and light red, and was deliberately not laid too flatly to give a feeling of surface. In any case, it would be overpainted for greater contrast at a later stage.

It is always useful to establish some of these larger washes in a painting first as they help to create a unity of colour (in this case a warm glow). The smaller details and stronger contrasts will be left until later.

Overpainting the darker portions of the fruit stand.

The cool grey shadow helps to create form and space.

The first details

The stand holding the fruit was painted next. This colour was a wash of neat burnt sienna, which was allowed to dry.. However, this left the stand without any sense of light and shade, so to create this impression I overpainted the darker portions with another wash of the same colour. I then started on the pears, initially applying a wash of viridian mixed with cadmium yellow. The quince was also painted with a wash, this time made up of a mixture of cadmium yellow and a little cadmium red. While this was still wet, a little of the green used on the pears was gently blended in. I used a wet-into-wet technique in this area to avoid any harsh contrasts. The softly blurred yellow and green here were intended eventually to contrast with, and complement, both in colour and feeling, the dark, crisply and freshly painted leaves.

At this stage, although I intended the finished painting to be warm, I felt that everything in the picture was getting *too* warm, so I added some cool grey to the upper left-hand side of the picture, deliberately leaving the wash uneven to emphasize the smooth wash of the background. I also used the same colour for the shadow of the quince. The yellow of the foreground was added next – a wash of cadmium yellow.

Applying an initial wash to the pears.

The first details have now been established.

Stippling the pears adds texture.

This completes the painting of the fruit.

The darker leaves are the last details to be painted.

Adding texture

The painting was beginning to appear but was still flat, and so now was the time to give it dimension by adding the textures. The orange was painted with a wash of cadmium yellow and a little cadmium red, which was allowed to dry. I then added more cadmium red to the colour on my palette and painted on this darker colour, leaving small islands of the paler colour showing through to create the impression of the fruit's texture. The darker colour on the pears – a mixture of viridian and raw sienna – was applied with a stipple technique, leaving some of the lighter colour showing through. At this stage too the shadow on the white jug was painted. This was a wash of indigo with a touch of raw sienna added, and while it was still wet, I softened the edge with a clean moist brush to enhance the shadow effect.

The darker details

The darker details will bring the picture to life, so they need to be painted crisply and freshly. For this reason, I have left them until last. The colour for the leaves was made with prussian blue and burnt sienna, which I painted over all the leaves and stalks. Then, to give variety and depth, I created the darker areas by putting a mixture of indigo and viridian wet into wet. I also used a dilute mixture of this colour to paint loosely over the left-hand side of the picture, since I felt that the grey I had previously painted did not bring that area of the picture alive enough.

The final touches

Finishing details are added to sharpen the image, and bring the whole painting together. The blue of the jug handle was cobalt blue and the richer brown on the table was overpainted to give that area more texture and life. The shadow of the quince was then moved. I did this by dampening it with clean water and sponging it down. Finally, I loosely laid a pale green wash in horizontal stripes to indicate the shadows of the leaves, and to help create the horizontal plane of the table.

Mounting (Matting) your work

When the painting is finished, decide where you want the mount (mat) to cut it. A mount defines the boundaries of your painting (and hides the rather untidy edges). Generally, I would suggest you use a 2-sheet white mounting card next to the watercolour with a 4-sheet off-white mounting card 6mm (¼in.) larger laid over the first one. For a painting of this size, margins of about 75mm (3in.) at the top and sides, and 90mm (3½in.) at the bottom will be about right.

Don't forget the old adage: if at first you don't succeed, try try and try again. Watercolour is not an exact medium – there will always be an element of chance about anything you paint. A painting can be going quite well and then suddenly something goes wrong – a colour runs badly, for example, or goes dirty. You can sometimes resurrect a painting in cases like this, but often I find it's best to start again. (This is why I suggest you should have two sheets of paper ready stretched.) I can assure you that all the practice you do will be worth while. As you become increasingly familiar with the medium you will gain in confidence and find that your work is improving.

The finishing details, painted crisply and freshly, bring the painting to life.

Further techniques

The kit of the artist is not confined to just paints and brushes, but blotting paper, sponges, hairdryers and many other household objects have their uses. The applications of these are not intended as tricks – they are part of the genuine vocabulary of the watercolour painter, to be used if and when they are considered necessary to strengthen an image. All painters develop their own techniques; the following demonstrations represent only a small selection of those possible.

This does not mean that you should ever try to use all these techniques in a single painting, any more than it would be advisable to use all the colours in your box on one watercolour. Perhaps you would only use one or two of these techniques in any one painting. I have tried not to include a lot of fringe materials and techniques, because they may just confuse. However do experiment, perhaps try drawing with a stick dipped in watercolour, or use washing-up (dishwashing) liquid to obtain a texture or try scratching a wet colour with the back of your brush. There is no need to use good paper, cartridge (drawing) will do, but just try as many effects as you can devise.

Some artists like using an old-fashioned shaving brush for large washes or even an airbrush. Sometimes in the excitement of making a watercolour you are tempted to try some wonderful techniques like one of these. It might come off, or it might completely ruin your work, but that I'm afraid is the nature of the beast we call watercolour! Do remember, too, that all these techniques are only of use if they help you to express your idea in a stronger way: they are of little or no use as an end in themselves.

You will need
☐ a drawing board with stretched paper
☐ two jars of clean water
☐ paints
☐ brushes
☐ a white plate or palette
☐ blotting paper
☐ natural sponges
☐ masking fluid
☐ razor or craft knife blades
☐ a hairdryer
☐ white candle wax
☐ tissue paper

This sketch (right) is made up of only flat washes and sponged texture. For the three larger trees, I laid a flat wash which I allowed to dry. I then painted some of this same colour on to a natural sponge and gently dabbed the area of the trees – this gives two tones. The darker shadows on these large trees were created by dabbing some of the colour I had mixed for the small tree into the still wet texture. I then just touched some red into this still wet paint to add highlights. The different texture on the small tree was created in exactly the same way but using a finer sponge.

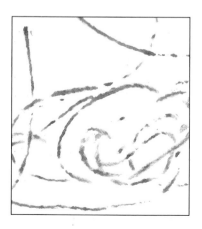 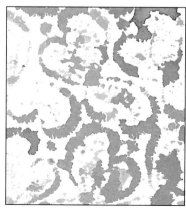

Left: Alternative patterns can be created using string (far left) and lace, pressed into paint and on to paper.

Sponging

Sponging is usually used to add texture to a painting and is a particularly useful technique for adding foliage to trees and bushes, and for creating the impression of greenery (see also pages 110–11). Sponge gives a random, exciting effect, which is not easily produced with a brush. It is a good idea to build up a collection of sponges of different sizes and different degrees of coarseness – also, I find natural sponge far better than synthetic. The area to be textured dictates the size and coarseness of the sponge to use.

For a small area, you can apply the paint to the sponge with a brush, but for larger areas prepare the wash in a saucer or deep palette and dip the sponge in lightly. If you get the sponge too wet, the texture will be almost non–existent. If the sponging is applied to a damp area of paper, it will tend to spread and you will get a softer effect; if the surface is dry, it will give a crisp and much more pronounced texture. A tone or colour can also be darkened by successive dabbing with the colour on the sponge and you can, of course, apply two colours, but again if you want the end result to be a crisp texture, allow the first to dry before applying the second.

Sometimes a wash which is too flat and uninteresting can be brought to life by sponging a light texture on to it. A touch of a dark colour dabbed with a sponge into still wet paint adds a random lively feel to an area of a painting. I achieved the highlights in the picture below by dabbing touches of red into the still wet sponging.

Drying and blowing

Blowing the paint surface while it is still wet spreads the colour, but is very difficult to control, and so is not used very often. Sometimes, you can achieve a happy accident, but I rarely use this method myself.

Lay a flat wash over the whole area, and while it is still wet use a hairdryer close to the surface to blow the paint where you want it to go. As it dries, it tends to granulate the colour, which can be very attractive. You can also blow wet paint through a drinking straw, although this again is a rather random technique.

Controlled drying, on the other hand, can be very useful. If you dry off an area rapidly, the colour doesn't have time to spread or run back on itself. You can use a hairdryer for this too, but don't put it too near the paper surface or you risk moving the paint. I use an electric fire (space-heater) with a guard. It seems to suit my technique better – it also helps me to keep warm in my garden studio! Obviously, you should only use a safe fire that is easy to handle, and be confident that you know what you are doing.

Scratching

If a wash, or succession of washes, has gone dull, or their transparency has been lost, you can bring some life back to the surface by scratching the paint off the pinnacles of the paper's surface texture using a single-sided razor blade or a sharp craft knife blade. If the edge is used, either will give an all-over textured effect; if only the point is applied, it will give a more linear quality. However, it is difficult to put a wash over an area you have scratched as the surface of the paper has been destroyed. Also, this technique is only suitable on a heavyweight paper.

It is also possible to take an area of wash back to the white paper with sandpaper. Use a fine-grained sandpaper and rub in a gentle circular motion at the area of paint you wish to remove. Don't be impatient – take the paint off gradually. Depending on the quality of the paper you use and the area of colour you have removed, the destroyed surface will take a wash, although not very well. Small areas of white, however, can be flicked out with a blade or painted on with Chinese white watercolour.

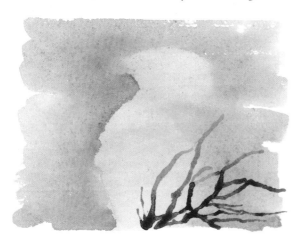

The granular effect here was achieved by blowing a wash of viridian with a hairdryer. When this was dry, I applied the dark green blobs, and then blew the wet paint through a straw. Some control over the general direction in which the paint goes is possible but this is a rather random technique.

This exercise shows how scratching can be used. Two simple flat washes were applied to the paper, and left to dry. A craft knife blade was scratched flatly over the water area to create the broken effect. The point of the blade was used to give the sharper white lines and the lighthouse.

Wax resist

When you draw with candle wax it doesn't completely cover the surface of the paper, particularly on a Rough or textured paper. Use a piece of ordinary white candle and rub it on to the parts you want to keep white. A subsequent wash cannot penetrate the wax but will lie in the crevices between, thereby giving a mottled broken effect. It is therefore unlike masking fluid, which will give you a clean, hard line (see pages 106-7). As the wax will stay on the paper you cannot change your mind and try to put a wash where the wax remains.

This technique is more suitable for larger, broader watercolours, because, although it can be controlled, it is only done so with difficulty. It is more usually used in a random or haphazard way; it does, however, produce interesting results on occasions.

Similar results can also be achieved with white wax crayons.

Above: Using wax as a resist repels a subsequent wash.

These poppies demonstrate how wax resist can be used. After sketching the design in pencil, I roughly drew in vertical lines using a piece of white candle. This acted as a wax resist and granulated the green wash which I laid over it. I then laid a light flat wash of raw sienna and cadmium red for the poppies. When this was completely dry, I again drew in a rather random way with my piece of candle to suggest the growth of the petals. This wax resist was overlaid with a wash of cadmium red mixed with a little cadmium yellow. Finally, the leaves were laid as a flat wash and parts of the flowers accentuated with darker streaks of red and purple.

Dabbing off and blotting

Apart from its use in removing colour, blotting paper is a real necessity for the watercolour artist. If you keep moistening an area of paint with water and blotting off you can almost eliminate a colour. Also, it is very useful to have a sheet of blotting paper on your work surface so that if you overcharge your brush you can lose some of the surplus by touching the blotting paper with your brush. In an emergency, such as a colour running or a drip of paint, blotting paper is indispensable.

Although you can use very absorbent tissue paper in the same way as blotting paper, it is more often used for creating texture. It gives a random effect, particularly useful in creating foliage. It is possible to use any absorbent material in this way – muslin, rags, string, or natural objects such as leaves. All of these can be either pressed into paint, placed on to the paper and rubbed on the back to create a texture, rather like using a stencil. Alternatively, place the dry material over wet paint on the paper to lift off areas of paint, thus creating a texture.

Scumbling

Although more widely used in oil painting, scumbling can also be useful to the watercolourist. Scumbling is really a dry-brush technique, used mainly for breaking one colour over another without obliterating the first. Many artists, including Eric Ravillious and Edward Bawden, have used it very successfully.

Load a brush with paint, keeping it fairly dry, and apply the pigment with a circular movement. It often helps if you pinch out the brush to splay

Blotting paper removes areas of wet paint.

HOW TO SCUMBLE

Splay out the brush hairs and comb the colour on.

Blotting with crumpled tissue creates a texture.

the hairs and virtually comb the colour on. Areas of white paper or a previous colour will show through. This effect does not work so well on a smooth-surfaced paper.

Similar effects can also be achieved by dragging the brush over the surface of the paper. For this the colour needs to be fairly dry. You can also achieve this dry-brush look by lifting the brush from the paper rapidly at the end of a stroke – the paint will leave a wispy dry-brush trail.

Lifting colour

Variations of this technique are used considerably by artists. Basically, when you have laid a wash of colour and while the paint is still wet, lift out the required area by wetting a large brush, squeezing it dry and mopping out the colour. The following are some common adaptations of this idea:

1 The edges of a wash can be softened by using a brush or sponge moistened in clean water and squeezed out to enable it to mop up surplus wet paint. This is illustrated on page 96.

2 If a wash has dried with a hard edge and it needs to be softened, wet inside the edge for about 6–12mm (¼–½in.), then, with a brush, work the paint in a circular motion until you can see the edge disappear. Blot off the water either with a squeezed-out brush or blotting paper.

3 If a colour has dried too dark and needs to be lightened, sponge over the whole surface with clean water and mop up with a squeezed-out sponge or brush. The harder you sponge, the more colour you will remove. This technique can be used over fairly large areas to lighten the colour a little overall. You will not, however, be able to get back to pure white paper because the watercolour will have left some stain.

4 Small areas and lines of paint can be lifted off with cottonwool buds (cotton swabs).

5 When the paint surface is completely dry you can lighten part or the whole of an area by using a soft eraser. However, if you rub too hard you will render the surface unusable for a further wash.

LIFTING TECHNIQUES

Use a cottonwool bud (swab) to blot small areas.

A brush can be used to mop out areas of wet paint.

A sponge is useful for lightening larger areas.

Masking fluid

Masking fluid is a liquid rubber solution which can be applied to areas of your painting where you don't want a wash to go. Its main value is that it will enable you to achieve clean crisp edges and, after it has been rubbed off, the surface can be painted over or left white. In this it differs from wax resist (see page 103). Masking fluid can be applied with an old watercolour brush, an oil hog-hair brush, a stippling brush, the edge of a piece of cardboard, a dip pen for lines and dots, or a ruling pen for long straight lines. Shake the bottle well. A word of warning: always clean your brush or pen in clean water immediately after use to remove the fluid completely.

The masking fluid can be applied to the white surface of the paper, or it can be used over an existing wash to preserve parts of that when you intend to paint another wash over the top. In both cases, the surface of the paper must be completely dry when you apply the fluid.

Right: In this instance, masking fluid was used to create a texture of tiny flowers in the foreground, and also on the frames of the greenhouse. After the masking fluid had been rubbed off, leaving white paper, watercolour was applied over some of these areas.

Left: The impact of the breaking wave in this illustration is created with masking fluid. I used masking fluid and a brush to draw in what would be the white of the breaking wave and dabbed on the white spots of the foreground. I then painted in the sky area and the water, creating the darker shadow under the wave, added wet into wet, and the foreground. When all the washes were dry, I rubbed off the masking fluid. At that stage I felt that there should be more white in the breaking wave, so I scratched a little of the colour away from the top of the wave.

USING MASKING FLUID

Paint with masking fluid those areas you wish to remain white.

When the fluid is dry, apply washes to the paper in the normal way – the unpainted surface will be protected.

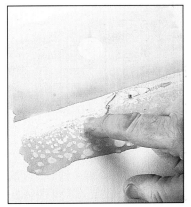

When the washes are completely dry, rub off the mask. Make sure your finger is clean!

Project: Painting a landscape

For this project, I decided to use an existing drawing that was made 'on the spot' as a basis from which to paint. The original was drawn in charcoal and pencil without any colour. This was backed up at the time with a sketch and colour notes. This

demonstration offers the chance of using many of the techniques outlined so far. Don't try to copy it exactly – it is important to select a subject that interests you and one that you feel confident enough to tackle – but try to pick a subject that will give you the opportunity to try out as many techniques as possible. Finally, don't worry if this doesn't turn out to be a masterpiece. As an artist, these are early days for you: the

> **You will need**
> ◾ a drawing board with stretched paper
> ◾ two jars of clean water
> ◾ paints
> ◾ brushes
> ◾ a white plate or palette
> ◾ a stick of charcoal
> ◾ a soft pencil and eraser
> ◾ natural sponges
> ◾ masking fluid
> ◾ razor or craft knife blades
> ◾ a toothbrush
> ◾ a ruler
> ◾ drinking straws
> ◾ a piece of cardboard

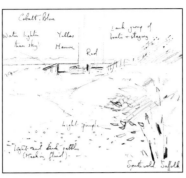

The notes on colour (above) and original 'on the spot' drawing.

important thing at this stage is that you enjoy your painting. The paper selected for this project was Arches 140lb (295gsm) and I stretched two ½ Imperial sheets as described on page 78. It is always worth having a spare sheet of paper ready stretched when you start on a project. If you do find that you want to start again, it is very annoying to have to wait several hours for a newly stretched sheet to dry naturally. The size of the painting here is 300 × 430mm (13 × 17in.) so there will be a margin inside the gumstrip.

An initial wash of raw sienna over most of the painting.

Sponging in the areas of grass.

The initial stippling on the trees.

Preliminary sketches

To start with, I lightly sketched the main lines of the composition on the stretched paper in charcoal; this enabled me to correct the drawing or composition easily with an eraser. After I was satisfied, I dusted off the charcoal with a rag, then established the drawing more carefully in pencil. Treat the paper with care – don't draw too heavily or rub out too vigorously and use a fairly soft pencil, such as a 2B.

The first washes

I then laid a flat wash of raw sienna over the whole composition, except for the sky and the water. This was done to help unify the subsequent colours and to give an overall warm glow to the painting. If there are a few islands of white left, however, it will give more variety to the colours you use in overpainting.

Don't be fussy about the painting's edges; run the colour beyond the limit of your composition – the mount (mat) will cover this anyway.

The sky area was put in next. I first sponged over it with clean water, then prepared the three washes on separate palettes. I started at the top with a wash of cobalt blue. This was allowed to run down for about half the sky area, then, while this was still wet, one horizontal brush stroke of cadmium yellow was flooded into it and allowed to run down. While this was still wet the mauve colour was put in with two horizontal strokes. This produces the variegated wet-into-wet wash. I mopped up the excess wash that had accumulated at the bottom with a squeezed-out brush, then allowed this to dry.

The broad details

The grass was a mixture of viridian and cadmium yellow, applied with a large size sponge. Painting leaves or grass in detail is tedious. An open-textured sponge creates a texture which parallels that of grass and leaves more easily. I gave some areas a second dab of colour after the first was dry for added depth. When all this was dry, I put a few

The range of tones from light to dark is established at this early stage.

strokes of paint on to the staging. I then started to stipple in the trees with a mixture of prussian blue and raw sienna. This helped me to establish the range of tones, from light to dark, at a fairly early stage of the painting.

Adding texture

I used masking fluid on the path, and applied it with a brush in blobs. After allowing it to dry, I put a wash of indigo and alizarin crimson over the path area with some raw sienna run into the foreground. When all this was dry, the masking fluid was rubbed off. The texture resembling stones was created by putting a few darker blobs of colour over the top of this whole area.

I used masking fluid on the path.

Maintaining unity

Normally in a painting it helps to keep the unity if you work over the whole surface and don't finish off one part at a time. For this reason, I added more interest to the foreground by applying some splatter and scratching areas away. I then intensified the stippling on the trees to make it darker, and added more colour and texture to the grass. I also did some more work on the staging, including painting an area of cadmium red on one of the boats. This ensured that the staging area did not fall behind the rest of the painting. The distance was added in grey and some brush strokes of pale cobalt blue in the water.

Scratching here is used to create a flat plane.

The darker details

At this stage, I did some preliminary work on the masts. I painted the edge of a piece of cardboard and used this as a template for them.

   Although my original 'on-the-spot' drawing did not have the bush in the foreground I decided to add it to the painting. I find it often helps to have something fairly large and dark in the foreground to make the distance lie back. The bush was made by mixing a dark wash of burnt umber, putting a few wet blobs at the bottom edge, then blowing it with a drinking straw; the leaves are the natural shape of brush strokes applied very freshly and allowed to dry.

The principal areas of texture completed.

Unifying the composition

Towards the completion of a painting, it is helpful to stand back and assess what needs to be done additionally to unify the composition. At this stage, I was able to see what the final effect of the painting was going to be, and decide how I should finish it.

   I decided that the focal point of the staging and the boats still needed quite a lot of attention. The focal point of a painting is often finished to a higher degree than the rest of the composition but it is difficult to ascertain exactly what needs to be done until the rest of the painting is finished. The staging needed to be painted crisply since to a

Preliminary work on the masts.

Blowing through a straw to indicate branches.

certain extent the success or failure of the finished watercolour depended on it.

The contrast of the dark staging and the feeling of light, particularly on the water, is one of the major factors in the success of the painting and one of my main reasons for selecting this subject. I enhanced the feeling of light by increasing the contrast between the banks and the water, and between the water and the masts and rigging of the boats. I painted these details with a fine brush to ensure that they had the crispness and freshness that I wanted to achieve. To finish off, I added a few darker touches here and there to give sparkle.

The darker touches, painted last, add contrast and sparkle to the painting.

Subjects for the watercolourist

Almost any subject is suitable for making a watercolour – the success of a painting depends on your vision as an artist and your ability to express your feelings. It is through these feelings, expressed in a visual form, that you can help others to see and appreciate the world about them in a new way.

Painting familiar things like your garden or the view from your window, even your pet (top), has many advantages.

Flower studies make interesting paintings.

Choosing your subject

It is important in selecting your subject to see things freshly and in terms of painting – that is, in terms of tones, colours, textures and lines, rather than objectively or figuratively.

There is no need to go miles from home in order to find a subject to paint; in fact, you will probably produce a more successful painting if the subject is something you know intimately, in your own home or garden, or an area of the countryside you know well and love. Until you have had more experience, it is not advisable to try to paint the figure, particularly nude, in watercolour. Flesh tones are more difficult to achieve in watercolour than, say, in oils. There is the added problem of trying to paint a subject that moves about, and you will have enough problems without worrying about a model who will not stay still. This also applies if you'd like to paint your pets – choose a time when they are asleep!

It is not always possible to sit down with your watercolour kit and paint just when you feel like it, but if you carry a sketchbook around with you you can always make a note of something that interests you. This is also a good way of improving your drawing. Buy a sketchbook that will fit into your pocket or bag and whenever you have a spare moment draw whatever you can see – a pair of shoes, a line of washing, the kitchen sink, the breakfast table, an apple, and so on. Drawing is fundamental to art and it needs to be practised constantly. It does need discipline, however, to enable you to develop the necessary hand-eye co-ordination.

While you are still familiarizing yourself with the medium, don't always work on the same size paper – if you are close to what you intend to paint, try working on a larger scale. Whatever your subject and size of painting, you will need something in the composition that you can use to measure scale; in a still life it could be a particular pot, it may be a tree in a landscape, or just the length of a particular line. This then becomes your module and everything is related to it in scale.

When you are selecting objects to paint, don't worry too much about arranging them: a good painting can be made from a completely haphazard group of items or indeed from something in itself quite insignificant.

Portraits, full or head and shoulders, though difficult, are worth trying.

The choice of subject for still lifes is endless – items in themselves insignificant can make interesting compositions.

Finally, although being an artist is fascinating, fulfilling and rewarding, remember that you will always be learning. The more you know, the less you seem to know. But, like anything worth while, you must work at it to reap the rewards. You cannot, therefore, learn to paint simply by reading about it. You must produce lots of paintings to become familiar with what you can (and can't) do. If you develop a love of the medium, and a desire to paint, all the effort and possible disappointments will seem unimportant.

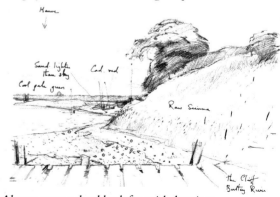

Always carry a sketchbook for quick drawings.

Approaches to watercolour

The paintings on these pages are a selection of historical and contemporary works by artists in watercolour. They show different treatments and different subjects and emphasize that there is no one way to approach a subject – there are as many ways as there are artists. Similarly, there is no one way to use watercolour paint. Andrew Wyeth, Hans Schwarz, Olwen Jones and I use watercolour transparently (this is known as the 'English' method), but Samuel Palmer and Christa Gaa in their works have used gouache (or body colour) – which is not transparent – mixed with the transparent watercolour.

I hope that these examples will demonstrate that watercolour is by no means a precious isolated medium, it is another way of expressing yourself. Most artists are not solely watercolourists or oil painters or draughtsmen they use whichever medium they feel best expresses their ideas at any particular time.

Samuel Palmer 'In a Shoreham Garden' 275 × 218mm (11 × 8¼in.). This example shows how the combination of transparent watercolour with gouache and pen lends itself to a decorative and textural approach. The gouache is used most thickly in the lighter areas.

Christa Gaa 'Still Life with Nepalese Bird' 192 × 216mm (8 × 9in.). This watercolour looks deceptively simple, but the quality of light, composition and colour are carefully considered. The combination of watercolour and gouache expresses the feeling of intense overhead light and atmosphere. The losing and finding of the tones and edge qualities also contribute to making this a very lovely painting.

Andrew Wyeth 'Southern Comfort'
563 × 750mm (21¾ × 30in.).
This watercolour was painted in
1987 and is typical of the work of
Andrew Wyeth. Obviously, the
painting has a strong illustrational
content yet it is so much more. The
very strong composition and limited
use of colour, and the artist's
understanding and care over edge
qualities, give this painting a great
sense of poetry. The texture of the
paint surface, the transparent use of
watercolour and the use of dry
brushwork typify his work.

Hans Schwarz 'Kitchen Jars and
Bottles on a White Table' 500 ×
675mm (20 × 27in.). 'I have only
a white piece of paper and a few
tubes of watercolour to represent this
complex arrangement of jars and
bottles. Faithful representation is
less important to me than a rich
colour pattern and a lively flow of
paint. Green becomes the
predominant colour. From the left
background it threads its way to the
jars on the right. Red, blue, orange,
violet and yellow interrupt the
green, bringing forward and
defining the objects in space.
Juxtaposed complementary colours
– red and green, violet and yellow,
give recession and sparkle.'

Olwen Jones 'Winter Geraniums' 600 × 475mm (24 × 19in.). 'This watercolour was painted with an afternoon light in my greenhouse. It depicts geranium cuttings overwintering, looking rather sad among the netting used for diffusing light and several odd panes of glass. The light and reflections from the panes were what first attracted me to the subject. The whole composition had a transparent quality with plenty of texture, which I always use a lot in my paintings. I also liked the contrast between the soft shapes of the geraniums and foliage, and the sharp hard edges of the glass. Reflections, whether in glass or a mirror, give an added dimension to a composition; you are never quite sure whether an image is real or reflected. In this painting I used only transparent watercolour and some masking fluid.'

Charles Bartlett 'Lakeside' 437 × 575mm (17½ × 23in.). 'This watercolour was painted in the studio from drawings and notes made on the spot. By working in this way I am able to consider and organize my composition. The feeling I got for the subject was the poetry of place, of tranquillity and stillness and a soft feeling of light on the reeds and in the water. It is not essential in watercolour to use a broken "washy" technique always. The dark silhouette of the distant trees accentuated the light shining on the feathery heads of the reeds. I used masking fluid fairly extensively on the reeds.'

Project: Still life

Art is about expressing oneself and not just copying what happens to be in front of you; it is about ideas and feelings. Above all, it is to be enjoyed. Once you have mastered the basic techniques of watercolour painting, expressing emotion through creating a feeling of light, freshness, sparkle and texture, for example, becomes more important than an accurate representation of what you see in front of you. This is what I try to achieve in my painting. This project interested me for a number of reasons. Probably the most important is the quality of light – I painted against the light on a windowsill in my studio – but I was also attracted by the colour and variety of textures, the light showing through the lace curtains and the stripes on the cloth, which also introduce perspective (the vanishing point is the centre of vision). The purple stripes are a complementary colour to the green of the landscape and apples. This subject also demonstrates the importance of choosing an appropriate eye-level. I selected a high eye-level so that I would be looking down on the striped cloth and into the basket, and also enough of the landscape over the windowsill to give a different dimension to the picture. This watercolour is painted on T.H. Saunders 140lb (295gsm) paper which I had stretched, and the image size is 380 × 310mm (16 × 13in.).

> **You will need**
> - ☐ a drawing board with stretched paper
> - ☐ two jars of clean water
> - ☐ paints
> - ☐ brushes
> - ☐ a white plate or palette
> - ☐ a sponge
> - ☐ a toothbrush
> - ☐ a knife
> - ☐ masking tape

Initial stages

The composition of this watercolour was decided after I had made several preliminary sketches. The drawing was first laid in with charcoal which was then dusted down, and the image was drawn in in pencil. Although the drawing is fairly accurate, I didn't want to labour it as I intended to keep the watercolour free. If you are over-careful with the drawing there is a tendency to fill in the shapes with paint in local areas, and this can produce a very stilted picture.

The sky was painted wet into wet, starting with cobalt blue, grading to pale raw sienna and then purple. The green (a mix of cadmium yellow and cobalt blue) was laid in as a flat wash. Raw sienna was loosely painted on parts of the basket and the foreground, and while this was still wet burnt sienna was flooded into the foreground.

The palest washes were put in first.

The trees were added over the flat wash of the landscape, then a paler wash of thin light prussian blue and a little burnt sienna was carried over the lace curtains and blotted off with blotting paper. The frames of the windows were added after the landscape was dry. I used burnt sienna, indigo and crimson lake for this wash. The apple and the shadow from the vase and plate were also indicated at this stage.

First details

I decided to finish the flowers and vase completely at this stage. Normally I like to keep the whole painting going but flowers move and die, so although the drawing of the flowers was fairly detailed, I painted them broadly to try to keep the feeling of light. The colours I used on the flowers were cadmium yellow, burnt sienna and purple (mixed from prussian blue and alizarin crimson). The cut glass vase was painted using cadmium yellow and cobalt blue, keeping the edges and contrasts sharp. I then lightly indicated the plate and knife.

Creating the flat planes

At this stage, I was anxious to establish the flat plane of the table and create a feeling of space. I felt that the stripes on the tablecloth would achieve this so I decided to tackle them next. Once they were done, I could see that they had achieved the perspective and plane of the table top.

The painting was now beginning to take shape and it was easier to appreciate what was needed next. I decided I could not delay work on the curtain and basket as these would establish if the painting was going to be successful or not.

The background completed.

The flowers nearly completed.

Painting the purple striped tablecloth.

The tablecloth establishes the plane of the table top.

Adding warmth

The pattern on the lace curtain was painted using masking fluid. I tried to consider the counter-change brought about by the holes in the lace being seen against the sky and landscape. I put a warm pale wash over the curtain (once the masking fluid was dry), and when the wash was dry, rubbed off the mask. I now felt that the purple stripes made the table top too cold so I added some broken raw sienna to the lace mat.

Creating light

To help establish the overall feeling of light in the painting the dark note of the basket was added next; this was important as it balanced the composition. I painted it in warm dark tones (burnt umber and burnt sienna) to help bring it forward from the landscape and background.

The curtain was painted with a wash of raw sienna.

The basket is the darkest note of the painting.

The basket's shadow makes it 'sit down' on the table.

Covering the final areas of white paper.

As I was painting against the light, the basket cast a deep shadow and I put this in next as it helped to make the basket 'sit down' on the plane of the table.

Covering the paper surface

In any painting before you can really begin to see the final result it is necessary to get all the white paper covered. The fruit in the basket was the last unpainted area and so I tackled this next. I was careful to retain a light top edge to the basket since it would help to convey a feeling of light. The shadow from the window frame falling on the cloth was put in with a simple wash of cobalt blue – blue is a colour that will lie back in a painting.

The finishing touches

At this stage, the painting was nearly finished; the surface was all covered and I felt the unity of the composition was coming together. I could now see what was needed to finish the painting – the curtain was not dark enough, the flowers and vase needed some strengthening, the foreground wasn't dark enough, and the lace table mat required work. These final touches are vital in any composition, they often bring the painting to life. At this stage, you may want to link the dark areas together, or to emphasize a particular movement.

The lace on the table mat was suggested rather delicately so as not to lose the overall feeling of whiteness and so I used a very fine brush. The outline shape was created by the dark stripes of the cloth; I felt it would be more satisfactory painted in this way as in this kind of painting outlining the shapes themselves may flatten the composition. Also I did not want to lose the feeling of light and the delicacy of the painting – where the far edge of the plate melts into the lace mat, for example.

The darker details

It now seemed to me that the landscape and background were too light for the weight of colour in the foreground. I decided to darken the curtain and also fill in the light hole behind the basket. Having done that, I felt that the flowers didn't seem to take their correct place in space because they were so pale, and so I darkened under their front edges. This pulled them forward, and linked the dark of the basket to the dark horizontal frame of the window. I did some scratching on the curtain and on the tablecloth to give small flecks of white which you often get when you are looking into strong light. This also helped the basket's shadow 'lie down'. Finally, I painted the foreground vigorously in a dark warm colour to pull the table edge forward.

When you finish a painting and stand back to look at it, you will probably always feel that some parts are more successful than others. Do try to restrain yourself from starting to niggle at these areas – this is the easiest way to destroy the feeling of freshness and light you have achieved.

The lace is suggested delicately.

The flowers needed darkening at this stage.

The painting is nearly finished at this stage.

The warm foreground pulls the table edge forward.

PART THREE

Starting in Oils

Introduction

Oil painting is one of the oldest and most widely used methods of painting, and because of the number of examples reproduced in books and on display in public art galleries, it has become the most familiar way of painting to us. This is probably one of the initial reasons why many people who wish to take up painting choose to work in oils. However once this decision has been made, one quickly realizes that there are many good reasons why the medium has survived for so long – oil has been widely used since the fifteenth century – and retained its popularity in the face of such modern alternatives as acrylics and resin-based paints.

'Frosted Grass' 500 × 600mm (20 × 24in.). This picture shows how the palette knife can be used as an expressive way of making marks which relate to the subject matter, in this case frosty grass. By using the edge of the knife I was able to give that sharp, crisp quality needed to convey the feeling and surface texture of frost on the rather linear shapes of the grass.

Oil paint is pigment that has been ground in an oil-based medium, usually 'linseed'. The actual pigment is often the same one that is used in watercolour or gouache (body colour or poster paint); it is the preparation that gives it certain unique qualities not present in other paints. Firstly, it tends to impart a richer feeling to the colour. It also makes it a very flexible medium, allowing it to be used in a variety of ways ranging from very thick (called 'impasto') to thin paint which is almost the consistency of watercolour. This also means that the application of oil paint has endless possibilities. It can be applied in almost any way one wishes – by brush, knives, rags and even fingers. There are also notable examples of the paint having been thrown on to the surface.

Although the beginner may feel somewhat intimidated by the long history of oil painting and the high degree of technical craftsmanship of most of the more familiar pictures, due to its flexibility oil paint is, in fact, an ideal medium for the beginner.

J.M.W. Turner 'Norham Castle'
908 × 1219mm (33¾ × 48in.).
This beautiful example of painting shows thin transparent paint throughout the whole picture. It has the quality of watercolour which gives the light translucence to the subject. The few impasto areas of paint are reserved for accents of light, catching clouds or water and act as a complement to the thin paint, and give a sparkle within the hazy sunlit atmosphere.

Martin Baldwin 'Portrait of a French Girl' 860 × 610mm (33 × 24in.). In this portrait the artist's careful build up using thin paint on a precise drawing base allows him to explore in detail the smaller forms of the head and drapery. Once the large areas had been broadly laid in, the artist used smaller and finer brushes such as sables for the fine detail. It is a painting which shows that the artist derives obvious pleasure in the pursuit of close observation and carefully modelled forms. Although this example is a portrait, the same approach can be used in any form of painting such as landscape, still life, or even abstract work.

One advantage that it has over most other paints is its drying time, which is considerably longer than water- or acrylic-based paints. This means that one can put the paint on to the canvas, then scrape it off, and work and rework areas of the painting over a much longer period of time.

Oil painting can have a certain air of mystery about it when you come to it as a total beginner, even though you may have worked with other mediums. There is no real reason why this should be so. By applying a practical and logical step-by-step approach to the subject, I will show that anyone who is interested enough to want to try can develop the skills and techniques through which to enhance their natural creativity and enjoy the fresh experience that can be gained by working with oil paints.

The great age of oil painting from which many of the most familiar examples date is probably the Renaissance, although there are also notable Impressionist and Modern paintings. This goes some way to supporting the idea that if the rules are adhered to, the other great quality that oil paint possesses is durability. There are many paintings now hundreds of years old that still retain the freshness of a new work. Sadly there are also many that are in a bad state of decay and preservation due either to neglect or to bad craftsmanship and materials.

There are some good examples of the use of oil techniques set out in these pages, but the most inspirational experience to be had is to go out and look at the real thing. They do not necessarily have to be works by great masters, and while looking at paintings in books can and does whet the appetite, this cannot be compared with the direct experience. No matter how good the reproduction is, you can never really experience fully the textural aspects of the brush or knife marks or the translucent qualities of the paint. By looking at paintings in galleries or museums and seeing and trying to understand how the artist actually executed them, not only will you give yourself hours of enjoyment, but you will also learn a great deal about oil-painting technique.

'Sleeping Dog' 900 × 1200mm (36 × 48in.). This painting gives a feeling of the gestural quality that painting can have. The large format allows the artist to make broad bold marks with large brushes. It is a painting which combines many aspects of applying paint; some has been painted wet into wet, while other areas have brush marks dragged across thick dry paint. The paint has been built up in this way throughout and gives the picture a richness of surface and colour.

Materials and equipment

The wide range of materials available to the oil painter, most of which are manufactured to a high standard, can be a source of difficulty and confusion for the beginner: where to start? what to choose? how much to spend? In this section, the various materials available and how to use them is outlined and clarified. This will enable you to make choices based on your knowledge of the products and, as you become more experienced, your own personal needs.

Oil colours: (clockwise from bottom left) flake white, cobalt blue, cadmium yellow, cadmium red, viridian, burnt sienna, raw umber, alizarin crimson, burnt umber – all Artists' colours; yellow ochre, terre verte and raw sienna – Students' colours.

Oil paints

Oil paints are produced in two qualities – Artists' colour and Students' colour. Artists' colour is very much more expensive, due to the origin of the pigments themselves: the very best are used in Artists' colours. You will also notice that there is a price variation within the range of colour; this is because of the rarity of some of the pigments, which affects the cost of manufacture. The texture of the paint is also generally smoother, although this is hardly noticeable to the beginner and does not significantly affect the look of the painting.

Tubes of Artists' colour usually have a coding denoting the price range of the particular colour.

Students' colour is manufactured using synthetic dyes and inexpensive pigments as substitutes for the rarer more expensive ones. The texture of these paints is also coarser as the pigments are not as finely ground. Although the Students' range is much cheaper than the Artists' range, there are some colours which are not normally available in it (such as the cadmium colours, cobalt blue and green, and vermilion) because of costs. If you compare Artists' colours with the Students' range you will notice a marked difference in strength and brightness, particularly when mixed with white; Artists' colour will need less to maintain the density of colour.

When you start painting, you will notice that certain colours take longer to dry than others: earth colours dry fairly quickly, while some reds

can take three or four days. The earth colours are: yellow ochre, red ochre, raw umber, burnt umber, terre verte, raw sienna and burnt sienna.

With the exception of white (which can be purchased in a large tube), tubes of colour are produced in two sizes. The 37ml (1¼oz./No. 14) size is the most practical for the majority of colours, but because one tends to use far more white than any other colour it is advisable to buy white in the larger (56ml/2oz./No. 20) size. Students' quality paints are also available in 200ml (8oz.) size tins, which unless used fairly quickly will skin over and dry out. They also tend to contain more oil than the tube equivalent.

Having described the basic differences between the two qualities of paint, I think that for the beginner Students' colours are perfectly adequate (to start with). The last thing you want is to feel inhibited by the cost and wastage of your materials, and, at this stage, the difference in results will not be noticeable. However as you progress and gain confidence you can increase your range by adding Artists' colours, as the two types of paint mix perfectly well together. This will also help to keep your initial costs down.

Paintboxes

There are many pre-selected paintboxes on the market. Some of the more expensive ones are beautifully made and can be rather seductive to the beginner. Their big disadvantage, however, is that the selection of colours has been put together by someone else. I think it is important for beginners to make their own selection based on their personal needs and development, and at a realistic cost. Eventually most artists need a container of some sort for all their painting paraphernalia, especially if they paint out of doors. When that time comes the decision will be one of personal preference. You may choose to buy a purpose-made paintbox and supply the materials yourself, or find a convenient-sized plastic or wooden box, or a stout canvas bag to hold all your equipment.

Brushes

There are several types and qualities of brush on the market for the painter to choose from. The most popular brushes for oil painting are bristle made from bleached hog's-hair, and soft brushes made from sable hair. Hog's-hair bristle brushes are fairly stiff, hold the paint well and are manufactured in three different shapes:

Flat brushes have a square-ended shape that is good for applying dabs of colour. If you use the edge, it will give a nice sharp linear mark, useful for drawing.

Round brushes in the larger sizes are good for covering large areas; smaller ones are ideal for initial drawing in.

Filberts are a cross between a flat and a round, except that the shape tapers to a point.

Sable brushes are usually used for detailed work or for thin fine glazes, and they are also ideal for the first drawing in. Some artists prefer to execute a whole painting with this type of brush. These brushes are extremely expensive and unless looked after carefully, they will deteriorate in a

very short time. These brushes are not really suited to a rough surface or ground, and will soon show signs of wear if used on one – the hairs tend to become brittle and break off and the brush soon loses its shape.

Synthetic bristle and hair brushes, usually made from nylon, are now also available. They come in the same shapes as the hog's-hair and sable types but are considerably cheaper and for the most part, are very good and hard-wearing. When choosing your brushes it is very much a personal preference, rather in the way that you build up your range of colours. Some artists will use a great many brushes, others will paint with just a few. As a beginner you really need to try various shapes and sizes to enable you to decide what suits your way of working. You may even find that you prefer the synthetic fibre brushes to the more traditional bristle.

The size of the brush is indicated by a number on the handle; the same size numbers do not apply to both hog's-hair and sable brushes, however, so a No. 1 bristle will not be the same actual size as No. 1 in a sable.

Whereas with paints, you can get away with mixing Students' and Artists' colours, I think that brushes should always be of the best quality from the start. If looked after properly they will last for years and keep their shape.

Brush care

Caring for your brush is of the utmost importance, not only to your pocket but to the quality of your painting. Brushes should be thoroughly cleaned at the end of each day's painting. Wipe the excess oil paint off with a rag or tissue and then rinse with turpentine (white spirit/paint thinner will do for this) until you feel that it is as clean as you can get it. Finally, wash with soap and water by rubbing the brush on to an ordinary household bar of soap and then working up a lather in the palm of your hand. Repeat until the soap suds show no sign of colour and then rinse with warm water. If you shape the brush while it is still wet, when it dries you will find it has kept its shape.

Palette knives

Palette knives have two main functions: applying the paint to the picture surface and scraping it off. It is possible to paint either a part or the whole of the picture with a knife if you desire a rich, textured surface. It is essential for scraping areas of paint from the picture surface to enable them to be reworked if necessary. Its use also extends to mixing colour and cleaning the palette. A wide range of shapes and sizes is available, the choice you make is again (rather like your brushes) a matter of preference. However, you certainly would not need more than one to start with. The most practical type for the beginner is the trowel shape or painting knife, recognizable by its cranked handle and more flexible blade.

Brushes: (left to right) hog's-hair flats, rounds and filberts of varying widths, large sable wash brush, sable flats and rounds of different sizes.

Right: Palette knives are available in various sizes and shapes – a trowel shape is probably the most practical for a beginner.

Palettes

The first thing to remember about a palette is that it is only the surface on which you set out and mix your paints. There is a wide variety of shapes and sizes available to the artist: you will need to decide at the outset whether you wish to hold the palette or rest it on the table or on some other convenient flat surface.

Most palettes are made to be held, and have a hole for the thumb. They come in two main shapes: kidney shape, sometimes called a studio palette, and rectangular shape. Rectangular ones are usually smaller and will fit into a paintbox. More expensive ones are usually made from mahogany but there are many made from other woods, from plastic or even from paper.

It is not essential to have either of the traditional shapes as long as you have a clean smooth surface. As you will find for most of your basic materials, there are cheap alternatives: a piece of hardboard (Masonite), plywood or perspex (plastic) will suit just as well as long as you seal the surface. The traditional way of doing this is to rub linseed oil into the wood and repeat the process over two or three days. This will prevent the surface soaking up the oil from the paint. However, a quicker way to seal the surface is to use shellac or button polish, either of which can be painted on, or rubbed in. Paper palettes are very practical when you are in a hurry; by simply tearing off the top layer of paper and disposing of it, you are left with a clean white surface for next time.

Diluents

As well as being used to clean your palette and brushes, the function of diluents is to thin or dilute the paint and help it spread over the painting surface.

It is essential that the solvent used should evaporate from the paint as it dries. Turpentine is the best solvent and there are two types: distilled turpentine (the more expensive) is pure turpentine made from pine resin and gives off a strong and distinctive although not unpleasant smell; turpentine substitute (or white spirit) is made from petroleum oils. Both can be used safely to thin paint but pure turpentine is best for painting, and white spirit is best kept for cleaning purposes.

It is worth pointing out that both sorts of turpentine have a strong smell and that some people are either allergic to turpentine products or just cannot stand the smell. To overcome this, manufacturers Pelican introduced Master Colour, a paint which has all the properties of oil paint, but it is soluble in water and is completely odourless. At present, the colour range is rather more limited than the traditional oil paints.

Mediums

The subject of mediums is a complex one for beginners. To start with, quite a number are produced. Some are very traditional mediums and binders of oil and varnishes of varying recipes, others are more modern acrylics and resins, produced by various manufacturers. Like diluents, mediums can be used to thin the paint, but they are also used to modify the paint in some way – perhaps to improve its consistency for impasto painting or to increase its drying time. Linseed oil has been the most popular medium through the ages, but other oils such as poppy are also used. However, I feel that the standard of paint manufacture today is of such a high level and consistency that unless you need a specific quality – a very glossy paint, for example, or an absence of brush marks – as a beginner, you need not concern yourself with the problem of what to use at this point. Later you can experiment with different kinds – nearly all the bottles have labels which explain the different attributes of the particular mediums. For example, pure linseed oil slows drying, and increases the gloss of the paint; poppy oil gives the paint a creamy consistency, good for *alla prima* – the method of oil painting used for the projects in this section; Wingel is good for glazing and thicker paint; and Liquin is good for glazing, gives gloss and increases the drying time.

A dipper (palette cup) is simply a receptacle for the painting medium and cleaning agent. They are usually made of metal, can be clipped on to the palette, and are especially useful if you are painting outdoors. For cleaning brushes, have a jar or old tin for the cleaning agent.

Easels

There are several types of easel available to the artist: the main point to remember is that the purpose of the easel is to provide a firm and stable support to your picture while you are working, so make sure that you pick the right one for the job. The most versatile is the radial or studio easel, which are manufactured by most of the well-known art suppliers. All are made to a similar pattern, and although fairly expensive will last a lifetime. They will support your smallest picture to a work about 1.75m (6ft) high comfortably.

A light sketching easel is ideal for outside work. These are folding and can be easily carried, but obviously the size of picture they can support is limited. Sketching easels are made in either wood or metal: the metal ones are lighter but slightly more expensive.

The table easel is a useful way of supporting a painting, especially if you are working in an area with limited floor space.

In the absence of an easel it is possible to use the back of an old chair as a support for a small painting.

You may find some or all of these items useful in your work. An easel provides a firm support for your paintings, and a palette and dippers of some kind are necessary. You will also need a diluent although you will probably not need to worry about mediums at this stage.

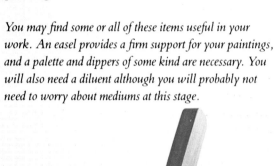

Painting supports

The painting support is the surface on to which
you apply your paint. For oil painting, this has to
be a non-porous surface and have sufficient tooth
to hold the paint. To achieve this the surface of
most supports has to be sealed. The most
traditional material for painting is canvas which
has been in use as a support since the fifteenth
century. As well as its pleasing natural qualities of
weave and texture, it has the advantage of being
light and easy to carry. There are several different
textures or weights of canvas available and what
you decide on really does depend on the way you

Oil painting supports: (from left) smooth cartridge paper,
rough cartridge paper, canvas board, Daler board,
unprimed canvas, primed canvas, ready stretched canvas,
strengthened hardboard and muslin.

prefer to work. If you paint thinly and with a great deal of detail, then you will find that a smooth-grain canvas will suit you best. On the other hand, a heavier coarse grain will be better for the thicker impasto way of working. All art suppliers sell ready prepared canvases in a variety of shapes and sizes but you will find that they are expensive. A much cheaper way of working with canvas is to buy the canvas by the metre or yard and stretch and prepare it yourself. Stretching the canvas is not difficult. The wooden stretcher pieces you will need are available either at the art suppliers or canvas stockists.

When you buy your canvas you will find that you have a wide choice. The best quality and therefore most expensive is linen canvas, easily recognizable by its darker brown colour. A cheaper version is cotton canvas which is also available in various textures and weights and is generally the most popular. You will notice that it is also much whiter than linen canvas.

Priming a canvas

Having stretched it, you are ready to prime the canvas. The purpose of priming is to separate the painting from the canvas – if the paint is applied to the raw canvas it will soak into the fibres of the material and eventually rot them. It will also have an effect on the look of the painting: paint used in this way has a dull, rather dry look. There are many examples of modern paintings which have been carried out in this way because this quality has been deliberately looked for, and the artist has stained the raw canvas. This will no doubt pose some interesting problems for future picture restorers and conservationists.

Sealing the surface is the first task, this is done with glue size (coating). Rabbit skin size is the finest and tends to be more flexible than other sizes, but really most commercial glue size will do the job. Two coats should be applied to the canvas, the first of which should be well brushed in; ideally a day should be left between each coat.

STRETCHING A CANVAS

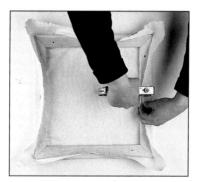

1 Lay the stretcher frame on a flat surface on top of the canvas. Mark off the amount of canvas you require, allowing a minimum of 5cm (2in.) overlap on all four sides. Remove the stretcher and cut the canvas parallel to the weave. Replace the stretcher on top of the canvas, making sure all the angles of the frame are square.

2 Starting on one side, fold the canvas over the stretcher and tack it with a staple gun in the centre. Pull the canvas taut and repeat this on the opposite side, then do the two remaining sides. Continue round the stretcher in this way, always working on opposite sides, and from the centre to the corners.

3 When you come to the corners, pull the corner of the canvas over, keeping it taut.

The next stage is to apply the ground. This will be the surface for your painting and will also serve as a further protection for the support. The ground should be an oil-based one which when dry should remain flexible to prevent the surface from cracking. There are many ready prepared grounds which can be purchased in artists' materials shops. They are always white, and at least two coats should be applied, but again this will depend on personal preferences as to the quality of surface you wish to achieve.

Another, quicker, method of preparing the canvas is to use acrylic primer which is water based and should be applied directly to the canvas without the glue size. This requires three or four coats, the first of which should be thinner and thoroughly brushed into the canvas. Priming in this way results in a good flexible ground which will take oil paint or acrylic paints equally well.

It is also possible to buy newly primed canvas by the metre or yard; this is fairly expensive but is still a good deal cheaper than buying ready stretched canvases.

The most commonly used support apart from canvas is hardboard (Masonite). This is a much cheaper alternative and has the advantage of strength – it will take more knocks than canvas. It is, however, far heavier and a larger size will need wooden supports to prevent it bending and warping. Hardboard still has to be sealed and given a ground in the same way as canvas. The most popular method is to use acrylic primer or plain white emulsion (latex) paint which eliminates the need for glue size and is cheaper by far. The finished surface is, obviously, hard and smooth, unlike canvas.

Never use the rough side of the hardboard to paint on, for although it superficially has the appearance of canvas, it is entirely unsuitable, due to its unsympathetic mechanical surface. It is almost impossible to get rid of paint if you do paint on it. If you do want a canvas type of

4 Fold one section of the canvas neatly into the frame, then fold the other section over it.

5 Staple through all the layers. It is important not to pull the canvas too tight, it should be taut and smooth. If it is too tight when you prime it the shrinkage caused by the priming will warp the shape and if really tight can split the canvas.

6 When you purchased your stretcher pieces you should have been given eight little wedges, two for each corner. These should be gently pushed into the slots on the inside of the corners. They enable you to tighten the canvas if it should slacken off due to atmospheric changes in the course of painting.

COVERING HARDBOARD

1 Cut a piece of muslin approximately 5cm (2in.) larger all round than the piece of hardboard you intend to use.

2 Glue the muslin to the shiny side of the hardboard with acrylic or emulsion primer. Brush through the fabric.

3 Turn the board over and glue the muslin to the hardboard supports. Make sure you glue well into the corners.

surface, muslin can be attached to the hardboard. Use the acrylic or emulsion primer to glue the muslin to the hardboard, making sure that you leave enough material (about 5cm/2in.) to turn over round the edges. This will need several coats of priming but will produce an interesting surface at low cost.

There are other ready prepared supports available in the form of oil painting papers, some bound like sketchbooks, and canvas boards or Daler boards which have a canvas-like surface. These are fairly inexpensive, and readily available. Lastly, plain heavy cartridge (drawing) paper and card can be used for oil painting if you treat the surface with emulsion paint before you start. This will provide a good working surface for quick sketches out of doors or in the studio.

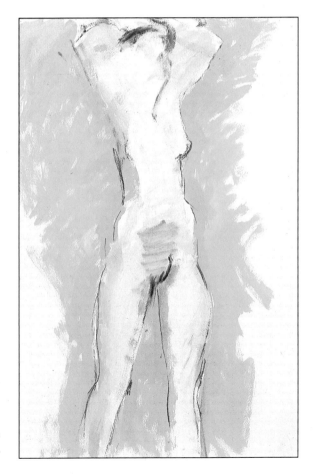

This is an example of oil paint used on cartridge (drawing) paper. It was a quick study, and the paint was kept thin, almost like a wash of watercolour except that, by using oil paint, the study has the vibrancy and strength needed without having to rely on the whiteness of the paper as one would with watercolour. It will also remain wet enough to work in for the duration of the drawing. Charcoal is used to define direction and shape.

Cheryl Gould 'Flowers' 770 × 550mm (30 × 21½in.). This painting was carried out on a heavy watercolour paper. This forms a tough surface and also has a pleasing texture which holds brush marks well. The paint has been applied in a wide range of ways, from thin staining in places, building up to thick impasto. Flowers provide a good range of colours and tones, and although each flower shape is composed of small petal shapes, great care has been taken to ensure that the overall form of flowers is not lost.

143

Recommended kit

In order to complete the exercises and projects in this section, you will need:

Paints For the exercises and first project you will need the following oil colours: yellow ochre, raw sienna, raw umber, burnt umber (these can be Students' colours), alizarin crimson, cadmium red, cadmium yellow, cobalt blue, viridian green and flake white. For the second project you would probably need in addition light red, magenta, geranium rose, cadmium orange, lemon yellow, terre verte, cerulean blue, ultramarine, mauve, indian red and black.

Brushes Initially, you should have four bristle brushes – a No. 10 filbert and No. 10 flat, No. 6 round, and a No. 4 filbert – and one 'soft' brush for drawing in. A No. 3 mix of sable and ox or soft nylon is probably most suitable.

Knives A flat palette knife will be adequate for the first project, and a trowel type for the second. Either is suitable for the exercises.

Supports A pad of oil-sketching or painting paper (canvasette) is adequate for the exercises. For the first project, a Daler board is probably the most suitable support; for the second, hardboard (Masonite) or canvas board, or the largest size Daler board available (60 × 72cm/25 × 30in.), may be more appropriate.

Additional items An easel, either sketching or table, or failing that use the back of an old chair; a palette, either a ready-made wooden one, or one from glass, hardboard, plastic or paper, the important thing is to have a clean surface on which to lay out and mix your paints; rags for wiping; and a dipper or jar for turpentine.

A beginner's basic oil-painting kit.

Starting to paint

The list of materials given on pages 144-5 is fairly comprehensive and eventually you will certainly need most, if not all, of them. At the beginning, however, this is not necessary. The first really important thing to do in oil painting is to get the feel of the paint and enjoy the qualities that are specified to oil paint, and explore the range of marks you can make with your various brushes. The idea of carrying out exercises before you make a proper painting is rather like doing finger exercises in music, limbering up without the complication of trying to paint objects or a landscape.

At this stage, I would suggest a series of small exercises (say 15 × 15cm/6 × 6in.) exploring the qualities of the paint and surface. You may wish to expand on these and develop them in further exercises of your own.

> **You will need**
> ☐ paints
> ☐ brushes
> ☐ painting knife
> ☐ a pad of oil-sketching paper or some Daler boards
> ☐ a palette
> ☐ a dipper (palette cup) containing turpentine
> ☐ rags

Use of brushes

Explore the range of marks that your brushes are capable of: this can either be in the form of a random doodle or a more organized chart which you can refer back to – it is really a matter of personal choice. The main object is to familiarize yourself with various brush marks. This will soon give you the confidence to select an appropriate brush for a particular task when you are working on a painting and will help you to enlarge your range of techniques.

The marks made by different brushes: (from top) flat, filbert, round, nylon and sable.

Laying out your palette

Obviously the way you lay out your palette is a matter of personal preference, but to enable you to work with more speed and fluency, it is advisable to establish an order for the colours on the palette, and stick to it. This will ensure that you can find them without having to spend time looking for them. The two small palettes illustrated here are laid out from warm to cool, with white as the divider, then the earth colours. One alternative would be to lay the colours out from light to dark, with white first, then moving through the colour range, as shown in the photograph of my palette.

My palette: white, raw sienna, naples yellow, cadmium yellow, lemon yellow, chrome yellow, cadmium orange, viridian, terre verte, emerald green, cinnabar green, chrome green, cerulean blue, alizarin crimson, magenta, cobalt violet, cadmium red, bright red, cobalt blue, ultramarine, black.

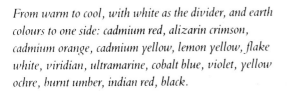

From warm to cool, with white as the divider, and earth colours to one side: cadmium red, alizarin crimson, cadmium orange, cadmium yellow, lemon yellow, flake white, viridian, ultramarine, cobalt blue, violet, yellow ochre, burnt umber, indian red, black.

Again from warm to cool, an extended palette: cadmium red, light red, crimson, magenta, geranium rose, cadmium orange, cadmium yellow, lemon yellow, viridian, terre verte, cerulean blue, cobalt blue, ultramarine, mauve, yellow ochre, burnt umber, indian red, black, flake white.

Colour

Although, at this stage, it is not necessary to go too deeply into colour theory, it is useful for the beginner to know about warm and cool colours. The phrase is used a great deal by artists when describing techniques or talking about the use of colour in a painting. The best place to start is with the colour wheel, a man-made device used to illustrate and explain colour theory. It is rather like a chart based on the colour spectrum found by passing light through a prism, but the important point to remember is that the artist is dealing with pigments which derive their colour through reflected, rather than direct, light.

The colour wheel illustrated is based on pigments. It was devised by Johannes Itten, who taught colour theory and practice to artists at the Bauhaus, in the 1930s. It starts with the three primary colours – red, yellow, and blue. These are pure colour and cannot be made by mixing together other pigments, but they do form the basis of the rest of the colour wheel. Surrounding these primaries are the secondary colours, which are a mixture of the primaries – red and yellow

produce orange, yellow and blue produce green, and red and blue give violet. The colours of the outer circle are known as tertiary colours. These are mixtures of the primary and secondary colours which give different strengths of colour. Red and orange, for example, will produce a red-orange, due to the predominance of the primary red in the two colours when mixed. Yellow and orange will produce a yellow-orange, and so on.

If the circle is divided in half, two groups of colour are formed – cool colours and warm colours. That is to say the colours of one half are warm in feeling compared with the rest of the colours which are cool in feeling. The word feeling is very important because it is an emotional response to the colours which makes us decide that they are warm or cool, although obviously there are associations within the range – reds, yellows and oranges make us think of fire, sun, heat, and so on, while in the cool range blues, greens and blue-violets make us think of sky, water and ice. This way of looking at colour is used extensively in the advertising industry where a particular mood or feeling is important.

Within the broad general terms 'warm' and 'cool', however, it is possible to find warmer and cooler variations – there are warmer greens and colder blues, and so on. A touch of red or violet in a blue will make it slightly warmer than a pure blue. These variations are infinite and very finely balanced. The degree of warmth or coolness also depends on the colours that surround a particular colour – chrome yellow placed next to lemon yellow will make the lemon yellow look cooler; viridian green next to lemon yellow will make the lemon yellow look warm.

There are examples of paintings which are predominantly warm or cool, and have been deliberately painted as such by the artists to convey a particular emotion to the spectator. In this way colour is as important as line or form in a composition. Specific use of warm or cool colours can also create a sense of space in a painting. You will notice in nature that distance tends to make

The colour wheel.

colours appear cooler – they take on a blue, hazy quality, because of the way the atmosphere affects how we see the colours. You will notice, however, that even in many old landscape paintings the artists used blues and other cool colours for backgrounds to create a feeling of distance, and warmer colours in the foreground to create the feeling of nearness. The Impressionists, too, used colour theory to create the feeling of light and vibrancy in their paintings. Today, abstract painters who may be unconcerned with any figurative elements in their works will achieve the feeling of space through their manipulation of colour theory.

Colour mixing

According to the colour wheel, it should be possible to produce all the colours you need from the primaries – red, yellow and blue. Unfortunately, this is not strictly true; there are some colours it is just not possible to create and the more intense violets, purples, greens and some blues have to come from a tube.

When you choose your oil colours you will find that there are various types of red, yellow and blue. It is very important to know the differences between them. Cadmium red, for example, is very near the primary red in the colour wheel. You will find that when you mix cadmium red with cadmium yellow you can achieve a good orange, near to the orange in the colour wheel. However if you use a crimson red with the cadmium yellow, the orange goes brown and the brilliance goes from it. The same applies with the yellows. Cadmium yellow is as good a primary as you will get, and mixed with cadmium red it gives a good orange, but lemon yellow will give a dull orange lacking in brightness.

These differences run through to the blues when mixed with reds. Our primary red (the cadmium), when mixed with cobalt blue, according to the colour circle should give us a good violet, but it will in fact make brown. To achieve violet, mix crimson red with blue.

Practise mixing colours so that you begin to get the feel of how the various pigments will react together and the colours you can make: (from top) cadmium red + cadmium yellow (this is a 'true' orange); cadmium red + lemon yellow; crimson red + cadmium yellow; crimson red + lemon yellow; cobalt blue + cadmium yellow (the 'truest' green); cobalt blue + lemon yellow; crimson red + cobalt blue (a 'true' violet); and cadmium red + cobalt blue.

149

Mixing primary and secondary complementaries plus increasing amounts of white. Orange and cobalt blue make a cool grey, violet and cadmium yellow, and green and cadmium red make warm greys, almost flesh tints.

It is useful at this stage to try small mixes of these colours and note the different results for future reference. The more you play with your paints and become familiar with the way they behave, the quicker you build up a knowledge which will become second nature as you work.

Wet into wet

There are many examples of the use of this technique, most often by abstract painters. It is an exciting way to explore the qualities, properties and possibilities of oil paint.

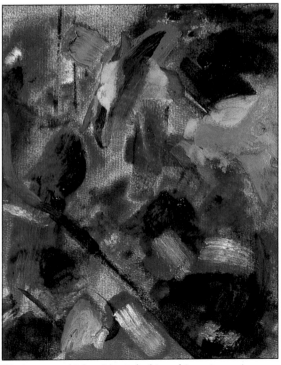

Wet into wet, thick paint worked into thin.

Mix a small quantity of thin paint to the consistency of watercolour. Then lay it on the surface quite freely. While this is still wet, add some thicker paint, of another colour, into the wet surface, perhaps scrubbing it around with a brush in some areas.

You will notice that the colour tends to bleed into the wet background, giving soft fuzzy edges in the areas where it is thinnest. Where it is slightly thicker, it will sit on top of the surface. You can also see how the colours will intermix on the surface in varying degrees of intensity.

Overall, this method gives a soft, translucent quality to the shapes, and a magical atmosphere and almost dreamlike aspect to the paint. In the areas where the paint is thicker, it seems to have a depth to it.

Glazing

Glazing is a very useful technique in many ways. It will give parts of a painting a rich glowing effect, and can also be used to overpaint and unify areas without having to repaint them totally.

Prepare an area of solid random shapes and let them dry off – this should take about 24 hours. When the paint is dry, overlay thin transparent paint of different colours. Use a soft brush for this so that you avoid any brush marks. The thinness of the overpainting will allow the colour beneath the glazed paint to show through, and it is this that gives the glowing effect to the painting.

You will notice that the colours have a brilliance which can only be achieved in this way. A green which is painted over a more solid area of green and blue, for example, intensifies in richness;

GLAZING

1 Green glazed over yellow tends to become sharper and brighter.

2 Blue over yellow. The colours mix on the surface, not on the palette.

3 Yellow over blue; yellow over darker colours often appears more solid.

4 Areas of purple glazed over other colours enhance the feeling of space.

Glazed colours have a unique brilliance.

painted over bright yellow, it becomes sharper and brighter. This is also true of the reds and blues.

The colours used for the solid shapes in this example have been thinned down and overlaid across each other. It is interesting to note that some colours, like the yellow, when painted over darker shapes, actually appear more solid – this can be seen, for instance, on the green and purple shapes. This overlaying can also enhance the feeling of space; even in this small exercise, the special aspect has emerged quite naturally.

Dragged brush techniques

In this exercise, keep the paint fairly thick and stiff in consistency. Start by dragging the brush strokes across the surface, noticing the texture made by the brush and surface together. Also, mix the brush marks together, enjoying the feeling of fluidity of the thick wet paint.

While this is drying, drag some more paint over the surface of the brush marks. You will find that the wet paint will move uncontrollably. This effect can be used consciously in your paintings.

You will also notice that the paint sticks to the raised texture and gives a gritty or dry feeling. It can also add a sparkle to the surface, and gives a completely different effect from the previous exercise. This sparkle can be very useful in the finishing stages of a painting.

Using a painting knife

Many people find thick paint more exciting to work with than thin, and the element of chance involved in knife painting – it is not so controllable as a brush mark – is in itself stimulating to many artists.

There are many ways to use a painting knife. The paint can be laid on to the surface very thickly to lose the surface texture of the ground

Paint dragged over surface brush marks.

completely. Alternatively, it can be lightly scraped or dragged over the surface to create a broken, sparkling feeling. It can also be used in conjunction with a brush. The contrast of marks adds extra interest.

The colour lies on the surface of the canvas or board in a different way from paint that is brushed on and there are no brush marks. The paint also usually has sharper edges than you could achieve with a brush.

There are many examples of well-known artists who have made extensive use of the knife in their paintings; a notable example is John Constable.

KNIFE PAINTING

1 Using the edge of the knife will give a sharp linear mark.

2 Using the whole blade flat allows a full gestural movement.

3 Knife painting gives a surface free from brush marks.

SCUMBLING

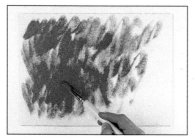

A colour scumbled over the support will mean areas of the white ground will show through.

Scumbling light over dark, the previous colour is still visible and changes the lighter colour.

Dark over light – the eye tends to mix the colours on the surface of the painting.

Scumbling

Scumbling is applying thick paint loosely and freely over the surface of a painting. It can be used to add interest to large plain areas of work, it can also give a glowing effect to the surface, tone down passages of a painting, produce a softness in places, and can add freshness and light.

Scumbling can be used on a surface that is already painted, or applied over an untinted ground. The colour underneath the scumble will show through. This gives an exciting broken, dappled effect. Different effects can be achieved, according to whether the scumble is lighter or darker than the ground. Also, depending on the colours you use, laying broken colours over one another can mean that the eye will mix the colours on the surface of the painting.

You can achieve interesting effects by scumbling the paint on with a rag or tissue, rather than a brush. This can give a variety of textures and effects to the surface of the painting.

The doodle

The doodle incorporates all or most of the elements in the smaller single exercises. The advantage of it is that the elements all interact and the various qualities complement each other. The only organization I allowed myself was that on one side the colour is thin and transparent in feeling, and on the other side the paint is thick and gestural with more intermixing of the colours and white so that you notice the subtle tonal variation. What is also interesting in this doodle is the quality of the thin transparent paints. They seem to float and create space and distance of a different kind from the thicker areas.

The way to learn from this exercise and also the smaller ones is to stop and really examine what you have done. At this stage, there will be a good many accidental qualities which are sometimes quite magical and can be used and made to work for you in a more considered situation later on.

The elements of the doodle interact with each other.

153

Project: A still life 1

The simple still-life group is an excellent way for the newcomer to oil painting to experiment and learn about the medium. By working indoors, you don't have all the problems encountered outside, such as changing light, and unwanted spectators. At this stage, it is more important to learn to manipulate the paint and experiment with different brushes and ways of applying the paint. It is only by doing this that you find the ways that suit you best and develop your own technique, which eventually becomes as personal and unique as handwriting. For this painting, I will show how to build from thin paint to thick in one sitting. By keeping the first areas thinly painted, the surface remains in a good state to make alterations and adjustments.

You will need

- [ ] paints
- [ ] brushes
- [ ] painting knife
- [ ] a Daler board, about 40 × 50cm (16 × 20in.)
- [ ] a palette
- [ ] a dipper (palette cup) containing turpentine
- [ ] rags
- [ ] a pencil and cartridge (drawing) paper

The still-life arrangement of objects.

Choice of subject

For this first project, I have set up a very simple still life using objects that are easily found around the home. Coloured paper creates areas of tone and colour in the simplest possible way. This avoids the complexities of folds and texture which you will find with drapery.

I have used the fruit and the plate because of their simplicity of shape. All are almost round, but have the variation and subtlety of colour needed to help you to see the changes of colour and tone in an individual object. You will also notice here that there is a relationship of colour which connects the objects and background throughout the picture. The predominant colour is established by the green background. The colour then ranges through a variety of greens in the apples and bottle, working its way through to the palest apple which is almost yellow to the full yellow of the lemon. Then, from the yellow of the lemon it is a natural step to the yellow-orange and full orange of the oranges themselves which intensify into the reds of the red apple. The blue of the small piece of drapery seems to act as an accent due to its opposition to the orange colour. I used the egg because of its simple smooth shape which when placed on the blue seemed to pick up the blues and grey-pinks of the colours around it.

Preliminary sketches

The viewpoint I have chosen is a flat and straight on view. This means that there are almost no perspective problems. It is a good idea before you start to make one or two very simple sketches just to get the composition right. As you will see from the first little drawing that I made, the composition was not satisfactory. The bottle and plate were practically central to the picture, thus creating a rather obvious viewpoint, but moving this focus over to the right of centre and adding the light strip to the left-hand side achieves a better balance and more interest. This will only take a few minutes of your time but it is invaluable when planning your picture.

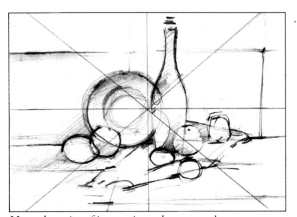

Here, the point of interest is much too central.

Moving the bottle makes a more interesting grouping.

The initial drawing in in raw umber.

Painting areas of background.

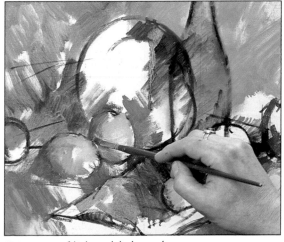

Paint areas of light and dark together.

When sketching in your composition on your board, use the minimum amount of drawing. Remember that almost all of the drawing will eventually be covered up. You only need to indicate, as accurately as possible, the sizes and shapes of the objects and their relationship to each other. Draw with sable using a neutral colour, in this case I used raw umber. The first drawn lines can be sketched in in pencil before the paint is used. Charcoal is sometimes used, but it tends to mix in with the first application of paint, which could present problems for the beginner.

I arranged my group of objects so that the light source comes into the picture from the side; this enhances the dramatic effect of light and dark and, more importantly for the beginner, it simplifies the way we see the forms. You will find that when you come to paint out of doors, the light source can present difficult handling problems (see pages 171-2), particularly if you work on a single painting all day, as the light is constantly changing. It requires a good deal of skill to organize the pace and tone of the picture right from the start to take this into account.

Painting the background

The second stage of the painting is to paint in thinly and in a general way the broad areas of colour and tone, letting the drawing show through. Don't worry about the colours overlapping, and don't try to paint each object separately – remember that it is the whole of the painting that you are concerned with. Use fairly large brushes so that you keep the surface free in feeling. This will also stop you fiddling with small details at this early stage.

I started with the background first only because it is the largest single area, but once a general statement was made, I quickly moved on to the smaller areas. It is important to try and paint these together, by that I mean if you are painting one area of the plate, you will look and make a decision regarding the colour and tone of a corresponding area next to it, which might be the bottle or background. In this way, the whole painting will gradually build up and you will avoid painting objects singularly. Paint lights and darks together, this will help you to make judgements as to the relative value of light and dark. You will also notice that although there are colour changes, as in the green pepper next to the blue drapery, the tones at their darkest are about the same. This is also true of the oranges and apples and the corresponding backgrounds. This is an important point to learn. While colours may change, tones may well come together. This is what will give a painting atmosphere and will get away from the feeling that the objects exist completely separately.

Initial areas of colour scrubbed in.

Re-establishing the drawing

You will probably find at this stage that some of the drawing has either got lost (because you have painted over it) or gone wrong in the painting. Don't worry about this – it happens in the course of a painting. All it means is that at this stage it is a good idea to re-establish the drawing in those areas where you feel it needs it. I found in this painting that it was necessary to re-draw the bottle and refine its shape, which had become clumsy. The fruit was also generally too round and was beginning to lose its character. I was able to change these without difficulty because I had kept the paint loose and thin, and like this it is easily overpainted.

The drawing has now been re-established.

The first details

By this stage, I am being more specific and looking in more detail at shapes and the small colour changes within the objects, paying particular attention to the way the colours reflect the different colours around them. You can see that I have carried some of the warmth of the orange on the left of the lemon into the lemon itself, so that a part of the lemon is almost orange. The orange also reflects down on to the surface of the table, giving off a warmer half-tone around it. The lemon was a particularly good choice for this

The fruit lends warm tones to the table.

157

Thicker paint is used in the lighter areas.

Almost all the board is now covered.

creates an accent and seems to balance the picture more satisfactorily. I have also found that the brightness of the orange at that point is useful in bringing the eye over to that side of the painting.

Adding the highlights

It is at this final stage that I have started to look at the highlights or lightest parts of the objects. I have carefully avoided adding these until now since they require a good deal of thought and restraint. You will find that there is a great temptation to over-emphasize the highlights and add flecks of white all over the place. When this occurs in a picture, these highlights usually look as though they are on the surface of the painting rather than on the objects themselves; in other words, they look totally unrelated to the whole.

Being more specific about edges.

project because as you will see it seems to pick up a great deal of the colour around it – greens, oranges and browns.

I am now able to use thicker paint, particularly in the light areas. The heavier paint strokes seem to give a feeling of surfaces reflecting light while the thin dark areas give a feeling of shadow.

I have kept the paint thinner on the bottle to give more of the feeling of transparency of glass and only where the light is reflected have I allowed the paint to become thicker. In this last stage, I have defined some of the lines of the composition more fully. For example, the folds on the green background paper are important directional lines and the light shape of the wall is crucial to the balance of the composition, particularly where the light meets the dark of the table and orange. This

Beginning to look at the lightest areas.

Building up the highlights.

Try to see highlights as areas of lightness of colour rather than as white reflections. I have noticed by now that the lightest points in the picture are the lemon, part of the apple next to it, the strip down the left-hand side, and the egg. All the other tones gradually come closer together so that the picture is predominantly dark and half-tones. This gives a bit of drama to the objects but, more importantly, if you can learn to look at your painting in this way, trying to sum up its whole feeling, stage by stage, you will find that you will begin to do this before you actually start painting. You will begin to apply this same sort of looking to the objects themselves.

This part of the apple is one of the lightest areas of the whole painting.

Underpainting

In all the little exercises that you carried out, and in the first project, you will have noticed that the paint has stayed wet for a considerable length of time, probably all day. This is one of the basic qualities of oil paint, which gives it the advantage over water-based pigments of being flexible for change and alteration over a long period. There are two basic methods of working in oils. The first, which is the approach taken in the first project, is called *alla prima*. This simply means working the paint directly on to the canvas into wet paint. The colour is mixed on the canvas as well as on the palette. This way of working is the most usual when you are doing a painting at one sitting – a landscape, for instance – when you can only spend a short time working, or a portrait where your time is limited to a day or part of a day. The second method is a more considered approach in that you have to have decided on the relative tones of the areas of the canvas or board before you start to paint. This is a very structured approach to picture-making and requires a good deal of time and a strong idea of how the paint will look to be successful.

> **You will need**
> - [ ] paints
> - [ ] brushes
> - [ ] oil-sketching paper or a Daler board
> - [ ] a palette
> - [ ] a dipper (palette cup) containing turpentine
> - [ ] rags

Ken Howard 'Homage to Sir William Orpen' 1500 × 1350mm (60 × 50in.). This picture is a beautiful example of underpainting cool greys and whites with a warm colour. You can see the full orange on the vertical edges of the picture. The colour filters through giving a vibrancy to the cool areas and cleverly lead us to the warm tones of the head and hands.

Underpainting technique

This approach to oil painting has a strong tradition. The picture is usually begun with a more detailed drawing than in *alla prima* painting on the canvas, and is then built up in a variety of ways. Sometimes strong glazes are laid on top of the drawing and when they are dry, they are worked into with thicker paint, and perhaps over-glazed again.

The whole of this method can be carried out on the white ground, although some artists prefer to stain the ground with a colour to give extra vibrancy to the colours applied later. The colour chosen to stain the surface ground can either set the mood of the picture from the start (either warm or cool), or act as a contrast to the colours added as the painting continues.

Thinned oil paint is usually used for underpainting, although some artists use acrylics, which dry quickly.

Monochrome underpainting

There is a further way of starting a painting, called underpainting in monochrome (monochrome meaning one colour). The reason for underpainting in this way is broadly to create the light and dark areas and build up the three-dimensional aspect of your picture before using colour. It is best to use a neutral colour (in the example illustrated here I used burnt umber and blue), since these have the advantage of drying quickly. Don't add white but thin the pigment down with turpentine, almost to the consistency of watercolour. For the areas you wish to be light in the finished painting, leave the ground white, and build up the layers of pigment for the darkest areas of your painting. In this way you will create the light and dark tonal areas.

UNDERPAINTING IN MONOCHROME

1 *Drawing in the main lines and directions using burnt umber, or raw umber. Remember to keep the drawing as simple as possible.*

2 *The next stage is to lay in quickly a thin wash of paint to indicate the feeling of shape and tone.*

3 *Here, I am starting to vary the lights and darks of the trees, keeping a general feeling of shape to preserve the dramatic quality of the trees.*

4 *Colour is now introduced on to the tonal underpainting; the tone of the colour relates to the first underpainting.*

Project: A still life 2

One of the outstanding advantages of painting still lifes is that you, the artist, are in complete control. You select the format, and choose and arrange the objects right from the start. You could say that it is at this point that the painting really begins. It is always a good idea to make your choice with a theme in mind. This could be the relationship of colour running through the objects and background, maybe a range of predominantly warm or cool colours. Shape could also be a strong element, for example, the linking of curved lines throughout, or the

The more complex still-life arrangement for this project allows a larger format.

contrast of curves against straight lines, which will often produce a dramatic effect in a composition. The use of texture in a painting heightens the feeling of surfaces – this can be achieved by contrasting textural qualities within the picture, such as drapery with glass, or a piece of natural form such as bark against paper or metal. Try to avoid the idea of a picture telling a story by using objects that are only connected in the literal sense. Remember that the picture's strength lies in its composition and colour. If there is another connection, it will be secondary to these considerations. There is such a wide choice of approaches open to the artist that it is only by experimenting that you will begin to develop your own ideas about the sort of image you prefer.

> **You will need**
> - paints, extended colour range
> - brushes
> - trowel-type painting knife
> - hardboard or canvas board, 65 × 75cm (26 × 30in.)
> - a palette
> - a dipper (palette cup) containing turpentine
> - rags

Choice of objects

The format for this second still life is larger than the first, which will allow me to make a more complex grouping of objects and be more adventurous in the way the objects are arranged. Instead of flat areas of colour as in the first project, here I have used drapery, the folds of which will give me strong directional lines running through the composition. I have used fruit again because of its colour content and the way it naturally seems to relate to the colours surrounding it. The plant is an important element. Apart from being an exciting organic shape, it encompasses a great deal of the colour that occurs in the rest of the painting. Also, its overall shape and tone, seen against the light background, help to balance the strong red area on the right of the picture. The sheep's skull in the foreground is also an object which picks up all the subtle half-tones and greys of the colours around it.

I also incorporated objects with reflective surfaces – the bottle and metal fruit stand. Finally, I used the check-patterned cloth to create interest in the foreground area; this helps to give a feeling of space because of the way the checks diminish in size as they recede through the picture.

When choosing objects, try to select them from the point of view of colour and see if you can trace links of colour between them. All the objects I have chosen have these colour links, from the warm reds of the drapery and fruit through to the orange and orange-yellows of the orange and apples, then to the full yellow of the grapefruit and the green of the apples and bottle. The green of the plant is moving towards the blue of the cloth. The aubergine (eggplant) acts as a focal point of colour, because its purple quality forms a link between the blue and the red. Choice of colour is also important in creating a sense of rhythm in a composition. A good sense of rhythm means that the eye will travel through the picture from one area to another, guided by the juxtapositions between them as they overlap and cross each other. In this way, painters control how you look at their pictures, perhaps leading you gently to an important focal point.

If you consciously think in these terms when you paint, you will find that it quickly becomes second nature and it will form part of your intuitive colour sense. This applies to landscape or any other form of painting; you will see these links in almost everything in the course of everyday life, whether you are painting or not.

Choice of eye level

It is advisable for the beginner to choose an eye level either straight on or just above; in other words, if the group is set up at table height you either stand or sit to paint. If you set the group up on the floor, although visually exciting, you will create drawing problems, such as foreshortening, which at this stage are best avoided. Here, by taking a slightly higher eye level than in the first still life more of the picture surface is broken up by shape and colour.

Arranging and lighting your objects

When arranging your composition you need to consider shape, not just the shapes of the individual elements but the shape of the spaces between them. These areas are called negative shapes. They are often ignored by beginners, although they are just as important as the objects themselves. If you think of the flat surface of the picture, and then think of the pattern quality of the drawing on that surface, you can realize that the negative shapes play an important part in the whole design. You will select objects for your painting for a number of reasons, one of which will probably be that they have interesting shapes, so it should follow that all the shapes created in the picture are as interesting as possible. Lighting can also help in describing the shapes and forms of your objects. The light source can heighten the dramatic effect of a picture by casting strong dark shadows. On the other hand, a strong overall light can achieve a brilliant sparkling effect, with areas of intense highlights.

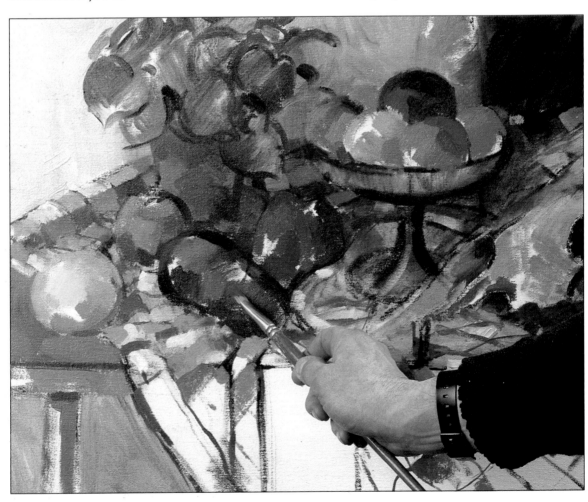

The initial scrubbing in of related areas of colour.

Initial stages

The start of the painting was the same as in the first still life, except that as the grouping was more complicated, I sketched in very lightly in pencil before making my first drawn marks in paint. This gave me more flexibility when trying to arrive at a satisfactory composition. At this stage, the painting has been kept very broad, with the paint as thin as possible, so that should I need to make changes, it will be very easy to wipe or scrape clean. You will notice that although the plant is made up of a number of elements, I have deliberately seen it as a simple overall shape and painted it loosely, rather than getting involved with the individual shapes themselves. This will come at a later stage.

The painting at this stage is very broad.

Covering the canvas

It is also important at this early stage to try to relate the tones and colours as closely as you can, although they will almost certainly be altered and adjusted as the painting progresses. Most of the canvas is covered by now and statements of colour and tone have been made regarding all the objects and their surroundings. The only outstanding area is the checked cloth; this requires more time due to the formal nature of the pattern and needs to be drawn with some accuracy. The important thing at this stage is to establish the mood and atmosphere of the picture; this is usually through the colour and tonal relationships.

The fruit stand reflects colour around it.

The first details

By now, I am beginning to look in more detail at individual parts of the painting. The metal fruit stand as well as the area surrounding its base show how reflective surfaces provide a wide range of colours, but you must beware of and try to avoid the temptation to over-state the highlights. At this point it is more important to see how the tones are very closely related to each other and the edges almost disappear into shadow. I have also developed the other parts of the picture, notably the skull and the fruit on the stand.

Form and colour are now developing.

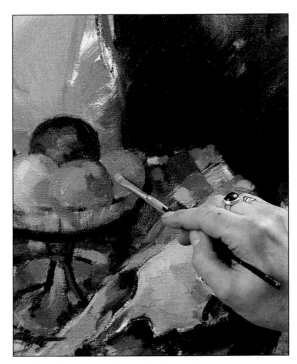

Looking in more detail at the fruit stand.

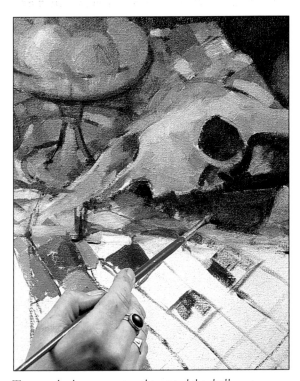

Tones and colours come together round the skull.

At this stage, I am more confident of colour and tone.

Colour and tonal relationships

It may be necessary at this point to re-establish the drawing in certain areas. At this stage, I am looking at the colours in the fruit stand and how they reflect into each other and change the nature of orange and yellow. You can see how the very yellow apple has taken into its shadow the orange quality of the orange fruit next to it. I am beginning to use thicker paint now, because I am confident about the colour and tonal relationships and I know that some of my marks will remain unchanged throughout the painting of the picture.

It can be seen by looking at the sheep's skull in the picture how all the subtle tones and colours seem to come together in this form. Because it is the lightest object in the group, it absorbs many of the shades surrounding it, and we can see the wonderful variety of greys which occur on the surface, warm pinky greys moving into cool green-blue greys.

Warm and cool areas

I am now working on the left-hand side of the picture. The grapefruit is an important element in the balance of the composition. The bright yellow helps to counterbalance the dark red passage in the opposite side of the picture, so the degree of

The brightness of the grapefruit is critical.

brightness is critical. If I make it too light, it will stand out too much; if I understate it, the point of it in the composition will be lost. The only immediate part of the painting which connects with it from the point of view of colour is the table top which has the same warm glow. It is also surrounded by a contrasting cool blue, so I have to relate the yellow to these colours. To do this, I notice that some of the yellow reflects down into the table top and there are areas of the yellow which take on a greeny quality which helps to bridge the gap from blue to yellow, as well as forming a link with the green apple just beyond.

At this stage, I am also beginning to paint into the checked cloth. At first sight, I am sure this complicated cloth pattern can appear daunting to the beginner, but don't be put off from using pattern in your pictures just because you feel it is too difficult. They create interesting and exciting areas in the picture, as well as being very useful in terms of composition. The best approach is to paint what you see, for instance, if you have an area of dark which is made because of the dark checks, just paint them. Don't think of them as checks, just as areas where you see definite patterns of light and dark, then it is easy to draw and paint them. If you look closely at parts of my

painting you will find it hard to define precisely the check pattern, but because it is well defined in other areas, you willingly accept that the pattern runs all through the picture, even though it can't always be seen in a precise way.

Establishing the planes

At this stage, I have drawn the cloth pattern more accurately with a fine brush, and I shall now be looking closely at the way the blues change. There are basically three blues, the dark blue, lighter blue and the blue-grey. Once the formal layout has been understood, the most important aspect is how they change due to the folds and how they describe the horizontal plane of the table top and the vertical plane down the front of the table. You will notice that I am developing the front edge of the table where this change in direction takes place. The light falls mainly from above and to the side so the top plane of the table is light. I have therefore emphasized this edge by making the white checks on the top surface strong where they change direction and become darker on the vertical drop.

More detailed work on the cloth.

167

Balance and movement

By now I feel that it is necessary to work on the plant. This, like the grapefruit, is an important compositional element. It is important as an overall shape to balance the picture. This is achieved by the contrast in tone of dark on light and its mauve-red flowers form a link with the red drapery. This link is helped by the red of the bottle top and the red apple in the fruit stand leading the eye over to the red drapery. I am now also developing the drawing of the leaf shapes, keeping the tones close together so as not to break down the overall feeling of the plant. The sharp pointed nature of the flowers takes the eye up from the busy lower half of the picture and helps to create movement through the composition.

The folds of drapery are almost completed.

The plant is an important element in balancing the picture.

Finishing touches

As the picture is nearing completion, it is important to stop and have a good look at the whole painting so far to see if there are any parts which are not working – the drawing might need re-establishing or it might be that certain parts have become over-stated or under-stated. In my painting, at this point, I can see that the orange on the right-hand side against the red appears to be jumping forward in the picture. I could re-paint it so that it recedes, or I could try glazing it down. This is, in fact, what I have done. By glazing thin red paint over the painted orange I was able to pull it back into the drapery. I left the very centre of the orange showing through so that the edges almost disappeared. I then lightened the horn of the sheep's skull to bring it forward. It was also at this point that I painted some detail into the fruit stand and finished off the check pattern. I also felt that the table top needed lightening to give more contrast with the dark shadow underneath. This helps to bring that edge forward.

Because the light background is a large plain area I painted some of the soft tones with a palette knife to give the area a textural interest, without making it too prominent.

Glazing the orange pulls it back into the drapery.

Varnishing pictures

Varnishes are used for two main reasons. The first, and most important, is to protect the painted surface from damage caused by atmospheric pollution, which can cause discoloration and eventually do irreparable harm to the pigments themselves, and from minor scratches and marks. Secondly, varnishes are used to restore the original quality of colour and tone to your picture.

You will probably have noticed during the course of your work on the exercises and projects that in many cases the colour has gone dull or patchy. This is due to the way some colours dry. If they have plenty of oil ground with them they will probably stay shiny; if you have mixed a lot of turpentine with your paint it will probably have dried dull and matt. This patchy quality is irritating and distracting. To overcome it, you can use re-touching varnish. This is an ideal temporary measure and can be used straight away to restore the brilliance of the paint.

In the longer term, however, a clear picture varnish will be necessary, although you shouldn't apply this for at least nine months to a year after the picture has been completed, since it takes this amount of time for the paint to dry and harden fully. If varnish is applied before the paint is fully dry, cracking or crazing will almost certainly occur, due to the different drying times of the paint and varnish.

When you come to apply the picture varnish make sure that your painting is clean and free from dust particles. To do this, wash it gently with a soft rag or cottonwool (absorbent cotton) dipped in mild soapy water, then rinse the rag with clean water and go over the surface again to get rid of all the soap. Let it dry thoroughly. Apply the varnish with a soft varnish brush, which can be obtained from art suppliers. Start from the top and apply the varnish thinly and evenly over the whole surface at one go. If you allow one area of varnish to dry and then continue you will find that there is an edge where the two varnished layers overlap.

Subjects for the oil painter

The choice of subject for the painter is endless and what moves one person to paint a particular subject will not necessarily have the same effect on another. It is, however, a strange phenomenon about painting that someone else's interpretation of a subject which is not particularly to our liking can have the power to move us – it is not so much what you paint as how you interpret the subject. If you are drawn to a subject, do not be put off by what might seem like problems at the time, have a go. You will find that your enthusiasm will help you to surmount many of the technical difficulties, and, the more you do it, the more your technique will improve.

Oil is very suitable for many subjects for the beginner due to its flexibility. If a painting is going wrong, or proving difficult, oil will allow you to scrape or rub it off the surface and rework it again and again. The technique is obviously different from, say, watercolour, which requires a more careful and considered approach, and won't allow for much pushing around the surface. Scale also plays a part. Very large watercolours require technical know-how and time, whereas a fairly large oil painting can be tackled more readily by an enthusiastic beginner.

John Constable 'Sketch for Leaping Horses' 1294 × 1880mm (51 × 71in.). This full-size sketch shows how Constable ironed out many of the problems of composition and colour before he committed himself to the final painting. Although this is referred to as a sketch, this only means that it was a loosely painted preparatory work – it has all the completeness of a finished painting.

Ken Howard 'Studio Interior' 625 × 750mm (25 × 30in.). This painting of Ken Howard's is an interesting example which shows that one does not necessarily have to go far for subjects. Very often the immediate environment in which you live and work can be just as stimulating pictorially as anything which you deliberately search out.

Painting out of doors

Although as we have seen, the simple still-life group is an excellent way for the newcomer to oil painting to experiment and learn about the medium, sooner or later many people (probably the majority) will feel that landscape is the subject that inspires them to want to paint most of all. So, the problems which I have outlined – light, spectators, and so on – will eventually have to be faced; the early work at home will have prepared you with the basic use of oil painting materials and the medium itself.

A clear advantage of working directly from nature is that you can compile a selection of studies of a location or subject and build them into a more considered composition. This also allows you to increase the scale to a size that would not be possible out of doors. There are many examples of this way of working. Constable made endless colour studies and drawings which he then developed into full-size sketches, then turned these into a finished painting.

The problem of light can be approached in several ways. Usually if you start painting out of doors and you intend to spend the best part of the day at it, you can assume that choosing your subject and the initial drawing will take an hour or so. During the time spent drawing and blocking in the large masses, you will not have to make major decisions about the light, except to bear in mind that it is changing very slowly. When you come to make specific decisions, save them until you are well on into the painting. Details can also be left until near the end as often the overall light won't affect how you paint them greatly.

Another way of dealing with the light is to paint on a small scale and do several paintings in a

This study is formed by the rather warm sultry day making dark shadows which push the white screens in to dramatic prominence.

The paint in this picture varies from very thin to thicker light scumbling in the sky area to convey the light misty atmosphere of this kind of subject.

day. By doing this, you will gradually begin to catch the light and build up a series of little paintings, telling the story of the changing light over a period of time. It would then be interesting to compare how changes in light affect the feeling of the landscape over the period of a day.

If the weather is fine and sunny you will notice that the paint, especially if you put it on thinly, will dry off more quickly than indoors. This is one of the major advantages of working outside.

There are also logistical problems to working out of doors. It is advisable to keep equipment down to the absolute essentials. Make sure that the size of canvas or board is one that you can

handle – remember that you are going to be going home with a wet painting so it has to be easy to carry. Art shops sell special carrying straps for wet paintings. As for the critical spectators, well you just have to learn to live with them.

Alternatively, it is nearly always possible to paint from a window or in your garden. The window can give the picture an extra dimension, since by including it as part of the composition you convey the feeling of looking through a vista. The garden has certain advantages: you can go where you like, you can always be sure of getting the same spot again, and you can spend as much time as you wish on the painting.

This little study was carried out on a piece of mounting card, one of many oil sketches made on the spot. Obviously it is necessary to work fast with a subject like a sunset so I have kept the scale small and the paint is very thin and washy in places.

Using photographs

You might prefer to paint portraits of people or animals, although they always pose a problem simply because they move. This is where a camera can be a useful aid. I use the word 'aid' deliberately, as there does not seem much point in taking a photograph and just reproducing in paint what was probably better as a photograph anyway! But there are times when certain information is needed, either as a supplement to a drawing, or as a way to capture quickly the feeling that you want in the picture. This, combined with quick sketches, will give added information for you to use.

Photographs can also provide the stimulus for an idea. The photograph reproduced here, for example, was taken by me on a walk in Wales. I was attracted by the colour of the moss-grown stump which was bright green, and the odd, interesting shapes of the decaying wood surrounded by spiky brambles and roots. Although I had the photograph to work from, my first impressions and memories of that encounter were more important as they formed the basis of the idea for the painting. I first made several small scribbles on paper, trying to formulate my idea. The next stage was to make a larger, more detailed drawing, working towards that precise composition. This I carried out in colour, using paint and inks. You will see that the picture has now moved away from the photograph: the basic composition has changed, and the colour is also changing. I have heightened the green of the stump and, to emphasize this, I have introduced the orange.

The photograph is now totally discarded as my drawing is to form the basis of the projected painting. I began to realize that the shapes had a sinister, almost animal-like, quality to them which was not in the photograph. This aspect I developed further in the painting. You will also see that the final painting differs from the drawing in many ways. It is not just a question of doing a

The photograph that was the starting point for the painting below.

The detailed colour drawing.

The finished painting.

painting of the drawing – there must be room for development in the painting itself. I have retained the feeling of the dark woodland but there is almost a feeling of a fantastic stage set emerging which is far from the original photograph. In this sequence I have tried to show that there are ways of working from photographs that are more than just copying them.

Painting from sketches

One of the most enjoyable and satisfying ways to acquire subjects for oil paintings is through using a sketchbook. You should never be without one, either at work or at home – think of it as a visual notebook. When you see a subject that you find interesting, jot it down. Drawings made on holiday, or on a normal day-to-day basis, will provide endless material for paintings carried out in the studio. (They will also help you to improve your drawing technique.) Obviously making the sketch studies is the first step, but when you are sketching you do not always have a finished painting in mind. So, how do you set about translating a drawing from your sketchbook into a finished painting?

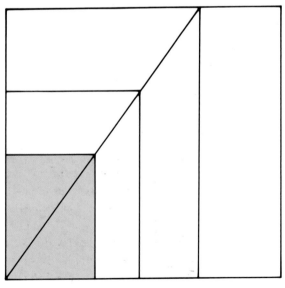

Any of the rectangles is in proportion to the original sketch.

Your first consideration will be to compose that initial sketch into a pleasing and well-constructed picture. You will also probably find that your first sketch is a different shape from the final format you have in mind, so you will have to alter or 'translate' your sketch to fit your new shape. The easiest way to do this is to redraw the main shapes and directions of your sketch on to another piece of paper, altering and adjusting them until you arrive at the arrangement that is most satisfying to you, and seems to work best.

The next stage is to transfer this image on to the larger shape that is to be your finished painting. For this, a system called 'gridding up' or 'squaring up' is used. This is simple to carry out. First, make sure that your small study is the same proportion as the painting is going to be. An easy method of reproducing the exact proportion from a small scale to a larger one is to lay the small shape (your drawing) on to the larger area (your painting support) tight into a corner and draw a diagonal line through the small shape, continuing it until it meets the edge of the painting support. Any rectangle drawn with that same diagonal will be in direct proportion to your smaller shape, and the area outside the point where it strikes the edge is waste. In the illustration here, any one of the coloured rectangles would be in direct proportion to the original drawing.

Having settled on the scale and proportion of your painting, you now need to transfer the drawing to the painting surface. To do this, you impose a grid structure on top of your study by drawing in two diagonals from corner to corner, then dividing it horizontally and vertically into four equal rectangles. This grid can then be subdivided as many times as you wish just by halving the shapes diagonally, horizontally and vertically. The number of times you repeat the process, obviously, depends on the complexity of the drawing you are transferring; the more detail you have the more reference points you will need. You will probably find it helps to number the grid lines.

The final step is to repeat this grid-making process on your painting support. You will now have a series of grid lines which correspond exactly to your small grid. These are the reference points which will enable you to transfer the marks from your small drawing to your final picture.

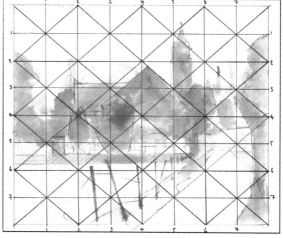

This is a pen and wash drawing made on the spot for a later painting. There are some colour notes on the actual sketch – this is often a useful addition to drawings made outside.

This small version of the original drawing has been made to improve the composition. The adjustments here are minor, mainly to give more room for the sky; this slightly increases the feeling of distance.

The drawing on to the support – in this case, hardboard (Masonite) – has been kept very simple. Just outlining the main shapes and directions is all that is needed at this stage, the rest will come with the painting.

Composing a picture

The important thing to remember about painting is that it is not just about technical skill and knowledge. You learn and develop your skills in order to convey the excitement you feel through painting. In the first two projects I dealt with painting a picture in a fairly objective way through still life, which has involved composition, colour, and, most of all, looking. Here, I shall deal with putting together a picture from various elements to make an imaginative composition. The picture I have decided to use as an example is totally different from the previous ones in subject matter and intention. Nevertheless, the considerations which are made have a great deal in common with those involved in the first two projects.

Sketchbook drawing for the eagle's head.

Problems of scale

The first point to note is the picture's scale and size. This picture is painted on a large format; this is an important step away from the first two pictures which were both small scale. The reason I make a point of this is that when you up the scale, there has to be much more information contained in the forms. The first two pictures were composed of small objects – fruit, and so on. Now we are dealing with large human figures – almost life size in the foreground – and a large space from front to back of the picture. The foreground figure occupies almost half of the picture space. One of the main pictorial problems was to relate the foreground figure to the background figure in a space almost devoid of objects. This has been done by the use of directional lines and points throughout the picture, and the direction of the figure's arms, which is echoed by the line of the square red shape at the top as well as the direction of the bottom line of the same red shape echoed again by the line of her breasts. These imaginary and real lines direct the eye to follow through to the seated background figure. This has to be a strong movement as each figure is contained in its own shape within the picture. This was an important aspect of the composition as the picture is about the isolation of the human figure. The curve of the bird's wing on the left of the picture is a movement to keep the eye contained in the shape. The spatial feeling is enhanced by the light tone of the foreground figure compared to the dark lost tones of the seated figure.

Choice of colour

The setting has the unreal quality of a stage set about it to give it a non-specific time and place setting. The colour is pervadingly warm, the figure in the foreground is warm in colour and tone compared to the background. To set about a picture of this nature, you need plenty of preparation. The size of the picture means that mistakes will be expensive in both time and

The body of the eagle.

The dark form of the eagle emerging.

energy. So, a number of preparatory drawings and paintings were necessary before embarking on such a large project.

Formulating an idea

If this is an aspect of picture making that interests you there are some things which you must be sure about before you start. With still lifes, landscapes or portraits your subject is there before you and there is a direct physical link between you, but once you move away from that situation then

Above and left: Sketchbook drawings for the torso, defining the main directional lines.

This painting was done from life in one short sitting of about two hours. The main purpose of this study was to gather information and also to build into the painting some of the qualities that I wanted in the final picture. The approach has been kept freer than in the large picture as this is still only a study.

there are other considerations. Firstly, and most importantly, is the idea. This is the foundation of your picture. If your idea is not sufficiently strong, then no matter how well you paint it, the painting will never stand up for long, in terms of the interest and intensity the spectator requires of a painting. Having satisfied yourself that the idea merits further development then your next requirement is to gather together more than enough information about the subject or content of the picture. This could be figures, architecture, landscape, atmosphere, or a combination of all these elements. When I say more than enough, it is necessary to be able to sieve through and discard what you don't need, rather than feel that you are scraping the barrel for information.

Painting the picture
When you have arrived at this point, then the process of painting the picture is almost the same as described for the previous projects in terms of composition, colour, shape, and line. The only

This is a sketchbook idea for parts of the larger painting, and was carried out to clarify my thoughts about the mood of the picture, rather than to make specific drawings about form and shape.

Below: This was one of many quick ideas for the painting in which colour was introduced into the sketches. These sketches are deliberately kept loose to allow for flexibility within the drawing and also to enable me to move quickly on to another sketch to develop ideas further.

difference is that this time you can do anything with your picture – you are completely in charge. It's rather like playing with plasticine (modelling clay), you can push and pull it into any shape you like, make spaces, close them off or change scale to suit your idea. It's a wonderful feeling to have this freedom in the creative process.

There are many painters who work in this vein. Graham Sutherland, one of the great English painters of the twentieth century, merits attention. The most interesting aspect of his work for us to consider is that a great deal of his work is landscape based but composed entirely in the studio. He used landscape, and took from it various aspects, changed them and set them back down in the landscape from which they had come. There is, however, an absolute authenticity about his work, due to direct observation. He changed, composed, and re-defined shapes, but they are always believable, and the considerations of composition and colour which you have been making throughout the projects and exercises in this section relate as much to his work as they will to yours.

To learn the rules and properties of oil painting is absolutely essential to you if you are to progress and develop your talent, and at the same time, liberate your creative spirit.

Graham Sutherland 'Horned Forms' 813 × 641mm (32 × 25¼in.). Sutherland is a painter who uses landscape rather than a painter of landscape. To use his own definition, he paraphrases landscape and forms which means that although his art is firmly based in landscape as his source of inspiration, he composes his pictures from various elements not necessarily from the same location. In this painting, one can see very definite landscape elements; the horizon line in the distance divides the sky and land mass, for example. The horned forms in the foreground have a menacing dramatic quality which, although their scale is large in the picture, probably came from quite small forms such as gorse thorns. This is essentially a picture composed of landscape and natural elements to express a particular personal feeling about an environment, and would have been arrived at through an acute personal observation using sketchbook studies and drawings.

PART FOUR

Composition
and
Perspective

Introduction

*This vase from the fourth century BC
is an example of the Greeks' use of
perspective.*

*(Artist unknown) Japanese print
370 × 228mm (14½ × 9in.).
None of the traditional Western
methods of creating form by using
tone or perspective has been used in
this print. Emotion is expressed
through the conflicting and powerful
angles of the flat design.*

Composition and perspective are powerful tools in artists'
hands, once you have understood how to employ them. They
are both concerned with the way that shapes and forms are
ordered on the page and with creating works that make visual
sense to the viewer and which have in-depth structure.

Composition is the organization of the shapes and forms
into an expressive whole, whereas perspective produces the
illusion of three dimensions on a two-dimensional surface. In
most Western art the two work together, in a relationship that
can perhaps be understood by an analogy with literature. In
this, the role of perspective is like that of grammar, and
composition like that of vocabulary. The compositional
elements – line, shape, tone and colour – need to be ordered
into coherent phrases and sentences, and this is the function of
perspective – reproducing those elements in a form that can be
'read'. The roots of the two words also throw some light on
their meaning. Composition derives from the Latin *compositus*,
which means well-arranged, whereas perspective comes from a
word concerned with looking – *perspicere*, to look through.

An artist, then, uses composition and perspective to present
a coherent pictorial representation of elements of life and
scenery from the world of our visual experience. Composition
is present in any painting, from the moment you put two blobs
of colour down next to each other, but perspective has only
been conventional in painting from the late Middle Ages, and
was to remain so until the early years of our own century. It is
still a powerful tool in representational art. Simply put,
perspective enables us to differentiate between forms of
different sizes and at different distances from the viewer and to
grasp immediately what those relationships are. Take a simple
drawing by a child of two people against a background. The
child will probably draw the two people in different sizes
against some other objects, and it will not be possible to tell
whether the smaller of the two is merely smaller than the other
one, or is the same size, but is further away. Perspective enables
you to establish such relationships in your work.

Although formal rules of perspective were not developed
until the Renaissance, a simple form was known earlier. It was
used by the Greeks in decorations on their pots and by the
Romans in the mural paintings in their villas. But the
Renaissance architects' use of space in their great buildings

challenged painters to find a means of equalling this concept of space on a two-dimensional surface, and this led to the great discoveries in perspective.

A study of perspective alone, however, does not make a work of art more (or less) beautiful. For centuries artists managed without it and more recently, since the experiments of the Cubists and the consequent development of abstraction, many artists have had no need for it. However, if you want to produce drawings and paintings that represent the visual world as you see it, a grasp of the principles of perspective will be invaluable.

The studies of composition and perspective are equally applicable, whether you are drawing or painting, but here the more direct approach will be studied through drawing. As in most disciplines knowledge and understanding give confidence, and in art this is as important as observation and sensitivity to form and colour. As you gain an improved understanding of these principles, you will find that your work will gain in confidence and that you will be better able to create a finished work from your sketches.

Valerie Thornton 'Cley Hall Farm' 400 × 572mm (15¾ × 22½in.). This sensitively balanced etching illustrates how depth is created without resorting to perspective in a composition in which the forms have been flattened, creating an almost abstract design. Depth is achieved by tone, and the scale of the textures. The carefully calculated lines on the left of the design are less intended to contribute to the feeling of depth than to give variation to the shapes created by the vertical and horizontal structure of the etching.

Many amateur artists and students fear that perspective is an abstruse subject, but in fact a grasp of the three-dimensional world is fundamental to our existence, and also to the mechanics of the eye and the way we perceive. It is a very straightforward process to gain a working understanding of the principles and to be able to use them to solve most visual problems concerning the size of shapes in distance. This section aims to teach the basic rules which will solve most problems, and at the same time to convey the principles of composition. It does this through giving a series of exercises, which are designed to be followed and put into practice. If they are read on the page without being tried out, they may sometimes appear to be complex and difficult, but if you actually do the drawings yourself, you should find that they are quite straightforward.

Another word of warning is to do them in sequence. They are designed to follow from one another, and if you skip or dip you may find that you are missing a vital piece of information that was given earlier.

Ultimately, however, your surest route to expressing the third dimension successfully in well-composed works is intense observation of your subject, careful study of angles and relative shapes and a feeling for space. Mastery of composition and perspective does not derive from learning a series of rules to which you have to adhere slavishly, but from the knowledge that gives the confidence to respond with spontaneity and excitement to the beauty of things you see around you.

'Hauled Out for a Polish'. This chalk study for a painting was done to establish the composition. The original view of the boats that I had was horizontal. From this study, however, I decided that a vertical shape was more appropriate for the purpose of the finished painting, which was to emphasize the unstable shape of boats out of the water.

Materials and equipment

A few simple tools will be needed to practice the exercises in this section: an A2 (594 × 420mm/ 24 × 18in.) or ½ Imperial (559 × 381mm/ 22 × 15in.) drawing board; A2 (594 × 420mm/ 24 × 18in.) white cartridge (drawing) paper; flat-headed drawing pins or masking tape for securing the corners of your paper to the board; a T-square to fit your drawing board; a 45° and 30°/ 60° set square (triangle), preferably of thick plastic and no less than 200mm (8in.) along the longest side – thin plastic bends and is liable to slip under a ruler or T-square; a pair of compasses for taking off measurements; H or F (2½-3) grade pencils – softer grades smudge easily; a 300mm (12in.) ruler – again, plastic is preferable to wood.

To use your instruments correctly requires no special skills. Hold your T-square arm hard up against the left side of your board to draw a horizontal line at any height across the board.

Slide the set square along the T-square, or along a firmly held ruler, or hold it underneath a horizontal line to locate the centre of vision and vanishing points of either a 45° or 30°/60° projection. The larger you make a perspective drawing with instruments, the easier you will find it to be accurate.

A useful hint when you are drawing a line to get it just where you want it is to put the point of a sharp pencil on the exact place you wish to start the line, slide your ruler, T- or set square up to it until it touches, then draw along. This is a great deal easier than trying to put the ruler in exactly the right point first.

Always keep your instruments clean, otherwise your drawing soon becomes dirty.

To prevent a plastic ruler or set square sliding about independently, stick a narrow strip of masking tape along the back.

You won't need a vast array of tools and equipment to practice the perspective exercises suggested: the most useful items are illustrated here.

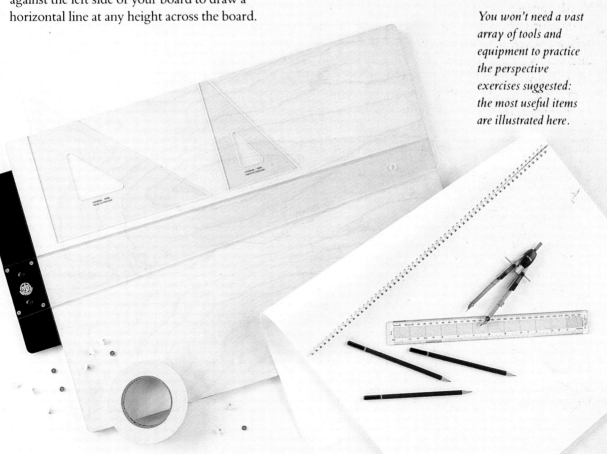

1 Composition

In his 'Notes on the Art of Painting' given to the Royal Academy in 1783 Sir Joshua Reynolds wrote:

'Composition, which is the principal part of the invention of a Painter, is by far the greatest difficulty he has to encounter. Every man that can paint at all, can execute individual parts; but to keep those parts in due subordination as relative to a whole, requires a comprehensive view of the art, that more strongly implies genius, than perhaps any other quality.'

In spite of Reynolds' rather pessimistic view, the principles of composition – arranging shapes within the picture area – once understood, can be mastered to good effect.

Sir Joshua Reynolds 'Self Portrait', painted 1753 or 1754.

The shape of the surface

For most artists the flat, two-dimensional surface is the stage on which they act out and convey all their emotional and intellectual ideas. Therefore, the size, shape and proportion of this surface have an important effect on a picture.

Artists' papers, boards and canvases are available in a very wide range of sizes and proportions and if you are making up your own canvases from stretchers there is an even greater choice of size. There is no objection either to cutting a board or piece of paper to the size and shape you would like it to be, so there is no need to feel inhibited by materials that come in stock sizes. You can work to any size and shape you feel comfortable with.

One of the most common shapes for easel paintings is the horizontal rectangle (diagram 1). Since its base is greater than its vertical sides, it produces a very stable shape. One feels it would be difficult to knock it over. The eye can roam

Diagram 1. The horizontal (or landscape) rectangle.

'Dangerous Reef' 485 × 700mm (19 × 27½in.). The powerful line of the horizon in this long composition is offset by the curves of the waves and the stern plates to exploit fully the overall shape.

Cosimo Tura 'The Virgin and Child Enthroned' 2390 × 1016mm (94¼ × 40in.). This painting shows Tura's mastery of design and creative use of perspective. He exploits the vertical format to the full, by repeating the arch at the top of the painting with the niche in which the Madonna sits, and underlining the height of the throne by the supporting figures and pillars on each side, which are emphasized by the two figures beneath.

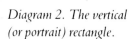

Diagram 2. The vertical (or portrait) rectangle.

expansively from side to side and also back into the picture (this is termed 'recession'). This has been and still is a favourite shape of the English and Dutch landscape painters, among them John Constable, J.M.W. Turner, and Meyndert Hobbema; indeed it is known as 'landscape' shape in art circles. However, it does not invite the eye to travel up and down.

The same rectangle up-ended (diagram 2) presents a very different feeling. It is less stable and could be knocked over easily, the eye cannot move much from side to side and is inhibited from going deep into the shape. However, the eye can roam up and down. It can soar, and consequently this became the favourite shape of the great religious painters, like Botticelli, Crivelli, and Tura, whose subjects like the 'Assumption of the Virgin', or 'Christ in Majesty' or the 'Ascension' were perfectly conveyed by this format. It has also been the format of descents into Hell and a hilarious drawing of a Royal Academy soirée by Rowlandson of an avalanche of inebriated members and their ladies tumbling down the main staircase. It is not such an easy shape to fill as the landscape, but is ideal for portraits and has earned the name throughout the art world as 'portrait' shape.

The square (diagram 3) is the least evocative and most neutral shape, although it has great stability. It invites the viewer to look into its centre and the eye tends to roam in a spiral around that point. This tendency was exploited by the great

Venetian painters, Veronese and Tintoretto, the former in 'Unfaithfulness' from his 'Allegory of Love' series and the latter in 'The Origin of the Milky Way'. More recently, Pieter Mondrian used the square because of its neutral qualities and relied upon his sensitivity to shape and the space within it to overcome that inherent neutrality.

The diamond shape (diagram 4) has little equilibrium; it is just balanced and presents a challenge to the artist to create a balanced stable design within it. More complex variations of shape than even the diamond are being tried today, with artists assembling different shapes and sizes of canvases to produce very large paintings of dynamic and arresting designs.

The final shape we will look at is typical of a painting designed for an architectural setting (diagram 5). Its half-round, arched top cuts off the top corners of the rectangle, but artists frequently incorporate the surrounding architectural features outside the picture area as anchorages and fulcrums for the main directional lines when employing this shape.

Paolo Veronese 'Unfaithfulness' 1850 × 1850mm (74 × 74in.). In this brilliant example of the square format, vertical and horizontal lines through the centre of the picture intersect where the figure's hip joins her torso.

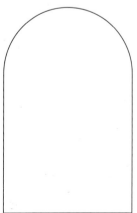

*Diagram 3.
The square.*

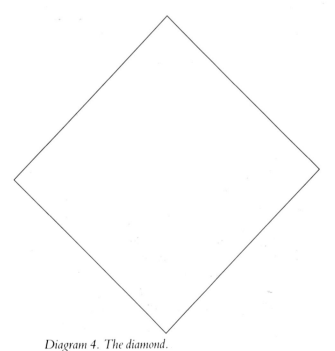

Diagram 4. The diamond.

*Diagram 5.
The arched rectangle.*

Dividing the surface

The first impact that any work of art has upon the spectator is usually made by the arrangement of the main shapes on the surface and the divisions of the total space. Having considered which shape is most suitable for the idea you want to express, you need to think about how best to arrange or 'compose' your picture within the space. In any work the subject matter will be arranged in such a way as to impose some sort of basic division of the painting surface. What this is going to be is one of the first decisions to be made.

Taking a horizontal rectangle as the chosen shape (although many of the considerations that follow are equally applicable, whichever shape of surface you have chosen), the simplest division is by one line only. The most common way is a horizontal line right across the centre (as shown in diagram 6). This can be used by a skilful artist to good effect, but because each rectangle is equal, it is probably the least interesting of all arrangements. (Have a look at your own drawings and paintings and see if you have ever done this.)

The same rectangle, although still cut across by only one line as in diagram 7, is much more

interesting when the two proportions are different. A division nearer the bottom of the painting gives you plenty of space for a fine sky or an interesting background. The foreground is reduced, so this division is ideal when the foreground presents you with several problems, since it allows you to cut out as much as possible.

The reverse of this (where the horizontal division is nearer the top of the painting, as shown in diagram 8), however, invites the artist to create an exciting foreground since it gives plenty of ground to cover to the horizon (assuming that you make the division coincide with the horizon). There is the opportunity to create a feeling of

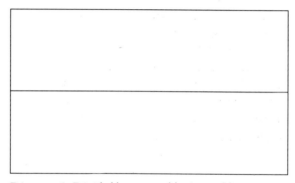

Diagram 6. Divided by a central horizontal line.

Diagram 7. The low horizon.

Jacob van Ruisdael 'Landscape with Ruins' 1075 × 1440mm (43 × 57½in.). Van Ruisdael was a master of composition. In this painting the low horizon gives room for the billowing clouds in the sky, which disappears beyond and below the horizon.

great recession, and for the interesting development of things near to.

Many artists content themselves with a simple horizontal division of their surface, but more often than not they will make a vertical division of their compositions as well. The most obvious division, into four rectangles (as shown in diagram 9), can be made to work in the hands of a great artist, but is very dull otherwise. This arrangement demands that something very exciting is put into each rectangle to make the whole work. This can be a handicap. However, a vertical and horizontal division producing a juxtaposition of rectangles (diagram 10) makes a more interesting framework for a composition.

Perhaps your decisions as an artist in composing your work have so far been intuitive and this is right, but why not review your work and see if these simple suggestions may help to give greater interest to your compositions?

Diagram 8. The high horizon.

'Bathing Huts' 395 × 525mm *(15½ × 21½in.). In this long composition the high horizon gives room for a full foreground. The study shows severe recession that takes the eye back in a rather lurching way into the design.*

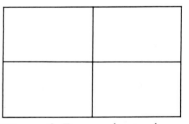

Diagram 9. Four equal rectangles.

'The Glebe Cottage' 405 × *550mm (16 × 22½in.). Here, the horizontal and repetitive lines of horizon, roof and walls are counterbalanced by the strong vertical through the chimney, gable and centre of the wall.*

Diagram 10. Four
rectangles of different
sizes.

James McNeill Whistler 'Old Battersea
Bridge: Nocturne in Blue and Gold'
679 × 508mm (26¾ × 20in.). It is not
only to horizontal rectangles that the
considerations on dividing the picture
surface apply. In this upright painting,
Whistler uses the deliberately heightened
bridge to create the simple but dramatic
vertical and horizontal divisions and force
the eye upward to take in the firework
display. Although he is ostensibly
concerned with colour and tone to create the
atmosphere, he needed space for the display
on the right. He achieves this, and makes a
satisfying composition, through the four
unequal rectangles.

Harmonious proportion

Artists have always looked for both an ideal shape on which to work, and ideal proportions for that shape and several theories have evolved, two of which we will look at. The first is based on the relationship of squares and rectangles.

Construct a square ABCD (as shown in diagram 11). Produce the lines AB and DC. Using diagonal DB, describe an arc so that it intersects the produced line DC at F. From F draw a line at right angles to DF to intersect the produced line AB at E. The constructed rectangle AEFD has a harmonious relationship with the square ABCD. Repeat the procedure, using diagonal DE, to construct a further rectangle. This rectangle AHID has a harmonious relation with the square ABCD and the rectangle AEFD. This principle has long provided a rule-of-thumb method for artists seeking good proportion.

The second method of establishing fine proportion we will look at developed from the discovery of the Golden Mean, a direct result of the widespread interest in geometry and classical art in the Renaissance. The Golden Mean is also called the 'divine' proportion because while it is provable and demonstrable geometrically it cannot be resolved arithmetically, since it always results in an irrational fraction, .618 recurring.

Diagram 12 demonstrates how to discover the ideal proportion of a line AB (which could be the base or upright of a rectangle). Produce the line to C, so that CA is half the length of AB. From A draw a 90° vertical line AD the same length as AB. With the point of a pair of compasses at C describe an arc from D to intersect AB. The point of intersection G marks the Golden Mean of AB.

Diagram 13 is an extension of diagram 12. In it, the Golden Means of the rectangle ABCD are drawn in (in order not to make the diagram too unwieldy, the calculation lines of three sides, AB, BC, and CD only are shown). The points of intersection of the Golden Means W, X, Y and Z are also indicated.

It is interesting to look at how one of the great artists put the theory of the Golden Mean into practice. A study of the works of the English artist John Constable reveals that his paintings constructed and developed in the studio from studies made in the field always show his understanding of the Golden Mean. So familiar was he with this proportion that he used it instinctively when working on location and the knowledge never interfered with his spontaneity and freshness. His respect for the ideal or 'divine'

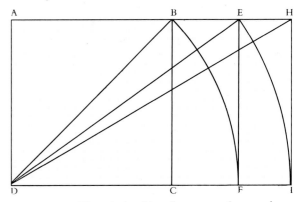

Diagram 11. The relationship of squares and rectangles.

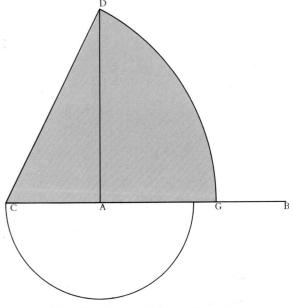

Diagram 12. The Golden Mean of a line AB.

proportion is evident from a detailed analysis of many of his works.

Constable regarded his painting 'The Cornfield', an upright design, as one of his best researched works, making studies beforehand of every detail, before building it into a fine satisfying painting. The parts did not appear in nature in the same positions as they do in the picture, since Constable has brought Dedham Church into view, in the background. The Golden Means have been calculated along with the main directional lines. It becomes very obvious that intersecting lines, whether within the main picture area or on the edges, assume a greater importance than disconnected lines which do not touch other lines or the edges of the picture. It is usually on these intersections that centres of interest are placed to great effect; those placed on the intersections of the Golden Means have the greatest effect. Try this exercise yourself with a reproduction of a great painting.

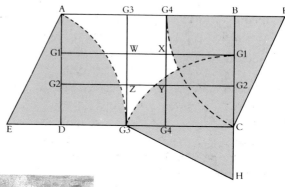

Above: Diagram 13. The Golden Means of a horizontal rectangle. These are found by taking each of the sides of the rectangle and determining its Golden Mean, as shown in diagram 12.

John Constable 'The Cornfield' 1429 × 1219mm (56¼ × 48in.). This painting shows Constable's understanding of the Golden Mean. The overlaid lines G1, G2, G3 and G4 mark the main Golden Sections, and it is along these lines that Constable placed his major points of interest, including the dog. The church, placed on an intersection of two of these lines has even greater prominence. The boy in the bottom left of the picture is exactly at the intersections of the Golden Sections of that rectangle: G5, G6, G7 and G8.

Creating a composition

Composition also involves arranging shapes within your picture area. Excited by a knowledge of proportion and shape it is tempting to be over-ambitious and use far too great a variety of shape within your composition. When three simple shapes, such as a triangle, rhomboid and circle, are placed separately in a composition or overlap each other (as shown in diagram 14), the viewer can identify each shape, read what it is and enjoy the interplay. The addition of one more shape, particularly an irregular one as shown in diagram 15, obscures their identities, however, and while the design may still hold up it would require only one more shape to create incoherence or confusion.

The last two points to consider here are, firstly, that a horizontal shape with easy flowing directional lines gives a sense of passivity or tranquillity, whereas strongly opposed lines and lines not parallel to the edges convey a sense of agitation, dynamism, or activity. Secondly, directional lines leading into corners take the viewer's eye out of the design. Avoid them unless you wish to create an impression of explosion.

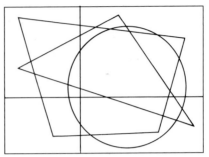

Diagram 14. Three shapes are readable.

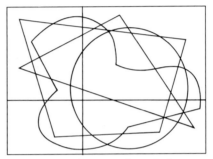

Diagram 15. One more is confusing.

PROVING MOUNTS (MATS)

Proving mounts are indispensable when designing a drawing or painting. Cut two L shapes from a piece of card (as shown in diagram 16). Gather all the work you have so far done, including those sketches you thought insignificant, and place the mounts around them. Then adjust the sizes and shape, taking pieces out of the picture, making square compositions long and upright from square. You may find, for instance, that instead of the horizon dividing your composition across the middle it looks much more interesting with less sky or even very little foreground.

Keep these proving mounts handy while composing your pictures – they will be of great assistance.

Viewing frames are also useful. Make three from dark-faced card – the first with a rectangular aperture of the proportions 3:5, based on the Golden Mean; the second with a square aperture

J.M.W. Turner 'The Evening Star' 900 × 1200mm (36 × 48in.). Although unfinished, this painting expresses a great sense of tranquillity. The equilibrium of the design creates a very still atmosphere.

Paolo Uccello 'Battle of San Romano' (detail) 1790 × 2950mm (71½ × 126in.). In this dynamic design, the conflicting angles of the lances and juxtapositions of each feature lead the eye out of the canvas.

3:3; and the third with a rectangular aperture of the proportions 3:4¼ based lengthwise on the diagonal of the square.

Practice is necessary to use viewing frames successfully; they can, however, be invaluable in helping you create a composition.

Close one eye and hold the frame a few centimetres from your open eye, then move it away until it is at arm's length. You will notice that the closer it is to the eye the greater the breadth of view you have through it, and the further away it is from your eye the narrower and more restricted is the view. Cut paper or prepare boards on which you are going to work to exactly the same proportions, for example, 30 × 50cm (12 × 20in.), 30 × 30cm (12 × 12in.) and 30 × 43cm (12 × 17in.). Find interesting still lifes or views from your window, and move your viewing frame until you see through the aperture how much you wish to draw. Then arrange the shapes as you see them through your viewing frame. (At this stage, work only in line. Don't try to add a third dimension.) Try moving your viewpoint lower or higher, and make drawings from these positions. Immediately your compositions will take on greater originality, and you will see shapes more clearly and use them more effectively than before.

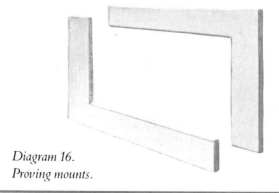

Diagram 16.
Proving mounts.

2 Approaching perspective

We have so far only looked at the linear aspect of composition, although we all know that gradations of tone of light to dark from white to black will add to the drama of fine composition. We are also aware, however, that we expect this flat composition – the two-dimensional structure of the surface – to be supported by an understandable structure in the third dimension. This can be achieved by tonal changes, by the use of colour or by an awareness of the principles of perspective. Perspective exists all around us – vanishing points, for example, can be traced from buildings and your eye level is a constant. Before we turn to the principles of perspective, and how they are applied in drawing and painting, however, it is necessary to become familiar with the technical terms that are used in dealing with perspective. These are not purely academic but have a practical value for the artist because they relate to and clarify the visual assumptions we make about the world around us.

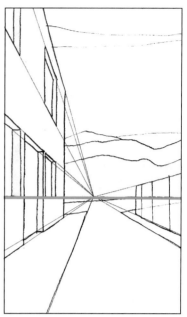

Diagram 17. In all diagrams, the blue line is the eye level.

Key terms

Almost everyone who has written about perspective, or who has taught it, has invented their own terms for the different elements. Some are widely used and well known, but others seem less familiar. To prevent confusion for those with some knowledge of perspective, and to establish these elements for those who are coming to it fresh, here is a list of the terms that I shall be using, together with definitions and alternatives you may meet elsewhere. The abbreviations are those used throughout the rest of this section.

Angle of Incidence   The angle formed between a ray of light as it strikes an object and the object's surface.

Angle of Reflection   The angle between a ray of light and the surface of an object as it bounces off that object. It equals the angle of incidence.

Centre of Vision – CV   Also termed Central Vanishing Point (CVP), Point of Sight (PS), Principal Vanishing Point (PVP). This is the nearest point on the picture plane (see below)

opposite your eye. It is found at the intersection of the lines of sight and eye level. Imagine that you are looking down the sights of a rifle held horizontally; the point of aim would be the centre of vision.

Elevation   A drawing of what you would see if you were standing directly in front of the subject.

Eye – E (black bullet)   Sometimes termed the Spectator (S) or Viewer (V). This is the point from which your eye views the subject.

Eye Level – EL (blue line)   This is a complete horizontal circle at your eye level as you turn your head or the horizon if you are at sea level. Everything in perspective is related to this line.

Ground Line – GL   A measuring line, this is a line running along the ground parallel to the eye level. A measured scale can be marked on it and projected back to the CV or VPs to give lateral measurements.

Ground Plane – GP   An imaginary horizontal flat extension of the ground on which you stand, it extends forwards from your feet to the eye level on the picture plane.

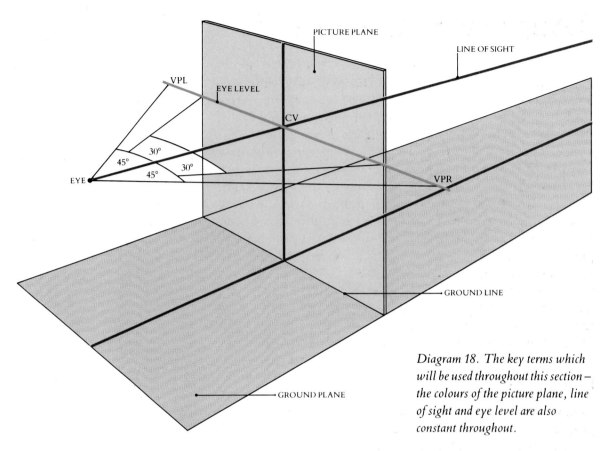

Diagram 18. The key terms which will be used throughout this section – the colours of the picture plane, line of sight and eye level are also constant throughout.

Horizon – H   In mountainous or hilly country it is the dividing line between sky and land and may be well above the eye level (or below in three-point perspective).

Line of Sight – LS (red lines)   Also termed Distance Line (DL). This is the line from the eye to the picture plane and which intersects it at 90°. Measuring it establishes the distance you are from the picture plane.

Parallels of Perspective   The term Vanishing Parallels (VP) is also used. These are lines seen on a plan as parallel, but in perspective they appear to converge at a point on the eye level at infinity.

Picture Plane – PP (solid blue)   This is an imaginary vertical plane at right angles to the line of sight upon which a drawing or painting is drafted. It can be regarded as the surface of your board or canvas. To help understand it, think of it

as a vertical sheet of clear glass at a short distance from you, through which you view your subject. What is seen on the picture plane is shaped by two factors: the height that the eye is from the ground line and the distance the subject is from the eye. The distance between eye and subject is usually equal to the greater dimension of your picture.

Plan   A drawing of something done as if you were looking at it from directly above.

Trace Lines   Lines which plot one point on a form to another, or the path of a shadow on an object on the ground plane or across the object.

Vanishing Points – VP   Also termed Distance Points (DP). These are points on the eye level on either side of the centre of vision to which parallel lines going away from you converge and appear to vanish. They can be extended to infinity to left and right – known as vanishing point left (VPL) and vanishing point right (VPR). While for your subject the natural vanishing points may occur on or about the extremes of your board, it is likely that they may be some distance outside the edges. A piece of card pinned along the foot of the board can be fixed at an inclined angle, and two lines from a central point at the bottom drawn upwards in the approximate directions of the vanishing

points as shown in diagram 19. This is a very inaccurate guide, but can be of use if you extend the lines in your imagination or point in the appropriate directions. You can persuade people looking at your work to stand back from the picture to the position from which you want it to be seen by placing your vanishing points further away from the edges of the painting.

Diagram 19. Determining vanishing points.

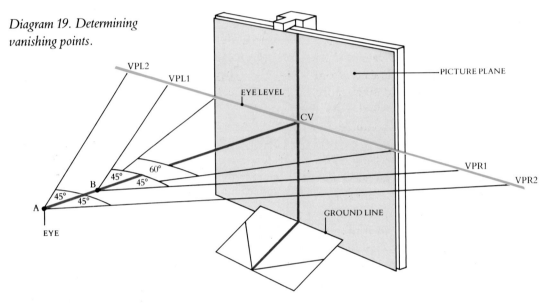

How we see

Lines in a composition that slope inwards away from the edge of the picture immediately create the illusion of depth. In diagram 20 in real life the

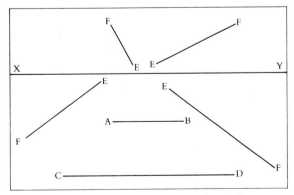

Diagram 20. We assume CD is nearer than AB.

lines represented by AB and CD are assumed to be the same length, but AB appears further away than CD. On a similar assumption the points labelled E appear further away than F. This illusion is heightened by the line XY which we visually assume is a distant horizon. This diagram could be a drawing on a flat vertical wall.

In diagram 21 a similar visual assumption is made. AB appears much nearer than CD and EF. We tend to assume that each line is really the same height, and that the smaller ones are further away. This time XY leaves us in less doubt that it is a distant horizon. The three figures in diagram 22 are even more compelling in the way they assume their positions in space. We immediately think that figure C is nearest and A and B further away.

Let us now look at *how* these 'optical illusions' happen. Close one eye, then stand or sit upright and fix your gaze on a spot straight in front, level with your eye. Raise and extend both your arms and hands in front of you, then open your arms until you can no longer see your hands with any definition. Most people open their arms to about 60° before being unable to see the hands in clear focus, so the average 'cone of vision' is taken to be 60°. Perspective, in theory, does not work if both your eyes are open.

Imagine you are looking through a pane of glass at two identical vertical pegs in the ground outside as shown in diagram 23. The rays of light from the pegs converge on the eye. The rays from the one furthest away have converged much more than the nearer one so the further peg will appear smaller on the glass pane, and correspondingly the nearer peg will appear larger and below the one further away. Diagram 24 shows two lengths of timber lying on the ground first in plan view and then seen through a pane of glass. The lines of sight converging on the eye show the piece of timber GH appearing much shorter than EF where they pass through the glass.

Now imagine that the pane of glass you have been looking through is a piece of paper or board. The way in which your eyes have perceived the lengths of timber through the glass is the way you should draw them, measuring off their heights and lengths on to the paper.

Diagram 22. C is obviously nearer than A or B.

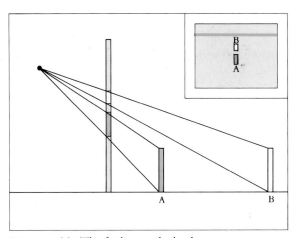

Diagram 23. The farther peg looks shorter.

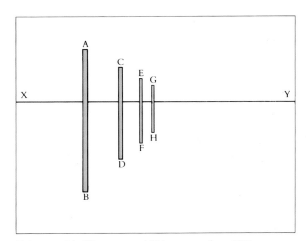

Diagram 21. We assume AB is nearer than CD.

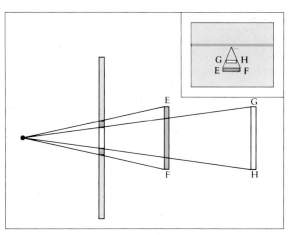

Diagram 24. The farther length looks shorter.

A classic example of these principles put into practice is the drawing of parallel railway lines disappearing into the distance (as shown in diagram 25). The tracks get smaller and closer together as they recede until the lines meet at a point on the horizon on the eye level – at infinity.

Left: Diagram 25. The tracks get smaller and closer together as they recede.

Aids to drawing

Over the years, artists, illustrators and draughtsmen have developed various ways to help them represent accurately what they see in front of them. These 'aids' to drawing, and you should remember that they are only that (not rules to follow slavishly or devices you must buy or make), vary from the simple and familiar to the more mechanical and technical. You may, however, find some of them very useful.

Measuring by eye with a pencil

A simple means of estimating and comparing proportions, particularly vertical and horizontal distances, is by using a pencil as a measure. Select the object you wish to use as a yardstick for your drawing, then hold your pencil out, making sure your arm is fully extended. Align the top of the pencil with the top of the object and your finger with the bottom (as shown in diagram 26). This 'measurement' will allow you to estimate the other objects in proportion. Ensure when

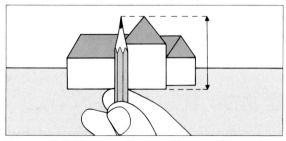

Diagram 26. Measuring by eye with a pencil.

measuring depths that the pencil is absolutely vertical. When estimating pitch or measuring horizontally, the pencil has to be at right angles to your line of vision. When estimating an angle, start with the pencil horizontal, then rotate it until it lies along the line. This will establish the angle.

Sight size

Working 'sight size' is a useful technique to employ. Diagram 27 shows how this system would work when tackling a 'still life' of a cube on a small table. If you are right-handed, you will need to look round the left side of the drawing board so that your drawing hand does not cross the lines of sight and obscure your vision. With the board vertical and one eye closed, move your head slightly to left and right so that the board's edge can be used as a plumb line to determine the varying heights of each part of the objects, and mark these points on the edge of the board. This is particularly useful when figure drawing, but can also be used to good effect when drawing a landscape or, as here, a still life. This is a time-honoured method, proved by the ticks to be seen down the edge of many a master's drawing, indicating he was drawing sight size.

We perceive objects in a plane which is at right angles to our line of vision. In the case of looking straight ahead the plane is vertical, as if it were a sheet of glass suspended in front of us. However, when you are drawing your board may be on your knees or on a sloping easel, so that you will have to look down; the tendency, nevertheless, is still to visualize the vertical plane before your eye. To 'translate' this vertical image to a board at an angle requires complex mental adjustments of proportion. There is a danger that you may overadjust, making the bottom half of what you are drawing much too big. If you are a beginner, it is probably easier to use a vertical board until you have had more practice and are more proficient.

The obvious exception to using a vertical board is when drawing a horizontal subject, say a landscape-shaped still life or, indeed, a real landscape. It is then much easier to look over the top (as shown in diagram 28). Hold the board horizontally beneath your subject, but close up against it, with one eye closed. Then, with your free hand, tick off the widths of the details of your subject along the top edge of your paper.

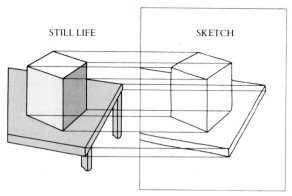

Diagram 27. Working sight size.

Your drawings might at first appear stilted or stiff using these methods; however, with practice the techniques will become instinctive and no longer inhibit your style.

Diagram 28. The principle of working sight size applied to a landscape.

Mechanical aids

Albrecht Dürer used a drawing frame with a rather elaborate mechanism. The eyepiece could be moved laterally with a thread and turnbuckle, and backwards or forwards, keeping it square with the table top. The glazed frame was also held vertically. A simpler version can be constructed with a picture frame, without its backing but with its glass, clamped on to a table. The critical part of this piece of equipment is the eyepiece. It must be steady for you to be able to produce accurate results. Position the frame and eyepiece so your arm and hand holding a brush loaded with permanent white gouache colour, or a chinagraph pencil (china marker), can reach the glass comfortably (this may take practice).

You will find that, as one eye is closed, it will, at first, be difficult to judge the distance your hand is from the glass. You then draw what you see on to the framed glass. Once the image has been completed, it can be traced off on to thin paper, giving you precise angles, shape and proportion for your drawing.

There are other mechanical aids to drawing, such as the Camera Obscura, which basically consists of a box with a magnifying lens. This produces an upside-down image on a screen which can then be traced off. A Camera Ottica is similar to a Camera Obscura but since it has a mirror inside, it rights the image produced by the lens; it does take some experimentation to make it work. Many eighteenth-century artists, including the great Venetian master Canaletto, are believed to have used such an instrument extensively. Such mechanical aids are fun to make and use, but are no real substitute for the judgements of your eye. Similarly a camera, although it can be a useful tool and reminder, and is to some people a source of inspiration, cannot give you the reasoned sensitivity to space that can be developed by keen observation and expressed by a sound understanding of perspective.

This illustration reproduced from Underweyssung der Messung, *first published in 1525, shows Albrecht Dürer's drawing frame in use. The artist moves the eyepiece back and forth until he can see through the glass as much or as little of his subject (here a figure) as he wishes to paint or draw. He can then trace the outline on to the glass. If he wants to paint a picture from this, he simply transfers the tracing on to his canvas.*

3 Principles of perspective

We now understand how converging rays make us see objects that we know to be the same size as varying sizes because of the different distances they are from the eye. The next step is to know how by applying the rules of perspective these variations can be expressed and appreciated in your drawings and paintings. You may find it useful to keep referring to the definitions of terms on pages 198–200, initially at least.

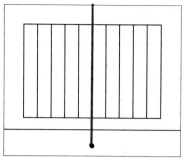

Diagram 29. Plan of floorboards.

Parallel perspective

Parallel perspective is employed when one side of what is facing you is parallel to the picture plane.

Take a plan view of floorboards, seen from above. As diagram 29 shows, they are all parallel and recede, and they are also all equal in width. When viewed on the picture plane, however (diagram 30), they converge and if extended meet at one point on the eye level which is at the viewer's centre of vision. As they are equal in width, their width measurements can be marked along the ground line at the foot of the picture plane. At any other point in their length the relative measurement of any board's width will be as it would be seen in perspective.

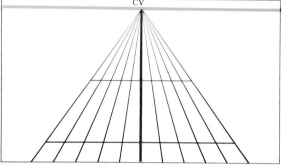

Diagram 30. On the PP, the boards converge.

The position of the viewer alters the appearance of the floorboards (as shown in diagrams 31 and 32). However, there is a limit as to how far you can move to right or left and still employ the rules of parallel perspective. As soon as you have to turn your head to see the whole object then you must use the rules of oblique perspective (see pages 213–16). At this stage we can summarize the first rules of parallel perspective:

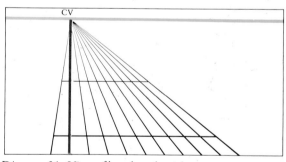

Diagram 31. View of boards to the right.

1 Parallel lines receding from the eye appear to converge and meet at a point at infinity. If these lines are in a horizontal plane and parallel to the line of sight, that point at which they meet is the centre of vision and is on the eye level.

2 Lines which are parallel to the picture plane, that is at right angles to the line of sight, have no vanishing point.

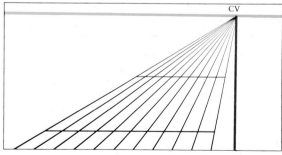

Diagram 32. View of boards to the left.

DRAWING AN INTERIOR

Having constructed a floor following the rules of parallel perspective, it is a very simple procedure to erect a vertical to any size you like at each corner and create an interior. Always start your drawings by establishing an eye level and a centre of vision. All the vanishing lines to the centre of vision are then fairly simple to plot.

The only new feature in the drawing below is the door ajar. Both the top and bottom of the door, since they are parallel, will vanish to a point on the eye level to the left of the CV. Once you have decided how far open you want the door to be, the vanishing lines of the top and the bottom can then be determined.

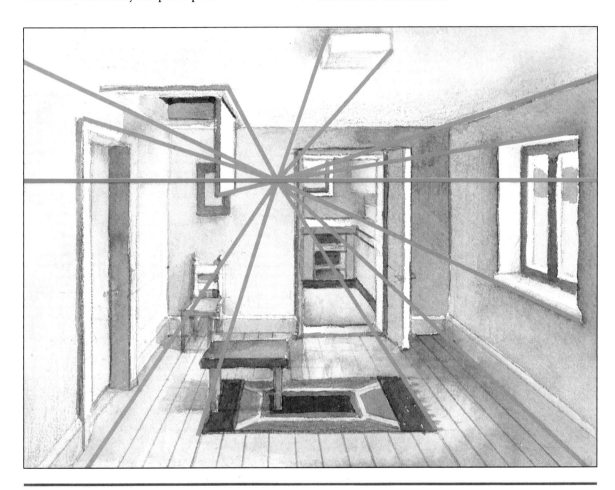

Using diagonals

It is useful to know how to find the centre of a rectangle or square whether in plan view or perspective. This is done by simply drawing in the diagonals. You will notice from the elevation of diagram 33 that the perspective centre makes the back half of square ABFE narrower than the front half EFCD. The diagonals of the square have their common vanishing point on the eye level outside the area of the picture plane. The real advantage of constructing these diagonals is that they allow you to measure the depth of each rectangle in

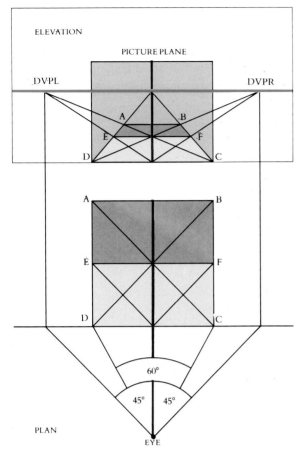

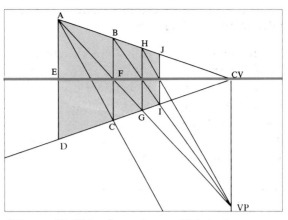

Diagram 34. Using diagonals to establish depth.

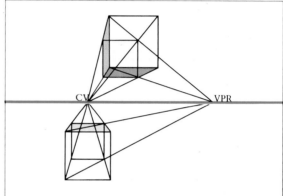

Diagram 33. The centre of a square, plan and elevation.

Diagram 35. Cubes above and below the eye level.

perspective, without resort to holding your pencil at arm's length, when you are drawing from objects or constructing forms from imagination or memory. In this way, you can achieve a convincing feeling of depth in your drawings and paintings.

It is not just horizontal distances that can be measured. It is also possible to measure the equal spaces between verticals in perspective (suppose, for example, you wanted to draw a receding row of vertical posts alongside a flat, straight road as in diagram 34). Decide where you want your first two posts to be. Then, establish a diagonal VP for the space between the posts, this will be immediately below the centre of vision. The diagonal AC produced will make a very long line

before it intersects a vertical dropped from the CV. Lack of space may make it impractical. A diagonal dropped through the eye level (E to CV), however, will work just as well. AF produced to meet a vertical dropped from the CV gives you your VP and the base of your third post (G). A vertical from G to H is your third post. A line from your VP to B gives the base of your fourth post (I) and so on.

Cubic shapes above and below the eye level can also be constructed by using diagonals (you may need the principles in order to put clouds in one of your pictures). A diagonal to the VPR in diagram 35 tells you where the back of the cube should be placed. The backs and faces are, obviously, drawn in parallel perspective.

207

A SIMPLE COMPOSITION

You should now be able to make very interesting drawings using simple parallel perspective and diagonal parallels. Establish your eye level, then decide compositionally what you want to appear facing you (here the ends of the buildings). Draw those in (here, since all the roofs are parallel, their slopes are also parallel). Diagonals are used here to establish the spacing of the fence posts on the right, although they too recede to the CV. The fence posts on the left are parallel to the PP, so don't recede.

Calculating depth

The calculation of depth (that is, where the 'back' of the room should be placed, or how far away the next fence post should be) of a shape in perspective initially seems a problem. If you are working on sight, you can measure it with your eye, or if in doubt with a vertically held pencil. If you can confine the shape you are drawing in a square or rectangle, the diagonal vanishing points can be fixed and depths established in that way. A simple way when working in the studio or to gain

a clear understanding is to make a plan as in diagram 36. This shows how a shape ABCD behind the picture plane and ground line can be accurately placed. The lines of sight intersecting the picture plane establish the widths of the back of the shape. When the width of the back is dropped vertically on to the vanishing parallels, you can establish the precise depth of the square.

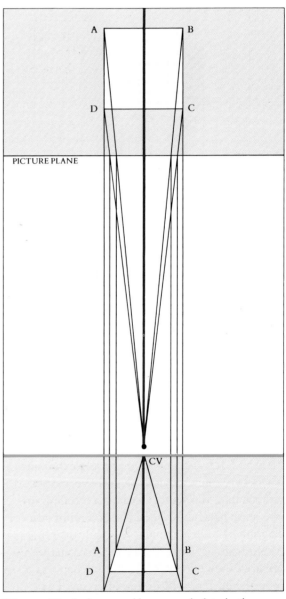

Diagram 36. A plan to enable you to calculate depth.

Placing figures in a landscape

A common problem is to depict people scattered on a flat surface and to establish their relative sizes. Draw a measuring line vertically on the left side of your board. In diagram 37, our artist standing with his sketch pad is 1.8m (6ft) tall and the other seated artist is 1.1m (3ft 6in.) high. These two measurements are projected back to the centre of vision and they represent a 1.8m (6ft) and 1.1m (3ft 6in.) height from the ground for the whole depth of the drawing. By carrying horizontals to left or right the whole area is covered by these measurements. The figures are placed between those lines where they compositionally fit.

Diagram 37. Relative heights of figures in a landscape.

A more common problem, and one over which students and experienced artists stumble, is how to place a figure or an object accurately in front of the picture plane (without making it appear that they are standing in a trench or on a chair).

Diagram 38 illustrates what we see with a normal eye level at 1.5m (5ft) from the ground. This is fixed by a measuring line, once again up the left-hand side of the picture plane. This time the receding lines on the ground have been extended forward of the picture plane as well as back to the centre of vision. From this, it is clear how much of the figures in front of the picture plane should logically be included in the composition.

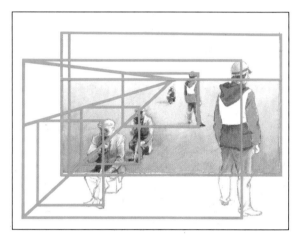

Diagram 38. Placing figures in front of the picture plane.

Inclined and declined planes

Many artists have used inclines and declines in their compositions to create an almost giddy feeling of recession in their designs. The principles involved in creating inclines and declines are the same as those used with a flat horizontal plane with the exception that if the vanishing points are parallel to the horizontal plane, they will appear immediately above or below the centre of vision on which parallel receding lines will converge.

Normally you would not have to calculate the angle of slope but would rely on the sureness of your eye viewing the subject. However, in a composition in the studio, the angle may well

'Holiday Chalet'. An example of inclined planes.

have as much to do with your compositional need for a line going in that direction as the precise angle of slope.

Diagram 39 shows three shapes A, B and C. All are the same width, and in parallel perspective all would recede to the CV. However, if you wanted A to slope downwards and C to slope up, you have to establish vanishing points immediately above and below the CV. The descending slope from A to D in this diagram from the position of the decline vanishing point (VPD) shows how little of this plane would be seen.

Slopes can be established by incline and decline VPs. In diagram 40, the straight road first runs level (A) then slopes down (section B). The vanishing point for the decline (VPD) is indicated. The road then runs level again (section C). This section vanishes at the CV. The road then ascends gently (section D) and the vanishing point for the incline (VPI) is indicated. Finally the road levels off and disappears to the centre of vision at the eye

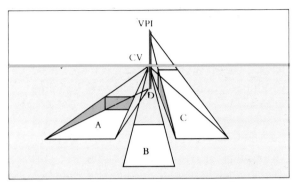

Diagram 39. Establishing vanishing points for slopes.

level. The fencing and wall slope at the same angle as the road, and because they are parallel to it, their vanishing points coincide.

Roofs, of course, are inclined planes and where they appear in recession (roofs A, C and D in diagram 41), they will have an incline vanishing point above the CV. The slopes of roofs B and E will not have vanishing points as they are parallel to the ground line and picture plane.

'Northern Suburb' 375 × 612mm (15 × 24½in.). Receding roofs create a convincing feeling of space.

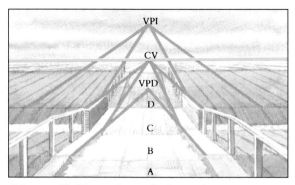

Diagram 40. How to draw a sloping road.

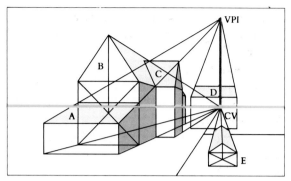

Diagram 41. Establishing VPs for roofs.

A STREET SCENE

You now have almost all the knowledge you need in order to be able to create a design with a descending and ascending road in recession, lined by buildings. There are two further points to understand.

Firstly, houses nearly always appear to go down in steps. Secondly, roofs, doors, windowsills and lintels are usually horizontal and so vanish to the CV, not the VPD. Establish your eye level and centre of vision, then decide how much of a decline you want in your street. Decide on a decline vanishing point, immediately below the CV. The tops and bottoms of the houses on the slope will vanish to the VPD.

Drawing circles and ellipses

We know that circles fit into squares and from diagram 33 we know how to draw a square in perspective. Circles or ellipses always have to be constructed in parallel perspective. Diagram 42 shows how ellipses can be constructed. Draw a square in perspective, and draw in the diagonals. Draw the front half of a circle from A to B freehand, touching C. Lines to the CV through where the half circle crosses the diagonals will give you the points through which to draw the back half of the circle.

There is one important point to remember if you are using this knowledge of ellipses to draw cylinders. You will remember from diagram 33 that the perspective centre of a square made the front half look bigger than the back. This is also, obviously, true of the centre line of an ellipse – it will make the back look smaller than the front. For this reason, you do not find the width of a cylinder by dropping verticals from the extremities of the perspective centre line, but from the widest portion of the ellipse. This is shown in diagram 43. The contours or edges that you would see are the lines XY and WZ.

When you are drawing cylindrical objects, it is better at the start to draw the whole ellipse, although only a portion of it may be seen. In this way the smooth rhythm of a compressed circle is best obtained. When you are satisfied with your shapes, erase those lines you don't need.

Once you have mastered drawing ellipses, all sorts of round and curved items – bicycles, pots, cups and glasses – can be included with effect in your compositions.

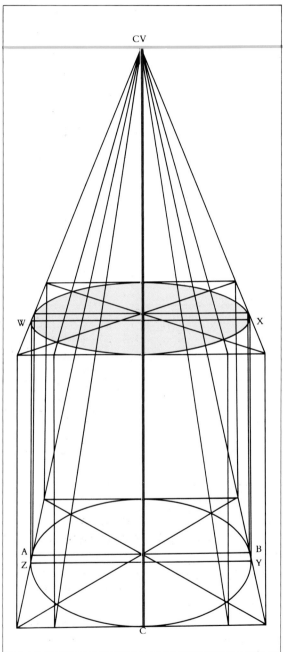

Diagram 43. Drawing a cylinder.

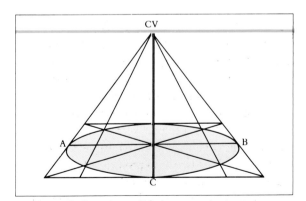

Diagram 42. Drawing a circle in perspective.

Oblique perspective

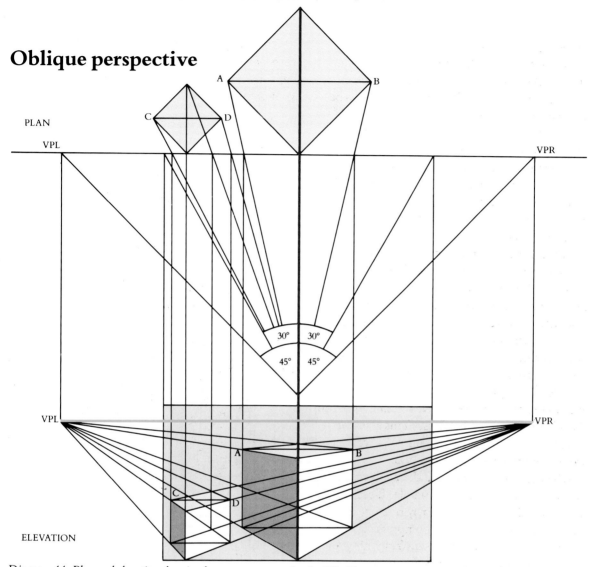

Diagram 44. Plan and elevation showing how to construct cubes in 45° oblique perspective.

A moment's observation reveals that objects in nature rarely oblige by lying parallel and at right angles to the eye level. They are nearly always at angles to it. Rules of perspective still govern these random dispositions, however, and, when applied, they help artists to create convincing form and space, and make a forceful contribution to composing a picture.

We have seen (pages 206-8) that by creating a 45° angle on either side of the line of vision vanishing points can be located that are in fact the points to which diagonals of squares in the design converge. This gives a geometrically calculated and convincing depth. Vanishing points are not necessarily at this 45° angle from the line of sight, but perspective (rather like some games) works well if you make rules from convenient assumptions. A useful set of rules can also be assumed if a 60°/30° perspective is used. They again will allow you to establish relative depths coherently and yet they will produce a totally different viewpoint and appearance.

Diagram 44 is similar to diagram 36 on page 208. It shows a 45° perspective from a top plan

213

projection and an elevation. It is very unusual for a creative artist to use a projection like this and I wouldn't recommend that you do either, but it does help you to understand how the lengths of the sides of the two squares are seen on the picture plane by the lines of sight passing through it, to the eye. These sizes projected down to the elevation form the basis for constructing the cubes. The size of the picture is governed by the 60° cone of vision.

One important point to notice is that where the edges of the squares are parallel to the vanishing parallels, the diagonals of each square AB and CD are parallel to the picture plane, that is, they are horizontal. The second point to notice is that the closer you get to the edges of the 60° field of

vision, the more distorted the cube appears. Outside that field of vision objects become progressively more distorted as the smaller cube illustrates. This looks more like a rectangular attaché case than a cube (to have avoided drawing it like this, you would have to have been standing further away). Perspective, then, has its limitations. As an artist, you must understand and either compensate for, or decide to exploit, these limitations.

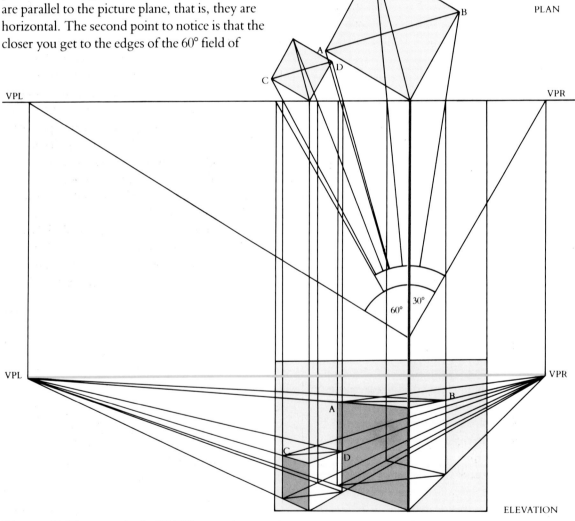

Diagram 45. The same cubes in 60°/30° perspective.

Diagram 45 demonstrates what happens to these cubes in 60°/30° perspective. The differences are obvious. Firstly, far more of the near side of the cubes is visible. Secondly, the vanishing parallels are again parallel to the sides of the squares, but these are more oblique to the eye level and picture plane than they were in 45° perspective. Also, the distortion of the smaller cube does not look so great due to the greater distance it is from the VPL. Finally, you can see that the diagonals of the cubes are not parallel to the picture plane or to eye level.

Diagrams 46 and 47 show these points in a 'real' situation. The first uses a high eye level and is drawn in 45° perspective. We are viewing the buildings from a distance, so no distortion occurs.

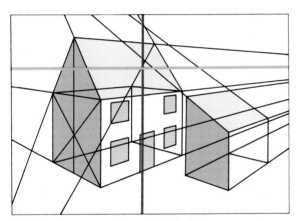

Diagram 46. View of houses in 45° oblique perspective.

Gable ends and fronts are equally seen. In the second, although the centre of vision is in almost the same place, the buildings are angled at 60°/30°. Their structure is still right-angled but because of the acute angle of vision we can see the front more fully and the gable ends less so. The gap between the buildings has also disappeared and the sharper angles give a less symmetrical look to the group than in the 45° perspective drawing.

Depth in oblique perspective

As we saw in the section on parallel perspective, ascertaining convincing depths in perspective, at first, seems difficult. There are many ways of doing this (as discussed on pages 206-8), and here ways to establish depth in oblique perspective are shown. The square WXYZ in diagram 48 has been constructed in 45° perspective, its depth established by the diagonal XZ. The diamond-shaped square ABCD is simply put into WXYZ, its diagonal corresponding with the perspective centre of WXYZ and parallel to the eye level.

Occasionally, however, you will want to establish the depth of a square that is less conveniently angled to your line of sight and eye level. The square ABCD in diagram 49 is more typical of the kind of problem you will find! Draw WXYZ in as a guide. From points A and C, draw lines parallel to the sides of the square XY and WZ, then draw in the diagonal of WXYZ (ZX).

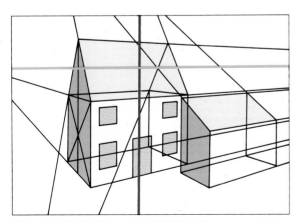

Diagram 47. The houses in 60°/30° oblique perspective.

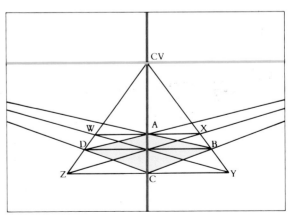

Diagram 48. Depth of a square in 45° oblique perspective.

From the points where these lines AE and CF intersect the diagonal (G and H) draw horizontals to WZ and XY to create the small interior squares FXBG and DHEZ. This can now be drafted into WXYZ which in diagram 50 has been constructed in parallel perspective. The lines EA and CF (measured along the foot of square WXYZ) recede. From the intersection of EA and CF with the diagonal XZ, the position of D and B can be ascertained. The square ABCD can then be constructed. DA and CB converge and if produced can be checked for accuracy. They meet on the eye level at VP.

This knowledge of oblique perspective should now enable you to create an interesting composition. Always decide first on an eye level

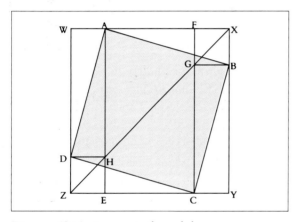

Diagram 49. An inconveniently angled square.

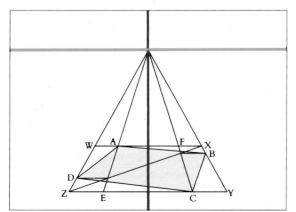

Diagram 50. The same square in plan view.

and place your vanishing points and centre of vision where you wish them to be. A simple rule of thumb if you wish to be accurate is, when using 45° perspective, to make your vanishing points equal distances from the centre of vision. The further apart you place them, the further away you are from your picture plane. If you are using 30°/60° perspective, the 60° vanishing point is roughly three times further from the centre of vision than the 30° vanishing point is. Although this is not a strictly accurate figure, it is a reasonable working estimate, and if you apply it you will find that it will generally produce convincing drawings.

Inclines and declines

Inclined and declined planes were discussed on pages 209–10. A knowledge of oblique perspective, however, enables a more convincing use of inclines and declines. Diagram 51 illustrates the way they could appear in a small harbour. Since this is in 45° oblique perspective, the right and left vanishing points are equal distances from the centre of vision on each side. The VPs are a long way outside the picture plane to left and right, indicating that the artist was standing well back. Also, because this is a sea view, the eye level is also the horizon. The ramps or hards incline and decline and their vanishing points lie immediately above and below the right-hand VP.

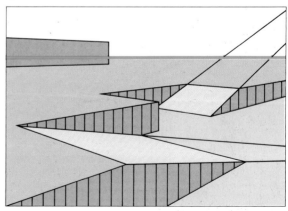

Diagram 51. Inclines and declines in oblique perspective.

A KITCHEN SCENE

This illustration is a very simplified version of the corner of a kitchen projected in 30°/60° perspective, and you now have all the knowledge you need in order to draw something like this. As already stated it was necessary to establish the eye level, the centre of vision and the 30° vanishing point on the left and the 60° vanishing point to the right. Such drawings can be put together even away from the subject without difficulty, if each point is established and logically constructed.

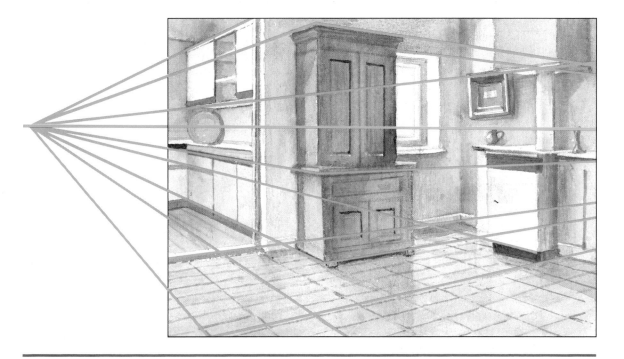

'Dinghies on the Hard' 473 × 640mm (19 × 25½in.). The almost random ridges along the inclined slopes – formed by planks being set on the still wet concrete – contribute to a powerful impression of recession. The boats, under covers, create a lateral rocking rhythm, but do not cut the composition in two because the lines of the foreground extend upwards to the top of the picture through the masts.

217

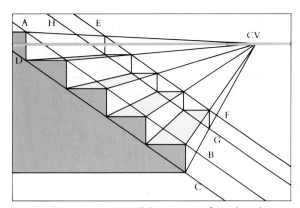

Diagram 52. Stairs in parallel perspective from the side.

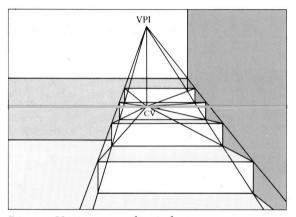

Diagram 53. Stairs, seen from in front.

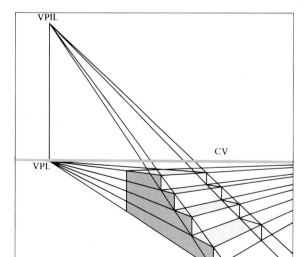

Diagram 54. A staircase in 45° oblique perspective.

Stairs

The perspective of stairs and of steps, rather like that of the roofs of buildings, is based on the presence of inclined and declined planes. Diagram 52 shows a series of stairs seen from the side and in parallel perspective. The lines connecting the treads (AB and CD) are parallel to EF and GH, although due to the recession of the stair treads,

'Mortlake Steps' 398 × 440mm (16 × 17½in.). Here, bank, causeway, wall and steps all contribute to recession.

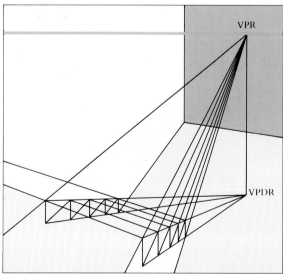

Diagram 55. Stairs in 30°/60° oblique perspective.

EF and GH are much closer than AB and CD. In stairs viewed from the front and in parallel perspective, however, these tread lines all converge on the VPI (incline), which is immediately above the CV (diagram 53).

In a staircase seen in 45° oblique perspective (diagram 54), the tread lines converge on the VPI left which is immediately above the VP left. As in diagram 52, the lines connecting the front treads are farther apart than those connecting the rear.

Normally, we view stairs in very sharp perspective when we are about to go down them, as we are not only looking straight down from above, but have the added height of our own bodies. The visual effect of this is shown clearly in the 30°/60° projection of diagram 55.

AN ARRANGEMENT OF STAIRS

A complex and fanciful arrangement of stairs, like this one, should now be within your capabilities. These are in a 30°/60° projection. Establish your eye level, and decide where you want the stairs to come into your drawing. Next decide on the height of your stairs. Indicate the slopes of the stairs by deciding on the VPI and VPD. Constructing the arrangement should not now present you with any problems if you follow the preceding principles.

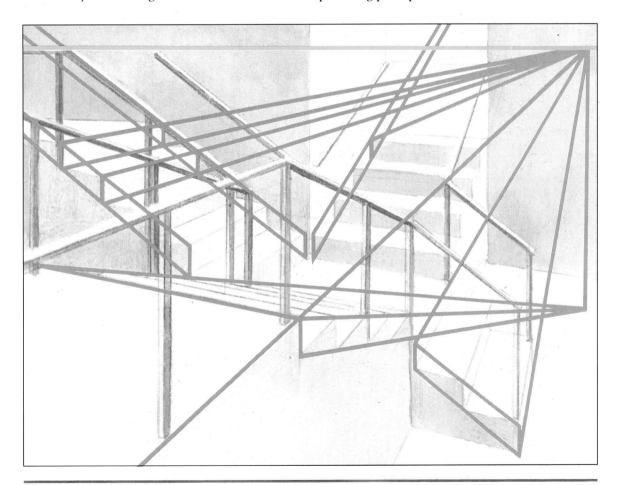

4 Shadows

When you are drawing or painting objectively, shadows cannot be ignored. They make shapes which are compositionally as important and as interesting as the objects from which they are cast (sometimes more so). They can often clarify the shapes and forms of these objects, which may otherwise be ill defined. They can also compel the artist to create tonal pattern, which must be co-ordinated with the other design elements to make an effective contribution to the emotional or descriptive content of the picture.

At various periods in the history of art, shadows have been employed to produce a romantic effect called 'chiaroscuro' (meaning light and shade), which enabled the artist to make some features of his design clear and distinct while others were shaded in gloom. This created a sense of mystery. Rembrandt was one of the great masters of this technique, and although the light and dark passages in his paintings defy perspective logic, they are totally convincing.

Sunlight usually gives better defined shadows over the whole of the picture plane than artificial light and the sun's shadows have a logic which can be seen as incorrect by any viewer if it is ignored. It takes masterful handling (composing) to use such light and shadow creatively and correctly.

'Fleet Sunset' 369 × 419mm (14³⁄₄ × 16³⁄₄in.). The recession along the beach is here reinforced by the diminishing scale of the mooring posts. Not only do the posts give the feeling of distance, they also help to explain the relative sizes of the boats.

Sunlight shadows

The size and extent of shadows produced by sunlight depend on the position of the sun in relation to the artist and the picture plane, on the time of day, and on the shape of the objects illuminated. An important point to remember about shadows produced by sunlight is that they are continually moving. After a few hours' work in front of a subject in sunlight, you will find that the position and size of the shadows have altered considerably. A few quick notes in a sketchbook from time to time will enable you to decide later where they are most appropriate compositionally.

Rays parallel to the picture plane

Shadows cast by the sun's rays falling on an object in parallel perspective on to a level surface are also parallel. The sun's rays in diagram 56 are parallel to the picture plane and the sun is on the left. The length of the shadows is determined by the point at which the sun's rays intersect the lines AB and DC extended along the ground plane, at X and Y.

   This applies to any object in parallel perspective. Diagram 57 shows a cylinder. Again, the sun's rays can be traced on the ground plane from lines parallel to the picture plane. In this case, the length of the shadows is determined by the distance from the cylinder's edge, hence the elliptical shape to the end of the shadow. This diagram also shows how the shadow reinforces the description of the shape upon which the sun's rays are falling.

   This is demonstrated more forcefully in diagram 58 in which a cube has been turned through 45° and projected in oblique perspective. The sun's rays, which are again on the left-hand side and parallel to the picture plane, determine the length and shape of the shadow by their intersection with lines drawn from A, B and C parallel to the ground line. The shape of the shadow explains the form and angle of the cube.

   As we have said, obviously the time of day and to some extent the season in which you are working influence the length of the shadows that

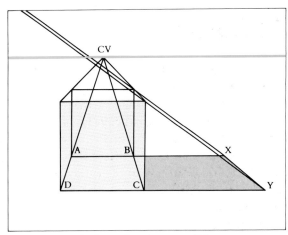

Diagram 56. Shadows of a cube in parallel perspective.

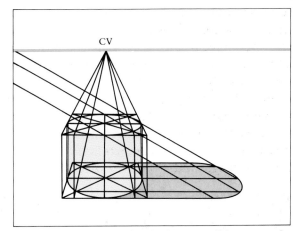

Diagram 57. Shadows of a cylinder in parallel perspective.

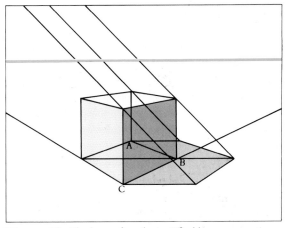

Diagram 58. Shadows of a cube in 45° oblique perspective.

221

will be cast. In winter, sunlight produces long shadows; a high noonday sun, however, produces very short shadows.

Shadows cast on an inclined slope are longer than those cast on a declined slope. In diagrams 59 and 60, the sun's rays are parallel to the picture plane. To find the length of the shadow on an incline (a pitched roof, for example), first find the horizontal plane. Extend lines from the CV through C and D to the edge of the roof and then around and down the sides of the building until they reach the horizontal line XY (parallel to the eye level). Extend the sides of the chimney AD and BC downwards until they reach the horizontal plane. Extend lines from points W and Z back to the CV; where they intersect AD extended to E, and BC extended to F gives you the forward plane of the shadow. Extend EF to G (drawn back also to the CV) and parallel to the ground plane. G is the point of intersection of the sun's rays, and the bottom extent of the shadow.

Shadows on declined planes are simpler. Extend DC up the slope, parallel to the angle of the roof, until it is intersected by a sun's ray from B at E. Trace from E back to the centre of vision. A line from A to the line ECV gives point F. Then, trace the far side of the chimney up the incline to F. This gives you the length and width of the shadow.

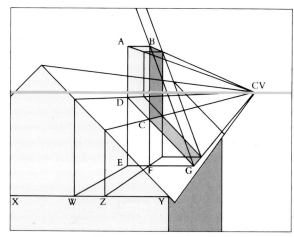

Diagram 59. Shadows on an inclined slope or plane.

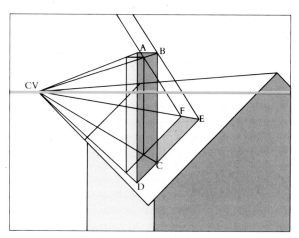

Diagram 60. Shadows on a declined slope or plane.

Sun immediately above the CV

Different phenomena occur when the sun is immediately above the centre of vision. In diagram 61, the sides of the shadow on the ground plane appear to incline inwards and when extended meet at the centre vision on the eye level. If, on the other hand, you were looking down on this cube, you would see the sides of the shadow, in fact, as parallel.

Diagram 62 demonstrates what happens to a wall with doorway and window when the sun is immediately above the CV, seen from directly in front. The sides of the shadow converge along the ground plane to the centre of vision.

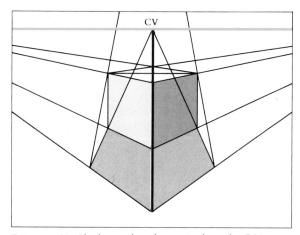

Diagram 61. Shadows when the sun is above the CV.

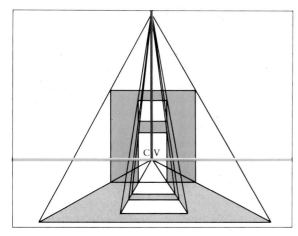

Diagram 62. Shadows of a doorway and window.

Sun to the left or right

Since the sun moves continually, you can't rely on it being directly to your left or right (and parallel to the picture plane) or straight above you. You will often have to cope with it in other situations and may in any case choose, compositionally, to place it elsewhere. In diagram 63, the sun is in front and to the artist's left. What is interesting now is that the vanishing point for the shadow

(VPS) is on the eye level and immediately beneath the sun. It would stay immediately beneath the sun even if the ground sloped. If it sloped upwards, the VP would be above the eye level; if it sloped downwards, the VP would be below the eye level, but in both cases, directly beneath the sun. Because the prism is drawn in oblique perspective, its vanishing points are out to the left and right of the diagram on the eye level.

Diagram 64 demonstrates how you would calculate the length and shape of a shadow if the sun were behind your left shoulder, just opposite to where it was in diagram 63. In this case you have to assume a position of the sun below the eye level; this will allow you to place the vanishing point of the shadow on the eye level. The assumed position of the sun should be as far below the EL as the sun really was above and as far to the right of the CV as the sun was to the left. Rays from the assumed sun to the top of the prism intersect with lines back from the base of the prism to the VPS. This determines the length and shape of the shadow. The vanishing points for the prism are on the eye level outside the diagram area.

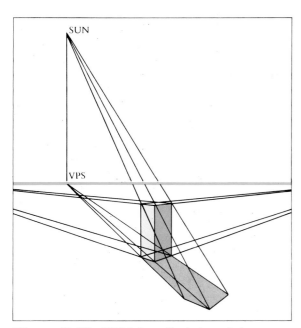

Diagram 63. The VPS is immediately beneath the sun.

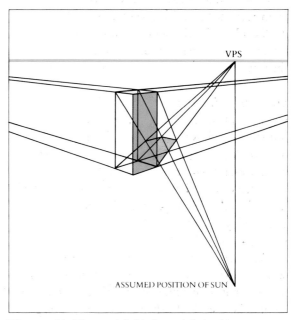

Diagram 64. The sun is behind your left shoulder.

Still with the sun behind your left shoulder, diagram 65 shows what happens to our wall pierced by a window and a door and its shadow. Again, to give the appearance of the sun being behind your left shoulder, the assumed position of the sun is the same distance from the centre of vision to the right as the real sun is to the left.

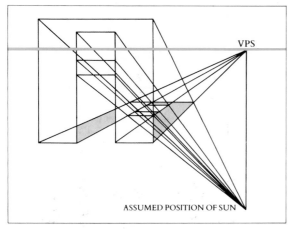

Diagram 65. Again, sun is behind your left shoulder.

Assuming that you are on flat ground, then the sun must be the same distance below the eye level as the real one would appear above. The vanishing point for the shadow is directly above the assumed sun's position on the eye level. The length of the shadows is determined by rays from the sun to the various points of the wall intersecting the vanishing lines to the VPS (shadow).

Shadows of a building with a sloping roof and chimney are illustrated in diagram 66. The chimney's shadow is cast on the sloping roof and on to the level ground. The shadow of the chimney on the roof has a vanishing point as far above the eye level as the vanishing point for the incline but immediately below the sun at VPS1. The vanishing point for the shadows on the ground plane (annotated VPS2) is on the eye level, directly beneath the sun. The length of the chimney's cast shadow was calculated by taking the trace lines of the chimney down to the ground plane and then back to VPS2. Trace lines were then drawn to the right until intersected by the sun's rays at A. It is interesting to note that the shadow of the chimney on the inclined slope of the roof does not appear immediately above the one on the ground plane. You have to calculate each one separately. The drawing is in 45° oblique perspective.

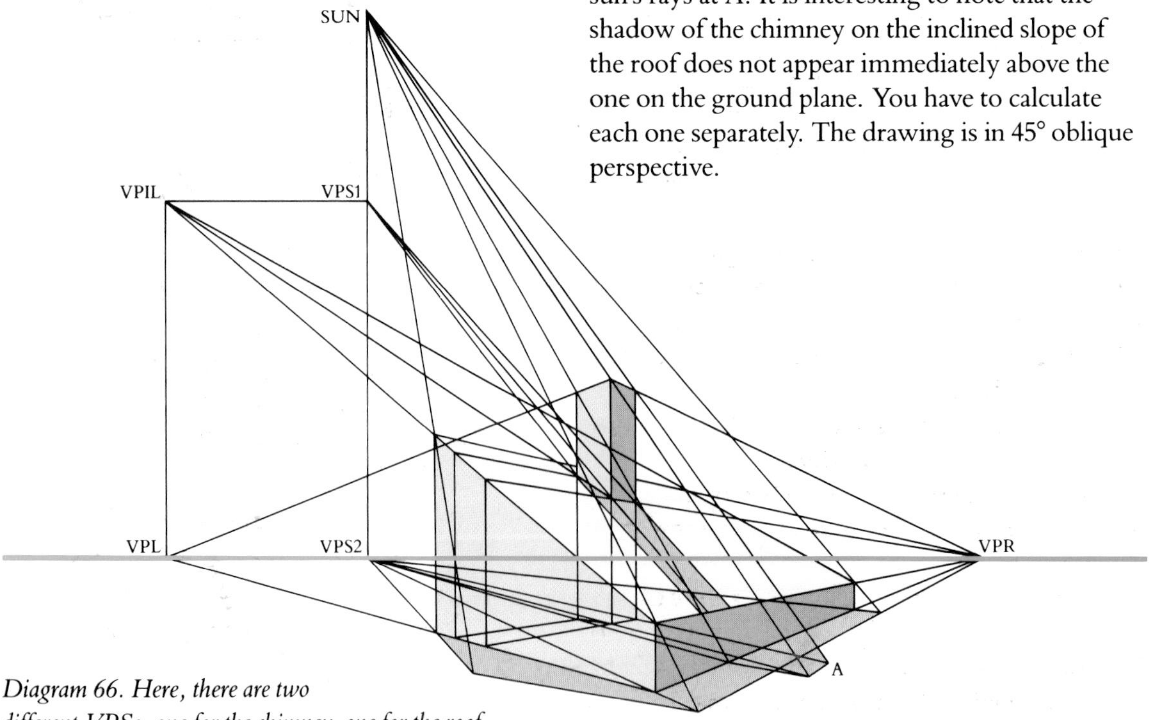

Diagram 66. Here, there are two different VPSs, one for the chimney, one for the roof.

Artificial light

Shadows cast by artificial light radiate from a point immediately below the light itself. These shadows, although well defined when near to, and in the main direction of, the light, become diffused as they get further away. They also are more distorted than shadows cast by sunlight.

Shadows produced by artificial light (the source of the light is indicated in these diagrams as ALS) have vanishing points immediately beneath the light and on the same plane as the objects which cast the shadow. This gives two radiating shadows.

Diagram 67 shows a cylinder. The extent of its shadow is determined by the intersection of the light rays and the vanishing point. The curved top of the cylinder can be determined either from points on the arc, or from diagonals of the square into which it fits (see page 212).

When the objects that cast the shadow are higher than the light source, the vanishing point of the shadow, obviously, is immediately above the light source.

Very often what we see is illuminated from more than one light source, so shadows form improbable shapes and, where they overlap, varied tones. Diagram 68 illustrates how that occurs. The vanishing points for the shadows are immediately below each of the two light sources. The trace and extent of the shadows is determined by the intersection of the light rays and the VPSs. The edges of the shadows appear much softer than those caused by direct light. Also, you will find two distinct tonal values in the area of shadow. The outer, lighter shadow is known as the penumbra and the darker central area of shadow as the umbra. The larger the light source, the smaller the umbra.

You will find a similar effect with a large or long source of light such as a tube light or even (if it is not in direct sunlight) a window with daylight passing through it. Because the light rays are emitted from the whole length of the source, you

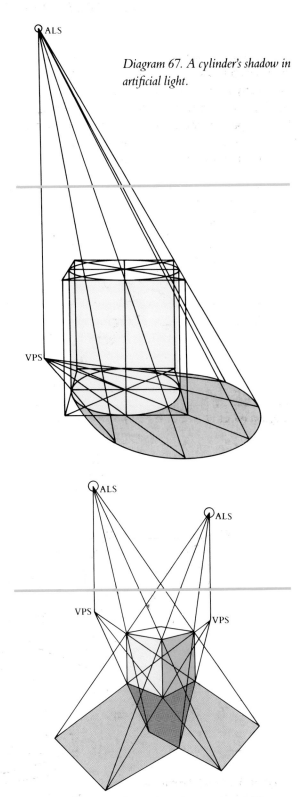

Diagram 67. A cylinder's shadow in artificial light.

Diagram 68. The cube illuminated from two sources.

225

get what may, at first sight, appear to be a confused shadow. For practical purposes, in a case like this, to construct the shadow take light rays from the centre of the tube or window and each end. Consequently you will have three vanishing points on the plane on which the object stands, immediately beneath each source point.

A ROOM IN SHADOW

This drawing with furniture reduced to fairly basic shapes shows the shadows produced by artificial light in a common situation. To draw a room like the one illustrated here, a vanishing point for shadows has to be established on each plane. The first is on the ground plane immediately below the light, and a second is on the chimney breast at the same height as the light. This establishes the shadows cast from the picture and fire surround. The third is level with the light but on the alcove wall, and is used to establish the depths of shadow from the shelving. A fourth, above the door, fixes the length of shadows from the pictures and chest of drawers on the wall facing you. A fifth would be on the far right wall outside the picture plane. This has to be plotted in order to give the length of shadow beneath the curtain. The radiation of shadow, which is the result of one central light source, is very typical of indoor artificial lighting.

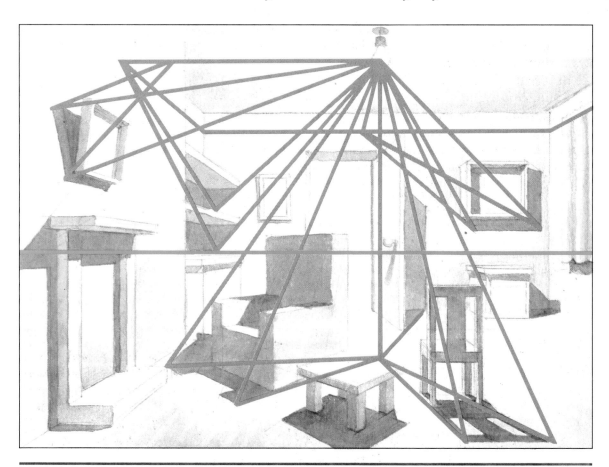

5 Reflections

To many artists the word reflection suggests water. There are, however, many other surfaces that reflect to a greater or lesser degree. The very best reflecting surface is mercury or mirror, but polished metal, a glazed picture or window, some plastics and even gloss-painted surfaces will give interesting reflections. Wet slates will reflect chimneys and wet pavements, figures and lampposts, lights and anything else on them. Sand along the shore, when wet, also gives a reflection. Often these surfaces are not level and slope at angles, which can complicate the reflection, but once the principles are understood the reflected shapes are not difficult to determine.

Agitated water reproduces images at improbable angles, the concavities actually reflecting objects the right way up, while swirls of lines cross, recross or zigzag across the surface. Surfaces are sometimes classified as producing regular and irregular reflections, but it is often difficult to know how to differentiate. Here, we will discuss flat water as a reflecting surface but rippled water is a large and complex subject. One of the major attractions of water that is near is that it reflects less light and, because it is transparent when clear, the bottom becomes visible (if you are in deep water, it takes on the hue of the ocean). The further away you view the reflection the clearer it appears. Vertical objects appear better defined, whereas horizontal ones may not seem to be reflected at all. Lights (such as the moon) on still water give a constant width reflection.

'Low Tide' 232 × 345mm (9¼ × 13¾in.). This chalk drawing on pale blue paper was done quickly on the quayside at Looe in Cornwall. The very shallow water reflects the warehouses and the high harbour wall.

227

Reflections in water

Most of the examples given here are illustrated in relation to boats, since they are more often associated with water than any other objects.

An object reflected in water is seen as far below the surface as it is in reality above. The reflecting ray to the eye cuts the surface and produces an angle (the angle of reflection, R) which is equal to the angle made from the point on the surface to the object (the angle of incidence, I). This principle governs all reflections, no matter what size the objects are or how far away they are. This is shown in diagram 69.

The reflecting surface is not necessarily the eye level, or even the horizon at sea. Diagram 70 shows a navigation mark, which extends exactly the same distance below the reflecting surface as it is above. More solid objects (a mooring post, for example) can create reflections whose sides appear to be of a different length. In diagram 71, for example, A and B are clearly the same length, but C and D appear different. They are not. They appear so because the angles of recession, extended, converge on the eye level at the centre of vision. An object which is not parallel to the

picture plane, however (like the length of timber in diagram 72) does have a reflection that is a different length from the object. The reflecting surface is projected forward from the CV to a point vertically below the nearest end of the timber (where a pebble dropped from C would strike the water at E); D is exactly the same distance below the surface. Both the object's and its reflection's lines of direction when extended will, if produced far enough, converge at a point immediately above and below the centre of vision and equidistant from it.

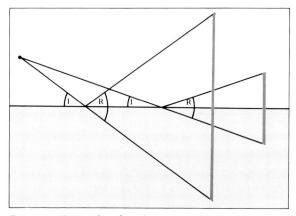

Diagram 69. Angles of incidence and reflection.

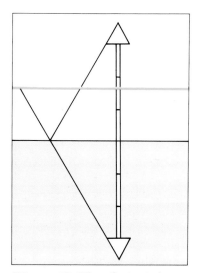

Diagram 70. The reflection is the same depth as the mark.

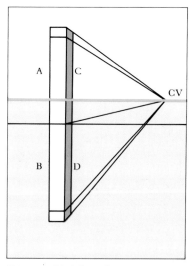

Diagram 71. The reflection appears longer, although it is not.

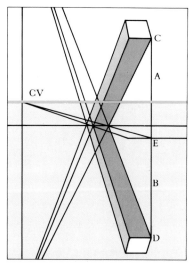

Diagram 72. The reflection is a different length from the object.

Diagram 73 illustrates a very common phenomenon of a flagstaff on the stern of a motorboat. The top of the staff is precisely the same distance above the reflecting surface as its reflection is below. This has to include the height of the stern of the boat. Note how the lines of recession converge on the centre of vision. The reflection of the stern shows a much steeper angle than the object itself because it is in parallel perspective. The same principles apply to buildings on a riverbank or at the seashore. Diagram 74 illustrates equal sized buildings at different distances from a riverbank and their reflections. A piece of the bank has been cut into like a dock to show how this works. Each vertical has to be brought down to the reflecting surface and then continued just as far below as it is above – this includes the height of the bank. Had we not

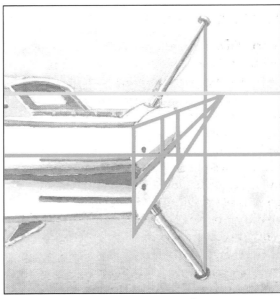

Diagram 73. The reflection of a flagstaff in water.

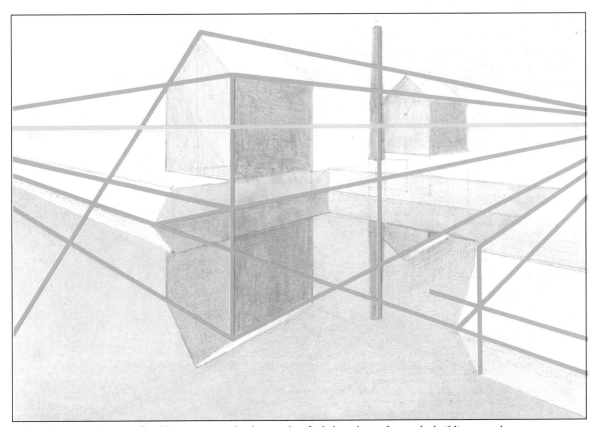

Diagram 74. Reflections of buildings on a riverbank extend as far below the surface as the buildings are above.

cut away the little dock all that would have been reflected of the rear building would have been the tip of its chimney. Note how the reflection of a sloping bank is ascertained by again taking back the level of the reflecting surface until it is vertically beneath the top of the slope. This is then extended the same distance downwards and the points connected.

The reflections of bridges show more of the underside of the constructions than does the direct view. Diagram 75 is projected in parallel perspective, so all the lines vanish to the same point. Those below the reflecting surface are the same distance from it as those above. A bridge in oblique perspective (diagram 76) has vanishing points outside the picture plane. For this reason,

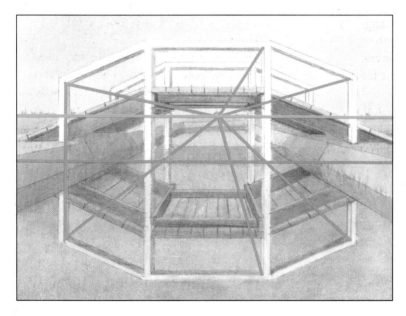

'Derelict Houseboat' 310 × 455mm (12½ × 18¼in.). This study for a painting gave many compositional opportunities to create improbable shapes from the derelict boat and its reflection in the river.

Diagram 75. In parallel perspective, all the lines vanish to the same point.

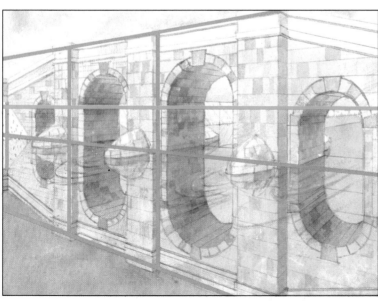

Diagram 76. In both parallel (above left) and oblique perspective (left), more of the underside of the bridges than the direct view is visible.

230

we can see through the arches. Each arch was constructed from a half square in perspective (see page 212). From then on, the construction is the same as for the bridge in parallel perspective.

Reflections on a wet surface – the reflection of a chimney on a sloping wet roof, for example – give shapes rather like shadows. The area of the reflection is determined in the same way as described in diagram 59. The only difference is that the reflecting surface slopes at an angle and the object is vertical. The easiest way to cope with this is to turn your drawing on its side and visualize the reflecting surface as being level, with the chimney tilting.

When the eye level is below the roof, it is still easier to turn your drawing on its side.

Reflections in glass

Reflections in a mirror are rather like looking through a hole in the wall into another room. The halfway marks between objects and their reflections occur on the mirror wall. Once you have established these marks, use a pair of compasses to describe an arc from the object to its reflection. In parallel perspective, everything slides across from the room into the looking glass. Don't forget, though, that objects will be laterally inverted: the position of the door knob changes, and you see the front of the chairback in the room and its back in the reflection. Remember too that in this situation the angles at which pictures tilt will be reversed.

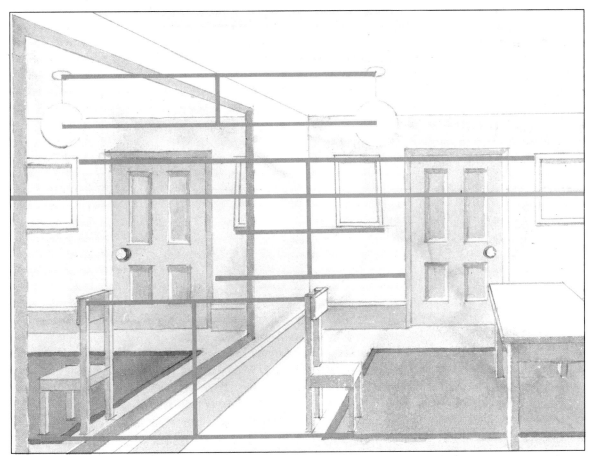

Diagram 77. Reflections in a mirror are rather like looking through a hole in a wall into another room.

6 Composition in practice

It is impossible to place a line on a piece of paper without attempting to draw it in the right place. All pictures have a compositional element. They have in common a sense of the third dimension and are strengthened by the feeling that the design and drawing go on behind the picture plane.

One of the most emotive elements of composition can be the planes which direct our eyes back into, up and across the picture. For this reason, planes are well worth establishing very early in your design, in fact second only to the horizontal and vertical arrangement of shapes and other main movements within the design and the shape you consider best communicates what you have to say.

Your picture's unity (which includes the shapes, tones and colours you use) is indissolubly linked to what you have to say. Remember that it is better to say one thing strongly and unequivocally than to try to say many things. That approach can make the painting fussy, splintered and without unity. Even a painting of a single object needs composing so that the very character and essence of the object are distilled in every shape. Consider your viewpoint, try sitting low on the floor or ground, look at your subject through undergrowth or the back of a chair. Climb high, sit on a table and look down upon your subject. See it in full light with the sun or a window behind you, or stand your subject directly in front of the light. Each position will have something of interest, so choose what, to you, is most exciting and best communicates your intentions. Make sketches, then detailed studies from nature and finally reconstruct the experience into a composition, when all your knowledge and skills of perspective and composition can be brought into play.

The advice and illustrations that follow will help you to employ your knowledge of perspective to create satisfying and meaningful pictures. However, the finest study of composition is to look closely at your favourite paintings by great masters. Trace the designs, find the Golden Sections, then the proportion of the rectangle, then the linear structure. Determine the eye level and principal vanishing points by tracing back the lines of recession, then look at the tonal shapes and masses. These studies will demonstrate that there are as many ways of composing as there are artists: the suggestions given here should not be seen as rules but as guidelines.

Ken Howard 'Saskia, Morning Light' 600 × 500mm (24 × 20in.). This masterly painting is held together by a well-considered geometric design. Although light is as much the subject of the painting as the model, there is a well-conceived spatial relationship between the two- and three-dimensional aspects of the picture. It is interesting to note that the vertical division of the composition is broken by the bent legs of the model, giving excitement to the painting. Note too how the areas of greatest highlights are juxtaposed against the darkest tones and perfectly balanced. There is also a subsidiary linear rhythm of light lines. The light shining on the model's chemise is echoed on the bottle on the table in the foreground and adds a further highlight to the painting.

232

Creating space

You have probably used, and must certainly have seen works by artists who use, the device illustrated in diagram 78 – putting one object in front of another – to create a feeling of space. By overlapping these shapes a sense of recession is created. This can, however, be ambiguous: you may just be putting a series of inverted 'L' shapes together. To give the impression of putting flat squares one in front of the other, another element is needed. Employing simple parallel perspective in the design, however, leaves no doubt which form is in front of the other and what that form is. Although cubic shapes are used in diagram 79, the principle can easily be applied to a sky filled with great cumulus clouds one in front of another, for example.

Symmetry and balance

Total symmetry and balance, although a common compositional ploy, need not be shunned. Many great pieces of architecture are designed symmetrically and it was used extensively in the fifteenth and sixteenth centuries for paintings of crucifixions, annunciations and other religious subjects. In diagram 80, the fulcrum (F) locates what we know instinctively as the centre of interest. This is a very convenient point around which to compose and on which to centre the action of a painting. It may be at the centre of vision or fulcrum of a mechanically structured design, or at the intersection of the important dividing lines of the painting (see pages 191-3). Many ploys can be used to assemble the directions and forms to direct attention to this spot. There

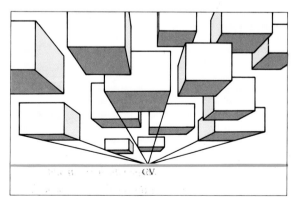

Diagram 78. Overlapping helps to create recession.

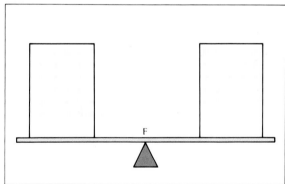

Diagram 80. A completely symmetrical arrangement.

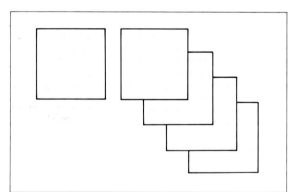

Diagram 79. Parallel perspective reinforces it.

Diagram 81. How to use the arrangement above.

may be possibly very little of importance at that point, it could just be a pinion, or it may be the most interesting point of the picture.

In diagram 81, the fulcrum, the centre of vision and centre of interest are focused at this one point.

Diagram 82 shows an alternative way of achieving equilibrium. The greater mass has the shorter arm of leverage, and the smaller form has the longer arm. This ensures that they remain in balance. In a composition based on this framework (diagram 83), the centre of interest is at the fulcrum and the most compelling centre of interest of all is employed, one of figures.

However small a figure is in a composition, it commands greater attention than more inanimate and elaborate forms. If you link a figure with the fulcrum and/or centre of vision, the eye gravitates straight to it.

In diagram 84, the centre of interest is again at the centre of vision and fulcrum. The mass nearest the fulcrum is hanging below the horizon and is a satisfactory balance to the object above it.

These masses can be made to balance by not necessarily being of greater or smaller area but by being of light or dark tone, or of subdued or vivid colour, or of intense subject interest and detail.

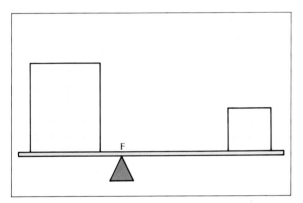

Diagram 82. A different way to achieve balance.

Diagram 83. How to use the arrangement on the left.

Diagram 84. Here, the centre of interest is at the centre of vision and fulcrum, but the larger mass (the boat) is below the horizon and balances the smaller mass above the horizon.

Achieving movement

There are many interesting possibilities in giving a painting or drawing movement. In a static piece of work actual movement is out of the question, but skilful use of shapes, repeated with progressively slight variations, will bounce the eye around a composition. Spots of similar colour or tone placed at intervals over the surface of a painting will cause the eye to move from one to the other, and lines, whether real or simply divisions between one tone and another, can compel the eye to move around wherever you wish.

Tone

Distance affects the tonal values of objects, as well as their colours. Before the nineteenth century, painters made distant passages of their work progressively more blue, without understanding the atmospheric changes that made this appear correct. If there were no atmospheric interference with light rays, black rocks, for example, would look black, and snow peaks white. Now we know that the very light and most reflective areas at a distance – snow-capped mountains, for instance – are not modified by the weaker, short-waved ultra-violet colours, so leave the red and infra-red long waves to penetrate the atmosphere. Thus, snow peaks look pink. The very darkest areas which reflect little or no light will appear at a distance lighter than they really are, so that black rocks will look blue. This is because the diffused ultra-violet short waves reach the dark areas, making them look blue or blue-violet. Half-toned colours depend upon the circumstances of light at the moment. If comparatively dark they will appear lighter, if fairly light they may seem warmer and darker.

'Work Boat' 512 × 705mm (20½ × 28¼in.). This study in gouache was composed on location. I chose the viewpoint that I felt showed the character of the boat to best advantage.

Index

Acknowledgements

Swallow Publishing wish to thank the following people and organizations for their help in preparing *Art Class*. We apologise to anyone we may have omitted to mention.

Unless indicated otherwise, all artwork is by the authors of the respective sections of this book: Jason Bowyer, Charles Bartlett, Roy Rodgers, and T. W. Ward.

Martin Baldwin, p. 130; Stephen Bitti, p. 148; The British Library, p. 204; The British Museum, pp. 17, 50; Christa Gaa, p. 117 (foot); Ken Howard, pp. 7, 8, 150, 170, 233; Olwen Jones, pp. 107, 119; The Provost and Fellows of Eton College, Windsor, p. 73 (top); By kind permission of the Henry Moore Foundation, p.53; Reproduced by courtesy of the Trustees, the National Gallery, London, pp. 189, 190, 191, 195, 196, 197; The National Portrait Gallery, p. 188 (top); Hans Schwarz, p. 118 (foot); The Tate Gallery, London, pp. 53, 62, 129, 181 © DACS, 193; Valerie Thornton, p. 185; Reproduced by kind permission of the Trustees of the Victoria and Albert Museum, London, pp. 117 (top), 171; The Wyeth Collection © Andrew Wyeth, p. 118 (top).

The equipment on pp. 18–20, 22, 76–84, 132–45 and 187 was kindly loaned by C J Graphic Supplies, 35–39 Old Street, London EC1 and 2–3 Great Pulteney Street, London W1, and Daler-Rowney, 12 Percy Street, London W1.

Thanks to Stephen Mansfield for testing the drawing projects, Richmond College of Adult Education for testing the watercolour and oils projects, and Kenneth Dear for testing the composition and perspective exercises.

JAVA PROGRAMMING

FROM PROBLEM ANALYSIS TO PROGRAM DESIGN

FOURTH EDITION

D.S. MALIK

Australia • Brazil • Jap   d Kingdom • United States

COURSE TECHNOLOGY
CENGAGE Learning

Java Programming: From Problem Analysis to Program Design, Fourth Edition
D.S. Malik

Executive Editor: Marie Lee

Acquisitions Editor: Amy Jollymore

Senior Product Manager: Alyssa Pratt

Editorial Assistant: Julia Leroux-Lindsey

Marketing Manager: Bryant Chrzan

Senior Content Project Manager: Catherine DiMassa

Art Director: Marissa Falco

Compositor: Integra

For product information and technology assistance, contact us at
Cengage Learning Customer & Sales Support, 1-800-354-9706
For permission to use material from this text or product, submit all requests online at **cengage.com/permissions**
Further permissions questions can be emailed to **permissionrequest@cengage.com**

International Student Edition:

ISBN-13: 978-1-4390-4034-8

ISBN-10: 1-4390-4034-6

Course Technology
20 Channel Center
Boston, MA 02210
USA

Cengage Learning is a leading provider of customized learning solutions with office locations around the globe, including Singapore, the United Kingdom, Australia, Mexico, Brazil, and Japan. Locate your local office at:
international.cengage.com/region

Cengage Learning products are represented in Canada by Nelson Education, Ltd.

For your lifelong learning solutions, visit
course.cengage.com
Visit our corporate website at **cengage.com**

Some of the product names and company names used in this book have been used for identification purposes only and may be trademarks or registered trademarks of their respective manufacturers and sellers.

Any fictional data related to persons or companies or URLs used throughout this book is intended for instructional purposes only. At the time this book was printed, any such data was fictional and not belonging to any real persons or companies.

Course Technology, a part of Cengage Learning, reserves the right to revise this publication and make changes from time to time in its content without notice.

The programs in this book are for instructional purposes only.

They have been tested with care, but are not guaranteed for any particular intent beyond educational purposes. The author and the publisher do not offer any warranties or representations, nor do they accept any liabilities with respect to the programs.

Printed in Canada
1 2 3 4 5 6 7 12 11 10 09

TO

My Daughter

Shelly Malik

BRIEF CONTENTS

TABLE OF CONTENTS

PREFACE TO THE FOURTH EDITION

Welcome to *Java Programming: From Problem Analysis to Program Design, Fourth Edition*. Designed for a first Computer Science (CS1) Java course, this text will provide a breath of fresh air to you and your students. The CS1 course serves as the cornerstone of the Computer Science curriculum. My primary goal is to motivate and excite all programming students, regardless of their level. Motivation breeds excitement for learning. Motivation and excitement are critical factors that lead to the success of the programming student. This text is the culmination and development of my classroom notes throughout more than fifty semesters of teaching successful programming.

Warning: This text can be expected to create a serious reduction in the demand for programming help during your office hours. Other side effects include significantly diminished student dependency on others while learning to program.

The primary focus in writing this text is on student learning. Therefore, in addition to clear explanations, we address the key issues that otherwise impede student learning. For example, a common question that arises naturally during an early programming assignment is: "How many variables and what kinds are needed in this program?" We illustrate this important and crucial step by helping students learn why variables are needed and how data in a variable is manipulated. Next students learn that the analysis of the problem will spill the number and types of the variables. Once students grasp this key concept, control structures, (selection and loops) become easier to learn. The second major impediment in learning programming is parameter passing. We pay special attention to this topic. First students learn how to use predefined methods and how actual and formal parameters relate. Next students learn about user-defined methods. They see visual diagrams that help them learn how methods are called and how formal parameters affect actual parameters. Once students have a clear understanding of these two key concepts, they readily assimilate advanced topics.

The topics are introduced at a pace that is conducive to learning. The writing style is friendly, engaging, and straightforward. It parallels the learning style of the contemporary CS1 student. Before introducing a key concept, the student learns why the concept is needed, and then sees examples illustrating the concept. Special attention is paid to topics that are essential in mastering the Java programming language and in acquiring a foundation for further study of computer science.

Other important topics include debugging techniques and techniques for avoiding programming bugs. When a beginner compiles his/her first program and sees that the number of errors exceeds the length of this first program, he/she becomes frustrated by the plethora of errors, only some of which can be interpreted. To ease this frustration and help students learn to produce correct programs, debugging and bug avoidance techniques are presented systematically throughout the text.

Changes In The Fourth Edition

In the fourth edition, the main changes are:

- In the fourth edition, throughout the text sections on debugging techniques and techniques on avoiding programming bugs are included.

- Chapter 10 of the third edition, which includes searching and sorting algorithms, is now Chapter 14. Sequential search algorithm and the **class** Vector, which were covered in Chapter 10, have been moved to Chapter 9. The additional methods of the **class** String, which were covered in Chapter 10 of the third edition, are now covered in Chapter 3. The OOD version of the programming example of Chapter 14 is available on the Web site and the CD accompanying this book. Furthermore, Chapter 14 also contains bubble sort and quick sort algorithms, which are provided on the Web site and the CD accompanying this book.

- Chapters 11, 12, 13, and 14 in the third edition are now Chapters 10, 11, 12, and 13, respectively, in the fourth edition.

- In the third edition, Chapter 7 contains user-defined classes so that primitive type values can be passed as objects and methods can manipulate and pass those values back to the calling environment. In the fourth edition, this discussion is taken out of Chapter 7 and put in a separate section, entitled "Chapter_7_PassingPrimitiveTypeAsObjects". This section is available on the Web site and the CD accompanying this book. Furthermore, as suggested by the reviewers, additional examples are included in this chapter.

- The fourth addition contains more than 30 new programming exercises.

- In Chapter 5, the Programming Example, Checking Account Balance, is available on the Web site and the CD accompanying this book.

- In Appendix D, a new section on how to create Java style documentation of user-defined classes has been added.

These changes were implemented based on comments from the text reviewers of the third edition. The source code and the programming exercises are developed and tested using Java 6.0 and the version of Java 7.0 available at the time the book was being typeset.

Approach

Once conceived as a Web programming language, Java slowly but surely found its way into classrooms where it now serves as a first programming language in computer science curricula (CS1). Java is a combination of traditional style programming—programming with a non-graphical user interface—and modern style programming with a graphical user interface (GUI). This book introduces you to both styles of programming. After giving a brief description of each chapter, we discuss how to read this book.

Chapter 1 briefly reviews the history of computers and programming languages. The reader can quickly skim and become familiar with some of the hardware and software components of the computer. This chapter also gives an example of a Java program and describes how a Java program is processed. The two basic problem-solving techniques, structured programming and object-oriented design, are also presented.

After completing Chapter 2, students become familiar with the basics of Java and are ready to write programs that are complicated enough to do some computations.

The three terms that you will encounter throughout the book are—primitive type variables, reference variables, and objects. Chapter 3 makes clear distinctions between these terms and sets the tone for the rest of the book. An object is a fundamental entity in an object-oriented programming language. This chapter further explains how an object works. The `class String` is one of the most important classes in Java. This chapter introduces this class and explains how various methods of this class can be used to manipulate strings. Because input/output is fundamental to any programming language, it is introduced early, and is covered in detail in Chapter 3.

Chapters 4 and 5 introduce control structures used to alter the sequential flow of execution.

Java is equipped with powerful yet easy-to-use graphical user interface (GUI) components to create user-friendly graphical programs. Chapter 6 introduces various GUI components and gives examples of how to use these components in Java application programs. Because Java is an object-oriented programming language, the second part of Chapter 6 discusses and gives examples of how to solve various problems using object-oriented design methodology.

Chapter 7 discusses user-defined methods. Parameter passing is a fundamental concept in any programming language. Several examples, including visual diagrams, help readers understand this concept. It is recommended that readers with no prior programming background spend extra time on this concept.

Chapter 8 discusses user-defined classes. In Java, a class is an important and widely used element. It is used to create Java programs, group related operations, and it allows users to create their own data types. This chapter uses extensive visual diagrams to illustrate how objects of classes manipulate data.

Chapter 9 describes arrays. This chapter also introduces variable length formal parameter lists. In addition, this chapter introduces foreach loops and explains how this loop can be used to process the elements of an array. This chapter also discusses the sequential searching algorithm and the `class Vector`.

Inheritance is an important principle of object-oriented design. It encourages code reuse. Chapter 10 discusses inheritance, and gives various examples to illustrate how classes are derived from existing classes. In addition, this chapter also discusses polymorphism, abstract classes, inner classes, and composition.

An occurrence of an undesirable situation that can be detected during program execution is called an exception. For example, division by zero is an exception. Java provides extensive support for handing exceptions. Chapter 11 shows how to handle exceptions in a program. Chapter 11 also discusses event handling, which was introduced in Chapter 6. Chapter 12 picks up the discussion of GUI components started in Chapter 6. This chapter introduces additional GUI components and discusses how to create applets.

Chapter 13 introduces recursion. Several examples illustrate how recursive methods execute.

Chapter 14 discusses a binary search algorithm as well as bubble sort, selection sort, insertion sort, and quick sort algorithms. The sorting algorithms: bubble sort and quick sort are provided on the Web site and the CD accompanying this book.

Appendix A lists the reserved words in Java. Appendix B shows the precedence and associativity of the Java operators. Appendix C lists the ASCII (American Standard Code for Information Interchange) portion of the Unicode character set as well as the EBCDIC (Extended Binary Code Decimal Interchange) character set.

Appendix D contains additional topics in Java. The topics covered are converting a base 10 number to binary (base 2) number and vice versa, converting a number from base 2 to base 8 (base 16) and vice versa, how to compile and execute a Java program using command line statements, how to create Java style documentation of the user-defined classes, how to create packages, how to use user-defined classes in a Java program, and `enum` type. Appendix E gives answers to all the odd-numbered exercises in the text.

How To Use This Book

Java is a complex and very powerful language. In addition to traditional (non-GUI) programming, Java provides extensive support for creating programs that use a graphical user interface (GUI). Chapter 3 introduces graphical input and output dialog boxes. Chapter 6 introduces most commonly used GUI components such as labels, buttons, and text fields. More extensive coverage of GUI components is provided in Chapter 12.

This book can be used in two ways. One way is an integrated approach in which readers learn how to write both non-GUI and GUI programs as they learn basic programming concepts and skills. The other approach focuses on illustrating fundamental programming concepts with non-GUI programming first, and later incorporating GUI components. The recommended chapter sequence for each of these approaches is as follows:

- **Integrated approach:** Study all chapters in sequence.
- **Non–GUI first, then GUI:** Study Chapters 1–5 in sequence. Then study Chapters 7–11 and Chapters 13 and 14. This approach initially skips Chapters 6 and 12, the primary GUI chapters. After studying Chapters 1–5, 7–11, 13, and 14, the reader can come back to study Chapters 6 and 12, the GUI chapters. Also note that Chapter 14 can be studied after Chapter 9.

If you choose the second approach, it should also be noted that the Programming Examples in Chapters 8 and 10 are developed first without any GUI components, and then the programs are extended to incorporate GUI components. Also, if Chapter 6 is skipped, the reader can skip the event handling part of Chapter 11. Chapter 13 (recursion) contains two Programming Examples: one creates a non-GUI application program, while the other creates a program that uses GUI. If you skip Chapters 6 and 12, you can skip the GUI part of the Programming Examples in Chapters 8, 10, 11, and 13. Once you have studied Chapter 6 and 12, you can study the GUI part of the Programming Examples of Chapters 8, 10, 11, and 13.

Figure 1 shows a chapter dependency diagram for this book. Solid arrows indicate that the chapter at the beginning of the arrow is required before studying the chapter at the end of the arrow. A dotted arrow indicates that the chapter at the beginning of the arrow is not essential to studying the chapter at the end of the dotted arrow.

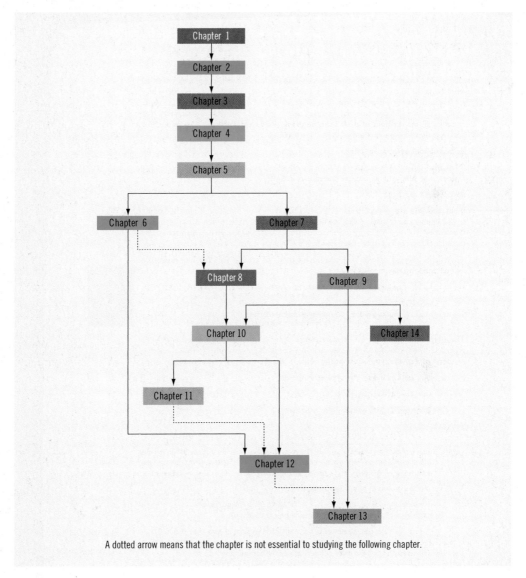

A dotted arrow means that the chapter is not essential to studying the following chapter.

FIGURE 1   Chapter dependency diagram

All source code and solutions have been written, compiled, and quality assurance tested with Java 6.0 and the version of Java 7.0 available at the time the book was being typeset.

FEATURES OF THE BOOK

called a **nonstatic** method. Similarly, the heading of a method may contain the reserved word `public`. In this case, it is called a `public` method. An important property of a `public` and `static` method is that (in a program) it can be used (called) using the name of the class, the dot operator, the method name, and the appropriate parameters. For example, all the methods of the `class` **Math** are `public` and `static`. Therefore, the general syntax to use a method of the `class` **Math** is:

```
Math.methodName(parameters)
```

(Note that, in fact, the parameters used in a method call are called actual parameters.) For example, the following expression determines $2.5^{3.5}$:

```
Math.pow(2.5, 3.5)
```

(In the previous statement, **2.5** and **3.5** are actual parameters.) Similarly, if a method of the `class` **Character** is `public` and `static`, you can use the name of the `class`, which is **Character**, the dot operator, the method name, and the appropriate parameters. The methods of the `class` **Character** listed in Table 7-2 are `public` and `static`.

To simplify the use of (`public`) `static` methods of a class, Java 5.0 introduces the following import statements:

```
import static pakageName.ClassName.*; //to use any (public)
                                      //static method of the class

import static pakageName.ClassName.methodName; //to use a
                                               //specific method of the class
```

These are called `static import` **statements**. After including such statements in your program, when you use a (`public`) `static` method (or any other `public static` member) of a `class`, you can omit the name of the `class` and the dot operator.

For example, after including the `import` statement:

```
import static java.lang.Math.*;
```

you can determine $2.5^{3.5}$ by using the expression:

```
pow(2.5, 3.5)
```

 NOTE After including the `static import` statement, in reality, you have a choice. When you use a (`public`) `static` method of a `class`, you can either use the name of the `class` and the dot operator or omit them. For example, after including the `static import` statement:

```
import static java.lang.Math.*;
```

in a program, you can determine $2.5^{3.5}$ by using either the expression **Math.pow(2.5, 3.5)** or the expression **pow(2.5, 3.5)**.

The `static import` statement is *not* available in versions of Java lower than 5.0. Therefore, if you are using, say, Java 4.0, then you must use a `static` method of the `class` **Math** using the name of the `class` and the dot operator.

Four-color interior design shows accurate code and related comments.

7

The preceding program works as follows: The statement in Line 5 declares **str** to be a reference variable of the **StringBuffer** type and assigns the string **"Hello"** to it (see Figure 7-13).

FIGURE 7-13 Variable after the statement in Line 5 executes

The statement in Line 6 outputs the first line of output. The statement in Line 7 calls the method **stringBufferParameter**. The actual parameter is **str** and the formal parameter is **pStr**. The value of **str** is copied into **pStr**. Because both of these parameters are reference variables, **str** and **pStr** point to the same string, which is **"Hello"** (see Figure 7-14).

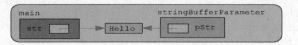

FIGURE 7-14 Variable before the statement in Line 7 executes

Then control is transferred to the method **stringBufferParameter**. The next statement executed is in Line 12, which produces the second line of the output. The statement in Line 13 produces the third line of the output. This statement also outputs the string to which **pStr** points, and the printed value is that string. The statement in Line 14 uses the method **append** to append the string **" There"** to the string pointed to by **pStr**. After this statement executes, **pStr** points to the string **"Hello There"**. However, this also changes the string that was assigned to the variable **str**. When the statement in Line 14 executes, **str** points to the same string as **pStr** (see Figure 7-15).

FIGURE 7-15 Variable after the statement in Line 14 executes

ACTUAL PARAMETER LIST

An actual parameter list has the following syntax:

```
expression or variable, expression or variable, ...
```

As with value-returning methods, in a method call the number of actual parameters, together with their data types, must match the formal parameters in the order given. Actual and formal parameters have a one-to-one correspondence. A method call causes the body of the called method to execute. Two examples of void methods with parameters follow.

EXAMPLE 7-5

Consider the following method heading:

```
public static void funexp(int a, double b, char c, String name)
```

The method **funexp** has four formal parameters: (1) **a**, a parameter of type int;, (2) **b**, a parameter of type double;, (3) **c**, a parameter of type char, and (4) **name**, a parameter of type **String**.

EXAMPLE 7-6

Consider the following method heading:

```
public static void expfun(int one, char two, String three, double four)
```

The method **expfun** has four formal parameters: (1) **one**, a parameter of type int;, (2) **two**, a parameter of type char;, (3) **three**, a parameter of type **String**, and (4) **four**, a parameter of type double.

Parameters provide a communication link between the calling method (such as **main**) and the called method. They enable methods to manipulate different data each time they are called.

EXAMPLE 7-7

Suppose that you want to print a pattern (a triangle of stars) similar to the following:

```
      *
    *  *
  *  *  *
*  *  *  *
```

The first line has one star with some blanks before the star, the second line has two stars, some blanks before the stars, and a blank between the stars, and so on. Let's write the

Because this is a value-returning method of type `int`, it must return a value of type `int`. Suppose the value of **x** is **10**. Then, the expression, **x > 5**, in Line 1, evaluates to `true`. So the `return` statement in Line 2 returns the value **20**. Now suppose that **x** is **3**. The expression, **x > 5**, in Line 1, now evaluates to `false`. The `if` statement therefore fails and the `return` statement in Line 2 *does not* execute. However, the body of the method has no more statements to be executed. It thus follows that if the value of **x** is less than or equal to **5**, the method does not contain any valid `return` statements to return the value of **x**. In this case, in fact, the compiler generates an error message such as **missing return statement**.

The correct definition of the method **secret** is:

```
public static int secret(int x)
{
    if (x > 5)                    //Line 1
        return 2 * x;             //Line 2

    return x;                     //Line 3
}
```

Here, if the value of **x** is less than or equal to 5, the `return` statement in Line 3 executes, which returns the value of **x**. On the other hand, if the value of **x** is, say, **10**, the `return` statement in Line 2 executes, which returns the value **20** and also terminates the method.

> **NOTE** (`return` statement: A precaution) If the compiler can determine that during execution certain statements in a program can never be reached, then it will generate syntax errors. For example, consider the following methods:
>
> ```
> public static int funcReturnStatementError(int z)
> {
>     return z;
>
>     System.out.println(z);
> }
> ```
>
> The first statement in the method **funcReturnStatementError** is the `return` statement. Therefore, if this method executes, then the output statement, **System.out.println(z);**, will never be executed. In this case, when the compiler compiles this method, it will generate two syntax errors, one specifying that the statement **System.out.println(z);** is unreachable, and the second specifying that there is a missing `return` statement after the output statement. Even if you include a `return` statement after the output statement, the compiler will still generate the error that the statement **System.out.println(z);** is unreachable. Therefore, you should be careful when writing the definition of a method. The Web site, *www.course.com*, and the CD accompanying this book contain additional methods illustrating such errors. The name of the program is **TestReturnStatement.java**.

PROGRAMMING EXAMPLE: Data Comparison

Two groups of students at a local university are enrolled in special courses during the summer semester. The courses are offered for the first time and are taught by different teachers. At the end of the semester, both groups are given the same tests for the same courses and their scores are recorded in separate files. The data in each file is in the following form:

```
courseID  score1, score2, ..., scoreN -999
courseID  score1, score2, ..., scoreM -999
  .
  .
  .
```

This programming example illustrates:

1. How to read data from more than one file in the same program.
2. How to send the output to a file.
3. How to generate bar graphs.
4. With the help of methods and parameter passing, how to use the same program segment on different (but similar) sets of data.
5. How to use structured design to solve a problem and how to perform parameter passing.

This program is broken into two parts. First, you learn how to read data from more than one file. Second, you learn how to generate bar graphs.

Next we write a program that finds the average course score for each course for each group. The output is of the following form:

```
Course ID   Group No   Course Average
  CSC          1            83.71
               2            80.82

  ENG          1            82.00
               2            78.20
  .
  .
  .
Avg for group 1: 82.04
Avg for group 2: 82.01
```

Input: Because the data for the two groups is recorded in separate files, the input data appears in two separate files

Output: As shown above

7

Programming Examples are complete programs featured in each chapter. These examples include the accurate, concrete stages of Input, Output, Problem Analysis and Algorithm Design, and a Complete Program Listing.

- An identifier **x** declared within a method (block) is accessible:
  - Only within the block from the point at which it is declared until the end of the block.
  - By those blocks that are nested within that block.
- Suppose **x** is an identifier declared within a class and outside every method's definition (block):
  - If **x** is declared without the reserved word `static` (such as a named constant or a method name), then it cannot be accessed within a `static` method.
  - If **x** is declared with the reserved word `static` (such as a named constant or a method name), then it can be accessed within a method (block), provided the method (block) does not have any other identifier named **x**.

38. Two methods are said to have different formal parameter lists if both methods have:
    - A different number of formal parameters, or
    - If the number of formal parameters is the same, then the data type of the formal parameters, in the order you list, must differ in at least one position.

39. The signature of a method consists of the method name and its formal parameter list. Two methods have different signatures if they have either different names or different formal parameter lists.

40. If a method is overloaded, then in a call to that method the signature, that is, the formal parameter list of the method, determines which method to execute.

EXERCISES

1. Mark the following statements as true or false.

   a. To use a predefined method of a `class` contained in the package `java.lang` in a program, you only need to know what the name of the method is and how to use it.

   b. A value-returning method returns only one value via the return statement.

   c. Parameters allow you to use different values each time the method is called.

   d. When a `return` statement executes in a user-defined method, the method immediately exits.

   e. A value-returning method returns only integer values.

PROGRAMMING EXERCISES

Programming
Exercises challenge
students to write
Java programs with
a specified
outcome.

1. Write a value-returning method, **isVowel**, that returns the value `true` if a given character is a vowel, and otherwise returns `false`. Also write a program to test your method.

2. Write a program that prompts the user to input a sequence of characters and outputs the number of vowels. (Use the method **isVowel** written in Programming Exercise 1.)

3. Consider the following program segment:

```java
public class Ch7_PrExercise3
{
    public static void main(String[] args)
    {
        int    num;
        double dec;
        .
        .
        .
    }

    public static int one(int x, int y)
    {
        .
        .
        .
    }

    public static double two(int x, double a)
    {
        int first;
        double z;
        .
        .
        .
    }
}
```

a. Write the definition of method **one** so that it returns the sum of **x** and **y** if **x** is greater than **y**; otherwise, it should return **x** minus **2** times **y**.

b. Write the definition of method **two** as follows:

   i. Read a number and store it in **z**.

   ii. Update the value of **z** by adding the value of **a** to its previous value.

   iii. Assign the variable **first** the value returned by method **one** with the parameters **6** and **8**.

Supplemental Resources

The following supplemental materials are available when this book is used in a classroom setting.

All instructor teaching tools, outlined below, are available with this book on a single CD-ROM.

Electronic Instructor's Manual

The Instructor's Manual that accompanies this textbook includes:

- Additional instructional material to assist in class preparation, including suggestions for lecture topics.

- Solutions to all the end-of-chapter materials, including the Programming Exercises.

ExamView®

This textbook is accompanied by ExamView, a powerful testing software package that allows instructors to create and administer printed, computer (LAN-based), and Internet exams. ExamView includes hundreds of questions that correspond to the topics covered in this text, enabling students to generate detailed study guides that include page references for further review. These computer-based and Internet testing components allow students to take exams at their computers, and save the instructor time because each exam is graded automatically.

PowerPoint Presentations

This book comes with Microsoft PowerPoint slides for each chapter. These slides are included as a teaching aid for classroom presentations, either to make available to students on the network for chapter review, or to be printed for classroom distribution. Instructors can add their own slides for additional topics that they introduce to the class.

Distance Learning

Cengage Course Technology is proud to present online courses in WebCT and Blackboard to provide the most complete and dynamic learning experience possible. For more information on how to bring distance learning to your course, contact your local Cengage Course Technology sales representative.

Source Code

The source code is available at *http://www.cengage.com/highered/*, and is also available on the Instructor Resources CD-ROM and the CD accompanying this text. The input files needed to run some of the programs are also included with the source code.

Solution Files

The solution files for all programming exercises are available at *http://www.cengage.com/highered/*, and are also available on the Instructor Resources CD-ROM. The input files needed to run some of the programming exercises are also included with the solution files.

ACKNOWLEDGMENTS

There are many people I must thank who, one way or another, contributed to the success of this book. First, I would like to thank those who e-mailed numerous comments to improve on the third edition. I am thankful to Professors S.C. Cheng, Randall Crist, and John N. Mordeson, for constantly supporting this project.

I owe a great deal to the following reviewers, who patiently read each page of every chapter of the current version and made critical comments to improve on the book: Atef Bader, DePaul University; Rajwant Gill, Anne Arundel Community College; Gerard Gordon, DePaul University; Jenneth Honeycutt, Fayetteville Technical Community College; and John Mill, Spokane Falls Community College. Additionally, I would like to thank the reviewers of the proposal package: Lemond Hall, South Georgia Technical College and Hemand Pendharkar, Worcester State College. The reviewers will recognize that their suggestions have not been overlooked and, in fact, made this a better book.

Next, I express thanks to Amy Jollymore, Acquisitions Editor, for recognizing the importance and uniqueness of this project. All this would not have been possible without the careful planning of Senior Product Manager Alyssa Pratt. I extend my sincere thanks to Alyssa, as well as to Senior Content Project Manager, Catherine DiMassa. I also thank Tintu Thomas of Integra Software Services for assisting us in keeping the project on schedule. I would like to thank Chris Scriver and Serge Palladino of the QA department of Course Technology for patiently and carefully proofreading the text, testing the code, and discovering typos and erros.

I am thankful to my parents for their blessings.

Finally, I am thankful to the support of my wife Sadhana, and especially my daughter Shelly, to whom this book is dedicated. They cheered me up whenever I was overwhelmed during the writing of this book.

We welcome any comments concerning the text. Comments may be forwarded to the following e-mail address: `malik@creighton.edu`.

D.S. Malik

AN OVERVIEW OF COMPUTERS AND PROGRAMMING LANGUAGES

IN THIS CHAPTER, YOU WILL:

- Learn about different types of computers
- Explore the hardware and software components of a computer system
- Learn about the language of a computer
- Learn about the evolution of programming languages
- Examine high-level programming languages
- Discover what a compiler is and what it does
- Examine how a Java program is processed
- Learn about the Internet and World Wide Web
- Learn what an algorithm is and explore problem-solving techniques
- Become familiar with structured and object-oriented programming design methodologies

Introduction

Terms such as "the Internet," which was unfamiliar just a few years ago, are now common. Elementary school students regularly "surf" the Internet and use computers to design their classroom projects. Many people use the Internet to look up information and to communicate with others. These Internet activities are all made possible by the availability of different software, also known as computer programs. Software is developed by using programming languages. The programming language Java is especially well suited for developing software to accomplish specific tasks. Our main objective is to teach you how to write programs in the Java programming language. Before you begin programming, it is useful if you understand some of the basic terminology and different components of a computer. We begin with an overview of the history of computers.

An Overview of the History of Computers

The first device known to carry out calculations was the abacus. The abacus was invented in Asia but was used in ancient Babylon, China, and throughout Europe until the late middle ages. The abacus uses a system of sliding beads on a rack for addition and subtraction. In 1642, the French philosopher and mathematician Blaise Pascal invented the calculating device called the Pascaline. It had eight movable dials on wheels that could calculate sums up to eight figures long. Both the abacus and Pascaline could perform only addition and subtraction operations. Later in the seventeenth century, Gottfried von Leibniz invented a device that was able to add, subtract, multiply, and divide. In 1819, Joseph Jacquard, a French weaver, discovered that the weaving instructions for his looms could be stored on cards with holes punched in them. While the cards moved throughout the loom in sequence, needles passed through the holes and picked up threads of the correct color and texture. A weaver could rearrange the cards and change the pattern being woven. In essence, the cards programmed a loom to produce patterns in cloth. The weaving industry seems to have little in common with the computer industry. However, the idea of storing information by punching holes on a card turned out to be of great importance in the later development of computers.

In the early and mid-1800s, Charles Babbage, an English mathematician and physical scientist, designed two calculating machines—the difference engine and the analytical engine. The difference engine could automatically perform complex operations, such as squaring numbers. Babbage built a prototype of the difference engine, but the actual device was never produced. The analytical engine's design included input device, memory storage, a control unit that allowed processing instructions in any sequence, and output devices. However, the designs remained in blueprint stage. Most of Babbage's work is known through the writings of the colleague Ada Augusta, Countess of Lovelace. Augusta is considered to be the first computer programmer.

At the end of the 19th century, U.S. Census officials needed help in accurately tabulating the census data. Herman Hollerith invented a calculating machine that ran on electricity and used punched cards to store data. Hollerith's machine was immensely successful.

Hollerith founded the Tabulating Machine Company, which later became the computer and technology corporation known as IBM.

The first computer-like machine was the Mark I. It was built, in 1944, jointly by IBM and Harvard University under the leadership of Howard Aiken. Punched cards were used to feed data into the machine. Mark I was 52 feet long, weighed 50 tons, and had 750,000 parts. In 1946, ENIAC (Electronic Numerical Integrator and Calculator) was built at the University of Pennsylvania. It contained 18,000 vacuum tubes and weighed some 30 tons.

The computers that we know today use the design rules given by John von Neumann in the late 1940s. His design included components such as arithmetic logic unit, control unit, memory, and input/output devices. These components are described in the next section. Von Neumann computer design makes it possible to store the programming instruction and the data in the same memory space. In 1951, the UNIVAC (Universal Automatic Computer) was built and sold to the U.S. Census Bureau.

In 1956, the invention of the transistors resulted in smaller, faster, more reliable, and more energy-efficient computers. This era also saw the emergence of the software development industry with the introduction of FORTRAN and COBOL, two early programming languages. In the next major technological advancement, transistors were replaced by tiny integrated circuits or "chips." Chips are smaller and cheaper than transistors and can contain thousands of circuits on a single chip. They give computers tremendous processing speed.

In 1970, the microprocessor, an entire CPU on a single chip, was invented. In 1977, Stephen Wozniak and Steven Jobs designed and built the first Apple computer in their garage. In 1981, IBM introduced its personal computer (PC). In the 1980s, clones of the IBM PC made the personal computer even more affordable. By the mid-1990s, people from many walks of life were able to afford them. Computers continue to become faster and less expensive as technology advances.

Modern-day computers are very powerful, reliable, and easy to use. They can accept spoken-word instructions and imitate human reasoning through artificial intelligence. Expert systems assist doctors in making diagnoses. Mobile computing applications are growing significantly. Using hand-held devices, delivery drivers can access global positioning satellites (GPS) to verify customer locations for pickups and deliveries. Cell phones can check your e-mail, make airline reservations, see how stocks are performing, and access your bank accounts.

Although there are several categories of computers, such as mainframe, midsize, and micro, all computers share some basic elements.

Elements of a Computer System

A computer is an electronic device capable of performing commands. The basic commands that a computer performs are input (get data), output (display results), storage, and performance of arithmetic and logical operations.

In today's market, personal computers are sold with descriptions such as a Pentium 4 Processor 2.80 GHz, 1 GB RAM, 100 GB HD, VX750 17" Silver Flat CRT Color Monitor, preloaded with software such as an operating system, games, encyclopedias, and application software such as word processors or money management programs. These descriptions represent two categories: hardware and software. Items such as "Pentium 4 Processor 2.80 GHz, 1 GB RAM, 100 GB HD, VX750 17" Silver Flat CRT Color Monitor" fall into the hardware category; items such as "operating system, games, encyclopedias, and application software" fall into the software category. Let's look at the hardware first.

Hardware

Major hardware components include the central processing unit (CPU); main memory (MM), also called random access memory (RAM); input/output devices; and secondary storage. Some examples of input devices are the keyboard, mouse, and secondary storage. Examples of output devices are the monitor, printer, and secondary storage.

CENTRAL PROCESSING UNIT AND MAIN MEMORY

The **central processing unit (CPU)** is the "brain" of the computer and the single most expensive piece of hardware in a computer. The more powerful the CPU, the faster the computer. Arithmetic and logical operations are carried out inside the CPU. Figure 1-1(a) shows some hardware components.

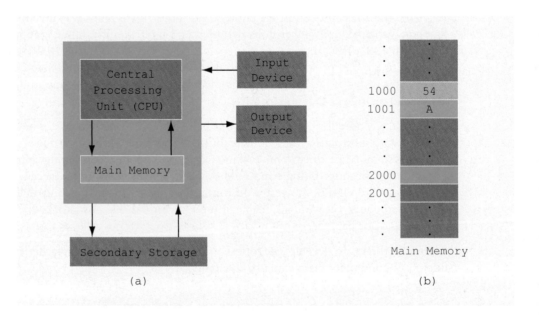

FIGURE 1-1 Hardware components of a computer and main memory

Main memory, or random access memory (RAM), is connected directly to the CPU. All programs must be loaded into main memory before they can be executed. Similarly, all data must be brought into main memory before a program can manipulate it. When the computer is turned off, everything in main memory is lost.

Main memory is an ordered sequence of cells, called **memory cells**. Each cell has a unique location in main memory, called the **address** of the cell. These addresses help you access the information stored in the cell. Figure 1-1(b) shows main memory with some data.

Today's computers come with main memory consisting of millions to billions of cells. Although Figure 1-1(b) shows data stored in cells, the content of a cell can be either a programming instruction or data. Moreover, this figure shows the data as numbers and letters. However, as explained later in this chapter, main memory stores everything as sequences of 0s and 1s. The memory addresses are also expressed as sequences of 0s and 1s.

SECONDARY STORAGE

Because programs and data must be stored in main memory before processing, and because everything in main memory is lost when the computer is turned off, information stored in main memory must be transferred to some other device for longer-term storage. A device that stores longer-term information (unless the device becomes unusable or you change the information by rewriting it) is called **secondary storage**. To be able to transfer information from main memory to secondary storage, these components must be connected directly to each other. Examples of secondary storage are hard disks, floppy disks, flash memory, ZIP disks, CD-ROMs, and tapes.

INPUT/OUTPUT DEVICES

For a computer to perform a useful task, it must be able to take in data and programs and display the results of the manipulation of the data. The devices that feed data and programs into computers are called **input devices**. The keyboard, mouse, and secondary storage are examples of input devices. The devices that the computer uses to display and store results are called **output devices**. A monitor, printer, and secondary storage are examples of output devices. Figure 1-2 shows some input and output devices.

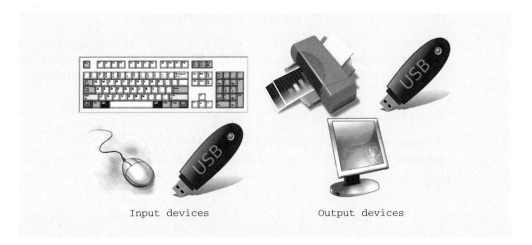

Input devices   Output devices

FIGURE 1-2 Some input and output devices

Software

Software consists of programs written to perform specific tasks. For example, you use word-processing programs to write letters, papers, and books. The two types of programs are system programs and application programs.

System programs control the computer. The system program that loads first when you turn on your PC is called the **operating system**. Without an operating system, the computer is useless. The operating system monitors the overall activity of the computer and provides services, such as memory management, input/output activities, and storage management. The operating system has a special program that organizes secondary storage so that you can access information conveniently. The operating system is the program that runs the application programs. **Application programs** perform specific tasks. Word processors, spreadsheets, and games are examples of application programs. Both operating systems and application programs are written in programming languages.

Language of a Computer

When you press A on your keyboard, the computer displays A on the screen, but what is actually stored inside the computer's main memory? What is the language of the computer? How does it store whatever you type on the keyboard?

Remember that a computer is an electronic device. Electrical signals move along channels inside the computer. There are two types of electrical signals: analog and digital. **Analog signals** are continuous waveforms used to represent things, such as sound. Audio tapes, for example, store data in analog signals. **Digital signals** represent information with a sequence of 0s and 1s. A 0 represents a low voltage, and a 1 represents a high voltage. Digital signals are more reliable carriers of information than analog signals and can be copied from one device to another with exact precision. You might have noticed that when you make a copy of an audio tape, the sound quality of the copy is not as good as that on the original tape. Computers use digital signals.

Because digital signals are processed inside a computer, the language of a computer, called **machine language**, is a sequence of 0s and 1s. The digit 0 or 1 is called a **binary digit**, or **bit**. Sometimes a sequence of 0s and 1s is referred to as a **binary code** or a **binary number**.

Bit: A binary digit 0 or 1.

A sequence of eight bits is called a **byte**. Moreover, $2^{10} = 1024$ bytes and is called a **kilobyte (KB)**. Table 1-1 summarizes the terms used to describe the various numbers of bytes.

TABLE 1-1 Binary Units

Unit	Symbol	Bits/Bytes
Byte		8 bits
Kilobyte	KB	2^{10} bytes = 1024 bytes
Megabyte	MB	1024 KB = 2^{10} KB = 2^{20} bytes = 1,048,576 bytes
Gigabyte	GB	1024 MB = 2^{10} MB = 2^{30} bytes = 1,073,741,824 bytes
Terabyte	TB	1024 GB = 2^{10} GB = 2^{40} bytes = 1,099,511,627,776 bytes
Petabyte	PB	1024 TB = 2^{10} TB = 2^{50} bytes = 1,125,899,906,842,624 bytes
Exabyte	EB	1024 PB = 2^{10} PB = 2^{60} bytes = 1,152,921,504,606,846,976 bytes
Zettabyte	ZB	1024 EB = 2^{10} EB = 2^{70} bytes = 1,180,591,620,717,411,303,424 bytes

Every letter, number, or special symbol (such as * or {) on your keyboard is encoded as a sequence of bits, each having a unique representation. The most commonly used encoding scheme on personal computers is the seven-bit **American Standard Code for Information Interchange (ASCII)**. The ASCII data set consists of 128 characters, numbered 0 through 127. (Note that $2^7 = 128$ and $2^8 = 256$.) That is, in the ASCII data set, the position of the first character is 0, the position of the second character is 1, and so on. In this scheme, A is encoded as 1000001. In fact, A is the 66th character in the ASCII character code, but its position is 65 because the position of the first character is 0. Furthermore, 1000001 is the binary representation of 65. The character 3 is encoded as 0110011. For a complete list of the printable ASCII character set, refer to Appendix C.

NOTE The number system that we use in our daily life is called the **decimal system** or **base 10**. Because everything inside a computer is represented as a sequence of 0s and 1s, that is, binary numbers, the number system that a computer uses is called binary or **base 2**. We indicated in the preceding paragraph that the number 1000001 is the binary representation of 65. Appendix D describes how to convert a number from base 10 to base 2 and vice versa. Appendix D also describes how to convert a number between base 2 and base 16 (hexadecimal) and between base 2 and base 8 (octal).

Inside the computer, every character is represented as a sequence of eight bits, that is, as a byte. Because ASCII is a seven-bit code, you must add 0 to the left of the ASCII encoding of a character. Hence, inside the computer, the character A is represented as 01000001, and the character 3 is represented as 00110011.

Other encoding schemes include Unicode, which is a more recent development. **Unicode** consists of 65,536 characters. To store a Unicode character, you need two bytes. Java uses the Unicode character set. Therefore, in Java, every character is represented as a sequence of 16 bits, that is, 2 bytes. In Unicode, the character **A** is represented as 0000000001000001.

The ASCII character set is a subset of Unicode; the first 128 characters of Unicode are the same as the characters in ASCII. If you are dealing with only the English language, the ASCII character set is sufficient to write Java programs. The advantage of the Unicode character set is that symbols from languages other than English can be handled easily.

Evolution of Programming Languages

The most basic computer language, machine language, provides program instructions in bits. Even though most computers perform the same kinds of operations, the designers of different CPUs sometimes choose different sets of binary codes to perform those operations. Therefore, the machine language of one computer is not necessarily the same as the machine language of another computer. The only consistency among computers is that in any computer, all data are stored and manipulated as a binary code.

Early computers were programmed in machine language. To see how instructions are written in machine language, suppose you want to use the equation:

wages = rate · hours

to calculate weekly wages. Assume that the memory locations of `rate`, `hours`, and `wages` are 010001, 010010, and 010011, respectively. Further suppose that the binary code 100100 stands for load, 100110 stands for multiplication, and 100010 stands for store. In machine language, you might need the following sequence of instructions to calculate the weekly wages:

```
100100 010001
100110 010010
100010 010011
```

To represent the weekly wages equation in machine language, the programmer had to remember the machine language codes for various operations. Also, to manipulate data, the programmer had to remember the locations of the data in main memory. Remembering specific codes made programming difficult and error prone.

Assembly languages were developed to make the programmer's job easier. In **assembly language**, an instruction is an easy-to-remember form called a **mnemonic**. Table 1-2 shows some examples of instructions in assembly language and their corresponding machine language code.

TABLE 1-2 Examples of Instructions in Assembly Language and Machine Language

Assembly Language	Machine Language
LOAD	100100
STOR	100010
MULT	100110
ADD	100101
SUB	100011

Using assembly language instructions, you can write the equation to calculate the weekly wages as follows:

```
LOAD    rate
MULT    hours
STOR    wages
```

As you can see, it is much easier to write instructions in assembly language. However, a computer cannot execute assembly language instructions directly. The instructions first have to be translated into machine language. A program called an **assembler** translates the assembly language instructions into machine language.

Assembler: A program that translates a program written in assembly language into an equivalent program in machine language.

Moving from machine language to assembly language made programming easier, but a programmer was still forced to think in terms of individual machine instructions. The next step toward making programming easier was to devise **high-level languages** that were closer to spoken languages, such as English and Spanish. Basic, FORTRAN, COBOL, Pascal, C, C++, and Java are all high-level languages. You will learn the high-level language Java in this book.

In Java, you write the weekly wages equation as follows:

```
wages = rate * hours;
```

The instruction written in Java is much easier to understand and is self-explanatory to a novice user who is familiar with basic arithmetic. As in the case of assembly language, however, the computer cannot directly execute instructions written in a high-level language. To run on a computer, these Java instructions first need to be translated into an intermediate language called **bytecode** and then interpreted into a particular machine language. A program called a **compiler** translates instructions written in Java into bytecode.

Compiler: A program that translates a program written in a high-level language into the equivalent machine language. (In the case of Java, this machine language is the bytecode.)

Recall that the computer understands only machine language. Moreover, different types of CPUs use different machine languages. To make Java programs **machine independent**, that is, able to run on many different types of computer platforms, the designers of Java introduced a hypothetical computer called the **Java Virtual Machine (JVM)**. In fact, bytecode is the machine language for the JVM.

 NOTE   In languages such as C and C++, the compiler translates the source code directly into the machine language of your computer's CPU. For such languages, a different compiler is needed for each type of CPU. Therefore, programs in these languages are not easily portable from one type of machine to another. The source code must be recompiled for each type of CPU. To make Java programs machine independent and easily portable, and to allow them to run on a Web browser, the designers of Java introduced the Java Virtual Machine (JVM) and bytecode as the (machine) language of this machine. It is easier to translate a bytecode into a particular type of CPU. This concept is covered further in the following section, Processing a Java Program.

Processing a Java Program

Java has two types of programs—applications and applets. The following is an example of a Java application program:

```
public class MyFirstJavaProgram
{
    public static void main(String[] args)
    {
        System.out.println("My first Java program.");
    }
}
```

At this point you need not be too concerned with the details of this program. However, if you run (execute) this program, it will display the following line on the screen:

```
My first Java program.
```

Recall that a computer can understand only machine language. Therefore, in order to run this program successfully, the code must first be translated into the machine language. In this section we review the steps required to execute programs written in Java.

To process a program written in Java, you carry out the following steps, as illustrated in Figure 1-3.

1. You use a text editor, such as Notepad, to create (that is, type) a program in Java following the rules, or syntax, of the language. This program is called the **source program**. The program must be saved in a text file named `ClassName.java`, where `ClassName` is the name of the Java class contained in the file. For example, in the Java program

given above, the name of the (`public`) class containing the Java program is `MyFirstJavaProgram`. Therefore, this program must be saved in the text file named `MyFirstJavaProgram.java`. Otherwise an error will occur.

Source program: A program written in a high-level language.

2. You must verify that the program obeys the rules of the programming language—that is, the program must be syntactically correct—and translate the program into the equivalent bytecode. The compiler checks the source program for syntax errors and, if no error is found, translates the program into bytecode. The bytecode is saved in the file with the `.class` extension. For example, the bytecode for `MyFirstJavaProgram.java` is stored in the `MyFirstJavaProgram.class` file by the compiler.

3. To run a Java application program, the `.class` file must be loaded into computer memory. To run a Java applet, you must use either a Web browser or an applet viewer, a stripped-down Web browser for running applets. The programs that you write in Java are typically developed using an **integrated development environment (IDE)**. The IDE contains many programs that are useful in creating your program. For example, it contains the necessary code to display the results of the program and several mathematical functions to make the programmer's job somewhat easier. Because certain code is already available to you, you can use this code rather than writing your own. You can also develop your own libraries (called *packages* in Java). (Note that in Java, typically, a package is a set of related classes. So, typically, a Java program is a collection of classes. We will explain this further in Chapters 2 and 8. At this point, you need not be too concerned with these details.) In general, to successfully run a Java program, the bytecode for classes used in the program must be connected. The program that automatically does this in Java is known as the **loader**.

4. The next step is to execute the Java program. In addition to connecting the bytecode from various classes, the loader also loads your Java program's bytecode into main memory. As the classes are loaded into main memory, the *bytecode verifier* verifies that the bytecode for the classes is valid and does not violate Java's security restrictions. Finally, a program called an **interpreter** translates each bytecode instruction into your computer's machine language, and then executes it.

Interpreter: A program that reads and translates each bytecode instruction into your computer's machine language, and then executes it.

Note that the Java interpreter translates and executes one bytecode instruction at a time. It does not first translate the entire bytecode into your computer's machine language. As noted earlier, in languages such as C++, a different compiler is needed for each type of CPU, whereas a Java compiler translates a Java source program into bytecode, the machine language of JVM, which is independent of any particular type of CPU.

The Java interpreter translates each bytecode instruction into a particular type of CPU machine language and then executes the instruction. Thus, in the case of the Java language, a different type of interpreter is needed for a particular type of CPU. However, interpreters are programs that are simpler than compilers. Because the Java interpreter translates one bytecode instruction at a time, Java programs run more slowly.

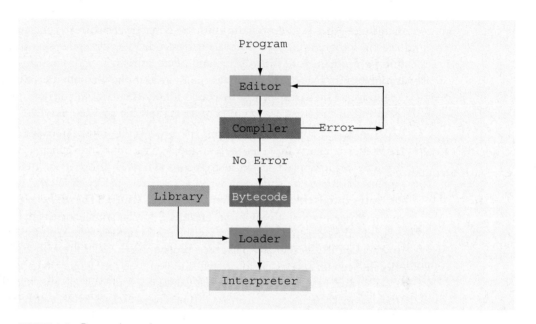

FIGURE 1-3 Processing a Java program

As a programmer, one of your primary concerns is with Step 1. That is, you must learn, understand, and master the rules of the programming language to create source programs. Programs are developed using an IDE. Well-known IDEs used to create programs in Java include JBuilder (from Borland), CodeWarrior (Metrowerks), and jGrasp (Auburn University). These IDEs contain an editor to create the program, a compiler to check the program for syntax errors, a program to load the object codes of the resources used from the IDE, and a program to execute the program. These IDEs are also quite user friendly. When you compile your program, the compiler not only identifies the syntax errors, but also typically suggests how to correct them.

NOTE   Other software that can be used to develop Java programs include Eclipse, TextPad, JCreator, BlueJ, and DrJava.

In Chapter 2, after being introduced to some basic elements of Java, you will see how a Java program is created.

Internet, World Wide Web, Browser, and Java

We often hear the terms Internet, World Wide Web (or simply, Web) and Web browser (or simply, browser). What do these terms mean, and what is Java's connection with them?

The *Internet* is an interconnection of networks that allows computers around the world to communicate with each other. In 1969, the U.S. Department of Defense's Advanced Research Project Agency (ARPA) funded research projects to investigate and develop techniques and technologies to interlink networks. The objective was to develop communication protocols so that networked computers could communicate with each other. This was called the *internetting* project, and the funding resulted into ARPANET, which eventually became known as the "Internet."

Over the last four decades, the Internet has grown manyfold. In 1973, approximately 25 computers were connected via the Internet. This number grew to 700,000 computers by 1991, and to over 10,000,000 by 2000. Each day, more and more computers are getting connected via the Internet.

The terms Internet and World Wide Web are often used interchangeably. However, there is a difference between the two. The Internet allows computers to be connected and communicate with each other. On the other hand, the *World Wide Web* (WWW), or Web, uses software programs that enable computer users to access documents and files (including images, audio, and video) on almost any subject over the Internet with the click of a mouse. Undoubtedly, the Internet has become one of the world's leading communication mechanisms. Computers around the world communicate via the Internet; the World Wide Web makes that communication a fun activity.

The primary language for the Web is known as *Hypertext Markup Language* (HTML). It is a simple language for laying out and linking documents, as well as for viewing images and listening to sound. However, HTML is not capable of interacting with the user, except to collect information via simple forms. Therefore, Web pages are essentially static. As noted previously, Java has two types of programs—applications and applets. In terms of programming, both types are similar. Application programs are stand-alone programs that can run on your computer. Java applets are programs that run from a *Web browser* and make the Web responsive and interactive. Two well-known *browsers* are Netscape and Internet Explorer. Java applets can run in either browser. Moreover, through the use of applets, the Web becomes responsive, interactive, and fun to use. (Note that to run applets, the browser you use must be Java enabled.)

Programming with the Problem Analysis–Coding– Execution Cycle

Programming is a process of problem solving. Different people use different techniques to solve problems. Some techniques are clearly outlined and easy to follow; they solve the problem and give insight into how the solution was reached. Such problem-solving techniques can be easily modified if the domain of the problem changes.

To be a skillful problem solver, and, therefore, to become a skillful programmer, you must use good problem-solving techniques. One common problem-solving technique includes analyzing a problem, outlining the problem requirements, and designing steps, called an **algorithm**, to solve the problem.

Algorithm: A step-by-step problem-solving process in which a solution is arrived at in a finite amount of time.

In the programming environment, the problem-solving process involves the following steps:

1. Analyze the problem and outline the problem and its solution requirements.
2. Design an algorithm to solve the problem.
3. Implement the algorithm in a programming language, such as Java.
4. Verify that the algorithm works.
5. Maintain the program by using and improving it, and modifying it if the problem domain changes.

Figure 1-4 summarizes this programming process.

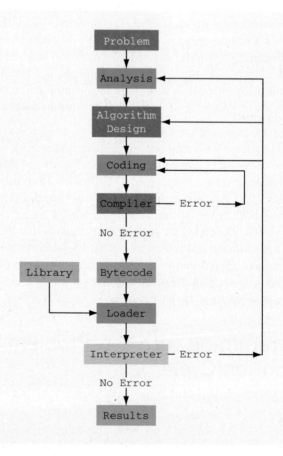

FIGURE 1-4 Problem analysis–coding–execution cycle

1

To develop a program to solve a problem, you start by analyzing the problem, then outlining the problem and the options for a solution. You then design the algorithm; write the program instructions in a high-level language, or code the program; and enter the program into a computer system.

Analyzing the problem is the first, and most important, step in the process. This step requires that you do the following:

- Thoroughly understand the problem.

- Understand the problem requirements. Requirements can include whether the program requires interaction with the user, whether it manipulates data, whether it produces output, and what the output looks like. If the program manipulates data, the programmer must know what the data are and how they are represented. To do this, you need to look at sample data.

- If the program produces output, you should know how the results should be generated and formatted.

- If the problem is complex, divide the problem into subproblems and repeat Steps 1 and 2 by analyzing each subproblem and understanding each subproblem's requirements. You also need to know how the subproblems relate to each other.

After you carefully analyze the problem, the next step is to design an algorithm to solve it. If you broke the problem into subproblems, you need to design an algorithm for each subproblem. Once you design an algorithm, you must check it for correctness. You can sometimes do this using sample data; other times, you might need to perform some mathematical analysis to test the algorithm's correctness. You also need to integrate the subproblem solutions.

Once you have designed the algorithm and verified its correctness, the next step is to convert the algorithm into a high-level language. You use a text editor to enter the program into a computer, making sure that the program follows the language's syntax. To verify the correctness of the syntax, you run the code through a compiler. If the compiler generates error messages, you must identify the errors in the code, resolve them, and then run the code through the compiler again. When all syntax errors are removed, the compiler generates the machine code (bytecode in Java).

The final step is to execute the program. The compiler guarantees only that the program follows the language's syntax; it does not guarantee that the program will run correctly. During execution, the program might terminate abnormally due to logical errors, such as division by zero. Even if the program terminates normally, it may still generate erroneous results. Under these circumstances, you may have to reexamine the code, the algorithm, or even your analysis of the problem.

Your overall programming experience will benefit if you spend enough time to thoroughly complete the problem analysis before attempting to write the programming instructions. Usually, you do this work on paper using a pen or pencil. Taking this careful approach to programming has a number of advantages. It is much easier to discover errors in a program that is well analyzed and well designed. Furthermore, a thoroughly analyzed and carefully designed program is much easier to follow and modify. Even the most experienced programmers spend a considerable amount of time analyzing a problem and designing an algorithm.

Throughout this book, you will learn not only the rules of writing programs in Java, but also problem-solving techniques. Each chapter discusses several programming problems, each of which is clearly marked as a Programming Example. The Programming Examples teach techniques to analyze and solve the problems and also help you understand the concepts discussed in the chapter. To gain the full benefit of this book, we recommend that you work through the Programming Examples at the end of each chapter.

EXAMPLE 1-1

In this example, we design an algorithm to find the perimeter and area of a rectangle.

To find the perimeter and area of a rectangle, you need to know the rectangle's length and width. The perimeter and area of the rectangle are then given by the following formulas:

```
perimeter = 2 · (length + width)
area = length · width
```

The algorithm to find the perimeter and area of the rectangle is:

1. Get the length of the rectangle.
2. Get the width of the rectangle.
3. Find the perimeter using the following equation:

   ```
   perimeter = 2 · (length + width)
   ```

4. Find the area using the following equation:

   ```
   area = length · width
   ```

EXAMPLE 1-2

In this example, we design an algorithm that calculates the monthly paycheck of a salesperson at a local department store.

Every salesperson has a base salary. The salesperson also receives a bonus at the end of each month, based on the following criteria: If the salesperson has been with the store for five years or less, the bonus is $10 for each year that he or she has worked there. If the salesperson has been with the store for more than five years, the bonus is $20 for each year that he or she has worked there. The salesperson can earn an additional bonus as follows: If the total sales made by the salesperson for the month are more than $5,000 but less than $10,000, he or she receives a 3% commission on the sale. If the total sales made by the salesperson for the month are at least $10,000, he or she receives a 6% commission on the sale.

To calculate a salesperson's monthly paycheck, you need to know the base salary, the number of years that the salesperson has been with the company, and the total sales made by the salesperson for that month. Suppose baseSalary denotes the base salary, noOfServiceYears denotes the number of years that the salesperson has been with the store, bonus denotes the bonus, totalSales denotes the total sales made by the salesperson for the month, and additionalBonus denotes the additional bonus.

You can determine the bonus as follows:

```
if (noOfServiceYears is less than or equal to five)
    bonus = 10 · noOfServiceYears
otherwise
    bonus = 20 · noOfServiceYears
```

Next, you can determine the additional bonus of the salesperson as follows:

```
if (totalSales is less than 5000)
    additionalBonus = 0
otherwise
    if (totalSales is greater than or equal to 5000 and
                    totalSales is less than 10000)
        additionalBonus = totalSales · (0.03)
    otherwise
        additionalBonus = totalSales · (0.06)
```

Following the above discussion, you can now design the algorithm to calculate a salesperson's monthly paycheck:

1. Get baseSalary.

2. Get noOfServiceYears.

3. Calculate bonus using the following formula:

```
if (noOfServiceYears is less than or equal to five)
    bonus = 10 · noOfServiceYears
otherwise
    bonus = 20 · noOfServiceYears
```

4. Get totalSales.

5. Calculate additionalBonus using the following formula:

```
if (totalSales is less than 5000)
    additionalBonus = 0
otherwise
    if (totalSales is greater than or equal to 5000 and
        totalSales is less than 10000)
        additionalBonus = totalSales · (0.03)
otherwise
        additionalBonus = totalSales · (0.06)
```

6. Calculate payCheck using the following equation:

```
payCheck = baseSalary + bonus + additionalBonus
```

EXAMPLE 1-3

In this example, we design an algorithm to play a number-guessing game.

The objective is to randomly generate an integer greater than or equal to 0 and less than 100. Then, prompt the player (user) to guess the number. If the player guesses the number correctly, output an appropriate message. Otherwise, check whether the guessed number is less than the random number. If the guessed number is less than the random number generated, output the message, "Your guess is lower than the number. Guess again!"; otherwise, output the message, "Your guess is higher than the number. Guess again!". Then, prompt the player to enter another number. The player is prompted to guess the random number until the player enters the correct number.

The first step is to generate a random number, as described above. Java provides the means to do so, which is discussed in Chapter 5. Suppose num stands for the random number and guess stands for the number guessed by the player.

After the player enters the guess, you can compare the guess with the random number as follows:

```
if (guess is equal to num)
    Print "You guessed the correct number."
otherwise
    if guess is less than num
        Print "Your guess is lower than the number. Guess again!"
otherwise
        Print "Your guess is higher than the number. Guess again!"
```

You can now design an algorithm as follows:

1. Generate a random number and call it num.

2. *Repeat* the following steps until the player has guessed the correct number:

    a. Prompt the player to enter guess.

    b. ```
        if (guess is equal to num)
            Print "You guessed the correct number."
        otherwise
            if guess is less than num
                Print "Your guess is lower than the number. Guess again!"
        otherwise
                Print "Your guess is higher than the number. Guess again!"
        ```

In Chapter 5, we write a program that uses this algorithm to play the number-guessing game.
        ```

The type of coding used in Examples 1-1 to 1-3 is called **pseudocode**, which is an "outline" of a program that could be translated into actual code. Pseudocode is not written in a particular language, nor does it have syntax rules; it is mainly a technique to show the programming steps.

Programming Methodologies

Two popular approaches to programming design are the structured approach and the object-oriented approach, which are outlined below.

Structured Programming

Dividing a problem into smaller subproblems is called **structured design**. Each subproblem is then analyzed, and a solution for the subproblem is obtained. The solutions to all the subproblems are then combined to solve the overall problem. This process of implementing a structured design is called **structured programming**. The structured design approach is also known as **top-down design**, **bottom-up design**, **stepwise refinement**, and **modular programming**.

Object-Oriented Programming

Object-oriented design (OOD) is a widely used programming methodology. In OOD, the first step in the problem-solving process is to identify the components called **objects**, which form the basis of the solution, and to determine how these objects interact with one another. For example, suppose you want to write a program that automates the video rental process for a local video store. The two main objects in this problem are the video and the customer.

After identifying the objects, the next step is to specify for each object the relevant data and possible operations to be performed on that data. For example, for a video object, the *data* might include:

- movie name
- starring actors
- producer
- production company
- number of copies in stock

Some of the operations on a video object might include:

- checking the name of the movie
- reducing the number of copies in stock by one after a copy is rented
- incrementing the number of copies in stock by one after a customer returns a copy

This illustrates that each **object** consists of data and the operations on those data. An object combines data and operations on that data into a single unit. In OOD, the final program is a collection of interacting objects. A programming language that implements OOD is called an **object-oriented programming (OOP)** language. You will learn about the many advantages of OOD in later chapters.

Because an object consists of data and operations on the data, before you can design and use objects, you need to learn how to represent data in computer memory, how to manipulate data, and how to implement operations. In Chapter 2, you will learn the basic data types of Java and discover how to represent and manipulate data in computer memory. Chapter 3 discusses how to input data into a Java program and output the results generated by a Java program.

To create operations, you write algorithms and implement them in a programming language. Because a data element in a complex program usually has many operations, to separate operations from each other and use them effectively and in a convenient manner, you use **methods** to implement algorithms. You will learn the details of methods in Chapter 7. Certain algorithms require that a program make decisions, a process called selection. Other algorithms might require that certain statements be repeated until certain conditions are met, a process called repetition. Still other algorithms might require both selection and repetition. You will learn about selection and repetition mechanisms, called control structures, in Chapters 4 and 5.

Finally, to work with objects, you need to know how to combine data and operations on that data into a single unit. In Java, the mechanism that allows you to combine data and operations on the data into a single unit is called a **class**. In Chapter 8, you will learn how to create your own classes.

In Chapter 9, using a mechanism called an array, you will learn how to manipulate data when data items are of the same type, such as the items in a list of sales figures. As you can see, you need to learn quite a few things before working with the OOD methodology.

For some problems, the structured approach to program design is very effective. Other problems are better addressed by OOD. For example, if a problem requires manipulating sets of numbers with mathematical functions, you might use the structured design approach and outline the steps required to obtain the solution. The Java library supplies a wealth of functions that you can use to manipulate numbers effectively. On the other hand, if you want to write a program that would make a candy machine operational, the OOD approach is more effective. Java was designed especially to implement OOD. Furthermore, OOD works well and is used in conjunction with structured design. Chapter 6 explains how to use an existing class to create a Graphical User Interface (GUI) and then gives several examples explaining how to solve problems using OOD concepts.

Both the structured design and OOD approaches require that you master the basic components of a programming language to be an effective programmer. In the next few chapters, you will learn the basic components of Java required by either approach to programming.

QUICK REVIEW

1. A computer is an electronic device capable of performing arithmetic and logical operations.

2. A computer system has two kinds of components: hardware and software.

3. The central processing unit (CPU) and the main memory are examples of hardware components.

4. All programs must be brought into main memory before they can be executed.

5. When the power to the computer is switched off, everything in main memory is lost.

6. Secondary storage provides permanent storage for information. Hard disks, floppy disks, flash-memory, ZIP disks, CD-ROMs, and tapes are examples of secondary storage.

7. Input to the computer is done via an input device. Two common input devices are the keyboard and the mouse.

8. The computer sends output to an output device, such as the computer monitor.

9. Software refers to programs run by the computer.

10. The operating system monitors the overall activity of the computer and provides services.

11. Application programs perform a specific task.

12. The most basic language of a computer is a sequence of 0s and 1s called machine language. Every computer directly understands its own machine language.

13. A bit is a binary digit, 0 or 1.

14. A sequence of 0s and 1s is called a binary code or a binary number.

15. A byte is a sequence of eight bits.

16. One kilobyte (KB) is $2^{10} = 1024$ bytes; one megabyte (MB) is $2^{20} = 1,048,576$ bytes; one gigabyte (GB) is $2^{30} = 1,073,741,824$ bytes; one terabyte (TB) is $2^{40} = 1,099,511,627,776$ bytes; one petabyte (PB) is $2^{50} = 1,125,899,906,842,624$ bytes; one exabyte (EB) is $2^{60} = 1,152,921,504,606,846,976$ bytes; and one zettabyte (ZB) is $2^{70} = 1,180,591,620,717,411,303,424$ bytes.

17. Assembly language uses easy-to-remember instructions called mnemonics.

18. Assemblers are programs that translate a program written in assembly language into machine language.

19. To run a Java program on a computer, the program must first be translated into an intermediate language called bytecode and then interpreted into a particular machine language.

20. To make Java programs machine independent, the designers of the Java language introduced a hypothetical computer called the Java Virtual Machine (JVM).

21. Bytecode is the machine language for the JVM.

22. Compilers are programs that translate a program written in a high-level language into an equivalent machine language. In the case of Java, this machine language is the bytecode.

23. In Java, the necessary steps to process a program are edit, compile, load, and execute.

24. A Java loader transfers into main memory the bytecode of the classes needed to execute the program.

25. An interpreter is a program that reads, translates each bytecode instruction into the machine language of your computer, and then executes it.

26. The Internet is a network of networks through which computers around the world are connected.

27. The World Wide Web, or Web, uses software programs that allow computer users to view documents on almost any subject over the Internet with the click of a mouse.

28. Java application programs are stand-alone programs that can run on your computer. Java applets are programs that run from a Web browser, or simply a browser.

29. A problem-solving process for programming has five steps: analyze the problem, design an algorithm, implement the algorithm in a programming language, verify that the algorithm works, and maintain the program.

30. An algorithm is a step-by-step problem-solving process in which a solution is arrived at in a finite amount of time.

31. The two basic approaches to programming design are structured design and object-oriented design.

32. In structured design, a problem is divided into smaller subproblems. Each subproblem is solved, and the subproblem solutions are integrated.

33. In object-oriented design (OOD), the programmer identifies components called objects, which form the basis of the solution, and determines how these objects interact with one another. In OOD, a program is a collection of interacting objects.

34. An object consists of data and the operations on those data.

EXERCISES

1. Mark the following statements as true or false.

   a. Assembly language is the language that uses mnemonics for its instructions.

   b. The arithmetic operations are performed inside CPU and, if an error is found, it outputs the logical errors.

   c. A Java compiler is a program that translates a Java program into bytecode.

   d. Bytecode is the machine language of the JVM.

   e. The CPU stands for command performing unit.

   f. RAM stands for readily available memory.

   g. A program written in a high-level programming language is called a source program.

   h. The operating system is the first program loaded into the computer when the power is turned on.

   i. The first step in the problem-solving process is to analyze the problem.

2. Name two input devices.

3. Name two output devices.

4. Why is secondary storage needed?

5. What is the function of an operating system?

6. What is a source program?

7. What kind of errors are reported by a compiler?

8. Why do you need to translate a program written in a high-level language into machine language?

9. Why would you prefer to write a program in a high-level language rather than a machine language?

10. What are the advantages of problem analysis and algorithm design over directly writing a program in a high-level language?

11. Design an algorithm to find the weighted average of four test scores. The four test scores and their respective weights are given in the following format:

    ```
    testscore1 weight1
    ...
    ```

    For example, a sample data is as follows:

    ```
    75 0.20
    95 0.35
    85 0.15
    65 0.30
    ```

12. Given the radius, in inches, and price of a pizza, design an algorithm and write the pseudocode to find the price of the pizza per square inch.

13. To make a profit, prices of the items sold in a furniture store are marked up 60%. Design an algorithm to find the selling price of an item sold at the furniture store. What information do you need to find the selling price?

14. Suppose a, b, and c denote the lengths of the sides of a triangle. Then, the area of the triangle can be calculated using the formula:

$$\sqrt{s(s - a)(s - b)(s - c)}$$

where $s = (1/2)(a + b + c)$. Design an algorithm that uses this formula to find the area of a triangle. What information do you need to find the area?

15. A triangle ABC is inscribed in a circle, that is, the vertices of the triangle are on the circumference of the circle. Suppose the triangle ABC divides the circumference into lengths of a, b, and c inches. Design an algorithm that asks the user to specify the values of a, b, and c and then calculates the radius of the circle. Note that if r is the radius of the circle, then $2\pi r = a + b + c$.

16. You are given a list of students' names and their test scores. Design an algorithm that does the following:

   a. Calculates the average test scores.

   b. Determines and prints the names of all the students whose test score is below the average test score.

   c. Determines the highest test score.

   d. Prints the names of all the students whose test score is the same as the highest test score.

   (You must divide this problem into subproblems as follows: The first subproblem determines the average test score. The second subproblem determines and prints the names of all the students whose test score is below the average test score. The third subproblem determines the highest test score. The fourth subproblem prints the names of all the students whose test score is the same as the highest test score. The main algorithm combines the solutions of the subproblems.)

BASIC ELEMENTS OF JAVA

IN THIS CHAPTER, YOU WILL:

- Become familiar with the basic components of a Java program, including methods, special symbols, and identifiers
- Explore primitive data types
- Discover how to use arithmetic operators
- Examine how a program evaluates arithmetic expressions
- Explore how mixed expressions are evaluated
- Learn about type casting
- Become familiar with the `String` type
- Learn what an assignment statement is and what it does
- Discover how to input data into memory by using input statements
- Become familiar with the use of increment and decrement operators
- Examine ways to output results using output statements
- Learn how to import packages and why they are necessary
- Discover how to create a Java application program
- Explore how to properly structure a program, including using comments to document a program
- Learn how to avoid bugs using consistent and proper formatting
- Learn how to do a code walk-through

In this chapter, you will learn the basics of Java. As you begin to learn the Java programming language, two questions naturally arise: First, what is a computer program? Second, what is programming? A **computer program**, or a program, is a sequence of statements intended to accomplish a task. **Programming** is a process of planning and creating a program. These two definitions tell the truth, but not the whole truth, about programming. It might take an entire book to give a satisfactory definition of programming. An analogy might help you gain a better grasp of the nature of programming, so we'll use a topic on which almost everyone has some knowledge—cooking. A recipe is also a program, and everyone with some cooking experience can agree on the following:

1. It is usually easier to follow a recipe than to create one.
2. There are good recipes and there are bad recipes.
3. Some recipes are easy to follow and some are difficult to follow.
4. Some recipes produce reliable results and some do not.
5. You must have some knowledge of how to use cooking tools to follow a recipe to completion.
6. To create good new recipes, you must have significant knowledge and understanding of cooking.

These same six points can also be applied to programming. Let us take the cooking analogy one step further. Suppose you want to teach someone how to become a chef. How would you go about it? Would you introduce the person to good food, hoping the person develops a taste for it? Would you have the person follow recipe after recipe in the hope that some of the techniques rub off? Or, would you first teach the use of the tools, the nature of ingredients and foods and spices, and then explain how these concepts fit together?

Just as there are many ways to teach cooking, there are also different ways to teach programming. However, some fundamentals apply to programming, just as they do to cooking or other activities, such as music.

Learning a programming language is like learning to become a chef or learning to play a musical instrument. All three skills require direct interaction with the tools. You cannot become a good chef just by reading recipes. Similarly, you cannot learn to play musical instruments by reading books about musical instruments. The same is true of programming. You must have a fundamental knowledge of the language, and you must test your programs on the computer to make sure that each program does what it is supposed to do.

A Java Program

In this and the next chapter, you will learn the basic elements and concepts of the Java programming language used to create a Java program. In addition to giving examples to illustrate various concepts, we also include Java programs to help clarify the concepts. This section gives an example of a Java program. At this point you need not be too concerned with the details of this program. You only need to understand the effect of an *output* statement, which is introduced in the program.

Consider the following Java (application) program:

```
//*********************************************************
// This is a simple Java program. It displays three lines
// of text, including the sum of two numbers.
//*********************************************************

public class ASimpleJavaProgram
{
    public static void main(String[] args)
    {
        System.out.println("My first Java program.");
        System.out.println("The sum of 2 and 3 = " + 5);
        System.out.println("7 + 8 = " + (7 + 8));
    }
}
```

Sample Run: (When you compile and execute this program, the following three lines are displayed on the screen.)

```
My first Java program.
The sum of 2 and 3 = 5
7 + 8 = 15
```

This output is displayed on the screen when the following three lines are executed:

```
System.out.println("My first Java program.");
System.out.println("The sum of 2 and 3 = " + 5);
System.out.println("7 + 8 = " + (7 + 8));
```

To explain how this happens, let's first consider the statement:

```
System.out.println("My first Java program.");
```

This is an example of a Java *output* statement. It causes the program to evaluate whatever is in the parentheses and display the result on the screen. Typically, anything in double quotation marks, called a *string*, evaluates to itself, that is, its value is the string itself. Therefore, the statement causes the system to display the following line on the screen:

```
My first Java program.
```

(In general, when a string is printed, it is printed without the double quotation marks.) Now let's consider the statement:

```
System.out.println("The sum of 2 and 3 = " + 5);
```

In this output statement, the parentheses contain the string `"The sum of 2 and 3 = "`, + (the plus sign), and the number 5. Here the symbol + is used to concatenate (join) the operands. In this case, the system automatically converts the number 5 into a string, joins that string with the first string, and displays the following line on the screen:

```
The sum of 2 and 3 = 5
```

Now let's consider the statement:

```
System.out.println("7 + 8 = " + (7 + 8));
```

In this output statement, the parentheses contain the string **"7 + 8 = "**, + (the plus sign), and the expression **(7 + 8)**. In the expression **(7 + 8)**, notice the parentheses around **7 + 8**. This causes the system to add the numbers 7 and 8, resulting in 15. The number 15 is then converted to the string **"15"** and then joined with the string **"7 + 8 = "**. Therefore, the output of this statement is:

```
7 + 8 = 15
```

In this and the next chapter, until we explain how to construct a Java program properly, we will use output statements such as the preceding ones to explain concepts.

Before closing this section, let's look at some other features of the preceding Java program. The basic unit of a Java program is a **class**. Typically, every Java **class** consists of one or more methods. Roughly speaking, a method is a sequence of statements or instructions whose objective is to accomplish something. The first line of the program is:

```
public class ASimpleJavaProgram
```

ASimpleJavaProgram is the name of the Java **class**. The second line of the program consists of the left brace, which is matched with the second right brace (the very last brace). These braces together mark the beginning and end of (the body of) the **class** **ASimpleJavaProgram**. The third line consists of:

```
public static void main(String[] args)
```

This is the heading of the method named **main**. A Java **class** can have at most one method **main**. If a Java **class** contains an application program, such as the preceding program, it must contain the method **main**. When you execute (run) a Java (application) program, execution always begins with the method **main**.

The eighth line consists of a left brace (the second left brace of the program). This marks the beginning of (the body of) the method **main**. The first right brace (on the 12th line of the program) matches this left brace and marks the end of (the body of) the method **main**. The method **main** is indented to set it apart.

In the next section, you will learn about the purpose of the lines shown in green in the program.

Basics of a Java Program

As we stated in the previous chapter, the two types of Java programs are Java applets and Java application programs. Java applets are programs designed to run on a Web browser. Java application programs do not require a Web browser. To introduce the basic Java components, in the next few chapters we develop Java application programs. Java applets are considered later.

If you have never seen a program written in a programming language, the Java program, `ASimpleJavaProgram`, given in the previous section, may seem to be written in a foreign language. To make meaningful sentences in any foreign language, you must learn its alphabet, words, and grammar. The same is true of a programming language. To write meaningful programs, you must learn the programming language's special symbols, words, and syntax rules. The **syntax rules** tell you which statements (instructions) are legal, or accepted by the programming language, and which are not. You must also learn the **semantic rules**, which determine the meaning of the instructions. The programming language's rules, symbols, special words, and their meanings enable you to write programs to solve problems.

Programming language: A set of rules, symbols, and special words used to construct programs.

In the remainder of this section, you will learn about some of the special symbols used in a Java program. Additional symbols are introduced as other concepts are encountered in later chapters. Similarly, syntax and semantic rules are introduced and discussed throughout the book.

Comments

The program that you write should be clear not only to you, but also to the reader of your program. Part of good programming is the inclusion of comments in the program. Typically, comments can be used to identify the authors of the program, give the date when the program is written or modified, give a brief explanation of the program, and explain the meaning of key statements in a program. In the programming examples, for the programs that we write, we will not include the date when the program is written, consistent with the standard convention for writing such books.

Comments are for the reader, not for the compiler. So when a compiler compiles a program to check for the syntax errors, it completely ignores comments. Throughout this book, comments are shown in green.

`ASimpleJavaProgram`, given in the previous section, contains the following comments:

```
//********************************************************
// This is a simple Java program. It displays three lines
// of text, including the sum of two numbers.
//********************************************************
```

A Java program has two common types of comments—single-line comments and multiple-line comments.

Single-line comments begin with `//` and can be placed anywhere in the line. Everything encountered in that line after `//` is ignored by the compiler. For example, consider the following statement:

```
System.out.println("7 + 8 = " + (7 + 8));
```

You can put comments at the end of this line as follows:

```
System.out.println("7 + 8 = " + (7 + 8)); //prints: 7 + 8 = 15
```

This comment could be meaningful for a beginning programmer.

Multiple-line comments are enclosed between /* and */. The compiler ignores anything that appears between /* and */. For example, the following is an example of a multiple-line comment:

```
/*
   You can include comments that can
   occupy several lines.
*/
```

Special Symbols

Following are some of the special symbols:

```
+    -    *    /
.    ;    ?    ,
<=   !=   ==   >=
```

The first row includes mathematical symbols for addition, subtraction, multiplication, and division. The second row consists of punctuation marks taken from English grammar. Note that the comma is a special symbol. In Java, commas are used to separate items in a list. Semicolons are used to end a Java statement. The third row contains symbols used for comparisons. Note that a blank, which is not shown above, is also a special symbol. You create a blank symbol by pressing the spacebar (only once) on the keyboard. The third row consists of tokens made up of two characters, but which are regarded as single symbols. No character can come between the two characters in these symbols, not even a blank.

Reserved Words (Keywords)

A second category of tokens is reserved words. Some reserved words include the following:

```
int, float, double, char, void, public, static, throws, return
```

Reserved words are also called **keywords**. The letters in a reserved word are always lowercase. Like the special symbols, each reserved word is considered a single symbol. Furthermore, reserved words cannot be redefined within any program; that is, they cannot be used for anything other than their intended use. For a complete list of reserved words in Java, see Appendix A.

> **NOTE** Throughout this book, the reserved words are shown in blue.

Identifiers

A third category of tokens is identifiers. **Identifiers** are names of things, such as variables, constants, and methods, that appear in programs. Some identifiers are predefined; others are defined by the user. All identifiers must obey Java's rules for identifiers.

Identifier: A Java identifier consists of letters, digits, the underscore character (_), and the dollar sign ($) and must begin with a letter, underscore, or the dollar sign.

Identifiers can be made of only letters, digits, the underscore character (_), and the dollar sign ($); no other symbols are permitted to form an identifier.

 NOTE Java is case sensitive—uppercase and lowercase letters are considered different. Thus, the identifier NUMBER is not the same as the identifier number or the identifier Number. Similarly, the identifiers X and x are different.

In Java, identifiers can be any length. Some predefined identifiers that you will encounter frequently are `print`, `println`, and `printf`, which are used when generating output, and `nextInt`, `nextDouble`, `next`, and `nextLine`, which are used to input data. Unlike reserved words, predefined identifiers can be redefined, but it would be unwise to do so.

EXAMPLE 2-1

The following are legal identifiers in Java:

```
first
conversion
payRate
counter1
$Amount
```

Table 2-1 shows some illegal identifiers and explains why they are illegal.

TABLE 2-1 Examples of Illegal Identifiers

Illegal Identifier	Description
employee Salary	There can be no space between employee and Salary.
Hello!	The exclamation mark cannot be used in an identifier.
one+two	The symbol + cannot be used in an identifier.
2nd	An identifier cannot begin with a digit.

Data Types

The objective of a Java program is to manipulate data. Different programs manipulate different data. A program designed to calculate an employee's paycheck will add, subtract, multiply, and divide numbers; some of the numbers might represent hours worked and pay rate. Similarly, a program designed to alphabetize a class list will manipulate names. You wouldn't expect a cherry pie recipe to help you bake cookies. Similarly, you wouldn't manipulate alphabetic characters with a program designed to perform arithmetic calculations. Furthermore, you wouldn't multiply or subtract names. Reflecting such underlying differences, Java categorizes data into different types, and only certain operations can be performed on a particular type of data. At first, it may seem confusing, but by being so type conscious, Java has built-in checks to guard against errors.

Data type: A set of values together with a set of operations on those values.

Primitive Data Types

The primitive data types are the fundamental data types in Java. There are three categories of primitive data types:

- **Integral**, which is a data type that deals with integers, or numbers without a decimal part (and characters)
- **Floating-point**, which is a data type that deals with decimal numbers
- **Boolean**, which is a data type that deals with logical values

Integral data types are further classified into five categories: `char`, `byte`, `short`, `int`, and `long`.

Why are there so many categories of integral data types? Every data type has a different set of values associated with it. For example, the `int` data type is used to represent integers between -2147483648 ($= -2^{32}$) and 2147483647 ($= 2^{32} - 1$). The data type `short` is used to represent integers between -32768 ($= -2^{15}$) and 32767 ($= 2^{15} - 1$).

Which data type you use depends on how big a number your program needs to deal with. In the early days of programming, computers and main memory were very expensive. Only a small amount of memory was available to execute programs and manipulate data. As a result, programmers had to optimize the use of memory. Because writing a program and making it work is already a complicated process, not having to worry about the size of the memory makes for one less thing to think about. To effectively use memory, a programmer can look at type of data used in a program and figure out which data type to use. (Memory constraints may still be a concern for programs written for applications such as a wrist watch.)

Table 2-2 gives the range of possible values associated with the five integral data types and the size of memory allocated to manipulate these values.

TABLE 2-2 Values and Memory Allocation for Integral Data Types

Data Type	Values	Storage (in bytes)
char	0 to 65535 ($= 2^{16} - 1$)	2 (16 bits)
byte	-128 ($= -2^7$) to 127 ($= 2^7 - 1$)	1 (8 bits)
short	-32768 ($= -2^{15}$) to 32767 ($= 2^{15} - 1$)	2 (16 bits)
int	-2147483648 ($= -2^{31}$) to 2147483647 ($= 2^{31} - 1$)	4 (32 bits)
long	-9223372036854775808 ($= -2^{63}$) to 9223372036854775807 ($= 2^{63} - 1$)	8 (64 bits)

The most commonly used integral data type is int. Note that the following discussion of the int data type also applies to the integral types byte, short, and long.

int DATA TYPE

This section describes the int data type, but this discussion also applies to other integral data types. Integers in Java, as in mathematics, are numbers such as the following:

```
-6728, -67, 0, 78, 36782, +763
```

Note the following two rules from these examples:

- Positive integers do not require a + sign in front of them.
- No commas are used within an integer. Recall that in Java, commas are used for separating items in a list. Thus, 36,782 is interpreted as two integers: 36 and 782.

char DATA TYPE

As indicated in Table 2-2, the char data type has 65536 values, 0 to 65535. However, the main purpose of this data type is to represent single characters—that is, letters, digits, and special symbols. Therefore, the char data type can represent any key on your keyboard. When using the char data type, you enclose each character represented within single quotation marks. Examples of values belonging to the char data type include the following:

```
'A', 'a', '0', '*', '+', '$', '&', ' '
```

Note that a blank space is a character and is written as ' ', with a space between the single quotation marks.

The data type char *allows only one symbol* to be placed between the single quotation marks. Thus, the value 'abc' is not of type char. Furthermore, even though != and similar special symbols are considered to be one symbol, they are not regarded as possible values of the data type `char` when enclosed in single quotation marks. All the individual symbols located on the keyboard that are printable are considered possible values of the `char` data type.

As stated in Chapter 1, each character has a specific representation in computer memory, and there are several different coding schemes for characters. Java uses the Unicode character set, which contains 65536 values numbered 0 to 65535. The position of the first character is 0, the position of the second character is 1, and so on. Other commonly used character data sets are the American Standard Code for Information Interchange (ASCII) and Extended Binary-Coded Decimal Interchange Code (EBCDIC). The ASCII character set has 128 values. ASCII is a subset of Unicode. That is, the first 128 characters of Unicode are the same as the characters in ASCII. The EBCDIC character set has 256 values and was created by IBM.

Each of the 65536 values of the Unicode character set represents a different character. For example, the value 65 represents `'A'`, and the value 43 represents `'+'`. Thus, each character has a specific non-negative integer value in the Unicode character set, which is called a **collating sequence**, of the character. It follows that the collating sequence of `'A'` is 65. The collating sequence is used when you compare characters. For example, the value representing `'B'` is 66, so `'A'` is smaller than `'B'`. Similarly, `'+'` is smaller than `'A'` because 43 is smaller than 65.

The 14th character in the Unicode (and ASCII) character set is called the newline character and is represented as `'\n'`. (Note that the position of the newline character in the Unicode and ASCII character sets is 13 because the position of the first character is 0.) Even though the newline character is a combination of two characters, it is treated as one character. Similarly, the horizontal tab character is represented in Java as `'\t'`, and the null character is represented as `'\0'` (a backslash followed by zero). (Later in this chapter, we elaborate on these special characters.) Furthermore, the first 32 characters in the Unicode and ASCII character sets are nonprintable. (See Appendix C for a list of these characters.)

boolean DATA TYPE

The data type `boolean` has only two values: `true` and `false`. Also, `true` and `false` are called the logical (Boolean) values. The primary purpose of this data type is to manipulate logical (Boolean) expression. An expression that evaluates to `true` or `false` is called a **logical (Boolean) expression**. Logical (Boolean) expressions are formally defined and discussed in detail in Chapter 4. In Java, `boolean`, `true`, and `false` are reserved words. The memory allocated for the `boolean` data type is 1 bit.

FLOATING-POINT DATA TYPES

To deal with decimal numbers, Java provides the floating-point data type. To facilitate our discussion of this data type, we will review a concept from a high school or college algebra course.

You may be familiar with scientific notation. For example:

```
43872918 = 4.3872918 * 10^7
.0000265 = 2.65 * 10^-5
47.9832 = 4.7983 * 10^1
```

To represent real numbers, Java uses a form of scientific notation called **floating-point notation**. Table 2-3 shows how Java might print a set of real numbers. In the Java floating-point notation, the letter E stands for the exponent.

TABLE 2-3 Examples of Real Numbers Printed in Java Floating-Point Notation

Real Number	Java Floating-Point Notation
75.924	7.592400E1
0.18	1.800000E-1
0.0000453	4.530000E-5
-1.482	-1.482000E0
7800.0	7.800000E3

Java provides two data types to represent decimal numbers: `float` and `double`. As in the case of integral data types, the data types `float` and `double` differ in the set of values.

`float`: The data type `float` is used in Java to represent any real number between $-3.4E+38$ and $3.4E+38$. The memory allocated for the `float` data type is 4 bytes.

`double`: The data type `double` is used in Java to represent any real number between $-1.7E+308$ and $1.7E+308$. The memory allocated for the `double` data type is 8 bytes.

Other than the set of values, there is one more difference between the data types `float` and `double`. The maximum number of significant digits—that is, the number of decimal places—in `float` values is 6 or 7. The maximum number of significant digits in values belonging to the `double` type is typically 15. The maximum number of significant digits is called the **precision**. Sometimes `float` values are called **single precision**, and values of type `double` are called **double precision**.

 NOTE In Java, by default, floating-point numbers are considered to be of type `double`. Therefore, if you use the data type `float` to represent floating-point numbers in a program, you might get a warning or an error message, such as "truncation from double to float" or "possible loss of data." To avoid such messages, you should use the `double` data type. For illustration purposes and to avoid such messages in programming examples, this book mostly uses the data type `double` to represent floating-point numbers.

LITERALS (CONSTANTS)

Some authors call values such as 23 and −67 **integer literals** or **integer constants** or simply **integers**; values such as 12.34 and 25.60 are called **floating-point literals** or **floating-point constants** or simply **floating-point numbers**; and values such as 'a' and '5' are called **character literals**, **character constants**, or simply **characters**.

Arithmetic Operators and Operator Precedence

One of the most important features of a computer is its ability to calculate. You can use the standard arithmetic operators to manipulate integral and floating-point data types.

Java has five arithmetic operators:

Arithmetic Operators: + (addition), − (subtraction or negation), * (multiplication), / (division), % (**mod**, (**modulus** or **remainder**))

You can use these operators with both integral and floating-point data types. When you use / with the integral data type, it gives the quotient in integer form. That is, integral division truncates any fractional part; there is no rounding. Similarly, when you use % with the integral data type, it gives the remainder in integer form. (Examples 2-2 and 2-3 clarify how the operators / and % work with integral and floating-point data types.)

Since junior high school, you have probably worked with arithmetic expressions such as the following:

    (i)   −5
   (ii)   8 − 7
  (iii) 3 + 4
  (iv) 2 + 3 * 5
   (v) 5.6 + 6.2 * 3
  (vi) x + 2 * 5 + 6 / y

In expression (vi), **x** and **y** are some unknown numbers. Formally, an **arithmetic expression** is constructed by using arithmetic operators and numbers. The numbers and alphabetical symbols in the expression are called **operands**. Moreover, the numbers and alphabetical symbols used to evaluate an operator are called the operands for that operator.

In expression (i), the operator − (subtraction) is used to specify that the number 5 is negative. Moreover, in the expression −5, − has only one operand, which is 5. Operators that have only one operand are called **unary operators**.

In expression (ii), the symbol − is used to subtract 7 from 8. In this expression, − has two operands, 8 and 7. Operators that have two operands are called **binary operators**.

Unary operator: An operator that has only one operand.

Binary operator: An operator that has two operands.

In the expression (iii), 3 and 4 are the operands for the operator +. Because the operator + has two operands, in this expression, + is a binary operator. Now consider the following expression:

+27

In this expression, the operator + is used to indicate that the number 27 is positive. Here, because + has only one operand, it acts as a unary operator.

From the preceding discussion, it follows that – and + can be unary or binary arithmetic operators. However, the arithmetic operators *, /, and % are binary and must have two operands.

The following examples show how arithmetic operators—especially / and %—work with integral data types. As you can see from these examples, the operator / represents the quotient in ordinary division when used with integral data types.

EXAMPLE 2-2

Arithmetic Expression	Result	Description
2 + 5	7	
13 + 89	102	
34 – 20	14	
45 – 90	–45	
2 * 7	14	
5 / 2	2	In the division 5 / 2, the quotient is 2 and the remainder is 1. Therefore, 5 / 2 with the integral operands evaluates to the quotient, which is 2.
14 / 7	2	
34 % 5	4	In the division 34 / 5, the quotient is 6 and the remainder is 4. Therefore, 34 % 5 evaluates to the remainder, which is 4.
4 % 6	4	In the division 4 / 6, the quotient is 0 and the remainder is 4. Therefore, 4 % 6 evaluates to the remainder, which is 4.

The following Java program evaluates the preceding expressions:

```java
// This program illustrates how integral expressions evaluate.

public class Example2_2
{
    public static void main(String[] args)
    {
        System.out.println("2 + 5 = " + (2 + 5));
        System.out.println("13 + 89 = " + (13 + 89));
        System.out.println("34 - 20 = " + (34 - 20));
        System.out.println("45 - 90 = " + (45 - 90));
```

```
            System.out.println("2 * 7 = " + (2 * 7));
            System.out.println("5 / 2 = " + (5 / 2));
            System.out.println("14 / 7 = " + (14 / 7));
            System.out.println("34 % 5 = " + (34 % 5));
            System.out.println("4 % 6 = " + (4 % 6));
        }
    }
```

Sample Run:

```
2 + 5 = 7
13 + 89 = 102
34 - 20 = 14
45 - 90 = -45
2 * 7 = 14
5 / 2 = 2
14 / 7 = 2
34 % 5 = 4
4 % 6 = 4
```

NOTE   You should be careful when evaluating the mod operator with negative integer operands. You might not get the answer you would expect. For example, −34 % 5 = −4, because in the division −34 / 5, the quotient is −6 and the remainder is −4. Similarly, 34 % −5 = 4, because in the division −34 / 5, the quotient is −6 and the remainder is 4. Also −34 % −5 = −4, because in the division −34 / −5, the quotient is 6 and the remainder is −4.

EXAMPLE 2-3

The following Java program evaluates various floating-point expressions. (The details are left as an exercise for you.)

```
// This program illustrates how floating-point expressions evaluate.

public class Example2_3
{
    public static void main(String[] args)
    {
        System.out.println("5.0 + 3.5 = " + (5.0 + 3.5));
        System.out.println("3.0 + 9.4 = " + (3.0 + 9.4));
        System.out.println("16.4 - 5.2 = " + (16.4 - 5.2));
        System.out.println("4.2 * 2.5 = " + (4.2 * 2.5));
        System.out.println("5.0 / 2.0 = " + (5.0 / 2.0));
        System.out.println("34.5 / 6.0 = " + (34.5 / 6.0));
        System.out.println("34.5 % 6.0 = " + (34.5 % 6.0));
        System.out.println("34.5 / 6.5 = " + (34.5 / 6.5));
        System.out.println("34.5 % 6.5 = " + (34.5 % 6.5));
    }
}
```

Sample Run:

```
5.0 + 3.5 = 8.5
3.0 + 9.4 = 12.4
16.4 - 5.2 = 11.2
4.2 * 2.5 = 10.5
5.0 / 2.0 = 2.5
34.5 / 6.0 = 5.75
34.5 % 6.0 = 4.5
34.5 / 6.5 = 5.3076923076923075
34.5 % 6.5 = 2.0
```

Order of Precedence

When more than one arithmetic operator is used in an expression, Java uses the operator precedence rules to determine the order in which the operations are performed to evaluate the expression. According to the order of precedence rules for arithmetic operators:

```
*,    /,    %
```

have a higher level of precedence than:

```
+,    -
```

Note that the operators *, /, and % have the same level of precedence. Similarly, the operators + and - have the same level of precedence.

When arithmetic operators have the same level of precedence, operations are performed from left to right. To avoid confusion, you can use parentheses to group arithmetic expressions.

EXAMPLE 2-4

Using the order of precedence rules,

```
3 * 7 - 6 + 2 * 5 / 4 + 6
```

means the following:

```
    (((3 * 7) - 6) + ((2 * 5) / 4 )) + 6
=  ((21 - 6) + (10 / 4)) + 6      (Evaluate *)
=  ((21 - 6) + 2) + 6             (Evaluate /. Note that this is an integer division.)
=  (15 + 2) + 6                   (Evaluate -)
=   17 + 6                        (Evaluate first +)
=   23                            (Evaluate +)
```

Note that using parentheses in the preceding expression clarifies the order of precedence.

Because arithmetic operators are evaluated from left to right, unless parentheses are present, the **associativity** of arithmetic operators is said to be from left to right.

 NOTE **Character arithmetic:** Since the `char` data type is also an integral data type, Java allows you to perform arithmetic operations on `char` data. You should use this ability carefully. There is a difference between the character `'8'` and the integer 8. The integer value of 8 is 8. The integer value of `'8'` is 56, which is the Unicode collating sequence of the character `'8'`.

When evaluating arithmetic expressions, 8 + 7 = 15, `'8'` + `'7'` = 56 + 55, yields 111, and `'8'` + 7 = 56 + 7, yields 63. Furthermore, `'8'` * `'7'` = 56 * 55 = 3080.

These examples illustrate that many things can go wrong when you perform character arithmetic. If you must use arithmetic operations on the `char` type data, do so with caution.

Expressions

To this point, we have discussed only arithmetic operators. In this section, we discuss arithmetic expressions in detail. (Arithmetic expressions were introduced in the last section.)

If all operands (that is, numbers) in an expression are integers, the expression is called an **integral expression**. If all operands in an expression are floating-point numbers, the expression is called a **floating-point** or **decimal expression**. An integral expression yields an integral result; a floating-point expression yields a floating-point result. Looking at some examples will help clarify these definitions.

EXAMPLE 2-5

Consider the following Java integral expressions:

```
2 + 3 * 5
3 + x - y / 7
x + 2 * (y - z) + 18
```

In these expressions, **x**, **y**, and **z** represent variables of the integral type; that is, they can hold integer values. (Variables are discussed later in this chapter.)

EXAMPLE 2-6

Consider the following Java floating-point expressions:

```
12.8 * 17.5 - 34.50
x * 10.5 + y - 16.2
```

Here, x and y represent variables of the floating-point type; that is, they can hold floating-point values. (Variables are discussed later in this chapter.)

Evaluating an integral or a floating-point expression is straightforward. As already noted, when operators have the same precedence, the expression is evaluated from left to right. To avoid confusion, you can always use parentheses to group operands and operators.

Mixed Expressions

An expression that has operands of different data types is called a **mixed expression**. A mixed expression contains both integers and floating-point numbers. The following expressions are examples of mixed expressions:

```
2 + 3.5
6 / 4 + 3.9
5.4 * 2 - 13.6 + 18 / 2
```

In the first expression, the operand + has one integer operand and one floating-point operand. In the second expression, both operands for the operator / are integers; the first operand of + is the result of 6 / 4, and the second operand of + is a floating-point number. The third example is a more complicated mix of integers and floating-point numbers. How does Java evaluate such mixed expressions?

Two rules apply when evaluating a mixed expression:

1. When evaluating an operator in a mixed expression:

   a. If the operator has the same types of operands (that is, both are integers or both are floating-point numbers), the operator is evaluated according to the type of the operand. Integer operands yield an integer result; floating-point numbers yield a floating-point number result.

   b. If the operator has both types of operands (that is, one is an integer and the other is a floating-point number), during calculation the integer is treated temporarily as a floating-point number with the decimal part of zero, and then the operator is evaluated. The result is a floating-point number.

2. The entire expression is evaluated according to the precedence rules. The multiplication, division, and modulus operators are evaluated before the addition and subtraction operators. Operators having the same level of precedence are evaluated from left to right. Grouping is allowed for clarity.

Following these rules, when you evaluate a mixed expression, you concentrate on one operator at a time, using the rules of precedence. If the operator to be evaluated has operands of the same data type, evaluate the operator using Rule 1(a). That is, an operator with integer operands yields an integer result, and an operator with floating-point operands yields a floating-point result. If the operator to be evaluated has one integer operand and one floating-point operand, before evaluating this operator, you treat the integer operand as a floating-point number with a decimal part of zero. Example 2-7 shows how to evaluate mixed expressions.

EXAMPLE 2-7

Mixed Expression	Evaluation	Rule Applied
3 / 2 + 5.0	= 1 + 5.0	3 / 2 = 1 (integer division; Rule 1(a))
	= 6.0	(1 + 5.0 = 1.0 + 5.0 (Rule 1(b))
		= 6.0)
15.6 / 2 + 5	= 7.8 + 5	15.6 / 2 = 15.6 / 2.0 (Rule 1(b))
		= 7.8
	= 12.8	7.8 + 5 = 7.8 + 5.0 (Rule1(b))
		= 12.8
4 + 5 / 2.0	= 4 + 2.5	5 / 2.0 = 5.0 / 2.0 (Rule 1(b))
		= 2.5
	= 6.5	4 + 2.5 = 4.0 + 2.5 (Rule 1(b))
		= 6.5
4 * 3 + 7 / 5 - 25.5	= 12 + 7 / 5 - 25.6	4 * 3 = 12; (Rule 1(a))
	= 12 + 1 - 25.6	7 / 5 = 1 (integer division; Rule 1(a))
	= 13 - 25.5	12 + 1 = 13; (Rule 1(a))
	= -12.5	13 - 25.5 = 13.0 - 25.5 (Rule 1(b))
		= -12.5

The following Java program evaluates the preceding expressions:

```java
// This program illustrates how mixed expressions are evaluated.

public class Example2_7
{
    public static void main(String[] args)
    {
        System.out.println("3 / 2 + 5.0 = " + (3 / 2 + 5.0));
        System.out.println("15.6 / 2 + 5 = " + (15.6 / 2 + 5));
        System.out.println("4 + 5 / 2.0 = " + (4 + 5 / 2.0));
        System.out.println("4 * 3 + 7 / 5 - 25.5 = "
                          + (4 * 3 + 7 / 5 - 25.5));
    }
}
```

Sample Run:

```
3 / 2 + 5.0 = 6.0
15.6 / 2 + 5 = 12.8
4 + 5 / 2.0 = 6.5
4 * 3 + 7 / 5 - 25.5 = -12.5
```

These examples illustrate that an integer is not treated as a floating-point number unless the operator to be evaluated has one integer and one floating-point operand.

Type Conversion (Casting)

In the previous section, you learned that when evaluating an arithmetic expression if the operator has mixed operands, the integer value is treated as a floating-point value with the zero decimal part. When a value of one data type is automatically treated as another data type, an **implicit type coercion** has occurred. As the examples in the preceding section illustrate, if you are not careful about data types, implicit type coercion can generate unexpected results.

To avoid implicit type coercion, Java provides for explicit type conversion through the use of a cast operator. The **cast operator**, also called **type conversion** or **type casting**, takes the following form:

```
(dataTypeName) expression
```

First, the `expression` is evaluated. Its value is then treated as a value of the type specified by `dataTypeName`.

When using the cast operator to treat a floating-point (decimal) number as an integer, you simply drop the decimal part of the floating-point number. That is, the floating-point number is truncated. The following examples show how cast operators work. Be sure you understand why the last two expressions evaluate as they do.

EXAMPLE 2-8

Expression	Evaluates to
(int) (7.9)	7
(int) (3.3)	3
(double) (25)	25.0
(double) (5 + 3)	= (double) (8) = 8.0
(double) (15) / 2	= 15.0 / 2 (because (double) (15) = 15.0)
	= 15.0 / 2.0 = 7.5

```
(double)(15 / 2)                        = (double)(7) (because 15 / 2 = 7)
                                        = 7.0


(int)(7.8 + (double)(15) / 2)           = (int)(7.8 + 7.5)
                                        = (int)(15.3)
                                        = 15


(int)(7.8 + (double)(15 / 2))           = (int)(7.8 + 7.0)
                                        = (int)(14.8)
                                        = 14
```

The following Java program evaluates the preceding expressions:

```java
// This program illustrates how explicit type conversion works.

public class Example2_8
{
    public static void main(String[] args)
    {
        System.out.println("(int)(7.9) = " + (int)(7.9));
        System.out.println("(int)(3.3) = " + (int)(3.3));
        System.out.println("(double)(25) = " + (double)(25));
        System.out.println("(double)(5 + 3) = "
                            + (double)(5 + 3));
        System.out.println("(double)(15) / 2 = "
                            + ((double)(15) / 2));
        System.out.println("(double)(15 / 2) = "
                            + ((double)(15 / 2)));
        System.out.println("(int)(7.8 + (double)(15) / 2) = "
                            + ((int)(7.8 + (double)(15) / 2)));
        System.out.println("(int)(7.8 + (double)(15 / 2)) = "
                            + ((int)(7.8 + (double)(15 / 2))));
    }
}
```

Sample Run:

```
(int)(7.9) = 7
(int)(3.3) = 3
(double)(25) = 25.0
(double)(5 + 3) = 8.0
(double)(15) / 2 = 7.5
(double)(15 / 2) = 7.0
(int)(7.8 + (double)(15) / 2) = 15
(int)(7.8 + (double)(15 / 2)) = 14
```

2

You can also use cast operators to explicitly treat `char` data values as `int` data values, and `int` data values as `char` data values. To treat `char` data values as `int` data values, you use a collating sequence. For example, in the Unicode character set, `(int) ('A')` is 65 and `(int) ('8')` is 56. Similarly, `(char) (65)` is `'A'` and `(char) (56)` is `'8'`.

class String

In the preceding sections, we discussed primitive types to deal with data consisting of numbers and characters. What about data values such as a person's name? A person's name contains more than one character. Such values are called strings. More formally, a **string** is a sequence of zero or more characters. Strings in Java are enclosed in double quotation marks (not in single quotation marks, as are the `char` data types).

Most often, we process strings as a single unit. To process strings effectively, Java provides the `class String`. The `class String` contains various operations to manipulate a string. You will see this class used throughout the book. Chapter 3 discusses various operations provided by the `class String`. Moreover, technically speaking, the `class String` is not a primitive type.

A string that contains no characters is called a **null** or **empty** string. The following are examples of strings. Note that `""` is the empty string.

```
"William Jacob"
"Mickey"
""
```

A string, such as `"hello"`, is sometimes called a **character string** or **string literal** or **string constant**. However, if no confusion arises, we refer to characters between double quotation marks simply as strings.

Every character in a string has a specific position in the string. The position of the first character is 0, the position of the second character is 1, and so on. The **length** of a string is the number of characters in it.

EXAMPLE 2-9

String	"Sunny Day"								
Character in the string	`'S'`	`'u'`	`'n'`	`'n'`	`'y'`	`' '`	`'D'`	`'a'`	`'y'`
Position of the character in the string	0	1	2	3	4	5	6	7	8

The length of the string `"Sunny Day"` is 9.

When determining the length of a string, you must also count any spaces contained in the string. For example, the length of the string `"It is a beautiful day."` is 22.

Strings and the Operator +

One of the most common operations performed on strings is the concatenation operation, which allows a string to be appended at the end of another string. The operator + can be used to concatenate (or join) two strings as well as a string and a numeric value or a character.

Next we illustrate how the operator + works with strings. Consider the following expression:

```
"Sunny" + " Day"
```

This expression evaluates to

```
"Sunny Day"
```

Now consider the following expression:

```
"Amount Due = $" + 576.35
```

When the operator + evaluates, the numeric value 576.35 is converted to the string "576.35", which is then concatenated with the string:

```
"Amount Due = $"
```

Therefore, the expression `"Amount Due = $" + 576.35` evaluates to

```
"Amount Due = $576.35"
```

Example 2-10 further explains how the operator + works with the `String` data type.

EXAMPLE 2-10

Consider the following expression:

```
"The sum = " + 12 + 26
```

This expression evaluates to

```
"The sum = 1226"
```

This is not what you might have expected. Rather than adding 12 and 26, the values 12 and 26 are concatenated. This is because the associativity of the operator + is from left to right, so the operator + is evaluated from left to right. The expression

```
"The sum = " + 12 + 26
```

is evaluated as follows:

```
"The sum = " + 12 + 26    = ("The sum = " + 12) + 26
                          = "The sum = 12" + 26
                          = "The sum = 12" + 26
                          = "The sum = 1226"
```

Now consider the following expression:

```
"The sum = " + (12 + 26)
```

This expression evaluates as follows:

```
    "The sum = " + (12 + 16)
=   "The sum = " + 38
=   "The sum = 38"
```

Next, consider the expression:

```
12 + 26 + " is the sum"
```

This expression evaluates as follows:

```
    12 + 26 + " is the sum"
=   (12 + 26) + " is the sum"
=   38 + " is the sum"
=   "38 is the sum"
```

Now consider the expression:

```
"The sum of " + 12 + " and " + 26 + " = " + (12 + 26)
```

Notice the parentheses around 12 + 26. This expression evaluates as follows:

```
    "The sum of " + 12 + " and " + 26 + " = " + (12 + 26)
=   "The sum of 12" + " and " + 26 + " = " + (12 + 26)
=   "The sum of 12 and " + 26 + " = " + (12 + 26)
=   "The sum of 12 and 26" + " = " + (12 + 26)
=   "The sum of 12 and 26 = " + (12 + 26)
=   "The sum of 12 and 26 = " + 38
=   "The sum of 12 and 26 = 38"
```

The following Java program shows the effect of the preceding statements:

```java
// This program illustrates how the String concatenation works.

public class Example2_10
{
    public static void main(String[] args)
    {
        System.out.println("The sum = " + 12 + 26);

        System.out.println("The sum = " + (12 + 26));

        System.out.println(12 + 26 + " is the sum");

        System.out.println("The sum of " + 12 + " and " + 26
                       + " = " + (12 + 26));
    }
}
```

Sample Run:

```
The sum = 1226
The sum = 38
38 is the sum
The sum of 12 and 26 = 38
```

 NOTE The **class** String contains many useful methods to manipulate strings. We will take a closer look at this class in Chapter 3 and illustrate how to manipulate strings. The complete description of this class can be found at the Web site *http://java.sun.com/javase/6/docs/api/*.

Input

As noted earlier, the main objective of Java programs is to perform calculations and manipulate data. Recall that the data must be loaded into main memory before it can be manipulated. In this section, you learn how to put data into the computer's memory. Storing data in the computer's memory is a two-step process:

1. Instruct the computer to allocate memory.
2. Include statements in the program to put the data into the allocated memory.

Allocating Memory with Named Constants and Variables

When you instruct the computer to allocate memory, you tell it what names to use for each memory location and what type of data to store in those locations. Knowing the location of the data is essential because data stored in one memory location might be needed at several places in the program. As you learned earlier, knowing what data type you have is crucial for performing accurate calculations. It is also critical to know whether your data must remain constant throughout program execution or whether it could change.

Some data must not be changed. For example, the pay rate might be the same for all part-time employees. The value in a conversion formula that converts inches into centimeters is fixed, because 1 inch is always equal to 2.54 centimeters. When stored in memory, this type of data must be protected from accidental changes during program execution. In Java, you can use a **named constant** to instruct a program to mark those memory locations in which data is constant throughout program execution.

Named constant: A memory location whose content is not allowed to change during program execution.

To allocate memory, we use Java's declaration statements. The syntax to declare a named constant is:

```
static final dataType IDENTIFIER = value;
```

In Java, `static` and `final` are reserved words. The reserved word `final` specifies that the value stored in the identifier is fixed and cannot be changed.

NOTE In syntax, the shading indicates the part of the definition that is optional.

Because the reserved word `static` is shaded, it may or may not appear when a named constant is declared. The section, Creating a Java Application Program, later in this chapter, explains when this reserved word might be required. Also, notice that the identifier for a named constant is in uppercase letters. This is because Java programmers typically use uppercase letters for a named constant. (If the name of a named constant is a combination of more than one word, called a *run-together-word*, then the words are separated using an underscore; see the next example.)

EXAMPLE 2-11

Consider the following Java statements:

```
final double CENTIMETERS_PER_INCH = 2.54;
final int NO_OF_STUDENTS = 20;
final char BLANK = ' ';
final double PAY_RATE = 15.75;
```

The first statement tells the compiler to allocate enough memory to store a value of type `double`, call this memory space `CENTIMETERS_PER_INCH`, and store the value `2.54` in it. Throughout a program that uses this statement, whenever the conversion formula is needed, the memory space `CENTIMETERS_PER_INCH` can be accessed. The other statements have similar meanings.

NOTE As noted earlier, the default type of floating-point numbers is `double`. Therefore, if you declare a named constant of type `float`, then you must specify that the value is of type `float` as follows:

```
final float PAY_RATE = 15.75f;
```

otherwise, the compiler will generate an error message. Notice that in `15.75f`, the letter `f` at the end specifies that `15.75` is a `float` value. Recall that the memory size for `float` values is 4 bytes; for `double` values, 8 bytes. We will mostly use the type `double` to work with floating-point values.

Using a named constant to store fixed data, rather than using the data value itself, has one major advantage. If the fixed data changes, you do not need to edit the entire program and change the old value to the new value. Instead, you can make the change at just one place, recompile the program, and execute it using the new value throughout. In addition, by storing a value and referring to that memory location whenever the value is needed, you avoid typing the same value again and again and you prevent typos. If you misspell the name of the location, the computer might warn you through an error message, but it will not warn you if the value is mistyped.

Certain data must be modifiable during program execution. For example, after each test, a student's average test score may change; the number of tests also changes. Similarly, after each pay increase, an employee's salary changes. This type of data must be stored in memory cells whose contents can be modified during program execution. In Java, memory cells whose contents can be modified during program execution are called **variables**.

Variable: A memory location whose content may change during program execution.

The syntax for declaring one variable or multiple variables is:

```
dataType identifier1, identifier2, ..., identifierN;
```

EXAMPLE 2-12

Consider the following statements:

```
double amountDue;
int counter;
char ch;
int num1, num2;
```

The first statement tells the compiler to allocate enough memory to store a value of type `double` and call it `amountDue`. Statements 2 and 3 have similar conventions. The fourth statement tells the compiler to allocate two different memory spaces (each large enough to store a value of the type `int`), name the first memory space `num1`, and name the second memory space `num2`.

 NOTE Java programmers typically use lowercase letters to declare variables. If a variable name is a combination of more than one word, then the first letter of each word, except the first word, is uppercase. (For example, see the variable `amountDue` in the preceding example.)

From now on, when we say "variable," we mean a variable memory location.

> **NOTE** In Java (within a method), you must declare all identifiers before you can use them. If you refer to an identifier without declaring it, the compiler will generate an error message indicating that the identifier is not declared.

2

Putting Data into Variables

Now that you know how to declare variables, the next question is: How do you put data into those variables? The two common ways to place data into a variable are:

1. Use an assignment statement.
2. Use input (read) statements.

ASSIGNMENT STATEMENT

The assignment statement takes the following form:

```
variable = expression;
```

In an assignment statement, the value of the **expression** should match the data type of the **variable**. The expression on the right side is evaluated, and its value is assigned to the variable (and thus to a memory location) on the left side.

A variable is said to be **initialized** the first time a value is placed in the variable.

In Java, = (the equal sign) is called the **assignment operator**.

EXAMPLE 2-13

Suppose you have the following variable declarations:

```
int num1;
int num2;
double sale;
char first;
String str;
```

Now consider the following assignment statements:

```
num1 = 4;
num2 = 4 * 5 - 11;
sale = 0.02 * 1000;
first = 'D';
str = "It is a sunny day.";
```

For each of these statements, the computer first evaluates the expression on the right and then stores that value in a memory location named by the identifier on the left. The first statement stores the value 4 in num1, the second statement stores 9 in num2, the third statement stores 20.00 in sale, and the fourth statement stores the character 'D' in first. The fifth statement assigns the string "It is a sunny day." to the variable str.

The following Java program shows the effect of the preceding statements:

```java
// This program illustrates how data in the variables are
// manipulated.

public class Example2_13
{
    public static void main(String[] args)
    {
        int num1;
        int num2;

        double sale;

        char first;

        String str;

        num1 = 4;
        System.out.println("num1 = " + num1);

        num2 = 4 * 5 - 11;
        System.out.println("num2 = " + num2);

        sale = 0.02 * 1000;
        System.out.println("sale = " + sale);

        first = 'D';
        System.out.println("first = " + first);

        str = "It is a sunny day.";
        System.out.println("str = " + str);
    }
}
```

Sample Run:

```
num1 = 4
num2 = 9
sale = 20.0
first = D
str = It is a sunny day.
```

For the most part, the preceding program is straightforward. Let us take a look at the output statement:

```java
System.out.println("num1 = " + num1);
```

This output statement consists of the string "num1 = ", +, and the variable num1. Here, the value of num1 is concatenated with the string "num1 = ", resulting in the string "num1 = 4", which is then output. The meanings of other output statements are similar.

A Java statement such as:

```
num = num + 2;
```

means "evaluate whatever is in num, add 2 to it, and assign the new value to the memory location num." The expression on the right side must be evaluated first; that value is then assigned to the memory location specified by the variable on the left side. Thus, the sequence of Java statements:

```
num = 6;
num = num + 2;
```

and the statement:

```
num = 8;
```

both assign 8 to num. Note that the statement num = num + 2 is meaningless if num has not been initialized.

The statement num = 5; is read as "num becomes 5" or "num gets 5" or "num is assigned the value 5." Each time a new value is assigned to num, the old value is erased.

NOTE   Suppose that num is an `int` variable. Consider the statement: num = num + 2;. This statement adds 2 to the value of num, and the new value is assigned to the variable num. If the variable num is not properly initialized, then the Java complier will generate a syntax error. So to use the value of a variable in an expression, the variable must be properly initialized. Variable initialization is further covered in the next section, "Declaring and initializing variables."

EXAMPLE 2-14

Suppose that num1, num2, and num3 are `int` variables and the following statements are executed in sequence.

1.   num1 = 18;
2.   num1 = num1 + 27;
3.   num2 = num1;
4.   num3 = num2 / 5;
5.   num3 = num3 / 4;

The following table shows the values of the variables after the execution of each statement. (A ? indicates that the value is unknown. The orange color in a box shows that the value of that variable is changed.)

TABLE 2-4 Values of the Variables `num1`, `num2`, and `num3`

Values of the Variables	Variables			Statement/Explanation
Before Statement 1	num1 ?	num2 ?	num3 ?	
After Statement 1	num1 18	num2 ?	num3 ?	`num1 = 18;` Store 18 into `num1`.
After Statement 2	num1 45	num2 ?	num3 ?	`num1 = num1 + 27;` `num1 + 27 = 18 + 27 = 45`. This value is assigned to `num1`, which replaces the old value of `num1`.
After Statement 3	num1 45	num2 45	num3 ?	`num2 = num1;` Copy the value of `num1` into `num2`.
After Statement 4	num1 45	num2 45	num3 9	`num3 = num2 / 5;` `num2 / 5 = 45 / 5 = 9`. This value is assigned to `num3`. So `num3 = 9`.
After Statement 5	num1 45	num2 45	num3 2	`num3 = num3 / 4;` `num3 / 4 = 9 / 4 = 2`. This value is assigned to `num3`, which replaces the old value of `num3`.

Thus, after the execution of the statement in Line 5, num1 = 45, num2 = 45, and num3 = 2.

NOTE The Java language is strongly typed, which means that you cannot assign a value to a variable that is not compatible with its data type. For example, a string cannot be stored in an `int` variable. If you try to store an incompatible value in a variable, an error is generated when you compile the program or during program execution. Therefore, in an assignment statement, the expression on the right side must evaluate to a value compatible with the data type of the variable on the left side.

NOTE Suppose that **x**, **y**, and **z** are `int` variables. The following is a legal statement in Java:

```
x = y = z;
```

In this statement, first the value of **z** is assigned to **y**, and then the new value of **y** is assigned to **x**. Because the assignment operator = is evaluated from right to left, the **associativity** of the **assignment operator** is said to be from right to left.

Earlier, you learned that if a variable is used in an expression, the expression yields a meaningful value only if the variable has been initialized previously. You also learned that after declaring a variable, you can use an assignment statement to initialize it. It is possible to initialize and declare variables simultaneously. Before we discuss how to use an input (read) statement, we address this important issue.

Declaring and Initializing Variables

When a variable is declared, Java might not automatically put a meaningful value into it. In other words, Java might not automatically initialize all the variables you declare. For example, the `int` and `double` variables might not be initialized to 0, as happens in some programming languages.

If you declare a variable and then use it in an expression without first initializing it, when you compile the program you are likely to get an error. To avoid these pitfalls, Java allows you to initialize variables while they are being declared. Consider the following Java statements, in which variables are first declared and then initialized:

```
int first;
int second;
char ch;
double x;
double y;
first = 13;
second = 10;
ch = ' ';
x = 12.6;
y = 123.456;
```

You can declare and initialize these variables at the same time using the following Java statements:

```
int first = 13;
int second = 10;
char ch = ' ';
double x = 12.6;
double y = 123.456;
```

The first Java statement declares the `int` variable `first` and stores 13 in it. The second Java statement declares the `int` variable `second` and stores 10 in it. The other statements have similar meanings. Declaring and initializing variables simultaneously is another way to place meaningful data into a variable.

NOTE Not all variables are initialized during declaration. The nature of the program or the programmer's choice dictates which variables should be initialized during declaration.

Input (Read) Statement

In an earlier section, you learned how to put data into variables using the assignment statement. In this section, you learn how to put data into variables from the standard input device using Java's input (or read) statements.

NOTE In most cases, the standard input device is the keyboard.

When the computer gets the data from the keyboard, the user is said to be acting interactively.

READING DATA USING THE `Scanner class`

To put data into variables from the standard input device, Java provides the `class Scanner`. Using this class, first we create an input stream object and associate it with the standard input device. The following statement accomplishes this:

```
static Scanner console = new Scanner(System.in);
```

This statement creates the input stream object `console` and associates it with the standard input device. (Note that `Scanner` is a predefined Java class and the preceding statement creates `console` to be an object of this class.) The object `console` reads the next input as follows:

a. If the next input token can be interpreted as an integer, then the expression:

```
console.nextInt()
```

retrieves that integer; that is, the value of this expression is that integer.

b. If the next input token can be interpreted as a floating-point number, then the expression:

```
console.nextDouble()
```

retrieves that floating-point number; that is, the value of this expression is that floating-point number. (Note that an integer can be treated as a floating-point number with 0 decimal part.)

c. The expression:

```
console.next()
```

retrieves the next input token as a string; that is, the value of this expression is the next input string. (Note that if the next input token is a number, this expression interprets that number as a string.)

d. The expression:

```
console.nextLine()
```

retrieves the next input as a string until the end of the line; that is, the value of this expression is the next input line. (Note that this expression also reads the newline character, but the newline character is not stored as part of the string.)

While scanning for the next input, the expressions `console.nextInt()`, `console.nextDouble()`, and `console.next()` skip whitespace characters. Whitespace characters are blanks and certain nonprintable characters, such as newline and tab.

 NOTE `System.in` is called a **standard input stream object** and is designed to input data from the standard input device. However, the object `System.in` extracts data in the form of bytes from the input stream. Therefore, using `System.in`, we first create a `Scanner` object, such as `console`, as shown previously, so that the data can be extracted in a desired form. (The meaning of the word `new` is explained in Chapter 3.)

 NOTE The `class Scanner` is added to the Java library in Java version 5.0. Therefore, this class is *not* available in Java versions lower than 5.0.

EXAMPLE 2-15

Suppose that `miles` is a variable of type `double`. Further suppose that the input is 73.65. Consider the following statements:

```
miles = console.nextDouble();
```

This statement causes the computer to get the input, which is 73.65, from the standard input device, and stores it in the variable `miles`. That is, after the execution of this statement, the value of the variable `miles` is 73.65.

Example 2-16 further explains how to input numeric data into a program.

EXAMPLE 2-16

Suppose we have the following declaration:

```
static Scanner console = new Scanner(System.in);
```

Consider the following statements:

```
int feet;
int inches;
```

Suppose the input is:

23 7

Next, consider the following statements:

```
feet = console.nextInt();          //Line 1
inches = console.nextInt();        //Line 2
```

The statement in Line 1 stores the number 23 into the variable feet. The statement in Line 2 stores the number 7 into the variable inches. Notice that when these numbers are entered at the keyboard, they are separated with a blank. In fact, they can be separated with one or more blanks, lines, or even the tab character. (Note that we have numbered the statements as Line 1 and Line 2, so that we can conveniently refer to a particular statement and explain its meaning.)

The following Java program shows the effect of the preceding input statements:

```
// This program illustrates how input statements work.

import java.util.*;

public class Example2_16
{
    static Scanner console = new Scanner(System.in);

    public static void main(String[] args)
    {
        int feet;
        int inches;

        System.out.println("Enter two integers separated by spaces.");

        feet = console.nextInt();
        inches = console.nextInt();

        System.out.println("feet = " + feet);
        System.out.println("inches = " + inches);
    }
}
```

Sample Run: (In this sample run, the user input is shaded.)

```
Enter two integers separated by spaces.
23 7
feet = 23
inches = 7
```

In the preceding program, notice the first line:

```
import java.util.*;
```

This line is required to use the class Scanner.

NOTE If the next input token cannot be expressed as an appropriate number, then the expressions `console.nextInt()` and `console.nextDouble()` will cause the program to terminate with an error message (unless some care is taken in the program), indicating an input mismatch. For example, if the next input cannot be expressed as an integer, then the expression `console.nextInt()` will cause the program to terminate, with the error message indicating an input mismatch. Examples of invalid integers are `24w5` and `12.50`. Chapter 12 explains why the program terminates with the error message indicating an input mismatch and how to include the necessary code to handle this problem. Until then, we assume that the user enters valid numbers.

The Java program in Example 2-17 illustrates how to read strings and numeric data.

EXAMPLE 2-17

```java
// This program illustrates how to read strings and numeric data.

import java.util.*;

public class Example2_17
{
    static Scanner console = new Scanner(System.in);

    public static void main(String[] args)
    {
        String firstName;                              //Line 1
        String lastName;                               //Line 2

        int age;                                       //Line 3
        double weight;                                 //Line 4

        System.out.println("Enter first name, last name, "
                    + "age, and weight separated "
                    + "by spaces.");                    //Line 5

        firstName = console.next();                    //Line 6
        lastName = console.next();                     //Line 7
        age = console.nextInt();                       //Line 8
        weight = console.nextDouble();                 //Line 9

        System.out.println("Name: " + firstName
                    + " " + lastName);                 //Line 10

        System.out.println("Age: " + age);            //Line 11
        System.out.println("Weight: " + weight);      //Line 12
    }
}
```

Sample Run: (In this sample run, the user input is shaded.)

```
Enter first name, last name, age, and weight separated by spaces.
Sheila Mann 23 120.5
Name: Sheila Mann
Age: 23
Weight: 120.5
```

The preceding program works as follows: The statements in Lines 1 to 4 declare the variables `firstName` and `lastName` of type `String`, `age` of type `int`, and `weight` of type `double`. The statement in Line 5 is an output statement and tells the user what to do. (Such output statements are called prompt lines.) As shown in the sample run, the input to the program is:

```
Sheila Mann 23 120.5
```

The statement in Line 6 reads and assigns the string `Sheila` to the variable `firstName`; the statement in Line 7 skips the space after `Sheila` and reads and assigns the string `Mann` to the variable `lastName`. Next, the statement in Line 8 skips the blank after `Mann` and reads and stores `23` into the variable `age`. Similarly, the statement in Line 9 skips the blank after `23` and reads and stores `120.5` into the variable `weight`.

The statements in Lines 10, 11, and 12 produce the third, fourth, and fifth lines of the sample run.

VARIABLE INITIALIZATION

Consider the following declaration:

```
int feet;
```

You can initialize the variable `feet` to a value of `35` either by using the assignment statement:

```
feet = 35;
```

or by executing the following statement and entering `35` during program execution:

```
feet = console.nextInt();
```

If you use the assignment statement to initialize `feet`, then you are stuck with the same value each time the program runs unless you edit the source code, change the value, recompile, and run. By using an input statement, each time the program runs you can enter a different value, and the value entered is stored in `feet`. Therefore, a read statement is much more versatile than an assignment statement.

Sometimes it is necessary to initialize a variable by using an assignment statement. This is especially true if the variable is used only for internal calculation and not for reading and storing data.

NOTE Recall that Java might not automatically initialize all the variables when they are declared. Some variables can be initialized when they are declared, whereas others must be initialized using either an assignment statement or a read statement. (Variable initialization is covered in more detail in Chapter 8.)

NOTE Suppose you want to store a character into a `char` variable using an input statement. During program execution, when you input the character, you do not include the single quotation marks. Suppose that `ch` is a `char` variable. Consider the following input statement:

```
ch = console.next().charAt(0);
```

If you want to store K in `ch` using this statement, during program execution you type K without the single quotation marks. Similarly, if you want to store a string in a `String` variable using an input statement, during program execution you enter only the string without the double quotation marks.

Reading a Single Character

Suppose the next input is a single printable character, say, A. Further suppose that `ch` is a `char` variable. To input A into `ch`, you can use the following statement:

```
ch = console.next().charAt(0);
```

where `console` is as declared previously.

When something goes wrong in a program and the results it generates are not what you expect, you should do a walk-through of the statements that assign values to your variables. Example 2-18 illustrates how to do this. The walk-through is an effective debugging technique.

EXAMPLE 2-18

This example further illustrates how assignment statements and input statements manipulate variables. Consider the following declarations:

```
static Scanner console = new Scanner(System.in);

int firstNum;
int secondNum;
char ch;
double z;
```

Also suppose that the following statements execute in the order given:

1. `firstNum = 4;`
2. `secondNum = 2 * firstNum + 6;`
3. `z = (firstNum + 1) / 2.0;`

```
4.  ch = 'A';
5.  secondNum = console.nextInt();
6.  z = console.nextDouble();
7.  firstNum = (int)(z) + 8;
8.  secondNum = secondNum + 1;
9.  ch = console.next().charAt(0);
10. firstNum = firstNum + (int)(ch);
```

In addition, suppose the input is:

`8 16.3 D`

Let's now determine the values of the declared variables after the last statement executes. To show explicitly how a particular statement changes the value of a variable, the values of the variables after each statement executes are shown. (In the following table, a question mark, `?`, in a box indicates that the value in the box is unknown.)

Values of the Variables	Variables				Statement/Explanation
Before Statement 1	firstNum `?`	secondNum `?`	ch `?`	z `?`	
After Statement 1	firstNum `4`	secondNum `?`	ch `?`	z `?`	`firstNum = 4;` Store 4 into `firstNum`.
After Statement 2	firstNum `4`	secondNum `14`	ch `?`	z `?`	`secondNum = 2 * firstNum + 6;` `2 * firstNum + 6 = 2 * 4 + 6 = 14.` Store 14 into `secondNum`.
After Statement 3	firstNum `4`	secondNum `14`	ch `?`	z `2.5`	`z = (firstNum + 1) / 2.0;` `(firstNum + 1) / 2.0 = (4 + 1) / 2.0 = 5 / 2.0 = 2.5.` Store 2.5 into `z`.
After Statement 4	firstNum `4`	secondNum `14`	ch `A`	z `2.5`	`ch = 'A';` Store `'A'` into `ch`.
After Statement 5	firstNum `4`	secondNum `8`	ch `A`	z `2.5`	`secondNum = console.nextInt();` Read a number from the keyboard (which is 8) and store it into `secondNum`. This statement replaces the old value of `secondNum` with the new value.

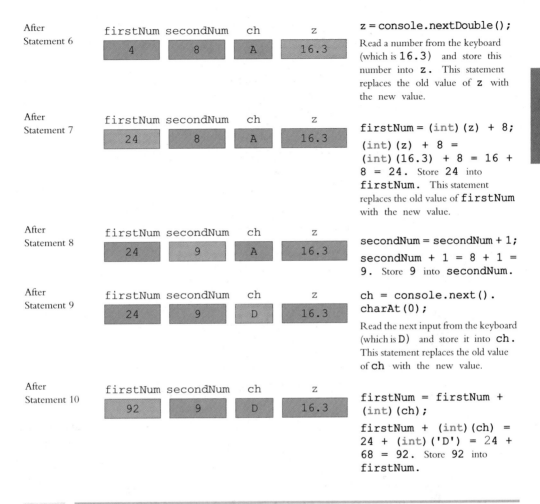

After Statement 6

firstNum secondNum ch z

| 4 | 8 | A | 16.3 |

z = console.nextDouble();

Read a number from the keyboard (which is **16.3**) and store this number into **z**. This statement replaces the old value of **z** with the new value.

2

After Statement 7

firstNum secondNum ch z

| 24 | 8 | A | 16.3 |

firstNum = (int)(z) + 8;

(int)(z) + 8 = (int)(16.3) + 8 = 16 + 8 = 24. Store **24** into firstNum. This statement replaces the old value of firstNum with the new value.

After Statement 8

firstNum secondNum ch z

| 24 | 9 | A | 16.3 |

secondNum = secondNum + 1;

secondNum + 1 = 8 + 1 = 9. Store **9** into secondNum.

After Statement 9

firstNum secondNum ch z

| 24 | 9 | D | 16.3 |

ch = console.next().charAt(0);

Read the next input from the keyboard (which is **D**) and store it into ch. This statement replaces the old value of ch with the new value.

After Statement 10

firstNum secondNum ch z

| 92 | 9 | D | 16.3 |

firstNum = firstNum + (int)(ch);

firstNum + (int)(ch) = 24 + (int)('D') = 24 + 68 = 92. Store **92** into firstNum.

NOTE The Web site (*www.course.com*) and the CD accompanying this book contain a Java program that shows the effect of the 10 statements listed at the beginning of Example 2-18. The program is named **Example2_18.java**.

NOTE If you assign the value of an expression that evaluates to a floating-point value—without using the cast operator—to a variable of type **int**, then a (syntax) error will occur.

Increment and Decrement Operators

Now you know how to declare a variable and enter data into a variable. In this section, you learn about two more operators: the increment and decrement operators. These operators are used frequently by Java programmers and are useful programming tools.

Suppose `count` is an `int` variable. The statement:

```
count = count + 1;
```

increments the value of `count` by 1. To execute this assignment statement, the computer first evaluates the expression on the right, which is `count + 1`. It then assigns this value to the variable on the left, which is `count`.

As you will see in later chapters, such statements are frequently used to keep track of how many times certain things have happened. To expedite the execution of such statements, Java provides the **increment operator**, ++, which increases the value of a variable by 1, and the **decrement operator**, --, which decreases the value of a variable by 1. Increment and decrement operators each have two forms: pre and post. The syntax of the increment operator is:

Pre-increment:	`++variable`
Post-increment:	`variable++`

The syntax of the decrement operator is:

Pre-decrement:	`--variable`
Post-decrement:	`variable--`

Let's look at some examples. The statement:

```
++count;
```

or:

```
count++;
```

increments the value of count by 1. Similarly, the statement:

```
--count;
```

or:

```
count--;
```

decrements the value of count by 1.

Because increment and decrement operators are built into Java, the value of a variable is quickly incremented or decremented without having to use the form of an assignment statement.

As you can see from these examples, both the pre- and post-increment operators increment the value of the variable by 1. Similarly, the pre- and post-decrement operators decrement the value of the variable by 1. What is the difference between the pre and post forms of these operators? The difference becomes apparent when the variable using these operators is employed in an expression.

Suppose that **x** is a variable of type `int`. If **++x** is used in an expression, first the value of **x** is incremented by 1, and then the new value of **x** is used to evaluate the expression. On the other hand, if **x++** is used in an expression, first the current value of **x** is used in the expression, and then the value of x is incremented by 1. The following example clarifies the difference between the pre- and post-increment operators.

Suppose that **x** and **y** are `int` variables. Consider the following statements:

```
x = 5;
y = ++x;
```

The first statement assigns the value 5 to **x**. To evaluate the second statement, which uses the pre-increment operator, first the value of **x** is incremented to 6, and then this value, 6, is assigned to **y**. After the second statement executes, both **x** and **y** have the value 6.

Now consider the following statements:

```
x = 5;
y = x++;
```

As before, the first statement assigns 5 to **x**. In the second statement, the post-increment operator is applied to **x**. To execute the second statement, first the value of **x**, which is 5, is used to evaluate the expression, and then the value of **x** is incremented to 6. Finally, the value of the expression, which is 5, is stored in **y**. After the second statement executes, the value of **x** is 6, and the value of **y** is 5.

The following example further illustrates how the pre- and post-increment operators work.

EXAMPLE 2-19

Suppose **a** and **b** are `int` variables and:

```
a = 5;
b = 2 + (++a);
```

The first statement assigns 5 to **a**. To execute the second statement, first the expression 2 + (++a) is evaluated. As the pre-increment operator is applied to **a**, first the value of a is incremented to 6. Then, 2 is added to 6 to get 8, which is then assigned to **b**. Therefore, after the second statement executes, **a** is 6 and **b** is 8. On the other hand, after the execution of:

```
a = 5;
b = 2 + (a++);
```

the value of a is 6 while the value of b is 7.

NOTE This book most often uses the increment and decrement operators with a variable in a stand-alone statement. That is, the variable using the increment or decrement operator will not be part of any expression.

Output

In the preceding sections, you have seen how to put data into the computer's memory and how to manipulate that data. We also used certain output statements to show the results. This section explains, in some detail, how to further use output statements to generate the desired results.

NOTE The standard output device is usually the monitor.

In Java, output on the standard output device is accomplished by using the **standard output object** System.out. The object System.out has access to two methods, print and println, to output a string on the standard output device.

NOTE As of Java 5.0, you can also use the method printf to generate the output of a program. Chapter 3 discusses this method in detail.

The syntax to use the object System.out and the methods print and println is:

```
System.out.print(expression);
System.out.println(expression);
System.out.println();
```

These are **output statements**. The expression is evaluated, and its value is printed at the current insertion point on the output device. After outputting the value of **expression**, the method print leaves the insertion point after the last character of the value of **expression**, while the method println positions the insertion point at the beginning of the next line. Moreover, the statement:

```
System.out.println();
```

only positions the insertion point at the beginning of the next line. In this statement, notice the empty parentheses after println. They are still needed even though there is no expression between them.

NOTE On the screen, the insertion point is where the cursor is.

In an output statement, if **expression** consists of only one string or a single constant value, then **expression** evaluates to itself. If **expression** consists of only one variable, then **expression** evaluates to the value of the variable. Also note, as explained in this chapter, how the operator + works with strings and numeric values. Example 2-20 illustrates how the output statements work and also gives examples of **expressions**.

When an output statement outputs `char` values, it outputs the character without the single quotation marks (unless the single quotation marks are part of the output statement). For example, suppose `ch` is a `char` variable and `ch = 'A';`. The statement:

```
System.out.println(ch);
```

or:

```
System.out.println('A');
```

outputs:

A

Similarly, when an output statement outputs the value of a string, it outputs the string without the double quotation marks (unless you include double quotation marks as part of the string, using an escape sequence).

EXAMPLE 2-20

Consider the following statements. The output is shown to the right of each statement.

	Statement	Output
1	`System.out.println(29 / 4);`	7
2	`System.out.println("Hello there.");`	Hello there.
3	`System.out.println(12);`	12
4	`System.out.println("4 + 7");`	4 + 7
5	`System.out.println(4 + 7);`	11
6	`System.out.println('A');`	A
7	`System.out.println("4 + 7 = " + (4 + 7));`	4 + 7 = 11
8	`System.out.println(2 + 3 * 5);`	17
9	`System.out.println("Hello \nthere.");`	Hello there.

Look at the output of statement 9. Recall that in Java, the newline character is `'\n'`; it causes the insertion point to move to the beginning of the next line before printing. Therefore, when `\n` appears in a string in an output statement, it moves the insertion point to the beginning of the next line on the output device. This explains why `Hello` and `there.` are printed on separate lines.

NOTE In Java, \ is called the **escape character** and \n is called the **newline escape sequence**.

Let's take a closer look at the newline character, '\n'. Consider the following Java statements:

```
System.out.print("Hello there. ");
System.out.print("My name is James.");
```

If these statements are executed in sequence, the output is:

```
Hello there. My name is James.
```

Consider the following Java statements:

```
System.out.print("Hello there.\n");
System.out.print("My name is James.");
```

The output of these Java statements is:

```
Hello there.
My name is James.
```

When \n is encountered in the string, the insertion point is positioned at the beginning of the next line. Note also that \n may appear anywhere in the string. For example, the output of the statement:

```
System.out.print("Hello \nthere. \nMy name is James.");
```

is:

```
Hello
there.
My name is James.
```

Also, note that the output of the statement:

```
System.out.print("\n");
```

is the same as the output of the statement:

```
System.out.println();
```

Thus, the output of the sequence of statements:

```
System.out.print("Hello there.\n");
System.out.print("My name is James.");
```

is equivalent to the output of the sequence of statements:

```
System.out.println("Hello there.");
System.out.print("My name is James.");
```

EXAMPLE 2-21

Consider the following Java statements:

```
System.out.print("Hello there.\nMy name is James.");
```

or:

```
System.out.print("Hello there.");
System.out.print("\nMy name is James.");
```

or:

```
System.out.println("Hello there.");
System.out.print("My name is James.");
```

In each case, the output of the statements is:

```
Hello there.
My name is James.
```

EXAMPLE 2-22

Suppose you want to output the following sentence in one line as part of a message:

```
It is sunny, warm, and not a windy day. We can go golfing.
```

Obviously, you will use the methods print and/or println to produce this output. However, in the programming code, this statement may not fit in one line as part of the output statement. Of course, you can use more than one output statement, as follows:

```
System.out.print("It is sunny, warm, and not a windy day. ");
System.out.println("We can go golfing.");
```

Two output statements are used to output the sentence in one line. You can also use the following statement to output this sentence:

```
System.out.println("It is sunny, warm, and not a windy day. " +
                   "We can go golfing.");
```

In this statement, note that because there is no semicolon at the end of the first line, this output statement continues at the second line. Also, note that the first line is followed by the operator +, and there is a double quotation mark at the beginning of the second line. The string is broken into two strings, but both strings are part of the same output statement.

If a string appearing in an output statement is long and you want to output the string in one line, you can break the string by using either of these two approaches. However, the following statement using the Enter (or return) key would be incorrect:

```
System.out.println("It is sunny, warm, and not a windy day.
              We can go golfing.")
```

The Enter (or return) key on your keyboard cannot be part of the string—in program-ming code, a string *cannot* be broken into more than one line by using the Enter (return) key.

Recall that the newline character is \n, which moves the insertion point to the beginning of the next line. In Java, there are many other escape sequences that allow you to control the output. Table 2-5 lists some of the commonly used escape sequences.

TABLE 2-5 Commonly Used Escape Sequences

	Escape Sequence	Description
\n	Newline	Cursor moves to the beginning of the next line
\t	Tab	Cursor moves to the next tab stop
\b	Backspace	Cursor moves one space to the left
\r	Return	Cursor moves to the beginning of the current line (not the next line)
\\	Backslash	Backslash is printed
\'	Single quotation	Single quotation mark is printed
\"	Double quotation	Double quotation mark is printed

Example 2-23 shows the effect of some of these escape sequences.

EXAMPLE 2-23

The output of the statement:

```
System.out.println("The newline escape sequence is \\n");
```

is:

```
The newline escape sequence is \n
```

The output of the statement:

```
System.out.println("The tab character is represented as \'\\t\'");
```

is:

```
The tab character is represented as '\t'
```

Note that the single quote can also be printed without using the escape sequence. Therefore, the preceding statement is equivalent to the following output statement:

```
System.out.println("The tab character is represented as '\\t'");
```

The output of the statement:

```
System.out.println("The string \"Sunny\" contains five characters");
```

is:

```
The string "Sunny" contains five characters
```

NOTE The Web site (*www.course.com*) and the CD accompanying this book contain the Java program that shows the effect of the statements in Example 2-23. (The program is named `Example2_23.java`.)

Packages, Classes, Methods, and the `import` Statement

Only a small number of operations, such as arithmetic and assignment operations, are explicitly defined in Java. Many of the methods and identifiers needed to run a Java program are provided as a collection of libraries, called packages. A **package** is a collection of related classes. Moreover, every package has a name.

In Java, *class* is a broadly used term. The term **class** is used to create Java programs, either application or applet; it is used to group a set of related operations; and it is used to allow users to create their own data types. For example, there are various mathematical operations, such as determining the absolute value of a number, determining one number raised to the power of another number, and determining the logarithm of a number. Each of these operations is implemented using the Java mechanism of *methods*. Think of a **method** as a set of instructions designed to accomplish a specific task. For example, the name of the method implementing the operation of one number raised to the power of another number is `pow`. This and other mathematical methods are contained in the `class Math`. The name of the package containing the `class Math` is `java.lang`.

The package `java.util` contains the `class Scanner`. This class contains the methods `nextInt`, `nextDouble`, `next`, and `nextLine` for inputting data into a program. In the next section, you learn how class(es) are used to create a Java application program.

NOTE To see the complete definitions of the (predefined) Java classes, such as `String`, `Math`, and `Scanner`, as well as the class hierarchy, you can visit the Web site *http://java.sun.com/javase/6/docs/api/*.

To make use of the existing classes, methods, and identifiers, you must tell the program which package contains the appropriate information. The `import` statement helps you do this.

The general syntax to import the contents of a package in a Java program is:

```
import packageName.*;
```

In Java, `import` is a reserved word. For example, the following statement imports the necessary classes from the package `java.util`:

```
import java.util.*;
```

To import a specific class from a package, you can specify the name of the class in place of the `*`. The following statement imports the `class` `Scanner` from the package `java.util`:

```
import java.util.Scanner;
```

Import statements are placed at the top of the program.

NOTE If you use the character `*` in the `import` statement, as in the statement:

```
import java.util.*;
```

then the compiler determines the relevant class(es) used in the program.

NOTE The primitive data types are directly part of the Java language and do not require that any package be imported into the program. Also, the `class` `String` is contained in the package `java.lang`. You do not need to import classes from the package `java.lang`. The system automatically does it for you.

Creating a Java Application Program

In previous sections, you learned enough Java concepts to write meaningful programs. In this section, you learn how to create a complete Java application program.

The basic unit of a Java program is called a class. A Java application program is, therefore, a collection of one or more classes. Roughly speaking, a class is a collection of methods and data members. As described in the previous section, a method is a set of instructions designed to accomplish a specific task. Some **predefined** or **standard** methods, such as `nextInt`, `print`, and `println`, are already written and are provided as part of the system. But to accomplish most tasks, programmers must learn to write their own methods.

One of the classes in a Java application program must have the method called `main`. Moreover, there can only be one method `main` in a Java class. If a Java application program has only one class, it *must* contain the method `main`. Until Chapter 6, other than

2

using some predefined methods, you will mainly deal with Java application programs that have only one class.

Statements to declare memory spaces (named constants and variables), statements to create input stream objects, statements to manipulate data (such as assignments), and statements to input and output data will be placed within the class.

Statements to declare named constants and input stream objects are usually placed outside the method `main`, and statements to declare variables are usually placed within the method `main`. Statements to manipulate data and input and output statements are placed within the method `main`.

The syntax of a class to create a Java application program is:

```
public class ClassName
{
        classMembers
}
```

where `ClassName` is a user-defined Java identifier; `classMembers` consists of the data members and methods (such as the method `main`). In Java, `public` and `class` are reserved words. (Typically, the name of a class begins with an uppercase letter.)

A typical syntax of the method `main` is:

```
public static void main(String[] args)
{
        statement1
        .
        .
        .
        statementn
}
```

Recall that in a syntax example, the shading indicates the part of the definition that is optional.

A Java application program might be using the resources provided by the IDE, such as the necessary code to input data, which require your program to import certain packages. You can, therefore, divide a Java application program into two parts: import statements and the program itself. The import statements tell the compiler which packages are needed by the program. The program contains statements (placed in a class) that accomplish some meaningful results. Together, the import statements and the program statements constitute the Java **source code**. To be useful, this source code must be saved in a file, called a **source file**, that has the file extension `.java`. Moreover, the name of the class and the name of the file containing the Java program must be the same. For example, if the name of the class to create the Java program is `Welcome`, then the name of the source file must be `Welcome.java`.

Because the programming instructions are placed in the method `main`, let us elaborate on the method `main` a bit more.

The basic parts of the method `main` are the heading and the body. The first line of the method `main`:

```
public static void main(String[] args)
```

is called the **heading** of the method `main`.

The statements enclosed between braces ({ and }) form the **body** of the method `main`. The body of the method `main` contains two types of statements:

- Declaration statements
- Executable statements

Declaration statements are used to declare things such as variables.
Executable statements perform calculations, manipulate data, create output, accept input, and so on.

In Java, variables or identifiers can be declared anywhere within a method, but they must be declared before they can be used.

EXAMPLE 2-24

The following statements are examples of variable declarations:

```
int     num1;
int     num2;
double  salary;
String  name;
```

EXAMPLE 2-25

Some executable statements that you have encountered so far are the assignment, input, and output statements.

Suppose that `num1` and `num2` are `int` variables. The following statements are examples of executable statements:

```
num1 = 4;                          //assignment statement
num2 = console.nextInt();          //input and
                                   //assignment statement

System.out.println(num1 + " " + num2);   //output statement
```

2

In skeleton form, a Java application program looks like the following:

```
import statements if any

public class ClassName
{
    named constants and/or stream objects declarations

    public static void main(String[] args)
    {
        variable declaration

        statements
    }
}
```

> **NOTE**
>
> Notice that the heading of the method `main` contains the reserved word `static`. The statements to declare the named constants and the input stream objects are placed outside the definition of the method `main`. Therefore, to use these named constants and stream objects in the method `main`, Java requires that you declare the named constants and the input stream objects with the reserved word `static`. Example 2-26 illustrates this concept.

EXAMPLE 2-26

The following is a simple Java application program showing where in a Java program the import statements, the method **main**, and statements such as named constants, declarations, assignment statements, and input and output statements typically appear.

```
//************************************************************
// Author: D.S. Malik
//
// This program shows where the import statements, named constants,
// variable declarations, assignment statements, and input and
// output statements typically appear.
//************************************************************

import java.util.*;                                    //Line 1

public class FirstJavaProgram                          //Line 2
{                                                      //Line 3
    static final int NUMBER = 12;                      //Line 4

    static Scanner console = new Scanner(System.in);   //Line 5

    public static void main(String[] args)             //Line 6
    {                                                  //Line 7
        int firstNum;                                  //Line 8
        int secondNum;                                 //Line 9

        firstNum = 18;                                 //Line 10
        System.out.println("Line 11: firstNum = "
                       + firstNum);                     //Line 11
```

```
        System.out.print("Line 12: Enter an integer: ");    //Line 12
        secondNum = console.nextInt();                       //Line 13
        System.out.println();                                //Line 14

        System.out.println("Line 15: secondNum = "
                        + secondNum);                        //Line 15

        firstNum = firstNum + NUMBER + 2 * secondNum;        //Line 16

        System.out.println("Line 17: The new value of " +
                        "firstNum = " + firstNum);           //Line 17
    }                                                        //Line 18
}                                                            //Line 19
```

Sample Run: (In this sample run, the user input is shaded.)

```
Line 11: firstNum = 18
Line 12: Enter an integer: 15

Line 15: secondNum = 15
Line 17: The new value of firstNum = 60
```

The preceding program works as follows: The statement in Line 1 imports the `class` Scanner. The statement in Line 2 names the `class` containing statements of the program as `FirstJavaProgram`. The left brace in Line 3 marks the beginning of the `class FirstJavaProgram`.

The statement in Line 4 declares the named constant `NUMBER` and sets its value to 12. The statement in Line 5 declares and initializes the object `console` to input data from the keyboard.

The statement in Line 6 contains the heading of the method `main`, and the left brace in Line 7 marks the beginning of the method `main`. The statements in Lines 8 and 9 declare the variables `firstNum` and `secondNum`.

The statement in Line 10 sets the value of `firstNum` to 18, and the statement in Line 11 outputs the value of `firstNum`.

Next, the statement in Line 12 prompts the user to enter an integer. The statement in Line 13 reads and stores the integer into the variable `secondNum`, which is 15 in the sample run. The statement in Line 14 positions the insertion point on the screen at the beginning of the next line. The statement in Line 15 outputs the value of `secondNum`.

The statement in Line 16 evaluates the expression:

```
firstNum + NUMBER + 2 * secondNum
```

and assigns the value of this expression to the variable `firstNum`, which is 60 in the sample run. The statement in Line 17 outputs the new value of `firstNum`. The right brace in Line 18 marks the end of the method `main`, and the right brace in Line 19 marks the end of the `class FirstJavaProgram`.

Programming Style and Form

In previous sections, you learned how to create a Java application program. Here, we describe the proper structure of a program. Using the proper structure makes a Java program easier to understand and modify. It is frustrating trying to follow, and perhaps modify, a program that is syntactically correct but has no structure.

Every Java application program must satisfy certain language rules. It must also satisfy the syntax rules, which, like grammar rules, tell what is correct and what is incorrect, and what is legal and what is illegal in the language. Other rules give precise meaning to the language; that is, they support the language's semantics. The sections that follow are designed to help you learn more about how to put together the Java programming elements you have learned so far and how to create a functioning program. These sections cover syntax; the use of blanks; the use of semicolons, brackets, and commas; semantics; prompt lines; documentation, including comments and naming identifiers; and form and style.

Syntax

As remarked earlier, the syntax rules of a language tell what is legal and what is illegal. Errors in syntax are detected during compilation. Consider the following Java statements:

```
int     x;          //Line 1
int     y           //Line 2
double  z;          //Line 3

y = w + x;          //Line 4
```

When these statements are compiled, a compilation error will occur at Line 2 because there is no semicolon after the declaration of the variable **y**. A second compilation error will occur at Line 4 because the identifier **w** is used but has not been declared. (If **w** has been declared and **x** has not been properly initialized, then a syntax error will occur at Line 4.)

As discussed in Chapter 1, you enter a program into the computer by using an editor. When a program is typed, errors are almost unavoidable. Therefore, when the program is compiled, you most likely will see syntax errors. It is possible that a syntax error at a particular place might lead to syntax errors in several subsequent statements. It is common for the omission of a single character to cause four or five error messages. However, when the first syntax error is removed and the program is recompiled, subsequent syntax errors caused by the first syntax error may disappear. Therefore, you should correct syntax errors in the order in which the compiler lists them. As you become more experienced with Java, you will learn how to spot and fix syntax errors quickly. Note that compilers not only discover syntax errors, but also provide hints and sometimes tell the user where the syntax errors are and how to fix them.

USE OF BLANKS

In Java, you use one or more blanks to separate numbers when data is input. Blanks are also used to separate reserved words and identifiers from each other and from other symbols. Blanks must never appear within a reserved word or identifier.

USE OF SEMICOLONS, BRACES, AND COMMAS

In Java, a semicolon is used to terminate a statement. The semicolon is also called a **statement terminator**.

Note that braces, { and }, are not Java statements, even though they often appear on a line with no other code. You might regard braces as delimiters because they enclose the body of a method and set it off from other parts of the program. (Braces have other uses, which will be explained in Chapter 4.)

Recall that commas are used to separate items in a list. For example, you use commas when you declare more than one variable following a data type.

SEMANTICS

The set of rules that gives meaning to a language is called **semantics**. For example, the order-of-precedence rules for arithmetic operators are semantic rules.

If a program contains syntax errors, the compiler will warn you. What happens when a program contains semantic errors? It is quite possible to eradicate all syntax errors in a program and still not have it run. And if it runs, it may not do what you meant it to do. For example, the following two expressions are both syntactically correct expressions, but they have different meanings:

2 + 3 * 5

and:

(2 + 3) * 5

If you substitute one of these expressions for the other in a program, you will not get the same results—even though the numbers are the same, the semantics are different. You will learn about semantics throughout this book.

PROMPT LINES

Part of good documentation is the use of clearly written prompts so that users will know what to do when they interact with a program. It is frustrating for a user to sit in front of a running program and not have the foggiest notion of whether to enter something, and if so, what to enter. **Prompt lines** are executable statements that inform the user what to do. Consider the following Java statements, in which num is an **int** variable:

```
System.out.println("Please enter a number between 1 and 10 and "
                  + "then press Enter");
num = console.nextInt();
```

When these two statements execute in the order given, first the output statement causes the following line of text to appear on the screen:

```
Please enter a number between 1 and 10 and then press Enter
```

After seeing this line, an example of a prompt line, users know that they must enter a number and press the Enter key. If the program contained only the second statement, users would not know that they must enter a number, and the computer would wait indefinitely for the input. The preceding output statement is an example of a prompt line.

In a program, whenever users must provide input, you should include the necessary prompt lines. The prompt lines should include sufficient information about what input is acceptable. For example, the preceding prompt line not only tells the user to input a number, but also informs the user that the number should be between 1 and 10.

FORM AND STYLE

You might think that Java has too many rules. However, in practice, the rules give Java a great degree of freedom. For example, consider the following two ways of declaring variables:

```
int feet;
int inch;

double x;
double y;
```

and:

```
int feet; int inch;double x;double y;
```

The computer has no difficulty understanding either of these formats, but the first form is easier for a person to read and follow.

What about blank spaces? Where are they significant and where are they meaningless?

Consider the following two statements:

```
int a;
```

and:

```
int     a;
```

Both of these declarations mean the same thing. Here, the extra blanks between the identifiers in the second statement are meaningless. On the other hand, consider the following statement:

```
inta;
```

This statement contains a syntax error. The lack of a blank between the t in int and the identifier a changes the reserved word int and the identifier a into a new identifier, inta.

The clarity provided by the rules of syntax and semantics frees you to adopt formats that are pleasing to you and easier to understand.

The following example further elaborates on form and style.

EXAMPLE 2-27

Consider the following Java program:

```
//An improperly formatted Java program.

import java.util.*;

public class Example2_27A
{
        static Scanner console = new Scanner(System.in);
public static void main(String[] args)
{
int num; double height;
String name;
System.out.print("Enter an integer: ");
num=console.nextInt(); System.out.println();
    System.out.println("num: "+num);
System.out.print("Enter first name: ");
name=console.next();
    System.out.println();System.out.print("Enter height: ");
height = console.nextDouble(); System.out.println();

System.out.println("Name: "+name);System.out.println("Height: "
+height);
}}
```

This program is syntactically correct; the Java compiler would have no difficulty reading and compiling this program. However, this program is very hard for a human to read. The program that you write should be properly indented and formatted. Next, we rewrite the preceding program and properly format it.

```
//Properly formatted Java program.

import java.util.*;

public class Example2_27B
{
    static Scanner console = new Scanner(System.in);

    public static void main(String[] args)
    {
        int num;
        double height;
        String name;

        System.out.print("Enter an integer: ");
        num = console.nextInt();
        System.out.println();
```

2

```
        System.out.println("num: " + num);

        System.out.print("Enter first name: ");
        name = console.next();
        System.out.println();

        System.out.print("Enter height: ");
        height = console.nextDouble();
        System.out.println();

        System.out.println("Name: " + name);
        System.out.println("Height: " + height);
    }
}
```

As you can see, this program is easier to read. Your programs should be properly indented and formatted. To document the variables, programmers typically declare one variable per line. Also, always put a space before and after an operator.

Avoiding Bugs: Consistent, Proper Formatting

Consistent, proper formatting of a report, term paper, or dissertation helps an author communicate her or his message. Consistent, proper formatting is just as important when you are writing programs. By using consistent, proper formatting, it becomes easier to develop, debug, and maintain programs. In all the examples presented in this book, you will see consistent and predictable use of blanks, tabs, and newline characters to separate the elements of these programs. You will also see consistent, predictable use of uppercase and lowercase letters. This makes it easy to discover the nature and function of the elements of a program and how they fit together. In addition to learning how the examples behave, observe how they are formatted and carefully copy this style in the programs you create.

Debugging—Code Walk-throughs

As you write programs, you will create unintentional bugs. Every programmer creates bugs. Bugs are aspects of programs that cause the programs to do other than what you intended. The Java compiler will find the aspects of your program that violate Java's syntax rules so that you can correct them. Sometimes a syntactically correct program (one that compiles successfully) has other problems that cause it to produce incorrect results or even to crash. Almost all the time, these problems are due to bugs in the program.

Programmers usually try to find and fix these problems themselves. They do so by walking carefully through their programs—identifying what actually is done and comparing it with what should be done at each step and in each section of the program. Often this approach reveals the problem so the programmer can fix it.

Sometimes, however, especially after multiple readings of a program in search of the bug, the programmer begins to gloss over sections of code, one of which may contain the elusive bug. At this point, it can be advantageous to invite the assistance of someone else who is learning to program or who has already learned to program.

Before you invite someone to examine your program, you'll probably make sure that it is formatted properly, that you have used uppercase and lowercase letters correctly, and that you have chosen good names for identifiers. In the process, you may find the bug. If not, as you explain your program to this person, you will not be able to gloss over sections of code as you might have done when you are reading your program to yourself. As you explain your program to someone else, you will be surprised how often you find the problem, even with the other person just listening.

Finally, the person looking at your program will hear your explanation of what you intended to do while looking at what you actually wrote your program to do. The person may be able to detect the inconsistency between what you intended to code and what you actually coded. Each of these processes (the private examination of your code, the preparation of your code for review by another person, and the review of your code with another person) is a walk-through. A presentation to a larger group, such as your study group, is also called a walk-through. A walk-through can be helpful for all phases of the software development process.

More on Assignment Statements (Optional)

Corresponding to the five arithmetic operators +, −, *, /, and %, Java provides five compound operators +=, −=, *=, /=, and %=, respectively. Consider the following simple assignment statement, where x and y are int variables:

```
x = x * y;
```

Using the compound operator *=, this statement can be written as:

```
x *= y;
```

In general, using the compound operator *=, you can rewrite the simple assignment statement:

```
variable = variable * (expression);
```

as:

```
variable *= expression;
```

2

Similar conventions apply to the other arithmetic compound operators. For example, using the compound operator +=, you can rewrite the simple assignment statement

```
variable = variable + (expression);
```

as:

```
variable += expression;
```

Thus, the compound assignment statement lets you write simple assignment statements in a concise fashion by combining an arithmetic operator with an assignment operator.

EXAMPLE 2-28

This example shows several compound assignment statements that are equivalent to simple assignment statements.

Simple Assignment Statement
```
i = i + 5;
counter = counter + 1;
sum = sum + number;
amount = amount * (interest + 1);
x = x / ( y + 5);
```

Compound Assignment Statement
```
i += 5;
counter += 1;
sum += number;
amount *= interest + 1;
x /= y + 5;
```

NOTE Any compound assignment statement can be converted into a simple assignment statement. However, a simple assignment statement may not be (easily) converted into a compound assignment statement. Consider the following simple assignment statement:

```
x = x * y + z - 5;
```

To write this statement as a compound assignment statement, the variable **x** must be a common factor in the right side, which is not the case. Therefore, you cannot immediately convert this statement into a compound assignment statement. In fact, the equivalent compound assignment statement is:

```
x *= y + (z - 5)/x;
```

which is more complicated than the simple assignment statement. Furthermore, in the preceding compound statement, **x** cannot be zero. We recommend avoiding such compound expressions.

PROGRAMMING EXAMPLE: Convert Length

Write a program that takes as input given lengths expressed in feet and inches. The program should then convert and output the lengths in centimeters. Assume that the lengths given in feet and inches are integers.

Input: Length in feet and inches

Output: Equivalent length in centimeters

PROBLEM
ANALYSIS
AND
ALGORITHM
DESIGN

The lengths are given in feet and inches, and you need to find the equivalent length in centimeters. One inch is equal to 2.54 centimeters. The first thing the program needs to do is convert the length given in feet and inches to all inches. To convert the length from feet and inches to inches, you multiply the number of feet by 12 (1 foot is equal to 12 inches), and add your answer to the given inches. Then you can use the conversion formula, 1 inch = 2.54 centimeters, to find the equivalent length in centimeters.

Suppose the input is 5 feet and 7 inches. You find the total inches as follows:

```
totalInches = (12 * feet) + inches
            = 12 * 5 + 7
            = 67
```

You can then apply the conversion formula, 1 inch = 2.54 centimeters, to find the length in centimeters.

```
centimeters = totalInches * 2.54
            = 67 * 2.54
            = 170.18
```

Based on this analysis, you can design an algorithm as follows:

1. Get the length in feet and inches.
2. Convert the length into total inches.
3. Convert total inches into centimeters.
4. Output centimeters.

VARIABLES

The input for the program is two numbers: one for feet and one for inches. Thus, you need two variables: one to store feet and the other to store inches. Because the program will first convert the given length into inches, you need a third variable to store the total inches. You need a fourth variable to store the equivalent length in centimeters. In summary, you need the following variables:

```
int feet;          //variable to store feet
int inches;        //variable to store inches
int totalInches;   //variable to store total inches

double centimeters; //variable to store length in centimeters
```

NAMED CONSTANTS

Recall that to calculate the equivalent length in centimeters, you need to multiply the total inches by 2.54. Instead of using the value 2.54 directly in the program, you will declare this value as a named constant. Similarly, to find the total inches, you need to multiply the feet by 12 and add the inches. Instead of using 12 directly in the program, you will also declare this value as a named constant. Using named constants makes it easier to modify the program later. Because the named constants will be placed before the method main, you must use the modifier static to declare these named constants (see the earlier section, Creating a Java Application Program).

```
static final double CENTIMETERS_PER_INCH = 2.54;
static final int INCHES_PER_FOOT = 12;
```

MAIN ALGORITHM

In the preceding sections, we analyzed the problem and determined the formulas to perform the calculations. We also determined the necessary variables and named constants. We can now expand the algorithm given in the section Problem Analysis and Algorithm Design to solve the problem given at the beginning of this programming example (converting feet and inches to centimeters).

1. Prompt the user for the input. (Without a prompt line, the user will stare at a blank screen and not know what to do.)
2. Get feet.
3. Prompt the user to enter a value for inches.
4. Get inches.
5. Echo the input by outputting what the program read as input. (Without this step, after the program has executed, you will not know what the input was.)
6. Find the length in inches.
7. Output the length in inches.
8. Convert the length to centimeters.
9. Output the length in centimeters.

PUTTING IT TOGETHER

Now that the problem has been analyzed and the algorithm has been designed, the next step is to translate the algorithm into Java code. Because this is the first complete Java program you are writing, let's review the necessary steps in sequence.

The program will begin with comments that document its purpose and functionality. Because there is both input to this program (the length in feet and inches) and output (the equivalent length in centimeters), you will use the system resources for input/output. In other words, the program will use input statements to get the data into the program and output statements to print the results. Because the data will be entered from the keyboard, the program must import the class Scanner from the package java.util. Thus, the first statement of the program, following the comments described previously, will be the `import` statement to import the `class` `Scanner` from the package `java.util`.

This program requires two types of memory locations for data manipulation: named constants and variables. Recall that named constants are usually placed before the method `main` so that they can be used throughout the program.

This program has only one class, which contains the method `main`. The method `main` will contain all of the programming instructions in its body. In addition, the program needs variables to manipulate the data; these variables will be declared in the body of the method `main`. (The reasons for declaring variables in the body of the method `main` are explained in Chapter 7.) The body of the method `main` will also contain the Java statements that implement the algorithm. Therefore, for this program, the definition of the method `main` has the following form:

```
public static void main(String[] args)
{
    declare variables
    statements
}
```

To write the complete conversion program, follow these steps:

1. Begin the program with comments for documentation.
2. Use `import` statements to import the classes required by the program.
3. Declare the named constants, if any.
4. Write the definition of the method `main`.

COMPLETE PROGRAM LISTING

```
//**********************************************************
// Author: D. S. Malik
//
// Program Convert: This program converts measurements
// in feet and inches into centimeters using the formula
// that 1 inch is equal to 2.54 centimeters.
//**********************************************************

import java.util.*;

public class Conversion
{
    static Scanner console = new Scanner(System.in);

    static final double CENTIMETERS_PER_INCH = 2.54;
    static final int INCHES_PER_FOOT = 12;
```

```java
public static void main(String[] args)
{
        //declare variables
    int feet;
    int inches;
    int totalInches;

    double centimeters;

    System.out.print("Enter feet: ");                     //Step 1
    feet = console.nextInt();                             //Step 2
    System.out.println();
    System.out.print("Enter inches: ");                   //Step 3
    inches = console.nextInt();                           //Step 4
    System.out.println();
    System.out.println("The numbers you entered are "
                    + feet + " for feet and "
                    + inches + " for inches.");           //Step 5

    totalInches = INCHES_PER_FOOT * feet + inches;        //Step 6

    System.out.println();
    System.out.println("The total number of inches = "
                    + totalInches);                       //Step 7

    centimeters = totalInches * CENTIMETERS_PER_INCH;     //Step 8

    System.out.println("The number of centimeters = "
                    + centimeters);                       //Step 9
    }
}
```

Sample Run: (In this sample run, the user input is shaded.)

```
Enter feet: 15

Enter inches: 7

The numbers you entered are 15 for feet and 7 for inches.

The total number of inches = 187
The number of centimeters = 474.98
```

The programming code of this program must be saved in the file `Conversion.java` because we named the `class` containing the method `main Conversion`.

> **NOTE** The preceding program uses comments such as `//Step 1`, `//Step 2`, and so on. The only purpose of these comments is to show which step of the algorithm (shown before the program listing) corresponds to which statement in the program. We typically use this convention in all the programming examples in this book.

PROGRAMMING EXAMPLE: Make Change

Write a program that takes as input any change expressed in cents. It should then compute the number of half-dollars, quarters, dimes, nickels, and pennies to be returned, using as many half-dollars as possible, then quarters, dimes, nickels, and pennies, in that order. For example, 483 cents would be returned as 9 half-dollars, 1 quarter, 1 nickel, and 3 pennies.

Input: Change in cents

Output: Equivalent change in half-dollars, quarters, dimes, nickels, and pennies

PROBLEM
ANALYSIS
AND
ALGORITHM
DESIGN

Suppose the given change is 646 cents. To find the number of half-dollars, you divide 646 by 50, the value of a half-dollar, and find the quotient, which is 12, and the remainder, which is 46. The quotient, 12, is the number of half-dollars, and the remainder, 46, is the remaining change.

Next, divide the remaining change by 25, to find the number of quarters. The remaining change is 46, so division by 25 gives the quotient 1, which is the number of quarters, and a remainder of 21, which is the remaining change. This process continues for dimes and nickels. To calculate the remainder (pennies) in integer division, you use the mod operator, %.

Applying this discussion to 646 cents yields the following calculations:

1. Change = 646
2. Number of half-dollars = 646 / 50 = 12
3. Remaining change = 646 % 50 = 46
4. Number of quarters = 46 / 25 = 1
5. Remaining change = 46 % 25 = 21
6. Number of dimes = 21 / 10 = 2
7. Remaining change = 21 % 10 = 1
8. Number of nickels = 1 / 5 = 0
9. Number of pennies = remaining change = 1 % 5 = 1

This discussion translates into the following algorithm:

1. Get the change in cents.
2. Find the number of half-dollars.
3. Calculate the remaining change.
4. Find the number of quarters.
5. Calculate the remaining change.
6. Find the number of dimes.

7. Calculate the remaining change.

8. Find the number of nickels.

9. Calculate the remaining change.

10. The remaining change is the number of pennies.

VARIABLES

From the previous discussion and algorithm, it appears that the program needs variables to hold the number of half-dollars, quarters, and so on. However, the numbers of half-dollars, quarters, and so on are not used in later calculations, so the program can simply output these values without saving them in variables. The only thing that keeps changing is the change, so the program needs only one variable:

```
int change;
```

NAMED
CONSTANTS

The program performs calculations using the values of a half-dollar, 50; a quarter, 25; a dime, 10; and a nickel, 5. Because these data are special and the program uses these values more than once, it makes sense to declare them as named constants. (Using named constants also simplifies later modification of the program.)

```
static final int HALFDOLLAR = 50;
static final int QUARTER  = 25;
static final int DIME = 10;
static final int NICKEL = 5;
```

MAIN
ALGORITHM

In the preceding sections, we analyzed the problem and determined the formulas to do the calculations. We also determined the necessary variables and named constants. We can now expand the algorithm given in the section Problem Analysis and Algorithm Design to solve the problem given at the beginning of this programming example (expressing change in cents).

1. Prompt the user for the input.

2. Get the input.

3. Echo the input by displaying the entered change on the screen.

4. Compute and print the number of half-dollars.

5. Calculate the remaining change.

6. Compute and print the number of quarters.

7. Calculate the remaining change.

8. Compute and print the number of dimes.

9. Calculate the remaining change.

10. Compute and print the number of nickels.

11. Calculate the remaining change.

12. Print the remaining change.

COMPLETE PROGRAM LISTING

```java
//***********************************************************
//  Author: D. S. Malik
//
// Program Make Change: Given any amount of change expressed
// in cents, this program computes the number of half-dollars,
// quarters, dimes, nickels, and pennies to be returned,
// returning as many half-dollars as possible, then quarters,
// dimes, nickels, and pennies, in that order.
//***********************************************************

import java.util.*;

public class MakeChange
{
    static Scanner console = new Scanner(System.in);

    static final int HALFDOLLAR = 50;
    static final int QUARTER = 25;
    static final int DIME = 10;
    static final int NICKEL = 5;

    public static void main(String[] args)
    {
        //declare variables
        int change;

        //Statements: Step 1 - Step 12
        System.out.print("Enter the change in cents: ");    //Step 1
        change = console.nextInt();                         //Step 2
        System.out.println();

        System.out.println("The change you entered is "
                    + change);                              //Step 3

        System.out.println("The number of half dollars "
                    + "to be returned is "
                    + change / HALFDOLLAR);                 //Step 4

        change = change % HALFDOLLAR;                       //Step 5

        System.out.println("The number of quarters to be "
                    + "returned is "
                    + change / QUARTER);                    //Step 6

        change = change % QUARTER;                          //Step 7

        System.out.println("The number of dimes to be "
                        + "returned is "
                        + change / DIME);                   //Step 8
```

```
        change = change % DIME;                              //Step 9

        System.out.println("The number of nickels to be "
                          + "returned is "
                          + change / NICKEL);                //Step 10

        change = change % NICKEL;                            //Step 11

        System.out.println("The number of pennies to be "
                          + "returned is " + change);        //Step 12
    }
}
```

2

Sample Run: (In this sample run, the user input is shaded.)

```
Enter the change in cents: 583

The change you entered is 583
The number of half dollars to be returned is 11
The number of quarters to be returned is 1
The number of dimes to be returned is 0
The number of nickels to be returned is 1
The number of pennies to be returned is 3
```

Debugging: Understanding Error Messages

The Java compiler will find syntactic errors in your program and will provide messages describing the errors. These messages do not always describe the problem exactly, nor do they always describe all the syntactic problems in your program at once, but they provide a good indication of where to look for the problem(s). Look carefully in the immediate vicinity of the reported error for anything that might be causing the problem. Often the correction of a single syntactic error will result in the reporting of multiple new syntactic errors, but there is no need for concern. Finding and reporting errors is like peeling away layers of an onion. By finding and correcting the sources of errors as they are reported, ultimately you will be able to find and correct all the syntactic errors in your program.

QUICK REVIEW

1. A Java program is a collection of classes.
2. Every Java application program has a method called `main`.
3. A single line comment starts with the pair of symbols // anywhere in the line. Multiple line comments are enclosed between /* and */.
4. The compiler ignores comments.
5. In Java, identifiers are names of things.

6. A Java identifier consists of letters, digits, the underscore character (_), and the dollar sign ($) and must begin with a letter, underscore, or the dollar sign.

7. Reserved words cannot be used as identifiers in a program.

8. All reserved words in Java consist of lowercase letters (see Appendix A).

9. Java is case sensitive.

10. A data type is a set of values with a set of operations.

11. The three categories of primitive data types are integral, floating-point, and Boolean.

12. Integral data types are used to deal with integers.

13. There are five categories of integral data types—char, byte, short, int, and long.

14. The int data type is used to represent integers between -2147483648 $(= -2^{31})$ and $2147483647 = (2^{31} - 1)$. The memory allocated for the int data type is 4 bytes.

15. The data type short is used to represent integers between -32768 $(= -2^{15})$ and 32767 $(2^{15} - 1)$. The memory allocated for the short data type is 2 bytes.

16. Java uses the Unicode character set, which is a set of 65536 characters. The ASCII character set, which has 128 values, is a subset of Unicode. The first 128 characters of Unicode, 0–127, are the same as those of ASCII.

17. The collating sequence of a character is its preset number in the Unicode character data set.

18. The data types float and double are used to deal with floating-point numbers.

19. The data type float can be used in Java to represent any real number between $-3.4E+38$ and $3.4E+38$. The memory allocated for the float data type is 4 bytes.

20. The data type double can be used in Java to represent any real number between $-1.7E+308$ and $1.7E+308$. The memory allocated for the double data type is 8 bytes.

21. The maximum number of significant digits—that is, the number of decimal places—in float values is 6 or 7. The maximum number of significant digits in values belonging to the double type is 15. The maximum number of significant digits is called the precision.

22. Values of type float are called single precision, and values of type double are called double precision.

23. The arithmetic operators in Java are addition (+), subtraction (-), multiplication (*), division (/), and mod (%).

24. The mod operator, %, gives the remainder upon division.

25. All operands in an integral expression, or integer expression, are integers, and all operands in a floating-point expression are decimal numbers.

26. A mixed expression is an expression that consists of both integers and decimal numbers.

27. When evaluating an operator in an expression, an integer is treated as a floating-point number, with a decimal part of zero, only if the operator has mixed operands.

28. You can use the cast operator to explicitly treat values of one data type as another.

29. The class `String` is used to manipulate strings.

30. A string is a sequence of zero or more characters.

31. Strings in Java are enclosed in double quotation marks.

32. A string containing no characters is called a null or empty string.

33. The operator + can be used to concatenate two strings.

34. During program execution, the contents of a named constant cannot be changed.

35. A named constant is declared by using the reserved word `final`.

36. A named constant is initialized when it is declared.

37. All variables must be declared before they can be used.

38. Java may not automatically initialize all the variables you declare.

39. Every variable has a name, a value, a data type, and a size.

40. When a new value is assigned to a variable, the old value is overwritten.

41. Only an assignment statement or an input (read) statement can change the value of a variable.

42. Input from the standard input device is accomplished by using a `Scanner` object initialized to the standard input device.

43. If `console` is a `Scanner` object initialized to the standard input device, then the expression `console.nextInt()` retrieves the next integer from the standard input device. Similarly, the expression `console.nextDouble()` retrieves the next floating number, and the expression `console.next()` retrieves the next string from the standard input device.

44. When data is input in a program, the data items, such as numbers, are usually separated by blanks, lines, or tabs.

45. The increment operator, ++, increases the value of its operand by 1.

46. The decrement operator, --, decreases the value of its operand by 1.

47. Output of the program to the standard output device is accomplished by using the standard output object `System.out` and the methods `print` and `println`.

48. The character \ is called the escape character.

49. The sequence \n is called the newline escape sequence.

50. A package is a collection of related classes. A class consists of methods, and a method is designed to accomplish a specific task.

51. The `import` statement is used to import the components of a package into a program. For example, the statement:

    `import java.util.*;`

    imports the (components of the) `package java.util` into the program.

52. In Java, `import` is a reserved word.

53. Because the primitive data types are directly part of the Java language, they do not require any import statement to use them.

54. The `class String` is contained in the package `java.lang`. You do not need to import classes from the package `java.lang`. The system automatically does it for you.

55. In Java, a semicolon is used to terminate a statement. The semicolon in Java is called the statement terminator.

56. A file containing a Java program always ends with the extension `.java`.

57. Prompt lines are executable statements that tell the user what to do.

58. Corresponding to five arithmetic operators +, −, *, /, and %, Java provides five compound operators +=, −=, *=, /=, and %=, respectively.

EXERCISES

1. Mark the following statements as true or false.

    a. An identifier can be any sequence of digits and letters.

    b. In Java, there is no difference between a reserved word and a pre-defined identifier.

    c. A Java identifier can start with a digit.

    d. The operands of the modulus operator must be integers.

    e. If the value of a is 4 and the value of b is 3, then after the statement a = b; the value of b is still 3.

    f. In an output statement, the newline character may be a part of the string.

    g. The following is a legal Java program:

    ```
    public class JavaProgram
    {
        public static void main(String[] args)
        {
        }
    }
    ```

    h. In a mixed expression, all operands are converted to floating-point numbers.

    i. Suppose x = 5. After the statement y = x++; executes, y is 5 and x is 6.

    j. Suppose a = 5. After the statement ++a; executes, the value of a is still 5 because the value of the expression is not saved in another variable.

2. Which of the following are valid Java identifiers?

    a. `myFirstProgram`   b. `MIX-UP`   c. `JavaProgram2`

    d. `quiz7` e. `ProgrammingLecture2`   f. `1footEquals12Inches`

    g. `Mike'sFirstAttempt`   h. `Update Grade`   i. `4th`

    j. `New_Student`

3. Which of the following is a reserved word in Java?

    a. `int`   b. `INT`   c. `Char`   d. `CHAR`

4. Evaluate the following expressions.

    a. `13 / 4`

    b. `2 + 12 / 4`

    c. `21 % 5`

    d. `3 - 5 % 7`

    e. `17.0 / 4`

    f. `8 - 5 * 2.0`

    g. `14 + 5 % 2 - 3`

    h. `15.0 + 3.0 / 2.0`

5. If `x = 5`, `y = 6`, `z = 4`, and `w = 3.5`, evaluate each of the following expressions, if possible. If it is not possible, state the reason.

    a. `(x + z) % y`

    b. `(x + y) % w`

    c. `(y + w) % x`

    d. `(x + y ) * w`

    e. `(x % y) % z`

    f. `(y % z) % x`

    g. `(x * z) % y`

    h. `((x * y) * w) * z`

6. Given:

```
int num1, num2, newNum;
double x, y;
```

Which of the following assignments are valid? If an assignment is not valid, state the reason. When not given, assume that each variable is declared.

    a. `num1 = 15;`

    b. `num2 = num1 - 18;`

    c. `num1 = 5; num2 = 2 + 6; num1 = num2 / 3;`

    d. `num1 + num2 = newNum;`

e.   `x = 12 * num1 - 15.3;`

f.   `num1 * 2 = newNum;`

g.   `x / y = x * y;`

h.   `num2 = num1 % 1.0;`

i.   `newNum = (int) (x) % 5;`

j.   `x = x + 5;`

k.   `newNum = num1 + (int) (4.6 / 2);`

7. Do a walk-through to find the value assigned to e. Assume that all variables are properly declared.

```
a = 3;
b = 4;
c = (a % b) * 6;
d = c / b;
e = (a + b + c + d)/ 4;
```

8. Which of the following variable declarations are correct? If a variable declaration is not correct, give the reason(s) and provide the correct variable declaration.

```
n = 12;                //Line 1
char letter = ;        //Line 2
int one = 5, two;      //Line 3
double x, y, z;        //Line 4
```

9. Which of the following are valid Java assignment statements? Assume that i, x, and `percent` are `double` variables.

a.   `i = i + 5;`

b.   `x + 2 = x;`

c.   `x = 2.5 * x;`

d.   `percent = 10%`

10. Write Java statements that accomplish the following.

a.   Declare `int` variables x and y.

b.   Initialize an `int` variable x to 10 and a `char` variable ch to `'B'`.

c.   Update the value of an `int` variable x by adding 5 to it.

d.   Declare and initialize a `double` variable `payRate` to 12.50.

e.   Copy the value of an `int` variable `firstNum` into an `int` variable `tempNum`.

f.   Swap the contents of the `int` variables x and y. (Declare additional variables, if necessary.)

g.   Suppose x and y are `double` variables. Output the contents of x, y, and the expression $x + 12 / y - 18$.

h.   Declare a `char` variable `grade` and set the value of `grade` to `'A'`.

i.   Declare `int` variables to store four integers.

j.   Copy the value of a `double` variable z to the nearest integer into an `int` variable x.

11. Write each of the following as a Java expression.

    a. 10 times a

    b. The character that represents 8

    c. $(b^2 - 4ac) / 2a$

    d. $(-b + (b^2 - 4ac)) / 2a$

12. Suppose x, y, z, and w are `int` variables. What value is assigned to each variable after the last statement executes?

    ```
    x = 5;
    z = 3;
    y = x - z;
    z = 2 * y + 3;
    w = x - 2 * y + z;
    z = w - x;
    w++;
    ```

13. Suppose x, y, and z are `int` variables and w and t are `double` variables. What is the value of each variable after the last statement executes?

    ```
    x = 17;
    y = 15;
    x = x + y / 4;
    z = x % 3 + 4;
    w = 17 / 3 + 6.5;
    t = x / 4.0 + 15 % 4 - 3.5;
    ```

14. Suppose x and y are `int` variables and x = 25 and y = 35. What is the output of each of the following statements?

    a. `System.out.println(x + ' ' + y);`

    b. `System.out.println(x + " " + y);`

15. Suppose x, y, and z are `int` variables and x = 2, y = 5, and z = 6. What is the output of each of the following statements?

    a. `System.out.println("x = " + x + ", y = " + y + ", z = " + z);`

    b. `System.out.println("x + y = " + (x + y));`

    c. `System.out.println("Sum of " + x + " and " + z + " is " + (x + z));`

    d. `System.out.println("z / x = " + (z / x));`

    e. `System.out.println(" 2 times " + x + " = " + (2 * x));`

16. What is the output of the following statements? Suppose a and b are `int` variables, c is a `double` variable, and a = 13, b = 5, and c = 17.5.

    a. `System.out.println(a + b - c);`

    b. `System.out.println(15 / 2 + c);`

    c. `System.out.println(a / (double)(b) + 2 * c);`

    d. `System.out.println(14 % 3 + 6.3 + b / a);`

    e. `System.out.println((int)(c) % 5 + a - b);`

    f. `System.out.println(13.5 / 2 + 4.0 * 3.5 + 18);`

17. How do you print the carriage return?

18. Which of the following are correct Java statements?

    a. `System.out.println("Hello There!");`

    b. `System.out.println("Hello");`
       `(" There!");`

    c. `System.out.println("Hello" +`
       `" There!");`

    d. `System.out.println('Hello There!');`

19. The following two programs have syntax errors. Correct them. On each successive line, assume that any preceding error has been corrected. After you have corrected the syntax errors, type and compile these programs to check if all errors have been found.

    a.
    ```java
    public class ProgWithErrorsA
    {
        static final int  SECRET_NUM = 11,213;
        static final PAY_RATE = 18.35
        public void main(String[] arg)
        {
            int one, two;
            double first, second;

            one = 18;
            two = 11;

            first = 25;
            second = first * three;

            second = 2 * SECRET_NUM;
            SECRET_NUM = SECRET_NUM + 3;
            System.out.println(first + " " + second + " " + SECRET_NUM);

            paycheck = hoursWorked * PAY_RATE

            System.out.println("Wages = "  paycheck);
        }
    }
    ```

    b.
    ```java
    public class ProgWithErrorsB
    {
        static final char = STAR = '*'
        static final int  PRIME = 71;

        public static void main(String[] arg)
        {
            count = 1;
            sum = count + PRIME;
            x := 25.67;
            newNum = count * ONE + 2;
            sum + count = sum;
    ```

```
            x = x + sum * COUNT;
            System.out.println(" count = " + count + ", sum = "
                              + sum + ", PRIME = " + Prime);

        }
    }
```

20. Write equivalent compound statements for the following, if possible.

    a.   `x = 2 * x;`

    b.   `x = x + y - 2;`

    c.   `sum = sum + num;`

    d.   `z = z * x + 2 * z;`

    e.   `y = y / (x + 5);`

21. Write the following compound statements as equivalent simple statements.

    a.   `x += 5 - z;`

    b.   `y *= 2 * x + 5 - z;`

    c.   `w += 2 * z + 4;`

    d.   `x -= z + y - t;`

    e.   `sum += num;`

    f.   `x /= y - 2;`

22. Suppose a, b, and c are `int` variables and a = 5 and b = 6. What value is assigned to each variable after each statement executes? If a variable is undefined at a particular statement, report UND (undefined).

	a	b	c
`a = (b++) + 3;`			
`c = 2 * a + (++b);`			
`b = 2 * (++c) - (a++);`			

23. Suppose a, b, and sum are `int` variables and c is a `double` variable. What value is assigned to each variable after each statement executes? Suppose a = 3, b = 5, and c = 14.1.

	a	b	c	sum
`sum = a + b + (int) c;`				
`c /= a;`				
`b += (int) c - a;`				
`a *= 2 * b + (int) c;`				

24. What is printed by the following program? Suppose the input is:

    20 15

```
import java.util.*;
public class Mystery
{
    static Scanner console = new Scanner(System.in);

    static final int NUM = 10;
    static final double X = 20.5;
```

```java
public static void main(String[] arg)
{
    int a, b;
    double z;
    char grade;

    a = 25;

    System.out.println("a = " + a);

    System.out.print("Enter the first integers: ");
    a = console.nextInt();
    System.out.println();

    System.out.print("Enter the second integers: ");
    b = console.nextInt();
    System.out.println();

    System.out.println("The numbers you entered are "
                        + a + " and " + b);

    z = X + 2 * a - b;

    System.out.println("z = " + z);

    grade = 'A';
    System.out.println("Your grade is " + grade);

    a = 2 * NUM + (int) z;
    System.out.println("The value of a = " + a);
    }
}
```

25. What is printed by the following program? Suppose the input is:

```
Miller
34
340
```

```java
import java.util.*;

public class Exercise25
{
    static Scanner console = new Scanner(System.in);

    static final int PRIME_NUM = 11;

    public static void main(String[] arg)
    {
        final int SECRET = 17;
```

```
            String name;
            int id;
            int num;
            int mysteryNum;

            System.out.print("Enter last name: ");
            name = console.next();
            System.out.println();

            System.out.print("Enter a two digit number: ");
            num = console.nextInt();
            System.out.println();

            id = 100 * num + SECRET;

            System.out.print("Enter a positive integer less than 1000: ");
            num = console.nextInt();
            System.out.println();

            mysteryNum = num * PRIME_NUM - 3 * SECRET;

            System.out.println("Name: " + name);
            System.out.println("Id: " + id);
            System.out.println("Mystery number: " + mysteryNum);
        }
    }
```

26. Rewrite the following program so that it is formatted properly.

```
import java.util.*;
public class Exercise26
{ static Scanner console = new Scanner(System.in);
static final double X = 13.45; static final int Y=34;
static final char BLANK= ' ';
public static void main(String[] arg)
{String firstName,lastName;int num;
double salary;
System.out.print("Enter first name: "); firstName=
console.next();System.out.println();
System.out.print("Enter last name: ");
lastName=console.next();System.out.println();
    System.out.print("Enter a positive integer less than 70:";
num = console.nextInt();System.out.println();salary=num*X;
 System.out.println("Name: " + firstName + BLANK + lastName);
System.out.println("Wages: $"+salary); System.out.println("X = " + X);
 System.out.println("X+Y = " + (X+Y));
}}
```

27. What type of input does the following program require, and in what order must the input be provided?

```
import java.util.*;

public class Strange
```

```
{
    static Scanner console = new Scanner(System.in);

    public static void main(String[] arg)
    {
        int x;
        int y;

        String name;

        x = console.nextInt();
        name = console.nextLine();
        y = console.nextInt();
    }
}
```

PROGRAMMING EXERCISES

1. Write a program that produces the following output:

```
**********************************
*     Programming Assignment 1    *
*       Computer Programming I     *
*         Author: Duffy Ducky      *
*     Due Date: Thursday, Jan. 24  *
**********************************
```

2. Write a program that prints the following banner:

```
JJJJJJJJJJJJ      AAA      VV          VV      AAA
      JJ        AA AA     VV          VV     AA AA
      JJ        AA   AA     VV        VV     AA    AA
      JJ      AAAAAAAAA      VV      VV    AAAAAAAAA
 JJ   JJ      AA      AA      VV VV       AA        AA
 JJJJJ        AA        AA      VVV       AA          AA
```

3. Consider the following program segment:

```
//import classes

public class Exercise3
{
    public static void main(String[] args)
    {
        //variable declaration

        //executable statements
    }
}
```

a. Write Java statements that declare the following variables: num1, num2, and num3, and average of type int.

b. Write Java statements that store 125 into num1, 28 into num2, and -25 into num3.

c. Write a Java statement that stores the average of num1, num2, and num3 into average.

d. Write Java statements that output the values of num1, num2, num3, and average.

e. Compile and run your program.

4. Repeat Exercise 3 by declaring num1, num2, and num3, and average of type double. Store 75.35 into num1, -35.56 into num2, and 15.76 into num3.

5. Consider the following program segment:

```
//import classes

public class Exercise5
{
    public static void main(String[] args)
    {
        //variable declaration

        //executable statements
    }
}
```

a. Write a Java statement that imports the class Scanner.

b. Write a Java statement that declares console to be a Scanner object for inputting data from the standard input device.

c. Write Java statements that declare and initialize the following named constants: SECRET of type int initialized to 11; RATE of type double initialized to 12.50.

d. Write Java statements that declare the following variables: num1, num2, and newNum of type int; name of type String; hoursWorked and wages of type double.

e. Write Java statements that prompt the user to input two integers and store the first number into num1 and the second number into num2.

f. Write a Java statement(s) that outputs the value of num1 and num2, indicating which is num1 and which is num2. For example, if num1 is 8 and num2 is 5, then the output is:

```
The value of num1 = 8 and the value of num2 = 5.
```

g. Write a Java statement that multiplies that value of num1 by 2, adds the value of num2 to it, and then stores the result in newNum. Then write a Java statement that outputs the value of newNum.

h. Write a Java statement that updates the value of `newNum` by adding the value of the named constant `SECRET`. Then, write a Java statement that outputs the value of `newNum` with an appropriate message.

i. Write Java statements that prompt the user to enter a person's last name and then store the last name into the variable `name`.

j. Write Java statements that prompt the user to enter a decimal number between 0 and 70 and then store the number entered into `hoursWorked`.

k. Write a Java statement that multiplies that value of the named constant `RATE` with the value of `hoursWorked` and stores the result into the variable `wages`.

l. Write Java statements that produce the following output:

```
Name:            //output the value of the variable name
Pay Rate: $      //output the value of the named constant RATE
Hours Worked:    //output the value of the variable hoursWorked
Salary: $        //output the value of the variable wages
```

For example, if the value of `name` is `"Rainbow"` and `hoursWorked` is `45.50`, then the output is:

```
Name: Rainbow
Pay Rate: $12.50
Hours Worked: 45.50
Salary: $568.75
```

m. Write a Java program that tests each of the Java statements in parts (a)—(l). Place the statements at the appropriate place in the preceding Java program segment. Test run your program (twice) on the following input data:

  i. `num1 = 13, num2 = 28; name = "Jacobson"; hoursWorked = 48.30.`

  ii. `num1 = 32, num2 = 15; name = "Cynthia"; hoursWorked = 58.45.`

6. Write a program that prompts the user to input a decimal number and outputs the number rounded to the nearest integer.

7. Write a program that prompts the user to input the length and width of a rectangle and then prints the rectangle's area and perimeter.

8. Write a program that prompts the user to enter five test scores and then prints the average test score.

9. Write a program that prompts the user to input five decimal numbers. The program should then add the five decimal numbers, convert the sum to the nearest integer, and print the result.

10. Write a program that does the following:

  a. Prompts the user to input five decimal numbers

  b. Prints the five decimal numbers

2

c. Converts each decimal number to the nearest integer

d. Adds the five integers

e. Prints the sum and average of the five integers

11. Write a program that prompts the user to input a four-digit positive integer. The program then outputs the digits of the number, one digit per line. For example, if the input is 3245, the output is:

```
3
2
4
5
```

12. Write a Java program that prompts the user to input the elapsed time for an event in seconds. The program then outputs the elapsed time in hours, minutes, and seconds. (For example, if the elapsed time is 9630 seconds, then the output is 2:40:30.)

13. Write a Java program that prompts the user to input the elapsed time for an event in hours, minutes, and seconds. The program then outputs the elapsed time in seconds.

14. To make a profit, a local store marks up the prices of its items by a certain percentage. Write a Java program that reads the original price of the item sold, the percentage of the marked-up price, and the sales tax rate. The program then outputs the original price of the item, the marked-up percentage of the item, the store's selling price of the item, the sales tax rate, the sales tax, and the final price of the item. (The final price of the item is the selling price plus the sales tax.)

15. Write a program to implement and test the algorithm that you designed for Exercise 15 of Chapter 1. (You may assume that the value of $\pi = 3.141593$. In your program, declare a named constant PI to store this value.)

16. A milk carton can hold 3.78 liters of milk. Each morning, a dairy farm ships cartons of milk to a local grocery store. The cost of producing one liter of milk is $0.38, and the profit of each carton of milk is $0.27. Write a program that does the following:

a. Prompts the user to enter the total amount of milk produced in the morning

b. Outputs the number of milk cartons needed to hold milk (Round your answer to the nearest integer.)

c. Outputs the cost of producing milk

d. Outputs the profit for producing milk

17. Redo Programming Exercise 16 so that the user can also input the cost of producing one liter of milk and the profit on each carton of milk.

18. You found an exciting summer job for five weeks. It pays $15.50 per hour. Suppose that the total tax you pay on your summer job income is 14%. After paying the taxes, you spend 10% of your net income to buy new clothes and other accessories for the next school year and 1% to buy school supplies. After buying clothes and school supplies, you use 25% of the remaining money to buy savings bonds. For each dollar you spend to buy savings bonds, your parents spend $0.50 to buy additional savings bonds for you. Write a program that prompts the user to enter the pay rate for an hour and the number of hours you worked each week. The program then outputs the following:

   a. Your income before and after taxes from your summer job

   b. The money you spend on clothes and other accessories

   c. The money you spend on school supplies

   d. The money you spend to buy savings bonds

   e. The money your parents spend to buy additional savings bonds for you

19. A permutation of three objects, *a*, *b*, and *c*, is any arrangement of these objects in a row. For example, some of the permutations of these objects are *abc*, *bca*, and *cab*. The number of permutations of three objects is 6. Suppose that these three objects are strings. Write a program that prompts the user to enter three strings. The program then outputs the six permutations of those strings.

20. Write a program that computes the cost of painting and installing carpet in a room. Assume that the room has one door, two windows, and one book-shelf. Your program must do the following:

   a. Prompts the user to enter, in feet, the length, width, and height of a room. Read the dimensions of the room.

   b. Prompts the user to enter the widths and heights, in feet, of the door, each window, and the bookshelf. Read these quantities.

   c. Prompts the user to enter the cost, per square foot, of painting the walls. Read these quantities.

   d. Prompts the user to enter of cost, per square foot, of installing carpet. Read these quantities.

   e. Outputs the cost of painting the walls and installing the carpet.

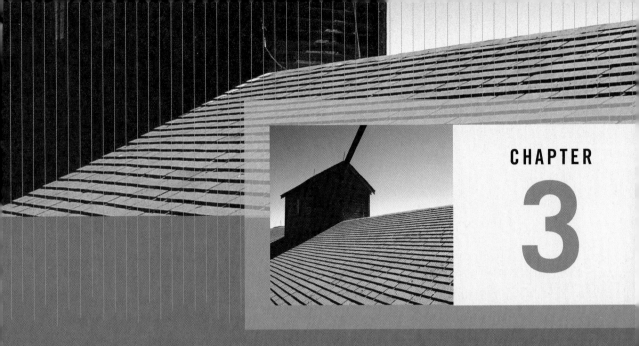

INTRODUCTION TO OBJECTS AND INPUT/OUTPUT

IN THIS CHAPTER, YOU WILL:

- Learn about objects and reference variables
- Explore how to use predefined methods in a program
- Become familiar with the `class String`
- Explore how to format output using the method `printf`
- Learn how to use input and output dialog boxes in a program
- Become familiar with the `String` method `format`
- Become familiar with file input and output
- Learn debugging by understanding error messages

Chapter 2 introduced you to the basic elements of Java programs, including special symbols and identifiers, primitive data types, arithmetic operators, and the order of precedence of arithmetic operators. You were briefly introduced to the `class` `String` for processing strings, the `class` `Scanner` for inputting data into a program, and general rules on programming style. In this chapter, you will learn more about input and output and how to use predefined methods in your programs. You will also learn, in some detail, how to use the `class` `String` to process strings.

Objects and Reference Variables

Three terms that you will encounter repeatedly throughout this book are variables, reference variables, and objects. We define these terms now so you will be familiar with them.

In Chapter 2, you learned about the primitive data types, such as `int`, `double`, and `char`. You also worked with strings. We used `String` variables to manipulate or process strings.

Consider the following statement:

```
int x;              //Line 1
```

This statement declares `x` to be an `int` variable. Now consider the statement:

```
String str;         //Line 2
```

This statement declares `str` to be a variable of type `String`.

The statement in Line 1 allocates memory space to store an `int` value and calls this memory space `x`. The variable `x` can store an `int` value in its memory space. For example, the following statement stores 45 in `x`, as shown in Figure 3-1:

```
x = 45;             //Line 3
```

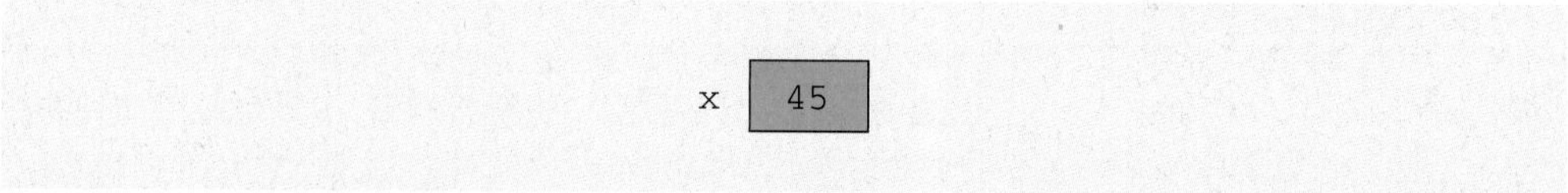

$$x \quad \boxed{45}$$

FIGURE 3-1 Variable x and its data

Next, let us see what happens with the statement in Line 2. This statement allocates memory space for the variable `str`. However, unlike the variable `x`, the variable `str` *cannot* directly store data in its memory space. The variable `str` stores the memory location, that is, the address of the memory space where the actual data is stored. For example, the effect of the statement:

```
str = "Java Programming";      //Line 4
```

is shown in Figure 3-2.

```
                                    2500
          str    2500          Java Programming
```

FIGURE 3-2 Variable `str` and the data it points to

For the `String` variable `str`, the statement in Line 4 causes the system to allocate memory space starting at, say, location 2500, stores the string (literal) `"Java Programming"` in this memory space, and then stores the address 2500 in the memory space of `str`.

The next obvious question is: How does this happen? In reality, *for the most part*, the effect of the statement in Line 4 is the same as the effect of the following statement:

```
str = new String("Java Programming");    //Line 5
```

In Java, `new` is an operator. It causes the system to allocate memory space of a specific type, store specific data in that memory space, and return the address of the memory space. Therefore, the statement in Line 4 causes the system to allocate memory space large enough to store the string (literal) `"Java Programming"`, stores this string in that memory space, and returns the address of the allocated memory space. The assignment operator stores the address of that memory space into the variable `str`.

NOTE As noted, for the most part the effects of the statements in Lines 4 and 5 are the same. In both the cases, the `String` variable `str` will point to a memory location that contains the string `"Java Programming"`. Note that in the statement in Line 5, the operator `new` is used explicitly, while the statement in Line 4 does not explicitly use the operator `new`. In reality, when the statement in Line 4 executes, it first looks if the program has already created the string `"Java Programming"`. If this is the case, then the `String` variable `str` will point to that memory location. However, when the statement in Line 5 executes, the system will allocate a memory space, store the string `"Java Programming"` into that memory space, and then store the address of that memory space into `str`. This is a key difference and plays an important role when strings and `String` variables are compared, which we will explain in Chapter 4.

`String` is not a primitive data type. In Java terminology, the data type `String` is defined by the `class` String. In this and subsequent chapters, you will encounter some other classes provided by the Java system. In Chapter 8, you will learn how to create your own classes.

In Java, variables such as `str` are called **reference variables**. More formally, reference variables are variables that store the address of a memory space. In Java, any variable declared using a `class` (such as the variable `str`) is a reference variable. Because `str` is a reference variable declared using the `class` String, we say that `str` is a reference variable of the `String` type.

The memory space 2500, where the string (literal) **"Java Programming"** is stored, is called a **String object**. We call String objects **instances** of the **class** String.

Because str is a reference variable of the String type, str can store the address of any String object. In other words, str can point to or refer to any String object. Moreover, it follows that we are dealing with two different things—the reference variable str and the String object that str points to. We call the String object that str points to, which is at memory space 2500 in Figure 3-2, the object str.

To emphasize that the String object at memory space 2500 is the object str, we can redraw Figure 3-2 as Figure 3-3.

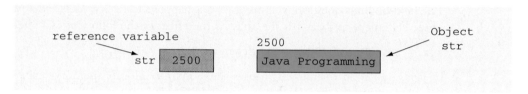

FIGURE 3-3 Variable str and object str

Using the operator **new** to create a **class** object is called **instantiating** an object of that **class**.

Let us summarize the Java terminology used in the preceding paragraphs, especially the use of the terms *variable* and *object*. While working with classes, we declare a reference variable of a **class** type and then, typically, we use the operator **new** to instantiate an object of that **class** type and store the address of the object into the reference variable. For example, suppose that refVar is a reference variable of a **class** type. When we use the term *variable* refVar, we mean the value of refVar, that is, the address stored in refVar. When we use the term *object* refVar, we mean the object whose address is stored in refVar. The object that refVar points to can be accessed via the variable refVar.

The next question is: How can you change the value of the object from **"Java Programming"**, as shown in Figure 3-3, to **"Hello there!"**? To do so, you must look at the **class** String and see if it provides a method that allows you to change the value of the (*existing*) object from **"Java Programming"** to **"Hello there!"**. (The next section briefly describes what a method is.) Unfortunately, the **class** String does not provide any such method. (The **class** String is discussed in some detail later in this chapter.) In other words, the value of the String object at memory space 2500 cannot be altered. It thus follows that String objects are *immutable*; that is, once they are created, they cannot be changed.

You could execute another statement, similar to the statement in Line 4, with the value **"Hello there!"**. Suppose that the following statement is executed:

```
str = "Hello there!";
```

This statement would again cause the system to allocate memory space to store the string **"Hello there!"**, if no such string already exists, and the address of that memory space would be stored in str. However, the address of the allocated memory space will be different from that in the first statement. To be specific, suppose that the address of the allocated memory space is 3850. Figure 3-4 illustrates the result.

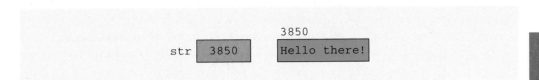

FIGURE 3-4 Variable str, its value, and the object str

This is an important property of reference variables of the **String** type and **String** objects, and must be recognized and understood. Furthermore, it is especially important to understand this property when we start comparing strings.

To simplify Figure 3-4, we usually use the format shown in Figure 3-5.

FIGURE 3-5 Variable str and the object str

In Figure 3-5, the arrow originating in the box **str** means that **str** contains an address. The arrow pointing to the memory space containing the value **"Hello there!"** means that the variable **str** contains the address of the object containing the value **"Hello there!"**. We will use this arrow notation to help explain various examples.

You might ask: What happened to memory space 2500 and the string **"Java Programming"** stored in it? If no other **String** variable refers to it, then sometime during program execution, the Java system reclaims this memory space for later use. This is called **garbage collection**.

NOTE If you do not want to depend on the system to choose when to perform garbage collection, then you can include the statement:

```
System.gc();
```

in your program to instruct the computer to run the garbage collector (immediately). In general, it is not necessary to do so.

We can now summarize the discussion of the preceding sections. You can declare two types of variables in Java: primitive type variables and reference variables, as shown in Figure 3-6.

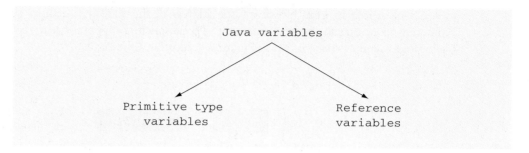

FIGURE 3-6 Java variables

Primitive type variables store data *directly* into their own memory spaces. Reference variables store the address of the object containing the data. An object is an instance of a `class` and the operator `new` is used to instantiate an object. In some languages, such as C++, reference variables are called *pointers*.

Before discussing the `class` `String`, we first discuss how to use predefined methods in a program.

Using Predefined Classes and Methods in a Program

Recall that a **method** is a collection of instructions. When a method executes, it accomplishes something. The method `main`, which you used in Chapter 2, executes automatically when you run a Java program. Other methods execute only when they are activated—that is, called. Java comes with a wealth of classes called **predefined classes**. In addition, every predefined `class` contains many predefined methods, which accomplish useful results. In this section, you do not learn how to write your own methods, but you do learn how to use some of the predefined classes and methods that accompany Java.

Recall from Chapter 2 that predefined classes are organized as a collection of packages, called **class libraries**. A particular `package` can contain several classes and each `class` can contain several methods. Therefore, to use a predefined `class` and/or a method, you need to know the name of the `package`, the name of the `class`, and the name of the method. To use a method, you also need to know a few other things, which are described shortly.

There are two types of methods in a `class`: `static` and non-`static`. A `static` method can be used, that is, called, using the name of the `class` containing the method. (Chapter 8 describes these methods in detail. At this point, you need to know only how to use predefined methods, which may be `static` or non-`static`.)

The Java system contains the `class` `Math`, which in turn contains powerful and useful mathematical functions. The `class` `Math` is contained in the `package` `java.lang`. Every method of the `class` `Math` is a `static` method. Therefore, you can use every method of the `class` `Math` using the name of the `class`, which is `Math`.

The **class** Math contains a very useful method, pow, called the method **power**, which is used to calculate x^y in a program, that is, Math.pow(x, y) = x^y. For example, Math.pow(2,3) = 2^3 = 8 and Math.pow(4, 0.5) = $4^{0.5}$ = $\sqrt{4}$ = 2. The numbers x and y used in the method pow are called the (*actual*) **parameters** of the method pow. For example, in Math.pow(2, 3), the parameters are 2 and 3.

An expression such as Math.pow(2, 3) is called a method call, and causes the code attached to the method pow to execute and, in this case, computes 2^3. The method pow computes a value of type **double**. Therefore, we say that the return type of the method pow is **double** or the method pow is of type **double**.

In general, to use a predefined method in a program:

1. You need to know the name of the **class** containing the method.
2. You need to know the name of the **package** containing the **class** and import this **class** from the **package** in the program.
3. You need to know the name of the method as well as the number of parameters the method takes, the type of each parameter, and the order of the parameters. You must also be aware of the return type of the method or, loosely speaking, what the method produces.

For example, to use the method nextInt, you import the **class** Scanner from the **package** java.util.

> **NOTE**
>
> As noted in Chapter 2, the Java system automatically imports methods and **classes** from the **package** java.lang. Therefore, you do not need to import any contents of the **package** java.lang explicitly. Because the **class** Math is contained in the **package** java.lang, to use the method pow, you need to know that the name of the method is pow, that the method pow has two parameters, both of which are numbers, and that the method calculates the first parameter to the power of the second parameter.

The program in the following example illustrates how to use predefined methods in a program. More specifically, we use some math methods. Later in this chapter, after introducing the **class** String, we will show how to use String methods in a program.

EXAMPLE 3-1

```
public class PredefinedMethods
{
    public static void main(String[] args)
    {
        double u, v;

        System.out.println("Line 1: 2 to the power "
                    + "of 6 = " + Math.pow(2, 6));    //Line 1
```

```
        u = 12.5;                                          //Line 2
        v = 3.0;                                           //Line 3
        System.out.println("Line 4: " + u + " to "
                     + "the power of " +  v
                     + " = " + Math.pow(u, v));            //Line 4

        System.out.println("Line 5: Square root of "
                     + "42.25 = "
                     + Math.sqrt(42.25));                  //Line 5

        u = Math.pow(8.5, 2.0);                            //Line 6
        System.out.println("Line 7: u = " + u);            //Line 7
    }
}
```

Sample Run:

```
Line 1: 2 to the power of 6 = 64.0
Line 4: 12.5 to the power of 3.0 = 1953.125
Line 5: Square root of 42.25 = 6.5
Line 7: u = 72.25
```

The preceding program works as follows. The statement in Line 1 uses the function pow to determine and output 2^6. The statement in Line 2 sets u to 12.5, and the statement in Line 3 sets v to 3.0. The statement in Line 4 determines and outputs u^v. The statement in Line 5 uses the method sqrt, of the **class** Math, to determine and output the square root of 42.25. The statement in Line 6 determines and assigns 8.5^2 to u. The statement in Line 7 outputs the value of u.

Dot Between Class (Object) Name and Class Member: A Precaution

In Chapter 2, you learned how to use the method nextInt of the **class** Scanner to input the next token, which can be expressed as an integer. In the preceding section, you learned how to use the method pow of the **class** Math.

Consider the following statement:

```
x = console.nextInt();
```

where x is a variable of type int. Notice the dot between console and nextInt; the name of the object console and the name of the method nextInt are separated by the dot.

In Java, the dot (.) is an operator called the **member access operator**.

Omitting the dot between console and nextInt results in a syntax error. In the statement:

```
x = consolenextInt();
```

`consolenextInt` becomes a new identifier. If you used `consolenextInt` in a program, the compiler (could) generate an undeclared identifier syntax error. Similarly, omitting the parentheses, as in `console.nextInt`, also results in a syntax error.

Usually, several methods and/or variables are associated with a particular `class`, each doing a specific job. In the dot notation, the dot separates the `class` variable name, that is, the object name from the member, or method, name. *It is also worth noting that* `methods` *are distinguished from (reference) variables by the presence of parentheses, and methods that have no parameters must have empty parentheses* (like in `nextInt()`). For example, `console` is the name of a (reference) variable, and `nextInt` is the name of a method.

3

class String

This section explains how to use `String` methods to manipulate strings. First, we review some terminology that we typically use while working with strings and the `class` `String`.

Consider the following statements:

```
String name;           //Line 1
name = "Lisa Johnson"; //Line 2
```

The statement in Line 1 declares `name` to be a `String` variable. The statement in Line 2 creates the string `"Lisa Johnson"` and assigns it to `name`.

In the statement in Line 2, we usually say that the `String` object, or the string `"Lisa Johnson"`, is assigned to the `String` variable or the variable `name`. In reality, as explained before, a `String` *object* with the value `"Lisa Johnson"` is instantiated (if it has not already been created) and the address of the object is stored in `name`. Whenever we use the term "the string `name`", we are referring to the object containing the string `"Lisa Johnson"`. Similarly, when we use the terms (reference) variable `name` or `String` variable `name`, we simply mean `name`, whose value is an address.

The remainder of this section describes various features of the `class` `String`. In Chapter 2, you learned that two strings can be joined using the operator +. The `class` `String` provides various methods that allow us to process strings in various ways. For example, we can find the length of a string, extract part of a string, find the position of a particular string in another string, convert a number into a string, and convert a numeric string into a number.

Each method associated with the `class` `String` implements a specific operation and has a specific name. For example, the method for determining the length of a string is named `length`, and the method for extracting a string from within another string is named `substring`.

As explained in the earlier section, Using Predefined Classes and Methods in a Program, in general, to use a method you must know the name of the `class` containing the method and the name of the `package` containing the `class`, you must import the `class`, and you must know the method name, its parameters, and what the method does. However, because the Java system automatically makes the `class` String available, you do not need to import this `class`. Therefore, in order to use a `String` method, you need to know its name, parameters, and what the method does.

Recall that a string (literal) is a sequence of 0 or more characters, and string literals are enclosed in double quotation marks. The **index** (position) of the first character is 0, the index of the second character is 1, and so on. The length of a string is the number of characters in it, not the largest index.

 NOTE If `length` denotes the length of a string and `length` is not zero (that is, string is not null), then `length` − 1 gives the index of the last character in the string.

The general expression to use a `String` method on a `String` variable is:

`StringVariable.StringMethodName(parameters)`

In this statement, the variable name and the method name are separated with the dot (`.`). For example, if `name` is a `String` variable, and `name = "Lisa Johnson"`, then the value of the expression

`name.length()`

is 12.

Table 3-1 lists commonly used methods of the `class` String. Suppose that `sentence` is a `String`. Suppose that `sentence = "Programming with Java";`. Then each character in `sentence` and its position is as follows:

sentence = "Programming with Java";																				
P	r	o	g	r	a	m	m	i	n	g	' '	w	i	t	h	' '	J	a	v	a
0	1	2	3	4	5	6	7	8	9	10	11	12	13	14	15	16	17	18	19	20

TABLE 3-1 Some Commonly Used `String` Methods

```
char charAt(int index)
   //Returns the character at the position specified by index
   //Example: sentence.charAt(3) returns 'g'

int indexOf(char ch)
   //Returns the index of the first occurrence of the character
   //specified by ch; If the character specified by ch does not
   //appear in the string, it returns -1
   //Example: sentence.indexOf('J') returns 17
   //         sentence.indexOf('a') returns 5
```

TABLE 3-1 Some Commonly Used `String` Methods (continued)

```
int indexOf(char ch, int pos)
   //Returns the index of the first occurrence of the character
   //specified by ch; The parameter pos specifies where to
   //begin the search; If the character specified by ch does not
   //appear in the string, it returns -1
   //Example: sentence.indexOf('a', 10) returns 18
```

```
int indexOf(String str)
   //Returns the index of the first occurrence of the string
   //specified by str; If the string specified by str does not
   //appear in the string, it returns -1
   //Example: sentence.indexOf("with") returns 12
   //          sentence.indexOf("ing") returns 8
```

```
int indexOf(String str, int pos)
   //Returns the index of the first occurrence of the String
   //specified by str; The parameter pos specifies where to begin
   //the search; If the string specified by str does not appear
   //in the string, it returns -1
   //Example: sentence.indexOf("a", 10) returns 18
   //          sentence.indexOf("Pr", 10) returns -1
```

```
String concat(String str)
   //Returns the string that is this string concatenated with str
   //Example: The expression
   //          sentence.concat(" is fun.")
   //          returns the string "Programming with Java is fun."
```

```
int compareTo(String str)
   //Compares two strings character by character
   //Returns a negative value if this string is less than str
   //Returns 0 if this string is same as str
   //Returns a positive value if this string is greater than str
```

```
boolean equals(String str)
   //Returns true if this string is same as str
```

```
int length()
   //Returns the length of the string
   //Example: sentence.length() returns 21, the number of characters in
   //          "Programming with Java"
```

```
String replace(char charToBeReplaced, char charReplacedWith)
   //Returns the string in which every occurrence of
   //charToBeReplaced is replaced with charReplacedWith
   //Example: sentence.replace('a', '*') returns the string
   //          "Progr*mming with J*v*"
   //          Each occurrence of a is replaced with *
```

TABLE 3-1 Some Commonly Used `String` Methods (continued)

```
String substring(int beginIndex)
  //Returns the string which is a substring of this string
  //beginning at beginIndex until the end of the string.
  //Example: sentence.substring(12) returns the string
  //          "with Java"

String substring(int beginIndex, int endIndex)
  //Returns the string which is a substring of this string
  //beginning at beginIndex until endIndex - 1

String toLowerCase()
  //Returns the string that is the same as this string, except
  //that all uppercase letters of this string are replaced with
  //their equivalent lowercase letters
  //Example: sentence.toLowerCase() returns "programming with java"

String toUpperCase()
  //Returns the string that is the same as this string, except
  //that all lowercase letters of this string are replaced with
  //their equivalent uppercase letters
  //Example: sentence.toUpperCase() returns "PROGRAMMING WITH JAVA"

boolean startsWith(String str)
  //Returns true if the string begins with the string specified by str;
  //otherwise, this methods returns false.

boolean endsWith(String str)
  //Returns true if the string ends with the string specified by str
  //otherwise, this methods returns false.

boolean regionMatches(int ind, String str, int strIndex, int len)
  //Returns true if the substring of str starting at strIndex and length
  //specified by len is same as the substring of this String
  //object starting at ind and having the same length

boolean regionMatches(boolean ignoreCase, int ind,
                      String str, int strIndex, int len)
  //Returns true if the substring of str starting at strIndex and length
  //specified by len is same as the substring of this String
  //object starting at ind and having the same length. If ignoreCase
  //is true, then during character comparison, case is ignored.
```

NOTE Table 3-1 lists only some of the methods for string manipulation. Moreover, the table gives only the name of the method, the number of parameters, and the type of the method. The reader can find a list of `String` methods at the Web site *http://java.sun.com/javase/6/docs/api/*. The methods `equals` and `compareTo` are explained in Chapter 4 and the methods, `startsWith`, `endsWith`, and `regionMatches` are explained in Example 3-3.

EXAMPLE 3-2

Consider the following statements:

```
String sentence;
String str1;
String str2;
int index;

sentence = "Now is the time for the birthday party.";
```

The following statements further show how String methods work.

Statement	Effect / Explanation
sentence.charAt(16)	Returns: 'f' In sentence, the character at position 16 is 'f'.
sentence.length()	Returns: 38 The number of characters in sentence is 38.
sentence.indexOf('t')	Returns: 7 This is the index of the first 't' in sentence.
sentence.indexOf("for")	Returns: 16 In sentence, the starting index of the string "for".
sentence.substring(0, 6)	Returns: "Now is" In sentence, the substring starting at index 0 until the index 5 (= 6 – 1) is "Now is".
sentence.substring(7, 12)	Returns: "the t" In sentence, the substring starting at index 7 until the index 11 (= 12 – 1) is "the t".
sentence.substring(7, 22)	Returns: "the time for th" In sentence, the substring starting at index 7 until the index 21 (= 22 – 1) is "the time for th".
sentence.substring(4, 10)	Returns: "is the" In sentence, the substring starting at index 4 until the index 9 (= 10 – 1) is "is the".
str1 = sentence.substring(0, 8);	str1 = "Now is t" In sentence, the substring starting at index 0 until the index 7 (= 8 – 1) is "Now is t". So the value assigned to str1 is "Now is t".

Statement	Effect / Explanation
`str2 = sentence.substring(2, 12);`	`str2 = "w is the t"`
	In `sentence`, the substring starting at index 2 until the index $11 (= 12 - 1)$ is `"w is the t"`. So the value assigned to `str2` is `"w is the t"`.
`index = sentence.indexOf("birthday");` `str1 = sentence.substring(index, index + 14);`	`index = 24` `str1 = "birthday party"`
	The starting index of `"birthday"` in `sentence` is 24. So the value of index is 24. Now index is 24, so index + 14 is 38. The substring starting at the position 24 until the position $37 (= 38 - 1)$ is `"birthday party"`.
`sentence.replace('t', 'T')`	Returns: `"Now is The Time for The birThday parTy"`
`sentence.toUpperCase()`	Returns: `"NOW IS THE TIME FOR THE BIRTHDAY PARTY"`

The following program tests the preceding statements:

```java
// This program illustrate how various String methods work.

public class VariousStringMethods
{
    public static void main(String[] args)
    {
        String sentence;
        String str1;
        String str2;
        String str3;
        int index;

        sentence = "Now is the time for the birthday party";

        System.out.println("sentence = \"" + sentence + "\"");
        System.out.println("The length of sentence = "
                        + sentence.length());

        System.out.println("The character at index 16 in "
                        + "sentence = " + sentence.charAt(16));

        System.out.println("The index of first t in sentence = "
                        + sentence.indexOf('t'));

        System.out.println("The index of for in sentence = "
                        + sentence.indexOf("for"));
```

```
            System.out.println("sentence.substring(0, 6) = \""
                            + sentence.substring(0, 6) + "\"");

            System.out.println("sentence.substring(7, 12) = \""
                            + sentence.substring(7, 12) + "\"");

            System.out.println("sentence.substring(7, 22) = \""
                            + sentence.substring(7, 22) + "\"");

            System.out.println("sentence.substring(4, 10) = \""
                            + sentence.substring(4, 10) + "\"");

            str1 = sentence.substring(0, 8);

            System.out.println("str1 = \"" + str1 + "\"");

            str2 = sentence.substring(2, 12);
            System.out.println("str2 = \"" + str2 + "\"");

            System.out.println("sentence in uppercase = \""
                            + sentence.toUpperCase() + "\"");

            index = sentence.indexOf("birthday");

            str1 = sentence.substring(index, index + 14);

            System.out.println("str1 = \"" + str1 + "\"");

            System.out.println("sentence.replace('t', 'T') = \""
                            + sentence.replace('t', 'T') + "\"");
    }
}
```

Sample Run:

```
sentence = "Now is the time for the birthday party"
The length of sentence = 38
The character at index 16 in sentence = f
The index of first t in sentence = 7
The index of for in sentence = 16
sentence.substring(0, 6) = "Now is"
sentence.substring(7, 12) = "the t"
sentence.substring(7, 22) = "the time for th"
sentence.substring(4, 10) = "is the"
str1 = "Now is t"
str2 = "w is the t"
sentence in uppercase = "NOW IS THE TIME FOR THE BIRTHDAY PARTY"
str1 = "birthday party"
sentence.replace('t', 'T') = "Now is The Time for The birThday parTy"
```

EXAMPLE 3-3

Consider the following statements:

```
String sentence;
String str1;
String str2;
String str3;
String str4;

sentence = "It is sunny and warm.";
str1 = "warm.";
str2 = "Programming with Java";
str3 = "sunny";
str4 = "Learning Java Programming is exciting";
```

The following statements show how `String` methods `startsWith`, `endsWith`, and `regionMatches` work.

Expression	Effect
`sentence.startsWith("It")`	Returns `true`
`sentence.startsWith(str1)`	Returns `false`
`sentence.endsWith("hot")`	Returns `false`
`sentence.endsWith(str1)`	Returns `true`
`sentence.regionMatches(6, str3, 0, 5)`	Returns `true`
`sentence.regionMatches(true, 6, "Sunny", 0, 5)`	Returns `true`
`str4.regionMatches(9, str2, 17, 4)`	Returns `true`

For the most part, the statements are straightforward. Let's look at the last three statements, which use the method `regionMatches`:

```
sentence.regionMatches(6, str3, 0, 5)
```

In this statement, we want to determine whether `str3` appears as a substring in the string `sentence` starting at position 6. Notice that the last three arguments, `str3`, 0, and 5, specify that in `str3` the starting index is 0 and the length of the substring is 5. The substring in `sentence` starting at position 6 and of length 5 matches `str3`. So this expression returns `true`.

The expression:

```
sentence.regionMatches(true, 6, "Sunny", 0, 5)
```

is similar to the previous expression, except that when the substrings are compared, the case is ignored, that is, uppercase and lowercase letters are considered the same. Next, let's look at the expression:

```
str4.regionMatches(9, str2, 17, 4)
```

In this expression, we want to determine whether the substring in str2 starting at position 17 and of length 4 is the same as the substring in str4 starting at position 9 and of length 4. This expression returns true because these substrings are the same.

The Web site and the CD accompanying this book contains the program, Ch3_SomeStringMethods.java, that shows the effect of preceding statements.

To summarize the preceding discussion of the class String:

1. String variables are reference variables.
2. A string object is an instance of the class String.
3. The class String contains various methods to process strings.
4. A String variable invokes a String method using the dot operator, the method name, and the set of arguments (if any) required by the method.

Input/Output

A program performs three basic operations: it gets data into the program, it manipulates the data, and it outputs the results. In Chapter 2, you learned how to manipulate numeric data using arithmetic operations. Because writing programs for input/output (I/O) is quite complex, Java offers extensive support for I/O operations by providing a substantial number of I/O classes, such as the class Scanner. In the remainder of this chapter, you will:

- Learn how to format output using the method printf.
- Learn other ways to input data and output results in Java.
- Learn how to format the output of decimal numbers to a specific number of decimal places.
- Learn how to instruct the program to read data from, or write output to, a file. If there is a large amount of data, inputting data from the keyboard every time you execute your program is not practical. Similarly, if the output is large or you want to save the output for later use, you must save a program's output to a file.

Formatting Output with printf

In Chapter 2, you learned how to show the output of a program on the standard output device using the standard output object System.out and the methods print and println. More specifically, to output the results, you used statements such as System.out.print(expression) and/or System.out.println(expression), where expression is evaluated and its value is output. However, the methods print and println cannot *directly* format certain outputs in a specific manner. For example, the default output of floating-point numbers is typically up to 6 decimal places for float values and up to 15 decimal places for double values. Moreover, sometimes we would like to align the output in certain columns. To format the output in a specific manner, you can use the method `printf`.

A syntax to use the method `printf` to produce the output on the standard output device is:

```
System.out.printf(formatString);
```

or:

```
System.out.printf(formatString, argumentList);
```

where `formatString` is a string specifying the format of the output and `argumentList` is a list of arguments. The `argumentList` is a list of arguments that consists of constant values, variables, or expressions. If `argumentList` has more than one argument, then the arguments are separated with commas.

For example, the statement:

```
System.out.printf("Hello there!");                          //Line 1
```

consists of only the format string, and the statement:

```
System.out.printf("There are %.2f inches in %d centimeters.%n",
                  centimeters / 2.54, centimeters);         //Line 2
```

consists of both the format string and `argumentList`, where `centimeters` is a variable of type `int`. Notice that the argument list consists of the expression `centimeters / 2.54` and the variable `centimeters`. Also notice that the format string consists of the two expressions, `%.2f` and `%d`; these are called **format specifiers**. By default, format specifiers and the arguments in `argumentList` have a one-to-one correspondence. Here, the first format specifier `%.2f` is matched with the first argument, which is the expression `centimeters / 2.54`. It says to output the value of the expression `centimeters / 2.54` to two decimal places. The second format specifier `%d` is matched with the second argument, which is `centimeters`. It says to output the value of `centimeters` as a (decimal) integer. (The format specifier `%n` positions the insertion point at the beginning of the next line.)

The output of the statement in Line 1 is:

```
Hello there!
```

Suppose that the value of `centimeters` is 150. Now (to 14 decimal places):

```
centimeters / 2.54 = 150 / 2.54 = 59.05511811023622
```

Therefore, the output of the statement in Line 2 is:

```
There are 59.06 inches in 150 centimeters.
```

Notice that the value of the expression `centimeters / 2.54` is rounded and printed to two decimal places.

It follows that when outputting the format string, the format specifiers are replaced with the formatted values of the corresponding arguments.

A format specifier for general, character, and numeric types has the following syntax:

```
%[argument_index$][flags][width][.precision]conversion
```

The expressions in square brackets are optional. That is, they may or may not appear in a format specifier.

The option *argument_index* is a (decimal) integer indicating the position of the argument in the argument list. The first argument is referenced by `"1$"`, the second by `"2$"`, and so on.

The option *flags* is a set of characters that modifies the output format. The set of valid flags depends on the conversion.

The option *width* is a (decimal) integer indicating the minimum number of characters to be written to the output.

The option *precision* is a (decimal) integer usually used to restrict the number of characters. The specific behavior depends on the conversion.

The required *conversion* is a character indicating how the argument should be formatted. The set of valid conversions for a given argument depends on the argument's data type. Table 3-2 summarizes some of the supported conversions.

TABLE 3-2 Some of Java's Supported Conversions

`'s'`	general	The result is a string
`'c'`	character	The result is a Unicode character
`'d'`	integral	The result is formatted as a (decimal) integer
`'e'`	floating point	The result is formatted as a decimal number in computerized scientific notation
`'f'`	floating point	The result is formatted as a decimal number
`'%'`	percent	The result is `'%'`
`'n'`	line separator	The result is the platform-specific line separator

The method `printf` is available in Java 5.0 and higher versions.

EXAMPLE 3-4

The following program illustrates how to format the output of decimal numbers using the method `printf`:

```
//Program to illustrate how to format the outputting of
//decimal numbers.

public class FormattingDecimalNum
{
    public static void main (String[] args)
    {
        double x = 15.674;                              //Line 1
        double y = 235.73;                             //Line 2
        double z = 9525.9864;                          //Line 3

        System.out.println("Line 4: The values of x, "
                        + "y, and z with two decimal "
                        + "places.");                   //Line 4
        System.out.printf("Line 5: x = %.2f %n", x);    //Line 5
        System.out.printf("Line 6: y = %.2f %n", y);    //Line 6
        System.out.printf("Line 7: z = %.2f %n", z);    //Line 7

        System.out.println("Line 8: The values of x, "
                        + "y, and z with three decimal "
                        + "places.");                   //Line 8
        System.out.printf("Line 9: x = %.3f %n", x);    //Line 9
        System.out.printf("Line 10: y = %.3f %n", y);   //Line 10
        System.out.printf("Line 11: z = %.3f %n", z);   //Line 11
    }
}
```

Sample Run:

```
Line 4: The values of x, y, and z with two decimal places.
Line 5: x = 15.67
Line 6: y = 235.73
Line 7: z = 9525.99
Line 8: The values of x, y, and z with three decimal places.
Line 9: x = 15.674
Line 10: y = 235.730
Line 11: z = 9525.986
```

Notice that in Lines 5, 6, and 7, the format specifier is %.2f, which causes the values of x, y, and z to be output to two decimal places. Also notice that the values of x and z are rounded. Moreover, the format specifier %n positions the insertion point at the beginning of the next line.

In Lines 9, 10, and 11, the format specifier is %.3f, which causes the values of x, y, and z to be output to three decimal places. Notice that the given value of y has only two decimal places. Therefore, to output the value of y to three decimal places, 0 is shown at the thousandth place.

In a format specifier, by using the option *width* you can also specify the number of columns to be used to output the value of an expression. For example, suppose num is an `int` variable and rate is a `double` variable. Furthermore, suppose that:

```
num = 96;
rate = 15.50;
```

Consider the following statements:

```
System.out.println("123456789012345");        //Line 1
System.out.printf("%5d %n", num);              //Line 2
System.out.printf("%5.2f %n", rate);           //Line 3
System.out.printf("%5d%6.2f %n", num, rate);   //Line 4
System.out.printf("%5d %6.2f %n", num, rate);  //Line 5
```

The output of the statement in Line 1 shows the column positions. The statement in Line 2 outputs the value of num in five columns. Because the value of num is 96, we need only two columns to output the value of num. The (*default*) output is right justified, so the first three columns are left blank.

The statement in Line 3 outputs the value of **rate** in five columns with two decimal places. Note that the decimal point also requires a column. That is, the width specifiers for floating-point values also include a column for the decimal point.

The statements in Lines 4 and 5 output the values of num in five columns, followed by the value of **rate** in six columns with two decimal places. The output of these statements is:

```
123456789012345
   96
15.50
   96 15.50
   96  15.50
```

Let us take a close look at the output of the statements in Lines 4 and 5. First, consider the statement in Line 4, that is:

```
System.out.printf("%5d%6.2f %n", num, rate);
```

In this statement, the format string is `"%5d%6.2f %n"`. Notice that there is no space between the format specifiers `%5d` and `%6.2f`. Therefore, after outputting the value of num in the first five columns, the value of **rate** is output starting at column 6 (see the fourth line of output). Because only five columns are needed to output the value of **rate** and the output is right justified, column 6 is left blank.

Now consider the statement in Line 5. Here, the format string is `"%5d %6.2f %n"`. Notice that there is a space between the format specifiers `%5d` and `%6.2f`. Therefore, after outputting the value of num in the first five columns, the sixth column is left blank. The value of **rate** is output starting at column 7 (see the fifth line of output). Because only five columns are needed to output the value of **rate** and the output is right justified, column 7 is (also) left blank.

> **NOTE** In a format specifier, if the number of columns in the option *width* is less than the number of columns required to output the value of the expression, the output is expanded to the required number of columns. That is, the output is not truncated. For example, the output of the statement:
>
> `System.out.printf("%2d", 8756);`
>
> is:
>
> 8756
>
> even though only two columns are specified to output 8756, which requires four columns.

Example 3-5 further illustrates the use of the method `printf`.

EXAMPLE 3-5

The following program illustrates how to format output using the `printf` method and format specifier:

```
public class FormattingOutputWithprintf
{
    public static void main(String[] args)
    {
        int num = 763;                              //Line 1

        double x = 658.75;                          //Line 2

        String str = "Java Program.";               //Line 3

        System.out.println("1234567890123456789"
                     + "01234567890");              //Line 4
        System.out.printf("%5d%7.2f%15s%n",
                     num, x, str);                  //Line 5
        System.out.printf("%15s%6d%9.2f%n",
                     str, num, x);                  //Line 6
        System.out.printf("%8.2f%7d%15s%n",
                     x, num, str);                  //Line 7

        System.out.printf("num = %5d%n", num);      //Line 8
        System.out.printf("x = %10.2f%n", x);       //Line 9
        System.out.printf("str = %15s%n", str);     //Line 10
        System.out.printf("%10s%7d%n",
                     "Program No.", 4);             //Line 11
    }
}
```

Sample Run:

```
123456789012345678901234567890
   763 658.75  Java Program.
   Java Program.    763    658.75
   658.75     763  Java Program.
num =    763
x =      658.75
str =    Java Program.
Program No.      4
```

For the most part, the preceding output is self-explanatory. Let us consider some of these statements. Notice that for each output statement, the output is right justified.

The statement in Line 4 outputs the first line of the sample run, which shows the column positions. The statements in Lines 5 through 11 produce the remaining lines of output. Let us consider the statement in Line 5, that is:

```
System.out.printf("%5d%7.2f%15s%n", num, x, str);
```

In this statement, the format string is `"%5d%7.2f%15s%n"` and the argument list is `num, x, str`. The value of `num` is output in five columns, the value of `x` is output in seven columns with two decimal places, and the value of `str` is output in 15 columns. Because only three columns are needed to output the value of `num`, the first two columns are left blank. There is no space between the format specifiers `%5d` and `%7.2f`; therefore, the output of `x` begins at column 6. Because only six columns are needed to output the value of `x` and the format specifier `%7.2f` specifies seven columns, column 6 is left blank. Once again, there is no space between the format specifiers `%7.2f` and `%15s`. The output of the object's value that `str` points to begins at column 13. The reference variable `str` refers to the `String` object with the value `"Java Program."`. Because the format specifier `%15s` specifies 15 columns and only 13 columns are needed to output the string `"Java Program."`, the first two columns, columns 13 and 14, are left blank. The format specifier `%n` positions the insertion point at the beginning of the next line. The statements in Lines 6 and 7 work similarly.

Let us consider the statement in Line 8, that is:

```
System.out.printf("num = %5d%n", num);
```

Note that in this statement, the format string, `"num = %5d%n"`, consists of a string and the format specifier. This statement first outputs the string `"num = "`, which requires six columns. Then, starting at column 7, the value of `num` is output in five columns. Because only three columns are needed to output the value of `num`, columns 7 and 8 are left blank.

If the number of columns specified in a format specifier is more than the number of columns needed to output the result, then the (default) output is right justified. However, strings such as names, typically, are left justified. To force the output to be left justified, you can use the format specifier flag. If the flag is set to `'-'`, then the output of the result is left justified.

For example, consider the following statements:

```
System.out.println("12345678901234567890123456 7890");    //Line 1
System.out.printf("%-15s ***%n", "Java Program.");        //Line 2
```

The output of these statements is:

```
123456789012345678901234567890
Java Program.    ***
```

Notice that the string `"Java Program."` is printed in 15 columns and the output is left justified. Because in Line 2, in the format specifier, there is a space between s and ***, the sixteenth column is left blank. Then, *** is printed.

The following example further clarifies this.

EXAMPLE 3-6

```
public class Example3_6
{
    public static void main(String[] args)
    {
        int num = 763;                              //Line 1
        double x = 658.75;                          //Line 2
        String str = "Java Program.";               //Line 3

        System.out.println("1234567890123456789"
                        + "01234567890");            //Line 4
        System.out.printf("%-5d%-7.2f%-15s ***%n",
                        num, x, str);                //Line 5
        System.out.printf("%-15s%-6d%-9.2f ***%n",
                        str, num, x);                //Line 6
        System.out.printf("%-8.2f%-7d%-15s ***%n",
                        x, num, str);                //Line 7

        System.out.printf("num = %-5d ***%n", num); //Line 8
        System.out.printf("x = %-10.2f ***%n", x);  //Line 9
        System.out.printf("str = %-15s ***%n", str); //Line 10
        System.out.printf("%-10s%-7d ***%n",
                        "Program No.", 4);           //Line 11
    }
}
```

Sample Run:

```
123456789012345678901234567890
763   658.75 Java Program.    ***
Java Program.   763    658.75     ***
658.75  763     Java Program.    ***
num = 763    ***
x = 658.75      ***
str = Java Program.   ***
Program No.4        ***
```

The output of this program is similar to the output of the program in Example 3-5. Here, the output is left justified. Notice that in the Sample Run, Lines 2 through 8 contain ***. This is to show how the value of the last argument is printed. The details are left as an exercise for you.

Soon, we will explain how to use input/output dialog boxes to input data into a program and then display the output of the program. However, input to a program using input dialog boxes is in string format. Even numeric data is input as strings. Therefore, you first need to learn how to convert numeric strings, called **parsing numeric strings**, into numeric form.

PARSING NUMERIC STRINGS

A string consisting of only an integer or a floating-point number, optionally preceded by a minus sign, is called a **numeric string**. For example, the following are numeric strings:

```
"6723"
"-823"
"345.78"
"-782.873"
```

To process these strings as numbers for addition or multiplication, we first must convert them into numeric form. Java provides special methods to convert numeric strings into their equivalent numeric form.

1. To convert a string consisting of an integer to a value of the type `int`, we use the following expression:

   ```
   Integer.parseInt(strExpression)
   ```

   For example:

   ```
   Integer.parseInt("6723") = 6723
   Integer.parseInt("-823") = -823
   ```

2. To convert a string consisting of a floating-point number to a value of the type `float`, we use the following expression:

   ```
   Float.parseFloat(strExpression)
   ```

   For example:

   ```
   Float.parseFloat("34.56") = 34.56
   Float.parseFloat("-542.97") = -542.97
   ```

3. To convert a string consisting of a floating-point number to a value of the type `double`, we use the following expression:

   ```
   Double.parseDouble(strExpression)
   ```

   For example:

   ```
   Double.parseDouble("345.78") = 345.78
   Double.parseDouble("-782.873") = -782.873
   ```

Note that Integer, Float, and Double are classes that contain methods to convert a numeric string into a number. These classes are called **wrapper** classes. Moreover, parseInt is a method of the class Integer, which converts a numeric integer string into a value of the type int. Similarly, parseFloat is a method of the class Float and is used to convert a numeric decimal string into an equivalent value of the type float, and the method parseDouble is a method of the class Double, which is used to convert a numeric decimal string into an equivalent value of the type double. At this point, do not be overly concerned with the details of these classes and methods; just continue to use them as shown previously whenever you need them. (Chapter 6 discusses these wrapper classes in some detail.)

EXAMPLE 3-7

1.
```
Integer.parseInt("34")                      = 34
Integer.parseInt("-456")                     = -456
Double.parseDouble("754.89")                 = 754.89
```

2.
```
Integer.parseInt("34") + Integer.parseInt("75")        = 34 + 75 = 109
Integer.parseInt("87") + Integer.parseInt("-67")       = 87 - 67 = 20
```

3.
```
     Double.parseDouble("754.89") - Double.parseDouble("87.34")
=    754.89 - 87.34
=    667.55
```

Using Dialog Boxes for Input/Output

Recall that you have already used the class Scanner to input data into a program from the keyboard, and you used the object System.out to output the results to the screen.

Another way to gather input and output results is to use a graphical user interface (GUI). Java provides the class JOptionPane, which allows the programmer to use GUI components for I/O. This section describes how to use these facilities to make I/O more efficient and the program more attractive.

The class JOptionPane is contained in the package javax.swing. The two methods of this class that we use are: showInputDialog and showMessageDialog. The method showInputDialog allows the user to input a string from the keyboard; the method showMessageDialog allows the programmer to display the results.

The syntax to use the method showInputDialog is:

```
str = JOptionPane.showInputDialog(stringExpression);
```

where `str` is a `String` variable and `stringExpression` is an expression evaluating to a string. When this statement executes, a dialog box containing `stringExpression` appears on the screen prompting the user to enter the data. (The `stringExpression` usually informs the user what to enter.) The data entered is returned as a string and assigned to the variable `str`.

Consider the following statement (suppose that `name` is a `String` variable):

`name = JOptionPane.showInputDialog("Enter your name and press OK");`

3

When this statement executes, the dialog box shown in Figure 3-7 appears on the screen. (The arrow and the words `Text Field` are not part of the dialog box.)

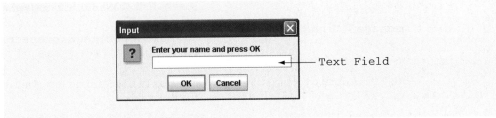

FIGURE 3-7   Input dialog box prompting the user to input name

The user enters the name in the white area, called a **text field**, as shown in Figure 3-8.

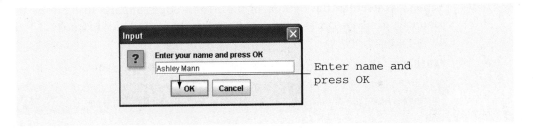

FIGURE 3-8   Input dialog box with user input

After you enter a name and click the OK button (or press the Enter key), the dialog box disappears and the entered name is assigned to the variable `name`. In this case, the string `"Ashley Mann"` is assigned to `name`.

Now that you know how to use an input dialog box, let's turn to the method `showMessageDialog` for output.

The syntax to use the method `showMessageDialog` is:

```
JOptionPane.showMessageDialog(parentComponent,
                             messageStringExpression,
                             boxTitleString, messageType);
```

The method **showMessageDialog** has four parameters, which are described in Table 3-3.

TABLE 3-3 Parameters for the Method showMessageDialog

Parameter	Description
parentComponent	This is an object that represents the parent of the dialog box. For now, we will specify the parentComponent to be null, in which case the program uses a default component that causes the dialog box to appear in the middle of the screen. Note that null is a reserved word in Java.
messageStringExpression	The messageStringExpression is evaluated and its value appears in the dialog box.
boxTitleString	The boxTitleString represents the title of the dialog box.
messageType	An int value representing the type of icon that will appear in the dialog box. Alternatively, you can use certain JOptionPane options described below.

Table 3-4 describes the options of the **class** JOptionPane that can be used with the parameter **messageType**. The option name is shown in bold. Examples 3-9 through 3-11 illustrate these options.

TABLE 3-4 JOptionPane Options for the Parameter messageType

messageType	Description
JOptionPane.**ERROR_MESSAGE**	The error icon, , is displayed in the dialog box.
JOptionPane.**INFORMATION_MESSAGE**	The information icon, , is displayed in the dialog box.
JOptionPane.**PLAIN_MESSAGE**	No icon appears in the dialog box.
JOptionPane.**QUESTION_MESSAGE**	The question icon, , is displayed in the dialog box.
JOptionPane.**WARNING_MESSAGE**	The warning icon, , is displayed in the dialog box.

EXAMPLE 3-8

The output of the statement:

```
JOptionPane.showMessageDialog(null, "Hello World!", "Greetings",
                              JOptionPane.INFORMATION_MESSAGE);
```

is shown in Figure 3-9.

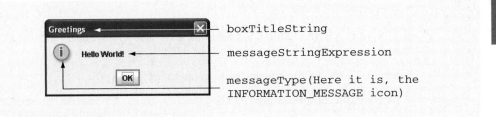

FIGURE 3-9   Message dialog box showing its various components

Notice the `INFORMATION_MESSAGE` icon to the left of `Hello World!` and the word `Greetings` in the title bar. After you click the OK button, the dialog box disappears.

EXAMPLE 3-9

Figure 3-10 shows the output of the following statement:

```
JOptionPane.showMessageDialog(null, "Amount Due = $" + 500.45,
                              "Invoice", JOptionPane.PLAIN_MESSAGE);
```

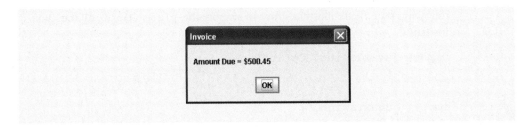

FIGURE 3-10   Message box with no icon

In the message dialog box in Figure 3-10, no icon appears to the left of the `messageStringExpression`. This is because the `messageType` is `JOptionPane.PLAIN_MESSAGE`.

EXAMPLE 3-10

Consider the following statements:

```
String str;
int num1 = 45;
int num2 = 56;
int sum;

str = "The two numbers are: " + num1 + " and " + num2 + "\n";
sum = num1 + num2;

str = str + "The sum of the numbers is: " + sum  + "\n";
str = str + "That is all for now!";
```

Figure 3-11 shows the output of the statement:

```
JOptionPane.showMessageDialog(null, str, "Summing Numbers",
                              JOptionPane.ERROR_MESSAGE);
```

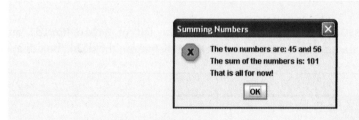

FIGURE 3-11   Message dialog box showing the output of the string `str`

The **class** JOptionPane is contained in the **package** javax.swing. Therefore, to use this **class** in a program, the program must import it from the **package** javax.swing. The following statements illustrate how to import the **class** JOptionPane (you can use either format):

```
import javax.swing.JOptionPane;
```

or:

```
import javax.swing.*;
```

`System.exit`

In order to use the input/output dialog boxes and properly terminate program execution, the program must include the following statement:

```
System.exit(0);
```

Note that th...
input/output...

Example 3-11 s...
uses input/output an...

EXAMPLE 3-11

The following program prompts the user ...
then outputs the circle's radius, area, and circu...
named constant PI (π), which is PI = 3.1415926... ...
find the area and circumference. (Note that to use th... ...
Math.PI.)

```java
//Program to determine the area and circumfer... ...

import javax.swing.JOptionPane;

public class AreaAndCircumferenceProgram
{
    public static void main(String[] args)             //Line 1
    {
        double radius;                                 //Line 2
        double area;                                   //Line 3
        double circumference;

        String radiusString;                           //Line 4
        String outputStr;                              //Line 5

        radiusString =
            JOptionPane.showInputDialog               //Line 6
                    ("Enter the radius: "
                                                       //Line 7
        radius = Double.parseDouble(radiusString);
                                                       //Line 8
        area = Math.PI * radius * radius;              //Line 9
        circumference = 2 * Math.PI * radius;

        outputStr = "Radius: " + radius + "\n" +
                "Area: " + area + " square units\n" +
                "Circumference: " + circumference +
                " units";                              //Line 10

        JOptionPane.showMessageDialog(null, outputStr,
                            "Circle",
                JOptionPane.INFORMATION_MESSAGE);      //Line 11

                                                       //Line 12

        System.exit(0);
    }
}
```

...un of this program. The input screen is

...pter 3: I...

Run: ...first, th...

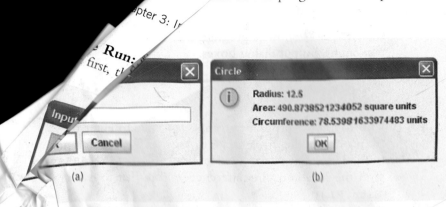

(a)   (b)

...E 3... Sa...run of program to calculate a circle's area and perimeter

The p...eding ...am...works as follows. The statements in Lines 1 through 5 declare the app...riate ...riable to manipulate the data. The statement in Line 6 displays the input di...box with th... message Enter the radius: (in Figure 3–12(a), the entered value is 12.50)...

The strin...

The state...ining the input data is assigned to the String variable radiusString. double an...Line 7 converts the string containing the radius into a value of the type The statemen...it in the variable radius.

store them in ...ines 8 and 9 calculate the area and circumference of the circle and Line 10 const...riables area and circumference, respectively. The statement in The string is a...string containing the radius, area, and circumference of the circle. message dialog b...to the variable outputStr. The statement in Line 11 uses the Figure 3–12(b). ...display the circle's radius, area, and circumference, as shown in

The statement in Lin...eminates the program after the user clicks the OK button in the dialog box.

The program in Example 11 does not output the area and circumference to two decimal places. The next section explains how to format the output in an output dialog box.

NOTE If the amount of input data is small and the output is small, dialog boxes are an effective and attractive way to build an application.

Formatting the Output Using the `String` Meth.

Earlier in this chapter, you learned how to format the output of[39]
device using the stream method `printf`. However, the method pri.
with output dialog boxes. Formatting the output in an output dialog
decimal numbers, can be done using the `String` method `format`
`DecimalFormat`. Next, we describe how to use the `String` meth.
Appendix D describes the `class DecimalFormat`.

An expression to use the `String` method `format` is:

```
String.format(formatString, argumentList)
```

where the meaning of the parameters `formatString` and `argumentList` is the same as
in the method `printf`. The value of the expression is a formatted string. The following
example shows how the method `format` works.

EXAMPLE 3-12

Suppose we have the following declarations and initializations:

```
double x = 15.674;
double y = 235.73;
double z = 9525.9864;

int num = 83;

String str;
```

Expression	Value
`String.format("%.2f", x)`	`"15.67"`
`String.format("%.3f", y)`	`"235.730"`
`String.format("%.2f", z)`	`"9525.99"`
`String.format("%7s", "Hello")`	`"  Hello"`
`String.format("%5d%7.2f", num, x)`	`"   83   15.67"`
`String.format("The value of num = %5d", num)`	`"The value of num =   83"`
`str = String.format("%.2f", z)`	`str = "9525.99"`

Because the value of the `String` method `format` is a string, the method `format` can also
be used as an argument to the methods `print`, `println`, or `printf`. Example 3-13
illustrates this concept.

EXAMPLE 3-13

```
public class StringMethodformat
{
    public static void main (String[] args)
```

```
    {
        double x = 15.674;
        double y = 235.73;
        double z = 9525.9864;
        int num = 83;
        String str;

        System.out.println("123456789012345678901234567890");
        System.out.println(String.format("%.2f", x));
        System.out.println(String.format("%.3f", y));
        System.out.println(String.format("%.2f", z));

        System.out.println(String.format("%7s", "Hello"));
        System.out.println(String.format("%5d%7.2f", num, x));
        System.out.println(String.format("The value of "
                                   + "num = %5d", num));

        str = String.format("%.2f", z);

        System.out.println(str);
    }
}
```

Sample Run:

```
123456789012345678901234567890
15.67
235.730
9525.99
  Hello
   83  15.67
The value of num =      83
9525.99
```

The preceding sample run is self-explanatory. The details are left as an exercise for you.

The following example illustrates how the **String** method **format** can be used to format the output in an output dialog box.

EXAMPLE 3-14

```
import javax.swing.JOptionPane;

public class Example3_14
{
    public static void main(String[] args)
    {
        double x = 15.674;
        double y = 235.73;
        double z = 9525.9864;
        String str;
```

```
      str = String.format("The value of x with two decimal "
                        + "places = %.2f%n", x)
          + String.format("The value of y with two decimal "
                        + "places = %.2f%n", y)
          + String.format("The value of z with two decimal "
                        + "places = %.2f%n", z);

      JOptionPane.showMessageDialog(null, str,
                  "Formatting with the String Method format",
                  JOptionPane.INFORMATION_MESSAGE);

      System.exit(0);
   }
}
```

Sample Run: (Figure 3-13 shows the output of this program.)

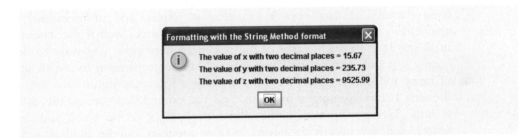

FIGURE 3-13 Output dialog box showing the values of x, y, and z with two decimal places

Note that in the preceding program, first we constructed str using the String method format and then used str in the output dialog box. However, you could have used the String method format directly in the output dialog box. That is, you can replace the statements:

```
str = String.format("The value of x with two decimal "
                  + "places = %.2f%n", x)
    + String.format("The value of y with two decimal "
                  + "places = %.2f%n", y)
    + String.format("The value of z with two decimal "
                  + "places = %.2f%n", z);

JOptionPane.showMessageDialog(null, str,
            "Formatting with the String Method format",
            JOptionPane.INFORMATION_MESSAGE);
```

with the following statement:

```
JOptionPane.showMessageDialog(null,
      String.format("The value of x with two decimal "
                  + "places = %.2f%n", x)
```

```
     + String.format("The value of y with two decimal "
               + "places = %.2f%n", y)
     + String.format("The value of z with two decimal "
               + "places = %.2f%n", z),
   "Formatting with the String Method format",
   JOptionPane.INFORMATION_MESSAGE);
```

File Input/Output

The previous sections discussed in some detail how to get input from the keyboard (standard input device) and send output to the screen (standard output device). However, getting input from the keyboard and sending output to the screen has limitations. If the amount of input data is large, it is inefficient to type it at the keyboard each time you run a program. In addition to the inconvenience of typing large amounts of data, typing can generate errors, and unintentional typos cause erroneous results. Sending output to the screen works well if the amount of data is small (no larger than the size of the screen), but suppose you want to distribute the output in a printed format? The solution to these problems is to use an alternate form of input and output: files. By using a file as a source of input data, you can prepare the data before running a program, and the program can access the data each time it runs. Saving output to a file allows the output to be saved and distributed to others, and the output produced by one program can be used as input to other programs.

This section discusses how to obtain data from other input devices, such as a disk (that is, secondary storage), and how to save the output to a disk. Java allows a program to get data from, and save output to, secondary storage. A program can use the file I/O and read data from or write data to a file. Formally, a **file** is defined as follows:

File: An area in secondary storage used to hold information.

In Chapter 2, you learned how to use a `Scanner` object to input data from the standard input device. Recall that the following statement creates the `Scanner` object `console` and initializes it to the standard input device:

`Scanner console = new Scanner(System.in);`

You can also initialize a `Scanner` object to input sources other than the standard input device by passing an appropriate argument in place of the object `System.in`. To do this, we use the `class FileReader` as follows. (The `class FileReader` is contained in the `package java.io`.) Suppose that the input data is stored in a file, say, `prog.dat`. The following statement creates the `Scanner` object `inFile` and initializes it to the file `prog.dat`:

```
Scanner inFile = new Scanner(new FileReader("prog.dat"));   //Line 1
```

Next, you use the object `inFile` to input the data from the file `prog.dat`, just the way you used the object `console` to input the data from the standard input device using the methods `next`, `nextInt`, `nextDouble`, and so on.

NOTE The statement in Line 1 assumes that the file `prog.dat` is in the same directory (subdirectory) as your program. However, if this is in a different directory (subdirectory), then you must specify the path where the file is located, along with the name of the file. For example, suppose that the file `prog.dat` is on a flash memory in drive H. Then, the statement in Line 1 should be modified as follows:

```
Scanner inFile = new Scanner(new FileReader("h:\\prog.dat"));
```

Note that there are two \ after `h:`. Recall from Chapter 2 that in Java \ is the escape character. Therefore, to produce a \ within a string you need \\. (Moreover, to be absolutely sure about specifying the source where the input file is stored, such as the flash drive `h:\\`, check your system's documentation.)

NOTE Suppose that a program reads data from a file. Because different computers have drives labeled differently, for simplicity, throughout the book we assume that the file containing the data and the program reading data from the file are in the same directory (subdirectory).

To send the output to a file, you use the **class** `PrintWriter`. This class is contained in the **package** `java.io`.

To summarize, Java file I/O is a four-step process:

1. Import the necessary classes from the **packages** `java.util` and `java.io` into the program.
2. Create and associate the appropriate objects with the input/output sources.
3. Use the appropriate methods associated with the variables created in Step 2 to input/output the data.
4. Close the files.

We now explain these four steps and then provide a skeleton program that shows how the steps might appear in a program.

Step 1 requires that the necessary classes be imported from the **packages** `java.util` and `java.io`. The following statements accomplish this task:

```
import java.util.*;
import java.io.*;
```

Step 2 requires that you create and associate appropriate `class` variables with the input/output sources. We already discussed how to declare and associate `Scanner` objects for inputting the data from a file. The next section describes how to create the appropriate objects to send the output to a file.

Step 3 requires us to read the data from the input file using the variables created in Step 2. Example 3-15 describes how to read the data from a file.

In Step 4, you close the input and output files. To do so, you use the method `close`, as described later in this section.

EXAMPLE 3-15

Suppose an input file, say `employeeData.txt`, consists of the following data:

```
Emily Johnson 45 13.50
```

The file consists of an employee's name, the number of hours the employee worked, and the pay rate. The following statements declare the appropriate variables to read and store the data into the variables:

```
    //Create and associate the Scanner object to the input source
Scanner inFile = new Scanner(new FileReader("employeeData.txt"));

String firstName;    //variable to store first name
String lastName;     //variable to store last name

double hoursWorked;  //variable to store hours worked
double payRate;      //variable to store pay rate
double wages;        //variable to store wages

firstName = inFile.next();  //get the first name
lastName = inFile.next();   //get the last name

hoursWorked = inFile.nextDouble(); //get hours worked
payRate = inFile.nextDouble();     //get pay rate

wages = hoursWorked * payRate;
```

The following statement closes the input file to which `inFile` is associated:

```
inFile.close();  //close the input file
```

Storing (Writing) Output to a File

To store the output of a program in a file, you use the **class** PrintWriter. You declare a PrintWriter variable and associate this variable with the destination, that is, the file where the output will be stored. Suppose the output is to be stored in the file prog.out. Consider the following statement:

```
PrintWriter outFile = new PrintWriter("prog.out");
```

This statement creates the PrintWriter object outFile and associates it with the file prog.out. (This statement assumes that the file prog.out is to be created in the directory [subdirectory] where the main program is.)

 NOTE If you want the output file to be stored, say, on a flash memory in drive H, then the previous statement takes the following form:

```
PrintWriter outFile = new PrintWriter("h:\\prog.out");
```

You can now use the methods print, println, and printf with outFile in the same way they have been used with the object System.out.

For example, the statement:

```
outFile.println("The paycheck is: $" + pay);
```

stores the output—The paycheck is: $565.78—in the file prog.out. This statement assumes that the value of the variable pay is 565.78.

Once the output is completed, Step 4 requires closing the file. You close the input and output files by using the method close. For example, assuming that inFile and outFile are as declared before, the statements to close these files are:

```
inFile.close();
outFile.close();
```

Closing the output file ensures that the buffer holding the output will be emptied, that is, the entire output generated by the program will be sent to the output file.

Step 3 requires that you create appropriate objects for file I/O. In the case of an input file, the file must exist before the program executes. If the input file does not exist, then the statement to associate the object with the input file fails and it **throws** a FileNotFoundException. At this time, we will not require the program to handle this exception, so the method main will also throw this exception. Therefore, the heading of the method main must contain an appropriate command to throw a FileNotFoundException.

An output file does not have to exist before it is opened; if the output file does not exist, the computer prepares an empty file for output. *If the designated output file already exists, by default, the old contents are erased (lost) when the file is opened.* Note that if the program is not able to create or access the output file, it throws a FileNotFoundException.

NOTE (`throws` **clause**) During program execution, various things can happen—for example, division by zero or inputting a letter for a number. If such things happen, the system would not tolerate it. In such cases, we say that an exception has occurred. If an exception occurs in a method, then the method should either handle the exception or *throw* it for the calling environment to handle. If an input file does not exist, the program throws a **FileNotFoundException**. Similarly, if an output file cannot be created or accessed, the program throws a **FileNotFoundException**. For the next few chapters, we will not be concerned with the handling of the exceptions; we will simply throw the exceptions. Because we do not need the method **main** to handle the **FileNotFoundException**, we will include a command in the heading of the method **main** to throw the **FileNotFoundException**. Chapter 11 describes exception handling.

In skeleton form, a program that uses file I/O is usually of the following form:

```java
import java.io.*;
import java.util.*;

//Add additional import statements as needed

public class ClassName
{
    //Declare appropriate variables
    public static void main(String[] args)
                            throws FileNotFoundException
    {
            //Create and associate the stream objects
        Scanner inFile =
            new Scanner(new FileReader("prog.dat"));

        PrintWriter outFile = new PrintWriter("prog.out");

         //Code for data manipulation

            //Close file
        inFile.close();
        outFile.close();
    }
}
```

The remainder of this chapter gives two programming examples—one illustrates dialog boxes for input/output; the other illustrates file input/output.

PROGRAMMING EXAMPLE: Movie Ticket Sale and Donation to Charity

A movie in a local theater is in great demand. The theater owner has decided to donate to a local charity a portion of the gross amount generated from the movie. This example designs and implements a program that prompts the user to input the movie name, adult ticket price, child ticket price, number of adult tickets sold, number of child tickets sold, and percentage of the gross amount to be donated to the charity. The output of the program is shown in Figure 3-14.

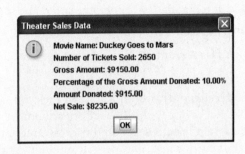

FIGURE 3-14 Output of theater sales program

Note that the decimal numbers are output with two decimal places.

Input: The input to the program consists of the movie name, adult ticket price, child ticket price, number of adult tickets sold, number of child tickets sold, and percentage of the gross amount to be donated to the charity.

Output: The output is as shown in Figure 3-14.

PROBLEM ANALYSIS AND ALGORITHM DESIGN

To calculate the amount donated to the local charity and the net sale, you first need to determine the gross amount. To calculate the gross amount, you multiply the number of adult tickets sold by the price of an adult ticket, multiply the number of child tickets sold by the price of a child ticket, and then add these two numbers:

```
grossAmount = adultTicketPrice * noOfAdultTicketsSold
            + childTicketPrice * noOfChildTicketsSold;
```

Next, you determine the percentage of the amount donated to the charity, and then calculate the net sale amount by subtracting the amount donated from the gross amount. The formulas to calculate the amount donated and the net sale amount are given below. This analysis leads to the following algorithm:

1. Get the movie name.
2. Get the price of an adult ticket.
3. Get the price of a child ticket.
4. Get the number of adult tickets sold.
5. Get the number of child tickets sold.
6. Get the percentage of the gross amount donated to the charity.
7. Calculate the gross amount using the following formula:

```
grossAmount = adultTicketPrice * noOfAdultTicketsSold
            + childTicketPrice * noOfChildTicketsSold;
```

8. Calculate the amount donated to the charity using the following formula:

```
amountDonated = grossAmount * percentDonation / 100;
```

9. Calculate the net sale amount using the following formula:

```
netSaleAmount = grossAmount - amountDonated;
```

VARIABLES From the preceding discussion, it follows that you need variables to store the movie name, adult ticket price, child ticket price, number of adult tickets sold, number of child tickets sold, percentage of the gross amount donated to the charity, gross amount, amount donated, and net sale amount. You also need a variable to get the string containing the sales data and a string to format the output. Therefore, the following variables are needed:

```
String movieName;
String inputStr;
String outputStr;

double adultTicketPrice;
double childTicketPrice;
int noOfAdultTicketsSold;
int noOfChildTicketsSold;

double percentDonation;
double grossAmount;
double amountDonated;
double netSaleAmount;
```

FORMATTING THE OUTPUT To show the desired output, you first create the string consisting of the strings and the values required. The following string accomplishes this:

```
outputStr = "Movie Name: " + movieName + "\n"
          + "Number of Tickets Sold: "
          + (noOfAdultTicketsSold +
```

```
          noOfChildTicketsSold) + "\n"
   + "Gross Amount: $"
   + String.format("%.2f", grossAmount) + "\n"
   + "Percentage of Gross Amount Donated: "
   + String.format("%.2f", percentDonation) + "\n"
   + "Amount Donated: $"
   + String.format("%.2f", amountDonated) + "\n"
   + "Net Sale: $"
   + String.format("%.2f", netSaleAmount);
```

Notice that we have used the method format of the class String to output decimal numbers to two decimal places.

MAIN
ALGORITHM

In the preceding sections, we analyzed the problem and determined the formulas to do the calculations. We also determined the necessary variables and the output string. We can now expand the algorithm given in the section Problem Analysis and Algorithm Design to solve the problem given at the beginning of this programming example.

1.   Declare the variables.
2.   Display the input dialog box to enter a movie name and retrieve the movie name.
3.   Display the input dialog box to enter the price of an adult ticket.
4.   Retrieve the price of an adult ticket.
5.   Display the input dialog box to enter the price of a child ticket.
6.   Retrieve the price of a child ticket.
7.   Display the input dialog box to enter the number of adult tickets sold.
8.   Retrieve the number of adult tickets sold.
9.   Display the input dialog box to enter the number of child tickets sold.
10. Retrieve the number of child tickets sold.
11. Display the input dialog box to enter the percentage of the gross amount donated.
12. Retrieve the percentage of the gross amount donated.
13. Calculate the gross amount.
14. Calculate the amount donated.
15. Calculate the net sale amount.
16. Format the output string.
17. Display the message dialog box to show the output.
18. Terminate the program.

COMPLETE PROGRAM LISTING

```java
//*****************************************************************
// Author D.S. Malik
//
// Program: Movie ticket sale and donation to charity.
// This program prompts the user to input the movie name, adult
// ticket price, child ticket price, number of adult tickets
// sold, number of child tickets sold, and the percentage of the
// gross amount to be donated to the charity.
// The program outputs the movie name, the number of tickets
// sold, the gross amount, the percentage of the gross amount
// donated to the charity, the amount donated to the charity,
// and the net amount.
//*****************************************************************

import javax.swing.JOptionPane;

public class MovieTicketSale
{
    public static void main(String[] args)
    {
            //Step 1
        String movieName;
        String inputStr;
        String outputStr;

        double adultTicketPrice;
        double childTicketPrice;

        int noOfAdultTicketsSold;
        int noOfChildTicketsSold;

        double percentDonation;
        double grossAmount;
        double amountDonated;
        double netSaleAmount;

        movieName = JOptionPane.showInputDialog
                ("Enter the movie name");                      //Step 2

        inputStr = JOptionPane.showInputDialog
                ("Enter the price of an adult ticket"); //Step 3
        adultTicketPrice = Double.parseDouble(inputStr);   //Step 4

        inputStr = JOptionPane.showInputDialog
                ("Enter the price of a child ticket");  //Step 5
        childTicketPrice = Double.parseDouble(inputStr);   //Step 6
```

```
inputStr = JOptionPane.showInputDialog
        ("Enter the number of adult tickets sold");   //Step 7
noOfAdultTicketsSold = Integer.parseInt(inputStr);    //Step 8

inputStr = JOptionPane.showInputDialog
        ("Enter the number of child tickets sold");   //Step 9
noOfChildTicketsSold = Integer.parseInt(inputStr);    //Step 10

inputStr = JOptionPane.showInputDialog
        ("Enter the percentage of the donation");     //Step 11
percentDonation = Double.parseDouble(inputStr);       //Step 12

grossAmount = adultTicketPrice * noOfAdultTicketsSold +
        childTicketPrice * noOfChildTicketsSold;      //Step 13

amountDonated = grossAmount * percentDonation / 100;  //Step 14
netSaleAmount = grossAmount - amountDonated;          //Step 15

outputStr = "Movie Name: " + movieName + "\n"
        + "Number of Tickets Sold: "
        + (noOfAdultTicketsSold +
          noOfChildTicketsSold) + "\n"
        + "Gross Amount: $"
        + String.format("%.2f", grossAmount) + "\n"
        + "Percentage of the Gross Amount Donated: "
        + String.format("%.2f%%", percentDonation) + "\n"
        + "Amount Donated: $"
        + String.format("%.2f", amountDonated) + "\n"
        + "Net Sale: $"
        + String.format("%.2f", netSaleAmount);       //Step 16
JOptionPane.showMessageDialog(null, outputStr,
            "Theater Sales Data",
            JOptionPane.INFORMATION_MESSAGE);          //Step 17
System.exit(0);                                        //Step 18
    }
}
```

Sample Run: (In this sample run, the user input is in the input dialog boxes.)

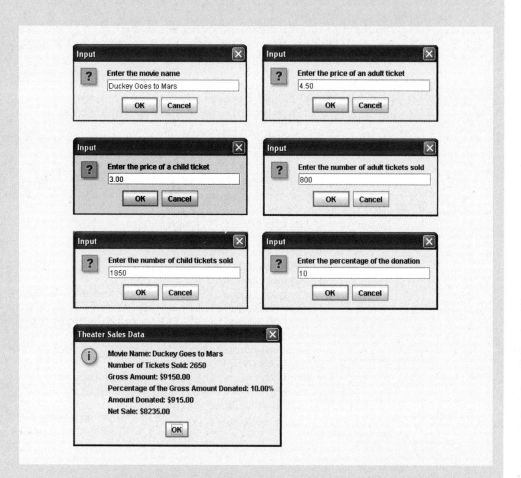

FIGURE 3-15 Sample run of movie sales program

In this output (see Figure 3–15), the first six dialog boxes (from left to right) get the necessary data to generate the last message dialog box.

PROGRAMMING EXAMPLE: Student Grade

Write a program that reads a student's first and last names followed by five test scores. The program should output the student's first name, last name, the five test scores, and the average test score. Output the average test score with two decimal places.

The data to be read is stored in a file named **test.txt**; the output should be stored in a file named **testavg.out**.

Input: A file containing the student's first name, last name, and the five test scores

Output: The student's first name, last name, five test scores, and the average of the five test scores, saved to a file

PROBLEM ANALYSIS AND ALGORITHM DESIGN

To find the average of the five test scores, you add the test scores and divide the sum by 5. The input data is in the following form: the student's first name, followed by the last name, followed by the five test scores. Therefore, we read the student's first name, followed by the last name, followed by the five test scores. This problem analysis translates into the following algorithm:

1. Get the student's first name, last name, and the five test scores.
2. Output the student's first name, last name, and the five test scores.
3. Calculate the average.
4. Output the average.

You output the average test score in the fixed-decimal format with two decimal places.

VARIABLES

The program needs to read a student's first name, last name, and five test scores. Therefore, you need two variables to store the student's first name and last name, and five variables to store the five test scores. To find the average, you must add the five test scores and then divide the sum by 5. Thus, you also need a variable to store the average test score. Furthermore, because the input data is in a file and the output is to be stored in a file, you must declare and initialize the appropriate variables. The program needs at least the following variables:

```java
double test1, test2, test3, test4, test5; //variables to store
                                           //five test scores
double average;        //variable to store average test score

String firstName;      //variable to store the first name
String lastName;       //variable to store the last name

Scanner inFile = new Scanner(new FileReader("test.txt"));

PrintWriter outFile = new PrintWriter("testavg.out");
```

MAIN
ALGORITHM

In the preceding sections, we analyzed the problem and determined the formulas to perform the calculations. We also determined the necessary variables. Now we can expand the algorithm given in the Problem Analysis and Algorithm Design section to solve the Student Grade problem given at the beginning of this programming example.

1. Declare the variables.
2. Create a `Scanner` object and associate it with the input source.
3. Create a `PrintWriter` object and associate it with the output source.
4. Get the student's first name and last name.
5. Output the student's first name and last name.
6. Read the five test scores.
7. Output the five test scores.
8. Find the average test score.
9. Output the average test score.
10. Close the files.

This program reads the data from a file and outputs the data to a file, so it must import the necessary classes from the packages `java.io` and `java.util`.

COMPLETE PROGRAM LISTING

```java
//**************************************************************
// Author D.S. Malik
//
// Program to calculate the average test score.
// Given a student's name and five test scores, this program
// calculates the average test score. The student's name, the
// five test scores, and the average test score is stored in the
// file testavg.out. The data is input from the file test.txt.
//**************************************************************
import java.io.*;
import java.util.*;

public class StudentGrade
{
    public static void main(String[] args) throws
                                        FileNotFoundException
    {
        //declare and initialize the variables        //Step 1
        double test1, test2, test3, test4, test5;
        double average;
```

```
        String firstName;
        String lastName;

        Scanner inFile =
            new Scanner(new FileReader("test.txt"));        //Step 2

        PrintWriter outFile = new
                        PrintWriter("testavg.out");         //Step 3

        firstName = inFile.next();                          //Step 4
        lastName = inFile.next();                           //Step 4

        outFile.println("Student Name: "
                    + firstName + " " + lastName);          //Step 5

            //Step 6 - retrieve the five test scores
        test1 = inFile.nextDouble();
        test2 = inFile.nextDouble();
        test3 = inFile.nextDouble();
        test4 = inFile.nextDouble();
        test5 = inFile.nextDouble();

        outFile.printf("Test scores: %5.2f %5.2f %5.2f "
                    + "%5.2f %5.2f %n", test1, test2,
                        test3, test4, test5);               //Step 7

        average = (test1 + test2 + test3 + test4
                + test5) / 5.0;                             //Step 8
        outFile.printf("Average test score: %5.2f %n",
                        average);                           //Step 9

        inFile.close();                                     //Step 10
        outFile.close();                                    //Step 10
    }
}
```

Sample Run:

Input File (contents of the file test.txt):

```
Andrew Miller 87.50 89 65.75 37 98.50
```

Output File (contents of the file testavg.out):

```
Student Name: Andrew Miller
Test scores: 87.50 89.00 65.75 37.00 98.50
Average test score: 75.55
```

The preceding program uses five variables: test1, test2, test3, test4, and test5 to read the five test scores and then find the average test score. The Web site (*www.course.com*) and the CD accompanying this book contain a modified version of this program that uses only one variable, testscore, to read the test scores and another variable, sum, to find the sum of the test scores. The program is named StudentGradeVersion2.java.

Debugging—Understanding Error Messages

The Java compiler will find syntactic errors in your program and will provide messages describing the errors. These messages do not always describe the problem exactly, nor do they always describe all the syntactic problems in your program at once, but they provide a good indication of where to look for the problem(s). Look carefully in the immediate vicinity of the reported error for anything that might be causing the problem. Often the correction of a single syntactic error will result in the reporting of multiple new syntactic errors, but there is no need for concern. Finding and reporting errors is like peeling away the layers of an onion. By finding and correcting the sources of errors as they are reported, ultimately you will be able to find and correct all the syntactic errors in your program.

QUICK REVIEW

1. A reference variable is a variable that stores the address of a memory space.
2. In Java, all variables declared using a `class` are reference variables.
3. A reference variable does not directly store data in its memory space. It stores the address of the memory space where the actual data is stored.
4. Class objects are instances of that `class`.
5. Using the operator `new` to create a `class` object is called instantiating an object of that `class`.
6. To use a predefined method in a program, you need to know the name of the `class` containing the method (unless the class, such as the `class` `String`, is automatically imported) and the name of the `package` containing the `class`, and then you need to import the `class` into the program. In addition, you need to know the name of the method, the number of parameters the method takes, and the type of each parameter. You must also be aware of the method's return type or, loosely speaking, what the method produces.
7. In Java, the dot (.) is called the member access operator. The dot separates the `class` name from the member, or method, name. Dot notation is also used when a reference variable of a `class` type accesses a member of that `class`.
8. The `class` `String` is used to process strings.
9. The assignment operator is defined for the `class` `String`.
10. The method `substring` of the `class` `String` returns a substring from another string.
11. The `class` `String` contains many other useful methods, such as: `charAt`, `indexOf`, `concat`, `length`, `replace`, `toLowerCase`, and `toUpperCase`.
12. You can use the method `printf` to format the output in a specific manner.
13. A format specifier for general, character, and numeric types has the following syntax:

```
%[argument_index$][flags][width][.precision]conversion
```

The expressions in square brackets are optional. The required `conversion` is a character indicating how the argument should be formatted.

14. The method `printf` is available in Java 5.0 and its higher versions.

15. In a format specifier, using the option `width` you can also specify the number of columns to be used to output the value of an expression. The (*default*) output is right justified.

16. In a format specifier, if the number of columns in the option `width` is less than the number of columns required to output the value of the expression, the output is expanded to the required number of columns. That is, the output is not truncated.

17. To force the output to be *left* justified, you use the format specifier flag. If the flag is set to `'-'`, then the output of the result is left justified.

18. A numeric string consists of an integer or a decimal number with an optional minus sign.

19. To convert a numeric integer string into an integer, you use the expression:

`Integer.parseInt(strExpression)`

where `strExpression` is an expression containing a numeric integer string.

20. To convert a numeric decimal string into a `double` value, you use the expression:

`Double.parseDouble(strExpression)`

where `strExpression` is an expression containing a numeric string.

21. The method `showInputDialog` of the `class JOptionPane` is used to create an input dialog box.

22. The method `showMessageDialog` of the `class JOptionPane` is used to create an output message dialog box.

23. The `class JOptionPane` is contained in the `package javax.swing`.

24. If a program uses input and output dialog boxes, it must also use the statement:

`System.exit(0);`

25. To format a floating-point number to a specific number of decimal places, you can use the `String` method `format`.

26. To input data from a file, you use the `classes Scanner` and `FileReader`; to send output to a file, you use the `class PrintWriter`.

27. File I/O is a four-step process: (i) import the necessary classes from the `packages java.util` and `java.io` into the program; (ii) create and associate the appropriate objects with the input/output sources; (iii) use the appropriate methods associated with the objects created in Step ii to input/output the data; and (iv) close the file(s).

EXERCISES

1. Mark the following statements as true or false.

   a. A variable declared using a `class` is called an object.

   b. In the statement x = `console.nextInt() ;`, x must be a variable.

   c. You generate the newline character by pressing Enter (return) on the keyboard.

   d. The methods `printf` and `format` are used to format a decimal number to a specific number of decimal places.

2. How does a variable of a primitive type differ from a reference variable?

3. What is an object?

4. What does the operator `new` do?

5. Suppose that `str` is a `String` variable. Write a Java statement that uses the operator `new` to instantiate the object `str` and assign the string `"Java Programming"` to `str`.

6. Consider the following statements:

```
String str = "Going to the amusement park";
char ch;
int len;
int position;
```

   a. What value is stored in ch by the following statement?
   ```
   ch = str.charAt(0);
   ```

   b. What value is stored in ch by the following statement?
   ```
   ch = str.charAt(10);
   ```

   c. What value is stored in len by the following statement?
   ```
   len = str.length();
   ```

   d. What value is stored in position by the following statement?
   ```
   position = str.indexOf('t');
   ```

   e. What value is stored in position by the following statement?
   ```
   position = str.indexOf("park");
   ```

7. Assume the declaration in Exercise 6. What is the output of the following statements?

   a. `System.out.println(str.substring(0, 5));`

   b. `System.out.println(str.substring(13, 22));`

   c. `System.out.println(str.toUpperCase());`

   d. `System.out.println(str.toLowerCase());`

   e. `System.out.println(str.replace('t', '*'));`

8. Suppose that you have the following statements:

```
String str;
str = "Java programming: from problem analysis to program design";
```

What is the value of the following expressions?

   a. `str.indexOf("analysis")`

   b. `str.substring(5, 16)`

   c. `str.startsWith("Java")`

   d. `str.startsWith("J")`

   e. `str.endsWith(".")`

9. Suppose that you have the following statements:

```
String str;
String str1 = "programming";
str = "Java programming: from problem analysis to program design";
```

What is the value of the following expressions?

   a. `str.regionMatches(6, str1, 0, str1.length())`

   b. `str.regionMatches(true, 31, "Analysis", 0, 8)`

10. a. What method is used to create an input dialog box?

    b. What method is used to create an output dialog box?

    c. What is the name of the `class` that contains the methods to create input and output dialog boxes?

    d. What is the name of the `package` that contains the `class` described in part c?

11. What does the following statement do? (Assume that `scoreStr` is a `String` variable.)

```
scoreStr = JOptionPane.showInputDialog("Enter the score:");
```

12. Write a Java statement that creates the output dialog box in Figure 3-16.

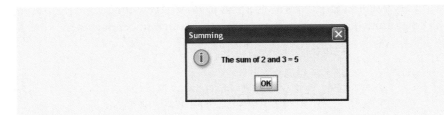

FIGURE 3-16 Figure for Exercise 12, Chapter 3

13. Write a Java statement that creates the output dialog box in Figure 3-17.

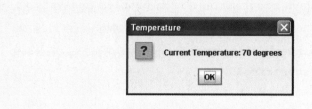

FIGURE 3-17   Figure for Exercise 13, Chapter 3

14. Consider the statements:

```
double x = 75.3987;
double y = 982.89764;
```

What is the output of the following statements?

a. `System.out.printf("%.2f %n", x);`

b. `System.out.printf("%.2f %n", y);`

c. `System.out.printf("%.3f %n", x);`

d. `System.out.printf("%.3f %n", y);`

15. Consider the statements:

```
int x, y;
char ch;
```

and the input:

`46 A 49`

Write the Java statements that would store 46 into x, 'A' into ch, and 49 into y.

16. The following program is supposed to read two numbers from a file named Ex16Input.txt, and write the sum of the numbers to a file named Ex16Output.dat. However, it fails to do so. Rewrite the program so that it performs correctly. (You may assume that both numbers are on the same line.)

```
import java.util.*;

public class Ch3Ex16
{
    public static void main(String[] args)
    {
        Scanner inFile =
            new Scanner(new FileReader("Ex16Input.txt"));

        int num1, num2;
```

```
        num1 = inFile.nextInt();
        num2 = inFile.nextInt();

        outFile.println("Sum = " + (num1 + num2));

        outFile.close();
    }
}
```

17. A program reads data from a file called `inputFile.dat` and, after doing some calculations, writes the results to a file called `outFile.dat`. Answer the following questions:

   a. After the program executes, what are the contents of the file `inputFile.dat`?

   b. After the program executes, what are the contents of the file `outFile.dat` if this file was empty before the program executed?

   c. After the program executes, what are the contents of the file `outFile.dat` if this file contained 100 numbers before the program executed?

   d. What would happen if the file `outFile.dat` did not exist before the program executed?

PROGRAMMING EXERCISES

1. Consider the following incomplete Java program:

```
public class Ch3_PrExercise1
{
    public static void main(String[] args)
    {
        .
        .
        .
    }
}
```

   a. Write Java statements that import the classes `Scanner`, `FileReader`, and `PrintWriter` from the packages `java.util` and `java.io`.

   b. Write statements that declare `inFile` to be a reference variable of type `Scanner` and `outFile` to be a reference variable of type `PrintWriter`.

   c. The program will read data from the file `inData.txt` and write output to the file `outData.dat`. Write statements to open both these files, associate `inFile` with `inData.txt`, and associate `outFile` with `outData.dat`.

d. Suppose that the file `inData.txt` contains the following data:

```
10.20 5.35
15.6
Randy Gill 31
18500 3.5
A
```

The numbers in the first line represent the length and width, respectively, of a rectangle. The number in the second line represents the radius of a circle. The third line contains the first name, last name, and the age of a person. The first number in the fourth line is the savings account balance at the beginning of the month and the second number is the interest rate per year. (Assume that $\pi = 3.1416$.) The fifth line contains an uppercase letter between A and Y (inclusive). Write statements so that after the program executes, the contents of the file `outData.txt` are as shown below. If necessary, declare additional variables. Your statements should be general enough so that if the content of the input file changes and the program is run again (without editing and recompiling), it outputs the appropriate results.

```
Rectangle:
Length = 10.20, width = 5.35, area = 54.57, parameter = 31.10

Circle:
Radius = 15.60, area = 764.54, circumference = 98.02

Name: Randy Gill, age: 31
Beginning balance = $18500.00, interest rate = 3.50
Balance at the end of the month = $18553.96

The character that comes after A in the ASCII set is B
```

e. Write the statement that closes the output file.

f. Write a Java application program that tests the Java statements that you wrote in parts a–e.

2. Write a program that prompts the user to enter a decimal number and then outputs this number rounded to two decimal places.

3. The manager of a football stadium wants you to write a program that calculates the total ticket sales after each game. There are four types of tickets—box, sideline, premium, and general admission. After each game, data is stored in a file in the following form:

```
ticketPrice    numberOfTicketsSold
 .
 .
 .
```

Sample data are shown below:

```
250 5750
100 28000
50 35750
25 18750
```

The first line indicates that the box ticket price is $250 and that 5750 tickets were sold at that price. Output the number of tickets sold and the total sale amount. Format your output with two decimal places.

4. Write a program to calculate the property tax. Property tax is calculated on 92% of the assessed value of the property. For example, if the assessed value is $100000, the property tax is on $92000. Assume that the property tax rate is $1.05 for each $100 of the assessed value. Your program should prompt the user to enter the assessed value of the property. Store the output in a file in the following sample format:

```
Assessed Value:              $ 100000.00
Taxable Amount:              $  92000.00
Tax Rate for each $100.00: $      1.05
Property Tax:                $    966.00
```

Format your output to have two decimal places.

5. Write a program that converts a temperature from degrees Fahrenheit to degrees Celsius. The formula for converting the temperature from degrees Fahrenheit to degrees Celsius is:

```
C = (5.0 / 9.0) (F - 32)
```

Your program should prompt the user to enter a temperature given in degrees Fahrenheit. The program should output the temperature both in degrees Fahrenheit and in degrees Celsius. Format your output to have two decimal places.

6. Write a program that calculates and prints the monthly paycheck for an employee. The net pay is calculated after taking the following deductions:

```
Federal Income Tax:        15%
State Tax:                 3.5%
Social Security Tax:       5.75%
Medicare/Medicaid Tax:     2.75%
Pension Plan:              5%
Health Insurance:          $75.00
```

Your program should prompt the user to input the gross amount and the employee name. The output will be stored in a file. Format your output to have two decimal places. A sample output follows:

```
Bill Robinson
Gross Amount:        $ 3575.00
Federal Tax:         $  536.25
State Tax:           $  125.13
```

```
Social Security Tax:    $   205.56
Medicare/Medicaid Tax: $    98.31
Pension Plan:           $   178.75
Health Insurance:       $    75.00
Net Pay:                $ 2356.00
```

7. Three employees in a company are up for a special pay increase. You are given a file, say Ch3_Ex7Data.txt, with the following data:

```
Miller Andrew 65789.87 5
Green Sheila 75892.56 6
Sethi Amit 74900.50 6.1
```

Each input line consists of an employee's last name, first name, current salary, and percent pay increase. For example, in the first input line, the last name of the employee is Miller, the first name is Andrew, the current salary is 65789.87, and the pay increase is 5%. Write a program that reads data from the specified file and stores the output in the file Ch3_Ex7Output.dat. For each employee, the data must be output in the following form: firstName lastName updatedSalary. Format the output of decimal numbers to two decimal places.

8. Write a program that accepts as input the mass (in grams) and density (in grams per cubic centimeters), and outputs the volume of the object using the formula: *density = mass / volume*. Format your output to two decimal places.

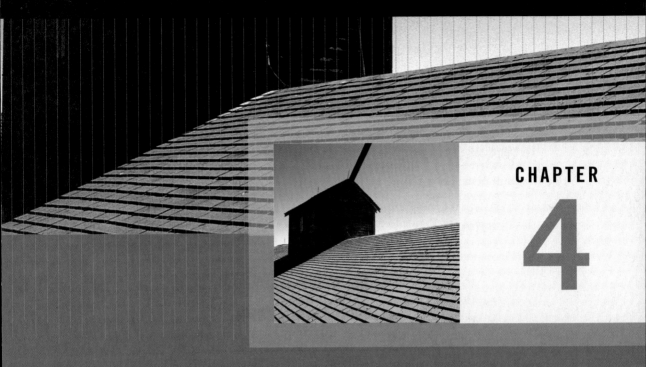

CONTROL STRUCTURES I: SELECTION

IN THIS CHAPTER, YOU WILL:

- Learn about control structures
- Examine relational and logical operators
- Explore how to form and evaluate logical (boolean) expressions
- Learn how to use the selection control structures **if**, **if...else**, and **switch** in a program
- Learn how to avoid bugs by avoiding partially understood concepts and techniques
- Explore how to compare strings

Chapter 2 defined a program as a sequence of statements whose objective is to accomplish some task. The programs you have examined so far have been simple and straightforward. In executing programs, the computer starts at the first (executable) statement and executes the statements in order until it comes to the end. In this chapter and in Chapter 5, you will learn how to tell a computer that it does not have to follow a simple sequential order of statements; it can also make decisions and/or repeat certain statements over and over until certain conditions are met.

Control Structures

A computer can process a program in one of three ways:

- In **sequence**
- By making a selection or a choice, which is also called a **branch**
- By repetition, executing a statement over and over using a structure called a **loop**

These three types of program flow are shown in Figure 4-1. The programming examples in Chapters 2 and 3 show simple sequential programs. With such a program, the computer starts at the beginning and follows the statements in order. No decisions are made and there is no repetition.

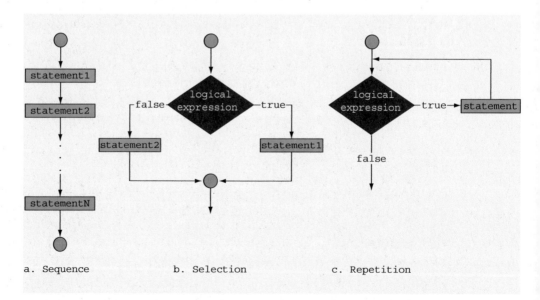

FIGURE 4-1 Flow of execution

Control structures provide alternatives to sequential program execution and are used to alter the flow of execution. The two most common control structures are selection and repetition. In **selection**, the program executes particular statements depending on one or more conditions. In **repetition**, the program repeats particular statements a certain number of times depending on one or more conditions. This chapter introduces selection (branching); Chapter 5 introduces repetition (looping).

Branch: Altering the flow of program execution by making a selection or choice.

Loop: Altering the flow of program execution by the repetition of statement(s).

Before you can learn about selection and repetition, you must understand the nature of conditional expressions and how to use them. Consider the following three statements (notice that these are not Java statements):

1.  ```
    if (score is greater than or equal to 90)
        grade is A
    ```

2.  ```
    if (hours worked are less than or equal to 40)
        wages = rate * hours
    otherwise
        wages = (rate * 40) + 1.5 * (rate * (hours - 40))
    ```

3.  ```
    if (temperature is greater than 50 degrees and it is not
        raining)
        recommended activity is golfing
    ```

These statements include conditional expressions. For example, in 1, the conditional expression is: `score is greater than or equal to 90`.

You can see that a statement such as `grade is A` is to be executed only if a certain condition is met.

A condition is met if it evaluates to `true`. For example, in statement 1:

`score is greater than or equal to 90`

is `true` if the value of `score` is greater than or equal to 90; it is `false` otherwise. For example, if the value of `score` is 95, the statement evaluates to `true`. Similarly, if the value of `score` is 86, the statement evaluates to `false`. So if the value of `score` is greater than or equal to 90, then the statement, `grade is A`, executes.

It is useful for the computer to be able to recognize expressions, such as `score is greater than or equal to 90`, to be `true` for appropriate values. Furthermore, in certain situations, the truth of a statement could depend on more than one condition. For example, in statement 3, both `temperature is greater than 50 degrees` and `it is not raining` must be `true` for the recommended activity to be `golfing`.

As you can see from these examples, to make decisions, the computer must be able to react to conditions that exist when the program executes. The next few sections discuss how to represent and evaluate conditional statements in Java.
    ```

Relational Operators

To make decisions, you must be able to express conditions and make comparisons. For example, the interest rate paid and service charges imposed on a checking account might depend on the balance at the end of the month. If the balance is less than some minimum balance, not only is the interest rate lower, but there is also usually a service charge. Therefore, to determine the interest rate, you must be able to state the minimum balance (a condition) and compare the account balance with the minimum balance. The premium on an insurance policy is also determined by determining conditions and making comparisons. For example, to determine an insurance premium, you must be able to check the smoking behavior of the policyholder. Nonsmokers (the condition) receive lower premiums than smokers. Both of these examples involve comparing items. Items can be compared in various ways. For example, you can compare items for equality or inequality. You can also determine whether one item is greater than another item, and so on.

An expression that has a value of either `true` or `false` is called a **logical (boolean) expression**. The values `true` and `false` are called **logical (boolean) values**. In Java, a condition is represented by a logical (boolean) expression; conditions are either `true` or `false`.

Logical (boolean) expression: An expression that has a value of either `true` or `false`.

Suppose `i` and `j` are integers. Consider the expression:

`i > j`

This is a logical expression. It will have the value `true` if the value of `i` is greater than the value of `j`; otherwise, it will have the value `false`. The symbol > is called a **relational operator** because the value of `i > j` is `true` only when the relationship "greater than" holds for `i` relative to `j`.

Relational operator: An operator that allows you to make comparisons in a program.

Java includes six relational operators that enable you to make comparisons. Table 4-1 lists the relational operators.

TABLE 4-1 Relational Operators in Java

Operator	Description
==	equal to
!=	not equal to
<	less than
<=	less than or equal to
>	greater than
>=	greater than or equal to

NOTE In Java, the symbol ==, which consists of two equal signs, is called the **equality operator**. Recall that the symbol = is called the assignment operator. The equality operator, ==, determines whether two expressions are equal, whereas the assignment operator, =, assigns the value of an expression to a variable.

Each of the relational operators is a binary operator; that is, it requires two operands. Because the result of a comparison is `true` or `false`, expressions using these operators evaluate to `true` or `false`.

4

Relational Operators and Primitive Data Types

You can use the relational operators with integral and floating-point primitive data types. For example, the following expressions use both integers and floating-point numbers:

Expression	Meaning	Value
8 < 15	8 is less than 15	true
6 != 6	6 is not equal to 6	false
2.5 > 5.8	2.5 is greater than 5.8	false
5.9 <= 7.5	5.9 is less than or equal to 7.5	true

 NOTE It is important to remember that the comparison of floating-point numbers for equality may not behave as you would expect. See Example 4-1.

EXAMPLE 4-1

Consider the following program:

```
public class FloatingPointNumbers
{
    public static void main(String[] args)
    {
        System.out.println("3.0 / 7.0 = " + (3.0 / 7.0));
        System.out.println("2.0 / 7.0 = " + (2.0 / 7.0));
        System.out.println("3.0 / 7.0 + 2.0 / 7.0 + 2.0 / 7.0 = "
                           + (3.0 / 7.0 + 2.0 / 7.0 + 2.0 / 7.0));
    }
}
```

Sample Run:

```
3.0 / 7.0 = 0.42857142857142855
2.0 / 7.0 = 0.2857142857142857
3.0 / 7.0 + 2.0 / 7.0 + 2.0 / 7.0 = 0.9999999999999999
```

From the output, it follows that the following equality evaluates to `false`:

```
1.0 == 3.0 / 7.0 + 2.0 / 7.0 + 2.0 / 7.0
```

NOTE The preceding program and its output show that you should be careful when comparing floating-point numbers for equality. One way to check whether two floating-point numbers are virtually equal is to check whether the absolute value of their difference is less than a certain tolerance. For example, suppose **x** and **y** are floating-point numbers and the tolerance is 0.000001. Then x and y are equal if the absolute value of **(x − y)** is less than 0.000001. To find the absolute value, you can use the method **abs** of the **class** Math. For example, the expression Math.abs(x − y) gives the absolute value of **x − y**. Therefore, the expression Math.abs(x − y) < 0.000001 determines whether the absolute value of **(x − y)** is less than 0.000001.

For **char** values, whether an expression using relational operators evaluates to **true** or **false** depends on the collating sequence of the Unicode character set. Table 4-2 gives the collating sequence (Unicode value as a decimal integer) of some of the characters in the character set.

TABLE 4-2 Some Characters of the Unicode Character Set and their Unicode Value as a Decimal Integer

Unicode Value	Character	Unicode Value	Character	Unicode Value	Character	Unicode Value	Character
32	' '	61	=	81	Q	105	i
33	!	62	>	82	R	106	j
34	"	65	A	83	S	107	k
42	*	66	B	84	T	108	l
43	+	67	C	85	U	109	m
45	−	68	D	86	V	110	n
47	/	69	E	87	W	111	o
48	0	70	F	88	X	112	p
49	9	71	G	89	Y	113	q
50	2	72	H	90	Z	114	r
51	3	73	I	97	a	115	s
52	4	74	J	98	b	116	t
53	5	75	K	99	c	117	u
54	6	76	L	100	d	118	v

TABLE 4-2 Some Characters of the Unicode Character Set and their Unicode Value as a Decimal Integer (continued)

Unicode Value	Character	Unicode Value	Character	Unicode Value	Character	Unicode Value	Character
55	7	77	M	101	e	119	w
56	8	78	N	102	f	120	x
57	9	79	O	103	g	121	y
60	<	80	P	104	h	122	z

The first 128 characters of the Unicode character set are described in Appendix C. Table 4-3 shows how expressions using the Unicode character set are evaluated.

TABLE 4-3 Evaluating Expressions Using Relational Operators and the Unicode (ASCII) Collating Sequence

Expression	Value of the Expression	Explanation
' ' < 'a'	true	The Unicode value of ' ' is 32, and the Unicode value of 'a' is 97. Because 32 < 97 is true, it follows that ' ' < 'a' is true.
'R' > 'T'	false	The Unicode value of 'R' is 82, and the Unicode value of 'T' is 84. Because 82 > 84 is false, it follows that 'R' > 'T' is false.
'+' < '*'	false	The Unicode value of '+' is 43, and the Unicode value of '*' is 42. Because 43 < 42 is false, it follows that '+' < '*' is false.
'6' <= '>'	true	The Unicode value of '6' is 54, and the Unicode value of '>' is 62. Because 54 <= 62 is true, it follows that '6' <= '>' is true.

NOTE Consider the following expression:

8 < '5'

You might think that 8 is being compared with 5. This is not the case. Here, the integer 8 is being compared with the character 5. That is, 8 is being compared with the Unicode collating sequence of '5', which is 53. The Java system uses implicit type conversion, changes '5' to 53, and compares 8 with 53. Therefore, the expression 8 < '5' always evaluates to true. However, the expression 8 < 5 always evaluates to false. Note that char and int are of integral type and using explicit or implicit type conversion, values of char type can be converted to int type and vice versa.

Expressions such as 4 < 6 and `'R' > 'T'` are examples of logical (boolean) expressions. When Java evaluates a logical expression, it returns the `boolean` value `true` if the logical expression evaluates to `true`; it returns the `boolean` value `false` otherwise.

Logical (Boolean) Operators and Logical Expressions

This section describes how to form and evaluate logical expressions that are combinations of other logical expressions. **Logical (Boolean) operators** enable you to combine logical expressions. Java has three logical (boolean) operators, as shown in Table 4-4.

TABLE 4-4   Logical (Boolean) Operators in Java

Operator	Description
!	not
&&	and
||	or

Logical operators take only logical values as operands and yield only logical values as results. The operator ! is unary, so it has only one operand. The operators && and || are binary.

Table 4-5 shows that when you use the ! operator, `!true` is `false` and `!false` is `true`. Putting ! in front of a logical expression reverses the value of that logical expression. Table 4-5 is called the **truth table** of the operator !. Example 4-2 gives examples of the ! operator.

TABLE 4-5   ! (not) Operator

Expression	!(Expression)
true	false
false	true

EXAMPLE 4-2

Expression	Value	Explanation
`!('A' > 'B')`	true	Because `'A' > 'B'` is `false`, `!('A' > 'B')` is `true`.
`!(6 <= 7)`	false	Because `6 <= 7` is `true`, `!(6 <= 7)` is `false`.

Table 4–6 defines the operator `&&` (and). From this table, it follows that `Expression1 && Expression2` is `true` if and only if both `Expression1` and `Expression2` are `true`; otherwise, `Expression1 && Expression2` evaluates to `false`. Table 4–6 is called the **truth table** of the operator `&&`. Example 4–3 gives examples of the `&&` operator.

TABLE 4-6 `&&` (and) Operator

Expression1	Expression2	Expression1 `&&` Expression2
true	true	true
true	false	false
false	true	false
false	false	false

EXAMPLE 4-3

Expression	Value	Explanation
`(14 >= 5) && ('A' < 'B')`	true	Because `(14 >= 5)` is `true`, `('A' < 'B')` is `true`, and `true && true` is `true`, the expression evaluates to `true`.
`(24 >= 35) && ('A' < 'B')`	false	Because `(24 >= 35)` is `false`, `('A' < 'B')` is `true`, and `false && true` is `false`, the expression evaluates to `false`.

Table 4–7 defines the operator `||` (or). From this table, it follows that `Expression1 || Expression2` is `true` if and only if at least one of the expressions, `Expression1` or `Expression2`, is `true`; otherwise, `Expression1 || Expression2` evaluates to `false`. Table 4–7 is called the **truth table** of the operator `||`. Example 4–4 gives examples of the `||` operator.

TABLE 4-7 `||` (or) Operator

Expression1	Expression2	Expression1 `||` Expression2
true	true	true
true	false	true
false	true	true
false	false	false

EXAMPLE 4-4

Expression	Value	Explanation
(14 >= 5) || ('A' > 'B')	true	Because (14 >= 5) is true, ('A' > 'B') is false, and true || false is true, the expression evaluates to true.
(24 >= 35) || ('A' > 'B')	false	Because (24 >= 35) is false, ('A' > 'B') is false, and false || false is false, the expression evaluates to false.
('A' <= 'a') || (7 != 7)	true	Because ('A' <= 'a') is true, (7 != 7) is false, and true || false is true, the expression evaluates to true.

Order of Precedence

To work with complex logical expressions, there must be some priority scheme for determining which operators to evaluate first. Because an expression might contain arithmetic, relational, and logical operators, as in the expression 5 + 3 <= 9 && 2 > 3, an order of precedence for the Java operators must be established. Table 4–8 shows the order of precedence of some Java operators, including the arithmetic, relational, and logical operators. (See Appendix B for the precedence of all Java operators.)

TABLE 4-8 Precedence of Operators

Operators	Precedence
!, +, − (unary operators)	first (highest)
*, /, %	second
+, −	third
<, <=, >=, >	fourth
==, !=	fifth
&&	sixth
||	seventh
= (assignment operator)	last (lowest)

Using the precedence rules given in Table 4–8, in an expression, relational and logical operators are evaluated from left to right, and consequently the **associativity** of these operators is said to be from left to right.

You can insert parentheses into an expression to clarify its meaning or to affect the predence.

EXAMPLE 4-5

Evaluate the following expression:

(17 < 4 * 3 + 5) || (8 * 2 == 4 * 4) && !(3 + 3 == 6)

Now:

Therefore, the value of the original logical expression is `false`.

```
      (17 < 4 * 3 + 5)  ||  (8 * 2 == 4 * 4)  && !(3 + 3 == 6)
=     (17 < 12 + 5)  ||  (16 == 16)  && !(6 == 6)
=     (17 < 17)  ||  true && !(true)
=     false || true && false
=     false || false (because true && false is false)
=     false
```

You can also use parentheses to override the precedence of operators. For example, in the expression:

(7 >= 8 || 'A' < 'B') && 5 * 4 == 20

the operator || evaluates before the operator &&; whereas, in the expression:

7 >= 8 || 'A' < 'B' && 5 * 4 == 20

the operator && evaluates before the operator ||.

Example 4–6 illustrates how logical expressions consisting of variables are evaluated.

EXAMPLE 4-6

Suppose you have the following declarations:

```
boolean found = true;
boolean flag = false;
double x = 5.2;
double y = 3.4;
int a = 5, b = 8;
int n = 20;
char ch = B;
```

Consider the following expressions:

Expression	Value	Explanation
!found	false	Because found is true, !found is false.
x > 4.0	true	Because x is 5.2 and 5.2 > 4.0 is true, the expression x > 4.0 evaluates to true.
!found && (x >= 0)	false	In this expression, !found is false. Also, because x is 5.2 and 5.2 >= 0 is true, x >= 0 is true. Therefore, the value of the expression !found && (x >= 0) is false && true, which evaluates to false.
!(found && (x >= 0))	false	In this expression, found && (x >= 0) is true && true, which evaluates to true. Therefore, the value of the expression !(found && (x >= 0)) is !true, which evaluates to false.
x + y <= 20.5	true	Because x + y = 5.2 + 3.4 = 8.6 and 8.6 <= 20.5 is true, it follows that x + y <= 20.5 evaluates to true.
(n >= 0) && (n <= 100)	true	Here, n is 20. Because 20 >= 0 is true, n >= 0 is true. Also, because 20 <= 100 is true, n <= 100 is true. Therefore, the value of the expression (n >= 0) && (n <= 100) is true && true, which evaluates to true.
('A' <= ch && ch <= 'Z')	true	In this expression, the value of ch is 'B'. Because 'A' <= 'B' is true, 'A' <= ch evaluates to true. Also, because 'B' <= 'Z' is true, ch <= 'Z' evaluates to true. Therefore, the value of the expression ('A' <= ch && ch <= 'Z') is true && true, which evaluates to true.
(a + 2 <= b) && !flag	true	Now a + 2 = 5 + 2 = 7 and b is 8. Because 7 < 8 is true, the expression a + 2 <= b evaluates to true. Also, because flag is false, !flag is true. Therefore, the value of the expression (a + 2 <= b) && !flag is true && true, which evaluates to true.

You can also write a Java program to evaluate and output the logical expressions given in Example 4-6, as shown in Example 4-7.

EXAMPLE 4-7

```java
//Logical operators

public class LogicalOperators
{
    public static void main(String[] args)
    {
        boolean found = true;
        boolean flag = false;
        double x = 5.2;
        double y = 3.4;
        int a = 5;
        int b = 8;
        int n = 20;
        char ch = 'B';

        System.out.println("Line 1: !found evaluates to "
                        + !found);                          //Line 1
        System.out.println("Line 2: x > 4.0 evaluates to "
                        + (x > 4.0));                       //Line 2
        System.out.println("Line 3: !found && (x >= 0) "
                        + "evaluates to "
                        + (!found && (x >= 0)));            //Line 3
        System.out.println("Line 4: !(found && (x >= 0)) "
                        + "evaluates to "
                        + !(found && (x >= 0)));            //Line 4
        System.out.println("Line 5: x + y <= 20.5 evaluates to "
                        + (x + y <= 20.5));                 //Line 5
        System.out.println("Line 6: (n >= 0) && (n <= 100) "
                        + "evaluates to "
                        + ((n >= 0) && (n <= 100)));        //Line 6
        System.out.println("Line 7: ('A' <= ch && ch <= 'Z') "
                        + "evaluates to "
                        + ('A' <= ch && ch <= 'Z'));        //Line 7
        System.out.println("Line 8: (a + 2 <= b) && !flag "
                        + "evaluates to "
                        + ((a + 2 <= b) && !flag));         //Line 8
    }
}
```

Sample Run:

```
Line 1: !found evaluates to false
Line 2: x > 4.0 evaluates to true
Line 3: !found && (x >= 0) evaluates to false
Line 4: !(found && (x >= 0)) evaluates to false
Line 5: x + y <= 20.5 evaluates to true
Line 6: (n >= 0) && (n <= 100) evaluates to true
Line 7: ('A' <= ch && ch <= 'Z') evaluates to true
Line 8: (a + 2 <= b) && !flag evaluates to true
```

NOTE Be careful when forming logical expressions. Some beginners make the following common mistake: Suppose that num is an `int` variable. Further suppose that you want to write a logical expression that evaluates to `true` if the value of num is between 0 and 10, including 0 and 10, and that evaluates to `false` otherwise. The following expression appears to represent a comparison of 0, num, and 10 that will yield the desired result:

```
0 <= num <= 10
```

This statement is *not* legal in Java and you will get a syntax error. This is because the associativity of the operator `<=` is from left to right. Therefore, the preceding expression is equivalent to:

```
(0 <= num) <= 10
```

The value of the expression `(0 <= num)` is either `true` or `false`. Because you cannot compare the **boolean** values `true` and `false` with other data types, the expression would result in a syntax error. A correct way to write this expression in Java is:

```
0 <= num && num <= 10
```

When creating a complex logical expression, take care to use the proper logical operators.

Short-Circuit Evaluation

Logical expressions in Java are evaluated using an efficient algorithm. This algorithm is illustrated with the help of the following statements:

```
(x > y) || (x == 5)
(a == b) && (x >= 7)
```

In the first statement, the two operands of the operator `||` are the expressions `(x > y)` and `(x == 5)`. This expression evaluates to `true` if either the operand `(x > y)` is `true` or the operand `(x == 5)` is `true`. With **short-circuit evaluation**, the computer evaluates the logical expression from left to right. As soon as the value of the entire logical expression can be determined, the evaluation stops. For example, in the first statement, if the operand `(x > y)` evaluates to `true`, then the entire expression evaluates to `true` because `true || true` is `true` and `true || false` is `true`. Therefore, the value of the operand `(x == 5)` has no bearing on the final outcome.

Similarly, in the second statement, the two operands of the operator `&&` are `(a == b)` and `(x >= 7)`. Now, if the operand `(a == b)` evaluates to `false`, then the entire expression evaluates to `false` because `false && true` is `false` and `false && false` is `false`.

Short-circuit evaluation (of a logical expression): A process in which the computer evaluates a logical expression from left to right and stops as soon as the value of the expression is determined.

EXAMPLE 4-8

Consider the following expressions:

```
(age >= 21) || (x == 5)      //Line 1
(grade == 'A') && (x >= 7)   //Line 2
```

For the expression in Line 1, suppose that the value of **age** is 25. Because **(25 >= 21)** is **true** and the logical operator used in the expression is **||**, the expression evaluates to **true**. Due to short-circuit evaluation, the computer does not evaluate the expression **(x == 5)**. Similarly, for the expression in Line 2, suppose that the value of **grade** is **'B'**. Because **('A' == 'B')** is **false** and the logical operator used in the expression is **&&**, the expression evaluates to **false**. The computer does not evaluate **(x >= 7)**.

4

NOTE   In Java, **&** and **|** are also operators. You can use the operator **&** in place of the operator **&&** in a logical expression. Similarly, you can use the operator **|** in place of the operator **||** in a logical expression. However, there is no short-circuit evaluation of the logical expressions if **&** is used in place of **&&** or **|** is used in place of **||**. For example, suppose that **a** and **b** are **int** variables, and **a = 10** and **b = 18**. After the evaluation of the expression **(a > 10) && (b++ < 5)**, the value of **b** is still 18. This is because the expression **a > 10** evaluates to **false**, and **false && false** is **false** as well as **false && true** is **false**, so using short circuit evaluation the expression **(a > 10) && (b++ < 5)** evaluates to **false** and the expression **(b++ < 5)** does not get evaluated.

`boolean` Data Type and Logical (Boolean) Expressions

Recall that Java contains the built-in data type **boolean**, which has the logical (boolean) values **true** and **false**. Therefore, you can manipulate logical (boolean) expressions using the **boolean** data type. Also, recall that in Java, **boolean**, **true**, and **false** are reserved words.

Suppose that you have the following statements:

```
boolean legalAge;
int age;
```

The statement:

```
legalAge = true;
```

sets the value of the variable **legalAge** to **true**. The statement:

```
legalAge = (age >= 21);
```

assigns the value **true** to **legalAge** if the value of **age** is greater than or equal to 21. This statement assigns the value **false** to **legalAge** if the value of **age** is less than 21. For example, if the value of **age** is 25, the value assigned to **legalAge** is **true**. Similarly, if the value of **age** is 16, the value assigned to **legalAge** is **false**.

Selection: `if` and `if...else`

Although there are only two logical values, `true` and `false`, they are extremely useful because they permit programs to incorporate decision making that alters the processing flow. The remainder of this chapter discusses ways to incorporate decisions into a program. Java has three selection or branch control structures: `if` and `if...else` statements, and the `switch` structure. This section discusses how `if` and `if...else` statements can be used to create one-way selection, two-way selection, and multiple selections. The `switch` structure is discussed later in this chapter.

One-Way Selection

A bank wants to send a notice to a customer if her or his checking account balance falls below the required minimum balance. That is, if the balance is below the required minimum, the bank should send a notice to the customer; otherwise, it should do nothing. Similarly, if the policyholder of an insurance policy is a nonsmoker, the company wants to apply a 10% discount to the policy premium. Both of these examples involve one-way selection. In Java, one-way selections are incorporated using the `if` statement. The syntax of one-way selection is:

```
if (logical expression)
    statement
```

Note the elements of this syntax. It begins with the reserved word `if`, followed by a **logical expression** contained within parentheses, followed by a **statement**. The **logical expression** is also called a **condition**; it decides whether to execute the **statement** that follows it. If **logical expression** is `true`, the **statement** executes. If it is `false`, the **statement** does not execute and the computer goes on to the next statement in the program. The **statement** following the **logical expression** is sometimes called the **action statement**. (Note the indentation of the action **statement**. We have indented it four spaces to the right of the `if` statement in the previous line.)

Figure 4-2 shows the flow of execution of the `if` statement (one-way selection).

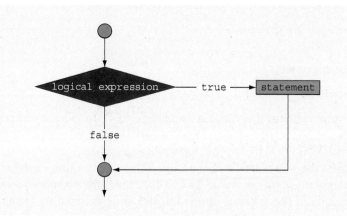

FIGURE 4-2 One-way selection

Next, we give various examples to show how an if statement works. We also show some common syntax and/or semantic errors that beginning programmers often make.

EXAMPLE 4-9

```
if (score >= 90)
    grade = 'A';
```

In this code, if the logical expression, score >= 90, evaluates to true, the assignment statement, grade = 'A';, executes. If score >= 90 evaluates to false, the assignment statement, grade = 'A';, is skipped. For example, if the value of score is 95, the value assigned to the variable grade is A.

EXAMPLE 4-10

The following Java program finds the absolute value of an integer.

```
//Program to determine the absolute value of an integer.

import javax.swing.JOptionPane;

public class AbsoluteValue
{
    public static void main(String[] args)
    {
        int number;
        int temp;

        String numString;

        numString =
          JOptionPane.showInputDialog("Enter an integer:"); //Line 1

        number = Integer.parseInt(numString);               //Line 2
        temp = number;                                      //Line 3

        if (number < 0)                                     //Line 4
            number = -number;                               //Line 5

        JOptionPane.showMessageDialog(null,
                    "The absolute value of " + temp
                  + " is " + number,
                    "Absolute Value",
                    JOptionPane.INFORMATION_MESSAGE);       //Line 6
        System.exit(0);
    }
}
```

Sample Run: Figure 4–3 shows a sample run of this program.

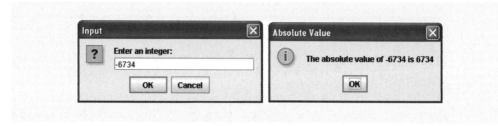

FIGURE 4-3 Sample run of Example 4-10

The statement in Line 1 displays the input dialog box and prompts the user to enter an integer. The entered number is stored as a string in `numString`. The statement in Line 2 uses the method `parseInt` of the `class` `Integer`, converts the value of `numString` into the number, and stores the number in the variable `number`. The statement in Line 3 copies the value of `number` into `temp`. The statement in Line 4 checks whether `number` is negative. If `number` is negative, the statement in Line 5 changes `number` to a positive number. The statement in Line 6 displays the message dialog box and shows the original number, stored in `temp`, and the absolute value of the number stored in `number`.

EXAMPLE 4-11

Consider the following statement:

```
if score >= 90
    grade = 'A';
```

This statement illustrates an incorrect version of an `if` statement. The parentheses around the logical expression are missing, which is a syntax error.

Putting a semicolon after the parentheses following the logical expression in an `if` statement (that is, before the statement) is a semantic error. If the semicolon immediately follows the closing parenthesis, the `if` statement will operate on the empty statement.

EXAMPLE 4-12

Consider the following Java statements:

```
if (score >= 90);            //Line 1
    grade = 'A';             //Line 2
```

This statement represents a one-way selection. Because there is a semicolon at the end of the logical expression in Line 1, the `if` statement terminates at Line 1, the action of the `if` statement is null, and the statement in Line 2 is not part of the `if` statement. The statement in Line 2 executes regardless of how the `if` statement evaluates. Note that the semicolon in Line 1 is a logical error and this can be hard to debug. So be careful when forming one-way selection.

Two-Way Selection

In the previous section, you learned how to implement one-way selections in a program. There are many situations in which you must choose between two alternatives. For example, if a part-time employee works overtime, the paycheck is calculated using the overtime payment formula; otherwise, the paycheck is calculated using the regular formula. This is an example of two-way selection. To choose between two alternatives—that is, to implement two-way selections—Java provides the `if...else` statement. Two-way selection uses the following syntax:

```
if (logical expression)
     statement1
else
     statement2
```

Take a moment to examine this syntax. It begins with the reserved word `if`, followed by a `logical expression` contained within parentheses, followed by a statement, followed by the reserved word `else`, followed by a second statement. Statements 1 and 2 can be any valid Java statements. In a two-way selection, if the value of the `logical expression` is `true`, then `statement1` executes. If the value of the `logical expression` is `false`, then `statement2` executes. Figure 4–4 shows the flow of execution of the `if...else` statement (two-way selection).

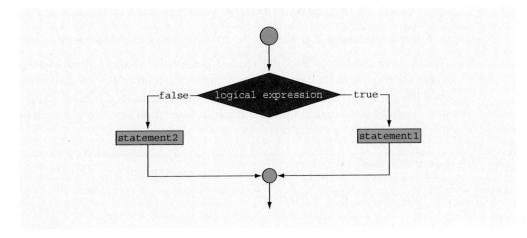

FIGURE 4-4 Two-way selection

EXAMPLE 4-13

Consider the following statements:

```
if (hours > 40.0)                                  //Line 1
    wages = 40.0 * rate +
            1.5 * rate * (hours - 40.0);           //Line 2
else                                               //Line 3
    wages = hours * rate;                          //Line 4
```

If the value of the variable `hours` is greater than `40.0`, then the `wages` include overtime payment. Suppose that `hours` is 50. The logical expression in the `if` statement in Line 1 evaluates to `true`, so the statement in Line 2 executes. On the other hand, if `hours` is 30, or any number less than or equal to 40, the logical expression in the `if` statement in Line 1 evaluates to `false`. In this case, the program skips the statement in Line 2 and executes the statement in Line 4—that is, the statement following the reserved word `else` executes.

In a two-way selection statement, putting a semicolon after the right parenthesis and before `statement1` creates a syntax error. If the `if` statement ends with a semicolon, `statement1` is no longer part of the `if` statement, and the `else` part of the `if...else` statement stands by itself. There is no stand-alone `else` statement in Java; that is, the `else` statement cannot be separated from the `if` statement. This also creates a syntax error.

EXAMPLE 4-14

The following statements show an example of a syntax error:

```
if (hours > 40.0);                                 //Line 1
    wages = 40.0 * rate +
            1.5 * rate * (hours - 40.0);           //Line 2
else                                               //Line 3
    wages = hours * rate;                          //Line 4
```

Because a semicolon follows the closing parenthesis of the `if` statement (Line 1), the `else` statement stands alone. The semicolon at the end of the `if` statement (see Line 1) ends the `if` statement, so the statement in Line 2 separates the `else` clause from the `if` statement. That is, `else` is by itself. Because there is no separate `else` statement in Java, this code generates a syntax error.

EXAMPLE 4-15

The following program determines an employee's weekly wages. If the **hours** worked exceed 40, then **wages** include overtime payment.

```
//Weekly Wages

import java.util.*;

public class WeeklyWages
{
    static Scanner console = new Scanner(System.in);

    public static void main(String[] args)
    {
        double wages, rate, hours;                      //Line 1

        System.out.print("Line 2: Enter the working "
                        + "hours: ");                   //Line 2
        hours = console.nextDouble();                   //Line 3
        System.out.println();                           //Line 4

        System.out.print("Line 5: Enter the pay "
                        + "rate: ");                     //Line 5
        rate = console.nextDouble();                    //Line 6
        System.out.println();                           //Line 7

        if (hours > 40.0)                               //Line 8
            wages = 40.0 * rate +
                1.5 * rate * (hours - 40.0);            //Line 9
        else                                            //Line 10
            wages = hours * rate;                       //Line 11

        System.out.printf("Line 12: The wages are $%.2f %n",
                        wages);                         //Line 12
        System.out.println();                           //Line 13
    }
}
```

Sample Run: (In this sample run, the user input is shaded.)

Line 2: Enter working hours: `60`

Line 5: Enter pay rate: `10`

Line 12: The wages are $700

The statement in Line 1 declares the appropriate variables. The statement in Line 2 prompts the user to input the number of hours worked. The statement in Line 3 inputs and stores the working hours in the variable **hours**. The statement in Line 5 prompts the user to input the pay rate. The statement in Line 6 inputs and stores the pay rate into the variable `rate`. The statement in Line 8 checks whether the value of the variable `hours` is greater than `40.0`. If `hours` is greater than `40.0`, then the wages are calculated by the statement in Line 9, which includes overtime payment; otherwise, the wages are calculated by the statement in Line 11. The statement in Line 12 outputs the wages.

Let's now consider more examples of `if` statements and examine some of the common errors made by beginning programmers.

EXAMPLE 4-16

Consider the following statements:

```
if (score >= 90)                                    //Line 1
    grade = 'A';                                    //Line 2
    System.out.println("The grade is " + grade);    //Line 3
```

Here, you might think that because the statements in Lines 2 and 3 are aligned, both statements are the action statements of the `if` statement. However, this is not the case. The `if` statement acts on only one statement, which is `grade = 'A';`. The output statement executes regardless of whether `(score >= 90)` is `true` or `false`.

Example 4-17 illustrates another common mistake.

EXAMPLE 4-17

Consider the following statements:

```
if (score >= 60)
    System.out.println("Passing");
    System.out.println("Failing");
```

If the logical expression, `score >= 60`, evaluates to `false`, the output would be `Failing`. That is, this set of statements performs the same action as an `else` statement. It will execute the second output statement rather than the first. For example, if the value of `score` is 50, these statements will output the following line:

```
Failing
```

However, if the logical expression, `score >= 60`, evaluates to `true`, the program will write both statements, giving an unsatisfactory result. For example, if the value of `score` is 70, these statements will output the following lines:

```
Passing
Failing
```

The correct code to print `Passing` or `Failing`, depending on the value of `score`, is:

```
if (score >= 60)
    System.out.println("Passing");
else
    System.out.println("Failing");
```

Compound (Block of) Statements

The `if` and `if...else` structures select only one statement at a time. Suppose, however, that you want to execute more than one statement if the `logical expression` in an `if` or `if...else` statement evaluates to `true`. To permit more complex statements, Java provides a structure called a **compound statement** or a **block** of statements. A compound statement takes the following form:

```
{
    statement1
    statement2
        .
        .
        .
    statementn
}
```

That is, a compound statement or block consists of a sequence of statements enclosed in braces. In an `if` or `if...else` structure, a compound statement functions as if it were a single statement. Thus, instead of having a simple two-way selection similar to the following code:

```
if (age > 18)
    System.out.println("Eligible to vote.");
else
    System.out.println("Not eligible to vote.");
```

you could include compound statements, similar to the following code:

```
if (age > 18)
{
    System.out.println("Eligible to vote.");
    System.out.println("No longer a minor.");
}
else
{
    System.out.println("Not eligible to vote.");
    System.out.println("Still a minor.");
}
```

The compound statement is useful and will be used in most of the ensuing structured statements in this chapter.

Multiple Selections: Nested `if`

In the previous sections, you learned how to implement one-way and two-way selections in a program. However, some problems require the implementation of more than two alternatives. For example, suppose that if the checking account balance is greater than or equal to $50000, the interest rate is 5%; if the balance is greater than or equal to $25000 and less than $50000, the interest rate is 4%; if the balance is greater than or equal to $1000 and less than $25000, the interest rate is 3%; otherwise, the interest rate is 0%. This particular problem has four alternatives—that is, multiple selection paths. You can include multiple selection paths in a program by using an `if...else` structure—if the action statement itself is an `if` or `if...else` statement. When one control statement is located within another, it is said to be **nested**.

EXAMPLE 4-18

Suppose that `balance` and `interestRate` are variables of type `double`. The following statements determine the `interestRate` depending on the value of `balance`:

```
if (balance >= 50000.00)                    //Line 1
    interestRate = 0.05;                    //Line 2
else                                        //Line 3
    if (balance >= 25000.00)                //Line 4
        interestRate = 0.04;                //Line 5
    else                                    //Line 6
        if (balance >= 1000.00)             //Line 7
            interestRate = 0.03;            //Line 8
        else                                //Line 9
            interestRate = 0.00;            //Line 10
```

Suppose that the value of `balance` is `60000.00`. Then, the expression `balance >= 50000.00` in Line 1 evaluates to `true` and the statement in Line 2 executes. Now suppose the value of `balance` is `40000.00`. Then, the expression `balance >= 50000.00` in Line 1 evaluates to `false`. So the `else` part at Line 3 executes. The statement part of this `else` is an `if...else` statement. Therefore, the expression `balance >= 25000.00` is evaluated, which evaluates to `true` and the statement in Line 5 executes. Note that the expression in Line 4 is evaluated only when the expression in Line 1 evaluates to `false`. The expression in Line 1 evaluates to `false` if `balance < 50000.00` and then the expression in Line 4 is evaluated. It follows that the expression in Line 4 determines if the value of `balance` is greater than or equal to `25000` and less than `50000`. In other words, the expression in Line 4 is equivalent to the expression `(balance >= 25000.00 && balance < 50000.00)`. The expression in Line 7 works the same way.

The statements in Example 4–18 illustrate how to incorporate multiple selections using a nested `if...else` structure.

A nested `if...else` structure presents an important question: How do you know which `else` is paired with which `if`? Recall that in Java there is no stand-alone `else` statement. Every `else` must be paired with an `if`. The rule to pair an `else` with an `if` is as follows:

Pairing an `else` with an `if`: In a nested `if` statement, Java associates an `else` with the most recent incomplete `if`—that is, the most recent `if` that has not been paired with an `else`.

Using this rule, in Example 4–18, the `else` in Line 3 is paired with the `if` in Line 1. The `else` in Line 6 is paired with the `if` in Line 4, and the `else` in Line 9 is paired with the `if` in Line 7.

To avoid excessive indentation, the code in Example 4–18 can be rewritten as follows:

```
if (balance >= 50000.00)              //Line 1
    interestRate = 0.05;              //Line 2
else if (balance >= 25000.00)         //Line 3
    interestRate = 0.04;              //Line 4
else if (balance >= 1000.00)          //Line 5
    interestRate = 0.03;              //Line 6
else                                  //Line 7
    interestRate = 0.00;              //Line 8
```

EXAMPLE 4-19

Assume that `score` is a variable of type `int`. Based on the value of `score`, the following code determines the grade:

```
if (score >= 90)
    System.out.println("The grade is A");
else if (score >= 80)
    System.out.println("The grade is B");
else if (score >= 70)
    System.out.println("The grade is C");
else if (score >= 60)
    System.out.println("The grade is D");
else
    System.out.println("The grade is F");
```

The following examples will further help you see the various ways in which you can use nested `if` structures to implement multiple selection.

EXAMPLE 4-20

Assume that all variables are properly declared, and consider the following statements:

```
if (temperature >= 50)                              //Line 1
    if (temperature >= 80)                          //Line 2
        System.out.println("Good day for swimming."); //Line 3
    else                                            //Line 4
        System.out.println("Good day for golfing.");  //Line 5
else                                                //Line 6
    System.out.println("Good day to play tennis."); //Line 7
```

In this Java code, the `else` in Line 4 is paired with the `if` in Line 2, and the `else` in Line 6 is paired with the `if` in Line 1. Note that the `else` in Line 4 cannot be paired with the `if` in Line 1. If you pair the `else` in Line 4 with the `if` in Line 1, the `if` in Line 2 becomes the action statement part of the `if` in Line 1, leaving the `else` in Line 6 dangling. Also, the statements in Lines 2 though 5 form the statement part of the `if` in Line 1.

EXAMPLE 4-21

Assume that all variables are properly declared, and consider the following statements:

```
if (temperature >= 60)                              //Line 1
    if (temperature >= 80)                          //Line 2
        System.out.println("Good day for swimming."); //Line 3
    else                                            //Line 4
        System.out.println("Good day for golfing.");  //Line 5
```

In this code, the `else` in Line 4 is paired with the `if` in Line 2. Note that for the `else` in Line 4, the most recent incomplete `if` is the `if` in Line 2. In this code, the `if` in Line 1 has no `else` and is a one-way selection.

EXAMPLE 4-22

Assume that all variables are properly declared, and consider the following statements:

```
if (gpa >= 2.0)                                     //Line 1
    if (gpa >= 3.9)                                 //Line 2
        System.out.println("Dean\'s Honor List.");  //Line 3
else                                                //Line 4
    System.out.println("Current GPA below graduation "
                    + "requirement."   +
                    "\nSee your academic advisor."); //Line 5
```

This code won't work the way we want it to work. Let us explore why. Following the rule of pairing an `else` with an `if`, the `else` in Line 4 is paired with the `if` in Line 2. However, this pairing produces an unintended result. Suppose that the gpa is 3.8. The logical expression, gpa >= 2.0, in the `if` at Line 1 evaluates to `true`, and the statement part of the `if`, which is an `if...else` structure, executes. Because gpa is 3.8, the logical expression in the `if` in Line 2 evaluates to `false`, and the `else` associated with this `if` executes, producing the following output:

```
Current GPA below graduation requirement.
See your academic advisor.
```

However, a student with a gpa of 3.8 would graduate with some type of honor. In fact, we intended for the code to print the message:

```
Current GPA below graduation requirement.
See your academic advisor.
```

only if the GPA is less than 2.0, and the message:

```
Dean's Honor List.
```

if gpa is greater than or equal to 3.9. To achieve that result, the `else` in Line 4 must be paired with the `if` in Line 1. To pair the `else` in Line 4 with the `if` in Line 1, you must use a compound statement, as follows:

```
if (gpa >= 2.0)                                          //Line 1
{
    if (gpa >= 3.9)                                      //Line 2
        System.out.println("Dean\"s Honor List.");       //Line 3
}
else                                                     //Line 4
        System.out.println("Current GPA below graduation "
                    + "requirement."   +
                    "\nSee your academic advisor.");     //Line 5
```

In cases such as this one, the general rule is that you cannot look inside a block (that is, inside the braces) to pair an `else` with an `if`. The `else` in Line 4 cannot be paired with the `if` in Line 2 because the `if` statement in Line 2 is enclosed within braces, and the `else` in Line 4 cannot look inside those braces. Therefore, the `else` in Line 4 is paired with the `if` in Line 1.

Comparing `if...else` Statements with a Series of `if` Statements

Consider the following Java program segments, both of which accomplish the same task:

(a)
```
if (month == 1)                                 //Line 1
    System.out.println("January");              //Line 2
else if (month == 2)                            //Line 3
    System.out.println("February");             //Line 4
```

```
else if (month == 3)                    //Line 5
    System.out.println("March");        //Line 6
else if (month == 4)                    //Line 7
    System.out.println("April");        //Line 8
else if (month == 5)                    //Line 9
    System.out.println("May");          //Line 10
else if (month == 6)                    //Line 11
    System.out.println("June");         //Line 12
```

(b)
```
if (month == 1)
    System.out.println("January");
if (month == 2)
    System.out.println("February");
if (month == 3)
    System.out.println("March");
if (month == 4)
    System.out.println("April");
if (month == 5)
    System.out.println("May");
if (month == 6)
    System.out.println("June");
```

Program segment (a) is written as a sequence of if...else statements; program segment (b) is written as a series of if statements. Both program segments accomplish the same thing. If month is 3, then both program segments output March. If month is 1, then in program segment (a), the expression in the if statement in Line 1 evaluates to true. The statement (in Line 2) associated with this if then executes. The rest of the structure, which is the else of this if statement, is skipped, and the remaining if statements are not evaluated. In program segment (b), the computer has to evaluate the logical expression in each if statement because there is no else statement. As a consequence, program segment (b) executes more slowly than does program segment (a).

Conditional Operator (? :) (Optional)

Certain if...else statements can be written more concisely by using Java's conditional operator. The **conditional operator**, written as ? :, is a **ternary operator**, which means that it takes three arguments. The syntax for using the conditional operator is:

```
expression1 ? expression2 : expression3
```

This type of statement is called a **conditional expression**. The conditional expression is evaluated as follows: If expression1 evaluates to true, the result of the conditional expression is expression2; otherwise, the result of the conditional expression is expression3. Note that expression1 is a logical expression.

Consider the following statements:

```
if (a >= b)
    max = a;
else
    max = b;
```

You can use the conditional operator to simplify the writing of this `if...else` statement as follows:

```
max = (a >= b) ? a : b;
```

switch Structures

Recall that there are three selection, or branch, structures in Java. The two-selection structure, which is implemented with `if` and `if...else` statements, usually requires the evaluation of a (logical) expression. The third selection structure, which does not require the evaluation of a logical expression, is called a `switch` structure. Java's `switch` structure gives the computer the power to choose from many alternatives.

The general syntax of a `switch` statement is:

```
switch (expression)
{
case value1:
     statements1
     break;

case value2:
     statements2
     break;

     .
     .
     .

case valuen:
     statementsn
     break;

default:
     statements
}
```

In Java, `switch`, `case`, `break`, and `default` are reserved words. In a `switch` structure, the **expression** is evaluated first. The value of the **expression** is then used to perform the actions specified in the statements that follow the reserved word `case`. (Recall that, in a syntax template, the shading indicates an optional part of the definition.)

Although it need not be, the **expression** is usually an identifier. Whether it is an identifier or an expression, *the value of the identifier or the expression can be only of type* `int`, `byte`, `short`, or `char`. The **expression** is sometimes called the selector. Its value determines which statements are selected for execution. A particular `case` value must appear only once. One or more statements may follow a `case` label, so you do not need to use braces to turn multiple statements into a single compound statement. The `break` statement may or may not appear after each `statements1`, `statements2`, ..., `statementsn`. A `switch` structure may or may not have the `default` label. Figure 4-5 shows the flow of execution of a `switch` statement.

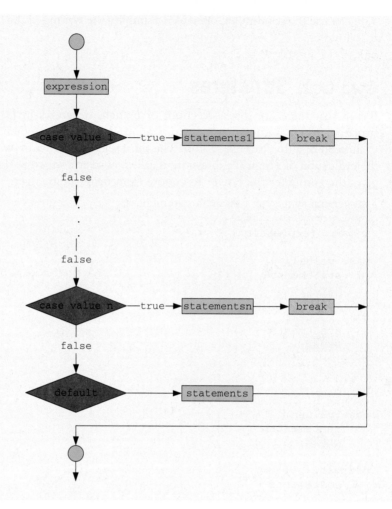

FIGURE 4-5 `switch` statement

A `switch` statement executes according to the following rules:

1. When the value of the **expression** is matched against a `case` value (also called a label), the statements execute until either a `break` statement is found or the end of the `switch` structure is reached.

2. If the value of the **expression** does not match any of the `case` values, the statements following the `default` label execute. If the `switch` structure has no `default` label, and if the value of the **expression** does not match any of the `case` values, the entire `switch` statement is skipped.

3. A `break` statement causes an immediate exit from the `switch` structure.

EXAMPLE 4-23

Consider the following statements (assume that `grade` is a `char` variable):

```
switch (grade)
{
case 'A':
   System.out.println("The grade is A.");
   break;

case 'B':
   System.out.println("The grade is B.");
   break;

case 'C':
   System.out.println("The grade is C.");
   break;

case 'D':
   System.out.println("The grade is D.");
   break;

case 'F':
   System.out.println("The grade is F.");
   break;

default:
   System.out.println("The grade is invalid.");
}
```

In this example, the expression in the `switch` statement is a variable identifier. The variable `grade` is of type `char`, which is an integral type. The valid values of `grade` are `'A'`, `'B'`, `'C'`, `'D'`, and `'F'`. Each `case` label specifies a different action to take, depending on the value of `grade`. If the value of `grade` is `'A'`, the output is:

```
The grade is A.
```

EXAMPLE 4-24

The following program illustrates the effect of the `break` statement. It asks the user to input a number between 0 and 10.

```
//Effect of break statements in a switch structure

import java.util.*;

public class BreakStatementsInSwitch
{
    static Scanner console = new Scanner(System.in);

    public static void main(String[] args)
    {
        int num;

        System.out.print("Enter an integer between "
                        + "0 and 10: ");              //Line 1
        num = console.nextInt();                       //Line 2
        System.out.println();                          //Line 3

        System.out.println("The number you entered "
                        + "is " + num);                //Line 4

        switch (num)                                   //Line 5
        {
        case 0:                                        //Line 6
        case 1:                                        //Line 7
            System.out.print("Hello ");                //Line 8
        case 2:                                        //Line 9
            System.out.print("there. ");               //Line 10
        case 3:                                        //Line 11
            System.out.print("I am ");                 //Line 12
        case 4:                                        //Line 13
            System.out.println("Mickey.");             //Line 14
            break;                                     //Line 15

        case 5:                                        //Line 16
            System.out.print("How ");                  //Line 17
        case 6:                                        //Line 18
        case 7:                                        //Line 19
        case 8:                                        //Line 20
            System.out.println("are you?");            //Line 21
            break;                                     //Line 22

        case 9:                                        //Line 23
            break;                                     //Line 24

        case 10:                                       //Line 25
            System.out.println("Have a nice day.");    //Line 26
            break;                                     //Line 27
        default:                                       //Line 28
            System.out.println("Sorry the number is "
                            + "out of range.");        //Line 29
        }
```

```
        System.out.println("Out of switch "
                        + "structure.");            //Line 30
    }
}
```

Sample Runs

These outputs were obtained by executing the preceding program several times. In each of these outputs, the user input is shaded.

Sample Run 1:

```
Enter an integer between 0 and 10: 0

The number you entered is 0
Hello there. I am Mickey.
Out of switch structure.
```

Sample Run 2:

```
Enter an integer between 0 and 10: 3

The number you entered is 3
I am Mickey.
Out of switch structure.
```

Sample Run 3:

```
Enter an integer between 0 and 10: 4

The number you entered is 4
Mickey.
Out of switch structure.
```

Sample Run 4:

```
Enter an integer between 0 and 10: 7

The number you entered is 7
are you?
Out of switch structure.
```

Sample Run 5:

```
Enter an integer between 0 and 10: 9

The number you entered is 9
Out of switch structure.
```

A walk-through of this program, using certain values of the switch expression num, can help you understand how the break statement functions. If the value of num is 0, the value of the switch expression matches the case value 0. All statements following case 0: execute until a break statement appears.

The first **break** statement appears at Line 15, just before the **case** value of **5**. Even though the value of the **switch** expression does not match any of the **case** values (**1**, **2**, **3**, or **4**), the statements following these values execute.

When the value of the **switch** expression matches a **case** value, *all* statements execute until a **break** is encountered, and the program skips all **case** labels in between. Similarly, if the value of **num** is 3, it matches the **case** value of 3 and the statements following this label execute until the **break** statement is encountered at Line 15. If the value of **num** is 9, it matches the **case** value of 9. In this situation, the action is empty, because only the **break** statement, at Line 24, follows the **case** value of 9.

EXAMPLE 4-25

Although a **switch** structure's **case** values (labels) are limited, the **switch** statement **expression** can be as complex as necessary. Consider the following **switch** statement:

```
switch (score / 10)
{
case 0:
case 1:
case 2:
case 3:
case 4:
case 5:
    grade = 'F';
    break;

case 6:
    grade = 'D';
    break;

case 7:
    grade = 'C';
    break;

case 8:
    grade = 'B';
    break;

case 9:
case 10:
    grade = 'A';
    break;

default:
    System.out.println("Invalid test score.");
}
```

Assume that `score` is an `int` variable with values between 0 and 100. If `score` is 75, then `score / 10 = 75 / 10 = 7` and the grade assigned is `'C'`. If the value of `score` is between 0 and 59, then the grade is `'F'`. If `score` is between 0 and 59, `score / 10` is 0, 1, 2, 3, 4, or 5; each of these values corresponds to the grade `'F'`.

Therefore, in this `switch` structure, the action statements of `case` 0, `case` 1, `case` 2, `case` 3, `case` 4, and `case` 5 are all the same. Rather than write the statement `grade = 'F';` followed by the `break` statement for each of the `case` values of 0, 1, 2, 3, 4, and 5, you can simplify the programming code by first specifying all of the case values (as shown in the preceding code) and then specifying the desired action statement. The `case` values of 9 and 10 follow similar conventions.

4

CHOOSING BETWEEN AN `if...else` AND A `switch` STRUCTURE

As you can see from the preceding examples, the `switch` statement is an elegant way to implement multiple selections. You will see a `switch` statement used in the programming example in this chapter. There are no fixed rules that can be applied to decide whether to use an `if...else` structure or a `switch` structure to implement multiple selections, but you should remember the following consideration: If multiple selections involve a range of values, you should use either an `if...else` structure or a `switch` structure wherein you convert each range to a finite set of values.

For instance, in Example 4-25, the value of `grade` depends on the value of `score`. If `score` is between 0 and 59, `grade` is `'F'`. Because `score` is an `int` variable, 60 values correspond to the grade of `'F'`. If you list all 60 values as `case` values, the `switch` statement could be very long. However, dividing by 10 reduces these 60 values to only 6 values: 0, 1, 2, 3, 4, and 5.

If the range of values is infinite and you cannot reduce them to a set containing a finite number of values, you must use the `if...else` structure. For example, suppose that `score` is a `double` variable. The number of `double` values between 0 and 60 is (practically) infinite. However, you can use the expression `(int)(score) / 10` and reduce the infinite number of values to just six values.

Avoiding Bugs by Avoiding Partially Understood Concepts and Techniques

By now you've probably written enough programs to realize that even small errors can prevent a program from running correctly or from running at all. For example, the omission of parentheses around the condition associated with an `if` statement, such as

```
if score >= 90
```

or an unintended semicolon following the condition of an `if` statement, such as

```
if (hours > 40.0);
```

can prevent successful compilation or correct execution. As a Java programmer, it is not sufficient to be mostly correct in your use of concepts and techniques. Even though there are many ways to solve a problem, the approach you take must make correct use of concepts and techniques. If you fail to do so, either you will have no solution at all, or your solution will be deficient. If you have a partial understanding of a concept or technique, don't use it until your understanding is complete.

The problem of using partially understood concepts and techniques can be illustrated with the `switch` structure that you have just learned. Recall Example 4–23 and consider the following statements where we assume again that `grade` is an `int` variable:

```java
switch (grade)
{
case 5:
    System.out.println("The grade is A.");

case 4:
    System.out.println("The grade is B.");

case 3:
    System.out.println("The grade is C.");

case 2:
    System.out.println("The grade is D.");

case 1:
    System.out.println("The grade is F.");

default:
    System.out.println("The grade is invalid.");
}
```

If the value of `grade` is of type `int` with a value other than 5, 4, 3, 2, or 1, these statements will produce correct results, but if the value of `grade` is 5, 4, 3, 2, or 1, these statements will produce incorrect results. Can you see why?

Let's suppose that the value of `grade` is 4. The value of `grade` does not match case label 5, but it does match case label 4. So, as we intended,

```
The grade is B.
```

is printed. However,

```
The grade is C.
The grade is D.
The grade is F.
The grade is invalid.
```

also are printed. But why? It seems clear that only one `println` statement is associated with each case label. The problem is a partial understanding of how the `switch` structure works. Specifically, when no `break` statement is included, after executing the statement(s) associated with the matching case label, execution continues with the statement(s) associated with the next case label. In this example, this execution continues with all the remaining statements in the `switch` structure, resulting in the printing of four unintended lines.

The concepts and techniques associated with the Java programming language are simple enough to be understood completely when they are learned one at a time and in a logical order, as we do in this book. By taking the time to understand each concept and technique completely before using it, you will save yourself hours of debugging time.

PROGRAMMING EXAMPLE: Cable Company Billing

4

This programming example demonstrates a program that calculates a customer's bill for a local cable company. There are two types of customers: residential and business. There are two rates for calculating a cable bill: one for residential customers and one for business customers.

For residential customers, the following rates apply:

- Bill-processing fee: $4.50
- Basic service fee: $20.50
- Premium channels: $7.50 per channel
  For business customers, the following rates apply:
- Bill-processing fee: $15.00
- Basic service fee: $75.00 for the first 10 connections; $5.00 for each additional connection
- Premium channels: $50.00 per channel for any number of connections

The program should ask the user for an account number (an integer) and a customer code. Assume that R or r stands for a residential customer, and B or b stands for a business customer.

Input: Input to the program is the customer's account number, customer code, number of premium channels to which the customer subscribes and, in the case of business customers, the number of basic service connections.

Output: Customer's account number and the billing amount.

PROBLEM ANALYSIS AND ALGORITHM DESIGN

The purpose of this program is to calculate and print the billing amount. To calculate the billing amount, you need to know the customer for whom the billing amount is calculated (whether the customer is residential or business) and the number of premium channels to which the customer subscribes. In the case of a business customer, you also need to know the number of basic service connections. Other data needed to calculate the bill, such as bill-processing fees and the cost of a premium channel, are known quantities. The program should print the billing amount to two decimal places, which is standard for monetary amounts. This problem analysis translates into the following algorithm:

1. Prompt the user for the account number and customer type.

2. Determine the number of premium channels and basic service connections, compute the bill, and print the bill based on the customer type:

    a. If the customer type is R or r:

        i.   Prompt the user for the number of premium channels.

        ii. Compute the bill.

        iii. Print the bill.

    b. If the customer type is B or b:

        i.   Prompt the user for the number of basic service connections and number of premium channels.

        ii. Compute the bill.

        iii. Print the bill.

VARIABLES

Because the program will ask the user to input the customer account number, customer code, number of premium channels, and number of basic service connections, you need variables to store all of this information. Also, because the program will calculate the billing amount, you need a variable to store the billing amount. Thus, the program needs at least the following variables to compute and print the bill:

```
int accountNumber;       //variable to store customer's
                         //account number
char customerType;       //variable to store customer code
int noOfPremChannels;    //variable to store number
                         //of premium channels to which
                         //the customer subscribes
int noOfBasicServConn;   //variable to store number of
                         //basic service connections
                         //to which the customer subscribes
double amountDue;        //variable to store the billing amount
```

NAMED CONSTANTS

As you can see, the bill-processing fees, the cost of a basic service connection, and the cost of a premium channel are fixed; these values are needed to compute the bill. Although these values are constants in the program, they do change periodically. To simplify the process of modifying the program later, instead of using these values directly in the program, you should declare them as named constants. Based on the problem analysis, you need to declare the following named constants:

```
    //Named constants - residential customers
static final double R_BILL_PROC_FEE = 4.50;
static final double R_BASIC_SERV_COST = 20.50;
static final double R_COST_PREM_CHANNEL = 7.50;
```

```
                  //Named constants - business customers
static final double B_BILL_PROC_FEE = 15.00;
static final double B_BASIC_SERV_COST = 75.00;
static final double B_BASIC_CONN_COST = 5.00;
static final double B_COST_PREM_CHANNEL = 50.00;
```

FORMULAS

The program uses a number of formulas to compute the billing amount. To compute the residential bill, you need to know only the number of premium channels to which the user subscribes. The following statement calculates the billing amount for a residential customer:

```
amountDue = R_BILL_PROC_FEE + R_BASIC_SERV_COST +
            noOfPremChannels * R_COST_PREM_CHANNEL;
```

To compute the business bill, you need to know the number of basic service connections and the number of premium channels to which the user subscribes. If the number of basic service connections is less than or equal to 10, the cost of the basic service connections is fixed. If the number of basic service connections exceeds 10, you must add the cost for each connection over 10. The following statement calculates the business billing amount:

```
if (noOfBasicServConn <= 10)
    amountDue =  B_BILL_PROC_FEE + B_BASIC_SERV_COST +
                noOfPremChannels * B_COST_PREM_CHANNEL;
else
    amountDue =  B_BILL_PROC_FEE + B_BASIC_SERV_COST +
                (noOfBasicServConn - 10) *
                B_BASIC_CONN_COST +
                noOfPremChannels * B_COST_PREM_CHANNEL;
```

MAIN
ALGORITHM

Based on the preceding discussion, you can now write the main algorithm.

1. Prompt the user to enter the account number.
2. Get the customer account number.
3. Prompt the user to enter the customer code.
4. Get the customer code.
5. If the customer code is r or R:

   a. Prompt the user to enter the number of premium channels.
   b. Get the number of premium channels.
   c. Calculate the billing amount.
   d. Print the account number.
   e. Print the billing amount.

6. If the customer code is **b** or **B**:

   a. Prompt the user to enter the number of basic service connections.

   b. Get the number of basic service connections.

   c. Prompt the user to enter the number of premium channels.

   d. Get the number of premium channels.

   e. Calculate the billing amount.

   f. Print the account number.

   g. Print the billing amount.

7. If the customer code is something other than **r**, **R**, **b**, or **B**, output an error message.

For Steps 5 and 6, the program uses a `switch` statement to calculate the bill for the desired customer. (You can also use an `if...else` statement to implement Steps 5 and 6.)

COMPLETE PROGRAM LISTING

```
//**********************************************************
// Author: D.S. Malik
//
// Program: Cable Company Billing
// This program calculates and prints a customer's bill for
// a local cable company. The program processes two types of
// customers: residential and business.
//**********************************************************

import java.util.*;

public class CableCompanyBilling
{
    static Scanner console = new Scanner(System.in);

        //Named constants - residential customers
    static final double R_BILL_PROC_FEE = 4.50;
    static final double R_BASIC_SERV_COST = 20.50;
    static final double R_COST_PREM_CHANNEL = 7.50;

        //Named constants - business customers
    static final double B_BILL_PROC_FEE = 15.00;
    static final double B_BASIC_SERV_COST = 75.00;
    static final double B_BASIC_CONN_COST = 5.00;
    static final double B_COST_PREM_CHANNEL = 50.00;
```

```
public static void main(String[] args)
{
    //Variable declaration
    int accountNumber;
    char customerType;
    int noOfPremChannels;
    int noOfBasicServConn;
    double amountDue;

    System.out.println("This program computes "
                    + "a cable bill.");

    System.out.print("Enter the account "
                    + "number: ");                //Step 1
    accountNumber = console.nextInt();            //Step 2
    System.out.println();

    System.out.print("Enter the customer type: "
                    + "R or r (Residential), "
                    + "B or b(Business): ");       //Step 3
    customerType = console.next().charAt(0);       //Step 4
    System.out.println();

    switch (customerType)
    {
    case 'r':                                      //Step 5
    case 'R':
        System.out.print("Enter the number of "
                    + "premium channels: ");  //Step 5a
        noOfPremChannels = console.nextInt();     //Step 5b
        System.out.println();

        amountDue = R_BILL_PROC_FEE +             //Step 5c
                    R_BASIC_SERV_COST +
                    noOfPremChannels *
                    R_COST_PREM_CHANNEL;

        System.out.println("Account number = "
                    + accountNumber);       //Step 5d
        System.out.printf("Amount due = $%.2f %n",
                    amountDue);             //Step 5e
        break;

    case 'b':                                      //Step 6
    case 'B':
        System.out.print("Enter the number of "
                    + "basic service "
                    + "connections: ");      //Step 6a
        noOfBasicServConn = console.nextInt();    //Step 6b
        System.out.println();
```

4

```
            System.out.print("Enter the number of "
                        + "premium channels: ");   //Step 6c
            noOfPremChannels = console.nextInt();   //Step 6d
            System.out.println();

            if (noOfBasicServConn <= 10)                //Step 6e
                amountDue = B_BILL_PROC_FEE +
                            B_BASIC_SERV_COST +
                            noOfPremChannels *
                            B_COST_PREM_CHANNEL;
            else
                amountDue = B_BILL_PROC_FEE +
                            B_BASIC_SERV_COST +
                            (noOfBasicServConn - 10) *
                            B_BASIC_CONN_COST +
                            noOfPremChannels *
                            B_COST_PREM_CHANNEL;

            System.out.println("Account number = "
                        + accountNumber);       //Step 6f
            System.out.printf("Amount due = $%.2f %n",
                        amountDue);             //Step 6g
            break;
        default:                                    //Step 7
            System.out.println("Invalid customer type.");
        }//end switch
    }
}
```

Sample Run: (In this sample run, the user input is shaded.)

```
This program computes a cable bill.
Enter the account number: 12345

Enter the customer type: R or r (Residential), B or b (Business): b

Enter the number of basic service connections: 16

Enter the number of premium channels: 8

Account number = 12345
Amount due = $520.00
```

Comparing Strings

In Java, strings are compared character by character, starting with the first character and using the Unicode collating sequence. The character-by-character comparison continues until one of the following three conditions is met: a mismatch is found, the last characters have been compared and are equal, or one string is exhausted.

For example, the string **"Air"** is less than the string **"Big"** because the first character **'A'** of **"Air"** is less than the first character **'B'** of **"Big"**. The string **"Air"** is less than the string **"An"** because the first characters of **"Air"** and **"An"** are the same, but the second character **'i'** of **"Air"** is less than the second character **'n'** of **"An"**. The string **"Hello"** is less than the string **"hello"** because the first character **'H'** of **"Hello"** is less than the first character **'h'** of **"hello"**.

If two strings of different lengths are compared and the character-by-character comparison is equal through the last character of the shorter string, the shorter string is evaluated as less than the larger string. For example, the string **"Bill"** is less than the string **"Billy"** and the string **"Sun"** is less than the string **"Sunny"**.

The `class` String provides the method `compareTo` to compare objects of the `class` String. The syntax to use the method `compareTo` is:

`str1.compareTo(str2)`

where `str1` and `str2` are String variables. Moreover, `str2` can also be a String constant (literal). This expression returns an integer value as follows:

$$str1.compareTo(str2) = \begin{cases} \text{an integer value less than 0 if string } str1 \\ \quad \text{is less than string } str2 \\ 0 \text{ if string } str1 \text{ is equal to string } str2 \\ \text{an integer value greater than 0 if string } str1 \\ \quad \text{is greater than string } str2 \end{cases}$$

Consider the following statements:

```
String str1 = "Hello";
String str2 = "Hi";
String str3 = "Air";
String str4 = "Bill";
String str5 = "Bigger";
```

Using these variable declarations, Table 4-9 shows how the method `compareTo` works.

TABLE 4-9 Comparing Strings with the Method `compareTo`

Expression	Value	Explanation
`str1.compareTo(str2)`	< 0	`str1 = "Hello"` and `str2 = "Hi"`. The first character of `str1` and `str2` are the same, but the second character `'e'` of `str1` is less than the second character `'i'` of `str2`. Therefore, `str1.compareTo(str2) < 0`.
`str1.compareTo("Hen")`	< 0	`str1 = "Hello"`. The first two characters of `str1` and `"Hen"` are the same, but the third character `'l'` of `str1` is less than the third character `'n'` of `"Hen"`. Therefore, `str1.compareTo("Hen") < 0`.
`str4.compareTo(str3)`	> 0	`str4 = "Bill"` and `str3 = "Air"`. The first character `'B'` of `str4` is greater than the first character `'A'` of `str3`. Therefore, `str4.compareTo(str3) > 0`.
`str1.compareTo("hello")`	< 0	`str1 = "Hello"`. The first character `'H'` of `str1` is less than the first character `'h'` of `"hello"` because the Unicode value of `'H'` is 72, and the Unicode value of `'h'` is 104. Therefore, `str1.compareTo("hello") < 0`.
`str2.compareTo("Hi")`	= 0	`str2 = "Hi"`. The strings `str2` and `"Hi"` are of the same length and their corresponding characters are the same. Therefore, `str2.compareTo("Hi") = 0`.
`str4.compareTo("Billy")`	< 0	`str4 = "Bill"` has four characters and `"Billy"` has five characters. Therefore, `str4` is the shorter string. All four characters of `str4` are the same as the corresponding first four characters of `"Billy"`, and `"Billy"` is the larger string. Therefore, `str4.compareTo("Billy") < 0`.

TABLE 4-9 Comparing Strings with the Method `compareTo` (continued)

Expression	Value	Explanation
`str5.compareTo("Big")`	> 0	str5 = "Bigger" has six characters and "Big" has three characters. Therefore, str5 is the larger string. The first three characters of str5 are the same as the corresponding first three characters of "Big". Therefore, `str5.compareTo("Big")` > 0.
`str1.compareTo("Hello ")`	< 0	str1 = "Hello" has five characters and "Hello " has six characters. Therefore, str1 is the shorter string. All five characters of str1 are the same as the corresponding first five characters of "Hello ", and "Hello " is the larger string. Therefore, `str1.compareTo("Hello ")` < 0.

The program in Example 4-26 evaluates the expressions in Table 4-9.

EXAMPLE 4-26

```
//The String method compareTo

public class StringComparison
{
    public static void main(String[] args)
    {
        String str1 = "Hello";                          //Line 1
        String str2 = "Hi";                             //Line 2
        String str3 = "Air";                            //Line 3
        String str4 = "Bill";                           //Line 4
        String str5 = "Bigger";                         //Line 5

        System.out.println("Line 6: " +
                "str1.compareTo(str2) evaluates to "
            + str1.compareTo(str2));                    //Line 6

        System.out.println("Line 7: " +
                "str1.compareTo(\"Hen\") evaluates to "
            + str1.compareTo("Hen"));                   //Line 7
```

```
        System.out.println("Line 8: " +
                "str4.compareTo(str3) evaluates to "
                + str4.compareTo(str3));               //Line 8

        System.out.println("Line 9: " +
                "str1.compareTo(\"hello\") evaluates to "
                + str1.compareTo("hello"));            //Line 9

        System.out.println("Line 10: " +
                "str2.compareTo(\"Hi\") evaluates to "
                + str2.compareTo("Hi"));               //Line 10

        System.out.println("Line 11: " +
                "str4.compareTo(\"Billy\") evaluates to "
                + str4.compareTo("Billy"));            //Line 11

        System.out.println("Line 12: " +
                "str5.compareTo(\"Big\") evaluates to "
                + str5.compareTo("Big"));              //Line 12

        System.out.println("Line 13: " +
                "str1.compareTo(\"Hello \") evaluates to "
                + str1.compareTo("Hello "));           //Line 13
    }
}
```

Sample Run:

```
Line 6: str1.compareTo(str2) evaluates to -4
Line 7: str1.compareTo("Hen") evaluates to -2
Line 8: str4.compareTo(str3) evaluates to 1
Line 9: str1.compareTo("hello") evaluates to -32
Line 10: str2.compareTo("Hi") evaluates to 0
Line 11: str4.compareTo("Billy") evaluates to -1
Line 12: str5.compareTo("Big") evaluates to 3
Line 13: str1.compareTo("Hello ") evaluates to -1
```

Notice that the values, such as -4, -2, 1, and so on, printed in Lines 6 through 13 are the differences of the collating sequences of the first unmatched characters of the strings. The only thing we need to know is whether the value is positive, negative, or zero. The output is self-explanatory.

In addition to the method compareTo, you can also use the method equals of the class String to determine whether two String objects contain the same value. However, the method equals returns the value true or false. For example, the expression:

```
str1.equals("Hello")
```

evaluates to `true`, while the expression:

`str1.equals(str2)`

evaluates to `false`, where `str1` and `str2` are as defined in Example 4–26.

NOTE You can apply the relational operators `==` and `!=` to variables of the `String` type, such as the variables `str1` and `str2`. However, when these operators are applied to these variables they compare the values of the variables, not the values of the `String` objects they point to. For example, suppose, as in Figure 4-6:

```
str1 = "Hello";
str2 = "Hi";
```

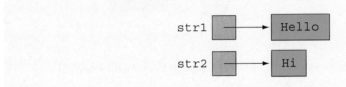

FIGURE 4-6 Variables `str1`, `str2`, and the objects to which they point

The expression (`str1 == str2`) determines whether the values of `str1` and `str2` are the same, that is, if `str1` and `str2` point to the same `String` object. Similarly, the expression (`str1 != str2`) determines whether the values of `str1` and `str2` are *not* the same, that is, if `str1` and `str2` do not point to the same `String` object.

Strings, the Assignment Operator, and the Operator new

Suppose that `str` is a `String` variable and we want to assign the string `"Sunny"` to `str`. As explained in Chapter 3, this can be accomplished by using the statement:

```
str = "Sunny";                //Line 1
```

or the statement:

```
str = new String("Sunny");    //Line 2
```

After the execution of the statement in Line 1 or Line 2, `str` will point to the `String` object with the value `"Sunny"`. Recall from Chapter 3 that the statement in Line 2 explicitly uses the operator `new`. Also recall that there is a slight difference in the way these statements execute. When the statement in Line 1 executes, the computer checks whether there already is a `String` object with the value `"Sunny"`; if so, then the address of that object is stored in `str`. On the other hand, when the statement in Line 2 executes, the computer will create a new `String` object with the value `"Sunny"` regardless of whether such a `String` object already exits. Let us further explain this concept.

Consider the following statements:

```
String str1 = "Hello";
String str2 = "Hello";
```

When the first statement executes, a `String` object with the value `"Hello"` is created and its address is assigned to `str1`. When the second statement executes, because there already exists a `String` object with the value `"Hello"`, the address of this `String` object is stored in `str2` (see Figure 4-7).

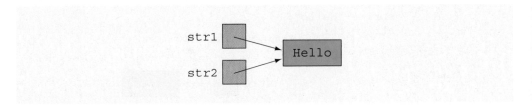

FIGURE 4-7 Variables `str1`, `str2`, and the objects to which they point

Therefore, if you evaluate the expression `(str1 == str2)` after these statements, this expression evaluates to `true`. Moreover, here the expression `str1.equals(str2)` also evaluates to `true`.

If you later assigned a different string, say, `"Cloudy"`, to `str2`, then if no `String` object exists with the value `"Cloudy"`, a `String` object with this value is created and its address is stored in `str2`. However, `str1` would still point to the string `"Hello"`. In other words, changing the value of the string `str2` does not change the value of the string `str1`.

Next, consider the following statements:

```
String str3 = new String("Hello");
String str4 = new String("Hello");
```

When the first statement executes, a `String` object with the value `"Hello"` is created and its address is assigned to `str3`. When the second statement executes, another `String` object with the value `"Hello"` is created and its address is assigned to `str4` (see Figure 4-8).

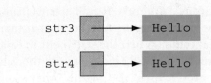

FIGURE 4-8 Variables `str3`, `str4`, and the objects to which they point

It follows that the expression (str3 == str4) evaluates to false. However, the expression str3.equals(str4) evaluates to true.

 NOTE The Web site (*www.course.com*) and the CD accompanying this book contain the program StringObjectsAndTheOprNew.java that shows the effect of the preceding statements.

QUICK REVIEW

4

1. Control structures alter the sequential flow of control.

2. The two most common activities provided by control structures are selection and repetition.

3. Selection structures incorporate decisions in a program.

4. The Java relational operators are == (equality), != (not equal to), < (less than), <= (less than or equal to), > (greater than), and >= (greater than or equal to).

5. Including a space within the relational operators ==, <=, >=, and != creates a syntax error. (For example, = = will create a syntax error.)

6. Characters are compared using the collating sequence of the Unicode character set.

7. Logical (boolean) expressions evaluate to true or false.

8. In Java, boolean variables are used to store the value of a logical expression.

9. In Java, the logical operators are ! (not), && (and), and || (or).

10. In Java, there are three selection structures.

11. One-way selection takes the following form:

```
if (logical expression)
    statement
```

If logical expression is true, then the statement executes; otherwise, the computer executes the statement following the if statement.

12. Two-way selection takes the following form:

```
if (logical expression)
    statement1
else
    statement2
```

If logical expression is true, then statement1 executes; otherwise, statement2 executes.

13. The expression in an if or if...else structure is a logical expression.

14. Including a semicolon before the **statement** in a one-way selection creates a semantic error. In this case, the action of the **if** statement is empty.

15. Including a semicolon before **statement1** in a two-way selection creates a syntax error.

16. There is no stand-alone **else** statement in Java. Every **else** has a related **if**.

17. An **else** is paired with the most recent **if** that has not been paired with any other **else**.

18. A sequence of statements enclosed between braces, { and }, is called a compound statement or block of statements. A compound statement is treated as a single statement.

19. A **switch** structure is used to handle multiple selections.

20. The **expression** in a **switch** statement must evaluate to an integral value.

21. A **switch** statement executes according to the following rules:

    a. When the value of the **expression** is matched against a **case** value, the statements execute until either a **break** statement is found or the end of the **switch** structure is reached.

    b. If the value of the **expression** does not match any of the **case** values, the statements following the **default** label execute. If the **switch** structure has no **default** label, and if the value of the **expression** does not match any of the **case** values, the entire **switch** statement is skipped.

    c. A **break** statement causes an immediate exit from the **switch** structure.

22. To compare strings, you use the method **compareTo** of the **class String**.

23. To use the method **compareTo**, you use the expression:

    str1.compareTo(str2)

    where **str1** and **str2** are **String** variables. Moreover, **str2** can also be a **String** constant (literal). The expression **str1.compareTo(str2)** evaluates as follows:

$$str1.compareTo(str2) = \begin{cases} \text{an integer value less than 0 if string } str1 \\ \quad \text{is less than string } str2 \\ 0 \text{ if string } str1 \text{ is equal to string } str2 \\ \text{an integer value greater than 0 if string } str1 \\ \quad \text{is greater than string } str2 \end{cases}$$

EXERCISES

1. Mark the following statements as true or false.

    a. The result of a logical expression cannot be assigned to an `int` variable.

    b. In a one-way selection, if a semicolon is placed after the expression in an `if` statement, the expression in the `if` statement is always `true`.

    c. Every `if` statement must have a corresponding `else`.

    d. The expression:

        (ch >= 'A' && ch <= 'Z')

    evaluates to `false` if either ch < 'A' or ch >= 'Z'.

    e. Suppose the input is 5. (Assume that all variables are properly declared.) The output of the code:

        num = console.nextInt();
        if (num > 5)
            System.out.println(num);
            num = 0;
        else
            System.out.println("Num is zero");

    is:

        Num is zero.

    f. The expression in a `switch` statement should evaluate to a value of any primitive data type.

    g. The expression ! (x > 0) is true only if x is a negative number.

    h. In Java, both ! and != are logical operators.

    i. The order in which statements execute in a program is called the flow of control.

2. Select the best answer.

    a. `if (6 < 2 * 5)`
        `System.out.print("Hello");`
        `System.out.print(" There");`

    outputs the following:

    i. `Hello There`   ii. `Hello`   iii. `Hello`   iv. `There`
                                              `There`

    b. `if ('a' > 'b' || 66 > (int)('A'))`
        `System.out.println("#*#");`

outputs the following:

i. #*#   ii. #   iii. *   iv. none of these

                    *

                    #

c.   `if (7 <= 7)`
```
     System.out.println(6 - 9 * 2 / 6);
```

outputs the following:

i. -1   ii. 3   iii. 3.0   iv. none of these

d.   `if (7 < 8)`
```
   {
       System.out.println("2 4 6 8");
       System.out.println("1 3 5 7");
   }
```

outputs the following:

i. 2 4 6 8   ii. 1 3 5 7   iii. none of these
    1 3 5 7

e.   `if (5 < 3)`
```
       System.out.println("*");
   else if (7 == 8)
       System.out.println("&");
   else
       System.out.println("$");
```

outputs the following:

i. *   ii. &   iii. $ iv. none of these

3. What is the output of the following Java code?
```
int x = 100;
int y = 200;

if (x > 100 && y <= 200)
    System.out.println(x + " " + y + " " + (x + y));
else
    System.out.println(x + " " + y + " " + (2 * x - y));
```

4. Write Java statements that output Democrat if the party affiliation code is 'D', Republican if the party affiliation code is 'R', and independent otherwise.

5. Correct the following code so that it prints the correct message.
```
if (score >= 60)
    System.out.println("You pass.");
else;
    System.out.println("You fail.");
```

6. Suppose that you have the following declaration:

    ```
    int j = 0;
    ```

    The output of the statement:

    ```
    if ((8 > 4) || (j++ == 7))
        System.out.println("j = = + j);
    ```

    is:

    ```
    j = 0
    ```

    while the output of the statement:

    ```
    if ((8 > 4) | (j++ == 7))
        System.out.println("j = " + j);
    ```

    is:

    ```
    j = 1
    ```

    Explain why.

7. State whether the following are valid `switch` statements. If not, explain why. Assume that n and `digit` are `int` variables.

    a.
    ```
    switch (n <= 2)
        {
        case 0:
            System.out.println("Draw.");
            break;

        case 1:
            System.out.println("Win.");
            break;

        case 2:
            System.out.println("Lose.");
            break;
        }
    ```

    b.
    ```
    switch (digit / 4)
        {
        case 0:
        case 1:
            System.out.println("low.");
            break;

        case 1:
        case 2:
            System.out.println("middle.");
            break;

        case 3:
            System.out.println("high.");
        }
    ```

c.
```
switch (n % 6)
{
case 1:
case 2:
case 3:
case 4:
case 5:
    System.out.println(n);
    break;

case 0:
    System.out.println();
    break;
}
```

d.
```
switch (n % 10)
{
case 0:
case 2:
case 4:
case 6:
case 8:
    System.out.println("Even");
    break;

case 1:
case 3:
case 5:
case 7:
    System.out.println("Odd");
    break;
}
```

8. Suppose the input is 5. What is the value of `alpha` after the following Java code executes? (Assume that `alpha` is an `int` variable and `console` is a `Scanner` object initialized to the keyboard.)

```
alpha = console.nextInt();

switch (alpha)
{
case 1:
case 2:
    alpha = alpha + 2;
    break;

case 4:
    alpha++;

case 5:
    alpha = 2 * alpha;
```

```
case 6:
    alpha = alpha + 5;
    break;
default:
    alpha--;
}
```

9. Suppose the input is 3. What is the value of beta after the following Java code executes? (Assume that all variables are declared properly.)

```
beta = console.nextInt();

switch (beta)
{
case 3:
    beta = beta + 3;
case 1:
    beta++;
    break;

case 5:
    beta = beta + 5;
case 4:
    beta = beta + 4;
}
```

10. Suppose the input is 6. What is the value of a after the following Java code executes? (Assume that all variables are declared properly.)

```
a = console.nextInt();

if (a > 0)
    switch (a)
    {
    case 1:
        a = a + 3;

    case 3:
        a++;
        break;

    case 6:
        a = a + 6;
    case 8:
        a = a * 8;
        break;

    default:
        a--;
    }
else
    a = a + 2;
```

11. In the following code, correct any errors that would prevent the program from compiling or running.

```java
public class Errors
{
    public static void main(String[] args)
    {
        int a, b;
        boolean found;
        System.out.print("Enter the first integer: ");
        a = console.nextInt();;
        System.out.println();

        System.out.print("Enter the second integer: ");
        b = console.nextInt();;

        if a > a * b && 10 < b
            found = 2 * a > b;
        else
        {
            found = 2 * a < b;
            if found
                a = 3;
                c = 15;
            if b
            {
                b = 0;
                a = 1;
            }
        }
    }
}
```

12. The following program contains errors. Correct them so that the program will run and output w = 21.

```java
public class Mystery
{
    static final int ONE = 5;

    public static void main(String[] args)
    {
        int  x, y, w, z;
        z = 9;

        if z > 10
            x = 12;  y = 5,   w = x + y + one;
        else
            x = 12;  y = 4,   w = x + y + one;

        System.out.println("w = " + w);
    }
}
```

PROGRAMMING EXERCISES

1. Write a program that prompts the user to input a number. The program should then output the number and a message saying whether the number is positive, negative, or zero.

2. Write a program that prompts the user to input three numbers. The program should then output the numbers in nondescending order.

3. Write a program that prompts the user to input an integer between 0 and 35. If the number is less than or equal to 9, the program should output the number; otherwise, it should output A for 10, B for 11, C for 12, ..., and Z for 35. (*Hint:* Use the cast operator, `(char)( )`, for numbers `>= 10`.)

4. In a right triangle, the square of the length of one side is equal to the sum of the squares of the lengths of the other two sides. Write a program that prompts the user to enter the lengths of three sides of a triangle and then outputs a message indicating whether the triangle is a right triangle.

5. A box of cookies can hold 24 cookies and a container can hold 75 boxes of cookies. Write a program that prompts the user to enter the total number of cookies. The program then outputs the number of boxes and the number of containers to ship the cookies. Note that each box must contain the specified number of cookies and each container must contain the specified number of boxes. If the last box of cookies contains less than the number of specified cookies, you can discard it, and output the number of leftover cookies. Similarly, if the last container contains less than the number of specified boxes, you can discard it, and output the number of leftover boxes.

6. The roots of the quadratic equation $ax^2 + bx + c = 0$, $a \neq 0$ are given by the following formula:

$$\frac{-b \pm \sqrt{b^2 - 4ac}}{2a}$$

In this formula, the term $b^2 - 4ac$ is called the **discriminant**. If $b^2 - 4ac = 0$, then the equation has a single (repeated) root. If $b^2 - 4ac > 0$, the equation has two real roots. If $b^2 - 4ac < 0$, the equation has two complex roots. Write a program that prompts the user to input the value of a (the coefficient of x^2), b (the coefficient of x), and c (the constant term), and outputs the type of roots of the equation. Furthermore, if $b^2 - 4ac \geq 0$, the program should output the roots of the quadratic equation. (*Hint:* Use the method `pow` or `sqrt` from the `class Math` to calculate the square root. Chapter 3 explains how to use these methods.)

7. Write a program that prompts the user to input the x-y coordinate of a point in a Cartesian plane. The program should then output a message indicating whether the point is the origin, is located on the x- (or y-) axis, or appears in a particular quadrant. For example:

```
(0, 0) is the origin
(4, 0) is on the x-axis
(0, -3) is on the y-axis
(-2, 3) is in the second quadrant
```

8. Write a program that mimics a calculator. The program should take as input two integers and an arithmetic operation (+, -, *, or /) to be performed. It should then output the numbers, the operator, and the result. (For division, if the denominator is zero, output an appropriate message.) Some sample outputs follow:

```
3 + 4 = 7
13 * 5 = 65
```

9. Redo Exercise 8 to handle floating-point numbers. (Format your output to two decimal places.)

10. Redo Programming Exercise 18 of Chapter 2, taking into account that your parents buy additional savings bonds for you as follows:

    a. If you do not spend any money to buy savings bonds, then because you had a summer job, your parents buy savings bonds for you in an amount equal to 1% of the money you save after paying taxes and buying clothes, school supplies, and other accessories.

    b. If you spend up to 25% of your net income to buy savings bonds, your parents spend $0.25 for each dollar you spend to buy savings bonds, plus money equal to 1% of the money you save after paying taxes and buying clothes, school supplies, and other accessories.

    c. If you spend more than 25% of your net income to buy savings bonds, your parents spend $0.40 for each dollar you spend to buy savings bonds, plus money equal to 2% of the money you save after paying taxes and buying clothes, school supplies, and other accessories.

11. A bank in your town updates its customers' accounts at the end of each month. The bank offers two types of accounts: savings and checking. Every customer must maintain a minimum balance. If a customer's balance falls below the minimum balance, there is a service charge of $10.00 for savings accounts and $25.00 for checking accounts. If the balance at the end of the month is at least the minimum balance, the account receives interest as follows:

    a. Savings accounts receive 4% interest.

    b. Checking accounts with balances of up to $5000 more than the minimum balance receive 3% interest; otherwise, the interest is 5%.

    Write a program that reads a customer's account number (int type), account type (char type; s or S for savings, c or C for checking), minimum balance that the account should maintain, and current balance. The program should then output the account number, account type, current balance, and an appropriate message. Test your program by running it five times, using the following data:

```
46728 S 1000 2700
87324 C 1500 7689
79873 S 1000 800
89832 C 2000 3000
98322 C 1000 750
```

12. Write a program that implements the algorithm given in Example 1-2 (Chapter 1), which determines the monthly wages of a salesperson.

13. The number of lines that can be printed on a paper depends on the paper size, the point size of each character in a line, whether lines are double-spaced or single-spaced, the top and bottom margin, and the left and right margins of the paper. Assume that all characters are of the same point size, and all lines are either single-spaced or double-spaced. Note that 1 inch = 72 points. Moreover, assume that the lines are printed along the width of the paper. For example, if the length of the paper is 11 inches and the width is 8.5 inches, then the maximum length of a line is 8.5 inches. Write a program that calculates the number of characters in a line and the number of lines that can be printed on a paper based on the following input from the user:

   a. The length and width, in inches, of the paper.

   b. The top, bottom, left, and right margins.

   c. The point size of a line.

   d. If the lines are double-spaced, then double the point size of each character.

14. Write a program that calculates and prints the bill for a cellular telephone company. The company offers two types of service: regular and premium. Rates vary based on the type of service and are computed as follows:

   Regular service: $10.00 plus first 50 minutes are free. Charges for over 50 minutes are $0.20 per minute.

   Premium service: $25.00 plus:

   a. For calls made from 6:00 a.m. to 6:00 p.m., the first 75 minutes are free; charges for over 75 minutes are $0.10 per minute.

   b. For calls made from 6:00 p.m. to 6:00 a.m., the first 100 minutes are free; charges for over 100 minutes are $0.05 per minute.

   Your program should prompt the user to enter an account number, a service code (type **char**), and the number of minutes the service was used. A service code of **r** or **R** means regular service; a service code of **p** or **P** means premium service. Treat any other character as an error. Your program should output the account number, type of service, number of minutes the telephone service was used, and the amount due from the user. For the premium service, the customer may be using the service during the day and the night. Therefore, to calculate the bill, you must ask the user to input the number of minutes the service was used during the day and the number of minutes the service was used during the night.

15. You have several pictures of different sizes that you would like to frame. A local picture framing store offers two types of frames—regular and fancy. The frames are available in white and can be ordered in any color the customer desires. Suppose that each frame is 1 inch wide. The cost of coloring the frame is $0.10 per inch. The cost of a regular frame is $0.15 per inch and the cost of a fancy frame is $0.25 per inch. The cost of putting a cardboard paper behind the picture is $0.02 per square inch and the cost of putting glass on top of the picture is $0.07 per square inch. The customer can also choose to put crowns on the corners, which costs $0.35 per crown. Write a program that prompts the user to input the following information and then output the cost of framing the picture:

a. The length and width, in inches, of the picture.

b. The type of the frame.

c. Customer's choice of color to color the frame.

d. If the user wants to add the crowns, then the number of crowns.

16. Samantha and Vikas are looking to buy a house in a new development. After looking at various models the three models they like are colonial, split-entry, and single-story. The builder gave them the base price and the finished area in square feet of the three models. They want to know the price per square foot of the three models and the model with the least price per square foot. Write a program that accepts as input the base price and the finished area in square feet of the three models. The program outputs the price per square foot of the three models and the model with the least price per square foot.

CONTROL STRUCTURES II: REPETITION

IN THIS CHAPTER, YOU WILL:

■ Learn about repetition (looping) control structures
■ Explore how to construct and use counter-controlled, sentinel-controlled, flag-controlled, and EOF-controlled repetition structures
■ Examine **break** and **continue** statements
■ Learn how to avoid bugs by avoiding patches
■ Discover how to form and use nested control structures

In Chapter 4, you learned how decisions are incorporated in programs. In this chapter, you learn how repetitions are incorporated in programs.

Why Is Repetition Needed?

Suppose you want to add five integers to find their average. From what you have learned so far, you know that you could proceed as follows (assume that all the variables are properly declared):

```
num1 = console.nextInt();   //get the first number
num2 = console.nextInt();   //get the second number
num3 = console.nextInt();   //get the third number
num4 = console.nextInt();   //get the fourth number
num5 = console.nextInt();   //get the fifth number

sum = num1 + num2 + num3 + num4 + num5;   //add the numbers
average = sum / 5;                        //find the average
```

But suppose you want to add and average 1000 or more numbers. You would have to declare that many variables, and list them again in the input statements, and perhaps again in the output statements. This would take an exorbitant amount of typing as well as time. Also, if you wanted to run this program again with a different number of values, you would have to rewrite the program.

Suppose you want to add the following numbers:

5 3 7 9 4

Assume that the input is these five numbers. Consider the following statements, in which sum and num are variables of type int:

```
sum = 0;                      //Line 1
num = console.nextInt();      //Line 2
sum = sum + num;              //Line 3
```

The statement in Line 1 initializes sum to 0. Let's execute the statements in Lines 2 and 3. The statement in Line 2 stores 5 in num; the statement in Line 3 updates the value of sum by adding num to it. After Line 3 executes, the value of sum is 5.

Let's repeat the statements in Lines 2 and 3. After the statement in Line 2 executes (after the programming code reads the next number):

num = 3

After the statement in Line 3 executes:

sum = sum + num = 5 + 3 = 8

At this point, **sum** contains the sum of the first two numbers. Let's repeat the statements in Lines 2 and 3 a third time. After the statement in Line 2 executes (after the programming code reads the next number):

```
num = 7
```

After the statement in Line 3 executes:

```
sum = sum + num = 8 + 7 = 15
```

Now, **sum** contains the sum of the first three numbers. If you repeat the statements in Lines 2 and 3 two more times, **sum** will contain the sum of all five numbers.

If you want to add 10 integers, you can repeat the statements in Lines 2 and 3 ten times. And if you want to add 100 numbers, you can repeat the statements 100 times. In either case, you do not have to declare any additional variables as you did in the code shown previously. By repeating the statements in Lines 2 and 3 you can add any set of integers, whereas the earlier code requires that you drastically change the code.

There are many situations in which it is necessary to repeat a set of statements. For example, for each student in a class, the formula to determine the course grade is the same. Java has three repetition, or looping, structures that let you repeat statements over and over until certain conditions are met: **while**, **for**, and **do...while**. The following sections discuss these three looping (repetition) structures.

while Looping (Repetition) Structure

In the previous section, you saw that sometimes it is necessary to repeat a set of statements several times. One way to do this is to type the set of statements in the program over and over. For example, if you want to repeat a set of statements 100 times, you type the set of statements 100 times in the program. However, this way of repeating a set of statements is impractical, if not impossible. Fortunately, there is a simpler approach. As noted earlier, Java has three repetition, or looping, structures that allow you to repeat a set of statements until certain conditions are met. This section discusses the first looping structure, a **while** loop.

The general form of the **while** statement is:

```
while (logical expression)
    statement
```

In Java, **while** is a reserved word. The **logical expression** is called a **loop condition** or simply a **condition**. The **statement** is called the body of the loop. Moreover, the **statement** can be either a simple or compound statement. Also, note that the parentheses around the **logical expression** are part of the syntax. Figure 5-1 shows the flow of execution of a **while** loop.

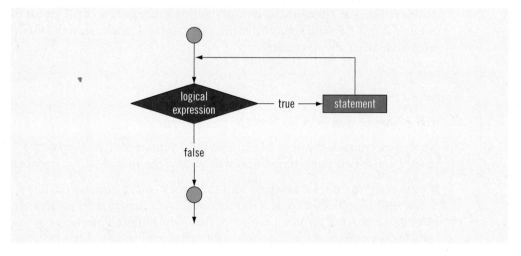

FIGURE 5-1 `while` loop

The `logical expression` provides an entry condition. If it initially evaluates to `true`, the `statement` executes. The loop condition—the `logical expression`—is then reevaluated. If it again evaluates to `true`, the `statement` executes again. The `statement` (body of the loop) continues to execute until the `logical expression` is no longer `true`. A loop that continues to execute endlessly is called an **infinite loop**. To avoid an infinite loop, make sure that the loop's body contains one or more statements that ensure that the loop condition—the `logical expression` in the `while` statement—will eventually be `false`.

EXAMPLE 5-1

Consider the following Java program segment:

```
int i = 0;                              //Line 1

while (i <= 20)                         //Line 2
{
    System.out.print(i + " ");          //Line 3
    i = i + 5;                          //Line 4
}

System.out.println();                   //Line 5
```

Sample Run:

0 5 10 15 20

In Line 1, the variable `i` is set to 0. The logical expression in the `while` statement (in Line 2), `i <= 20`, is then evaluated. Because the expression `i <= 20` evaluates to `true`, the body of the `while` loop executes next. The body of the `while` loop consists of the statements in

Lines 3 and 4. The statement in Line 3 outputs the value of i, which is 0; the statement in Line 4 changes the value of i to 5. After executing the statements in Lines 3 and 4, the logical expression in the while loop (Line 2) is evaluated again. Because i is 5, the expression i <= 20 evaluates to true and the body of the while loop executes again. This process of evaluating the logical expression and executing the body of the while loop continues until the expression i <= 20 (Line 2) no longer evaluates to true.

The variable i (Line 2) in the expression is called the **loop control variable**. Note the following from the preceding example:

1. Eventually, within the loop, i becomes 25, but is not printed because the entry condition is false.

2. If you omit the statement:

   ```
   i = i + 5;
   ```

   from the body of the loop, you will have an infinite loop, continually printing rows of zeros.

3. You must initialize the loop control variable i before you execute the loop. If the statement:

   ```
   i = 0;
   ```

   (in Line 1) is omitted, either the compiler will generate an error or the loop might not execute at all. (Recall that not all variables in Java are automatically initialized.)

4. In the previous program segment, if the two statements in the body of the loop are interchanged, the result may be altered. For example, consider the following statements:

   ```
   int i = 0;

   while (i <= 20)
   {
       i = i + 5;
       System.out.print(i + " ");
   }

   System.out.println();
   ```

   Here, the output is:

   ```
   5 10 15 20 25
   ```

   Typically, this would be a semantic error because you rarely want a condition to be true for i <= 20, and yet produce results for i > 20.

Designing `while` Loops

As shown in Example 5-1, the body of a `while` loop executes only when the `expression` in the `while` statement evaluates to `true`. Typically, the `expression` checks whether a variable(s), called the loop control variable (LCV), satisfies certain conditions. For example, in Example 5-1, the `expression` in the `while` statement checks whether i <= 20. (Recall that in Java, when variables are declared, they are not automatically initialized.) The LCV must be properly initialized before the `while` loop, and its value should eventually make the `logical expression` evaluate to `false`. We do this by updating the LCV in the body of the `while` loop. Therefore, `while` loops are typically written in the following form:

```
//initialize the loop control variable(s)

while (logical expression)      //expression tests the LCV
{
    .
    .
    .
    //update the loop control variable(s)
    .
    .
    .
}
```

For instance, in Example 5-1, the statement in Line 1 initializes the LCV i to 0. The expression i <= 20 in Line 2 checks whether i is less than or equal to 20, and the statement in Line 4 updates the value of i.

EXAMPLE 5-2

Consider the following Java program segment:

```
int i = 20;                              //Line 1

while (i < 20)                           //Line 2
{
    System.out.print(i + " ");           //Line 3
    i = i + 5;                           //Line 4
}

System.out.println();                    //Line 5
```

It is easy to overlook the difference between this example and Example 5-1. Here, in Line 1, i is set to 20. Because i is 20, the expression i < 20 in the `while` statement (Line 2) evaluates to `false`. Initially, the loop entry condition, i < 20, is `false`, so the body of the `while` loop never executes. Hence, no values are output and the value of i remains 20.

The next few sections describe the various forms of `while` loops.

Counter-Controlled `while` Loops

Suppose you know exactly how many times certain statements need to be executed. For example, suppose you know exactly how many pieces of data (or entries) need to be read. In such cases, the `while` loop assumes the form of a **counter-controlled `while` loop**. (If you know the number of iterations in advance, a `for` loop should be used.) Suppose that a set of statements needs to be executed N times. You can set up a `counter` (initialized to 0 before the `while` statement) to track how many items have been read. Before executing the body of the `while` statement, the `counter` is compared with N. If `counter < N`, the body of the `while` statement executes. The body of the loop continues to execute until the value of `counter >= N`. Thus, inside the body of the `while` statement, the value of `counter` increments after it reads a new item. In this case, the `while` loop might look like the following:

```
counter = 0;          //initialize the loop control variable

while (counter < N) //test the loop control variable
{
        .
        .
        .
        counter++;    //update the loop control variable
        .
        .
        .
}
```

If N represents the number of data items in a file, then the value of N can be determined several ways: The program can prompt you to specify the number of items in the file; an input statement can read the value; or you can specify the first item in the file as the number of items in the file, so that you need not remember the number of input values (items). This is useful if someone other than the programmer enters the data. Consider Example 5-3.

EXAMPLE 5-3

Suppose the input is:

8 9 2 3 90 38 56 8 23 89 7 2

Suppose you want to add these numbers and find their average. Consider the following program.

```
//Counter-controlled while loop

import java.util.*;

public class CounterControlledWhileLoop
{
    static Scanner console = new Scanner(System.in);
```

```
public static void main(String[] args)
{
    int limit;          //store the number of items
                        //in the list
    int number;         //variable to store the number
    int sum;            //variable to store the sum
    int counter;        //loop control variable

    System.out.print("Line 1: Enter the number of "
                    + "integers in the list: ");       //Line 1

    limit = console.nextInt();                          //Line 2
    System.out.println();                               //Line 3

    sum = 0;                                            //Line 4
    counter = 0;                                        //Line 5
    System.out.println("Line 6: Enter " + limit
                    + " integers.");                    //Line 6

    while (counter < limit)                             //Line 7
    {
        number = console.nextInt();                     //Line 8
        sum = sum + number;                             //Line 9
        counter++;                                      //Line 10
    }

    System.out.printf("Line 11: The sum of the %d " +
                    "numbers = %d%n", limit, sum);      //Line 11

    if (counter != 0)                                   //Line 12
        System.out.printf("Line 13: The average = %d%n",
                        (sum / counter));               //Line 13
    else                                                //Line 14
        System.out.println("Line 15: No input.");       //Line 15
}
}
```

Sample Run: In this sample run, the user input is shaded.

```
Line 1: Enter the number of integers in the list: 12

Line 6: Enter 12 integers.
8 9 2 3 90 38 56 8 23 89 7 2
Line 11: The sum of the 12 numbers = 335
Line 13: The average = 27
```

The preceding program works as follows: The statement in Line 1 prompts the user to input the data for processing. The statement in Line 2 reads the next input and stores it in the variable limit. The value of limit indicates the number of items to be read. The statements in Lines 4 and 5 initialize the variables sum and counter to 0. The **while** statement in Line 7 checks the value of counter to determine how many items have been read. If counter is less than limit, the **while** loop proceeds for the next iteration.

The statement in Line 8 stores the next number in the variable `number`. The statement in Line 9 updates the value of `sum` by adding the value of `number` to the previous value. The statement in Line 10 increments the value of `counter` by 1. The statement in Line 11 outputs the sum of the numbers. The statements in Lines 12 through 15 output either the average or the text: `Line 15: No input`.

Note that in this program, in Line 4, `sum` is initialized to 0. In Line 9, after storing the next number in `number` in Line 8, the program adds the next number to the sum of all the numbers scanned before the current number. The first number read is added to zero (because `sum` is initialized to 0), giving the correct sum of the first number. To find the average, divide `sum` by `counter`. If `counter` is 0, then dividing by 0 terminates the program and you get an error message. Therefore, before dividing `sum` by `counter`, you must check whether or not `counter` is 0.

Notice that in this program, the statement in Line 5 initializes the LCV `counter` to 0. The expression `counter < limit` in Line 7 evaluates whether `counter` is less than `limit`. The statement in Line 8 updates the value of `counter`. Note that in this program, the `while` loop can also be written without using the variable `number` as follows:

```
while (counter < limit)
{
    sum = sum + console.nextInt();
    counter++;
}
```

Sentinel-Controlled `while` Loops

You might not know exactly how many times a set of statements needs to be executed, but you do know that the statements need to be executed until a special value is met. This special value is called a **sentinel**. For example, while processing data, you might not know how many pieces of data (or entries) need to be read, but you do know that the last entry is a special value. In such cases, you read the first item before entering the `while` statement. If this item does not equal the sentinel, the body of the `while` statement executes. The `while` loop continues to execute as long as the program has not read the sentinel. Such a `while` loop is called a **sentinel-controlled** `while` **loop**. In this case, a `while` loop might look like the following:

```
input the first data item into variable //initialize the
                                         //loop control variable
while (variable != sentinel)     //test the loop control variable
{
    .
    .
    .
    input a data item into variable  //update the loop
                                     //control variable
}
```

EXAMPLE 5-4

Suppose you want to read some positive integers and average them, but you do not have a preset number of data items in mind. Suppose you choose the number −999 to mark the end of the data. You can proceed as follows:

```java
//Sentinel-controlled while loop

import java.util.*;

public class SentinelControlledWhileLoop
{
    static Scanner console = new Scanner(System.in);

    static final int SENTINEL = -999;

    public static void main(String[] args)
    {
        int number;        //variable to store the number
        int sum = 0;       //variable to store the sum
        int count = 0;     //variable to store the total
                           //numbers read

        System.out.println("Line 1: Enter positive integers "
                        + "ending with " + SENTINEL);    //Line 1

        number = console.nextInt();                      //Line 2

        while (number != SENTINEL)                       //Line 3
        {
            sum = sum + number;                          //Line 4
            count++;                                     //Line 5
            number = console.nextInt();                  //Line 6
        }

        System.out.printf("Line 7: The sum of %d " +
                    "numbers = %d%n", count, sum);       //Line 7

        if (count != 0)                                  //Line 8
            System.out.printf("Line 9: The average = %d%n",
                            (sum / count));              //Line 9
        else                                             //Line 10
            System.out.println("Line 11: No input.");    //Line 11
    }
}
```

Sample Run: (In this sample run, the user input is shaded.)

```
Line 1: Enter positive integers ending with -999
34 23 9 45 78 0 77 8 3 5 -999
Line 7: The sum of 10 numbers = 282
Line 9: The average = 28
```

This program works as follows: The statement in Line 1 prompts the user to enter numbers and to terminate by entering -999. The statement in Line 2 reads the first number and stores it in the variable number. The while statement in Line 3 checks whether number is not equal to SENTINEL. If number is not equal to SENTINEL, the body of the while loop executes. The statement in Line 4 updates the value of sum by adding number to it. The statement in Line 5 increments the value of count by 1. The statement in Line 6 stores the next number in the variable number. The statements in Lines 4 through 6 repeat until the program reads -999. The statement in Line 7 outputs the sum of the numbers, and the statements in Lines 8 through 11 output the average of the numbers.

Notice that the statement in Line 2 initializes the LCV number. The expression number != SENTINEL in Line 3 checks whether the value of number is not equal to SENTINEL. The statement in Line 6 updates the LCV number. Also, note that the program continues to read data as long as the user has not entered -999.

Next, consider another example of a sentinel-controlled while loop. In this example, the user is prompted to enter the value to be processed. If the user wants to stop the program, he or she can enter the value chosen for the sentinel.

EXAMPLE 5-5 TELEPHONE DIGITS

The following program reads the letter codes 'A' through 'Z' and prints the corresponding telephone digit. This program uses a sentinel-controlled while loop. To stop the program, the user is prompted for the sentinel, which is '#'. This is also an example of a nested control structure, where if... else, switch, and the while loop are nested.

```
//*******************************************************
// Program: Telephone Digits
// This is an example of a sentinel-controlled while loop.
// This program converts uppercase letters to their
// corresponding telephone digits.
//*******************************************************

import javax.swing.JOptionPane;

public class TelephoneDigitProgram
{
    public static void main (String[] args)
    {
        char letter;                          //Line 1

        String inputMessage;                  //Line 2
        String inputString;                   //Line 3
        String outputMessage;                 //Line 4
```

```
        inputMessage = "Program to convert uppercase "
                    + "letters to their corresponding "
                    + "telephone digits.\n"
                    + "To stop the program enter #.\n"
                    + "Enter a letter:";              //Line 5
        inputString =
              JOptionPane.showInputDialog(inputMessage); //Line 6

        letter = inputString.charAt(0);                 //Line 7

        while (letter != '#' )                          //Line 8
        {
            outputMessage = "The letter you entered is: "
                        + letter + "\n"
                        + "The corresponding telephone "
                        + "digit is: ";                 //Line 9

            if (letter >= 'A' && letter <= 'Z')         //Line 10
            {
                switch (letter)                         //Line 11
                {
                case 'A':
                case 'B':
                case 'C':
                    outputMessage = outputMessage
                                    + "2";              //Line 12
                    break;                              //Line 13

                case 'D':
                case 'E':
                case 'F':
                    outputMessage = outputMessage
                                    + "3";              //Line 14
                    break;                              //Line 15

                case 'G':
                case 'H':
                case 'I':
                    outputMessage = outputMessage
                                    + "4";              //Line 16
                    break;                              //Line 17

                case 'J':
                case 'K':
                case 'L':
                    outputMessage = outputMessage
                                    + "5";              //Line 18
                    break;                              //Line 19
```

```
        case 'M':
        case 'N':
        case 'O':
            outputMessage = outputMessage
                            + "6";                    //Line 20
            break;                                    //Line 21

        case 'P':
        case 'Q':
        case 'R':
        case 'S':
            outputMessage = outputMessage
                            + "7";                    //Line 22
            break;                                    //Line 23

        case 'T':
        case 'U':
        case 'V':
            outputMessage = outputMessage
                            + "8";                    //Line 24
            break;                                    //Line 25

        case 'W':
        case 'X':
        case 'Y':
        case 'Z':
            outputMessage = outputMessage
                            + "9";                    //Line 26
        }
    }
    else                                              //Line 27
        outputMessage = outputMessage
                    + "Invalid input";                //Line 28

    JOptionPane.showMessageDialog(null, outputMessage,
                "Telephone Digit",
                JOptionPane.PLAIN_MESSAGE); //Line 29

    inputMessage = "Enter another uppercase letter "
                + "to find its corresponding "
                + "telephone digit.\n"
                + "To stop the program enter #.\n"
                + "Enter a letter:";                  //Line 30

    inputString =
        JOptionPane.showInputDialog(inputMessage); //Line 31
    letter = inputString.charAt(0);                   //Line 32
}//end while

System.exit(0);                                       //Line 33
    }
}
```

Sample Run: (Figure 5-2 shows the sample run.)

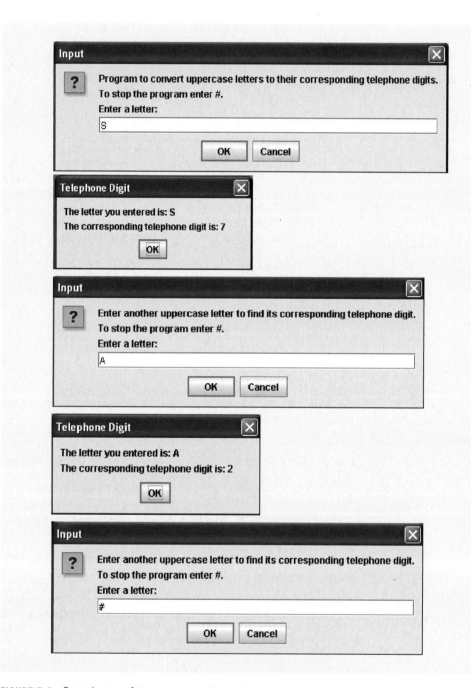

FIGURE 5-2 Sample run of `TelephoneDigitProgram`

The program in Example 5-5 works as follows: The statements in Lines 1 through 4 declare the appropriate variables. The statement in Line 5 creates the appropriate string to be included in the input dialog box. The statement in Line 6 displays the input dialog box informing the user what to do. This statement also retrieves the string entered by the user and assigns the string to the object `inputString`. (Notice that even though the user enters a single letter, it is still treated as a string.) The statement in Line 7 retrieves the letter from `inputString` and stores it in `letter`. The expression in the `while` statement in Line 8 checks that the letter is not #. If the letter entered by the user is not #, the body of the `while` loop executes. The statement in Line 9 creates the appropriate string to be displayed in the output dialog box.

The `if` statement in Line 10 checks whether the letter entered by the user is uppercase. If the letter entered by the user is uppercase, the `logical expression` in the `if` statement (in Line 10) evaluates to `true` and the `switch` statement executes, which determines the appropriate telephone digit and appends the telephone digit to `outputMessage` (see the statements in Lines 11 through 26). If the letter entered by the user is not uppercase, the `else` statement (in Line 27) executes and the statement in Line 28 appends the string `"Invalid input"` to `outputMessage`. The statement in Line 29 displays the output dialog box showing the result of the input.

Once the current letter is processed, the statement in Line 30 creates the message string, and the statement in Line 31 displays the input dialog box informing the user what to do next. The statement in Line 32 copies the letter entered by the user into `letter`. (Note that the statement in Line 30 is similar to the statement in Line 5, and that the statements in Lines 31 and 32 are the same as the statements in Lines 6 and 7.) After the statement in Line 32 (at the end of the `while` loop) executes, the control goes back to the top of the `while` loop and the same process begins again. When the user enters #, the program terminates.

NOTE In the program in Example 5-5, you can write the statements between Lines 10 and 28 using just a `switch` structure, that is, without the `if` in Line 10 and the `else` in Line 27. (See Programming Exercise 3 at the end of this chapter.)

Flag-Controlled `While` Loops

A **flag-controlled** `while` **loop** uses a `boolean` variable to control the loop. Suppose `found` is a `boolean` variable. The flag-controlled `while` loop takes the following form:

```
found = false;        //initialize the loop control variable

while (!found)        //test the loop control variable
{
    .
    .
    .

    if (logical expression)
        found = true; //update the loop control variable
    .
    .
    .
}
```

The variable, such as found, which is used to control the execution of the while loop, is called a **flag variable**.

Example 5-6 further illustrates the use of a flag-controlled while loop.

EXAMPLE 5-6 GUESSING THE NUMBER GAME

The following program randomly generates an integer greater than or equal to 0 and less than 100. The program then prompts the user to guess the number. If the user guesses the number correctly, the program outputs an appropriate message. Otherwise, the program checks whether the guessed number is less than the random number. If the guessed number is less than the random the number generated by the program, the program outputs the message, "Your guess is lower than the number"; otherwise, the program outputs the message, "Your guess is higher than the number". The program then prompts the user to enter another number. The user is prompted to guess the random number until the user enters the correct number.

The program uses the method random of the **class** Math to generate a random number. To be specific, the expression:

```
Math.random()
```

returns a value of type double greater than or equal to 0.0 and less than 1.0. To convert it to an integer greater than or equal to 0 and less than 100, the program uses the following expression:

```
(int) (Math.random() * 100);
```

Furthermore, the program uses the boolean variable done to control the loop. The boolean variable done is initialized to false. It is set to true when the user guesses the correct number.

```
//Flag-controlled while loop.
//Guessing the number game.

import java.util.*;
```

```java
public class FlagControlledLoop
{
    static Scanner console = new Scanner(System.in);

    public static void main(String[] args)
    {
            //declare the variables
        int num;        //variable to store the random number
        int guess;      //variable to store the number
                        //guessed by the user

        boolean done;   //boolean variable to control the loop

        num = (int) (Math.random() * 100);          //Line 1

        done = false;                               //Line 2

        while (!done)                               //Line 3
        {                                           //Line 4
            System.out.print ("Enter an integer greater"
                        + " than or equal to 0 and "
                        + "less than 100: ");       //Line 5
            guess = console.nextInt();              //Line 6
            System.out.println();                   //Line 7

            if (guess == num)                       //Line 8
            {                                       //Line 9
                System.out.println("You guessed the "
                            + "correct number.");   //Line 10
                done = true;                        //Line 11
            }                                       //Line 12
            else if (guess < num)                   //Line 13
                System.out.println("Your guess is "
                            + "lower than "
                            + "the number.\n"
                            + "Guess again!");       //Line 14
            else                                     //Line 15
                System.out.println("Your guess is "
                            + "higher than "
                            + "the number.\n"
                            + "Guess again!");       //Line 16
        } //end while                                //Line 17
    }                                                //Line 18
}
```

Sample Runs: (In the following sample run, the user input is shaded.)

Enter an integer greater than or equal to 0 and less than 100: 25

Your guess is higher than the number.
Guess again!
Enter an integer greater than or equal to 0 and less than 100: 5

Your guess is lower than the number.
Guess again!
Enter an integer greater than or equal to 0 and less than 100: 10

```
Your guess is higher than the number.
Guess again!
Enter an integer greater than or equal to 0 and less than 100: 8

Your guess is higher than the number.
Guess again!
Enter an integer greater than or equal to 0 and less than 100: 6

Your guess is lower than the number.
Guess again!
Enter an integer greater than or equal to 0 and less than 100: 7

You guessed the correct number.
```

The preceding program works as follows: The statement in Line 1 creates an integer greater than or equal to 0 and less than 100 and stores this number in the variable num. The statement in Line 2 sets the **boolean** variable done to **false**. The **while** loop starts at Line 3 and ends at Line 17. The expression in the **while** loop at Line 3 evaluates the expression !done. If done is **false**, then !done is **true** and the body of the **while** loop executes; if done is **true**, then !done is **false**, so the **while** loop terminates.

The statement in Line 5 prompts the user to enter an integer greater than or equal to 0 and less than 100. The statement in Line 6 stores the number entered by the user in the variable guess. The expression in the **if** statement in Line 8 determines whether the value of guess is the same as num , that is, if the user guessed the number correctly. If the value of guess is the same as num, then the statements in Lines 10 and 11 execute. The statement in Line 10 outputs the message:

```
You guessed the correct number.
```

The statement in Line 11 sets the variable done to **true**. The control then goes back to Line 3. Because done is **true**, !done is **false** and the **while** loop terminates.

If the expression in Line 8 evaluates to **false**, then the **else** statement in Line 13 executes. The statement part of this **else** is an **if...else** statement, starting at Line 13 and ending at Line 16. The **if** statement in Line 13 determines whether the value of guess is less than num. In this case, the statement in Line 14 outputs the message:

```
Your guess is lower than the number.
Guess again!
```

If the expression in the **if** statement in Line 13 evaluates to **false**, then the statement in Line 16 executes, which outputs the message:

```
Your guess is higher than the number.
Guess again!
```

The program then prompts the user to enter an integer greater than or equal to 0 and less than 100.

EOF-Controlled while Loops

If the data file is frequently altered (for example, if data is frequently added or deleted), it's best not to read the data with a sentinel value. Someone might accidentally erase the sentinel value or add data past the sentinel, especially if the programmer and data entry person are different people. Also, the programmer sometimes does not know what the sentinel is. In such situations, you can use an **EOF (End Of File)-controlled while loop**.

In Java, the form of the EOF-controlled while loop depends on the type of stream object used to input data into a program. Because we have been using the Scanner object to input data into a program, next we describe the EOF-controlled while loop that uses a Scanner object to input data.

Recall that the following statement creates the Scanner object console and initializes it to the standard input device:

```
static Scanner console = new Scanner(System.in);    //Line 1
```

This statement is equivalent to the following statements:

```
static Scanner console;              //Line 2
console = new Scanner(System.in);    //Line 3
```

The statement in Line 2 declares console to be the Scanner variable; the statement in Line 3 initializes console to the standard input device. On the other hand, the statement in Line 1 both declares and initializes the Scanner variable console.

The method hasNext, of the class Scanner, returns true if there is an input in the input stream, otherwise it returns false. In other words, the expression console.hasNext() evaluates to true if there is an input in the input stream, otherwise it returns false. Therefore, the expression console.hasNext() acts as the loop condition.

It now follows that a general form of the EOF-controlled while loop that uses the Scanner object console to input data is of the following form (we assume that console has been created and initialized using either the statement in Line 1 or the statements in Lines 2 and 3):

```
while (console.hasNext())
{
    //Get the next input (token) and store it in an
    //appropriate variable
    //Process the data
}
```

NOTE   In the Windows console environment, the end-of-file marker is entered using Ctrl+z. (Hold the Ctrl key and press z.) In the UNIX environment, the end-of-file marker is entered using Ctrl+d. (Hold the Ctrl key and press d.)

Suppose that `inFile` is a `Scanner` object initialized to the input file. In this case, the EOF-controlled `while` loop takes the following form:

```
while (inFile.hasNext())
{
    //Get the next input (token) and store it in an
    //appropriate variable
    //Process the data
}
```

EXAMPLE 5-7

The following code uses an EOF-controlled `while` loop to find the sum of a set of numbers:

```
static Scanner console = new Scanner(System.in);

int sum = 0;
int num;

while (console.hasNext())
{
    num = console.nextInt(); //Get the next number
    sum = sum + num;         //Add the number to sum
}

System.out.printf("Sum = %d%n", sum);
```

EXAMPLE 5-8

Suppose we are given a file consisting of students' names and their test scores, a number between 0 and 100 (inclusive). Each line in the file consists of a student name followed by the test score. We want a program that outputs each student's name followed by the test score and the grade. The program also needs to output the average test score for the class. Consider the following program.

```
// This program reads data from a file consisting of students'
// names and their test scores. The program outputs each
// student's name followed by the test score and the grade. The
// program also outputs the average test score for all students.

import java.io.*;                                        //Line 1
import java.util.*;                                      //Line 2

public class ClassAverage                                //Line 3
{                                                        //Line 4
    public static void main(String[] args)
                        throws FileNotFoundException      //Line 5
```

```
{                                                  //Line 6
    String firstName;                              //Line 7
    String lastName;                               //Line 8
    double testScore;                              //Line 9
    char grade = ' ';                              //Line 10
    double classAverage;                           //Line 11

    double sum = 0;                                //Line 12
    int count = 0;                                 //Line 13

    Scanner inFile =
        new Scanner(new FileReader("stData.txt"));  //Line 14

    PrintWriter outFile =
        new PrintWriter("stData.out");             //Line 15

    while (inFile.hasNext())                        //Line 16
    {                                              //Line 17
        firstName = inFile.next();//read the first name Line 18
        lastName = inFile.next(); //read the last name Line 19
        testScore =
            inFile.nextDouble(); //read the test score Line 20

        sum = sum + testScore; //update sum          Line 21
        count++;                  //increment count   Line 22

            //determine the grade
        switch ((int) testScore / 10)               //Line 23
        {                                          //Line 24
        case 0:                                     //Line 25
        case 1:                                     //Line 26
        case 2:                                     //Line 27
        case 3:                                     //Line 28
        case 4:                                     //Line 29
        case 5:                                     //Line 30
            grade = 'F';                            //Line 31
            break;                                  //Line 32

        case 6:                                     //Line 33
            grade = 'D';                            //Line 34
            break;                                  //Line 35

        case 7:                                     //Line 36
            grade = 'C';                            //Line 37
            break;                                  //Line 38

        case 8:                                     //Line 39
            grade = 'B';                            //Line 40
            break;                                  //Line 41

        case 9:                                     //Line 42
        case 10:                                    //Line 43
            grade = 'A';                            //Line 44
            break;                                  //Line 45
```

5

```
        default:                                          //Line 46
            System.out.println ("Invalid score.");        //Line 47
        }//end switch                                     //Line 48

        outFile.printf("%-12s %-12s %4.2f %c %n",
                       firstName, lastName,
                       testScore, grade);                 //Line 49
    }//end while                                          //Line 50

    outFile.println ();                                   //Line 51

    if (count != 0)                                       //Line 52
        outFile.printf("Class Average: %.2f %n",
                       sum / count);                      //Line 53
    else                                                  //Line 54
        outFile.println ("No data.");                     //Line 55

    outFile.close ();                                     //Line 56
    }                                                     //Line 57
}                                                         //Line 58
```

Sample Run:

Input File:

```
Steve Gill 89
Rita Johnson 91.5
Randy Brown 85.5
Seema Arora 76.5
Samir Mann 73
Samantha McCoy 88.5
```

Output File:

```
Steve       Gill         89.00 B
Rita        Johnson      91.50 A
Randy       Brown        85.50 B
Seema       Arora        76.50 C
Samir       Mann         73.00 C
Samantha    McCoy        88.50 B

Class Average: 84.00
```

The preceding program works as follows. The statements in Lines 7 to 11 declare variables required by the program. The statements in Lines 12 and 13 initialize the variables sum and count. The statement in Line 14 declares inFile to be a reference variable of type Scanner and associates it with the input file. The statement in Line 15 declares outFile to be a reference variable of type PrintWriter and associates it with the output file.

The while loop from Lines 16 to 50 reads each student's first name, last name, and test score, and outputs the name followed by the test score and grade. Specifically, the statement in Line 18 reads the first name, the statement in Line 19 reads the last name, and the statement in Line 20 reads the test score. The statement in Line 21 updates the value of sum. (After reading all the data, the value of sum stores the sum of all the test scores.) The statement in Line 22 updates the value of count. (The variable count stores the number of students in the class.) The switch statement from Lines 23 to 48 determines the grade from testScore and stores it in the variable grade. The statement in Line 49 outputs a student's first name, last name, test score, and grade.

The if...else statement in Lines 52 to 55 outputs the class average, and the statement in Line 56 closes the file associated with outFile, which is stData.out.

The Programming Example Checking Account Balance, available on the Web site and the CD accompanying this book, further illustrates how to use an EOF-controlled while loop in a program.

5

More on Expressions in while Statements

In the examples in the previous sections, the expression in the while statement is quite simple. In other words, the while loop is controlled by a single variable. However, there are situations where the logical expression in the while statement may be more complex.

For example, the program in Example 5-6 uses a flag-controlled while loop to implement the Guessing the Number game. However, the program gives as many tries as the user needs to guess the number. Suppose you want to give the user, at most, five tries to guess the number. If the user does not guess the number correctly within five tries, then the program outputs the random number generated by the program, as well as a message that they lost the game. In this case, you can write the while loop as follows. (Assume that numOfGuesses is an int variable initialized to 0.)

```
while ((numOfGuesses < 5) && (!done))
{
    System.out.print ("Enter an integer greater "
                    + "than or equal to 0 and "
                    + "less than 100: ");
    guess = console.nextInt();
    System.out.println();

    numOfGuesses++;

    if (guess == num)
    {
        System.out.println("Winner!. You guessed the "
                        + "correct number.");
        done = true;
    }
    else if (guess < num)
        System.out.println("Your guess is "
                        + "lower than "
                        + "the number.\n"
                        + "Guess again!");
```

```
    else
        System.out.println("Your guess is "
                            + "higher than "
                            + "the number.\n"
                            + "Guess again!");
}//end while
```

You also need the following code, to be included after the `while` loop, in case the user cannot guess the correct number in five tries:

```
if (!done)
    System.out.println("You lose! The correct "
                    + "number is " + num);
```

We leave it as an exercise for you to write a complete Java program to implement the Guessing the Number game in which the user has, at most, five tries to guess the number. (See Programming Exercise 14 at the end of this chapter.)

As you can see from the preceding `while` loop, the logical expression in a `while` statement can be complex. The main objective of a `while` loop is to repeat certain statement(s) until certain conditions are met.

PROGRAMMING EXAMPLE: Fibonacci Number

So far, you have seen several examples of loops. Recall that in Java, `while` loops are used when a certain statement(s) must be executed repeatedly until certain conditions are met. The following program uses a `while` loop to find a **Fibonacci number**.

Consider the following sequence of numbers:

```
1, 1, 2, 3, 5, 8, 13, 21, 34, ....
```

Given the first two numbers of the sequence (say, a_1 and a_2), the nth number a_n, $n >= 3$, of this sequence is given by:

$$a_n = a_{n-1} + a_{n-2}$$

Thus:

$$a_3 = a_2 + a_1 = 1 + 1 = 2,$$

$$a_4 = a_3 + a_2 = 2 + 1 = 3,$$

and so on.

Such a sequence is called a **Fibonacci sequence**. In the preceding sequence, $a_2 = 1$ and $a_1 = 1$. However, given any first two numbers, using this process, you can determine the nth number, a_n, $n >= 3$, of the sequence. The number determined this way is called the nth **Fibonacci number**. Suppose $a_2 = 6$ and $a_1 = 3$.

Then:

$$a_3 = a_2 + a_1 = 6 + 3 = 9; \; a_4 = a_3 + a_2 = 9 + 6 = 15.$$

Next, we write a program that determines the nth Fibonacci number given the first two numbers.

Input: The first two numbers of the Fibonacci sequence and the position of the desired Fibonacci number in the Fibonacci sequence

Output: The nth Fibonacci number

PROBLEM ANALYSIS AND ALGORITHM DESIGN

To find, say, the 10th Fibonacci number of a sequence, you must first find a_9 and a_8, which requires you to find a_7 and a_6 and so on. Therefore, to find a_{10}, you must first find $a_3, a_4, a_5, \ldots, a_9$. This discussion translates into the following algorithm:

1. Get the first two Fibonacci numbers.

2. Get the position of the desired number in the Fibonacci sequence. That is, get the position, n, of the number in the Fibonacci sequence.

3. Calculate the next Fibonacci number by adding the previous two elements of the Fibonacci sequence.

4. Repeat Step 3 until the nth Fibonacci number is found.

5. Output the nth Fibonacci number.

Note that the program assumes that the first number of the Fibonacci sequence is less than or equal to the second number of the Fibonacci sequence, and both numbers are non-negative. Moreover, the program also assumes that the user enters a valid value for the position of the desired number in the Fibonacci sequence; that is, it is a positive integer. (See Programming Exercise 12 at the end of this chapter.)

VARIABLES

Because you must know the last two numbers to find the current Fibonacci number, you need the following variables: two variables—say, `previous1` and `previous2`— to hold the previous two numbers of the Fibonacci sequence, and one variable—say, `current`—to hold the current Fibonacci number. The number of times that Step 2 of the algorithm repeats depends on the position of the Fibonacci number you are calculating. For example, if you want to calculate the 10th Fibonacci number, you must execute Step 3 eight times. (Remember, the user gives the first two numbers of the Fibonacci sequence.) Therefore, you need a variable to store the number of times that Step 3 should execute. You also need a variable—the loop control variable—to track the number of times that Step 3 has executed. Therefore, you need five variables for the data manipulation:

5

```
int previous1;    //Variable to store the first
                  //Fibonacci number
int previous2;    //Variable to store the second
                  //Fibonacci number
int current;      //Variable to store the current
                  //Fibonacci number
int counter;      //Loop control variable
int nthFibonacci; //Variable to store the desired
                  //Fibonacci number
```

To calculate the third Fibonacci number, add the value of **previous1** and **previous2** and store the result in **current**. To calculate the fourth Fibonacci number, add the value of the second Fibonacci number (that is, **previous2**) and the value of the third Fibonacci number (that is, **current**). Thus, when the fourth Fibonacci number is calculated, you no longer need the first Fibonacci number. Instead of declaring additional variables, which could be several, after calculating a Fibonacci number to determine the next Fibonacci number, **current** becomes **previous2** and **previous2** becomes **previous1**. Therefore, you can again use the variable **current** to store the next Fibonacci number. This process is repeated until the desired Fibonacci number is calculated. Initially, **previous1** and **previous2** are the first two numbers of the sequence, supplied by the user. From the preceding discussion, it follows that you need five variables.

MAIN ALGORITHM

1. Display the input dialog box to prompt the user for the first Fibonacci number—that is, **previous1**. Store the string representing **previous1** into **inputString**.

2. Retrieve the string from **inputString**, and store the first Fibonacci number into **previous1**.

3. Display the input dialog box to prompt the user for the second Fibonacci number—that is, **previous2**. Store the string representing **previous2** into **inputString**.

4. Retrieve the string from **inputString**, and store the second Fibonacci number into **previous2**.

5. Create the **outputString** and append **previous1** and **previous2**.

6. Display the input dialog box to prompt the user for the desired Fibonacci number, that is, **nthFibonacci**. Store the string representing **nthFibonacci** into **inputString**.

7. Retrieve the string from **inputString**, and store the desired *n*th Fibonacci number into **nthFibonacci**.

8. a. `if (nthFibonacci == 1)`

   the desired Fibonacci number is the first Fibonacci number. Copy the value of **previous1** into **current**.

b. `else if (nthFibonacci == 2)`

the desired Fibonacci number is the second Fibonacci number. Copy the value of `previous2` into `current`.

c. `else` calculate the desired Fibonacci number as follows:

Since you already know the first two Fibonacci numbers of the sequence, start by determining the third Fibonacci number.

i. Initialize `counter` to 3, to keep track of the calculated Fibonacci numbers.

ii. Calculate the next Fibonacci number, as follows:

`current = previous2 + previous1;`

iii. Assign the value of `previous2` to `previous1`.

iv. Assign the value of `current` to `previous2`.

v. Increment `counter`.

Repeat Steps 8c(ii) through 8c(v) until the Fibonacci number you want is calculated.

The following `while` loop executes Steps 8c(ii) through 8c(v) and determines the *n*th Fibonacci number:

```
while (counter <= nthFibonacci)
{
    current = previous2 + previous1;
    previous1 = previous2;
    previous2 = current;
    counter++;
}
```

9. Append the *n*th Fibonacci number to `outputString`. Notice that the *n*th Fibonacci number is stored in `current`.

10. Display the output dialog box showing the first two and the *n*th Fibonacci numbers.

COMPLETE PROGRAM LISTING

```
//****************************************************************
// Author: D.S. Malik
//
// Program: nth Fibonacci number
// Given the first two numbers of a Fibonacci sequence, this
// determines and outputs the desired number of the Fibonacci
// sequence.
//****************************************************************
```

```
import javax.swing.JOptionPane;

public class FibonacciNumber
{
    public static void main (String[] args)
    {
            //Declare variables

        String inputString;
        String outputString;

        int    previous1;
        int    previous2;
        int    current = 0;
        int    counter;
        int    nthFibonacci;

        inputString =
            JOptionPane.showInputDialog("Enter the first "
                              + "Fibonacci number: ");  //Step 1
        previous1 = Integer.parseInt(inputString);      //Step 2

        inputString =
            JOptionPane.showInputDialog("Enter the second "
                              + "Fibonacci number: "); //Step 3
        previous2 = Integer.parseInt(inputString);      //Step 4

        outputString = "The first two numbers of the "
                     + "Fibonacci sequence are: "
                     + previous1 + " and " + previous2;  //Step 5

        inputString =
            JOptionPane.showInputDialog("Enter the position "
                          + "of the desired number in "
                          + "the Fibonacci sequence: ");  //Step 6
        nthFibonacci = Integer.parseInt(inputString);    //Step 7

        if (nthFibonacci == 1)                           //Step 8.a
            current = previous1;
        else if (nthFibonacci == 2)                      //Step 8.b
            current = previous2;
        else                                             //Step 8.c
        {
            counter = 3;                                 //Step 8.c.1

                //Steps 8.c.2 - 8.c.5
            while (counter <= nthFibonacci)
            {
                current = previous2 + previous1;         //Step 8.c.2
                previous1 = previous2;                   //Step 8.c.3
```

```
                    previous2 = current;            //Step 8.c.4
                    counter++;                       //Step 8.c.5
            }
        }

        outputString = outputString + "\nThe "
                    + nthFibonacci
                    + "th Fibonacci number of "
                    + "the sequence is: "
                    + current;                       //Step 9

        JOptionPane.showMessageDialog(null, outputString,
                            "Fibonacci Number",
                    JOptionPane.INFORMATION_MESSAGE);  //Step 10
        System.exit(0);
    }
}
```

Sample Run: (Figure 5-3 shows the sample run.)

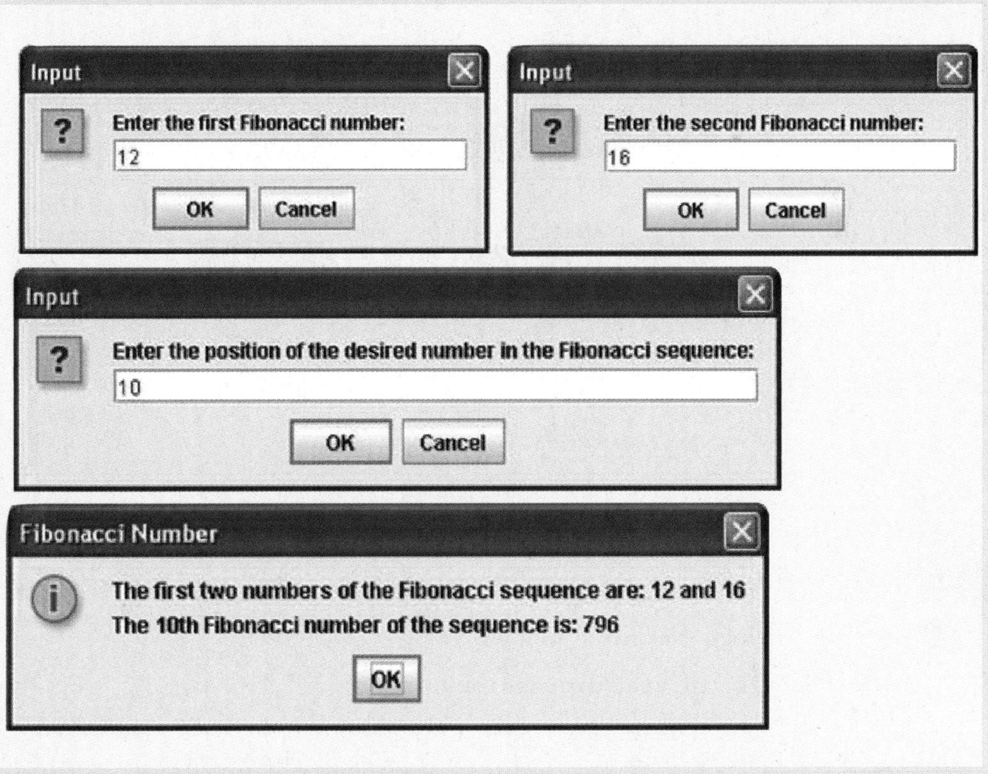

FIGURE 5-3 Sample run FibonacciNumber

`for` Looping (Repetition) Structure

The `while` loop discussed in the previous section is general enough to implement all forms of repetitions. As noted earlier, Java provides three looping structures. The previous section discussed `while` loops in detail. This section explains how to use Java's `for` loop.

The general form of the `for` statement is:

```
for (initial expression; logical expression; update expression)
    statement
```

In Java, `for` is a reserved word. The `logical expression` is called the **loop condition**. The `initial expression`, `logical expression`, and `update expression` (called `for` loop **control expressions**) are enclosed within parentheses and control the body (`statement`) of the `for` statement. Note that the `for` loop control expressions are separated by semicolons, and that the body of a `for` loop can have either a simple or compound statement. Figure 5-4 shows the flow of execution of a `for` loop.

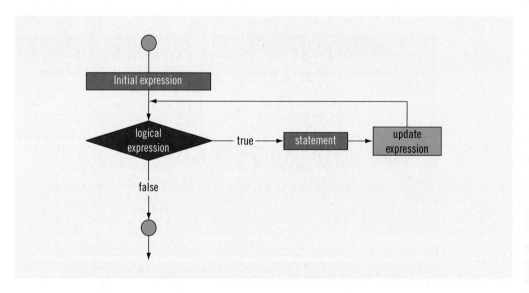

FIGURE 5-4 `for` loop

The `for` loop executes as follows:

1. The `initial expression` executes.
2. The `logical expression` is evaluated. If the `loop condition` evaluates to `true`:
   a. Execute the body of the `for` loop.
   b. Execute the `update statement` (the third expression in the parentheses).
3. Repeat Step 2 until the `loop condition` evaluates to `false`.

The `initial statement` usually initializes a variable (called the `for` loop control, or indexed, variable).

> **NOTE** As the name implies, the `initial expression` in the `for` loop is the first statement to execute; it executes only once.

Primarily, `for` loops are used to implement counter-controlled loops. For this reason, the `for` loop is typically called a **counted** or **indexed** `for` loop. Next, we give various examples to illustrate how a `for` loop works.

EXAMPLE 5-9

5

The following `for` loop prints the first 10 non-negative integers: (Assume that `i` is an `int` variable.)

```
for (i = 0; i < 10; i++)
    System.out.print(i + " " );

System.out.println();
```

The `initial expression`, i = 0;, initializes i to 0. Next, the `logical expression`, i < 10, is evaluated. Because 0 < 10 is `true`, the print statement executes and outputs 0. The `update expression`, i++, then executes, which sets the value of i to 1. Once again, the `logical expression` is evaluated, which is still `true`, and so on. When i becomes 10, the `logical expression` evaluates to `false`, the `for` loop terminates, and the statement following the `for` loop executes.

The following examples further illustrate how a `for` loop executes.

EXAMPLE 5-10

1. The following `for` loop outputs the word `Hello` and a star (on separate lines) five times:

```
for (i = 1; i <= 5; i++)
{
    System.out.println("Hello");
    System.out.println("*");
}
```

2. Now consider the following `for` loop:

```
for (i = 1; i <= 5; i++)
    System.out.println("Hello");
    System.out.println("*");
```

This loop outputs the word `Hello` five times and the star only once. In this case, the `for` loop controls only the first output statement because the two output statements are not made into a compound statement using braces. Therefore, the first output statement executes five times because the `for` loop executes five times. After the `for` loop executes, the second output statement executes only once.

EXAMPLE 5-11

The following `for` loop executes five empty statements:

```
for (i = 0; i < 5; i++);          //Line 1
    System.out.println("*");       //Line 2
```

The semicolon at the end of the `for` statement (before the output statement in Line 2) terminates the `for` loop. The action of this `for` loop is empty. The statement in Line 2 outputs a star.

The preceding examples show that care is required to get a `for` loop to perform the desired action.

Some additional comments on `for` loops follow:

- If the `logical expression` is initially `false`, the loop body does not execute.

- The update expression, when executed, should change the value of the loop control variable, which eventually sets the value of the loop condition to `false`. The `for` loop executes indefinitely if the loop condition is always `true`.

- If you put a semicolon at the end of a `for` statement (just before the body of the loop), the action of the `for` loop is empty.

- In a `for` statement, if the `logical expression` is omitted, it is assumed to be `true`.

- In a `for` statement, you can omit all three statements—initial expression, logical expression, and update expression. The following is a legal `for` loop:

```
for (;;)
    System.out.println("Hello");
```

This is an infinite `for` loop, continuously printing the world `Hello`.

More examples of `for` loops follow.

EXAMPLE 5-12

1. You can count backward using a `for` loop if the `for` loop control expressions are set correctly. For example, consider the following `for` loop:

```
for (i = 10; i >= 1; i--)
    System.out.print(i + " ");

System.out.println();
```

The output is:

```
10 9 8 7 6 5 4 3 2 1
```

In this `for` loop, the variable `i` is initialized to 10. After each iteration of the loop, `i` is decremented by 1. The loop continues to execute as long as `i >= 1`.

2. You can increment (or decrement) the loop control variable by any fixed number (or modify it in any way you please). In the following `for` loop, the variable is initialized to 0; at the end of the `for` loop, `i` is incremented by 2. This `for` loop outputs 10 even integers 0 through 18:

```
for (i = 0; i < 20; i = i + 2)
    System.out.print(i + " ");

System.out.println();
```

EXAMPLE 5-13

Consider the following examples, where `i` is an `int` variable.

1. ```
   for (i = 10; i <= 9; i++)
       System.out.print(i + " ");

   System.out.println();
   ```

   In this `for` loop, the initial expression sets `i` to 10. Because initially the logical expression (`i <= 9`) is `false`, the body of the `for` loop does not execute.

2. ```
   for (i = 9; i >= 10; i--)
       System.out.print(i + " ");

   System.out.println();
   ```

   In this `for` loop, the initial expression sets `i` to 9. Because initially the logical expression (`i >= 10`) is `false`, the body of the `for` loop does not execute.

3.  ```
    for (i = 10; i <= 10; i++)        //Line 1
        System.out.print(i + " ");    //Line 2

    System.out.println();             //Line 3
    ```

    In this **for** loop, the output statement in Line 2 executes once.

4.  ```
    for (i = 1; i <= 10; i++);
        System.out.print(i + " ");

    System.out.println();
    ```

    This **for** loop has no effect on the output statement. The semicolon at the end of the **for** statement terminates the **for** loop; the action of the **for** loop is thus empty. Both output statements are outside the scope of the **for** loop, so the **for** loop has no effect on them. Note that this code will output 11.

5.  ```
    for (i = 1; ; i++)
        System.out.print(i + " ");

    System.out.println();
    ```

    In this **for** loop, because the `logical expression` is omitted from the **for** statement, the loop condition is always **true**. This is an infinite loop.

EXAMPLE 5-14

In this example, a **for** loop reads five integers and finds their sum and average. Consider the following programming code, in which i, newNum, sum, and **average** are **int** variables:

```
sum = 0;

for (i = 0; i < 5; i++)
{
    newNum = console.nextInt();
    sum = sum + newNum;
}

average = sum / 5;
System.out.println("The sum is " + sum);
System.out.println("The average is " + average);
```

In the preceding **for** loop, after getting a newNum, this value is added to the previously calculated (partial) sum of all the numbers read before the current number. The variable sum is initialized to 0 before the **for** loop. Thus, after the program gets the first number and adds it to the value of sum, the variable sum holds the correct sum of the first number.

```

NOTE The syntax of the `for` loop, which is

```
for (initial expression; logical expression; update expression)
    statement
```

is functionally equivalent to the following `while` statement:

```
initial expression
while (logical expression)
{
    statement
    update expression
}
```

For example, the following `for` and `while` loops are equivalent:

```
for (int i = 0; i < 10; i++)        int i = 0;
    system.out.print(i + " ");      while (i < 10)
system.out.println();               {
                                        system.out.print(i + " ");
                                        i++;
                                    }
                                    system.out.println();
```

If the number of iterations of a loop is known or can be determined in advance, then typically, programmers use a `for` loop.

Recall that putting one control structure statement inside another is called **nesting**. The following programming example demonstrates a simple instance of nesting, and also nicely demonstrates counting.

PROGRAMMING EXAMPLE: Classify Numbers

This program reads a given set of integers and then prints the number of odd integers, the number of even integers, and the number of zeros.

The program reads 20 integers, but you can easily modify it to read any set of numbers. In fact, you can modify the program so that it first prompts the user to specify how many integers are to be read.

Input: 20 integers—positive, negative, or zeros

Output: The number of zeros, even numbers, and odd numbers

PROBLEM
ANALYSIS
AND
ALGORITHM
DESIGN

After reading a number, you need to check whether it is even or odd. Suppose the value is stored in the variable number. Divide number by 2 and check the remainder. If the remainder is zero, number is even. Increment the even count and then check whether number is zero. If it is, increment the zero count. If the remainder is not zero, increment the odd count.

The program uses a `switch` statement to decide whether number is odd or even. Suppose that number is odd. Dividing by 2 gives the remainder 1 if number is positive, and the remainder -1 if negative. If number is even, dividing by 2 gives the remainder 0 whether number is positive or negative. You can use the mod operator, %, to find the remainder. For example:

```
6 % 2 = 0, -4 % 2 = 0, -7 % 2 = -1, 15 % 2 = 1
```

Repeat the preceding process of analyzing a number for each number in the list.

This discussion translates into the following algorithm:

1. For each number in the list:

   a. Get the number.

   b. Analyze the number.

   c. Increment the appropriate count.

2. Print the results.

VARIABLES

Because you want to count the number of zeros, even numbers, and odd numbers, you need three variables of the type int—say, zeros, evens, and odds—to track the counts. You also need a variable—say, number—to read and store the number to be analyzed, and another variable—say, counter—to count the numbers analyzed. Your program thus needs the following variables:

```
int counter;    //loop control variable
int number;     //variable to store the number read
int zeros;      //variable to store the zero count
int evens;      //variable to store the even count
int odds;       //variable to store the odd count
```

Clearly, you must initialize the variables zeros, evens, and odds to zero. You can initialize these variables when you declare them.

MAIN
ALGORITHM

1. Initialize the variables.

2. Prompt the user to enter 20 numbers.

3. For each number in the list:

   a. Get the next number.

   b. Output the number (echo input).

c. If the number is even:

{

   i. Increment the even count.

   ii. If the number is zero, increment the zero count.

}

otherwise

Increment the odd count.

4. Print the results.

Before writing the Java program, let's describe Steps 1 through 4 in more detail. It will be much easier for you to then write the instructions in Java.

1. Initialize the variables. You can initialize the variables `zeros`, `evens`, and `odds` when you declare them.

2. Use an output statement to prompt the user to enter 20 numbers.

3. For Step 3, you can use a `for` loop to process and analyze the 20 numbers. In pseudocode, this step is written as follows:

```
for (counter = 1; counter <= 20; counter++)
{
    a.   get the number;
    b.   output the number;
    c.   switch (number % 2)      //check the remainder
         {
         case 0:
             increment the even count;
             if (number == 0)
                 increment the zero count;
             break;

         case 1:
         case -1:
             increment the odd count;
         } //end switch
} //end for
```

4. Print the result. Output the values of the variables `zeros`, `evens`, and `odds`.

COMPLETE PROGRAM LISTING

```java
//*********************************************************
// Author: D.S. Malik
//
// Program: Classify Numbers
// This program counts the number of odd and even numbers.
// The program also counts the number of zeros.
//*********************************************************

import java.util.*;

public class ClassifyNumbers
{
    static Scanner console = new Scanner(System.in);

    static final int N = 20;

    public static void main (String[] args)
    {
            //Declare the variables
        int counter;  //loop control variable
        int number;    //variable to store the new number

        int zeros = 0;                              //Step 1
        int odds = 0;                               //Step 1
        int evens = 0;                              //Step 1

        System.out.println("Please enter " + N
                        + " integers, positive, "
                        + "negative, or zeros.");   //Step 2

        for (counter = 1; counter <= N; counter++)  //Step 3
        {
            number = console.nextInt();             //Step 3a
            System.out.print(number + " ");         //Step 3b

                //Step 3c
            switch (number % 2)
            {
            case 0:
                evens++;
                if (number == 0)
                    zeros++;
                break;

            case 1:
            case -1:
                odds++;
            }//end switch

        }//end for loop
```

```
            System.out.println();

                //Step 4
            System.out.println("There are " + evens + " evens, "
                        + "which also includes "
                        + zeros + " zeros");
            System.out.println("Total number of odds is: " + odds);
        }
    }
```

Sample Run: (In this sample run, the user input is shaded.)

```
Please enter 20 integers, positive, negative, or zeros.
0 0 -2 -3 -5 6 7 8 0 3 0 -23 -8 0 2 9 0 12 67 54
0 0 -2 -3 -5 6 7 8 0 3 0 -23 -8 0 2 9 0 12 67 54
There are 13 evens, which also includes 6 zeros
Total number of odds is: 7
```

We recommend that you do a walk-through of this program using the above sample input.

Note that the `switch` statement in Step 3c can also be written as an `if...else` statement as follows:

```
if (number % 2 == 0)
{
    evens++;
    if (number == 0)
        zeros++;
}
else
    odds++;
```

do...while Looping (Repetition) Structure

This section describes the third type of looping or repetition structure—a `do...while` loop. The general form of a `do...while` statement is:

```
do
    statement
while (logical expression);
```

In Java, `do` is a reserved word. As with the other repetition structures, the `do...while` `statement` can be either a simple or compound statement. If it is a compound statement, enclose it between braces. The `logical expression` is called the **loop condition**. Figure 5-5 shows the flow of execution of a `do...while` loop.

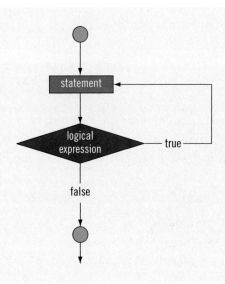

FIGURE 5-5 `do...while` loop

The `statement` executes first, and then the `logical expression` is evaluated. If the `logical expression` evaluates to `true`, the `statement` executes again. As long as the `logical expression` in a `do...while` statement is `true`, the `statement` executes. To avoid an infinite loop, you must, as before, make sure that the body of the loop contains a statement that ultimately makes the `logical expression` evaluate to `false` and assures that it exits properly.

EXAMPLE 5-15

```
i = 0;
do
{
    System.out.print(i + " ");
    i = i + 5;
}
while (i <= 20);
```

The output of this code is:

`0 5 10 15 20`

After the value 20 is output, the statement:

`i = i + 5;`

changes the value of i to 25, so i <= 20 becomes `false`, which halts the loop.

Because the `while` or `for` loops both have entry conditions, these loops might never activate. The `do...while` loop, on the other hand, has an exit condition; therefore, the body of the `do...while` loop always executes at least once.

In a `while` or `for` loop, the loop condition is evaluated before executing the body of the loop. Therefore, `while` and `for` loops are called **pretest loops**. On the other hand, the loop condition in a `do...while` loop is evaluated after executing the body of the loop. Therefore, `do...while` loops are called **post-test loops**.

EXAMPLE 5-16

Consider the following two loops:

```
a.  i = 11;
    while (i <= 10)
    {
            System.out.print(i + " ");
            i = i + 5;
    }

    System.out.println();

b.  i = 11;
    do
    {
        System.out.print(i + " ");
        i = i + 5;
    }
    while (i <= 10);

    System.out.println();
```

In (a), the `while` loop produces nothing. In (b), the `do...while` loop outputs the number 11 and also changes the value of i to 16.

The `do...while` loop is useful when it does not make sense to check a condition until after the action occurs. For example, a `do...while` loop can be used for input validation. Consider a program that prompts a user to enter a test score, which must be at least 12 but not more than 36. If the user enters a score less than 12 or greater than 36, he should be prompted to re-enter the score. The following `do...while` loop can be used to accomplish this objective.

```
int score;

do
{
    System.out.print(Enter a score between 12 and 36: ");
    score = console.nextInt();
    System.out.println();
}
while (score < 12 || score > 36);
```

EXAMPLE 5-17 DIVISIBILITY TEST BY 3 AND 9

Suppose that m and n are integers and m is nonzero. Then m is called a **divisor** of n if $n = mt$ for some integer t; that is, when m divides n, the remainder is 0.

Let $n = a_k a_{k-1} a_{k-2} \ldots a_1 a_0$ be an integer. Let $s = a_k + a_{k-1} + a_{k-2} + \ldots + a_1 + a_0$ be the sum of the digits of n. It is known that n is divisible by 3 and 9 if s is divisible by 3 and 9. In other words, an integer is divisible by 3 and 9 if and only if the sum of its digits is divisible by 3 and 9.

For example, suppose $n = 27193257$. Then, $s = 2 + 7 + 1 + 9 + 3 + 2 + 5 + 7 = 36$. Because 36 is divisible by both 3 and 9, it follows that 27193257 is divisible by both 3 and 9.

Next, we write a program that determines whether a positive integer is divisible by 3 and 9 by first finding the sum of its digits and then checking whether the sum is divisible by 3 and 9.

To find the sum of the digits of a positive integer, we need to extract each digit of the number. Consider the number 951372. Note that 951372 % 10 = 2, which is the last digit of 951372. Also note that 951372 / 10 = 95137, that is, when the number is divided by 10, it removes the last digit. Next, we repeat this process on the number 95137. Of course, we need to add the extracted digits.

Suppose that `sum` and `num` are `int` variables and the positive integer is stored in `num`. We thus have the following algorithm to find the sum of the digits:

```
sum = 0;

do
{
    sum = sum + num % 10; //extract the last digit
                          //and add it to sum
    num = num / 10;       //remove the last digit
}
while (num > 0);
```

Using this algorithm, we can write the following program that uses a `do...while` loop to implement the preceding divisibility test algorithm.

```
//Program: Divisibility test by 3 and 9

import java.util.*;

public class DivisibilityTest
{
    static Scanner console = new Scanner(System.in);
```

```java
public static void main (String[] args)
{
    int num;
    int temp;
    int sum;

    System.out.print("Enter a positive integer: ");
    num = console.nextInt();
    System.out.println();

    temp = num;

    sum = 0;

    do
    {
        sum = sum + num % 10;  //extract the last digit
                               //and add it to sum
        num = num / 10;        //remove the last digit
    }
    while (num > 0);

    System.out.println("The sum of the digits = " + sum);

    if (sum % 3 == 0)
        System.out.println(temp + " is divisible by 3");
    else
        System.out.println(temp + " is not divisible by 3");

    if (sum % 9 == 0)
        System.out.println(temp + " is divisible by 9");
    else
        System.out.println(temp + " is not divisible by 9");
}
}
```

Sample Runs: (In these sample runs, the user input is shaded.)

Sample Run 1:
```
Enter a positive integer: 27193257

The sum of the digits = 36
27193257 is divisible by 3
27193257 is divisible by 9
```

Sample Run 2:
```
Enter a positive integer: 609321

The sum of the digits = 21
609321 is divisible by 3
609321 is not divisible by 9
```

Sample Run 3:
```
Enter a positive integer: 161905102
```

```
The sum of the digits = 25
161905102 is not divisible by 3
161905102 is not divisible by 9
```

Choosing the Right Looping Structure

All three loops have a place in Java. If you know or the program can determine in advance the number of repetitions needed, the `for` loop is the correct choice. If you do not know, and the program cannot determine in advance, the number of repetitions needed, and it could be zero, the `while` loop is the right choice. If you do not know, and the program cannot determine in advance, the number of repetitions needed, and it is at least one, the `do...while` loop is the right choice.

break and continue Statements

The `break` and `continue` statements alter the flow of control in a program. As you have seen, the `break` statement, when executed in a `switch` structure, provides an immediate exit from the `switch` structure. Similarly, you can use the `break` statement in `while`, `for`, and `do...while` loops to immediately exit from these structures. The `break` statement is typically used for two purposes:

- To exit early from a loop

- To skip the remainder of the `switch` structure

After the `break` statement executes, the program continues to execute starting at the first statement after the structure.

Suppose that you have the following declaration:

```
static Scanner console = new Scanner(System.in);

int sum;
int num;

boolean isNegative;
```

The use of a `break` statement in a loop can eliminate the use of certain `boolean` variables. The following Java code segment helps illustrate this idea:

```
sum = 0;
isNegative = false;

while (console.hasNext() && !isNegative)
{
    num = console.nextInt();
```

```
        if (num < 0)    //if the number is negative, terminate the
                        //loop after this iteration
        {
            System.out.println("Negative number found in the data.");

            isNegative = true;
        }
        else
            sum = sum + num;
}
```

This `while` loop is supposed to find the sum of a set of positive numbers. If the data set contains a negative number, the loop terminates with an appropriate error message. This `while` loop uses the flag variable `isNegative` to accomplish the desired result. The variable `isNegative` is initialized to `false` before the `while` loop. Before adding num to sum, the code checks whether num is negative. If num is negative, an error message appears on the screen and `isNegative` is set to `true`. In the next iteration, when the expression in the `while` statement is evaluated, it evaluates to `false` because `!isNegative` is `false`. (Note that because `isNegative` is `true`, `!isNegative` is `false`.)

The following `while` loop is written without using the variable `isNegative`:

```
sum = 0;

while (console.hasNext())
{
    num = console.nextInt();

    if (num < 0)    //if the number is negative, terminate the loop
    {
        System.out.println("Negative number found in the data.");

        break;
    }

    sum = sum + num;
}
```

In this form of the `while` loop, when a negative number is found, the expression in the `if` statement evaluates to `true`; after printing an appropriate message, the `break` statement terminates the loop. (After executing the `break` statement in a loop, the remaining statements in the loop are skipped.)

The `continue` statement is used in `while`, `for`, and `do...while` structures. When the `continue` statement is executed in a loop, it skips the remaining statements in the loop and proceeds with the next iteration of the loop. In a `while` or `do...while` structure, the `logical expression` is evaluated immediately after the `continue` statement. In a `for` structure, the `update statement` is executed after the `continue` statement, and then the `logical expression` executes.

If the previous program segment encounters a negative number, the `while` loop terminates. If you want to ignore the negative number and read the next number rather than terminate the loop, replace the `break` statement with the `continue` statement, as shown in the following example:

```
sum = 0;

while (console.hasNext())
{
    num = console.nextInt();

    if (num < 0) //if the number is negative, go to the
                 //next iteration
    {
        System.out.println("Negative number found in the data.");

        continue;
    }

    sum = sum + num;
}
```

NOTE The `break` and `continue` statements are an effective way to avoid extra variables to control a loop and produce an elegant code. However, these statements must be used very sparingly within a loop. An excessive use of these statements in a loop will produce a spaghetti-code (loops with many exit conditions) and could be very hard to understand and manage.

NOTE As stated earlier, all three loops have their place in Java and one loop can often replace another. The execution of a `continue` statement, however, is where a `while` structure differs from a `for` structure. In a `while` loop, when the `continue` statement is executed, if the **update statement** appears after the `continue` statement, the **update statement** is not executed. In a `for` loop, the **update statement** always executes.

Avoiding Bugs by Avoiding Patches

A software patch is a piece of code written on top of an existing piece of code and intended to remedy a deficiency in the original code. Determining and correcting the original deficiency is a much better approach.

Consider, for example, the following lines of code, originally intended to print three rows of stars, with one star on the first row, two stars on the second row, and three stars on the third row:

```
for (i = 0; i <= 3; i++)              //Line 1
{                                      //Line 2
    for (j = 0; j <= i; j++)          //Line 3
        System.out.print("*");         //Line 4

    System.out.println();              //Line 5
}                                      //Line 6
```

These lines of code produce the following output:

```
*
**
***
****
```

The output consists of four rows of stars rather than three rows of stars, as intended originally.

Instead of addressing the problem, some programmers address the symptom of the problem by adding a software patch. The following example illustrates a software patch that might be produced by a beginning programmer:

```
for (i = 0; i <= 3; i++)              //Line 1
{                                      //Line 2
    if (i == 3)                        //Line p1
        break;                         //Line p2
    else                               //Line p3
        for (j = 0; j <= i; j++)      //Line 3
            System.out.print("*");     //Line 4

    System.out.println();              //Line 5
}                                      //Line 6
```

Here, the programmer has observed a symptom of the problem, namely the printing of an extra row of stars. Instead of addressing the problem, he has addressed the symptom by exiting the outer **for** loop during its fourth repetition. The patch on Lines **p1**, **p2**, and **p3** eliminates the symptom, but it represents poor programming practice. Instead, the programmer should find and fix the problem. Here, the code allows four values of the loop control variable i, in this case 0, 1, 2, and 3. This is an example of the classic "off by one" problem. The problem can be eliminated by allowing i to range from 0 to 2. The problem also can be eliminated by allowing i to range from 1 to 3, but this necessitates initializing j to 1 (rather than 0) in the inner **for** loop. However, the code becomes clearer by allowing i to range from 1 to 3 with j initialized to 1, so this is the better solution even though it requires more changes:

```
for (i = 1; i <= 3; i++)              //Line 1
{                                      //Line 2
    for (j = 1; j <= i; j++)          //Line 3
        System.out.print("*");         //Line 4

    System.out.println();              //Line 5
}                                      //Line 6
```

This piece of code fixes the original problem without using a software patch and represents good programming practice.

Nested Control Structures

In this section, we give examples that illustrate how to use nested loops to achieve useful results and process data.

EXAMPLE 5-18

Suppose you want to create the following pattern:

```
*
**
***
****
*****
```

Clearly, you want to print five lines of stars. In the first line you want to print one star, in the second line two stars, and so on. Because five lines will be printed, start with the following `for` statement:

```
for (i = 1; i <= 5; i++)
```

The value of i in the first iteration is 1, in the second iteration it is 2, and so on. You can use the value of i as the limiting condition in another `for` loop nested within this loop to control the number of stars in a line. A little more thought produces the following code:

```
for (i = 1; i <= 5; i++)          //Line 1
{                                 //Line 2
    for (j = 1; j <= i; j++)      //Line 3
        System.out.print("*");    //Line 4

    System.out.println();         //Line 5
}                                 //Line 6
```

A walk-through of this code shows that the `for` loop, in Line 1, starts with i = 1. When i is 1, the inner `for` loop, in Line 3, outputs one star and the insertion point moves to the next line. Then i becomes 2, the inner `for` loop outputs two stars, and the output statement in Line 5 moves the insertion point to the next line, and so on. This process continues until i becomes 6 and the loop stops.

What pattern does this code produce if you replace the `for` statement, in Line 1, with the following?

```
for (i = 5; i >= 1; i--)
```

EXAMPLE 5-19

Suppose you want to create the following multiplication table:

```
1  2  3  4  5  6  7  8  9 10
2  4  6  8 10 12 14 16 18 20
3  6  9 12 15 18 21 24 27 30
4  8 12 16 20 24 28 32 36 40
5 10 15 20 25 30 35 40 45 50
```

The multiplication table has five lines. Therefore, as in Example 5-18, we use a `for` statement to output these lines as follows:

```
for (i = 1; i <= 5; i++)
    //output a line of numbers
```

In the first line, we want to print the multiplication table of one, in the second line we want to print the multiplication table of 2, and so on. Notice that the first line starts with 1 and when this line is printed, `i` is 1. Similarly, the second line starts with 2 and when this line is printed, the value of `i` is 2, and so on. If `i` is 1, `i * 1` is 1; if `i` is 2, `i * 2` is 2; and so on. Therefore, to print a line of numbers we can use the value of `i` as the starting number and 10 as the limiting value. That is, consider the following `for` loop:

```
for (j = 1; j <= 10; j++)
    System.out.printf("%3d", i * j);
```

Let us take a look at this `for` loop. Suppose `i` is 1. Then we are printing the first line of the multiplication table. Also, `j` goes from 1 to 10 and so this `for` loop outputs the numbers 1 through 10, which is the first line of the multiplication table. Similarly, if `i` is 2, we are printing the second line of the multiplication table. Also, `j` goes from 1 to 10, and so this `for` loop outputs the second line of the multiplication table, and so on.

A little more thought produces the following nested loops to output the desired grid:

```
for (i = 1; i <= 5; i++)                        //Line 1
{                                               //Line 2
    for (j = 1; j <= 10; j++)                   //Line 3
        System.out.printf("%3d", i * j);        //Line 4

    System.out.println();                       //Line 5
}                                               //Line 6
```

EXAMPLE 5-20

Consider the following data residing in a file:

```
65 78 65 89 25 98 -999
87 34 89 99 26 78 64 34 -999
23 99 98 97 26 78 100 63 87 23 -999
62 35 78 99 12 93 19 -999
```

The number -999 at the end of each line acts as a sentinel and, therefore, it is not part of the data. Our objective is to find the sum of the numbers in each line and output the sum. Moreover, assume that this data is to be read from a file, say, Exp_5_20.txt. We assume that the input file has been opened using the input file stream variable inFile.

This particular data set has four lines of input. So we can use a for loop or a counter-controlled while loop to process each line of data. Let us use a for loop to process these four lines. The for loop takes the following form:

```
for (counter = 0; counter < 4; counter++;)    //Line 1
{                                              //Line 2
    //process the line
    //output the sum
}
```

Let us now concentrate on processing a line. Each line has a varying number of data items. For example, the first line has 6 numbers, the second line has 8 numbers, and so on. Because each line ends with -999, we can use a sentinel-controlled while loop to find the sum of the numbers in each line. Remember how a sentinel-controlled loop works. Consider the following while loop:

```
sum = 0;                            //Line 3
num = inFile.nextInt();             //Line 4

while (num != -999)                 //Line 5
{                                   //Line 6
    sum = sum + num;                //Line 7
    num = inFile.nextInt();         //Line 8
}                                   //Line 9
```

The statement in Line 3 initializes sum to 0, and the statement in Line 4 reads and stores the first number of the line into num. The logical expression, num != -999, in Line 5, checks whether the number is -999. If num is not -999, the statements in Lines 7 and 8 execute. The statement in Line 7 updates the value of sum; the statement in Line 8 reads and stores the next number into num. The loop continues to execute as long as num is not -999.

It now follows that the nested loop to process the data is as follows (assuming that all variables are properly declared):

```
for (counter = 0; counter < 4; counter++;)      //Line 1
{                                               //Line 2
    sum = 0;                                    //Line 3
    num = inFile.nextInt();                     //Line 4
```

```
    while (num != -999)                      //Line 5
    {                                        //Line 6
        sum = sum + num;                     //Line 7
        num = inFile.nextInt();              //Line 8
    }                                        //Line 9

    System.out.println("Line " + (counter + 1)
                    + ": Sum = " + sum);     //Line 10
}                                            //Line 11
```

EXAMPLE 5-21

Consider the following data:

```
101
Lance Smith
65 78 65 89 25 98 -999
102
Cynthia Marker
87 34 89 99 26 78 64 34 -999
103
Sheila Mann
23 99 98 97 26 78 100 63 87 23 -999
104
David Arora
62 35 78 99 12 93 19 -999
...
```

The number -999 at the end of a line acts as a sentinel and therefore is not part of the data.

Assume that this data describes certain candidates seeking the student council's presidential seat. For each candidate the data is in the following form:

```
ID
Name
Votes
```

The objective is to find the total number of votes received by each candidate.

We assume that the data is input from the file, Exp_5_21.txt, of unknown size. We also assume that the input file has been opened using the Scanner variable inFile.

Because the input file is of an unspecified length, we use an EOF-controlled while loop. For each candidate, the first data item is the ID of the type, say, int, on a line by itself; the second data item is the name, which may consist of more than one word; and the third line contains the votes received from the various departments.

To read the ID we use the method nextInt; to read the name we use the method nextLine. Notice that after reading the ID, the reading marker is after the ID and the character after the ID is the newline character. Therefore, after reading the ID, the reading marker is after the ID and at the newline character (of the line containing the ID).

The method nextLine reads until the end of the line. Therefore, if we read the name immediately after reading the ID, then the method nextLine will position the reading marker after the newline character following the ID, and nothing will be stored in the variable name. Because the reading marker is just before the name, if we use the method nextInt to read the voting data, the program will terminate with an error message. Therefore, it follows that to read the name, we must discard the newline character after the ID, which we can do using the method nextLine. (Assume that discard is a variable of type String.) Therefore, the statements to read the ID and name are as follows:

```
ID = inFile.nextInt();        //read the ID
discard = inFile.nextLine();  //discard the newline character
                              //after the ID
name = inFile.nextLine();     //read the name
```

The general loop to process the data is:

```
while (inFile.hasNext())                        //Line 1
{                                               //Line 2
    ID = inFile.nextInt();                      //Line 3
    discard = inFile.nextLine();                //Line 4
    name = inFile.nextLine();                   //Line 5
    //process the numbers in each line
}
```

The code to read and sum up the voting data is the same as in Example 5-20. That is, the required while loop is:

```
sum = 0;                  //Line 6
num = inFile.nextInt();   //Line 7; read the first number

while (num != -999)       //Line 8
{                         //Line 9
    sum = sum + num;      //Line 10; update sum
    num = inFile.nextInt();//Line 11; read the next number
}                         //Line 12
```

We can now write the following nested loop to process the data:

```
while (inFile.hasNext())                        //Line 1
{                                               //Line 2
    ID = inFile.nextInt();                      //Line 3
    discard = inFile.nextLine();                //Line 4
    name = inFile.nextLine();                   //Line 5

    sum = 0;                                    //Line 6
```

```
    num = inFile.nextInt();        //Line 7; read the first number

    while (num != -999)            //Line 8
    {                              //Line 9
        sum = sum + num;           //Line 10; update sum
        num = inFile.nextInt();    //Line 11; read the next number
    }                              //Line 12

    System.out.println("Name: " + name
                   + ", Votes: " + sum);   //Line 13
}                                          //Line 14
```

To learn more about the nesting of `for` loops, see Exercise 30 at the end of this chapter.

5

QUICK REVIEW

1. Java has three looping (repetition) structures: `while`, `for`, and `do...while`.

2. The syntax of the `while` statement is:

   `while (logical expression)`
   `    statement`

3. In Java, `while` is a reserved word.

4. In a `while` statement, the parentheses around the `logical expression`, the loop condition, are required; they mark the beginning and end of the expression.

5. The `statement` is called the body of the loop.

6. The body of the `while` loop typically contains statement(s) that eventually set the expression to `false` to terminate the loop.

7. A counter-controlled `while` loop uses a counter to control the loop.

8. In a counter-controlled `while` loop, you must initialize the counter before the loop, and the body of the loop must contain a statement that changes the value of the counter variable.

9. A sentinel is a special value that marks the end of the input data. The sentinel must be similar, yet different, from all the data items.

10. A sentinel-controlled `while` loop uses a sentinel to control the `while` loop. The `while` loop continues to execute until the sentinel is read.

11. An EOF-controlled `while` loop continues to execute until the program detects the end-of-file marker.

12. The method `hasNext` returns the value `true` if there is an input (token) in the input stream, otherwise it returns `false`.

13. In the Windows console environment, the end-of-file marker is entered using `Ctrl+z`. (Hold the `Ctrl` key and press z.) In the UNIX environment, the end-of-file marker is entered using `Ctrl+d`. (Hold the `Ctrl` key and press d.)

14. In Java, `for` is a reserved word.

15. A `for` loop simplifies the writing of a counter-controlled `while` loop.

16. The syntax of the `for` loop is:

```
for (initialize expression; logical expression; update expression)
    statement
```

The `statement` is called the body of the `for` loop.

17. If you put a semicolon at the end of the `for` loop (before the body of the `for` loop), the action of the `for` loop is empty.

18. The syntax of the `do...while` statement is:

```
do
    statement
while (logical expression);
```

19. The `statement` is called the body of the `do...while` loop.

20. The body of the `while` and `for` loops might not execute at all, but the body of a `do...while` loop always executes at least once.

21. In a `while` or `for` loop, the loop condition is evaluated before executing the body of the loop. Therefore, `while` and `for` loops are called pretest loops.

22. In a `do...while` loop, the loop condition is evaluated after executing the body of the loop. Therefore, `do...while` loops are called post-test loops.

23. Executing a `break` statement in the body of a loop immediately terminates the loop.

24. Executing a `continue` statement in the body of a loop skips the loop's remaining statements and proceeds with the next iteration.

25. When a `continue` statement executes in a `while` or `do...while` loop, the update statement in the body of the loop might not execute.

26. After a `continue` statement executes in a `for` loop, the update statement is the next statement executed.

EXERCISES

1. Mark the following statements as true or false.

   a. In a counter-controlled `while` loop, it is not necessary to initialize the loop control variable.

   b. It is possible that the body of a `while` loop might not execute at all.

   c. In an infinite `while` loop, the loop condition is initially false, but after the first iteration, it is always true.

   d. The `while` loop:

   ```
   j = 0;

   while (j <= 10)
       j++;
   ```

   terminates when j > 10.

   e. A sentinel-controlled `while` loop is an event-controlled `while` loop whose termination depends on a special value.

   f. A loop is a control structure that causes certain statements to execute over and over.

   g. To read data from a file of an unspecified length, an EOF-controlled loop is a good choice.

   h. When a `while` loop terminates, the control first goes back to the statement just before the `while` statement, and then the control goes to the statement immediately following the `while` loop.

2. What is the output of the following Java code?

   ```
   count = 1;
   y = 100;

   while (count < 100)
   {
       y = y - 1;
       count++;
   }

   System.out.println("y = " + y + " and count = " + count);
   ```

3. What is the output of the following Java code?

   ```
   num = 5;

   while (num > 5)
       num = num + 2;

   System.out.println(num);
   ```

4. What is the output of the following Java code?

```
num = 1;

while (num < 10)
{
    System.out.print(num + " ");
    num = num + 2;
}

System.out.println();
```

5. When does the following `while` loop terminate?

```
ch = 'D';

while ('A' <= ch && ch <= 'Z')
    ch = (char)((int)(ch) + 1));
```

6. Suppose that the input is:

   `38 45 71 4 -1`

   What is the output of the following code? Assume all variables are properly declared.

```
sum = console.nextInt();
num = console.nextInt();

for (j = 1; j <= 3; j++)
{
    num = console.nextInt();
    sum = sum + num;
}

System.out.println("Sum = " + sum);
```

7. Suppose that the input is:

   `38 45 71 4 -1`

   What is the output of the following code? Assume all variables are properly declared.

```
sum = console.nextInt();
num = console.nextInt();

while (num != -1)
{
    sum = sum + num;
    num = console.nextInt();
}

System.out.println("Sum = " + sum);
```

8. Suppose that the input is:

   38 45 71 4 -1

   What is the output of the following code? Assume all variables are properly declared.

   ```
   num = console.nextInt();
   sum = num;

   while (num != -1)
   {
       num = console.nextInt();
       sum = sum + num;
   }

   System.out.println("Sum = " + sum);
   ```

9. Suppose that the input is:

   38 45 71 4 -1

   What is the output of the following code? Assume all variables are properly declared.

   ```
   sum = 0;
   num = console.nextInt();

   while (num != -1)
   {
       sum = sum + num;
       num = console.nextInt();
   }

   System.out.println("Sum = " + sum);
   ```

10. Correct the following code so that it finds the sum of 10 numbers:

    ```
    sum = 0;

    while (count < 10)
        num = console.nextInt();
        sum = sum + num;
        count++;
    ```

11. What is the output of the following program?

    ```
    public class WhatIsTheOutput
    {
        public static void main(String[] args)
        {
            int x, y, z;

            x = 4;
            y = 5;
            z = y + 6;
    ```

5

```
        while (((z - x) % 4) != 0)
        {
            System.out.print(z + " ");
            z = z + 7;
        }
        System.out.println();
    }
}
```

12. Suppose that the input is:

    58 23 46 75 98 150 12 176 145 -999

    What is the output of the following program?

```
import java.util.*;

public class FindTheOutput
{
    static Scanner console = new Scanner(System.in);

    public static void main(String[] args)
    {
        int num;

        num = console.nextInt();

        while (num != -999)
        {
            System.out.print(num % 25 + "  ");
            num = console.nextInt();
        }

        System.out.println();
    }
}
```

13. Given the following code:

```
for (i = 12; i <= 25; i++)
    System.out.println(i);
System.out.println();
```

    Answer the following questions:

    a. The seventh integer printed is __.

    b. The for loop produces _____ lines of output.

    c. If i++ were changed to i--, a compilation error would result. True or False?

14. Given that the following code is correctly inserted into a program, state its entire output as to content and form:

```
num = 0;

for (i = 1; i <= 4; i++)
{
    num = num + 10 * (i - 1);
    System.out.print(num + " ");
}

System.out.println();
```

15. Given that the following code is correctly inserted into a program, describe the content and form of its entire output:

```
j = 2;

for (i = 0; i <= 5; i++)
{
    System.out.print(j + " ");
    j = 2 * j + 3;
}

System.out.println();
```

16. Assume that the following code is correctly inserted into a program:

```
s = 0;

for (i = 0; i < 5; i++)
{
    s = 2 * s + i;
    System.out.print(s + " ");
}

System.out.println();
```

a. What is the final value of s?

    i. 11 ii. 4 iii. 26 iv. none of these

b. If a semicolon is inserted after the right parenthesis in the for loop control expressions, what is the final value of s?

    i. 0 ii. 1 iii. 2 iv. 5 v. none of these

c. If the 5 is replaced with a 0 in the for loop control expression, what is the final value of s?

    i. 0 ii. 1 iii. 2 iv. none of these

17. State what output, if any, results in each of the following statements:

    a.
```
for (i = 1; i <= 1; i++)
    System.out.print ("* ");

System.out.println ();
```

    b.
```
for (i = 2; i >= 1; i++)
        System.out.print ("* ");

System.out.println ();
```

    c.
```
for (i = 1; i <= 1; i--)
    System.out.print ("* ");

System.out.println ();
```

    d.
```
for (i = 12; i >= 9; i--)
    System.out.print ("* ");
System.out.println ();
```

    e.
```
for (i = 0; i <= 5; i++)
    System.out.print ("* ");

System.out.println ();
```

    f.
```
for (i = 1; i <= 5; i++)
{

    System.out.print ("* ");
    i = i + 1;
}
System.out.println ();
```

18. Write a **for** statement to add all multiples of 3 between 1 and 100.

19. Write a **for** statement to find the sum of the squares of all multiples of 5 between 1 and 100.

20. Suppose that the input is:

    5 3 8

What is the output of the following code? Assume all variables are properly declared.

```
a = console.nextInt ();
b = console.nextInt ();
c = console.nextInt ();
```

```
for (j = 1; j < a; j++)
{
    d = b + c;
    b = c;
    c = d;

    System.out.print(c + "   ");
}

System.out.println();
```

21. What is the output of the following Java program segment? Assume all variables are properly declared.

```
for (j = 0; j < 8; j++)
{
    System.out.print(j * 25 + " - ");

    if (j != 7)
        System.out.println((j + 1) * 25 - 1);
    else
        System.out.println((j + 1) * 25);
}
```

22. The following program has more than five mistakes that prevent it from compiling and/or running. Correct all such mistakes.

```
public class Exercise22
{
    final int N = 2,137;

    public static main(String[] args)
    {
        int a, b, c, d:

        a := 3;
        b = 5;
        c = c + d;
        N = a + n;

        for (i = 3; i <= N; i++)
        {
            System.out.print(" " + i);
            i = i + 1;
        }

        System.out.println();
    }
}
```

23. Which of the following apply to the `while` loop only? To the `do...while` loop only? To both?

    a. It is considered a conditional loop.

    b. The body of the loop executes at least once.

    c. The logical expression controlling the loop is evaluated before the loop is entered.

    d. The body of the loop might not execute at all.

24. How many times will each of the following loops execute? What is the output in each case?

    a.
    ```
    x = 5;   y = 50;
    do
        x = x + 10;
    while (x < y);

    System.out.println(x + " " + y);
    ```

    b.
    ```
    x = 5;   y = 80;
    do
        x = x * 2;
    while (x < y);

    System.out.println(x + " " + y);
    ```

    c.
    ```
    x = 5;   y = 20;

    do
        x = x + 2;
    while (x >= y);

    System.out.println(x + " " + y);
    ```

    d.
    ```
    x = 5;   y = 35;

    while (x < y)
        x = x + 10;

    System.out.println(x + " " + y);
    ```

    e.
    ```
    x = 5;   y = 30;

    while (x <= y)
        x = x * 2;

    System.out.println(x + " " + y);
    ```

f. `x = 5;  y = 30;`

```
while (x > y)
    x = x + 2;

System.out.println(x + " " + y);
```

25. The do...while loop in the following program is intended to read some numbers until it reaches a sentinel (in this case, −1). It is supposed to add all of the numbers except for the sentinel. If the data looks like:

`12 5 30 48 −1`

the program fails to work as intended. Make any necessary corrections.

```
import java.util.*;

public class Strange
{
    static Scanner console = new Scanner(System.in);

    public static void main(String[] args)
    {
        int total = 0;
        int number;

        do
        {
            number = console.nextInt();
            total = total + number;
        }
        while (number != -1);

        System.out.println("The sum of the numbers entered is "
                        + total);
    }
}
```

26. Using the data from Exercise 25, the following two loops also fail. Correct them. Assume that all variables are properly declared.

a.
```
number = console.nextInt();

while (number != -1)
    total =  total + number;
    number = console.nextInt();
```

b.
```
number = console.nextInt();

while (number != -1)
{
    number = console.nextInt();
    total = total + number;
}
```

27. Given the following program segment:

```
for (number = 1; number <= 10; number++)
    System.out.print(number + " ");
System.out.println();
```

write a **while** loop and a **do...while** loop that have the same output.

28. Given the following program segment:

```
j = 2;

for (i = 1; i <= 5; i++)
{
    System.out.print(j + " ");
    j = j + 5;
}

System.out.println();
```

write a **while** loop and a **do...while** loop that have the same output.

29. What is the output of the following program?

```
public class Mystery
{
    public static void main(String[] args)
    {
        int  x, y, z;

        x = 4;
        y = 5;
        z = y + 6;

        do
        {
            System.out.print(z + " ");
            z = z + 7;
        }
        while(((z - x) % 4) != 0);

        System.out.println();
    }
}
```

30. To further learn how nested **for** loops work, do a walk-through of the following program segments and, in each case, determine the exact output.

a.
```
int i, j;

for (i = 1; i <= 5; i++)
{
    for (j = 1; j <= 5; j++)
        System.out.printf("%3d", i);
    System.out.println();
}
```

b.
```
int i, j;

for (i = 1; i <= 5; i++)
{
    for (j = 1; j <= i; j++)
        System.out.printf("%3d", j);
    System.out.println();
}
```

c.
```
int i, j;

for (i = 1; i <= 5; i++)
{
    for (j = (i + 1); j <= 5; j++)
        System.out.printf("%5d", j);
    System.out.println();
}
```

d.
```
final int m = 10;
final int n = 10;
int i, j;

for (i = 1; i <= m; i++)
{
    for (j = 1; j <= n; j++)
        System.out.printf("%4d", (m * (i - 1) + j));
    System.out.println();
}
```

e.
```
int i, j;

for (i = 1; i <= 9; i++)
{
    for (j = 1; j <= (9 - i); j++)
        System.out.print(" ");
    for (j = 1; j <= i; j++)
        System.out.print(j);
    for (j = (i - 1); j >= 1; j--)
        System.out.print(j);

    System.out.println();
}
```

PROGRAMMING EXERCISES

1. Write a program that prompts the user to input an integer and then outputs both the individual digits of the number and the sum of the digits. For example, the program should: output the individual digits of 3456 as 3 4 5 6 and the sum as 18, output the individual digits of 8030 as 8 0 3 0 and the sum as 11, output the individual digits of 2345526 as 2 3 4 5 5 2 6 and the sum as 27, output the individual digits of 4000 as 4 0 0 0 and the sum as 4, and output the individual digits of −2345 as 2 3 4 5 and the sum as 14.

2. Write a program that prompts the user to input an integer and then outputs the number with the digits reversed. For example, if the input is 12345, the output should be 54321. Your program must also output 5000 as 0005 and 980 as 089.

3. Rewrite the program of Example 5-5, Telephone Digits. Replace the statements from Lines 10 to 28 so that the program uses only a **switch** structure to find the digit that corresponds to an uppercase letter.

4. The program Telephone Digits outputs only telephone digits that correspond to uppercase letters. Rewrite the program so that it processes both uppercase and lowercase letters and outputs the corresponding telephone digit. If the input is other than an uppercase or lowercase letter, the program must output an appropriate error message.

5. To make telephone numbers easier to remember, some companies use letters to show their telephone number. For example, the telephone number 438-5626 can be shown as GET-LOAN. In some cases, to make a telephone number meaningful, companies might use more than seven letters. For example, 225-5466 can be displayed as CALL-HOME, which uses eight letters. Write a program that prompts the user to enter a telephone number expressed in letters and outputs the corresponding telephone number in digits. If the user enters more than eight letters, then process only the first seven letters. Also, output the − (hyphen) after the third digit. Allow the user to use uppercase and lowercase letters, as well as spaces between words. Moreover, your program should process as many telephone numbers as the user wants. (*Hint*: You can read the entered telephone number as a string and then use the **charAt** method of the **class String** to extract each character. For example, if **str** refers to a string, then the expression **str.charAt(i)** returns the character at the *i*th position. Recall that in a string, the position of the first character is 0.)

6. Write a program that reads a set of integers, and then finds and prints the sum of the even and odd integers.

7. Write a program that prompts the user to input a positive integer. It should then output a message indicating whether the number is a prime number. (*Note*: 2 is the only even number which is prime. An odd integer is prime if it is not divisible by any odd integer less than or equal to the square root of the number.)

8. Let $n = a_k a_{k-1} a_{k-2} \ldots a_1 a_0$ be an integer. Let $t = a_0 - a_1 + a_2 - \ldots + (-1)^k a_k$. It is known that n is divisible by 11 if and only if t is divisible by 11. For example, suppose that $n = 8784204$. Then, $t = 4 - 0 + 2 - 4 + 8 - 7 + 8 = 11$. Because 11 is divisible by 11, it follows that 8784204 is divisible by 11. If $n = 54063297$, then $t = 7 - 9 + 2 - 3 + 6 - 0 + 4 - 5 = 2$. Because 2 is not divisible by 11, 54063297 is not divisible by 11.

Write a program that prompts the user to enter a positive integer and then uses this criterion to determine whether the number is divisible by 11.

9. Write a program that uses `while` loops to perform the following steps:

   a. Prompt the user to input two integers: `firstNum` and `secondNum`. (`firstNum` must be less than `secondNum`.)

   b. Output all the odd numbers between `firstNum` and `secondNum` inclusive.

   c. Output the sum of all the even numbers between `firstNum` and `secondNum` inclusive.

   d. Output all the numbers and their squares between 1 and 10.

   e. Output the sum of the squares of all the odd numbers between `firstNum` and `secondNum` inclusive.

   f. Output all the uppercase letters.

10. Redo Exercise 9 using `for` loops.

11. Redo Exercise 9 using `do...while` loops.

12. The program in the Fibonacci Number programming example does not check whether the first number entered by the user is less than or equal to the second number and both the numbers are non-negative. Also, the program does not check whether the user entered a valid value for the position of the desired number in the Fibonacci sequence. Rewrite the program so that it checks for these conditions.

13. Suppose that m and n are integers and m is nonzero. Recall that m is called a *divisor* of n if $n = mt$ for some integer t; that is, when m divides n, the remainder is 0. The number m is called a **proper divisor** of n if $m < n$ and m divides n. A positive integer is called **perfect** if it is the sum of its positive proper divisors. For example, the positive proper divisors of 28 are 1, 2, 4, 7, and 14, and $1 + 2 + 4 + 7 + 14 = 28$. Therefore, 28 is perfect. Write a program that does the following:

   a. Outputs the first four perfect integers.

   b. Takes as input a positive integer and then outputs whether the integer is perfect.

14. The program in Example 5-6 implements the Guessing the Number game. However, in that program, the user is given as many tries as needed to guess the correct number. Rewrite that program so that the user has, at most, five tries to guess the correct number. Your program should print an appropriate message, such as "You win!" or "You lose!"

15. Example 5-6 implements the Guessing the Number game program. If the guessed number is not correct, the program outputs a message indicating whether the guess is low or high. Modify the program as follows: Suppose that the variables num and guess are as declared in Example 5-6 and diff is an int variable. Let diff = the absolute value of (num – guess). If diff is 0, then guess is correct and the program outputs a message indicating that the user guessed the correct number. Suppose diff is not 0. Then, the program outputs the message as follows:

   a. If diff is greater than or equal to 50, the program outputs the message indicating that the guess is very high (if guess is greater than num) or very low (if guess is less than num).

   b. If diff is greater than or equal to 30 and less than 50, the program outputs the message indicating that the guess is high (if guess is greater than num) or low (if guess is less than num).

   c. If diff is greater than or equal to 15 and less than 30, the program outputs the message indicating that the guess is moderately high (if guess is greater than num) or moderately low (if guess is less than num).

   d. If diff is greater than 0 and less than 15, the program outputs the message indicating that the guess is somewhat high (if guess is greater than num) or somewhat low (if guess is less than num).

   As in Programming Exercise 14, give the user, at most, five tries to guess the number. (To find the absolute value of num – guess, use the expression Math.abs(num – guess).)

16. A high school has 1000 students and 1000 lockers, one locker for each student. On the first day of school, the principal plays the following game: She asks the first student to open all the lockers. She then asks the second student to close all the even-numbered lockers. The third student is asked to check every third locker. If it is open, the student closes it; if it is closed, the student opens it. The fourth student is asked to check every fourth locker. If it is open, the student closes it; if it is closed, the student opens it. The remaining students continue this game. In general, the nth student checks every nth locker. If the locker is open, the student closes it; if it is closed, the student opens it. After all the students have taken their turns, some of the lockers are open and some are closed. Write a program that prompts the user to enter the number of lockers in a school. After the game is over, the program outputs the number of lockers and the locker numbers of the lockers that are open. Test run your program for the following inputs: 1000, 5000, and 10000. Do you see any pattern developing for the locker numbers that are open in the output?

   (*Hint*: Consider locker number 100. This locker is visited by student numbers 1, 2, 4, 5, 10, 20, 25, 50, and 100. These are the positive divisors of 100. Similarly, locker number 30 is visited by student numbers 1, 2, 3, 5,

6, 10, 15, and 30. Note that if the number of positive divisors of a locker number is odd, then at the end of the game the locker is open. If the number of positive divisors of a locker number is even, then at the end of the game the locker is closed.)

17. For research purposes and to assist students, the admissions office of your local university wants to determine the performance of female and male students in certain courses. You receive a file that contains female and male students' GPAs for certain courses. Due to confidentiality, the letter code f is used for female students; m is used for male students. Every file entry consists of a letter code followed by a GPA. Each line has one entry. The number of entries in the file is unknown. Write a program that computes and outputs the average GPA for both female and male students. Format your results to two decimal places.

18. When you borrow money to buy a house, a car, or for some other purpose, you repay the loan by making periodic payments over a certain time. Of course the lending company will charge interest on the loan. Every periodic payment consists of the interest on the loan and the payment toward the principal amount. To be specific, suppose that you borrow $1000 at the interest rate of 7.2% per year and the payments are monthly. Suppose that your monthly payment is $25. The interest is 7.2% per year and the payments are monthly, so the interest rate per month is $7.2/12 = 0.6\%$. The first month's interest on $1000 is $1000 \star 0.006 = 6$. Because the payment is $25 and interest for the first month is $6, the payment toward the principal amount is $25 - 6 = 19$. This means that after making the first payment, the loan amount is $1000 - 19 = 981$. For the second payment, the interest is calculated on $981. So the interest for the second month is $981 \star 0.006 = 5.886$, that is, approximately $5.89. This implies that the payment toward the principal is $25 - 5.89 = 19.11$, and the remaining balance after the second payment is $981 - 19.11 = 961.89$. This process is repeated until the loan is paid. Write a program that accepts as input, the loan amount, the interest rate per year, and the monthly payment. (Enter the interest rate as a percentage. For example, if the interest rate is 7.2% per year, then enter 7.2.) The program then outputs the number of months it would take to repay the loan. (*Note:* If the monthly payment is less then the first month's interest, then after each payment, the loan amount will increase. In this case, the program must warn the borrower that the monthly payment is too low and with this monthly payment the loan amount could not be repaid.)

19. Enhance your program of Exercise 18, by first telling the user the minimum monthly payment and then prompting the user to enter the monthly payment. The last payment might be more than the remaining loan amount and interest on it. In this case, output the loan amount before the last payment and the actual amount of the last payment. Also, output the total interest paid.

20. Write a complete program to generate the pattern given in Example 5-18.

21. Write a complete program to generate the grid of numbers given in Example 5-19.

22. Write a complete program to process the data given in Example 5-20.

23. Write a complete program to process the data given in Example 5-21.

24. You have been given the contract for making little conical cups that are used for bottled water. These cups are to be made from a circular waxed paper die of 4 inches in radius, by removing a sector of length x (see Figure 5-6). By closing the remaining part of the circle, a conical cup is made. Your objective is to remove the sector so that the cup is of maximum volume.

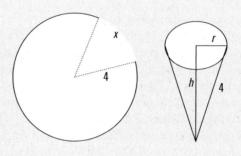

FIGURE 5-6 Conical paper cup

Write a program that prompts the user to enter the radius of the circular waxed paper. The program should then output the length of the removed sector so that the resulting cup is of maximum volume. Calculate your answer to two decimal places.

25. A real estate office handles 50 apartment units. When the rent is $600 per month, all the units are occupied. However, for each $40 increase in rent, one unit becomes vacant. Each occupied unit requires an average of $27 per month for maintenance. How many units should be rented to maximize the profit?

Write a program that prompts the user to enter:

a. The number of apartment units

b. The rent to occupy all the units

c. The increase in rent that results in a vacant unit

d. Amount to maintain a rented unit

The program then outputs the number of units to be rented to maximize the profit.

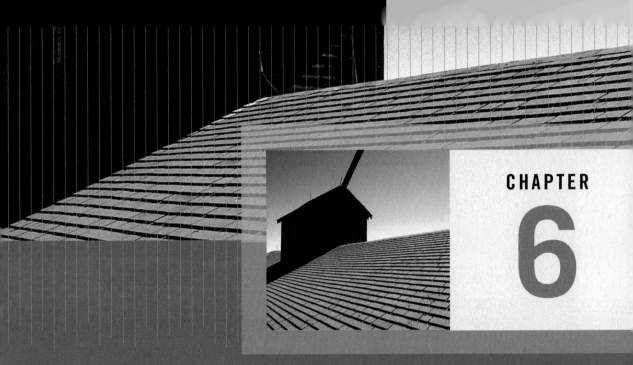

GRAPHICAL USER INTERFACE (GUI) AND OBJECT-ORIENTED DESIGN (OOD)

IN THIS CHAPTER, YOU WILL:

- Learn about basic GUI components
- Explore how the GUI components **JFrame**, **JLabel**, **JTextField**, and **JButton** work
- Become familiar with the concept of event-driven programming
- Discover events and event handlers
- Explore object-oriented design
- Learn how to identify objects, classes, and members of a class
- Learn about wrapper classes
- Become familiar with the autoboxing and auto-unboxing of primitive data types

Java is equipped with many powerful, yet easy-to-use graphical user interface (GUI) components, such as the input and output dialog boxes you learned about in Chapter 3. You can use these to make your programs attractive and user-friendly. The first half of this chapter introduces you to some basic Java GUI components. Chapter 12 covers GUI in some details.

In Chapter 1, you were introduced to the object-oriented design (OOD) problem-solving methodology. The second half of this chapter outlines a general approach to solving problems using OOD, and provides several examples to clarify this problem-solving methodology.

Graphical User Interface (GUI) Components

In Chapter 3, you learned how to use input and output dialog boxes to input data into a program and show the output of a program. Before introducing the various GUI components, we will use input and output dialog boxes to write a program to determine the area and perimeter of a rectangle. We will then discuss how to use additional GUI components to create a different graphical user interface to determine the area and perimeter of a rectangle.

The program in Example 6-1 prompts the user to input the length and width of a rectangle and then displays its area and perimeter. We will use the method **showInputDialog** to create an input dialog box and the method **showMessageDialog** to create an output dialog box. Recall that these methods are contained in the **class** JOptionPane and this class is contained in the package javax.swing.

EXAMPLE 6-1

```java
// This Java Program determines the area and
// perimeter of a rectangle.

import javax.swing.JOptionPane;

public class Rectangle
{
    public static void main(String[] args)
    {
        double width, length, area, perimeter;          //Line 1

        String lengthStr, widthStr, outputStr;           //Line 2

        lengthStr =
            JOptionPane.showInputDialog("Enter the length: "); //Line 3
        length = Double.parseDouble(lengthStr);          //Line 4
```

```
widthStr =
        JOptionPane.showInputDialog("Enter the width: ");  //Line 5
width = Double.parseDouble(widthStr);                     //Line 6

area = length * width;                                     //Line 7
perimeter = 2 * (length + width);                         //Line 8

outputStr = "Length: " + length + "\n" +
            "Width: " + width + "\n" +
            "Area: " + area + " square units\n" +
            "Perimeter: " + perimeter + " units\n";       //Line 9

JOptionPane.showMessageDialog(null, outputStr,
                    "Rectangle",
                    JOptionPane.INFORMATION_MESSAGE);     //Line 10

System.exit(0);                                           //Line 11
    }
}
```

Sample Run: (Figure 6-1 shows the sample run.)

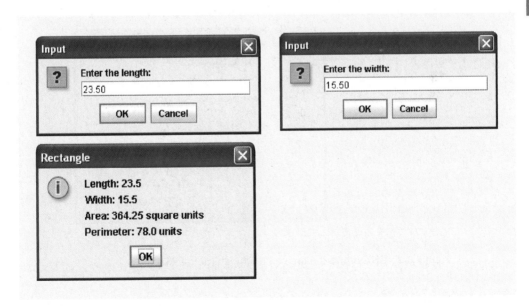

FIGURE 6-1 Sample run for `Rectangle`

The program in Example 6-1 works as follows: The statements in Lines 1 and 2 declare various variables to manipulate the data. The statement in Line 3 displays the first dialog box of the sample run and prompts the user to enter the length of the rectangle. The entered length is assigned as a string to `lengthStr`. The statement in Line 4 retrieves the length and stores it in the variable `length`.

The statement in Line 5 displays the second dialog box of the sample run and prompts the user to enter the width of the rectangle. The entered width is assigned as a string to `widthStr`. The statement in Line 6 retrieves the width and stores it in the variable `width`.

The statement in Line 7 determines the area, and the statement in Line 8 determines the perimeter of the rectangle. The statement in Line 9 creates the string containing the desired output and assigns it to `outputStr`. The statement in Line 10 uses the output dialog box to display the desired output, which is shown in the third dialog box of the sample run. Finally, the statement in Line 11 terminates the program.

The program in Example 6-1 uses input and output dialog boxes to accomplish its job. When you run this program, you see only one dialog box at a time.

However, suppose that you want the program to display all the input and output in one dialog box, as shown in Figure 6-2.

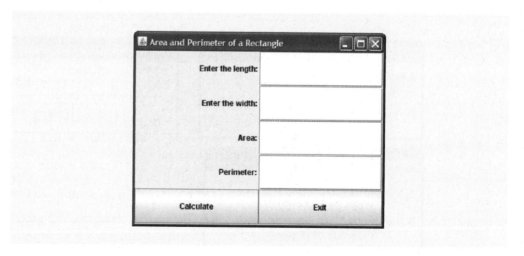

FIGURE 6-2 GUI to find the area and perimeter of a rectangle

In Java terminology, such a dialog box is called a **graphical user interface** (GUI), or simply a **user interface**. In this GUI, the user enters the length and width in the top two white boxes. When the user clicks the `Calculate` button, the program displays the area and the perimeter in their respective locations. When the user clicks the `Exit` button, the program terminates.

In this interface, the user can:

- See the entire input and output simultaneously
- Input values for length and width, in any order of preference
- Input values that can be corrected after entering them and before clicking the `Calculate` button
- Enter another set of input values and click the `Calculate` button to obtain the area and perimeter of another rectangle

The interface shown in Figure 6-2 contains various Java GUI components that are labeled in Figure 6-3.

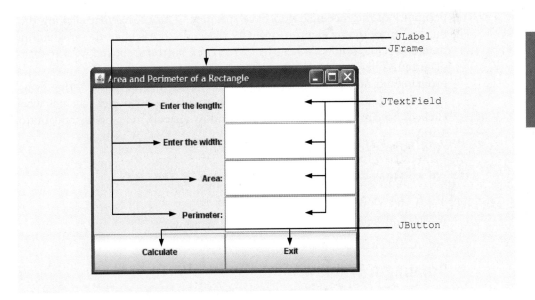

FIGURE 6-3 Java GUI components

As you can see in Figure 6-3, the white areas used to get the input and show the results are called `JTextFields`. The labels for these text fields, such as `Enter the length:`, are called `JLabels`; the buttons `Calculate` and `Exit` are each called a `JButton`. All these components are placed in a window, called `JFrame`.

Creating this type of user interface is not difficult. Java has done all the work; you merely need to learn how to use the tools provided by Java to create such an interface. For example, to create an interface like the one shown in Figures 6-2 and 6-3 that contains labels, text fields, buttons, and windows, you need to learn how to write the statements that create these components. The next sections describe how to create the following GUI components:

- Windows
- Labels
- Text fields
- Buttons

GUI components, such as labels, are placed in an area called the **content pane** of the window. You can think of a content pane as the inner area of the window, below the title bar and inside the border. You will also learn how to place these GUI components in the content pane of a window.

In Figure 6-2, when you click the `Calculate` button, the program displays the area and perimeter of the rectangle you have specified. This means that clicking the `Calculate` button causes the program to execute the code to calculate the area and perimeter and then display the results. When the `Calculate` button is clicked, we say that an **event** has occurred. The Java system is very prompt in listening for the events generated by a program and then reacting to those events. This chapter will describe how to write the code that needs to be executed when a particular event occurs, such as when a button is clicked. So, in addition to creating windows, labels, text fields, and buttons, you will learn:

- How to access the content pane
- How to create event listeners
- How to process or handle events

We begin by describing how to create a window.

Creating a Window

GUI components such as windows and labels are, in fact, objects. Recall that an object is an instance of a particular class. Therefore, these components (objects) are instances of a particular class type. `JFrame` is a `class` and the GUI component `window` can be created by using a `JFrame` object. Various attributes are associated with a window. For example:

- Every window has a title.
- Every window has width and height.

JFrame

The `class` `JFrame` provides various methods to control the attributes of a window. For example, it has methods to set the window title and methods to specify the height and width of the window. Table 6-1 describes some of the methods provided by the `class` `JFrame`.

TABLE 6-1 Some Methods Provided by the **class** JFrame

Method / Description / Example

```
public JFrame()
  //This is used when an object of type JFrame is
  //instantiated and the window is created without any title.
  //Example: JFrame myWindow = new JFrame();
  //          myWindow is a window with no title
```

```
public JFrame(String s)
  //This is used when an object of type JFrame is
  //instantiated and the title specified by the string s.
  //Example: JFrame myWindow = new JFrame("Rectangle");
  //          myWindow is a window with the title Rectangle
```

```
public void setSize(int w, int h)
  //Method to set the size of the window.
  //Example: The statement
  //          myWindow.setSize(400, 300);
  //          sets the width of the window to 400 pixels and
  //          the height to 300 pixels.
```

```
public void setTitle(String s)
  //Method to set the title of the window.
  //Example: myWindow.setTitle("Rectangle");
  //          sets the title of the window to Rectangle.
```

```
public void setVisible(boolean b)
  //Method to display the window in the program. If the value of b is
  //true, the window will be displayed on the screen.
  //Example: myWindow.setVisible(true);
  //    After this statement executes, the window will be shown
  //    during program execution.
```

```
public void setDefaultCloseOperation(int operation)
  //Method to determine the action to be taken when the user clicks
  //on the window closing button, ×, to close the window.
  //Choices for the parameter operation are the named constants —
  //EXIT_ON_CLOSE, HIDE_ON_CLOSE, DISPOSE_ON_CLOSE, and
  //DO_NOTHING_ON_CLOSE. The named constant EXIT_ON_CLOSE is defined
  //in the class JFrame. The last three constants are defined in
  //javax.swing.WindowConstants.
  //Example: The statement
  //          setDefaultCloseOperation(EXIT_ON_CLOSE);
  //sets the default close option of the window closing to close the
  //window and terminate the program when the user clicks the
  //window closing button, ×.
```

6

TABLE 6-1 Some Methods Provided by the **class** JFrame (continued)

Method / Description / Example
`public void` **addWindowListener**`(WindowEvent e)` `//Method to register a window listener object to a JFrame.`

NOTE The **class** JFrame also contains methods to set the color of a window. Chapter 12 describes these methods.

There are two ways to make an application program create a window. The first way is to declare an object of type JFrame, instantiate the object, and then use various methods to manipulate the window. In this case, the object created can use the various applicable methods of the class.

The second way is to create the class containing the application program by *extending* the definition of the **class** JFrame; that is, the class containing the application program is built "on top of" the **class** JFrame. In Java, this way of creating a class uses the mechanism of **inheritance**. Inheritance means that a new class can be derived from or based on an already existing class. The new class "inherits" features such as methods from the existing class, which saves a lot of time for programmers. For example, we could define a new **class** RectangleProgram that would extend the definition of JFrame. The class RectangleProgram would be able to use the variables and methods from JFrame, and also add some functionality of its own (such as the ability to calculate the area and perimeter of a rectangle).

When you use inheritance, the class containing your application program will have more than one method. In addition to the method main, you will have at least one other method that will be used to create a window object containing the required GUI components (such as labels and text fields). This additional method is a special type of method called a **constructor**. A constructor is a method of a class that is automatically executed when an object of the class is created. Typically, a constructor is used to initialize an object. The name of the constructor is always the same as the name of the class. For example, the constructor for the **class** RectangleProgram would be named RectangleProgram.

NOTE Chapter 10 discusses the principles of inheritance in detail. Constructors are covered in detail in Chapter 8.

Because inheritance is an important concept in programming languages such as Java, we will use the second way of creating a window. We will extend the definition of the class JFrame by using the modifier **extends**. For example, the definition of the `class RectangleProgram`, containing the application program to calculate the area and perimeter of a rectangle, is as follows:

```
public class RectangleProgram extends JFrame
{
    public RectangleProgram()        //constructor
    {
        //Necessary code
    }

    public static void main(String[] args)
    {
        //Code for the method main
    }
}
```

In Java, **extends** is a reserved word. The remainder of this section describes the necessary code to create a window.

An important property of inheritance is that the class (called a **subclass**) that extends the definition of an existing class (called a **superclass**) inherits all the properties of the superclass. For example, all **public** methods of the superclass can be *directly* accessed in the subclass. In our example, the `class RectangleProgram` is a subclass of the `class JFrame`, so it can access the **public** methods of the `class JFrame`. Therefore, to set the title of the window to `Area and Perimeter of a Rectangle`, you use the method `setTitle` of the `class JFrame` as follows:

```
setTitle("Area and Perimeter of a Rectangle");        //Line 1
```

Similarly, the statement:

```
setSize(400, 300);                                    //Line 2
```

sets the window's width to 400 pixels and its height to 300 pixels. (A **pixel** is the smallest unit of space on your screen. The term pixel stands for *picture element*.) Note that since the pixel size depends on the current monitor setting, it is impossible to predict the exact width and height of a window in centimeters or inches.

Next, to display the window, you must invoke the method `setVisible`. The following statement accomplishes this:

```
setVisible(true);                                     //Line 3
```

To terminate the application program when the user closes the window, use the following statement (as described in Table 6-1):

```
setDefaultCloseOperation(EXIT_ON_CLOSE);              //Line 4
```

The statements in Lines 1, 2, 3, and 4 will be placed in the constructor (that is, in the method whose heading is **public** `RectangleProgram()`). Thus, you can write the constructor as follows:

```
public RectangleProgram()
{
    setTitle("Area and Perimeter of a Rectangle");
    setSize(400, 300);
    setVisible(true);
    setDefaultCloseOperation(EXIT_ON_CLOSE);
}
```

You could create a window by using an object of type JFrame. However, for our program, if we do so, then the window created will not have a title or the required size unless we specify the necessary statements similar to the ones in the preceding code. Because RectangleProgram is also a class, we can create objects of type RectangleProgram. Because the class RectangleProgram extends the definition of the class JFrame, it inherits the properties of the class JFrame. If we create an object of type RectangleProgram, not only do we create a window, but the created window will also have a title and a specific size, and the window will be displayed when the program executes.

Consider the following statement:

RectangleProgram rectObject = new RectangleProgram();   //Line 5

This statement creates the object rectObject of type RectangleProgram.

The statement in Line 5 causes the window shown in Figure 6-4 to appear on the screen.

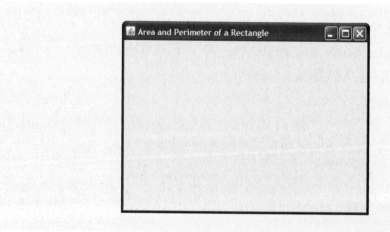

FIGURE 6-4 Window with the title Area and Perimeter of a Rectangle

You can close the window in Figure 6-4 by clicking the "close" button, the button containing the ×, in the upper-right corner. The window in Figure 6-4 is empty because we have not yet created labels, text fields, and so on.

The program to create the window shown in Figure 6-4 uses the class JFrame; this class is contained in the package javax.swing. Therefore, the program must include either of the following two statements:

```
import javax.swing.*;
```

or:

```
import javax.swing.JFrame;
```

After making the minor changes in the statements described in this section, the program to create the window shown in Figure 6-4 is as follows:

```java
//Java program to create a window.

import javax.swing.*;

public class RectangleProgramOne extends JFrame
{
    private static final int WIDTH = 400;
    private static final int HEIGHT = 300;

    public RectangleProgramOne()
    {
        setTitle("Area and Perimeter of a Rectangle");
        setSize(WIDTH, HEIGHT);

        setDefaultCloseOperation(EXIT_ON_CLOSE);
        setVisible(true);
    }

    public static void main(String[] args)
    {
        RectangleProgramOne rectProg = new RectangleProgramOne();
    }
}
```

Notice that the named constants `WIDTH` and `HEIGHT` are declared with the modifier `private`. This is because we want these named constants to be used only within the `class` `RectangleProgram`. In general, if a named constant, variable, or method is to be used only within the specified `class`, then it is declared with the modifier `private`. Also, note that `private` is a reserved word in Java. (Chapter 8 discusses the modifier `private` in detail.)

(Note that in the preceding program we have changed the name of the `class` to `RectangleProgramOne`. This is because we have not yet added all the GUI components to the program. After adding labels, we will call it `class` `RectangleProgramTwo`, and so on. After adding all the necessary GUI components, we will call it `class` `RectangleProgram`. The Web site, *www.course.com*, and the CD accompanying this book contain all these programs.)

Let's review the important points introduced in this section:

- The preceding program has exactly one class: `RectangleProgramOne`.
- The `class` `RectangleProgramOne` contains the constructor `RectangleProgramOne` and the `main` method.

- You created the new **class** `RectangleProgramOne` by extending the existing class, `JFrame`. Therefore, `JFrame` is the superclass of `RectangleProgramOne`, and `RectangleProgramOne` is a subclass of `JFrame`.

- Whenever there is a superclass–subclass relationship, the subclass inherits all the data members and methods of the superclass. The methods `setTitle`, `setSize`, `setVisible`, and `setDefaultCloseOperation` are methods of the **class** `JFrame`, and these methods can be inherited by its subclasses.

The next few sections describe how to create GUI labels, text fields, and buttons, which can all be placed in the content pane of a window. Before you can place GUI components in the content pane, you must learn how to access the content pane.

Getting Access to the Content Pane

If you can visualize `JFrame` as a window, think of the content pane as the inner area of the window (below the title bar and inside the border). The **class** `JFrame` has the method `getContentPane` that you can use to access the content pane of the window. However, the **class** `JFrame` does not have the necessary tools to manage the components of the content pane. The components of the content pane are managed by declaring a reference variable of the `Container` type and then using the method `getContentPane`, as shown next.

Consider the following statements:

```
Container pane;                    //Line 1
pane = getContentPane();           //Line 2
```

The statement in Line 1 declares **pane** to be a reference variable of the `Container` type. The statement in Line 2 gets the content pane of the window as a container, that is, the reference variable **pane** now points to the content pane. You can now access the content pane to add GUI components to it by using the reference variable **pane**.

The statements in Lines 1 and 2 can be combined into one statement:

```
Container pane = getContentPane();    //Line 3
```

If you look back at Figure 6-2, you will see that the labels, text fields, and buttons are arranged in five rows and two columns. To control the placement of GUI components in the content pane, you set the layout of the content pane. The layout used in Figure 6-2 is called the grid layout. The **class** `Container` provides the method `setLayout`, as described in Table 6-2, to set the layout of the content pane. To add components such as labels and text fields to the content pane, you use the method **add** of the **class** `Container`, which is also described in Table 6-2.

TABLE 6-2 Some Methods of the **class** Container

Method / Description
`public void add(Object obj)` `//Method to add an object to the pane.`
`public void setLayout(Object obj)` `//Method to set the layout of the pane.`

The **class** Container is contained in the package `java.awt`. To use this **class** in your program, you need to include one of the following statements:

```
import java.awt.*;
```

or:

```
import java.awt.Container;
```

As noted earlier, the method `setLayout` is used to set the layout of the content pane, **pane**. To set the layout of the container to a grid, you use the **class** GridLayout. Consider the following statement:

```
pane.setLayout(new GridLayout(5, 2));
```

This statement creates an object belonging to the **class** GridLayout and assigns that object as the layout of the content pane, **pane**, by invoking the **setLayout** method. Moreover, this statement sets the layout of the content pane, **pane**, to five rows and two columns. This allows you to add 10 components arranged in five rows and two columns.

Note that the GridLayout manager arranges GUI components in a matrix formation with the number of rows and columns defined by the constructor and that the components are placed left to right, starting with the first row. For example, in the statement `pane.setLayout(new GridLayout(5, 2));`, the expression `new GridLayout(5, 2)`, invokes the constructor of the **class** GridLayout and sets the number of rows to 5 and the number of columns to 2. Also, in this chapter, we only discuss the GridLayout manager; additional layout managers are discussed in Chapter 12. Layout managers allow you to manage GUI components in a content pane.

If you do not specify a layout, Java uses a default layout. If you specify a layout, you must set the layout before adding any components. Once the layout is set, you can use the method `add` to add the components to the pane; this process is described in the next section.

JLabel

Now you will learn how to create labels and add them to the pane. We assume the following statements:

```
Container pane = getContentPane();
pane.setLayout(new GridLayout(4, 1));
```

Labels are objects of a particular `class` type. The Java `class` that you use to create labels is `JLabel`. Therefore, to create labels, you instantiate objects of type `JLabel`. The `class` `JLabel` is contained in the package `javax.swing`.

Just like a window, various attributes are associated with a label. For example, every label has a title, width, and height. The `class` `JLabel` contains various methods to control the display of labels. Table 6-3 describes some of the methods provided by the `class` `JLabel`.

TABLE 6-3 Some Methods Provided by the `class` `JLabel`

Method / Description/ Example

``
public JLabel(String str)
  //Constructor to create a label with left-aligned text specified
  //by str.
  //Example: JLabel lengthL;
  //   lengthL = new JLabel("Enter the length:")
  //   Creates the label lengthL with the title Enter the length:
``

``
public JLabel(String str, int align)
  //Constructor to create a label with the text specified by str.
  //   The value of align can be any one of the following:
  //   SwingConstants.LEFT, SwingConstants.RIGHT,
  //   SwingConstants.CENTER
  //Example:
  // JLabel lengthL;
  // lengthL = new JLabel("Enter the length:",
  //   SwingConstants.RIGHT);
  // The label lengthL is right aligned.
``

``
public JLabel(String t, Icon icon, int align)
  //Constructs a JLabel with both text and an icon.
  //The icon is to the left of the text.
``

``
public JLabel(Icon icon)
  //Constructs a JLabel with an icon.
``

NOTE In Table 6-3, `SwingConstants.LEFT`, `SwingConstants.RIGHT`, and `SwingConstants.CENTER` are constants defined in the `class` `SwingConstants`. They specify whether to set the string describing the label as left-justified, right-justified, or centered.

Consider the statements:

```
JLabel lengthL;
lengthL = new JLabel("Enter the length:", SwingConstants.RIGHT);
```

After these statements execute, the label in Figure 6-5 is created.

FIGURE 6-5 JLabel with the text Enter the length:

Now consider the following statements:

```
private JLabel lengthL, widthL, areaL, perimeterL;          //Line 1

lengthL =
    new JLabel("Enter the length: ", SwingConstants.RIGHT); //Line 2

widthL =
    new JLabel("Enter the width: ", SwingConstants.RIGHT);  //Line 3

areaL = new JLabel("Area: ", SwingConstants.RIGHT);         //Line 4

perimeterL =
    new JLabel("Perimeter: ", SwingConstants.RIGHT);        //Line 5
```

The statement in Line 1 declares four reference variables, lengthL, widthL, areaL, and perimeterL, of the JLabel type. The statement in Line 2 instantiates the object lengthL, assigns it the title Enter the length:, and sets the title alignment to right-justified. The statements in Lines 3 through 5 instantiate the objects widthL, areaL, and perimeterL with appropriate titles and text alignment.

Next, we add these labels to the **pane** declared at the beginning of this section. The following statements accomplish this. (Recall from the preceding section that we use the method **add** to add components to a **pane**.)

```
pane.add(lengthL);
pane.add(widthL);
pane.add(areaL);
pane.add(perimeterL);
```

Because we have specified a grid layout for the **pane** with four rows and one column, the label `lengthL` is added to the first row, the label `widthL` is added to the second row, and so on.

Now that you know how to add the components to the **pane**, you can put together the program to create these labels. `RectangleProgramTwo` builds on the `RectangleProgramOne` of the preceding section and, like `RectangleProgramOne`, is a subclass of `JFrame`.

```java
//Java program to create a window and place four labels

import javax.swing.*;
import java.awt.*;

public class RectangleProgramTwo extends JFrame
{
    private static final int WIDTH = 400;
    private static final int HEIGHT = 300;

    private JLabel lengthL, widthL, areaL, perimeterL;

    public RectangleProgramTwo()
    {
        setTitle("Area and Perimeter of a Rectangle");

        lengthL =
            new JLabel("Enter the length: ", SwingConstants.RIGHT);
        widthL =
            new JLabel("Enter the width: ", SwingConstants.RIGHT);
        areaL = new JLabel("Area: ", SwingConstants.RIGHT);
        perimeterL =
            new JLabel("Perimeter: ", SwingConstants.RIGHT);

        Container pane = getContentPane();
        pane.setLayout(new GridLayout(4, 1));

        pane.add(lengthL);
        pane.add(widthL);
        pane.add(areaL);
        pane.add(perimeterL);

        setSize(WIDTH, HEIGHT);
        setVisible(true);
        setDefaultCloseOperation(EXIT_ON_CLOSE);
    }

    public static void main(String[] args)
    {
        RectangleProgramTwo rectObject = new RectangleProgramTwo();
    }
}
```

Sample Run: (Figure 6-6 shows a sample run.)

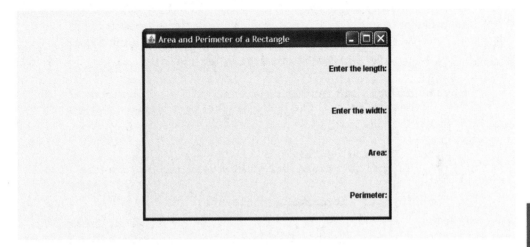

FIGURE 6-6 Sample run for `RectangleProgramTwo`

Now you are ready to create and place the text fields and buttons. The techniques for creating and placing components, such as `JTextField` and `JButton`, in a container are similar to the ones used for `JLabel`, and are described in the next two sections.

JTextField

As you may recall, text fields are objects belonging to the **class** `JTextField`. Therefore, you can create a text field by declaring a reference variable of type `JTextField` followed by an instantiation of the object.

Table 6-4 describes some of the methods of the **class** `JTextField`.

TABLE 6-4 Some Methods of the **class** JTextField

Method / Description
public **JTextField**(int columns)   //Constructor to set the size of the text field.

public **JTextField**(String str)
  //Constructor to initialize the object with the text specified
  //by str.

TABLE 6-4 Some Methods of the **class** JTextField (continued)

Method / Description

public **JTextField**(String str, int columns)
//Constructor to initialize the object with the text specified
//by str and to set the size of the text field.

public void **setText**(String str)
//Method to set the text of the text field to the string specified
//by str.

public **String** getText() //Method to return the text contained in the text field.

public void **setEditable**(boolean b)
//If the value of the boolean variable b is false, the user cannot
//type in the text field.
//In this case, the text field is used as a tool to display
//the result.

public void **addActionListener**(ActionListener obj) //Method to register a listener object to a JTextField.

Consider the following statements:

```
private JTextField lengthTF, widthTF, areaTF,
                   perimeterTF;                    //Line 1

lengthTF = new JTextField(10);                     //Line 2
widthTF = new JTextField(10);                      //Line 3
areaTF = new JTextField(10);                       //Line 4
perimeterTF = new JTextField(10);                  //Line 5
```

The statement in Line 1 declares four reference variables, lengthTF, widthTF, areaTF, and perimeterTF, of type JTextField. The statement in Line 2 instantiates the object lengthTF and sets the width of this text field to 10 characters. That is, this text field can display no more than 10 characters. The meaning of the other statements is similar.

Placing these objects involves using the add method of the **class** Container as described in the previous section. The following statements add these components to the container:

```
pane.add(lengthTF);
pane.add(widthTF);
pane.add(areaTF);
pane.add(perimeterTF);
```

The container **pane** now would contain eight objects—four labels and four text fields. We want to place the object **lengthTF** adjacent to the label **lengthL** in the same row, and use similar placements for the other objects. So we need to expand the grid layout to four rows and two columns. The following statements create the required grid layout and the necessary objects:

```
pane.setLayout(new GridLayout(4, 2));
pane.add(lengthL);
pane.add(lengthTF);
pane.add(widthL);
pane.add(widthTF);
pane.add(areaL);
pane.add(areaTF);
pane.add(perimeterL);
pane.add(perimeterTF);
```

The following program, RectangleProgramThree, summarizes our discussion so far:

```
//Java program to create a window
//and place four labels and four text fields

import javax.swing.*;
import java.awt.*;

public class RectangleProgramThree extends JFrame
{
    private static final int WIDTH = 400;
    private static final int HEIGHT = 300;

    private JLabel lengthL, widthL, areaL, perimeterL;
    private JTextField lengthTF, widthTF, areaTF,
                       perimeterTF;

    public RectangleProgramThree()
    {
        setTitle("Area and Perimeter of a Rectangle");

        lengthL =
            new JLabel("Enter the length: ", SwingConstants.RIGHT);
        widthL =
            new JLabel("Enter the width: ", SwingConstants.RIGHT);
        areaL =
            new JLabel("Area: ", SwingConstants.RIGHT);
        perimeterL =
            new JLabel("Perimeter: ", SwingConstants.RIGHT);
```

6

```java
        lengthTF = new JTextField(10);
        widthTF = new JTextField(10);
        areaTF = new JTextField(10);
        perimeterTF = new JTextField(10);

        Container pane = getContentPane();
        pane.setLayout(new GridLayout(4, 2));

        pane.add(lengthL);
        pane.add(lengthTF);
        pane.add(widthL);
        pane.add(widthTF);
        pane.add(areaL);
        pane.add(areaTF);
        pane.add(perimeterL);
        pane.add(perimeterTF);

        setSize(WIDTH, HEIGHT);
        setVisible(true);
        setDefaultCloseOperation(EXIT_ON_CLOSE);
    }

    public static void main(String[] args)
    {
        RectangleProgramThree rectObject =
                        new RectangleProgramThree();
    }
}
```

Sample Run: (Figure 6-7 shows the sample run.)

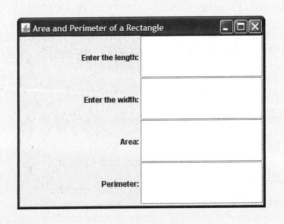

FIGURE 6-7 Sample run for `RectangleProgramThree`

To complete the design of the user interface, we will discuss how to create buttons.

JButton

To create a button, Java provides the **class** JButton. Thus, to create objects belonging to the **class** JButton, we use a technique similar to the one we used to create instances of **JLabel** and **JTextField**. Table 6-5 shows some methods of the **class** JButton.

TABLE 6-5 Commonly Used Methods of the **class** JButton

Method / Description

public **JButton**(Icon ic)
  //Constructor to initialize the button object with the icon
  //specified by ic.

public **JButton**(String str)
  //Constructor to initialize the button object to the text specified
  //by str.

public **JButton**(String str, Icon ic)
  //Constructor to initialize the button object to the text specified
  //by str and the icon specified by ic.

public void **setText**(String str)   //Method to set the text of the button to the string specified by str.
public String **getText**()   //Method to return the text contained in the button.
public void **addActionListener**(ActionListener obj)   //Method to register a listener object to the button object.

6

The following three lines will create two buttons, Calculate and Exit, shown earlier in Figure 6-2:

```
JButton calculateB, exitB;                //Line 1

calculateB = new JButton("Calculate");    //Line 2
exitB = new JButton("Exit");              //Line 3
```

The statement in Line 1 declares calculateB and exitB to be reference variables of type JButton. The statement in Line 2 instantiates the button object calculateB and sets the text for the button to the string Calculate. Similarly, the statement in Line 3 instantiates the button object exitB and sets the text for exitB to the string Exit.

The buttons `calculateB` and `exitB` can be placed into the container `pane` by using the method `add`. The following statements add these buttons to the `pane`:

```
pane.add(calculateB);
pane.add(exitB);
```

Now you have two more objects in the container, so you need to modify the `GridLayout` to accommodate five rows and two columns, and then add all the components. The following statements create the required grid layout and add the labels, text fields, and buttons to the container `pane`:

```
pane.setLayout(new GridLayout(5,2)); //specify the layout

pane.add(lengthL);        //add the label lengthL
pane.add(lengthTF);       //add the text field lengthTF
pane.add(widthL);         //add the label widthL
pane.add(widthTF);        //add the text field widthTF
pane.add(areaL);          //add the label areaL
pane.add(areaTF);         //add the text field areaTF
pane.add(perimeterL);     //add the label perimeterL
pane.add(perimeterTF);    //add the text field perimeterTF
pane.add(calculateB);     //add the button calculateB
pane.add(exitB);          //add the button exitB
```

Notice that the preceding `add` statements place the components from left to right and from top to bottom.

HANDLING AN EVENT

You have now learned how to create a window, how to create a container, and how to create labels, text fields, and buttons.

Now that you can create a button, such as `calculateB`, you need to specify how such a button should behave when you click it. For example, when you click the button `calculateB`, you want the program to calculate the area and perimeter of the rectangle and display these values in their respective text fields. Similarly, when you click the button `exitB`, the program should terminate.

Clicking a `JButton` creates an event, known as an **action event**, which sends a message to another object, known as an **action listener**. When the listener receives the message, it performs some action. Sending a message or an event to a listener object simply means that some method in the listener object is invoked with the event as the argument. This invocation happens automatically; you will not see the code corresponding to the method invocation. However, you must specify two things:

- For each JButton, you must specify the corresponding listener object. In Java, this is known as **registering** the listener.
- You must define the methods that will be invoked when the event is sent to the listener. Normally, you will write these methods and you will never write the code for invocation.

Java provides various classes to handle different kinds of events. The action event is handled by the class ActionListener, which contains only the method actionPerformed. In the method actionPerformed, you include the code that you want the system to execute when an action event is generated.

The class ActionListener that handles the action event is a special type of class, called an interface. In Java, interface is a reserved word. Roughly speaking, an interface is a class that contains only the method headings, and each method heading is terminated with a semicolon. For example, the definition of the interface ActionListener containing the method actionPerformed is:

```
public interface ActionListener
{
    public void actionPerformed(ActionEvent e);
}
```

Because the method actionPerformed does not contain a body, Java does not allow you to instantiate an object of type ActionListener. So how do you register an action listener with the object calculateB?

One way is as follows (there are other ways not discussed here): Because you cannot instantiate an object of type ActionListener, first you need to create a class on top of ActionListener so that the required object can be instantiated. The class created must provide the necessary code for the method actionPerformed. You will create the class CalculateButtonHandler to handle the event generated by clicking the button calculateB.

The class CalculateButtonHandler is created on top of the interface ActionListener. The definition of the class CalculateButtonHandler is:

```
private class CalculateButtonHandler implements
                                    ActionListener    //Line 1
{
   public void actionPerformed(ActionEvent e)        //Line 2
   {
      //The code for calculating the area and the perimeter
      //and displaying these quantities goes here
   }
}
```

6

Notice the following:

- The class CalculateButtonHandler starts with the modifier private. This is because you want this class to be used only within your RectangleProgram.

- This class uses another modifier, implements. This is how you build classes on top of classes that are interfaces. Notice that you have not yet provided the code for the method actionPerformed. You will do that shortly.

In Java, implements is a reserved word.

Next, we illustrate how to create a listener object of type CalculateButtonHandler. Consider the following statements:

```
CalculateButtonHandler cbHandler;

cbHandler = new CalculateButtonHandler();   //instantiate the object
```

As described, these statements create the listener object. Having created a listener, you next must associate (or in Java terminology, register) this handler with the corresponding JButton. The following line of code registers cbHandler as the listener object of calculateB:

```
calculateB.addActionListener(cbHandler);
```

The complete definition of the class CalculateButtonHandler, including the code for the method actionPerformed, is:

```
private class CalculateButtonHandler implements
                                    ActionListener    //Line 1
{
    public void actionPerformed(ActionEvent e)        //Line 2
    {
        double width, length, area, perimeter;        //Line 3

        length
            = Double.parseDouble(lengthTF.getText());  //Line 4
        width
            = Double.parseDouble(widthTF.getText());   //Line 5
        area = length * width;                         //Line 6
        perimeter = 2 * (length + width);              //Line 7

        areaTF.setText("" + area);                     //Line 8
        perimeterTF.setText("" + perimeter);           //Line 9
    }
}
```

In the preceding program segment, Line 1 declares the class CalculateButtonHandler and makes it an action listener by including the phrase implements ActionListener. Note that all of this code is just a new class definition.

This class has one method; Line 2 is the first statement of that method. Let us look at the statement in Line 4:

```
length = Double.parseDouble(lengthTF.getText());
```

The length of the rectangle is stored in the text field `lengthTF`. We use the method `getText` to retrieve the string from this text field, specifying the length. Now the value of the expression `lengthTF.getText()` is the length, but it is in a string form. So we need to use the method `parseDouble` to convert the length string into an equivalent decimal number. The length is then stored in the variable `length`. The statement in Line 5 works similarly for the width.

The statements in Lines 6 and 7 compute the area and the perimeter, respectively. The statement in Line 8 uses the method `setText` of the `class JTextField` to display the area. Because `setText` requires that the argument be a string, you need to convert the value of the variable `area` into a string. The easiest way to do this is to concatenate the value of `area` to an empty string. Similar conventions apply for the statement in Line 9.

It follows that the method `actionPerformed` displays the area and perimeter in the corresponding `JTextFields`.

Before creating an action listener for the `JButton exitB`, let us summarize what we've done so far to create and register an action event listener:

1. Created a class that implements the `interface ActionListener`. For example, for the `JButton calculateB` we created the `class CalculateButtonHandler`.

2. Provided the definition of the method `actionPerformed` within the class that you created in Step 1. The method `actionPerformed` contains the code that the program executes when a specific event is generated. For example, when you click the `JButton calculateB`, the program should calculate and display the area and perimeter of the rectangle.

3. Created and instantiated an object of the class type created in Step 1. For example, for the `JButton calculateB` we created the object `cbHandler`.

4. Registered the event handler created in Step 3 with the object that generates an action event using the method `addActionListener`. For example, for `JButton calculateB` the following statement registers the object `cbHandler` to listen and register the action event:

    ```
    calculateB.addActionListener(cbHandler);
    ```

6

We can now repeat these four steps to create and register the action listener with the JButton exitB.

```
private class ExitButtonHandler implements ActionListener
{
    public void actionPerformed(ActionEvent e)
    {
        System.exit(0);
    }
}
```

The following statements create the action listener object for the button exitB:

```
ExitButtonHandler ebHandler;

ebHandler = new ExitButtonHandler();
exitB.addActionListener(ebHandler);
```

The interface ActionListener is contained in the package java.awt.event. Therefore, to use this interface to handle events, your program must include the statement:

```
import java.awt.event.*;
```

or:

```
import java.awt.event.ActionListener;
```

The complete program to calculate the perimeter and area of a rectangle is:

```
//Given the length and width of a rectangle, this Java
//program determines its area and perimeter.

import javax.swing.*;
import java.awt.*;
import java.awt.event.*;

public class RectangleProgram extends JFrame
{
    private JLabel lengthL, widthL, areaL, perimeterL;

    private JTextField lengthTF, widthTF, areaTF, perimeterTF;

    private JButton calculateB, exitB;

    private CalculateButtonHandler cbHandler;
    private ExitButtonHandler ebHandler;

    private static final int WIDTH = 400;
    private static final int HEIGHT = 300;

    public RectangleProgram()
    {
            //Create the four labels
        lengthL = new JLabel("Enter the length: ",
                                SwingConstants.RIGHT);
```

```
widthL = new JLabel("Enter the width: ",
                             SwingConstants.RIGHT);
areaL = new JLabel("Area: ", SwingConstants.RIGHT);
perimeterL = new JLabel("Perimeter: ",
                             SwingConstants.RIGHT);

       //Create the four text fields
lengthTF = new JTextField(10);
widthTF = new JTextField(10);
areaTF = new JTextField(10);
perimeterTF = new JTextField(10);

       //Create Calculate Button
calculateB = new JButton("Calculate");
cbHandler = new CalculateButtonHandler();
calculateB.addActionListener(cbHandler);

       //Create Exit Button
exitB = new JButton("Exit");
ebHandler = new ExitButtonHandler();
exitB.addActionListener(ebHandler);

       //Set the title of the window
setTitle("Area and Perimeter of a Rectangle");

       //Get the container
Container pane = getContentPane();

       //Set the layout
pane.setLayout(new GridLayout(5, 2));

       //Place the components in the pane
pane.add(lengthL);
pane.add(lengthTF);
pane.add(widthL);
pane.add(widthTF);
pane.add(areaL);
pane.add(areaTF);
pane.add(perimeterL);
pane.add(perimeterTF);
pane.add(calculateB);
pane.add(exitB);

       //Set the size of the window and display it
setSize(WIDTH, HEIGHT);
setVisible(true);
setDefaultCloseOperation(EXIT_ON_CLOSE);
}
```

6

```java
private class CalculateButtonHandler implements ActionListener
{
    public void actionPerformed(ActionEvent e)
    {
        double width, length, area, perimeter;

        length = Double.parseDouble(lengthTF.getText());
        width = Double.parseDouble(widthTF.getText());
        area = length * width;
        perimeter = 2 * (length + width);

        areaTF.setText("" + area);
        perimeterTF.setText("" + perimeter);
    }
}

private class ExitButtonHandler implements ActionListener
{
    public void actionPerformed(ActionEvent e)
    {
        System.exit(0);
    }
}

public static void main(String[] args)
{
    RectangleProgram rectObject = new RectangleProgram();
}
}
```

Sample Run: (Figure 6-8 shows the sample run.)

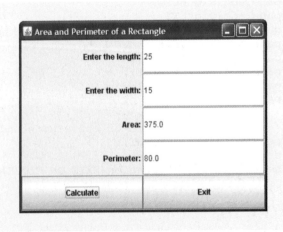

FIGURE 6-8 Sample run for the final `RectangleProgram`

PROGRAMMING EXAMPLE: Temperature Conversion

Write a program that creates the GUI shown in Figure 6-9, to convert the temperature from Fahrenheit to Celsius and from Celsius to Fahrenheit.

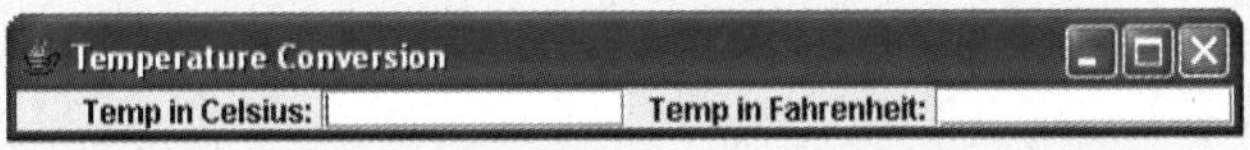

FIGURE 6-9 GUI for the temperature conversion program

When the user enters the temperature in the text field adjacent to the label `Temp in Celsius` and presses the `Enter` key, the program displays the equivalent temperature in the text field adjacent to the label `Temp in Fahrenheit`. Similarly, when the user enters the temperature in Fahrenheit and presses the `Enter` key, the program displays the equivalent temperature in Celsius.

Input: Temperature in Fahrenheit or Celsius

Output: Temperature in Celsius if the input is Fahrenheit; the temperature in Fahrenheit if the input is Celsius

PROBLEM
ANALYSIS,
GUI DESIGN,
AND
ALGORITHM
DESIGN

Suppose that the variable `celsius` represents the temperature in Celsius and the variable `fahrenheit` represents the temperature in Fahrenheit. If the user enters the temperature in Fahrenheit, the formula for calculating the equivalent temperature in Celsius is:

```
celsius = (5.0 / 9.0) * (fahrenheit - 32)
```

For example, if `fahrenheit` is `98.6`, then:

```
celsius = 5.0 / 9.0 * (98.6 - 32) = 37.00
```

Similarly, if the user enters the temperature in Celsius, then the formula for calculating the equivalent temperature in Fahrenheit is:

```
fahrenheit = 9.0 / 5.0 * celsius + 32
```

For example, if `celsius` is 20, then:

```
fahrenheit = 9.0 / 5.0 * 20 + 32 = 68.0
```

The GUI in Figure 6-9 contains a window, a container, two labels, and two text fields. The labels and text fields are placed in the container of the window. As we did in the rectangle program earlier in this chapter, we can create the window by making the application extend the `class JFrame`. To get access to the container, we will use a reference variable of the `Container` type. To create labels, we use objects of type `JLabel`; to create text fields, we use objects of type `JTextField`. Suppose that we have the following declarations:

```
JLabel celsiusLabel;        //label Celsius
JLabel fahrenheitLabel;     //label Fahrenheit

JTextField celsiusTF;       //text field Celsius
JTextField fahrenheitTF;    //text field Fahrenheit
```

When the user enters the temperature in the text field `celsiusTF` and presses the `Enter` key, we want the program to show the equivalent temperature in the text field `fahrenheitTF` and vice versa.

Recall that when you click a `JButton`, it generates an action event. Moreover, the action event is handled by the method `actionPerformed` of the `interface ActionListener`. Similarly, when you press the `Enter` key in a text field, it generates an action event. Therefore, we can register an action event listener with the text fields `celsiusTF` and `fahrenheitTF` to take the appropriate action.

Based on this analysis and the GUI shown in Figure 6-9, you can design an event-driven algorithm as follows:

1. Have a listener in each text field.
2. Register an event handler with each text field.
3. Let each event handler registered with a text field do the following:

   a. Get the data from the text field once the user presses `Enter`.
   b. Apply the corresponding formula to perform the conversion.
   c. Set the value of the other text field.

This process of adding an event listener and then registering the event listener to a text field is similar to the process we used to register an event listener to a `JButton` earlier in the chapter. (This process will be described later in this programming example.)

VARIABLES, OBJECTS, AND NAMED CONSTANTS

The input to the program is either the temperature in Celsius or the temperature in Fahrenheit. If the input is a value for Celsius, then the program calculates the equivalent temperature in Fahrenheit. Similarly, if the input is a value for Fahrenheit, then the program calculates the equivalent temperature in Celsius. Therefore, the program needs the following variables:

```
double celsius;      //variable to hold Celsius
double fahrenheit;   //variable to hold Fahrenheit
```

Notice that these variables are needed in each event handler.

The formulas to convert the temperature from Fahrenheit to Celsius and vice versa use the special values 32, 9.0/5.0, and 5.0/9.0, which we will declare as named constants as follows:

```
private static final double FTOC = 5.0 / 9.0;
private static final double CTOF = 9.0 / 5.0;
private static final int OFFSET = 32;
```

As in the GUI, you need two labels—one to label the text field corresponding to the Celsius value and another to label the text field corresponding to the Fahrenheit value. Therefore, the following statements are needed:

```
private JLabel celsiusLabel;        //label Celsius
private JLabel fahrenheitLabel;     //label Fahrenheit

celsiusLabel = new JLabel("Temp in Celsius: ",
                SwingConstants.RIGHT);//object instantiation

fahrenheitLabel = new JLabel("Temp in Fahrenheit: ",
                SwingConstants.RIGHT);//object instantiation
```

You also need two **JTextField** objects. The necessary Java code is:

```
private JTextField celsiusTF;        //text field Celsius
private JTextField fahrenheitTF;     //text field Fahrenheit

celsiusTF = new JTextField(7);       //object instantiation
fahrenheitTF = new JTextField(7);    //object instantiation
```

Now you need a window to display the labels and the text fields. Because a window is an object of type **JFrame**, the class containing the application program that we create will extend the definition of the **class JFrame**. We will set the width of the window to 500 pixels and the height to 50 pixels. We'll call the class containing the application program **TempConversion**. The application will look like this:

```
//Java program to convert the temperature from Celsius to
//Fahrenheit and vice versa.

import javax.swing.*;

public class TempConversion extends JFrame
{
    private static final int WIDTH = 500;
    private static final int HEIGHT = 50;

    private static final double FTOC = 5.0 / 9.0;
    private static final double CTOF = 9.0 / 5.0;
    private static final int OFFSET = 32;
```

6

```java
public TempConversion()
{
    setTitle("Temperature Conversion");
    setSize(WIDTH, HEIGHT);
    setVisible(true);
    setDefaultCloseOperation(EXIT_ON_CLOSE);
}

public static void main(String[] args)
{
    TempConversion tempConv = new TempConversion();
}
}
```

Now you need to access the container content pane to place the GUI components and set the required layout of the pane. Therefore, as before, you need the following statements:

```java
Container c = getContentPane();     //get the container

c.setLayout(new GridLayout(1, 4)); //create a new layout

c.add(celsiusLabel);               //add the label celsiusLabel
                                   //to the container
c.add(celsiusTF);                  //add the text field celsiusTF
                                   //to the container
c.add(fahrenheitLabel);            //add the label fahrenheitLabel
                                   //to the container
c.add(fahrenheitTF);               //add the text field fahrenheitTF
                                   //to the container
```

You want your program to respond to the events generated by JTextFields. Just as when you click a JButton an action event is generated, when you press Enter in a JTextField, it generates an action event. Therefore, to register event listeners with JTextFields, we use the four steps outlined in the section Handling an Event earlier in this chapter: (1) create a class that implements the interface ActionListener; (2) provide the definition of the method actionPerformed within the class that you created in Step 1; (3) create and instantiate an object of the class created in Step 1; and (4) register the event handler created in Step 3 with the object that generates an action event using the method addActionListener.

Next, we create and register an action listener with the JTextField celsiusTF.

First we create the class CelsHandler, implementing the interface ActionListener. Then, we provide the definition of the method actionPerformed of the class CelsHandler. When the user enters the temperature in the JTextField celsiusTF and presses Enter, the program needs to calculate and display the equivalent temperature in the JTextField

fahrenheitTF. The necessary code is placed within the body of the method actionPerformed.

We now describe the steps of the method actionPerformed. The temperature in Celsius is contained in the JTextField celsiusTF. We use the method getText of the class JTextField to retrieve the temperature in celsiusTF. However, the value returned by the method getText is in string form, so we use the method parseDouble of the class Double to convert the numeric string into a decimal value. It follows that we need a variable of type double, say, celsius, to store the temperature in Celsius. We accomplish this with the following statement:

```
celsius = Double.parseDouble(celsiusTF.getText());
```

We also need a variable of type double, say, fahrenheit, to store the equivalent temperature in Fahrenheit. Because we want to display the temperature to two decimal places, we use the method format of the class String.

We can now write the definition of the class CelsHandler as follows:

```
private class CelsHandler implements ActionListener
{
    public void actionPerformed(ActionEvent e)
    {
        double celsius, fahrenheit;

        celsius =
            Double.parseDouble(celsiusTF.getText());

        fahrenheit = celsius * CTOF + OFFSET;

        fahrenheitTF.setText(String.format("%.2f",
                                        fahrenheit));
    }
}
```

We can now create an object of type CelsHandler as follows:

```
private CelsHandler celsiusHandler;
celsiusHandler = new CelsHandler();
```

Having created a listener, you must associate this handler with the corresponding JTextField celsiusTF. The following code does this:

```
celsiusTF.addActionListener(celsiusHandler);
```

6

Similarly, we can create and register an action listener with the text field `fahrenheitTF`. The necessary code is:

```java
private class FahrHandler implements ActionListener
{
    public void actionPerformed(ActionEvent e)
    {
        double celsius, fahrenheit;

        fahrenheit =
            Double.parseDouble(fahrenheitTF.getText());

        celsius = (fahrenheit - OFFSET) * FTOC;

        celsiusTF.setText(String.format("%.2f",
                                        celsius));
    }
}

private FahrHandler fahrenheitHandler;

fahrenheitHandler = new FahrHandler(); //instantiate the object

fahrenheitTF.addActionListener(fahrenheitHandler);
                                //add the action listener
```

Now that we have created the necessary GUI components and the programming code, we can put everything together to create the complete program.

PUTTING IT
TOGETHER

You can start with the window creation program and then add all the components, handlers, and classes developed. You also need the necessary `import` statements. In this case, they are:

```java
import java.awt.*;          //for the class Container
import java.awt.event.*;    //for events
import javax.swing.*;       //for JLabel and JTextField
```

Thus, you have the following Java program:

```java
//********************************************************************
//Author: D.S. Malik
//
//Java program to convert the temperature between Celsius and
//Fahrenheit.
//********************************************************************

import java.awt.*;
import java.awt.event.*;
import javax.swing.*;
```

```java
public class TempConversion extends JFrame
{
    private JLabel celsiusLabel;
    private JLabel fahrenheitLabel;

    private JTextField celsiusTF;
    private JTextField fahrenheitTF;

    private CelsHandler celsiusHandler;
    private FahrHandler fahrenheitHandler;

    private static final int WIDTH = 500;
    private static final int HEIGHT = 50;
    private static final double FTOC = 5.0 / 9.0;
    private static final double CTOF = 9.0 / 5.0;
    private static final int OFFSET = 32;

    public TempConversion()
    {
        setTitle("Temperature Conversion");
        Container c = getContentPane();
        c.setLayout(new GridLayout(1, 4));

        celsiusLabel = new JLabel("Temp in Celsius: ",
                                   SwingConstants.RIGHT);
        fahrenheitLabel = new JLabel("Temp in Fahrenheit: ",
                                   SwingConstants.RIGHT);

        celsiusTF = new JTextField(7);
        fahrenheitTF = new JTextField(7);

        c.add(celsiusLabel);
        c.add(celsiusTF);
        c.add(fahrenheitLabel);
        c.add(fahrenheitTF);

        celsiusHandler = new CelsHandler();
        fahrenheitHandler = new FahrHandler();

        celsiusTF.addActionListener(celsiusHandler);
        fahrenheitTF.addActionListener(fahrenheitHandler);

        setSize(WIDTH, HEIGHT);
        setDefaultCloseOperation(EXIT_ON_CLOSE);
        setVisible(true);
    }
```

6

```java
private class CelsHandler implements ActionListener
{
    public void actionPerformed(ActionEvent e)
    {
        double celsius, fahrenheit;

        celsius =
                Double.parseDouble(celsiusTF.getText());

        fahrenheit = celsius * CTOF + OFFSET;

        fahrenheitTF.setText(String.format("%.2f",
                                            fahrenheit));
    }
}

private class FahrHandler implements ActionListener
{
    public void actionPerformed(ActionEvent e)
    {
        double celsius, fahrenheit;

        fahrenheit =
                Double.parseDouble(fahrenheitTF.getText());

        celsius = (fahrenheit - OFFSET) * FTOC;

        celsiusTF.setText(String.format("%.2f",
                                          celsius));
    }
}

public static void main(String[] args)
{
    TempConversion tempConv = new TempConversion();
}
}
```

Sample Run: (Figure 6-10 shows the display after the user typed 98.60 in the text field Temp in Fahrenheit and pressed Enter.)

FIGURE 6-10 Sample run for TempConversion

Object-Oriented Design

Chapter 3 discussed the class String in detail. Using the class String, you can create various String objects. Moreover, using the methods of the class String, you can manipulate the string stored in a String object. Recall that String objects are instances of the class String. Similarly, a Java program that uses GUI components also uses various objects. For example, in the first part of this chapter, you used the JFrame, JLabel, JTextField, and JButton objects. Labels are instances of the class JLabel, buttons are instances of the class JButton, and so on. In general, an object is an instance of a particular class.

In this section, we delve a little deeper into the general concept of objects and how they are used in object-oriented design (OOD). OOD is a major field of study in its own right. Most colleges and universities offer courses on this topic. This section by no means presents an in-depth treatise on OOD. Rather, we review its general concepts and give a simplified methodology for using the OOD approach to problem solving.

Since Chapter 2, you have used String objects. Moreover, in the first part of this chapter, you used objects belonging to various classes, such as JFrame, JLabel, JTextField, JButton, and String. In fact, in your daily life you use objects such as a VCR, CD player, and so on without realizing how they might be conceptualized as objects or classes. For example, regarding a VCR, note the following facts:

- To use a VCR, you do not need to know how the VCR is made. You do not need to know the internal parts of a VCR or how they work. These are hidden from you.

- To use a VCR, you do need to know the functions of various buttons and how to use them.

- Once you know how to use a VCR, you can use it either as a stand-alone device or you can combine it with other devices to create an entertainment system.

- You cannot modify the functions of a VCR. The Record button will always function as a Record button.

Any Java objects, such as String objects, that you have encountered also have the properties mentioned above. You can use the objects and their methods, but you don't need to know how they work.

The aim of OOD is to build software from components called classes so that if someone wants to use a class, all they need to know is the various methods provided by that class.

Recall that in OOD, an object combines data and operations on that data in a single unit, a feature called **encapsulation**. In OOD, we first identify the object, then identify the relevant data, and then identify the operations needed to manipulate the object.

For example, the relevant data for a String object is the actual string and the length of the string, that is, the number of characters in the string. Every String object must have memory space to store the relevant data, that is, the string and its length. Next, we must identify the type of operations performed on a string. Some of the operations on a string might be to replace a particular character of a string, extract part of a string, change a string from uppercase to lowercase, and so on. The `class` String provides the necessary operations to be performed on a string.

As another example of how an object contains both data and operations on that data, consider objects of type JButton. Because every button has a label, which is a string, every button must have memory space to store its label. Some of the operations on a button that you have encountered are to set the label of the button and to add a listener object to a button. Other operations that can be performed on a button are to set its size and location. These operations are the methods of a class. Thus, the `class` JButton provides the methods to set a button's size and location.

A Simplified OOD Methodology

Now that you have an overview of objects and the essential components of OOD, you may be eager to learn how to solve a particular problem using OOD methodology. The best way to learn is by practice. A simplified OOD methodology can be expressed as follows:

1. Write down a detailed description of the problem.
2. Identify all the (relevant) nouns and verbs.
3. From the list of nouns, select the objects. Identify the data components of each object.
4. From the list of verbs, select the operations.

In item 3, after identifying the objects or classes, usually you will realize that several objects function in the same way. That is, they have the same data components and same operations. In other words, they will lead to the construction of the same class.

Remember that objects are nothing but instances of a particular class. Therefore, to create objects you have to learn how to create classes. In other words, to create objects you first need to create classes; to know what type of classes to create, you need to know what an object stores and what operations are needed to manipulate an object's data. You can see that objects and classes are closely related. Because an object consists of data and operations on the data in a single unit, in Java we use the mechanism of classes to combine data and its operations in a single unit. In OOD methodology, we therefore identify classes, data members of classes, and operations. In Java, data members are also known as **fields**.

The remainder of this section gives various examples to illustrate how objects, data components of objects, and operations on data are identified. In these examples, nouns (objects) are in bold type, and verbs (operations) are in italics.

EXAMPLE 6-2

Consider the problem presented in Example 6-1. In simple terms, the problem can be stated as follows:

"Write a **program** to *input* the **length** and **width** of a **rectangle** and *calculate* and *print* the **perimeter** and **area** of the **rectangle**."

Step 1: Identify all the (relevant) nouns.

- Length
- Width
- Perimeter
- Area
- Rectangle

Step 2: Identify the class(es).

Considering all five nouns, it is clear that:

- Length is the length of a rectangle.
- Width is the width of a rectangle.
- Perimeter is the perimeter of a rectangle.
- Area is the area of a rectangle.

Notice that four of the five nouns are related to the fifth one, namely, `rectangle`. Therefore, choose `Rectangle` as a class. From the `class` `Rectangle`, you can instantiate rectangles of various dimensions. The `class` `Rectangle` can be graphically represented as in Figure 6-11.

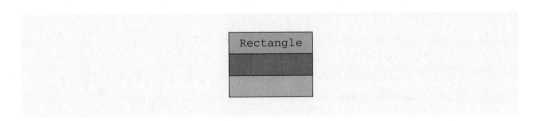

FIGURE 6-11 `class` Rectangle

Step 3: Identify the data members for each of the classes.

In this step, you evaluate the remaining nouns and determine the information that is essential to fully describing each class. Therefore, consider each noun—length, width, perimeter, and area—and ask: "Is each of these nouns essential for describing the rectangle?"

- Perimeter is not needed, because it can be computed from length and width. Perimeter is not a data member.
- Area is not needed, because it can be computed from length and width. Area is not a data member.
- Length is required. Length is a data member.
- Width is required. Width is a data member.

Having made these choices, the **class Rectangle** can be represented with data members, as shown in Figure 6-12.

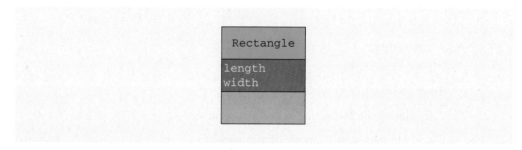

FIGURE 6-12 class Rectangle with data members

Step 4: Identify the operations for each of the classes.

Many operations for a class or an object can be determined by looking at the list of verbs. Let us consider the verbs *input*, *calculate*, and *print*. The possible operations on a rectangle object are *input* the length and width, *calculate* the perimeter and area, and *print* the perimeter and area. In this step, we focus on the functionalities of the class(es) involved. By carefully reading the problem statement, you may conclude that you need at least the following operations:

- **setLength**: Set the length of the rectangle.
- **setWidth**: Set the width of the rectangle.
- **computePerimeter**: Calculate the perimeter of the rectangle.
- **computeArea**: Calculate the area of the rectangle.
- **print**: Print the perimeter and area of the rectangle.

It is customary to include operations to retrieve the values of the data members of an object. Therefore, you also need the following operations:

- **getLength**: Retrieve the length of the rectangle.
- **getWidth**: Retrieve the width of the rectangle.

Figure 6-13 shows the **class Rectangle** with data members and operations.

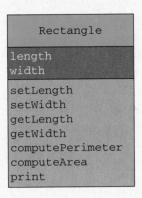

FIGURE 6-13 `class` Rectangle with data members and operations

6

With these steps completed, you can design an algorithm for each operation of an object (class) and implement each algorithm in Java.

 NOTE The diagram in Figure 6-13 is a form of a diagram known as the *class unified modeling language (UML) diagram.* After introducing a few more terms used in a class UML diagram, we formally introduce the class UML diagram in Chapter 8, when we discuss classes in general.

EXAMPLE 6-3

Consider the following problem:

A **place** to buy **candy** is from a **candy machine**. A new candy machine is purchased for the **cafeteria**, but it is not working properly. The candy machine has four **dispensers** to hold and release **items** sold by the candy machine as well as a **cash register**. The machine sells four products—**candies**, **chips**, **gum**, and **cookies**—each stored in a separate dispenser. You have been asked to write a program for this candy machine so that it can be put into operation.

The program should do the following:

- *Show* the **customer** the different **products** sold by the **candy machine**.
- Let the **customer** *make* the selection.
- *Show* the **customer** the **cost of the item** selected.
- *Accept* the **money** from the **customer**.
- *Return* the **change**.
- *Release* the **item**, that is, *make* the sale.

The OOD solution to this problem proceeds as follows:

Step 1: Identify all the nouns.

Place, **candy**, **candy machine**, **cafeteria**, **dispenser**, **items**, **cash register**, **chips**, **gum**, **cookies**, **customer**, **products**, **cost** (of the item), **money**, and **change**.

In this description of the problem, products stand for items such as candy, chips, gum, and cookies. In fact, the actual product in the machine is not that important. What is important is to note that there are four dispensers, each capable of dispensing one product. Further, there is one cash register. Thus, the candy machine consists of four dispensers and one cash register. Graphically, this can be represented as in Figure 6-14.

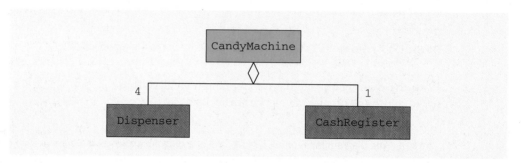

FIGURE 6-14   Candy Machine and its components

In Figure 6-14, the number 4 on top of the box `Dispenser` indicates that there are four dispensers in the candy machine. Similarly, the number 1 on top of the box `CashRegister` indicates that the candy machine has one cash register.

Step 2: Identify the class(es).

You can see that the program you are about to write is supposed to deal with dispensers and cash registers. That is, the main objects are four dispensers and a cash register. Because all the dispensers are of the same type, you need to create a class, say, `Dispenser`, to create the dispensers. Similarly, you need to create a class, say, `CashRegister`, to create a cash register. We will create the `class` `CandyMachine` containing the four dispensers, a cash register, and the application program.

Step 3: Identify the data members for each of the class(es).

Dispenser To make the sale, at least one item must be in the dispenser and the customer must know the cost of the product. Therefore, the data members of a dispenser are:

- Product cost
- Number of items in the dispenser

Cash Register The cash register accepts money and returns change. Therefore, the cash register has only one data member, which we call `cashOnHand`.

Candy Machine The `class` CandyMachine has four dispensers and a cash register. You can name the four dispensers by the items they store. Therefore, the candy machine has five data members—four dispensers and a cash register.

Step 4: Identify the operations for each of the objects (classes).

The relevant verbs are *show* (selection), *make* (selection), *show* (cost), *accept* (money), *return* (change), and *make* (sale).

The verbs *show* (selection) and *make* (selection) relate to the candy machine. The verbs *show* (cost) and *make* (sale) relate to the dispenser. Similarly, the verbs *accept* (money) and *return* (change) relate to the cash register.

Dispenser The verb *show* (cost) applies to either printing or retrieving the value of the data member `cost`. The verb *make* (sale) applies to reducing the number of items in the dispenser by 1. Of course, the dispenser has to be nonempty. You must also provide an operation to set the cost and the number of items in the dispenser. Thus, the operations for a dispenser object are:

- `getCount`: Retrieve the number of items in the dispenser.
- `getProductCost`: Retrieve the cost of the item.
- `makeSale`: Reduce the number of items in the dispenser by 1.
- `setCost`: Set the cost of the product.
- `setNumberOfItems`: Set the number of items in the dispenser.

Cash Register The verb *accept* (money) applies to updating the money in the cash register by adding the money deposited by the customer. Similarly, the verb *return* (change) applies to reducing the money in the cash register by returning the overpaid amount (by the customer) to the customer. You also need to (initially) set the money in the cash register and retrieve the money from the cash register. Thus, the possible operations on a cash register are:

- `acceptAmount`: Update the amount in the cash register.
- `returnChange`: Return the change.
- `getCashOnHand`: Retrieve the amount in the cash register.
- `setCashOnHand`: Set the amount in the cash register.

Candy Machine The verbs *show* (selection) and *make* (selection) apply to the candy machine. Thus, the two possible operations are:

- `showSelection`: Show the number of products sold by the candy machine.
- `makeSelection`: Allow the customer to select the product.

The result of the OOD for this problem is shown in Figure 6-15.

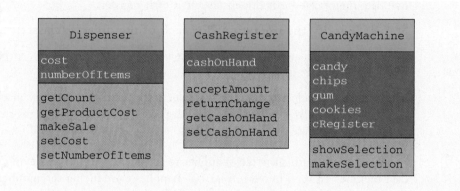

FIGURE 6-15 Classes `Dispenser`, `CashRegister`, `CandyMachine`, and their members

Implementing Classes and Operations

From the preceding examples, it is clear that once the relevant classes, data members of each class, and relevant operations for each class are identified, the next step is to implement these things in Java. Because objects are nothing but instances of classes, we need to learn how to implement classes in Java. Implementing data members, that is, fields, of classes is simple because you need variables to store the data.

What about operations? In Java, we write algorithms to implement operations. Because there is usually more than one operation on an object, each algorithm is implemented with the help of Java's methods. In Chapter 3, we briefly introduced methods and described some predefined methods. However, Java does not provide all the methods that you will ever need. Therefore, to learn how to design and implement classes, you first must learn how to construct and implement your own methods. Because methods are an essential part of Java (or any programming language), Chapter 7 is devoted to teaching you how to create methods.

Primitive Data Types and the Wrapper Classes

Chapter 3 discussed how to use the method `parseInt` of the `class` `Integer` to convert an integer string into an integer. Moreover, you learned that the `class` `Integer` is called a **wrapper** class, or simply a wrapper. It is used to wrap `int` values into `Integer` objects so that `int` values can be regarded as objects. Similarly, the `class` `Long` is used to wrap `long` values into `Long` objects, the `class` `Double` is used to wrap **double** values into **Double** objects, and the **class Float** is used to wrap **float** values into **Float** objects. In fact, Java provides a wrapper class corresponding to each primitive data type. For example, the wrapper class corresponding to the type **int** is **Integer**.

Next, we briefly discuss the **class Integer**. Table 6-6 describes some members of the **class Integer**.

TABLE 6-6 Some Members of the **class** Integer

Named Constants
`public static final int MAX_VALUE = 2147483647;`
`public static final int MIN_VALUE = -2147483648;`

Constructors

`public Integer(int num)`
`   //Creates an object initialized to the value specified`
`   //by num.`

`public Integer(String str)`
`   //Creates an object initialized to the value specified`
`   //by the num contained in str.`

Methods

`int compareTo(Integer anotherInteger)`
`   //Compares two Integer objects numerically.`
`   //Returns the value 0 if the value of this Integer object is`
`   //equal to the value of anotherInteger object, a value less`
`   //than 0 if the value of this Integer is less than the value of`
`   //anotherInteger object, and a value greater than 0 if the value`
`   //of this Integer object is greater than the value of`
`   //anotherInteger object.`

`public int intValue()` `   //Returns the value of the object as an int value.`
`public double doubleValue()` `   //Returns the value of the object as a double value.`

`public boolean equals(Object obj)`
`   //Returns true if the value of this object is equal`
`   //to the value of the object specified by obj;`
`   //otherwise returns false.`

6

TABLE 6-6 Some Members of the **class** Integer (continued)

```
public static int parseInt(String str)
  //Returns the value of the number contained in str.

public String toString()
  //Returns the int value, of the object, as a string.

public static String toString(int num)
  //Returns the value of num as a string.

public static Integer valueOf(String str)
  //Returns an Integer object initialized to the value
  //specified by str.
```

Consider the following statements:

```
Integer num;            //Line 1
num = new Integer(86)   //Line 2
```

The statement in Line 1 declares num to be a reference variable of type Integer. The statement in Line 2 creates an Integer object, stores the value 86 in it, and then stores the address of this object into num. (See Figure 6-16. Suppose that the address of the Integer object is 1350.)

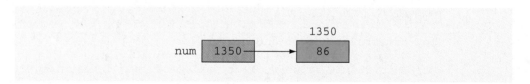

FIGURE 6-16 The reference variable num and the object it points to

As you can see, the int value 86 is wrapped into an Integer object. Just like the **class** String, the **class** Integer does not provide any method to change the value of an existing Integer object. That is, Integer objects are **immutable**. (In fact, wrapper class objects are immutable.)

As of Java 5.0, Java has simplified the wrapping and unwrapping of primitive type values, called the **autoboxing** and **auto-unboxing** of primitive types. For example, consider the following statements:

```
int x;         //Line 3
Integer num;   //Line 4
```

The statement in Line 3 declares the `int` variable `x`; the statement in Line 4 declares `num` to be a reference variable of type `Integer`.

Consider the statement:

```
num = 25;                    //Line 5
```

For the most part, this statement is equivalent to the statement:

```
num = new Integer(25);       //Line 6
```

That is, after the execution of either of these statements, `num` refers to or points to an `Integer` object with value 25. The expression in Line 5 is referred to as *autoboxing* of `int` type.

 NOTE In reality, for the statement in Line 5, if an `Integer` object with value 25 already exists, then `num` would point to that object. On the other hand, if the statement in Line 6 executes, then an `Integer` object with value 25 will be created, even if such an object exists, and `num` would point to that object. In either case, `num` would point to an `Integer` object with value 25.

Now consider the statement:

```
x = num;                     //Line 7
```

This statement is equivalent to the statement:

```
x = num.intValue();          //Line 8
```

After the execution of either the statement in Line 7 or Line 8, the value of `x` is 25. The statement in Line 7 is referred to as *auto-unboxing* of `int` type.

 NOTE Autoboxing and -unboxing of primitive types are features of Java 5.0 and are *not* available in Java versions lower than 5.0.

Next, consider the following statement:

```
x = 2 * num;                 //Line 9
```

This statement first unboxes the value of the object `num`, which is 25, multiplies this value by 2, and then stores the value, which is 50, into `x`. This illustrates that unboxing also occurs in an expression.

To compare the values of two `Integer` objects, you can use the method `compareTo`, described in Table 6-6. If you want to compare the values of two `Integer` objects only for equality, then you can use the method `equals`.

NOTE

Suppose you have the following statements:

```
Integer num1 = 24;
Integer num2 = 35;
```

Now consider the following statements:

```
if (num1.equals(num2))
    System.out.println("The values of the "
                    + "objects num1 and num2 "
                    + "are the same.");
else
    System.out.println("The values of the "
                    + "objects num1 and num2 "
                    + "are not the same.");
```

The expression in the `if` statement determines if the value of the object num1, which is 24, is the same as the value of the object num2, which is 35. Next, consider the following statements:

```
if (num1 == num2)
    System.out.println("Both num1 and num2 "
                    + "point to the same "
                    + "object.");
else
    System.out.println("num1 and num2 "
                    + "do not point to the "
                    + "same object.");
```

It follows that when the operator `==` is used with reference variables of the `Integer` type, it compares whether the objects point to the same object. Therefore, if you want to compare the values of two `Integer` objects, then you should use the method `equals` of the `class` Integer. On the other hand, if you want to determine whether two reference variables of `Integer` type points to the same `Integer` object, then you should use the operator `==`.

The preceding discussion of comparing Integer objects also applies to other wrapper classes' objects.

Autoboxing and –unboxing of primitive types is a new feature of Java and is available in Java 5.0 and higher versions. It automatically boxes and unboxes primitive type values into appropriate objects. For example, as explained above, `int` values can be automatically boxed and unboxed into `Integer` objects. Example 6-4 further illustrates autoboxing and auto-unboxing of `Integer` objects.

EXAMPLE 6-4

```java
//Programm illustrating autoboxing and -unboxing
//of Integer objects.

public class IntegerClassExample
{
    public static void main(String[] args)
    {
        int    x, y;                                    //Line 1

        Integer num1, num2;                             //Line 2

        num1 = 8;       //Autobox 8                     //Line 3
        num2 = 16;      //Autobox 16                    //Line 4

        System.out.println("Line 5: num1 = " + num1
                      + ", num2 = " + num2);            //Line 5

        x = num1 + 4;                                   //Line 6

        System.out.println("Line 7: x = " + x);         //Line 7

        y = num1 + num2;                                //Line 8

        System.out.println("Line 9: y = " + y);         //Line 9

        System.out.println("Line 10: The value of "
                      + "2 * num1 + num2 = "
                      + (2 * num1 + num2));             //Line 10

        System.out.println("Line 11: The value of "
                      + "x * num2 - num1 = "
                      + (x * num2 - num1));             //Line 11

        System.out.println("Line 12: The value of "
                      + "num1 <= num2 is "
                      + (num1 <= num2));                //Line 12

        System.out.println("Line 13: The value of "
                      + "2 * num1 <= x is "
                      + (2 * num1 <= x));               //Line 13

        System.out.println("Line 14: The value of "
                      + "2 * num1 >= num2 is "
                      + (2 * num1 >= num2));            //Line 14
    }
}
```

Sample Run:

```
Line 5: num1 = 8, num2 = 16
Line 7: x = 12
```

```
Line 9: y = 24
Line 10: The value of 2 * num1 + num2 = 32
Line 11: The value of x * num2 - num1 = 184
Line 12: The value of num1 <= num2 is true
Line 13: The value of 2 * num1 <= x is false
Line 14: The value of 2 * num1 >= num2 is true
```

For the most part, the preceding sample run is self-explanatory. Let us look at some of the statements. The statement in Line 3 autoboxes the value 8 into an `Integer` object and stores the address of that object into the reference variable `num1`. The meaning of the statement in Line 4 is similar.

The statement in Line 6 unboxes the value of the object to which `num1` points, adds 4 to that value, and stores the result in `x`. Similarly, the statement in Line 8 unboxes the values of objects pointed to by `num1` and `num2`, adds the values, and stores the result in `y`.

The statement in Line 12 unboxes the values of the objects pointed by `num1` and `num2`, and then compares the values using the relational operator `<=`. (Note that we are not using the operator `==`, so autoboxing occurs here.)

The `class Double` also has methods similar to the methods shown in Table 6-6. The Web site, *www.course.com*, and the CD accompanying this book contain a program that illustrates the autoboxing and –unboxing of `double` values into `Double` objects. The program is named `DoubleClassExample.java`. However, to compare the values, for equality, of the wrapper classes objects, you should use the method `equals`. See the following example.

EXAMPLE 6-5

```java
//Program illustrating how the operator == and the
//method equals works with Double objects.

public class DoubleClassMethodEquals
{
    public static void main(String[] args)
    {
        Double num1, num2;                            //Line 1

        num1 = 2567.58;                               //Line 2
        num2 = 2567.58;                               //Line 3

        System.out.println("Line 4: num1 = " + num1
                       + ", num2 = " + num2);         //Line 4

        System.out.println("Line 5: The value of "
                      + "num1.equals(num2) is "
                      + num1.equals(num2));           //Line 5
```

```
    System.out.println("Line 6: The value of "
                  + "num1 == num2 is "
                  + (num1 == num2));        //Line 6
    }
}
```

Sample Run:

```
Line 4: num1 = 2567.58, num2 = 2567.58
Line 5: The value of num1.equals(num2) is true
Line 6: The value of num1 == num2 is false
```

In the preceding program, the statements in Lines 2 and 3 create two objects, each with the value 2567.58 and make num1 and num2, respectively, point to these objects. The expression num1.equals(num2), in Line 5, compares the values stored in the objects to which num1 and num2 point. Because both objects contain the same value, this expression evaluates to true; see the output of the statement in Line 5. On the other hand, the expression num1 == num2, in Line 6, determines whether num1 and num2 point to the same object.

NOTE   Note that the program in Example 6-5 also illustrates that when you create a Double object using the assignment operator without explicitly using the operator new, the system always creates a different Double object even if one with a given value already exists. For example, see the statements in Lines 2 and 3, and the output of the statement in Line 6.

QUICK REVIEW

1. GUI stands for graphical user interface.
2. Every GUI program requires a window.
3. Various components are added to the content pane of the window and not to the window itself.
4. You must create a layout before you can add a component to the content pane.
5. Pixel stands for picture element. Windows are measured in pixels of height and width.
6. JFrame is a class and the GUI component window can be created as an instance of JFrame.
7. JLabel is used to label other GUI components and to display information to the user.
8. A JTextField can be used for both input and output.
9. A JButton generates an event.
10. An event handler is a Java method that determines the action to be performed as the event happens.
11. When you click a button, an action event is created and sent to another object known as an action listener.

12. An action listener must have a method called `actionPerformed`.

13. A `class` is a collection of data members and methods associated with those data members.

14. OOD starts with a problem statement and tries to identify the classes required by identifying the nouns appearing in the problem statement.

15. Methods of a class are identified with the help of verbs appearing in the problem statement.

16. To wrap values of primitive data types into objects corresponding to each primitive type, Java provides a `class`, called a wrapper class. For example, to wrap an `int` value into an object, the corresponding wrapper `class` is `Integer`. Similarly, to wrap a `double` value into an object, the corresponding wrapper `class` is `Double`.

17. Java 5.0 simplifies the wrapping and unwrapping of primitive type values, called the autoboxing and auto-unboxing of primitive data types.

18. `Integer` objects are immutable. (In fact, wrapper classes' objects are immutable.)

19. To compare the values of two `Integer` objects, you can use the method `compareTo`. If you want to compare the values of two `Integer` objects only for equality, then you can use the method `equals`.

EXERCISES

1. Mark the following statements as true or false.

   a. Every window has a width and height.

   b. In Java, `JFrame` is a class.

   c. To display the window, you need not invoke a method such as `setVisible`.

   d. In Java, the reserved word `extends` allows you to create a new class from an existing one.

   e. The window you see displayed on your screen is a class.

   f. Labels are used to display the output of a program.

   g. Every GUI component you need has to be created and added to a container.

   h. In Java, `implements` is a keyword.

   i. Clicking a button is an example of an action event.

   j. In a problem statement, every verb is a possible class.

   k. In a problem statement, every noun is a possible method.

   l. To use an object, you must know how it is implemented.

2. Name some commonly used GUI components and their uses.

3. Name a GUI component that can be used for both input and output.

4. Name two input GUI components.

5. Why do you need labels in a GUI program?

6. Why would you prefer a GUI program over a non-GUI version?

7. What are the advantages of problem analysis, GUI design, and algorithm design over directly writing a program?

8. Modify the temperature conversion program to convert centimeters to inches, and vice versa.

9. Modify the program to compute the area and perimeter of a rectangle so that your new program will compute the sum and product of two numbers.

10. Fill in the blanks in each of the following:

    a. A(n) _____ places GUI components in a container.

    b. Clicking a button is a(n)_____.

    c. The method _____ is invoked when a button is pressed and a(n) _____ is registered to handle the event.

    d. _____operator is needed to instantiate an object.

    e. A class has two types of members: _____ and _____.

    f. To create a window, you extend the _____class.

    g. Every GUI program is a(n)_____ program.

    h. The method _____ gets the string in the JTextField and the method _____ changes the string displayed in a JTextField.

    i. If Student is a class and you create a new **class** GradStudent by extending Student, then Student is a(n) _____ and GradStudent is a(n) _____.

    j. Event and event listener classes are contained in the package _____.

    k. The unit of measure of length in a window is _____.

11. Write necessary statements to create the following GUI components:

    a. A JLabel with the text string "Enter the number of courses"

    b. A JButton with the text string "Run"

    c. A JTextField that can display 15 characters

    d. A window with the title "Welcome Home!"

    e. A window with a width of 200 pixels and a height of 400 pixels

    f. A JTextField that displays the string "Apple tree"

12. Correct the syntax errors in the following program and add any additional statements necessary to make the program work:

```java
import javax.jswing.*;

public class ROne extends JFrame
{
    static private final int WIDTH = 400;
    static private final int HEIGHT = 300;

    public RectangleProgramOne()
    {
        setTitle("Welcome");
        setSize(WIDTH,HEIGHT);
        SetVisible(true);
        setDefaultCloseOperation(EXIT_ON_CLOSE);
    }

    public static void main(String args[])
    {
        ROne r1 = r1();
    }
}
```

13. Correct the syntax errors in the following program:

```java
public class RTwo extends JFrame
{
    public RTwoProgram()
    {
        private JLabel length, width, area;

        setTitle("Good day Area");

        length =   JLabel("Enter the length);
        width = JLabel("Enter the width);
        area = JLabel("Area: ");
        containerPane   = ContentPane();
        pane.setLayout(GridLayout(4,1));
        setSize(WIDTH,HEIGHT);
        setVisible();
        setDefaultCloseOperation(EXIT_ON_CLOSE);
    }

    public static void main(String args[])
    {
        RTwoProgram R2 = new RTwoProgram();
    }
}
```

14. Consider a common VCR. What are the methods of a VCR?

15. What are the methods of an ATM?

16. Do an OOD analysis of the following problem: Write a program to input the dimensions of a cylinder, and calculate and print the surface area and volume.

17. Lead County Credit Union (LCCU) has recently upgraded its software systems to an OOD design. List at least five classes that you think should be included in this design. For each class, identify some of the data members and methods.

18. Your local public library wants to design new software to keep track of patrons, books, and lending activity. List at least three classes you think should be in the design. For each class, identify some data members and methods.

19. The Custom Consulting Company (CCC) places temporary computer professionals in companies that request such employees. CCC's business can be explained as follows:

CCC keeps a list of professionals willing to work or currently working on a temporary assignment. A professional may have up to three qualifications, including programmer, senior programmer, analyst, tester, designer, and so on. A company always requests a professional with a single specific qualification. CCC keeps a list of all its clients (that is, a list of other companies) and their current needs. If CCC can find a match, a professional with the required qualification is assigned to a specific opening at one of CCC's clients.

Identify at least five classes and, for each class, list possible data members and methods.

PROGRAMMING EXERCISES

1. Design a GUI program to find the weighted average of four test scores. The four test scores and their respective weights are given in the following format:

```
testscore1 weight1
...
```

For example, the sample data is as follows:

```
75 0.20
95 0.35
85 0.15
65 0.30
```

The user is supposed to enter the data and press a Calculate button. The program must display the weighted average.

2. Write a GUI program that converts seconds to years, weeks, days, hours, and minutes. For this problem, assume 1 year is 365 days.

3. Design and implement a GUI program to compare two strings and display the larger one.

4. Write a GUI program to convert a character to a corresponding integer, and vice versa.

5. Write a GUI program to convert all letters in a string to uppercase letters. For example, `Alb34ert` will be converted to `ALB34ERT`.

6. Write a GUI program to convert all lowercase letters in a string to uppercase letters, and vice versa. For example, `Alb34eRt` will be converted to `aLB34ErT`.

7. Write a GUI program to compute the amount of a certificate of deposit on maturity. The sample data follows:

```
Amount deposited: 80000.00
Years: 15
Interest rate: 7.75
```

   Hint: To solve this problem, compute $80000.00 \ (1 + 7.75 \ / \ 100)^{15}$.

8. Write a GUI program that will accept three (integer) input values, say, x, y, and z, and then verify whether or not $x * x + y * y = z * z$.

9. Design and implement a GUI program to convert a positive number given in one base to another base. For this problem, assume that both bases are less than or equal to 10. Consider the sample data:

```
number = 2010, base = 3, and new base = 4.
```

   In this case, first convert 2010 in base 3 into the equivalent number in base 10 as follows:

   $$2 * 3^3 + 0 * 3^2 + 1 * 3 + 0 = 54 + 0 + 3 + 0 = 57$$

   To convert 57 to base 4, you need to find the remainders obtained by dividing by 4, as shown in the following:

```
57 % 4 = 1, quotient = 14
14 % 4 = 2, quotient = 3
3 % 4 = 3, quotient = 0.
```

   Therefore, 57 in base 4 is 321.

USER-DEFINED METHODS

IN THIS CHAPTER, YOU WILL:

- Understand how methods are used in Java programming
- Explore predefined methods and how to use them in a program
- Learn about user-defined methods
- Examine value-returning methods
- Understand actual and formal parameters
- Explore how to construct and use a value-returning, user-defined method in a program
- Learn how to construct and use user-defined void methods in a program
- Explore variables as parameters
- Learn about the scope of an identifier
- Become acquainted with method overloading
- Learn how to avoid bugs by doing one-piece-at-a-time coding
- Learn how to avoid bugs by using "stubs" as appropriate

In Chapter 2, you learned that a Java application program is a collection of classes, and that a class is a collection of methods and data members. One such method is `main`. The programs in Chapters 2 through 5 use only the method `main`; all the programming instructions are packed into one method. This technique, however, is appropriate only for short programs. For large programs, it is not practical (although it is possible) to put the entire programming instructions into one method, as you will soon discover. You must learn to break the problem into manageable pieces. This chapter first discusses previously defined methods and then user-defined methods.

Let's imagine an automobile factory. When an automobile is manufactured, it is not made from basic raw materials; it is put together from previously manufactured parts. Some parts are made by the company itself, others are manufactured by different companies at different locations.

Methods in Java are like automobile parts; they are building blocks. Methods are used to divide complicated programs into manageable pieces. There are both **predefined methods**, methods that are already written and provided by Java, and **user-defined methods**, methods that you create.

Using methods has several advantages:

- While working on one method, you can focus on just that part of the program and construct it, debug it, and perfect it.
- Different people can work on different methods simultaneously.
- If a method is needed in more than one place in a program, or in different programs, you can write it once and use it many times.
- Using methods greatly enhances the program's readability because it reduces the complexity of the method `main`.

Methods are often called *modules*. They are like miniature programs; you can put them together to form a larger program. When user-defined methods are discussed, you will see that this is the case. This ability is less apparent with predefined methods because their programming code is not available to us. However, because predefined methods are already written, you will learn these first so that you can use them when needed. To include a predefined method in your program(s), you only need to know how to use it.

Predefined Methods

Before formally discussing Java's predefined methods, let's review a concept from college algebra. In algebra, a function can be considered a rule or correspondence between values—called the function's arguments—and the unique value of the function associated with the arguments. Thus, if $f(x) = 2x + 5$, then $f(1) = 7$, $f(2) = 9$, and $f(3) = 11$, where 1, 2, and 3 are arguments of f, and 7, 9, and 11 are the corresponding values of the function f.

In Java, the concept of a method, whether predefined or user-defined, is similar to that of a function in algebra. For example, every method has a name and, depending on the values specified by the user, it does some computation. This section discusses various predefined methods.

Some of the predefined mathematical methods are `pow(x, y)` and `sqrt(x)`.

The *power* method, `pow(x, y)`, calculates x^y; that is, the value of `pow(x, y)` is x^y.

For example, `pow(2, 3)` is `8.0` and `pow(2.5, 3)` is `15.625`. Because the value of `pow(x, y)` is of type `double`, we say that the method `pow` is of type `double` or that the method `pow` returns a value of type `double`. Also, `x` and `y` are called the **parameters** (or **arguments**) of the method `pow`. The method `pow` has two parameters.

The *square root* method, `sqrt(x)`, calculates the nonnegative square root of `x` for `x >= 0.0`. For example, `sqrt(2.25)` is `1.5`. The method `sqrt` is of type `double` and has only one parameter.

In Java, predefined methods are organized as a collection of classes, called **class libraries**. For example, the `class` Math contains mathematical methods. Table 7-1 lists some of Java's predefined mathematical methods. The table gives the name of the method (in bold type), number of parameters, the data type of the parameters, and the method type. The **method type** is the data type of the value returned by the method. The table also shows how a method works. The `class` Math is contained in the package `java.lang`.

TABLE 7-1 Some Predefined Mathematical Methods and Named Constants

class Math (**Package:** java.lang)	
Named Constants	
double E;	E = 2.7182818284590455
double PI;	PI = 3.141592653589793
Methods	
Expression	**Description**
abs(x)	Returns the absolute value of **x**. If **x** is of type int, it returns a value of type int; if **x** is of type long, it returns a value of type long; if **x** is of type float, it returns a value of type float; if **x** is of type double, it returns a value of type double. **Example:** abs(-67) returns the value 67 abs(35) returns the value 35 abs(-75.38) returns the value 75.38

7

TABLE 7-1 Some Predefined Mathematical Methods and Named Constants (continued)

class Math (**Package:** java.lang)	
ceil(x)	x is of type double. Returns a value of type double, which is the smallest integer value that is not less than x. **Example:** ceil(56.34) returns the value 57.0
exp(x)	x is of type double. Returns e^x, where e is approximately 2.7182818284590455. **Example:** exp(3) returns the value 20.085536923187668
floor(x)	x is of type double. Returns a value of type double, which is the largest integer value less than x. **Example:** floor(65.78) returns the value 65.0
log(x)	x is of type double. Returns a value of type double, which is the natural logarithm (base e) of x. **Example:** log(2) returns the value 0.6931471805599453
log10(x)	x is of type double. Returns a value of type double, which is the common logarithm (base 10) of x. **Example:** log10(2) returns the value 0.3010299956639812
max(x, y)	Returns the larger of x and y. If x and y are of type int, it returns a value of type int; if x and y are of type long, it returns a value of type long; if x and y are of type float, it returns a value of type float; if x and y are of type double, it returns a value of type double. **Example:** max(15, 25) returns the value 25 max(23.67, 14.28) returns the value 23.67 max(45, 23.78) returns the value 45.00
min(x, y)	Returns the smaller of x and y. If x and y are of type int, it returns a value of type int; if x and y are of type long, it returns a value of type long; if x and y are of type float, it returns a value of type float; if x and y are of type double, it returns a value of type double. **Example:** min(15, 25) returns the value 15 min(23.67, 14.28) returns the value 14.28 min(12, 34.78) returns the value 12.00
pow(x, y)	x and y are of type double. Returns a value of type double, which is x^y. **Example:** pow(2.0, 3.0) returns the value 8.0 pow(4, 0.5) returns the value 2.0
round(x)	Returns a value which is the integer closest to x. **Example:** round(24.56) returns the value 25 round(18.35) returns the value 18

TABLE 7-1 Some Predefined Mathematical Methods and Named Constants (continued)

class Math (**Package:** java.lang)	
sqrt(x)	x is of type double. Returns a value of type double, which is the square root of **x**. **Example:** sqrt(4.0) returns the value 2.0 sqrt(2.25) returns the value 1.5
cos(x)	x is of type double. Returns the cosine of x measured in radians. **Example:** cos(0) returns the value 1.0 cos(PI / 3) returns the value 0.5000000000000001
sin(x)	x is of type double. Returns the sine of **x** measured in radians. **Example:** sin(0) returns the value 0.0 sin(PI / 2) returns the value 1.0
tan(x)	x is of type double. Returns the tangent of **x** measured in radians. **Example:** tan(0) returns the value 0.0

NOTE The method log10 is not available in Java versions lower than 5.0.

Java also provides methods, contained in the **class** Character, to manipulate characters. Table 7-2 describes some of the methods of the **class** Character contained in the package java.lang. As in Table 7-1, Table 7-2 shows the name of the method in bold and gives examples of how the methods work.

TABLE 7-2 Some Predefined Methods for Character Manipulation

class Character (**Package:** java.lang)	
Expression	**Description**
isDigit(ch)	ch is of type char. Returns true, if ch is a digit; false otherwise. **Example:** isDigit('8') returns the value true isDigit('*') returns the value false
isLetter(ch)	ch is of type char. Returns true, if ch is a letter; false otherwise. **Example:** isLetter('a') returns the value true isLetter('*') returns the value false

7

TABLE 7-2 Some Predefined Methods for Character Manipulation (continued)

class Character (Package: java.lang)	
Expression	**Description**
isLowerCase(ch)	ch is of type char. Returns true, if ch is a lowercase letter; false otherwise. **Example:** isLowerCase('a') returns the value true isLowerCase('A') returns the value false
isUpperCase(ch)	ch is of type char. Returns true, if ch is an uppercase letter; false otherwise. **Example:** isUpperCase('B') returns the value true isUpperCase('k') returns the value false
toLowerCase(ch)	ch is of type char. Returns the character that is the lowercase equivalent of ch. If ch does not have the corresponding lowercase letter, it returns ch. **Example:** toLowerCase('D') returns the value d toLowerCase('*') returns the value *
toUpperCase(ch)	ch is of type char. Returns the character that is the uppercase equivalent of ch. If ch does not have the corresponding uppercase letter, it returns ch. **Example:** toUpperCase('j') returns the value J toUpperCase('8') returns the value 8

Using Predefined Methods in a Program

In general, to use the predefined methods of a class in a program, you must import the class from the package containing the class. For example, to use the method nextInt of the class Scanner contained in the package java.util, we imported this class from the package java.util. However, as stated in Chapter 2, if a class is contained in the package java.lang and you want to use a (public) method of this class, Java does not require you to include an explicit import statement to import that class. For example, to use any (public) method of the class String contained in the package java.lang in a program, we do not need an import statement. By default, Java automatically imports classes from the package java.lang.

A method of a class may contain the reserved word static (in its heading). For example, the method main contains the reserved word static in its heading. If (the heading of) a method contains the reserved word static, it is called a static method; otherwise, it is called a **nonstatic** method. Similarly, the heading of a method may contain the reserved word `public`. In this case, it is called a `public` method. An important property of a `public` and `static` method is that (in a program) it can be used (called) using the name of the class, the dot operator, the method name, and the appropriate parameters. For example, all the methods of the `class Math` are `public` and `static`. Therefore, the general syntax to use a method of the `class Math` is:

```
Math.methodName(parameters)
```

(Note that, in fact, the parameters used in a method call are called actual parameters.) For example, the following expression determines $2.5^{3.5}$:

```
Math.pow(2.5, 3.5)
```

(In the previous statement, `2.5` and `3.5` are actual parameters.) Similarly, if a method of the `class Character` is `public` and `static`, you can use the name of the `class`, which is `Character`, the dot operator, the method name, and the appropriate parameters. The methods of the `class Character` listed in Table 7-2 are `public` and `static`.

To simplify the use of (`public`) `static` methods of a class, Java 5.0 introduces the following import statements:

```
import static pakageName.ClassName.*;  //to use any (public)
                                       //static method of the class

import static packageName.ClassName.methodName;  //to use a
                                       //specific method of the class
```

These are called `static import` **statements**. After including such statements in your program, when you use a (`public`) `static` method (or any other `public static` member) of a `class`, you can omit the name of the class and the dot operator.

For example, after including the `import` statement:

```
import static java.lang.Math.*;
```

you can determine $2.5^{3.5}$ by using the expression:

```
pow(2.5, 3.5)
```

NOTE After including the `static import` statement, in reality, you have a choice. When you use a (`public`) `static` method of a `class`, you can either use the name of the class and the dot operator or omit them. For example, after including the `static import` statement:

```
import static java.lang.Math.*;
```

in a program, you can determine $2.5^{3.5}$ by using either the expression `Math.pow(2.5, 3.5)` or the expression `pow(2.5, 3.5)`.

The `static import` statement is *not* available in versions of Java lower than 5.0. Therefore, if you are using, say, Java 4.0, then you must use a `static` method of the `class Math` using the name of the class and the dot operator.

NOTE Suppose that there are two classes Test1 and Test2. Both classes contain the static method printAll, and you want to use these classes in a program. To correctly use the method printAll, you should call this method using the name of the class and the dot operators.

The (public) static methods of the class Character have similar conventions. Example 7-1 illustrates how to use predefined methods.

EXAMPLE 7-1

This example shows you how to use some of the predefined methods:

```
//How to use the predefined methods

import static java.lang.Math.*;
import static java.lang.Character.*;

public class PredefinedMethods
{
    public static void main(String[] args)
    {
        int     x;
        double u;
        double v;

        System.out.println("Line 1: Uppercase a is "
                            + toUpperCase('a'));          //Line 1

        u = 4.2;                                          //Line 2
        v = 3.0;                                          //Line 3

        System.out.printf("Line 4: %.1f to the power "
                    + "of %.1f = %.2f%n",
                       u, v, pow(u, v));                  //Line 4

        System.out.printf("Line 5: 5 to the power of "
                        + "4 = %.2f%n", pow(5, 4));       //Line 5

        u = u + Math.pow(3, 3);                           //Line 6
        System.out.printf("Line 7: u = %.2f%n", u);       //Line 7

        x = -15;                                          //Line 8
        System.out.printf("Line 9: The absolute value "
                          + "of %d = %d%n", x, abs(x));   //Line 9
    }
}
```

Sample Run:

```
Line 1: Uppercase a is A
Line 4: 4.2 to the power of 3.0 = 74.09
Line 5: 5 to the power of 4 = 625.00
Line 7: u = 31.20
Line 9: The absolute value of -15 = 15
```

This program works as follows: The statement in Line 1 outputs the uppercase letter that corresponds to `'a'`, which is `'A'`. In the statement in Line 4, the method `pow` (of the `class` Math) is used to output u^v. In Java terminology, it is said that the method `pow` is called with the (actual) parameters u and v. In this case, the values of u and v are passed to the method `pow`. The statement in Line 5 uses the method `pow` to output 5^4. The statement in Line 6 uses the method `pow` to determine 3^3, adds this value to the value of u, and then stores the new value into u. Notice that in this statement, the method `pow` is called using the name of the `class`, which is Math, and the dot operator. The statement in Line 7 outputs the value of u. The statement in Line 8 stores −15 into x, and the statement in Line 9 outputs the absolute value of x.

 NOTE The Web site, *www.course.com*, and the CD accompanying this book contain additional programming examples that show how to use some of the other methods of the `class`es Math and Character.

7

User-Defined Methods

Because Java does not provide every method that you will ever need, and designers cannot possibly know a user's specific needs, you must learn to write your own methods.

User-defined methods in Java are classified into two categories:

- **Value-returning methods**—methods that have a return data type. These methods return a value of a specific data type using the `return` statement, which we will explain shortly.

- **Void methods**—methods that do not have a return data type. These methods *do not* use a `return` statement to return a value.

The next section discusses value-returning methods. Many concepts regarding value-returning methods also apply to void methods. Void methods are discussed later in this chapter.

Value-Returning Methods

The previous section introduced some predefined Java methods, such as `pow`, `sqrt`, `isLowerCase`, and `toUpperCase`. These are examples of value-returning methods, that is, methods that calculate and return a value. To use these methods in your programs, you must know the following properties:

1. The name of the method
2. The number of **parameters**, if any
3. The data type of each parameter
4. The data type of the value computed (that is, the value returned) by the method, called the type of the method

Typically, the value returned by a value-returning method is unique. So it is natural for you to use the value in one of three ways:

- Save the value for further calculation.
- Use the value in some calculation.
- Print the value.

This suggests that a value-returning method is used in either an assignment statement or an output statement. That is, a value-returning method is used in an expression.

In addition to the four properties just described, one more thing is associated with methods (both value-returning and void):

5. The code required to accomplish the task

Before we look at the syntax of a user-defined value-returning method, let's review the points associated with such methods. The first four properties become part of what is called the **heading** of the method; the fifth property (the code) is called the **body** of the method. Together, these five properties form what is called the **definition** of the method.

 NOTE For predefined methods, you only need to be concerned with the first four properties. Software companies typically do not give out the actual source code, which is the body of the method.

For example, for the method `abs` (*absolute*), the heading might look like:

```
public static int abs(int number)
```

Similarly, the method `abs` might have the following definition:

```
public static int abs(int number)
{
    if (number < 0)
        number = -number;

    return number;
}
```

The variable declared in the heading, within the parentheses, of the method `abs` is called the **formal parameter** of the method `abs`. Thus, the formal parameter of `abs` is `number`.

The program in Example 7-1 contains several statements that use the method `pow`. In Java terminology, we say that the method `pow` is *called* several times. Later in this chapter, we discuss what happens when a method is called.

Suppose that the heading of the method `pow` is:

```
public static double pow(double base, double exponent)
```

In this heading, you can see that the formal parameters of `pow` are `base` and `exponent`. Consider the following statements:

```
double u = 2.5;
double v = 3.0;
double x, y, w;

x = pow(u, v);          //Line 1
y = pow(2.0, 3.2);      //Line 2
w = pow(u, 7);          //Line 3
```

In Line 1, the method `pow` is called with the parameters u and v. In this case, the values of u and v are passed to the method `pow`. In fact, the value of u is copied into `base` and the value of v is copied into `exponent`. The variables u and v that appear in the call to the method `pow` in Line 1 are called **actual parameters** of that call. In Line 2, the method `pow` is called with the parameters 2.0 and 3.2. In this call, the value 2.0 is copied into `base` and 3.2 is copied into `exponent`. In this call to the method `pow`, the actual parameters are 2.0 and 3.2, respectively. Similarly, in Line 3, the actual parameters of the method `pow` are u and 7. The value of u is copied into `base`, and 7.0 is copied into `exponent`.

We now present the following two definitions:

Formal parameter: A variable declared in the method heading.

Actual parameter: A variable or expression listed in a call to a method.

SYNTAX: VALUE-RETURNING METHOD

The syntax of a value-returning method is:

```
modifier(s) returnType methodName(formal parameter list)
{
    statements
}
```

In this syntax:

- **`modifier(s)`** indicates the visibility of the method, that is, where in a program the method can be used (called). Some of the modifiers are `public`, `private`, `protected`, `static`, `abstract`, and `final`. If you include more than one modifier, they must be separated with spaces. You can select one modifier among `public`, `protected`, and `private`. The modifier `public` specifies that the method can be called outside the class; the modifier `private` specifies that the method cannot be used outside the class. Similarly, you can choose one of the modifiers `static` or `abstract`. More information about these modifiers is provided in Chapter 8. Meanwhile, we will use the modifiers `public` and/or `static`, as used in the method `main`.

- **returnType** is the type of value that the method returns. This type is also called the type of the value-returning method.
- **methodName** is a Java identifier, giving a name to the method.
- Statements enclosed between braces form the body of the method.

In Java, `public`, `protected`, `private`, `static`, and `abstract` are reserved words.

 NOTE Abstract methods are covered in Chapter 10. Chapter 8 describes, in detail, the meaning of the modifiers `public`, `private`, and `static`.

SYNTAX: FORMAL PARAMETER LIST

The syntax of a formal parameter list is:

```
dataType identifier, dataType identifier,....
```

METHOD CALL

The syntax to call a value-returning method is:

```
methodName(actual parameter list)
```

SYNTAX: ACTUAL PARAMETER LIST

The syntax of an actual parameter list is:

```
expression or variable, expression or variable, ...
```

Thus, to call a value-returning method, you use its name, with the actual parameters (if any) in parentheses.

A method's formal parameter list can be empty, but the parentheses are still needed. If the formal parameter list is empty, the method heading of the value-returning method takes the following form:

```
modifier(s) returnType methodName()
```

If the formal parameter list is empty, in a method call, the actual parameter list is also empty. In the case of an empty formal parameter list, in a method call, the empty parentheses are still needed. Thus, a call to a value-returning method with an empty formal parameter list is:

```
methodName ()
```

In a method call, the number of actual parameters, together with their data types, must match the formal parameters in the order given. That is, actual and formal parameters have a one-to-one correspondence.

As stated previously, a value-returning method is called in an expression. The expression can be part of an assignment statement, or an output statement, or a parameter in a method call. A method call in a program causes the body of the called method to execute.

 NOTE   Recall that the heading of the method `main` contains the modifier `static`. The main objective of this chapter is to learn how to write your own methods and use them in a Java application program. Therefore, the methods that you will learn to write in this chapter will be called (used) within the method `main` and/or in other methods of the `class` containing the application program. Because a `static` method cannot call another nonstatic method of the `class`, the heading of the methods that you will learn to write in this chapter will contain the modifier `static`. Chapter 8 discusses the `static` methods (members) of a `class` in detail.

Next, we describe how a value-returning method returns its value.

`return` Statement

A value-returning method uses a `return`(s) statement to return its value; that is, it passes a value back when the method completes its task.

SYNTAX: `return` STATEMENT

The `return` statement has the following syntax:

```
return expr;
```

where **expr** is a variable, constant value, or expression. The **expr** is evaluated and its value is returned. The data type of the value that **expr** computes should be compatible with the return type of the method.

In Java, `return` is a reserved word.

When a `return` statement executes in a method, the method immediately terminates and the control goes back to the caller.

To put the ideas of this section to work, we'll write a method that determines the larger of two numbers. Because the method compares two numbers, it follows that this method has two parameters and that both parameters are numbers. Assume that the data type of these numbers is a floating-point number—say, `double`. Because the larger number is of type `double`, the method's data type is also `double`. Let's name this method `larger`. The only thing you need to complete this method is the body of the method. Thus, following the syntax of a method, you can write this method as follows:

```
public static double larger(double x, double y)
{
    double max;

    if (x >= y)
        max = x;
    else
        max = y;

    return max;
}
```

Note that the method `larger` requires that you use an additional variable `max` (called a **local declaration**, where `max` is a variable local to the method `larger`); the second form does not. Figure 7-1 describes the various parts of the method `larger`.

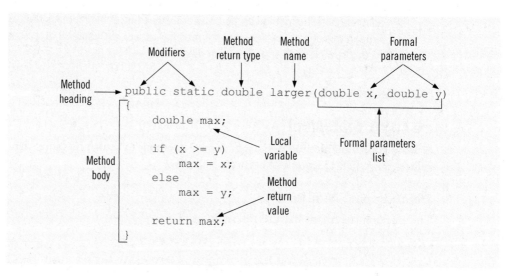

FIGURE 7-1 Various parts of the method `larger`

Suppose that `num`, `num1`, and `num2` are `int` variables. Also suppose that `num1 = 45.75` and `num2 = 35.50`. Figure 7-2 shows various calls to the method `larger`.

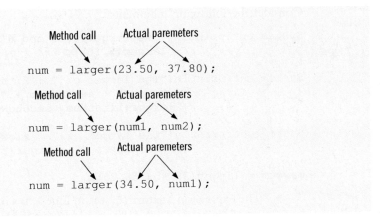

FIGURE 7-2 Method calls

Note that you can write the method `larger` as follows:

```java
public static double larger(double x, double y)
{
    if (x >= y)
        return x;
    else
        return y;
}
```

Because the execution of a `return` statement in a method terminates the method, the preceding definition of the method `larger` can also be written (without the word `else`) as:

```java
public static double larger(double x, double y)
{
    if (x >= y)
        return x;

    return y;
}
```

NOTE   The `return` statement can appear anywhere in the method. Recall that once a `return` statement executes, all subsequent statements are skipped. Thus, it's a good idea to return the value as soon as it is computed.

Example 7-2 further shows how to use the method `larger`.

EXAMPLE 7-2

Now that the method `larger` is written, the following Java code further illustrates how to use it.

```java
double firstNum = 13;
double secondNum = 36;
double maxNum;
```

Consider the following statements:

```
System.out.println("The larger of 5 and 6 is "
                + larger(5, 6));                              //Line 1

System.out.println("The larger of " + firstNum
              +  " and " + secondNum + " is "
              + larger(firstNum, secondNum));                 //Line 2

System.out.println("The larger of " + firstNum
             + " and 29 is " + larger(firstNum, 29));  //Line 3

maxNum = larger(38.45, 56.78);                               //Line 4
```

- The expression larger(5, 6), in Line 1, is a method call, and 5 and 6 are actual parameters. This statement outputs the larger of 5 and 6, which is 6.

- The expression larger(firstNum, secondNum), in Line 2, is a method call. Here, firstNum and secondNum are actual parameters. This statement outputs the larger of firstNum and secondNum, which is 36.

- The expression larger(firstNum, 29), in Line 3, is also a method call. Here, firstNum and 29 are actual parameters.

- The expression larger(38.45, 56.78), in Line 4, is a method call. In this call, the actual parameters are 38.45 and 56.78. In this statement, the value returned by the method larger is assigned to the variable maxNum.

NOTE   In a method call, you specify only the actual parameter, not its data type. For example, in Example 7-2, the statements in Lines 1, 2, 3, and 4 show how to call the method larger with the actual parameters. However, the following statements contain incorrect calls to the method larger and would result in syntax errors. (Assume that all variables are properly declared.)

```
x = larger(int one, 29);                      //illegal
y = larger(int one, int 29);                  //illegal
System.out.println(larger(int one, int two));     //illegal
```

Final Program

You now know enough to write the entire program, compile it, and run it. The following program uses the method larger and main to determine the larger of two numbers:

```
//Program: Larger of two numbers

import java.util.*;

public class LargerNumber
{
    static Scanner console = new Scanner(System.in);

    public static void main(String[] args)
```

```
    {
        double num1;                                      //Line 1
        double num2;                                      //Line 2

        System.out.println("Line 3: The larger of "
                        + "5.6 and 10.8 is "
                        + larger(5.6, 10.8));             //Line 3

        System.out.print("Line 4: Enter two "
                        + "numbers: ");                  //Line 4
        num1 = console.nextDouble();                     //Line 5
        num2 = console.nextDouble();                     //Line 6
        System.out.println();                            //Line 7

        System.out.println("Line 8: The larger of "
                        + num1 + " and " + num2 + " is "
                        + larger(num1, num2));           //Line 8
    }

    public static double larger(double x, double y)
    {
        double max;

        if (x >= y)
            max = x;
        else
            max = y;

        return max;
    }
}
```

Sample Run: In this sample run, the user input is shaded.

```
Line 3: The larger of 5.6 and 10.8 is 10.8
Line 4: Enter two numbers: 34 43

Line 8: The larger of 34.0 and 43.0 is 43.0
```

NOTE You can put methods within a class in any order.

NOTE A value-returning method must return a value. Consider the following method, `secret`, which takes as a parameter an `int` value. If the value of the parameter, `x`, is greater than 5, it should return twice the value of `x`; otherwise, it should return the value of `x`.

```
public static int secret(int x)
{
    if (x > 5)                 //Line 1
        return 2 * x;          //Line 2
}
```

Because this is a value-returning method of type `int`, it must return a value of type `int`. Suppose the value of **x** is 10. Then, the expression, **x** > 5, in Line 1, evaluates to `true`. So the `return` statement in Line 2 returns the value 20. Now suppose that **x** is 3. The expression, **x** > 5, in Line 1, now evaluates to `false`. The `if` statement therefore fails and the `return` statement in Line 2 *does not* execute. However, the body of the method has no more statements to be executed. It thus follows that if the value of **x** is less than or equal to 5, the method does not contain any valid `return` statements to return the value of **x**. In this case, in fact, the compiler generates an error message such as `missing return statement`.

The correct definition of the method `secret` is:

```
public static int secret(int x)
{
    if (x > 5)                  //Line 1
        return 2 * x;           //Line 2

    return x;                   //Line 3
}
```

Here, if the value of **x** is less than or equal to 5, the `return` statement in Line 3 executes, which returns the value of **x**. On the other hand, if the value of **x** is, say, 10, the `return` statement in Line 2 executes, which returns the value 20 and also terminates the method.

NOTE (`return` statement: A precaution) If the compiler can determine that during execution certain statements in a program can never be reached, then it will generate syntax errors. For example, consider the following methods:

```
public static int funcReturnStatementError(int z)
{
    return z;

    System.out.println(z);
}
```

The first statement in the method `funcReturnStatementError` is the `return` statement. Therefore, if this method executes, then the output statement, `System.out.println(z);`, will never be executed. In this case, when the compiler compiles this method, it will generate two syntax errors, one specifying that the statement `System.out.println(z);` is unreachable, and the second specifying that there is a missing `return` statement after the output statement. Even if you include a `return` statement after the output statement, the compiler will still generate the error that the statement `System.out.println(z);` is unreachable. Therefore, you should be careful when writing the definition of a method. The Web site, *www.course.com*, and the CD accompanying this book contain additional methods illustrating such errors. The name of the program is `TestReturnStatement.java`.

The following is an example of a method that returns a boolean value.

EXAMPLE 7-3 ROLLING A PAIR OF DICE

In this example, we write a method that rolls a pair of dice until the sum of the numbers rolled is a specific number. We also want to know the number of times the dice are rolled to get the desired sum.

The smallest number on each die is 1 and the largest number is 6. So the smallest sum of the numbers rolled is 2 and the largest sum of the numbers rolled is 12. Suppose that we have the following declarations:

```
int die1;
int die2;
int sum;
int rollCount = 0;
```

We use the random number generator, discussed in Chapter 5, to randomly generate a number between 1 and 6. Then the following statement randomly generates a number between 1 and 6 and stores that number into `die1`, which becomes the number rolled by `die1`.

```
die1 = (int) (Math.random() * 6) + 1;
```

Similarly, the following statement randomly generates a number between 1 and 6 and stores that number into `die2`, which becomes the number rolled by `die2`.

```
die2 = (int) (Math.random() * 6) + 1;
```

The sum of the numbers rolled by two dice is

```
sum = die1 + die2;
```

Next, we determine whether `sum` contains the desired sum of the numbers rolled by the dice. If `sum` does not contain the desired sum, then we roll the dice again. This can be accomplished by the following `do...while` loop. (Assume that the `int` variable `num` contains the desired sum to be rolled.)

```
do
{
    die1 = (int) (Math.random() * 6) + 1;
    die2 = (int) (Math.random() * 6) + 1;
    sum = die1 + die2;
    rollCount++;
}
while (sum == num);
```

We can now write the method `rollDice` that takes as a parameter the desired sum of the numbers to be rolled and returns the number of times the dice are rolled to roll the desired sum.

```
public static int rollDice(int num)
{
    int die1;
    int die2;
    int sum;
    int rollCount = 0;
```

```
    do
    {
        die1 = (int) (Math.random() * 6) + 1;
        die2 = (int) (Math.random() * 6) + 1;
        sum = die1 + die2;
        rollCount++;
    }
    while (sum == num);

    return rollCount;
}
```

The following program shows how to use the method `rollDice` in a program.

```
//Program: Roll dice

public class RollDice
{
    public static void main(String[] args)
    {
        System.out.println("The number of times the dice are "
                + "rolled to get the sum 10 = " + rollDice(10));
        System.out.println("The number of times the dice are "
                + "rolled to get the sum 6 = " + rollDice(6));
    }

    public static int rollDice(int num)
    {
        int die1;
        int die2;
        int sum;
        int rollCount = 0;

        do
        {
            die1 = (int) (Math.random() * 6) + 1;
            die2 = (int) (Math.random() * 6) + 1;
            sum = die1 + die2;
            rollCount++;
        }
        while (sum != num);

        return rollCount;
    }
}
```

Sample Run:

```
The number of times the dice are rolled to get the sum 10 = 91
The number of times the dice are rolled to get the sum 6 = 7
```

We leave it as an exercise for you to modify this program so that it allows the user to enter the desired sum of the numbers to be rolled. (See Programming Exercise 5 at the end of this chapter.)

The following is an example of a method that returns a boolean value.

EXAMPLE 7-4

In this example, we write a method that determines whether a string is a palindrome. A string is a **palindrome** if it reads the same forward and backward. For example, the strings `"madam"` and `"789656987"` are both palindromes.

The method `isPalindrome` takes a string as a parameter and returns `true` if the string is a palindrome, `false` otherwise. Suppose that the `String` variable `str` refers to the string. To be specific, suppose that `str` refers to the string `"845548"`. The length of this string is 6. Recall that the position of the first character of a string is 0, the position of the second character is 1, and so on.

To determine whether the string `str` `"madam"` is a palindrome, first we compare the character at position 0 with the character at position 4. If these two characters are the same, then we compare the character at position 1 with the character at position 3; if these two characters are the same, then we compare the characters at position 2 and 2. If we find mismatched characters, the string `str` is not a palindrome, and the method returns `false`. It follows that we need two variables, `i` and `j`; `i` is initialized to 0 and `j` is initialized to the position of the last character of the string. We then compare the characters at positions `i` and `j`. If the characters at positions `i` and `j` are the same, we then increment `i` and decrement `j`, and continue this process. If the characters at positions `i` and `j` are not the same, then the method returns `false`. Note that we only need to compare the characters in the first half of the string with the characters in the second half of the string in the order described above. This discussion translates into the following algorithm:

1. Find the length of the string. Because `str` is a `String` variable, we can use the method `length` of the `class` `String` to find the length of the string. Suppose `len = str.length();`.

2. Set `j = len - 1`. (Recall that in a string, the position of the first character is 0, the position of the second character is 1, and so on. Therefore, the position of the last character in the string `str` is `len - 1`.)

3. Use a `for` loop to compare the characters in the first half of the string with those in the second half. Now `len` specifies the length of the string, so `len - 1` specifies the position of the last character in the string. Therefore, `(len - 1) / 2` gives the position of the character immediately in front of the midposition in the string. Initially, `j` is set to `len - 1` and we will use a variable, `i` (`for` loop control variable), initialized to 0. After each iteration, `i` is incremented by 1 and `j` is decremented by 1. Therefore, when `i` is `(len - 1) / 2`, the value of `i` gives the position of the character immediately in front of the midposition in the string. When `i` is at the last character of the first half of the string, `j` is at the first character of the second half of the string. The required `for` loop is:

7

```
for (i = 0; i <= (len - 1)/2; i++)
{
 a. if (str.charAt(i) is not equal to str.charAt(j))
        return false;
 b. j--;
}
```

4. Return true.

The following method implements this algorithm:

```
public static boolean isPalindrome(String str)
{
    int len = str.length();                    //Step 1
    int i, j;

    j = len - 1;                               //Step 2

    for (i = 0; i <= (len - 1)/2; i++)         //Step 3
    {
        if (str.charAt(i) !=  str.charAt(j))   //Step 3.a
            return false;
        j--;                                   //Step 3.b
    }

    return true;                               //Step 4
}
```

We leave it as an exercise for you to write a program to test the method isPalindrome. (See Programming Exercise 6 at the end of this chapter.)

Flow of Execution

As you know, a Java application program is a collection of classes, and a class is a collection of methods and data members. In a Java program, methods can appear in any order. However, when a (class containing the main) program executes, the first statement in the method main (of that class) always executes first, regardless of where in the program the method main is placed. Other methods execute only when they are called.

A method call statement transfers control to the first statement in the body of the method. In general, after the last statement of the called method executes, control is passed back to the point immediately following the method call. A value-returning method returns a value. *Therefore, for value-returning methods, after executing the method control goes back to the caller, and the value that the method returns replaces the method call statement.* The execution then continues at the point immediately following the method call.

PROGRAMMING EXAMPLE: Largest Number

In this programming example, the method `larger` is used to determine the largest number from a set of numbers, in this case, the largest number from a set of 10 numbers. You can easily modify this program to accommodate any set of numbers.

Input: A set of 10 numbers

Output: The largest of 10 numbers

PROBLEM
ANALYSIS
AND
ALGORITHM
DESIGN

Suppose that the input data is:

15 20 7 8 28 21 43 12 35 3

Read the first number of the data set. Because this is the only number read to this point, you can assume that it is the largest number and call it `max`. Next, read the second number and call it `num`. Now compare `max` and `num`, and store the larger number into `max`. Now `max` contains the larger of the first two numbers. Next, read the third number. Compare it with `max` and store the larger number into `max`. At this point, `max` contains the largest of the first three numbers. Read the next number, compare it with `max`, and store the larger into `max`. Repeat this process for each remaining number in the data set. Eventually, `max` will contain the largest number in the data set. This discussion translates into the following algorithm:

1. Get the first number. Because this is the only number that you have read so far, it is the largest number so far. Save it in a variable called `max`.

2. For each remaining number in the list:

   a. Get the next number. Store it in a variable called `num`.

   b. Compare `num` and `max`. If `max` < `num`, then `num` is the new largest number; update the value of `max` by copying `num` into `max`. If `max` >= `num`, discard `num`; that is, do nothing.

3. Because `max` now contains the largest number, print it.

To find the larger of two numbers, the program uses the method `larger`.

COMPLETE PROGRAM LISTING

```
//*************************************************************
// Author D.S. Malik
//
// Program: Largest number
// This program determines the largest number of a set of
// 10 numbers.
//*************************************************************
```

```java
import java.util.*;

public class LargestNumber
{
    static Scanner console = new Scanner(System.in);

    public static void main(String[] args)
    {
        double num;    //variable to hold the current number
        double max;    //variable to hold the larger number
        int count;     //loop control variable

        System.out.println("Enter 10 numbers:");

        num = console.nextDouble();                   //Step 1
        max = num;                                    //Step 1

        for (count = 1; count < 10; count++)          //Step 2
        {
            num = console.nextDouble();               //Step 2a
            max = larger(max, num);                   //Step 2b
        }

        System.out.println("The largest number is "
                           + max);                    //Step 3
    }

    public static double larger(double x, double y)
    {
        double max;

        if (x >= y)
            max = x;
        else
            max = y;

        return max;
    }
}
```

Sample Run: (In this sample run, the user input is shaded.)

```
Enter 10 numbers:
10.5 56.34 73.3 42 22 67 88.55 26 62 11
The largest number is 88.55
```

Void Methods

Void methods (methods that do not have a `return` data type) and value-returning methods have similar structures. Both have a heading part and a statement part. You can place user-defined void methods either before or after the method `main`. However, program execution always begins with the first statement in the method `main`. Because a void method does not return a value of a specific data type using the `return` statement, the return type of these methods can be considered `void`. In a void method, you can use the `return` statement without any value; it is typically used to exit the method early. Like value-returning methods, void methods may or may not have formal parameters.

Because void methods do not return a value of a data type, they are not used (that is, called) in an expression. A call to a void method is a stand-alone statement. Thus, to call a void method, you use the method name together with the actual parameters (if any) in a stand-alone statement. When a void method exits, control goes back to the calling environment at the statement immediately following the point where it was called. Before giving examples of void methods, next we give the syntax of void methods.

7

METHOD DEFINITION

The definition of a void method with parameters has the following syntax:

```
modifier(s) void methodName(formal parameter list)
{
     statements
}
```

The formal parameter list may be empty, in which case, in the method heading, the empty parentheses are still needed.

FORMAL PARAMETER LIST

A formal parameter list has the following syntax:

```
dataType variable, dataType variable, ...
```

METHOD CALL

A method call has the following syntax:

```
methodName(actual parameter list);
```

If the formal parameter list is empty, then in the method call statement, empty parentheses are still needed, that is, in this case the method call is: `methodName();`.

ACTUAL PARAMETER LIST

An actual parameter list has the following syntax:

```
expression or variable, expression or variable, ...
```

As with value-returning methods, in a method call the number of actual parameters, together with their data types, must match the formal parameters in the order given. Actual and formal parameters have a one-to-one correspondence. A method call causes the body of the called method to execute. Two examples of void methods with parameters follow.

EXAMPLE 7-5

Consider the following method heading:

```
public static void funexp(int a, double b, char c, String name)
```

The method `funexp` has four formal parameters: (1) a, a parameter of type `int;`, (2) b, a parameter of type `double;`, (3) c, a parameter of type `char`, and (4) name, a parameter of type `String`.

EXAMPLE 7-6

Consider the following method heading:

```
public static void expfun(int one, char two, String three, double four)
```

The method `expfun` has four formal parameters: (1) one, a parameter of type `int;`, (2) two, a parameter of type `char;`, (3) three, a parameter of type `String`, and (4) four, a parameter of type `double`.

Parameters provide a communication link between the calling method (such as `main`) and the called method. They enable methods to manipulate different data each time they are called.

EXAMPLE 7-7

Suppose that you want to print a pattern (a triangle of stars) similar to the following:

```
   *
  * *
 * * *
* * * *
```

The first line has one star with some blanks before the star, the second line has two stars, some blanks before the stars, and a blank between the stars, and so on. Let's write the method `printStars`, which has two parameters: a parameter to specify the number of blanks before the stars in a line and another parameter to specify the number of stars in a line. The definition of the method `printStars` is:

```
public static void printStars(int blanks, int starsInLine)
{
    int count = 1;

        //print the number of blanks before the stars in a line
    for (count <= blanks; count++)
        System.out.print(" ");

        //print the number of stars with a blank between stars
    for (count = 1; count <= starsInLine; count++)
        System.out.print(" *");

    System.out.println();
} //end printStars
```

The first parameter, `blanks`, determines how many blanks to print preceding the star(s); the second parameter, `starsInLine`, determines how many stars to print in a line. If the value of the parameter `blanks` is 30, for instance, then the first `for` loop in the method `printStars` executes 30 times and prints 30 blanks. Also, because you want to print spaces between the stars, every iteration of the second `for` loop in the method `printStars` prints the string `" *"` (Line 30)—a blank followed by a star.

Next consider the following statements:

```
int numberOfLines = 15;
int numberOfBlanks = 30;
int counter = 1;

for (counter = 1; counter <= numberOfLines; counter++)
{
    printStars(numberOfBlanks, counter);
    numberOfBlanks--;
}
```

The `for` loop calls the method `printStars`. Every iteration of this `for` loop specifies the number of blanks followed by the number of stars to print in a line, using the variables `numberOfBlanks` and `counter`. Every invocation of the method `printStars` receives one fewer blank and one more star than the previous call. For example, the first iteration of the `for` loop in the method `main` specifies 30 blanks and 1 star (which are passed as the parameters, `numberOfBlanks` and `counter`, to the method `printStars`). The `for` loop then decrements the number of blanks by 1 by executing the statement, `numberOfBlanks--;`. At the end of the `for` loop, the number of stars is incremented by 1 for the next iteration. This is done by executing the update statement, `counter++`, in the `for` statement, which increments the value of the variable `counter` by 1. In other words, the second call of the method `printStars` receives 29 blanks and 2 stars as parameters. Thus, the previous statements will print a triangle of stars consisting of 15 lines.

The complete program is as follows:

```java
// Program: Print a triangle of stars
// Given the number of lines, this program prints a triangle of
// stars.

import java.util.*;

public class TriangleOfStars
{
    static Scanner console = new Scanner(System.in);

    public static void main(String[] args)
    {
        int numberOfLines;
        int numberOfBlanks;
        int counter = 1;

        System.out.print("Enter the number of star lines "
                         + "(1 to 20) to be printed: ");
        numberOfLines = console.nextInt();
        System.out.println();

        while (numberOfLines < 0 || numberOfLines > 20)
        {
            System.out.println("The number of star lines should "
                               + "be between 1 and 20");
            System.out.print("Enter the number of star lines "
                             + "(1 to 20) to be printed: ");
            numberOfLines = console.nextInt();
            System.out.println ();
        }

        numberOfBlanks = 30;

        for (counter = 1; counter <= numberOfLines; counter++)
        {
            printStars(numberOfBlanks, counter);
            numberOfBlanks--;
        }
    } // end main

    public static void printStars(int blanks, int starsInLine)
    {
        int count = 1;

        for (count = 1; count <= blanks; count++)
            System.out.print(" ");

        for (count = 1; count <= starsInLine; count++)
            System.out.print(" *");

        System.out.println();
    } //end printStars

}
```

Sample Run: In this sample run, the user input is shaded.

```
Enter the number of star lines (1 to 20) to be printed: 10
```

In the method `main`, the user is first asked to specify how many lines of stars to print. (In this program, the user is restricted to 20 lines because a triangular grid of up to 20 lines fits nicely on the screen.) Because the program is restricted to only 20 lines, the `while` loop in the method `main` ensures that the program prints the triangular grid of stars only if the number of lines is between 1 and 20.

7

Primitive Data Type Variables as Parameters

In Chapter 3, you learned that Java has two categories of variables—primitive type variables and reference variables. Before considering examples of void methods with parameters, let's make the following observation about variables of primitive types and reference variables. When a method is called, the value of the actual parameter is copied into the corresponding formal parameter. If a formal parameter is a variable of a primitive data type, then after copying the value of the actual parameter, there is no connection between the formal parameter and the actual parameter. That is, the formal parameter has its own copy of the data. Therefore, during program execution, the formal parameter manipulates the data stored in its own memory space. The program in Example 7-8 further illustrates how a formal parameter of a primitive data type works.

EXAMPLE 7-8

```java
//Example 7-8
//Program illustrating how a formal parameter of a
//primitive data type works.

public class PrimitiveTypeParameters          //Line 1
{                                             //Line 2
    public static void main(String[] args)    //Line 3
```

```
{                                                          //Line 4
    int number = 6;                                        //Line 5

    System.out.println("Line 6: Before calling"
                  + "the method "
                  + "primFormalParam, "
                  + "number = " + number);                 //Line 6

    primFormalParam(number);                               //Line 7

    System.out.println("Line 8: After calling "
                  + "the method "
                  + "primFormalParam, "
                  + "number = " + number);                 //Line 8
} //end main                                               //Line 9

public static void primFormalParam(int num)                //Line 10
{                                                          //Line 11
    System.out.println("Line 12: In the method "
                  + "primFormalParam, "
                  + "before changing, num = "
                  + num);                                  //Line 12

    num = 15;                                              //Line 13

    System.out.println("Line 14: In the method "
                  + "primFormalParam, "
                  + "after changing, num = "
                  + num);                                  //Line 14
} //end primFormalParam                                    //Line 15
}                                                          //Line 16
```

Sample Run:

```
Line 6: Before calling the method primFormalParam, number = 6
Line 12: In the method primFormalParam, before changing, num = 6
Line 14: In the method primFormalParam, after changing, num = 15
Line 8: After calling the method primFormalParam, number = 6
```

The preceding program works as follows. The execution begins at the method main. The statement in Line 5 declares and initializes the int variable number (see Figure 7-3).

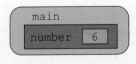

FIGURE 7-3 The method main and its variable number

The statement in Line 6 outputs the value of number before calling the method primFormalParam. The statement in Line 7 calls the method primFormalParam. The value of the variable **number** is passed to the formal parameter **num**. Control now transfers to the method **primFormalParam** (see Figure 7-4).

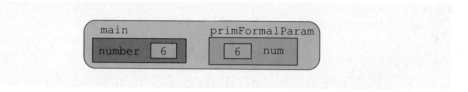

FIGURE 7-4 The variables number and num before execution of the statement in Line 13

The statement in Line 12 outputs the value of **num** before changing its value. The statement in Line 13 changes the value of **num** to **15** (see Figure 7-5).

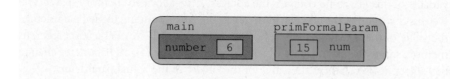

FIGURE 7-5 The variables number and num after execution of the statement in Line 13

The statement in Line 14 outputs the value of **num**. After this statement executes, the method **primFormalParam** exits and control goes back to the method **main** at Line 8 (see Figure 7-6).

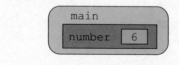

FIGURE 7-6 The variables number and num after execution of the statement in Line 13

The statement in Line 8 outputs the value of **number** after calling the method **primFormalParam**. As you can see from the output, the value of **number**, as shown by the output of the statements in Lines 6 and 8, remains the same even though the value of its corresponding formal parameter **num** was changed within the method **primFormalParam**.

After copying data, a formal parameter of the primitive data type has no connection with the actual parameter, so a formal parameter of the primitive data type cannot pass any result back to the calling method. When the method executes, any changes made to the formal parameters do not, in any way, affect the actual parameters. The actual parameter has no knowledge of what is happening to the formal parameter. Thus, formal parameters of the primitive data types cannot pass information outside the method; formal parameters of the primitive data types only provide a one-way link between the actual parameters and formal parameters.

Reference Variables as Parameters

The program in Example 7-8 illustrates how a formal parameter of a primitive data type works. Now suppose that a formal parameter is a reference variable. Here, also, the value of the actual parameter is copied into the corresponding formal parameter, but there is a slight difference. Recall that a reference variable does not store data directly in its own memory space. We use the operator new to allocate memory for an object belonging to a specific class, and a reference variable of that class type contains the address of the allocated memory space. Therefore, when we pass the value of the actual parameter to the corresponding formal parameter, after copying the value of the actual parameter, both the actual and the formal parameters refer to the same memory space, that is, the same object. Therefore, if the formal parameter changes the value of the object, it also changes the value of the object of the actual parameter.

Because a reference variable contains the address (that is, memory location) of the actual data, both the formal and the value parameters refer to the same object. Therefore, reference variables can pass one or more values from a method and can change the value of the actual parameter.

Reference variables as parameters are useful in three situations:

- When you want to return more than one value from a method
- When the value of the actual object needs to be changed
- When passing the address would save memory space and time, relative to copying a large amount of data

Parameters and Memory Allocation

When a method is called, memory for its formal parameters and variables declared in the body of the method, called **local variables**, is allocated in the method data area. The value of the actual parameter is copied into the memory cell of its corresponding formal parameter. If the parameter is an object (of a class type), both the actual parameter and the formal parameter refer to the same memory space.

Reference Variables of the String Type as Parameters: A Precaution

Recall that reference variables do not directly contain the data. Reference variables contain the address of the memory space where the data is stored. We use the operator new to allocate memory space of a specific type. However, in the case of reference variables of type `String`, we can also use the assignment operator to allocate memory space to store a string and assign the string to a `String` variable. Consider the following statements:

```
String str;                      //Line 1
```

The statement:

```
str = "Hello";                   //Line 2
```

creates a `String` object with the value `"Hello"`, if one does not exist, and stores the reference of that object in `str` (see Figure 7-7).

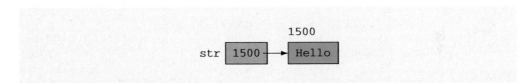

FIGURE 7-7   Variable `str` and the `string` object

We assume that the address of the memory space where the string `"Hello"` is stored is 1500. Now suppose that you execute either the statement:

```
str = "Hello There";
```

or the statement:

```
str = str + " There";
```

The effect of either of these statements is illustrated by Figure 7-8.

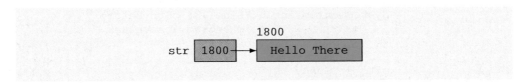

FIGURE 7-8   `str` after the statement `str = "Hello There";` or `str = str + " There";` executes

Note that the string `"Hello There"` is stored at a different location. It is now clear that any time you assign a different string to a `String` variable, the `String` variable points to a different object. In other words, when a string is created and assigned to a `String` variable, the *string cannot be changed*. Note that the **class** `String` does not contain any method that allows you to change an existing string.

If you pass a `String` variable, that is, a reference variable of the `String` type, as a parameter to a method, and within the method you use the assignment operator to change the string, you might think that you have changed the string assigned to the actual parameter. But this does not happen. The string of the actual parameter remains unchanged; a new string is assigned to the formal parameter. The following example further illustrates this concept.

EXAMPLE 7-9 String OBJECTS AS PARAMETERS

Consider the following program:

```java
// This program illustrates how String objects as parameters work.

public class StringObjectsAsParameters              //Line 1
{                                                   //Line 2
    public static void main(String[] args)          //Line 3
    {                                               //Line 4
        String str = "Hello";                       //Line 5

        System.out.println("Line 6: str before "
                    + "calling the method "
                    + "stringParameter: "+ str);    //Line 6

        stringParameter(str);                       //Line 7

        System.out.println("Line 8: str after "
                    + "calling the method "
                    + "stringParameter: " + str);   //Line 8
    } //end main                                    //Line 9

    public static void stringParameter(String pStr) //Line 10
    {                                               //Line 11
        System.out.println("Line 12: In the method "
                    + "stringParameter");           //Line 12
        System.out.println("Line 13: pStr before "
                    + "changing its value: "
                    + pStr);                        //Line 13

        pStr = "Sunny Day";                         //Line 14

        System.out.println("Line 15: pStr after "
                    + "changing its value: "
                    + pStr);                        //Line 15
    } //end stringParameter                         //Line 16
}                                                   //Line 17
```

Sample Run:

```
Line 6: str before calling the method stringParameter: Hello
Line 12: In the method stringParameter
Line 13: pStr before changing its value: Hello
Line 15: pStr after changing its value: Sunny Day
Line 8: str after calling the method stringParameter: Hello
```

The preceding program works as follows: The statement in Line 5 declares `str` to be a `String` variable and assigns the string `"Hello"` to it (see Figure 7-9).

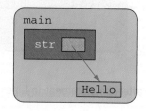

FIGURE 7-9 Variable after the statement in Line 5 executes

The statement in Line 6 outputs the first line of output. The statement in Line 7 calls the method `stringParameter`. The actual parameter is `str` and the formal parameter is `pStr`, so the value of `str` is copied into `pStr`. Because both these parameters are reference variables, `str` and `pStr` point to the same string, which is `"Hello"` (see Figure 7-10).

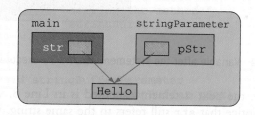

FIGURE 7-10 Variable before the statement in Line 7 executes

The control is transferred to the method `stringParameter`. The next statement executed is in Line 12, which outputs the second line of the output. The statement in Line 13 outputs the third line of the output. Notice that this statement also outputs the string referenced by `pStr` and the printed value is the string `"Hello"`. The next statement executed is in Line 14. This statement uses the assignment operator and assigns the string `"Sunny Day"` to `pStr`. After the execution of the statement in Line 14, `str` no longer refers to the same string as does `pStr` (see Figure 7-11).

The preceding program works as follows: The statement in Line 5 declares `str` to be a reference variable of the `StringBuffer` type and assigns the string `"Hello"` to it (see Figure 7-13).

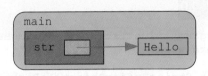

FIGURE 7-13 Variable after the statement in Line 5 executes

The statement in Line 6 outputs the first line of output. The statement in Line 7 calls the method `stringBufferParameter`. The actual parameter is `str` and the formal parameter is `pStr`. The value of `str` is copied into `pStr`. Because both of these parameters are reference variables, `str` and `pStr` point to the same string, which is `"Hello"` (see Figure 7-14).

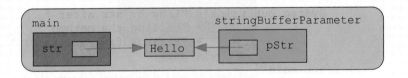

FIGURE 7-14 Variable before the statement in Line 7 executes

Then control is transferred to the method `stringBufferParameter`. The next statement executed is in Line 12, which produces the second line of the output. The statement in Line 13 produces the third line of the output. This statement also outputs the string to which `pStr` points, and the printed value is that string. The statement in Line 14 uses the method `append` to append the string `" There"` to the string pointed to by `pStr`. After this statement executes, `pStr` points to the string `"Hello There"`. However, this also changes the string that was assigned to the variable `str`. When the statement in Line 14 executes, `str` points to the same string as `pStr` (see Figure 7-15).

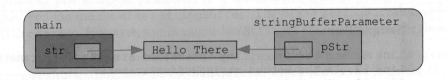

FIGURE 7-15 Variable after the statement in Line 14 executes

The statement in Line 15 produces the fourth line of output. Notice that the printed value is the string **"Hello There"**, which is the string pointed to by **pStr**. After this statement executes, control goes back to the method **main** at Line 8 (see Figure 7-16).

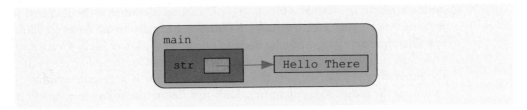

FIGURE 7-16 Variable after the statement in Line 7 executes

The next statement executed is in Line 8, which produces the last line of the output. Note that **str** points to the string **"Hello There"**.

Primitive Type Wrapper Classes as Parameters

As illustrated by the program in Example 7-8, if a formal parameter is of the primitive data type and the corresponding actual parameter is a variable, then the formal parameter cannot change the value of the actual parameter. In other words, changing the value of a formal parameter of the primitive data type has no effect on the actual parameter. So, how do we pass the values of primitive data types outside the method? As stated earlier, only reference variables can pass values outside the method (except, of course, for the return value). Corresponding to each primitive data type, Java provides a class so that the values of primitive data types can be wrapped in objects. For example, you can use the **class Integer** to wrap **int** values in objects, the **class Double** to wrap **double** values in objects, and so on. These wrapper classes were introduced in Chapter 6, "Graphical User Interface (GUI) and Object-Oriented Design (OOD)." Even though you can use the **class Integer** to wrap **int** values in objects, the **class Integer** does not provide a method to change the value of an existing **Integer** object. The same is true of other wrapper classes. That is, when passed as parameters, objects of wrapper classes have the same limitations as objects of the **class String**. If we want to pass a **String** object as a parameter and also change that object, we can use the **class StringBuffer**. However, Java does not provide any class that wraps primitive type values in objects and when passed as parameters change their values. If a method returns only one value of a primitive type, then you can write a value–returning method. However, if you encounter a situation that requires you to write a method that needs to pass more than one value of a primitive type, then you should design your own classes. Appendix D provides the definitions of such classes and shows how to use them in a program.

The Web site, *www.course.com*, and the CD accompanying this book contains the file, Chapter_7_PassingPrimitiveTypeAsObjects, illustrating how to use user–defined classes to pass primitive type values as objects and change their values.

Scope of an Identifier Within a Class

The previous sections presented several examples of programs with user–defined methods. In these examples, and in Java in general, identifiers are declared in a method heading, within a block, or outside a block. (Recall that an identifier is the name of something in Java, such as a variable or method.) A question naturally arises: Are you allowed to access any identifier anywhere in the program? The general answer is no. Certain rules exist that you must follow to access an identifier. The **scope** of an identifier refers to what parts of the program can "see" an identifier, that is, where it is accessible (visible). This section examines the scope of an identifier. Let's first define the following widely used term:

Local identifier: An identifier declared within a method or block that is visible only within that method or block.

Before giving the scope rules of an identifier, let us note the following:

- Java does not allow the nesting of methods. That is, you cannot include the definition of one method in the body of another method.

- Within a method or a block, an identifier must be declared before it can be used. Note that a block is a collection of statements enclosed within braces. A method's definition can contain several blocks. The body of a loop or an `if` statement also forms a block.

- Within a class, outside every method definition (and every block), an identifier can be declared anywhere.

- Within a method, an identifier used to name a variable in the outer block of the method cannot be used to name any other variable in an inner block of the method. For example, in the following method definition, the second declaration of the variable **x** is illegal:

```java
public static void illegalIdentifierDeclaration()
{
    int x;

    //block
    {
        double x;    //illegal declaration, x is already declared
        ...
    }
}
```

Next, we describe the scope rules of an identifier declared within a class and accessed within a method (block) of the class. (In Chapter 8, we describe the rules for an *object* to access the identifiers of its class.)

- An identifier, say, **x**, declared within a method (block) is accessible:

  - Only within the block from the point at which it is declared until the end of the block.

  - By those blocks that are nested within that block.

- Suppose **x** is an identifier declared within a class and outside every method's definition (block):
  - If **x** is declared *without* the reserved word `static` (such as a named constant or a method name), then it *cannot* be accessed within a `static` method.
  - If **x** is declared *with* the reserved word `static` (such as a named constant or a method name), then it *can* be accessed within a method (block), provided the method (block) does not have any other identifier named **x**.

Before considering an example that illustrates these scope rules, first note the scope of the identifier declared in the `for` statement. Java allows the programmer to declare a variable in the initialization statement of the `for` statement. For example, the following `for` statement:

```
for (int count = 1; count < 10; count++)
    System.out.println(count);
```

declares the variable `count` and initializes it to 1. The scope of the variable `count` is only limited to the body of the `for` loop.

Example 7-11 illustrates the scope rules.

7

EXAMPLE 7-11

```java
public class ScopeRules
{
    static final double rate = 10.50;
    static int z;
    static double t;

    public static void main(String[] args)
    {
        int num;
        double x, z;
        char ch;

        //...
    }

    public static void one(int x, char y)
    {
        //...
    }

    public static int w;

    public static void two(int one, int z)
    {
        char ch;
        int a;
```

```
        //block three
        {
            int x = 12;

            //...
        }//end block three
        //...
    }
}
```

Table 7-3 summarizes the scope (visibility) of the identifiers in Example 7-11.

TABLE 7-3 Scope (Visibility) of the Identifiers

Identifier	Visibility in one	Visibility in two	Visibility in block three	Visibility in main
rate (before main)	Y	Y	Y	Y
z (before main)	Y	N	N	N
t (before main)	Y	Y	Y	Y
main	Y	Y	Y	Y
local variables of main	N	N	N	Y
one (method name)	Y	Y	Y	Y
x (one's formal parameter)	Y	N	N	N
y (one's formal parameter)	Y	N	N	N
w (before method two)	Y	Y	Y	Y
two (method name)	Y	Y	Y	Y
one (two's formal parameter)	N	Y	Y	N
z (two's formal parameter)	N	Y	Y	N
local variables of two	N	Y	Y	N
x (Block three's local variable)	N	N	Y	N

The Web site, *www.course.com*, and the CD accompanying this book contain the programs ScopeRuleA.java and ScopeRuleB.java, and further demonstrates the scope of variables.

Before we look at some programming examples, we will explore the concept of method overloading.

Method Overloading: An Introduction

In Java, several methods can have the same name within a `class`. This is called **method overloading** or **overloading a method name**. Before we state the rules to overload a method, let us define the following:

Two methods are said to have **different formal parameter lists** if both methods have:

- A different number of formal parameters, or
- If the number of formal parameters is the same, then the data type of the formal parameters, in the order you list, must differ in at least one position.

For example, consider the following method headings:

```
public void methodOne(int x)
public void methodTwo(int x, double y)
public void methodThree(double y, int x)
public int methodFour(char ch, int x, double y)
public int methodFive(char ch, int x, String name)
```

These methods all have different formal parameter lists.

Now consider the following headings:

```
public void methodSix(int x, double y, char ch)
public void methodSeven(int one, double u, char firstCh)
```

The methods `methodSix` and `methodSeven` both have three formal parameters, and the data type of the corresponding parameters is the same. Therefore, these methods have the same formal parameter list.

To overload a method name, within a `class`, any two definitions of the method must have different formal parameter lists.

Method overloading: Creating several methods, within a `class`, with the same name.

The **signature** of a method consists of the method name and its formal parameter list. Two methods have different signatures if they have either different names or different formal parameter lists. (Note that the signature of a method does not include the return type of the method.)

If a method's name is overloaded, then all the methods (with the same name) have different signatures if they have different formal parameter lists. Thus, the following method headings correctly overload the method `methodXYZ`:

```
public void methodXYZ()
public void methodXYZ(int x, double y)
public void methodXYZ(double one, int y)
public void methodXYZ(int x, double y, char ch)
```

Consider the following method headings to overload the method `methodABC`:

```
public void methodABC(int x, double y)
public int methodABC(int x, double y)
```

Both method headings have the same name and same formal parameter list. Therefore, these method headings to overload the method `methodABC` are incorrect. In this case, the compiler will generate a syntax error. (Note that the return types of these method headings are different.)

If a method's name is overloaded, then in a call to that method, the formal parameter list of the method determines which method to execute.

NOTE Some authors define the signature of a method as the formal parameter list; other authors consider the entire heading of the method as its signature. In this book, the signature of a method consists of the method's name and its formal parameter list. If the method names are different, then, of course, the compiler would have no problem identifying which method is called and correctly translating the code. However, if a method name is overloaded, then, as noted, the method's formal parameter list determines which method's body executes.

Suppose you need to write a method that determines the larger of two items. Both items can be integers, floating-point numbers, characters, or strings. You could write several methods as follows (we give only the method heading):

```
int largerInt(int x, int y)
char largerChar(char first, char second)
double largerDouble(double u, double v)
String largerString(String first, String second)
```

The method `largerInt` determines the larger of two integers, the method `largerChar` determines the larger of two characters, and so on. All of these methods perform similar operations. Instead of giving different names to these methods, you can use the same name—say, `larger`—for each method; that is, you can overload the method `larger` as follows:

```
int larger(int x, int y)
char larger(char first, char second)
double larger(double u, double v)
String larger(String first, String second)
```

If the call is `larger(5, 3)`, for example, the first method executes because the actual parameters match the formal parameters of the first method. If the call is `larger('A', '9')`, the second method executes, and so on.

Method overloading is used when you have the same action for different types of data. Of course, for method overloading to work, you must give the definition of each method.

PROGRAMMING EXAMPLE: Data Comparison

Two groups of students at a local university are enrolled in special courses during the summer semester. The courses are offered for the first time and are taught by different teachers. At the end of the semester, both groups are given the same tests for the same courses and their scores are recorded in separate files. The data in each file is in the following form:

```
courseID   score1, score2, ..., scoreN -999
courseID   score1, score2, ..., scoreM -999
   .
   .
   .
```

This programming example illustrates:

1. How to read data from more than one file in the same program.
2. How to send the output to a file.
3. How to generate bar graphs.
4. With the help of methods and parameter passing, how to use the same program segment on different (but similar) sets of data.
5. How to use structured design to solve a problem and how to perform parameter passing.

This program is broken into two parts. First, you learn how to read data from more than one file. Second, you learn how to generate bar graphs.

Next we write a program that finds the average course score for each course for each group. The output is of the following form:

```
Course ID   Group No   Course Average
   CSC         1           83.71
               2           80.82

   ENG         1           82.00
               2           78.20
   .
   .
   .
Avg for group 1: 82.04
Avg for group 2: 82.01
```

Input: Because the data for the two groups is recorded in separate files, the input data appears in two separate files

Output: As shown above

PROBLEM
ANALYSIS AND
ALGORITHM
DESIGN

Reading the input data from both files is straightforward. Suppose the data is stored in the file `group1.txt` for group 1 and in the file `group2.txt` for group 2. After processing the data for one group, we can process the data for the second group for the same course, and continue until we run out of data. Processing the data for each course is similar and uses the following process:

a. Sum the scores for the course.

b. Count the number of students in the course.

c. Divide the total score by the number of students to find the course average.

d. Output the results.

We are only comparing the averages of the corresponding courses in each group. The data in each file is ordered according to the course ID. To ensure that only the averages of the corresponding courses are compared, we compare the course IDs for each group. If the corresponding course IDs are not the same, we output an error message and terminate the program.

This discussion suggests that we should write a method, `calculateAverage`, to find the course average. We should also write another method, `printResult`, to output the data in the form given. By passing the appropriate parameters, we can use the same methods, `calculateAverage` and `printResult`, to process each course's data for both groups. (In the second part of the program, we modify the method `printResult`.)

The preceding discussion translates into the following algorithm:

1. Initialize the variables.

2. Get the course IDs for group 1 and group 2.

3. If the course IDs are different, print an error message and exit the program.

4. Calculate the course average for group 1 and group 2.

5. Print the results in the form given earlier.

6. Repeat Steps 2 through 5 for each course.

7. Print the final results.

Variables
(Method
main)

The preceding discussion suggests that the program needs the following variables for data manipulation in the method `main`:

```
String courseId1;                    //course ID for group 1
String courseId2;                    //course ID for group 2
```

```
int numberOfCourses;

double avg1; //average for a course in group 1
double avg2; //average for a course in group 2

double avgGroup1;
double avgGroup2;

Scanner group1 =
        new Scanner(new FileReader("group1.txt"));
Scanner group2 =
        new Scanner(new FileReader("group2.txt"));

PrintWriter outfile = new PrintWriter("student.out");
```

Next, we discuss the methods `calculateAverage` and `printResult`. Then, we will put the method `main` together.

Method calculate Average

This method calculates the average for a course. Because the input is stored in a file and the input file is opened in the method `main`, we must pass the variable associated with the input file to this method. Furthermore, after calculating the course average, this method must pass the course average to the method `main`. Therefore, this method has one parameter.

To find the course average, we must first find the sum of all the scores for the course and the number of students who took the course; we then divide the sum by the number of students. Thus, we need a variable to find the sum of the scores, a variable to find the number of students, a variable to find the course average, and a variable to read and store a score. Of course, we must initialize the variables to zero to find the sum and the number of students.

Local Variables (Method calculate Average)

In the previous discussion of data manipulation, we identified four variables for the method `calculateAverage`:

```
double totalScore;      //to store the sum of scores
int numberOfStudents;   //to store the number of students
int score;              //to read and store a course score
double courseAvg;       //to store the course average
```

The preceding discussion translates into the following algorithm for the method `calculateAverage`:

    a. Declare the variables.

    b. Initialize `totalScore` to `0.0`.

    c. Initialize `numberOfStudents` to `0`.

    d. Get the (next) course score.

e. while (score != -999)

    i. Update `totalScore` by adding the course score read in Step d.

    ii. Increment `numberOfStudents` by 1.

    iii. Get the next course score.

f. `courseAvg = totalScore / numberOfStudents;`

g. `return courseAvg;`

We are now ready to write the definition of the method `calculateAverage`.

```
public static double calculateAverage(Scanner inp)
{
    double totalScore = 0.0;
    int numberOfStudents = 0;
    int score = 0;
    double courseAvg;

    score = inp.nextInt();

    while (score != -999)
    {
        totalScore = totalScore + score;
        numberOfStudents++;
        score = inp.nextInt();
    }//end while

    courseAvg = totalScore / numberOfStudents;

    return courseAvg;
}//end calculate Average
```

Method printResult

The method `printResult` prints the group's course ID, group number, and course average. The output is stored in a file. We must pass four parameters to this method: the variable associated with the output file, the group number, the course ID, and the course average for the group. Also, from the output, it is clear that we print the course ID only before group 1. In pseudocode, the algorithm is:

```
if (group number == 1)
    print course ID
else
    print a blank

print group number and course average
```

The definition of the method `printResult` follows:

```
public static void printResult(PrintWriter outp, String courseId,
                               int groupNo, double avg)
```

```
{
    if (groupNo == 1)
        outp.print("  " + courseId + "    ");
    else
        outp.print("            ");

    outp.printf("%9d %15.2f%n", groupNo, avg);
}
```

Now that we have designed and defined the methods `calculateAverage` and `printResults`, we can describe the algorithm for the method `main`. Before outlining the algorithm, however, note the following: It is quite possible that in both input files the data is ordered according to the course IDs, but one file might have fewer courses than the other. We discover this error only after we have processed both files and discover that one file has unprocessed data. Make sure to check for this error before printing the final answer—that is, the average for group 1 and group 2.

Main Algorithm: Method main

1. Declare the variables (local declaration).
2. Create and initialize the variables to open the input and output files.
3. Initialize the course average for group 1 to `0.0`.
4. Initialize the course average for group 2 to `0.0`.
5. Initialize the number of courses to `0`.
6. Print the heading.
7. For each course in group 1 and group 2:

   a. Get `courseId1` for group 1.

   b. Get `courseId2` for group 2.

   c. `if (courseId1 != courseId2)`
      ```
      {
          System.out.println("Data error: Course IDs do not match");
          return;
      }
      ```

   d. `else`
      ```
      {
      ```
      i. Calculate the course average for group 1 (call the method `calculateAverage` and pass the appropriate parameters).

      ii. Calculate the course average for group 2 (call the method `calculateAverage` and pass the appropriate parameters).

iii. Print the results for group 1 (call the method printResult and pass the appropriate parameters).

iv. Print the results for group 2 (call the method printResult and pass the appropriate parameters).

v. Update the average for group 1.

vi. Update the average for group 2.

vii. Increment the number of courses.

}

8. a. if not_end_of_file on group 1 and end_of_file on group 2

print "Ran out of data for group 2 before group 1"

b. else if end_of_file on group 1 and not_end_of_file on group 2

print "Ran out of data for group 1 before group 2"

c. else

print the average of group 1 and group 2.

9. Close the files.

COMPLETE PROGRAM LISTING

```
//********************************************************
// Author: D.S. Malik
//
// Program: Comparison of Class Averages
// This program computes and compares the class averages of
// two groups of students.
//********************************************************

import java.io.*;
import java.util.*;

public class DataComparison
{
    public static void main (String[] args)
                            throws FileNotFoundException
    {
                //Step 1
        String courseId1;      //course ID for group 1
        String courseId2;      //course ID for group 2

        int numberOfCourses;

        double avg1; //average for a course in group 1
        double avg2; //average for a course in group 2
        double avgGroup1;  //average group 1
        double avgGroup2;  //average group 2
```

```
                    //Step 2 Open the input and output files
Scanner group1 =
            new Scanner(new FileReader("group1.txt"));
Scanner group2 =
            new Scanner(new FileReader("group2.txt"));

PrintWriter outfile = new PrintWriter("student.out");


avgGroup1 = 0.0;                                      //Step 3
avgGroup2 = 0.0;                                      //Step 4

numberOfCourses = 0;                                  //Step 5

                //print heading: Step 6
outfile.println("Course ID   Group No"
            + "    Course Average");

while (group1.hasNext() && group2.hasNext()) //Step 7
{
    courseId1 = group1.next();                        //Step 7a
    courseId2 = group2.next();                        //Step 7b

    if (!courseId1.equals(courseId2))                 //Step 7c
    {
        System.out.println("Data error: Course IDs "
                        + "do not match.");
        System.out.println("Program terminates.");
        outfile.println("Data error: Course IDs "
                    + "do not match.");
        outfile.println("Program terminates.");
        outfile.close();
        return;
    }
    else                                              //Step 7d
    {
        avg1 = calculateAverage(group1);              //Step 7d.i
        avg2 = calculateAverage(group2);              //Step 7d.ii
        printResult(outfile, courseId1,
                1, avg1);                             //Step 7d.iii
        printResult(outfile, courseId2,
                2, avg2);                             //Step 7d.iv
        avgGroup1 = avgGroup1 + avg1;                 //Step 7d.v
        avgGroup2 = avgGroup2 + avg2;                 //Step 7d.vi
        outfile.println();
        numberOfCourses++;                            //Step 7d.vii
    }
}//end while

if (group1.hasNext() && !group2.hasNext())            //Step 8a
    System.out.println("Ran out of data for group 2 "
                + "before group 1.");
```

7

```
Group 1 -- ****
Group 1 -- ####

Avg for group 1: 82.04
Avg for group 2: 82.01
```

Each symbol (* or #) in the bar graph represents 2 points. If a course average is less than 2, no symbol is printed.

Because the output is in the form of a bar graph, we need to modify the method `printResult`.

Method printResult   The method `printResult` prints the course ID and the bar graph representing the average for a course. The output is stored in a file. So we must pass four parameters to this method: the variable associated with the output file, the group number (to print * or #), the course ID, and the course average for the department.

To print the bar graph, we can use a loop to print a symbol for each two points. If the average is `78.45`, for example, we must print 39 symbols to represent this average. To find the number of symbols to print, we can use integer division as follows:

```
numberOfSymbols = (int)(average) / 2;
```

For example, `(int)(78.45) / 2 = 78 / 2 = 39`.

Following this outline, the definition of the method `printResult` is:

```java
public static void printResult(PrintWriter outp,
                               String courseId,
                               int groupNo, double avg)
{
    int noOfSymbols;
    int count;

    if (groupNo == 1)
        outp.print(" " + courseId + "      ");
    else
        outp.print("            ");

    noOfSymbols = (int)(avg)/2;

    if (groupNo == 1)
        for (count = 1; count <= noOfSymbols; count++)
            outp.print("*");
    else
        for (count = 1; count <= noOfSymbols; count++)
            outp.print("#");

    outp.println();
}//end printResults
```

We also include a method, printHeading, to print the first two lines of the output. The definition of this method is:

```
public static void printHeading(PrintWriter outp)
{
    outp.println("Course          Course Average");
    outp.println("  ID     0   10   20   30   40   50   60   70"
             + "   80   90   100");
    outp.println("         |....|....|....|....|....|....|....|"
             + "....|....|....|");
}//end printHeading
```

If you replace the method printResult in the preceding program, include the method printHeading, include the statements to output—Group 1 -- **** and Group 2 -- ####—and rerun the program, then the output for the previous data is as follows:

Sample Output:

```
Course          Course Average
  ID     0   10   20   30   40   50   60   70   80   90   100
         |....|....|....|....|....|....|....|....|....|....|
  CSC    **************************************
         ####################################

  ENG    **************************************
         ####################################

  HIS    *************************************
         ######################################

  MTH    ***************************************
         ######################################

  PHY    ***************************************
         ######################################

Group 1 -- ****
Group 2 -- ####

Avg for group 1: 82.04
Avg for group 2: 82.01
```

Compare both outputs. Which one do you think is better?

7

Avoiding Bugs: One-Piece-at-a-Time Coding

Except for the simplest problems, a solution consists of several pieces that work together. In Java, classes and objects—consisting of data, methods, and sometimes inner classes—are the pieces that work together to provide a solution.

After the problem is understood fully, the solution is designed. All design decisions should be made during the design phase, before any code is written. This includes the design of every class needed to solve the problem, the determination of how the classes relate to each other, and often, the determination of the specific objects of each class needed to solve the problem. The design of each class includes the determination of the data elements and methods of each class, including which methods provide services to the user and which methods provide support for other methods.

It would be a mistake to attempt to design all or several of the pieces at once. Instead, we can begin at level 0, the level of the original problem. We ask ourselves how this problem can be broken down into a few subproblems, which we can call level 1 problems. Chances are, the level 1 problems will need to be broken down into smaller subproblems, which we can call level 2 problems. We do this by picking one of the level 1 problems for further subdivision into level 2 problems. Then we have a choice: We can subdivide one of the level 2 problems, or we can subdivide one of the remaining level 1 problems. A good rule of thumb is to pick a remaining problem whose subdivision is obvious. Subdivision continues in this manner until the solution to each subproblem is so clear that it can be designed directly. By picking a problem where the subdivision is obvious, we are tackling a relatively easy task from among the remaining tasks. After having tackled a relatively easy task, the solution to one or more of the remaining tasks often becomes clear, and we find that we are able to complete all the tasks without ever encountering a task that seems overly challenging. Designing a solution by starting with the original problem and subdividing into smaller problems reflects a divide-and-conquer and top-down design approach. Both are proven techniques that work for many kinds of problems, including most or all of the problems you will encounter as a beginning programmer.

Coding proceeds in a similar manner. The method `main` corresponds to level 0 of the problem solution. The method `main` often contains calls to other methods, each of which corresponds to a solution to one of the level 1 problems. Similarly, each of the methods representing the solution to a level 1 problem often contains calls to other methods, each of which represents a solution to one of the level 2 problems, and so on until we reach levels where solutions can be coded directly without further subdivision. The implementation reflects the design exactly.

Again, it would be a mistake to attempt to code all or several of the pieces at once, so we code one piece at a time. Neither classes nor methods need to be coded in the order used to design them. Nevertheless, the same rule of thumb applies: Pick a remaining task whose implementation is clear and code it. As before, we tackle a relatively easy task from among the remaining tasks. Having done so, the solution to one or more of the remaining tasks often becomes obvious, and we find that we are able to complete all the tasks without encountering a particularly challenging task.

The divide-and-conquer approach should really be called the divide-conquer-and-reassemble approach. If we want to build an automobile, it is not sufficient simply to identify the parts that make up an automobile, and then build each part, making sure that it is exactly as we intended. It is necessary to make all the parts of the automobile work together. Similarly, it is not sufficient simply to code all the required classes with their data and methods, and to instantiate all the necessary objects. We need to make them work together to provide the intended solution. This is achieved by calling the intended methods at the intended times, as specified in the design, passing the intended parameter(s) when a method is called, returning the intended value from each value-returning method, and manipulating the instance variables of any objects passed to the method, as intended.

The task of building a solution (a program) that consists of several pieces is simplified when we code it one piece at a time. The first version of a solution should be a working program with perhaps only a single feature—generally one that is easy to provide. That program is saved. Then, work continues by adding the next easy-to-provide feature, saving the revised program using a different name. After all, a working program with fewer features is better than a nonworking program with more features; we do not want to overwrite our working program with a nonworking program, even if the nonworking program has more features. This process continues, adding perhaps just one feature at a time until all the intended features are present and the solution is complete.

Avoiding Bugs: Using "Stubs" as Appropriate

Sometimes a method or a class can be tested in isolation. Other times, for example when one method relies on another method, testing in isolation is not possible until the other method is written. Does this dictate the order in which the completed pieces of a program must be written? Not necessarily. A **method stub** is a method that is not fully coded. Sometimes a method stub consists of only a method header and a set of empty braces, {}, which is sufficient to permit it to be called, at least for a void method. Sometimes a stub merely produces a plausible return value. For example, a stub for method `calculateCost` that accepts `item` as a parameter might simply return 100.00, independent of the value associated with `item`. This permits method `calculateCost` to be called while the program is being coded. To complete the coding of the program, the stub for method `calculateCost` is ultimately replaced with a method that properly calculates cost based on the value of `item` passed in as a parameter. In the meantime, the method stub permits work to progress on other parts of the solution that call method `calculateCost`.

QUICK REVIEW

1. Methods enable you to divide a program into manageable tasks.
2. The Java system provides standard (predefined) methods.

3. In general, to use a predefined method, you must:

   a. Know the name of the class containing the method, and the name of the package containing the class that contains the method.

   b. Import the class into the program.

   c. Know the name and type of the method, and the number and types of the parameters (arguments).

4. To use a method of a class contained in the package `java.lang` in a program, you do not need to explicitly import these classes into your program.

5. To simplify the use of `static` methods (members) of a class, Java 5.0 and higher versions provide the `static import` statement.

6. The two types of user-defined methods are value-returning methods and void methods.

7. Variables defined in a method heading are called formal parameters.

8. Expressions, variables, or constant values used in a method call are called actual parameters.

9. In a method call, the number of actual parameters and their types must match the formal parameters in the order given.

10. To call a method, use its name together with the actual parameter list.

11. A value-returning method returns a value. Therefore, a value-returning method is typically used (called) in either an expression or an output statement, or as a parameter in a method call.

12. The general syntax of a value-returning method is:

```
modifier(s) returnType  methodName(formal parameter list)
{
     statements
}
```

13. The line:

```
modifier(s) returnType methodName(formal parameter list)
```

   is called the method heading (or method header). Statements enclosed between braces, { and }, are called the body of the method.

14. The method heading and the body of the method are called the definition of the method.

15. If a method has no parameters, you still need the empty parentheses in both the method heading and the method call.

16. A value-returning method returns its value via the `return` statement.

17. A method can have more than one `return` statement. However, whenever a `return` statement executes in a method, the remaining statements are skipped and the method exits.

18. When a program executes, the execution always begins with the first statement in the method `main`.

19. User-defined methods execute only when they are called.

20. A call to a method transfers control from the caller to the called method.

21. In a method call statement, you specify only the actual parameters, not their data type or the method type.

22. When a method exits, control goes back to the caller.

23. A method that does not have a return data type is called a `void` method.

24. A return statement without any value can be used in a `void` method.

25. If a return statement is used in a `void` method, it is typically used to exit the method early.

26. In Java, `void` is a reserved word.

27. A `void` method may or may not have parameters.

28. To call a `void` method, you use the method name together with the actual parameters in a stand-alone statement.

29. A formal parameter receives a copy of its corresponding actual parameter.

30. If a formal parameter is of the primitive data type, it directly stores the value of the actual parameter.

31. If a formal parameter is a reference variable, it copies the value of its corresponding actual parameter, which is the address of the object where the actual data is stored. Therefore, if a formal parameter is a reference variable, both the formal and actual parameters refer to the same object.

32. The scope of an identifier refers to those parts of the program where it is accessible.

33. Java does not allow the nesting of methods. That is, you cannot include the definition of one method in the body of another method.

34. Within a method or a block, an identifier must be declared before it can be used. Note that a block is a set of statements enclosed within braces. A method's definition can contain several blocks. The body of a loop or an `if` statement also forms a block.

35. Within a class, outside every method definition (and every block), an identifier can be declared anywhere.

36. Within a method, an identifier used to name a variable in the outer block of the method cannot be used to name any other variable in an inner block of the method.

37. The scope rules of an identifier declared within a class and accessed within a method (block) of the class are as follows:

7

- An identifier **x** declared within a method (block) is accessible:
  - Only within the block from the point at which it is declared until the end of the block.
  - By those blocks that are nested within that block.
- Suppose **x** is an identifier declared within a class and outside every method's definition (block):
  - If **x** is declared without the reserved word `static` (such as a named constant or a method name), then it cannot be accessed within a `static` method.
  - If **x** is declared with the reserved word `static` (such as a named constant or a method name), then it can be accessed within a method (block), provided the method (block) does not have any other identifier named **x**.

38. Two methods are said to have different formal parameter lists if both methods have:

- A different number of formal parameters, or
- If the number of formal parameters is the same, then the data type of the formal parameters, in the order you list, must differ in at least one position.

39. The signature of a method consists of the method name and its formal parameter list. Two methods have different signatures if they have either different names or different formal parameter lists.

40. If a method is overloaded, then in a call to that method the signature, that is, the formal parameter list of the method, determines which method to execute.

EXERCISES

1. Mark the following statements as true or false.

   a. To use a predefined method of a `class` contained in the package `java.lang` in a program, you only need to know what the name of the method is and how to use it.

   b. A value-returning method returns only one value via the return statement.

   c. Parameters allow you to use different values each time the method is called.

   d. When a `return` statement executes in a user-defined method, the method immediately exits.

   e. A value-returning method returns only integer values.

f. If a Java method does not use parameters, parentheses around the empty parameter list are still needed.

g. In Java, the names of the corresponding formal and actual parameters must be the same.

h. In Java, method definitions can be nested; that is, the definition of one method can be enclosed in the body of another method.

2. What is the output of the following Java program?

```java
import static java.lang.Math.*;

public class Exercise2
{
    public static void main(String[] args)
    {
        for (int counter = 1; counter <= 100; counter++)
            if (pow(floor(sqrt(counter)), 2) == counter)
                System.out.print(counter + " ");

        System.out.println();
    }
}
```

3. Which of the following method headings are valid? If they are invalid, explain why.

```java
public static one(int a, int b)
public static int thisone(char x)
public static char another(int a, b)
public static double yetanother
```

4. Consider the following statements:

```java
double num1, num2, num3;
int int1, int2, int3;
double value;

num1 = 5.0; num2 = 6.0; num3 = 3.0;
int1 = 4; int2 = 7; int3 = 8;
```

and the method heading:

```java
public static double cube(double a, double b, double c)
```

Which of the following statements are valid? If they are invalid, explain why.

a. `value = cube (num1, 15.0, num3);`

b. `System.out.println(cube(num1, num3, num2));`

c. `System.out.println(cube(6.0, 8.0, 10.5));`

d. `System.out.println(num1 + " " + num3);`

e. `System.out.println(cube(num1, num3));`

f. `value = cube(num1, int2, num3);`

g. `value = cube(7, 8, 9);`

7

5. Consider the following methods:

```java
public static int secret(int x)
{
    int i, j;

    i = 2 * x;

    if (i > 10)
        j = x / 2;
    else
        j = x / 3;

    return j - 1;
}

public static int another(int a, int b)
{
    int i, j;

    j = 0;

    for (i = a; i <= b; i++)
        j = j + i;

    return j;
}
```

What is the output of each of the following program segments?

a. ```java
x = 10;
System.out.println(secret(x));
```

b. ```java
x = 5; y = 8;
System.out.println(another(x, y));
```

c. ```java
x = 10; k = secret(x);
System.out.println(x + " " + k + " "
                        + another(x, k));
```

d. ```java
x = 5; y = 8;
System.out.println(another(y, x));
```

6. Consider the following method headings:

```java
public static int test(int x, char ch, double d, int y)
public static double two(double d1, double d2)
public static char three(int x, int y, char ch, double d)
```

Answer the following questions.

a. How many parameters does the method test have? What is the type of the method test?

b. How many parameters does method two have? What is the type of the method two?

c. How many parameters does method `three` have? What is the type of the method `three`?

d. How many actual parameters are needed to call the method `test`? What is the type of each parameter, and in what order should you use these parameters in a call to the method `test`?

e. Write a Java statement that prints the value returned by the method `test` with the actual parameters 5, 5, 7.3, and `'z'`.

f. Write a Java statement that prints the value returned by method `two` with the actual parameters 17.5 and 18.3, respectively.

g. Write a Java statement that prints the next character returned by the method `three`. (Use your own actual parameters.)

7. Consider the following method:

```java
public static int mystery(int x, double y, char ch)
{
    int u;

    if ('A' <= ch && ch <= 'R')
        return (2 * x + (int)(y));
    else
        return ((int)(2 * y) - x);
}
```

What is the output of the following Java statements?

a. `System.out.println(mystery(5, 4.3, 'B'));`

b. `System.out.println(mystery(4, 9.7, 'v'));`

c. `System.out.println(2 * mystery(6, 3.9, 'D'));`

8. Consider the following method:

```java
public static int secret(int one)
{
    int i;
    int prod = 1;

    for (i = 1; i <= 3; i++)
        prod = prod * one;

    return prod;
}
```

a. What is the output of the following Java statements?

i. `System.out.println(secret(5));`

ii. `System.out.println(2 * secret(6));`

b. What does the method `secret` do?

9. Show the output of the following program:

```java
public class MysteryClass
{
    public static void main(String[] args)
    {
        int n;

        for (n = 1; n <= 5; n++)
            System.out.println(mystery(n));
    }

    public static int mystery(int k)
    {
        int x, y;

        y = k;

        for (x = 1; x <= (k - 1); x++)
            y = y * (k - x);

        return y;
    }
}
```

10. Show the output of the following program:

```java
public class StrangeClass
{
    public static void main(String[] args)
    {
        int num = 0;

        while (num <= 29)
        {
            if (strange(num))
                System.out.println("True");
            else
                System.out.println("False");

            num = num + 4;
        }
    }

    public static boolean strange(int n)
    {
        if (n % 2 == 0 && n % 3 == 0)
            return true;
        else
            return false;
    }
}
```

11. In the program fragment shown on the next page, identify the following items: method heading, method body, method definition, formal parameters, actual parameters, method call, and local variables.

```
public class Exercise11                                   //Line 1
{                                                         //Line 2
    public static void main(String[] args)                //Line 3
    {                                                     //Line 4
        int x;                                            //Line 5
        double y;                                         //Line 6
        char z;                                           //Line 7
        //...                                             //Line 8
        hello(x, y, z);                                   //Line 9
        //...                                             //Line 10
        hello(x + 2, y - 3.5, 'S');                       //Line 11
        //...                                             //Line 12
    }                                                     //Line 13

    public static void hello(int first, double second,   //Line 14
                             char ch)                     //Line 15
    {                                                     //Line 16
        int num;                                          //Line 17
        double y;                                         //Line 18
        //...                                             //Line 19
    }                                                     //Line 20
}                                                         //Line 21
```

7

12. For the program in Exercise 11, fill in the blanks below with variable names to show the matching that occurs between the actual and the formal parameter list in each of the two calls.

First Call to hello				**Second Call to hello**	
Formal	**Actual**			**Formal**	**Actual**
1. _____	_____		1.	_____	_____
2. _____	_____		2.	_____	_____
3. _____	_____		3.	_____	_____

13. What is the output of the following program?

```
public class Exercise13
{
    public static void main(String[] args)
    {
        int num1;
        int num2;

        num1 = 5;
        num2 = 10;
        num2 = test(24, num2);
        num2 = test(num1, num2);
        num2 = test(num1 * num1, num2);
        num2 = test(num1 + num1, num2);
    }
```

```
public static int test(int first, int second)
{
    int third;

    third = first + second * second + 2;
    first = second - first;
    second = 2 * second;
    System.out.println(first + " " + second + " "
                        + third);
    return second;
}
}
```

14. In the following program, number the marked statements to show the order in which they will execute (the logical order of execution).

```
import java.util.*;

public class Exercise14
{
    static Scanner console = new Scanner(System.in);

    public static void main(String[] args)
    {
        int num1;
        int num2;

_____    System.out.println("Please enter two integers "
                                + "on separate lines";

_____    num1 = console.nextInt();

_____    num2 = console.nextInt();

_____    func (num1, num2);

_____    System.out.println("The two integers are " + num1
                                + ", " + num2);
    }

    public static void func (int val1, int val2)
    {
        int val3;
        int val4;

_____    val3 = val1 + val2;

_____    val4 = val1 * val2;

_____    System.out.println("The sum and product are " + val3
                                + " and " + val4);
    }
}
```

15. Consider the following program. What is its exact output?

```
public class Exercise15
{
    public static void main(String[] args)
    {
        int num1;
        int num2;

        num1 = 10;                                      //Line 1
        num2 = 20;                                      //Line 2

        System.out.println("Line 3: In main: num1 = "
                        + num1 + ", num2 = "
                        + num2);                        //Line 3

        num2 = funcOne(num1, num2);                     //Line 4

        System.out.println("Line 5: In main after funcOne: "
                        + "num1 = " + num1 + ", num2 = "
                        + num2);                        //Line 5
    }

    public static int funcOne(int a, int b)
    {
        int x;
        int z;

        x = b;                                          //Line 6

        z = a + x;                                      //Line 7

        System.out.println("Line 8: In funcOne: a = " + a
                        + ", b = " + b + ", x = " + x
                        + ", and z = " + z);            //Line 8

        x = x + 5;                                      //Line 9

        System.out.println("Line 10: In funcOne: a = " + a
                        + ", b = " + b + ", x = " + x
                        + ", and z = " + z);            //Line 10

        a = a + 8;                                      //Line 11

        b = a + x + z;                                  //Line 12

        System.out.println("Line 13: In funcOne: a = " + a
                        + ", b = " + b + ", x = " + x
                        + ", and z = " + z);            //Line 13
        return b;
    }
}
```

7

PROGRAMMING EXERCISES

1. Write a value-returning method, `isVowel`, that returns the value `true` if a given character is a vowel, and otherwise returns `false`. Also write a program to test your method.

2. Write a program that prompts the user to input a sequence of characters and outputs the number of vowels. (Use the method `isVowel` written in Programming Exercise 1.)

3. Consider the following program segment:

```
public class Ch7_PrExercise3
{
    public static void main(String[] args)
    {
        int     num;
        double dec;
        .
        .
        .
    }

    public static int one(int x, int y)
    {
        .
        .
        .
    }

    public static double two(int x, double a)
    {
        int first;
        double z;
        .
        .
        .
    }
}
```

a. Write the definition of method `one` so that it returns the sum of `x` and `y` if `x` is greater than `y`; otherwise, it should return `x` minus 2 times `y`.

b. Write the definition of method `two` as follows:

  i. Read a number and store it in `z`.

  ii. Update the value of `z` by adding the value of `a` to its previous value.

  iii. Assign the variable `first` the value returned by method `one` with the parameters 6 and 8.

iv. Update the value of **first** by adding the value of **x** to its previous value.

v. If the value of **z** is more than twice the value of **first**, return **z**; otherwise, return 2 times **first** minus **z**.

c. Write a Java program that tests parts a and b. (Declare additional variables in the method **main**, if necessary.)

4. Write a method, **reverseDigit**, that takes an integer as a parameter and returns the number with its digits reversed. For example, the value of **reverseDigit(12345)** is **54321**. Also, write a program to test your method.

5. Modify the **RollDice** program, Example 7-3, so that it allows the user to enter the desired sum of the numbers to be rolled. Also allow the user to call the **rollDice** method as many times as the user desires.

6. Write a program to test the method **isPalindrome** discussed in Example 7-4.

7. The following formula gives the distance between two points (x_1, y_1) and (x_2, y_2) in the Cartesian plane:

$$\sqrt{(x_2 - x_1)^2 + (y_2 - y_1)^2}.$$

Given the center and a point on a circle, you can use this formula to find the radius of the circle. Write a program that prompts the user to enter the center and a point on the circle. The program should then output the circle's radius, diameter, circumference, and area. Your program must have at least the following methods:

a. **distance**: This method takes as its parameters four numbers that represent two points in the plane and returns the distance between them.

b. **radius**: This method takes as its parameters four numbers that represent the center and a point on the circle, calls the method **distance** to find the radius of the circle, and returns the circle's radius.

c. **circumference**: This method takes as its parameter a number that represents the radius of the circle and returns the circle's circumference. (If r is the radius, the circumference is $2\pi r$.)

d. **area**: This method takes as its parameter a number that represents the radius of the circle and returns the circle's area. (If r is the radius, the area is πr^2.)

e. Assume that $\pi = 3.1416$.

8. Rewrite the Cable Company Billing programming example (from Chapter 4) so that it uses the following methods to calculate the billing amount:

a. **residentialCustomer**: This method calculates and returns the billing amount for the residential customer.

b. **businessCustomer**: This method calculates and returns the billing amount for the service business customer.

7

9. Rewrite the program in Programming Exercise 14 from Chapter 4 (cell phone) so that it uses the following methods to calculate the billing amount. (In this programming exercise, do not output the number of minutes during which the service is used.)

   a. `regularBill`: This method calculates and returns the billing amount for regular service.

   b. `premiumBill`: This method calculates and returns the billing amount for premium service.

10. A nonnegative integer is called a **palindrome** if it reads forward and backward in the same way. For example, the numbers 5, 121, 3443, and 123454321 are palindromes. Write a method that takes as input a nonnegative integer and returns `true` if the number is a palindrome; otherwise, it returns `false`. (When determining whether the number is a palindrome, do not convert the number into a string.) Also write a program to test your method.

11. Programming Exercise 7 (Chapter 5) asks you to write a program that determines whether a positive integer is a prime number. Redo this programming exercise by writing a method that takes as input a positive integer and returns `true` if the number is a prime number; otherwise, it returns `false`.

12. Write a program that determines whether a positive is a prime number. If the number is a prime number, then the program also outputs whether the number is a palindrome. Use the methods developed in Programming Exercises 10 and 11 of this chapter.

13. Write a program that takes as input five numbers and outputs the mean (average) and standard deviation of the numbers. If the numbers are x_1, x_2, x_3, x_4, and x_5, then the mean is $x = (x_1 + x_2 + x_3 + x_4 + x_5) / 5$ and the standard deviation is:

$$s = \sqrt{\frac{(x_1 - x)^2 + (x_2 - x)^2 + (x_3 - x)^2 + (x_4 - x)^2 + (x_5 - x)^2}{5}}.$$

Your program must contain at least the following method: A method that calculates and returns the mean and a method that calculates the standard deviation.

14. When you borrow money to buy a house, a car, or for some other purpose, then you typically repay it by making periodic payments. Suppose that the loan amount is L, r is the interest rate per year, m is the number of payments in a year, and the loan is for t years. Suppose that $i = (r / m)$ and r is in decimal. Then the periodic payment is:

$$R = \frac{Li}{1 - (1 + i)^{-mt}}.$$

You can also calculate the unpaid loan balance after making certain payments. For example, the unpaid balance after making k payments is:

$$L' = R\left[\frac{1 - (1+i)^{-(mt-k)}}{i}\right],$$

where R is the periodic payment. (Note that if the payments are monthly, then $m = 12$.)

15. Write a program that prints the day number of the year, given the date is in the form month day year. For example, if the input is 1 1 09, the day number is 1; if the input is 12 25 09, the day number is 359. The program should check for a leap year. A year is a leap year if it is divisible by 4 but not divisible by 100. For example, 1992 and 2008 are divisible by 4 but not by 100. A year that is divisible by 100 is a leap year if it is also divisible by 400. For example, 1600 and 2000 are divisible by 400. However, 1800 is not a leap year because 1800 is not divisible by 400.

16. Write a program that reads a student's name together with his or her test scores. The program should then compute the average test score for each student and assign the appropriate grade. The grade scale is as follows: 90–100,A; 80–89,B; 70–79,C;60–69,D; 0–59,F.

Your program must use the following methods:

a. A value-returning method, `calculateAverage`, to determine and return the average of five test scores for each student. Use a loop to read and sum the five test scores. (This method does not output the average test score. That task must be done in the method `main`.)

b. A value-returning method, `calculateGrade`, to determine and return each student's grade. (This method does not output the grade. That task must be done in the method `main`.)

Test your program on the following data. Read the data from a file and send the output to a file. Do not use any global variables. Use the appropriate parameters to pass values in and out of methods.

```
Johnson 85 83 77 91 76
Aniston 80 90 95 93 48
Cooper 78 81 11 90 73
Gupta 92 83 30 69 87
Blair 23 45 96 38 59
Clark 60 85 45 39 67
Kennedy 77 31 52 74 83
Bronson 93 94 89 77 97
Sunny 79 85 28 93 82
Smith 85 72 49 75 63
```

Sample Output: The output should be in the following form. Fill the last two columns and the last line showing the class average. (Output test average and class average with two decimal places.)

Student	Test1	Test2	Test3	Test4	Test5	Average	Grade
Johnson	85	83	77	91	76		
Aniston	80	90	95	93	48		
Cooper	78	81	11	90	73		
Gupta	92	83	30	69	87		
Blair	23	45	96	38	59		
Clark	60	85	45	39	67		
Kennedy	77	31	52	74	83		
Bronson	93	94	89	77	97		
Sunny	79	85	28	93	82		
Smith	85	72	49	75	63		

Class Average =

17. (**The box problem**) You have been given a flat cardboard of area, say, 70 square inches, to make an open box by cutting a square from each corner and folding the sides (see Figure 7-17). Your objective is to determine the dimension, that is, the length and width, and the side of the square to be cut from the corners so that the resulting box is of maximum volume.

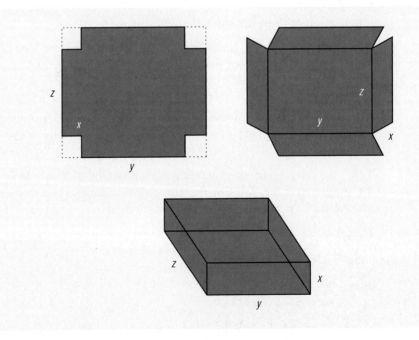

FIGURE 7-17 Cardboard box

Write a program that prompts the user to enter the area of the flat card-board. The program then outputs the length and width of the cardboard and the length of the side of the square to be cut from the corner so that the resulting box is of maximum volume. Calculate your answer to three decimal places. Your program must contain a method that takes as input the length and width of the cardboard and returns the side of the square that should be cut to maximize the volume. The method also returns the maximum volume.

18. **(The Power Station Problem)** A power station is on one side of a river that is one-half miles wide, and a factory is 8 miles downstream on the other side of the river (see Figure 7-18). It costs $7 per foot to run power lines overland and $9 per foot to run them underwater. Your objective is to determine the most economical path to lay the power line. That is, determine how long the power line should run underwater and how long it should run over land, to achieve the minimum total cost of laying the power line.

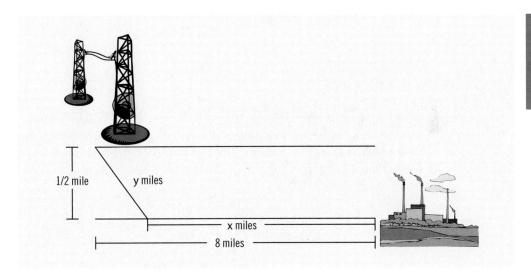

FIGURE 7-18 Power station, river, and factory

Write a program that prompts the user to enter the following:

a. The width of the river.

b. The distance of the factory downstream on the other side of the river.

c. Cost of laying the power line underwater.

d. Cost of laying the power line overland.

The program then outputs the length of the power line that should run underwater and the length that should run over land, so the cost of constructing the power line is at the minimum. The program should also output the total cost of constructing the power line.

19. **(Pipe Problem, requires trigonometry)** A pipe is to be carried around the right-angled corner of two intersecting corridors. Suppose that the widths of the two intersecting corridors are 5 feet and 8 feet (see Figure 7-19). Your objective is to find the length of the longest pipe, rounded to the nearest foot, that can be carried level around the right-angled corner.

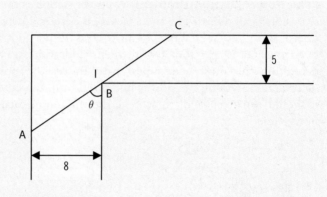

FIGURE 7-19 Pipe problem

Write a program that prompts the user to input the widths of both the hallways. The program then outputs the length of the longest pipe, rounded to the nearest foot, that can be carried level around the right-angled corner. (Note that the length of the pipe is given by $l = AB + BC = 8 / \sin \theta + 5 / \cos \theta$, where $0 < \theta < \pi/2$.)

USER-DEFINED CLASSES AND ADTS

IN THIS CHAPTER, YOU WILL:

- Learn about user-defined classes
- Learn about **private**, **protected**, **public**, and **static** members of a class
- Explore how classes are implemented
- Learn about various operations on classes
- Examine constructors
- Examine the method **toString**
- Become aware of accessor methods and mutator methods
- Learn how to avoid bugs by preparing a class design document
- Learn how to do a walk-through of a class design
- Become aware of the reference **this**
- Learn about abstract data types (ADTs)

In the preceding chapters, you learned how to use various classes and their methods to manipulate data. Java does not provide all the classes that you will ever need, so it permits you to design and implement your own classes. Therefore, you must learn how to create your own classes. This chapter discusses how to create classes and objects of those classes.

Classes and Objects

Recall, from Chapter 1, that the first step in problem-solving using object-oriented design (OOD) is to identify the components called classes and objects. An *object* of a class has both data and operations that can be performed on that data. The mechanism in Java that allows you to combine data and operations on the data in a single unit is called a *class*. (Combining data and operations on the data is called *encapsulation*—the first principle of OOD.) Now that you know how to store and manipulate data in computer memory and how to construct your own methods, you are ready to learn how classes and objects are constructed.

In Chapter 3, we described the `class String` and illustrated how to use the various `String` methods. Using the `class String`, you can create various `String` objects, each storing a different string, and using the methods of the `class String`, each object can manipulate its string. The `class String` allows us to group data, which are strings, and operations on that data in a convenient way. We can use the `class String` in any Java program that requires the manipulation of strings, without re-creating it for a specific program. In fact, the Java programming language provides a wealth of pre-defined classes that can be effectively used in any program. For example, in Chapter 7 we discussed how to use the `classes Math` and `Character`, and in Chapter 6, we used various classes, such as `JFrame`, `JText`, and `JLabel`, to create GUI programs. However, Java does not provide all the classes that we will ever need as it does not know the specific needs of a programmer. Therefore, we must learn how to create our own classes.

Before discussing how to design your own classes, let's first learn how the `class String` looks. In skeleton form the `class String` has the following form:

```
public final class String
{
    //variables to store a string
    ...

    public int compareTo(String anotherString)
    {
        //code to compare two strings
    }

    public String concat(String str)
    {
        //code to join two strings
    }
```

```
public String toLowerCase()
{
    //code to convert all the characters of a string to lowercase
}

...
}
```

As you can see, the `class String` has quite a few members. It has methods to implement operations such as compare strings and concatenation operations to join strings. In general, to design a class you must know what data you need to manipulate and what operations you need to manipulate the data. For example, suppose that you want to design the `class Circle` that implements the basic properties of a circle. Now every circle has a radius, which can be a floating-point value. Therefore, when you created an object of the `class Circle`, then you must store the radius of the circle into that object. Next, the two basic operations that are performed on a circle are to find the area and circumference of the circle. Thus, the `class Circle` must provide these two operations. This class needs to provide a few other operations to effectively use this class in a program. In skeleton form, the definition of the `class Circle` looks as follows:

```
public class Circle
{
    private double radius;

    public double area()
    {
        //code to determine the area of the circle
    }

    public double perimeter()
    {
        //code to determine the perimeter of the circle
    }

    //Additional methods as needed
    ...
}
```

At this point you don't need to be concerned with this definition of the `class Circle`. We will create such a class in Example 8-3, of this chapter.

Considering the definition of the `class Circle`, it is apparent that to design your own class you need to be familiar with several things. For example, in the definition of the `class Circle`, the variable `radius` is declared with the keyword `private` and the methods `area` and `perimeter` are declared with the keyword `public`. Also, notice that the methods `area` and `perimeter` have no parameters. You will learn these and various other characteristics of a class in this chapter.

Next, we give the syntax of a Java class and describe its various parts.

A **class** is a collection of a specific number of components. The components of a `class` are called the **members** of the `class`.

The general syntax for defining a `class` is:

```
modifier(s) class ClassIdentifier modifier(s)
{
    classMembers
}
```

where `modifier(s)` are used to alter the behavior of the class and, usually, `classMembers` consist of named constants, variable declarations, and/or methods, but can even include other classes. That is, usually a member of a `class` can be a variable (to store data) or a method or an inner class. Some of the modifiers that we have encountered are `public`, `private`, and `static`.

- If a member of a class is a named constant, you declare it just like any other named constant.
- If a member of a class is a variable, you declare it just like any other variable.
- If a member of a class is a method, you define it just like any other method.
- If a member of a class is a method, it can (directly) access any member of the class—both data members and methods. Therefore, when you write the definition of a method, you can directly access any data member of the class (without passing it as a parameter).
- Later, we'll describe class members, which themselves are classes, called inner classes.

In Java, `class` is a reserved word. It only defines a data type and it announces the declaration of a class. In Java, the data members of a `class` are also called **fields**.

The members of a `class` are classified into four categories. The three typically used categories are `private`, `public`, and `protected`. (The fourth category is described in the next note.) This chapter discusses the `private` and `public` categories. Chapter 10 discusses `protected` members.

The following are some facts about `private` and `public` members of a class:

- If a member of a class is `private`, you *cannot* access it outside the class.
- If a member of a class is `public`, you *can* access it outside the class.

 NOTE Recall that a package is a collection of related classes. Appendix D describes how to create your own packages. If a class member is declared/defined without any modifiers, then that class member can be accessed from anywhere in the package. (This is the fourth category of class members and is called the *default* visibility of class members. However, this type of visibility should be avoided.)

In Java, `private`, `protected`, and `public` are reserved words.

Suppose that we want to define the `class Clock` to represent the time of day in a program. Further suppose that the time is represented as a set of three integers: one to represent the hours, one to represent the minutes, and one to represent the seconds. We also want to perform the following operations on the time:

1. Set the time.
2. Return the hours.
3. Return the minutes.
4. Return the seconds.
5. Print the time.
6. Increment the time by one hour.
7. Increment the time by one minute.
8. Increment the time by one second.
9. Compare the two times for equality.
10. Copy the time.
11. Return a copy of the time.

To implement these 11 operations, we write algorithms, which we implement as methods—11 methods to implement 11 operations. So far, the `class Clock` has 14 members: 3 data members and 11 methods. Suppose that the 3 data members are `hr`, `min`, and `sec`, each of type `int`.

Some members of the `class Clock` will be `private`, others will be `public`. Deciding which members to make `private` and which to make `public` depends on the nature of each member. The general rule is that any member that needs to be accessed from outside the class is declared `public`; any member that should not be accessed directly by the user should be declared `private`. For example, the user should be able to set the time and print the time. Therefore, the methods that set the time and print the time should be declared `public`.

Similarly, the method to increment the time and compare the times for equality should be declared `public`. On the other hand, users should not control the *direct* manipulation of the data members `hr`, `min`, and `sec`, so we will declare them `private`. Note that if the user has direct access to the data members, methods such as `setTime` are not needed. (However, in general, the user should never be provided with direct access to the variables.)

The data members for the `class Clock` are:

```
private int hr;  //store the hours
private int min; //store the minutes
private int sec; //store the seconds
```

The (non-`static`) data members—variables declared without using the modifier (reserved word) `static`—of a `class` are called **instance variables**. Therefore, the variables `hr`, `min`, and `sec` are the instance variables of the `class Clock`.

Suppose that the 11 methods to implement the 11 operations are as follows (we also specify the headings of the methods):

1. `setTime` sets the time to the time specified by the user. The method heading is:

   `public void setTime(int hours, int minutes, int seconds)`

2. `getHours` returns the hours. The method heading is:

   `public int getHours()`

3. `getMinutes` returns the minutes. The method heading is:

   `public int getMinutes()`

4. `getSeconds` returns the seconds. The method heading is:

   `public int getSeconds()`

5. `printTime` prints the time in the form `hh:mm:ss`. The method heading is:

   `public void printTime()`

6. `incrementHours` increments the time by one hour. The method heading is:

   `public void incrementHours()`

7. `incrementMinutes` increments the time by one minute. The method heading is:

   `public void incrementMinutes()`

8. `incrementSeconds` increments the time by one second. The method heading is:

   `public void incrementSeconds()`

9. `equals` compares two times to determine whether they are equal. The method heading is:

   `public boolean equals(Clock otherClock)`

10. `makeCopy` copies the time of one `Clock` object into another `Clock` object. The method heading is:

    `public void makeCopy(Clock otherClock)`

11. `getCopy` returns a copy of the time. A copy of the object's time is created and a reference to the copy is returned. The method heading is:

    `public Clock getCopy()`

The objective of the method `setTime` is to set the values of the instance variables. In other words, it changes the values of the instance variables. Such methods are called *mutator* methods. On the other hand, the method `getHours` only accesses the value of an instance variable; that is, it does not change the value of the instance variable. Such methods are called *accessor* methods. These methods are described in detail later in this chapter.

The (non-`static`) methods of a class are called the **instance methods** of the class.

NOTE In the definition of the `class Clock`, all the data members are `private` and all the method members are `public`. However, a method can also be `private`. For example, if a method is only used to support other methods of the class, and the user of the class does not need to access this method, you make it `private`.

Notice that we have not yet written the definitions of the methods of the `class Clock`. (You will learn how to write them in the section Definitions of the Constructors and Methods of the `class Clock`.) Also notice that the method `equals` has only one parameter, although you need two things to make a comparison. Similarly, the method `makeCopy` has only one parameter. An example later in this chapter will help explain why.

Before giving the definition of the `class Clock`, we first introduce another important concept related to classes—constructors.

Constructors

In addition to the methods necessary to implement operations, every class can have *special* types of methods called constructors. A **constructor** has the same name as the class, and it executes automatically when an object of that class is created. Constructors are used to guarantee that the instance variables of the class are initialized.

There are two types of constructors: those with parameters and those without parameters. The constructor without parameters is called the **default constructor**.

Constructors have the following properties:

- The name of a constructor is the same as the name of the class.
- A constructor, even though it is a method, has no return type. That is, it is neither a value-returning method nor a `void` method.
- A class can have more than one constructor. However, all constructors of a class have the same name. That is, the constructors of a class can be overloaded.
- If a class has more than one constructor, the constructors must have different *signatures*.
- Constructors execute automatically when class objects are instantiated. Because they have no types, they cannot be called like other methods.
- If there are multiple constructors, the constructor that executes depends on the type of values passed to the class object when the class object is instantiated.

For the `class Clock`, we will include two constructors: the default constructor and a constructor with parameters. The default constructor initializes the instance variables used to store the hours, minutes, and seconds, each to `0`. Similarly, the constructor with parameters initializes the instance variables to the values specified by the user. We will illustrate shortly how constructors are invoked.

8

The heading of the default constructor is:

`public Clock()`

The heading of the constructor with parameters is:

`public Clock(int hours, int minutes, int seconds)`

The definition of the `class Clock` has 16 members: 11 methods to implement the 11 operations, 2 constructors, and 3 instance variables to store the hours, minutes, and seconds.

 NOTE If you do not include any constructor in a class, then Java *automatically* provides the default constructor. Therefore, when you create an object, the instance variables are initialized to their default values. For example, `int` variables are initialized to 0. If you provide at least one constructor and do not include the default constructor, then Java *will not automatically* provide the default constructor. Generally, if a class includes constructors, you should also include the default constructor.

Unified Modeling Language Class Diagrams

A class and its members can be described graphically using **Unified Modeling Language (UML)** notation. For example, Figure 8-1 shows the UML diagram of the `class` Clock. Also, what appears in the figure is called the **UML class diagram** of the class.

```
                    Clock
-hr:  int
-min: int
-sec: int

+Clock()
+Clock(int, int, int)
+setTime(int, int, int): void
+getHours(): int
+getMinutes(): int
+getSeconds(): int
+printTime(): void
+incrementSeconds(): int
+incrementMinutes(): int
+incrementHours(): int
+equals(Clock): boolean
+makeCopy(Clock): void
+getCopy(): Clock
```

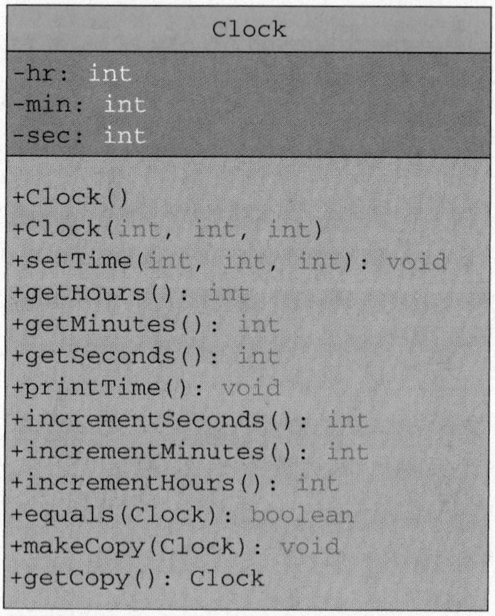

FIGURE 8-1 UML class diagram of the `class` clock

The top box in the UML diagram contains the name of the class. The middle box contains the data members and their data types. The last box contains the method names, parameter list, and return types. The + (plus) sign in front of a member indicates that it is a `public` member; the – (minus) sign indicates that it is a `private` member. The # symbol before a member name indicates that it is a `protected` member.

Variable Declaration and Object Instantiation

Once a `class` is defined, you can declare reference variables of that `class` type. For example, the following statements declare `myClock` and `yourClock` to be reference variables of type `Clock`:

```
Clock myClock;          //Line 1
Clock yourClock;        //Line 2
```

These statements *do not* allocate memory spaces to store the hours, minutes, and seconds. Next, we explain how to allocate memory space to store the hours, minutes, and seconds, and how to access that memory space using the variables `myClock` and `yourClock`.

The `class` `Clock` has three instance variables. To store the hours, minutes, and seconds, we need to create a `Clock` object, which is accomplished by using the operator `new`.

The general syntax for using the operator `new` is:

```
new className()
```
//Line 3

or:

```
new className(argument1, argument2, ..., argumentN)
```
//Line 4

The expression in Line 3 instantiates the object and initializes the instance variables of the object using the default constructor. The expression in Line 4 instantiates the object and initializes the instance variables using a constructor with parameters.

For the expression in Line 4:

- The number of arguments and their type should match the formal parameters (in the order given) of one of the constructors.
- If the type of the arguments does not match the formal parameters of any constructor (in the order given), Java uses type conversion and looks for the best match. For example, an integer value might be converted to a floating-point value with a zero decimal part. Any ambiguity will result in a compile-time error.

Consider the following statements (notice that `myClock` and `yourClock` are as declared in Lines 1 and 2):

```
myClock = new Clock();              //Line 5
yourClock = new Clock(9, 35, 15);   //Line 6
```

The statement in Line 5 allocates memory space for a `Clock` object, initializes each instance variable of the object to 0, and stores the address of the object into `myClock`. The statement in Line 6 allocates memory space for a `Clock` object; initializes the instance variables `hr`, `min`, and `sec` of the object to 9, 35, and 15, respectively; and stores the address of the object into `yourClock` (see Figure 8-2).

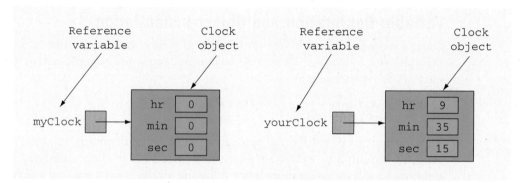

FIGURE 8-2 Variables `myClock` and `yourClock` and associated `Clock` objects

To be specific, we call the object to which `myClock` points the object `myClock` and the object to which `yourClock` points the object `yourClock` (see Figure 8-3).

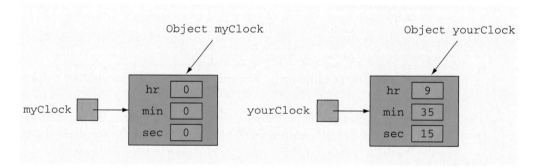

FIGURE 8-3 Objects `myClock` and `yourClock`

Of course, you can combine the statements to declare the variable and instantiate the object into one statement. For example, the statements in Lines 1 and 5 can be combined as:

```
Clock myClock = new Clock();    //declare and instantiate myClock
```

That is, the preceding statement declares `myClock` to be a reference variable of type `Clock` and instantiates the object `myClock` to store the hours, minutes, and seconds. Each instance variable of the object `myClock` is initialized to 0 by the default constructor.

Similarly, the statements in Lines 2 and 6 can be combined as:

```
Clock yourClock = new Clock(9, 35, 15);   //declare and
                                          //instantiate yourClock
```

That is, the preceding statement declares `yourClock` to be a reference variable of type `Clock` and instantiates the object `yourClock` to store the hours, minutes, and seconds. The instance variables `hr`, `min`, and `sec` of the object `yourClock` are initialized to 9, 35, and 15, respectively, by the constructor with parameters.

 NOTE When we use phrases such as "create an object of a `class` type" we mean to: (i) declare a reference variable of the `class` type, (ii) instantiate the `class` object, and (iii) store the address of the object into the reference variable declared. For example, the following statements create the object `tempClock` of the `Clock` type:

```
Clock tempClock = new Clock();
```

The object `tempClock` is accessed via the reference variable `tempClock`.

Recall from Chapter 3 that a `class` object is called an **instance** of that `class`.

Accessing Class Members

Once an object of a class is created, the object can access the members (as explained in the next paragraph, after the syntax) of the `class`. The general syntax for an object to access a data member or a method is:

```
referenceVariableName.memberName
```

The class members that the class object can access depend on where the object is created.

- If the object is created in the definition of a method of the class, then the object can access both the `public` and `private` members. We will elaborate on this when we write the definitions of the methods `equals`, `makeCopy`, and `getCopy` of the `class` `Clock` later in this chapter.

- If the object is created elsewhere (for example, in a user's program), then the object can access *only* the `public` members of the class.

Recall that in Java, the dot **.** (period) is called the **member access operator**.

Example 8-1 illustrates how to access the members of a class.

EXAMPLE 8-1

Suppose that the objects `myClock` and `yourClock` have been created as before. Consider the following statements:

```
myClock.setTime(5, 2, 30);
myClock.printTime();
yourClock.setTime(x, y, z);   //Assume x, y, and z are variables
                              //of type int that have been
                              //initialized.
```

```
if (myClock.equals(yourClock))
.
.
.
```

These statements are legal; that is, they are syntactically correct. Note the following:

- In the first statement, `myClock.setTime(5, 2, 30);`, the method `setTime` is executed. The values 5, 2, and 30 are passed as parameters to the method `setTime`, and the method uses these values to set the values of `hr`, `min`, and `sec` of the object `myClock` to 5, 2, and 30, respectively.
- Similarly, the second statement executes the method `printTime` and outputs the values of `hr`, `min`, and `sec` of the object `myClock`.
- In the third statement, the values of the variables `x`, `y`, and `z` are used to set the values of `hr`, `min`, and `sec` of the object `yourClock`.
- In the fourth statement, the method `equals` executes and compares the instance variables of the object `myClock` with the corresponding instance variables of the object `yourClock`. Because in this statement the method `equals` is invoked by the variable `myClock`, it has direct access to the instance variables of the object `myClock`. So it needs one more object to compare, which, in this case, is the object `yourClock`. This explains why the method `equals` has only one parameter.

The objects `myClock` and `yourClock` can access only `public` members of the class. The following statements are illegal because `hr` and `min` are `private` members of the `class Clock` and, therefore, cannot be accessed by `myClock` and `yourClock`:

```
myClock.hr = 10;                    //illegal
myClock.min = yourClock.min;        //illegal
```

Built-in Operations on Classes

Most of Java's built-in operations do not apply to classes. You cannot perform arithmetic operations on class objects. For example, you cannot use the operator + to add the values of two `Clock` objects. Also, you cannot use relational operators to compare two class objects in any meaningful way.

The built-in operation that is valid for classes is the dot operator (.). A reference variable uses the dot operator to access `public` members; classes can use the dot operator to access `public static` members.

Assignment Operator and Classes: A Precaution

This section discusses how the assignment operator works with reference variables and objects.

Suppose that the objects `myClock` and `yourClock` are as shown in Figure 8-4.

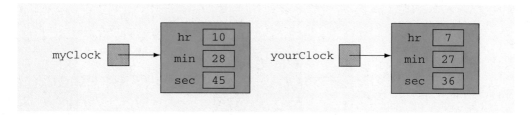

FIGURE 8-4 myClock and yourClock

The statement:

```
myClock = yourClock;
```

copies the value of the reference variable `yourClock` into the reference variable `myClock`. After this statement executes, both `yourClock` and `myClock` refer to the same object. Figure 8-5 illustrates this situation.

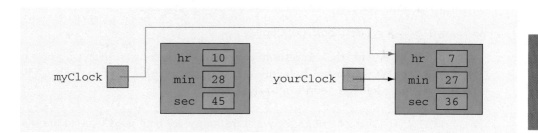

FIGURE 8-5 myClock and yourClock after the statement myClock = yourClock; executes

This is called the shallow copying of data. In **shallow copying**, two or more reference variables of the same type point to the same object; that is, two or more reference variables become aliases. Note that the object originally referred to by `myClock` becomes inaccessible.

To copy the instance variables of the object `yourClock` into the corresponding instance variables of the object `myClock`, you need to use the method `makeCopy`. This is accomplished by the following statement:

```
myClock.makeCopy(yourClock);
```

After this statement executes:

1. The value of `yourClock.hr` is copied into `myClock.hr`.
2. The value of `yourClock.min` is copied into `myClock.min`.
3. The value of `yourClock.sec` is copied into `myClock.sec`.

In other words, the values of the three instance variables of the object yourClock are copied into the corresponding instance variables of the object myClock, as shown in Figure 8-6.

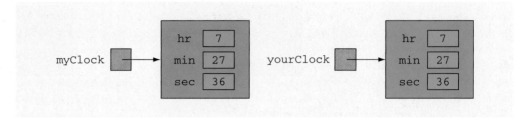

FIGURE 8-6 Objects myClock and yourClock after the statement myClock.makeCopy(yourClock); executes

This is called the deep copying of data. In **deep copying**, each reference variable refers to its *own* object, as in Figure 8-6, *not* the same object, as in Figure 8-5.

Another way to avoid the shallow copying of data is to have the object being copied create a copy of itself, and then return a reference to the copy. This is accomplished by the method getCopy. Consider the following statement:

myClock = yourClock.getCopy();

In this statement, the expression yourClock.getCopy() makes a copy of the object yourClock and returns the address, that is, the reference, of the copy. The assignment statement stores this address into myClock.

NOTE
The methods makeCopy and getCopy are both used to avoid the shallow copying of data. The main difference between these two methods is: To use the method makeCopy, both objects—the object whose data is being copied and the object that is copying the data—must be instantiated before invoking this method. To use the method getCopy, the object whose data is being copied must be instantiated before invoking this method, while the object of the reference variable receiving a copy of the data need not be instantiated. Note that makeCopy and getCopy are *user-defined* methods.

It is important to understand the difference between the shallow and deep copying of data and when to use which. Shallow copying can produce unintended results, especially by beginning Java programmers.

Class Scope

A reference variable follows the same scope rules as other variables. A member of a class is local to the class. You access a **public class** member outside the **class** through the reference variable name or the **class** name (for **static** members) and the member access operator (.).

Methods and Classes

Reference variables can be passed as parameters to methods and returned as method values. Recall from Chapter 7 that when a reference variable is passed as a parameter to a method, both the formal and actual parameters point to the same object.

Definitions of the Constructors and Methods of the `class Clock`

We now give the definitions of the methods of the `class Clock`, then we will write the complete definition of this class. First, note the following:

1. The `class Clock` has 11 methods: `setTime`, `getHours`, `getMinutes`, `getSeconds`, `printTime`, `incrementHours`, `incrementMinutes`, `incrementSeconds`, `equals`, `makeCopy`, and `getCopy`. It has two constructors and three instance variables: `hr`, `min`, and `sec`.

2. The three instance variables—`hr`, `min`, and `sec`—are `private` to the `class` and cannot be accessed directly outside the `class`.

3. The 11 methods—`setTime`, `getHours`, `getMinutes`, `getSeconds`, `printTime`, `incrementHours`, `incrementMinutes`, `incrementSeconds`, `equals`, `makeCopy`, and `getCopy`—can directly access the instance variables (`hr`, `min`, and `sec`). In other words, we do not pass instance variables or data members as parameters to these methods. Similarly, constructors directly access the instance variables.

Let's first write the definition of the method `setTime`. The method `setTime` has three parameters of type `int`. This method sets the instance variables to the values specified by the user, which are passed as parameters to this function. The definition of the method `setTime` follows:

```
public void setTime(int hours, int minutes, int seconds)
{
    if (0 <= hours && hours < 24)
        hr = hours;
    else
        hr = 0;

    if (0 <= minutes && minutes < 60)
        min = minutes;
    else
        min = 0;

    if (0 <= seconds && seconds < 60)
        sec = seconds;
    else
        sec = 0;
}
```

8

Note that the definition of the method `setTime` checks for the valid values of hours, minutes, and seconds. If any of these values is out of range, the corresponding instance variable is initialized to 0. Now let's look at how the method `setTime` works.

The method `setTime` is a **void** method and has three parameters. Therefore:

- A call to this method is a stand–alone statement.
- We must use three parameters in a call to this method.

Furthermore, recall that because `setTime` is a member of the **class** `Clock`, it can directly access the instance variables `hr`, `min`, and `sec`, as shown in the definition of `setTime`.

Suppose that the object `myClock` is as shown in Figure 8-7.

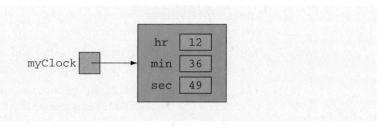

FIGURE 8-7 Object `myClock`

Consider the following statement:

```
myClock.setTime(3, 48, 52);
```

The variable `myClock` accesses the member `setTime`. In the statement `myClock.setTime(3, 48, 52);`, `setTime` is accessed by the variable `myClock`. Therefore, the three variables—`hr`, `min`, and `sec`—referred to in the body of the method `setTime` are the three instance variables of the object `myClock`. Thus, the values 3, 48, and 52, which are passed as parameters in the preceding statement, are assigned to the three instance variables of the object `myClock` by the method `setTime` (see the body of the method `setTime`). After the previous statement executes, `myClock` is as shown in Figure 8-8.

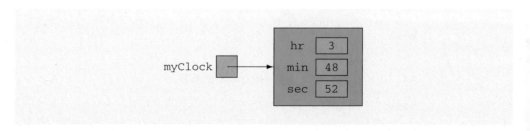

FIGURE 8-8 `myClock` after statement `myClock.setTime(3,48,52);` executes

Next, let's give the definitions of the other methods of the class Clock. These definitions are simple and easy to follow.

```java
public int getHours()
{
    return hr;          //return the value of hr
}

public int getMinutes()
{
    return min;         //return the value of min
}

public int getSeconds()
{
    return sec;         //return the value of sec
}

public void printTime()
{
    if (hr < 10)
        System.out.print("0");
    System.out.print(hr + ":");

    if (min < 10)
        System.out.print("0");
    System.out.print(min + ":");

    if (sec < 10)
        System.out.print("0");
    System.out.print(sec);
}

public void incrementHours()
{
    hr++;               //increment the value of hr by 1

    if (hr > 23)        //if hr is greater than 23,
        hr = 0;         //set hr to 0
}

public void incrementMinutes()
{
    min++;              //increment the value of min by 1

    if (min > 59)       //if min is greater than 59
    {
        min = 0;            //set min to 0
        incrementHours();   //increment hours
    }
}
```

8

```
public void incrementSeconds()
{
    sec++;                    //increment the value of sec by 1

    if (sec > 59)     //if sec is greater than 59
    {
        sec = 0;                  //set sec to 0
        incrementMinutes();   //increment minutes
    }
}
```

From the definitions of the methods incrementMinutes and incrementSeconds, you can see that a method of a class can call other methods of the class.

The method equals has the following definition:

```
public boolean equals(Clock otherClock)
{
    return (hr == otherClock.hr
            && min == otherClock.min
            && sec == otherClock.sec);
}
```

Let's see how the method equals works.

Suppose that myClock and yourClock are as shown in Figure 8-9.

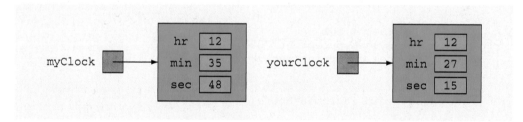

FIGURE 8-9 Objects myClock and yourClock

Consider the following statement:

```
if (myClock.equals(yourClock))
    .
    .
    .
```

In the expression:

```
myClock.equals(yourClock)
```

myClock accesses the method equals. The value of the parameter yourClock is passed to the formal parameter otherClock, as shown in Figure 8-10.

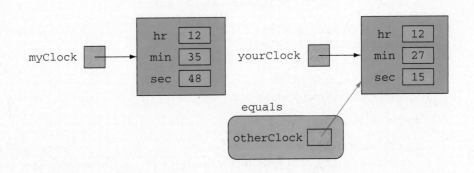

FIGURE 8-10 Object `myClock` and parameter `otherClock`

Note that `otherClock` and `yourClock` refer to the same object. The instance variables `hr`, `min`, and `sec` of the object `otherClock` have the values 12, 27, and 15, respectively. In other words, when the body of the method `equals` executes, the value of `otherClock.hr` is 12, the value of `otherClock.min` is 27, and the value of `otherClock.sec` is 15. The method `equals` is a member of `myClock`. When the method `equals` executes, the variables `hr`, `min`, and `sec` in the body of the method `equals` are the instance variables of the object `myClock`. Therefore, the instance variable `hr` of the object `myClock` is compared with `otherClock.hr`, the instance variable `min` of the object `myClock` is compared with `otherClock.min`, and the instance variable `sec` of the object `myClock` is compared with `otherClock.sec`.

Once again, in the expression:

`myClock.equals(yourClock)`

the method `equals` is invoked by `myClock` and compares the object `myClock` with the object `yourClock`. It follows that the method `equals` needs only one parameter.

Let us again take a look at the definition of the method `equals`. Notice that within the definition of this method, the object `otherClock` accesses the data members `hr`, `min`, and `sec`. However, these data members are `private`. So is there any violation? The answer is no. The method `equals` is a member of the `class Clock` and `hr`, `min`, and `sec` are the data members. Moreover, `otherClock` is an object of the `class Clock`. Therefore, the object `otherClock` can access its `private` data members within the definition of the method `equals`. The same is true for any method of a class.

That is, in general, when you write the definition of a method, say, `dummyMethod`, of a `class`, say, `DummyClass`, and the method uses an object, `dummyObject` of the `class DummyClass`, then within the definition of `dummyMethod` the object `dummyObject` can access its `private` data members (in fact, any `private` member of the class).

The method `makeCopy` copies the instance variables of its parameter, `otherClock`, into the corresponding instance variables of the object referenced by the variable using this method. Its definition is:

```
public void makeCopy(Clock otherClock)
{
    hr = otherClock.hr;
    min = otherClock.min;
    sec = otherClock.sec;
}
```

Consider the following statement:

```
myClock.makeCopy(yourClock);
```

In this statement, the method makeCopy is invoked by myClock. The three instance variables hr, min, and sec in the body of the method makeCopy are the instance variables of the object myClock. The variable yourClock is passed as a parameter to makeCopy. Therefore, yourClock and otherClock refer to the same object, which is the object yourClock. Thus, after the preceding statement executes, the instance variables of the object yourClock are copied into the corresponding instance variables of the object myClock. (Note that as in the case of the method equals, the parameter otherClock can directly access the private data members of the object it points to.)

The method getCopy creates a copy of an object's hr, min, and sec and returns the address of the copy of the object. That is, the method getCopy creates a new Clock object, initializes the instance variables of the object, and returns the address of the object created. The definition of the method getCopy is:

```
public Clock getCopy()
{
    Clock temp = new Clock();      //Line 1

    temp.hr = hr;                  //Line 2
    temp.min = min;                //Line 3
    temp.sec = sec;                //Line 4

    return temp;                   //Line 5
}
```

The following illustrates how the method getCopy works. Suppose that yourClock is as shown in Figure 8-11.

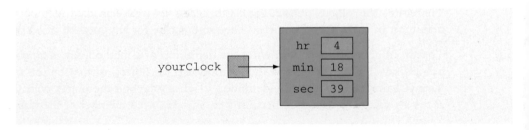

FIGURE 8-11 Object yourClock

Consider the following statement:

```
myClock = yourClock.getCopy();          //Line A
```

In this statement, because the method `getCopy` is invoked by `yourClock`, the three variables `hr`, `min`, and `sec` in the body of the method `getCopy` are the instance variables of the object `yourClock`. The body of the method `getCopy` executes as follows. The statement in Line 1 creates the `Clock` object `temp`. The statements in Lines 2 through 4 copy the instance variables of the object `yourClock` into the corresponding instance variables of `temp`. In other words, the object referenced by `temp` is a copy of the object `yourClock` (see Figure 8-12).

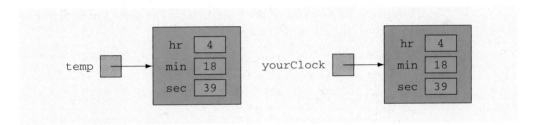

FIGURE 8-12 Objects `temp` and `yourClock`

The statement in Line 5 returns the value of `temp`, which is the address of the object holding a copy of the data. The value returned by the method `getCopy` is copied into `myClock`. Therefore, after the statement in Line A executes, `myClock` and `yourClock` are as shown in Figure 8-13.

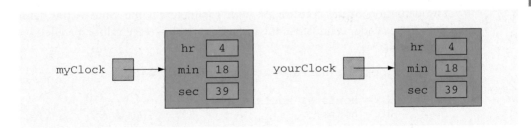

FIGURE 8-13 Objects `myClock` and `yourClock`

Note that as in the case of the methods `equals` and `makeCopy`, the reference variable `temp`—in the definition of the method `getCopy`—can directly access the private data members of the object it points to because `getCopy` is a method of the **class** `Clock`.

NOTE The definition of the method `getCopy` can also be written as:

```
public Clock getCopy()
{
    Clock temp = new Clock(hr, min, sec);

    return temp;
}
```

This definition of the method `getCopy` uses the constructor with parameters, described below, to initialize the instance variables of the object `temp`.

Next, we give the definitions of the constructors. The default constructor initializes each instance variable to 0. Its definition is:

```
public Clock()
{
    hr = 0;
    min = 0;
    sec = 0;
}
```

You can also write the definition of the default constructor using the method `setTime` as follows:

```
public Clock()
{
    setTime(0, 0, 0);
}
```

The definition of the constructor with parameters is the same as the definition of the method `setTime`. It initializes the instance variables to the values specified by the user. Its definition is:

```
public Clock(int hours, int minutes, int seconds)
{
    if (0 <= hours && hours < 24)
        hr = hours;
    else
        hr = 0;

    if (0 <= minutes && minutes < 60)
        min = minutes;
    else
        min = 0;

    if (0 <= seconds && seconds < 60)
        sec = seconds;
    else
        sec = 0;
}
```

As in the case of the default constructor, you can write the definition of the constructor with parameters using the method `setTime` as follows:

```
public Clock(int hours, int minutes, int seconds)
{
    setTime(hours, minutes, seconds);
}
```

This definition of the constructor with parameters makes debugging easier, because only the code for the method `setTime` needs to be checked.

DEFINITION OF THE Class Clock

Now that we have defined the methods of the **class** `Clock`, we can give the complete definition of the **class** `Clock`. Before the definition of a method, we include comments specifying the preconditions and/or postconditions.

Precondition: A statement specifying the condition(s) that must be true before the function is called.

Postcondition: A statement specifying what is true after the function call is completed.

The definition of the **class** `Clock` is:

```
public class Clock
{
    private int hr;   //store hours
    private int min;  //store minutes
    private int sec;  //store seconds

        //Default constructor
        //Postcondition: hr = 0; min = 0; sec = 0
    public Clock()
    {
        setTime(0, 0, 0);
    }

        //Constructor with parameters, to set the time
        //The time is set according to the parameters.
        //Postcondition: hr = hours; min = minutes;
        //               sec = seconds
    public Clock(int hours, int minutes, int seconds)
    {
        setTime(hours, minutes, seconds);
    }


        //Method to set the time
        //The time is set according to the parameters.
        //Postcondition: hr = hours; min = minutes;
        //               sec = seconds
```

```java
public void setTime(int hours, int minutes, int seconds)
{
    if (0 <= hours && hours < 24)
        hr = hours;
    else
        hr = 0;

    if (0 <= minutes && minutes < 60)
        min = minutes;
    else
        min = 0;

    if (0 <= seconds && seconds < 60)
        sec = seconds;
    else
        sec = 0;
}

    //Method to return the hours
    //Postcondition: the value of hr is returned
public int getHours()
{
    return hr;
}

    //Method to return the minutes
    //Postcondition: the value of min is returned
public int getMinutes()
{
    return min;
}

    //Method to return the seconds
    //Postcondition: the value of sec is returned
public int getSeconds()
{
    return sec;
}

    //Method to print the time
    //Postcondition: Time is printed in the form hh:mm:ss
public void printTime()
{
    if (hr < 10)
        System.out.print("0");
    System.out.print(hr + ":");

    if (min < 10)
        System.out.print("0");
    System.out.print(min + ":");
```

```
        if (sec < 10)
            System.out.print("0");
        System.out.print(sec);
    }


        //Method to increment the time by one second
        //Postcondition: The time is incremented by one second
        //If the before-increment time is 23:59:59, the time
        //is reset to 00:00:00
    public void incrementSeconds()
    {
        sec++;

        if (sec > 59)
        {
            sec = 0;
            incrementMinutes(); //increment minutes
        }
    }


        //Method to increment the time by one minute
        //Postcondition: The time is incremented by one minute
        //If the before-increment time is 23:59:53, the time
        //is reset to 00:00:53
    public void incrementMinutes()
    {
        min++;

        if (min > 59)
        {
            min = 0;
            incrementHours(); //increment hours
        }
    }


        //Method to increment the time by one hour
        //Postcondition: The time is incremented by one hour
        //If the before-increment time is 23:45:53, the time
        //is reset to 00:45:53
    public void incrementHours()
    {
        hr++;

        if (hr > 23)
            hr = 0;
    }


        //Method to compare two times
        //Postcondition: Returns true if this time is equal to
        //               otherClock; otherwise returns false
    public boolean equals(Clock otherClock)
```

8

```
    {
        return (hr == otherClock.hr
                && min == otherClock.min
                && sec == otherClock.sec);
    }

        //Method to copy time
        //Postcondition: The instance variables of otherClock
        //               copied into the corresponding data
        //               are members of this time.
        //               hr = otherClock.hr;
        //               min = otherClock.min;
        //               sec = otherClock.sec;
    public void makeCopy(Clock otherClock)
    {
        hr = otherClock.hr;
        min = otherClock.min;
        sec = otherClock.sec;
    }

        //Method to return a copy of time
        //Postcondition: A copy of the object is created and
        //               a reference of the copy is returned
    public Clock getCopy()
    {
        Clock temp = new Clock();

        temp.hr = hr;
        temp.min = min;
        temp.sec = sec;

        return temp;
    }
}
```

> **NOTE**   In a class definition, it is a common practice to list all the instance variables, named constants, other data members, or variable declarations first, then the constructors, and then the methods.

Once a class is properly defined and implemented, it can be used in a program. A program or software that uses and manipulates the objects of a class is called a **client** of that class.

EXAMPLE 8-2

```
//Program to test various operations of the class Clock

import java.util.*;

public class TestProgClock
```

```
{
    static Scanner console = new Scanner(System.in);

    public static void main(String[] args)
    {
        Clock myClock = new Clock(5, 4, 30);                     //Line 1
        Clock yourClock = new Clock();                          //Line 2

        int hours;                                              //Line 3
        int minutes;                                            //Line 4
        int seconds;                                            //Line 5

        System.out.print("Line 6: myClock: ");                 //Line 6
        myClock.printTime();                                   //Line 7
        System.out.println();                                  //Line 8
        System.out.print("Line 9: yourClock: ");               //Line 9
        yourClock.printTime();                                 //Line 10
        System.out.println();                                  //Line 11

        yourClock.setTime(5, 45, 16);                          //Line 12

        System.out.print("Line 13: After setting "
                       + "the time - yourClock: ");             //Line 13
        yourClock.printTime();                                 //Line 14
        System.out.println();                                  //Line 15

        if (myClock.equals(yourClock))                         //Line 16
            System.out.println("Line 17: Both the "
                             + "times are equal.");             //Line 17
        else                                                   //Line 18
            System.out.println("Line 19: The two "
                             + "times are not "
                             + "equal.");                       //Line 19

        System.out.print("Line 20: Enter hours, "
                       + "minutes, and seconds: ");             //Line 20
        hours = console.nextInt();                             //Line 21
        minutes = console.nextInt();                           //Line 22
        seconds = console.nextInt();                           //Line 23
        System.out.println();                                  //Line 24

        myClock.setTime(hours, minutes, seconds);              //Line 25

        System.out.print("Line 26: New time of "
                       + "myClock: ");                          //Line 26
        myClock.printTime();                                   //Line 27
        System.out.println();                                  //Line 28

        myClock.incrementSeconds();                            //Line 29

        System.out.print("Line 30: After "
                       + "incrementing the time by "
                       + "one second, myClock: ");              //Line 30
```

8

```
        myClock.printTime();                              //Line 31
        System.out.println();                             //Line 32

        yourClock.makeCopy(myClock);                      //Line 33

        System.out.print("Line 34: After copying "
                    + "myClock into yourClock, "
                    + "yourClock: ");                      //Line 34
        yourClock.printTime();                            //Line 35
        System.out.println();                             //Line 36
    }//end main
}
```

Sample Run: (In this sample run, the user input is shaded.)

```
Line 6: myClock: 05:04:30
Line 9: yourClock: 00:00:00
Line 13: After setting the time - yourClock: 05:45:16
Line 19: The two times are not equal.
Line 20: Enter hours, minutes, and seconds: 11 22 59

Line 26: New time of myClock: 11:22:59
Line 30: After incrementing the time by one second, myClock: 11:23:00
Line 34: After copying myClock into yourClock, yourClock: 11:23:00
```

A walk-through of the preceding program is left as an exercise for you.

Classes and the Method toString

Suppose that **x** is an **int** variable and the value of **x** is 25. The statement:

```
System.out.println(x);
```

outputs:

25

However, the output of the statement:

```
System.out.println(myClock);
```

is:

Clock@11b86e7

which looks strange. (Note that when you execute a similar statement, you are likely to get a different but similar output.) This is because whenever you create a **class**, the Java system provides the method **toString** to that **class**. The method **toString** is used to convert an object to a **String** object. When an object reference is provided as a parameter to the methods **print**, **println**, and **printf**, the **toString** method is called.

The default definition of the method `toString` creates a string that is the name of the object's `class`, followed by the hash code of the object. For example, in the preceding statement, `Clock` is the name of the object `myClock`'s `class` and the hash code for the object referenced by `myClock` is `@11b86e7`.

The method `toString` is a `public` value-returning method. It does not take any parameters and returns the address of a `String` object. The heading of the method `toString` is:

`public String toString()`

You can *override* the default definition of the method `toString` to convert an object to a desired string. Suppose that for the objects of the `class Clock` you want the method `toString` to create the string hh:mm:ss—the string consists of the object's hour, minutes, seconds, and the colons as shown. The string created by the method `toString` is the same as the string output by the method `printTime` of the `class Clock`. This is easily accomplished by providing the following definition of the method `toString`:

```
public String toString()
{
    String str = "";

    if (hr < 10)
        str = "0";
    str = str + hr + ":";

    if (min < 10)
        str = str + "0" ;
    str = str + min + ":";

    if (sec < 10)
        str = str + "0";
    str = str + sec;

    return str;
}
```

In the preceding code, `str` is a `String` variable used to create the required string.

The preceding definition of the method `toString` must be included in the `class Clock`. In fact, after including the method `toString` in the `class Clock`, we can remove the method `printTime`. If the values of the instance variables `hr`, `min`, and `sec` of `myClock` are 8, 25, and 56, respectively, then the output of the statement:

`System.out.println(myClock)`

is:

`08:25:56`

You can see that the method `toString` is useful for outputting the values of the instance variables. Note that the method `toString` only returns the (formatted) string; the methods `print`, `println`, or `printf` output the string.

EXAMPLE 8-3

In this example, we give the complete definition of the **class** Circle, which was briefly discussed in the beginning of this chapter.

```java
public class Circle
{
    private double radius;

      //Default constructor
      //Sets the radius to 0
    Circle()
    {
        radius = 0;
    }

      //Constructor with a parameter
      //Sets the radius to the value specified by the parameter r.
    Circle(double r)
    {
        radius = r;
    }

      //Method to set the radius of the circle.
      //Sets the radius to the value specified by the parameter r.
    public void setRadius(double r)
    {
        radius = r;
    }

      //Method to return the radius of the circle.
      //Returns the radius of the circle.
    public double getRadius()
    {
        return radius;
    }

      //Method to compute and return the area of the circle.
      //Computes and returns the area of the circle.
    public double area()
    {
        return Math.PI * Math.PI * radius;
    }

      //Method to compute and return the perimeter of the circle.
      //Computes and returns the area of the circle.
    public double perimeter()
    {
        return 2 * Math.PI * radius;
    }

      //Method to return the radius, area, perimeter of the circle
      //as a string.
```

```java
    public String toString()
    {
        return String.format("Radius = %.2f, Perimeter = %.2f"
                    + ", Area = %.2f%n", radius, perimeter(),
                    area());
    }
}
```

We leave the UML class diagram of the `class Circle` as an exercise for you.

The following program shows how to use the `class Circle` in a program.

```java
// Program to test various operations of the class Circle.

import java.util.*;                                    //Line 1

public class TestProgCircle                            //Line 2
{                                                      //Line 3
    static Scanner console = new Scanner(System.in);   //Line 4

    public static void main(String[] args)             //Line 5
    {                                                  //Line 6
        Circle firstCircle = new Circle();             //Line 7
        Circle secondCircle = new Circle(12);          //Line 8

        double radius;                                 //Line 9

        System.out.println("Line 10: firstCircle: "
                        + firstCircle);                //Line 10

        System.out.println("Line 11: secondCircle: "
                        + secondCircle);               //Line 11

        System.out.print("Line 12: Enter the radius: "); //Line 12
        radius = console.nextDouble();                 //Line 13
        System.out.println();                          //Line 14

        firstCircle.setRadius(radius);                 //Line 15

        System.out.println("Line 16: firstCircle: "
                        + firstCircle );               //Line 16

        if (firstCircle.getRadius()
                > secondCircle.getRadius())            //Line 17
            System.out.println("Line 18: The radius of "
                + "the first circle is greater than "
                + "the radius of the second circle. "); //Line 18
        else if (firstCircle.getRadius()
                < secondCircle.getRadius())            //Line 19
            System.out.println("Line 20: The radius of "
                + "the first circle is less than the "
                + "radius of the second circle. ");    //Line 20
```

8

```
        else                                          //Line 21
            System.out.println("Line 22: The radius of "
                + "both the circles are the same.");   //Line 22
    }//end main                                        //Line 23
}                                                      //Line 24
```

Sample Run: (In this sample run, the user input is shaded.)

Line 10: firstCircle: Radius = 0.00, Perimeter = 0.00, Area = 0.00

Line 11: secondCircle: Radius = 12.00, Perimeter = 75.40, Area = 118.44

Line 12: Enter the radius: 10

Line 16: firstCircle: Radius = 10.00, Perimeter = 62.83, Area = 98.70

Line 20: The radius of the first circle is less than the radius of the second circle.

The preceding program works as follows. The statement in Line 7 creates the object firstCircle and using the default constructor sets the radius to 0. The statement in Line 8 creates the object secondCircle and sets the radius to 12. The statement in Line 9 declares the double variable radius. The statement in Line 10 outputs the radius, area, and perimeter of the firstCircle. Similarly, the statement in Line 11 outputs the radius, area, and perimeter of the secondCircle The statement in Line 12 prompts the user to enter the value of radius. The statement in Line 13 stores the value entered by the user in the variable radius. The statement in Line 15 uses the value of radius to set the radius of firstCircle. The statement in Line 16 outputs the radius, area, and perimeter of the firstCircle. The statements in Lines 17 to 23 compare the radius of firstCircle and secondCircle and output the appropriate result.

EXAMPLE 8-4

In Example 7-3, the method rollDice rolls a pair of dice until the sum of the numbers rolled is a given number and returns the number of times the dice are rolled to get the desired sum. In fact, we can design a class that implements the basic properties of a die. Consider the definition of the following class RollDie.

```
public class RollDie
{
    private int num;

        //Default constructor
        //Sets the default number rolled by a die to 1
    RollDie()
    {
        num = 1;
    }
```

```
    //Method to roll a die.
    //This method uses a random number generator to randomly
    //generate a number between 1 and 6, and stores the number
    //in the instance variable num and returns the number.
public int roll()
{
    num = (int) (Math.random() * 6) + 1;

    return num;
}

    //Method to return the number on the top face of the die.
    //Returns the value of the instance variable num.
public int getNum()
{
    return num;
}

    //Returns the value of the instance variable num as a string.
public String toString()
{
    return "" + num;
}
}
```

We leave the UML class diagram of the **class** RollDie as an exercise for you.

The following program shows how to use the **class** RollDie in a program.

```
// Program to test various operations of the class RollDie.

import java.util.*;                                    //Line 1

public class TestProgRollDie                           //Line 2
{                                                      //Line 3
    static Scanner console = new Scanner(System.in);   //Line 4

    public static void main(String[] args)             //Line 5
    {                                                  //Line 6
        RollDie die1 = new RollDie();                  //Line 7
        RollDie die2 = new RollDie();                  //Line 8

        System.out.println("Line 9: die1: " + die1);   //Line 9

        System.out.println("Line 10: die2: " + die2);  //Line 10

        System.out.println("Line 11: After rolling "
                    + "die1: " + die1.roll());          //Line 11

        System.out.println("Line 12: After rolling "
                    + "die2: " + die2.roll());          //Line 12

        System.out.println("Line 13: Sum of the "
                + "numbers rolled by the dice is: "
                + (die1.getNum() + die2.getNum()));     //Line 13
```

8

```
        System.out.println("Line 14: After again rolling "
                + "the sum of the numbers rolled is: "
                + (die1.roll() + die2.roll()));        //Line 14
    }//end main                                        //Line 15
}                                                      //Line 16
```

Sample Run:

```
Line 9: die1: 1
Line 10: die2: 1
Line 11: After rolling die1: 5
Line 12: After rolling die2: 3
Line 13: Sum of the numbers rolled by the dice is: 8
Line 14: After again rolling the sum of the numbers rolled is: 4
```

The preceding program works as follows. The statements in Lines 7 and 8 create the objects die1 and die2, and using the default constructor set both the dice to 1. The statements in Lines 9 and 10 output the number of both the dice. The statement in Line 11 rolls die1 and outputs the number rolled. Similarly, the statement in Line 12 rolls die2 and outputs the number rolled. The statement in Line 13 outputs the sum of the numbers rolled by die1 and die2. The statement in Line 14 again rolls both the dice and outputs the sum of the numbers rolled.

Copy Constructor

Suppose that you have the following statement:

```
Clock myClock = new Clock(8, 45, 22);        //Line 1
```

You can use the object myClock to declare and instantiate another Clock object. Consider the following statement:

```
Clock aClock = new Clock(myClock);        //Line 2
```

This statement declares aClock to be a reference variable of type Clock, instantiates the object aClock, and initializes the instance variables of the object aClock using the values of the corresponding instance variables of the object myClock. However, to successfully execute the statement in Line 2, you need to include a special constructor, called a **copy constructor**, in the class Clock. The copy constructor executes when an object is instantiated and initialized using an existing object.

The syntax of the heading of the copy constructor is:

```
public ClassName(ClassName otherObject)
```

For example, the heading of the copy constructor for the **class** Clock is:

```
public Clock(Clock otherClock)
```

The definition of the copy constructor for the **class** Clock is:

```
public Clock(Clock otherClock)
{
    hr = otherClock.hr;
    min = otherClock.min;
    sec = otherClock.sec;
}
```

If you include this definition of the copy constructor in the **class** Clock, then the statement in Line 2 declares aClock to be a reference variable of type Clock, instantiates the object aClock, and initializes the instance variables of the object aClock using the values of the instance variables of the object myClock.

NOTE   The definition of the copy constructor of the **class** Clock can also be written as:

```
public Clock(Clock otherClock)
{
    setTime(otherClock.hr, otherClock.min, otherClock.sec);
}
```

The copy constructor is useful and will be included in most of the classes.

Static Members of a Class

In Chapter 7, we described the **class**es Math and Character. In Example 7-1 (of Chapter 7), we used several methods of the **class**es Math and Character; however, we did not need to create any objects to use these methods. We simply used the import statement:

```
import static java.lang.Math.*;
```

and then called the method with an appropriate actual parameter list. For example, to use the method pow of the **class** Math, we used expressions such as:

```
pow(5, 3)
```

Recall from Chapter 7 that if you are using versions of Java lower than Java 5.0 or you do not include the preceding **import** statement, then you call the method pow as follows:

```
Math.pow(5, 3)
```

That is, we can simply call the method using the name of the class and the dot operator.

We cannot use the same approach with the **class** Clock. Although the methods of the **class** Math are **public**, they also are defined using the modifier **static**. For example, the heading of the method pow of the **class** Math is:

```
public static double pow(double base, double exponent)
```

The modifier **static** in the heading specifies that the method can be invoked by using the name of the **class**. Similarly, if a data member of a **class** is declared using the modifier **static**, it can be accessed by using the name of the **class**.

The following example clarifies the effect of the modifier `static`.

EXAMPLE 8-5

Consider the following definition of the `class Illustrate`:

```
public class Illustrate
{
    private int x;
    private static int y;
    public static int count;

        //Default constructor
        //Postcondition: x = 0;
    public Illustrate()
    {
        x = 0;
    }

        //Constructor with parameters
        //Postcondition: x = a;
    public Illustrate(int a)
    {
        x = a;
    }

        //Method to set x.
        //Postcondition: x = a;
    void setX(int a)
    {
        x = a;
    }

        //Method to return the values of the instance
        //and static variables as a string
        //The string returned is used by the methods
        //print, println, or printf to print the values
        //of the instance and static variables.
        //Postcondition: The values of x, y, and count
        //are returned as a string.
    public String toString()
    {
        return("x = " + x + ", y = " + y
            + ", count = " + count);
    }

        //Method to increment the value of the private
        //static member y
        //Postcondition: y is incremented by 1.
```

```
public static void incrementY()
{
    y++;
}
}
```

Suppose that you have the following declaration:

```
Illustrate illusObject = new Illustrate();
```

The reference variable `illusObject` can access any `public` member of the `class` `Illustrate`.

The method `incrementY` is `static` and `public`, so the following statement is legal:

```
Illustrate.incrementY();
```

Similarly, because the data member `count` is `static` and `public`, the following statement is legal:

```
Illustrate.count++;
```

___

In essence, `public` `static` members of a `class` can be accessed either by an object, that is, by using a reference variable of the `class` type, or using the `class` name and the dot operator.

static **Variables (Data Members) of a Class**

Suppose that you have a `class`, say, `MyClass`, with data members (`static` and non-`static`). When you instantiate the objects of type `MyClass`, only the non-`static` data members of the `class` `MyClass` become the data members of each object. What about the memory for the `static` data members of `MyClass`? For each `static` data member of the `class`, Java allocates memory space only once. All `MyClass` objects refer to the same memory space. In fact, `static` data members of a `class` *exist* even when no object of the `class` type is instantiated. Moreover, `static` variables are initialized to their default values. You can access the `public` `static` data members outside the `class`, as explained in the previous section.

The following example further clarifies how memory space is allocated for `static` and non-`static` data members of a class.

Suppose that you have the `class` `Illustrate`, as given in Example 8-5. Then, memory space exists for the `static` data members `y` and `count`.

Consider the following statements:

```
Illustrate illusObject1 = new Illustrate(3);      //Line 1
Illustrate illusObject2 = new Illustrate(5);      //Line 2
```

The statements in Lines 1 and 2 declare `illusObject1` and `illusObject2` to be reference variables of type `Illustrate` and instantiate these objects (see Figure 8-14).

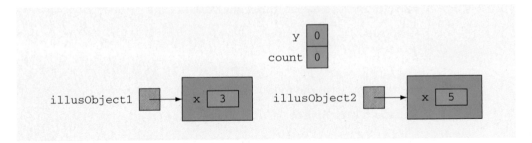

FIGURE 8-14 illusObject1 and illusObject2

Now consider the following statement:

```
Illustrate.incrementY();
Illustrate.count++;
```

After these statements execute, the objects and static members are as shown in Figure 8-15.

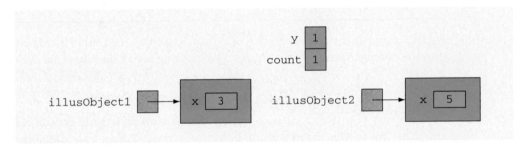

FIGURE 8-15 illusObject1 and illusObject2 after the statements Illustrate.incrementY(); and Illustrate.count++; execute

The output of the statement:

```
System.out.println(illusObject1);            //Line 3
```

is:

```
x = 3, y = 1, count = 1
```

Similarly, the output of the statement:

```
System.out.println(illusObject2);            //Line 4
```

is:

```
x = 5, y = 1, count = 1
```

Now consider the statement:

```
Illustrate.count++;
```

After this statement executes, the objects and static members are as shown in Figure 8-16.

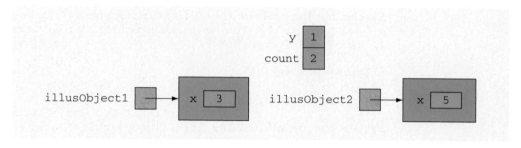

FIGURE 8-16 illusObject1 and illusObject2 after the statement Illustrate.count++; executes

The output of the statements:

```
System.out.println(illusObject1);
System.out.println(illusObject2);
```

is:

```
x = 3, y = 1, count = 2
x = 5, y = 1, count = 2
```

The program in Example 8-6 further illustrates how **static** members of a class work.

8

EXAMPLE 8-6

```
public class StaticMembers
{
    public static void main(String[] args)
    {
        Illustrate illusObject1 = new Illustrate(3);   //Line 1
        Illustrate illusObject2 = new Illustrate(5);   //Line 2

        Illustrate.incrementY();                        //Line 3
        Illustrate.count++;                             //Line 4

        System.out.println("Line 5: illusObject1: "
                      + illusObject1);                  //Line 5
        System.out.println("Line 6: illusObject2: "
                      + illusObject2);                  //Line 6

        System.out.println("Line 7: ***Increment y "
                      + "using illusObject1***");       //Line 7
        illusObject1.incrementY();                      //Line 8

        illusObject1.setX(8);                           //Line 9

        System.out.println("Line 10: illusObject1: "
                      + illusObject1);                  //Line 10
```

```
        System.out.println("Line 11: illusObject2: "
                    + illusObject2);                //Line 11

        System.out.println("Line 12: ***Increment y "
                    + "using illusObject2***");     //Line 12
        illusObject2.incrementY();                  //Line 13

        illusObject2.setX(23);                      //Line 14

        System.out.println("Line 15: illusObject1: "
                    + illusObject1);                //Line 15
        System.out.println("Line 16: illusObject2: "
                    + illusObject2);                //Line 16
    }
}
```

Sample Run:

```
Line 5: illusObject1: x = 3, y = 1, count = 1
Line 6: illusObject2: x = 5, y = 1, count = 1
Line 7: ***Increment y using illusObject1***
Line 10: illusObject1: x = 8, y = 2, count = 1
Line 11: illusObject2: x = 5, y = 2, count = 1
Line 12: ***Increment y using illusObject2***
Line 15: illusObject1: x = 8, y = 3, count = 1
Line 16: illusObject2: x = 23, y = 3, count = 1
```

The preceding program works as follows: The static data members y and count are initialized to 0. The statements in Lines 1 and 2 create the Illustrate objects illusObject1 and illusObject2. The instance variable x of illusObject1 is initialized to 3; the instance variable x of illusObject2 is initialized to 5.

The statement in Line 3 uses the name of the class Illustrate and the method incrementY to increment y. Because count is a public static member of the class Illustrate, the statement in Line 4 uses the name of the class Illustrate to directly access count, and increments it by 1. The statements in Lines 5 and 6 output the data stored in the objects illusObject1 and illusObject2. Note that the value of y for both objects is the same. Similarly, the value of count for both objects is the same.

The statement in Line 7 is an output statement. The statement in Line 8 uses the object illusObject1 and the method incrementY to increment y. The statement in Line 9 sets the value of the instance variable x of illusObject1 to 8. Lines 10 and 11 output the data stored in the objects illusObject1 and illusObject2. Note that the value of y for both objects is the same. Similarly, the value of count for both objects is the same. Moreover, notice that the statement in Line 9 only changes the value of the instance variable x of illusObject1 because x is *not* a static member of the class Illustrate.

The statement in Line 13 uses the object illusObject2 and the method incrementY to increment y. The statement in Line 14 sets the value of the instance variable x of illusObject2 to 23. Lines 15 and 16 output the data stored in the objects illusObject1 and illusObject2. Notice that the value of y for both objects is the same. Similarly, the value of count for both objects is the same. Note that the statement in Line 14 only changes the value of the instance variable x of illusObject2 because x is *not* a static member of the class Illustrate.

NOTE Here are some additional comments on static members of a class. As you have seen in this section, a static method of a class does not need any object to be invoked. It can be called using the name of the class and the dot operator. Therefore, a static method cannot use anything that depends on a calling object. In other words, in the definition of a static method, you cannot use a non-static data member or a non-static method, unless there is a locally declared object that accesses the non-static data member or the non-static method.

Finalizers

Like constructors, **finalizers** are also special types of methods. However, a finalizer is a void method. A class can have only one finalizer, and the finalizer cannot have any parameters. The name of the finalizer is finalize. The method finalize automatically executes when the class object goes out of scope. A typical use of a finalizer is to free up the memory allocated by the object of a class.

Accessor and Mutator Methods

Earlier in this chapter, we defined the terms mutator method and accessor method. This section discusses these terms in detail and explains why such methods are needed to construct a class.

Let us look at the methods of the class Clock. The method setTime sets the values of the data members to the values specified by the user. In other words, it alters or modifies the values of the instance variables. Similarly, the methods incrementHours, incrementMinutes, and incrementSeconds also modify the instance variables. However, methods such as getHours, getMinutes, getSeconds, printTime, and equals only access the values of the data members; they *do not* modify the data members. We can, therefore, divide the methods of the class Clock into two categories: methods that modify the data members, and methods that access, but do not modify, the data members.

This is typically true for any class. That is, almost every class has methods that only access and do not modify the data members, called **accessor methods**, and methods that modify the data members, called **mutator methods**.

Accessor Method: A method of a class that only accesses (that is, does not modify) the value(s) of the data member(s).

Mutator Method: A method of a class that modifies the value(s) of one or more data member(s).

Typically, the instance variables of a class are declared `private` so that the user of a class does not have direct access to them. In general, every class has a set of accessor methods to work with the instance variables. If the data members need to be modified, then the class also has a set of mutator methods. Conventionally, mutator methods begin with the word `set` and accessor methods begin with the word `get`. You might wonder why we need both mutator and accessor methods when we can simply make the instance variables `public`. However, look closely, for example, at the mutator method `setTime` of the `class` `Clock`. Before setting the time, it validates the time. On the other hand, if the instance variables are all `public`, then the user of the class can put any values in the instance variables. Similarly, the accessor methods only return the value(s) of an instance variable(s); that is, they do not modify the values. A well-designed class uses `private` instance variables, accessor methods, and (if needed) mutator methods to implement the OOD principle of encapsulation.

Example 8-7 further illustrates how classes are designed and implemented. The `class` `Person` that we create in this example is very useful; we will use this `class` in subsequent chapters.

EXAMPLE 8-7

Two common attributes of a person are the person's first name and last name. The typical operations on a person's name are to set the name and print the name. The following statements define a `class` with these properties (see Figure 8-17).

```
public class Person
{
    private String firstName; //store the first name
    private String lastName;  //store the last name

        //Default constructor;
        //Initialize firstName and lastName to empty string.
        //Postcondition: firstName = ""; lastName = "";
    public Person()
    {
        firstName = "";
        lastName = "";
    }

        //Constructor with parameters
        //Set firstName and lastName according to the parameters.
        //Postcondition: firstName = first; lastName = last;
    public Person(String first, String last)
    {
        setName(first, last);
    }
```

```
    //Method to output the first name and last name
    //in the form firstName lastName
public String toString()
{
    return (firstName + " " + lastName);
}

    //Method to set firstName and lastName according to
    //the parameters
    //Postcondition: firstName = first; lastName = last;
public void setName(String first, String last)
{
    firstName = first;
    lastName = last;
}

    //Method to return the firstName
    //Postcondition: the value of firstName is returned
public String getFirstName()
{
    return firstName;
}

    //Method to return the lastName
    //Postcondition: the value of lastName is returned
public String getLastName()
{
    return lastName;
}
}
```

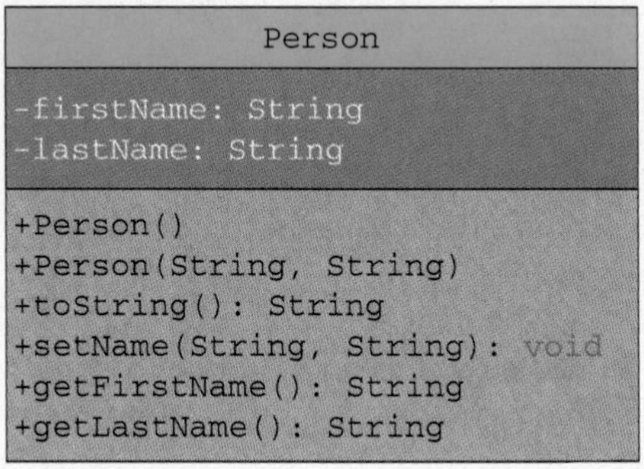

8

Person

-firstName: String
-lastName: String

+Person()
+Person(String, String)
+toString(): String
+setName(String, String): void
+getFirstName(): String
+getLastName(): String

FIGURE 8-17 UML class diagram of the class Person

The following program tests the `class Person`:

```
public class TestProgPerson
{
    public static void main(String[] args)
    {
        Person name = new Person();                         //Line 1

        Person emp = new Person("Donald", "Jackson");       //Line 2

        System.out.println("Line 3: name: " + name);        //Line 3

        name.setName("Ashley", "Blair");                    //Line 4
        System.out.println("Line 5: name: " + name);        //Line 5

        System.out.println("Line 6: emp: " + emp);          //Line 6

        emp.setName("Sandy", "Smith");                      //Line 7
        System.out.println("Line 8: emp: " + emp);          //Line 8
    }//end main
}
```

Sample Run:

```
Line 3: name:
Line 5: name: Ashley Blair
Line 6: emp: Donald Jackson
Line 8: emp: Sandy Smith
```

Debugging—Designing a Class and Documenting the Design

Some beginning programmers mistakenly assume that problem-solving is about coding. These individuals either never become competent programmers, or they come to appreciate the fact that design is a critical step that always precedes coding. By the time we reach the design phase, we already know what the problem is and we focus our attention on how to solve it. Good programmers learn how to solve a problem completely before they write a single line of code. The solution should be understood so thoroughly that, given only pencil, paper, and enough time, the programmer could solve the problem without the use of a computer.

The design is not something that exists only in the programmer's head. It is written down in enough detail that another programmer with the same level of programming skill can take the design and produce the Java code without having to do additional problem-solving.

Let's review the approach we took in designing the `class Clock`. First we identified the operations that the class needed to perform. We determined that each operation should have its own method and identified the data members required by each of these operations. We determined the type and value, if any, produced and returned by each of these operations. We determined which members should be `private` and which members should be `public`, and wrote method headings for each member, each beginning with the word `public` or `private`. Following the word `public` or `private`, we stated the return type—except for the constructors, which never have a return type. Then we provided the name of the method followed by parentheses. Any needed parameters, each preceded by its type, were included between the parentheses.

Sometimes, the means by which a method achieves the intended objective is obvious, requiring only a simple statement. Sometimes it takes a great deal of thought to discover the best means of achieving the intended objective, occasionally requiring a more complex statement. Often several means of achieving the objective are considered before one is selected. Determining how to achieve the intended objective should be completed during the design phase, not the coding phase. An **algorithm** describes the means for achieving the intended objective.

An algorithm can be described in many different ways. Algorithms are often described using *pseudocode*. Pseudocode is a mixture of English, Java, and useful symbols, but usually without regard for formal syntax. Whatever form is used to describe the algorithm, it should be sufficiently clear so that a programmer can code the algorithm in Java without having to make any further decisions about how to solve the problem.

The means by which each method achieves its objective is written down as part of the design phase. At one extreme, only a single line is required. At the other extreme, a complicated process with complicated formulas might need to be described. But, in all cases, the means should be clear and complete.

Our design of the `class` `Clock` might look like the following:

```java
public class Clock
{
// data members

    private int hr;
    private int min;
    private int sec;

// methods

    public Clock()
    {
        // set time to 0,0,0
    }

    public Clock(int hours, int minutes, int seconds)
    {
        // set time to according to the parameters
    }

    public void setTime(int hours, int minutes, int seconds)
    {
        // set time to according to the parameters

    }
```

```
    public int getHours()
    {
        // return hr
    }

    public int getMinutes()
    {
        // return min
    }

    public int getSeconds()
    {
        //return sec
    }

    public void printTime()
    {
        // print hr:min:sec
    }

    public void incrementSeconds()
    {
        // increment sec by 1
    }

    public void incrementMinutes()
    {
        // increment min by 1
    }

    public void incrementHours()
    {
        // increment hr by 1
    }

    public boolean equals(Clock otherClock)
    {
        // compare this time with the time of otherClock
    }

    public void makeCopy(Clock otherClock)
    {
        // copy time of otherClock
    }

    public Clock getCopy()
    {
        // return a copy of this time
    }
}
```

The current version of the `class Clock` can be coded directly from this design.

Avoid the temptation to skip the design phase. Even though the first programs you write can be made to run by going directly to the coding phase, this approach works only for very small programs. More importantly, it creates a bad habit, which is easy to form but hard to live with—whereas good habits are hard to form but easy to live with. Experience demonstrates consistently that the total time required to produce, debug, and maintain a properly designed program is significantly less than the total time required to produce, debug, and maintain a program with an incomplete design or with no design at all. In fact, programs with incomplete designs, or no designs at all, often never achieve their intended objectives.

Debugging—Design Walk-Throughs

In Chapter 2, you learned about using code walk-throughs to find and remove bugs from programs. The same principles apply to design walk-throughs. Typically, a design walk-through takes place as the design is being finalized and before any code is written.

Except for the syntactic bugs that show up in your program, many of the bugs that you encounter in your programs creep in at design time. Sometimes an important operation is omitted. Sometimes we fail to consider potential future use of the class, and we make a class needlessly specialized. Sometimes too much is expected of a single method, when instead two or more methods should be written to achieve the intended objective. Sometimes not all the data members required by the method are identified and provided. Sometimes the value to be produced and returned by the method is characterized improperly. Sometimes the `public` or `private` status of a member is determined incorrectly. For example, a `public` data member is seldom if ever appropriate. All of these problems can be corrected at design time before a single line of code is written.

Sometimes, in the interest of generality, programmers provide methods that are unlikely to ever be used. This creates excess baggage that can make it difficult to design, implement, test, and maintain programs. Occasionally data members are passed into a method even though the method makes no use of them, or a method returns a value that is never used. All of these excesses make programs more difficult to develop. As a programmer, you should take steps to avoid them.

With a code walk-through, a programmer begins by trying to find and fix these problems himself. The programmer should verify that each intended operation is represented by one or more methods. He should verify that each method receives only the data members needed to achieve its intended objective. The programmer should verify that any intended value is returned by the method. He should also review the `public` or `private` status of each member. Next, the programmer should think through the ranges of data that could be passed to each method. By walking through it in his mind, he verifies that, in every case, the method performs as intended with each variety of data that could be passed to it.

At this point, it may be prudent for the programmer to repeat the design walk-through process with someone who is learning to design programs or who has learned to design programs already. As always, the programmer should be sure that he has prepared his design carefully before presenting it to someone else. In the process of doing so, he may find and correct one or more bugs that he missed during his previous design review. As the programmer explains his design, both he and his audience will have an opportunity to look carefully and methodically at each aspect.

As before, avoid the temptation to shortchange the design phase by "cutting to the chase." Deficiencies encountered at design time are much easier to correct than deficiencies encountered after coding has begun.

Reference `this` (Optional)

In this chapter, we defined the `class` `Clock`. Suppose that `myClock` is a reference variable of type `Clock`. Suppose that the object `myClock` has been created. Consider the following statements:

```
myClock.setTime(5, 6, 59);        //Line 1
myClock.incrementSeconds();       //Line 2
```

The statement in Line 1 uses the method `setTime` to set the instance variables `hr`, `min`, and `sec` of the object `myClock` to 5, 6, and 59, respectively. The statement in Line 2 uses the method `incrementSeconds` to increment the time of the object `myClock` by one second. The statement in Line 2 also results in a call to the method `incrementMinutes` because, after incrementing the value of `sec` by 1, the value of `sec` becomes 60, which then is reset to 0, and the method `incrementMinutes` is invoked.

How do you think Java makes sure that the statement in Line 1 sets the instance variables of the object `myClock` and not of another `Clock` object? How does Java make sure that when the method `incrementSeconds` calls the method `incrementMinutes`, the method `incrementMinutes` increments the value of the instance variable `min` of the object `myClock` and not of another `Clock` object?

The answer is that every object has access to a reference of itself. The name of this reference is `this`. In Java, `this` is a reserved word.

Java implicitly uses the reference `this` to refer to both the instance variables and the methods of a class. Recall that the definition of the method `setTime` is:

```
public void setTime(int hours, int minutes, int seconds)
{
    if (0 <= hours && hours < 24)
        hr = hours;
    else
        hr = 0;
```

```
    if (0 <= minutes && minutes < 60)
        min = minutes;
    else
        min = 0;

    if (0 <= seconds && seconds < 60)
        sec = seconds;
    else
        sec = 0;
}
```

In the method setTime, the statement:

```
hr = hours;
```

is, in fact, equivalent to the statement:

```
this.hr = hours;
```

In this statement, the reference this is used explicitly. You can explicitly use the reference this and write the equivalent definition of the method setTime as follows:

```
public void setTime(int hr, int min, int sec)
{
    if (0 <= hr && hr < 24)
        this.hr = hr;
    else
        this.hr = 0;

    if (0 <= min && min < 60)
        this.min = min;
    else
        this.min = 0;

    if (0 <= sec && sec < 60)
        this.sec = sec;
    else
        this.sec = 0;
}
```

Notice that in the preceding definition of the method setTime, the name of the formal parameters and the name of the instance variables are the same. In this definition of the method setTime, the expression this.hr means the instance variable hr, not the formal parameter hr, and so on. Because the code explicitly uses the reference this, the compiler can distinguish between the instance variables and the formal parameters. Of course, you could have kept the name of the formal parameters as before and still used the reference this as shown in the code.

Similarly, explicitly using the reference `this`, you can write the definition of the method `incrementSeconds` as follows:

```
public void incrementSeconds()
{
    this.sec++;

    if (this.sec > 59)
    {
        this.sec = 0;
        this.incrementMinutes(); //increment minutes
    }
}
```

Cascaded Method Calls (Optional)

In addition to explicitly referring to the instance variables and methods of an object, the reference `this` has another use—to implement cascaded method calls. We explain this with the help of an example.

In Example 8-7, we designed the `class` Person to implement a person's name in a program. Here, we extend the definition of the `class` Person to individually set a person's first name and last name, and then return a reference to the object, using `this`. The following code is the extended definition of the `class` Person. (The methods `setFirstName` and `setLastName` are added to this definition of the `class` Person.)

```
public class Person
{
    private String firstName; //store the first name
    private String lastName;  //store the last name

        //Default constructor;
        //Initialize firstName and lastName to empty string.
        //Postcondition: firstName = ""; lastName = "";
    public Person()
    {
        firstName = "";
        lastName = "";
    }

        //Constructor with parameters
        //Set firstName and lastName according to the parameters.
        //Postcondition: firstName = first; lastName = last;
    public Person(String first, String last)
    {
        setName(first, last);
    }
```

```java
    //Method to return the first name and last name
    //in the form firstName lastName
public String toString()
{
    return (firstName + " " + lastName);
}

    //Method to set firstName and lastName according to
    //the parameters
    //Postcondition: firstName = first; lastName = last;
public void setName(String first, String last)
{
    firstName = first;
    lastName = last;
}

    //Method to set the last name
    //Postcondition: lastName = last;
    //       After setting the last name, a reference
    //       of the object is returned.
public Person setLastName(String last)
{
    lastName = last;

    return this;
}

    //Method to set the first name
    //Postcondition: firstName = first;
    //       After setting the first name, a reference
    //       of the object is returned.
public Person setFirstName(String first)
{
    firstName = first;

    return this;
}

  //Method to return the firstName
  //Postcondition: the value of firstName is returned
public String getFirstName()
{
    return firstName;
}

  //Method to return the lastName
  //Postcondition: the value of lastName is returned
public String getLastName()
{
    return lastName;
}
}
```

8

Consider the following method `main`:

```
public class CascadedMethodCalls
{
   public static void main(String[] args)
   {
      Person student1 =
               new Person("Angela", "Smith");        //Line 1

      Person student2 = new Person();                //Line 2

      Person student3 = new Person();                //Line 3
      System.out.println("Line 4 -- Student 1: "
                         + student1);                //Line 4

      student2.setFirstName("Shelly").
                         setLastName("Malik");       //Line 5

      System.out.println("Line 6 -- Student 2: "
                         + student2);                //Line 6

      student3.setFirstName("Chelsea");              //Line 7

      System.out.println("Line 8 -- Student 3: "
                         + student3);                //Line 8

      student3.setLastName("Tomek");                 //Line 9

      System.out.println("Line 10 -- Student 3: "
                         + student3);                //Line 10

   }
}
```

Sample Run:

```
Line 4 -- Student 1: Angela Smith
Line 6 -- Student 2: Shelly Malik
Line 8 -- Student 3: Chelsea
Line 10 -- Student 3: Chelsea Tomek
```

The statements in Lines 1, 2, and 3 declare the variables `student1`, `student2`, and `student3` and also instantiate the objects. The instance variables of the objects `student2` and `student3` are initialized to empty strings. The statement in Line 4 outputs the value of `student1`. The statement in Line 5 works as follows. In the statement:

```
student2.setFirstName("Shelly").setLastName("Malik");
```

first the expression:

```
student2.setFirstName("Shelly")
```

is executed because the associativity of the dot operator is from left to right. This expression sets the first name to **"Shelly"** and returns a reference to the object, which is the object **student2**. Thus, the next expression executed is:

```
student2.setLastName("Malik")
```

which sets the last name of the object **student2** to **"Malik"**. The statement in Line 6 outputs the value of **student2**. The statement in Line 7 sets the first name of **student3** to **"Chelsea"**, and the statement in Line 8 outputs **student3**. Notice the output in Line 8. The output shows only the first name, not the last name, because we have not yet set the last name of the object **student3**. The last name of the object **student3** is still empty, which was set by the statement in Line 3 when **student3** was declared. Next, the statement in Line 9 sets the last name of the object **student3**, and the statement in Line 10 outputs **student3**.

Inner Classes

The classes defined thus far in this chapter are said to have file scope, that is, they are contained within a file, but not within another class. In Chapter 6, while designing the **class RectangleProgram**, we defined the **class CalculateButtonHandler** to handle an action event. The definition of the **class CalculateButtonHandler** is contained within the **class RectangleProgram**. Classes that are defined within other classes are called **inner classes**.

An inner class can be either a complete class definition, such as the **class CalculateButtonHandler**, or an anonymous inner class definition. Anonymous classes are classes with no name.

One of the main uses of inner classes is to handle events—as we did in Chapter 6. A full discussion of inner classes is beyond the scope of this book. In this book, our main use of inner classes is to handle events in a GUI program. For example, see the programming example in Chapter 6 and the GUI part of the programming example in this chapter.

Abstract Data Types

To help you understand an abstract data type (ADT) and how it might be used, we'll provide an analogy. The following items seem unrelated:

- A deck of playing cards
- A set of index cards containing contact information
- Telephone numbers stored in your cellular phone

All three of these items share the following structural properties:

- Each one is a collection of elements.
- There is a first element.

- There is a second element, third element, and so on.
- There is a last element.
- Given an element other than the last element, there is a "next" element.
- Given an element other than the first element, there is a "previous" element.
- An element can be removed from the collection.
- An element can be added to the collection.
- A specified element can be located in the collection by systematically going through the collection.

In your programs, you may want to keep a collection of various elements, such as addresses, students, employees, departments, and projects. This structure commonly appears in various applications, and it is worth studying in its own right. We call this organization a *list*, which is an example of an ADT.

There is a data type called `Vector` (discussed in Chapter 9) with basic operations such as:

- Insert an item.
- Delete an item.
- Find an item.

You can use a `Vector` object to create an address book. You would not need to write a program to insert an address, delete an address, or find an item in your address book. Java also allows you to create your own abstract data types through classes.

An ADT is an abstraction of a commonly appearing data structure, along with a set of defined operations on the data structure.

Abstract data type (ADT): A data type that specifies the logical properties without concern for the implementation details.

Historically, the concept of ADT in computer programming developed as a way of abstracting the common data structure and the associated operations. Along the way, ADT provided **information hiding**. That is, ADT *hides* the implementation details of the operations and the data from the users of the ADT. Users can use the operations of an ADT without knowing how the operation is implemented.

PROGRAMMING EXAMPLE: Candy Machine

A new candy machine is bought for the cafeteria and a program is needed to make the machine function properly. The machine sells candies, chips, gum, and cookies. In this programming example, we write a program to create a Java application program for the candy machine so that it can be put into operation.

We implement this program in two ways. First, we show how to design a non-GUI application program. Then, we show how to design an application program that will create a GUI to make the candy machine operational.

The non-GUI application program should do the following:

1. Show the customer the different products sold by the candy machine.
2. Let the customer make the selection.
3. Show the customer the cost of the item selected.
4. Accept the money from the customer.
5. Release the item.

Input: The item selection and the cost of the item

Output: The selected item

In the next section, we design the candy machine's basic components, which are required by either type of application program—GUI or non-GUI. The difference between the two types is evident when we write the main program to put the candy machine into operation.

PROBLEM ANALYSIS AND ALGORITHM DESIGN

A candy machine has three main components: a built-in cash register, several dispensers to hold and release the products, and the candy machine itself. Therefore, we need to define a class to implement the cash register, a class to implement the dispenser, and a class to implement the candy machine. First, we describe the classes to implement the cash register and dispenser, and then we use these classes to describe the candy machine.

Cash Register

Let's first discuss the properties of a cash register. The register has some cash on hand, it accepts the amount from the customer, and if the amount entered is more than the cost of the item, then—if possible—it returns the change. For simplicity, we assume that the user enters the exact amount for the product. The cash register should also be able to show the candy machine's owner the amount of money in the register at any given time. Let's call the class implementing the cash register `CashRegister`.

8

The members of the **class CashRegister** are listed below and shown in Figure 8-18.

Instance
Variables

```
private int cashOnHand;
```

Constructors
and Methods

```
public CashRegister()
    //Default constructor
    //To set the cash in the register 500 cents
    //Postcondition: cashOnHand = 500;

public CashRegister(int cashIn)
    //Constructor with parameters
    //Postcondition: cashOnHand = cashIn;

public int currentBalance()
    //Method to show the current amount in the cash register
    //Postcondition: The value of the instance variable
    //               cashOnHand is returned

public void acceptAmount(int amountIn)
    //Method to receive the amount deposited by
    //the customer and update the amount in the register
    //Postcondition: cashOnHand = cashOnHand + amountIn
```

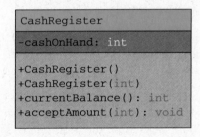

FIGURE 8-18 UML class diagram of the **class** CashRegister

Next, we give the definitions of the methods to implement the operations of the **class CashRegister**. The definitions of these methods are simple and easy to follow.

The method **currentBalance** shows the current amount in the cash register. The amount stored in the cash register is in cents. Its definition is:

```
public int currentBalance()
{
    return cashOnHand;
}
```

The method `acceptAmount` accepts the amount entered by the customer. It updates the cash in the register by adding the amount entered by the customer to the previous amount in the cash register. The definition of this method is:

```java
public void acceptAmount(int amountIn)
{
    cashOnHand = cashOnHand + amountIn;
}
```

The constructor with the parameter sets the value of the instance variable to the value specified by the user. The value is passed as a parameter to the constructor. The definition of the constructor with the parameter is:

```java
public CashRegister(int cashIn)
{
    if (cashIn >= 0)
        cashOnHand = cashIn;
    else
        cashOnHand = 500;
}
```

Note that the definition of the constructor checks for valid values of the parameter `cashIn`. If the value of `cashIn` is less than 0, the value assigned to the instance variable `cashOnHand` is 500.

The default constructor sets the value of the instance variable `cashOnHand` to 500 cents. Its definition is:

```java
public CashRegister()
{
    cashOnHand = 500;
}
```

Now that we have the definitions of all the methods necessary to implement the operations of the class `CashRegister`, we can give the definition of `CashRegister`. Its definition is:

```java
//class cashRegister

public class CashRegister
{
    private int cashOnHand;    //variable to store the cash
                               //in the register

        //Default constructor to set the cash
        //in the register to 500 cents
        //Postcondition: cashOnHand = 500
    public CashRegister()
    {
        cashOnHand = 500;
    }
```

8

```java
        //Constructor with parameters to set the cash in
        //the register to a specific amount
        //Postcondition: cashOnHand = cashIn
    public CashRegister(int cashIn)
    {
        if (cashIn >= 0)
            cashOnHand = cashIn;
        else
          cashOnHand = 500;
    }


        //Method to show the current amount in the cash register
        //Postcondition: The value of the instance variable
        //               cashOnHand is returned.
    public int currentBalance()
    {
        return cashOnHand;
    }


        //Method to receive the amount deposited by
        //the customer and update the amount in the register
        //Postcondition: cashOnHand = cashOnHand + amountIn
    public void acceptAmount(int amountIn)
    {
        cashOnHand = cashOnHand + amountIn;
    }
}
```

Dispenser   The dispenser releases the selected item if it is not empty. It should show the number of items in the dispenser and the cost of the item. Let's call the class implementing a dispenser `Dispenser`. The members necessary to implement the **class** `Dispenser` are listed next and shown in Figure 8-19.

Instance Variables

```java
private int numberOfItems; //variable to store the number of
                           //items in the dispenser

private int cost;   //variable to store the cost of an item
```

Constructors and Methods

```java
public Dispenser()
    //Default constructor to set the cost and number of
    //items to the default values
    //Postcondition: numberOfItems = 50; cost = 50;

public Dispenser(int setNoOfItems, int setCost)
    //Constructor with parameters to set the cost and number
    //of items in the dispenser specified by the user
    //Postcondition: numberOfItems = setNoOfItems;
    //               cost = setCost;
```

```
public int getCount()
    //Method to show the number of items in the dispenser
    //Postcondition: The value of the instance variable
    //                numberOfItems is returned

public int getProductCost()
    //Method to show the cost of the item
    //Postcondition: The value of the instance
    //                variable cost is returned

public void makeSale()
    //Method to reduce the number of items by 1
    //Postcondition: numberOfItems = numberOfItems - 1;
```

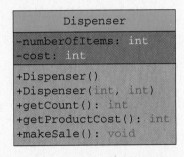

FIGURE 8-19 UML class diagram of the **class** Dispenser

Because the candy machine sells four types of items, we will create four objects of type **Dispenser**. The statement:

```
Dispenser chips = new Dispenser(100, 65);
```

creates the object **chips**, sets the number of chip bags in this dispenser to **100**, and sets the cost of each chip bag to **65** cents (see Figure 8-20).

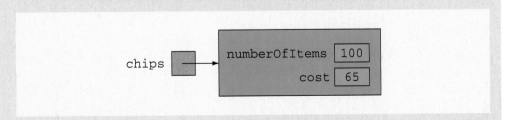

FIGURE 8-20 The object **chips**

Next, we discuss the definitions of the methods to implement the operations of the class Dispenser.

The method getCount returns the number of items of a particular product. Because the number of items currently in the dispenser is stored in the instance variable numberOfItems, the method getCount returns the value of the instance variable numberOfItems. The definition of this method is:

```
public int getCount()
{
    return numberOfItems;
}
```

The method getProductCost returns the cost of a product. Because the cost of a product is stored in the instance variable cost, it returns the value of the instance variable cost. The definition of this method is:

```
public int getProductCost()
{
    return cost;
}
```

When a product is sold, the number of items in that dispenser is reduced by 1. Therefore, the method makeSale reduces the number of items in the dispenser by 1. That is, it decrements the value of the instance variable numberOfItems by 1. The definition of this method is:

```
public void makeSale()
{
    numberOfItems--;
}
```

The definition of the constructor checks for valid values of the parameters. If these values are less than 0, the default values are assigned to the instance variables. The definition of the constructor is:

```
    //constructor with parameters
public Dispenser(int setNoOfItems, int setCost)
{
    if (setNoOfItems >= 0)
       numberOfItems = setNoOfItems;
    else
        numberOfItems = 50;

    if (setCost >= 0)
        cost = setCost;
    else
        cost = 50;
}
```

The default constructor assigns the default values to the instance variables:

```
public Dispenser()
{
    numberOfItems = 50;
    cost = 50;
}
```

The definition of the class Dispenser is:

```
//class Dispenser

public class Dispenser
{
    private int numberOfItems;   //variable to store the number of
                                 //items in the dispenser
    private int cost;     //variable to store the cost of an item

        //Default constructor to set the cost and number of
        //items to the default values
        //Postcondition: numberOfItems = 50; cost = 50;
    public Dispenser()
    {
        numberOfItems = 50;
        cost = 50;
    }

        //Constructor with parameters to set the cost and number
        //of items in the dispenser specified by the user
        //Postcondition: numberOfItems = setNoOfItems;
        //               cost = setCost;
    public Dispenser(int setNoOfItems, int setCost)
    {
        if (setNoOfItems >= 0)
            numberOfItems = setNoOfItems;
        else
            numberOfItems = 50;

        if (setCost >= 0)
            cost = setCost;
        else
            cost = 50;
    }

        //Method to show the number of items in the dispenser
        //Postcondition: The value of the instance variable
        //               numberOfItems is returned.
    public int getCount()
    {
        return numberOfItems;
    }
```

8

```
        //Method to show the cost of the item
        //Postcondition: The value of the instance
        //                variable cost is returned.
    public int getProductCost()
    {
        return cost;
    }

        //Method to reduce the number of items by 1
        //Postcondition: numberOfItems = numberOfItems - 1
    public void makeSale()
    {
        numberOfItems--;
    }
}
```

Main Program   When the program executes, it must do the following:

1. Show the different products sold by the candy machine.
2. Show how to select a particular product.
3. Show how to terminate the program.

Furthermore, these instructions must be displayed after processing each selection (except when exiting the program), so that the user need not remember what to do if he or she wants to buy additional items. Once the user makes the appropriate selection, the candy machine must act accordingly. If the user opts to buy an available product, the candy machine should show the cost of the product and ask the user to deposit the money. If the money deposited is at least the cost of the item, the candy machine should sell the item and display an appropriate message.

This discussion translates into the following algorithm:

1. Show the selection to the customer.
2. Get the selection.
3. If the selection is valid and the dispenser corresponding to the selection is not empty, sell the product.

We divide this program into three functions—showSelection, sellProduct, and main.

Method showSelection   This method displays the necessary information to help the user select and buy a product. Essentially, it contains the following output statements (we assume that the candy machine sells four types of products):

```
*** Welcome to Shelly's Candy Shop ***"
To select an item, enter
1 for Candy
2 for Chips
```

```
3 for Gum
4 for Cookies
9 to exit
```

The definition of the function showSelection is:

```
public static void showSelection()
{
    System.out.println("*** Welcome to Shelly's "
                    + "Candy Shop ***");
    System.out.println("To select an item, enter ");
    System.out.println("1 for Candy");
    System.out.println("2 for Chips");
    System.out.println("3 for Gum");
    System.out.println("4 for Cookies");
    System.out.println("9 to exit");
}//end showSelection
```

Next, we describe the method sellProduct.

Method sellProduct This method attempts to sell a particular product selected by the customer. The candy machine contains four dispensers, which correspond to the four products. The first thing this method does is check whether the dispenser holding the product is empty. If the dispenser is empty, the method informs the customer that this product is sold out. If the dispenser is not empty, it tells the user to deposit the necessary amount to buy the product. For simplicity, we assume that this program does not return the extra money deposited by the customer. Therefore, the cash register is updated by adding the money entered by the user.

From this discussion, it follows that the method sellProduct must have access to the dispenser holding the product (to decrement the number of items in the dispenser by 1 and to show the cost of the item) as well as access to the cash register (to update the cash). Therefore, this method has two parameters: one corresponding to the dispenser and the other corresponding to the cash register.

In pseudocode, the algorithm for this method is:

1. If the dispenser is not empty

   a. Get the product cost.

   b. Set the variable coinsRequired to the price of the product.

   c. Set the variable coinsInserted to 0.

   d. While coinsRequired is greater than 0:

      i. Show and prompt the customer to enter the additional amount.

      ii. Calculate the total amount entered by the customer.

      iii. Determine the amount needed.

  e. Update the amount in the cash register.

  f. Sell the product—that is, decrement the number of items in the dispenser by 1.

  g. Display an appropriate message.

 2. If the dispenser is empty, tell the user that this product is sold out.

The definition of the method `sellProduct` is:

```
public static void sellProduct(Dispenser product,
                               CashRegister cRegister)
{
    int price;          //variable to hold the product price
    int coinsInserted;  //variable to hold the amount entered
    int coinsRequired;  //variable to show the extra amount
                        //needed

    if (product.getCount() > 0)                      //Step 1
    {
        price = product.getProductCost();            //Step 1a
        coinsRequired = price;                        //Step 1b
        coinsInserted = 0;                            //Step 1c

        while (coinsRequired > 0)                     //Step 1d
        {
            System.out.print("Please deposit "
                             + coinsRequired
                             + " cents: ");           //Step 1d.i

            coinsInserted = coinsInserted
                            + console.nextInt();      //Step 1d.ii

            coinsRequired = price
                            - coinsInserted;          //Step 1d.iii
        }

        System.out.println();

        cRegister.acceptAmount(coinsInserted);        //Step 1e
        product.makeSale();                           //Step 1f

        System.out.println("Collect your item "
                           + "at the bottom and "
                           + "enjoy.\n");             //Step 1g
    }
    else
        System.out.println("Sorry this item "
                           + "is sold out.\n");       //Step 2
}//end sellProduct
```

Method
main

The algorithm for the method `main` follows:

1. Create the cash register—that is, create and initialize a `CashRegister` object.

2. Create four dispensers—that is, create and initialize four objects of type `Dispenser`. For example, the statement:

   ```
   Dispenser candy = new Dispenser(100, 50);
   ```

   creates a dispenser object, `candy`, to hold the candies. The number of items in the dispenser is 100, and the cost of an item is 50 cents.

3. Declare additional variables as necessary.

4. Show the selection; call the method `showSelection`.

5. Get the selection.

6. While not done (a selection of 9 exits the program):

   a. Sell the product; call the method `sellProduct`.

   b. Show the selection; call the method `showSelection`.

   c. Get the selection.

The definition of the method `main` follows:

```java
public static void main(String[] args)
{
    CashRegister cashRegister = new CashRegister();   //Step 1
    Dispenser candy = new Dispenser(100, 50);         //Step 2
    Dispenser chips = new Dispenser(100, 65);         //Step 2
    Dispenser gum = new Dispenser(75, 45);            //Step 2
    Dispenser cookies = new Dispenser(100, 85);       //Step 2

    int choice;  //variable to hold the selection     //Step 3

    showSelection();                                  //Step 4
    choice = console.nextInt();                       //Step 5

    while (choice != 9)                               //Step 6
    {
        switch (choice)                               //Step 6a
        {
        case 1:
            sellProduct(candy, cashRegister);
            break;

        case 2:
            sellProduct(chips, cashRegister);
            break;
```

8

```
                case 3:
                    sellProduct(gum, cashRegister);
                    break;

                case 4:
                    sellProduct(cookies, cashRegister);
                    break;

                default:
                    System.out.println("Invalid Selection");
            }//end switch

            showSelection();                              //Step 6b
            choice = console.nextInt();                   //Step 6c
        }//end while
}//end main
```

MAIN PROGRAM LISTING

```
//Program: Candy Machine

import java.util.*;

public class CandyMachine
{
    static Scanner console = new Scanner(System.in);

    //Place the definition of the method main as given above here.

    //Place the definition of the method showSelection as
    //given above here.

    //Place the definition of the method sellProduct as
    //given above here.
}
```

Sample Run: (In this sample run, the user input is shaded.)

```
*** Welcome to Shelly's Candy Shop ***
To select an item, enter
1 for Candy
2 for Chips
3 for Gum
4 for Cookies
9 to exit
1
Please deposit 50 cents: 50

Collect your item at the bottom and enjoy.
```

```
*** Welcome to Shelly's Candy Shop ***
To select an item, enter
1 for Candy
2 for Chips
3 for Gum
4 for Cookies
9 to exit
3
Please deposit 45 cents: 45

Collect your item at the bottom and enjoy.

*** Welcome to Shelly's Candy Shop ***
To select an item, enter
1 for Candy
2 for Chips
3 for Gum
4 for Cookies
9 to exit
9
```

CANDY
MACHINE:
CREATING
A GUI

 NOTE If you skipped the GUI part of Chapter 6, you can skip this section.

8

We will now design an application program that creates the GUI shown in Figure 8-21.

FIGURE 8-21 GUI for the candy machine

The program should do the following:

1. Show the customer the above GUI.
2. Let the customer make the selection.
3. When the user clicks on a product, show the customer its cost, and prompt the customer to enter the money for the product using an input dialog box, as shown in Figure 8-22.

FIGURE 8-22 Input dialog box to enter money for the candy machine

4. Accept the money from the customer.
5. Make the sale and display a dialog box, as shown in Figure 8-23.

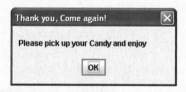

FIGURE 8-23 Output dialog box to show the output of the candy machine

In the first part of this programming example, we designed and implemented the classes CashRegister and Dispenser. Our final step is to revise the main program of the first part to create a GUI.

MAIN
PROGRAM

We now describe how to create the candy machine using the classes CashRegister and Dispenser and the GUI components. When the program executes, it must display the GUI shown earlier in Figure 8-21.

The GUI contains a window, two labels, and five buttons. The labels and buttons are placed in the content pane of the window. As you learned in Chapter 6, to create the window, the application program is created by extending the definition of the class JFrame. Thus, we need the following GUI components:

```
private JLabel headingMainL;    //label for the first line

private JLabel selectionL;      //label for the second line

private JButton exitB, candyB, chipsB, gumB, cookiesB;
```

The following statements create and instantiate these labels and button objects:

```
headingMainL = new JLabel("WELCOME TO SHELLY'S CANDY SHOP",
                    SwingConstants.CENTER);

selectionL = new JLabel("To Make a Selection, "
                + "Click on the Product Button",
                    SwingConstants.CENTER);

candyB = new JButton("Candy");

chipsB = new JButton("Chips");

gumB = new JButton("Gum");

cookiesB = new JButton("Cookies");

exitB = new JButton("Exit");
```

These components are to be placed in the content pane of the window. The seven components—labels and buttons—are arranged in seven rows. Therefore, the content pane layout will be a grid of 7 rows and 1 column. The following statements get the content pane and add these components to the content pane:

```
Container pane = getContentPane();
setSize(300, 300);

pane.setLayout(new GridLayout(7,1));

pane.add(headingMainL);
pane.add(selectionL);
pane.add(candyB);
pane.add(chipsB);
pane.add(gumB);
pane.add(cookiesB);
pane.add(exitB);
```

EVENT HANDLING When the user clicks on a product button, it generates an action event. There are five buttons, each generating an action event. To handle these action events, we use the same process that we used in Chapter 6. That is:

1. Create a class implementing the `interface ActionListener`.
2. Provide the definition of the method `actionPerformed`.
3. Create and instantiate an object, action listener, of the class type created in Step 1.
4. Register the listener of Step 3 to each button.

In Chapter 6, we created a separate class for each of the buttons and then created a separate listener for each button. In this new program, rather than create a separate class for each button, we create only one class. Recall that the heading of the method `actionPerformed` is:

```
public void actionPerformed(ActionEvent e)
```

In Chapter 6, while providing the definition of this method, we ignored the formal parameter `e`. The formal parameter `e` is a reference variable of the `ActionEvent` type. The `class ActionEvent` contains `getActionCommand` (a method without parameters), which can be used to identify which button generated the event. For example, the expression:

```
e.getActionCommand()
```

returns the string containing the label of the component generating the event. We can now use the appropriate `String` method to determine the button generating the event.

If the user clicks on one of the product buttons, then the candy machine attempts to sell the product. Therefore, the action of clicking on a product button is to sell. For this, we write the method `sellProduct` (discussed later in this programming example). If the user clicks on the `Exit` button, the program should terminate. Let's call the class to handle these events `ButtonHandler`. Its definition is:

```
private class ButtonHandler implements ActionListener
{
    public void actionPerformed (ActionEvent e)
    {
        if (e.getActionCommand().equals("Exit"))
            System.exit(0);
        else if (e.getActionCommand().equals("Candy"))
            sellProduct(candy, "Candy");
        else if (e.getActionCommand().equals("Chips"))
            sellProduct(chips, "Chips");
        else if (e.getActionCommand().equals("Gum"))
            sellProduct(gum, "Gum");
        else if (e.getActionCommand().equals("Cookies"))
            sellProduct(cookies, "Cookies");
    }
}
```

You can now declare, instantiate, and register the listener as follows:

```
private ButtonHandler pbHandler;   //declare the listener

pbHandler = new ButtonHandler();   //instantiate the object

    //register the listener with each button
candyB.addActionListener(pbHandler);
chipsB.addActionListener(pbHandler);
gumB.addActionListener(pbHandler);
cookiesB.addActionListener(pbHandler);
exitB.addActionListener(pbHandler);
```

Next, we describe the method sellProduct.

**Method
sellProduct**

The definition of this method is similar to the one we designed for the non-GUI program. (We give the definition here for the sake of completeness.) This method attempts to sell a particular product selected by the customer. The candy machine contains four dispensers, which correspond to the four products. These dispensers will be declared as instance variables. Therefore, the dispenser of the product to be sold and the name of the product are passed as parameters to this method. Because the cash register will be declared as an instance variable, this method can directly access the cash register.

This definition of the method sellProduct is:

```
private void sellProduct(Dispenser product, String productName)
{
    int coinsInserted = 0;
    int price;
    int coinsRequired;
    String str;

    if (product.getCount() > 0)
    {
        price = product.getProductCost();
        coinsRequired = price - coinsInserted;

        while (coinsRequired > 0)
        {
            str = JOptionPane.showInputDialog("To buy "
                            + productName
                            + " please insert "
                            + coinsRequired + " cents");
```

8

```
                        coinsInserted = coinsInserted
                                        + Integer.parseInt(str);
                        coinsRequired = price - coinsInserted;
        }

        cashRegister.acceptAmount(coinsInserted);
        product.makeSale();

        JOptionPane.showMessageDialog(null,"Please pick up your "
                                + productName + " and enjoy",
                                "Thank you, Come again!",
                                JOptionPane.PLAIN_MESSAGE);
    }
    else            //dispenser is empty
        JOptionPane.showMessageDialog(null,"Sorry "
                                + productName
                                + " is sold out\n" +
                                "Make another selection",
                                "Thank you, Come again!",
                                JOptionPane.PLAIN_MESSAGE);
}//end sellProduct
```

We have described the method `sellProduct` and the other necessary components, so next we will write the Java application program for the candy machine.

The algorithm is as follows:

1. Create the cash register—that is, declare a reference variable of type `CashRegister` and instantiate the object.

2. Create four dispensers—that is, declare four reference variables of type `Dispenser` and instantiate the appropriate `Dispenser` objects. For example, the statement:

```
Dispenser candy = new Dispenser(100, 50);
```

declares `candy` to be a reference variable of the `Dispenser` type and instantiates the object `candy` to hold the candies. The number of items in the object `candy` is 100, and the cost of a candy is 50 cents.

3. Create the other objects, such as labels and buttons, as previously described.

4. Display the GUI showing the candy machine, as described at the beginning of this programming example.

5. Get and process the selection.

The complete programming listing is available on the Web site and the CD accompanying this book.

QUICK REVIEW

1. A `class` is a collection of a specific number of components.
2. Components of a `class` are called the members of the class.
3. Members of a `class` are accessed by name.
4. In Java, `class` is a reserved word, and it defines only a data type; no memory is allocated.
5. Members of a class are classified into four categories. The three typically used categories are `private`, `protected`, or `public`.
6. The `private` members of a class are not directly accessible outside the class.
7. The `public` members of a class are accessible outside the class.
8. The `public` members are declared using the modifier `public`.
9. The `private` members are declared using the modifier `private`.
10. A member of a class can be a method, a variable, or an inner class.
11. If any member of a class is a variable, it is declared like any other variable.
12. In Java, a `class` is a definition.
13. Non-`static` variables of a `class` are called instance variables of that `class`.
14. Non-`static` methods of a class are called instance methods.
15. Constructors permit the data members to be initialized when an object is declared.
16. The name of a constructor is the same as the name of the class.
17. A class can have more than one constructor.
18. A constructor without parameters is called the default constructor.
19. Constructors automatically execute when a class object is created.
20. In a UML class diagram, the top box contains the name of the class. The middle box contains the data members and their data types. The bottom box contains the methods' names, parameter list, and return type. A + (plus) sign in front of a member indicates that the member is a `public` member; a − (minus) sign indicates that this is a `private` member. The # symbol before a member name indicates that the member is a `protected` member.
21. In shallow copying, two or more reference variables of the same type refer to the same object.
22. In deep copying, each reference variable refers to its own object.
23. A reference variable follows the same scope rules as other variables.
24. A member of a class is local to the class.
25. You access a `public` `class` member outside the `class` through the reference variable name or the `class` name (for `static` members) and the member access operator (`.`).

8

26. The copy constructor executes when an object is instantiated and initialized using an existing object.

27. The method toString is a public value-returning method. It does not take any parameters and returns the address of a String object.

28. The methods print, println, and printf output the string created by the method toString.

29. The default definition of the method toString creates a String that is the name of the object's class name followed by the object's hash code.

30. The modifier static in the heading of the method of a class specifies that the method can be invoked by using the name of the class.

31. If a data member of a class is declared using the modifier static, that data member can be invoked by using the name of the class.

32. static data members of a class *exist* even when no object of the class type is instantiated. Moreover, static variables are initialized to their default values.

33. Finalizers automatically execute when a class object goes out of scope.

34. A class can have only one finalizer, and the finalizer has no parameters.

35. The name of the finalizer is finalize.

36. A method of a class that only accesses (that is, does not modify) the value(s) of the data member(s) is called an accessor method.

37. A method of a class that modifies the value(s) of the data member(s) is called a mutator method.

38. Java implicitly uses the reference this to refer to both the instance variables and the methods of a class.

39. Classes that are defined within another class are called inner classes.

40. A data type that specifies the logical properties without the implementation details is called an abstract data type (ADT).

EXERCISES

1. Mark the following statements as true or false:

   a. The instance variables of a class must be of the same type.

   b. The methods of a class must be public.

   c. A class can have more than one constructor.

   d. A constructor can return a value of the int type.

   e. An accessor method of a class accesses and modifies the data members of the class.

2. Find the syntax errors in the definitions of the following classes:

a.
```
public class AA
{
    private int x;
    private int y;

    public void print()
    {
        System.out.println(x + " " + y);
    }
    public int sum()
    {
        return x + y;
    }

    public AA()
    {
        x = 0;
        y = 0;
    }

    public int AA(int a, int b)
    {
        x = a;
        y = b;
    }
}
```

b.
```
public class BB
{
    private int one;
    private int two;

    public boolean equal()
    {
        return (one == two);
    }

    public print()
    {
        System.out.println(one + " " + two);
    }

    public BB(int a, int b)
    {
        one = a;
        two = b;
    }
}
```

3. Consider the definition of the following class:

```
class CC
{
    private int u;
    private int v;
    private double w;

    public CC ()                              //Line 1
    {
    }

    public CC (int a)                         //Line 2
    {
    }

    public CC (int a, int b)                  //Line 3
    {
    }

    public CC (int a, int b, double d)    //Line 4
    {
    }
}
```

a. Give the line number containing the constructor that is executed in each of the following declarations:

   i.   `CC one = new CC();`

   ii. `CC two = new CC(5, 6);`

   iii. `CC three = new CC(2, 8, 3.5);`

b. Write the definition of the constructor in Line 1 so that the instance variables are initialized to 0.

c. Write the definition of the constructor in Line 2 so that the instance variable u is initialized according to the value of the parameter, and the instance variables v and w are initialized to 0.

d. Write the definition of the constructor in Line 3 so that the instance variables u and v are initialized according to the values of the parameters a and b, respectively, and the instance variable w is initialized to 0.0.

e. Write the definitions of the constructors in Line 4 so that the instance variables u, v, and w are initialized according to the values of the parameters a, b, and d, respectively.

4. Write a Java statement that creates the object mysteryClock of the Clock type and initializes the instance variables hr, min, and sec of mysteryClock to 7, 18, and 39, respectively.

5. Given the statements:

```
Clock firstClock = new Clock(2, 6, 35);
Clock secondClock = new Clock(6, 23, 17);
firstClock = secondClock;
```

what is the output of the following statements?

```
firstClock.print();
System.out.println();
secondClock.print();
System.out.println();
```

6. Consider the following declarations:

```
public class XClass
{
    private int u;
    private double w;

    public XClass()
    {
    }

    public XClass(int a, double b)
    {
    }

    public void func()
    {
    }

    public void print()
    {
    }
}

XClass x = new XClass(10, 20.75);
```

a. How many members does class XClass have?

b. How many private members does class XClass have?

c. How many constructors does class XClass have?

d. Write the definition of the member func so that u is set to 10 and w is set to 15.3.

e. Write the definition of the member print that prints the contents of u and w.

f. Write the definition of the default constructor of the class XClass so that the instance variables are initialized to 0.

g. Write the definition of the constructor with parameters of the class XClass so that the instance variable u is initialized to the value of a and the instance variable w is initialized to the value of b.

h. Write a Java statement that prints the values of the instance variables of x.

i. Write a Java statement that creates the XClass object t and initializes the instance variables of t to 20 and 35.0, respectively.

7. Explain shallow copying.

8. Explain deep copying.

9. Suppose that two reference variables, say aa and bb, of the same type point to two different objects. What happens when you use the assignment operator to copy the value of aa into bb?

10. Assume that the method toString is defined for the class Clock as given in this chapter. What is the output of the following statements?

```
Clock firstClock;
Clock secondClock = new Clock(6, 23, 17);

firstClock = secondClock.getCopy();

System.out.println(firstClock);
```

11. What is the purpose of the copy constructor?

12. How does Java use the reference this?

13. Can you use the relational operator == to determine whether two different objects of the same class type contain the same data?

14. Consider the definition of the following class:

```
class TestClass
{
    private int x;
    private int y;

        //Default constructor to initialize
        //the instance variables to 0
    public TestClass()
    {
    }

        //Constructors with parameters to initialize the
        //instance variables to the values specified by
        //the parameters
        //Postcondition: x = a; y = b;
    TestClass(int a, int b)
    {
    }

        //return the sum of the instance variables
    public int sum()
    {
    }

        //print the values of the instance variables
    public void print()
    {
    }
}
```

a. Write the definitions of the methods as described in the definition of the **class** TestClass.

b. Write a test program to test various operations of the **class** TestClass.

15. Write the definition of a class that has the following properties:

a. The name of the class is Secret.

b. The **class** Secret has four instance variables: name of type String, age and weight of type int, and height of type double.

c. The **class** Secret has the following methods:

print—outputs the data stored in the data members with the appropriate titles

setName—method to set the name

setAge—method to set the age

setWeight—method to set the weight

setHeight—method to set the height

getName—value-returning method to return the name

getAge—value-returning method to return the age

getWeight—value-returning method to return the weight

getHeight—value-returning method to return the height

default constructor—the default value of name is the empty string ""; the default values of age, weight, and height are 0

constructor with parameters—sets the values of the instance variables name, age, weight, and height to the values specified by the user

d. Write the definitions of the method members of the **class** Secret, as described in part c.

16. Consider the following definition of the **class** MyClass:

```
class MyClass
{
    private int x;
    private static int count;

        //default constructor
        //Postcondition: x = 0
    public MyClass()
    {
        //write the definition
    }

        //constructor with a parameter
        //Postcondition: x = a
    public MyClass(int a)
```

```
    {
        //write the definition
    }

        //Method to set the value of x
        //Postcondition: x = a
    public void setX(int a);
    {
        //write the definition
    }

        //Method to output x.
    public void printX()
    {
        //write the definition
    }

        //Method to output count
    public static void printCount()
    {
        //write the definition
    }

        //Method to increment count
        //Postcondition: count++
    public static int incrementCount()
    {
        //write the definition
    }
}
```

a. Write a Java statement that increments the value of count by 1.

b. Write a Java statement that outputs the value of count.

c. Write the definitions of the methods and the constructors of the class MyClass as described in its definition.

d. Write a Java statement that declares myObject1 to be a MyClass object and initializes its instance variable x to 5.

e. Write a Java statement that declares myObject2 to be a MyClass object and initializes its instance variable x to 7.

f. Which of the following statements are valid? (Assume that myObject1 and myObject2 are as declared in parts d and e.)

```
myObject1.printCount();        //Line 1
myObject1.printX();            //Line 2
MyClass.printCount();          //Line 3
MyClass.printX();              //Line 4
MyClass.count++;               //Line 5
```

g. Assume that myObject1 and myObject2 are as declared in parts d and e. After you have written the definition of the methods of the class MyClass, what is the output of the following Java code?

```
myObject1.printX();
myObject1.incrementCount();
MyClass.incrementCount();
myObject1.printCount();
myObject2.printCount();
myObject2.printX();
myObject1.setX(14);
myObject1.incrementCount();
myObject1.printX();
myObject1.printCount();
myObject2.printCount();
```

PROGRAMMING EXERCISES

1. The class Clock given in the chapter only allows the time to be incremented by one second, one minute, or one hour. Rewrite the definition of the class Clock by including additional members so that time can also be decremented by one second, one minute, or one hour. Also write a program to test your class.

2. Write a program that converts a number entered in Roman numerals to decimal. Your program should consist of a class, say, Roman. An object of type Roman should do the following:

   a. Store the number as a Roman numeral.

   b. Convert and store the number into decimal.

   c. Print the number as a Roman numeral or decimal number as requested by the user.

   The decimal values of the Roman numerals are:

M	1000
D	500
C	100
L	50
X	10
V	5
I	1

   d. Test your program using the following Roman numerals: MCXIV, CCCLIX, and MDCLXVI.

8

3. Design and implement the `class` Day that implements the day of the week in a program. The `class` Day should store the day, such as Sun for Sunday. The program should be able to perform the following operations on an object of type Day:

   a. Set the day.

   b. Print the day.

   c. Return the day.

   d. Return the next day.

   e. Return the previous day.

   f. Calculate and return the day by adding certain days to the current day. For example, if the current day is Monday and we add four days, the day to be returned is Friday. Similarly, if today is Tuesday and we add 13 days, the day to be returned is Monday.

   g. Add the appropriate constructors.

   h. Write the definitions of the methods to implement the operations for the `class` Day, as defined in a through g.

   i. Write a program to test various operations on the `class` Day.

4. a. Example 8-7 defined the `class` Person to store the name of a person. The methods that we included merely set the name and print the name of a person. Redefine the `class` Person so that, in addition to what the existing `class` does, you can:

      i. Set the last name only.

      ii. Set the first name only.

      iii. Set the middle name.

      iv. Check whether a given last name is the same as the last name of this person.

      v. Check whether a given first name is the same as the first name of this person.

      vi. Check whether a given middle name is the same as the middle name of this person.

   b. Add the method `equals` that returns true if two objects contain the same first, middle, and last name.

   c. Add the method `makeCopy` that copies the instance variables of a Person object into another Person object.

   d. Add the method `getCopy` that creates and returns the address of the object, which is a copy of another Person object.

   e. Add the copy constructor.

   f. Write the definitions of the methods of the `class` Person to implement the operations for this `class`.

   g. Write a program that tests various operations of the `class` Person.

5. Redo Example 7-3, Chapter 7, so that it uses the `class` `RollDie` to roll a die.

6. a. Some of the characteristics of a book are the title, author(s), publisher, ISBN, price, and year of publication. Design the `class` `Book` that defines the book as an ADT.

   Each object of the `class` `Book` can hold the following information about a book: title, up to four authors, publisher, ISBN, price, year of publication, and number of copies in stock. To keep track of the number of authors, add another instance variable.

   Include the methods to perform various operations on the objects of `Book`. For example, the usual operations that can be performed on the title are to show the title, set the title, and check whether a title is the actual title of the book. Similarly, the typical operations that can be performed on the number of copies in stock are to show the number of copies in stock, set the number of copies in stock, update the number of copies in stock, and return the number of copies in stock. Add similar operations for the publisher, ISBN, book price, and authors. Add the appropriate constructors.

   b. Write the definitions of the methods of the `class` `Book`.

   c. Write a program that uses the `class` `Book` and tests various operations on the objects of `class` `Book`.

7. In this exercise, you will design the `class` `Member`.

   a. Each object of `Member` can hold the name of a person, member ID, number of books bought, and amount spent.

   b. Include the methods to perform the various operations on the objects of the `class` `Member`—for example, modify, set, and show a person's name. Similarly, update, modify, and show the number of books bought and the amount spent.

   c. Write the definitions of the methods of the `class` `Member`. Also write a program to test your class.

8. The equation of a line in standard form is $ax + by = c$, where a and b both cannot be zero, and a, b, and c are real numbers. If $b \neq 0$, then $-a / b$ is the slope of the line. If $a = 0$, then it is a horizontal line, and if $b = 0$, then it is a vertical line. The slope of a vertical line is undefined. Two lines are parallel if they have the same slope or both are vertical lines. Two lines are perpendicular if one of the lines is horizontal and another is vertical, or if the product of their slopes is -1. Design the `class` `lineType` to store a line. To store a line, you need to store the values of a (coefficient of x), b (coefficient of y), and c. Your class must contain the following operations:

   a. If a line is nonvertical, then determine its slope.

   b. Determine if two lines are equal. (Two lines $a_1x + b_1y = c_1$ and $a_2x + b_2y = c_2$ are equal if either $a_1 = a_2$, $b_1 = b_2$, and $c_1 = c_2$ or $a_1 = ka_2$, $b_1 = kb_2$, and $c_1 = kc_2$ for some real number k.)

c. Determine if two lines are parallel.

d. Determine if two lines are perpendicular.

e. If two lines are not parallel, then find the point of intersection.

Add appropriate constructors to initialize variables of `lineType`. Also write a program to test your class.

9. Rational fractions are of the form a / b, where a and b are integers and $b \neq 0$. In this exercise, by "fractions" we mean rational fractions. Suppose that a / b and c / d are fractions. Arithmetic operations on fractions are defined by the following rules:

$a / b + c / d = (ad + bc) / bd$
$a / b - c / d = (ad - bc) / bd$
$a / b \times c / d = ac / bd$
$(a / b) / (c / d) = ad / bc$, where $c / d \neq 0$

Fractions are compared as follows: a / b *op* c / d if ad *op* bc, where *op* is any of the relational operations. For example, $a / b < c / d$ if $ad < bc$.

Design the **class** `Fraction` that can be used to manipulate fractions in a program. Among others, the **class** `Fraction` must include methods to add, subtract, multiply, and divide fractions. When you add, subtract, multiply, or divide fractions, your answer need not be in the lowest terms. Also, override the method `toString` so that the fractions can be output using the output statement.

Write a Java program that, using the **class** `Fraction`, performs operations on fractions.

ARRAYS

IN THIS CHAPTER, YOU WILL:

- Learn about arrays
- Explore how to declare and manipulate data in arrays
- Learn about the instance variable `length`
- Understand the meaning of "array index out of bounds"
- Become aware of how the assignment and relational operators work with array names
- Discover how to pass an array as a parameter to a method
- Learn how to search an array
- Discover how to manipulate data in a two-dimensional array
- Learn about multidimensional arrays
- Become acquainted with the `class` Vector

In previous chapters, you worked with primitive data types and learned how to construct your own classes. Recall that a variable of a primitive data type can store only one value at a time; on the other hand, a `class` can be defined so that its objects can store more than one value at a time. This chapter introduces a special data structure called an array, which allows the user to group data items of the same type and process them in a convenient way.

Why Do We Need Arrays?

Before we formally define an array, let's consider the following problem. We want to write a Java program that reads five numbers, finds their sum, and prints the numbers in reverse order.

In Chapter 5, you learned how to read numbers, print them, and find their sum. What's different here is that we want to print the numbers in reverse order. We cannot print the first four numbers until we have printed the fifth, and so on. This means that we need to store all the numbers before we can print them in reverse order. From what we have learned so far, the following program accomplishes this task:

```java
//Program to read five numbers, find their sum, and print the
//numbers in the reverse order.

import java.util.*;

public class ReversePrintI
{
    static Scanner console = new Scanner(System.in);

    public static void main(String[] args)
    {
        int item0, item1, item2, item3, item4;
        int sum;

        System.out.println("Enter five integers: ");
        item0 = console.nextInt();
        item1 = console.nextInt();
        item2 = console.nextInt();
        item3 = console.nextInt();
        item4 = console.nextInt();

        sum = item0 + item1 + item2 + item3 + item4;

        System.out.println("The sum of the numbers = " + sum);
        System.out.print("The numbers in reverse order are: ");
        System.out.println(item4 + " " + item3 + " " + item2
                        + " " + item1 + " " + item0);
    }
}
```

This program works fine. However, to read 100 (or more) numbers and print them in reverse order, you would have to declare 100 or more variables and write many input and output statements. Thus, for large amounts of data, this type of program is not desirable.

Note the following in the preceding program:

1. Five variables must be declared because the numbers are to be printed in reverse order.
2. All variables are of type `int`—that is, of the same data type.
3. The way in which these variables are declared indicates that the variables to store these numbers have the same name except for the last character, which is a number.

From 1, it follows that you have to declare five variables. From 3, it follows that it would be convenient if you could somehow put the last character, which is a number, into a counter variable and use one `for` loop to count from 0 to 4 for reading, and use another `for` loop to count from 4 to 0 for printing. Finally, because all the variables are of the same type, you should be able to specify how many variables must be declared—as well as their data type—with a simpler statement than the one used previously.

The data structure that lets you do all of these things in Java is called an array.

Arrays

An **array** is a collection (sequence) of a fixed number of variables called **elements** or **components**, wherein all the elements are of the same data type. A **one-dimensional array** is an array in which the elements are arranged in a list form. The remainder of this section discusses one-dimensional arrays. Arrays of two or more dimensions are discussed later in this chapter.

The general form to declare a one-dimensional array is:

```
dataType[] arrayName;        //Line 1
```

where `dataType` is the element type.

In Java, an array is an object, just like the objects discussed in Chapter 8. Because an array is an object, `arrayName` is a reference variable. Therefore, the preceding statement only declares a reference variable. Before we can store the data, we must instantiate the array object.

The general syntax to instantiate an array object is:

```
arrayName = new dataType[intExp];        //Line 2
```

where `intExp` is any expression that evaluates to a positive integer. Also, the value of `intExp` specifies the number of elements in the array.

You can combine the statements in Lines 1 and 2 into one statement as follows:

```
dataType[] arrayName = new dataType[intExp];    //Line 3
```

We typically use statements similar to the one in Line 3 to create arrays to manipulate data.

> **NOTE**   When an array is instantiated, Java automatically initializes its elements to their default values. For example, the elements of numeric arrays are initialized to 0, the elements of `char` arrays are initialized to the null character, which is `'\u0000'`, the elements of `boolean` arrays are initialized to `false`.

EXAMPLE 9-1

The statement:

```
int[] num = new int[5];
```

declares and creates the array `num` consisting of 5 elements. Each element is of type `int`. The elements are accessed as `num[0]`, `num[1]`, `num[2]`, `num[3]`, and `num[4]`. Figure 9-1 illustrates the array `num`.

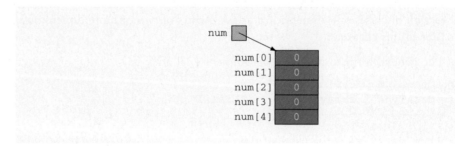

FIGURE 9-1   Array `num`

> **NOTE** To save space, we also draw an array, as shown in Figure 9-2(a) and 9-2(b).

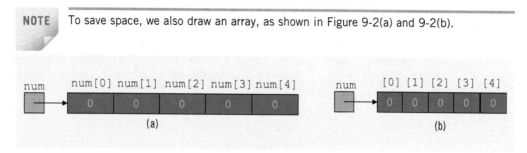

FIGURE 9-2 Array num

Alternate Ways to Declare an Array

Java allows you to declare arrays as follows:

```
int list[];          //Line 1
```

Here, the operator `[]` appears after the identifier `list`, not after the data type `int`.

You should be careful when declaring arrays as in Line 1. Consider the following statements:

```
int alpha[], beta;    //Line 2
int[] gamma, delta;   //Line 3
```

The statement in Line 2 declares the variables `alpha` and `beta`. Similarly, the statement in Line 3 declares the variables `gamma` and `delta`. However, the statement in Line 2 declares only `alpha` to be an array reference variable, while the variable `beta` is an `int` variable. On the other hand, the statement in Line 3 declares both `gamma` and `delta` to be array reference variables.

Traditionally, Java programmers declare arrays as shown in Line 3. We recommend that you do the same.

Accessing Array Elements

The general form (syntax) used to access an array element is:

```
arrayName[indexExp]
```

where `indexExp`, called the **index**, is an expression whose value is a nonnegative integer less than the size of the array. The index value specifies the position of the element in the array. In Java, the array index starts at 0.

In Java, `[]` is an operator called the **array subscripting operator**.

Consider the following statement:

```
int[] list = new int[10];
```

This statement declares an array `list` of 10 elements. The elements are `list[0]`, `list[1]`, ..., `list[9]`. In other words, we have declared 10 variables of type `int` (see Figure 9-3).

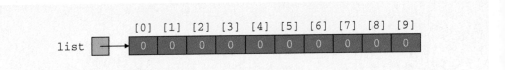

FIGURE 9-3 Array `list`

The assignment statement:

```
list[5] = 34;
```

stores 34 into `list[5]`, which is the sixth element of the array `list` (see Figure 9-4).

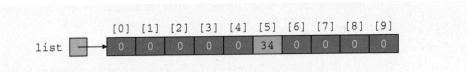

FIGURE 9-4 Array `list` after the execution of the statement `list[5]= 34;`

Suppose `i` is an `int` variable. Then, the assignment statement:

```
list[3] = 63;
```

is equivalent to the assignment statements:

```
i = 3;
list[i] = 63;
```

If `i` is 4, then the assignment statement:

```
list[2 * i - 3] = 58;
```

stores 58 into `list[5]`, because `2 * i - 3` evaluates to 5. The index expression is evaluated first, giving the position of the element in the array.

Next, consider the following statements:

```
list[3] = 10;
list[6] = 35;
list[5] = list[3] + list[6];
```

The first statement stores 10 into `list[3]`, the second statement stores 35 into `list[6]`, and the third statement adds the contents of `list[3]` and `list[6]` and stores the result into `list[5]` (see Figure 9-5).

FIGURE 9-5 Array `list` after the execution of the statements `list[3]= 10;`, `list[6]= 35;`, and `list[5] = list[3] + list[6];`

EXAMPLE 9-2

You can also declare arrays as follows:

```
final int ARRAY_SIZE = 10;
int[] list = new int[ARRAY_SIZE];
```

That is, you can first declare a named constant of an integral type, such as `int`, and then use the value of the named constant to specify the size of the array.

Specifying Array Size during Program Execution

When you include a statement in a program to instantiate an array object, it is not necessary to know the size of the array at compile time. During program execution, you can first prompt the user to specify the size of the array and then instantiate the object. The following statements illustrate this concept (suppose that `console` is a `Scanner` object initialized to the standard input device):

```
int arraySize;                                  //Line 1

System.out.print("Enter the size of the array: ");  //Line 2
arraySize = console.nextInt();                  //Line 3
System.out.println();                           //Line 4

int[] list = new int[arraySize];                //Line 5
```

The statement in Line 2 asks the user to enter the size of the array when the program executes. The statement in Line 3 inputs the size of the array into `arraySize`. During program execution, the system uses the value of the variable `arraySize` to instantiate the object `list`. For example, if the value of `arraySize` is 15, `list` is an array of size 15.

Array Initialization during Declaration

Like any other primitive data type variable, an array can also be initialized with specific values when it is declared. For example, the following Java statement declares an array, `sales`, of five elements and initializes those elements to specific values:

```
double[] sales = {12.25, 32.50, 16.90, 23, 45.68};
```

The **initializer list** contains values, called **initial values**, that are placed between braces and separated by commas. Here, `sales[0] = 12.25`, `sales[1] = 32.50`, `sales[2] = 16.90`, `sales[3] = 23.00`, and `sales[4]= 45.68`.

Note the following about declaring and initializing arrays:

- When declaring and initializing arrays, the size of the array is determined by the number of initial values in the initializer list within the braces.
- If an array is declared and initialized simultaneously, we *do not* use the operator `new` to instantiate the array object.

Arrays and the Instance Variable `length`

Recall that an array is an object; therefore, to store data, the array object must be instantiated. Associated with each array that has been instantiated (that is, for which memory has been allocated to store data), there is a `public` (`final`) instance variable `length`. The variable `length` contains the size of the array. Because `length` is a `public` member, it can be directly accessed in a program using the array name and the dot operator.

Consider the following declaration:

```
int[] list = {10, 20, 30, 40, 50, 60};
```

This statement creates the array `list` of six elements and initializes the elements using the values given. Here, `list.length` is 6.

Consider the following statement:

```
int[] numList = new int[10];
```

This statement creates the array `numList` of 10 elements and initializes each element to 0. Because the number of elements of `numList` is 10, the value of `numList.length` is 10. Now consider the following statements:

```
numList[0] = 5;
numList[1] = 10;
numList[2] = 15;
numList[3] = 20;
```

These statements store 5, 10, 15, and 20, respectively, in the first four elements of `numList`. Even though we put data into only the first four elements, the value of `numList.length` is 10, the total number of array elements.

You can store the number of filled elements (that is, the actual number of elements) in the array in a variable, say numOfElements. Programs commonly keep track of the number of filled elements in an array. Also, the filled elements are, typically, in the front of the array, and the empty elements are at the bottom.

NOTE   Once an array is instantiated, its size remains fixed. In other words, if you have instantiated an array of 5 elements, the number of elements of the array remains 5. If you need to increase the size of the array, then you must instantiate another array of the desired size and copy the data stored in the first array into the new array. In the next section, we show how to copy the elements of one array into another array.

Processing One-Dimensional Arrays

Some basic operations performed on a one-dimensional array are initializing the array, reading data into the array, storing output data in the array, and finding the largest and/ or smallest element in the array. If the data type of an array element is numeric, some common operations are to find the sum and average of the elements of the array. Each of these operations requires the ability to step through the elements of the array, which is easily accomplished by using a loop. Suppose that we have the following statements:

```
int[] list = new int[100];   //list is an array of size 100
```

The following for loop steps through each element of the array list, starting at the first element of list:

```
for (int i = 0; i < list.length; i++)                //Line 1
   //process list[i], the (i + 1)th element of list //Line 2
```

If processing list requires inputting data into list, the statement in Line 2 takes the form of an input statement, such as in the following code. The following statements read 100 numbers from the keyboard and store the numbers into list:

```
for (int i = 0; i < list.length; i++)     //Line 1
    list[i] = console.nextInt();          //Line 2
```

Similarly, if processing list requires outputting data, then the statement in Line 2 takes the form of an output statement. The following for loop outputs the elements of list:

```
for (int i = 0; i < list.length; i++)     //Line 1
    System.out.print(list[i] + " ");      //Line 2
```

Example 9-3 further illustrates how to process one-dimensional arrays.

EXAMPLE 9-3

This example shows how loops are used to process arrays. The following declaration is used throughout this example:

```
double[] sales = new double[10];
double largestSale, sum, average;
```

The first statement creates the array `sales` of 10 elements, with each element of type `double`. The meaning of the other statements is clear. Also, notice that the value of `sales.length` is 10.

Loops can be used to process arrays in several ways:

1. **Initializing an array to a specific value:** Suppose that you want to initialize every element of the array `sales` to `10.00`. You can use the following loop:

    ```
    for (int index = 0; index < sales.length; index++)
        sales[index] = 10.00;
    ```

2. **Reading data into an array:** The following loop inputs data into the array `sales`. For simplicity, we assume that the data is entered at the keyboard one number per line.

    ```
    for (int index = 0; index < sales.length; index++)
        sales[index] = console.nextDouble();
    ```

3. **Printing an array:** The following loop outputs the elements of array `sales`. For simplicity, we assume that the output goes to the screen.

    ```
    for (int index = 0; index < sales.length; index++)
        System.out.print(sales[index] + " ");
    ```

4. **Finding the sum and average of an array:** Because the array `sales`, as its name implies, represents certain sales data, it may be desirable to find the total sale and average sale amounts. The following Java code finds the sum of the elements of the array `sales` (total sales) and the average sale amount:

    ```
    sum = 0;

    for (int index = 0; index < sales.length; index++)
        sum = sum + sales[index];

    if (sales.length != 0)
        average = sum / sales.length;
    else
        average = 0.0;
    ```

5. **Determining the largest element in the array:** We now discuss an algorithm to find the largest element in an array—that is, the array element with the largest value. However, the user is typically more interested in determining the location of the largest element in the array. Of course, if you know the location (the index of the largest element in the array), you can easily determine the value of the largest element in the array. Let's describe the algorithm to determine the index of the largest element in an array—in particular, the index of the largest sale amount in the array `sales`.

We assume that `maxIndex` will contain the index of the largest element in the array `sales`. The general algorithm is as follows. Initially, we assume that the first element in the list is the largest element, so `maxIndex` is initialized to 0. We then compare the element to which `maxIndex` points with every element in the list. Whenever we find an element in the array larger than the element to which `maxIndex` points, we update `maxIndex` so that it stores the index of the new larger element. The code to implement this algorithm is as follows:

```
maxIndex = 0;

for (int index = 1; index < sales.length; index++)
    if (sales[maxIndex] < sales[index])
        maxIndex = index;

largestSale = sales[maxIndex];
```

The way this code works can be demonstrated with an example. Suppose the array `sales` is as given in Figure 9-6, and we want to determine the largest element in the array.

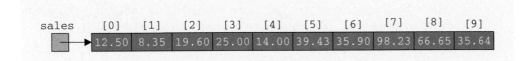

FIGURE 9-6 Array `sales`

Before the `for` loop begins, `maxIndex` is initialized to 0 and the `for` loop initializes `index` to 1. In Table 9-1, we show the values of `maxIndex`, `index`, and certain array elements during each iteration of the `for` loop:

TABLE 9-1 Values of `sales` Array Elements during `for` Loop Iterations

index	maxIndex	sales [maxIndex]	sales [index]	sales[maxIndex] < sales[index]
1	0	12.50	8.35	12.50 < 8.35 is false
2	0	12.50	19.60	12.50 < 19.60 is true; maxIndex = 2
3	2	19.60	25.00	19.60 < 25.00 is true; maxIndex = 3
4	3	25.00	14.00	25.00 < 14.00 is false
5	3	25.00	39.43	25.00 < 39.43 is true; maxIndex = 5
6	5	39.43	35.90	39.43 < 35.90 is false
7	5	39.43	98.23	39.43 < 98.23 is true; maxIndex = 7
8	7	98.23	66.65	98.23 < 66.65 is false
9	7	98.23	35.64	98.23 < 35.64 is false

After the `for` loop executes, `maxIndex` = 7, giving the index of the largest element in the array `sales`. Thus, `largestSale = sales[maxIndex] = 98.23`.

 NOTE In an array, if the largest element occurs more than once, then the previous algorithm will find the index of the first occurrence of the largest element. The algorithm to find the smallest element in an array is similar to the algorithm for finding the largest element in an array. (See Programming Exercise 2 at the end of this chapter.)

Now that we know how to declare and process arrays, let's rewrite the program that we discussed in the beginning of this chapter. Recall that this program reads five numbers, finds the sum, and prints the numbers in reverse order.

EXAMPLE 9-4

```java
//Program to read five numbers, find their sum, and
//print the numbers in the reverse order.

import java.util.*;

public class ReversePrintII
{
    static Scanner console = new Scanner(System.in);

    public static void main(String[] args)
    {
        int[] items = new int[5]; //declare an array item of
                                  //five elements
        int sum;

        System.out.println("Enter five integers:");

        sum = 0;

        for (int counter = 0; counter < items.length;
                                              counter++)
        {
            items[counter] = console.nextInt();
            sum = sum + items[counter];
        }

        System.out.println("The sum of the numbers = "
                           + sum);
        System.out.print("The numbers in the reverse "
                       + "order are: ");

            //print the numbers in the reverse order
        for (int counter = items.length - 1; counter >= 0;
                                              counter--)
            System.out.print(items[counter] + " ");

        System.out.println();

    }
}
```

Sample Run: (In this sample run, the user input is shaded.)

```
Enter five integers:
12 76 34 52 89
The sum of the numbers is: 263
The numbers in the reverse order are: 89 52 34 76 12
```

Array Index Out of Bounds Exception

Consider the following declaration:

```
double[] num = double[10];
int i;
```

The element num[i] is valid, that is, i is a valid index if i = 0, 1, 2, 3, 4, 5, 6, 7, 8, or 9.

The index—say, index—of an array is **in bounds** if index >= 0 and index <= arraySize - 1. If either index < 0 or index > arraySize - 1, then we say that the index is **out of bounds**.

In Java, if an array index goes out of bounds during program execution, it throws an ArrayIndexOutOfBoundsException exception. If the program does not handle this exception, the program terminates with an appropriate error message.

A loop such as the following can set the index out of bounds:

```
for (i = 0; i <= 10; i++)
    list[i] = 0;
```

Here, we assume that list is an array of 10 elements. When i becomes 10, the loop test condition i <= 10 evaluates to true, the body of the loop executes, and the program tries to access list[10], which does not exist.

BASE ADDRESS OF AN ARRAY

The **base address** of an array is the address (memory location) of the first array element. For example, if list is a one-dimensional array, then the base address of list is the address of the element list[0]. The value of the variable list is the base address of the array—the address of list[0]. It follows that when you pass an array as a parameter, the base address of the actual array is passed to the formal parameter.

Declaring Arrays as Formal Parameters to Methods

Just like other data types, you can declare arrays as formal parameters to methods. A general syntax to declare an array as a formal parameter is:

```
dataType[] arrayName
```

For example, consider the following method:

```
public static void arraysAsFormalParameter(int[] listA,
                                           double[] listB,
                                           int num)
{
    //...
}
```

This method has three formal parameters. The formal parameters listA and listB are arrays, and num is of type int.

Suppose that you have the following statements:

```
int[] intList = new int[10];

double[] doubleNumList = new double[15];

int number;
```

The following statement calls the method with actual parameters `intList`, `doubleNumList`, and `number`:

```
arraysAsFormalParameter(intList, doubleNumList, number);
```

Assignment Operator, Relational Operators, and Arrays: A Precaution

Consider the following statements:

```
int[] listA = {5, 10, 15, 20, 25, 30, 35};   //Line 1
int[] listB = new int[listA.length];          //Line 2
```

The statement in Line 1 creates the array `listA` of size 7 and also initializes the array. Note that the value of `listA.length` is 7. The statement in Line 2 uses the value of `listA.length` to create the array `listB` of size 7 (see Figure 9-7).

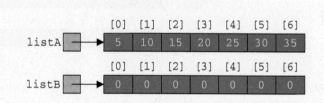

FIGURE 9-7 Arrays `listA` and `listB`

You can use the assignment operator to assign `listA` to `listB` and the relational operators to compare `listA` with `listB`. However, the results obtained might not be what you expect.

For example, consider the following statement:

```
listB = listA;
```

Here, you might expect that the elements of `listA` are copied into the corresponding elements of `listB`. However, this is not the case. Because `listA` is a reference variable, its value is a reference, that is, a memory address. Therefore, the preceding statement copies the value of `listA` into `listB`, and so after this statement executes, both `listA` and `listB` refer to the same array (see Figure 9-8).

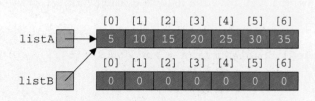

FIGURE 9-8 Arrays after the statement `listB = listA;` executes

Recall that this is called the *shallow copying* of data.

To copy the elements of `listA` into the corresponding elements of `listB`, you need to provide an element-by-element copy, as shown by the following loop:

```
for (int index = 0; index < listA.length; index++)
    listB[index] = listA[index];
```

After this statement executes, `listA` and `listB` each refers to its own array and the elements of `listA` are copied into the corresponding elements of `listB` (see Figure 9-9).

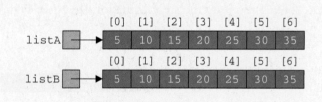

FIGURE 9-9 `listA` and `listB` after the `for` loop executes

Recall that this is called the *deep copying* of data.

In addition to the assignment operator, you can use the relational operators `==` and `!=` to compare arrays. However, you must be aware of what you are comparing. For example, in the statement:

```
if (listA == listB)
...
```

the expression `listA == listB` determines whether the values of `listA` and `listB` are the same, and thus determines whether `listA` and `listB` refer to the same array. That is, this statement does *not* determine whether `listA` and `listB` contain the same elements (when `listA` and `listB` refer to arrays stored at different locations).

To determine whether `listA` and `listB` contain the same elements when they refer to arrays stored at different locations, you need to compare them element by element. You can, in fact, write a method that returns `true` if two `int` arrays contain the same elements. For example, consider the following method:

```
boolean areEqualArrays(int[] firstArray, int[] secondArray)
{
    if (firstArray.length != secondArray.length)
        return false;

    for (int index = 0; index < firstArray.length; index++)
        if (firstArray[index] != secondArray[index]) //the
                                           //corresponding elements
                                           //are different
            return false;

    return true;
}
```

Now consider the following statement:

```
if (areEqualArrays(listA, listB))
...
```

The expression `areEqualArrays(listA, listB)` evaluates to `true` if the arrays `listA` and `listB` contain the same elements; `false` otherwise.

Arrays as Parameters to Methods

Just like other objects, arrays can be passed as parameters to methods. The following method takes as an argument any `int` array and outputs the data stored in each element:

```
public static void printArray(int[] list)
{
    for (int index = 0; index < list.length; index++)
        System.out.print(list[index] + " ");
}
```

Methods such as the preceding one process the data of an entire array. Sometimes the number of elements in the array might be less than the length of the array. For example, the number of elements in an array storing student data might increase or decrease as students drop or add courses. In situations like this, we only want to process the elements of the array that hold actual data. To write methods to process such arrays, in addition to declaring an array as a formal parameter, we declare another formal parameter specifying the number of valid elements in the array, as in the following method:

```
public static void printArray(int[] list, int numOfElements)
{
    for (int index = 0; index < numOfElements; index++)
        System.out.print(list[index] + " ");
}
```

The first parameter of the method `printArray` is an `int` array of any size. When the method `printArray` is called, the number of valid elements in the actual array is passed as the second parameter of the method `printArray`.

9

EXAMPLE 9-5

To access the methods to process a one-dimensional array conveniently, we create the class OneDimArrayMethods and put these methods in this class.

```java
// This class contains methods to manipulate data in a
// one-dimensional array.

import java.util.*;

public class OneDimArrayMethods
{
        //Method to input data and store in an int array.
        //The array to store the data and its size are passed as
        //parameters. The parameter numOfElements specifies the
        //number of elements to be read.
    public static void fillArray(int[] list, int numOfElements)
    {
        Scanner console = new Scanner(System.in);

        for (int index = 0; index < numOfElements; index++)
            list[index] = console.nextInt();
    }

        //Method to print the elements of an int array.
        //The array to be printed and the number of elements are
        //passed as parameters. The parameter numOfElements
        //specifies the number of elements to be printed.
    public static void printArray(int[] list, int numOfElements)
    {
        for (int index = 0; index < numOfElements; index++)
            System.out.print(list[index] + " ");
    }

        //Method to find and return the sum of the elements of an
        //int array. The parameter numOfElements specifies the
        //number of elements to be added.
    public static int sumArray(int[] list, int numOfElements)
    {
        int sum = 0;

        for (int index = 0; index < numOfElements; index++)
            sum = sum + list[index];

        return sum;
    }

        //Method to find and return the index of the first occurrence
        //of the largest element, if it repeats, in an int array.
        //The parameter numOfElements specifies the number of
        //elements in the array.
    public static int indexLargestElement(int[] list,
                                          int numOfElements)
```

```
    {
        int maxIndex = 0; //Assume first element is the largest

        for (int index = 1; index < numOfElements; index++)
            if (list[maxIndex] < list[index])
                maxIndex = index;

        return maxIndex;
    }

    //Method to copy some or all the elements of one array
    //into another array. Starting at the position specified
    //by src, the  elements of list1 are copied into list2
    //starting at the position specified by tar. The parameter
    //numOfElements specifies the number of elements of list1 to
    //be copied into list2. Starting at the position specified
    //by tar, list2 must have enough components to copy the
    //elements of list1. The following call copies all the
    //elements of list1 into the corresponding positions in
    //list2:  copyArray(list1, 0, list2, 0, numOfElements);.
    public static void copyArray(int[] list1, int src, int[] list2,
                                 int tar, int numOfElements)
    {
        for (int index = src; index < src + numOfElements; index++)
        {
            list2[index] = list1[tar];
            tar++;
        }
    }
}
```

Because the methods of the **class** OneDimArrayMethods are **public** and **static**, they can be called by using the name of the class and the dot operator. For example, if myList is an array of 10 elements of type **int**, the following statement outputs the elements of myList:

```
OneDimArrayMethods.printArray(myList, myList.length);
```

NOTE   Just as arrays can be passed as parameters to methods, individual elements of the array can also be passed as parameters to methods. For example, suppose that you have the following statement:

```
int[] list = {2, 3, 5};
```
and the method:

```
public static int sumNum(int firstNum, int secondNum)
{
    return firstNum + secondNum;
}
```

The following statement outputs the sum of the first two elements of the array list:

```
System.out.println("Sum = " + sumNum(list[0], list[1]));
```

The following program illustrates how arrays are passed as actual parameters in a method call.

EXAMPLE 9-6

```
// This program illustrates how arrays are passed as parameters
// to methods.

import java.util.*;                                        //Line 1

public class ArraysAsParameters                            //Line 2
{                                                          //Line 3
    static final int ARRAY_SIZE = 10;                      //Line 4

    public static void main(String[] args)                 //Line 5
    {                                                      //Line 6
        int[] listA = new int[ARRAY_SIZE];                 //Line 7
        int[] listB = new int[ARRAY_SIZE];                 //Line 8

        System.out.print("Line 9: listA elements: ");      //Line 9

            //output the elements of listA using
            //the method printArray
        OneDimArrayMethods.printArray(listA,
                              listA.length);                //Line 10
        System.out.println();                              //Line 11

        System.out.print("Line 12: Enter " + listA.length
                + " integers: ");                          //Line 12

            //input data into listA using the method fillArray
        OneDimArrayMethods.fillArray(listA,
                              listA.length);                //Line 13
        System.out.println();                              //Line 14

        System.out.print("Line 15: After filling "
                + "listA, the elements are:"
                + "\n         ");                           //Line 15

            //output the elements of listA
        OneDimArrayMethods.printArray(listA,
                              listA.length);                //Line 16
        System.out.println();                              //Line 17

            //find and output the sum of the elements of listA
        System.out.println("Line 18: The sum of the "
                + "elements of listA is: "
                + OneDimArrayMethods.sumArray(listA,
                              listA.length));               //Line 18

            //find and output the position of the (first)
            //largest element in listA
```

```
        System.out.println("Line 19: The position of "
                + "the largest element in "
                + "listA is: "
                + OneDimArrayMethods.indexLargestElement
                        (listA, listA.length));      //Line 19

            //find and output the largest element in listA
        System.out.println("Line 20: The largest element "
            + "in listA is: "
            + listA[OneDimArrayMethods.indexLargestElement
                        (listA, listA.length)]);  //Line 20

            //copy the elements of listA into listB
            //using the method copyArray
        OneDimArrayMethods.copyArray(listA, 0, listB, 0,
                            listA.length);       //Line 21
        System.out.print("Line 22: After copying the "
                + "elements of listA into listB\n"
                + "           listB elements are: ");   //Line 22

            //output the elements of listB
        OneDimArrayMethods.printArray(listB,
                            listB.length);       //Line 23
        System.out.println();                    //Line 24
    } //end main                                 //Line 25
}                                                //Line 26
```

Sample Run: In this sample run, the user input is shaded.

```
Line 9: listA elements: 0 0 0 0 0 0 0 0 0 0
Line 12: Enter 10 integers: 33 77 25 63 56 48 98 39 5 12

Line 15: After filling listA, the elements are:
         33 77 25 63 56 48 98 39 5 12
Line 18: The sum of the elements of listA is: 456
Line 19: The position of the largest element in listA is: 6
Line 20: The largest element in listA is: 98
Line 21: After copying the elements of listA into listB
         listB elements are: 33 77 25 63 56 48 98 39 5 12
```

The statement in Line 7 creates the array listA of 10 elements and initializes each element of listA to 0. Similarly, the statement in Line 8 creates the array listB of 10 elements and initializes each element of listB to 0. The statement in Line 10 calls the method printArray and outputs the values stored in listA. The statement in Line 13 calls the method fillArray to input the data into array listA. The statement in Line 18 calls the method sumArray and outputs the sum of all the elements of listA. The statement in Line 19 calls the method indexLargestElement to find the index of (the first occurrence of) the largest element in listA. Similarly, the statement in Line 20 outputs the value of the largest element in listA. The statement in Line 21 calls the method copyArray to copy the elements of listA into listB, and the statement in Line 23 outputs the elements of listB.

Searching an Array for a Specific Item

Searching a list for a given item is one of the most common operations performed on a list. The search algorithm we describe is called the **sequential search** or **linear search**. As the name implies, you search the array sequentially starting from the first array element. You compare `searchItem` with the elements in the array (the list) and continue the search until either you find the item or no more data is left in the `list` to compare with `searchItem`.

Consider the list of seven elements shown in Figure 9-10.

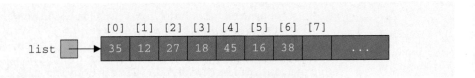

FIGURE 9-10 List of seven elements

Suppose that you want to determine whether 27 is in the list. A sequential search works as follows: First you compare 27 with `list[0]`, that is, compare 27 with 35. Because `list[0]` ≠ 27, you then compare 27 with `list[1]` (that is, with 12, the second item in the list). Because `list[1]` ≠ 27, you compare 27 with the next element in the list, that is, compare 27 with `list[2]`. Because `list[2]` = 27, the search stops. This search is successful.

Let's now search for 10. As before, the search starts at the first element in the list, that is, at `list[0]`. Proceeding as before, we see that this time the search item, which is 10, is compared with every item in the list. Eventually, no more data is left in the list to compare with the search item. This is an unsuccessful search.

It now follows that, as soon as you find an element in the list that is equal to the search item, you must stop the search and report success. (In this case, you usually also report the location in the list where the search item was found.) Otherwise, after the search item is unsuccessfully compared with every element in the list, you must stop the search and report failure.

The following method performs a sequential search on a list. To be specific, and for illustration purposes, we assume that the list elements are of type `int`.

```java
public static int seqSearch(int[] list, int listLength,
                            int searchItem)
{
    int loc;
    boolean found = false;
    loc = 0;

    while (loc < listLength && !found)
        if (list[loc] == searchItem)
            found = true;
        else
            loc++;
```

```
    if (found)
        return loc;
    else
        return -1;
}
```

If the method `seqSearch` returns a value greater than or equal to 0, it is a successful search; otherwise, it is an unsuccessful search.

As you can see from this code, you start the search by comparing `searchItem` with the first element in the `list`. If `searchItem` is equal to the first element in the `list`, you exit the loop; otherwise, `loc` is incremented by 1 to point to the next element in the `list`. You then compare `searchItem` with the next element in the `list`, and so on.

You can also include the method `seqSearch` in the `class OneDimArrayMethods` just like other methods. Suppose that you have included the method `seqSearch` in this `class`. Example 9-7 shows how to use the method `seqSearch` in a program.

EXAMPLE 9-7

```java
// This program illustrates how to use a sequential search in a
// program.

import java.util.*;                                      //Line 1

public class TestSeqSearch                               //Line 2
{                                                        //Line 3
    static Scanner console = new Scanner(System.in);     //Line 4

    public static void main(String[] args)               //Line 5
    {                                                    //Line 6
        int[] intList = new int[10];                     //Line 7
        int number;                                      //Line 8
        int index;                                       //Line 9

        System.out.println("Line 10: Enter "
                    + intList.length + " integers.");    //Line 10

        for (index  = 0; index < intList.length; index++) //Line 11
            intList[index] = console.nextInt();          //Line 12

        System.out.println();                            //Line 13

        System.out.print("Line 14: Enter the number "
                    + "to be searched: ");               //Line 14
        number  = console.nextInt();                     //Line 15
        System.out.println();                            //Line 16

        index = OneDimArrayMethods.seqSearch(intList,
                        intList.length, number);         //Line 17
```

```
        if (index != -1)                            //Line 18
            System.out.println("Line 19: " + number
                                + " is found at position "
                                + index);            //Line 19
        else                                         //Line 20
            System.out.println("Line 21: " + number
                                + " is not in the list.");  //Line 21
    }                                                //Line 22
}                                                    //Line 23
```

Sample Run 1: In this sample run, the user input is shaded.

```
Line 10: Enter 10 integers.
2 56 34 25 73 46 89 10 5 16

Line 14: Enter the number to be searched: 25

Line 19: 25 is found at position 3
```

Sample Run 2:

```
Line 10: Enter 10 integers.
2 56 34 25 73 46 89 10 5 16

Line 14: Enter the number to be searched: 38

Line 21: 38 is not in the list.
```

In this program, the statement in Line 7 creates `intList` to be an array of 10 elements. The `for` loop in Lines 11 and 12 inputs the data into `intList`. The statement in Line 14 prompts the user to enter the search item; the statement in Line 15 inputs this search item into `number`. The statement in Line 17 uses the method `seqSearch` to search `intList` for the search item. In Sample Run 1, the search item is `25`; in Sample Run 2, it is `38`. The statements in Lines 18 through 21 output the appropriate message. Notice that the search in Sample Run 1 is successful and in Sample Run 2 it is unsuccessful.

Arrays of Objects

In the previous sections, you learned how to use an array to store and manipulate values of the primitive data types, such as `int` and `double`. You can also use arrays to manipulate objects. This section explains how to create and work with arrays of objects.

Arrays of `string` Objects

This section discusses how to create and work with an array of `String` objects. To create an array of strings, you declare an array as follows:

```
String[] nameList = new String[5];    //Line 1
```

This statement declares and instantiates `nameList` to be an array of 5 elements, wherein each element of `nameList` is a reference to a `String` object. (Note that this statement only creates the array `nameList`, which is an array of references. At this point, no `String` object has been created. We will create `String` objects and assign them to array elements next.)

Next, consider the statement:

```
nameList[0] = "Amanda Green";          //Line 2
```

This statement creates a `String` object with the value `"Amanda Green"` and stores the address of the object into `nameList[0]`. Similarly, the following statements assign `String` objects, with the given values, to the other elements of `nameList`:

```
nameList[1] = "Vijay Arora";           //Line 3
nameList[2] = "Sheila Mann";           //Line 4
nameList[3] = "Rohit Sharma";          //Line 5
nameList[4] = "Mandy Johnson";         //Line 6
```

After the statements in Lines 2 through 6 execute, each element of `nameList` is a reference to a `String` object, as shown in Figure 9-11.

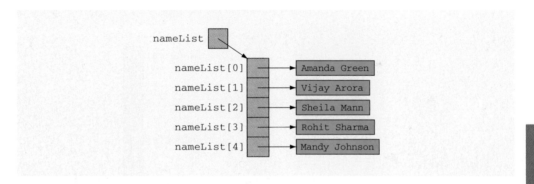

FIGURE 9-11 Array `nameList`

To output the names, you can use a `for` loop as follows:

```
for (int index = 0; index < nameList.length; index++)
    System.out.println(nameList[index]);
```

You can use `String` methods to work with the objects of `nameList`. For example, the expression:

```
nameList[0].equals("Amanda Green")
```

evaluates to `true`, while the expression:

```
nameList[3].equals("Randy Blair")
```

evaluates to `false`.

Similarly, the expression:

```
nameList[4].substring(0, 5)
```

returns a reference to the `String` object with the string `"Mandy"`.

Arrays of Objects of Other Classes

This section discusses, in general, how to create and work with an array of objects.

Suppose that you have 100 employees who are paid on an hourly basis, and you need to keep track of their arrival and departure times. In Chapter 8, we designed and implemented the **class** Clock to implement the time of day in a program. You can declare two arrays—arrivalTimeEmp and departureTimeEmp—of 100 elements each, wherein each element is a reference variable of Clock type. Consider the following statement:

```
Clock[] arrivalTimeEmp = new Clock[100];          //Line 1
```

The statement in Line 1 creates the array shown in Figure 9-12.

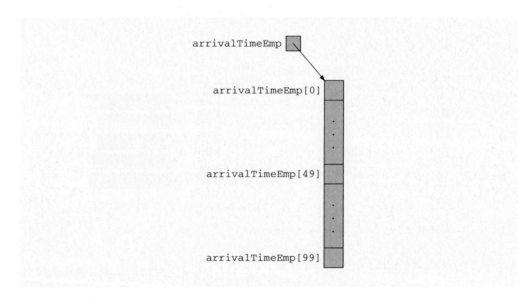

FIGURE 9-12 Array arrivalTimeEmp

The statement in Line 1 creates only the array, not the objects arrivalTimeEmp[0], arrivalTimeEmp[1], ..., arrivalTimeEmp[99]. We still need to instantiate Clock objects for each array element. Consider the following statements:

```
for (int j = 0; j < arrivalTimeEmp.length; j++)  //Line 2
    arrivalTimeEmp[j] = new Clock();              //Line 3
```

The statements in Lines 2 and 3 instantiate the objects arrivalTimeEmp[0], arrivalTimeEmp[1], ..., arrivalTimeEmp[99], as shown in Figure 9-13.

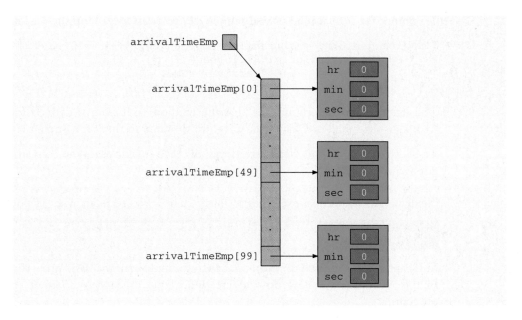

FIGURE 9-13 Array `arrivalTimeEmp` after instantiating objects for each element

You can now use the methods of the **class** `Clock` to manipulate the time for each employee. For example, the following statement sets the arrival time—that is, `hr`, `min`, and `sec`—of employee **49** to 8, 5, and 10, respectively (see Figure 9-14).

```
arrivalTimeEmp[49].setTime(8, 5, 10);                    //Line 4
```

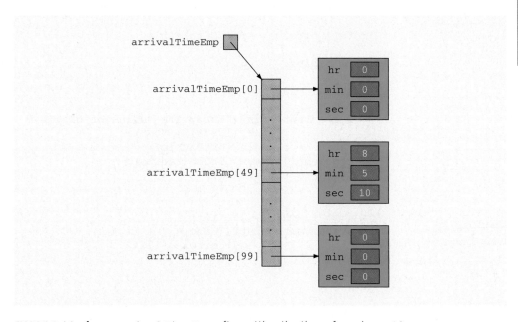

FIGURE 9-14 Array `arrivalTimeEmp` after setting the time of employee 49

To output the arrival time of each employee, you can use a loop such as the following:

```
for (int j = 0; j < arrivalTimeEmp.length; j++)        //Line 5
    System.out.println("Employee " +  (j + 1)
                + " arrival time: "
                + arrivalTimeEmp[j]);                   //Line 6
```

The statement in Line 6 assumes that the method toString is defined for the class Clock, as described in Chapter 8, to return the time in the form hr:min:sec.

To keep track of the departure time of each employee, you can use the array departureTimeEmp.

Next we give additional examples to illustrate how to create an array of objects.

EXAMPLE 9-8

In Chapter 8, we created the class Circle to implement the basic properties of a circle. In this example, we show how to create an array of circles. Consider the following program:

```
// Program to create an array of circles.

import java.util.*;                                     //Line 1

public class TestProgArrayOfCircles                     //Line 2
{                                                       //Line 3
    static Scanner console = new Scanner(System.in);    //Line 4

    public static void main(String[] args)              //Line 5
    {                                                   //Line 6
        Circle[] circles = new Circle[5];               //Line 7

        double radius;                                  //Line 8

        for (int i = 0; i < 5; i++)                     //Line 9
        {                                               //Line 10
            System.out.print("Enter the radius of circle "
                    + (i + 1) + ": ");                  //Line 11
            radius = console.nextDouble();              //Line 12
            circles[i] = new Circle(radius);            //Line 13
            System.out.println();                       //Line 14
        }                                               //Line 15

        for (int i = 0; i < 5; i++)                     //Line 16
            System.out.printf("Circle " + (i + 1) + ": "
                    + circles[i]);                      //Line 17
    }//end main                                         //Line 18
}                                                       //Line 19
```

Sample Run: In this sample run, the user input is shaded.

```
Enter the radius of circle 1: 7

Enter the radius of circle 2: 4

Enter the radius of circle 3: 8

Enter the radius of circle 4: 9

Enter the radius of circle 5: 6

Circle 1: Radius = 7.00, Perimeter = 43.98, Area = 69.09
Circle 2: Radius = 4.00, Perimeter = 25.13, Area = 39.48
Circle 3: Radius = 8.00, Perimeter = 50.27, Area = 78.96
Circle 4: Radius = 9.00, Perimeter = 56.55, Area = 88.83
Circle 5: Radius = 6.00, Perimeter = 37.70, Area = 59.22
```

The preceding program works as follows. The statement in Line 7 creates the array circles of 5 Circle objects. The for loop in Line 9 prompts the user to enter the radius of 5 circles (Line 11), inputs the radius of each circle (Line 12), and instantiates and sets the radius of circles (Line 13). The for loop in Line 16 outputs the radius, perimeter, and area of each circle. Note that in the class Circle, the toString method returns the radius, perimeter, and area of a circle.

EXAMPLE 9-9

9

In Chapter 8, we created the class RollDie to roll a die. The following program uses this class to roll 100 dice and outputs the number of times each number is rolled, the number(s) that are rolled the maximum number of times, and the maximum roll count.

```java
// This program rolls 100 dice. It outputs the number of times
// each number is rolled, the number(s) that are rolled the
// maximum number of times, and the maximum roll count.

import java.util.*;                                      //Line 1

public class TestProgArrayofDice                         //Line 2
{                                                        //Line 3
    static Scanner console = new Scanner(System.in);     //Line 4

    public static void main(String[] args)               //Line 5
    {                                                    //Line 6
        RollDie[] dice = new RollDie[100];               //Line 7

        int[] rollCount = new int[6];                    //Line 8
        int maxNumRoll = 0;                              //Line 9

        for (int i = 0; i < 100; i++)                    //Line 10
```

```
    {                                                //Line 11
        dice[i] = new RollDie();                     //Line 12
        dice[i].roll();                              //Line 13
    }                                                //Line 14

    System.out.println("Numbers rolled: ");          //Line 15
    for (int i = 0; i < 100; i++)                    //Line 16
    {                                                //Line 17
        int num = dice[i].getNum();                  //Line 18

        System.out.print(" " + num);                 //Line 19
        rollCount[num - 1]++;                        //Line 20
        if ((i + 1) % 34 == 0)                       //Line 21
            System.out.println();                    //Line 22
    }                                                //Line 23

    System.out.println();                            //Line 24
    System.out.println("Num  Roll_Count");           //Line 25

    for (int i = 0; i < 6; i++)                      //Line 26
    {                                                //Line 27
        System.out.println(" " + (i + 1) + "       "
                      + rollCount[i]);               //Line 28
        if (rollCount[i] > rollCount[maxNumRoll])    //Line 29
            maxNumRoll = i;                          //Line 30
    }                                                //Line 31

    System.out.print("The number(s) ");              //Line 32
    for (int i = 0; i < 6; i++)                      //Line 33
        if (rollCount[i] == rollCount[maxNumRoll])   //Line 34
            System.out.print((i + 1) + " ");         //Line 35

    System.out.println("is (are) rolled maximum "
                  + "number of times, which is "
                  + rollCount[maxNumRoll] + ".");    //Line 36
    }//end main                                      //Line 37
}                                                    //Line 38
```

Sample Run:

```
Numbers rolled:
 4 6 2 6 5 4 5 2 6 4 2 5 3 1 6 6 1 2 4 5 1 6 6 4 6 3 2 5 3 2 3 5 1 5
 1 6 5 2 1 5 1 6 4 2 4 4 1 1 6 2 4 2 1 3 4 3 5 3 5 1 2 3 5 2 2 2 1 4
 5 1 4 5 6 6 3 6 2 5 5 3 1 4 4 2 3 5 6 4 5 2 3 6 5 3 2 4 2 6 1 3
Num  Roll_Count
 1     15
 2     19
 3     14
 4     16
 5     19
 6     17
The number(s) 2 5 is (are) rolled maximum number of times, which is 19.
```

This program works as follows. The statement in Line 7 creates the array `dice` of 100 elements and each element is a reference to an object of the `class` `RollDie`. The statement in Line 8 creates the array `rollCount` to store the number of times each number is rolled. The `for` loop in Line 10 instantiates and initializes each element of the array `dice`. The `for` loop in 16 retrieves the number rolled by each die and also counts the number of times each number is rolled. This loop also outputs the numbers rolled with 34 numbers per line. The `for` loop in Line 26 outputs the number of times each number is rolled and also determines the maximum roll count. The `for` loop in Line 33 outputs the numbers that are rolled the maximum number of times.

Arrays and Variable Length Parameter List (Optional)

In Chapter 7, we wrote the method `larger` to determine the larger of two numbers. Similarly, we can write methods to determine the largest of three numbers, four numbers, five numbers, and so on. Moreover, using the mechanism of method overloading, each of these methods can be called `largest`. For example, we can write several such methods with the following headings:

```
public static double largest(double x, double y)
public static double largest(double x, double y, double z)
public static double largest(double x, double y, double z,
                             double u)
public static double largest(double x, double y, double z,
                             double u, double w)
```

9

However, this requires us to write the definitions of each of these methods. Java simplifies this by providing a variable length formal parameter (list). The syntax to declare a variable length formal parameter (list) is:

```
dataType ... identifier
```

where `dataType` is the name of a type, such as the primitive data type or a Java class or a user-defined data type. Note the ellipsis in this syntax; it is part of the syntax. For example, consider the following formal parameter declaration:

```
double ... numList
```

This statement declares `numList` to be a variable length formal parameter. In fact, `numList` is an array wherein each element is of type `double`, and the number of elements in `list` depends on the number of arguments passed to `numList`.

Consider the following method definition:

```
public static double largest(double ... list)
{
    double max;

    if (list.length != 0)
    {
        max = list[0];

        for (int index = 1; index < list.length; index++)
        {
            if (max < list[index])
                max = list[index];
        }

        return max;
    }

    return 0.0;
}
```

The formal parameter `list` of the method `largest` is of variable length. In a call to the method `largest`, you can specify either any number of actual parameters of type `double` or an array of type `double`. If the actual parameters of the method `largest` are of type `double`, then the values of the actual parameters are put in the array `list`. Because the number of actual parameters can be zero, in which case the length of `list` is 0, before determining the largest number in `list` we check whether the length of `list` is 0.

Consider the following statements:

```
double num1 = largest(34, 56);                  //Line 1
double num2 = largest(12.56, 84, 92);           //Line 2
double num3 = largest(98.32, 77, 64.67, 56);    //Line 3
System.out.println(largest(22.50, 67.78,
                    92.58, 45, 34, 56));        //Line 4


double[] numberList = {18.50, 44, 56.23, 17.89,
                    92.34, 112.0, 77, 11, 22,
                    86.62);                     //Line 5
System.out.println(largest(numberList));        //Line 6
```

In Line 1, the method `largest` is called with two parameters; in Line 2 it is called with three parameters; in Line 3 it is called with four parameters; and in Line 4 it is called with six parameters. In Line 6, the actual parameter of the method `largest` is the array `numberList`.

Example 9-10 further illustrates how the method largest can be used in a program.

EXAMPLE 9-10

```java
//Program: Largest of a set of numbers

import java.util.*;

public class LargestNumber
{
    public static void main(String[] args)
    {
        double[] numberList = {23, 45.5, 89, 34, 92.78,
                               36, 90, 120.89, 97, 23,
                               90, 89};                //Line 1

        System.out.println("Line 2: The larger of 5.6 "
                    + "and 10.8 is "
                    + largest(5.6, 10.8));             //Line 2

        System.out.println("Line 3: The largest of 23, "
                    + "78, and 56 is "
                    + largest(23, 78, 56));            //Line 3

        System.out.println("Line 4: The largest of 93, "
                    + "28, 83, and 66 is "
                    + largest(93, 28, 83, 66));        //Line 4

        System.out.println("Line 5: The largest of 22.5, "
                    + "12.34, 56.34, 78, "
                    + "\n         "
                    + "98.45, 25, 78, 23 and 36 is "
                    + largest(22.5, 12.34, 56.34,
                              78, 98.45, 25, 78,
                              23, 36));                //Line 5

        System.out.println("Line 6: The largest "
                    + "number in numList is "
                    + largest(numberList));            //Line 6

        System.out.println("Line 7: A call to the method "
                    + "largest with an empty \n"
                    + "          parameter "
                    + "list returns the value "
                    + largest());                      //Line 7
    }

    public static double largest(double ... numList)
    {
        double max;
```

```
        if (numList.length != 0)
        {
            max = numList[0];

            for (int index = 1; index < numList.length; index++)
            {
                if (max < numList [index])
                    max = numList [index];
            }

            return max;
        }

        return 0.0;
    }
}
```

Sample Run:

```
Line 2: The larger of 5.6 and 10.8 is 10.8
Line 3: The largest of 23, 78, and 56 is 78.0
Line 4: The largest of 93, 28, 83, and 66 is 93.0
Line 5: The largest of 22.5, 12.34, 56.34, 78,
        98.45, 25, 78, 23 and 36 is 98.45
Line 6: The largest number in numList is 120.89
Line 7: A call to the method largest with an empty
        parameter list returns the value 0.0
```

In the preceding program, in Line 2, the method `largest` is called with two parameters; in Line 3 it is called with three parameters; in Line 4 it is called with four parameters; and in Line 5 it is called with nine parameters. Note that in Line 6, the method `largest` is called using an array of numbers, and in Line 7 it is called with no parameters.

Just as you can create a method using the primitive data type as a variable length formal parameter, you can also create a method with objects as a variable length formal parameter (list). Examples 9-11 and 9-12 show you how to do this. First, we specify some rules to follow when using a variable length formal parameter list.

1. A method can have both a variable length formal parameter and other formal parameters. For example, consider the following method heading:

```
public static void myMethod(String name, double num,
                            int ... intList)
```

The formal parameter `name` is of type `String`, the formal parameter `num` is of type `double`, and the formal parameter `intList` is of variable length. The actual parameter corresponding to `intList` can be an `int` array or any number of `int` variables and/or `int` values.

2. A method can have, at most, one variable length formal parameter.

3. If a method has both a variable length formal parameter and other types of formal parameters, then the variable length formal parameter must be the last formal parameter of the formal parameter list.

Before giving more examples of methods with a variable length formal parameter list, we note the following.

One way to process the elements of an array one-by-one, starting at the first element, is to use an index variable, initialized to 0, and a loop. For example, to process the elements of an array, `list`, you can use a `for` loop, such as the following:

```
for (int index; index < list.length; index++)
    //process list[index]
```

In fact, this chapter uses these types of loops to process the elements of an array. The most recent version of Java provides a special type of `for` loop to process the elements of an object, such as an array. The syntax to use this `for` loop to process the elements of an array is:

```
for (dataType identifier : arrayName)
    statements
```

where `identifier` is a variable and the data type of `identifier` is the same as the data type of the array elements. This form of the `for` loop is called a **foreach** loop.

For example, suppose `list` is an array and each element is of type `double`, and `sum` is a `double` variable. The following code finds the sum of the elements of `list`:

```
sum = 0;                        //Line 1

for (double num : list)         //Line 2
    sum = sum + num;            //Line 3
```

The `for` statement in Line 2 is read for each num in `list`. The identifier num is initialized to `list[0]`. In the next iteration, the value of num is `list[1]`, and so on.

Using the foreach loop, the `for` loop in the method `largest`, in Example 9-10, can be written as:

```
for (double num : list)
{
    if (max < num)
        max = num;
}
```

(The Web site, *www.course.com*, and the CD accompanying this book contain the modified program, named `LargestNumberVersionII.java`, that uses the foreach loop to determine the largest element in `list`.)

Example 9-11 shows that the variable length formal parameters (list) of a method can be objects. This example uses the `class` `Clock` designed in Chapter 8.

EXAMPLE 9-11

```java
public class ObjectsAsVariableLengthParameters
{
    public static void main(String[] args)
    {
        Clock myClock = new Clock(12, 5, 10);          //Line 1
        Clock yourClock = new Clock(8, 15, 6);         //Line 2

        Clock[] arrivalTimeEmp = new Clock[10];        //Line 3

        for (int j = 0; j < arrivalTimeEmp.length;
                        j++)                           //Line 4
            arrivalTimeEmp[j] = new Clock();           //Line 5

        arrivalTimeEmp[5].setTime(8, 5, 10);           //Line 6

        printTimes(myClock, yourClock);                //Line 7

        System.out.println("\n*****************"
                        + "****** \n");                //Line 8

        printTimes(arrivalTimeEmp);                    //Line 9
    }

    public static void printTimes(Clock ... clockList)
    {
        for (int i = 0; i < clockList.length; i++)     //Line 10
            System.out.println(clockList[i]);          //Line 11
    }
}
```

Sample Run:

```
12:05:10
08:15:06

************************

00:00:00
00:00:00
00:00:00
00:00:00
00:00:00
08:05:10
00:00:00
00:00:00
00:00:00
00:00:00
```

In this program, the statements in Lines 1 and 2 create the objects myClock and yourClock. The statement in Line 3 creates the array arrivalTimeEmp of 10 elements, wherein each element is a reference variable of the Clock type. The for loop in the statements in Lines 4 and 5 instantiates the objects of the array arrivalTimeEmp. The statement in Line 6 sets the arrival time of employee 5, which is the sixth element of the array. The statement in Line 7 calls the method printTimes with two actual parameters, and the statement in Line 9 calls this method with arrivalTimeEmp as the actual parameter, an array of 10 elements.

Note that the for loop in Lines 10 and 11 can be replaced with the following foreach loop:

```
for (Clock clockObject : clockList)        //Line 10
    System.out.println(clockObject);    //Line 11
```

Example 9-12 illustrates that a constructor of a class can have a variable length formal parameter list.

EXAMPLE 9-12

Consider the class StudentData:

```
public class StudentData
{
    private String firstName;
    private String lastName;

    private double[] testScores; //array to store
                                 //the test scores
    private char grade;

        //Default constructor
    public StudentData()
    {
        firstName = "";
        lastName = "";
        grade = '*';
        testScores = new double[5];
    }

        //Constructor with parameters
        //The parameter list is of varying length.
        //Postcondition: firstName = fName; lastName = lName;
        //               testScores = list;
        //               Calculate and assign the grade to
        //               grade.
    public StudentData(String fName, String lName,
                       double ... list)
    {
        firstName = fName;
        lastName = lName;
        testScores = list;
```

9

```
        grade = courseGrade(list); //calculate and store
                                   //the grade in grade
    }

    //Method to calculate the grade
    //Postcondition: The grade is calculated and
    //                    returned.
    public char courseGrade(double ... list)
    {
        double sum = 0;
        double average = 0;

        for (double num : list)
            sum = sum + num;    //sum the test scores

        if (list.length != 0)   //find the average
            average = sum / list.length;

        if (average >= 90)      //determine the grade
            return 'A';
        else if (average >= 80)
            return 'B';
        else if (average > 70)
            return 'C';
        else if (average > 60)
            return 'D';
        else
            return 'F';
    }

    //Method to return student's name, test scores,
    //and grades as a string.
    //Postcondition: The string consisting of the first
    //                    name, last name, followed by the
    //                    test scores, and the course grade is
    //                    constructed and returned.
    public String toString()
    {
        String str;

        str = String.format("%-10s %-10s ", firstName,
                            lastName);

        for (double score : testScores)
            str = str + String.format("%7.2f", score);

        str = str + "    " + grade;

        return str;
    }
}
```

Note that the constructor with parameters of the **class** StudentData has a variable length formal parameter. The method **courseGrade** also consists of a variable length formal parameter. The following program uses the **class** Student to keep track of students' names, test scores, and course grades:

```
public class TestProgStudentData
{
    public static void main(String[] args)
    {
        StudentData student1 =
                    new StudentData("John", "Doe",
                            89, 78, 95, 63, 94);

        StudentData student2 =
                    new StudentData("Lindsay", "Green",
                            92, 82, 90, 70, 87, 99);

        System.out.println(student1);
        System.out.println(student2);
    }
}
```

Sample Run:

```
John        Doe        89.00  78.00  95.00  63.00  94.00  B
Lindsay     Green      92.00  82.00  90.00  70.00  87.00  99.00  B
```

We leave the details of the preceding output as an exercise.

NOTE   To learn more about constructors with a variable length formal parameter list, see Exercise 8 at the end of this chapter.

Two-Dimensional Arrays

In the previous section, you learned how to use one-dimensional arrays to manipulate data. If the data is provided in a list form, you can use one-dimensional arrays. However, sometimes data is provided in a table form.

Suppose you want to keep track of how many cars of a particular color a local dealership has in stock. The dealership sells six types of cars in five different colors. Figure 9-15 shows a sample data table.

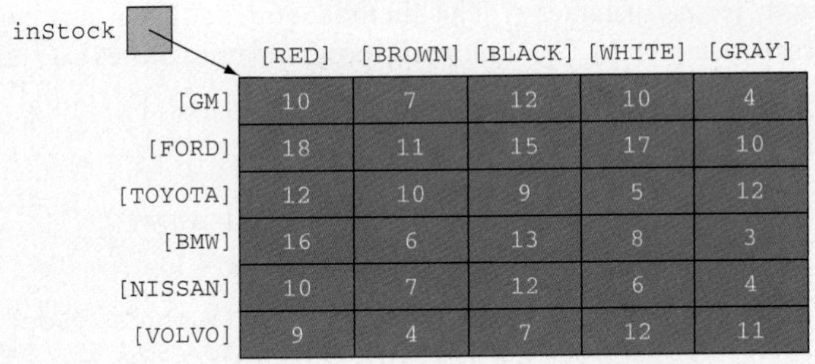

FIGURE 9-15 Table inStock

You can see that the data is in a table format. The table has 30 entries, and every entry is an integer. Because all the table entries are of the same type, you could declare a one-dimensional array of 30 elements of type int. The first five elements of the one-dimensional array could store the data of the first row of the table, the next five elements of the one-dimensional array could store the data of the second row of the table, and so on. In other words, you could simulate the data given in a table format in a one-dimensional array.

If you do so, the algorithms to manipulate the data in the one-dimensional array will be somewhat complicated, because you must carefully note where one row ends and another begins. Also, you would need to correctly compute the index of a particular element from its row and column location. Java simplifies manipulating data in a table format by using **two-dimensional arrays**. This section first discusses how to declare two-dimensional arrays, and then looks at ways to manipulate the data in a two-dimensional array.

Two-dimensional array: A collection of a fixed number of elements arranged in rows and columns (that is, in two dimensions), wherein all the elements are of the same type.

A syntax for declaring a two-dimensional array is:

```
dataType[][] arrayName;
```

where **dataType** is the data type of the array elements.

Because an array is an object, we must instantiate the object to allocate memory space to store the data. The general syntax to instantiate a two-dimensional array object is:

```
arrayName = new dataType[intExp1][intExp2];
```

where **intExp1** and **intExp2** are expressions yielding positive integer values. The two expressions, **intExp1** and **intExp2**, specify the number of rows and the number of columns, respectively, in the array.

The preceding two statements can be combined into one statement, as follows:

```
dataType[][] arrayName = new dataType[intExp1][intExp2];
```

For example, the statement:

```
double[][] sales = new double[10][5];
```

declares a two-dimensional array `sales` of 10 rows and 5 columns, wherein every element is of type `double` initialized to the default value of `0.0`. As in a one-dimensional array, the rows are numbered `0...9` and the columns are numbered `0...4` (see Figure 9-16).

	[0]	[1]	[2]	[3]	[4]
[0]	0.0	0.0	0.0	0.0	0.0
[1]	0.0	0.0	0.0	0.0	0.0
[2]	0.0	0.0	0.0	0.0	0.0
[3]	0.0	0.0	0.0	0.0	0.0
[4]	0.0	0.0	0.0	0.0	0.0
[5]	0.0	0.0	0.0	0.0	0.0
[6]	0.0	0.0	0.0	0.0	0.0
[7]	0.0	0.0	0.0	0.0	0.0
[8]	0.0	0.0	0.0	0.0	0.0
[9]	0.0	0.0	0.0	0.0	0.0

FIGURE 9-16   Two-dimensional array `sales`

9

NOTE   From this point forward, whenever we instantiate a two-dimensional array and draw its diagram, all the default values may not be shown as they are in Figure 9-16.

Accessing Array Elements

To access the elements of a two-dimensional array, you need a pair of indices: one for the row position, and one for the column position.

The syntax to access an element of a two-dimensional array is:

```
arrayName[indexExp1][indexExp2]
```

where `indexExp1` and `indexExp2` are expressions yielding nonnegative integer values. `indexExp1` specifies the row position and `indexExp2` specifies the column position. Moreover, the value of `indexExp1` must be nonnegative and less than the number of rows, and the value of `indexExp2` must be nonnegative and less than the number of columns in the array.

The statement:

```
sales[5][3] = 25.75;
```

stores 25.75 into row number 5 and column number 3 (the 6th row and the 4th column) of the array **sales** (see Figure 9-17).

FIGURE 9-17 sales[5][3]

Suppose that:

```
int i = 5;
int j = 3;
```

Then, the previous statement:

```
sales[5][3] = 25.75;
```

is equivalent to:

```
sales[i][j] = 25.75;
```

So the indices can also be variables.

TWO-DIMENSIONAL ARRAYS AND THE INSTANCE VARIABLE length

Just as in one-dimensional arrays, you can use the instance variable **length** to determine the number of rows as well as the number of columns (in each row). Consider the following statement:

```
int[][] matrix = new int[20][15];
```

This statement declares and instantiates a two-dimensional array **matrix** of 20 rows and 15 columns. The value of the expression:

```
matrix.length
```

is 20, the number of rows.

Each row of `matrix` is a one-dimensional array; `matrix[0]`, in fact, refers to the first row. Therefore, the value of the expression:

`matrix[0].length`

is 15, the number of columns in the first row. Similarly, `matrix[1].length` gives the number of columns in the second row, which in this case is 15, and so on.

TWO-DIMENSIONAL ARRAYS: SPECIAL CASES

The two-dimensional arrays created in the preceding sections are quite straightforward; each row has the same number of columns. However, Java allows you to specify a different number of columns for each row. In this case, each row must be instantiated separately. Consider the following statement:

`int[][] board;`

Suppose that you want to create the array `board`, as shown in Figure 9-18.

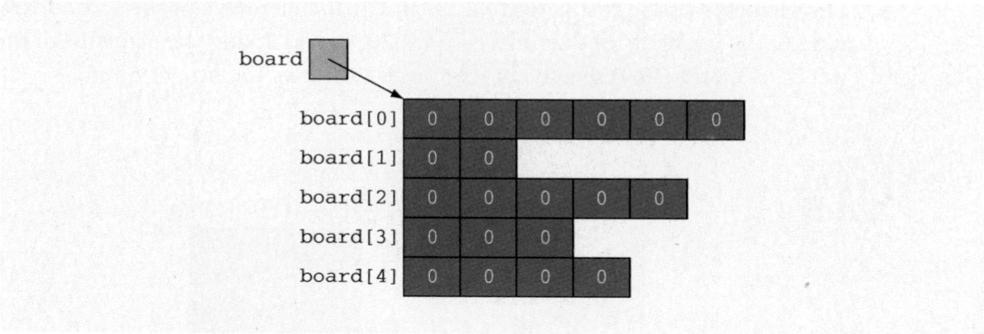

FIGURE 9-18 Array `board`

It follows from Figure 9-18 that the number of rows in `board` is 5, the number of columns in the first row is 6, the number of columns in the second row is 2, the number of columns in the third row is 5, the number of columns in the fourth row is 3, and the number of columns in the fifth row is 4. To create this two-dimensional array, first we create the one-dimensional array `board` of 5 rows. Then, we instantiate each row, specifying the required number of columns, as follows:

```
board = new int[5][];    //Create the number of rows

board[0] = new int[6];   //Create the columns for the first row
board[1] = new int[2];   //Create the columns for the second row
board[2] = new int[5];   //Create the columns for the third row
board[3] = new int[3];   //Create the columns for the fourth row
board[4] = new int[4];   //Create the columns for the fifth row
```

Because the number of columns in each row is not the same, such arrays are called **ragged arrays**. To process these types of two-dimensional arrays, you must know the exact number of columns for each row.

Notice that here `board.length` is 5, the number of rows in the array `board`. Similarly, `board[0].length` is 6, the number of columns in the first row; `board[1].length` is 2, the number of columns in the second row; `board[2].length` is 5, the number of columns in the third row; `board[3].length` is 3, the number of columns in the fourth row; and `board[4].length` is 4, the number of columns in the fifth row.

Two-Dimensional Array Initialization during Declaration

Like one-dimensional arrays, two-dimensional arrays can be initialized when they are declared. The example in the following statement helps illustrate this concept:

```
int[][] board = {{2, 3, 1},
                 {15, 25, 13},
                 {20, 4, 7},
                 {11, 18, 14}};        //Line 1
```

This statement declares `board` to be a two-dimensional array of 4 rows and 3 columns. The elements of the first row are 2, 3, and 1; the elements of the second row are 15, 25, and 13; the elements of the third row are 20, 4, and 7; and the elements of the fourth row are 11, 18, and 14, respectively. Figure 9-19 shows the array `board`.

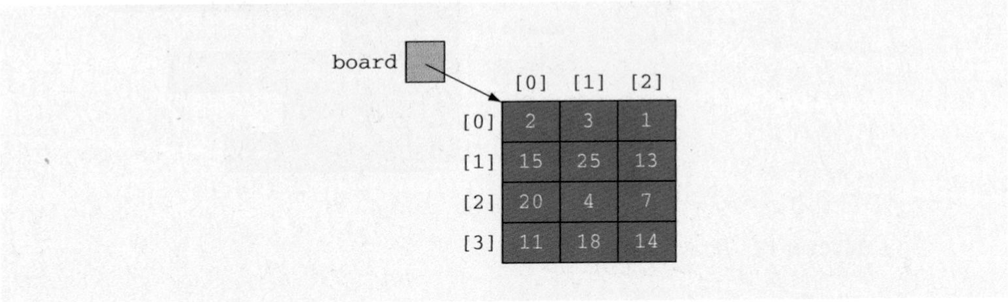

FIGURE 9-19 Two-dimensional array `board`

To initialize a two-dimensional array when it is declared:

- The elements of each row are enclosed within braces and separated by commas.
- All rows are enclosed within braces.

Now consider the following statement:

```
int[][] table = {{2, 1, 3, 5},
                 {15, 25},
                 {4, 23, 45}};
```

Here, you see that the number of values specified for the first row of the array `table` is 4, the number of values specified for the second row is 2, and the number of values specified for the third row is 3. Because the number of values specified for the first row is 4, only four columns are assigned to the first row. Similarly, the number of columns assigned to the second and third rows are 2 and 3, respectively (see Figure 9-20).

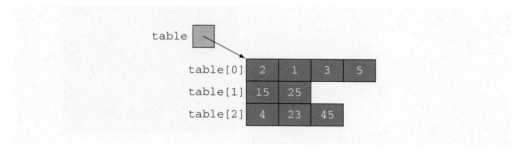

FIGURE 9-20 Array `table`

Processing Two-Dimensional Arrays

In the remainder of this chapter, we assume that the two-dimensional arrays that are being considered are not ragged.

A two-dimensional array can be processed in three common ways:

1. Process the entire array.
2. Process a particular row of the array, called **row processing**.
3. Process a particular column of the array, called **column processing**.

Initializing and printing the array are examples of processing the entire two-dimensional array. Finding the largest element in a row or column, or finding the sum of a row or column, are examples of row (column) processing. We will use the following declarations for our discussion:

```
static final int ROWS = 7;    //this can be set to any number
static final int COLUMNS = 6; //this can be set to any number

int[][] matrix = new int[ROWS][COLUMNS];

int sum;
int largest;
int temp;
```

Figure 9-21 shows the array `matrix`.

9

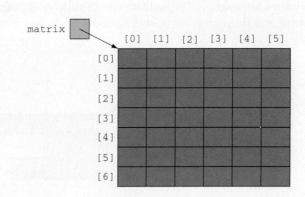

FIGURE 9-21 Two-dimensional array `matrix`

NOTE For the two-dimensional array `matrix`, the value of `matrix.length` is 7, which is the same as the value of the named constant ROWS. Also, the values of `matrix[0].length, matrix[1].length, ..., matrix[6].length` give the number of columns in row 0, row 1, . . ., row 6, respectively. Notice that the number of columns in each row is 6.

Because all the elements of a two-dimensional array are of the same type, the elements of any row or column are of the same type. This means that in a two-dimensional array, the elements of each row and each column can be processed as a one-dimensional array. Therefore, when processing a particular row or column of a two-dimensional array, we use algorithms similar to those that process one-dimensional arrays. We explain this concept further with the help of the two-dimensional array `matrix`, as declared previously.

Suppose that we want to process row number 5 of `matrix` (the **sixth** row of `matrix`). The elements of row number 5 of `matrix` are:

`matrix[5][0], matrix[5][1], matrix[5][2], matrix[5][3], matrix[5][4], matrix[5][5]`

In these elements, the first index (the row position) is fixed at 5. The second index (the column position) ranges from 0 to 5. Therefore, we can use the following `for` loop to process row number 5:

```
for (int col = 0; col < matrix[5].length; col++)
    //process matrix[5][col]
```

This `for` loop is equivalent to the following `for` loop:

```
int row = 5;

for (int col = 0; col < matrix[row].length; col++)
    //process matrix[row][col]
```

Similarly, suppose that we want to process column number 2 (the third column) of `matrix`. The elements of this column are:

```
matrix[0][2], matrix[1][2], matrix[2][2], matrix[3][2], matrix[4][2],
matrix[5][2], matrix[6][2]
```

Here, the second index (the column position) is fixed at 2. The first index (the row position) ranges from 0 to 6. In this case, we use the following `for` loop to process column 2 of `matrix`:

```
for (int row = 0; row < matrix.length; row++)
    //process matrix[row][2]
```

This `for` loop is equivalent to the following `for` loop:

```
int col = 2;

for (int row = 0; row < matrix.length; row++)
    //process matrix[row][col]
```

Next, we discuss some specific algorithms for processing two-dimensional arrays.

INITIALIZATION

Suppose that you want to initialize the elements of row number 4 (the fifth row) to 10. As explained earlier, the following `for` loop initializes the elements of row number 4 to 10:

```
int row = 4;
for (int col = 0; col < matrix[row].length; col++)
    matrix[row][col] = 10;
```

If you want to initialize the elements of the entire `matrix` to 10, you can also put the first index (the row position) in a loop. By using the following nested `for` loops, you can initialize each element of `matrix` to 10:

```
for (int row = 0; row < matrix.length; row++)
    for (int col = 0; col < matrix[row].length; col++)
        matrix[row][col] = 10;
```

PRINT

By using a nested `for` loop, you can output the elements of `matrix`. The following nested `for` loops print the elements of `matrix`, one row per line:

```
for (int row = 0; row < matrix.length; row++)
{
    for (int col = 0; col < matrix[row].length; col++)
        System.out.printf("%7d", matrix[row][col]);

    System.out.println();
}
```

9

INPUT

The following `for` loop inputs data into row number 4 (the fifth row) of `matrix`:

```
int row = 4;

for (int col = 0; col < matrix[row].length; col++)
    matrix[row][col] = console.nextInt();
```

As before, by putting the row number in a loop, you can input data into each element of `matrix`. The following `for` loop inputs data into each element of `matrix`:

```
for (int row = 0; row < matrix.length; row++)
    for (int col = 0; col < matrix[row].length; col++)
        matrix[row][col] = console.nextInt();
```

SUM BY ROW

The following `for` loop finds the sum of the elements of row number 4 of `matrix`; that is, it adds the elements of row number 4:

```
sum = 0;
int row = 4;
for (int col = 0; col < matrix[row].length; col++)
    sum = sum + matrix[row][col];
```

Once again, by putting the row number in a loop, you can find the sum of each row separately. The Java code to find the sum of each individual row follows:

```
    //Sum of each individual row
for (int row = 0; row < matrix.length; row++)
{
    sum = 0;

    for (int col = 0; col < matrix[row].length; col++)
        sum = sum + matrix[row][col];

    System.out.println("The sum of the elements of row "
                    + (row + 1) + " = " + sum);
}
```

SUM BY COLUMN

As in the case of sum by row, the following nested `for` loop finds the sum of the elements of each individual column. (Notice that `matrix[0].length` gives the number of columns in each row.)

```
    //Sum of each individual column
for (int col = 0; col < matrix[0].length; col++)
{
    sum = 0;
    for (int row = 0; row < matrix.length; row++)
        sum = sum + matrix[row][col];
```

```
System.out.println("The sum of the elements of column "
                   + (col + 1) + " = " + sum);
}
```

(Note that the preceding code to find the sum of the elements of each column assumes that the number of columns in each row is the same. In other words, the two-dimensional array is *not* ragged.)

LARGEST ELEMENT IN EACH ROW AND EACH COLUMN

As stated earlier, another possible operation on a two-dimensional array is finding the largest element in each row and each column. Next, we give the Java code to perform this operation.

The following `for` loop determines the largest element in row number 4:

```
int row = 4;
largest = matrix[row][0]; //assume that the first element of the
                          //row is the largest
for (int col = 1; col < matrix[row].length; col++)
    if (largest < matrix[row][col])
        largest = matrix[row][col];
```

The following Java code determines the largest element in each row and each column:

```
    //The largest element of each row
for (int row = 0; row < matrix.length; row++)
{
    largest = matrix[row][0]; //assume that the first element
                              //of the row is the largest
    for (int col = 1; col < matrix[row].length; col++)
        if (largest < matrix[row][col])
            largest = matrix[row][col];

    System.out.println("The largest element of row "
                       + (row + 1) + " = " + largest);
}

    //The largest element of each column
for (int col = 0; col < matrix[0].length; col++)
{
    largest = matrix[0][col]; //assume that the first element
                              //of the column is the largest
    for (int row = 1; row < matrix.length; row++)
        if (largest < matrix[row][col])
            largest = matrix[row][col];

    System.out.println("The largest element of col "
                       + (col + 1) + " = " + largest);
}
```

Passing Two-Dimensional Arrays as Parameters to Methods

Just like one-dimensional arrays, references to two-dimensional arrays can be passed as parameters to a method.

In the section, Processing Two–Dimensional Arrays, we described various algorithms to process the elements of a two-dimensional array. Using those algorithms, we can write methods that can be used in a variety of applications. In this section, we write some of these methods. For simplicity, we assume that we are processing the entire two-dimensional array.

The following method outputs the elements of a two-dimensional array, one row per line:

```java
public static void printMatrix(int[][] matrix)
{
    for (int row = 0; row < matrix.length; row++)
    {
        for (int col = 0; col < matrix[row].length; col++)
            System.out.printf("%7d", matrix[row][col]);

        System.out.println();
    }
}
```

Similarly, the following method outputs the sum of the elements of each row of a two-dimensional array whose elements are of type int:

```java
public static void sumRows(int[][] matrix)
{
    int sum;

        //sum of each individual row
    for (int row = 0; row < matrix.length; row++)
    {
        sum = 0;

        for (int col = 0; col < matrix[row].length; col++)
            sum = sum + matrix[row][col];

        System.out.println("The sum of the elements of row "
                        + (row + 1) + " = " + sum);
    }
}
```

The following method determines the largest element in each row:

```java
public static void largestInRows(int[][] matrix)
{
    int largest;

        //The largest element in each row
    for (int row = 0; row < matrix.length; row++)
```

```
    {
        largest = matrix[row][0]; //assume that the first
                                  //element of the row is
                                  //the largest
        for (int col = 1; col < matrix[row].length; col++)
            if (largest < matrix[row][col])
                largest = matrix[row][col];

        System.out.println("The largest element of row "
                        + (row + 1) + " = " + largest);
    }
}
```

In a similar fashion, you can write methods to find the sum of the elements of each column, read data into a two-dimensional array, find the largest and/or smallest element in each row or each column, and so on.

As in the case of one-dimensional arrays, to conveniently use the methods to process data in a two-dimensional array, we put the definitions of the methods printArray, sumRows, largestInRows, and other such methods in the class TwoDimArraysMethods. The definition of this class is:

```
// This class contains methods to process elements in two-
// dimensional arrays.

public class TwoDimArraysMethods
{
    public static void printMatrix(int[][] matrix)
    {
        for (int row = 0; row < matrix.length; row++)
        {
            for (int col = 0; col < matrix[row].length; col++)
                System.out.printf("%7d", matrix[row][col]);

            System.out.println();
        }
    } //end printMatrix

    public static void sumRows(int[][] matrix)
    {
        int sum;

        //sum of each individual row
        for (int row = 0; row < matrix.length; row++)
        {
            sum = 0;

            for (int col = 0; col < matrix[row].length; col++)
                sum = sum + matrix[row][col];
```

```
            System.out.println("The sum of the elements of row "
                               + (row + 1) + " = " + sum + ".");
        }
    } //end sumRows

    public static void largestInRows(int[][] matrix)
    {
        int largest;

            //Largest element in each row
        for (int row = 0; row < matrix.length; row++)
        {
            largest = matrix[row][0]; //assume that the first
                                      //element of the row is
                                      //largest
            for (int col = 1; col < matrix[row].length; col++)
                if (largest < matrix[row][col])
                    largest = matrix[row][col];

            System.out.println("The largest element of row "
                               + (row + 1) + " = " + largest + ".");
        }
    } //end largestInRows
}
```

Example 9-13 shows how the preceding methods are used in a program.

EXAMPLE 9-13

The following program illustrates how (references to) two-dimensional arrays are passed as parameters to methods:

```
// This program illustrates how two-dimensional arrays are
// passed as parameters to methods.

public class TwoDimArraysAsParam                        //Line 1
{                                                       //Line 2
    public static void main(String[] args)              //Line 3
    {                                                   //Line 4
        int[][] board ={{23,5,6,15,18},
                        {4,16,24,67,10},
                        {12,54,23,76,11},
                        {1,12,34,22,8},
                        {81,54,32,67,33},
                        {12,34,76,78,9}};                //Line 5

        TwoDimArraysMethods.printMatrix(board);         //Line 6
        System.out.println();                           //Line 7

        TwoDimArraysMethods.sumRows(board);             //Line 8
        System.out.println();                           //Line 9
```

```
        TwoDimArraysMethods.largestInRows(board);    //Line 10
    } //end main                                     //Line 11
}                                                    //Line 12
```

Sample Run:

```
23      5      6     15     18
 4     16     24     67     10
12     54     23     76     11
 1     12     34     22      8
81     54     32     67     33
12     34     76     78      9
```

```
The sum of the elements of row 1 = 67.
The sum of the elements of row 2 = 121.
The sum of the elements of row 3 = 176.
The sum of the elements of row 4 = 77.
The sum of the elements of row 5 = 267.
The sum of the elements of row 6 = 209.

The largest element of row 1 = 23.
The largest element of row 2 = 67.
The largest element of row 3 = 76.
The largest element of row 4 = 34.
The largest element of row 5 = 81.
The largest element of row 6 = 78.
```

In the preceding program, the statement in Line 5 declares and initializes **board** to be a two-dimensional array of 6 rows and 5 columns. The statement in Line 6 uses the method **printMatrix** to output the elements of **board** (see the first six lines of the Sample Run). The statement in Line 8 uses the method **sumRows** to calculate and print the sum of each row. The statement in Line 10 uses the method **largestInRows** to find and print the largest element in each row.

9

When storing a two-dimensional array in computer memory, Java uses the **row order form**. That is, the first row is stored first, followed by the second row, followed by the third row, and so on.

Multidimensional Arrays

Earlier in this chapter, we defined an array as a collection of a fixed number of variables called elements or components of the same type. A one-dimensional array is an array in which the elements are arranged in a list form; in a two-dimensional array, the elements are arranged in a table form. We can also define three-dimensional or larger arrays. In Java, there is no limit on the dimensions of arrays. The following is the general definition of an array:

n-**dimensional array:** A collection of a fixed number of variables, called elements or components, arranged in n dimensions (n >= 1).

The general syntax for declaring and instantiating an n-dimensional array is:

```
dataType[][]...[] arrayName
                = new dataType[intExp1][intExp2] ... [intExpn];
```

where `intExp1`, `intExp2`, ..., and `intExpn` are constant expressions yielding positive integer values.

The syntax to access an element of an n-dimensional array is:

```
arrayName[indexExp1][indexExp2] ... [indexExpn]
```

where `indexExp1`, `indexExp2`, ..., and `indexExpn` are expressions yielding nonnegative integer values. Moreover, for each `i`, the value of `indexExpi` must be nonnegative and less than the size of the `i`th dimension. `indexExpi` gives the position of the array element in the `i`th dimension.

For example, the statement:

```
double[][][] carDealers = new double[10][5][7];
```

declares `carDealers` to be a three-dimensional array. The size of the first dimension is 10, the size of the second dimension is 5, and the size of the third dimension is 7. The first dimension ranges from 0 to 9, the second dimension ranges from 0 to 4, and the third dimension ranges from 0 to 6. The base address of the array `carDealers` is the address of the first array element—the address of `carDealers[0][0][0]`. The total number of elements in the array `carDealers` is 10 * 5 * 7 = 350.

The statement:

```
carDealers[5][3][2] = 15564.75;
```

sets the value of the element `carDealers[5][3][2]` to `15564.75`.

You can use loops to process multidimensional arrays. For example, the nested `for` loops:

```
for (int i = 0; i < 10; i++)
    for (int j = 0; j < 5; j++)
        for (int k = 0; k < 7; k++)
            carDealers[i][j][k] = 10.00;
```

initialize each element of the array to `10.00`.

During program execution, if an array index goes out of bounds, the program throws an `ArrayIndexOutOfBoundsException`. Exception handling is discussed in detail in Chapter 11.

PROGRAMMING EXAMPLE: Code Detection

When a message is transmitted in secret code over a transmission channel, it is usually transmitted as a sequence of bits, that is, 0s and 1s. Due to noise in the transmission channel, the transmitted message may become corrupted. That is, the message received at the destination is not the same as the message transmitted; some of the bits may have been changed. There are several techniques to check the validity of the transmitted message at the destination. One technique is to transmit the same message twice. At the destination, both copies of the message are compared bit-by-bit. If the corresponding bits are the same, the message is assumed to have been received error-free.

Let's write a program to check whether the message received at the destination is likely error-free. For simplicity, assume that the secret code representing the message is a sequence of digits (0 to 9). Also, the first number in the message is the length of the message. For example, if the secret code is:

7 9 2 7 8 3 5 6

then the actual message is 7 digits long, and it is transmitted twice.

The above message is transmitted as:

7 9 2 7 8 3 5 6 7 9 2 7 8 3 5 6

Input: The secret code and its copy.

Output: The secret code, its copy, and a message—if the received code is error-free—in the following form:

```
Code Digit      Code Digit Copy
    9                   9
    2                   2
    7                   7
    8                   8
    3                   3
    5                   5
    6                   6
Message transmitted OK.
```

The preceding output is to be stored in a file.

PROBLEM ANALYSIS AND ALGORITHM DESIGN

Because we have to compare the corresponding digits of the secret code and its copy, you first read the secret code and store it in an array. Then you read the first digit of the copy and compare it with the first digit of the secret code, and so on. If any corresponding digits are not the same, you indicate this fact by printing a message next to the digits. We use an array to store the secret code. The first number in the secret code, and in the copy of the secret code, indicates the length of the code. This discussion translates into the following algorithm:

1. Prompt and read the length of the secret code.

2. Create an array of appropriate length to store the secret code.

3. Read and store the secret code into an array.

4. Read the length of the copy.

5. If the length of the secret code and its copy are the same, compare the codes. Otherwise, print an error message.

To simplify the definition of the method main, let us write the method, readCode, to read the secret code and another method, compareCode, to compare the codes. Next, we describe these two methods.

readCode   The method readCode reads and stores the secret code in an array. This method has one parameter: an array to store the secret code. The definition of the method readCode is as follows:

```
public static void readCode(int[] list)
{
    System.out.print("Enter the secret code: ");

    for (int count = 0; count < list.length; count++)
        list[count] = console.nextInt();

    System.out.println();
}
```

compareCode   This method compares the secret code with its copy and prints an appropriate message. Therefore, it must have access to the array containing the secret code. Thus, this method has one parameter: the array containing the secret code. This discussion translates into the following algorithm for the method compareCode:

a. Declare the variables.

b. Set a boolean variable codeOk to true.

c. Read the length of the copy of the secret code.

d. If the length of the secret code and its copy are not the same, output an appropriate error message and terminate the method.

e. Output the heading: Code Digit   Code Digit Copy

f. For each digit in the secret code:

    i. Read the next digit of the copy of the secret code.

    ii. Output the corresponding digits from the secret code and its copy.

    iii. If the corresponding digits are not the same, output an error message and set the boolean variable codeOk to false.

g. if the `boolean` variable `codeOk` is `true`

Output a message indicating that the secret code was transmitted correctly.

`else`

Output an error message.

Following this algorithm, the definition of the method `compareCode` is

```java
public static void compareCode(int[] list)
{
        //Step a: Declare the variables
    int length2;
    int digit;
    boolean codeOk;

    codeOk = true;                               //Step b

    System.out.println("Enter the length of the copy of "
                    + "the secret code \nand a copy of "
                    + "the secret code: ");

     length2 = console.nextInt();                //Step c

    if (list.length != length2)                  //Step d
    {
        System.out.println("The original code and "
                        + "its copy are not of "
                        + "the same length.");
        return;
    }

    System.out.println("Code Digit    Code Digit "
                    + "Copy");                    //Step e

    for (int count = 0; count < list.length; count++) //Step f
    {
        digit = console.nextInt();               //Step f(i)

        System.out.printf("%5d %15d",
                        list[count], digit);     //Step f(ii)

        if (digit != list[count])                //Step f(iii)
        {
            System.out.println("  corresponding code "
                            + "digits not the same");
            codeOk = false;
        }
    }
```

```
                else
                    System.out.println();
            }

            if (codeOk)                                   //Step g
                System.out.println("Message transmitted OK.");
            else
                System.out.println("Error in transmission. "
                                    + "Retransmit!!");
        }
```

The following is the algorithm for the method `main`.

Main
Algorithm

1. Declare the variable to store the length of the secret code.
2. Prompt the user to enter the length of the secret code.
3. Get the length of the secret code.
4. Create the array to store the secret code.
5. Call the method `readCode` to read the secret code.
6. Call the method `compareCode` to compare the codes.

PROGRAM LISTING

```
//*************************************************************
// Author: D. S. Malik
//
// Program: Code Detection
// This program checks whether the message received at the
// destination is error-free. If there is an error in the
// message, then the program outputs an error message and
// asks for retransmission.
//*************************************************************

import java.util.*;

public class CodeDetection
{
    static Scanner console = new Scanner(System.in);

    public static void main(String[] args)
    {
        int codeLength;                               //Step 1

        System.out.print("Enter the length "
                        + "of the code: ");           //Step 2
```

```
        codeLength = console.nextInt();        //Step 3
        System.out.println();

        int[] codeArray = new int[codeLength];  //Step 4

        readCode(codeArray);                    //Step 5
        compareCode(codeArray);                 //Step 6
    }

    //Place the definition of the method readCode as
    //described earlier here.
    //Place the definition of the method compareCode as
    //described earlier here.
}
```

Sample Run: (In this sample run, the user input is shaded.)

Enter the length of the code: 7

Enter the secret code: 9 2 7 8 3 5 6

Enter the length of the copy of the secret code
and a copy of the secret code:
7 9 2 7 8 3 5 6

```
Code Digit   Code Digit Copy
    9              9
    2              2
    7              7
    8              8
    3              3
    5              5
    6              6
Message transmitted OK.
```

9

PROGRAMMING EXAMPLE: Text Processing

Let's now write a program that reads a given text, outputs the text as is, and prints the number of lines and the number of times each letter appears in the text. An uppercase letter and a lowercase letter are treated as being the same; that is, they are tallied together.

Because there are 26 letters, we use an array of 26 elements to perform the letter count. We also need a variable to store the line count.

The text is stored in a file, which we will call text.txt. The output will be stored in a file, which we will call textCh.out.

Input: A file containing the text to be processed.

Output: A file containing the text, number of lines, and the number of times a letter appears in the text.

PROBLEM
ANALYSIS
AND
ALGORITHM
DESIGN

Based on the desired output, it is clear that we must output the text as is. That is, if the text contains any whitespace characters, they must be output as well.

Let's first describe the variables that are necessary to develop the program. This will simplify the discussion that follows.

Variables

We need to store the letter count and the line count. Therefore, we need a variable to store the line count and 26 variables to store the letter count. We will use an array of 26 elements to perform the letter count. We also need a variable to read and store each character in turn, because the input file will be read character-by-character. Because the data will be read from an input file and the output will be saved in a file, we need an input stream object to open the input file and an output stream object to open the output file. Because the program needs to do a character count, the program should read the input file character-by-character. Moreover, the program should also count the number of lines. Therefore, while reading the data from the input file, the program must capture the newline character. The `Scanner class` does not contain any method that can only read the next character in the input stream, unless the character is delimited by whitespace characters such as blanks. Moreover, using the `Scanner class`, the program should read the entire line or else the newline character will be ignored.

To simplify the character-by-character reading of the input file, we use the Java `class FileReader`. (In Chapter 3, we introduced this class to create and initialize a `Scanner` object to the input source.) The `class FileReader` contains the method `read` that returns the integer value of the next character. For example, if the next input character is `A`, the method `read` returns 65. We can use the cast operator to change the value 65 to the character `A`. Notice that the method `read` *does not* skip whitespace characters. Also, the method `read` returns −1 when the end of the input file has been reached. We can, therefore, use the value returned by the method `read` to determine whether the end of the input file is reached.

Consider the following statement:

```
FileReader inputStream = new FileReader("text.txt");
```

This statement creates the `FileReader` object `inputStream` and initializes it to the input file `text.txt`. If `nextChar` is a `char` variable, then the following statement reads and stores the next character from the input file into `nextChar`:

```
ch = (char) inputStream.read();
```

It now follows that the method `main` needs (at least) the following variables:

```
int lineCount = 0;      //variable to store the line count

int[] letterCount = new int[26]; //array to store the letter
                                 //count

int next;   //variable to read a character

FileReader inputStream = new FileReader("text.txt");

PrintWriter outfile = new PrintWriter("textCh.out");
```

(Note that the method `read` throws an `IOException` when something goes wrong. At this point, we will ignore this exception by throwing it in the program. Exceptions are covered in detail in Chapter 11.)

In this declaration, `letterCount[0]` stores the `A` count, `letterCount[1]` stores the `B` count, and so on. Clearly, the variable `lineCount` and the array `letterCount` must be initialized to `0`.

The algorithm for the program is:

1. Declare and initialize the variables.
2. Create objects to open the input and output files.
3. While there is more data in the input file:

    a. For each character in a line:

        i. Read and write the character.
        ii. Increment the appropriate letter count.

    b. Increment the line count.

4. Output the line count and letter counts.
5. Close the files.

To simplify the method `main`, we divide it into three methods:

1. Method `copyText`
2. Method `chCount`
3. Method `writeTotal`

The following sections describe each method in detail. Then, with the help of these methods, we describe the algorithm for the method `main`.

copyText   This method reads a line and outputs the line. Whenever a nonblank character is found, it calls the method `chCount` to update the letter count. Clearly, this method has four parameters: an input stream object, an output stream object, a variable to read the character, and the array to update the letter count.

Note that the method `copyText` does not perform the letter count, but we still pass the array `letterCount` to it. We do this because this method calls the method `chCount`, which needs the array `letterCount` to update the appropriate letter count. Therefore, we must pass the array `letterCount` to the `copyText` method so that it can pass the array to the method `chCount`.

```
static int copyText(FileReader infile, PrintWriter outfile,
                    int next, int[] letterC) throws IOException
{
    while (next != (int)'\n')
    {
        outfile.print((char)(next));
        chCount((char)(next), letterC);
        next = infile.read();
    }

    outfile.println();

    return next;
}
```

chCount   This method increments the letter count. To increment the appropriate letter count, the method must know what the letter is. Therefore, the `chCount` method has two parameters: a `char` variable and the array to update the letter count. In pseudocode, this method is:

  a. Convert the letter to uppercase.

  b. Find the index of the array corresponding to this letter.

  c. If the index is valid, increment the appropriate count. At this step, we must ensure that the character is a letter. We are only counting letters, so other characters—such as commas, hyphens, and periods—are ignored.

Following this algorithm, the definition of the method is:

```
static void chCount(char ch, int[] letterC)
{
    int index;

    ch = Character.toUpperCase(ch);    //Step a

    index = (int) ch - 65;             //Step b

    if (index >= 0 && index < 26)      //Step c
        letterC[index]++;
}
```

riteTotal

This method outputs the line count and the letter count. It has three parameters: the output stream object, the line count, and the array to output the letter count. The definition of this method is:

```
static void writeTotal(PrintWriter outfile, int lines,
                       int[] letters)
{

    outfile.println();
    outfile.println("The number of lines = " + lines);

    for (int i = 0; i < 26; i++)
        outfile.println((char)(i + 65) + " count = "
                        + letters[i]);
}
```

We now describe the algorithm for the method main.

MAIN
ALGORITHM

1. Declare and initialize the variables.
2. Open the input and output files.
3. Read the first character.
4. while (not end of the input file):
   a. Process the next line; call the method copyText.
   b. Increment the line count. (Increment the variable lineCount.)
   c. Read the next character.
5. Output the line count and letter count. Call the method writeTotal.
6. Close the files.

COMPLETE PROGRAM LISTING

```
//****************************************************************
// Author: D. S. Malik
//
// Program: Line and letter count
// This program reads a given text, outputs the text as
// is, and prints the number of lines and the number of times
// each letter appears in the text. An uppercase letter and a
// lowercase letter are treated as being the same; that is,
// they are tallied together.
//****************************************************************
```

```
import java.io.*;

public class CharacterCount
{
    public static void main(String[] args)
                  throws FileNotFoundException, IOException
    {
        int lineCount = 0;
        int[] letterCount = new int[26];

        int next;

        FileReader inputStream = new FileReader("text.txt");

        PrintWriter outfile = new PrintWriter("textCh.out");

        next = inputStream.read();

        while (next != -1)
        {
            next = copyText(inputStream, outfile,
                            next, letterCount);
            lineCount++;
            next = inputStream.read();
        } //end while loop

        writeTotal(outfile, lineCount, letterCount);

        outfile.close();
    }

    //Place the definition of the method copyText, chCount,
    //and writeTotal as described earlier here.
}
```

Sample Run:

Input file (text.txt)

Today we live in an era where information is processed
almost at the speed of light. Through computers, the
technological revolution is drastically changing the way we
live and communicate with one another. Terms such as
"the Internet," which was unfamiliar just a few years ago, are
very common today. With the help of computers you can send
letters to, and receive letters from, loved ones within
seconds. You no longer need to send a resume by mail to apply
for a job; in many cases you can simply submit your job
application via the Internet. You can watch how stocks perform
in real time, and instantly buy and sell them. Students
regularly "surf" the Internet and use computers to design

their classroom projects. They also use powerful word
processing software to complete their term papers. Many
people maintain and balance their checkbooks on computers.

Output file (textCh.txt)

Today we live in an era where information is processed
almost at the speed of light. Through computers, the
technological revolution is drastically changing the way we
live and communicate with one another. Terms such as
"the Internet," which was unfamiliar just a few years ago, are
very common today. With the help of computers you can send
letters to, and receive letters from, loved ones within
seconds. You no longer need to send a resume by mail to apply
for a job; in many cases you can simply submit your job
application via the Internet. You can watch how stocks perform
in real time, and instantly buy and sell them. Students
regularly "surf" the Internet and use computers to design
their classroom projects. They also use powerful word
processing software to complete their term papers. Many
people maintain and balance their checkbooks on computers.

The number of lines = 15
A count = 53
B count = 7
C count = 30
D count = 19
E count = 83
F count = 11
G count = 10
H count = 29
I count = 41
J count = 4
K count = 3
L count = 31
M count = 26
N count = 50
O count = 59
P count = 21
Q count = 0
R count = 45
S count = 48
T count = 62
U count = 24
V count = 7
W count = 15
X count = 0
Y count = 20
Z count = 0

9

class Vector (Optional)

In addition to arrays, Java provides the **class** Vector to implement a list. Unlike an array, the size of a Vector object can grow and shrink during program execution. Therefore, you need not be concerned about the number of data elements. Before describing how a Vector object is used to manage a list, Table 9-2 describes some of the members of the **class** Vector.

TABLE 9-2 Some Members of the **class** Vector

Instance variables

```
protected int elementCount;

protected Object[] elementData; //Array of references
```

Constructors

```
public Vector()
   //Creates an empty vector of size 0

public Vector(int size)
   //Creates an empty vector of the length specified by size
```

Methods

```
public void addElement(Object insertObj)
   //Add the object insertObj at the end

public void insertElementAt(Object insertObj, int index)
   //Inserts the object insertObj at the position specified by index
   //If index is out of range, this method throws
   //ArrayIndexOutOfBoundsException.

public boolean contains(Object obj)
   //Returns true if the Vector object contains the element specified
   //by obj; otherwise it returns false

public Object elementAt(int index)
   //Returns the element of the vector at location specified by index

public int indexOf(Object obj)
   //Returns the position of the first occurrence of the element
   //specified by obj in the vector
   //If item is not in the vector, the method returns -1.
```

```
public int indexOf(Object obj, int index)
   //Starting at index, the method returns the position of the
   //first occurrence of the element specified by obj in the vector.
   //If item is not in the vector, the method returns -1.

public boolean isEmpty()
   //Returns true if the vector is empty; otherwise it returns false

public void removeAllElements()
   //Removes all elements of the vector

public void removeElementAt(int index)
   //If an element at position specified by index exists, it is
   //removed from the vector.
   //If index is out of range, this method throws an
   //ArrayIndexOutOfBoundsException.

public int size()
   //Returns the number of elements in the vector

public String toString()
   //Returns a string representation of this vector
```

From Table 9-2, it follows that every element of a `Vector` object is a reference variable of type `Object`. In Java, `Object` is a predefined class, and a reference variable of the `Object` type can store the address of any object. Because every element of a `Vector` object is a reference, to add an element to a `Vector` object, you must first create the appropriate object and store the data into that object. You can then store the address of the object holding the data into a `Vector` object element. Because every string in Java is considered a `String` object, we will illustrate some of the operations on a `Vector` object using string data.

Consider the following statement:

```
Vector<String> stringList = new Vector<String>();        //Line 1
```

This statement declares `stringList` to be a reference variable of the `Vector` type, instantiates an empty `Vector` object, and stores the address of this object into `stringList`. The `Vector` object `stringList` is used to create a `Vector` of `String` objects.

 NOTE   In Java 5.0 and higher versions, whenever you declare a `Vector` object, you should also specify the reference type of the objects that the `Vector` object will hold. To do this, enclose the reference type of the objects between < and > after the word `Vector`. For example, in the statement in Line 1, `Vector<String>` specifies that the `Vector` object `stringList` is a `Vector` of the `String` object. If you do not specify the reference type after the word `Vector`, the compiler will generate a warning message indicating an unchecked or unsafe operation.

Next, consider the following statements:

```
stringList.addElement("Spring");
stringList.addElement("Summer");
stringList.addElement("Fall");
stringList.addElement("Winter");
```

After these statements execute, `stringList` is as shown in Figure 9-22.

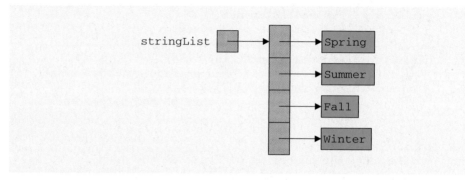

FIGURE 9-22 `stringList` after adding four strings

The statement:

```
System.out.println(stringList);
```

outputs the elements of `stringList` in the following form:

```
[Spring, Summer, Fall, Winter]
```

The **class** Vector is contained in the package `java.util`. Therefore, to use the **class** Vector, your program must include either the statement:

```
import java.util.*;
```

or the statement:

```
import java.util.Vector;
```

The program in Example 9-14 further illustrates how a **Vector** object works.

EXAMPLE 9-14

```
//StringVectorExample

import java.util.Vector;                              //Line 1

public class StringVectorExample                      //Line 2
{                                                     //Line 3
    public static void main(String[] arg)             //Line 4
```

```
    {                                                       //Line 5
        Vector<String> stringList =
                        new Vector<String>();               //Line 6

        System.out.println("Line 7: Empty stringList?: "
                        + stringList.isEmpty());            //Line 7
        System.out.println("Line 8: Size stringList?: "
                        + stringList.size());               //Line 8
        System.out.println();                               //Line 9

        stringList.addElement("Spring");                    //Line 10
        stringList.addElement("Summer");                    //Line 11
        stringList.addElement("Fall");                      //Line 12
        stringList.addElement("Winter");                    //Line 13
        stringList.addElement("Sunny");                     //Line 14

        System.out.println("Line 15: **** After adding "
                        + "elements to stringList ****");    //Line 15
        System.out.println("Line 16: Empty stringList?: "
                        + stringList.isEmpty());            //Line 16
        System.out.println("Line 17: Size stringList?: "
                        + stringList.size());               //Line 17
        System.out.println("Line 18: stringList: "
                        + stringList);                      //Line 18

        System.out.println("Line 19: stringList contains Fall?: "
                        + stringList.contains("Fall"));      //Line 19
        System.out.println();                               //Line 20

        stringList.removeElement("Fall");                   //Line 21
        stringList.removeElementAt(2);                      //Line 22
        System.out.println("Line 23: **** After the remove"
                        + " operations ****");              //Line 23
        System.out.println("Line 24: stringList: "
                        + stringList);                      //Line 24
    }                                                       //Line 25
}                                                           //Line 26
```

Sample Run:

```
Line 7: Empty stringList?: true
Line 8: Size stringList?: 0

Line 15: **** After adding elements to stringList ****
Line 16: Empty stringList?: false
Line 17: Size stringList?: 5
Line 18: stringList: [Spring, Summer, Fall, Winter, Sunny]
Line 19: stringList contains Fall?: true

Line 23: **** After the remove operations ****
Line 24: stringList: [Spring, Summer, Sunny]
```

Primitive Data Types and the `class` Vector

As described in the preceding section, every element of a `Vector` object is a reference. Therefore, to create a `Vector` of, say integers, the integers must be wrapped in an object. Recall that Java provides a wrapper class corresponding to each primitive data type. For example, the wrapper class corresponding to type `int` is `Integer`. Therefore, an `int` value can be wrapped in an `Integer` object. As explained in Chapter 6, as of Java 5.0, Java has simplified the wrapping and unwrapping of primitive type values, called the *autoboxing* and *auto-unboxing* of primitive data types. For example, suppose that `x` is an `int` variable and `num` is an `Integer` object.

Consider the statements:

```
num = 25;
num = new Integer(25);
```

After the execution of either of these statements, `num` would point to an `Integer` object with the value 25. Recall that the expression, `num = 25;`, is called the *autoboxing* of the `int` type.

Next, we illustrate how to create a `Vector` of `Integer` objects to store `int` values.

Suppose that you have the declaration:

```
Vector<Integer> list = new Vector<Integer>();
```

The following statements create `Integer` objects with the `int` values 13 and 25 (if there are no other `Integer` objects with these values), and the `Integer` objects are assigned to `list`:

```
list.addElement(13);
list.addElement(25);
```

You can use other `Vector` operations to manipulate the objects of `list`. The Web site, *www.course.com*, and the CD accompanying this book contain the program `IntVectorExample.java`, which shows how to create and manipulate a `Vector` of `Integer` objects. Also, recall that the wrapper class corresponding to type `char` is `Character`, type `double` is `Double`, type `float` is `Float`, and type `boolean` is `Boolean`.

Vector Objects and the foreach Loop

Recall that a foreach loop can be used to process the elements of a collection object one at a time. Because each `Vector` object is a collection of elements, you can use a foreach loop to process the elements of a `Vector` object. The syntax to use this type of `for` loop to process the elements of a `Vector` object is:

```
for (type identifier : vectorObject)
    statements
```

where `identifier` is a (reference) variable and the data type of (the object that) `identifier` (points to) is the same as the data type of the objects that each `vectorObject` element points to. Also, `type` is either a primitive type or the name of a class.

For example, suppose that you have the following statements:

```
Vector<String> stringList = new Vector<String>();     //Line 1

stringList.addElement("One");                          //Line 2
stringList.addElement("Two");                          //Line 3
stringList.addElement("Three");                        //Line 4

System.out.println("stringList: " + stringList);       //Line 5

for (String str : stringList)                          //Line 6
    System.out.println(str.toUpperCase());             //Line 7
```

The statement in Line 1 creates the `Vector` object `stringList` to create a list of `String` objects. The statements in Lines 2 through 4 add the string objects with the values `"One"`, `"Two"`, and `"Three"`, respectively, to `stringList`. The statement in Line 5 outputs the values of the string objects of `stringList`. Note that the output of the statement in Line 5 is:

```
stringList: [One, Two, Three]
```

The foreach loop in Lines 6 and 7 processes each element of `stringList` one at a time and outputs each string in uppercase letters. More specifically, the output is:

```
ONE
TWO
THREE
```

The Web site and the CD accompanying this book contain the program `StringVectorExampleII.java`, which shows how to use a foreach loop to process string `Vector` lists. The program `IntVectorExampleII.java` shows how a foreach loop, using the auto-unboxing feature of primitive data types, can be used to process the elements of a `Vector` object of `int` values.

QUICK REVIEW

1. An array is a structured data type with a fixed number of elements. Every element is of the same type, and the elements are accessed using their relative positions in the array.

2. Elements of a one-dimensional array are arranged in the form of a list.

3. An array index can be any expression that evaluates to a nonnegative integer. The value of the index must always be less than the size of the array.

4. In Java, an array index starts with 0.

5. In Java, `[]` is an operator, called the array subscripting operator.

6. When an array object is instantiated, its elements are initialized to their default values.

7. Arrays that are created, that is, instantiated, during program execution are called dynamic arrays.

8. Arrays can be initialized when they are created.

9. A `public` (`final`) instance variable `length` is associated with each array that has been instantiated (that is, for which memory has been allocated to store the data). The variable `length` contains the size of the array.

10. If an array index goes out of bounds, the program throws an `ArrayIndexOutOfBoundsException`.

11. The base address of an array is the address (that is, memory location) of the first array element.

12. Arrays can be passed as parameters to methods.

13. In a method call statement, when passing an array as an actual parameter, you use only its name.

14. Individual array elements can be passed as parameters to methods.

15. The sequential search searches the array sequentially starting from the first array element.

16. You can create an array of objects.

17. The syntax to declare a variable length formal parameter is:

    `dataType ... identifier`

18. A method can have both a variable length formal parameter and other formal parameters.

19. A method can have, at most, one variable length formal parameter.

20. If a method has both a variable length formal parameter and other types of formal parameters, then the variable length formal parameter must be the last formal parameter of the formal parameter list.

21. The most recent version of Java provides a special type of `for` loop, called a foreach loop, to process the elements of an object, such as an array.

22. The syntax to use a foreach loop to process the elements of an array is:

    `for (dataType identifier : arrayName)`

    `    statements`

    where `identifier` is a variable and the data type of `identifier` is the same as the data type of the array elements.

23. A two-dimensional array is an array in which the elements are arranged in a table form.

24. To access an element of a two-dimensional array, you need a pair of indices: one for the row position and one for the column position.

25. In row processing, a two-dimensional array is processed one row at a time.

26. In column processing, a two-dimensional array is processed one column at a time.

27. Java stores two-dimensional arrays in a row order form in computer memory.

28. In addition to arrays, Java provides the `class Vector` to implement a list.

29. Unlike an array, the size of a `Vector` object can grow and shrink during program execution.

EXERCISES

1. Mark the following statements as true or false.

   a. A `double` type is an example of a primitive data type.

   b. A one-dimensional array is an example of a structured data type.

   c. Arrays can be passed as parameters to a method.

   d. A method can return a value of the type `array`.

   e. The size of an array is determined at compile time.

   f. Given the declaration:

      ```
      int[] list = new int[10];
      ```

      the statement:

      ```
      list[5] = list[3] + list[2];
      ```

      updates the content of the fifth element of the array `list`.

   g. If an array index goes out of bounds, the program terminates in an error.

2. Write Java statements that do the following:

   a. Declare an array `alpha` of 15 elements of type `int`.

   b. Output the value of the tenth element of the array `alpha`.

   c. Set the value of the fifth element of the array `alpha` to 35.

   d. Set the value of the ninth element of the array `alpha` to the sum of the sixth and thirteenth elements of the array `alpha`.

   e. Set the value of the fourth element of the array `alpha` to three times the value of the eighth element, minus 57.

   f. Output `alpha` so that five elements per line are printed.

3. Consider the method headings:

   ```
   void funcOne(int[] alpha, int size)
   int funcSum(int x, int y)
   void funcTwo(int[] alpha, int[] beta)
   ```

and the declarations:

```
int[] list = new int[50];
int[] AList = new int[60];
int num;
```

Write Java statements that do the following:

a. Call the method funcOne with the actual parameters, list and 50, respectively.

b. Print the value returned by the method funcSum with the actual parameters, 50 and the fourth element of list, respectively.

c. Print the value returned by the method funcSum with the actual parameters, the thirtieth and tenth elements of list, respectively.

d. Call the method funcTwo with the actual parameters, list and AList, respectively.

4. Suppose list is an array of five elements of type int. What is stored in list after the following Java code executes?

```
for (int i = 0; i < 5; i++)
{
    list[i] = 2 * i + 5;

    if (i % 2 == 0)
        list[i] = list[i] - 3;
}
```

5. Suppose list is an array of six elements of type int. What is stored in list after the following Java code executes?

```
list[0] = 5;

for (int i = 1; i < 6; i++)
{
    list[i] = i * i + 5;

    if (i > 2)
        list[i] = 2 * list[i] - list[i - 1];
}
```

6. What is the output of the following program?

```
public class Exercise6
{
    public static void main(String[] args)
    {
        int[] alpha = new int[5];

        alpha[0] = 5;
        for (int count = 1; count < 5; count++)
        {
            alpha[count] = 5 * count + 10;
            alpha[count - 1] = alpha[count] - 4;
        }
```

```
        System.out.print("List elements: ");

        for (int count = 0; count < 5; count++)
            System.out.print(alpha[count] + " ");
        System.out.println();
    }
}
```

7. What is the output of the following program?

```
public class Exercise7
{
    public static void main(String[] args)
    {
        int[] one = new int[5];
        int[] two = new int[10];

        for (int j = 0; j < 5; j++)
            one[j] = 5 * j + 3;

        System.out.print("One contains: ");

        for (int j = 0; j < 5; j++)
            System.out.print(one[j] + " ");

        System.out.println();

        for (int j = 0; j < 5; j++)
        {
            two[j] = 2 * one[j] - 1;
            two[j + 5] = one[4 - j] + two[j];
        }

        System.out.print("Two contains: ");

        for (int j = 0; j < 10; j++)
            System.out.print(two[j] + " ");

        System.out.println();
    }
}
```

8. Suppose you have the following class:

```
public class NamesList
{
    private String[] namesList;

        //Constructor with a variable length
        //formal parameter
    public NamesList(String ... names)
    {
        namesList = names;
    }
```

```
        //Method to return namesList as a string
    public String toString()
    {
        String str = "";
        for (String name : namesList)
            str = str + name + "\n";

        return str;
    }
}
```

What is the output of the following program?

```
public class Exercise8
{
    public static void main(String[] args)
    {
        String[] days = {"Sunday", "Monday", "Tuesday",
                         "Wednesday", "Thursday",
                         "Friday", "Saturday"};
        NamesList familyMember =
                new NamesList("William Johnson",
                              "Linda Johnson",
                              "Susan Johnson",
                              "Alex Johnson");
        NamesList friends =
                new NamesList("Amy Miller",
                              "Bobby Gupta",
                              "Sheila Mann",
                              "Chris Green",
                              "Silvia Smith",
                              "Randy Arora");
        NamesList seasons =
                new NamesList("Winter", "Spring",
                              "Summer", "Fall");
        NamesList emptyList = new NamesList();
        NamesList weekDays = new NamesList(days);
        System.out.println("*****  Family Members  "
                    + "*****");
        System.out.println(familyMember);
        System.out.println("\n*****  Friends  "
                    + "*****");
        System.out.println(friends);
        System.out.println("\n*****  Seasons  "
                    + "*****");
        System.out.println(seasons);
        System.out.println("\n*****  Empty Names List  "
                    + "*****");
        System.out.println(emptyList);
        System.out.println("\n*****  Week Days  "
                    + "*****");
        System.out.println(weekDays);
    }
}
```

9. Consider the following declarations:

```
static final int CAR_TYPES = 5;
static final int COLOR_TYPES = 6;

double[][] sales = new double[CAR_TYPES][COLOR_TYPES];
```

    a.   How many elements does the array `sales` have?

    b.   What is the number of rows in the array `sales`?

    c.   What is the number of columns in the array `sales`?

    d.   To sum the sales by `CAR_TYPES`, what kind of processing is required?

    e.   To sum the sales by `COLOR_TYPES`, what kind of processing is required?

10. Write Java statements that do the following:

    a.   Declare an array `alpha` of 10 rows and 20 columns of type `int`.

    b.   Initialize each element of the array `alpha` to 5.

    c.   Store 1 in the first row and 2 in the remaining rows.

    d.   Store 5 in the first column, and the value in each remaining column is twice the value of the previous column.

    e.   Print the array `alpha` one row per line.

    f.   Print the array `alpha` one column per line.

11. Consider the following declaration:

```
int[][] beta = new int[3][3];
```

What is stored in `beta` after each of the following statements executes?

    a.
```
for (int i = 0; i < 3; i++)
    for (int j = 0; j < 3; j++)
        beta[i][j] = 0;
```

    b.
```
for (int i = 0; i < 3; i++)
    for (int j = 0; j < 3; j++)
        beta[i][j] = i + j;
```

    c.
```
for (int i = 0; i < 3; i++)
    for (int j = 0; j < 3; j++)
        beta[i][j] = i * j;
```

    d.
```
for (int i = 0; i < 3; i++)
    for (int j = 0; j < 3; j++)
        beta[i][j] = 2 * (i + j) % 4;
```

12. What is the effect of the following statement?

```
Vector<Double> list = new Vector<Double>();
```

13. Suppose that you have the following `Vector` object `list`:

```
list = ["One", "Two", "Three", "Four"];
```

What are the elements of `list` after the following statements execute?

```
list.addElement("Five");
list.insertElementAt("Six", 1);
```

9

14. Suppose that you have the following `Vector` object `names`:

    names = ["Gwen", "Donald", "Michael", "Peter", "Susan"];

    What are the elements of `names` after the following statements execute?

    names.removeElementAt(1);
    names.removeElement("Peter");

15. What is the output of the following program?

```java
import java.util.Vector;

public class Exercise15
{
    public static void main(String[] arg)
    {
        Vector<String> strList = new Vector<String>();
        Vector<Integer> intList = new Vector<Integer>();

        strList.addElement("Hello");
        intList.addElement(10);
        strList.addElement("Happy");
        intList.addElement(20);
        strList.addElement("Sunny");
        intList.addElement(30);

        System.out.println("strList: " + strList);
        System.out.println("intList: " + intList);

        strList.insertElementAt("Joy", 2);

        intList.removeElement(20);

        System.out.println("strList: " + strList);
        System.out.println("intList: " + intList);
    }
}
```

PROGRAMMING EXERCISES

1. Write a Java program that declares an array `alpha` of 50 elements of type `double`. Initialize the array so that the first 25 elements are equal to the square of the index variable, and the last 25 elements are equal to three times the index variable. Output the array so that 10 elements per line are printed.

2. Write a Java method, `smallestIndex`, that takes as its parameters an `int` array and its size, and returns the index of the (first occurrence of the) smallest element in the array. Also, write a program to test your method.

3. Write a program that reads a file consisting of students' test scores in the range 0-200. It should then determine the number of students having scores in each of

the following ranges: 0–24, 25–49, 50–74, 75–99, 100–124, 125–149, 150–174, and 175–200. Output the score ranges and the number of students. Run your program with the following input data: 76, 89, 150, 135, 200, 76, 12, 100, 150, 28, 178, 189, 167, 200, 175, 150, 87, 99, 129, 149, 176, 200, 87, 35, 157, 189.

4. In a gymnastics or diving competition, each contestant's score is calculated by dropping the lowest and highest scores and then adding the remaining scores. Write a program that allows the user to enter eight judges' scores and then outputs the points received by the contestant. Format your output with two decimal places. A judge awards points between 1 and 10, with 1 being the lowest and 10 being the highest. For example, if the scores are 9.2, 9.3, 9.0, 9.9, 9.5, 9.5, 9.6, and 9.8, the contestant receives a total of 56.90 points.

5. Write a program that prompts the user to input a string and then outputs the string in uppercase letters. (Use an array of characters [or char] to store the string.)

6. The history teacher at your school needs help grading a True/False test. The students' IDs and test answers are stored in a file. The first entry in the file contains the answers to the test in the form:

```
TFFTFFTTTTFFTFTFTFTT
```

Every other entry in the file is the student's ID, followed by a blank, followed by the student's response. For example, the entry:

```
ABC54301 TFTFTFTT TFTFTFFTTFT
```

indicates that the student's ID is ABC54301 and the answer to question 1 is True, the answer to question 2 is False, and so on. This student did not answer question 9. The exam has 20 questions, and the class has more than 150 students. Each correct answer is awarded two points, each wrong answer gets -1 point, and no answer gets 0 points. Write a program that processes the test data. The output should be the student's ID, followed by the answers, followed by the test score, followed by the test grade. Assume the following grade scale: 90% – 100%, A; 80% – 89.99%, B; 70% – 79.99%, C; 60% – 69.99%, D; and 0% – 59.99%, F.

7. Write a program that allows the user to enter the last names of five candidates in a local election and the votes received by each candidate. The program should then output each candidate's name, the votes received by that candidate, and the percentage of the total votes received by the candidate. Your program should also output the winner of the election. A sample output is:

```
Candidate      Votes Received      % of Total Votes
Johnson             5000                 25.91
Miller              4000                 20.72
Duffy               6000                 31.09
Robinson            2500                 12.95
Ashtony             1800                  9.33
Total              19300
The Winner of the Election is Duffy.
```

8. Write a program that allows the user to enter students' names followed by their test scores and outputs the following information (assume that the maximum number of students in the class is 50):

a. Class average

b. Names of all the students whose test scores are below the class average, with an appropriate message

c. Highest test score and the names of all the students having the highest score

9. Programming Exercise 13, in Chapter 7, asks you to find the mean and standard deviation of five numbers. Extend this programming exercise to find the mean and standard deviation of up to 100 numbers. Suppose that the mean (average) of n numbers $x_1, x_2, \ldots, x_n$ is x. Then the standard deviation of these numbers is:

$$s = \sqrt{\frac{(x_1-x)^2+(x_2-x)^2+\cdots+(x_i-x)^2+\cdots+(x_n-x)^2}{n}}.$$

10. **(Adding Large Integers)** In C++, the largest `int` value is 2147483647. So an integer larger than this cannot be stored and processed as an integer. Similarly, if the sum or product of two positive integers is greater than 2147483647, then the result will be incorrect. One way to store and manipulate large integers is to store each individual digit of the number in an array. Write a program that inputs two positives and outputs the sum of the numbers. Your program must contain a method to find and output the sum of the numbers. (*Hint*: Read numbers as strings and store the digits of the number in the reverse order.)

11. Consider the following method `main`:

```java
public static void main(String[] args)
{
    int[][] inStock = new int[10][4];
    int[] alpha = new int[20];
    int[] beta = new int[20];
    int[] gamma = {11, 13, 15, 17};
    int[] delta = {3, 5, 2, 6, 10, 9, 7, 11, 1, 8};
        .
        .
        .
}
```

a. Write the definition of the method `inputArray` that prompts the user to input 20 numbers and stores the numbers in `alpha`.

b. Write the definition of the method `doubleArray` that initializes the elements of `beta` to two times the corresponding elements of `alpha`.

c. Write the definition of the method `copyGamma` that sets the elements of the first row of `inStock` to `gamma` and the remaining rows of `inStock` to three times the previous row of `inStock`.

d. Write the definition of the method `copyAlphaBeta` that stores `alpha` into the first five rows of `inStock` and `beta` into the last five rows of `inStock`. Make sure that you prevent the method from modifying the elements of `alpha` and `beta`.

e. Write the definition of the method `printArray` that prints any one-dimensional array of type `int`. Print 15 elements per line.

f. Write the definition of the method `setInStock` that prompts the user to input the elements for the first column of `inStock`. The method should then set the elements in the remaining columns to two times the corresponding element in the previous column, minus the corresponding element in `delta`.

g. Write Java statements that call each of the methods in parts a through f.

h. Write a Java program that tests the method `main` and the methods discussed in parts a through f.

12. Write a program that uses a two-dimensional array to store the highest and lowest temperatures for each month of the year. The program should output the average high, average low, and highest and lowest temperatures of the year. Your program must consist of the following methods:

a. Method `getData`: This method reads and stores the data in the two-dimensional array.

b. Method `averageHigh`: This method calculates and returns the average high temperature of the year.

c. Method `averageLow`: This method calculates and returns the average low temperature of the year.

d. Method `indexHighTemp`: This method returns the index of the highest temperature in the array.

e. Method `indexLowTemp`: This method returns the index of the lowest temperature in the array.

(These methods must all have the appropriate parameters.)

13. Write a program that reads in a set of positive integers and outputs how many times a particular number appears in the list. You may assume that the data set has, at most, 100 numbers and -999 marks the end of the input data. The numbers must be output in increasing order. For example, for the data:

15 40 28 62 95 15 28 13 62 65 48 95 65 62 65 95 95 -999

the output is:

```
Number    Count
13        1
15        2
28        2
40        1
48        1
62        3
65        3
95        4
```

14. Write a program that uses the **class RollDie** to roll a pair of dice 1000 times (or 1000 pairs of dice). The program then outputs the pair of numbers rolled by the dice, the sum of the numbers rolled by each pair of dice, the number of times each sum is rolled, and the sums that are rolled the maximum number of times. (Use a two dimensional array to create 1000 pairs of dice and to store the pairs of numbers rolled by each pair of dice).

15. **Airplane Seating Assignment:** Write a program that can be used to assign seats for a commercial airplane. The airplane has 13 rows, with 6 seats in each row. Rows 1 and 2 are first class, rows 3 to 7 are business class, and rows 8 to 13 are economy class. Your program prompts the user to enter the following information:

    a. Ticket type (first class, business class, or economy class)

    b. Desired seat

    Output the seating plan in the following format:

```
         A B C   D E F
Row 1    * * X   * X X
Row 2    * X *   X * X
Row 3    * * X   X * X
Row 4    X * X   * X X
Row 5    * X *   X * *
Row 6    * X *   * * X
Row 7    X * *   * X X
Row 8    * X *   X X *
Row 9    X * X   X * X
Row 10   * X *   X X X
Row 11   * * X   * X *
Row 12   * * X   X * X
Row 13   * * *   * X *
```

    Here, * indicates that the seat is available; X indicates that the seat has been assigned. Make this a menu-driven program; show the user's choices and allow the user to make the appropriate choices.

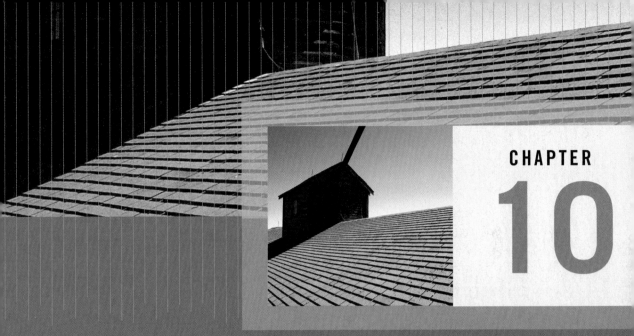

INHERITANCE AND POLYMORPHISM

IN THIS CHAPTER, YOU WILL:

- Learn about inheritance
- Learn about subclasses and superclasses
- Explore how to override the methods of a superclass
- Examine how constructors of superclasses and subclasses work
- Learn about polymorphism
- Examine abstract classes
- Become familiar with interfaces
- Learn about composition

Classes were introduced in Chapter 8. Using classes, you can combine data and operations on that data in a single unit, a process called *encapsulation*. Through encapsulation, an object becomes a self-contained entity. Operations can (directly) access the data, but the internal state of an object cannot be manipulated directly.

In addition to implementing encapsulation, classes have other capabilities. For instance, you can create new classes from existing classes. This important feature encourages code reuse and saves programmers an enormous amount of time. In Java, you can relate two or more classes in more than one way. This chapter examines two common ways to relate classes:

- **Inheritance** ("is-a" relationship)
- **Composition** (aggregation) ("has-a" relationship)

Inheritance

Suppose that you want to design a `class`, `PartTimeEmployee`, to implement and process the characteristics of a part-time employee. The main features associated with a part-time employee are the name, pay rate, and number of hours worked. In Example 8-7 (Chapter 8), we designed the `class` `Person` to implement a person's name. Every part-time employee is a person. Therefore, rather than design the `class` `PartTimeEmployee` from scratch, we want to be able to extend the definition of the `class` `Person` from Example 8-7 by adding additional members (data and/or methods).

Of course, we do not want to make the necessary changes directly to the `class` `Person`—that is, edit the `class` `Person` and add and/or delete members. We want to create a new `class` `PartTimeEmployee` without making any physical changes to the `class` `Person`, by adding only the members that are necessary to `class` `PartTimeEmployee`. For example, because the `class` `Person` already has data members to store the first name and last name, we will not include any such members in the `class` `PartTimeEmployee`. In fact, these data members will be *inherited* from the `class` `Person`. (We will design the `class` `PartTimeEmployee` in Example 10-3.)

In Chapter 8, we extensively studied and designed the `class` `Clock` to implement the time of day in a program. The `class` `Clock` has three data members (instance variables) to store the hours, minutes, and seconds. Certain applications might require that we also store the time zone. In this case, we want to *extend* the definition of the `class` `Clock` and create a `class`, `ExtClock`, to accommodate this new information. That is, we want to derive the `class` `ExtClock` by adding a data member—`timeZone`—and the necessary method members to manipulate the time.

In Java, the mechanism that allows us to extend the definition of a class without making any physical changes to the existing class is **inheritance**. Inheritance implies an "is-a" relationship. For example, every (part-time) employee *is a* person. Similarly, every extended clock, `ExtClock`, *is a* `Clock`.

Inheritance lets you create new classes from existing classes. Any new class that you create from an existing class is called a **subclass** or **derived class**; existing classes are called

superclasses or **base classes**. The inheritance relationship enables a subclass to inherit features from its superclass. Furthermore, the subclass can add new features of its own. Therefore, rather than create completely new classes from scratch, you can take advantage of inheritance and reduce software complexity.

Inheritance can be viewed as a treelike, or hierarchical, structure wherein a superclass is shown with its subclasses. Consider the diagram in Figure 10-1, which shows the relationship between various shapes.

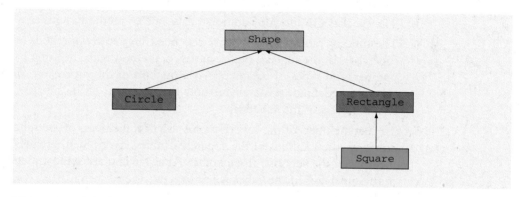

FIGURE 10-1 Inheritance hierarchy

In this diagram, `Shape` is the superclass. The `class`es `Circle` and `Rectangle` are derived from `Shape`, and the `class` `Square` is derived from `Rectangle`. Every `Circle` and every `Rectangle` is a `Shape`. Every `Square` is a `Rectangle`.

The general syntax to derive a class from an existing class is:

```
modifier(s) class ClassName extends ExistingClassName modifier(s)
{
    memberList
}
```

In Java, `extends` is a reserved word.

EXAMPLE 10-1

Suppose that we have defined a `class` called `Shape`. The following statements specify that the `class` `Circle` is derived from `Shape`:

```
public class Circle extends Shape
{
    .
    .
    .
}
```

The following rules about superclasses and subclasses should be kept in mind:

1. The `private` members of the superclass are `private` to the superclass; hence, the members of the subclass(es) cannot access them directly. In other words, when you write the definitions of the methods of the subclass, you cannot access the `private` members of the superclass directly. (The next section explains how to access the `private` members of a superclass in its subclass.)

2. The subclass can directly access the `public` members of the superclass.

3. The subclass can include additional data and/or method members.

4. The subclass can override, that is, redefine, the `public` methods of the superclass. In the subclass, you can have a method with the same name, number, and types of parameters as a method in the superclass. However, this redefinition is available only to the objects of the subclass, not to the objects of the superclass.

5. All data members of the superclass are also data members of the subclass. Similarly, the methods of the superclass (unless overridden) are also the methods of the subclass. (Remember Rule 1 when accessing a member of the superclass in the subclass.)

Each subclass, in turn, may become a superclass for a future subclass. Inheritance can be either single or multiple. In **single inheritance**, the subclass is derived from a single superclass; in **multiple inheritance**, the subclass is derived from more than one superclass. Java *supports only single inheritance*; that is, in Java a class can *extend* the definition of only one class.

The next sections describe two important issues related to inheritance. The first issue is using the methods of a superclass in its subclass. While discussing this issue, we will also address how to access the `private` (data) members of the superclass in the subclass. The second key inheritance issue is related to the constructor. The constructor of a subclass *cannot directly access* the `private` data members of the superclass. Thus, you must ensure that `private` data members that are inherited from the superclass are initialized when a constructor of the subclass executes.

Using Methods of the Superclass in a Subclass

Suppose that a `class SubClass` is derived from a `class SuperClass`. Further assume that both `SubClass` and `SuperClass` have some data members. It then follows that the data members of the `class SubClass` are its own data members, together with the data members of `SuperClass`. Similarly, in addition to its own methods, the subclass also inherits the methods of the superclass. The subclass can give some of its methods the same signature as given by the superclass. For example, suppose that `SuperClass` contains a method, `print`, that prints the values of the data members of `SuperClass`. `SubClass` contains data members in addition to the data members inherited from `SuperClass`.

Suppose that you want to include a method in `SubClass` that prints the data members of `SubClass`. You can give any name to this method. However, in the `class SubClass`, you can also name this method `print` (the same name used by `SuperClass`). This is called **overriding**, or **redefining**, the method of the superclass.

To override a `public` method of the superclass in the subclass, the corresponding method in the subclass must have the same name, the same type, and the same formal parameter list. That is, to override a method of a superclass, in the subclass the method must be defined using the same signature and the same return type as in its superclass. If the corresponding method in the superclass and the subclass has the same name but different parameter lists, then this is method *overloading* in the subclass, which is also allowed.

Whether you override or overload a method of the superclass in the subclass, you must know how to specify a call to the method of the superclass that has the same name as that used by a method of the subclass. We illustrate these concepts with the help of an example.

Consider the definition of the following class:

```java
public class Rectangle
{
    private double length;
    private double width;

    public Rectangle()
    {
        length = 0;
        width = 0;
    }

    public Rectangle(double l, double w)
    {
        setDimension(l, w);
    }

    public void setDimension(double l, double w)
    {
        if (l >= 0)
            length = l;
        else
            length = 0;

        if (w >= 0)
            width = w;
        else
            width = 0;
    }

    public double getLength()
    {
        return length;
    }
```

```
public double getWidth()
{
    return width;
}

public double area()
{
    return length * width;
}

public double perimeter()
{
    return 2 * (length + width);
}

public String toString()
{
    return ("Length = " + length + "; Width = " + width);
}
}
```

Figure 10-2 shows the UML class diagram of the **class** Rectangle.

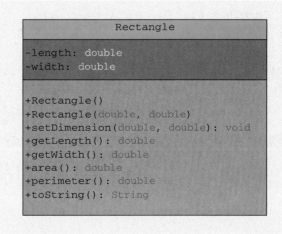

FIGURE 10-2 UML class diagram of the **class** Rectangle

The **class** Rectangle has 10 members.

Now consider the following definition of the **class** Box, derived from the **class** Rectangle:

```
public class Box extends Rectangle
{
    private double height;

    public Box()
    {
        //The definition is as given below
    }

    public Box(double l, double w, double h)
    {
        //The definition is as given below
    }

    public void setDimension(double l, double w, double h)
    {
        //Sets the length, width, and height of the box
        //The definition is as given below
    }

    public double getHeight()
    {
        return height;
    }

    public double area()
    {
        //Returns the surface area
        //The definition is as given below
    }

    public double volume()
    {
        //Returns the volume
        //The definition is as given below
    }

    public String toString()
    {
        //Returns length, width, and height of the box as
        //a string. The definition is as given below.
    }
}
```

Figure 10-3 shows the UML class diagram of the class Box and the inheritance hierarchy.

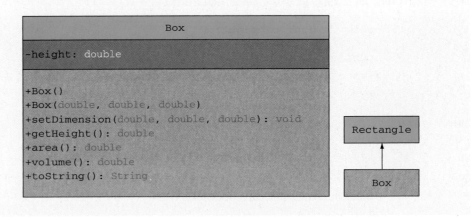

FIGURE 10-3 UML class diagram of the **class** Box and the inheritance hierarchy

From the definition of the **class** **Box**, it is clear that the **class** **Box** is derived from the **class** **Rectangle**. Therefore, all **public** members of **Rectangle** are **public** members of **Box**. The **class** **Box** overrides the methods **toString** and **area**, and overloads the method **setDimension**.

In general, when writing the definitions of the methods of a subclass to specify a call to a **public** method of a superclass, you do the following:

- If the subclass overrides a **public** method of the superclass, then you must specify a call to that **public** method of the superclass by using the reserved word **super**, followed by the dot operator, followed by the method name with an appropriate parameter list. In this case, the general syntax to call a method of the superclass is:

```
super.methodName(parameters);
```

- If the subclass does not override a **public** method of the superclass, you can specify a call to that **public** method by using the name of the method and an appropriate parameter list.

Next, let's write the definition of the method **toString** of the **class** **Box**.

The **class** **Box** has three instance variables: **length**, **width**, and **height**. The method **toString** of the **class** **Box** prints the values of these three instance variables. To write the definition of the method **toString** of the **class** **Box**, remember the following:

- The instance variables **length** and **width** are **private** members of the **class** **Rectangle** and so cannot be directly accessed in the **class** **Box**. Therefore, when writing the definition of the method **toString** of the **class** **Box**, you cannot directly reference **length** and **width**.

- The instance variables `length` and `width` of the `class Rectangle` are accessible in the `class Box` through the `public` methods of the `class Rectangle`. Therefore, when writing the definition of the method `toString` of the `class Box`, you first call the method `toString` of the `class Rectangle` to print the values of `length` and `width`. After printing the values of `length` and `width`, you output the value of `height`.

As stated above, to call the method `toString` of `Rectangle` in the definition of the method `toString` of `Box`, you must use the following statement:

```
super.toString ();
```

This statement ensures that you call the method `toString` of the superclass `Rectangle`, not of the `class Box`.

The definition of the method `toString` of the `class Box` is:

```
public String toString()
{
    return super.toString()      //retrieve length and width
            + "; Height = " + height;
}
```

Let's write the definitions of the remaining methods of the `class Box`.

```
public void setDimension(double l, double w, double h)
{
    super.setDimension(l, w);

    if (h >= 0)
        height = h;
    else
        height = 0;
}
```

NOTE The `class Box` overloads the method `setDimension` of the `class Rectangle`. Therefore, in the preceding definition of the method `setDimension` of the `class Box`, you can also specify a call to the method `setDimension` of the `class Rectangle` without the reserved word `super` and the dot operator.

The definition of the method `getHeight` is:

```
public double getHeight()
{
    return height;
}
```

The method **area** of the `class Box` determines the surface area of the box. To do so, we need to access the length and width of the box, which are declared as `private` members of the `class Rectangle`. Therefore, we use the methods `getLength` and `getWidth` of the `class Rectangle` to retrieve the length and width, respectively. Because the `class`

`Box` does not override the methods `getLength` and `getWidth`, we can call these methods of the `class Rectangle` without using the reserved word `super`.

```
public double area()
{
    return  2 * (getLength() * getWidth()
                + getLength() * height
                + getWidth() * height);
}
```

The method `volume` of the `class Box` determines the volume of the box. To determine the box's volume, you multiply the length, width, and height of the box or multiply the area of the base of the box by its height. Let's write the definition of the method `volume` by using the second alternative. To do so, you can use the method `area` of the `class Rectangle` to determine the area of the base. Because the `class Box` overrides the method `area`, to specify a call to the method `area` of the `class Rectangle`, we use the reserved word `super`, as shown in the following definition:

```
public double volume()
{
    return super.area() * height;
}
```

In the next section, we discuss how to specify a call to the constructor of the superclass when writing the definition of a constructor of the subclass.

Constructors of the Superclass and Subclass

A subclass can have its own `private` data members, so a subclass can also have its own constructors. A constructor typically serves to initialize the instance variables. When we instantiate a subclass object, this object inherits the instance variables of the superclass, but the subclass object cannot directly access the `private` instance variables of the superclass. The same is true for the methods of a subclass. That is, the methods of the subclass cannot directly access the `private` members of the superclass.

As a consequence, the constructors of the subclass can and should (directly) initialize only the instance variables of the subclass. Thus, when a subclass object is instantiated, to initialize the (`private` and other) instance variables—both its own and its ancestor class(es)—the subclass object must also automatically execute one of the constructors of the superclass. A call to a constructor of the superclass is specified in the definition of a subclass constructor by using the reserved word `super`. The general syntax to call a constructor of a superclasss is:

```
super(parameters);
```

In the preceding section, we defined the `class Rectangle` and derived the `class Box` from it. Moreover, we illustrated how to override a method of the `class Rectangle`. We now discuss how to write the definitions of the constructors of the `class Box`.

The **class** Rectangle has two constructors and two instance variables. The **class** Box has three instance variables: length, width, and height. The instance variables length and width are inherited from the **class** Rectangle.

To write the definitions of the constructors of the **class** Box, we first write the definition of the default constructor of the **class** Box. Recall that if a class contains the default constructor and no values are specified during object instantiation, the default constructor executes and initializes the object. Because the **class** Rectangle contains the default constructor, when we write the definition of the default constructor of the **class** Box, to (explicitly) specify a call to the default constructor of the **class** Rectangle, we use the reserved word **super** with no parameters, as shown in the following code. Also, a call to the (default) constructor of the superclass *must* be the first statement.

```
public Box()
{
    super();
    height = 0;
}
```

Next, we discuss how to write the definitions of the constructors with parameters. (Note that if you do not include the statement **super();**, then, by default, the default constructor of the superclass (if any), will be called.)

To specify a call to a constructor with parameters of the superclass, we use the reserved word **super** with the appropriate parameters. A call to the constructor of the superclass must be the first statement.

Consider the following definition of the constructor with parameters of the **class** Box:

```
public Box(double l, double w, double h)
{
    super(l, w);
    height = h;
}
```

This definition specifies the constructor of Rectangle with two parameters. When this constructor of Box executes, it triggers the execution of the constructor with two parameters of type **double** of the **class** Rectangle.

(Note that invoking a superclass constructor's name in a subclass will result in a syntax error. Also, because a call to a constructor of the superclass must be the first statement, within the definition of a constructor of a subclass only one constructor of the superclass can be invoked.)

As an exercise, try writing the complete definition of the **class** Box.

Consider the following statements:

```
Rectangle myRectangle = new Rectangle(5, 3);    //Line 1
Box myBox = new Box(6, 5, 4);                   //Line 2
```

1
0

The statement in Line 1 creates the `Rectangle` object `myRectangle`. Thus, the object `myRectangle` has two instance variables: `length` and `width`. The statement in Line 2 creates the `Box` object `myBox`. Thus, the object `myBox` has three instance variables: `length`, `width`, and `height` (see Figure 10-4).

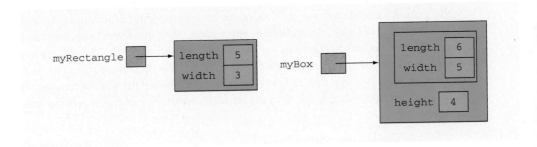

FIGURE 10-4   Objects `myRectangle` and `myBox`

Consider the following statements:

```
System.out.println(myRectangle);  //Line 3
System.out.println(myBox);        //Line 4
```

In the statement in Line 3, the method `toString` of the **class** `Rectangle` is executed; in the statement in Line 4, the method `toString` associated with the **class** `Box` is executed. Recall that if a subclass overrides a method of the superclass, the redefinition applies only to the objects of the subclass. Thus, the output of the statement in Line 3 is:

```
Length = 5.0; Width = 3.0
```

The output of the statement in Line 4 is:

```
Length = 6.0; Width = 5.0; Height = 4.0
```

The program in Example 10-2 shows how the objects of a superclass and a base class work.

EXAMPLE 10-2

Consider the following Java application program:

```
// This program illustrates how the objects of a superclass and a
// base class work.

public class SubClassSuperClassMethods                //Line 1
{                                                      //Line 2
    public static void main(String[] args)            //Line 3
    {                                                  //Line 4
        Rectangle myRectangle1 = new Rectangle();     //Line 5
        Rectangle myRectangle2 = new Rectangle(8, 6); //Line 6
```

```
    Box myBox1 = new Box();                                //Line 7
    Box myBox2 = new Box(10, 7, 3);                        //Line 8

    System.out.println("Line 9: myRectangle1: "
                + myRectangle1);                           //Line 9

    System.out.println("Line 10: Area of myRectangle1: "
                + myRectangle1.area());                    //Line 10

    System.out.println("Line 11: myRectangle2: "
                + myRectangle2);                           //Line 11
    System.out.println("Line 12: Area of myRectangle2: "
                + myRectangle2.area());                    //Line 12

    System.out.println("Line 13: myBox1: " + myBox1); //Line 13

    System.out.println("Line 14: Surface Area of myBox1: "
                + myBox1.area());                          //Line 14
    System.out.println("Line 15: Volume of myBox1: "
                + myBox1.volume());                        //Line 15

    System.out.println("Line 16: myBox2: " + myBox2); //Line 16

    System.out.println("Line 17: Surface Area of myBox2: "
                + myBox2.area());                          //Line 17
    System.out.println("Line 18: Volume of myBox2: "
                + myBox2.volume());                        //Line 18
  }                                                        //Line 19
}                                                          //Line 20
```

Sample Run:

```
Line 9: myRectangle1: Length = 0.0; Width = 0.0
Line 10: Area of myRectangle1: 0.0
Line 11: myRectangle2: Length = 8.0; Width = 6.0
Line 12: Area of myRectangle2: 48.0
Line 13: myBox1: Length = 0.0; Width = 0.0; Height = 0.0
Line 14: Surface Area of myBox1: 0.0
Line 15: Volume of myBox1: 0.0
Line 16: myBox2: Length = 10.0; Width = 7.0; Height = 3.0
Line 17: Surface Area of myBox2: 242.0
Line 18: Volume of myBox2: 210.0
```

The preceding program works as follows: The statement in Line 5 creates the Rectangle object myRectangle1 and initializes its instance variables to 0. The statement in Line 6 creates the Rectangle object myRectangle2 and initializes its instance variables length and width to 8.0 and 6.0, respectively.

The statement in Line 7 creates the Box object myBox1 and initializes its instance variables to 0. The statement in Line 8 creates the Box object myBox2 and initializes its instance variables length, width, and height to 10.0, 7.0, and 3.0, respectively.

The statements in Lines 9 and 10 output the length, width, and area of myRectangle1. Because the instance variables of myRectangle1 are initialized to 0 by the default constructor, the area of the rectangle is 0.0 square units, as shown in the output of Line 10.

The statements in Lines 11 and 12 output the length, width, and area of myRectangle2. Because the instance variables length and width of myRectangle2 are initialized to 8.0 and 6.0, respectively, by the constructor with parameters, this rectangle's area is 48.0 square units. See the output of Line 12.

The statements in Lines 13, 14, and 15 output the length, width, height, surface area, and volume of myBox1. Because the instance variables of myBox1 are initialized to 0.0 by the default constructor, this box's surface area is 0.0 square units and the volume is 0.0 cubic units. See the output of Lines 14 and 15.

The statements in Lines 16, 17, and 18 output the length, width, height, surface area, and volume of myBox2. Because the instance variables length, width, and height of myBox2 are initialized to 10.0, 7.0, and 3.0, respectively, by the constructor with parameters, this box's surface area is 242.0 square units and the volume is 210.0 cubic units. See the output of Lines 17 and 18.

The output of this program demonstrates that the redefinition of the methods toString and area in the class Box applies only to the objects of type Box.

NOTE | **(Shadowing Variables)** Suppose that the class SubClass is derived from the class SuperClass and SuperClass has a variable named temp. You can declare a variable named temp in the class SubClass. In this case, the variable temp of SubClass is called a **shadowing variable**. The concept of a shadowing variable is similar to the concept of overriding a method, but it causes confusion. Now the SubClass is derived from SuperClass, so it inherits the variable temp of SuperClass. Because a variable named temp is already available in SubClass, there is seldom if ever any reason to override it. Furthermore, it is poor programming practice to override a variable in the SubClass. Anyone reading code with a shadowed variable will have two different declarations of a variable seeming to apply to the shadowed variable of the SubClass. This causes confusion and should be avoided. In general, you should avoid shadowing variables.

Next, we give another example illustrating how to create a subclass.

EXAMPLE 10-3

Suppose that you want to define a class to group the attributes of an employee. There are full-time employees and part-time employees. Part-time employees are paid based on the number of hours worked and an hourly rate. Suppose that you want to define a class to keep track of a part-time employee's information, such as the name, pay rate, and hours worked. You can then print the employee's name, together with his or her wages. Recall that Example 8-7 (Chapter 8) defined the class Person to store the first name and the last name together with the necessary operations on name. Because every employee is a person, we can define a class PartTimeEmployee derived from the class Person. You can also override the method toString of the class Person to print the appropriate information.

The members of the class PartTimeEmployee are as follows:

Instance Variables:

```
private double payRate;      //store the pay rate

private double hoursWorked;  //store the hours worked
```

Instance Methods:

```
public void setNameRateHours(String first, String last,
                             double rate, double hours)
   //Method to set the first name, last name, payRate,
   //and hoursWorked according to the parameters.
   //The parameters first and last are passed to the
   //superclass.
   //Postcondition: firstName = first; lastName = last;
   //               payRate = rate; hoursWorked = hours;

public double getPayRate()
   //Method to return the pay rate
   //Postcondition: The value of payRate is returned

public double getHoursWorked()
   //Method to return the number of hours worked
   //Postcondition: The value of hoursWorked is returned

public double calculatePay()
   //Method to calculate and return the wages

public String toString()
   //Method to return the string consisting of the
   //first name, last name, and the wages in the form:
   //firstName lastName wages are $$$$.$$

public PartTimeEmployee(String first, String last,
                        double rate, double hours)
   //Constructor with parameters
   //Set the first name, last name, payRate, and
   //hoursWorked according to the parameters.
   //Parameters first and last are passed to the
   //superclass.
   //Postcondition: firstName = first; lastName = last;
   //               payRate = rate; hoursWorked = hours;
```

```
public PartTimeEmployee()
    //Default constructor
    //Set the first name, last name, payRate, and
    //hoursWorked to the default values.
    //The first name and last name are initialized to an empty
    //string by the default constructor of the superclass.
    //Postcondition: firstName = ""; lastName = "";
    //                payRate = 0; hoursWorked = 0;
```

Figure 10-5 shows the UML class diagram of the **class** `PartTimeEmployee` and the inheritance hierarchy.

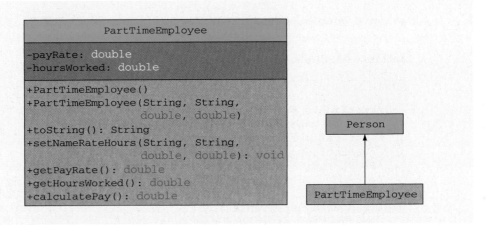

FIGURE 10-5 UML class diagram of the **class** `PartTimeEmployee` and the inheritance hierarchy

The definitions of the member methods of the **class** `PartTimeEmployee` are as follows:

```
public String toString()
{
    return (super.toString() + " wages are: $" + calculatePay());
}

public double getPayRate()
{
    return payRate;
}

public double getHoursWorked()
{
    return hoursWorked;
}

public double calculatePay()
{
    return (payRate * hoursWorked);
}
```

```
public void setNameRateHours(String first, String last,
                             double rate, double hours)
{
    setName(first, last);
    payRate = rate;
    hoursWorked = hours;
}
```

The definition of the constructor with parameters is as follows. (Note that the body contains a call to the superclass's constructor with parameters.)

```
public PartTimeEmployee(String first, String last,
                        double rate, double hours)
{
    super(first, last);
    payRate = rate;
    hoursWorked = hours;
}
```

The definition of the default constructor is:

```
public PartTimeEmployee()
{
    super();
    payRate = 0;
    hoursWorked = 0;
}
```

The definition of the class PartTimeEmployee is:

```
public class PartTimeEmployee extends Person
{
   private double payRate;      //store the pay rate
   private double hoursWorked;  //store the hours worked

     //Default constructor
     //Set the first name, last name, payRate, and
     //hoursWorked to the default values.
     //The first name and last name are initialized to an empty
     //string by the default constructor of the superclass.
     //Postcondition: firstName = ""; lastName = "";
     //                payRate = 0; hoursWorked = 0;
   public PartTimeEmployee()
   {
       super();
       payRate = 0;
       hoursWorked = 0;
   }

     //Constructor with parameters
     //Set the first name, last name, payRate, and
     //hoursWorked according to the parameters.
     //Parameters first and last are passed to the
     //superclass.
```

1
0

```
    //Postcondition: firstName = first; lastName = last;
    //               payRate = rate; hoursWorked = hours;
public PartTimeEmployee(String first, String last,
                        double rate, double hours)
{
    super(first, last);
    payRate = rate;
    hoursWorked = hours;
}

    //Method to return the string consisting of the
    //first name, last name, and the wages in the form:
    //firstName lastName wages are $$$$.$$
public String toString()

    return (super.toString() + " wages are: $" + calculatePay());
}

    //Method to calculate and return the wages
public double calculatePay()
{
    return (payRate * hoursWorked);
}

    //Method to set the first name, last name, payRate,
    //and hoursWorked according to the parameters.
    //The parameters first and last are passed to the
    //superclass.
    //Postcondition: firstName = first; lastName = last;
    //               payRate = rate; hoursWorked = hours;
public void setNameRateHours(String first, String last,
                             double rate, double hours)

{
    setName(first, last);
    payRate = rate;
    hoursWorked = hours;
}

    //Method to return the pay rate
    //Postcondition: The value of payRate is returned
public double getPayRate()
{
    return payRate;
}

    //Method to return the number of hours worked
    //Postcondition: The value of hoursWorked is returned
public double getHoursWorked()
{
    return hoursWorked;
}
}
```

NOTE The definition of the subclass is typically placed in a separate file. Recall that the name of the file must be the same as the name of the class, and the file extension must be `java`.

Protected Members of a Class

The `private` members of a class are `private` to the class and cannot be directly accessed outside the class. Only methods of that class can access the `private` members directly. As discussed previously, the subclass cannot access the `private` members of the superclass directly. However, sometimes it may be necessary for a subclass to access a `private` member of a superclass. If you make a `private` member `public`, then anyone can access that member. Recall that the members of a class are classified into three categories: `public`, `private`, and `protected`. So, if a member of a superclass needs to be (directly) accessed in a subclass and yet still prevent its direct access outside the class, such as in a user program, you must declare that member using the modifier `protected`. Thus, the accessibility of a `protected` member of a class falls between `public` and `private`. A subclass can directly access the `protected` member of a superclass.

To summarize, if a member of a superclass needs to be accessed directly (only) by a subclass, that member is declared using the modifier `protected`.

Example 10-4 illustrates how the methods of a subclass can directly access a `protected` member of the superclass.

EXAMPLE 10-4

1
0

Consider the following definitions of the `classes BClass` and `DClass`:

```java
public class BClass
{
    protected char bCh;
    private double bX;

        //Default constructor
    public BClass()
    {
        bCh = '*';
        bX = 0.0;
    }

        //Constructor with parameters
    public BClass(char ch, double u)
    {
        bCh = ch;
        bX = u;
    }
```

```java
    public void setData(double u)
    {
        bX = u;
    }

    public void setData(char ch, double u)
    {
        bCh = ch;
        bX = u;
    }

    public String toString()
    {
        return ("Superclass: bCh = " + bCh + ", bX = "
                + bX + '\n');
    }
}
```

The definition of the **class** BClass contains the **protected** instance variable bCh of type **char**, and the **private** instance variable bX of type **double**. It also contains an overloaded method setData; one version of setData is used to set both the instance variables, and the other version is used to set only the **private** instance variable. The **class** BClass also has a constructor with default parameters.

Next, we derive a **class** DClass from the **class** BClass. The **class** DClass contains a **private** instance variable dA of type **int**. It also contains a method setData, with three parameters, and the method toString.

```java
public class DClass extends BClass
{
    private int dA;

    public DClass()
    {
        //The definition is as shown later in this section
    }

    public DClass(char ch, double v, int a)
    {
        //The definition is as shown later in this section
    }

    public void setData(char ch, double v, int a)
    {
        //The definition is as shown later in this section
    }

    public String toString()
    {
        //The definition is as shown later in this section
    }
}
```

Let's now write the definition of the method `setData` of the `class DClass`. Because `bCh` is a `protected` instance variable of the `class BClass`, it can be directly accessed in the definition of the method `setData`. However, because `bX` is a `private` instance variable of the `class BClass`, the method `setData` of the `class DClass` *cannot* directly access `bX`. Thus, the method `setData` of the `class DClass` must set `bX` by using the method `setData` of the `class BClass`. The definition of the method `setData` of the `class DClass` can be written as follows:

```
public void setData(char ch, double v, int a)
{
    super.setData(v);

    bCh = ch;     //initialize bCh using the assignment
                  //statement
    dA = a;
}
```

Note that the definition of the method `setData` contains the statement:

```
super.setData(v);
```

to call the method `setData` with one parameter (of the superclass), to set the instance variable `bX`, and then directly set the value of `bCh`.

Next, let's write the definition of the method `toString` (of the `class DClass`):

```
public String toString()
{
    return (super.toString() + "Subclass dA = " + dA + '\n');
}
```

The constructors' definitions are:

```
public DClass()
{
    super();
    dA = 0;
}
```

```
public void DClass(char ch, double v, int a)
{
    super(ch, v);
    dA = a;
}
```

The following program shows how the objects of `BClass` and `DClass` work:

```
public class ProtectedMemberProg
{
    public static void main(String[] args)
    {
        BClass bObject = new BClass();              //Line 1

        DClass dObject = new DClass();              //Line 2
```

10

```
        System.out.println("Line 3: " + bObject);      //Line 3

        System.out.println("Line 4: ***   "
                        + "Subclass object ***");       //Line 4

        dObject.setData('&', 2.5, 7);                   //Line 5

        System.out.println("Line 6: " + dObject);       //Line 6
    }
}
```

Sample Run:

```
Line 3: Superclass: bCh = *, bX = 0.0

Line 4: ***   Subclass object ***
Line 6: Superclass: bCh = &, bX = 2.5
Subclass dA = 7
```

When you write the definitions of the methods of the class DClass, the protected instance variable bCh can be accessed directly. However, DClass objects *cannot* directly access bCh. That is, the following statement is illegal (it is, in fact, a syntax error):

```
dObject.bCh = '&';  //Illegal
```

 NOTE In an inheritance hierarchy, the public and protected members of a superclass are directly accessible, in a subclass, across any number of generations, that is, at any level. To be explicit, if class Three is derived from class Two and class Two is derived from class One, then the protected and public members of class One are directly accessible in class Two as well as in class Three. Even though the (public and) protected data members of a super class are directly accessible in a subclass, in the inheritance hierarchy, it should be the responsibility of the superclass to properly initialize these data members. (Also note that, in fact, a class member declared with the modifier protected may be accessed by any class in the same package.)

---

class object

In Chapter 8, we defined the class Clock and later included the method toString to return the time as a string. When we included the method toString, we noted that every Java class (built-in or user-defined) is automatically provided the method toString. If a user-defined class does not provide its own definition of the method toString, then the default definition of the method toString is invoked. The methods print and println use the method toString to determine what to print. As shown in Chapter 8, the default definition of the method toString returns the class name followed by the hash code of the object. You might ask, where is the method toString defined?

The method toString comes from the Java **class** Object, and it is a **public** member of this class. In Java, if you define a class and do not use the reserved word **extends** to derive it from an existing class, then the class you define is automatically considered to be derived from the **class** Object. Therefore, the **class** Object directly or indirectly becomes the superclass of every class in Java. From this, it follows that the definition of the **class** Clock (previously given in Chapter 8):

```
public class Clock
{
    //Declare instance variables as given in Chapter 8
    //Definition of instance methods as given in Chapter 8
    //...
}
```

is, in fact, equivalent to the following:

```
public class Clock extends Object
{
    //Declare instance variables as given in Chapter 8
    //Definition of instance methods as given in Chapter 8
    //...
}
```

Using the mechanism of inheritance, every **public** member of the **class** Object can be overridden and/or invoked by every object of any class type. Table 10-1 describes some of the constructors and methods of the **class** Object.

TABLE 10-1 Constructors and Methods of the **class** Object

```
public Object()
//Constructor
```

```
public String toString()
//Method to return a string to describe the object
```

```
public boolean equals(Object obj)
//Method to determine if two objects are the same
//Returns true if the object invoking the method and the object
//specified by the parameter obj refer to the same memory space;
//otherwise it returns false.
```

```
protected Object clone()
//Method to return a reference to a copy of the object invoking
//this method
```

```
protected void finalize()
//The body of this method is invoked when the object goes out of scope.
```

1
0

Because every Java class is directly or indirectly derived from the `class Object`, it follows from Table 10-1 that the method `toString` becomes a `public` member of every Java class. Therefore, if a class does not override this method, whenever this method is invoked, the method's default definition executes. As indicated previously, the default definition returns the class name followed by the hash code of the object as a string. Usually, every Java class overrides the method `toString`. The `class String` overrides it so that the string stored in the object is returned. The `class Clock` overrides it so that the string containing the time in the form `hh:mm:ss` is returned. Similarly, the `class Person` also overrides it.

The method `equals` is also a very useful method of the `class Object`. This method's definition, as given in the `class Object`, determines whether the object invoking this method and the object passed as a parameter refer to the same memory space, that is, whether they point to data in the same memory space. The method `equals` determines whether the two objects are aliases. As in the case of the method `toString`, to implement its own needs, every user-defined `class` also usually overrides the method `equals`. For example, in the `class Clock`, in Chapter 8, the method `equals` was overridden to determine whether the instance variables (`hr`, `min`, and `sec`) of two `Clock` objects contained the same value. (You may review the definition of the method `equals` of the `class Clock` to see how this method may be written for a class.)

As usual, the default constructor is used to initialize an object. The method `clone` makes a copy of the object and returns a reference to the copy. However, the method `clone` makes only a memberwise (that is, field-by-field) copy of the object. In other words, the method `clone` provides a shallow copy of the data.

Java Stream Classes

In Chapter 2, we used the `class Scanner` for inputting data from the standard input device. Chapter 3 described in detail how to perform input/output (I/O) using Java stream classes, such as `FileReader` and `PrintWriter`. In Java, stream classes are implemented using the inheritance mechanism, as shown in Figure 10-6.

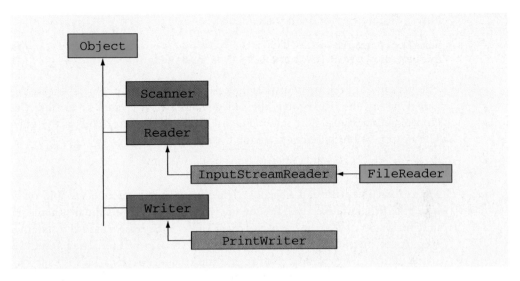

FIGURE 10-6 Java stream classes hierarchy

From Figure 10-6, it follows that the `classes` `Scanner`, `Reader`, and `Writer` are derived from the `class` `Object`. The `class` `InputStreamReader` is derived from the `class` `Reader`, and the `class` `FileReader` is derived from the `class` `InputStreamReader`. Similarly, the `class` `PrintWriter` is derived from the `class` `Writer`.

Polymorphism

Java allows us to treat an object of a subclass as an object of its superclass. In other words, a reference variable of a superclass type can point to an object of its subclass. There are situations when this feature of Java can be used to develop generic code for a variety of applications.

Consider the following statements. (The `classes` `Person` and `PartTimeEmployee` are as previously defined.)

```
Person name, nameRef;                          //Line 1
PartTimeEmployee employee, employeeRef;        //Line 2

name = new Person("John", "Blair");            //Line 3
employee = new PartTimeEmployee("Susan", "Johnson",
                        12.50, 45);            //Line 4
```

The statement in Line 1 declares `name` and `nameRef` to be reference variables of type `Person`. Similarly, the statement in Line 2 declares `employee` and `employeeRef` to be reference variables of type `PartTimeEmployee`. The statement in Line 3 instantiates the object `name` and the statement in Line 4 instantiates the object `employee`.

Now consider the following statements:

```
nameRef = employee;                               //Line 5
System.out.println("nameRef: " + nameRef);        //Line 6
```

The statement in Line 5 makes `nameRef` point to the object `employee`. After the statement in Line 5 executes, the object `nameRef` is treated as an object of the `class PartTimeEmployee`. The statement in Line 6 outputs the value of the object `nameRef`. The output of the statement in Line 6 is:

```
nameRef: Susan Johnson's wages are: $562.5
```

Notice that even though `nameRef` is declared as a reference variable of type `Person`, when the program executes, the statement in Line 6 outputs the first name, the last name, and the wages of a `PartTimeEmployee`. This is because when the statement in Line 6 executes to output `nameRef`, the method `toString` of the `class PartTimeEmployee` executes, not the method `toString` of the `class Person`. This is called **late binding**, **dynamic binding**, or **run-time binding**; that is, the method that gets executed is determined at execution time, not at compile time.

 NOTE Suppose that the `class` C is a subclass of the `class` B and that the `class` B is a subclass of the `class` A. Then, a reference variable of `class` A can point to an object of `class` B as well as to an object of `class` C. Thus, a reference variable of a superclass can point to an object of any of its descendent classes.

In a class hierarchy, several methods may have the same name and the same formal parameter list. Also, a reference variable of a class can refer to either an object of its own class or an object of its subclass. Therefore, a reference variable can invoke, that is, execute, a method of its own class or of its subclass(es). Binding means associating a method definition with its invocation, that is, determining which method definition gets executed. In *early binding*, a method's definition is associated with its invocation when the code is compiled. In *late binding*, a method's definition is associated with the method's invocation at execution time, that is, when the method is executed. Except for a few (special) cases (noted following Example 10-5), Java uses late binding for all methods. Furthermore, the term **polymorphism** means associating multiple (potential) meanings with the same method name. In Java, polymorphism is implemented using late binding.

The reference variable `name` or `nameRef` can point to any object of the `class Person` or the `class PartTimeEmployee`. Loosely speaking, we say that these reference variables have many forms, that is, they are **polymorphic reference** variables. They can refer to objects of their own class or to objects of the subclasses inherited from their class.

The following example further illustrates polymorphism.

EXAMPLE 10-5

```
public class RectangleFigure
{
    private double length;
    private double width;

    public RectangleFigure()
    {
        length = 0;
        width = 0;
    }

    public RectangleFigure(double l, double w)
    {
        setDimension(l, w);
    }

    public void setDimension(double l, double w)
    {
        if (l >= 0)
            length = l;
        else
            length = 0;

        if (w >= 0)
            width = w;
        else
            width = 0;
    }

    public double getLength()
    {
        return length;
    }

    public double getWidth()
    {
        return width;
    }

    public double area()
    {
        return length * width;
    }

    public double perimeter()
    {
        return 2 * (length + width);
    }
```

```java
    public String toString()
    {
        return ("Length = "  + length
                + "; Width = " + width + "\n"
                + "Area = " + area());
    }
}
```

Note that the definition of the class RectangleFigure is similar to the definition of the class Rectangle given previously. The method toString of the class RectangleFigure, in addition to returning the length and width, also prints the area of the rectangle.

```java
public class BoxFigure extends RectangleFigure
{
    private double height;

    public BoxFigure()
    {
        super();
        height = 0;
    }

    public BoxFigure(double l, double w, double h)
    {
        super(l, w);
        if (h >= 0)
            height = h;
        else
            height = 0;
    }

    public void setDimension(double l, double w, double h)
    {
        super.setDimension(l, w);

        if (h >= 0)
            height = h;
        else
            height = 0;
    }

    public double getHeight()
    {
        return height;
    }

    public double area()
    {
        return 2 * (getLength() * getWidth()
                    + getLength() * height
                    + getWidth() * height);
    }
```

```
    public double volume()
    {
        return super.area() * height;
    }

    public String toString()
    {
        return ("Length = "  + getLength()
                + "; Width = " + getWidth()
                + "; Height = " + height
                + "\n"
                + "Surface Area = " + area()
                + "; Volume = " + volume());
    }
}
```

Note that the class BoxFigure is derived from the class RectangleFigure. The definition of the class BoxFigure is similar to the definition of the class Box given previously. The method toString of the class BoxFigure, in addition to returning the length, width, and height, also returns the surface area and volume of the box.

Consider the following application program:

```
// This program illustrates how polymorphic reference variables
// work.

public class Polymorphism                          //Line 1
{                                                  //Line 2
    public static void main(String[] args)         //Line 3
    {                                              //Line 4
        RectangleFigure rectangle, shapeRef;       //Line 5

        BoxFigure box;                             //Line 6

        rectangle  = new RectangleFigure(8, 5);    //Line 7
        box = new BoxFigure(10, 7, 3);             //Line 8

        shapeRef = rectangle;                      //Line 9
        System.out.println("Line 10: Rectangle:\n"
                        + shapeRef);               //Line 10
        System.out.println();                      //Line 11

        shapeRef = box;                            //Line 12
        System.out.println("Line 13: Box:\n"
                        + shapeRef);               //Line 13
        System.out.println();                      //Line 14
    } //end main                                   //Line 15
}                                                  //Line 16
```

Sample Run:

```
Line 10: Rectangle:
Length = 8.0; Width = 5.0
Area = 40.0
```

```
Line 13: Box:
Length = 10.0; Width = 7.0; Height = 3.0
Surface Area = 242.0; Volume = 210.0
```

In the preceding program, `shapeRef` is a reference variable of the `RectangleFigure` type. Because the `class BoxFigure` is derived from the `class RectangleFigure`, the reference variable `shapeRef` can point to an object of the `class RectangleFigure` or to an object of the `class BoxFigure`.

The statement in Line 7 instantiates a `RectangleFigure` object and stores the address of this object in the reference variable `rectangle`. Similarly, the statement in Line 8 instantiates a `BoxFigure` object and stores the address of this object in the reference variable `box`.

After the statement in Line 9 executes, `shapeRef` points to the object `rectangle`. The statement in Line 10 executes the method `toString`. Because `shapeRef` points to an object of the `class RectangleFigure`, the method `toString` of the `class RectangleFigure` executes. When the method `toString` of the `class RectangleFigure` executes, it also executes the method `area`. In this case, the method `area` of the `class RectangleFigure` executes.

After the statement in Line 12 executes, `shapeRef` points to the object `box`. The statement in Line 13 executes the method `toString`. Because `shapeRef` points to an object of the `class BoxFigure`, the method `toString` of the `class BoxFigure` executes. When the method `toString` of the `class BoxFigure` executes, it also executes the method `area`. In this case, the method `area` of the `class BoxFigure` executes, which outputs the surface area of the box.

 NOTE If a method of a `class` is declared final, it cannot be overridden with a new definition in a derived class. You declare a method of a class final by using the keyword `final`. For example, the following method is final:

```
public final void doSomeThing()
{
    //...
}
```

Similarly, you can also declare a `class` final using the keyword `final`. If a class is declared final, then no other `class` can be derived from this `class`; that is, it cannot be the superclass of any other classes.

Java does *not* use late binding for methods that are marked `private`, `final`, or `static`.

As illustrated above, a reference variable of a superclass type can point to an object of its subclass. However, you cannot automatically consider a superclass object to be an object of a subclass. In other words, you *cannot* automatically make a reference variable of a subclass type point to an object of its superclass.

Suppose that `supRef` is a reference variable of a superclass type. Moreover, suppose that `supRef` points to an object of its subclass. You can use an appropriate cast operator on `supRef` and make a reference variable of the subclass point to the object. On the other hand, if `supRef` does not point to a subclass object and you use a cast operator on `supRef` to make a reference variable of the subclass point to the object, then Java will throw a `ClassCastException`—indicating that the `class` cast is not allowed.

Suppose `name`, `nameRef`, `employee`, and `employeeRef` are as declared in the begining of this section, that is:

```
Person name, nameRef;                               //Line 1
PartTimeEmployee employee, employeeRef;             //Line 2

name = new Person("John", "Blair");                 //Line 3
employee = new PartTimeEmployee("Susan", "Johnson",
                          12.50, 45);               //Line 4
nameRef = employee;                                 //Line 5
```

Now consider the following statement:

```
employeeRef = (PartTimeEmployee) name;       //Illegal
```

This statement will throw a `ClassCastException` because `name` points to an object of the `class` `Person`. It does not refer to an object of the `class` `PartTimeEmployee`. However, the following statement is legal:

```
employeeRef = (PartTimeEmployee) nameRef;
```

Because `nameRef` refers to the object `employee` (as set by the statement in Line 5), and `employee` is a reference variable of the `PartTimeEmployee` type, this statement would make `employeeRef` point to the object `employee`. Therefore, the output of the statement:

```
System.out.println(employeeRef);
```

is:

```
Susan Johnson's wages are: $562.50
```

Operator `instanceof`

As previously described, an object of a subclass type can be considered an object of the superclass type. Moreover, by using an appropriate cast operator, you can treat an object of a superclass type as an object of a subclass type. To determine whether a reference variable that points to an object is of a particular class type, Java provides the operator `instanceof`. Consider the following expression (suppose that `p` is an object of a class type):

```
p instanceof BoxShape
```

This expression evaluates to true if p points to an object of the class BoxShape; otherwise, it evaluates to false. The class BoxShape is defined in Example 10-6, which further illustrates how the operator instanceof works.

EXAMPLE 10-6

Consider the following classes: (The classes RectangleShape and BoxShape are the same as the classes Rectangle and Box given earlier in this chapter. The only difference is that the instance variables of the classes Rectangle and Box are private. Because the instance variables of the class RectangleShape are protected, they can be directly accessed in the class BoxShape. Therefore, the definitions of the methods area and volume of the class BoxShape directly access the instance variables length and width of the class RectangleShape.)

```
public class RectangleShape
{
    protected double length;
    protected double width;

    public RectangleShape()
    {
        length = 0;
        width = 0;
    }

    public RectangleShape(double l, double w)
    {
        setDimension(l, w);
    }

    public void setDimension(double l, double w)
    {
        if (l >= 0)
            length = l;
        else
            length = 0;

        if (w >= 0)
            width = w;
        else
            width = 0;
    }

    public double getLength()
    {
        return length;
    }
```

```java
    public double getWidth()
    {
        return width;
    }

    public double area()
    {
        return length * width;
    }

    public double perimeter()
    {
        return 2 * (length + width);
    }

    public String toString()
    {
        return("Length = "  + length
            + ", Width = " + width
            + ", Perimeter = " + perimeter()
            + ", Area = " + area());
    }
}
```

The class BoxShape, given next, is derived from the class RectangleShape.

```java
public class BoxShape extends RectangleShape
{
    protected double height;

    public BoxShape()
    {
        super();
        height = 0;
    }

    public BoxShape(double l, double w, double h)
    {
        super(l, w);
        height = h;
    }

    public void setDimension(double l, double w, double h)
    {
        super.setDimension(l, w);

        if (h >= 0)
            height = h;
        else
            height = 0;
    }
```

10

```java
public double getHeight()
{
    return height;
}

public double area()
{
    return  2 * (length * width + length * height + width * height);
}

public double volume()
{
    return length * width * height;
}

public String toString()
{
    return ("Length = "  + length
           + ", Width = " + width
           + ", Height = " + height
           + ", Surface Area = " + area()
           + ", Volume = " + volume());
}
}
```

Next, consider the following application program:

```java
public class SuperSubClassObjects
{
    public static void main(String[] args)
    {
        RectangleShape   rectangle, rectRef;            //Line 1
        BoxShape box, boxRef;                           //Line 2

        rectangle = new RectangleShape(12, 4);          //Line 3
        System.out.println("Line 4: Rectangle \n"
                          + rectangle+ "\n");            //Line 4
        box = new BoxShape(13, 7, 4);                   //Line 5
        System.out.println("Line 6: Box\n"
                          + box+ "\n");                  //Line 6
        rectRef = box;                                  //Line 7
        System.out.println("Line 8: Box via rectRef\n"
                          + rectRef+ "\n");              //Line 8


        boxRef = (BoxShape) rectRef;                    //Line 9
        System.out.println("Line 10: Box via boxRef\n"
                          + boxRef + "\n");              //Line 10

        if (rectRef instanceof BoxShape)                //Line 11
            System.out.println("Line 12: rectRef is "
                          + "an instance of BoxShape");  //Line 12
```

```
        else                                          //Line 13
            System.out.println("Line 14: rectRef is not "
                        + "an instance of BoxShape");   //Line 14

        if (rectangle instanceof BoxShape)             //Line 15
            System.out.println("Line 16: rectangle is "
                        + "an instance of BoxShape");   //Line 16
        else                                           //Line 17
            System.out.println("Line 18: rectangle is not "
                        + "an instance of BoxShape");   //Line 18
    }
}
```

Sample Run:

```
Line 4: Rectangle
Length = 12.0, Width = 4.0, Perimeter = 32.0, Area = 48.0

Line 6: Box
Length = 13.0, Width = 7.0, Height = 4.0, Surface Area = 342.0, Volume = 364.0

Line 8: Box via rectRef
Length = 13.0, Width = 7.0, Height = 4.0, Surface Area = 342.0, Volume = 364.0

Line 10: Box via boxRef
Length = 13.0, Width = 7.0, Height = 4.0, Surface Area = 342.0, Volume = 364.0

Line 12: rectRef is an instance of BoxShape
Line 18: rectangle is not an instance of BoxShape
```

The preceding program works as follows: The statement in Line 1 declares rectangle and rectRef to be reference variables of the RectangleShape type. Similarly, the statement in Line 2 declares box and boxRef to be reference variables of the BoxShape type.

The statement in Line 3 instantiates the object rectangle and initializes the instance variables length and width to 12.0 and 4.0, respectively. The statement in Line 4 outputs the length, width, perimeter, and area of rectangle.

The statement in Line 5 instantiates the object box and initializes the instance variables length, width, and height to 13.0, 7.0, and 4.0, respectively. The statement in Line 6 outputs the length, width, height, surface area, and volume of box.

The statement in Line 7 copies the value of box into rectRef. After this statement executes, rectRef points to the object box. Notice that rectRef is a reference variable of the RectangleShape (the superclass) type and box is a reference variable of the BoxShape (the subclass of RectangleShape) type.

The statement in Line 8 outputs the length, width, height, surface area, and volume of box via the reference variable rectRef. Notice that rectRef is a reference variable of the RectangleShape type. However, when the statement in Line 8 executes to output rectRef, the method toString of the **class** BoxShape executes, not the method toString of the **class** RectangleShape.

10

Because the reference variable `rectRef` points to an object of `BoxShape`, the statement in Line 9 uses the cast operator and copies the value of `rectRef` into `boxRef`. (If the reference variable `rectRef` did not point to an object of type `BoxShape`, then the statement in Line 9 would result in an error.) The statement in Line 10 outputs the length, width, height, surface area, and volume of the object to which `boxRef` points.

The statements in Lines 11 through 14 determine whether `rectRef` is an instance of `BoxShape`, that is, if `rectRef` points to an object of the `BoxShape` type. Similarly, the statements in Lines 15 through 18 determine whether the reference variable `rectangle` is an instance of `BoxShape`.

Abstract Methods and Classes

An **abstract method** is a method that has only the heading with no body. The heading of an abstract method contains the reserved word `abstract` and ends with a semicolon. The following are examples of abstract methods:

```
public void abstract print();
public abstract object larger(object, object);
void abstract insert(int insertItem);
```

An **abstract class** is a class that is declared with the reserved word `abstract` in its heading. Following are some facts about abstract classes:

- An abstract class can contain instance variables, constructors, the finalizer, and nonabstract methods.
- An abstract class can contain an abstract method(s).
- If a class contains an abstract method, then the class must be declared abstract.
- You cannot instantiate an object of an abstract class. You can only declare a reference variable of an abstract class type.
- You can instantiate an object of a subclass of an abstract class, but only if the subclass gives the definitions of *all* the abstract methods of the superclass.

The following is an example of an abstract class:

```
public abstract class AbstractClassExample
{
    protected int x;

    public abstract void print();

    public void setX(int a)
    {
        x = a;
    }
```

```
    public AbstractClassExample()
    {
        x = 0;
    }
}
```

Abstract classes are used as superclasses from which other subclasses within the same context can be derived. They serve as placeholders to store members common to all subclasses. They can be used to force subclasses to provide certain methods, as illustrated in Example 10-7.

EXAMPLE 10-7

Banks offer various types of accounts, such as savings, checking, certificate of deposits, and money market, to attract customers as well as to meet their specific needs. In this example, we illustrate how to use abstract classes and polymorphism for processing different kinds of bank accounts.

Two of the most commonly used accounts are savings and checking. Each of these accounts has various options. For example, you may have a savings account that requires no minimum balance, but has a lower interest rate. Similarly, you may have a checking account that limits the number of checks that you can write each month. Another type of account that is used to save money for the long term is a certificate of deposit (CD). To illustrate how abstract classes are designed and how polymorphism works we assume that the bank offers three types of accounts—savings, checking, and certificate of deposit, as described next.

Savings accounts: Suppose that the bank offers two types of savings accounts: one that has no minimum balance and has a lower interest rate and another that requires a minimum balance and has a higher interest rate.

Checking accounts: Suppose that the bank offers three types of checking accounts: one with a monthly service charge, a limited number of monthly checking writing, no minimum balance, and no interest; another with no monthly service charge, requires a minimum balance, allows an unlimited number of monthly check writing, pays lower interest; and a third with no monthly service charge, requires a higher minimum balance, has a higher interest rate, and allows an unlimited number of monthly check writing.

Certificate of deposit (CD): In an account of this type, money is left for some time and these accounts draw higher interest rates than either savings or checking accounts. Suppose that you purchase a CD for six months. Then we say that the CD will mature in six months. Furthermore, the penalty for early withdrawal is stiff.

Figure 10-7 shows the inheritance hierarchy of these bank accounts.

10

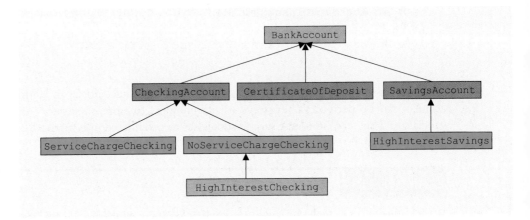

FIGURE 10-7 Inheritance hierarchy of banking accounts

Note that the classes `BankAccount` and `CheckingAccount` are abstract. That is, we cannot instantiate objects of these classes. Typically, common characteristics are placed as high as possible in the inheritance hierarchy and these characteristics are inherited by the subclasses. The other classes in Figure 10-7 are not abstract. Next we describe each of these classes in more detail.

`BankAccount`: Every bank account has an account number, the name of the owner, and a balance. Therefore, instance variables `name`, `accountNumber`, and `balance` are declared in the abstract `class` `BankAccount`. Some operations common to all types of accounts are to retrieve the account owner's name, the account number, the account balance, make deposits, withdraw money, and create a monthly statement. So we include methods to implement these operations. Furthermore, some of these methods will be abstract. We also include the method `toString` to return the appropriate information about the class as a string. The UML class diagram of the `class` `BankAccount` is shown in Figure 10-8.

BankAccount (Abstract class)
#accountNumber: int #name: String #balance: double
+BankAccount(String, int, double) +getAccountNumber(): int +getBalance(): double +getName(): String +setName(String): void +withdraw(double): void +deposit(double): void +createMonthlyStatement(): abstract void +String toString()

FIGURE 10-8 UML class diagram of the `class` BankAccount

CheckingAccount: A checking account *is a* bank account. Therefore, it inherits all the properties of a bank account. Because one of the objectives of a checking account is to be able to write checks, we include the abstract method **writeCheck** to write checks. The UML class diagram for **class CheckingAccount** is shown in Figure 10-9.

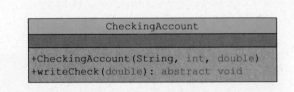

FIGURE 10-9 UML class diagram of the **class** CheckingAccount

ServiceChargeChecking: A service charge checking account *is a* checking account. Therefore, it inherits all the properties of a checking account. For simplicity we assume that this type of account does not pay any interest, allows the account holder to write a limited number of checks each month, and does not require any minimum balance. The named constants, instance variables, and methods of this class are described in Figure 10-10, which also shows the UML class diagram of the **class ServiceChargeChecking**.

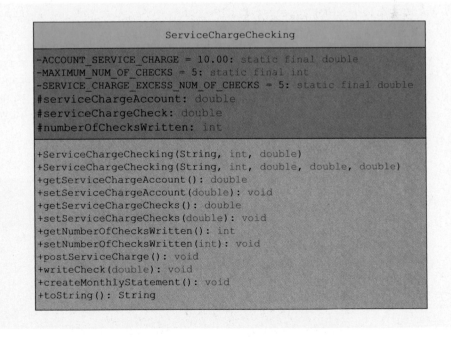

FIGURE 10-10 UML class diagram of the **class** ServiceChargeChecking

1
0

`NoServiceChargeChecking`: A checking account with no monthly service charge *is a* checking account. Therefore, it inherits all the properties of a checking account. Furthermore, this type of account pays interest, allows the account holder to write checks, and requires a minimum balance. The named constants, instance variables, and methods of this class are described in Figure 10-11, which also shows the UML class diagram of the **class** `NoServiceChargeChecking`.

```
                         NoServiceChargeChecking
-MIN_BALANCE = 1000.00: static final double
-INTEREST_RATE = 0.02: static final double
#minimumBalance: double
#interestRate: double

+NoServiceChargeChecking(String, int, double)
+NoServiceChargeChecking(String, int, double, double, double)
+getMinimumBalance(): double
+setMinimumBalance(double): void
+verifyMinimumumBalance(double): boolean
+writeCheck(double): void
+withdraw(double): void
+createMonthlyStatement(): void
+toString(): String
```

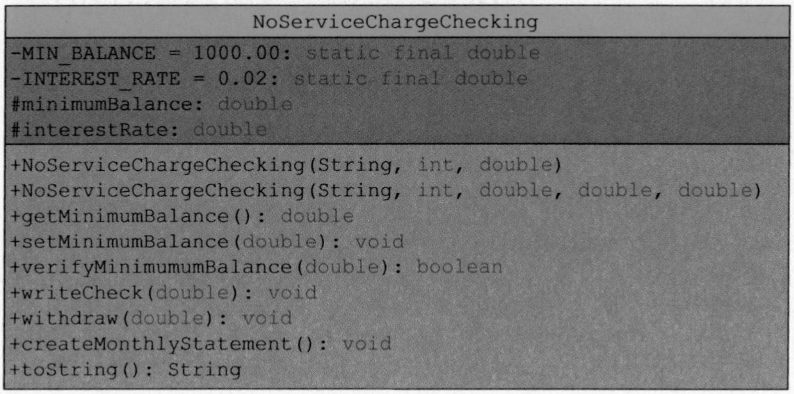

FIGURE 10-11 UML class diagram of the **class** NoServiceChargeChecking

`HighInterestChecking`: A checking account with high interest *is a* checking account with no monthly service charge. Therefore, it inherits all the properties of a no service charge checking account. Furthermore, this type of account pays higher interest and requires higher minimum balance than the no service charge checking account. The named constants, instance variables, and methods of this class are described in Figure 10-12, which also shows the UML class diagram of the **class** `HighInterestChecking`.

```
                         HighInterestChecking
-INTEREST_RATE = 0.05: static final double
-MIN_BALANCE = 5000.00: static final double

+HighInterestChecking(String, int, double)
+HighInterestChecking(String, int, double, double, double)
+getInterestRate(): double
+setInterestRate(double): void
+postInterest(): void
+createMonthlyStatement(): void
+toString(): String
```

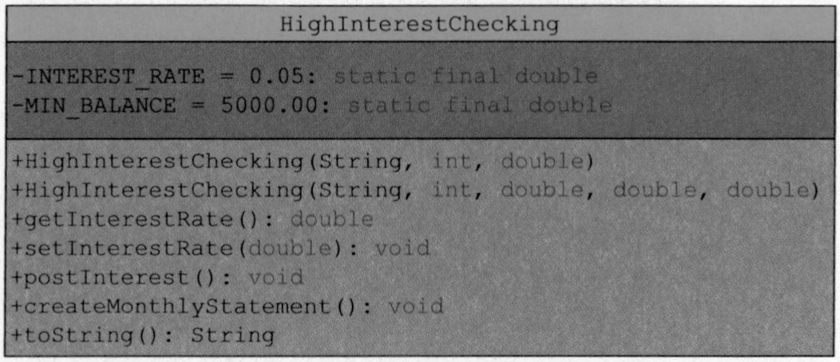

FIGURE 10-12 UML class diagram of the **class** HighInterestChecking

SavingsAccount: A savings account *is a* bank account. Therefore, it inherits all the properties of a bank account. Furthermore, a savings account also pays interest. The named constants, instance variables, and methods of this class are described in Figure 10-13, which also shows the UML class diagram of the class SavingsAccount.

```
                  SavingsAccount

-INTEREST_RATE = 0.03: static final double
#interestRate: double

+SavingsAccount(String, int, double)
+SavingsAccount(String, int, double, double)
+getInterestRate(): double
+setInterestRate(double): void
+postInterest(): void
+createMonthlyStatement(): void
+toString(): String
```

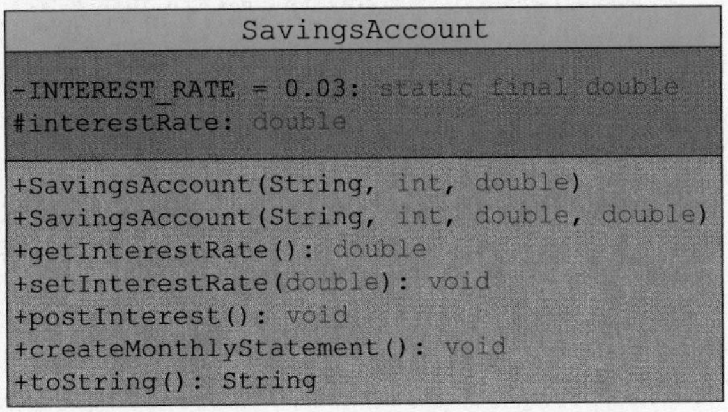

FIGURE 10-13 UML class diagram of the class SavingsAccount

HighInterestSavings: A high interest savings account *is a* savings account. Therefore, it inherits all the properties of a savings account. It also requires a minimum balance. The named constants, instance variables, and methods of this class are described in Figure 10-14, which also shows the UML class diagram of the class HighInterestSavings.

```
                HighInterestSavings

-MINIMUM_BALANCE = 2500.00: static final double
-INTEREST_RATE = 0.05: static final double
#minimumBalance: double

+HighInterestSavings(String, int, double)
+HighInterestSavings(String, int, double, double, double)
+getMinimumBalance(): double
+verifyMinimumBalance(double): boolean
+withdraw(double): void
+toString(): String
```

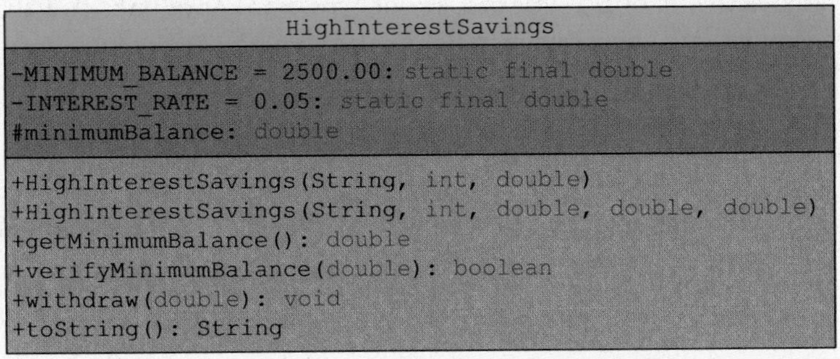

FIGURE 10-14 UML class diagram of the class HighInterestSavings

CertificateOfDeposit: A certificate of deposit account *is a* bank account. Therefore, it inherits all the properties of a bank account. In addition, it has instance variables to store the number of CD maturity months, the interest rate, and the current CD month. The named constants, instance variables, and methods of this class are listed in Figure 10-15, which also shows the UML class diagram of the `class` `CertificateOfDeposit`.

```
CertificateOfDeposit
-INTEREST_RATE = 0.05: static final double
-NUMBER_OF_MATURITY_MONTHS = 6: static final int
-interestRate: double
-maturityMonths: int
-cdMonth: int
+CertificateOfDeposit(String, int, double)
+CertificateOfDeposit(String, int, double, double, int)
+getInterestRate(): double
+setInterestRate(double): void
+getCurrentCDMonth(): double
+setCurrentCDMonth(int): void
+getMaturityMonths(): double
+setMaturityMonths(int): void
+postInterest():void
+withdraw(double): void
+withdraw(): void
+createMonthlyStatement(): void
+toString(): String
```

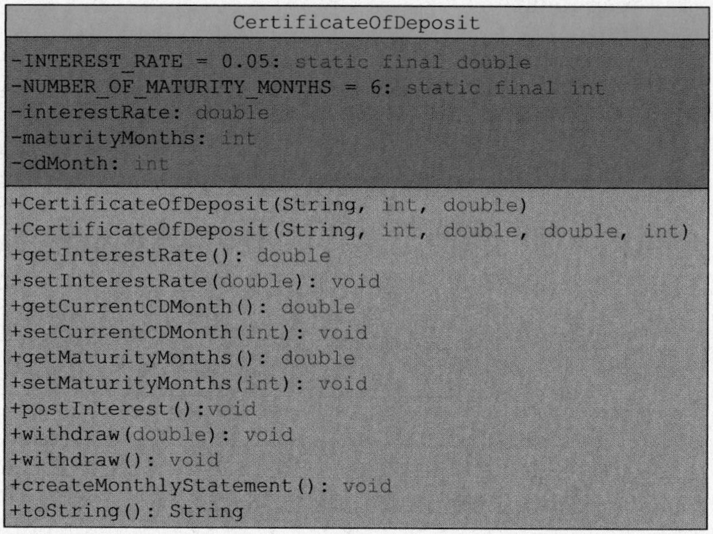

FIGURE 10-15 UML class diagram of the `class` `CertificateOfDeposit`

To create various types of accounts, we can use a **Vector** object. Recall from Chapter 9 that a **Vector** object can increase in size if additional accounts are needed to be created. The elements of the **Vector** are of type **BankAccount**, and six different kinds of bank accounts can be instantiated. The following statement created the **Vector** object **accountsList** and the element type is **BankAccount**.

`Vector <BankAccount> accountsList = new Vector <BankAccount>();`

We leave it as an exercise for you to write the definitions of the classes described in this example as well as a program to test these classes. (See Programming Exercise 13 at the end of this chapter.)

Interfaces

In Chapter 6, you learned that the **class** **ActionListener** is a special type of class called an **interface**. Several other classes in Java are similar to the **interface** **ActionListener**. For example, window events are handled by the **interface** **WindowListener**, and mouse events are handled by the interface MouseListener. The obvious question is: Why does Java have these interfaces? After all, they are similar to classes. The answer is that Java *does not* support multiple inheritance; a class can extend the definition of only one class. In other words, a class can be derived from *only* one existing class. However, a Java program might contain a variety of GUI components and thus generate a variety of events, such as window events, mouse events, and action events. These events are handled by separate interfaces. Therefore, a program might need to use more than one such interface.

Until now, we have handled events by using the mechanism of the inner class. For example, action events were processed by using inner classes. There are two more ways, discussed in Chapter 11, to process events in a Java program—by using anonymous classes and by making the class containing the application program implement the appropriate interface.

When we created an inner class to process an action event, the inner class was built on top of the interface ActionListener by using the mechanism of implements. Rather than use the inner class mechanism, the class containing the Java program can itself be created on top of ("by implementing") an interface, just as we created the GUI program by extending the class JFrame. For example, for the RectangleProgram in Chapter 6, we could have defined the class RectangleProgram as follows:

```
public class RectangleProgram extends JFrame implements
                                         ActionListener
{
    //...
}
```

Of course, doing so would also require us to register the listener using the reference this, which was explained in Chapter 8.

To be able to handle a variety of events, Java allows a class to implement more than one interface. This is, in fact, how Java implements a *form* of multiple inheritance, *which is not true multiple inheritance*. In the remainder of this section, we provide a few facts about interfaces.

You already know that an interface is a special type of class. How does an interface differ from an actual class?

An **interface** is a type of class that contains only abstract methods and/or named constants. Interfaces are defined using the reserved word interface in place of the reserved word class. For example, the definition of the interface WindowListener is:

```
public interface WindowListener
{
    public void windowOpened(WindowEvent e);
    public void windowClosing(WindowEvent e);
    public void windowClosed(WindowEvent e);
    public void windowIconified(WindowEvent e);
```

1
0

```
    public void windowDeiconified(WindowEvent e);
    public void windowActivated(WindowEvent e);
    public void windowDeactivated(WindowEvent e);
}
```

The definition of the `interface` `ActionListener` is:

```
public interface ActionListener
{
    public void actionPerformed(ActionEvent e);
}
```

EXAMPLE 10-8

The following `class` implements the `interfaces` `ActionListener` and `WindowListener`:

```
public class ExampleInterfaceImp implements ActionListener,
                                            WindowListener
{
    //....
}
```

 NOTE   Recall that if a `class` contains an `abstract` method, it must be declared `abstract`. Moreover, you cannot instantiate an object of an `abstract class`. Therefore, if a `class` implements an `interface`, it must provide definitions for each of the methods of the `interface`; otherwise, you cannot instantiate an object of that class type.

Polymorphism Via Interfaces

As stated above, one of the main uses of interfaces is to allow GUI programs to handle more than one type of event such as window events, mouse events, and action events. These events are handled by separate interfaces. An interface can also be used in the implementation of abstract data types. Like some other languages, such as C++, you cannot separate the definition of a class from the definitions of its methods. If the user of a class looks at the definition of the class, the user can also look at the definitions of the methods. That is, implementation details of a class cannot be (directly) separated from its specification details. In reality, the user of a class should only be concerned with the specification, not the implementation. One way to accomplish this is to define an interface that contains the methods headings and/or named constants. Then you can define the class that implements the interface. The user can look at the interface and see what operations are implemented by the class.

Just as you can create polymorphic references to classes in an inheritance hierarchy, you can also create polymorphic references using interfaces. You can use an interface name as the type of a reference variable, and the reference variable can point to any object of any class that implements the interface. However, because an interface contains only method headings and/or named constants, *you cannot create an object of an interface.*

Suppose that you have the following interface:

```
public interface Employee
{
    public double wages();
    public String department();
}
```

Now you declare a reference variable using the interface Employee. For example, the following statement declares newEmployee to be a reference variable of type Employee:

```
Employee newEmployee;
```

However, the following statement is illegal because you cannot instantiate an object of an interface:

```
newEmployee = new Employee();      //illegal
```

Suppose that you have two types of employees—part-time and full-time. You can define the class FullTimeEmployee that implements the interface Employee. You can use the reference variable newEmployee to create an object of the class FullTimeEmployee. For example, the following statement creates an object of this class.

```
newEmployee = new FullTimeEmployee();
```

The following statement invokes the methods wages:

```
double salary = newEmployee.wages();
```

In a similar manner, if the class PartTimeEmployee implements the interface Employee, the following statement creates an object of this class:

```
newEmployee = new PartTimeEmployee();
```

In addition to implementing methods of the interface Employee, the class FullTimeEmployee can contain additional methods. Suppose that the class FullTimeEmployee contains the method

```
public void upDatePayRate(double increment)
{
    //...
}
```

Then the following statement will generate a compiler error:

```
newEmployee.upDatePayRate(25);    //causes compiler error
```

The reason for this error is that, because newEmployee is a reference variable of type Employee, it can point to an object of the class FullTimeEmployee or an object of the class PartTimeEmployee, but it can only guarantee that the object it points to can use the methods `wages` and `department`. However, if we know that `newEmployee` points to an object of the `class FullTimeEmployee`, then using an appropriate cast operator, we can call the method `upDatePayRate` as follows:

```
((FullTimeEmployee)newEmployee).upDatePayRate(25);
```

You can expand or extend the hierarchy as needed to accommodate additional kinds of employees. For example, a board member might be another kind of employee, expanding the hierarchy. Or, there might be two kinds of full-time employees: those who receive a fixed salary and those who are paid by the hour. Java provides the flexibility to accommodate the expansion and extension, and to represent these kinds of class relationships.

You can also use an `interface` name to declare a parameter to a method. In this case, any reference variable of any class that implements that interface can be passed as an (actual) parameter to that method.

Composition (Aggregation)

Composition is another way to relate two classes. In **composition (aggregation)**, one or more members of a class are objects of one or more other classes. Composition is a "has-a" relation; for example, "every person has a date of birth."

The `class Person`, as defined in Chapter 8, Example 8-7, stores a person's first name and last name. Suppose we want to keep track of additional information, such as a personal ID and date of birth. Because every person has a personal ID and a date of birth, we can define a new `class PersonalInfo`, in which one of the members is an object of type `Person`. We can declare additional members to store the personal ID and date of birth for the `class PersonalInfo`.

First, we define another `class`, `Date`, to store only a person's date of birth, and then construct the `class PersonalInfo` from the `classes Person` and `Date`. This way, we can demonstrate how to define a new class using two classes.

To define the `class Date`, we need three instance variables to store the month, day number, and year. Some of the operations that need to be performed on a date are to set the date and to print the date. The following statements define the `class Date`:

```
public class Date
{
    private int dMonth;      //variable to store the month
    private int dDay;        //variable to store the day
    private int dYear;       //variable to store the year

        //Default constructor
        //The instance variables dMonth, dDay, and dYear are set to
        //the default values.
        //Postcondition: dMonth = 1; dDay = 1; dYear = 1900;
```

```java
public Date()
{
    dMonth = 1;
    dDay = 1;
    dYear = 1900;
}

    //Constructor to set the date
    //The instance variables dMonth, dDay, and dYear are set
    //according to the parameters.
    //Postcondition: dMonth = month; dDay = day;
    //               dYear = year;
public Date(int month, int day, int year)
{
    dMonth = month;
    dDay = day;
    dYear = year;
}

    //Method to set the date
    //The instance variables dMonth, dDay, and dYear are set
    //according to the parameters.
    //Postcondition: dMonth = month; dDay = day;
    //               dYear = year;
public void setDate(int month, int day, int year)
{
    dMonth = month;
    dDay = day;
    dYear = year;
}

    //Method to return the month
    //Postcondition: The value of dMonth is returned.
public int getMonth()
{
    return dMonth;
}

    //Method to return the day
    //Postcondition: The value of dDay is returned.
public int getDay()
{
    return dDay;
}

    //Method to return the year
    //Postcondition: The value of dYear is returned.
public int getYear()
{
    return dYear;
}
```

10

```
        //Method to return the date in the form mm-dd-yyyy
    public String toString()
    {
        return (dMonth + "-" + dDay + "-" + dYear);
    }
}
```

Figure 10-16 shows the UML diagram of the class Date.

```
┌─────────────────────────────┐
│            Date             │
├─────────────────────────────┤
│ -dMonth: int                │
│ -dDay: int                  │
│ -dYear:int                  │
├─────────────────────────────┤
│ +Date()                     │
│ +Date(int, int, int)        │
│ +setDate(int, int, int): void│
│ +toString(): String         │
│ +getMonth(): int            │
│ +getDay(): int              │
│ +getYear(): int             │
└─────────────────────────────┘
```

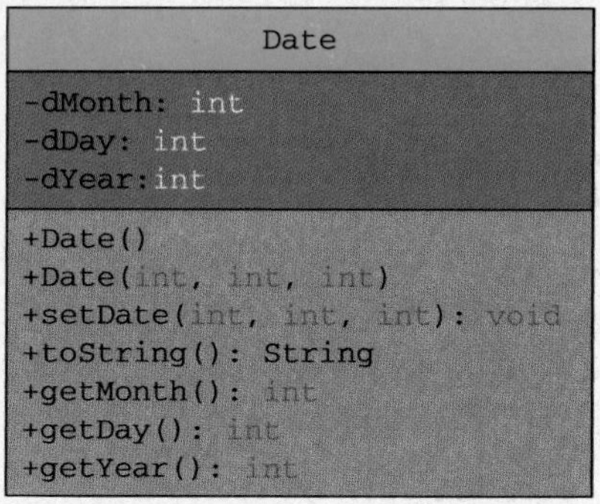

FIGURE 10-16 UML class diagram of the class Date

The definition of the method setDate, before storing the date into the data members, does not check to see if the date is valid. That is, it does not confirm that month is between 1 and 12, year is greater than 0, and day is valid (for example, for January, day should be between 1 and 31). In Programming Exercise 2 at the end of this chapter, you are asked to rewrite the definition of the method setDate so that the date is validated before storing it in the data members. Similarly, in Programming Exercise 2, you are asked to rewrite the definition of the constructor with parameters so that it checks for valid values of month, day, and year before storing the date into the data members.

Next, we specify the members of the class PersonalInfo.

Instance Variables:

```
private Person name;
private Date bDay;
private int personID;
```

Constructors and Instance Methods:

```
public void setPersonalInfo(String first, String last, int month,
                            int day, int year, int ID)
    //Method to set the personal information
    //Instance variables are set according to the parameters
    //Postcondition: firstName = first; lastName = last;
    //         dMonth = month; dDay = day; dYear = year;
    //         personID = ID;
```

```
public String toString()
   //Method to return the string containing personal information

public PersonalInfo(String first, String last, int month,
                    int day, int year, int ID)
   //Constructor with parameters
   //Instance variables are set according to the parameters
   //Postcondition: firstName = first; lastName = last;
   //    dMonth = month; dDay = day; dYear = year;
   //    personID = ID;

public PersonalInfo()
   //Default constructor
   //Instance variables are set to the default values
   //Postcondition: firstName = ""; lastName = "";
   //               dMonth = 1; dDay = 1; dYear = 1900;
   //               personID = 0;
```

Figure 10-17 shows the UML class diagram of the **class** `PersonalInfo`.

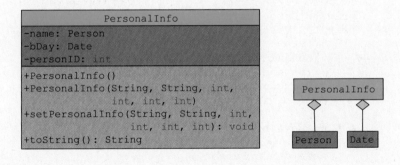

FIGURE 10-17 UML class diagram of the **class** `PersonalInfo`

The definitions of the methods of the **class** `PersonalInfo` follow:

```
public void setPersonalInfo(String first, String last, int month,
                            int day, int year, int ID)
{
    name.setName(first, last);
    bDay.setDate(month, day, year);
    personID = ID;
}

public String toString()

    return ("Name: " + name.toString() + "\n"
        + "Date of birth: " + bDay.toString() + "\n"
        + "Personal ID: " + personID);
}
```

```java
public PersonalInfo(String first, String last, int month,
                    int day, int year, int ID)
{
    name = new Person(first, last);   //instantiate and
                                      //initialize the object name
    bDay = new Date(month, day, year);   //instantiate and
                                         //initialize the object bDay

    personID = ID;
}

public PersonalInfo()
{
    name = new Person();
    bDay = new Date();
    personID = 0;
}
```

Next, we give the definition of the **class** **PersonalInfo**:

```java
public class PersonalInfo
{
    private Person name;
    private Date bDay;
    private int personID;

        //Default constructor
        //Instance variables are set to the default values
        //Postcondition: firstName = ""; lastName = "";
        //               dMonth = 1; dDay = 1; dYear = 1900;
        //               personID = 0;
    public PersonalInfo()
    {
        name = new Person();
        bDay = new Date();
        personID = 0;
    }

        //Constructor with parameters
        //Instance variables are set according to the parameters
        //Postcondition: firstName = first; lastName = last;
        //               dMonth = month; dDay = day; dYear = year;
        //               personID = ID;
    public PersonalInfo(String first, String last, int month,
                        int day, int year, int ID)
    {
        name = new Person(first, last);   //instantiate and
                                          //initialize the object name
        bDay = new Date(month, day, year);//instantiate and
                                          //initialize the object bDay

        personID = ID;
    }
```

```
    //Method to set the personal information
    //Instance variables are set according to the parameters
    //Postcondition: firstName = first; lastName = last;
    //               dMonth = month; dDay = day; dYear = year;
    //               personID = ID;
public void setPersonalInfo(String first, String last, int month,
                            int day, int year, int ID)
{
    name.setName(first, last);
    bDay.setDate(month, day, year);
    personID = ID;
}


    //Method to return the string containing personal information
public String toString()
{
    return ("Name: " + name.toString() + "\n"
        + "Date of birth: " + bDay.toString() + "\n"
        + "Personal ID: " + personID);
}
}
```

NOTE   The Web site and CD accompanying this book contain the definitions of the classes
Person, Date, and PersonalInfo, as well as a program that shows how to use these
classes. The folder Composition contains the necessary files.

PROGRAMMING EXAMPLE: Grade Report

1
0

This programming example further illustrates the concepts of inheritance and composition.

The midsemester point at your college or university is approaching. The registrar's office wants to prepare the grade reports as soon as the students' grades are recorded. Some of the enrolled students have not yet paid their tuition, however.

If a student has paid the tuition, the student's grades are shown on the grade report with the grade-point average (GPA).

If a student has not paid the tuition, the grades are not printed. For these students, the grade report contains a message indicating that the grades are being held for non-payment of tuition. The grade report also shows the billing amount.

The registrar's office and the business office want you to help write a program that can analyze the students' data and print the appropriate grade reports.

The program is divided into two parts. In the first part, we create the application program that generates the grade report in the window's console environment and stores the output in a file.

In the second part, which is available at the Web site and the CD accompanying this book, we create a GUI to display the students' grade reports, as shown in the section Student Grade Report: GUI Design.

For this report, the data is stored in a file in the following form:

PART I:
STUDENT
GRADE
REPORT:
CONSOLE
DISPLAY

```
noOfStudents tuitionRate
studentName studentID isTuitionPaid numberOfCourses
courseName courseNumber creditHours grade
courseName courseNumber creditHours grade
   .
   .
   .

studentName studentID isTuitionPaid numberOfCourses
courseName courseNumber creditHours grade
courseName courseNumber creditHours grade
   .
   .
   .
```

The first line indicates the number of students enrolled and the tuition rate per credit hour. The students' data is given thereafter.

A sample input file follows:

```
3 345
Lisa Miller 890238 Y 4
Mathematics MTH345 4 A
Physics PHY357 3 B
ComputerSci CSC478 3 B
History HIS356 3 A
   .
   .
   .
```

The first line indicates that 3 students are enrolled and the tuition rate is $345 per credit hour. Next, the course data for student Lisa Miller is given: Lisa Miller's ID is 890238, she has paid the tuition, and is taking 4 courses. The course number for the mathematics class she is taking is MTH345, the course has 4 credit hours, her mid-semester grade is A, and so on. The output of the program is of the following form:

```
Student Name: Lisa Miller
Student ID: 890238
Number of courses enrolled: 4
```

```
Course No   Course Name  Credits Grade
CSC478      ComputerSci     3      B
HIS356      History         3      A
MTH345      Mathematics     4      A
PHY357      Physics         3      B

Total number of credit hours: 13
Midsemester GPA: 3.54
```

It is clear from this output that the courses must be ordered according to the course number. To calculate the GPA, we assume that the grade A is equivalent to 4 points, B is equivalent to 3 points, C is equivalent to 2 points, D is equivalent to 1 point, and F is equivalent to 0 points.

Input: A file containing the data in the form given previously. For easy reference in the rest of the discussion, let's assume that the name of the input file is stData.txt.

Output: A file containing the output of the form given previously.

ROBLEM
NALYSIS AND
LGORITHM
ESIGN

We must first identify the main components of the program. The college or university has students, and every student takes courses. Thus, the two main components are the student and the course.

Let's first describe the component Course.

Course

The main characteristics of a course are the course name, course number, and number of credit hours.

Some of the basic operations that need to be performed on an object of the course type are:

1. Set the course information.
2. Print the course information.
3. Show the credit hours.
4. Show the course number.

Next, we define the members of the class Course.

Instance Variables:

```
private String courseName;    //object to store the course name
private String courseNo;      //object to store the course number
private int courseCredits;    //variable to store the course
                              //credits
```

Constructors and Instance Methods:

```
public void setCourseInfo(String cName, String cNo,
                          int credits)
   //Method to set the course information
   //The course information is set according to the
   //incoming parameters.
   //Postcondition: courseName = cName; courseNo = cNo;
   //               courseCredits = credits;

public void setCourseName(String cName)
   //Method to set the course Name
   //Postcondition: courseName = cName;

public void setCourseNumber(String cNo)
   //Method to set the course Number
   //Postcondition: courseNo = cNo;

public void setCourseCredits(int credits)
   //Method to set the course credits
   //Postcondition: courseCredits = credits;

public String toString()
   //Method to return the course information as a string
   //Postcondition: The course information is returned
   //               as a string.

public String getCourseName()
   //Method to return the course name
   //Postcondition: The value of courseName is returned.

public String getCourseNumber()
   //Method to return the course number
   //Postcondition: The value of courseNo is returned.

public int getCredits()
   //Method to return the credit hours
   //Postcondition: The value of courseCredits is returned.

public void copyCourseInfo(Course otherCourse)
   //Method to copy a course's information.
   //otherCourse is copied into this course
   //Postcondition: courseName = otherCourse.courseName;
   //               courseNo = otherCourse.courseNo;
   //               courseCredits = otherCourse.courseCredits;

public Course()
   //Default Constructor
   //The object is initialized to the default values.
   //Postcondition: courseName = ""; courseNo = "";
   //               courseCredits = 0;
```

```
public Course(String cName, String cNo, int credits)
   //Constructor
   //The object is initialized according to the parameters.
   //Postcondition: courseName = cName; courseNo = cNo;
   //                courseCredits = credits;
```

Figure 10-18 shows the UML class diagram of the class Course.

```
                    Course
-courseName: String
-courseNo: String
-courseCredits: int

+Course()
+Course(String, String, int)
+setCourseInfo(String, String, int): void
+setCourseName(String): void
+setCourseNumber(String): void
+setCourseCredits(int): void
+toString(): String
+getCourseName(): String
+getCourseNumber(): String
+getCredits(): int
+copyCourseInfo(Course): void
```

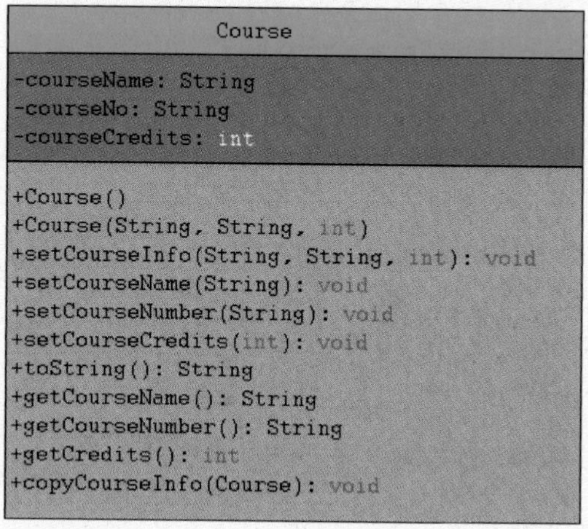

FIGURE 10-18 UML class diagram of the class Course

Next, we discuss the definition of the methods to implement the operations of the class Course.

The method setCourseInfo sets the values of the instance variables according to the values of the parameters. Its definition is:

```
public void setCourseInfo(String cName, String cNo,
                          int credits)
{
    courseName = cName;
    courseNo = cNo;
    courseCredits = credits;
}
```

The definitions of the methods setCourseName, setCourseNumber, and setCourseCredits are similar to the method setCourseInfo. Their definitions are:

```java
public void setCourseName(String cName)
{
    courseName = cName;
}

public void setCourseNumber(String cNo)
{
    courseNo = cNo;
}

public void setCourseCredits(int credits)
{
    courseCredits = credits;
}
```

The method toString returns the course information as a string. Its definition is:

```java
public String toString()
{
    return String.format("%-12s%-15s%4s", courseNo,
                         courseName, courseCredits);
} //end toString
```

The definitions of the remaining methods and constructors are as follows:

```java
public Course(String cName, String cNo, int credits)
{
    courseName = cName;
    courseNo = cNo;
    courseCredits = credits;
}

public Course()
{
    courseName = "";
    courseNo = "";
    courseCredits = 0;
}

public String getCourseName()
{
    return courseName;
}

public String getCourseNumber()
{
    return courseNo;
}
```

```java
public int getCredits()
{
    return courseCredits;
}

public void copyCourseInfo(Course otherCourse)
{
    courseName = otherCourse.courseName;
    courseNo = otherCourse.courseNo;
    courseCredits = otherCourse.courseCredits;
}
```

The definition of the **class** Course looks like the following: (You can complete the definition of this class as an exercise.)

```java
import java.io.*;

public class Course
{
    private String courseName;    //object to store the
                                  //course name
    private String courseNo;      //object to store the
                                  //course number
    private int courseCredits;    //variable to store the
                                  //course credits
        //Place the definitions of the instance methods
        //as discussed here.
}
```

Next, we discuss the component **Student**.

The main characteristics of a student are the student name, student ID, number of courses in which the student is enrolled, courses in which the student is enrolled, and the grade for each course. Because every student must pay tuition, we also include a member to indicate whether the student has paid the tuition.

Every student is a person, and every student takes courses. We have already designed a **class** Person to process a person's first and last name. We have also designed a class to process the course information. Thus, we see that we can derive the **class** Student to keep track of a student's information from the **class** Person, and one member of the **class** Student is of type Course. We can add more members as needed.

The basic operations to be performed on an object of type **Student** are as follows:

1. Set the student information.
2. Print the student information.
3. Calculate the number of credit hours taken.

4. Calculate the GPA.

5. Calculate the billing amount.

6. Because the grade report will print the courses in ascending order, sort the courses according to the course number.

Next, we define the members of the class Student.

Instance Variables:

```
private int sId;                //variable to store the
                                //student ID
private int numberOfCourses;    //variable to store the number
                                //of courses
private boolean isTuitionPaid;  //variable to indicate if
                                //the tuition is paid

private Course [] coursesEnrolled; //array to store
                                      //the courses
private char [] courseGrades;   //array to store the
                                //course grades
```

Constructors and Instance Methods:

```
public void setInfo(String fName, String lName, int ID,
               int nOfCourses, boolean isTPaid,
               Course[] courses, char[] cGrades)
   //Method to set a student's information
   //Postcondition: The instance variables are set according
   //               to the parameters.

public void setStudentId(int ID)
   //Method to set a student ID
   //Postcondition: sId = ID;

public void setIsTuitionPaid(boolean isTPaid)
   //Method to set whether tuition is paid
   //Postcondition: isTuitionPaid = isTPaid;

public void setNumberOfCourses(int nOfCourses)
   //Method to set number of courses taken
   //Postcondition: numberOfCourses = nOfCourses;

public void setCoursesEnrolled(Course[] courses,
                               char[] cGrades)
   //Method to set courses enrolled
   //Postcondition: array courses is copied into the array
   //        coursesEnrolled, array cGrades is copied into
   //        the array courseGrades, and these arrays are
   //        sorted.
```

```java
public String toString()
    //Method to return a student's grade report as a string
    //Postcondition: If the instance variable isTuitionPaid
    //          is true, the grades are returned; otherwise
    //          three stars are returned.

public int getStudentId()
    //Method to get a student ID
    //Postcondition: The value of sId is returned.

public boolean getIsTuitionPaid()
    //Method to return a value specifying if the tuition is paid
    //Postcondition: The value of isTuitionPaid is returned.

public int getNumberOfCourses()
    //Method to get the number of courses taken
    //Postcondition: The value of numberOfCourses is returned.

public char getGrade(int i)
    //Method to return a course grade
    //Postcondition: The value of courseGrades[i] is returned.

public Course getCourse(int i)
    //Method to get a copy of a course taken
    //Postcondition: A copy of coursesEnrolled[i]
    //              is returned.

public int getHoursEnrolled()
    //Method to return the credit hours in which a
    //student is enrolled
    //Postcondition: Total credits are calculated
    //              and returned.

public double getGpa()
    //Method to return the grade point average
    //Postcondition: GPA is calculated and returned.

public double billingAmount(double tuitionRate)
    //Method to return the tuition fees
    //Postcondition: The billing amount is calculated
    //              and returned.

private void sortCourses()
    //Method to sort the courses
    //Postcondition: The array coursesEnrolled is sorted.
    //              The grades for each course, in the
    //              array courseGrades, are also reorganized.

public Student()
    //Default constructor
    //Postcondition: The instance variables are initialized.
```

10

Figure 10-19 shows the UML class diagram of the **class** Student.

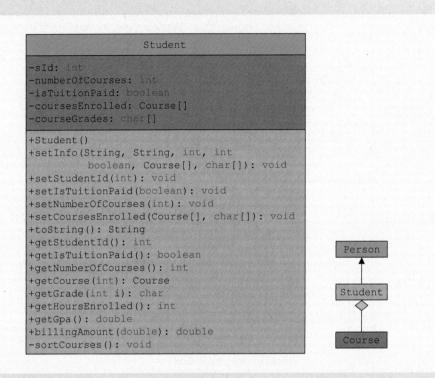

FIGURE 10-19 UML class diagram of the **class** Student

Note that the method **sortCourses** to sort the array **coursesEnrolled** is a **private** member of the **class** Student. This is because this method is needed for internal data manipulation, and the user of the class does not need to access this member.

Next, we discuss the definitions of the methods to implement the operations of the **class** Student.

The method **setInfo** first initializes the **private** data members according to the incoming parameters. This method then calls the method **sortCourses** to sort the array **coursesEnrolled** by course number. The **class** Student is derived from the **class** Person, and the variables to store the first and last name are **private** members of that class. Therefore, we call the method **setName** of the **class** Person, and we pass the appropriate variables to set the first and last names. The definition of the method **setInfo** is as follows:

```java
public void setInfo(String fName, String lName, int ID,
                    int nOfCourses, boolean isTPaid,
                    Course[] courses, char[] cGrades)
{
    setName(fName, lName);              //set the name

    sId = ID;                           //set the student ID
    isTuitionPaid = isTPaid;            //set isTuitionPaid
    numberOfCourses = nOfCourses ;      //set the number of courses

    for (int i = 0; i < numberOfCourses; i++) //set the array
    {
        coursesEnrolled[i].copyCourseInfo(courses[i]);
        courseGrades[i] = cGrades[i];
    }

    sortCourses();          //sort the array coursesEnrolled
}
```

The definitions of the methods setStudentId, setIsTuitionPaid, setNumberOfCourses, and setCoursesEnrolled are similar to the definition of the method setInfo, and are given next.

```java
public void setStudentId(int ID)
{
    sId = ID;
}

public void setIsTuitionPaid(boolean isTPaid)
{
    isTuitionPaid = isTPaid;
}

public void setNumberOfCourses(int nOfCourses)
{
     numberOfCourses = nOfCourses ;
}

public void setCoursesEnrolled(Course[] courses,
                               char[] cGrades)
{
    for (int i = 0; i < numberOfCourses; i++)
    {
        coursesEnrolled[i].copyCourseInfo(courses[i]);
        courseGrades[i] = cGrades[i];
    }

    sortCourses();
}
```

The default constructor initializes the instance variables to their default values.

```java
public Student()
{
    super();
    numberOfCourses = 0;
    sId = 0;
    isTuitionPaid = false;

    coursesEnrolled = new Course[6];

    for (int i = 0; i < 6; i++)
        coursesEnrolled[i] = new Course();

    courseGrades = new char[6];

    for (int i = 0; i < 6; i++)
        courseGrades[i] = '*';
}
```

The method `toString` returns the grade report as a string. If the student has paid his or her tuition, the grades and the GPA are returned. Otherwise, three stars are returned in place of each grade. The definition of this method is:

```java
public String toString()
{
    String gReport;

    gReport = "Student Name: "
            + super.toString() + "\r\n"
            + "Student ID: " + sId + "\r\n"
            + "Number of courses enrolled: "
            + numberOfCourses + "\r\n"
            + String.format("%-12s%-15s%-8s%-6s%n",
                            "Course No", "Course Name",
                            "Credits", "Grade");

    for (int i = 0; i < numberOfCourses; i++)
    {
        gReport = gReport + coursesEnrolled[i];

        if (isTuitionPaid)
            gReport = gReport
                    + String.format("%8s%n", courseGrades[i]);
        else
            gReport = gReport
                    + String.format("%8s%n", "***");
    }

    gReport = gReport
            + "\r\nTotal number of credit hours: "
            + getHoursEnrolled() + "\r\n";

    return gReport;
} //end toString
```

The definitions of the methods `getStudentId`, `getIsTuitionPaid`, `getNumberOfCourses`, `getCourse`, and `getGrade` are given next:

```
public int getStudentId()
{
    return sId;
}

public boolean getIsTuitionPaid()
{
    return isTuitionPaid;
}

public int getNumberOfCourses()
{
    return numberOfCourses;
}

public Course getCourse(int i)
{
    Course temp = new Course();

    temp.copyCourseInfo(coursesEnrolled[i]);

    return temp;
}

public char getGrade(int i)
{
    return courseGrades[i];
}
```

The method `getHoursEnrolled` calculates and returns the total credit hours that a student is taking. These credit hours are needed to calculate both the GPA and the billing amount. The total credit hours are calculated by adding the credit hours of each course in which the student is enrolled. Because the credit hours for a course are in the `private` data member of an object of type `Course`, we use the method `getCredits` of the `class` `Course` to retrieve the credit hours. The definition of this method is:

```
public int getHoursEnrolled()
{
    int totalCredits = 0;

    for (int i = 0; i < numberOfCourses; i++)
        totalCredits += coursesEnrolled[i].getCredits();

    return totalCredits;
}
```

If a student has not paid the tuition, the method `billingAmount` calculates and returns the amount due, based on the number of credit hours enrolled. The definition of this method is:

```
public double billingAmount(double tuitionRate)
{
    return tuitionRate * getHoursEnrolled();
}
```

We now discuss the method `getGpa`. This method calculates a student's GPA. To find the GPA, we find the equivalent points for each grade, add the points, and then divide the sum by the total credit hours the student is taking. The definition of this method is:

```
public double getGpa()
{
    double sum = 0.0;

    for (int i = 0; i < numberOfCourses; i++)
    {
        switch (courseGrades[i])
        {
        case 'A':
            sum += coursesEnrolled[i].getCredits() * 4;
            break;

        case 'B':
            sum += coursesEnrolled[i].getCredits() * 3;
            break;

        case 'C':
            sum += coursesEnrolled[i].getCredits() * 2;
            break;

        case 'D':
            sum += coursesEnrolled[i].getCredits() * 1;
            break;

        case 'F':
            sum += coursesEnrolled[i].getCredits() * 0;
            break;

        default:
            System.out.println("Invalid Course Grade");
        }
    }

    return sum / getHoursEnrolled();
}
```

The method `sortCourses` sorts the array `coursesEnrolled` by course number. To sort the array, we use a selection sort algorithm. Because we will compare the course numbers, which are the strings and `private` data members of the `class` Course, we first retrieve and store the course numbers in the local variables. Moreover, this method also rearranges the course grades because the course grades are stored in a separate array. The definition of this method is:

```java
private void sortCourses()
{
    int minIndex;
    Course temp = new Course();    //variable to swap data
    String course1;
    String course2;

    char tempGrade;

    for (int i = 0; i < numberOfCourses - 1; i++)
    {
        minIndex = i;

        for (int j = i + 1; j < numberOfCourses; j++)
        {
                //get course numbers
            course1 =
                    coursesEnrolled[minIndex].getCourseNumber();
            course2 = coursesEnrolled[j].getCourseNumber();

            if (course1.compareTo(course2) > 0)
                minIndex = j;
        }//end for

        temp.copyCourseInfo(coursesEnrolled[minIndex]);
        coursesEnrolled[minIndex].copyCourseInfo(coursesEnrolled[i]);
        coursesEnrolled[i].copyCourseInfo(temp);

        tempGrade = courseGrades[minIndex];
        courseGrades[minIndex] = courseGrades[i];
        courseGrades[i] = tempGrade;
    }//end for
}//end sortCourses
```

The definition of the `class` Student has the following form: (You can complete the definition of this class as an exercise.)

```java
import java.io.*;

public class Student extends Person
{
    private int sId;                 //variable to store the
                                     //student ID
    private int numberOfCourses;     //variable to store the number
                                     //of courses
    private boolean isTuitionPaid;   //variable to indicate if
                                     //the tuition is paid
```

```
            private Course [] coursesEnrolled; //array to store
                                               //the courses
            private char [] courseGrades;  //array to store the
                                           //course grades
            //Place the definitions of the instance methods
            //as discussed here.
            //...
    }
```

MAIN
PROGRAM

Now that we have designed the classes Course and Student, we will use these classes to complete the program.

Because the toString method of the class Student does the necessary computations to print the final grade report, the main program has very little work to do. In fact, all the main program must do is create the objects to hold the students' data, load the data into these objects, and then print the grade reports. Because the input is in a file and the output will be sent to a file, we create appropriate objects to access the input and output files. Essentially, the main algorithm for the program is:

1. Declare the variables.
2. Open the input file.
3. Open the output file.
4. Get the number of students registered and the tuition rate.
5. Load the students' data.
6. Print the grade reports.

Variables

This program first reads the number of students from the input file and then creates the array, studentList, to hold the students' data. The size of studentList is equal to the number of students.

```
Student[] studentList;

int noOfStudents;
double tuitionRate;

Scanner inFile = new Scanner(new FileReader("stData.txt"));
PrintWriter outFile = new PrintWriter("sDataOut.out");
```

To simplify the complexity of the method main, we write a method, getStudentData, to load the students' data.

Method
getStudent
Data

This method has two parameters: one to access the input file and one to access the array studentList. In pseudocode, the definition of this method is as follows:

For each student in the university:

1. Get the first name, last name, student ID, and isPaid.

2. if isPaid is 'Y'
      set isTuitionPaid to true
   else
      set isTuitionPaid to false

3. Get the number of courses the student is taking.

4. For each course:

   a. Get the course name, course number, credit hours, and grade.

   b. Load the course information into a Course object.

5. Load the data into a Student object.

We need to declare several local variables to read and store the data. The definition of the method getStudentData is:

```
public static void getStudentData(Scanner inpFile,
                                  Student[] sList)
{
        //Local variables
    String fName;       //variable to store the first name
    String lName;       //variable to store the last name
    int ID;             //variable to store the student ID
    int noOfCourses;    //variable to store the number of courses
    char isPaid;        //variable to store Y/N; that is,
                        //is the tuition paid?

    boolean isTuitionPaid;    //variable to store true/false

    String cName;   //variable to store the course name
    String cNo;     //variable to store the course number
    int credits;    //variable to store the course credit hours
    char grade;     //variable to store the course grade

    Course[] courses = new Course[6]; //array of objects to
                                      //store the course
                                      //information
    char[] courseGrades = new char[6];

    for (int i = 0; i < 6; i++)
        courses[i] = new Course();

    for (int count = 0; count < sList.length; count++)
    {
            //Step 1
        fName = inpFile.next();
        lName = inpFile.next();
        ID = inpFile.nextInt();
        isPaid = inpFile.next().charAt(0);
```

1
0

```
        if (isPaid == 'Y')                         //Step 2
            isTuitionPaid = true;
        else
            isTuitionPaid = false;

        noOfCourses = inpFile.nextInt();           //Step 3

        for (int i = 0; i < noOfCourses; i++)      //Step 4
        {
            cName = inpFile.next();
            cNo = inpFile.next();
            credits = inpFile.nextInt();
            courseGrades[i] = inpFile.next().charAt(0);

            courses[i].setCourseInfo(cName, cNo, credits);
        }

        sList[count].setInfo(fName, lName, ID,
                        noOfCourses, isTuitionPaid,
                        courses, courseGrades);   //Step 5
    }//end for
} //end getStudentData
```

Method printGrade Reports

This method prints the grade reports. The definition of the method printGradeReports is:

```
public static void printGradeReports(PrintWriter outpFile,
                                        Student[] sList,
                                        double tuitionRate)
{
    for (int count = 0; count < sList.length; count++)
    {
        outpFile.print(sList[count]);

        if (sList[count].getIsTuitionPaid())
            outpFile.printf("Midsemester GPA: %.2f%n",
                            sList[count].getGpa());
        else
        {
            outpFile.println("*** Grades are being held for "
                        + "not paying the tuition. ***");
            outpFile.printf("Amount Due: $%.2f%n",
                        sList[count].billingAmount(tuitionRate));
        }

        outpFile.println("-*-*-*-*-*-*-*-*-*-*-*-*-*-"
                        + "*-*-*-*-*-*-*-*-*-*-*-\r\n");
    }
} //end printGradeReports
```

PROGRAM LISTING

```java
//****************************************************************
// Author: D.S. Malik
//
// Program: Student Grade Report
// This program reads students' data from a file and outputs
// the grades. If a student has not paid the tuition, the
// grades are not shown, and an appropriate message is output.
// The output is stored in a file.
//****************************************************************

import java.io.*;
import java.util.*;

public class GradeReportProgram
{
    public static void main(String[] args) throws
                                    FileNotFoundException
    {
        int noOfStudents;
        double tuitionRate;

        Scanner inFile =
                new Scanner(new FileReader("stData.txt"));
        PrintWriter outFile =
                new PrintWriter("sDataOut.out");

        noOfStudents = inFile.nextInt();      //get the number
                                              //of students
        tuitionRate = inFile.nextDouble();    //get the tuition
                                              //rate

        Student[] studentList =
                new Student[noOfStudents];

        for (int i = 0; i < studentList.length; i++)
            studentList[i] = new Student();

        getStudentData(inFile, studentList);
        printGradeReports(outFile, studentList, tuitionRate);

        inFile.close();
        outFile.close();
    }

    //Place the definition of the method getStudentData as
    //described above

    //Place the definition of the method printGradeReports as
    //described above
}
```

1
0

Sample Run:

```
Student Name: Lisa Miller
Student ID: 890238
Number of courses enrolled: 4
Course No   Course Name   Credits Grade
CSC478      ComputerSci      3      B
HIS356      History          3      A
MTH345      Mathematics      4      A
PHY357      Physics          3      B

Total number of credit hours: 13
Midsemester GPA: 3.54
-*-*-*-*-*-*-*-*-*-*-*-*-*-*-*-*-*-*-*-*-*-*-*-

Student Name: Bill Wilton
Student ID: 798324
Number of courses enrolled: 5
Course No   Course Name   Credits Grade
BIO234      Biology          4      ***
CHM256      Chemistry        4      ***
ENG378      English          3      ***
MTH346      Mathematics      3      ***
PHL534      Philosophy       3      ***

Total number of credit hours: 17
*** Grades are being held for not paying the tuition. ***
Amount Due: 5865.00
-*-*-*-*-*-*-*-*-*-*-*-*-*-*-*-*-*-*-*-*-*-*-*-

Student Name: Dandy Goat
Student ID: 746333
Number of courses enrolled: 6
Course No   Course Name   Credits Grade
BUS128      Business         3      C
CHM348      Chemistry        4      B
CSC201      ComputerSci      3      B
ENG328      English          3      B
HIS101      History          3      A
MTH137      Mathematics      3      A

Total number of credit hours: 19
Midsemester GPA: 3.16
-*-*-*-*-*-*-*-*-*-*-*-*-*-*-*-*-*-*-*-*-*-*-*-
```

Input File

```
3 345
Lisa Miller 890238 Y 4
Mathematics MTH345 4 A
Physics PHY357 3 B
ComputerSci CSC478 3 B
History HIS356 3 A
```

```
Bill Wilton 798324 N 5
English ENG378 3 B
Philosophy PHL534 3 A
Chemistry CHM256 4 C
Biology BIO234 4 A
Mathematics MTH346 3 C

Dandy Goat 746333 Y 6
History HIS101 3 A
English ENG328 3 B
Mathematics MTH137 3 A
Chemistry CHM348 4 B
ComputerSci CSC201 3 B
Business BUS128 3 C
```

> **NOTE** A GUI version of this program is available on the Web site and CD accompanying this book.

QUICK REVIEW

1. Inheritance and composition (aggregation) are meaningful ways to relate two or more classes.

2. Inheritance is an "is-a" relationship.

3. Composition (aggregation) is a "has-a" relationship.

4. In single inheritance, the subclass is derived from only one existing class, called the superclass.

5. In multiple inheritance, a subclass is derived from more than one superclass. Java does not support true multiple inheritance; that is, in Java, a class can only *extend* the definition of one class.

6. The `private` members of a superclass are `private` to the superclass. The subclass cannot directly access them.

7. A subclass can override the methods of a superclass, but this redefinition is available only to the objects of the subclass.

8. In general, while writing the definitions of the methods of a subclass to specify a call to a `public` method of a superclass, we do the following:

   - If the subclass overrides a `public` method of a superclass, then you specify a call to that `public` method of the superclass by using the reserved word `super`, followed by the dot operator, followed by the method name with an appropriate parameter list.

   - If the subclass does not override a `public` method of the superclass, you can specify a call to that `public` method by using the name of the method and an appropriate parameter list.

9. While writing the definition of a constructor of a subclass, a call to a constructor of the superclass is specified using the reserved word `super` with an appropriate parameter list. Moreover, the call to a constructor of the superclass must be the first statement.

10. For a superclass to give direct access to its member(s), to its subclass(es), and still prevent its direct access outside the class, such as in a user program, you must declare that member using the modifier `protected`. In fact, a class member declared with the modifier `protected` may be accessed by any class in the same package.

11. If you define a class and do not use the reserved word `extends` to derive it from an existing class, then the class you define is automatically considered to be derived from the `class` `Object`.

12. The `class` `Object` directly or indirectly becomes the superclass of every class in Java.

13. The `classes` `Scanner`, `Reader`, and `Writer` are derived from the `class` `Object`. The `class` `InputStreamReader` is derived from the `class` `Reader`, and the `class` `FileReader` is derived from the `class` `InputStreamReader`. Similarly, the `class` `PrintWriter` is derived from the `class` `Writer`.

14. Java allows us to treat an object of a subclass as an object of a superclass; that is, a reference variable of a superclass type can point to an object of a subclass type.

15. In a class hierarchy, several methods can have the same name and the same formal parameter list.

16. A reference variable of a class can refer to either an object of its own class or an object of its subclass.

17. In early binding, a method's definition is associated with its invocation when the code is compiled.

18. In late binding, a method's definition is associated with its invocation at execution time, that is, when the method is executed.

19. Except for a few (special) cases, Java uses late binding for all methods.

20. The term polymorphism means assigning multiple meanings to the same method. In Java, polymorphism is implemented using late binding.

21. You *cannot* automatically consider a superclass object to be an object of a subclass. In other words, you *cannot* automatically make a reference variable of a subclass type point to an object of a superclass type.

22. Suppose that `supRef` is a reference variable of a superclass type. Moreover, suppose that `supRef` points to an object of a subclass. You can use an appropriate cast operator on `supRef` and make a reference variable of the subclass point to the object. On the other hand, if `supRef` does not point to a subclass object, and you use a cast operator on `supRef` to make a

reference variable of the subclass point to the object, then Java will throw a `ClassCastException`—indicating that the class cast is not allowed.

23. An abstract method is a method that has only the heading, not the body. Moreover, the heading of an abstract method is terminated with a semicolon.

24. An abstract class is a class that is declared with the reserved word `abstract` in its heading.

25. The following are some of the facts about abstract classes:

- An abstract class can contain instance variables, constructors, a finalizer, and nonabstract methods.
- An abstract class can contain an abstract method(s).
- If a class contains an abstract method, then the class must be declared abstract.
- You cannot instantiate an object of an abstract class. You can only declare a reference variable of an abstract class type.
- You can instantiate an object of a subclass of an abstract class, but only if the subclass gives the definitions of *all* the abstract methods of the superclass.

26. An `interface` is a class that contains only abstract methods and/or named constants.

27. Java allows a class to implement more than one interface. This is, in fact, the way to implement a form of multiple inheritance in Java.

28. In composition, one or more members of a class are objects of one or more other classes.

EXERCISES

1. Mark the following statements as true or false.

   a. The constructor of a subclass specifies a call to the constructor of the superclass in the heading of the constructor's definition.

   b. The constructor of a subclass specifies a call to the constructor of the superclass using the name of the class.

   c. A subclass must define a constructor.

   d. In Java, polymorphism is implemented using late binding.

2. Draw a class hierarchy in which several classes are subclasses of a single superclass.

3. Suppose that a `class Employee` is derived from the `class Person` (see Example 8-7, in Chapter 8). Give examples of data and method members that can be added to the `class Employee`.

4. Explain the difference between the `private` and `protected` members of a class.

5. What is the difference between overloading a method name and overriding a method name?

6. Name two situations in which you would use the reserved word `super`.

7. Consider the following class definition:

```java
public class AClass
{
    private int u;
    private int v;

    public void print()
    {
    }

    public void set(int x, int y)
    {
    }

    public AClass()
    {
    }

    public AClass(int x, int y)
    {
    }
}
```

What is wrong with the following class definition?

```java
class BClass AClass
{
    private int w;

    public void print()
    {
        System.out.println("u + v + w = " + (u + v + w));
    }

    public BClass()
    {
        super();
        w = 0;
    }

    public BClass(int x, int y, int z)
    {
        super(x, y);
        w = z;
    }
}
```

8. Consider the following statements:

```java
public class YClass
{
    private int a;
    private int b;

    public void one()
    {
    }

    public void two(int x, int y);
    {
    }

    public YClass()
    {
    }
}

class XClass extends YClass
{
    private int z;

    public void one()
    {
    }

    public XClass()
    {
    }
}

YClass yObject;
XClass xObject;
```

a. The **private** members of YClass are **public** members of XClass. True or False?

b. Mark the following statements as valid or invalid. If a statement is invalid, explain why.

   i. The following is a valid definition of the method one of YClass.
   ```java
   public void one()
   {
       System.out.println(a + b);
   }
   ```

   ii. yObject.a = 15;

   iii. xObject.b = 30;

iv. The following is a valid definition of the method one of XClass:

```
public void one()
{
    a = 10;
    b = 15;
    z = 30;
    System.out.println(a + b + z);
}
```

v.
```
System.out.println(yObject.a + " " + yObject.b + " "
                   + xObject.z);
```

9. Assume the declaration of Exercise 8.

a. Write the definition of the default constructor of YClass so that the instance variables of YClass are initialized to 0.

b. Write the definition of the default constructor of XClass so that the instance variables of XClass are initialized to 0.

c. Write the definition of the method two of YClass so that the instance variable a is initialized to the value of the first parameter of two and the instance variable b is initialized to the value of the second parameter of two.

10. Suppose that you have the following class:

```
public class classA
{
    private int x;                        //Line 1
    protected void setX(int a)            //Line 2
    {                                     //Line 3
        x = a;                            //Line 4
    }
}
```

What is wrong with the following code?

```
public class Exercise10                   //Line 5
{
    public static void main(String[] args) //Line 6
    {
        classA aObject;                   //Line 7

        aObject.setX(4);                  //Line 8
    }
}
```

11. Suppose that you have the following class definition:

```
public class One
{
    private int x;
    private int y;

    public void print()
    {
        System.out.println(x + " " + y);
    }
```

```
protected void setData(int u, int v)
{
    x = u;
    y = v;
}
}
```

Consider the following class definition:

```
public class Two extends One
{
    private int z;

    public void setData(int a, int b, int c)
    {
        //Postcondition: x = a; y = b; z = c;
    }

    public void print()
    {
        //Output the values of x, y, and z
    }
}
```

a. Write the definition of the method setData of the class Two as described in the class definition.

b. Write the definition of the method print of the class Two as described in the class definition.

12. Suppose that you have the following class definitions:

```
public class SuperClass
{
    protected int x;

    private String str;

    public void print()
    {
        System.out.println(x + " " + str);
    }

    public SuperClass()
    {
        str = "";
        x = 0;
    }

    public SuperClass(String s, int a)
    {
        str = s;
        x = a;
    }
}
```

1
0

```java
public class SubClass extends SuperClass
{
    private int y;

    public void print()
    {
        System.out.println("SubClass: " + y);
        super.print();
    }

    public SubClass()
    {
        super();
        y = 0;
    }

    public SubClass(String s, int a, int b)
    {
        super("Hello Super", a + b);
        y = b;
    }
}
```

What is the output of the following Java code?

```java
SuperClass superObject = new SuperClass("This is superclass", 2);
SubClass subObject = new SubClass("DDDDDD", 3, 7);

superObject.print();
subObject.print();
```

13. What does the operator `instanceof` do?

14. What is an abstract method?

15. What is the difference between an abstract class and an interface?

16. Why does Java allow a class to implement more than one interface?

PROGRAMMING EXERCISES

1. In Chapter 8, the `class Clock` was designed to implement the time of day in a program. Certain applications, in addition to hours, minutes, and seconds, might require you to store the time zone. Derive the `class ExtClock` from the `class Clock` by adding a data member to store the time zone. Add the necessary methods and constructors to make the class functional. Also, write the definitions of the methods and the constructors. Finally, write a test program to test your class.

2. In this chapter, the `class Date` was designed to implement the date in a program, but the method `setDate` and the constructor with parameters do not check whether the date is valid before storing the date in the data

members. Rewrite the definitions of the method `setDate` and the constructor with parameters so that the values of month, day, and year are checked before storing the date into the data members. Add a method `isLeapYear` to check whether a year is a leap year. Then, write a test program to test your class.

3. A point in the x-y plane is represented by its x-coordinate and y-coordinate. Design the **class** `Point` that can store and process a point in the x-y plane. You should then perform operations on a point, such as showing the point, setting the coordinates of the point, printing the coordinates of the point, returning the x-coordinate, and returning the y-coordinate. Also, write a test program to test various operations on a point.

4. Every circle has a center and a radius. Given the radius, we can determine the circle's area and circumference. Given the center, we can determine its position in the x-y plane. The center of a circle is a point in the x-y plane. Design the **class** `Circle` that can store the radius and center of the circle. Because the center is a point in the x-y plane and you designed the class to capture the properties of a point in Programming Exercise 3, you must derive the **class** `Circle` from the **class** `Point`. You should be able to perform the usual operations on a circle, such as setting the radius, printing the radius, calculating and printing the area and circumference, and carrying out the usual operations on the center.

5. Every cylinder has a base and height, where the base is a circle. Design the **class** `Cylinder` that can capture the properties of a cylinder and perform the usual operations on a cylinder. Derive this class from the **class** `Circle` designed in Programming Exercise 4. Some of the operations that can be performed on a cylinder are as follows: calculate and print the volume, calculate and print the surface area, set the height, set the radius of the base, and set the center of the base.

6. Using classes, design an online address book to keep track of the names, addresses, phone numbers, and birthdays of family members, close friends, and certain business associates. Your program should be able to handle a maximum of 500 entries.

    a. Define the **class** `Address` that can store a street address, city, state, and zip code. Use the appropriate methods to print and store the address. Also, use constructors to automatically initialize the data members.

    b. Define the **class** `ExtPerson` using the **class** `Person` (as defined in Example 8-7, Chapter 8), the **class** `Date` (as designed in this chapter's Programming Exercise 2), and the **class** `Address`. Add a data member to this class to classify the person as a family member, friend, or business associate. Also, add a data member to store the phone number. Add (or override) methods to print and store the appropriate information. Use constructors to automatically initialize the data members.

c. Define the **class AddressBook** using previously defined classes. An object of type **AddressBook** should be able to process a maximum of 500 entries.

The program should perform the following operations:

i. Load the data into the address book from a disk.

ii. Sort the address book by last name.

iii. Search for a person by last name.

iv. Print the address, phone number, and date of birth (if available) of a given person.

v. Print the names of the people whose birthdays are in a given month or between two given dates.

vi. Print the names of all the people between two last names.

7. In Programming Exercise 2, the **class Date** was designed and implemented to keep track of a date, but it has very limited operations. Redefine the **class Date** so that, in addition to the operations already defined, it can perform the following operations on a date:

a. Set the month.

b. Set the day.

c. Set the year.

d. Return the month.

e. Return the day.

f. Return the year.

g. Test whether the year is a leap year.

h. Return the number of days in the month. For example, if the date is 3-12-2011, the number of days to be returned is 31, because there are 31 days in March.

i. Return the number of days passed in the year. For example, if the date is 3-18-2011, the number of days passed in the year is 77. Note that the number of days returned also includes the current day.

j. Return the number of days remaining in the year. For example, if the date is 3-18-2011, the number of days remaining in the year is 288.

k. Calculate the new date by adding a fixed number of days to the date. For example, if the date is 3-18-2011 and the days to be added are 25, the new date is 4-12-2011.

l. Return a reference to the object containing a copy of the date.

m. Make a copy of another date. Given a reference to an object containing a date, copy the data members of the object into the corresponding data members of this object.

n. Write the definitions of the methods to implement the operations defined for the **class Date**.

8. The **class Date** defined in Programming Exercise 7 prints the date in numerical form. Some applications might require the date to be printed in another form, such as March 24, 2011. Derive the **class ExtDate** so that the date can be printed in either form.

Add a data member to the **class ExtDate** so that the month can also be stored in string form. Add a method to output the month in the string format followed by the year—for example, in the form March 2011.

Write the definitions of the methods to implement the operations for the **class ExtDate**.

9. Using the **classes ExtDate** (Programming Exercise 8) and **Day** (Chapter 8, Programming Exercise 3), design the **class Calendar** so that, given the month and the year, we can print the calendar for that month. To print a monthly calendar, you must know the first day of the month and the number of days in that month. Thus, you must store the first day of the month, which is of the form **Day**, and the month and the year of the calendar. Clearly, the month and the year can be stored in an object of the form **ExtDate** by setting the day component of the date to **1**, and the month and year as specified by the user. Thus, the **class Calendar** has two data members: an object of type **Day** and an object of type **ExtDate**.

Design the **class Calendar** so that the program can print a calendar for any month starting January 1, 1500. Note that the day for January 1 of the year 1500 was a Monday. To calculate the first day of a month, you can add the appropriate number of days to Monday, January 1, 1500.

For the **class Calendar**, include the following operations:

a. Determine the first day of the month for which the calendar will be printed. Call this operation **firstDayOfMonth**.

b. Set the month.

c. Set the year.

d. Return the month.

e. Return the year.

f. Print the calendar for the particular month.

g. Add the appropriate constructors to initialize the data members.

10. a. Write the definitions of the methods of the **class** **Calendar** (designed in Programming Exercise 9) to implement the operations of the **class** **Calendar**.

   b. Write a test program to print the calendar for either a particular month or a particular year. For example, the calendar for September 2014 is:

```
                       September 2014
   Sun    Mon    Tue    Wed    Thu    Fri    Sat
           1      2      3      4      5      6
    7      8      9     10     11     12     13
   14     15     16     17     18     19     20
   21     22     23     24     25     26     27
   28     29     30
```

11. In the Grade Report programming example, the **class** **Student** contains two array instance variables, **coursesEnrolled** and **courseGrades**, to store the courses a student is taking and the grades in those courses. Redo the Grade Report programming example by defining the **class** **CourseAndGrade** that has two instance variables—**courseEnrolled** of type **Course** and **courseGrade** of type **char**. Add appropriate constructors and methods in this **class** to manipulate the instance variables. In the **class** **Student**, use an array instance variable **coursesEnrolled** of type **CourseAndGrade** to store the courses a student is taking and the grade for each course.

12. In the Grade Report programming example, we created the **classes** **Course** and **Student**, and in the main program we created an array to hold student data. Redo this programming example by defining the **class** **StudentList** with an instance variable to hold students' data, an instance variable to store the number of students, and an instance variable to store the tuition rate. This class contains methods to load students' data in the array and output grade reports and the appropriate constructors. The method **main** in a separate class uses the **class** **StudentList** to create grade reports. Also, write a program to test your class.

13. Complete Example 10-7 by writing the definitions of the eight classes. Also write a program to test your classes.

HANDLING EXCEPTIONS AND EVENTS

IN THIS CHAPTER, YOU WILL:

- Learn what an exception is
- Learn how to use a **try/catch** block to handle exceptions
- Become acquainted with the hierarchy of exception classes
- Learn about checked and unchecked exceptions
- Learn how to handle exceptions within a program
- Discover how to throw and rethrow an exception
- Learn how to handle events in a program

The File Input/Output section in Chapter 3 defined an *exception* as an occurrence of an undesirable situation that can be detected during program execution. For example, division by zero and inputting invalid data are exceptions. Similarly, trying to open an input file that does not exist is an exception, as is an array index that is outside the bounds of the array.

Until now, our programs have not included any code to handle exceptions. If exceptions occurred during program execution, the program terminated with an appropriate error message. However, there are situations when an exception occurs and you don't want the program to simply ignore the exception and terminate. For example, a program that monitors stock performance should not automatically sell if the value of the stock exceeds a certain threshold. It should inform the stockholder and request an appropriate action.

This chapter provides more detail about exceptions and describes how they are handled in Java. You will learn about different kinds of exceptions and the options available to programmers for dealing with them. You'll also extend what you learned in Chapters 6 and 10 about event handling.

Handling Exceptions Within a Program

Chapter 2 stated that if you try to input incompatible data into a variable, the program will terminate with an error message indicating that an exception has occurred. For example, inputting a letter or number containing a nondigit character into an `int` variable would cause an exception to occur. Before we discuss how to handle exceptions, let us give some examples that show what can happen if an exception is not handled.

The program in Example 11-1 shows what happens when division by zero is attempted or an invalid input occurs and the problem is not addressed.

EXAMPLE 11-1

```java
import java.util.*;

public class ExceptionExample1
{
    static Scanner console = new Scanner(System.in);

    public static void main(String[] args)
    {
        int dividend, divisor, quotient;           //Line 1

        System.out.print("Line 2: Enter the "
                       + "dividend: ");             //Line 2
        dividend = console.nextInt();              //Line 3
        System.out.println();                      //Line 4
```

```
        System.out.print("Line 5: Enter the "
                        + "divisor: ");             //Line 5
        divisor = console.nextInt();                //Line 6
        System.out.println();                       //Line 7

        quotient = dividend / divisor;              //Line 8

        System.out.println("Line 9: Quotient = "
                        + quotient);                //Line 9
    }
}
```

Sample Run 1:

```
Line 2: Enter the dividend: 12

Line 5: Enter the divisor: 5

Line 9: Quotient = 2
```

Sample Run 2:

```
Line 2: Enter the dividend: 24

Line 5: Enter the divisor: 0

Exception in thread "main" java.lang.ArithmeticException: / by zero
        at ExceptionExample1.main(ExceptionExample1.java:22)
```

Sample Run 3:

```
Line 2: Enter the dividend: 2e
Exception in thread "main" java.util.InputMismatchException
        at java.util.Scanner.throwFor(Unknown Source)
        at java.util.Scanner.next(Unknown Source)
        at java.util.Scanner.nextInt(Unknown Source)
        at java.util.Scanner.nextInt(Unknown Source)
        at ExceptionExample1.main(ExceptionExample1.java:14)
```

In Sample Run 1, the value of `divisor` is nonzero, so no exception occurred. The program calculated and printed the quotient and terminated normally.

In Sample Run 2, the value entered for `divisor` is 0. The statement in Line 8 divides `dividend` by the divisor. However, the program does not check whether `divisor` is 0 before attempting to divide `dividend` by `divisor`. So the program terminates with the message as shown.

In Sample Run 3, the value entered is `2e`. This input cannot be expressed as an `int` value; therefore, the method `nextInt` in Line 3 throws an `InputMismatchException` and the program terminates with the error message as shown.

11

On some systems, you may get the following output for Sample Run 3:

```
Line 2: Enter the dividend: 2e
Exception in thread "main" java.util.InputMismatchException
        at java.util.Scanner.throwFor(Scanner.java:819)
        at java.util.Scanner.next(Scanner.java:1431)
        at java.util.Scanner.nextInt(Scanner.java:2040)
        at java.util.Scanner.nextInt(Scanner.java:2000)
        at ExceptionExample1.main(ExceptionExample1.java:14)
```

Next, consider Example 11-2. This is the same program as in Example 11-1, except that in Line 8, using an `if` statement, a common programming practice, the program checks whether `divisor` is zero. (Later in this chapter we will explain how to use Java's mechanism to handle an `InputMismatchException`.)

EXAMPLE 11-2

```java
import java.util.*;

public class ExceptionExample2
{
    static Scanner console = new Scanner(System.in);

    public static void main(String[] args)
    {
        int dividend, divisor, quotient;           //Line 1

        System.out.print("Line 2: Enter the "
                        + "dividend: ");            //Line 2
        dividend = console.nextInt();              //Line 3
        System.out.println();                      //Line 4

        System.out.print("Line 5: Enter the "
                        + "divisor: ");             //Line 5
        divisor = console.nextInt();               //Line 6
        System.out.println();                      //Line 7

        if (divisor != 0)                          //Line 8
        {
            quotient = dividend / divisor;         //Line 9
            System.out.println("Line 10: "
                            + "Quotient = "
                            + quotient);           //Line 10
        }
        else
            System.out.println("Line 11: Cannot "
                            + "divide by zero.");  //Line 11
    }
}
```

Sample Run 1:

```
Line 2: Enter the dividend: 12

Line 5: Enter the divisor: 5

Line 10: Quotient = 2
```

Sample Run 2:

```
Line 2: Enter the dividend: 24

Line 5: Enter the divisor: 0

Line 11: Cannot divide by zero.
```

In Sample Run 1, the value of `divisor` is nonzero, so no exception occurred. The program calculated and printed the quotient and terminated normally.

In Sample Run 2, the value entered for `divisor` is 0. In Line 8, the program checks whether `divisor` is 0. Because `divisor` is zero, the expression in the `if` statement fails and the `else` part executes, which outputs the third line of the sample run.

Java's Mechanism of Exception Handling

Example 11-1 shows what happens when a division by zero or an input mismatch exception occurs in a program and is not processed. Example 11-2 shows a way to handle a division by zero exception. However, suppose that division by zero occurs in more than one place within the same block. In this case, using `if` statements may not be the most effective way to handle the exception.

Next, we describe how to handle exceptions using Java's exception handling mechanism. However, first let's note the following.

When an exception occurs, an object of a particular exception `class` is created. For example, in Sample Run 2 of Example 11-1, an object of the `class` `ArithmeticException` is created. Java provides several exception classes to effectively handle certain common exceptions, such as division by zero, invalid input, and file not found. For example, division by zero is an arithmetic error and is handled by the `class ArithmeticException`. Therefore, when a division by zero exception occurs, the program creates an object of the `class ArithmeticException`. Similarly, when a `Scanner` object is used to input data into a program, any invalid input errors are handled using the `classInputMismatchException`. Note that the `class Exception` (directly or indirectly) is the superclass of all the exception classes in Java.

NOTE   The section titled Java Exception Hierarchy describes the hierarchy of Java's various built-in exception classes. The section titled Java's Exception Classes describes some of the built-in exception classes and their methods. Both sections appear later in this chapter.

try/catch/finally Block

Statements that might generate an exception are placed in a **try** block. The **try** block might also contain statements that should not be executed if an exception occurs. The **try** block is followed by zero or more **catch** blocks. A **catch** block specifies the type of exception it can catch and contains an exception handler. The last **catch** block may or may not be followed by a **finally** block. Any code contained in a **finally** block always executes, regardless of whether an exception occurs, except when the program exits early from a **try** block by calling the method **System.exit**. If a **try** block has no **catch** block, then it *must* have the **finally** block.

As noted previously, when an exception occurs, Java creates an object of a specific exception class. For example, if a division by zero exception occurs, then Java creates an object of the **ArithmeticException class**.

The general syntax of the **try/catch/finally** block is:

```
try
{
    //statements
}
catch (ExceptionClassName1 objRef1)
{
    //exception handler code
}
catch (ExceptionClassName2 objRef2)
{
    //exception handler code
}
...
catch (ExceptionClassNameN objRefN)
{
    //exception handler code
}
finally
{
    //statements
}
```

(A **try** block contains code for normal circumstances, while a **catch** block contains code to handle an exception(s).)

Note the following about `try/catch/finally` blocks:

- If no exception is thrown in a `try` block, all `catch` blocks associated with the `try` block are ignored and program execution resumes after the last `catch` block.

- If an exception is thrown in a `try` block, the remaining statements in the `try` block are ignored. The program searches the `catch` blocks in the order in which they appear after the `try` block and looks for an appropriate exception handler.

- If the type of the thrown exception matches the parameter type in one of the `catch` blocks, the code of that `catch` block executes and the remaining `catch` blocks after this `catch` block are ignored.

- If there is a `finally` block after the last `catch` block, the `finally` block executes regardless of whether an exception occurs.

As noted, when an exception occurs, an object of a particular exception class type is created. The type of exception handled by a `catch` block is declared in the `catch` block heading, which is the statement between the parentheses after the keyword `catch`.

Consider the following `catch` block:

```
catch (ArithmeticException aeRef)
{
    //exception handler code
}
```

This `catch` block catches an exception of type `ArithmeticException`. The identifier `aeRef` is a reference variable of type `ArithmeticException`. If an exception of type `ArithmeticException` is thrown by the `try` block associated with this `catch` block, and control reaches this `catch` block, then the reference parameter `aeRef` contains the address of the exception object thrown by the `try` block. Because `aeRef` contains the address of the exception object, you can access the exception object through the variable `aeRef`. The object `aeRef` stores a detailed description of the thrown exception. You can use the method `toString` (or the method `getMessage`) to retrieve the message containing the description of the thrown exception. Example 11-3 illustrates how to use the method `toString` to retrieve the description of the thrown exception.

ORDER OF `catch` BLOCKS

A `catch` block can catch either all exceptions of a specific type or all types of exceptions. The heading of a `catch` block specifies the type of exception it handles. As discussed in Chapter 10, a reference variable of a superclass type can point to an object of its subclass. Therefore, if in the heading of a `catch` block you declare an exception using the `class` `Exception`, then that `catch` block can catch all types of exceptions because the `class` `Exception` is the superclass of all exception classes.

Suppose that an exception occurs in a `try` block and that exception is caught by a `catch` block. Then, the remaining `catch` blocks associated with that `try` block are ignored.

Therefore, you should be careful about the order in which you list `catch` blocks following a `try` block (putting more specific exceptions before less specific exceptions). For example, consider the following sequence of `try/catch` blocks:

```
try                               //Line 1
{
    //statements
}
catch (Exception eRef)            //Line 2
{
    //statements
}
catch (ArithmeticException aeRef) //Line 3
{
    //statements
}
```

Suppose that an exception is thrown in the `try` block. Because the `catch` block in Line 2 can catch exceptions of all types, the `catch` block in Line 3 cannot be reached. This sequence of `try/catch` blocks would, in fact, result in a compile-time error. In general, if a `catch` block of a superclass appears before a `catch` block of a subclass, a compilation error will occur. Therefore, in a sequence of `catch` blocks following a `try` block, a `catch` block declaring an exception of a subclass type should be placed before `catch` blocks declaring exceptions of a superclass type. Often it is useful to make sure that all exceptions which might be thrown by a `try` block are caught. In this case, you should make the `catch` block that declares an exception of the `class Exception` type the last `catch` block.

USING `try/catch` BLOCKS IN A PROGRAM

Next, we give some examples to illustrate how `try/catch` blocks might appear in a program.

As shown in Example 11-1, a common error that might occur while inputting numeric data is typing a nonnumeric character, such as a letter. If the input is invalid, the methods `nextInt` and `nextDouble` throw an `InputMismatchException`. Similarly, another error that might occur when performing numeric calculations is division by zero with integer values. In this case, the program throws an exception of the `class ArithmeticException`. The following program shows how to handle these exceptions.

EXAMPLE 11-3

```java
import java.util.*;

public class ExceptionExample3
{
    static Scanner console = new Scanner(System.in);

    public static void main(String[] args)           //Line 1
    {
        int dividend, divisor, quotient;             //Line 2
```

```
    try                                              //Line 3
    {
        System.out.print("Line 4: Enter the "
                    + "dividend: ");                 //Line 4
        dividend = console.nextInt();                //Line 5
        System.out.println();                        //Line 6

        System.out.print("Line 7: Enter the "
                    + "divisor: ");                  //Line 7
        divisor = console.nextInt();                 //Line 8
        System.out.println();                        //Line 9

        quotient = dividend / divisor;               //Line 10
        System.out.println("Line 11: Quotient = "
                    + quotient);                     //Line 11
    }
    catch (ArithmeticException aeRef)                //Line 12
    {
        System.out.println("Line 13: Exception "
                    + aeRef.toString());             //Line 13
    }
    catch (InputMismatchException imeRef)            //Line 14
    {
        System.out.println("Line 15: Exception "
                    + imeRef.toString()); //Line 15
    }
}
}
```

Sample Run: (In these sample runs, the user input is shaded.)

Sample Run 1:

Line 4: Enter the dividend: 45

Line 7: Enter the divisor: 2

Line 11: Quotient = 22

Sample Run 2:

Line 4: Enter the dividend: 18

Line 7: Enter the divisor: 0

Line 13: Exception java.lang.ArithmeticException: / by zero

Sample Run 3:

Line 4: Enter the dividend: 2753

Line 7: Enter the divisor: 2f1
Line 15: Exception java.util.InputMismatchException

This program works as follows: The method main starts at Line 1. The statement in Line 2 declares the int variables dividend, divisor, and quotient. The try block starts at Line 3. The statement in Line 4 prompts the user to enter the value of the dividend; the statement in Line 5 stores this number in the variable dividend. The statement in Line 7 prompts the user to enter the value of divisor, and the statement in Line 8 stores this number in the variable divisor. The statement in Line 10 divides the value of dividend by the value of divisor and stores the result in quotient. The statement in Line 11 outputs the value of quotient.

The first catch block, which starts at Line 12, catches an ArithmeticException. The next catch block, which starts at Line 14, catches an InputMismatchException.

In Sample Run 1, the program did not throw any exceptions because the user entered valid data.

In Sample Run 2, the entered value of divisor is 0. Therefore, when the dividend is divided by the divisor, the statement in Line 10 throws an ArithmeticException, which is caught by the catch block starting at Line 12. The statement in Line 13 outputs the appropriate message.

In Sample Run 3, the value entered in Line 8 for the variable divisor contains the letter f, a nondigit character. Because this value cannot be converted to an integer, the statement in Line 8 throws an InputMismatchException. Notice that the InputMismatchException is thrown by the method nextInt of the class Scanner. The catch block starting at Line 14 catches this exception, and the statement in Line 15 outputs the appropriate message.

Consider again Sample Run 3. In this sample run, the input for the divisor is 2f1, which, of course, is invalid. When the expression:

```
console.nextInt()
```

in Line 8 executes, it throws an InputMismatchException because the input, 2f1, cannot be expressed as an integer. Note that because 2f1 cannot be expressed as an integer, it stays as the next input token in the input stream. That is, if the input token is invalid, then the method nextInt does not remove that input token from the input stream. To capture this invalid input and print it, you can read it as a string in the catch block, in Line 14, and then output the string. To be specific, if you replace the catch block starting at Line 14 with the following catch block:

```
catch (InputMismatchException imeRef)               //Line 14
{
    String str;                                     //Line 15

    str = console.next();                           //Line 16
    System.out.println("Line 17: Exception "
                    + imeRef.toString()
                    + " " + str );                  //Line 17
}
```

and rerun the program with the same input as in Sample Run 3, then this sample run is:

Sample Run 3 (with the modified catch block):

Line 4: Enter the dividend: `2753`

Line 7: Enter the divisor: `2f1`
Line 17: Exception java.util.InputMismatchException 2f1

The Web site, *www.course.com,* and the CD accompanying this book contain the modified program. It is named **ExceptionExample3A.java**.

As noted, when an exception occurs in a program, the program throws an object of a specific exception class. Example 11-3 illustrates how to handle an arithmetic exception and an input mismatch exception. We also noted that the `class` Exception (directly or indirectly) becomes the superclass of the exception classes. Because Java provides many classes for handling exceptions, before giving more examples of exception handling, the next few sections describe the hierarchy of Java's exception classes as well as some of the exception classes in more detail.

Java Exception Hierarchy

In the preceding sections, you learned ways to handle exceptions in a program. Chapter 8 discussed how to create your own classes. Every class you design can potentially cause exceptions. Java provides extensive support for exception handling by providing a number of exception classes. Java also allows users to create and implement their own exception classes to handle exceptions not covered by Java's exception classes. This section discusses the exception classes provided by Java.

The `class` Throwable, which is derived from the `class` Object, is the superclass of the `class` Exception, as shown in Figure 11-1.

1
1

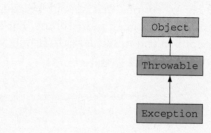

FIGURE 11-1 Java exception hierarchy

The **class** Throwable contains various constructors and methods, some of which are described in Table 11-1.

TABLE 11-1 Constructors and Methods of the **class** Throwable

```
public Throwable()
    //Default constructor
    //Creates an instance of Throwable with an empty message string

public Throwable(String strMessage)
    //Constructor with parameters
    //Creates an instance of Throwable with message string
    //specified by the parameter strMessage

public String getMessage()
    //Returns the detailed message stored in the object

public void printStackTrace()
    //Method to print the stack trace showing the sequence of
    //method calls when an exception occurs

public void printStackTrace(PrintWriter stream)
    //Method to print the stack trace showing the sequence of
    //method calls when an exception occurs. Output is sent
    //to the stream specified by the parameter stream.

public String toString()
    //Returns a string representation of the Throwable object
```

The methods getMessage, printStackTrace, and toString are **public** and are inherited by the subclasses of the **class** Throwable.

The **class** Exception and its subclasses, some of which are shown in Figures 11-2 to 11-4, are designed to catch exceptions that should be caught and processed during program execution, thus making a program more robust. The sections that follow discuss how to use the **class** Exception and its subclasses to handle various types of exceptions, and how to create your own exception classes.

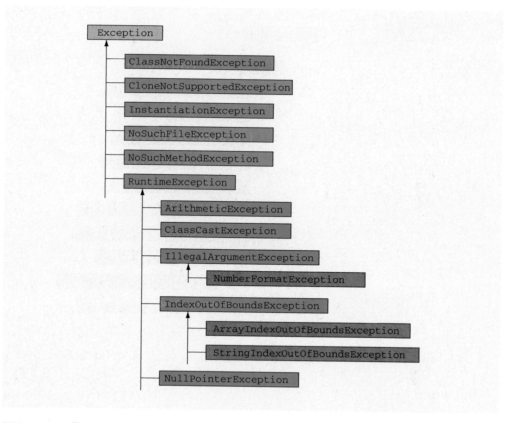

FIGURE 11-2 The **class** Exception and some of its subclasses from the **package** java.lang

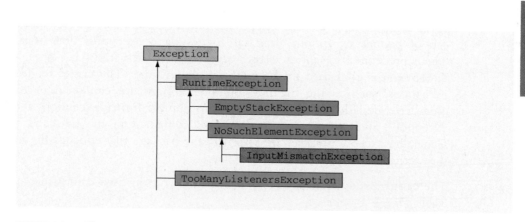

FIGURE 11-3 The **class** Exception and some of its subclasses from the **package** java.util. (Note that the **class** RuntimeException is in the **package** java.lang)

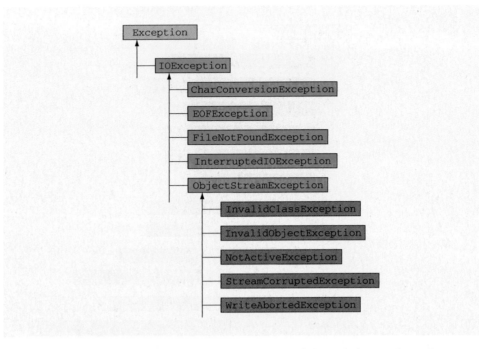

FIGURE 11-4 The **class** IOException and some of its subclasses from the **package** java.io

Java's Exception Classes

The **class** **Exception** is the superclass of the classes designed to handle exceptions. There are various types of exceptions, such as I/O exceptions, input mismatch exceptions, number format exceptions, file not found exceptions, and array index out of bounds exceptions. Java categorizes these exceptions into separate classes. These predefined exception classes are contained in various packages. The **class** **Exception** is contained in the **package** java.lang. The classes to deal with I/O exceptions, such as the file not found exception, are contained in the **package** java.io. Similarly, the classes to deal with number format exceptions and arithmetic exceptions, such as division by zero, are contained in the **package** java.lang. Generally, exception classes are placed in the package that contains the methods that throw these exceptions.

The **class** **Exception** is very simple. It only contains two constructors, as shown in Table 11-2.

TABLE 11-2 `class` Exception and its Constructors

```
public Exception()
 //Default constructor
 //Creates a new instance of the class Exception

public Exception(String str)
 //Constructor with parameters
 //Creates a new instance of the class Exception. The parameter
 //str specifies the message string.
```

Because the `class` Exception is a subclass of the `class` Throwable, the `class` Exception and its subclasses inherit the methods `getMessage`, `printStackTrace`, and `toString`. The method `getMessage` returns the string containing the detailed message stored in the exception object. The method `toString` returns the detailed message stored in the exception object as well as the name of the exception class. The method `printStackTrace` is discussed later in this chapter.

The `class` RuntimeException is the superclass of the classes designed to deal with exceptions, such as division by zero, array index out of bounds, and number format (see Figure 11-2).

Table 11-3 lists some of the exception classes and the type of exceptions they throw.

TABLE 11-3 Some of Java's Exception Classes

Exception Class	Description
ArithmeticException	Arithmetic errors such as division by zero
ArrayIndexOutOfBoundsException	Array index is either less than 0 or greater than or equal to the length of the array.
FileNotFoundException	Reference to a file that cannot be found
IllegalArgumentException	Calling a method with illegal arguments
IndexOutOfBoundsException	An array or a string index is out of bounds.
NullPointerException	Reference to an object that has not been instantiated

11

TABLE 11-3 Some of Java's Exception Classes (continued)

Exception Class	Description
NumberFormatException	Use of an illegal number format
StringIndexOutOfBoundsException	A string index is either less than 0 or greater than or equal to the length of the string.
InputMismatchException	Input (token) retrieved does not match the pattern for the expected type, or the token is out of range for the expected type.

The Java application programs in the preceding chapters used the **class** Scanner and its methods nextInt, nextDouble, next, and nextLine to input data into the programs. As shown by Sample Run 3 of Example 11-1, if the user enters an invalid value, the program terminates with an error message indicating an InputMismatchException. This exception is thrown by the method nextInt. In addition to the InputMismatchException, the methods nextInt and nextDouble can throw other exceptions, as shown in Tables 11-4 and 11-5.

TABLE 11-4 Exceptions Thrown by the Method nextInt

Exception Thrown	Description
InputMismatchException	If the next input (token) is not an integer or is out of range
NoSuchElementException	If the input is exhausted
IllegalStateException	If this scanner is closed

TABLE 11-5 Exceptions Thrown by the Method nextDouble

Exception Thrown	Description
InputMismatchException	If the next input (token) is not a floating-point number or is out of range
NoSuchElementException	If the input is exhausted
IllegalStateException	If this scanner is closed

The methods `nextInt` and `nextDouble` both throw an `InputMismatchException` if the input is invalid. The `class InputMismatchException` is a subclass of the `class NoSuchElementException`, which is a subclass of the `class RuntimeException`. The `class InputMismatchException` has only two constructors, as described in Table 11-6.

TABLE 11-6 `class` InputMismatchException and its Constructors

```
public InputMismatchException()
//Default constructor
//Creates a new instance of the class InputMismatchException.
//The error message is null.


public InputMismatchException(String str)
//Constructor with parameters
//Creates a new instance of the class InputMismatchException. The
//parameter str specifies the message string that is to be retrieved
//by the method getMessage.
```

Tables 11-7 and 11-8 show the exceptions thrown by the methods `next` and `nextLine` of the `class Scanner`.

TABLE 11-7 Exceptions Thrown by the Method next

Exception Thrown	Description
NoSuchElementException	If there is no more input (tokens)
IllegalStateException	If this scanner is closed

TABLE 11-8 Exceptions Thrown by the Method nextLine

Exception Thrown	Description
NoSuchElementException	If the input is exhausted
IllegalStateException	If this scanner is closed

In an end-of-file (EOF)-controlled `while` loop, we use the method `hasNext` of the `class Scanner` to determine whether there is a token in the input stream. Table 11-9 shows the exception thrown by the method `hasNext`.

TABLE 11-9 Exceptions Thrown by the Method hasNext

Exception Thrown	Description
IllegalStateException	If this scanner is closed

As we have seen in the previous chapters, as an input to a dialog box or a text field, Java programs accept only strings as input. Numbers, integer or decimal, are entered as strings. We then use the method `parseInt` of the `class Integer` to convert an integer string into the equivalent integer. If the string containing the integer contains only digits, the method `parseInt` will return the integer. However, if the string contains a letter or any other nondigit character, the method `parseInt` throws a `NumberFormatException`. Similarly, the method `parseDouble` also throws this exception if the string does not contain a (valid) number. The programs that we've written up to this point ignored these exceptions. Later in this chapter we show how to handle these and other exceptions.

Tables 11-10, 11-11, and 11-12 list some of the exceptions thrown by the methods of the `class`es `Integer`, `Double`, and `String`.

TABLE 11-10 Exceptions Thrown by the Methods of the `class` Integer

Method	Exception Thrown	Description
`parseInt(String str)`	`NumberFormatException`	The string `str` does not contain an `int` value.
`valueOf(String str)`	`NumberFormatException`	The string `str` does not contain an `int` value.

TABLE 11-11 Exceptions Thrown by the Methods of the `class` Double

Method	Exception Thrown	Description
`parseDouble(String str)`	`NumberFormatException`	The string `str` does not contain a `double` value.
`valueOf(String str)`	`NumberFormatException`	The string `str` does not contain a `double` value.

TABLE 11-12 Exceptions Thrown by the Methods of the **class** String

Method	Exception Thrown	Description
String(String str)	NullPointerException	str is null.
charAt(int a)	StringIndexOutOfBounds Exception	The value of a is not a valid index.
indexOf(String str)	NullPointerException	str is null.
lastIndexOf(String str)	NullPointerException	str is null.
substring(int a)	StringIndexOutOfBounds Exception	The value of a is not a valid index.
substring(int a, int b)	StringIndexOutOfBounds Exception	The value of a and/or b is not a valid index.

Checked and Unchecked Exceptions

In discussing file input/output, Chapter 3 stated that if an input file does not exist when the program executes, the program throws a FileNotFoundException. Similarly, if a program cannot create or access an output file, the program throws a FileNotFoundException. Until now, the program we have used ignored this type of exception by including the throws FileNotFoundException clause in the heading of the method. If we did not include this throws clause in the heading of the method main, the compiler would generate a syntax (compile-time) error.

On the other hand, in programs that used the methods nextInt and nextDouble, we did not include the code to check whether the input was valid or a throws clause (there was no need to do so) in the method heading to ignore these exceptions, and the compiler did not generate a syntax error. Also, we were not concerned about situations such as division by zero or array index out of bounds. If these types of errors occurred during program execution, the program terminated with an appropriate error message. For these types of exceptions, we did not need to include a throws clause in the heading of any method. So, the obvious question is: What types of exceptions need the throws clause in a method heading?

Java's predefined exceptions are divided into two categories: checked exceptions and unchecked exceptions. Any exception that the compiler can recognize is called a **checked exception**. For example, FileNotFoundExceptions are checked exceptions.

1
1

The constructors of the `classes` `FileReader` and `PrintWriter` that we used throw a `FileNotFoundException`. Therefore, these constructors throw a checked exception. When the compiler encounters the statements to open an input or output file, it checks whether the program handles `FileNotFoundExceptions`, or reports them by throwing them. Enabling the compiler to check for these types of exceptions reduces the number of exceptions not properly handled by the program. Because our programs so far were not required to handle `FileNotFoundExceptions` or other types of predefined exceptions, the programs handled the checked exceptions by throwing them. (Another common checked exception that can occur during program execution is known as `IOExceptions`. For example, the method `read` used in the Text Processing programming example, in Chapter 9, may throw an `IOException`.)

When a program is being compiled, the compiler may not be able to determine whether exceptions—such as division by zero, index out of bounds, or the next input is invalid—will occur. Therefore, the compiler does not check these types of exceptions, called **unchecked exceptions**. To significantly improve the correctness of programs, programmers must check for these types of exceptions.

Because the compiler does not check for unchecked exceptions, the program does not need to declare them using a `throws` clause or provide the code within the program to deal with them. The exceptions belonging to a subclass of the `class` `RuntimeException` are *unchecked exceptions*. Because `InputMismatchException` is a subclass of the `class` `RuntimeException`, the exceptions thrown by the methods `nextInt` and `nextDouble` are unchecked. Therefore, in all the programs that used the methods `nextInt` and `nextDouble`, we did not use the `throws` clause to throw these exceptions. If a program does not provide the code to handle an unchecked exception, the exception is handled by Java's default exception handler.

In the method heading, the `throws` clause lists the types of exceptions thrown by the method. The syntax of the `throws` clause is:

```
throws ExceptionType1, ExceptionType2, ...
```

where `ExceptionType1`, `ExceptionType2`, and so on, are the names of the exception classes.

For example, consider the following method:

```
public static void exceptionMethod()
                throws InputMismatchException, FileNotFoundException
{
    //statements
}
```

The method `exceptionMethod` throws exceptions of type `InputMismatchException` and `FileNotFoundException`.

More Examples of Exception Handling

Because Java accepts only strings as input in input dialog boxes and text fields, inputting data into a string variable won't cause any problems. However, when we use the methods `parseInt`, `parseFloat`, or `parseDouble` to convert a numeric string into its respective numeric form, the program may terminate with a number format error. This is because the methods `parseInt`, `parseFloat`, and `parseDouble` each `throw` a number format exception if the numeric string does not contain a number. For example, if the numeric string does not contain an `int` value, then when the method `parseInt` tries to determine the numeric form of the integer string, it throws a `NumberFormatException`.

EXAMPLE 11-4

This example shows how to catch and handle number format and division by zero exceptions in programs that use input dialog boxes and/or text fields.

```java
import javax.swing.JOptionPane;

public class ExceptionExample4
{
    public static void main(String[] args)              //Line 1
    {
        int dividend, divisor, quotient;                //Line 2
        String inpStr;                                  //Line 3

        try                                             //Line 4
        {
            inpStr =
                JOptionPane.showInputDialog
                    ("Enter the dividend: ");           //Line 5
            dividend = Integer.parseInt(inpStr);        //Line 6

            inpStr =
                JOptionPane.showInputDialog
                    ("Enter the divisor: ");            //Line 7
            divisor = Integer.parseInt(inpStr);         //Line 8

            quotient = dividend / divisor;              //Line 9

            JOptionPane.showMessageDialog(null,
                    "Line 10:\nDividend = " + dividend
                + "\nDivisor = " + divisor
                + "\nQuotient =" + quotient,
                    "Quotient",
                JOptionPane.INFORMATION_MESSAGE);       //Line 10
        }
```

11

```
    catch (ArithmeticException aeRef)                //Line 11
    {
        JOptionPane.showMessageDialog(null,
                "Line 12: Exception "
                + aeRef.toString(),
                "ArithmeticException",
                JOptionPane.ERROR_MESSAGE);           //Line 12
    }
    catch (NumberFormatException nfeRef)             //Line 13
    {
        JOptionPane.showMessageDialog(null,
                "Line 14: Exception "
                + nfeRef.toString(),
                "NumberFormatException",
                JOptionPane.ERROR_MESSAGE);           //Line 14
    }

    System.exit(0);                                  //Line 15
    }
}
```

Sample Runs: Figures 11-5 to 11-7 show various sample runs.

Sample Run 1:

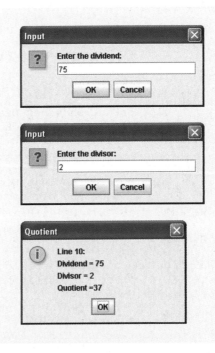

FIGURE 11-5 Sample Run 1 of the program ExceptionExample4

Sample Run 2:

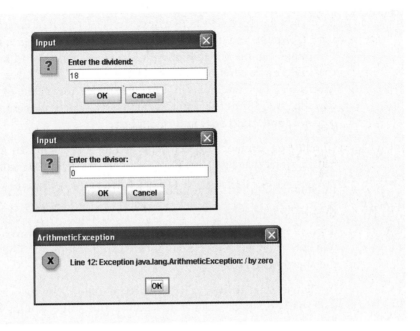

FIGURE 11-6   Sample Run 2 of the program `ExceptionExample4`

Sample Run 3:

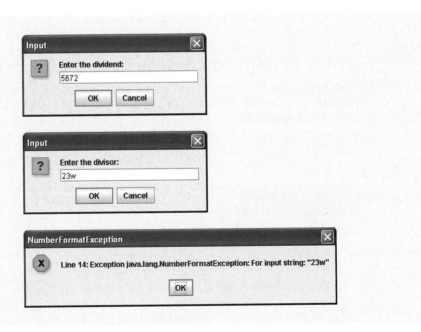

FIGURE 11-7   Sample Run 3 of the program `ExceptionExample4`

This program works as follows: The method `main` starts at Line 1. The statement in Line 2 declares the `int` variables `dividend`, `divisor`, and `quotient`. The statement in Line 3 declares the `String` variable `inpStr`. The `try` block starts at Line 4. The statement in Line 5 prompts the user to enter the value of the dividend; the statement in Line 6 stores this number in the variable `dividend`. The statement in Line 7 prompts the user to enter the value of the divisor, and the statement in Line 8 stores this number in the variable `divisor`. The statement in Line 9 divides the value of `dividend` by the value of `divisor` and stores the result in `quotient`. The statement in Line 10 outputs the values of `dividend`, `divisor`, and `quotient`.

The first `catch` block, which starts at Line 11, catches an `ArithmeticException`. The `catch` block that starts at Line 13 catches a `NumberFormatException`.

In Sample Run 1, the program did not throw any exceptions.

In Sample Run 2, the entered value of `divisor` is 0. Therefore, when the `dividend` is divided by the `divisor`, the statement in Line 9 throws an `ArithmeticException`, which is caught by the `catch` block starting at Line 11. The statement in Line 12 outputs the appropriate message.

In Sample Run 3, the value entered in Line 7 for the variable `divisor` contains the letter `w`, a nondigit character. Because this value cannot be converted to an integer, the statement in Line 8 throws a `NumberFormatException`. Note that the `NumberFormatException` is thrown by the method `parseInt` of the `class Integer`. The `catch` block starting at Line 13 catches this exception, and the statement in Line 14 outputs the appropriate message.

class Exception and the Operator instanceof

The program in Example 11-3 uses two `catch` blocks to handle two types of exceptions. Recall from Chapter 10 that a reference variable of a superclass type can point to the objects of its subclasses, and using the operator `instanceof`, you can determine whether a reference variable points to an object of a particular `class`. You can use this facility to combine the two `catch` blocks of the program in Example 11-3 into one `catch` block, as shown by the program in Example 11-5.

EXAMPLE 11-5

```java
import java.util.*;

public class ExceptionExample5
{
    static Scanner console = new Scanner(System.in);

    public static void main(String[] args)              //Line 1
```

```
{
    int dividend, divisor, quotient;                    //Line 2

    try                                                 //Line 3
    {
        System.out.print("Line 4: Enter the "
                        + "dividend: ");                //Line 4
        dividend = console.nextInt();                   //Line 5
        System.out.println();                           //Line 6

        System.out.print("Line 7: Enter the "
                        + "divisor: ");                 //Line 7
        divisor = console.nextInt();                    //Line 8
        System.out.println();                           //Line 9

        quotient = dividend / divisor;                  //Line 10
        System.out.println("Line 11: Quotient = "
                        + quotient);                    //Line 11
    }
    catch (Exception eRef)                              //Line 12
    {
        if (eRef instanceof ArithmeticException)        //Line 13
            System.out.println("Line 14: Exception "
                            + eRef.toString());         //Line 14
        else if (eRef instanceof InputMismatchException) //Line 15
            System.out.println("Line 16: Exception "
                            + eRef.toString());         //Line 16
    }
}
}
```

This program works the same way as the program in Example 11-3. This program, however, has only one **catch** block, which can catch all types of exceptions (see the statement in Line 12). This is because, directly or indirectly, the **class** Exception is the superclass of all the exception classes, and a reference variable of a superclass can point to an object of its subclasses. The parameter **eRef** of the **catch** block in Line 12 is a reference variable of the Exception type. The statement in Line 13 determines whether **eRef** is an instance of the **class** ArithmeticException—that is, if it points to an object of the **class** ArithmeticException. Similarly, the statement in Line 15 determines whether **eRef** is an instance of the **class** InputMismatchException. If **eRef** is an instance of ArithmeticException, then the statement in Line 14 executes, and so on.

EXAMPLE 11-6

The Student Grade programming example in Chapter 3 calculates a student's grade. It reads the data from a file and writes the output to a file. The program given in Chapter 3 throws a FileNotFoundException and other exceptions. Now that we know how to handle exceptions in a program, we can rewrite the program to handle the exceptions.

```
//Program: Calculate the average test score
//This program shows how to handle a FileNotFoundException
//or any other exception.

import java.io.*;
import java.util.*;

public class StudentGrade
{
    public static void main(String[] args)
    {

        //Declare and initialize the variables    //Step 1
        double test1, test2, test3, test4, test5;
        double average;
        String firstName;
        String lastName;

        try
        {
            Scanner inFile = new Scanner
                    (new FileReader("test.txt"));    //Step 2

            PrintWriter outFile =
                    new PrintWriter("testavg.out");    //Step 3

            firstName = inFile.next();                  //Step 4
            lastName = inFile.next();                   //Step 4

            outFile.println("Student Name: "
                            + firstName + " "
                            + lastName);             //Step 5

                //Step 6 - retrieve the five test scores
            test1 = inFile.nextDouble();
            test2 = inFile.nextDouble();
            test3 = inFile.nextDouble();
            test4 = inFile.nextDouble();
            test5 = inFile.nextDouble();

            outFile.printf("Test scores: %5.2f %5.2f %5.2f "
                    + "%5.2f %5.2f %n", test1,
                        test2, test3, test4,
                        test5);                      //Step 7

            average = (test1 + test2 + test3 + test4
                    + test5) / 5.0;                  //Step 8

            outFile.printf("Average test score: %5.2f %n",
                            average);                //Step 9

            outFile.close();                         //Step 10

        }
```

```
    catch (FileNotFoundException fnfeRef)
    {
        System.out.println(fnfeRef.toString());
    }
    catch (Exception eRef)
    {
        System.out.println(eRef.toString());
    }
  }
}
```

Sample Run: If the input file does not exist, the following message is printed:

```
java.io.FileNotFoundException: test.txt (The system cannot find the
file specified)
```

The `try` block contains statements that open both the input and output files. It also contains input and output statements. The first `catch` block catches a `FileNotFoundException`, the second `catch` block catches all types of exceptions. As shown in the sample run, if the input file does not exist, the statement in Step 2 in the `try` block throws a `FileNotFoundException`, which is caught and handled by the first `catch` block.

Rethrowing and Throwing an Exception

When an exception occurs in a `try` block, control immediately passes to the first matching `catch` block. Typically, a `catch` block does one of the following:

- Completely handles the exception.
- Partially processes the exception. In this case, the `catch` block either rethrows the same exception or throws another exception for the calling environment to handle the exception.
- Rethrows the same exception for the calling environment to handle the exception.

The `catch` blocks in Examples 11-3 to 11-6 handled the exception. The mechanism of rethrowing or throwing an exception is quite useful in cases when a `catch` block catches the exception, but the `catch` block is unable to handle the exception, or if the `catch` block decides that the exception should be handled by the calling environment. This allows the programmer to provide the exception handling code in one place.

Rethrowing an exception or throwing an exception is accomplished by the `throw` statement. A `throw` statement can throw either a checked or an unchecked exception.

Exceptions are objects of a specific `class` type. Therefore, if you have a reference to an exception object, you can use the reference to throw the exception. In this case, the general syntax to rethrow an exception caught by a `catch` block is:

```
throw exceptionReference;
```

Example 11-7 shows how to rethrow an exception caught by a `catch` block.

EXAMPLE 11-7

Consider the following Java code:

```
//RethrowExceptionExmp1

import java.util.*;

public class RethrowExceptionExmp1
{
    static Scanner console = new Scanner(System.in);

    public static void main(String[] args)          //Line 1
    {
        int number;                                 //Line 2

        try                                         //Line 3
        {
            number = getNumber();                   //Line 4
            System.out.println("Line 5: number = "
                            + number);              //Line 5
        }
        catch (InputMismatchException imeRef)       //Line 6
        {
            System.out.println("Line 7: Exception "
                            + imeRef.toString());   //Line 7
        }
    }

    public static int getNumber()
                throws InputMismatchException       //Line 8
    {
        int num;                                    //Line 9

        try                                         //Line 10
        {
            System.out.print("Line 11: Enter an "
                            + "integer: ");         //Line 11
            num = console.nextInt();                //Line 12
            System.out.println();                   //Line 13

            return num;                             //Line 14
        }
```

```
        catch (InputMismatchException imeRef)        //Line 15
        {
            throw imeRef;                            //Line 16
        }
    }
}
```

Sample Runs:

Sample Run 1: (In this sample run, the user input is shaded.)

```
Line 11: Enter an integer: 56

Line 5: number = 56
```

Sample Run 2: (In this sample run, the user input is shaded.)

```
Line 11: Enter an integer: 56t7
Line 7: Exception java.util.InputMismatchException
```

The preceding program contains the method `getNumber`, which reads an integer and returns it to the method `main`. If the number entered by the user contains a nondigit character, the method `getNumber` throws an `InputMismatchException`. The catch block in Line 15 catches this exception. Rather than handle this exception, the method `getNumber` rethrows this exception (see the statement in Line 16).

The `catch` block in Line 6 of the method `main` also catches the `InputMismatchException`.

In Sample Run 1, the method `getNumber` successfully reads the number and returns it to the method `main`. In Sample Run 2, the user enters an invalid number. The statement in Line 12 throws an `InputMismatchException`, which is caught and rethrown by the catch block starting at Line 15. After the statement in Line 16 executes, control goes back to the method `main` (Line 4), which throws an `InputMismatchException` thrown by the method `getNumber`. The `catch` block in Line 6 catches this exception, and the statement in Line 7 outputs the appropriate message.

Example 11-7 illustrates how to rethrow the same exception caught by a `catch` block. When an exception occurs, the system creates an object of a specific exception `class`. In fact, you can also create your own exception objects and throw them using the `throw` statement. In this case, the general syntax used for the `throw` statement is:

```
throw new ExceptionClassName(messageString);
```

Of course, you could have first created the object and then used the reference to the object in the `throw` statement.

Example 11-8 illustrates how to create and `throw` an exception object.

EXAMPLE 11-8

```
//RethrowExceptionExmp2

import java.util.*;

public class RethrowExceptionExmp2
{
    static Scanner console = new Scanner(System.in);

    public static void main(String[] args)          //Line 1
    {
        int number;                                 //Line 2

        try                                         //Line 3
        {
            number = getNumber();                   //Line 4
            System.out.println("Line 5: number = "
                              + number);            //Line 5
        }
        catch (InputMismatchException imeRef)       //Line 6
        {
            System.out.println("Line 7: Exception "
                              + imeRef.toString());  //Line 7
        }
    }

    public static int getNumber()
                throws InputMismatchException        //Line 8
    {
        int num;                                    //Line 9

        try                                         //Line 10
        {
            System.out.print("Line 11: Enter an "
                          + "integer: ");            //Line 11
            num = console.nextInt();                //Line 12
            System.out.println();                   //Line 13

            return num;                             //Line 14
        }
        catch (InputMismatchException imeRef)       //Line 15
        {
            System.out.println("Line 16: Exception "
                              + imeRef.toString());  //Line 16
            throw new InputMismatchException
                          ("getNumber");            //Line 17
        }
    }
}
```

Sample Run: (In this sample run, the user input is shaded.)

```
Line 11: Enter an integer: 563r9
Line 16: Exception java.util.InputMismatchException
Line 7: Exception java.util.InputMismatchException: getNumber
```

The preceding program works similarly to the program in Example 11-7. The difference is in the `catch` block starting at Line 15, in the method `getNumber`. The `catch` block in Line 15 catches an `InputMismatchException`, outputs an appropriate message in Line 16, and then in Line 17 creates an `InputMismatchException` object with the message string `"getNumber"` and throws the object. The `catch` block starting at Line 6 in the method `main` catches the thrown object. The statement in Line 7 outputs the appropriate message. Notice that the output of the statement in Line 16 (the second line of the sample run) does not output the string `getNumber`, whereas the statement in Line 7 (the third line of the sample run) does output the string `getNumber`. This is because the statement in Line 17 creates and throws an object that is different from the `InputMismatchException` object thrown by the statement in Line 12. The message string of the object thrown by the statement in Line 12 is null; the object thrown by the statement in Line 17 contains the message string `"getNumber"`.

The programs in Examples 11-7 and 11-8 illustrate how a method can rethrow the same exception object, or create an exception object and throw it for the calling method to handle. This mechanism is quite useful; it allows a program to handle all the exceptions in one location rather than spreading exception-handling code throughout the program.

Method `printStackTrace`

Suppose that method `A` calls method `B`, method `B` calls method `C`, and an exception occurs in method `C`. Java keeps track of this sequence of method calls. Recall that the `class` `Exception` is a subclass of the `class` `Throwable`. As shown in Table 11-1, the `class` `Throwable` contains the `public` method `printStackTrace`. Because the method `printStackTrace` is `public`, every subclass of the `class` `Throwable` inherits this method. When an exception occurs in a method, you can use the method `printStackTrace` to determine the order in which the methods were called and where the exception was handled.

EXAMPLE 11-9

This example shows the use of the method `printStackTrace` to show the order in which methods are called and exceptions handled.

```java
import java.io.*;

public class PrintStackTraceExample1
{
    public static void main(String[] args)
    {
        try
        {
            methodA();
        }
        catch (Exception e)
        {
            System.out.println(e.toString() + " caught in main");
            e.printStackTrace();
        }
    }

    public static void methodA() throws Exception
    {
        methodB();
    }

    public static void methodB() throws Exception
    {
        methodC();
    }

    public static void methodC() throws Exception
    {
        throw new Exception("Exception generated in method C");
    }
}
```

Sample Run:

```
java.lang.Exception: Exception generated in method C caught in main
java.lang.Exception: Exception generated in method C
        at PrintStackTraceExample1.methodC(PrintStackTraceExample1.java:30)
        at PrintStackTraceExample1.methodB(PrintStackTraceExample1.java:25)
        at PrintStackTraceExample1.methodA(PrintStackTraceExample1.java:20)
        at PrintStackTraceExample1.main(PrintStackTraceExample1.java:9)
```

The preceding program contains the methods methodA, methodB, methodC, and main. The method methodC creates and throws an object of the **class** Exception. The method methodB calls methodC, methodA calls methodB, and the method main calls methodA. Because the methods methodA and methodB do not handle the exception thrown by methodC, they contain the **throws** Exception clause in their heading. The method main handles the exception thrown by methodC, which was propagated first by methodB and then by methodA. The **catch** block in the method main first outputs the message contained in the exception object and the string " caught in main", then it calls the method printStackTrace to trace the method calls (see the last four lines of the output).

The program in Example 11-10 is similar to the program in Example 11-9. The main difference is that the exception thrown by `methodC` is caught and handled in `methodA`. Note that the heading of `methodA` does not contain any `throws` clause.

EXAMPLE 11-10

```java
import java.io.*;

public class PrintStackTraceExample2
{
    public static void main(String[] args)
    {
        methodA();
    }

    public static void methodA()
    {
        try
        {
            methodB();
        }
        catch (Exception e)
        {
            System.out.println(e.toString() + " caught in methodA");
            e.printStackTrace();
        }
    }

    public static void methodB() throws Exception
    {
        methodC();
    }

    public static void methodC() throws Exception
    {
        throw new Exception("Exception generated in method C");
    }
}
```

Sample Run:

```
java.lang.Exception: Exception generated in method C caught in methodA
java.lang.Exception: Exception generated in method C
        at PrintStackTraceExample2.methodC(PrintStackTraceExample2.java:30)
        at PrintStackTraceExample2.methodB(PrintStackTraceExample2.java:25)
        at PrintStackTraceExample2.methodA(PrintStackTraceExample2.java:14)
        at PrintStackTraceExample2.main(PrintStackTraceExample2.java:7)
```

Exception-Handling Techniques

When an exception occurs in a program, usually the programmer has three choices—terminate the program, fix the error and continue, or log the error and continue. The following sections discuss each situation.

Terminate the Program

In some cases, it is best to let the program terminate when an exception occurs. Suppose you have written a program that inputs data from a file. If the input file does not exist when the program executes, then there is no point in continuing with the program. In this case, the program can output an appropriate error message and terminate.

Fix the Error and Continue

In other cases, you will want to handle the exception and let the program continue. Suppose you have a program that takes as input an integer. If a user inputs a character in place of a digit, the program will throw an `InputMismatchException`. This is a situation where you can include the necessary code to keep prompting the user to input a number until the entry is valid. Example 11-11 illustrates this concept.

EXAMPLE 11-11

The following program continues to prompt the user until the user enters a valid integer.

```java
import java.util.*;

public class FixErrorAndContinue
{
    static Scanner console = new Scanner(System.in);

    public static void main(String[] args)
    {
        int number;                                     //Line 1
        boolean done;                                   //Line 2
        String str;                                     //Line 3

        done = false;                                   //Line 4

        do                                              //Line 5
        {
            try                                         //Line 6
            {
                System.out.print("Line 7: Enter an "
                        + "integer: ");                 //Line 7
                number = console.nextInt();             //Line 8
                System.out.println();                   //Line 9
                done = true;                            //Line 10
```

```
            System.out.println("Line 11: number = "
                            + number);          //Line 11
        }
        catch (InputMismatchException imeRef)    //Line 12
        {
            str = console.next();                //Line 13

            System.out.println("Line 14: Exception "
                            + imeRef.toString()
                            + " " + str);         //Line 14
        }
    }
    while (!done);                               //Line 15
    }
}
```

Sample Run: (In this sample run, the user input is shaded.)

```
Line 7: Enter an integer: 34t5
Line 14: Exception java.util.InputMismatchException 34t5
Line 7: Enter an integer: 398se2
Line 14: Exception java.util.InputMismatchException 398se2
Line 7: Enter an integer: r45
Line 14: Exception java.util.InputMismatchException r45
Line 7: Enter an integer: 56

Line 11: number = 56
```

In the preceding program, the statement in Line 7 prompts the user to enter an integer. The statement in Line 8 inputs the integer entered by the user into the variable number. If the user enters a valid integer, then that integer is stored in number. Then, the statement in Line 10 sets the boolean variable done to true. After the statement in Line 11 executes, the next statement executed is the expression !done in Line 15. If done is true, then !done is false, so the while loop terminates.

Suppose that the user does not enter a valid integer. Because the next input (token) cannot be expressed as an integer, the statement in Line 8 throws an InputMismatchException and control is transferred to the catch block starting at Line 12. Notice that the invalid number entered by the user is still the next input (token) in the input stream. Therefore, the statement in Line 13 reads that invalid number and assigns that input (token) to str. The statement in Line 14 outputs the exception as well as the invalid input. Notice that we can output the invalid input because the program captured the invalid input at Line 13. The do...while loop continues to prompt the user until the user inputs a valid integer.

Notice that in the sample run, the first, second, and third inputs are 34t5, 398se2, and r45, which contain nondigit characters. The fourth input, which is 56, is a valid integer.

Log the Error and Continue

A program that terminates when an exception occurs usually assumes that the termination is reasonably safe. On the other hand, if your program is designed to run a nuclear reactor or continuously monitor a satellite, it cannot be terminated if an exception occurs. These programs should report the exception, but the program must continue to run.

For example, consider a program that analyzes airline-ticketing transactions. Because a large number of ticketing transactions take place each day, a program is run daily to validate that day's transactions. This type of program would take an enormous amount of time to process the transactions. Therefore, when an exception occurs, the program should write the exception into a file and continue to analyze the transactions.

Creating Your Own Exception Classes

When you create your own classes or write programs, exceptions are likely to occur. As you have seen, Java provides a substantial number of exception classes to deal with these situations. However, it does not provide all the exception classes you will ever need. Therefore, Java enables programmers to create exception classes to handle the exceptions not covered by Java's exception classes or to handle their own exceptions. This section describes how to create your own exception classes.

Java's mechanism to process the exceptions you define is the same as that for built-in exceptions. However, you must throw your own exceptions using the `throw` statement.

The exception class that you define extends either the `class` `Exception` or one of its subclasses. Also, a subclass of the `class` `Exception` is either a predefined class or a user-defined class. In other words, if you have created an exception class, you can define other exception classes by extending the definition of the exception class you created.

Typically, constructors are the only methods that you include when you define your own exception class. Because the exception class you define is a subclass of an existing exception class, either built-in or user-defined, the exception class that you define inherits the members of the superclass. Therefore, objects of the exception classes can use the `public` members of the superclasses.

Because the `class` `Exception` is derived from the `class` `Throwable`, it inherits the methods `getMessage` and `toString` of the `class` `Throwable`. These methods are `public`, so they are also inherited by the subclasses of the `class` `Exception`.

EXAMPLE 11-12

This example shows how to create your own division by the zero exception class.

```java
public class MyDivisionByZeroException extends Exception
{
    public MyDivisionByZeroException()
    {
        super("Cannot divide by zero");
    }

    public MyDivisionByZeroException(String strMessage)
    {
        super(strMessage);
    }
}
```

The program in Example 11-13 uses the class MyDivisionByZeroException designed in Example 11-12.

EXAMPLE 11-13

```java
import java.util.*;

public class MyDivisionByZeroExceptionTestProg
{
    static Scanner console = new Scanner(System.in);

    public static void main(String[] args)
    {
        double numerator;                              //Line 1
        double denominator;                            //Line 2

        try                                            //Line 3
        {
            System.out.print("Line 4: Enter the "
                    + "numerator: ");                  //Line 4
            numerator = console.nextDouble();          //Line 5
            System.out.println();                      //Line 6

            System.out.print("Line 7: Enter the "
                    + "denominator: ");                //Line 7
            denominator = console.nextDouble();        //Line 8
            System.out.println();                      //Line 9

            if (denominator == 0.0)                    //Line 10
                throw new MyDivisionByZeroException(); //Line 11

            System.out.println("Line 12: Quotient = "
                    + (numerator / denominator));      //Line 12
        }
```

11

```
        catch (MyDivisionByZeroException mdbze)        //Line 13
        {
            System.out.println("Line 14: "
                                + mdbze.toString());     //Line 14
        }
        catch (Exception e)                              //Line 15
        {
            System.out.println("Line 16: "
                                + e.toString());         //Line 16
        }
    }
}
```

Sample Runs:

Sample Run 1: (In this sample run, the user input is shaded.)

Line 4: Enter the numerator: 25

Line 7: Enter the denominator: 4

Line 12: Quotient = 6.25

Sample Run 2: (In this sample run, the user input is shaded.)

Line 4: Enter the numerator: 20

Line 7: Enter the denominator: 0

Line 14: myDivisionByZeroException: Cannot divide by zero

 NOTE If the exception class you create is a direct subclass of the **class** Exception—or a direct subclass of an exception class whose exceptions are checked exceptions—then the exceptions of the class you created are checked exceptions.

Event Handling

The previous sections discussed in detail Java's mechanism of exception handling. You learned that Java offers extensive support for handling exceptions by providing a number of exception classes. In previous chapters, you learned that Java also provides powerful yet easy-to-use GUI components to create programs that can visually interact with the user. A major item that is required in creating a GUI is the handling of events. In Chapter 6, you learned that when you click a button or press the **Enter** key in a text field, it generates an action event. In fact, when you press a mouse button to click a button, in addition to generating an action event, a mouse event is generated. Similarly, when you press the **Enter** key in a text field, in addition to the action event, it generates a key event. Therefore, a GUI program can simultaneously generate more than one event. In the remainder of this section, you learn how to handle other action events, such as windows and mouse events.

As described in Chapter 6, Java provides various `interface`s to handle different events. For example, to handle action events, you use the `interface ActionListener` and to handle mouse events, you use the `interface MouseListener`. Key events are handled by the `interface KeyListener`; and window events are handled by the `interface WindowListener`. These and other interfaces contain methods that are executed when a particular event occurs. For example, when an action event occurs, the method `actionPerformed` of the `interface ActionListener` is executed.

To handle an event, we create an appropriate object and register it with the GUI component. Recall that the methods of an interface are `abstract`. That is, they contain only the headings of the methods. Therefore, you cannot instantiate an object of an interface. To create an object to handle an event, first you create a class that implements an appropriate interface.

Chapter 6 discussed in detail how to handle action events. Recall that to handle an action event, we do the following:

1. Create a class that implements the `interface ActionListener`. For example, in Chapter 6, for the `JButton calculateB`, we created the `class CalculateButtonHandler`.

2. Provide the definition of the method `actionPerformed` within the class that you created in Step 1. The method `actionPerformed` contains the code that the program executes when the specific event is generated. For example, in Chapter 6, when you click the `JButton calculateB`, the program should calculate and display the area and perimeter of the rectangle.

3. Create and instantiate an object of the class created in Step 1. For example, in Chapter 6, for the `JButton calculateB`, we created the object `cbHandler`.

4. Register the event handler created in Step 3 with the object that generates an action event using the method `addActionListener`. For example, in Chapter 6, for the `JButton calculateB`, the following statement registers the object `cbHandler` to listen for and register the action event:

```
calculateB.addActionListener(cbHandler);
```

Just as you create objects of the class that extends the `interface ActionListener` to handle action events, to handle window events you first create a class that implements the `interface WindowListener` and then create and register objects of that class. You take similar steps to handle mouse events.

In Chapter 6, to terminate the program when the close window button is clicked, we used the method `setDefaultCloseOperation` with the predefined named constant `EXIT_ON_CLOSE`. If you want to provide your own code to terminate the program when the window is closed, or if you want the program to take a different action when the window closes, then you use the `interface WindowListener`. That is, first you create a class that implements the `interface WindowListener`, provide the appropriate definition of the method `windowClosed`, create an appropriate object of that class, and then register the object created with the program.

Let's look at the definition of the `interface WindowListener`:

```
public interface WindowListener
{
    void windowActivated(WindowEvent e);
      //This method executes when a window is activated.
    void windowClosed(WindowEvent e);
      //This method executes when a window is closed.
    void windowClosing(WindowEvent e);
      //This method executes when a window is closing,
      //just before a window is closed.
    void windowDeactivated(WindowEvent e);
      //This method executes when a window is deactivated.
    void windowIconified(WindowEvent e);
      //This method executes when a window is iconified.
    void windowOpened(WindowEvent e);
      //This method executes when a window is opened.
}
```

As you can see, the `interface WindowListener` contains several `abstract` methods. Therefore, to instantiate an object of the class that implements the `interface WindowListener`, that class must provide the definition of each method of the `interface WindowListener`, even if a method is not used. Of course, if a method is not used, you could provide an empty body for that method. Recall that if a class contains an `abstract` method, you cannot instantiate an object of that class.

In Chapter 6, we used the mechanism of the inner class to handle events. That is, the class that implemented the interface was defined within the class containing the application program. Chapter 10 noted that rather than create an inner class to implement the interface, the class containing the application program can itself implement the interface. Now a program can generate various types of events, such as action events and window events. Java allows a class to implement more than one interface. However, Java does not allow a class to extend the definition of more than one class; that is, Java does not support multiple inheritance.

For interfaces such as `WindowListener` that contain more than one method, Java provides the `class WindowAdapter`. The `class WindowAdapter` implements the `interface WindowListener` by providing an empty body for each method of the `interface WindowListener`. The definition of the `class WindowAdapter` is:

```
public class WindowAdapter implements WindowListener
{
    void windowActivated(WindowEvent e)
    {
    }

    void windowClosed(WindowEvent e)
    {
    }
```

```
    void windowClosing(WindowEvent e)
    {
    }

    void windowDeactivated(WindowEvent e)
    {
    }

    void windowIconified(WindowEvent e)
    {
    }

    void windowOpened(WindowEvent e)
    {
    }
}
```

If you use the inner class mechanism to handle a window event, you can create the class by extending the definition of the **class** WindowAdapter and provide the definition of only the methods that the program needs. Similarly, to handle window events, if the class containing the application program does not extend the definition of another class, you can make that class extend the definition of the **class** WindowAdapter.

Chapter 6 discussed in detail how to use the inner class mechanism. The GUI part of the programming example in Chapter 10, provided with the CD accompanying this book, explained how to make the class containing the application program implement more than one interface. As stated in Chapter 10, there is one more way to handle events in a program—using the mechanism of anonymous classes. This mechanism is quite useful to handle events such as window and mouse events because the corresponding interfaces contain more than one method, and the program might want to use only one method.

Recall from Chapter 6 that to register an action listener object to a GUI component, you use the method addActionListener. To register a WindowListener object to a GUI component, you use the method addWindowListener. The WindowListener object being registered is passed as a parameter to the method addWindowListener.

Consider the following code:

```
this.addWindowListener(new WindowAdapter()
        {
            public void windowClosing(WindowEvent e)
            {
                System.exit(0);
            }
        }
);
```

The preceding statements create an object of the anonymous class, which extends the **class** WindowAdapter and overrides the method windowClosing. The object created is passed as an argument to the method addWindowListener. The method addWindowListener is invoked by explicitly using the reference this.

Similarly, you can handle mouse events by using the interface MouseListener. The definition of the interface MouseListener and the class MouseAdapter is:

```
public interface MouseListener
{
    void mouseClicked(MouseEvent e);
      //This method executes when a mouse button is clicked
      //on a component.
    void mouseEntered(MouseEvent e);
      //This method executes when the mouse enters a component.
    void mouseExited(MouseEvent e);
      //This method executes when the mouse exits a component.
    void mousePressed(MouseEvent e);
      //This method executes when a mouse button is
      //is pressed on a component.
    void mouseReleased(MouseEvent e);
      //This method executes when a mouse button is released
      //on a component.
}

public class MouseAdapter implements MouseListener
{
    void mouseClicked(MouseEvent e)
    {
    }

    void mouseEntered(MouseEvent e)
    {
    }

    void mouseExited(MouseEvent e)
    {
    }

    void mousePressed(MouseEvent e)
    {
    }

    void mouseReleased(MouseEvent e)
    {
    }
}
```

To register a MouseListener object to a GUI component, you use the method addMouseListener. The MouseListener object being registered is passed as a parameter to the method addMouseListener.

In addition to the GUI components with which you have worked, Chapter 12 introduces other GUI components such as check boxes, option buttons, menu items, and lists. These GUI components also generate events. Table 11-13 summarizes the various events generated by GUI components. It also shows the GUI component, the listener interface, and the name of the method of the interface to handle the event.

TABLE 11-13 Events Generated by a GUI Component, the Listener Interface, and the Name of the Method of the Interface to Handle the Event

GUI Component	Event Generated	Listener Interface	Listener Method
JButtton	ActionEvent	ActionListener	actionPerformed
JCheckBox	ItemEvent	ItemListener	itemStateChanged
JCheckboxMenuItem	ItemEvent	ItemListener	itemStateChanged
JChoice	ItemEvent	ItemListener	itemStateChanged
JComponent	ComponentEvent	ComponentListener	componentHidden
JComponent	ComponentEvent	ComponentListener	componentMoved
JComponent	ComponentEvent	ComponentListener	componentResized
JComponent	ComponentEvent	ComponentListener	componentShown
JComponent	FocusEvent	FocusListener	focusGained
JComponent	FocusEvent	FocusListener	focusLost
Container	ContainerEvent	ContainerListener	componentAdded
Container	ContainerEvent	ContainerListener	componentRemoved
JList	ActionEvent	ActionListener	actionPerformed
JList	ItemEvent	ItemListener	itemStateChanged
JMenuItem	ActionEvent	ActionListener	actionPerformed
JScrollbar	AdjustmentEvent	AdjustmentListener	adjustmentValueChanged
JTextComponent	TextEvent	TextListener	textValueChanged
JTextField	ActionEvent	ActionListener	actionPerformed
Window	WindowEvent	WindowListener	windowActivated
Window	WindowEvent	WindowListener	windowClosed
Window	WindowEvent	WindowListener	windowClosing
Window	WindowEvent	WindowListener	windowDeactivated
Window	WindowEvent	WindowListener	windowDeiconified
Window	WindowEvent	WindowListener	windowIconified
Window	WindowEvent	WindowListener	windowOpened

Even though key and mouse are not GUI components, they do generate events. Table 11-14 summarizes the events generated by the key and mouse components.

TABLE 11-14 Events Generated by `key` and `mouse` Components

	Event Generated	Listener Interface	Listener Method
key	KeyEvent	KeyListener	keyPressed
key	KeyEvent	KeyListener	keyReleased
key	KeyEvent	KeyListener	keyTyped
mouse	MouseEvent	MouseListener	mouseClicked
mouse	MouseEvent	MouseListener	mouseEntered
mouse	MouseEvent	MouseListener	mouseExited
mouse	MouseEvent	MouseListener	mousePressed
mouse	MouseEvent	MouseListener	mouseReleased
mouse	MouseEvent	MouseMotionListener	mouseDragged
mouse	MouseEvent	MouseMotionListener	mouseMoved

NOTE The section Key and Mouse Events in Chapter 12 gives examples of how to handle key and mouse events.

PROGRAMMING EXAMPLE: Calculator

In this programming example, we design a program that simulates a calculator. The program will provide the basic integer arithmetic operations +, −, *, and /. When the program executes, it displays the GUI shown in Figure 11-8.

FIGURE 11-8 Calculator program GUI

Input: Integers via pressing various digit buttons, arithmetic operations via pressing operation buttons, the equal sign via pressing the button containing the symbol = on the calculator panel, and clearing inputs by pressing the C button.

Output: The result of the operation or an appropriate error message if something goes wrong.

PROBLEM
ANALYSIS
AND GUI AND
ALGORITHM
DESIGN

As shown in Figure 11-8, the GUI contains 16 buttons, a text field, and a window. The buttons and the text field are placed in the content pane of the window. The user enters the input using the various buttons, and the program displays the result in the text field. To create the 16 buttons, you use 16 reference variables of type JButton, and to create the text field, you use a reference variable of type JTextField. You also need a reference variable to access the content pane of the window. As we did in previous GUI programs (in Chapters 6, 8, and 10), we create the class containing the application program by extending the definition of the class JFrame, which also allows you to create the necessary window to create the GUI. Thus, we use the following variables to create the GUI components and to access the content pane of the window:

```
private JTextField displayText = new JTextField(30);
private JButton[] button = new JButton[16];

Container pane = getContentPane(); //to access the content pane
```

As you can see from Figure 11-8, the GUI components are nicely organized. To place the GUI components as shown in the figure, we first set the layout of the content pane to null and then use the methods setSize and setLocation to place the GUI components at various locations in the content pane. The following statement instantiates the JTextField object displayText and places it in the content pane:

```
displayText.setSize(200, 30);
displayText.setLocation(10, 10);
pane.add(displayText);
```

The size of displayText is set to 200 pixels wide and 30 pixels high and it is placed at position (10, 10) in the content pane.

To assign labels to the buttons, rather than write 16 statements, we use an array of strings and a loop. Consider the following statement:

```
private String[] keys = {"7", "8", "9", "/",
                         "4", "5", "6", "*",
                         "1", "2", "3", "-",
                         "0", "C", "=", "+"};
```

Because the size of the displayText is 200 pixels wide and each row has four JButtons, we set the width of each JButton to 50 pixels wide. To keep the height of each JButton the same as the height of displayText, we set the height of each JButton to 30 pixels.

1
1

The user enters input via the buttons. Therefore, each button can generate an action event. To respond to the events generated by a button, we will create and register an appropriate object. In Chapters 6, 8, and 10, we used the mechanism of the inner class to create and register a listener object. In this program, we make the class containing the application program implement the **interface** `ActionListener`. Therefore, we need to provide only the definition of the method `actionPerformed`, which will be described later in this section. Because the class containing the application program implements the **interface** `ActionListener`, we do not need to explicitly instantiate a listener object. We can simply use the reference `this` as an argument to the method `addActionListener` to register the listener.

The following statements instantiate the 16 `JButtons`, place them in the content pane at the proper locations, and register the listener object:

```
int x, y;

x = 10;
y = 40;

for (int ind = 0; ind < 16; ind++)
{
    button[ind] = new JButton(keys[ind]); //instantiate the
                                          //JButton and assign
                                          //it a label
    button[ind].addActionListener(this);  //register the
                                          //listener object
    button[ind].setSize(50,30);           //set the size
    button[ind].setLocation(x, y);        //set the location
    pane.add(button[ind]);                //place the button
                                          //in the content pane

        //determine the coordinates of the next JButton
    x = x + 50;

    if ((ind + 1) % 4 == 0)
    {
        x = 10;
        y = y + 30;
    }
}
```

The inputs to the program are integers, various operations, and the equal symbol. The numbers are entered via the buttons whose labels are digits, and the operations are specified via the buttons whose labels are operations. When the user presses the button with the label =, the program displays the results. The user can also press the button with the label C to clear the numbers.

Because Java accepts only strings as inputs in a GUI component, we need two `String` variables to store the number strings. Before performing the operation, the strings will be converted to their numeric form.

To input numbers, the user presses various digit buttons, one at a time. For example, to specify that a number is 235, the user presses the buttons labeled 2, 3, and 5 in sequence. After pressing each button, the number is displayed in the text field. Each number is entered as a string and therefore concatenated with the previous string. When the user presses an operation button, it indicates that the user is about to enter the second number. Therefore, we use a `boolean` variable, which is set to `false` after the first number is input. We will need the following variables:

```
private String numStr1 = "";
private String numStr2 = "";

private char op;
private boolean firstInput = true;
```

When an event is generated by a button, the method `actionPerformed` is executed. So when the user clicks the = button, the program must display the result. Similarly, when the user clicks an operation button, the program should prepare to receive the second number, and so on. We, therefore, see that the instructions to receive the inputs and operations and display the results will be placed in the method `actionPerformed`. Next, we describe this method.

Method action Performed

As described above, the method `actionPerformed` is executed when the user presses any button. Several things can go wrong while using the calculator. For example, the user might press an operation button without specifying the first number, or the user might press the equal button either without specifying a number or after inputting the first number. Of course, we must also address division by zero. Therefore, the method `actionPerformed` must appropriately respond to the errors.

Suppose that the user wants to add three numbers. After adding the first two numbers, the third number can be added to the sum of the first two numbers. In this case, when the third number is added, the first number is the sum of the first two numbers and the second number becomes the third number. Therefore, after each operation, we will set the first number as the result of the operation. The user can click the C button to start a different calculation. This discussion translates into the following algorithm:

1. Declare the appropriate variables.
2. Use the method `getActionCommand` to identify the button clicked. Retrieve the label of the button, which is a string.
3. Retrieve the character specifying the button label and store it in the variable ch.
4. a. If ch is a digit and `firstInput` is `true`, append the character at the end of the first number string; otherwise, append the character at the end of the second number string.
    b. If ch is an operation, set `firstInput` to `false` and set the variable op to ch.

    c. If ch is = and there is no error, perform the operation, display the result, and set the first number as the result of the operation. If an error occurred, display an appropriate message.

    d. If ch is C, set both number strings to blank and clear the `displayText`.

To perform the operation, we write the method **evaluate**, which is described in the next section.

The definition of the method **actionPerformed** is:

```
public void actionPerformed(ActionEvent e)
{
    String resultStr;                                 //Step 1

    String str
       = String.valueOf(e.getActionCommand()); //Steps 1 and 2

    char ch = str.charAt(0);                          //Steps 1 and 3

    switch (ch)                                       //Step 4
    {
    case '0':                                         //Step 4a
    case '1':
    case '2':
    case '3':
    case '4':
    case '5':
    case '6':
    case '7':
    case '8':
    case '9':
        if (firstInput)
        {
            numStr1 = numStr1 + ch;
            displayText.setText(numStr1);
        }
        else
        {
            numStr2 = numStr2 + ch;
            displayText.setText(numStr2);
        }
        break;

    case '+':                                         //Step 4b
    case '-':
    case '*':
    case '/':
        op = ch;
        firstInput = false;
        break;
```

```
        case '=':                                    //Step 4c
            resultStr = evaluate();
            displayText.setText(resultStr);
            numStr1 = resultStr;
            numStr2 = "";
            firstInput = false;
            break;

        case 'C':
            displayText.setText("");                 //Step 4d
            numStr1 = "";
            numStr2 = "";
            firstInput = true;
        }
    }
```

Method evaluate The method **evaluate** performs an operation and returns the result of the operation as a string. This method also handles various exceptions, such as division by zero and number format error (which occurs if one of the number strings is empty). The definition of this method is:

```
private String evaluate()
{
    final char beep = '\u0007';

    try
    {
        int num1 = Integer.parseInt(numStr1);
        int num2 = Integer.parseInt(numStr2);
        int result = 0;

        switch (op)
        {
        case '+':
            result = num1 + num2;
            break;

        case '-':
            result = num1 - num2;
            break;

        case '*':
            result = num1 * num2;
            break;

        case '/':
            result = num1 / num2;
        }

        return String.valueOf(result);
    }
```

```
catch (ArithmeticException e)
{
    System.out.print(beep);
    return "E R R O R: " + e.getMessage();
}
catch (NumberFormatException e)
{
    System.out.print(beep);

    if (numStr1.equals(""))
        return "E R R O R: Invalid First Number" ;
    else
        return "E R R O R: Invalid Second Number" ;
}
catch (Exception e)
{
    System.out.print(beep);
    return "E R R O R";
}
}
```

Before writing the complete program, we must do one more thing. When the user clicks the window closing button, the program must terminate. Clicking the window closing button generates a window event. Therefore, we must create a WindowListener object and register the object of the class containing the application program because this class extends the definition of the class JFrame. The window events are handled by the interface WindowListener. To terminate the program when the user clicks the window closing button, we must provide the definition of the method windowClosing of the interface WindowListener. Because the interface WindowListener contains more than one method and we only want to use the method windowClosing, we use the mechanism of the anonymous class to create and register the window event object. To do so, we make the class containing the application program use the class WindowAdapter to create and register the window event object. Creating and registering the window event object is accomplished by the following statements:

```
this.addWindowListener(new WindowAdapter()
        {
            public void windowClosing(WindowEvent e)
            {
                System.exit(0);
            }
        }
);
```

We can now outline the program listing.

PROGRAM LISTING

```java
//*************************************************************
// Author: D.S. Malik
//
// GUI Calculator Program
// This program implements the arithmetic operations.
//*************************************************************

import javax.swing.*;
import java.awt.*;
import java.awt.event.*;
import java.io.*;

public class Calculator extends JFrame implements
                                       ActionListener
{
    private JTextField displayText = new JTextField(30);
    private JButton[] button = new JButton[16];

    private String[] keys = {"7", "8", "9", "/",
                             "4", "5", "6", "*",
                             "1", "2", "3", "-",
                             "0", "C", "=", "+"};

    private String numStr1 = "";
    private String numStr2 = "";

    private char op;
    private boolean firstInput = true;

    public Calculator()
    {
        setTitle("My Calculator");
        setSize(230, 200);
        Container pane = getContentPane();

        pane.setLayout(null);

        displayText.setSize(200,30);
        displayText.setLocation(10,10);
        pane.add(displayText);

        int x, y;

        x = 10;
        y = 40;
```

```java
    for (int ind = 0; ind < 16; ind++)
    {
        button[ind] = new JButton(keys[ind]);
        button[ind].addActionListener(this);
        button[ind].setSize(50,30);
        button[ind].setLocation(x, y);
        pane.add(button[ind]);
        x = x + 50;

        if ((ind + 1) % 4 == 0)
        {
            x = 10;
            y = y + 30;
        }
    }

    this.addWindowListener(new WindowAdapter()
        {
            public void windowClosing(WindowEvent e)
            {
                System.exit(0);
            }
        }
    );

    setVisible(true);
}

//Place the definition of the method actionPerformed
//as described here

//Place the definition of the method evaluate
//as described here

public static void main(String[] args)
{
    Calculator C = new Calculator();
}
}
```

Sample Run 1: In this sample run (see Figure 11-9), the user entered the numbers 34 and 25, the operation +, and =. The result is shown in the bottom screen.

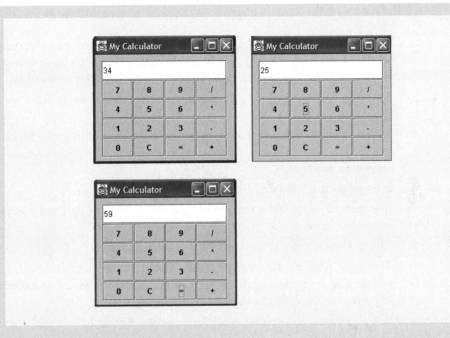

FIGURE 11-9 Adding numbers 34 and 25

Sample Run 2: In this sample run (see Figure 11-10), the user attempted to divide by 0, resulting in an error message.

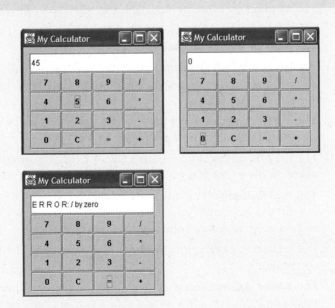

FIGURE 11-10 An attempt to divide by 0

QUICK REVIEW

1.   An exception is an object of a specific exception class. Java provides extensive support for exception handling by providing several exception classes. Java also allows users to create and implement their own exception classes.

2.   The `try/catch/finally` block is used to handle exceptions within a program.

3.   Statements that may generate an exception are placed in a `try` block. The `try` block also contains statements that should not be executed if an exception occurs.

4.   A `try` block is followed by zero or more `catch` blocks.

5.   A `catch` block specifies the type of exception it can catch and contains an exception handler.

6.   The last `catch` block may or may not be followed by a `finally` block.

7.   The code contained in the `finally` block always executes, regardless of whether an exception occurs, except when the program exits early from a `try` block by calling the method `System.exit`.

8.   If a `try` block is not followed by a `catch` block, then it must have the `finally` block.

9.   When an exception occurs, an object of a specific exception class is created.

10. A `catch` block can catch either all exceptions of a specific type or all types of exceptions.

11. The heading of a `catch` block specifies the type of exception it handles.

12. The `class Throwable`, which is derived from the `class Object`, is the superclass of the `class Exception`.

13. The methods `getMessage`, `printStackTrace`, and `toString` of the `class Throwable` are `public` and so are inherited by the subclasses of the `class Throwable`.

14. The method `getMessage` returns the string containing the detailed message stored in the exception object.

15. The method `toString` (in `class Exception`) returns the detailed message stored in the exception object as well as the name of the exception class.

16. The `class Exception` and its subclasses are designed to catch exceptions that should be caught and processed during program execution, and thus make a program more robust.

17. The `class Exception` is the superclass of the classes designed to handle exceptions.

18. The `class Exception` is contained in the package `java.lang`.

19. The classes to deal with I/O exceptions, such as the file not found exception, are contained in the `package java.io`.

20. The `class InputMismatchException` is contained in the package `java.util`.

21. The classes to deal with number format exceptions and arithmetic exceptions, such as division by zero, are contained in the `package java.lang`.

22. Generally, exception classes are placed in the package that contains the methods that throw these exceptions.

23. Java's predefined exceptions are divided into two categories—checked exceptions and unchecked exceptions.

24. Any exception that can be recognized by the compiler is called a checked exception.

25. Unchecked exceptions are exceptions that are not recognized by the compiler.

26. Typically, a `catch` block does one of the following:

    - Completely handles the exception.
    - Partially processes the exception. In this case, the `catch` block either rethrows the same exception or throws another exception for the calling environment to handle the exception.
    - Rethrows the same exception for the calling environment to handle the exception.

27. The general syntax to rethrow an exception caught by a `catch` block is:

    `throw exceptionReference;`

28. The general syntax to throw your own exception object is:

    `throw new ExceptionClassName(messageString);`

29. The method `printStackTrace` is used to determine the order in which the methods were called and where the exception was handled.

30. The exception class that you define extends the `class Exception` or one of its subclasses.

31. Action events are handled by appropriately implementing the `interface ActionListener`.

32. Window events are handled by appropriately implementing the `interface WindowListener`.

33. The `class WindowAdapter` implements the `interface WindowListener` by providing empty bodies to the methods.

34. To register a window listener object to a GUI component, you use the method `addWindowListener`. The window listener object being registered is passed as a parameter to the method `addWindowListener`.

35. Mouse events are handled by appropriately implementing the `interface MouseListener`.

36. The `class MouseListener` implements the `interface MouseListener` by providing empty bodies to the methods.

11

37. To register a mouse listener object to a GUI component, you use the method `addMouseListener`. The mouse listener object being registered is passed as a parameter to the method `addMouseListener`.

38. Key events are handled by appropriately implementing the `interface KeyListener`.

EXERCISES

1. Mark the following statements as true or false.

   a. The block `finally` is always executed.

   b. Division by zero is a checked exception.

   c. File not found is an unchecked exception.

   d. Exceptions are thrown either in a `try` block in a method or from a method called directly or indirectly from a `try` block.

   e. The order in which `catch` blocks are listed is not important.

   f. An exception can be caught either in the method where it occurred or in any one of the methods that led to the invocation of this method.

   g. One way to handle an exception is to print an error message and exit the program.

   h. All exceptions must be reported to avoid compilation errors.

   i. An event handler is a method.

   j. A GUI component can generate only one type of event.

2. Consider the following Java code:

```
int lowerLimit;
...
try
{
    System.out.println("Entering the try block.");

    if (lowerLimit < 100)
        throw new Exception("Lower limit violation.");

    System.out.println("Exiting the try block.");
}
catch (Exception e)
{
    System.out.println("Exception: " + e.getMessage());
}

System.out.println("After the catch block");
```

What is the output if:

   a. The value of `lowerLimit` is 50?

   b. The value of `lowerLimit` is 150?

3. Consider the following Java code:

```
int lowerLimit;
int divisor;
int result;

try
{
    System.out.println("Entering the try block.");

    result = lowerLimit / divisor;

    if (lowerLimit < 100)
        throw new Exception("Lower limit violation.");

    System.out.println("Exiting the try block.");
}
catch (ArithmeticException e)
{
    System.out.println("Exception: " + e.getMessage());

    result = 110;
}
catch (Exception e)
{
    System.out.println("Exception: " + e.getMessage());
}

System.out.println("After the catch block");
```

What is the output if:

a. The value of lowerLimit is 50 and the value of divisor is 10?

b. The value of lowerLimit is 50 and the value of divisor is 0?

c. The value of lowerLimit is 150 and the value of divisor is 10?

d. The value of lowerLimit is 150 and the value of divisor is 0?

4. Rewrite the Java code given in Exercise 3 so that the new equivalent code has exactly one catch block.

5. Correct any compile-time errors in the following code:

```
import java.io.*;
import java.util.*;

public class SAverage
{
    public static void main(String[] args)
    {
        double test1, test2, test3, test4;
        double average;
```

```
try
{
    Scanner inFile = new
            Scaner(new FileReader("test.txt"));

    PrintWriter outFile =
                new PrintWriter("testavg.out");

    test1 = inFile.nextDouble();
    test2 = inFile.nextDouble();
    test3 = inFile.nextDouble();
    test4 = inFile.nextDouble();

    outFile.printf("Test scores: %.2f %.2f %.2f %.2f %n",
                test1, test2, test3, test4);

    average = (test1 + test2 + test3 + test4) / 4.0;
    outFile.println("Average test score: %.2f",
                average);

    outFile.close();

}
catch (Exception e)
{
    System.out.println(e.toString());
}
catch (FileNotFoundException e)
{
    System.out.println(e.toString());
}
    }
}
```

6. Define the exception **class** `TornadoException`. The class should have two constructors, including one default constructor. If the exception is thrown with the default constructor, the method `getMessage` should return:

   `"Tornado! Take cover immediately!"`

   The other constructor has a single parameter, say, m, of type `int`. If the exception is thrown with this constructor, the method `getMessage` should return:

   `"Tornado m miles away and approaching!"`

7. Write a Java program to test the **class** `TornadoException` specified in Exercise 6.

8. Suppose the exception `class MyException` is defined as follows:

```
public class MyException extends Exception
{
    public MyException()
    {
        super("MyException thrown!");

        System.out.println("Immediate attention required!");
    }
    public MyException(String msg)
    {
        super(msg);

        System.out.println("Attention required!");
    }
}
```

What output will be produced if the exception is thrown with the default constructor? What output will be produced if the exception is thrown by the constructor with parameter with the actual parameter `"May Day, May Day"`?

9. What are the three different ways you can implement an interface?

PROGRAMMING EXERCISES

1. Write a program that prompts the user to enter the length in feet and inches and outputs the equivalent length in inches and in centimeters. If the user enters a negative number or a nondigit number, throw and handle an appropriate exception and prompt the user to enter another set of numbers.

2. Redo Programming Exercise 17 of Chapter 5 so that if the input file does not exist, the program handles the `FileNotFoundException`, outputs an appropriate message, and terminates normally.

3. Redo the Text Processing programming example in Chapter 9 so that if the array index goes out of bounds when the program accesses the array `letterCount`, it throws and handles the `ArrayIndexOutOfBoundsException`.

4. Redo Programming Exercise 9 of Chapter 8 so that your program handles exceptions such as division by zero.

5. Extend the Calculator programming example of this chapter by adding three buttons with the labels M, R, and E as follows: If the user clicks the button M, the number currently in the `displayText` field is stored in the variable, say, `memory`; if the user clicks the button R, the number stored in memory is displayed and also becomes the first number (so that another number can be added, subtracted, multiplied, or divided); and if the user clicks the button E, the program terminates.

11

6. The Calculator programming example of this chapter is designed to perform operations on integers. Write a similar program that can be used to perform operations on decimal numbers. (*Note*: If division by zero occurs with values of the `int` data type, the program throws a division by zero exception. However, if you divide a decimal number by zero, Java does not throw the division by zero exception; it returns the answer as `infinity`. However, if division by zero occurs, your calculator program must output the message `ERROR: / by zero`.)

7. In Programming Exercise 2 in Chapter 8, we defined a `class` `Roman` to implement Roman numerals in a program. In that exercise, we also implemented the method `romanToDecimal` to convert a Roman numeral into its equivalent decimal number.

   a. Modify the definition of the `class` `Roman` so that the data members are declared as `protected`. Also include the method `decimalToRoman`, which converts the decimal number (the decimal number must be a positive integer) to an equivalent Roman numeral format. Write the definition of the method `decimalToRoman`. Your definition of the `class` `Roman` must contain the method `toString`, which returns the string containing the number in Roman format. For simplicity, we assume that only the letter `I` can appear in front of another letter and that it appears only in front of the letters `V` and `X`. For example, `4` is represented as `IV`, `9` is represented as `IX`, `39` is represented as `XXXIX`, and `49` is represented as `XXXXIX`. Also, `40` is represented as `XXXX`, `190` is represented as `CLXXXX`, and so on.

   b. Derive the `class` `ExtendedRoman` from the `class` `Roman` to do the following. In the `class` `ExtendedRoman`, include the methods `add`, `subtract`, `multiply`, and `divide` so that arithmetic operations can be performed on Roman numerals.

   To add (subtract, multiply, or divide) Roman numerals, add (subtract, multiply, or divide, respectively) their decimal representations and then convert the result to the Roman numeral format. For subtraction, if the first number is smaller than the second number, throw the exception, "`Because the first number is smaller than the second, the numbers cannot be subtracted`". Similarly, for division, the numerator must be larger than the denominator.

   c. Write the definitions of the methods `add`, `subtract`, `multiply`, and `divide` as described in Part b. Also, your definition of the `class` `ExtendedRoman` must contain the method `toString` that returns the string containing the number in Roman format.

   d. Write a program to test various operations on your `class` `ExtendedRoman`.

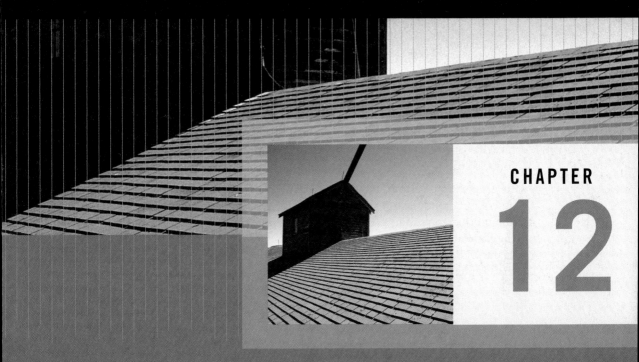

ADVANCED GUIS AND GRAPHICS

IN THIS CHAPTER, YOU WILL:

- Learn about applets
- Explore the **class** Graphics
- Learn about the **class** Font
- Explore the **class** Color
- Learn how to use additional Layout managers
- Become familiar with more GUI components
- Learn how to create menu-based programs
- Learn how to handle key and mouse events

There are two types of Java programs—applications and applets. Up to this point, we have created only application programs. Even the programs we've created that use GUI components are application programs. Java **applets** are small applications that can be embedded in an HTML page. In this chapter, you will learn how to create an applet. You will also learn how to convert a GUI application to a Java applet. This chapter also shows you how to use fonts, colors, and geometric shapes to enhance the output of your programs.

In Chapter 6, you learned how to use GUI components, such as `JFrame`, `JLabel`, `JTextField`, and `JButton`, to make your programs attractive and user-friendly. In this chapter, you learn about other commonly used GUI components. The `class` `JComponent` is the superclass of the classes used to create various GUI components. Figure 12-1 shows the inheritance hierarchy of the GUI classes that you have used in previous chapters, plus the ones you will encounter in this chapter. The package containing the definition of a particular class is also shown.

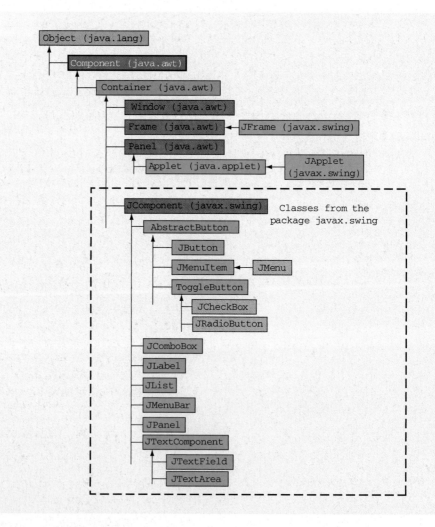

FIGURE 12-1 Inheritance hierarchy of GUI classes (classes shown in the dotted rectangle are from the **package** `javax.swing`)

As shown in Figure 12-1, the `class Container`, which is a subclass of the `class Component`, is the superclass of all the classes designed to provide GUIs—and, therefore, all `public` members of these classes are inherited by their subclasses. Moreover, both the `Container` and `Component` classes are `abstract`.

The `class Component` contains many methods that are inherited by its subclasses. You have used methods such as `setSize` and `setLocation` in various GUI programs. Table 12-1 describes some of the constructors and methods of the `class Component`.

TABLE 12-1 Constructors and Methods of the `class Component`

```
protected Component()
  //Constructor
  //Creates a new instance of a component.
public void addComponentListener(ComponentListener lis)
  //Adds the component listener specified by lis.
public void addFocusListener(FocusListener lis)
  //Adds the focus listener specified by lis.
public void addKeyListener(KeyListener lis)
  //Adds the key listener specified by lis.
public void addMouseListener(MouseListener lis)
  //Adds the mouse listener specified by lis.
public void addMouseMotionListener(MouseMotionListener lis)
  //Adds the mouse motion listener specified by lis.
public void removeComponentListener(ComponentListener lis)
  //Removes the component listener specified by lis.
public void removeKeyListener(KeyListener lis)
  //Removes the key listener specified by lis.
public void removeMouseListener(MouseListener lis)
  //Removes the mouse listener specified by lis.
public void removeMouseMotionListener(MouseMotionListener lis)
  //Removes the mouse motion listener specified by lis.
public Color getBackground()
  //Returns the background color of this component.
public Color getForeground()
  //Returns the foreground color of this component.
public void setBackground(Color c)
  //Sets the background color of this component to color c.
```

1
2

TABLE 12-1 Constructors and Methods of the **class** Component (continued)

```
public void setForeground(Color c)
  //Sets the foreground color of this component to color c.
```

```
public Font getFont()
  //Returns the font of this component.
```

```
public void setFont(Font ft)
  //Sets the font of this component to ft.
```

```
public void setSize(int w, int h)
  //Sets the size of this component to width w and height h
```

```
public boolean isVisible()
  //Returns true if the component is visible; false otherwise.
```

```
public void setVisible(boolean tog)
  //If tog is true, sets the component to visible;
  //if tog is false, the component is not shown.
```

```
public void paint(Graphics g)
  //Paints the component with the graphic component specified by g.
```

```
public void repaint()
  //Repaints the component.
```

```
public void repaint(int x, int y, int wid, int ht)
  //Repaints the rectangular portion of the component from (x, y)
  //to (x + wid, y + ht)
```

```
public void setLocation(int x, int y)
  //Sets the component at the location (x, y).
```

```
public String toString()
  //Returns a string representation of this component.
```

```
public void update(Graphics g)
  //Invokes the paint method.
```

```
public void validate()
  //Validates this container and all of its subcomponents; the
  //method validate is used to cause a container to lay out its
  //subcomponents once more. Typically called after the components
  //it contains have been added to or modified.
```

The **class** Container inherits all the methods of the **class** Component. In addition to the methods listed in Table 12-1, Table 12-2 shows some commonly used methods of the **class** Container.

TABLE 12-2 Methods of the **class** Container

```
public Component add(Component comp)
  //Appends the specified component to the end of this container.

public Component add(Component comp, int index)
  //Adds the specified component to this container at the
  //position specified by index.

public void paint(Graphics g)
  //Paints the container with the graphics component specified by g.

public void update(Graphics g)
  //Invokes the paint method.

public void validate()
  //Validates this container and all of its subcomponents. The
  //method validate is used to cause a container to lay out its
  //subcomponents once more. Typically called after the components
  //it contains have been added to or modified.
```

In the remainder of this chapter, whenever we list the methods of a class, we will not show the methods that are inherited from the **classes** Component and Container.

Next, we discuss how to create a Java applet. For the most part, the programs in this chapter are Java applets.

Applets

The term *applet* refers to a little application. In Java, an **applet** is a Java program that is embedded within an HTML document and executed by a Web browser. You create an applet by extending the **class** JApplet, which is contained in the **package** javax.swing.

Table 12-3 describes some commonly used methods of the **class** JApplet.

TABLE 12-3 Some Members of the **class** JApplet (**package** javax.swing)

```
public void init()
  //Called by the browser or applet viewer to inform this applet
  //that it has been loaded into the system.

public void start()
  //Called by the browser or applet viewer to inform this applet
  //that it should start its execution. It is called after the init
  //method and each time the applet is revisited in a Web page.

public void stop()
  //Called by the browser or applet viewer to inform this applet
  //that it should stop its execution. It is called before the
  //method destroy.
```

TABLE 12-3 Some Members of the **class** JApplet (**package** javax.swing) (continued)

```
public void destroy()
  //Called by the browser or applet viewer. Informs this applet that
  //it is being reclaimed and that it should destroy any resources
  //that it has allocated. The method stop is called before destroy.

public void showStatus(String msg)
  //Displays the string msg in the status bar.

public Container getContentPane()
  //Returns the ContentPane object for this applet.

public JMenuBar getJMenuBar()
  //Returns the JMenuBar object for this applet.

public URL getDocumentBase()
  //Returns the URL of the document that contains this applet.

public URL getCodeBase()
  //Returns the URL of this applet.

public void update(Graphics g)
  //Calls the paint() method.

protected String paramString()
  //Returns a string representation of this JApplet; mainly used
  //for debugging.
```

Unlike Java application programs, Java applets do not have the method `main`. Instead, when a browser runs an applet, the methods `init`, `start`, and `paint` are guaranteed to be invoked in sequence. Therefore, as a programmer, to develop an applet, all you have to do is override one or all of the methods `init`, `start`, and `paint`. Of these three methods, the `paint` method has one argument, which is a `Graphics` object. This allows you to use the **class** `Graphics` without actually creating a `Graphics` object. Later in this chapter, when the **class** `Graphics` is presented in detail, you will notice that it is an **abstract** class; therefore, you cannot create an instance of this class. For now, all you need to do is import the **package** `java.awt` so that you can use various methods of the **class** `Graphics` in the `paint` method. To do so, you need the following two **import** statements:

```
import java.awt.Graphics;
import javax.swing.JApplet;
```

Because you create an applet by extending the **class** `JApplet`, a Java applet in skeleton form looks something like this:

```
import java.awt.Graphics;
import javax.swing.JApplet;

public class WelcomeApplet extends JApplet
{

}
```

As a general rule, you keep all statements to be executed only once in the `init` method. The `paint` method is used to draw various items, including strings, in the content pane of the applet. Thus, in the applets presented in this chapter, we use `init` to:

- Initialize variables
- Get data from the user
- Place various GUI components

The `paint` method is used to create the output. The `init` and `paint` methods need to share common data items, so these items are the data members of the applet.

Let's now create an applet that will display a welcome message. Because no initialization is required, all you need to do is override the method `paint` so that it draws the welcome message. Sometimes when you override a method, it is a good idea to invoke the corresponding method of the parent `class`. Whenever you override the `paint` method, the first Java statement is:

```
super.paint(g);
```

where g is a `Graphics` object. Recall that `super` is a reserved word in Java and refers to the instance of the parent class.

To display the string containing the welcome message, we use the method `drawString` of the `class` `Graphics`. The method `drawString` is an overloaded method. One of the headings of the method `drawString` is:

```
public abstract void drawString(String str, int x, int y)
```

The method `drawString` displays the string specified by `str` at the horizontal position `x` pixels away from the upper-left corner of the applet, and the vertical position `y` pixels away from the upper-left corner of the applet. In other words, the applet has an x-y coordinate system, with `x` = 0, `y` = 0 at the upper-left corner; the `x` value increases from left to right and the `y` value increases from top to bottom. Thus, the method `drawString`, as given previously, draws the string `str` starting at the position `(x, y)`.

The following Java applet displays a welcome message:

```java
//Welcome Applet

import java.awt.Graphics;
import javax.swing.JApplet;

public class WelcomeApplet extends JApplet
{
    public void paint(Graphics g)
    {
        super.paint(g);                             //Line 1

        g.drawString("Welcome to Java Programming",
                     30, 30);                       //Line 2
    }
}
```

1
2

In the preceding applet, the statement in Line 1 invokes the `paint` method of the class `JApplet`. Notice that the method `paint` uses a `Graphics` object `g` as the argument. Recall that the `class Graphics` is an `abstract` class, and for this reason, you cannot create an instance of the `class Graphics`. The system will create a `Graphics` object for you; you need not be concerned about it. The statement in Line 2 draws the string `"Welcome to Java Programming"` at the coordinate position (30, 30).

Until now, when we created a GUI application program, we used methods such as `setTitle` and `setSize`. As you can see in the preceding applet, such methods are not used in an applet. Note the following about applets:

- The method `setTitle` is not used in applets because applets do not have titles. An applet is embedded in an HTML document, and the applet itself does not have a title. The HTML document may have a title, which is set by the document.

- The method `setSize` is not used in applets because the applet's size is determined in the HTML document, not by the applet. You do not need to set the size of the applet.

- You do not need to invoke the method `setVisible`.

- You do not need to close the applet. When the HTML document containing the applet is closed, the applet is destroyed.

- There is no method `main`.

As with an application, you compile an applet and produce a `.class` file. Once the `.class` file is created, you need to place it in a Web page to run the applet. For example, you can create a file with the `.html` extension, say, `WelcomeApplet.html`, with the following lines in the same folder where the `WelcomeApplet.class` file resides:

```
<HTML>
  <HEAD>
    <TITLE>WELCOME APPLET</TITLE>
  </HEAD>
  <BODY>
    <OBJECT code = "WelcomeApplet.class" width = "250"
                                         height = "60">
    </OBJECT>
  </BODY>
</HTML>
```

Once the HTML file is created, you can run your applet either by opening `WelcomeApplet.html` with a Web browser, or you can enter:

```
appletviewer WelcomeApplet.html
```

at a command-line prompt, if you are using the JDK (Java Development Kit).

Sample Run: Figure 12-2 shows the output of the `WelcomeApplet` produced by the Applet Viewer in Windows XP.

FIGURE 12-2 Output of the `WelcomeApplet`

You terminate the applet by clicking the close button in the upper-right corner of the Applet Viewer, or by closing the HTML document in which the applet is embedded.

Two ways to make your applets more attractive are to vary the type font and color. Next, we introduce the **classes** `Font` and `Color`, contained in the **package** `java.awt`.

class **Font**

The GUI programs we have created so far have used only the default font. To show text in different fonts when the program executes, Java provides the **class** `Font`. The **class** `Font` is contained in the **package** `java.awt`, so you need to use the following `import` statement in your program:

`import java.awt.*;`

The **class** `Font` contains various constructors, methods, and constants, some of which are described in Table 12-4.

TABLE 12-4 Some Constructors and Methods of the **class** `Font`

```
public Font(String name, int style, int size)
   //Constructor
   //Creates a new Font from the specified name, style, and point
   //size.

public String getFamily()
   //Returns the family name of this Font.

public String getFontName()
   //Returns the font face name of this Font.
```

Typically, you use only the constructor of the **class** Font. As shown in Table 12-4, the constructor of the **class** Font takes the following three arguments:

- A string specifying the font face name (or font name for short)
- An **int** value specifying the font style
- An **int** value specifying the font size expressed in points, where 72 points equal one inch

Fonts available on different systems vary widely. However, using the JDK guarantees the following fonts:

- Serif
- SanSerif
- Monospaced
- Dialog
- DialogInput

If you want to know which fonts are available on your system, you can run the program given next. (This program uses a graphics environment, which is covered later in this chapter.)

```java
import java.awt.*;

public class FontNames
{
    public static void main(String[] args)
    {
        String[] listOfFontNames =
            GraphicsEnvironment.getLocalGraphicsEnvironment()
                    .getAvailableFontFamilyNames();

        for (int i = 0; i < listOfFontNames.length; i++)
            System.out.println(listOfFontNames[i]);
    }
}
```

The **class** Font contains the constants Font.PLAIN, Font.ITALIC, and Font.BOLD, which you can apply to change the style of a font. For example, the Java statement:

```java
new Font("Serif", Font.ITALIC, 12)
```

creates a 12-point Serif italic font. Likewise, the statement:

```java
new Font("Dialog", Font.ITALIC + Font.BOLD, 36)
```

creates a 36-point Dialog italic and bold font.

The applet given in Example 12-1 illustrates how to change fonts in text.

EXAMPLE 12-1

```java
//FontsDisplayed Applet

import java.awt.*;
import javax.swing.JApplet;

public class FontsDisplayed extends JApplet
{
    public void paint(Graphics g)
    {
        super.paint(g);

        g.setFont(new Font("Courier", Font.BOLD, 24));
        g.drawString("Courier bold 24pt font", 30, 36);

        g.setFont(new Font("Arial", Font.PLAIN, 30));
        g.drawString("Arial plain 30pt font", 30, 70);

        g.setFont(new Font("Dialog", Font.BOLD + Font.ITALIC,
                            36));
        g.drawString("Dialog italic bold 36pt font", 30, 110);

        g.setFont(new Font("Serif", Font.ITALIC, 30));
        g.drawString("Serif italic 42pt font", 30, 156);
    }
}
```

The HTML file that invokes this applet contains the following code:

```html
<HTML>
  <HEAD>
    <TITLE>Four Fonts</TITLE>
  </HEAD>
  <BODY>
    <OBJECT code = "FontsDisplayed.class" width = "500"
                                          height = "190">
    </OBJECT>
  </BODY>
</HTML>
```

Sample Run: Figure 12-3 shows the output of the FontsDisplayed applet in Applet Viewer.

1
2

FIGURE 12-3 Output of the `FontsDisplayed` applet

class Color

So far, we have used only the default colors in our GUI programs. For example, the text always appeared as black. You may want to show the text in different colors or change the background color of a component. Java provides the **class** `Color` to accomplish this. The **class** `Color` is contained in the **package** `java.awt`, so you need to use the **import** statement:

```
import java.awt.*;
```

Table 12-5 shows various constructors and methods of the **class** `Color`.

TABLE 12-5 Some Constructors and Methods of the **class** `Color`

```
Color(int r, int g, int b)
//Constructor
//Creates a Color object with the red value r, green value g,
//and blue value b. In this case, r, g, and b can be
//between 0 and 255.
//Example: new  Color(0, 255, 0)
//         creates a color with no red or blue component.

Color(int rgb)
//Constructor
//Creates a Color object with the red value r, green value g,
//and blue value b; RGB value consisting of the red component
//in bits 16-23, the green component in bits 8-15, and the
//blue component in bits 0-7.
//Example: new  Color(255)
//         creates a color with no red or green component.
```

TABLE 12-5 Some Constructors and Methods of the **class** Color (continued)

```
Color(float r, float g, float b)
  //Constructor
  //Creates a Color object with the red value r, green value g,
  //and blue value b. In this case, r, g, and b can be between 0
  //and 1.0.
  //Example: new Color(1.0, 0, 0)
  //         creates a color with no green or blue component.

public Color brighter()
  //Returns a Color that is brighter.

public Color darker()
  //Returns a Color that is darker.

public boolean equals(Object o)
  //Returns true if the color of this object is the same as the
  //color of the object o; false otherwise.

public int getBlue()
  //Returns the value of the blue component.

public int getGreen()
  //Returns the value of the green component.

public int getRed()
  //Returns the value of the red component.

public int getRGB()
  //Returns the RGB value.

public String toString()
  //Returns a string with the information about the color.
```

You can use the methods `setBackground` and `setForeground`, described in Table 12-1, to set the background and foreground color of a component.

Java uses the color scheme known as RGB, where R stands for red, G for green, and B for blue, respectively. You create instances of `Color` by mixing red, green, and blue hues in various proportions. The **class** Color contains three constructors, as shown in Table 12-5. In the first constructor, an RGB value is represented as three `int` values. The second constructor specifies an RGB value as a single integer. In either form, the closer an r, g, or b value is to 255, the more hue is mixed into the color. For example, if you use the first constructor, pure red is produced by mixing red 255, green 0, and blue 0 parts each. To produce the color red, you use the first constructor as follows:

```
Color redColor = new Color(255, 0, 0);
```

Various tones of black, white, and gray can be created by mixing all three colors in the same proportion. For example, the color white has the RGB values 255, 255, 255, and black has the RGB values 0, 0, 0. An RGB value of 100, 100, 100 creates a gray color darker than one with an RGB value of 200, 200, 200.

In addition to the methods shown in Table 12-5, the class Color defines a number of standard colors as constants. Table 12-6 shows the color name in bold and its values for easy reference.

TABLE 12-6 Constants Defined in the class Color

Color.**black**: (0, 0, 0)	Color.**magenta**: (255, 0, 255)
Color.**blue**: (0, 0, 255)	Color.**orange**: (255, 200, 0)
Color.**cyan**: (0, 255, 255)	Color.**pink**: (255, 175, 175)
Color.**darkGray**: (64, 64, 64)	Color.**red**: (255, 0, 0)
Color.**gray**: (128, 128, 128)	Color.**white**: (255, 255, 255)
Color.**green**: (0, 255, 0)	Color.**yellow**: (255, 255, 0)
Color.**lightGray**: (192, 192, 192)	

A simple applet to illustrate the use of the class Color is given in Example 12-2. In this example, we use the class GridLayout, described in Chapter 6, to place the GUI components. Recall that GridLayout divides the container into a grid of rows and columns, allowing you to place the components in rows and columns. Every component placed in a GridLayout will have the same width and height. The components are placed from left to right in the first row, followed by left to right in the second row, and so on.

The class GridLayout is contained in the package java.awt. Most often, we use the following constructor of the class GridLayout:

GridLayout(int row, int col)

where row specifies the number of rows and col specifies the number of columns in the grid, respectively. For example, to create a grid with 10 rows and 5 columns, and set it as the layout of the container c, you use the following Java statement:

c.setLayout(new GridLayout(10, 5));

In our next applet, we use a grid with 2 rows and 2 columns. Therefore, we use the statement:

c.setLayout(new GridLayout(2, 2));

Example 12-2 uses the method random of the class Math that returns a random value between 0 and 1. For example, the statement:

Math.random();

returns a random `double` value between 0 and 1. Note that the third constructor of the `Color` class (see Table 12-5) takes three `float` values, each between 0 and 1, as parameters. Therefore, we use the explicit cast operator (`float`) to convert the `double` value returned by the `random` method. Thus, we use the following statements to randomly generate a value for the colors red, green, and blue:

```
red = (float) Math.random();
green = (float) Math.random();
blue = (float) Math.random();
```

These statements assign random `float` values between 0 and 1 to the `float` variables `red`, `green`, and `blue`. Suppose that `bottomrightJL` is a `JLabel`. The statement:

```
bottomrightJL.setForeground(new Color(red, green, blue));
```

creates a color and assigns it as the foreground color of the label `bottomrightJL`.

EXAMPLE 12-2

This example gives the complete program listing and a sample run that shows how to set the colors of a text and GUI components.

```
//ColorsDisplayed Applet

import java.awt.*;
import javax.swing.*;

public class ColorsDisplayed extends JApplet
{
    JLabel topleftJL, toprightJL, bottomleftJL, bottomrightJL;

    int i;
    float red, green, blue;

    public void init()
    {
        Container c = getContentPane();

        c.setLayout(new GridLayout(2, 2));
        c.setBackground(Color.white);

        topleftJL = new JLabel("Red", SwingConstants.CENTER);
        toprightJL = new JLabel("Green", SwingConstants.CENTER);
        bottomleftJL = new JLabel("Blue",
                                SwingConstants.CENTER);
        bottomrightJL = new JLabel("Random",
                                SwingConstants.CENTER);

        topleftJL.setForeground(Color.red);
        toprightJL.setForeground(Color.green);
        bottomleftJL.setForeground(Color.blue);
```

1
2

```
        red = (float) Math.random();
        green = (float) Math.random();
        blue = (float) Math.random();
        bottomrightJL.setForeground(new Color(red, green, blue));

        c.add(topleftJL);
        c.add(toprightJL);
        c.add(bottomleftJL);
        c.add(bottomrightJL);
    }
}
```

The HTML file that invokes this applet contains the following code:

```
<HTML>
  <HEAD>
    <TITLE>Four Colors</TITLE>
  </HEAD>
  <BODY>
    <OBJECT code = "ColorsDisplayed.class" width = "400"
                                           height = "200">
    </OBJECT>
  </BODY>
</HTML>
```

Sample Run: Figure 12-4 shows the output of the `ColorsDisplayed` applet.

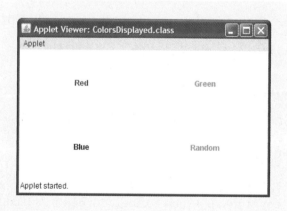

FIGURE 12-4   Output of the `ColorsDisplayed` applet

You can use both the **class** Font and the **class** Color to enhance your presentation of an applet. For example, consider the `GrandWelcome` applet given in Example 12-3, which shows the complete program listing followed by a sample run.

EXAMPLE 12-3

```
//GrandWelcome Applet

import java.awt.*;
import javax.swing.JApplet;

public class GrandWelcome extends JApplet
{
    public void paint(Graphics g)
    {
        super.paint(g);

        g.setColor(Color.red);
        g.setFont(new Font("Courier", Font.BOLD, 24));
        g.drawString("Welcome to Java Programming", 30, 30);
    }
}
```

The HTML file for this program contains the following code:

```
<HTML>
  <HEAD>
    <TITLE>WELCOME</TITLE>
  </HEAD>
  <BODY>
    <OBJECT code = "GrandWelcome.class" width = "440"
                                        height = "50">
    </OBJECT>
  </BODY>
</HTML>
```

Sample Run: Figure 12-5 shows the output of the GrandWelcome applet.

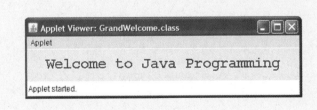

FIGURE 12-5 Output of the GrandWelcome applet

class Graphics

This section presents a glimpse of the **class** Graphics, which is contained in the **package** java.awt. The **class** Graphics provides methods for drawing items such as lines, ovals, and rectangles on the screen. Some methods of the **class** Graphics draw shapes; others draw bitmap images. This class also contains methods to set the properties of graphic elements including fonts and colors. Table 12-7 shows some of the constructors and methods of the **class** Graphics.

TABLE 12-7 Some Constructors and Methods of the **class** Graphics

```
protected Graphics()
    //Constructs a Graphics object that defines a context in which the
    //user can draw. This constructor cannot be called directly.
```

```
public void draw3DRect(int x, int y, int w, int h, boolean t)
    //Draws a 3D rectangle at (x, y) of the width w and height h. If t is
    //true, the rectangle will appear raised.
```

```
public abstract void drawArc(int x, int y, int w, int h,
                             int sangle, int aangle)
    //Draws an arc in the rectangle at the position (x, y) of width w
    //and height h. The arc starts at the angle sangle with an arc angle
    //aangle. Both angles are measured in degrees.
```

```
public abstract boolean drawImage(Image img, int xs1, int ys1,
                int xs2, int ys2, int xd1, int yd1,
                int xd2, int yd2, Color c, ImageObserver ob)
    //Draws the image specified by img from the area defined by the
    //bounding rectangle, (xs1, ys1) to (xs2, ys2), in the area defined
    //by the rectangle (xd1, yd1) to (xd2, yd2). Any transparent color
    //pixels are drawn in the color c. The ob monitors the progress of
    //the image.
```

```
public abstract void drawLine(int xs, int ys, int xd, int yd)
    //Draws a line from (xs, ys) to (xd, yd).
```

```
public abstract void drawOval(int x, int y, int w, int h)
    //Draws an oval at the position (x, y) of width w and height h.
```

```
public abstract void drawPolygon(int[] x, int[] y, int num)
    //Draws a polygon with the points (x[0], y[0]), ...,
    //(x[num - 1], y[num - 1]). Here num is the number of points in
    //the polygon.
```

```
public abstract void drawPolygon(Polygon poly)
    //Draws a polygon as defined by the object poly.
```

```
public abstract void drawRect(int x, int y, int w, int h)
    //Draws a rectangle at the position (x, y) of width w and
    //height h.
```

TABLE 12-7 Some Constructors and Methods of the **class** Graphics (continued)

```
public abstract void drawRoundRect(int x, int y, int w, int h,
                                    int arcw, int arch)
    //Draws a round-cornered rectangle at the position (x, y) having a
    //width w and height h. The shape of the rounded corners is
    //determined by the arc with the width arcw and the height arch.
```

```
public abstract void drawString(String s, int x, int y)
    //Draws the string s at (x, y).
```

```
public void fill3DRect(int x, int y, int w, int h, boolean t)
    //Draws a 3D filled rectangle at (x, y) of width w height h.
    //If t is true, the rectangle will appear raised. The rectangle is
    //filled with the current color.
```

```
public abstract void fillArc(int x, int y, int w, int h,
                             int sangle, int aangle)
    //Draws a filled arc in the rectangle at the position (x, y) of
    //width w and height h starting at angle sangle with the arc
    //angle aangle. Both angles are measured in degrees. The arc is
    //filled with the current color.
```

```
public abstract void fillOval(int x, int y, int w, int h)
    //Draws a filled oval at the position (x, y) having a width w and
    //height h. The oval is filled with the current color.
```

```
public abstract void fillPolygon(int[] x, int[] y, int num)
    //Draws a filled polygon with the points (x[0], y[0]), ...,
    //(x[num - 1], y[num - 1]). Here num is the number of points in
    //the polygon. The polygon is filled with the current color.
```

```
public abstract void fillPolygon(Polygon poly)
    //Draws a filled polygon as defined by the object poly. The polygon
    //is filled with the current color.
```

```
public abstract void fillRect(int x, int y, int w, int h)
    //Draws a filled rectangle at the position (x, y) of width w
    //and height h. The rectangle is filled with the current color.
```

```
public abstract void fillRoundRect(int x, int y, int w, int h,
                                    int arcw, int arch)
    //Draws a filled, round-cornered rectangle at the position (x, y)
    //of width w and height h. The shape of the rounded corners
    //is determined by the arc with the width arcw and the height arch.
    //The rectangle is filled with the current color.
```

```
public abstract Color getColor()
    //Returns the current color for this graphics context.
```

```
public abstract void setColor(Color c)
    //Sets the current color for this graphics context to c.
```

1
2

TABLE 12-7 Some Constructors and Methods of the **class** Graphics (continued)

```
public abstract Font getFont()
  //Returns the current font for this graphics context.

public abstract void setFont(Font f)
  //Sets the current font for this graphics context to f.

public void String toString()
  //Returns a string representation of this graphics context.
```

Before drawing in Java, let us first explain Java's coordinate system, which is used to identify every point on the screen. The coordinates of the upper-left corner of a GUI component, such as the content pane, are (0, 0); this point is called the **origin**. Every coordinate pair has an x-coordinate and a y-coordinate. The x-coordinate specifies the horizontal position, moving from left to right relative to the origin; the y-coordinate specifies the vertical position, moving from top to bottom relative to the origin. The x-axis specifies every x-coordinate and the y-axis specifies every y-coordinate. Figure 12-6 illustrates Java's coordinate system.

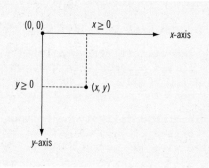

FIGURE 12-6 Java's coordinate system

You have already used the **drawString** method to output a string. Other draw methods are used in a similar manner. For example, to draw a line from (10, 10) to (10, 40), you use the method **drawLine** as follows:

```
g.drawLine(10, 10, 10, 40);      //left line
```

where g is a **Graphics** object.

Let us draw three more lines, so that our welcome message is inside a box.

```
g.drawLine(10, 40, 430, 40);    //bottom line
g.drawLine(430, 40, 430, 10);   //right line
g.drawLine(430, 10, 10, 10);    //top line
```

Placing these lines in our **GrandWelcome** applet of Example 12-3 gives us the program shown in Example 12-4.

EXAMPLE 12-4

```
//GrandWelcomeLine Applet

import java.awt.*;
import javax.swing.JApplet;

public class GrandWelcomeLine extends JApplet
{
    public void paint( Graphics g)
    {
        super.paint(g);

        g.setColor(Color.red);

        g.setFont(new Font("Courier", Font.BOLD, 24));
        g.drawString("Welcome to Java Programming", 30, 30);

        g.drawLine(10, 10, 10, 40);     //left line
        g.drawLine(10, 40, 430, 40);    //bottom line
        g.drawLine(430, 40, 430, 10);   //right line
        g.drawLine(430, 10, 10, 10);    //top line
    }
}
```

The HTML file for this program contains the following code:

```
<HTML>
  <HEAD>
    <TITLE>WELCOME</TITLE>
  </HEAD>
  <BODY>
    <OBJECT code = "GrandWelcomeLine.class" width = "440"
                                            height = "50">
    </OBJECT>
  </BODY>
</HTML>
```

Sample Run: Figure 12-7 shows the output of the GrandWelcomeLine applet.

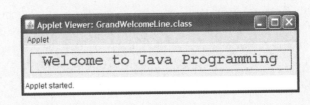

FIGURE 12-7 Output of the GrandWelcomeLine applet

In the applet of Example 12-4, you could have used the method `drawRect` to draw a rectangle rather than four lines. In that case, you could use the following statement:

```
g.drawRect(10, 10, 430, 40);    //draw rectangle
```

The program in Example 12-5 further illustrates how to use various methods of the `Graphics` class. In this example, we create a random collection of geometric shapes. The program uses the method `random` of the `class Math` to randomly determine the number of figures. We want to have at least 5 and at most 14 figures. Therefore, we declare an `int` variable and initialize it as follows:

```
int numOfFigures;

numOfFigures = 5 + (int)(Math.random() * 10); //determine the
                                              //number of figures
```

For each figure, we want a random color, random anchor point, random width, and random height. Further, we want a random shape from a set of possible options. This applies to all figures. Therefore, we need to have a loop similar to the following:

```
for (i = 0; i < numOfFigures; i++)
{
    //...
}
```

Inside the preceding loop, we determine a random color. We can use the method `random` of the `class Math` to get red, green, and blue values between 0 and 255 and use them to create a random color. Therefore, we need the following statements (assume that `g` is a reference variable of the `Graphics` type):

```
int red;
int green;
int blue;

red = (int)(Math.random() * 256);    //red component
green = (int)(Math.random() * 256);  //green component
blue = (int)(Math.random() * 256);   //blue component

g.setColor(new Color(red, green, blue));  //color for
                                          //this figure
```

We also need to compute four more values for `x`, `y`, and the width and height between, say, 0 and 200. Further, to make the program easier to modify, we use the named constant `SIZE`, initialized to 200. Thus, we need the following Java statements:

```
private final int SIZE = 200;
int x;
int y;
int width;
int height;
int red;
```

```
x = (int)(Math.random() * SIZE);          //x value
y = (int)(Math.random() * SIZE);          //y value
width = (int)(Math.random() * SIZE);      //width
height = (int)(Math.random() * SIZE);     //height
```

Now all that is left is to randomly select a shape among, say, rectangle, filled rectangle, oval, and filled oval. So let's assign the values:

- 0 for rectangle
- 1 for filled rectangle
- 2 for oval
- 3 for filled oval

A `switch` statement can be used to invoke the appropriate method, as shown in the following:

```
shape = (int)(Math.random() * 4);

switch (shape)
{
case 0 :
    g.drawRect(x, y, width, height);
    break;

case 1 :
    g.fillRect(x, y, width, height);
    break;

case 2 :
    g.drawOval(x, y, width, height);
    break;

case 3 :
    g.fillOval(x, y, width, height);
    break;
}
```

Putting it all together, we have the Java applet shown in Example 12-5.

EXAMPLE 12-5

```
//Java applet to draw ovals and rectangles

import java.awt.*;
import javax.swing.*;

public class OvalRectApplet extends JApplet
{
    private final int SIZE = 200;
```

```java
public void paint(Graphics g)
{
    int shape;
    int numOfFigures;
    int x;
    int y;
    int width;
    int height;
    int red;
    int green;
    int blue;

    int i;

            //determine the number of figures
    numOfFigures = 5 + (int)(Math.random() * 10);

    for (i = 0; i < numOfFigures; i++)
    {
        red = (int)(Math.random() * 256);   //red component
        green = (int)(Math.random() * 256);//green component
        blue = (int)(Math.random() * 256); //blue component

        g.setColor(new Color(red, green, blue)); //color for
                                                 //this figure

        x = (int)(Math.random() * SIZE);       //x value
        y = (int)(Math.random() * SIZE);       //y value
        width = (int)(Math.random() * SIZE);   //width
        height = (int)(Math.random() * SIZE);  //height

        shape = (int)(Math.random() * 4);

        /**
         *    0 : Rectangle
         *    1 : Filled Rectangle
         *    2 : Oval
         *    3 : Filled Oval
         *
         **/

        switch (shape)
        {
        case 0:
            g.drawRect(x, y, width, height);
            break;

        case 1:
            g.fillRect(x, y, width, height);
            break;
```

```
        case 2:
            g.drawOval(x, y, width, height);
            break;

        case 3:
            g.fillOval(x, y, width, height);
        }//end switch
    }//end for
    }
}
```

The HTML file for this program contains the following code:

```
<HTML>
  <HEAD>
    <TITLE>WELCOME APPLET</TITLE>
  </HEAD>
  <BODY>
    <OBJECT code = "OvalRectApplet.class" width = "400"
                                          height = "300">
    </OBJECT>
  </BODY>
</HTML>
```

Sample Run: Figure 12-8 shows a sample run of OvalRectApplet.

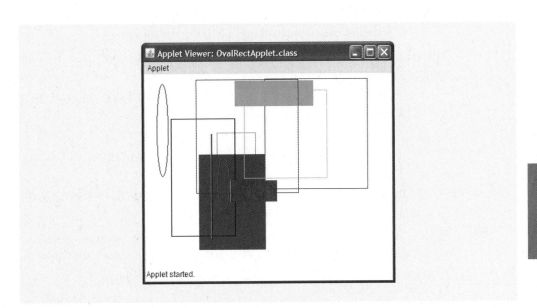

FIGURE 12-8 Sample Run of OvalRectApplet

Note that in this sample run, a figure drawn later has visual priority over a figure drawn earlier.

Converting an Application Program to an Applet

At this point, you might wonder whether there is a simple scheme to convert GUI applications to applets. An applet class shares many features of a GUI application. The main differences are:

- An applet class is derived from the `class JApplet`, whereas a GUI application class is created by extending the `class JFrame`.
- Applets do not have the method `main`. Instead, an applet invokes the `init`, `start`, `paint`, `stop`, and `destroy` methods in sequence. Quite often, you place the initialization code in `init` and the output is produced by the method `paint`.
- Applets do not use constructors. Instead, they use the method `init` to initialize various GUI components and data members.
- Applets do not require methods such as `setVisible`. Applets are embedded in HTML documents, and it is the HTML document that displays the applet.
- Applets do not use the method `setTitle`; the HTML document sets the title.
- Applets do not use the method `setSize`; the HTML document specifies the size of the applet.
- Applets do not have to be closed. In particular, there is no `Exit` button. The applet closes when the HTML document closes.

Therefore, in most cases, you perform the following five steps to convert a GUI application to an applet:

1. Make your `class` extend the definition of the `class JApplet`. In other words, change `JFrame` to `JApplet`.
2. Change the constructor to the method `init`.
3. Remove method calls such as `setVisible`, `setTitle`, and `setSize`.
4. Remove the method `main`.
5. Remove the `Exit` button, if you have one, and all code associated with it, such as the action listener, and so on.

As an example, we modify the temperature conversion program presented in Chapter 6 as a GUI application. The statements changed to create an applet are shown as comments.

```
//Java program to convert the temperature between
//Celsius and Fahrenheit.

import java.awt.*;
import java.awt.event.*;
import javax.swing.*;
```

```
    //public class TempConversion extends JFrame
    //
    //Replace JFrame with JApplet
    //
public class TempConvertApplet extends JApplet
{
    private JLabel celsiusLabel;
    private JLabel fahrenheitLabel;
    private JTextField celsiusTF;
    private JTextField fahrenheitTF;
    private CelsHandler celsiusHandler;
    private FahrHandler fahrenheitHandler;

    private static final int WIDTH = 500;
    private static final int HEIGHT = 50;
    private static final double FTOC = 5.0 / 9.0;
    private static final double CTOF = 1.8;      // 9 / 5
    private static final int OFFSET = 32;

     //public TempConversion()
     //
     //Replace this constructor with the init method
     //
    public void init()
    {
        //setTitle("Temperature Conversion");
        //
        //Delete setTitle
        //

        Container c = getContentPane();
        c.setLayout(new GridLayout(1, 4));

        celsiusLabel = new JLabel("Enter Celsius",
                            SwingConstants.RIGHT);
        fahrenheitLabel = new JLabel("Enter Fahrenheit ",
                            SwingConstants.RIGHT);

        celsiusTF = new JTextField(7);
        fahrenheitTF = new JTextField(7);

        c.add(celsiusLabel);
        c.add(celsiusTF);
        c.add(fahrenheitLabel);
        c.add(fahrenheitTF);

        celsiusHandler = new CelsHandler();
        fahrenheitHandler = new FahrHandler();
        celsiusTF.addActionListener(celsiusHandler);
        fahrenheitTF.addActionListener(fahrenheitHandler);
```

1
2

```
        //setSize(WIDTH, HEIGHT);
        //Delete: setSize(WIDTH, HEIGHT);

        //setDefaultCloseOperation(EXIT_ON_CLOSE);
        //Delete: setDefaultCloseOperation(EXIT_ON_CLOSE);

        //setVisible(true);
        //Delete: setVisible(true);
    }

    private class CelsHandler implements ActionListener
    {
        public void actionPerformed(ActionEvent e)
        {
            double celsius, fahrenheit;

            celsius =
                    Double.parseDouble(celsiusTF.getText());
            fahrenheit = celsius * CTOF + OFFSET;
            fahrenheitTF.setText(""+
                        String.format("%.2f", fahrenheit));
        }
    }

    private class FahrHandler implements ActionListener
    {
        public void actionPerformed(ActionEvent e)
        {
            double celsius, fahrenheit;

            fahrenheit =
                Double.parseDouble(fahrenheitTF.getText());

            celsius = (fahrenheit - OFFSET) * FTOC;
            celsiusTF.setText(""+
                        String.format("%.2f", celsius));
        }
    }

    //public static void main(String[] args)
    //{
    //     TempConversion tempConv = new TempConversion();
    //}
    //
    //Delete the method main
    //
}//end TempConvertApplet
```

The HTML file for this program contains the following code:

```
<HTML>
  <HEAD>
    <TITLE>TEMPCONVERT APPLET</TITLE>
  </HEAD>
  <BODY>
    <OBJECT code = "TempConvertApplet.class" width = "500"
                                              height = "50">
    </OBJECT>
  </BODY>
</HTML>
```

Additional GUI Components

The remainder of this chapter introduces GUI components in addition to those introduced in Chapter 6. For the most part, these additional GUI components are used in the same way as the ones introduced earlier. For example, you create an instance (or object) using the operator new. If the program needs to respond to an event occurring in a GUI component, such as JTextField or JButton, you must add an event listener and provide the associated method that needs to be invoked, commonly called the event handler. We will also illustrate the use of various methods of the class Graphics.

JTextArea

The GUI programs in previous chapters extensively used the class JTextField to display a line of text. However, there are situations when the program must display multiple lines of text. For example, an employee's address is shown in three or more lines. Because an object of the class JTextField can display only one line of text, you cannot use an object of this class to display multiple lines of text. Java provides the class JTextArea to either collect multiple lines of input from the user or to display multiple lines of output. Using an object of this class, the user can type multiple lines of text, which are separated by pressing the Enter key. In Java, each line ends with the newline character '\n'.

The GUI part of the Student Grade Report programming example in Chapter 10, (provided on the CD accompanying this book) uses a JTextArea to display multiple lines of text to show the various courses taken by a student and the student's grade for each course. This section discusses the capabilities of the class JTextArea in some detail.

Both JTextField and JTextArea are derived from the class JTextComponent and, as such, share many common methods. However, you cannot create an instance of the class JTextComponent because it is an abstract class. Table 12-8 lists some of the constructors and methods of the class JTextArea.

1
2

TABLE 12-8 Commonly Used Constructors and Methods of the **class** JTextArea

```
public JTextArea(int r, int c)
  //Constructor
  //Creates a new JTextArea with r number of rows and
  //c number of columns.

public JTextArea(String t, int r, int c)
  //Constructor
  //Creates a new JTextArea with r number of rows, c number
  //of columns, and the initial text t.

public void setColumns(int c)
  //Sets the number of columns to c.

public void setRows(int r)
  //Sets the number of rows to r.

public void append(String t)
  //Concatenates the text already in the JTextArea with t.

public void setLineWrap(boolean b)
  //If b is true, the lines are wrapped.

public void setTabSize(int c)
  //Sets tab stops every c columns.

public void setWrapStyleWord(boolean b)
  //If b is true, the lines are wrapped at the word boundaries.
  //If b is false, the word boundaries are not considered.
```

Table 12-9 shows the methods, which you have used with a JTextField object, that are inherited by the **class** JTextArea from the parent **class** JTextComponent.

TABLE 12-9 Methods Inherited by the **class** JTextArea from the Parent **class** JTextComponent

```
public void setText(String t)
  //Changes the text of the text area to t.

public String getText()
  //Returns the text contained in the text area.

public void setEditable(boolean b)
  //If b is false, the user cannot type in the text area. In this case,
  //the text area is used as a tool to display the result.
```

EXAMPLE 12-6

The program in this example illustrates the use of `JTextArea`. It creates the GUI shown in Figure 12-9.

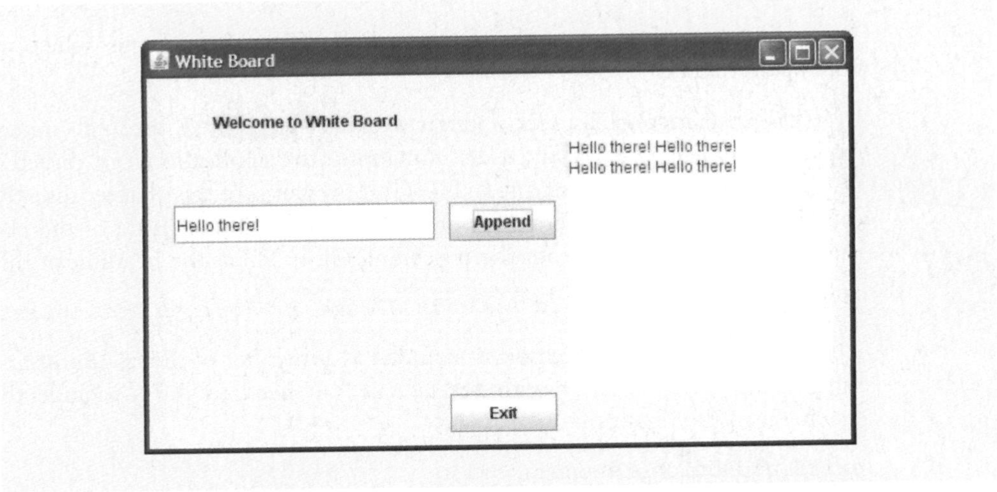

FIGURE 12-9 White Board GUI

As shown in Figure 12-9, the GUI contains a `JLabel`, two `JButtons`, a text field, and a text area. The user can type a line of text in the text field. Similarly, if the user clicks the `Append` button, the text in the text field is appended to the text in the text area. When the user clicks the `Exit` button, the program terminates.

In this example, we write the program as a GUI application. A corresponding applet is left as an exercise for you; see Programming Exercise 8 at the end of this chapter.

As in the previous GUI application program, we create the necessary labels, text fields, and text areas, and place them in the content pane. We also create and place two buttons, `exitB` and `appendB`, in the content pane. The following statements access the content pane, create the GUI components, and place the GUI components in the content pane:

```
private JLabel headingL;
headingL = new JLabel("Welcome to White Board");

private JTextField lineTF;
lineTF = new JTextField(20);

private JTextArea whiteBoardTA;
whiteBoardTA = new JTextArea(10, 20);

private JButton exitB, appendB;
exitB = new JButton("Exit");
appendB = new JButton("Append");
```

```
Container pane = getContentPane();

pane.add(headingL);
pane.add(lineTF);
pane.add(whiteBoardTA);
pane.add(appendB);
pane.add(exitB);
```

We will specify the sizes and locations of the GUI components when we write the complete program.

In Chapter 6, action listener interfaces are implemented through inner classes. As explained in Chapter 10, any class containing the application can directly implement the interface ActionListener. The GUI programs of this chapter directly implement the interfaces to handle events. Suppose WhiteBoard is the name of the class to implement the application to create the preceding GUI. Then, the heading of this class is:

```
public class WhiteBoard extends JFrame implements ActionListener
```

The method actionPerformed is included as a member of the class WhiteBoard. To register the action listener with exitB, all you need to do is include the following statement in the program:

```
exitB.addActionListener(this);
```

Of course, the necessary code is placed in the method actionPerformed.

Because action events are generated by the two buttons, the method actionPerformed uses the methods getActionCommand and equals to identify the source of the event. The definition of this method is:

```
public void actionPerformed(ActionEvent e)
{
    if (e.getActionCommand().equals("Append"))      //Line 1
        whiteBoardTA.append(lineTF.getText());      //Line 2
    else if (e.getActionCommand().equals("Exit"))   //Line 3
        System.exit(0);                             //Line 4
}
```

If the user clicks the Append button, the if statement in Line 1 evaluates to true. In this case, the statement in Line 2 retrieves the line of text from the text field object lineTF and appends it to the text in the text area object whiteBoardTA. When the user clicks the Exit button, the if statement in Line 3 evaluates to true and the statement in Line 4 terminates the program.

The complete program listing follows:

```
import javax.swing.*;
import java.awt.*;
import java.awt.event.*;
```

```java
public class WhiteBoard extends JFrame
                        implements ActionListener
{
    private static int WIDTH = 550;
    private static int HEIGHT = 350;

    private int row = 10;
    private int col = 20;

        //GUI components
    private JLabel headingL;
    private JTextField lineTF;
    private JTextArea whiteBoardTA;
    private JButton exitB, appendB;

    public WhiteBoard()
    {
        setTitle("White Board");
        Container pane  = getContentPane();
        setSize(WIDTH,HEIGHT);

        headingL = new JLabel("Welcome to White Board");
        lineTF = new JTextField(20);

        whiteBoardTA = new JTextArea(row, col);
        exitB = new JButton("Exit");
        exitB.addActionListener(this);

        appendB = new JButton("Append");
        appendB.addActionListener(this);

        pane.setLayout(null);

        headingL.setLocation(50, 20);
        lineTF.setLocation(20, 100);
        whiteBoardTA.setLocation(320, 50);
        appendB.setLocation(230, 100);
        exitB.setLocation(230, 250);

        headingL.setSize(200, 30);
        lineTF.setSize(200, 30);
        whiteBoardTA.setSize(200, 200);
        appendB.setSize(80, 30);
        exitB.setSize(80, 30);

        pane.add(headingL);
        pane.add(lineTF);
        pane.add(whiteBoardTA);
        pane.add(appendB);
        pane.add(exitB);
```

1
2

```
            setVisible(true);
            setDefaultCloseOperation(EXIT_ON_CLOSE);
    } //end of the constructor

    public static void main(String[] args)
    {
        WhiteBoard board = new WhiteBoard();
    }

    public void actionPerformed(ActionEvent e)
    {
        if (e.getActionCommand().equals("Append"))
            whiteBoardTA.append(lineTF.getText());
        else if (e.getActionCommand().equals("Exit"))
            System.exit(0);
    }
}
```

Sample Run: Figure 12-10 shows a sample run of this program. (To get the new line in the text area, click the mouse to position the insertion point in the text area, then press the Enter key. The next append should now be in the next line.)

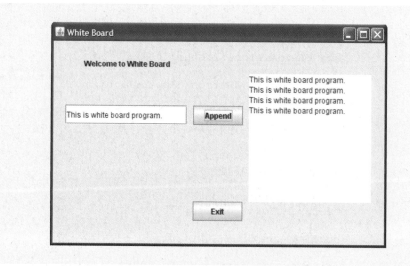

FIGURE 12-10   Sample run of the White Board program

JCheckBox

In the previous section, you learned how to use text fields and text areas to collect input from the user. When you use a text field or a text area to input data, users can type anything they want. However, sometimes you want the user to select from a set of predefined values. For example, to specify gender, the user would select either male or female; similarly, a student would select either undergraduate or graduate. In addition to freeing the user from typing in such values, to get precise input, you want the user to select a value from a given set.

The JCheckBox and JRadioButton classes allow a user to select a value from a set of given values. These classes are both subclasses of the abstract class ToggleButton. The class JCheckBox is described in this section; the class JRadioButton is discussed in the next section.

Table 12-10 shows some of the constructors and methods of the class JCheckBox.

TABLE 12-10 Some Constructors and Methods of the class JCheckBox

```
public JCheckBox()
   //Creates an initially unselected check box button
   //with no label and no icon.
   //Example: JCheckBox myJCheckBox = new JCheckBox()
   //         myJCheckBox points to the check box with no label
   //         and no icon.

public JCheckBox(Icon icon)
   //Creates an initially unselected check box button with
   //the specified icon and no label.
   //Example: JCheckBox myJCheckBox = new JCheckBox(anIcon);
   //         myJCheckBox points to the check box with the
   //         icon "anIcon".

public JCheckBox(Icon icon, boolean selected)
   //Creates a check box with the specified
   //image and selection state, but with no label.
   //Example: JCheckBox myJCheckBox =
   //                    new JCheckBox(anIcon, true);
   //         myJCheckBox points to the selected check box with
   //         anIcon as the icon.

public JCheckBox(String text)
   //Creates an unselected check box with
   //the specified label.
   //Example: JCheckBox myJCheckBox = new JCheckBox("Box");
   //         myJCheckBox points to the unselected check box with
   //         the label "Box".

public JCheckBox(String text, boolean selected)
   //Creates a check box with the specified
   //label and selection state.
   //Example: JCheckBox myJCheckBox =
   //                    new JCheckBox("Box", false);
   //         myJCheckBox points to the unselected check box with
   //         the label "Box".
```

TABLE 12-10 Some Constructors and Methods of the **class** JCheckBox (continued)

```
public JCheckBox(String text, Icon icon)
  //Creates a check box with the specified image
  //and specified label.
  //Example: JCheckBox myJCheckBox =
  //                   new JCheckBox("Box", anIcon,);
  //      myJCheckBox points to the unselected check box with
  //      the label "Box" and anIcon as the icon.

public JCheckBox(String text, Icon icon, boolean selected)
  //Creates a check box with the specified image
  //and selection state, and with the specified text.
  //Example: JCheckBox myJCheckBox =
  //                   new JCheckBox("Box", anIcon, true);
  //      myJCheckBox points to the selected check box with
  //      the label "Box" and anIcon as the icon.

public boolean isSelected()
  //This method is inherited from the AbstractButton class
  //and is used to retrieve the state of a button.
  //Example: if(myJCheckBox.isSelected() == true)
  //      The "if" block will be executed, provided that myJCheckBox
  //      is checked.

public boolean setSelected(boolean b)
  //This method is inherited from the AbstractButton class
  //and is used to set the state of a button.
  //Example: myJCheckBox.setSelected(true);
  //      myJCheckBox gets checked.
```

Similar to buttons, check boxes also come with their own identifying labels. Consider the following statements:

```
JCheckBox italicCB;                       //Line 1
italicCB = new JCheckBox("Italic");       //Line 2
```

The statement in Line 1 declares italicCB to be a reference variable of JCheckBox type. The statement in Line 2 creates the object italicCB and assigns it the label Italic. After the statement in Line 2 executes, the check box shown in Figure 12-11 results.

 Italic

FIGURE 12-11 Check box with label

In Figure 12-11, the box to the left of the label Italic is a check box. The user clicks it to select or deselect it. For example, clicking the check box in Figure 12-11 produces the result shown in Figure 12-12.

FIGURE 12-12 Result of clicking the check box

If you click the check box shown in Figure 12-12, the checkmark disappears. A check box is an example of a toggle button. If it is not selected and you click it, then the box is selected and a checkmark appears. If it is selected and you click it, the checkmark disappears.

When you click a JCheckBox, it generates an **item event**. Item events are handled by the interface ItemListener. The interface ItemListener contains only the abstract method itemStateChanged. The heading of the method is:

```
public void itemStateChanged(ItemEvent e)
```

To make the program respond to the event generated by clicking a check box, you write the code that needs to be executed in the body of the method itemStateChanged and register an item listener object to the check box.

Next, we write an applet that has two check boxes and also displays a line of text. The first check box is used to indicate the selection of bold style and the second to indicate the selection of italic style. The user can click the check boxes to change the font and style of the text. We create two check boxes with the labels "Bold" and "Italic" and place them in the content pane of the applet. The method init contains the statements needed for these initializations. Therefore, the init method can be written as follows:

```
public void init()
{
    Container c = getContentPane();   //get the container
    c.setLayout(null);                //set the layout to null
        //create the check boxes with the appropriate labels
    boldCB = new JCheckBox("Bold");
    italicCB = new JCheckBox("Italic");

        //set the sizes of the check boxes
    boldCB.setSize(100, 30);
    italicCB.setSize(100, 30);

        //set the location of the check boxes
    boldCB.setLocation(100, 100);
    italicCB.setLocation(300, 100);
```

1
2

```
        //register the item listener to the check boxes
    boldCB.addItemListener(this);
    italicCB.addItemListener(this);

        //add the check boxes to the pane
    c.add(boldCB);
    c.add(italicCB);
}
```

To specify the font and style of the text, we use two `int` variables: `intBold` and `intItalic`. These variables are set to `Font.PLAIN` when the check boxes are not checked. They are set to `Font.BOLD` and `Font.ITALIC`, respectively, if the corresponding check boxes are checked. To create bold and italic fonts, you simply add the values of the variables `bold` and `italic`. In other words, you can create desired fonts by just using `intBold + intItalic` as the style value. Note that because `Font.PLAIN` has a value of zero, `Font.PLAIN + Font.PLAIN` remains `Font.PLAIN`. The `paint` method can be used to set the color and font, and to display the welcome message. The definition of the method `paint` can be written as follows:

```
public void paint(Graphics g)
{
    super.paint(g);
    g.setColor(Color.red);
    g.setFont(new Font("Courier", intBold + intItalic, 24));
    g.drawString("Welcome to Java Programming", 30, 30);
}
```

To make the program respond to the events generated by the check boxes, next we write the definition of the method `itemStateChanged`. As shown earlier, the method `itemStateChanged` has one parameter, `e`, of the type `ItemEvent`. Because there are two check boxes, we use the method `getSource` to identify the box generating the event.

The expression:

```
e.getSource() == boldCB
```

is `true` if the check box associated with `boldCB` generated the event. Similarly, the expression:

```
e.getSource() == italicCB
```

is `true` if the check box associated with `italicCB` generated the event.

After identifying the check box that generated the event, we determine whether the user selected or deselected the check box. For this, we use the method `getStateChange` of the `class ItemEvent` that returns either the constant `ItemEvent.SELECTED` or the constant `ItemEvent.DESELECTED`, which are defined in the `class ItemEvent`. For example, the expression:

```
e.getStateChange() == ItemEvent.SELECTED
```

is `true` if the event `e` corresponds to selecting the check box.

Finally, every time an event happens, you want to change the font accordingly. This can be achieved by invoking the **paint** method. To call the **paint** method, you need a **Graphics** object. So, you invoke the **repaint** method, which in turn invokes the **paint** method. Therefore, you need to call the **repaint** method before leaving the event handler method.

The definition of the method **itemStateChanged** is:

```
public void itemStateChanged(ItemEvent e)
{
    if (e.getSource() == boldCB)
    {
        if (e.getStateChange() == ItemEvent.SELECTED)
            intBold = Font.BOLD;
        if (e.getStateChange() == ItemEvent.DESELECTED)
            intBold = Font.PLAIN;
    }

    if (e.getSource() == italicCB)
    {
        if (e.getStateChange() == ItemEvent.SELECTED)
            intItalic = Font.ITALIC;
        if (e.getStateChange() == ItemEvent.DESELECTED)
            intItalic = Font.PLAIN;
    }

    repaint();
}
```

Now that the necessary components are written, we can write the complete program.

```
//Welcome Applet with check boxes

import java.awt.*;
import java.awt.event.*;
import javax.swing.*;

public class GrandWelcomeCheckBox extends JApplet implements
                                                   ItemListener
{
    private int intBold = Font.PLAIN;
    private int intItalic = Font.PLAIN;
    private JCheckBox boldCB, italicCB;

    public void init()
    {
        Container c = getContentPane();
        c.setLayout(null);
        boldCB = new JCheckBox("Bold");
        italicCB = new JCheckBox("Italic");
```

```
        boldCB.setSize(100, 30);
        italicCB.setSize(100,30);

        boldCB.setLocation(100, 100);
        italicCB.setLocation(300, 100);

        boldCB.addItemListener(this);
        italicCB.addItemListener(this);

        c.add(boldCB);
        c.add(italicCB);
    }

    public void paint( Graphics g)
    {
        super.paint(g);
        g.setColor(Color.red);
        g.setFont(new Font("Courier", intBold + intItalic, 24));
        g.drawString("Welcome to Java Programming", 30, 30);
    }

    public void itemStateChanged(ItemEvent e)
    {
        if (e.getSource() == boldCB)
        {
            if (e.getStateChange() == ItemEvent.SELECTED)
                intBold = Font.BOLD;
            if (e.getStateChange() == ItemEvent.DESELECTED)
                intBold = Font.PLAIN;
        }

        if (e.getSource() == italicCB)
        {
            if (e.getStateChange() == ItemEvent.SELECTED)
                intItalic = Font.ITALIC;
            if (e.getStateChange() == ItemEvent.DESELECTED)
                intItalic = Font.PLAIN;
        }

        repaint();
    }
}
```

The HTML file for this program contains the following code:

```
<HTML>
  <HEAD>
    <TITLE>WELCOME</TITLE>
  </HEAD>
  <BODY>
    <OBJECT code = "GrandWelcomeCheckBox.class" width = "440"
                                                height = "200">
    </OBJECT>
  </BODY>
</HTML>
```

Sample Run: Figure 12-13 shows a sample run of the applet with check boxes.

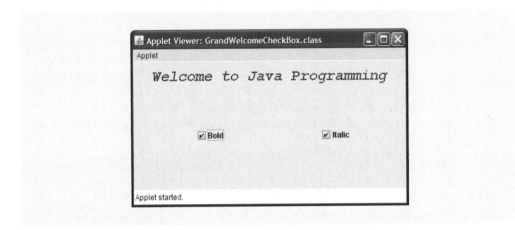

FIGURE 12-13 Welcome applet with check boxes

JRadioButton

Check boxes allow the user to select values from a given set of values. The program in the previous section used two check boxes. The user could select or deselect one or both check boxes. However, there are situations in which you want the user to make only one selection from a set of values. For example, if the user needs to select the gender of a person, the user selects either female or male, but not both. If you want the user to select only one of the options presented, you use radio buttons. To make such selections possible, Java provides the **class** JRadioButton.

Table 12-11 shows some of the constructors and methods of the **class** JRadioButton.

TABLE 12-11 Some Constructors and Methods of the **class** JRadioButton

```
public JRadioButton()
   //Creates an initially unselected radio button
   //with no label and no icon.
   //Example: JRadioButton myJRadioButton = new JRadioButton();
   //    myJRadioButton points to the radio button with no label
   //    and no icon.

public JRadioButton(Icon icon)
   //Creates an initially unselected radio button
   //with the specified icon and no label.
   //Example: JRadioButton myJRadioButton =
   //          new JRadioButton(anIcon);
   //    myJRadioButton points to the radio button with the
   //    icon "anIcon".
```

1
2

TABLE 12-11 Some Constructors and Methods of the **class** JRadioButton (continued)

```
public JRadioButton(Icon icon, boolean selected)
  //Creates a radio button with the specified
  //icon and selection state, but with no label.
  //Example:JRadioButton myJRadioButton =
  //                     new JRadioButton(anIcon, true);
  //    myJRadioButton points to the selected radio button
  //    with the icon "anIcon".
```

```
public JRadioButton(String text)
  //Creates an unselected radio button with the
  //specified text as the label.
  //Example: JRadioButton myJRadioButton =
  //                     new JRadioButton("Box");
  //    myJRadioButton points to the unselected radio button
  //    with the label "Box".
```

```
public JRadioButton(String text, boolean selected)
  //Creates a radio button with the specified
  //text as the label and selection state.
  //Example: JRadioButton myJRadioButton =
  //              new JRadioButton("Box", false);
  //        myJRadioButton points to the unselected radio
  //        button with the label "Box".
```

```
public JRadioButton(String text, Icon icon)
  //Creates a radio button with the specified
  //icon and the specified text as the label.
  //Example: RadioButton myJRadioButton =
  //                     new JRadioButton("Box", anIcon);
  //      myJRadioButton points to the unselected radio button
  //      with the label "Box" and the icon "anIcon".
```

```
public JRadioButton(String text, Icon icon, boolean selected)
  //Creates a radio button with the specified icon and
  //selection state, and with the specified text as the label
  //Example: JRadioButton myJRadioButton =
  //                 new JRadioButton("Box", anIcon, true);
  //      myJRadioButton points to the selected radio button
  //      with the label "Box" and the icon "anIcon".
```

```
public boolean isSelected()
  //This method is inherited from the AbstractButton class
  //and is used to retrieve the state of a button.
  //Example: if (myJRadioButton.isSelected() == true)
  //      The "if" block will be executed provided
  //      myJRadioButton is checked.
```

```
public boolean setSelected(boolean b)
  //This method is inherited from the AbstractButton class
  //and is used to set the state of a button.
  //Example: myJRadioButton.setSelected(true);
  //        myJRadioButton gets checked.
```

Radio buttons are created the same way check boxes are created. Consider the following statements:

```
private JRadioButton redRB, greenRB, blueRB;    //Line 1
redRB = new JRadioButton("Red");                //Line 2
greenRB = new JRadioButton("Green");            //Line 3
blueRB = new JRadioButton("Blue");              //Line 4
```

The statement in Line 1 declares redRB, greenRB, and blueRB to be reference variables of the JRadioButton type. The statement in Line 2 instantiates the object redRB and assigns it the label "Red". Similarly, the statements in Lines 3 and 4 instantiate the objects greenRB and blueRB and with the labels "Green" and "Blue", respectively.

As with check boxes, we create and place radio buttons in the content pane of the applet. However, in this case, to force the user to select only one radio button at a time, we create a button group and group the radio buttons. Consider the following statements:

```
private ButtonGroup ColorSelectBGroup;          //Line 5

ColorSelectBGroup = new ButtonGroup();          //Line 6
ColorSelectBGroup.add(redRB);                   //Line 7
ColorSelectBGroup.add(greenRB);                 //Line 8
ColorSelectBGroup.add(blueRB);                  //Line 9
```

The statements in Lines 5 and 6 create the object ColorSelectBGroup, and the statements in Lines 7, 8, and 9 add the radio buttons redRB, greenRB, and blueRB to this object. The statements in Lines 1 through 9 create and group the radio buttons, as shown in Figure 12-14.

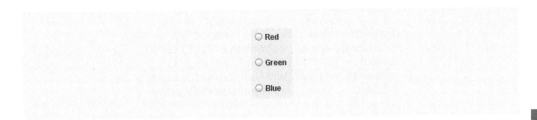

FIGURE 12-14 Radio buttons

Because the radio buttons redRB, greenRB, and blueRB are grouped, the user can select only one of these buttons. Similarly to JCheckBox, JRadioButton also generates an ItemEvent. So we use the interface ItemListener and its method itemStateChanged to handle the events.

In the following example, we start with the applet we created in the section JCheckBox and add three radio buttons so that the text color can be selected from the list: red, green, or blue.

Grouping buttons enforces the constraint that only one radio button can be selected at any time. This also affects how you write the event handler. Because only one button can be selected, once you know the source of the event, you can conclude that the associated radio button is selected. Thus, the relevant code for handling the events generated by these radio buttons can be written as follows:

```
if (e.getSource() == redRB)
    currentColor = Color.red;
else if (e.getSource() == greenRB)
    currentColor = Color.green;
else if (e.getSource() == blueRB)
    currentColor = Color.blue;
```

The complete program, along with the sample run, follows:

```
import java.awt.*;
import java.awt.event.*;
import javax.swing.*;

public class GrandWelcomeRButton extends JApplet implements
                                                    ItemListener
{
    private int intBold = Font.PLAIN;
    private int intItalic = Font.PLAIN;
    private Color currentColor = Color.black;
    private JCheckBox boldCB, italicCB;
    private JRadioButton redRB, greenRB, blueRB;
    private ButtonGroup ColorSelectBGroup;

    public void init()
    {
        Container c = getContentPane();
        c.setLayout(null);

        boldCB = new JCheckBox("Bold");
        italicCB = new JCheckBox("Italic");
        redRB = new JRadioButton("Red");
        greenRB = new JRadioButton("Green");
        blueRB = new JRadioButton("Blue");

        boldCB.setSize(100, 30);
        italicCB.setSize(100, 30);
        redRB.setSize(100, 30);
        greenRB.setSize(100, 30);
        blueRB.setSize(100, 30);

        boldCB.setLocation(100, 70);
        italicCB.setLocation(100, 150);
        redRB.setLocation(300, 70);
        greenRB.setLocation(300, 110);
        blueRB.setLocation(300, 150);

        boldCB.addItemListener(this);
        italicCB.addItemListener(this);
        redRB.addItemListener(this);
```

```java
        greenRB.addItemListener(this);
        blueRB.addItemListener(this);

        c.add(boldCB);
        c.add(italicCB);
        c.add(redRB);
        c.add(greenRB);
        c.add(blueRB);

        ColorSelectBGroup = new ButtonGroup();
        ColorSelectBGroup.add(redRB);
        ColorSelectBGroup.add(greenRB);
        ColorSelectBGroup.add(blueRB);
    }

    public void paint(Graphics g)
    {
        super.paint(g);
        g.setColor(Color.orange);
        g.drawRoundRect(75, 50, 125, 140, 10, 10);
        g.drawRoundRect(275, 50, 125, 140, 10, 10);
        g.setColor(currentColor);
        g.setFont(new Font("Courier", intBold + intItalic, 24));
        g.drawString("Welcome to Java Programming", 30, 30);
    }

    public void itemStateChanged(ItemEvent e)
    {
        if (e.getSource() == boldCB)
        {
            if (e.getStateChange() == ItemEvent.SELECTED)
                intBold = Font.BOLD;
            if (e.getStateChange() == ItemEvent.DESELECTED)
                intBold = Font.PLAIN;
        }

        if (e.getSource() == italicCB)
        {
            if (e.getStateChange() == ItemEvent.SELECTED)
                intItalic = Font.ITALIC;
            if (e.getStateChange() == ItemEvent.DESELECTED)
                intItalic = Font.PLAIN;
        }

        if (e.getSource() == redRB)
            currentColor = Color.red;
        else if (e.getSource() == greenRB)
            currentColor = Color.green;
        else if (e.getSource() == blueRB)
            currentColor = Color.blue;

        repaint();
    }
}
```

1
2

The HTML file for this program contains the following code:

```
<HTML>
  <HEAD>
    <TITLE>WELCOME</TITLE>
  </HEAD>
  <BODY>
    <OBJECT code = "GrandWelcomeRButton.class" width = "440"
                                               height = "200">
    </OBJECT>
  </BODY>
</HTML>
```

Sample Run: Figure 12-15 is a sample run showing check boxes and radio buttons.

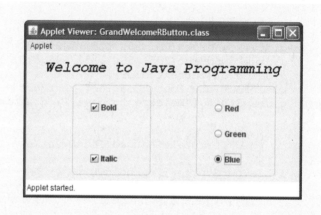

FIGURE 12-15 Sample run showing check boxes and radio buttons

JComboBox

A **combo box**, also known as a drop-down list, is used to select an item from a list of possibilities. A JComboBox generates an ItemEvent monitored by an ItemListener, which invokes the method itemStateChanged exactly as in JCheckBox or JRadioButton.

Table 12-12 lists some constructors of the class JComboBox.

TABLE 12-12 Some Constructors of the **class** JComboBox

```
public JComboBox()
   //Creates a JComboBox with no items to select.
   //Example: JComboBox selectionList = new JComboBox();
   //         selectionList is created but has no selectable items.

public JComboBox(Vector v)
   //Creates a JComboBox to display the elements
   //in the vector provided as an input parameter.
   //Example: JComboBox selectionList = new JComboBox(v);
   //         selectionList points to the combo box that lists the
   //         elements contained in Vector v.

public JComboBox(Object[] o)
   //Constructor:  Creates a JComboBox that displays the
   //elements in the object array provided as an input parameter.
   //Example: JComboBox selectionList = new JComboBox(o);
   //      creates the new combo box called selectionList and
   //      displays the selections. For an object list, would
   //      display o.toString() values.
```

In the previous two sections, we created an applet that uses check boxes and radio buttons to change the font and style of the text. In this section, we add a JComboBox to the program so that the user can select a font from a list of font names, and apply that font to the text.

To create a combo box, we first declare a reference variable as follows:

```
private JComboBox fontFaceDD;                          //Line 1
```

Next, we create an array of strings and initialize it with the list of font names. The corresponding Java statement is:

```
private String fontNames[] = {"Dialog", "Century Gothic",
                              "Courier", "Serif"};    //Line 2
```

Next, we use the variable fontFaceDD, declared in Line 1, and the array of strings fontNames, created in Line 2, to create a combo box. Consider the following statement:

```
fontFaceDD = new JComboBox(fontNames);                 //Line 3
```

This statement creates the object fontFaceDD and initializes this object using the strings in the array fontNames.

The object fontFaceDD has four items. When you click the combo box, it shows you the four choices. You can control the number of choices shown by using the method setMaximumRowCount. For example, the statement:

```
fontFaceDD.setMaximumRowCount(3);
```

sets the number of choices to be shown to 3. Because there are four choices in the combo box `fontFaceDD` and only three choices are shown, a vertical scroll bar appears to the right of the box. You can scroll this bar to see and select the other choices.

When you click an item in the combo box, it generates an item event. To process item events, we use the `interface ItemListener`. As described in the previous section, the item event handler code is placed in the body of the method `itemStateChanged`.

When the user selects an item from a combo box, the index of the selected item can be obtained by using the method `getSelectedIndex()`. For example, the statement:

```
currentFontName = fontNames[fontFaceDD.getSelectedIndex()];
```

assigns the current font name to the string variable `currentFontName`.

Example 12-7 gives the complete program listing for this `JComboBox` example.

EXAMPLE 12-7

```
//Welcome program with check boxes, radio buttons, and combo box

import java.awt.*;
import java.awt.event.*;
import javax.swing.*;

public class GrandWelcomeFinal extends JApplet implements
                                                   ItemListener
{
    private int intBold = Font.PLAIN;
    private int intItalic = Font.PLAIN;

    private Color currentColor = Color.black;
    private String currentFontName ="Courier";
    private JCheckBox boldCB, italicCB;
    private JRadioButton redRB, greenRB, blueRB;
    private ButtonGroup ColorSelectBGroup;
    private JComboBox fontFaceDD;

    private String[] fontNames
                = {"Dialog", "Century Gothic",
                   "Courier", "Serif"};

    public void init()
    {
        Container c = getContentPane();
        c.setLayout(null);
```

```java
        boldCB = new JCheckBox("Bold");
        italicCB = new JCheckBox("Italic");
        redRB = new JRadioButton("Red");
        greenRB = new JRadioButton("Green");
        blueRB = new JRadioButton("Blue");
        fontFaceDD = new JComboBox(fontNames);
        fontFaceDD.setMaximumRowCount(3);

        boldCB.setSize(80, 30);
        italicCB.setSize(80, 30);
        redRB.setSize(80, 30);
        greenRB.setSize(80, 30);
        blueRB.setSize(80, 30);
        fontFaceDD.setSize(80, 30);

        boldCB.setLocation(100, 70);
        italicCB.setLocation(100, 150);
        redRB.setLocation(300, 70);
        greenRB.setLocation(300, 110);
        blueRB.setLocation(300, 150);
        fontFaceDD.setLocation(200, 70);

        boldCB.addItemListener(this);
        italicCB.addItemListener(this);
        redRB.addItemListener(this);
        greenRB.addItemListener(this);
        blueRB.addItemListener(this);
        fontFaceDD.addItemListener(this);

        c.add(boldCB);
        c.add(italicCB);
        c.add(redRB);
        c.add(greenRB);
        c.add(blueRB);

        c.add(fontFaceDD);
        ColorSelectBGroup = new ButtonGroup();
        ColorSelectBGroup.add(redRB);
        ColorSelectBGroup.add(greenRB);
        ColorSelectBGroup.add(blueRB);
    }

public void paint(Graphics g)
{
        super.paint(g);

        g.setColor(Color.orange);
        g.drawRoundRect(75, 50, 324, 140, 10, 10);
        g.drawLine(183, 50, 183, 190);
        g.drawLine(291, 50, 291, 190);
```

1
2

```
        g.setColor(currentColor);
        g.setFont(new Font(currentFontName,
                          intBold + intItalic, 24));
        g.drawString("Welcome to Java Programming", 30, 30);
    }

    public void itemStateChanged(ItemEvent e)
    {
        if (e.getSource() == boldCB)
        {
            if (e.getStateChange() == ItemEvent.SELECTED)
                intBold = Font.BOLD;
            if (e.getStateChange() == ItemEvent.DESELECTED)
                intBold = Font.PLAIN;
        }

        if (e.getSource() == italicCB)
        {
            if (e.getStateChange() == ItemEvent.SELECTED)
                intItalic = Font.ITALIC;
            if (e.getStateChange() == ItemEvent.DESELECTED)
                intItalic = Font.PLAIN;
        }

        if (e.getSource() == redRB)
            currentColor = Color.red;
        else if (e.getSource() == greenRB)
            currentColor = Color.green;
        else if (e.getSource() == blueRB)
            currentColor = Color.blue;

        if (e.getSource() == fontFaceDD)
            currentFontName =
                        fontNames[fontFaceDD.getSelectedIndex()];

        repaint();
    }
}
```

The HTML file for this program contains the following code:

```
<HTML>
  <HEAD>
    <TITLE>WELCOME</TITLE>
  </HEAD>
  <BODY>
    <OBJECT code = "GrandWelcomeFinal.class" width = "440"
                                            height = "200">
    </OBJECT>
  </BODY>
</HTML>
```

Sample Run: Figure 12-16 shows a sample run of the Welcome applet with check boxes, a combo box, and radio buttons.

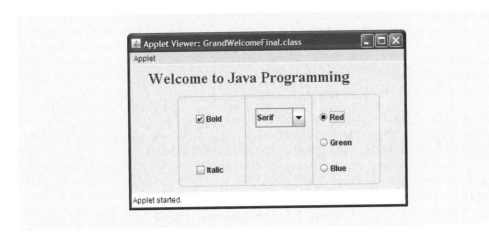

FIGURE 12-16 Welcome applet with check boxes, combo box, and radio buttons

JList

A **list** displays a number of items from which the user can select one or more items. This section illustrates the use of a single selection list. The programming example at the end of this chapter uses a multiple selection list. Table 12-13 shows some constructors and methods of the `class JList`.

TABLE 12-13 Some Constructors and Methods of the `class JList`

```
public JList()
   //Creates a JList with no items to select.
   //Example: JList selectionList = new JList();
   //         selectionList is created but has no selectable items.

public JList(Vector v)
   //Creates a JList to display the elements in the
   //vector provided as an input parameter.
   //Example: JList selectionList = new JList(v);
   //         selectionList is a new list that lists the elements
   //         contained in Vector v.
```

TABLE 12-13 Some Constructors and Methods of the **class** JList (continued)

```
public JList(Object[] o)
  //Creates a JList that displays the elements in the object
  //array provided as an input parameter.
  //Example: JList selectionList = new JList(o);
  //     creates the new list called selectionList and displays
  //     the selections. For an object list, would
  //     display o.toString() values.
```

```
public void setSelectionMode(ListSelectionModel listselectionmodel)
  //Method to set the model for managing the list selections.
  //Allows only one item to be selected or a range of
  //contiguous or noncontiguous items to be selected.
  //Example: pictureList.setSelectionMode
  //                (ListSelectionModel.SINGLE_SELECTION);
  //     limits pictureList to allow only a single selection
  //     at a time.
```

```
public void setSelectionBackground(Color sbColor)
  //Method to set the color of the background of a selected item
  //Example: myList.setSelectionBackground(myCustomColor);
  //   This statement sets the color that appears in the
  //   background of a selected item in myList to the color
  //   represented by the Color object myCustomColor.
```

```
public void addListSelectionListener(ListSelectionListener lsl)
  //Method to add a listener class to take action when an item
  //in the list is selected.
  //Example: pictureList.addListSelectionListener(handler);
  //   This statement adds a new ListSelectionListener object,
  //   named handler, to pictureList to process the events
  //   related to the selection of a list item.
```

```
public int getSelectedIndex()
  //When an item in the list is selected, this method returns
  //the index of that item (0 to the number of items - 1);
  //returns -1 if nothing is selected
  //Example: myLabel.setIcon
  //                (pictures[ pictureList.getSelectedIndex() ]);
  //   This statement sets an icon for a label to the item in
  //   an array of image icons specified by the index of the
  //   selected item in the list.
```

Let's write a program that uses a JList and JLabels to create the GUI as shown in Figure 12-17.

The GUI in Figure 12-17 contains four GUI components: a JList and three JLabels. The JList object contains the list of items, such as Pie Diagram, Line Graph, and Bar Graph. The first JLabel contains the string "Select an Image". Below this label is the JList object, and below the JList object is a JLabel that displays an image. For example, if the user selects Normal Curve, this JLabel object shows the image of a normal curve. Below the label showing an image is a `JLabel` that displays the name of the image. For example, in Figure 12-17, this label displays the text `Normal Curve`.

The top and the bottom labels display a line of text, so they are manipulated using strings as labels. The label showing an image is manipulated using images. For this program, we include five JPEG images. The following statement creates the `JLabel` object `promptJL` with `Select an Image` as its label and sets the justification of the label to center:

```
private JLabel promptJL = new JLabel("Select an Image",
                                     SwingConstants.CENTER);
```

The following statements declare `displayPicJL` and `infoJL` to be reference variables of the `JLabel` type:

```
private JLabel displayPicJL;
private JLabel infoJL;
```

We use `displayPicJL` to display the image and `infoJL` to display the name of the image, as shown in Figure 12-17. The following paragraphs explain how to change the text and image of these labels during program execution.

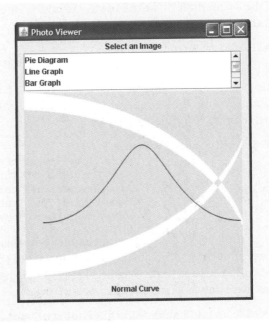

FIGURE 12-17 GUI using `JList` and `JLabel`

We now discuss how to create the `JList` with five items. For the most part, creating a `JList` is similar to creating a `JComboBox`. To create a `JList`, we first declare a reference variable as follows:

```
private JList pictureJList;
```

Next, we create an array of strings consisting of the names of the images. The following statement creates the array `pictureNames` of five components:

```
private String[] pictureNames = {"Pie Diagram",
                                 "Line Graph",
                                 "Bar Graph",
                                 "Table",
                                 "Normal Curve"};
```

Next, we use the array `pictureNames` to create the `JList` object `pictureJList` as follows:

```
pictureJList = new JList(pictureNames);
```

As in the case of combo boxes, you can use the method `setVisibleRowCount` to set the number of visible rows of a `JList`. For example, the following statement sets the number of visible rows of `pictureJList` to 3:

```
pictureJList.setVisibleRowCount(3);
```

In the program we are writing, we want the user to select only one item at a time from `pictureJList`, so we set `pictureJList` to the single selection mode by using the method `setSelectionMode` together with the constant `ListSelectionModel.SINGLE_SELECTION` as follows:

```
pictureJList.setSelectionMode
             (ListSelectionModel.SINGLE_SELECTION);
```

When the user selects an image from `pictureJList`, the program displays the corresponding image using the `JLabel` object `displayPicJL`. We use the **class** `ImageIcon` and create an array of images as follows:

```
private ImageIcon[] pictures =
                    {new ImageIcon("pieDiagram.jpg"),
                     new ImageIcon("lineGraph.jpg"),
                     new ImageIcon("barGraph.jpg"),
                     new ImageIcon("table.jpg"),
                     new ImageIcon("normalCurve.jpg")};
```

When the user clicks to select an item from the `JList` object `pictureJList`, `ListSelectionEvent` is generated. To process `ListSelectionEvent`, we use the **interface** `ListSelectionListener`. This **interface** has the method `valueChanged`, which executes when a `ListSelectionEvent` occurs. The heading of this method is:

```
public void valueChanged(ListSelectionEvent e)
```

We can put the code to display the required image and its name in this method. When the user clicks an item in the `JList`, we can determine the index of the selected item by using the method `getSelectedIndex`. We then use this index to select the corresponding image from the array `pictures` and the name of the image from the array `pictureNames`. We can now use the method `repaint` to repaint the pane. The definition of the method `valueChanged` is:

```java
public void valueChanged(ListSelectionEvent e)
{
    displayPicJL.setIcon(
            pictures[pictureJList.getSelectedIndex()]);
    infoJL.setText(
            pictureNames[pictureJList.getSelectedIndex()]);
    repaint();
}
```

Of course, we must register the list selection listener to the JList. The following statement accomplishes this:

```java
pictureJList.addListSelectionListener(this);
```

There are five items in pictureJList. When the program executes, it displays only three of these items in the list at a time. Therefore, we want to attach a vertical scroll bar to pictureJList, so that the user can scroll to select an item not currently shown in the list. To do so, we use the class JScrollPane as follows. First, we create the JScrollPane object selectionJS and initialize this object using the object pictureJList. We then add the object to the pane selectionJS. The following statements illustrate this concept:

```java
selectionJS = new JScrollPane(pictureJList);
pane.add(selectionJS);
```

We will set the pane layout to null and specify the size and location of the GUI components. The complete program listing contains the following statements:

```java
//Program to demonstrate JLIST

import java.awt.*;
import javax.swing.*;
import javax.swing.event.*;

public class JListPictureViewer extends JFrame implements
                                    ListSelectionListener
{
    private String[] pictureNames = {"Pie Diagram",
                                     "Line Graph",
                                     "Bar Graph",
                                     "Table",
                                     "Normal Curve"};

    private ImageIcon[] pictures =
                {new ImageIcon("pieDiagram.jpg"),
                 new ImageIcon("lineGraph.jpg"),
                 new ImageIcon("barGraph.jpg"),
                 new ImageIcon("table.jpg"),
                 new ImageIcon("normalCurve.jpg")};
```

1
2

```java
private JList pictureJList;
private JScrollPane selectionJS;
private JLabel promptJL;
private JLabel displayPicJL;
private JLabel infoJL;

public JListPictureViewer()
{
    super("Photo Viewer");

    Container pane = getContentPane();
    pane.setLayout(null);

    promptJL = new JLabel("Select an Image",
                          SwingConstants.CENTER);
    promptJL.setSize(350, 20);
    promptJL.setLocation(10, 0);
    pane.add(promptJL);

    pictureJList = new JList(pictureNames);
    pictureJList.setVisibleRowCount(3);
    pictureJList.setSelectionMode
                (ListSelectionModel.SINGLE_SELECTION);
    pictureJList.addListSelectionListener(this);

    selectionJS = new JScrollPane(pictureJList);
    selectionJS.setSize(350, 60);
    selectionJS.setLocation(10, 20);
    pane.add(selectionJS);

    displayPicJL = new JLabel(pictures[4]);
    displayPicJL.setSize(350, 350);
    displayPicJL.setLocation(10, 50);

    pane.add(displayPicJL);

    infoJL = new JLabel(pictureNames[4],
                        SwingConstants.CENTER);
    infoJL.setSize(350, 20);
    infoJL.setLocation(10, 380);
    pane.add(infoJL);

    setSize (380, 440);
    setVisible(true);
    setDefaultCloseOperation(EXIT_ON_CLOSE);
}

public static void main(String args[])
{
    JListPictureViewer picViewer = new JListPictureViewer();
}
```

```
    public void valueChanged(ListSelectionEvent e)
    {
        displayPicJL.setIcon(
            pictures[pictureJList.getSelectedIndex()]);
        infoJL.setText(
            pictureNames[pictureJList.getSelectedIndex()]);
        repaint();
    }
}
```

Sample Run: Figure 12-18 shows a sample run of the JListPictureViewer program.

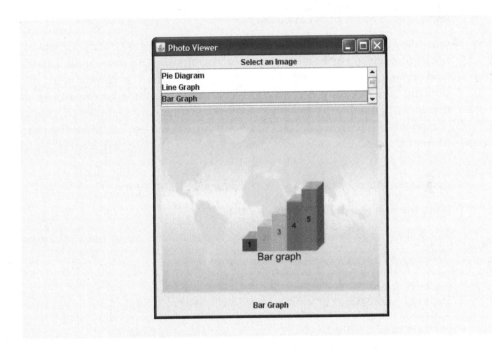

FIGURE 12-18 Sample run of the JListPictureViewer program

Layout Managers

In earlier chapters, you saw two layout managers, GridLayout and null. For GridLayout, you specify the number of rows and columns you want, and you can place your components from left to right, row-by-row, or from top to bottom. If you choose the null layout, you have to specify the size and location of each component. Java provides many layout managers; this section briefly introduces two more.

FlowLayout

FlowLayout is the default layout manager for a Java application. Creating a FlowLayout manager is similar to creating a GridLayout manager. For example, suppose that you have the following declaration:

```
Container pane = getContentPane();
```

The statement(s):

```
pane.setLayout(new FlowLayout());
```

or:

```
FlowLayout flowLayoutMgr = new FlowLayout();
pane.setLayout(flowLayoutMgr);
```

set(s) the layout of the container pane to FlowLayout. FlowLayout places the components from left to right and centered, by default, until no more items can be placed. The next item(s) will be placed in the second line. Thus, a FlowLayout manager works similarly to a GridLayout manager. The main difference between these two layouts is that in a GridLayout, all rows (columns) have the same number of components and all components have the same size. However, in a FlowLayout, there is no such guarantee. Moreover, in a FlowLayout, you can align each line left, center, or right using a statement such as:

```
flowLayoutMgr.setAlignment(FlowLayout.RIGHT);
```

Note that the default alignment is CENTERED.

The following Java application program illustrates the use of the FlowLayout manager:

```java
//Program to illustrate FlowLayout

import javax.swing.*;
import java.awt.*;

public class FlowLayoutExample extends JFrame
{
    private static int WIDTH = 350;
    private static int HEIGHT = 350;

        //Variables to create GUI components
    private JLabel labelJL;
    private JTextField textFieldTF;
    private JButton buttonJB;
    private JCheckBox checkboxCB;
    private JRadioButton radioButtonRB;
    private JTextArea textAreaTA;
```

```java
    private FlowLayout flowLayoutMgr;

    public FlowLayoutExample()
    {
        setTitle("FlowLayout Manager");              //Line 1
        Container pane = getContentPane();           //Line 2
        setSize(WIDTH,HEIGHT);                       //Line 3

        flowLayoutMgr = new FlowLayout();            //Line 4
        pane.setLayout(flowLayoutMgr);               //Line 5

        labelJL = new JLabel("First Component");     //Line 6
        textFieldTF = new JTextField(15);            //Line 7
        textFieldTF.setText("Second Component");     //Line 8
        buttonJB = new JButton("Third Component");   //Line 9

        checkboxCB = new JCheckBox("Fourth Component"); //Line 10

        radioButtonRB =
              new JRadioButton("Fifth Component");   //Line 11

        textAreaTA = new JTextArea(10, 20);          //Line 12

        textAreaTA.setText("Sixth Component.\n");    //Line 13

        textAreaTA.append(
            "Use the mouse to resize the window."); //Line 14

                //place the GUI components into the pane
        pane.add(labelJL);                           //Line 15
        pane.add(textFieldTF);                       //Line 16
        pane.add(buttonJB);                          //Line 17
        pane.add(checkboxCB);                        //Line 18
        pane.add(radioButtonRB);                     //Line 19
        pane.add(textAreaTA);                        //Line 20

        setVisible(true);                            //Line 21
        setDefaultCloseOperation(EXIT_ON_CLOSE);     //Line 22
    }

    public static void main(String[] args)           //Line 23
    {
        FlowLayoutExample flow =
                new FlowLayoutExample();             //Line 24
    }
}
```

1
2

Sample Run: Figure 12-19 shows a sample run of the `FlowLayoutExample` program.

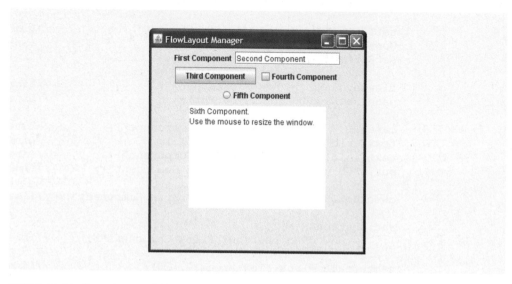

FIGURE 12-19 Sample run of the `FlowLayoutExample` program

The preceding program works as follows: The statement in Line 1 sets the title of the window. The statement in Line 2 accesses the content pane. The statement in Line 3 sets the size of the window. The statement in Line 4 creates the `FlowLayout` object `flowLayoutMgr`; the statement in Line 5 uses this object to set the layout of the pane to `FlowLayout`. (Because we did not specify the layout, the default layout, `CENTERED`, is assumed.) The statement in Line 6 instantiates the `JLabel` object `labelJL`. The statement in Line 7 instantiates the `JTextField` object `textFieldTF`, and the statement in Line 8 sets the text of the object `textFieldTF`. The statement in Line 9 instantiates the `JButton` object `buttonJB`. The statement in Line 10 instantiates the `JCheckBox` object `checkboxCB`. The statement in Line 11 instantiates the `JRadioButton` object `radioButtonRB`. The statement in Line 12 instantiates the `JTextArea` object `textAreaTA` with 10 rows and 20 columns. The statement in Line 13 places the text `Sixth Component` into the text area. The statement in Line 14 appends the text:

`Use the mouse to resize the window.`

The statements in Lines 15 through 20 place the GUI components in the pane. The statement in Line 21 sets the visibility of the window to `true`, and the statement in Line 22 sets the window closing option to close when the program terminates. When the program executes, the statement in Line 24 creates the window with the GUI components shown in the sample run.

BorderLayout

The `BorderLayout` manager allows you to place items in specific regions. This layout manager divides the container into five regions: NORTH, SOUTH, EAST, WEST, and CENTER. Components placed in the NORTH and SOUTH regions extend horizontally, completely spanning one edge to the other. EAST and WEST components extend vertically between the components in the NORTH and SOUTH regions. The component placed at the CENTER expands to occupy any unused regions.

In the following example, we create five components and place them in the content pane using the `BorderLayout` manager:

```
//Program to illustrate BorderLayout

import javax.swing.*;
import java.awt.*;

public class BorderLayoutExample extends JFrame
{
    private static int WIDTH = 350;
    private static int HEIGHT = 300;

        //GUI components
    private JLabel labelJL;
    private JTextField textFieldTF;
    private JButton buttonJB;
    private JCheckBox checkboxCB;
    private JRadioButton radioButtonRB;
    private JTextArea textAreaTA;

    private BorderLayout borderLayoutMgr;

    public BorderLayoutExample()
    {
        setTitle("BorderLayout Manager");
        Container pane  = getContentPane();
        setSize(WIDTH, HEIGHT);

        borderLayoutMgr = new BorderLayout(10, 10);
        pane.setLayout(borderLayoutMgr);

        labelJL = new JLabel("North Component");
        textAreaTA = new JTextArea(10, 20);
        textAreaTA.setText("South Component.\n");
        textAreaTA.append(
            "Use the mouse to change the size of the window.");
        buttonJB = new JButton("West Component");
        checkboxCB = new JCheckBox("East Component");
        radioButtonRB = new JRadioButton("Center Component");
```

```java
        pane.add(labelJL, BorderLayout.NORTH);
        pane.add(textAreaTA, BorderLayout.SOUTH);
        pane.add(buttonJB, BorderLayout.EAST);
        pane.add(checkboxCB, BorderLayout.WEST);
        pane.add(radioButtonRB, BorderLayout.CENTER);

        setVisible(true);
        setDefaultCloseOperation(EXIT_ON_CLOSE);
    }

    public static void main(String[] args)
    {
        BorderLayoutExample flow = new BorderLayoutExample();
    }
}
```

Sample Run: A sample run of the `BorderLayoutExample` program is shown in Figure 12-20.

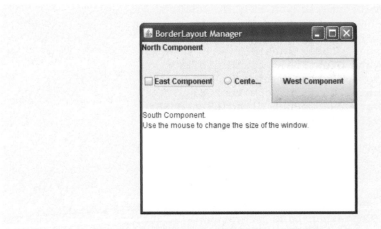

FIGURE 12-20 Sample run of the `BorderLayoutExample` program

Menus

Menus allow you to provide various functions without cluttering the GUI with too many components. Menus can be attached to objects, such as `JFrame` and `JApplet`.

The `classes` `JFrame` and `JApplet` both have the method `setJMenuBar` that allows you to set a menu bar. To set a menu bar, say, `menuMB`, you need statements such as the following:

```
private JMenuBar menuMB = new JMenuBar();   //creates a menu bar

setJMenuBar(menuMB);                        //sets the menu bar
```

Once you have created a menu bar, you can add menus, and in each menu you can add menu items. For instance, to create an `Edit` menu and add it to the menu bar created above, you need the following two statements:

```
JMenu editM = new JMenu("Edit");   //creates a menu "Edit"
menuMB.add(editM);                 //adds the menu to menu bar
                                   //menuMB created above
```

Likewise, if you need to create a `File` menu, you may do so by adding the following lines of code:

```
JMenu fileM = new JMenu("File");

menuMB.add(fileM);
```

Notice that the order in which you add menus to the menu bar determines the order in which they appear. For example, if you want the `File` menu to appear first, you must add it first.

The following program illustrates the use of menus:

```
import java.awt.*;
import java.awt.event.*;
import javax.swing.*;

public class TextEditor extends JFrame implements
                                        ActionListener
{
    private JMenuBar menuMB =
                    new JMenuBar(); //create the menu bar
    private JMenu fileM, editM, optionM;
    private JMenuItem exitI;
    private JMenuItem cutI, copyI, pasteI, selectI;
    private JTextArea pageTA = new JTextArea();
    private String scratchpad = "";

    public TextEditor()
    {
        setTitle("Simple Text Editor");

        Container pane = getContentPane();

        pane.setLayout(new BorderLayout());
        pane.add(pageTA, BorderLayout.CENTER);
        pane.add(new JScrollPane(pageTA));
        pageTA.setLineWrap(true);
```

```java
        setJMenuBar(menuMB);
        setFileMenu();
        setEditMenu();
        setSize(300, 200);

        setVisible(true);
        setDefaultCloseOperation(EXIT_ON_CLOSE);
    }

    private void setFileMenu()
    {
        fileM = new JMenu("File");
        menuMB.add(fileM);
        exitI = new JMenuItem("Exit");
        fileM.add(exitI);
        exitI.addActionListener(this);
    }

    private void setEditMenu()
    {
        editM = new JMenu("Edit");
        menuMB.add(editM);
        cutI = new JMenuItem("Cut");
        editM.add(cutI);
        cutI.addActionListener(this);
        copyI = new JMenuItem("Copy");
        editM.add(copyI);
        copyI.addActionListener(this);
        pasteI = new JMenuItem("Paste");
        editM.add(pasteI);
        pasteI.addActionListener(this);
        selectI = new JMenuItem("Select All");
        editM.add(selectI);
        selectI.addActionListener(this);
    }

    public void actionPerformed(ActionEvent e)
    {
        JMenuItem mItem = (JMenuItem) e.getSource();

        if (mItem == exitI)
        {
            System.exit(0);
        }
        else if (mItem == cutI)
        {
            scratchpad = pageTA.getSelectedText();
            pageTA.replaceRange("",
                        pageTA.getSelectionStart(),
                        pageTA.getSelectionEnd());
        }
```

```
        else if (mItem == copyI)
            scratchpad = pageTA.getSelectedText();
        else if (mItem == pasteI)
            pageTA.insert(scratchpad, pageTA.getCaretPosition());
        else if (mItem == selectI)
            pageTA.selectAll();
    }

    public static void main(String args[])
    {
        TextEditor texted = new TextEditor();
    }
}
```

Sample Run: A sample run of the program with menus is shown in Figure 12-21.

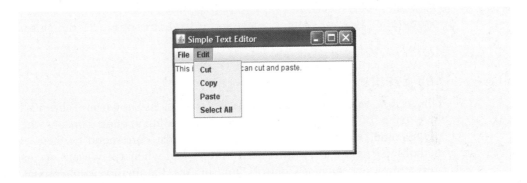

FIGURE 12-21 Sample run of the `TextEditor` program

Key and Mouse Events

In this chapter and in the preceding chapters, you learned how to handle action events when the user clicks a button. Moreover, Chapter 11 noted that when the `Enter` key is pressed in a text field, an action event is generated. Also, recall that when a mouse button is pressed to click a button, in addition to generating an action event, a mouse event is generated. Likewise, when the `Enter` key is pressed in a text field, in addition to the action event, a key event is generated. Therefore, a GUI program can simultaneously generate more than one event. This section includes various programs to show how to handle key and mouse events.

Recall from Chapter 11 that key events are handled by the `interface KeyListener`, and mouse events are handled by the `interfaces MouseListener` and `MouseMotionListener`. The key and mouse events and the corresponding event handlers were shown in Table 11-14 and are reproduced in Table 12-14.

TABLE 12-14 Events Generated by the Keyboard and Mouse

	Event Generated	Listener Interface	Listener Method
key	KeyEvent	KeyListener	keyPressed
key	KeyEvent	KeyListener	keyReleased
key	KeyEvent	KeyListener	keyTyped
mouse	MouseEvent	MouseListener	mouseClicked
mouse	MouseEvent	MouseListener	mouseEntered
mouse	MouseEvent	MouseListener	mouseExited
mouse	MouseEvent	MouseListener	mousePressed
mouse	MouseEvent	MouseListener	mouseReleased
mouse	MouseEvent	MouseMotionListener	mouseDragged
mouse	MouseEvent	MouseMotionListener	mouseMoved

Key Events

This section describes how to handle key events. As shown in Table 12-14, there are three types of key events. The interface KeyListener contains the methods—keyPressed, keyReleased, and keyTyped—that correspond to these events. These methods specify the action that needs to be taken when a key event occurs. When you press a meta key (such as Control, Shift, or Alt), the method keyPressed is executed; when you type a regular alphanumeric key, the method keyTyped is executed. When you release any key, the method keyReleased is executed. The program in Example 12-8 shows how to handle key events.

EXAMPLE 12-8

This program displays the character that corresponds to the key typed by the user. For example, if the user presses the key A, the program displays A. We use a JTextField object to display the character.

When you type an alphanumeric key, a key event is generated. The key event is handled by the method keyTyped. The necessary code to display the key is placed in the body of the method keyTyped. Before displaying the key typed by the user, the previous character is removed from the JTextField object. In other words, the program displays only one character at a time, corresponding to the key typed. In this program, the font of the character is set to Courier and the color of the character is randomly selected.

Because the interface keyListener contains three methods and we want to implement only one of these methods, we use the anonymous class mechanism to register a listener object. The complete program listing follows. (Notice that the program uses a message dialog box to inform the user what to do.)

```java
//Key Event

import java.awt.*;
import java.awt.event.*;
import javax.swing.*;

public class OneChar extends JApplet
{
    JTextField oneLetter = new JTextField(1);

    public void init()
    {
        Container c = getContentPane();

        //register the listener object
        oneLetter.addKeyListener(new KeyAdapter()
        {
            public void keyTyped(KeyEvent e)
            {
                float red, green, blue;

                Color fg, bg;

                oneLetter.setText(" ");

                red = (float) Math.random();
                green = (float) Math.random();
                blue = (float) Math.random();

                fg = new Color(red, green, blue);
                bg = Color.white;

                oneLetter.setForeground(fg);
                oneLetter.setBackground(bg);
                oneLetter.setCaretColor(bg);
                oneLetter.setFont(new Font("Courier",
                                    Font.BOLD, 200));
            }
        });

        c.setLayout(new GridLayout(1, 1));
        c.setBackground(Color.white);
        c.add(oneLetter);

        JOptionPane.showMessageDialog
            (null, "Click on the applet, then type a key ",
            "Information", JOptionPane.PLAIN_MESSAGE );
    }
}
```

The HTML file for this program contains the following code:

```
<HTML>
  <HEAD>
    <TITLE>ONECHAR APPLET</TITLE>
  </HEAD>
  <BODY>
    <OBJECT code = "OneChar.class" width = "350" height = "300">
    </OBJECT>
  </BODY>
</HTML>
```

Sample Run: Figure 12-22 shows a sample run of the `OneChar` applet. (Notice that Figure 12-22 does not show the message dialog box. However, when you execute this program, it first shows the message dialog box.)

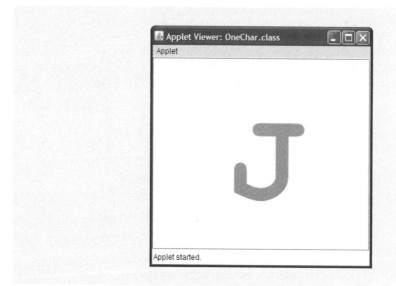

FIGURE 12-22 Sample run of the `OneChar` applet

Mouse Events

This section describes how to handle mouse events. A mouse can generate seven different types of events, as shown previously in Table 12-14. Some mouse events are handled by the `interface MouseListener` and others are handled by the `interface MouseMotionListener`. Table 12-14 also shows which listener method is executed when a particular mouse event occurs. Example 12-9 illustrates how to handle mouse events.

EXAMPLE 12-9

This example shows how to handle the following mouse events: mouse clicked, mouse entered, mouse exited, mouse pressed, and mouse released. To handle these events, we use the methods of the **interface** MouseListener. The MouseExample program contains six labels corresponding to the five mouse events and one label to display the mouse location. When you run this program and use the mouse, the foreground color of the label corresponding to the generated mouse event changes, and the mouse location where the event occurred is displayed.

```java
//Program to illustrate mouse events

import javax.swing.*;
import java.awt.*;
import java.awt.event.*;

public class MouseExample extends JFrame
                          implements MouseListener
{
    private static int WIDTH = 350;
    private static int HEIGHT = 250;

        //GUI components
    private JLabel[] labelJL;

    public MouseExample()
    {
        setTitle("Mouse Events");
        Container pane  = getContentPane();
        setSize(WIDTH,HEIGHT);

        GridLayout gridMgr = new GridLayout(6, 1, 10, 10);
        pane.setLayout(gridMgr);

        labelJL = new JLabel[6];

        labelJL[0] = new JLabel("Mouse Clicked",
                        SwingConstants.CENTER);
        labelJL[1] = new JLabel("Mouse Entered",
                        SwingConstants.CENTER);
        labelJL[2] = new JLabel("Mouse Exited",
                        SwingConstants.CENTER);
        labelJL[3] = new JLabel("Mouse Pressed",
                        SwingConstants.CENTER);
        labelJL[4] = new JLabel("Mouse Released",
                        SwingConstants.CENTER);
        labelJL[5] = new JLabel("",SwingConstants.CENTER);
```

1
2

```java
        for (int i = 0; i < labelJL.length; i++)
        {
           labelJL[i].setForeground(Color.gray);
           pane.add(labelJL[i]);
        }

        pane.addMouseListener(this);

        setVisible(true);
        setDefaultCloseOperation(EXIT_ON_CLOSE);
    }

    public void mouseClicked(MouseEvent event)
    {
        for (int i = 0; i < labelJL.length; i++)
        {
           if (i == 0)
              labelJL[i].setForeground(Color.yellow);
           else
              labelJL[i].setForeground(Color.gray);
        }

        labelJL[5].setText("["+ event.getX() + ","
                           + event.getY()+"]");

    }

    public void mouseEntered(MouseEvent event)
    {
        for (int i = 0; i < labelJL.length; i++)
        {
           if (i == 1)
              labelJL[i].setForeground(Color.green);
           else
              labelJL[i].setForeground(Color.gray);
        }

        labelJL[5].setText("["+ event.getX() + ","
                           + event.getY()+"]");
    }

    public void mouseExited(MouseEvent event)
    {
        for (int i = 0; i < labelJL.length; i++)
        {
           if (i == 2)
              labelJL[i].setForeground(Color.red);
           else
              labelJL[i].setForeground(Color.gray);
        }

        labelJL[5].setText("["+ event.getX() + ","
                           + event.getY()+"]");
    }
```

```java
public void mousePressed(MouseEvent event)
{
    for (int i = 0; i < labelJL.length; i++)
    {
        if (i == 3)
            labelJL[i].setForeground(Color.blue);
        else
            labelJL[i].setForeground(Color.gray);
    }

    labelJL[5].setText("["+ event.getX() + ","
                    + event.getY()+"]");
}

public void mouseReleased(MouseEvent event)
{
    for (int i = 0; i < labelJL.length; i++)
    {
        if (i == 4)
            labelJL[i].setForeground(Color.pink);
        else
            labelJL[i].setForeground(Color.gray);
    }

    labelJL[5].setText("["+ event.getX() + ","
                    + event.getY()+"]");
}

public static void main(String[] args)
{
    MouseExample flow = new MouseExample();
}
}
```

Sample Run: Figure 12-23 shows a sample run of the `MouseExample` program.

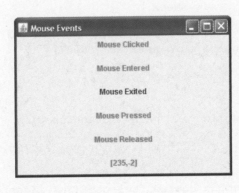

FIGURE 12-23 Sample run of the `MouseExample` program

EXAMPLE 12-10

The program in this example shows how to handle the mouse-dragged event. You can handle the mouse moved event similarly. These events are handled by the **interface** MouseMotionListener, which contains the methods mouseDragged and mouseMoved, which, in turn, are used to handle the mouse-dragged and mouse-moved events, respectively.

The program starts with some colored dots. If you drag a dot using the mouse, the dot turns into a line. This way, you can "freehand draw" different pictures. What is really happening is that we created small circle objects. The program contains the method selected to check whether or not the mouse is on a circle. If you drag a circle, the method mouseDragged is invoked and it paints a new circle. The sequence of circles gives the impression of drawing a line. The complete program listing follows:

```java
import javax.swing.*;
import java.awt.event.*;
import java.applet.*;
import java.awt.*;

public class FreeDrawApplet extends JApplet
                            implements MouseMotionListener
{
    //instance variables
    ColorCircle[] myGraph;

    final int NUM_CIRCLES = 7;
    final int WIDTH = 400;
    final int HEIGHT = 400;

    public class ColorCircle
    {
        private int x;
        private int y;

        public void setX(int iNewX)
        {
            x = iNewX;
        }

        public void setY(int iNewY)
        {
            y = iNewY;
        }

        public void paint (Graphics g)
        {
            g.fillOval(x - 10, y - 10, 20, 20);
        }

        public boolean selected(int iXcoord, int iYcoord)
        {
            if ((iXcoord >= x - 10) && (iXcoord <= x + 10)
                && (iYcoord >= y - 10) && (iYcoord <= y + 10))
                return true;
```

```
          else
              return false;
      }
}

public void init ()
{
    addMouseMotionListener(this);
    myGraph = new ColorCircle[NUM_CIRCLES];

    for (int i = 0; i < NUM_CIRCLES; i++)
    {
        ColorCircle myVertex = new ColorCircle();

        myVertex.setX((int)(Math.random() * (WIDTH-50)));

        myVertex.setY((int)(Math.random() * (HEIGHT - 100)));

        myGraph[i] = myVertex;
    }

    JOptionPane.showMessageDialog(null,
            "Try to drag any one of the colored circles ",
            "Information", JOptionPane.PLAIN_MESSAGE );

}

public void paint(Graphics g)
{
    Color[] myColor = {Color.black, Color.red, Color.blue,
                        Color.green, Color.cyan,
                        Color.orange, Color.yellow};

    if (NUM_CIRCLES > 0)
        for (int i = 0; i < NUM_CIRCLES; i++)
        {
            g.setColor(myColor[i]);
            myGraph[i].paint(g);
        }
}

public void mouseDragged(MouseEvent event)
{
    int iX = event.getX();
    int iY = event.getY();

    for (int i = 0; i < NUM_CIRCLES; i++)
        if (myGraph[i].selected(iX, iY))
        {
            myGraph[i].setX(iX);
            myGraph[i].setY(iY);
            break;
        }
```

```
        repaint();

    }

    public void mouseMoved(MouseEvent p1)
    {
    }
}
```

The HTML file for this program contains the following code:

```
<HTML>
  <HEAD>
    <TITLE>Drawing Board</TITLE>
  </HEAD>
  <BODY>
    <OBJECT code = "FreeDrawApplet.class" width = "400"
                                          height = "400">
    </OBJECT>
  </BODY>
</HTML>
```

Sample Run: Figure 12-24 shows a sample run of the `FreeDrawApplet`.

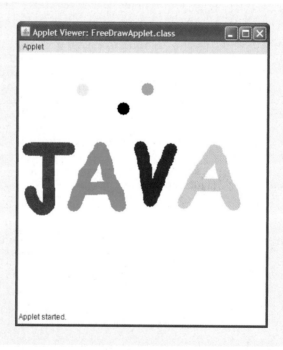

FIGURE 12-24 Sample run of the `FreeDrawApplet`

The program `FreeDrawApplet` uses small circles to draw lines. Because there is no GUI component we can use, we created the `class ColorCircle`. This class has two `private` members x and y of the type `int`. The point (x, y) specifies the center of the circle, and the radius of the circle is fixed at 10 pixels. In addition to the methods to set the values of x and y, the `class ColorCircle` has only two other methods: `paint` and `isSelected`. The `paint` method draws a filled circle of radius 10 at the point (x, y). The method `isSelected` returns `true` if and only if (iXcoord, iYcoord) lies inside a 20-by-20 square with the point (x, y) as the center. We use this method to check whether the mouse is at, say, (iXcoord, iYcoord) on the circle with the center (x, y). Note that because `ColorCircle` is not a GUI component, it can generate any event. Therefore, any time a `mouseDragged` event is generated, we must check whether the mouse is on any of the circles. We do so using the following `for` loop:

```
for (int i = 0; i < NUM_CIRCLES; i++)
    if (myGraph[i].selected(iX, iY))
    {
        myGraph[i].setX(iX);
        myGraph[i].setY(iY);
        break;
    }
```

Note that if a `mouseDragged` event occurs on a `ColorCircle` object, the preceding `for` loop sets the current mouse position as the new center of the `ColorCircle` object. This, in effect, moves the `ColorCircle` object. By continually moving a `ColorCircle` object, we create a line.

ROGRAMMING EXAMPLE: Java Kiosk

In this programming example, we design a program that simulates a fast food kiosk. The program displays a menu similar to one you might find in a fast food restaurant. The user makes a selection and then presses a `JButton` to mark the end of the selection process. The program then calculates and displays the bill. A sample output is shown in Figure 12-25.

1
2

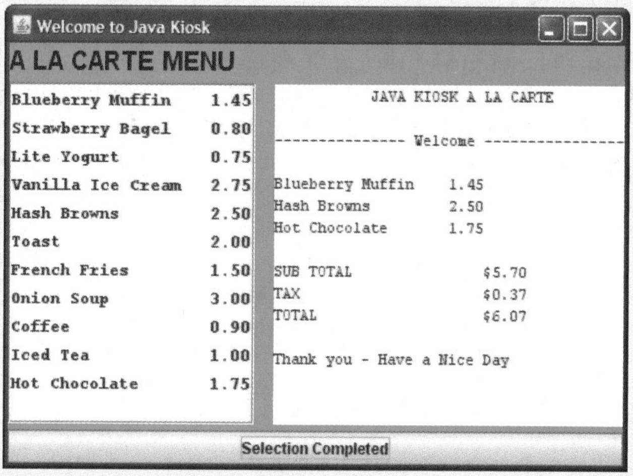

FIGURE 12-25 Sample output of the Java Kiosk program

Input: A list of selected items from the menu shown on the left in Figure 12-25.

Output: A bill shown on the right in Figure 12-25.

PROBLEM
ANALYSIS
AND GUI AND
ALGORITHM
DESIGN

As shown in Figure 12-25, there are five GUI components: a frame, a label, a list, a text area, and a button. All components other than the frame are placed into the content pane of the window. The user selects various list items and then presses the `Selection Completed` button. Recall that when you click a button, it generates an action event, which is processed by using the `interface ActionListener`. Therefore, we will create and register an action listener object with the button.

When the event is generated, the event handler computes the subtotal, tax, and total. The program then displays the result in the text area. To create the label, list, text area, and button, we use reference variables of the types `JLabel`, `JList`, `JTextArea`, and `JButton`, respectively. We also need a reference variable to access the content pane of the window. As in the GUI programs in previous chapters, we create the class containing the application program by extending the definition of the `class JFrame`; this also allows us to create the necessary window to create the GUI. Thus, we use the following reference variables to create the GUI components and to access the content pane of the window:

```
private JList yourChoices;
private JTextArea bill;
```

```
private Container pane;
JLabel yourChoicesJLabel;
JButton button;
```

The next step is to instantiate four GUI components and initialize the pane using the method `getContentPane`. Recall that, to create a list, we first create an array of strings and then use the array as the argument in the constructor of the `JList`. We can instantiate other GUI components the same way we have done previously. This program uses the `BorderLayout` to neatly place all four GUI components. We place the label in the NORTH region, the list in the WEST region, the text area in the EAST region, and the button in the SOUTH region.

The following statement creates the array of strings to create the menu:

```
static String[] yourChoicesItems =
                    {"Blueberry Muffin     1.45",
                     "Strawberry Bagel     0.80",
                     "Lite Yogurt          0.75",
                     "Vanilla Ice Cream    2.75",
                     "Hash Browns          2.50",
                     "Toast                2.00",
                     "French Fries         1.50",
                     "Onion Soup           3.00",
                     "Coffee               0.90",
                     "Iced Tea             1.00",
                     "Hot Chocolate        1.75"};
```

The following statements create the necessary GUI components and place them in the container:

```
private JList yourChoices;
private JTextArea bill;

private Container pane;

pane = getContentPane();
pane.setBackground(new Color(0, 200, 200));
pane.setLayout(new BorderLayout(5, 5));

        //Create a label and place it in the NORTH region
        //and set the font of this label.
JLabel yourChoicesJLabel = new JLabel("A LA CARTE MENU");
pane.add(yourChoicesJLabel, BorderLayout.NORTH);
yourChoicesJLabel.setFont(new Font("Dialog", Font.BOLD, 20));

        //Create a list and place it in the WEST region
        //and set the font of this list.
yourChoices = new JList(yourChoicesItems);
pane.add(new JScrollPane (yourChoices), BorderLayout.WEST);
yourChoices.setFont(new Font("Courier", Font.BOLD, 14));
```

1
2

```
        //Create a text area and place it in the EAST region
        //and set the font of this text area.
bill = new JTextArea();
pane.add(bill, BorderLayout.EAST);
bill.setFont(new Font("Courier", Font.PLAIN, 12));

        //Create a button and place it in the SOUTH region and
        //add an action listener.
JButton button = new JButton("Selection Completed");
pane.add(button, BorderLayout.SOUTH);
button.addActionListener(this);
```

We need another array to keep track of the prices of the various items.

```
static double[] yourChoicesPrices = {1.45, 0.80, 0.75, 2.75,
                                      2.50, 2.00, 1.50, 3.00,
                                      0.90, 1.00, 1.75};
```

The following statements set the size of the window and set its visibility to `true`:

```
setSize(500, 360);
setVisible(true);
```

Recall that when an action event is generated by a button, the method `actionPerformed` is invoked. When the user clicks the button, the program must compute the subtotal, tax, and total, and display the result in the text area. The instructions to perform these tasks are placed in the method `actionPerformed`, which is described next.

Method actionPerformed As noted previously, the method `actionPerformed` is executed when the user clicks the button. The method `actionPerformed` calculates and displays the bill. We write the method `displayBill` that computes the bill and displays it using the text area. The method `actionPerformed` invokes the method `displayBill` to display the bill. The definition of the method `actionPerformed` is:

```
public void actionPerformed(ActionEvent event)
{
    if (event.getActionCommand().equals("Selection Completed"))
    {
        displayBill();
    }
}
```

Method displayBill The method `displayBill` first needs to identify the items selected by the user. The method `getSelectedIndices` of the `JList` will return an array of indices. Because we need an integer array to hold these indices, we might need the following Java statements:

```
int[] listArray = yourChoices.getSelectedIndices();
double localTax = 0.065;
double tax;
double subtotal = 0;
double total;
```

Note that `listArray[0]`, `listArray[1]`, ..., `listArray[listArray.length - 1]` contains the indices of the items selected from the menu list. Therefore, the following `for` loop computes the total cost of the items selected from the menu:

```
for (int index = 0; index < listArray.length; index++)
    subTotal = subTotal + yourChoicesPrices[listArray[index]];
```

Next, we compute the tax and add it to `subTotal` to get the billing amount:

```
tax = localTax * subTotal;
total = subTotal + tax;
```

To display the bill, we append the necessary statements to the `JTextArea` and invoke the `repaint` method to redraw the GUI components. To place another order, we unselect the selected items. The definition of the method `displayBill` is:

```
// method to display the order and total cost
private void displayBill()
{
    int[] listArray = yourChoices.getSelectedIndices();
    double localTax = 0.065;
    double tax;
    double subtotal = 0;
    double total;

    //Set the text area to nonedit mode
    //and start with an empty string.
    bill.setEditable(false);
    bill.setText("");

    //Calculate the cost of the items ordered.
    for (int index = 0; index < listArray.length; index++)
        subTotal = subTotal + yourChoicesPrices[listArray[index]];

    tax = localTax * subTotal;
    total = subTotal + tax;

    //Display costs.
    bill.append("            JAVA KIOSK A LA CARTE\n\n");
    bill.append("-------------- Welcome ---------------\n\n");

    for (int index = 0; index < listArray.length; index++)
    {
        bill.append(yourChoicesItems[listArray[index]] + "\n");
    }
```

1

2

```
        bill.append("\n");
        bill.append("SUB TOTAL\t\t$"
                    + String.format("%.2f", subTotal) + "\n");
        bill.append("TAX     \t\t$"
                    + String.format("%.2f", tax) + "\n");
        bill.append("TOTAL   \t\t$"
                    + String.format("%.2f", total) + "\n\n");
        bill.append("Thank you - Have a Nice Day\n\n");

        //reset the list array
        yourChoices.clearSelection();

        repaint();
    }
```

The program listing is as follows:

```
//A la Carte

import java.awt.*;
import java.awt.event.*;
import javax.swing.*;
import javax.swing.event.*;

public class AlaCarte extends JFrame implements ActionListener
{
    static String[] yourChoicesItems =
                        {"Blueberry Muffin    1.45",
                         "Strawberry Bagel    0.80",
                         "Lite Yogurt         0.75",
                         "Vanilla Ice Cream   2.75",
                         "Hash Browns         2.50",
                         "Toast               2.00",
                         "French Fries        1.50",
                         "Onion Soup          3.00",
                         "Coffee              0.90",
                         "Iced Tea            1.00",
                         "Hot Chocolate       1.75"};

    static double[] yourChoicesPrices = {1.45, 0.80, 0.75, 2.75,
                         2.50, 2.00, 1.50, 3.00,
                         0.90, 1.00, 1.75};
    private JList yourChoices;
    private JTextArea  bill;

    private Container pane;
```

```java
public AlaCarte()
{
    super("Welcome to Java Kiosk");

        //Get the content pane and set its background color
        //and layout manager.
    pane = getContentPane();
    pane.setBackground(new Color(0, 200, 200));
    pane.setLayout(new BorderLayout(5, 5));

        //Create a label and place it at NORTH. Also
        //set the font of this label.
    JLabel yourChoicesJLabel = new JLabel("A LA CARTE MENU");
    pane.add(yourChoicesJLabel,BorderLayout.NORTH);
    yourChoicesJLabel.setFont(new Font("Dialog",Font.BOLD,20));

        //Create a list and place it at WEST. Also
        //set the font of this list.
    yourChoices = new JList(yourChoicesItems);
    pane.add(new JScrollPane (yourChoices),BorderLayout.WEST);
    yourChoices.setFont(new Font("Courier",Font.BOLD,14));

        //Create a text area and place it at EAST. Also
        //set the font of this text area.
    bill = new JTextArea();
    pane.add(bill,BorderLayout.EAST);
    bill.setFont(new Font("Courier",Font.PLAIN,12));

        //Create a button and place it in the SOUTH region
        //and add an action listener.
    JButton button = new JButton("Selection Completed");
    pane.add(button,BorderLayout.SOUTH);
    button.addActionListener(this);

    setSize(500, 360);
    setVisible(true);
    setDefaultCloseOperation(EXIT_ON_CLOSE);
}

    //method to display the order and the total cost
private void displayBill()
{
    int[] listArray = yourChoices.getSelectedIndices();
    double localTax = 0.065;
    double tax;
    double subTotal = 0;
    double total;

        //Set the text area to nonedit mode and start
        //with an empty string.
    bill.setEditable(false);
    bill.setText("");
```

1
2

```
        //Calculate the cost of the items ordered.
    for (int index = 0; index < listArray.length; index++)
        subTotal = subTotal
                    + yourChoicesPrices[listArray[index]];

    tax = localTax * subTotal;
    total = subTotal + tax;

        //Display the costs.
    bill.append("            JAVA KIOSK A LA CARTE\n\n");
    bill.append("--------------- Welcome ----------------\n\n");

    for (int index = 0; index < listArray.length; index++)
    {
        bill.append(yourChoicesItems[listArray[index]] + "\n");
    }

    bill.append("\n");
    bill.append("SUB TOTAL\t\t$"
                + String.format("%.2f", subTotal) + "\n");
    bill.append("TAX      \t\t$"
                + String.format("%.2f", tax) + "\n");
    bill.append("TOTAL     \t\t$"
                + String.format("%.2f", total) + "\n\n");
    bill.append("Thank you - Have a Nice Day\n\n");

        //Reset list array.
    yourChoices.clearSelection();

    repaint();
}

public void actionPerformed(ActionEvent event)
{
    if (event.getActionCommand().equals("Selection Completed"))
        displayBill();
}

public static void main(String[] args)
{
    AlaCarte alc = new AlaCarte();
}
}
```

Sample Run: Figure 12-26 shows a sample run of the program. (To make more than one selection, click the first selection, hold the Ctrl key, then click the left mouse button on the other selections. To make contiguous selections, click the first item, hold the Shift key, then click the last item you want to select.)

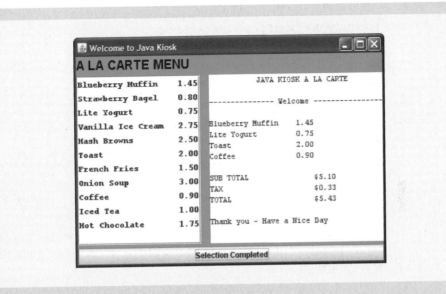

FIGURE 12-26 Sample run of the Java Kiosk program

QUICK REVIEW

1. The term applet means a little application.

2. An applet is a Java program that is embedded within a Web page and executed by a Web browser.

3. You create an applet by extending the **class** JApplet, which is contained in the **package** javax.swing.

4. Unlike a Java application program, a Java applet does not have the main method.

5. When a browser runs an applet, the methods init, start, and paint are guaranteed to be invoked in sequence.

6. All statements to be executed only once are kept in the init method of an applet.

7. An applet does not have a title.

8. The **classes** Font and Color are contained in the **package** java.awt.

9. Java uses the color scheme known as RGB, where R stands for red, G for green, and B for blue.

10. You create instances of the **class** Color by mixing red, green, and blue hues in various proportions.

11. An applet class is derived from the **class** JApplet, whereas a GUI application class is created by extending the **class** JFrame.

1
2

12. Applets do not use constructors.

13. Java provides the `class JTextArea` either to collect multiple lines of input from the user or to display multiple lines of output.

14. Java provides the `classes JCheckBox` and `JRadioButton` to allow a user to select a value from a set of given values.

15. A check box is also called a toggle button.

16. To force the user to select only one radio button at a time, you create a button group and add radio buttons to the group.

17. A combo box, also known as a drop-down list, is used to select an item from a list of possibilities.

18. A `JList` displays a number of items from which the user can select one or more items.

19. The `FlowLayout` manager places GUI components from left to right until no more items can be placed in a line. Then the next item is placed in the following line.

20. In the case of `BorderLayout` manager, the component placed at the center expands to occupy any unused regions.

21. Menus allow you to provide various functions without cluttering the GUI with components.

22. Menus can be attached to objects such as `JFrame` and `JApplet`.

23. Key events are handled by the `interface KeyListener`; mouse events are handled by the `interfaces MouseListener` and `MouseMotionListener`.

EXERCISES

1. Mark the following statements as true or false.

   a. An applet's width and height are specified in the HTML file.

   b. In Java, `JApplet` is a class.

   c. To display an applet, you do not need to invoke a method, such as `setVisible()`.

   d. You must include an exit button in all Java applets.

   e. When an applet is loaded, the method `start` is invoked before the method `init`.

   f. Check boxes are used to display the output of a program.

   g. A radio button always has a label.

   h. You use `JList` to create a combo box.

   i. `JTextField` can be used to output multiple lines of text.

2. Name four GUI components that can be used for input only.

3. Name two GUI components that can be used for both input and output.

4. Name a GUI component that can be used for output only.

5. Why do you need check boxes in a GUI program?

6. Fill in the blanks in each of the following:

   a. The _____ method of the `class` Graphics draws a rectangle.

   b. RGB is short for ____, ____, and _____.

   c. The method _____ is invoked when an item is selected from a combo box and a(n) _____ is registered to handle an event.

   d. The _____ method of the `class` Graphics can be used to draw a circle.

   e. Font sizes are specified in units called _____.

   f. Both `JTextField` and `JTextArea` inherit directly from the `class` _____.

   g. The method `Random` returns a value between _____ and _____.

   h. The method _____ gets the string in the `JTextArea`, and the method _____ changes the string displayed in a `JTextArea`.

   i. The `BorderLayout` manager divides the container into five regions: _____, _____, _____, _____, and _____.

   j. The _____ class is used to create a slider for _____.

   k. You cannot use `System.out.println` inside a(n) _____ method.

7. Write the necessary statements to create the following:

   a. A `JList` with the list items `orange`, `apple`, `banana`, `grape`, and `pineapple`

   b. A check box with the label `draft`

   c. A group of three radio buttons with the labels `home`, `visitor`, and `neutral`

   d. A menu bar

   e. A Courier bold 32-point font

   f. A new color that is not already defined in the `class` Color

8. Correct any syntax errors in the following program:

```
//Grand Welcome Problem Applet

import java.awt.*;
import javax.swing.JApplet;
```

1
2

```
public class GrandWelcomeProblem extends JApplet
{
    public int ()
    {
        JLabel myLabel = new JLabel("");
    }

    public void paint ( Graphics g)
    {
        super.paint(g);
        Container pane = g.getContentPane();
        pane.setLayout(BORDER_LAYOUT);
        pane.add(BORDER_LAYOUT.CENTER);

        myLabel.setText("A Grand Welcome to "
                        + "Java Programming! ");
    }
}
```

PROGRAMMING EXERCISES

1. Create an applet to draw a digit using the method `fillRect` of the `class Graphics`. For instance, if the input is 6, the applet will display the digit 6, as shown in Figure 12-27.

FIGURE 12-27 Figure for Programming Exercise 1

2. Modify the applet created in Programming Exercise 1 by adding eight radio buttons so the user can change the color of the digit drawn.

3. Modify the applet created in Programming Exercise 1 by adding a color menu to change the color of the digit drawn.

4. Modify the applet created in Programming Exercise 1 by adding a JList of eight items so the user can change the background color of the applet.

5. Create an applet that will draw a set of ovals similar to that shown in Figure 12-28. The user can specify the number of ovals.

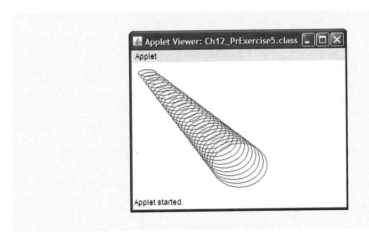

FIGURE 12-28 Figure for Programming Exercise 5

6. Modify the applet in Programming Exercise 5 by adding three different types of GUI components so the user can select from the following:

   a. Number of figures: 1, 2, 4, 8, 16, or various combinations of these numbers

   b. Type of figures: circle, oval, rectangle, or square

   c. Color: red, blue, green, yellow, pink, black, cyan, or magenta

7. Modify the applet in Programming Exercise 5 by adding the necessary menus so the user can select from the following:

   a. Number of figures: 1, 10, 20, 30, or 40

   b. Type of figures: circle, oval, rectangle, or square

   c. Color: red, blue, green, yellow, pink, black, cyan, or magenta

8. Convert the WhiteBoard program (presented earlier in this chapter) from an application to an applet.

9. Redo JListPictureViewer (presented earlier in this chapter) using one of the layout managers. For this exercise, use a JList and one JLabel to display the image.

10. Create an applet to draw lines. The user can choose the start and end points of the line to be drawn by clicking the mouse.

11. Create an application to illustrate mouse events, mouse motion events, and keyboard events. Figure 12-29 shows the user interface. The key code corresponding to a key event or the position of the mouse is displayed just above the text field.

FIGURE 12-29 Figure for Programming Exercise 11

12. Create an applet to draw lines, rectangles, squares, circles, and ovals. The user can select any one of these through a menu. The user can also choose the start and end points of the line to be drawn by clicking the mouse. For other geometric figures, the user chooses the upper-left and lower-right corners by clicking the mouse.

13. Convert the Java Kiosk programming example from an application to an applet.

14. Create an applet that starts with displaying several colored circles that can be moved to different places in the applet by dragging the mouse.

15. Convert the `GrandWelcomeFinal` program (presented earlier in this chapter) from an applet to an application.

16. Convert the `OneChar` program (presented earlier in this chapter) from an applet to an application.

17. Write a GUI program that produces the figure shown in Figure 12-30.

FIGURE 12-30 Target practice

18. Write a GUI program that produces the house shown in Figure 12-31.

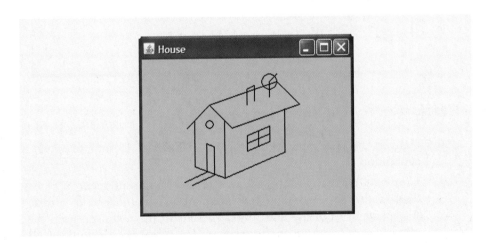

FIGURE 12-31 House

19. Write a GUI application program, to create a menu for a pizza shop. Use check boxes, radio buttons, and a JButton to allow a customer to make selections and process their order. Use a text area to display the customer's order and the amount due. A sample menu and a customer's order is shown in Figure 12-32.

FIGURE 12-32 Figure for Programming Exercise 19

20. Convert the Java application program of Exercise 19 into an applet to an application.

21. Create a GUI that prompts the user to enter a measurement in inches and displays the corresponding measurement in centimeters in a text area. Accept input from the user, display results in the text area, until the user presses an exit button or the program has processed 15 numbers. Before processing the 16th number, clear the text area. A sample addition to the text area might be `2.00 inches = 5.08 centimeters`.

22. Enhance the GUI of Programming Exercise 21 by omitting duplicate entries. Also add a scroll bar to the text area so that more than 15 lines can be viewed.

23. Enhance the GUI of Programming Exercises 22 by adding two buttons: one with the label `Inches to Centimeters` and the other with the label `Centimeters to Inches`. When the user enters a value and presses one of the two buttons, the appropriate calculation is performed and the results are appended to the text area.

13

RECURSION

IN THIS CHAPTER, YOU WILL:

- ◼ Learn about recursive definitions
- ◼ Determine the base case and general case of a recursive definition
- ◼ Learn about recursive algorithms
- ◼ Learn about recursive methods
- ◼ Become familiar with direct and indirect recursion
- ◼ Learn how to use recursive methods to implement recursive algorithms

In previous chapters, we used the common technique called iteration to devise problem solutions. For certain problems, however, using the iterative technique to obtain the solution is quite complicated. This chapter introduces another problem–solving technique called recursion and provides several examples demonstrating how recursion works.

Recursive Definitions

The process of solving a problem by reducing it to successively smaller versions of itself is called **recursion**. Recursion is a powerful way to solve certain problems for which the solution can otherwise be very complicated. Let's consider a familiar problem.

In mathematics, the factorial of a nonnegative integer is defined as follows:

$$0! = 1 \qquad\qquad\qquad (13\text{-}1)$$

$$n! = n \times (n - 1)! \text{ if } n > 0 \qquad\qquad\qquad (13\text{-}2)$$

In this definition, 0! is defined to be 1, and if n is an integer greater than 0, first we find $(n - 1)!$ and then multiply it by n. To find $(n - 1)!$, we apply the definition again. If $(n - 1) > 0$, we use Equation 13-2; otherwise, we use Equation 13-1. Thus, for an integer n greater than 0, $n!$ is obtained by first finding $(n - 1)!$ (that is, $n!$ is determined in part by a smaller, but similar problem) and then multiplying $(n - 1)!$ by n.

Let's apply this definition to find 3!. Here, $n = 3$. Because $n > 0$, we use Equation 13-2 to obtain:

$$3! = 3 \times 2!$$

Next we find 2!. Here, $n = 2$. Because $n > 0$, we use Equation 13-2 to obtain:

$$2! = 2 \times 1!$$

Now, to find 1!, we again use Equation 13-2 because $n = 1 > 0$. Thus:

$$1! = 1 \times 0!$$

Finally, we use Equation 13-1 to find 0!, which is 1. Substituting 0! into 1! gives $1! = 1$. This gives $2! = 2 \times 1! = 2 \times 1 = 2$, which in turn gives $3! = 3 \times 2! = 3 \times 2 = 6$.

Note that the solution in Equation 13-1 is direct—that is, the right side of the equation contains no factorial notation. The solution in Equation 13-2 is given in terms of a smaller version of itself. The definition of the factorial as given in Equations 13-1 and 13-2 is called a **recursive definition**. Equation 13-1 is called the **base case**, the case for which the solution is obtained directly; Equation 13-2 is called the **general case** or **recursive case**.

Recursive definition: A definition in which something is defined in terms of a smaller version of itself.

From the previous example, it is clear that:

1. Every recursive definition must have one (or more) base case(s).
2. The general case must eventually be reduced to a base case.
3. The base case stops the recursion.

The concept of recursion in computer science works similarly. Here, we talk about recursive algorithms and recursive methods. An algorithm that finds the solution to a given problem by reducing the problem to smaller versions of itself is called a **recursive algorithm**. The recursive algorithm must have one or more base cases, and the general solution must eventually be reduced to a base case.

A method that calls itself is called a **recursive method**. That is, the body of the recursive method contains a statement that causes the same method to execute before completing the current call. Recursive algorithms are implemented using recursive methods.

Next, let's write the recursive method that implements the factorial definition:

```
public static int fact(int num)
{
    if (num == 0)
        return 1;
    else
        return num * fact(num - 1);
}
```

Figure 13-1 traces the execution of the following statement:

```
System.out.println(fact(4));
```

1
3

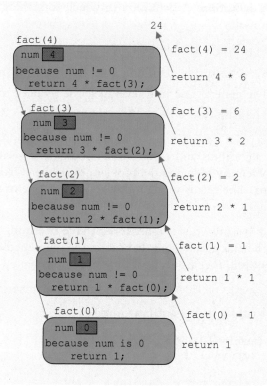

FIGURE 13-1 Execution of `fact(4)`

The output of the previous statement is **24**.

In Figure 13-1, the downward arrows represent the successive calls to the method **fact**, and the upward arrows represent the values returned to the caller, that is, the calling method.

While tracing the execution of the recursive method **fact**, note the following:

- Logically, you can think of a recursive method as having unlimited copies of itself.

- Every call to a recursive method—that is, every recursive call—has its own code and its own set of parameters and local variables.

- After completing a particular recursive call, control goes back to the calling environment, which is the previous call. The current (recursive) call must execute completely before control goes back to the previous call. The execution in the previous call begins from the point immediately following the recursive call.

Direct and Indirect Recursion

A method is called **directly recursive** if it calls itself. A method that calls another method and eventually results in the original method call is called **indirectly recursive**. For example, if method A calls method B and method B calls method A, then method A is indirectly recursive. Indirect recursion could be several layers deep. For example, if method A calls method B, method B calls method C, method C calls method D, and method D calls method A, then method A is indirectly recursive.

Indirect recursion requires the same careful analysis as direct recursion. The base cases must be identified and nonrecursive solutions to them must be provided. However, tracing through indirect recursion can be a tedious process. Therefore, extra care must be exercised when designing indirect recursive methods. For simplicity, this book considers only problems that involve direct recursion.

A recursive method in which the last statement executed is the recursive call is called a **tail recursive method**. The method `fact` is an example of a tail recursive method.

Infinite Recursion

Figure 13-1 shows that the sequence of recursive calls reached a call that made no further recursive calls. That is, the sequence of recursive calls eventually reached a base case. However, if every recursive call results in another recursive call, then the recursive method (algorithm) is said to have infinite recursion. In theory, infinite recursion executes forever. However, every call to a recursive method requires the system to allocate memory for the local variables and formal parameters. In addition, the system also saves the information so that after completing a call, control can be transferred back to the caller. Therefore, because computer memory is finite, if you execute an infinite recursive method on a computer, the method will execute until the system runs out of memory, which results in an abnormal termination of the program.

Designing Recursive Methods

Recursive methods (algorithms) must be designed and analyzed carefully. You must make sure that every recursive call eventually reduces to a base case. The following sections give various examples illustrating how to design and implement recursive algorithms.

To design a recursive method, you must:

1. Understand the problem requirements.
2. Determine the limiting conditions. For example, for a list, the limiting condition is determined by the number of elements in the list.
3. Identify the base cases and provide a direct (nonrecursive) solution to each base case.
4. Identify the general cases and provide a solution to each general case in terms of a smaller version of itself.

Typically, all recursive methods have the following characteristics: (a) they use an `if...else` or a `switch` statement that leads to different cases, (b) one or more base cases are used to stop recursion, and (c) each recursive call reduces the problem to a smaller version of itself.

Problem Solving Using Recursion

Examples 13-1 through 13-3 illustrate how recursive algorithms are developed and implemented in Java using recursive methods.

EXAMPLE 13-1 LARGEST ELEMENT IN THE ARRAY

In Chapter 9, we used a loop to find the largest element in an array. This example uses a recursive algorithm to find the largest element in an array. Consider the list given in Figure 13-2.

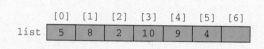

FIGURE 13-2   List with six elements

The largest element in the list given in Figure 13-2 is 10.

Suppose list is the name of the array containing the list elements. Also suppose that list[a]...list[b] stands for the array elements list[a], list[a + 1], ..., list[b]. For example, list[0]...list[5] represents the array elements list[0], list[1], list[2], list[3], list[4], and list[5]. Similarly, list[1]...list[5] represents the array elements list[1], list[2], list[3], list[4], and list[5]. To write an algorithm to find the largest element in list, let's think recursively.

If list is of length 1, then list has only one element, which is the largest element. Suppose the length of list is greater than 1. To find the largest element in list[a]...list[b], we first find the largest element in list[a + 1]...list[b] and then compare this largest element with list[a]. That is, the largest element in list[a]...list[b] is given by:

maximum(list[a], largest(list[a + 1]...list[b]))

Let's apply this formula to find the largest element in the list shown in Figure 13-2. This list has six elements, given by list[0]...list[5]. Now the largest element in list is:

maximum(list[0], largest(list[1]...list[5]))

That is, the largest element in list is the maximum of list[0] and the largest element in list[1]...list[5]. To find the largest element in list[1]...list[5], we use the same formula again because the length of this list is greater than 1. The largest element in list[1]...list[5] is then:

maximum(list[1], largest(list[2]...list[5]))

and so on. Note that every time we use the preceding formula to find the largest element in a sublist, the length of the sublist in the next call is reduced by one. Eventually, the sublist is of length 1, in which case the sublist contains only one element, which, in turn, is the largest element in the sublist. From this point onward, we backtrack through the recursive calls. This discussion translates into the following recursive algorithm, which is presented in pseudocode:

```
if the size of the list is 1
    the largest element in the list is the only element in the list
else
    to find the largest element in list[a]...list[b]
        a. find the largest element in list[a + 1]...list[b] and call
           it max
        b. compare list[a] and max
            if (list[a] >= max)
                the largest element in list[a]...list[b] is list[a]
            else
                the largest element in list[a]...list[b] is max
```

This algorithm translates into the following Java method to find the largest element in an array:

```java
public static int largest(int[] list,
                          int lowerIndex, int upperIndex)
{
    int max;

    if (lowerIndex == upperIndex)   //size of the sublist is 1
        return list[lowerIndex];
    else
    {
        max = largest(list, lowerIndex + 1, upperIndex);

        if (list[lowerIndex] >= max)
            return list[lowerIndex];
        else
            return max;
    }
}
```

Consider the list given in Figure 13-3.

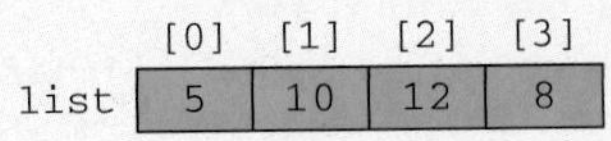

FIGURE 13-3 List with four elements

Let's trace the execution of the following statement:

```
System.out.println(largest(list, 0, 3));
```

Here, upperIndex = 3 and the list has four elements. Figure 13-4 traces the execution of largest(list, 0, 3).

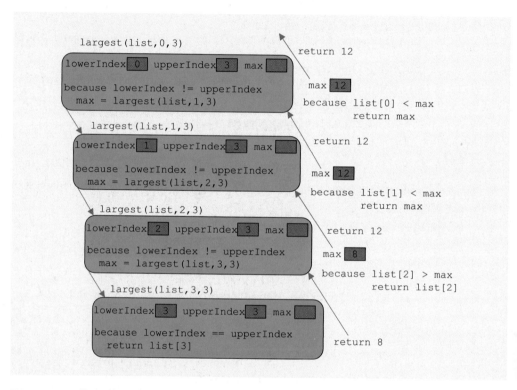

FIGURE 13-4 Execution of largest(list, 0, 3)

The value returned by the expression largest(list, 0, 3) is 12, which is the largest element in list.

The following Java program uses the method largest to determine the largest element in the list:

```
//Recursion: Largest Element in an Array

import java.io.*;

public class  LargestElementInAnArray
{
    public static void main(String[] args)
    {
        int[]  intArray = {23, 43, 35, 38, 67, 12, 76,
                            10, 34, 8};
```

```
        System.out.println("The largest element in intArray: "
                + largest(intArray, 0, intArray.length - 1));
    }

    public static int largest(int[] list,
                        int lowerIndex, int upperIndex)
    {
        int max;

        if (lowerIndex == upperIndex)
            return list[lowerIndex];
        else
        {
            max = largest(list, lowerIndex + 1, upperIndex);

            if (list[lowerIndex] >= max)
                return list[lowerIndex];
            else
                return max;
        }
    }
}
```

Sample Run:

```
The largest element in intArray: 76
```

EXAMPLE 13-2 FIBONACCI NUMBER

In Chapter 5, we designed a program to determine the desired Fibonacci number. In this example, we write a recursive method, rFibNum, to determine the desired Fibonacci number. The method rFibNum takes as parameters three numbers representing the first two numbers of the Fibonacci sequence and a number *n*, the desired *n*th Fibonacci number. The method rFibNum returns the *n*th Fibonacci number in the sequence.

Recall that the third Fibonacci number is the sum of the first two Fibonacci numbers. The fourth Fibonacci number in a sequence is the sum of the second and third Fibonacci numbers. Therefore, to calculate the fourth Fibonacci number, we add the second Fibonacci number and the third Fibonacci number (which itself is the sum of the first two Fibonacci numbers). The following recursive algorithm calculates the *n*th Fibonacci number, where *a* denotes the first Fibonacci number, *b* the second Fibonacci number, and *n* the *n*th Fibonacci number:

$$rFibNum(a, b, n) = \begin{cases} a & \text{if } n = 1 \\ b & \text{if } n = 2 \\ rFibNum(a, b, n-1) + rFibNum(a, b, n-2) & \text{if } n > 2. \end{cases} \quad (13\text{-}3)$$

Suppose that we want to determine the following:

1. rFibNum(2, 5, 4)

   Here, a = 2, b = 5, and n = 4. That is, we want to determine the fourth Fibonacci number of the sequence whose first number is 2 and whose second number is 5. Because n is 4 > 2:

   rFibNum(2, 5, 4) = rFibNum(2, 5, 3) + rFibNum(2, 5, 2)

   Next, we determine rFibNum(2, 5, 3) and rFibNum(2, 5, 2). Let's first determine rFibNum(2, 5, 3). Here, a = 2, b = 5, and n is 3. Because n is 3:

   1.a. rFibNum(2, 5, 3) = rFibNum(2, 5, 2) + rFibNum(2, 5, 1)

   This statement requires that we determine rFibNum(2, 5, 2) and rFibNum(2, 5, 1). In rFibNum(2, 5, 2), a = 2, b = 5, and n = 2. Therefore, from the definition given in Equation 13-3, it follows that:

   1.a.1. rFibNum(2, 5, 2) = 5

   To find rFibNum(2, 5, 1), note that a = 2, b = 5, and n = 1. Therefore, by the definition given in Equation 13-3:

   1.a.2. rFibNum(2, 5, 1) = 2

   We substitute the values of rFibNum(2, 5, 2) and rFibNum(2, 5, 1) into (1.a) to get:

   rFibNum(2, 5, 3) = 5 + 2 = 7

   Next, we determine rFibNum(2, 5, 2). As in (1.a.1), rFibNum(2, 5, 2) = 5. We can substitute the values of rFibNum(2, 5, 3) and rFibNum(2, 5, 2) into (1) to get:

   rFibNum(2, 5, 4) = 7 + 5 = 12

The following recursive method implements this algorithm:

```
public static int rFibNum(int a, int b, int n)
{
    if (n == 1)
        return a;
    else if (n == 2)
        return b;
    else
        return rFibNum(a, b, n - 1) + rFibNum(a, b, n - 2);
}
```

Let's trace the execution of the following statement:

```
System.out.println(rFibNum(2, 3, 5));
```

In this statement, the first number is 2, the second number is 3, and we want to determine the 5th Fibonacci number of the sequence. Figure 13-5 traces the execution of the expression `rFibNum(2, 3, 5)`. The value returned is 13, which is the 5th Fibonacci number of the sequence whose first number is 2 and whose second number is 3.

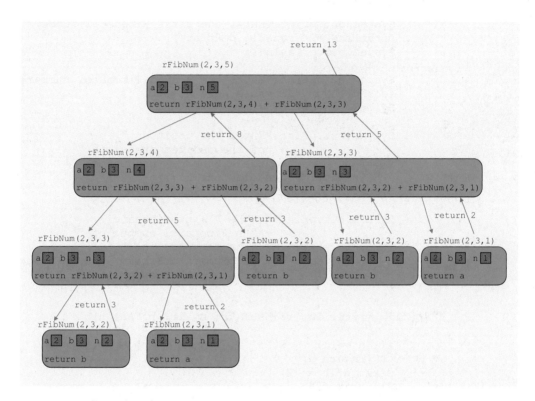

FIGURE 13-5 Execution of `rFibNum(2, 3, 5)`

From Figure 13-5, we can conclude that the recursive version of the program to calculate a Fibonacci number is not as efficient as the nonrecursive version. In the recursive version, some values are calculated more than once. For example, to calculate `rFibNum(2, 3, 5)`, the value `rFibNum(2, 3, 2)` is calculated three times. So a recursive method may be easier to write, but may not be very efficient. The section Recursion or Iteration?, presented later in this chapter, discusses the differences between these two alternatives.

The following Java program uses the method `rFibNum`:

```
//Recursion: Fibonacci Number

import java.util.*;

public class FibonacciNumber
{
    static Scanner console = new Scanner(System.in);
```

```java
public static void main(String[] args)
{
    int firstFibNum;
    int secondFibNum;
    int nthFibonacci;

    System.out.print("Enter the first Fibonacci number: ");
    firstFibNum = console.nextInt();
    System.out.println();

    System.out.print("Enter the second Fibonacci number: ");
    secondFibNum = console.nextInt();
    System.out.println();

    System.out.print("Enter the position "
                    + "of the desired number in "
                    + "the Fibonacci \nsequence: ");
    nthFibonacci = console.nextInt();
    System.out.println();

    System.out.println("The " + nthFibonacci
                    + "th Fibonacci number of "
                    + "the sequence is: "
                    + rFibNum(firstFibNum, secondFibNum,
                            nthFibonacci));
}

public static int rFibNum(int a, int b, int n)
{
    if (n == 1)
        return a;
    else if (n == 2)
        return b;
    else
        return rFibNum(a, b, n - 1) + rFibNum(a, b, n - 2);
}
}
```

Sample Run: (In this sample run, the user input is shaded.)

```
Enter the first Fibonacci number: 3

Enter the second Fibonacci number: 4

Enter the position of the desired number in the Fibonacci
sequence: 6

The 6th Fibonacci number of the sequence is: 29
```

EXAMPLE 13-3 TOWER OF HANOI

In the nineteenth century, a game called the Tower of Hanoi was popular in Europe. This game is based on a legend regarding the construction of the temple of Brahma. According to this legend, at the creation of the universe, priests in the temple of Brahma were given three diamond needles, with one needle containing 64 golden disks. Each golden disk is slightly smaller than the disk below it. The priests' task was to move all 64 disks from the first needle to the third needle. The rules for moving the disks are as follows:

1. Only one disk can be moved at a time.

2. The removed disk must be placed on one of the needles.

3. A larger disk cannot be placed on top of a smaller disk.

The priests were told that once they had moved all the disks from the first needle to the third needle, the universe would come to an end.

Our objective is to write a program that prints the sequence of moves needed to transfer the disks from the first needle to the third needle. Figure 13-6 shows the Tower of Hanoi problem with three disks.

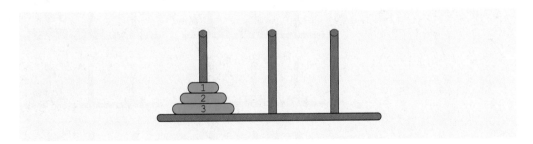

FIGURE 13-6 Tower of Hanoi problem with three disks

As before, we think in terms of recursion. Let's consider the case where the first needle contains only one disk. In this case, the disk can be moved directly from needle 1 to needle 3. Now let's consider the case when the first needle contains only two disks. In this case, we move the first disk from needle 1 to needle 2, and then we move the second disk from needle 1 to needle 3. Finally, we move the first disk from needle 2 to needle 3. Next, we consider the case where the first needle contains three disks, and then generalize this to the case of 64 disks (in fact, to an arbitrary number of disks).

Suppose that needle 1 contains three disks. To move disk number 3 to needle 3, the top two disks must first be moved to needle 2. Disk number 3 can then be moved from needle 1 to needle 3. To move the top two disks from needle 2 to needle 3, we use the same strategy as before. This time, we use needle 1 as the intermediate needle. Figure 13-7 shows a solution to the Tower of Hanoi problem with three disks.

1
3

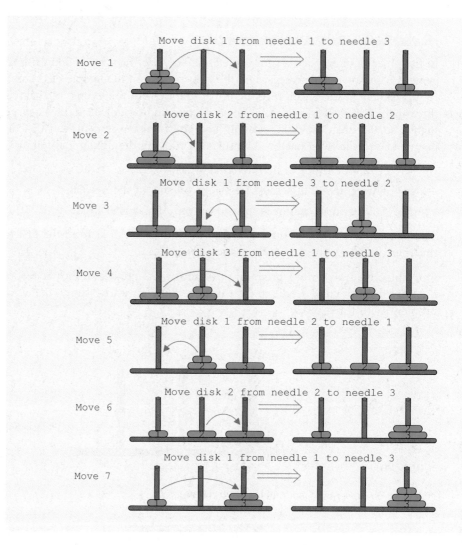

FIGURE 13-7 Solution to Tower of Hanoi problem with three disks

Let's now generalize this problem to the case of 64 disks. To begin, the first needle contains all 64 disks. Disk number 64 cannot be moved from needle 1 to needle 3 unless the top 63 disks are on the second needle. So first we move the top 63 disks from needle 1 to needle 2, and then we move disk number 64 from needle 1 to needle 3. Now the top 63 disks are all on needle 2. To move disk number 63 from needle 2 to needle 3, we first move the top 62 disks from needle 2 to needle 1, and then we move disk number 63 from needle 2 to needle 3. To move the remaining 62 disks, we use a similar procedure. This discussion translates into the following recursive algorithm, given in pseudocode. Suppose that needle 1 contains n disks, where $n \geq 1$.

1. Move the top $n - 1$ disks from needle 1 to needle 2, using needle 3 as the intermediate needle.
2. Move disk number n from needle 1 to needle 3.
3. Move the top $n - 1$ disks from needle 2 to needle 3, using needle 1 as the intermediate needle.

This recursive algorithm translates into the following Java method:

```java
public static void moveDisks(int count, int needle1,
                             int needle3, int needle2)
{
    if (count > 0)
    {
        moveDisks(count-1, needle1, needle2, needle3);
        System.out.println("Move disk " + count
                    + " from needle "
                    + needle1
                    + " to needle " + needle3 + ".");
        moveDisks(count-1, needle2, needle3, needle1);
    }
}
```

Tower of Hanoi: Analysis

Let us determine how long it would take to move all 64 disks from needle 1 to needle 3. If needle 1 contains 3 disks, then the number of moves required to move all 3 disks from needle 1 to needle 3 is $2^3 - 1 = 7$. Similarly, if needle 1 contains 64 disks, then the number of moves required to move all 64 disks from needle 1 to needle 3 is $2^{64} - 1$. Because $2^{10} = 1024 \approx 1000 = 10^3$, we have

$$2^{64} = 2^4 \times 2^{60} \approx 2^4 \times 10^{18} = 1.6 \times 10^{19}$$

The number of seconds in one year is approximately 3.2×10^7. Suppose the priests move one disk per second and they do not rest. Now:

$$1.6 \times 10^{19} = 5 \times 3.2 \times 10^{18} = 5 \times (3.2 \times 10^7) \times 10^{11} = (3.2 \times 10^7) \times (5 \times 10^{11})$$

The time required to move all 64 disks from needle 1 to needle 3 is roughly 5×10^{11} years. It is estimated that our universe is about 15 billion years old (1.5×10^{10}). Also, $5 \times 10^{11} = 50 \times 10^{10} \approx 33 \times (1.5 \times 10^{10})$. This calculation shows that our universe would last about 33 times as long as it already has.

Assume that a computer can generate 1 billion (10^9) moves per second. Then, the number of moves that the computer can generate in one year is:

$$(3.2 \times 10^7) \times 10^9 = 3.2 \times 10^{16}$$

So, the computer time required to generate 2^{64} moves is:

$$2^{64} \approx 1.6 \times 10^{19} = 1.6 \times 10^{16} \times 10^3 = (3.2 \times 10^{16}) \times 500$$

Thus, it would take about 500 years for the computer to generate 2^{64} moves at the rate of 1 billion moves per second.

Recursion or Iteration?

In Chapter 5, we designed a program to determine a desired Fibonacci number. That program used a loop to perform the calculation. In other words, the programs in Chapter 5 used an iterative control structure to repeat a set of statements. More formally, **iterative control structures** use a looping structure, such as `while`, `for`, or `do...while`, to repeat a set of statements. In Example 13-2, we designed a recursive method to calculate a Fibonacci number. From the examples in this chapter, it follows that in recursion, a set of statements is repeated by having the method call itself. Moreover, a selection control structure is used to control the repeated calls in recursion.

Similarly, in Chapter 9, we used an iterative control structure (a `for` loop) to determine the largest element in a list. In this chapter, we used recursion to determine the largest element in a list. In addition, this chapter began by designing a recursive method to find the factorial of a nonnegative integer. Using an iterative control structure, we can also write an algorithm to find the factorial of a nonnegative integer. The only reason we gave a recursive solution to a factorial problem is to illustrate how recursion works.

Often there are two ways to solve a particular problem—recursion or iteration. The obvious question is, Which method is better? There is no simple answer. In addition to the nature of the problem, the other key factor in determining the best solution method is efficiency.

When we traced the execution of the program in Example 7-11 (Chapter 7), we saw that whenever a method is called, memory space for its formal parameters and (automatic) local variables is allocated. When the method terminates, that memory space is then deallocated.

In this chapter, while tracing the execution of recursive methods, we saw that every (recursive) call also had its own set of parameters and local variables. That is, every (recursive) call required that the system allocate memory space for its formal parameters and local variables, and then deallocate the memory space when the method exited. Thus, overhead is associated with executing a (recursive) method, both in terms of memory space and computer time. Therefore, a recursive method executes more slowly than its iterative counterpart. On slower computers, especially those with limited memory space, the (slow) execution of a recursive method would be noticeable.

Today's computers, however, are fast and have ample memory. Therefore, the execution of a recursive method is not so noticeable. Keeping in mind the power of today's computers, the choice between iteration or recursion depends on the nature of the problem. Of course, for problems such as mission control systems, efficiency is absolutely critical and, therefore, the efficiency factor dictates the solution method.

As a general rule, if you think an iterative solution is more obvious and easier to understand than a recursive solution, use the iterative solution, which is more efficient. On the other hand, problems exist for which the recursive solution is more obvious or easier to construct, such as the Tower of Hanoi problem. (In fact, it is difficult to construct an iterative solution for the Tower of Hanoi problem.) Keeping in mind the power of recursion, if the definition of a problem is inherently recursive, then you should consider a recursive solution.

PROGRAMMING EXAMPLE: Decimal to Binary Conversion

This programming example discusses and designs a program that uses recursion to convert a nonnegative integer in decimal format—that is, base 10—into the equivalent binary number—that is, base 2. First, we define some terms.

Let x be a nonnegative integer. We call the remainder of x after division by 2 the **rightmost bit** of x.

Thus, the rightmost bit of 33 is 1 because 33 % 2 is 1, and the rightmost bit of 28 is 0 because 28 % 2 is 0.

We first use an example to illustrate the algorithm to convert an integer in base 10 to the equivalent number in binary format.

Suppose we want to find the binary representation of 35. First, we divide 35 by 2. The quotient is 17 and the remainder—that is, the rightmost bit of 35—is 1. Next, we divide 17 by 2. The quotient is 8 and the remainder—that is, the rightmost bit of 17—is 1. Next, we divide 8 by 2. The quotient is 4 and the remainder—that is, the rightmost bit of 8—is 0. We continue this process until the quotient becomes 0.

The rightmost bit of 35 cannot be printed until we have printed the rightmost bit of 17. The rightmost bit of 17 cannot be printed until we have printed the rightmost bit of 8, and so on. Thus, the binary representation of 35 is the binary representation of 17 (that is, the quotient of 35 after division by 2), followed by the rightmost bit of 35.

Thus, to convert a nonnegative integer num in base 10 into the equivalent binary number, we first convert the quotient num / 2 into an equivalent binary number, and then append the rightmost bit of num to the binary representation of num / 2.

This discussion translates into the following recursive algorithm, where binary(num) denotes the binary representation of num:

1. binary(num) = num if num = 0.
2. binary(num) = binary(num / 2), followed by num % 2 if num > 0.

The following recursive method implements this algorithm:

```java
public static void decToBin(int num, int base)
{
    if (num == 0)
        System.out.print(0);
    else if (num > 0)
    {
        decToBin(num / base, base);
        System.out.print(num % base);
    }
}
```

Figure 13-8 traces the execution of the following statement:

```java
decToBin(13, 2);
```

where num is 13 and base is 2.

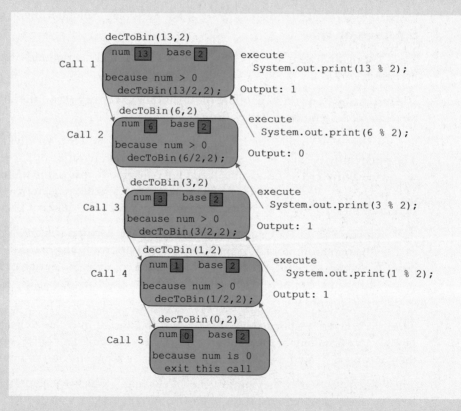

FIGURE 13-8 Execution of decToBin(13, 2)

Because the if statement in Call 5 succeeds, this call prints 0. The second output is produced by Call 4, which prints 1; the third output is produced by Call 3, which prints 1; the fourth output is produced by Call 2, which prints 0; and the fifth output is produced by Call 1, which prints 1. Thus, the output of the statement:

```
decToBin(13, 2);
```

is:

01101

The following Java program tests the method `decToBin`:

```java
//*********************************************************
// Author: D.S. Malik
//
// Recursion: Program - Decimal to Binary
// This program uses recursion to find the binary
// representation of a nonnegative integer.
//*********************************************************

import java.util.*;

public class DecimalToBinary
{
    static Scanner console = new Scanner(System.in);

    public static void main(String[] args)
    {
        int decimalNum;
        int base;

        base = 2;

        System.out.print("Enter a nonnegative integer in "
                        + "decimal: ");
        decimalNum = console.nextInt();
        System.out.println();

        System.out.print("Decimal " + decimalNum + " = ");
        decToBin(decimalNum, base);
        System.out.println(" binary");
    }

    public static void decToBin(int num, int base)
    {
        if (num == 0)
            System.out.print(0);
        else if (num > 0)
        {
            decToBin(num / base, base);
            System.out.print(num % base);
        }
    }
}
```

1
3

Sample Run: (In this sample run, the user input is shaded.)

```
Enter a nonnegative integer in decimal: 57

Decimal 57 = 0111001 binary
```

PROGRAMMING EXAMPLE: Sierpinski Gasket

To draw the shapes of natural scenes, such as mountains, trees, and clouds, graphic programmers typically use special mathematical tools, called **fractals**, related to fractal geometry. Fractal geometry is a major area of research in mathematics in its own right. The term fractal was introduced by the mathematician Benoit Mandelbrot in the mid-1970s. Mandelbrot is credited with the development of systematic fractal geometry, which provides a description of many seemingly complex forms found in nature. One kind of fractal, called a self-similar fractal, is a geometric shape in which certain patterns repeat, sometimes at different scales and with different orientations. Mandelbrot is recognized as the first person to demonstrate that fractals occur in various places in mathematics and nature.

Because certain patterns occur at various places in a fractal, a convenient and effective way to write programs to draw fractals is to use recursion. This section describes a special type of fractal called a **Sierpinski gasket**.

Suppose that you have the triangle *ABC* as given in Figure 13-9(a). Now determine the midpoints *P*, *Q*, and *R* of the sides *AB*, *AC*, and *BC*, respectively. Next, draw the lines *PQ*, *QR*, and *PR*. This creates three triangles, *APQ*, *BPR*, and *CRQ*, as shown in Figure 13-9(b), which have similar shapes as in the triangle *ABC*. The process of finding the midpoints of the sides and then drawing lines through those midpoints is now repeated on each of the triangles *APQ*, *BPR*, and *CRQ*, as shown in Figure 13-9(c). Figure 13-9(a) is called a Sierpinski gasket of order (or level) 0; Figure 13-9(b) is called a Sierpinski gasket of order (or level) 1; Figure 13-9(c) is called a Sierpinski gasket of order (or level) 2; and Figure13-9(d) shows a Sierpinski gasket of order (or level) 3.

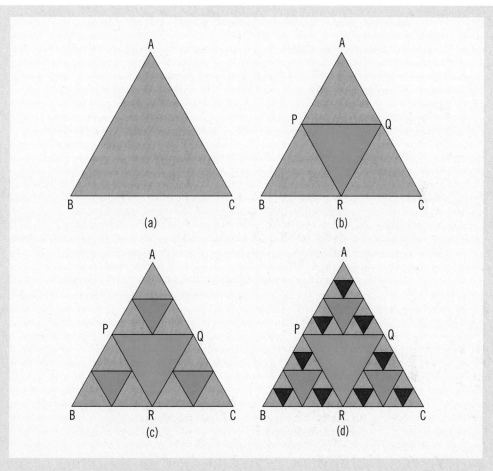

FIGURE 13-9 Sierpinski gaskets of various orders (levels)

Input: A nonnegative integer indicating the level of the Sierpinski gasket.

Output: A triangle shape displaying a Sierpinski gasket of the given order.

PROBLEM
ANALYSIS
AND
ALGORITHM
DESIGN

The problem is as described previously. Initially, we specify the coordinates of the first triangle and then draw the triangle. We use the **class** Point to store the *x-y* coordinates of a point. (The **class** point is a predefined Java class and is contained in the **package** java.awt.) We also use the method drawLine, as described in Chapter 12, to draw a line between two points.

For each triangle, we need three objects of the **class** Point to store the vertices of the triangle, and three more objects to store the midpoints of each side. Because we frequently need to find the midpoints of a line, we write the method midPoint, which returns the coordinates of the midpoint of a line. Its definition is:

```
private Point midPoint(Point pOne, Point pTwo)
{
    Point mid = new Point((pOne.x + pTwo.x) / 2,
                          (pOne.y + pTwo.y) / 2);

    return mid;
}
```

The recursive algorithm to draw a Sierpinski gasket is as follows:

Base case: If the level is 0, draw the first triangle.

Recursive case: If the level is greater than 0, then for each triangle in the Sierpinski gasket, find the midpoints of the sides and draw lines through those points.

Suppose that p1, p2, and p3 are the three vertices of a triangle, and lev denotes the number of levels of the Sierpinski gasket to be drawn. The following method implements the recursive algorithm to draw a Sierpinski gasket:

```
private void drawSierpinski(Graphics g, int lev,
                            Point p1, Point p2, Point p3)
{
    Point midP1P2;
    Point midP2P3;
    Point midP3P1;

    if (lev > 0)
    {
        g.drawLine(p1.x, p1.y, p2.x, p2.y);
        g.drawLine(p2.x, p2.y, p3.x, p3.y);
        g.drawLine(p3.x, p3.y, p1.x, p1.y);

        midP1P2 = midPoint(p1, p2);
        midP2P3 = midPoint(p2, p3);
        midP3P1 = midPoint(p3, p1);

        drawSierpinski(g, lev - 1, p1, midP1P2, midP3P1);
        drawSierpinski(g, lev - 1, p2, midP2P3, midP1P2);
        drawSierpinski(g, lev - 1, p3, midP3P1, midP2P3);
    }
}
```

The following program listing provides the complete algorithm to draw a Sierpinski gasket of a given order. Notice that the program uses an input dialog box to get the user's input.

COMPLETE PROGRAM LISTING

```java
//***********************************************************
// Author: D.S. Malik
//
// Program: Drawing a Sierpinski Gasket
// Given the order of a Sierpinski Gasket, this program
// draws a Sierpinski Gasket of that order.
//***********************************************************

import java.awt.*;
import javax.swing.*;

public class SierpinskiGasket extends JApplet
{
    int level = 0;

    public void init()
    {
        String levelStr = JOptionPane.showInputDialog
                         ("Enter the recursion depth: ");

        level = Integer.parseInt(levelStr);
    }

    public void paint(Graphics g)
    {
        Point pointOne = new Point(60, 160);
        Point pointTwo = new Point(220, 160);
        Point pointThree = new Point(140, 20);

        drawSierpinski(g, level, pointOne, pointTwo,
                   pointThree);
    }

    private void drawSierpinski(Graphics g, int lev,
                              Point p1, Point p2, Point p3)
    {
        Point midP1P2;
        Point midP2P3;
        Point midP3P1;

        if (lev > 0)
        {
            g.drawLine(p1.x, p1.y, p2.x, p2.y);
            g.drawLine(p2.x, p2.y, p3.x, p3.y);
            g.drawLine(p3.x, p3.y, p1.x, p1.y);

            midP1P2 = midPoint(p1, p2);
            midP2P3 = midPoint(p2, p3);
            midP3P1 = midPoint(p3, p1);
```

1
3

```
                        drawSierpinski(g, lev - 1, p1, midP1P2, midP3P1);
                        drawSierpinski(g, lev - 1, p2, midP2P3, midP1P2);
                        drawSierpinski(g, lev - 1, p3, midP3P1, midP2P3);
            }
        }

        private Point midPoint(Point pOne, Point pTwo)
        {
            Point mid = new Point((pOne.x + pTwo.x) / 2,
                                  (pOne.y + pTwo.y) / 2);

            return mid;
        }
    }
```

Sample Run: Figure 13-10 shows a sample run. In this sample run, the user input is entered in the input dialog box.

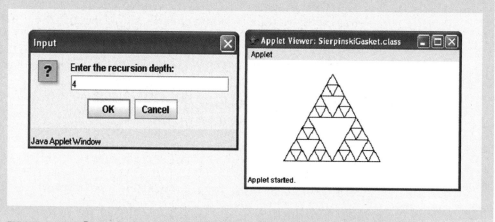

FIGURE 13-10   Recursion depth of 4 produces a Sierpinski gasket of order 3

QUICK REVIEW

1. The process of solving a problem by reducing it to smaller versions of itself is called recursion.

2. A recursive definition defines the problem in terms of smaller versions of itself.

3. Every recursive definition has one or more base cases.

4. A recursive algorithm solves a problem by reducing it to smaller versions of itself.

5. Every recursive algorithm has one or more base cases.

6. The solution to a problem in a base case is obtained directly.

7. A method is recursive if it calls itself.

8. Recursive algorithms are implemented using recursive methods.

9. Every recursive method must have one or more base cases.

10. The general solution breaks a problem into smaller versions of itself.

11. The general case must eventually be reduced to a base case.

12. The base case stops the recursion.

13. While tracing a recursive method:

    a. Logically, you can think of a recursive method as having unlimited copies of itself.

    b. Every call to a recursive method—that is, every recursive call—has its own code and its own set of parameters and local variables.

    c. After completing a particular recursive call, control goes back to the calling environment, which is the previous call. The current (recursive) call must execute completely before control goes back to the previous call. The execution in the previous call continues from the point immediately following the recursive call.

14. A method is directly recursive if it calls itself.

15. A method that calls another method and eventually results in the original method call is indirectly recursive.

16. A recursive method in which the last statement executed is the recursive call is called a tail recursive method.

17. To design a recursive method, you must do the following:

    a. Understand the problem requirements.

    b. Determine the limiting conditions.

    c. Identify the base cases and provide a direct solution to each base case.

    d. Identify the general case(s) and provide a solution to each general case in terms of a smaller version of itself.

EXERCISES

1. Mark the following statements as true or false.

    a. Every recursive definition must have one or more base cases.

    b. Every recursive method must have one or more base cases.

    c. The general case stops the recursion.

d. In the general case, the solution to the problem is obtained directly.

e. A recursive method always returns a value.

2. What is a base case?

3. What is a recursive case?

4. What is direct recursion?

5. What is indirect recursion?

6. What is tail recursion?

7. Consider the following recursive method:

```
public static int mystery(int number)          //Line 1
{
    if (number == 0)                            //Line 2
        return number;                          //Line 3
      else                                      //Line 4
        return(number + mystery(number - 1));   //Line 5
}
```

a. Identify the base case.

b. Identify the general case.

c. What valid values can be passed as parameters to the method mystery?

d. If mystery(0) is a valid call, what is its value? If it is not a valid call, explain why.

e. If mystery(5) is a valid call, what is its value? If not, explain why.

f. If mystery(-3) is a valid call, what is its value? If not, explain why.

8. Consider the following recursive method:

```
public static void funcRec(int u, char v)          //Line 1
{
    if (u == 0)                                     //Line 2
        System.out.print(v);                        //Line 3
    else if(u == 1)                                 //Line 4
        System.out.print((char)((int)(v) + 1);      //Line 5
    else                                            //Line 6
        funcRec(u - 1, v);                          //Line 7
}
```

a. Identify the base case.

b. Identify the general case.

c. What is the output of the following statement?

funcRec(5, 'A');

9. Consider the following recursive method:

```
public static void exercise(int x)
{
    if (x > 0 && x < 10)
```

```
    {
        System.out.print(x + " ");
        exercise(x + 1);
    }
}
```

What is the output of the following statements?

a. `exercise(0);`

b. `exercise(5);`

c. `exercise(10);`

d. `exercise(-5);`

10. Consider the following method:

```
public static int test(int x, int y)
{
    if (x == y)
        return x;
    else if (x > y)
        return (x + y);
    else
        return test(x + 1, y - 1);
}
```

What is the output of the following statements?

a. `System.out.println(test(5, 10));`

b. `System.out.println(test(3, 9));`

11. Consider the following method:

```
public static int func(int x)
{
    if (x == 0)
        return 2;
    else if (x == 1)
        return 3;
    else
        return (func(x - 1) + func(x - 2));
}
```

What is the output of the following statements?

a. `System.out.println(func(0));`

b. `System.out.println(func(1));`

c. `System.out.println(func(2));`

d. `System.out.println(func(5));`

12. Suppose that intArray is an array of integers and length specifies the number of elements in intArray. Also, suppose that low and high are two integers such that 0 <= low < length, 0 <= high < length, and low <= high. That is, low and high are two indices in intArray. Write a

recursive definition that reverses the elements in `intArray` between `low` and `high`.

13. Write a recursive definition to multiply two positive integers *m* and *n* using repeated addition.

PROGRAMMING EXERCISES

1. Write a recursive method that takes as a parameter a nonnegative integer and generates the following pattern of stars. If the nonnegative integer is 4, then the pattern generated is:

    ```
    ****
    ***
    **
    *
    *
    **
    ***
    ****
    ```

    Also, write a program that prompts the user to enter the number of lines in the pattern and uses the recursive method to generate the pattern. For example, specifying the number of lines to be 4 generates the preceding pattern.

2. Write a recursive method to generate a pattern of stars such as the following:

    ```
    *
    **
    ***
    ****
    ****
    ***
    **
    *
    ```

    Also, write a program that prompts the user to enter the number of lines in the pattern and uses the recursive method to generate the pattern. For example, specifying the number of lines to be 4 generates the preceding pattern.

3. Write a recursive method to generate the following pattern of stars:

    ```
       *
      * *
     * * *
    * * * *
     * * *
      * *
       *
    ```

Also, write a program that prompts the user to enter the number of lines in the pattern and uses the recursive method to generate the pattern. For example, specifying the number of lines to be 4 generates the preceding pattern.

4. Write a recursive method, `vowels`, that returns the number of vowels in a string. Also, write a program to test your method.

5. Write a recursive method that finds and returns the sum of the elements of an `int` array. Also, write a program to test your method.

6. A palindrome is a string that reads the same both forward and backward. For example, the string "`madam`" is a palindrome. Write a program that uses a recursive method to check whether a string is a palindrome. Your program must contain a value-returning recursive method that returns `true` if the string is a palindrome and `false` otherwise. Use appropriate parameters in your method.

7. Write a program that uses a recursive method to print a string backward. Your program must contain a recursive method that prints the string backward. Use appropriate parameters in your method.

8. Write a recursive method, `reverseDigits`, that takes an integer as a parameter and returns the number with the digits reversed. Also, write a program to test your method.

9. Write a recursive method, `power`, that takes as parameters two integers x and y such that x is nonzero and returns x^y. You can use the following recursive definition to calculate x^y. If $y \geq 0$:

$$power(x, y) = \begin{cases} 1 & \text{if } y = 0 \\ x & \text{if } y = 1 \\ x * power(x, y - 1) & \text{if } y > 1 \end{cases}$$

If $y < 0$:

$$power(x, y) = \frac{1}{power(x, -y)}$$

Also, write a program to test your method.

10. **Greatest Common Divisor.** Given two integers x and y, the following recursive definition determines the greatest common divisor of x and y, written gcd(x,y):

$$gcd(x, y) = \begin{cases} x & \text{if } y = 0 \\ gcd(y, x \% y) & \text{if } y \neq 0 \end{cases}$$

(*Note:* In this definition, % is the mod operator.)
(This algorithm to determine the gcd of two integers is called the **Euclidean algorithm**.) Write a recursive method, `gcd`, that takes as parameters

two integers and returns the greatest common divisor of the numbers. Also, write a program to test your method.

11. Write a recursive method to implement the recursive definition of Exercise 12 (reversing the elements of an array between two indices). Also, write a program to test your method.

12. Write a recursive method to implement the recursive definition of Exercise 13 (multiply two positive integers using repeated addition). Also, write a program to test your method.

13. In the Decimal to Binary Conversion programming example presented in this chapter, you learned how to convert a decimal number into its equivalent binary number. Two more number systems, octal (base 8) and hexadecimal (base 16), are of interest to computer scientists.

The digits in the octal number system are 0, 1, 2, 3, 4, 5, 6, and 7. The digits in the hexadecimal number system are 0, 1, 2, 3, 4, 5, 6, 7, 8, 9, A, B, C, D, E, and F. So, A in hexadecimal is 10 in decimal, B in hexadecimal is 11 in decimal, and so on.

The algorithm to convert a positive decimal number into an equivalent number in octal (or hexadecimal) is the same as that discussed for binary numbers. Here, we divide the decimal number by 8 (for octal) and by 16 (for hexadecimal). Suppose that a_b represents the number a to the base b. For example, 75_{10} means 75 to the base 10 (that is, decimal), and 83_{16} means 83 to the base 16 (that is, hexadecimal). Then:

$$753_{10} = 1361_8$$

$$753_{10} = 2F1_{16}$$

The method of converting a decimal number to base 2, or 8, or 16 can be extended to any arbitrary base. Suppose you want to convert a decimal number n into an equivalent number in base b, where b is between 2 and 36. You then divide the decimal number n by b, as in the algorithm for converting decimal to binary.

Note that the digits in, say, base 20, are 0, 1, 2, 3, 4, 5, 6, 7, 8, 9, A, B, C, D, E, F, G, H, I, and J.

Write a program that uses a recursive method to convert a number in decimal to a given base b, where b is between 2 and 36. Your program should prompt the user to enter the number in decimal and in the desired base.

Test your program on the following data:

9098 and base 20

692 and base 2

753 and base 16

14. **Binary to Decimal Conversion.** The language of a computer, called machine language, is a sequence of 0s and 1s. When you press the A key on the keyboard, 01000001 is stored in the computer. Note that the collating sequence of A in the Unicode character set is 65. In fact, the binary representation of A is 01000001 and the decimal representation of A is 65.

The numbering system we use is called the decimal system, or base 10 system. The numbering system that the computer uses is called the binary system, or base 2 system. This chapter described how to convert a decimal number into an equivalent binary number. The purpose of this exercise is to write a program to convert a number from base 2 to base 10.

To convert a number from base 2 to base 10, we first find the weight of each bit in the binary number. The weight of each bit in the binary number is assigned from right to left. The weight of the rightmost bit is 0. The weight of the bit immediately to the left of the rightmost bit is 1, the weight of the bit immediately to the left of it is 2, and so on. Consider the binary number 1001101. The weight of each bit is as follows:

```
weight   6  5  4  3  2  1  0
         1  0  0  1  1  0  1
```

We use the weight of each bit to find the equivalent decimal number. For each bit, we multiply the bit by 2 to the power of its weight and then add all of the numbers. For the above binary number, the equivalent decimal number is:

$$1 \times 2^6 + 0 \times 2^5 + 0 \times 2^4 + 1 \times 2^3 + 1 \times 2^2 + 0 \times 2^1 + 1 \times 2^0$$

$$= 64 + 0 + 0 + 8 + 4 + 0 + 1$$

$$= 77$$

To write a program that converts a binary number into the equivalent decimal number, we note two things: (1) the weight of each bit in the binary number must be known; and (2) the weight is assigned from right to left. Because we do not know in advance how many bits are in the binary number, we must process the bits from right to left. After processing a bit, we can add 1 to its weight, giving the weight of the bit immediately to its left. Also, each bit must be extracted from the binary number and multiplied by 2 to the power of its weight. To extract a bit, you can use the mod operator. Write a method that converts a binary number into an equivalent decimal number. Moreover, write a program and test your method for the following values: 11000101, 10101010, 11111111, 10000000, and 1111100000.

15. Write a program that uses recursion to draw a Koch snowflake fractal of any given order. A Koch snowflake of order 0 is an equilateral triangle. To create the next-higher-order fractal, each line segment in the shape is modified by replacing its middle third with a sharp protrusion made of two line segments, each having the same length as the replaced one, as shown in Figure 13-11.

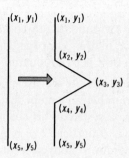

FIGURE 13-11 Line segments for Koch snowflakes

The following is the necessary information to compute the three new points (x_2, y_2), (x_3, y_3), and (x_4, y_4) in terms of (x_1, y_1) and (x_5, y_5).

Let:

$deltaX = x_5 - x_1$

$deltaY = y_5 - y_1$

Then:

$x_2 = x_1 + deltaX/3,$

$y_2 = y_1 + deltaY/3,$

$x_3 = 0.5(x_1 + x_5) + \sqrt{3}(y_1 - y_5)/6,$

$y_3 = 0.5(y_1 + y_5) + \sqrt{3}(x_5 - x_1)/6,$

$x_4 = x_1 + 2 \times deltaX/3,$

$y_4 = y_1 + 2 \times deltaY/3$

The first three Koch snowflakes produced by the program might look like Figure 13-12.

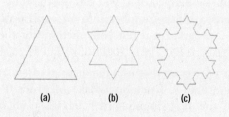

(a)   (b)   (c)

FIGURE 13-12 First three Koch snowflakes

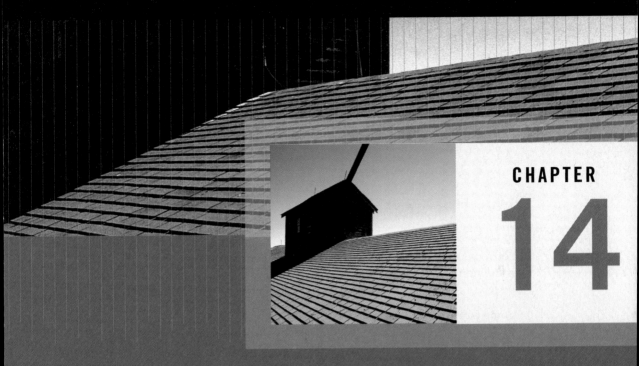

SEARCHING AND SORTING

IN THIS CHAPTER, YOU WILL:

- Explore how to sort an array using the selection sort algorithm
- Explore how to sort an array using the insertion sort algorithm
- Learn how to implement the binary search algorithm
- Learn how to avoid bugs by developing test suites in advance

Chapter 9 introduced arrays, a structured data type. Arrays are a convenient way to store and process data values of the same type. You learned how to use loops effectively with arrays for input/output, initialization, and other operations. You also learned how to pass an entire set of values as a single parameter. This chapter continues the discussion of arrays and shows you how to use them effectively for processing lists.

List Processing

A **list** is a set of values of the same type. Because all values are of the same type, it is convenient to store a list in an array, specifically a one-dimensional array. The size of a list is the number of elements in the list. Because a list's size can increase and decrease, the array you use to store the list should be declared to be the maximum size of the list.

Some basic operations performed on a list are:

- Search the list for a given item.
- Sort the list.
- Insert an item in the list.
- Delete an item from the list.

The following sections discuss algorithms to perform some of these operations.

Searching

Chapter 9 described a sequential search algorithm and also illustrated how to use it. Recall that the sequential search searches the array sequentially starting from the first array element.

Suppose that you have a list with 1000 elements, as shown in Figure 14-1.

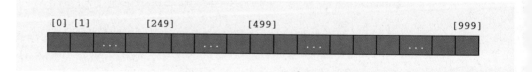

FIGURE 14-1 List of 1000 elements

If the search item is the second item in the list, the sequential search makes two **key comparisons** (also called **item comparisons**) to determine whether the search item is in the list. Similarly, if the search item is the 900th item in the list, the sequential search makes 900 key comparisons to determine whether the search item is in the list. If the search item is not in the list, the sequential search makes 1000 key comparisons.

If `searchItem` is always at the end of the `list`, it will take many comparisons to find `searchItem`. Also, if `searchItem` is not in the `list`, then we will compare `searchItem` with every element in the `list`. A sequential search is therefore not efficient for large lists. In fact, it can be proved that, on average, the number of comparisons (that is, key comparisons) made by a sequential search is equal to half the size of the list. So, for a list of size 1000, on average, the sequential search makes about 500 comparisons. Similarly, for a list of size 1,000,000, on average, the sequential search makes about 500,000 comparisons. (Imagine how much time it will take if you search a telephone book for "Smith" sequentially starting at A's and go through all the records until you find Smith.)

This search algorithm does not assume that the `list` is sorted. If the `list` is sorted, then you can improve the search algorithm. Next, we discuss how to sort a `list`.

Selection Sort

Many sorting algorithms are available in the literature. This section describes the sorting algorithm called the **selection sort**, to sort a list.

In a selection sort, a list is sorted by selecting elements in the list, one at a time, and moving them to their proper positions. This algorithm finds the location of the smallest element in the unsorted portion of the list and moves it to the top of the unsorted portion (i.e., the whole list) of the list. The first time we locate the smallest item in the entire list; the second time we locate the smallest item in the list starting from the second element in the list; and so on. For example, suppose you have the list shown in Figure 14-2.

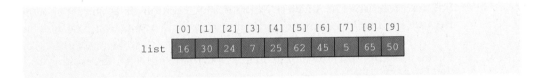

FIGURE 14-2 List of 10 elements

Figure 14-3 shows the elements of `list` in the first iteration.

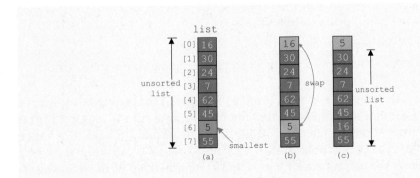

FIGURE 14-3 Elements of `list` during the first iteration

Initially, the entire list is unsorted. So we find the smallest item in the list. The smallest item is at position 6, as shown in Figure 14-3(a). Because this is the smallest item, it must be moved to position 0. So we swap 16 (that is, list[0]) with 5 (that is, list[6]), as shown in Figure 14-3(b). After swapping these elements, the resulting list is as shown in Figure 14-3(c).

Figure 14-4 shows the elements of list in the second iteration.

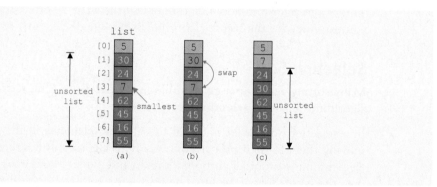

FIGURE 14-4 Elements of list during the second iteration

Now the unsorted list is list[1]...list[7]. So we find the smallest element in the unsorted list. The smallest element is at position 3, as shown in Figure 14-4(a). Because the smallest element in the unsorted list is at position 3, it must be moved to position 1. So we swap 7 (that is, list[3]) with 30 (that is, list[1]), as shown in Figure 14-4(b). After swapping list[1] with list[3], the resulting list is as shown in Figure 14-4(c).

Now the unsorted list is list[2]...list[7]. So we repeat the preceding process of finding the (position of the) smallest element in the unsorted portion of the list and moving it to the beginning of the unsorted portion of the list. The selection sort thus involves the following steps.

In the unsorted portion of the list:

    a.   Find the location of the smallest element.

    b.   Move the smallest element to the beginning of the unsorted list.

Initially, the entire list, that is, list[0]...list[listLength - 1], is the unsorted list. After executing steps a and b, the unsorted list is list[1]...list[listLength - 1]. After we execute steps a and b the second time, the unsorted list is list[2]...list[listLength - 1], and so on. We can keep track of the unsorted portion of the list and repeat steps a and b with the help of the following **for** loop:

```
for (index = 0; index < listLength - 1; index++)
{
    a. find the location, smallestIndex, of the smallest element in
       list[index]...list[listLength].
    b. Swap the smallest element with list[index]. That is, swap
       list[smallestIndex] with list[index].
}
```

The first time through the loop, we locate the smallest element in `list[0]...list[listLength - 1]` and swap this smallest element with `list[0]`. The second time through the loop, we locate the smallest element in `list[1]...list[listLength - 1]` and swap this smallest element with `list[1]`, and so on.

Step a is similar to the algorithm of finding the index of the largest item in the list, as discussed in Chapter 9. Here, we find the index of the smallest item in the list. (See Programming Exercise 2 in Chapter 9.) The general form of step a is:

```
smallestIndex = index; //assume that the first element
                       //is the smallest

for (minIndex = index + 1; minIndex < listLength; minIndex++)
    if (list[minIndex] < list[smallestIndex])
        smallestIndex = minIndex; //current element in the list
                                  //is smaller than the smallest so
                                  //far, so update smallestIndex
```

Step b swaps the contents of `list[smallestIndex]` with `list[index]`. The following statements accomplish this task:

```
temp = list[smallestIndex];
list[smallestIndex] = list[index];
list[index] = temp;
```

It follows that to swap these values, three item assignments are needed. The following method, **selectionSort**, implements the selection sort algorithm:

```
public static void selectionSort(int[] list, int listLength)
{
    int index;
    int smallestIndex;
    int minIndex;
    int temp;

    for (index = 0; index < listLength - 1; index++)
    {
            //Step a
        smallestIndex = index;

        for (minIndex = index + 1; minIndex < listLength;
                                   minIndex++)
            if (list[minIndex] < list[smallestIndex])
                smallestIndex = minIndex;
```

1
4

```
                    //Step b
            temp = list[smallestIndex];
            list[smallestIndex] = list[index];
            list[index] = temp;
        }
    }
```

Note that if the list contains duplicates, then while searching for the smallest element, the method selectionSort finds the position of the first occurrence of the smallest element, and in the successive iterations finds the positions of other occurrences of this smallest element. Example 14-1 shows how to use the selection sort algorithm in a program.

EXAMPLE 14-1(SELECTION SORT)

```
// This program illustrates how to use a selection sort algorithm
// in a program.

public class TestSelectionSort                      //Line 1
{                                                   //Line 2
    public static void main(String[] args)          //Line 3
    {
        int list[] = {2, 56, 34, 25, 73, 46, 89,
                      10, 5, 16};                    //Line 4

        selectionSort(list, list.length);           //Line 5

        System.out.println("After sorting, the "
                    + "list elements are:");         //Line 6

        for (int i = 0; i < list.length; i++)        //Line 7
            System.out.print(list[i] + " ");         //Line 8

        System.out.println();                        //Line 9
    }                                                //Line 10

    //Place the definition of the selection sort algorithm
    //given previously here.
}
```

Sample Run:

```
After sorting, the list elements are:
2 5 10 16 25 34 46 56 73 89
```

The statement in Line 4 creates and initializes list to be an array of 10 elements of type int. The statement in Line 5 uses the method selectionSort to sort list. Notice that both list and its length are passed as parameters to the method selectionSort. The for loop in Lines 7 and 8 outputs the elements of list.

In this program, to illustrate the selection sort algorithm, we declared and initialized the array list. However, you can also prompt the user to input the data during program execution.

For a list of length n, on average, a selection sort makes $\frac{n(n-1)}{2}$ key comparisons and $3(n-1)$ item assignments. Therefore, if $n = 1000$, then to sort the list, selection sort makes about 500,000 key comparisons and about 3000 item assignments. The next section presents the insertion sort algorithm that reduces the number of comparisons.

Insertion Sort

As noted in the previous section, for a list of length 1000, selection sort makes approximately 500,000 key comparisons, which is quite high. This section describes the sorting algorithm called the insertion sort, which attempts to reduce the number of key comparisons.

The insertion sort algorithm sorts a list by repeatedly inserting an element in its proper place into a sorted sublist until the whole list is sorted. Consider the list shown in Figure 14-5.

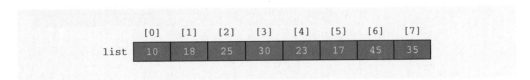

FIGURE 14-5 List

The length of the list is 8. In this list, the elements `list[0]`, `list[1]`, `list[2]`, and `list[3]` are in order. That is, `list[0]...list[3]` is sorted (see Figure 14-6).

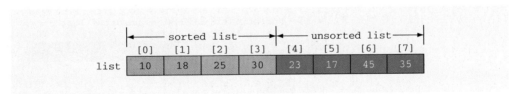

FIGURE 14-6 Sorted and unsorted portion of `list`

Next, we consider the element `list[4]`, the first element of the unsorted list. Because `list[4] < list[3]`, we need to insert the element `list[4]` in its proper location. From this list, it follows that element `list[4]` should be moved to `list[2]` (see Figure 14-7).

1
4

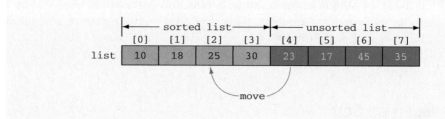

FIGURE 14-7 Move `list[4]` into `list[2]`

To move `list[4]` into `list[2]`, first we copy `list[4]` into `temp`, a temporary memory space (see Figure 14-8).

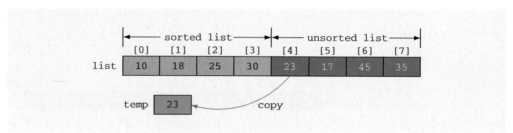

FIGURE 14-8 Copy `list[4]` into `temp`

Next, we copy `list[3]` into `list[4]`, and then `list[2]` into `list[3]` (see Figure 14-9).

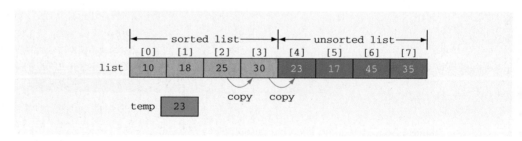

FIGURE 14-9 List before copying `list[3]` into `list[4]`, and then `list[2]` into `list[3]`

After copying `list[3]` into `list[4]` and `list[2]` into `list[3]`, the list is as shown in Figure 14-10.

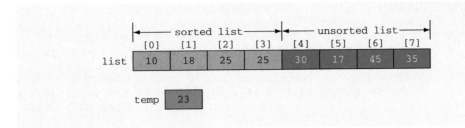

FIGURE 14-10 List after copying `list[3]` into `list[4]`, and then `list[2]` into `list[3]`

We now copy `temp` into `list[2]`. Figure 14-11 shows the resulting list.

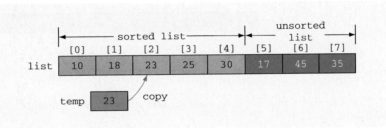

FIGURE 14-11 List after copying `temp` into `list[2]`

Now `list[0]...list[4]` is sorted and `list[5]...list[7]` is unsorted. We repeat this process on the resulting list by moving the first element of the unsorted list into the sorted list in the proper place.

From this discussion, it is clear that during the sorting phase the array containing the list is divided into two sublists, upper and lower. Elements in the upper sublist are sorted; elements in the lower sublist are to be moved to the upper sublist in their proper places one at a time. We use an index—say, `firstOutOfOrder`—to point to the first element in the lower sublist; that is, `firstOutOfOrder` gives the index of the first element in the unsorted portion of the array. Initially, `firstOutOfOrder` is initialized to 1.

This discussion translates into the following pseudoalgorithm:

```
for (firstOutOfOrder = 1; firstOutOfOrder < listLength;
                    firstOutOfOrder++)
   if (list[firstOutOfOrder] is less than list[firstOutOfOrder - 1])
   {
       copy list[firstOutOfOrder] into temp

       initialize location to firstOutOfOrder
```

```
do
{
    a. move list[location - 1] one array slot down
    b. decrement location by 1 to consider the next element
       sorted of the portion of the array
}
while (location > 0 && the element in the upper list at
                location - 1 is greater than temp)
}
copy temp into list[location]
```

Let us trace the execution of this algorithm on the list given in Figure 14-12.

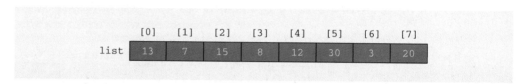

FIGURE 14-12 Unsorted list

The length of this list is 8; that is, `length = 8`. We initialize `firstOutOfOrder` to 1 (see Figure 14-13).

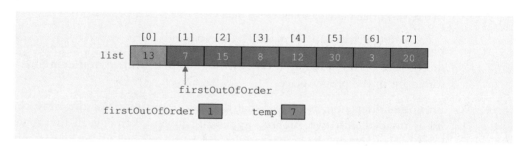

FIGURE 14-13 `firstOutOfOrder = 1`

Now `list[firstOutOfOrder]` = 7, `list[firstOutOfOrder - 1]` = 13 and 7 < 13, and the expression in the `if` statement evaluates to `true`, so we execute the body of the `if` statement.

```
temp = list[firstOutOfOrder] = 7
location = firstOutOfOrder = 1
```

Next, we execute the do...while loop.

```
list[1] = list[0] = 13    (copy list[0] into list[1])
location = 0              (decrement location)
```

The `do...while` loop terminates because `location = 0`. We copy `temp` into `list[location]`—that is, into `list[0]`. Figure 14-14 shows the resulting list.

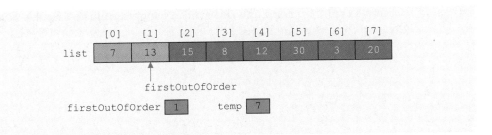

FIGURE 14-14 List after the first iteration of the insertion sort algorithm

Now suppose that we have the list given in Figure 14-15.

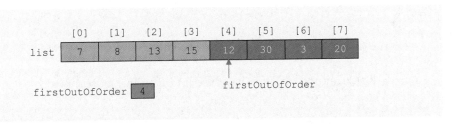

FIGURE 14-15 First out-of-order element is at position 4

Here, `list[0]...list[3]`, or the elements `list[0]`, `list[1]`, `list[2]`, and `list[3]`, are in order. Now `firstOutOfOrder = 4`. Because `list[4] < list[3]`, the element `list[4]`, which is 12, needs to be moved to its proper location.

As before:

```
temp = list[firstOutOfOrder] = 12
location = firstOutOfOrder = 4
```

First, we copy `list[3]` into `list[4]` and decrement `location` by 1. Then we copy `list[2]` into `list[3]` and again decrement `location` by 1. Now the value of `location` is 2. At this point, the list is as shown in Figure 14-16.

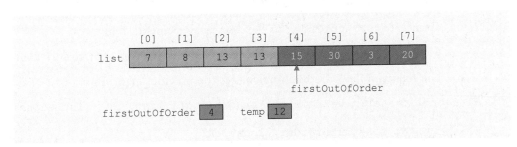

FIGURE 14-16 List after copying `list[3]` into `list[4]`, and then `list[2]` into `list[3]`

Because list[1] < temp, the do...while loop terminates. At this point, location is 2, so we copy temp into list[2]. That is:

list[2] = temp = 12

Figure 14-17 shows the resulting list.

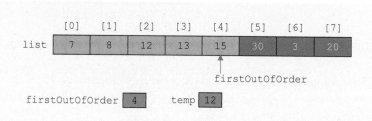

FIGURE 14-17 List after copying temp into list[2]

Next, suppose that we have the list given in Figure 14-18.

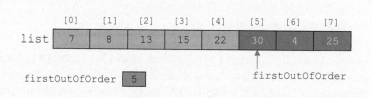

FIGURE 14-18 First out-of-order element is at position 5

Here, list[0]...list[4], or the elements list[0], list[1], list[2], and list[4], are in order. Now firstOutOfOrder = 5. Because list[5] > list[4], the if statement evaluates to false. So the body of the if statement does not execute, and the next iteration of the for loop, if any, takes place. Note that this is the case when the firstOutofOrder element is already at the proper place. So we simply need to advance firstOutofOrder to the next array element, if any.

We can repeat this process for the remaining elements of list to sort list.

The following Java method implements the previous algorithm:

```
public static void insertionSort(int[] list, int listLength)
{
    int firstOutOfOrder, location;
    int temp;
```

```
for (firstOutOfOrder = 1; firstOutOfOrder < listLength;
                          firstOutOfOrder++)
    if (list[firstOutOfOrder] < list[firstOutOfOrder - 1])
    {
        temp = list[firstOutOfOrder];
        location = firstOutOfOrder;

        do
        {
            list[location] = list[location - 1];
            location--;
        }
        while (location > 0 && list[location - 1] > temp);

        list[location] = temp;
    }
} //end insertionSort
```

We leave it as an exercise for you to write a program to test the insertion sort algorithm.

It is known that for a list of length n, on average, an insertion sort makes about $\dfrac{n^2 + 3n - 4}{4}$ key comparisons and about $\dfrac{n(n-1)}{4}$ item assignments. Therefore, if $n = 1000$, then to sort the list, an insertion sort makes about 250,000 key comparisons and about 250,000 item assignments.

This chapter has presented two sorting algorithms, but there are many others. (For example, the Web site and the CD accompanying this book contains a bubble sort and a quick sort algorithms.) Why are there so many different sorting algorithms? The answer is that the performance of each sorting algorithm is different. Some algorithms make more comparisons, some make fewer item assignments, and some algorithms make fewer comparisons as well as fewer item assignments. The preceding sections gave the average number of comparisons and item assignments for this chapter's three sorting algorithms. By analyzing the number of key comparisons and item assignments, the user can decide which algorithm to use in a particular situation.

Binary Search

A sequential search, as described in the preceding section, performs better on a sorted list but is still not efficient for large lists. It typically still searches about half the list. However, if the list is sorted, you can use another search algorithm, called a **binary search**. A binary search is much faster than a sequential search, but a binary search can be performed only on a sorted list. A binary search uses the *divide and conquer* technique to search the list. First, the search item is compared with the middle element of the list. If the search item is not equal to the middle element, and is less than the middle element of the list, the search is restricted to the first half of the list; otherwise, the second half of the list is searched.

Consider the following sorted list of length 12, shown in Figure 14-19.

FIGURE 14-19 List of length 12

Suppose that we want to determine whether 75 is in the list. Initially, the entire list is the search list (see Figure 14-20).

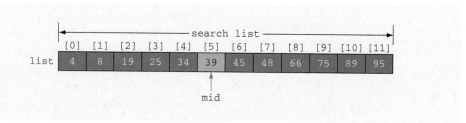

FIGURE 14-20 Search list, `list[0]...list[11]`

First, we compare 75 with the middle element, `list[5]` (which is 39), in the list. Because 75 ≠ `list[5]` and 75 > `list[5]`, next we restrict our search to the list `list[6]...list[11]`, as shown in Figure 14-21.

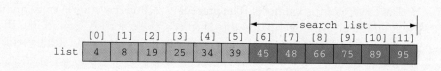

FIGURE 14-21 Search list, `list[6]...list[11]`

The above process is now repeated on the list `list[6]...list[11]`, which is a list of length 6.

Because we frequently need to determine the middle element of the list, the binary search algorithm is usually implemented for array-based lists. To determine the middle element of the list, we add the starting index, `first`, and the ending index, `last`, of the search list and divide by 2 to calculate its index. That is, $mid = \dfrac{first + last}{2}$.

Initially, `first = 0` and (because the array index in Java starts at 0 and `listLength` denotes the number of elements in the list) `last = listLength - 1`.

The following Java method implements the binary search algorithm. If the search item is found in the list, its location is returned. If the search item is not in the list, −1 is returned.

```java
public static int binarySearch(int[] list, int listLength,
                               int searchItem)
{
    int first = 0;
    int last = listLength - 1;
    int mid;

    boolean found = false;

    while (first <= last && !found)
    {
        mid = (first + last) / 2;

        if (list[mid] == searchItem)
            found = true;
        else if (list[mid] > searchItem)
            last = mid - 1;
        else
            first = mid + 1;
    }

    if (found)
        return mid;
    else
        return -1;
}//end binarySearch
```

Note that in the binary search algorithm, two key (item) comparisons are made each time through the loop, except in the successful case the last time through the loop, when only one key comparison is made.

Next, we do a walk-through of the binary search algorithm on the list shown in Figure 14-22.

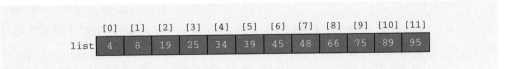

	[0]	[1]	[2]	[3]	[4]	[5]	[6]	[7]	[8]	[9]	[10]	[11]
list	4	8	19	25	34	39	45	48	66	75	89	95

FIGURE 14-22 Sorted list for binary search

The size of the list in Figure 14-22 is 12, that is, listLength = 12. Suppose that the item for which we are searching is 89, that is, searchItem = 89. Before the while loop executes, first = 0, last = 11, and found = false. In the following, we trace the execution of the `while` loop, showing the values of `first`, `last`, and `mid`, and the number of key comparisons during each iteration:

Iteration	first	last	mid	list[mid]	Number of key comparisons
1	0	11	5	39	2
2	6	11	8	66	2
3	9	11	10	89	1 (found is true)

The item is found at location 10 and the total number of key comparisons is 5.

Next, let's search the list for 34, that is, `searchItem = 34`. Before the `while` loop executes, `first = 0`, `last = 11`, and `found = false`. In the following, as before, we trace the execution of the `while` loop, showing the values of `first`, `last`, and `mid`, and the number of key comparisons during each iteration:

Iteration	first	last	mid	list[mid]	Number of key comparisons
1	0	11	5	39	2
2	0	4	2	19	2
3	3	4	3	25	2
4	4	4	4	34	1 (found is true)

The item is found at location 4 and the total number of key comparisons is 7.

Let's now search for 22, that is, `searchItem = 22`. Before the `while` loop executes, `first = 0`, `last = 11`, and `found = false`. In the following, as before, we trace the execution of the `while` loop, showing the values of `first`, `last`, and `mid`, and the number of key comparisons during each iteration:

Iteration	first	last	mid	list[mid]	Number of key comparisons
1	0	11	5	39	2
2	0	4	2	19	2
3	3	4	3	25	2
4	3	2		the loop stops (because first > last) unsuccessful search	

This is an unsuccessful search. The total number of key comparisons is 6.

From these tracings of the binary search algorithm, you can see that every time you go through the loop, you cut the size of the sublist by half. That is, the size of the sublist you search the next time through the loop is half the size of the previous sublist.

PERFORMANCE OF THE BINARY SEARCH

Suppose that L is a sorted list of size 1000 and we want to determine if an item x is in L. From the binary search algorithm, it follows that every iteration of the `while` loop cuts the size of the search list by half. (For example, see Figures 14-20 and 14-21.) Because $1000 \approx 1024 = 2^{10}$, the `while` loop will have, at most, 11 iterations to determine whether x is in L. (Note that the symbol $\approx$ means approximately equal to.) Because every iteration of the `while` loop makes two item (key) comparisons, that is, x is compared twice with the elements of L, the binary search will make, at most, 22 comparisons to determine whether x is in L. On the other hand, recall that a sequential search on average will make 500 comparisons to determine whether x is in L.

To better understand how fast binary search is compared to sequential search, suppose that L is of size 1000000. Since $1000000 \approx 1048576 = 2^{20}$, it follows that the `while` loop in binary search will have at most *21* iterations to determine whether an element is in L. Every iteration of the `while` loop makes two key (that is, item) comparisons. Therefore, to determine whether an element is in L, binary search makes at most 42 item comparisons. On the other hand, on average, a sequential search will make 500,000 key (item) comparisons to determine whether an element is in L. (Because a telephone book is in alphabetical order, it can be searched using a binary search. For example, to search for "Smith," you open the telephone book in the middle to start the search.)

In general, if L is a sorted list of size n, to determine whether an element is in L, the binary search makes at most $2\log_2 n + 2$ key (item) comparisons.

Avoiding Bugs: Developing Test Suites in Advance

It can be tempting to conclude that a program is working correctly when it outputs a correct result for the first time. A program that outputs a correct result is correct for that set of input, but it may be incorrect for other sets of input. However, it is seldom practical to test a program with all possible input sets. So how do we determine that a program is correct without testing every possible input set? We develop an efficient test suite intended to test every kind of input, with special attention to boundary values.

For example, suppose we write a program to find the square root of a whole number, but without using method `sqrt` from `class Math`. In our first attempt to determine if our program is working, we might input the value 16. If our program outputs the value 4, we know that our program works at least for the input value 16, but it may not work for other input values. Next, we might be inclined to try 4 or 25 or 36, because we know the square roots of each of these numbers. But these numbers all are perfect squares (each is the square of some integer). Instead, it may be safe to assume that, if our program works for one perfect square, it probably works for other perfect squares. Hence, we should try our program on a number such as 5, which is not a perfect square. Let's assume it works correctly if the input value is 5. So far, all of the numbers we have tested are positive. We should try our program on one or more negative numbers, to see if our program outputs the correct imaginary number. Then, even though 0 is a perfect square, we ought to try our program on 0. We can say that negative numbers, 0, and positive numbers are different kinds of numbers, and we should make certain that our program works properly on each kind of number. Finally, we should check numbers on the boundaries. The number on the boundary between the negative numbers and 0 is the number –1. The number on the boundary between 0 and the positive numbers is the number 1. Finally, we should try our program on the largest positive integer and the smallest negative integer, which are also boundary values. By checking one number of each kind and at each boundary, we maximize the return on our investment of time to determine if our program is working correctly.

A test suite is a collection of input values (often together with a corresponding set of expected outputs), determined in advance, to be used to verify that a program is working correctly once it is written. At this stage, you are still learning the fundamentals of programming. As you become comfortable with the fundamentals of programming, you should begin to establish test suites as part of the software development process. A test suite should be established as soon as the requirements are known. After familiarizing ourselves with the requirements, we should be able to determine input values (and corresponding output values) that we will use to test our program. At this early development stage, our focus is undiluted by the attention that we must ultimately devote to design and implementation.

Sometimes a programmer establishes a set of objectives for a program, only to realize that the designed and coded program satisfies only a subset of those objectives. Sometimes, in the process of designing and implementing, the programmer even loses track of some of the objectives. Instead of designing and coding program features to satisfy the remaining objectives, the programmer intentionally (or subconsciously) changes the objectives to match what the program actually does. This is seldom if ever a suitable approach to programming. By establishing a test suite before beginning to tackle the challenges of design and implementation, the programmer fortifies himself/herself against the temptation to shortchange or to inadvertently omit some of the objectives from the solution.

Let's apply these concepts to determine a test suite for the binary search algorithm. We do so by identifying all the kinds of lists to which the user might apply the binary search algorithm. The list will be either empty or not. Hence, one member of our test suite is the empty list. If the list is not empty, it might consist of a single element (a boundary case), or it could have as many as MAXINT elements (another boundary case). Further, it might consist of an even number of elements greater than zero or an odd number of elements greater than 1. In each of these cases, the element for which we are searching may or may not be present. If the element is present, it may be the first element in the list, the last element in the list, or it may be neither the first nor the last element in the list. If the element is not present, it may be smaller than the first item in the list, larger than the last element in the list, or, except in the case of a list of only one element, it may be larger than the first element in the list and smaller than the last element in the list. Thus, we have identified nine different kinds of lists on which we should test our binary search algorithm and the method implementing our binary search algorithm, six of which have three subcases each and one of which has two subcases, for a total of 22 different lists on which we should test our binary search algorithm and the method that implements it. They are:

- an empty list
- a list of one element that is the element for which we are searching
- a list of one element that is not the element for which we are searching, and the element for which we are searching is smaller or larger than the element
- a list with MAXINT elements that contains the element for which we are searching in the first position, the last position, or in an intermediate position
- a list with MAXINT elements that does not contain the element for which we are searching, and the element for which we are searching is smaller than the smallest element, larger than the largest element, or neither smaller than the smallest element nor larger than the largest element
- a list with an even number of elements (other than 0) that contains the element for which we are searching in the first position, the last position, or in an intermediate position
- a list with an even number of elements (other than 0) that does not contain the element for which we are searching, and the element for which we are searching is smaller than the smallest element, larger than the largest element, or neither smaller than the smallest element nor larger than the largest element
- a list with an odd number of elements (other than 1 or MAXINT) that contains the element for which we are searching in the first position, the last position, or in an intermediate position
- a list with an odd number of elements (other than 1 or MAXINT) that does not contain the element for which we are searching, and the element for which we are searching is smaller than the smallest element, larger than the largest element, or neither smaller than the smallest element nor larger than the largest element

For the most part, test suites are beyond the scope of this text, and are not discussed further. However, to the extent that you include them as part of the software development process, you will increase your confidence in the quality of the software you develop.

1
4

PROGRAMMING EXAMPLE: Election Results

The election for president of the student council of your local university is about to be held. To ensure confidentiality, the election committee chair wants to computerize the voting. The chair is looking for someone to write a program to process the data and report the winner. Let's write a program to help the chair of the election committee.

The university has four major colleges, and each college has several departments. For election purposes, the four colleges are labeled Region 1, Region 2, Region 3, and Region 4. Each department in each college holds its own voting and directly reports the votes received by each candidate to the election committee. The voting is reported in the form:

```
candidate_name region# number_of_votes_for_this_candidate
```

The election committee wants the output in the following tabular form:

```
--------------Election Results--------------

Candidate                 Votes
Name        Region1 Region2 Region3 Region4  Total
----        ------- ------- ------- -------  -----
Ashley          23      89       0     160    272
Danny           25      71      89      97    282
Donald         110     158       0       0    268
 .
 .
 .


Winner: ???,  Votes Received: ???
Total votes polled: ???
```

The names of the candidates in the output must be in alphabetical order.

For this program, we assume that six candidates are running for student council president. This program can be enhanced to any number of candidates. Also, we assume that no two candidates receive the same number of votes, that is, there is no tie. We will leave it as an exercise for you to modify the program so that if more than one candidate receives the maximum number of votes, then the program outputs the names of all such candidates.

The data is provided in two files. One file, candData.txt, consists of the names of the candidates. The names of the candidates in the file are in no particular order. In the second file, voteData.txt, each line consists of the voting results in the following form:

```
candidateName regionNumber numberOfVotesForTheCandidate
```

That is, each line in the file **voteData.txt** consists of the candidate's name, region number, and the votes received by the candidate in this region. There is one entry per line. For example, the input file containing the voting data looks like:

```
Mia 2 34
Mickey 1 56
Donald 2 56
Mia 1 78
Danny 4 29
Ashley 4 78
    .
    .
    .
```

The first line indicates that **Mia** received **34** votes from region **2**.

Input: Two files, one containing the candidates' names and the other containing the voting data, as described previously.

Output: The election results in a tabular form, as described previously, and the winner.

PROBLEM ANALYSIS AND ALGORITHM DESIGN

Looking at the output, it is clear that the program must organize the voting data by regions. The program must also calculate the total votes received by each candidate and the total votes polled for the election. Furthermore, the names of the candidates must appear in alphabetical order.

Because the data type of a candidate's name (which is a string) and the data type of the number of votes (which is an integer) are different, we need separate arrays—one to hold the candidates' names and the other to hold the voting data. The array to hold the names of the candidates is a one-dimensional array, and each element of this array is a string. Instead of using one two-dimensional array to hold the voting data, we will use a two-dimensional array to hold the next four columns of the output, that is, the regional voting data, and we will use a one-dimensional array to hold the total votes received by each candidate. These three arrays are parallel arrays (see Figure 14-23).

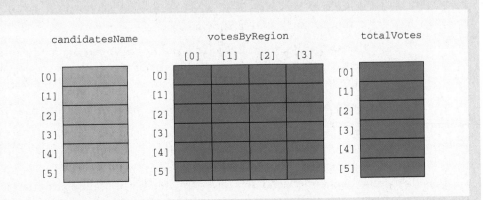

FIGURE 14-23 Parallel arrays `candidatesName`, `votesByRegion`, and `totalVotes`

The data in the first row of these three arrays correspond to the candidate whose name is stored in the first row of the array `candidatesName`, and so on. In the voting-by-region array, column 1 corresponds to Region 1, column 2 corresponds to Region 2, and so on. Recall that, in Java, an array index starts at 0. Therefore, if the name of this array in the program is, say, `votesByRegion`, `votesByRegion[][0]` refers to the first column and thus Region 1, and so on.

For easy reference, for the remainder of this discussion, assume that in the program we are writing, the name of the candidates' name array is `candidatesName`, the name of the voting-by-region array is `votesByRegion`, and the name of the array containing the total votes is `totalVotes`.

The first thing we must do in this program is read the candidates' names from the input file `candData.txt` into the array `candidatesName`. Once the candidates' names are stored in the array `candidatesName`, we must sort this array.

Next, we process the voting data. Every entry in the file `voteData.txt` contains `candidatesName`, `regionNumber`, and `numberOfVotesForTheCandidate`. To process this entry, we find the appropriate entry in the array `votesByRegion` and update this entry by adding `numberOfVotesForTheCandidate` to this entry. Therefore, it follows that the array `votesByRegion` must be initialized to zero. Processing the voting data is described in detail later in this section.

After processing the voting data, the next step is to calculate the total votes received by each candidate. This is accomplished by adding the votes received in each region. Therefore, we must initialize the array `totalVotes` to zero. Finally, we output the results as shown earlier.

This discussion translates into the following algorithm:

1. Read the candidates' names into the array `candidatesName`.
2. Sort the array `candidatesName`.
3. Process the voting data.
4. Calculate the total votes received by each candidate.
5. Output the results as shown earlier.

Note that the arrays `votesByRegion` and `totalVotes` are automatically initialized when they are created. Because the input data is provided in two separate files, in this program, we must open two input files. We open both input files in the method `main`.

To implement the preceding five steps, the program consists of several methods, which are described next.

Method getCandidatesName This method reads the data from the input file `candData.txt` and fills the array `candidatesName`. The input file is opened in the method `main`. Note that this method has two parameters: a parameter corresponding to the input file and a parameter corresponding to the array candidatesName. Essentially, this method is:

```
public static void getCandidatesName(Scanner inp,
                                     String[] cNames)
{
    int i;

    for (i = 0; i < cNames.length; i++)
        cNames[i] = inp.next();
}
```

After a call to this method, the arrays to hold the data are as shown in Figure 14-24.

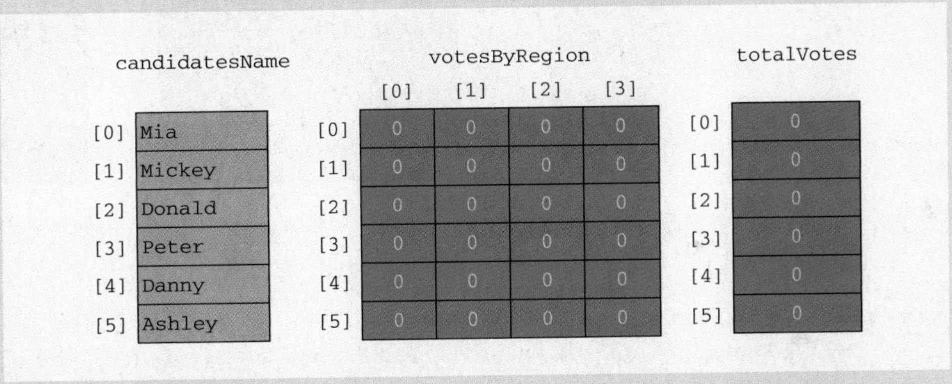

FIGURE 14-24 Arrays candidatesName, votesByRegion, and totalVotes after reading candidates' names

Method
Candidates
Name

This method uses a selection sort algorithm to sort the array candidatesName. This method has only one parameter: the parameter corresponding to the array candidatesName. Essentially, this method is:

```
public static void sortCandidatesName(String[] cNames)
{
    int i, j;
    int min;
    String temp;

        //selection sort
    for (i = 0; i < cNames.length - 1; i++)
    {
        min = i;

        for (j = i + 1; j < cNames.length; j++)
            if (cNames[j].compareTo(cNames[min]) <  0)
                min = j;
```

14

```
            temp = cNames[i];
            cNames[i] = cNames[min];
            cNames[min] = temp;
        }
    }
```

After a call to this method, the arrays are as shown in Figure 14-25.

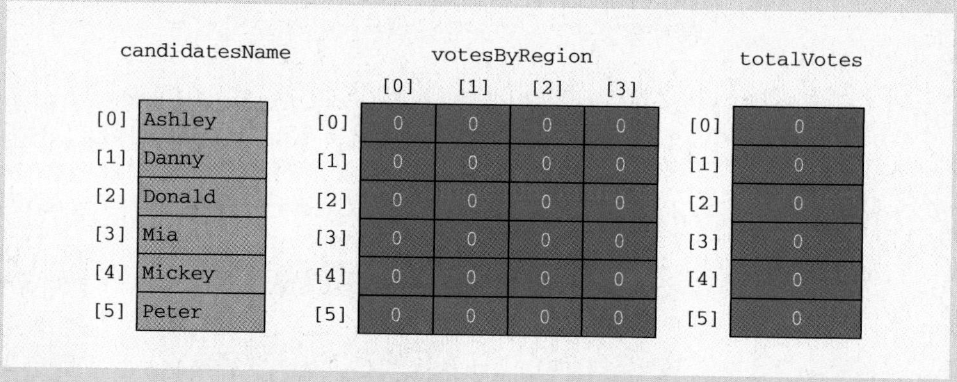

FIGURE 14-25 Arrays `candidatesName`, `votesByRegion`, and `totalVotes` after sorting names

Process Voting Data Processing the voting data is quite straightforward. Each entry in the file **voteData.txt** is in the following form:

candidatesName regionNumber numberOfVotesForTheCandidate

The general algorithm to process the voting data follows.

For each entry in the file **voteData.txt**:

1. Get the candidatesName, regionNumber, and numberOfVotesForTheCandidate.
2. Find the row number in the array **candidatesName** corresponding to this candidate. This will give the corresponding row number in the array **votesByRegion** for this candidate.
3. Find the column number in the array **votesByRegion** corresponding to this **regionNumber**.
4. Update the appropriate entry in the array **votesByRegion** by adding **numberOfVotesForTheCandidate**.

Step 2 requires us to search the array **candidatesName** to find the location, that is, row number, of a particular candidate. Because the array **candidatesName** is sorted, we can use the binary search algorithm to find the row number corresponding to a particular candidate. Therefore, the program also includes the method **binSearch** to implement the binary search algorithm on the array `candidatesName`. We will write the definition of the method `binSearch` shortly. First we discuss how to update the array `votesByRegion`.

Suppose that the three arrays are as shown in Figure 14-26.

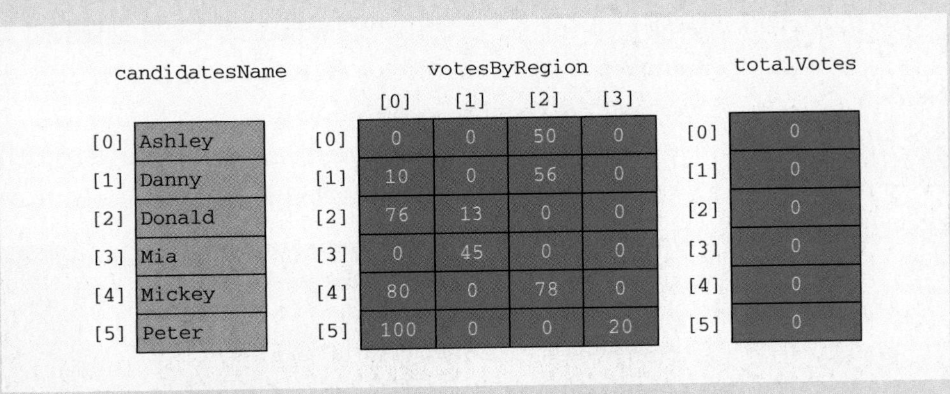

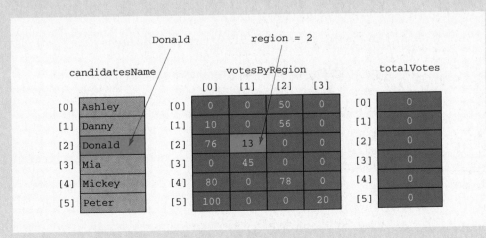

FIGURE 14-26 Arrays `candidatesName`, `votesByRegion`, and `totalVotes`

Further suppose that the next entry read from the input file is:

`Donald 2 35`

Next, we locate the row in the preceding grid that corresponds to this candidate. To find the row, we search the array `candidatesName` to find the row that corresponds to this name. Now `Donald` corresponds to row number 2 in the array `candidatesName`, as shown in Figure 14-27.

FIGURE 14-27 Position of `Donald` and `region = 2`

1
4

To process this entry, we access row number 2 of the array **votesByRegion**. Because Donald received 35 votes from Region 2, we access row number 2 and column number 1, that is, **votesByRegion[2][1]**, and update this entry by adding 35 to its previous value. The following statement accomplishes this:

```
votesByRegion[2][1] = votesByRegion[2][1] + 35;
```

After processing this entry, the three arrays are as shown in Figure 14-28.

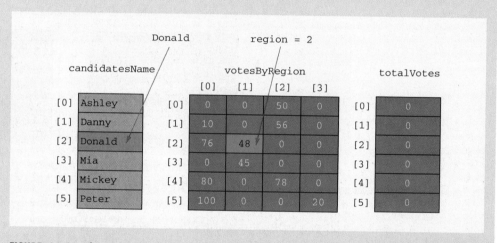

FIGURE 14-28 Arrays `candidatesName`, `votesByRegion`, and `totalVotes` after processing the entry `Donald 2 35`

We now describe the method **binSearch** and the method **processVotes** to process the voting data.

Method binSearch This method implements the binary search algorithm on the array **candidatesName**. It is similar to the method **binarySearch**. Its definition is:

```
public static int binSearch(String[] cNames, String name)
{
    int first, last;
    int mid = 0;

    boolean found;

    first = 0;
    last = cNames.length - 1;
    found = false;

    while (first <= last && !found)
    {
        mid = (first + last) / 2;
```

```
                    if (cNames[mid].equals(name))
                        found = true;
                    else if (cNames[mid].compareTo(name) > 0)
                        last = mid - 1;
                    else
                        first = mid + 1;
            }

            if (found)
                return mid;
            else
                return -1;
    }
```

Method processVotes This method processes the voting data. Clearly, this method must have access to the arrays `candidatesName` and `votesByRegion`, and to the input file `voteData.txt`. Thus, this method has three parameters: a parameter to access the input file `voteData.txt`, a parameter corresponding to the array `candidatesName`, and a parameter corresponding to the array `votesByRegion`. The definition of this method is:

```
public static void processVotes(Scanner inp,
                                String[] cNames,
                                int[][] vbRegion)
{
    String candName;
    int region;
    int noOfVotes;
    int loc;

    while (inp.hasNext())
    {
        candName = inp.next();
        region = inp.nextInt();
        noOfVotes = inp.nextInt();

        loc = binSearch(cNames, candName);

        if (loc != -1)
            vbRegion[loc][region - 1] =
                vbRegion[loc][region - 1] + noOfVotes;
    }
}
```

Calculate Total Votes (Method calculateRegionsVote) After processing the voting data, the next step is to calculate the total votes for each candidate. Suppose that after processing the voting data, the arrays are as shown in Figure 14-29.

1
4

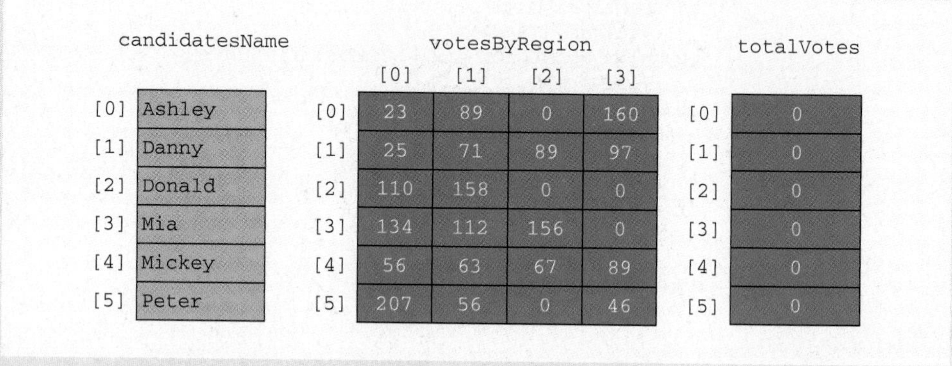

	candidatesName		votesByRegion					totalVotes
			[0]	[1]	[2]	[3]		
[0]	Ashley	[0]	23	89	0	160	[0]	0
[1]	Danny	[1]	25	71	89	97	[1]	0
[2]	Donald	[2]	110	158	0	0	[2]	0
[3]	Mia	[3]	134	112	156	0	[3]	0
[4]	Mickey	[4]	56	63	67	89	[4]	0
[5]	Peter	[5]	207	56	0	46	[5]	0

FIGURE 14-29 Arrays candidatesName, votesByRegion, and totalVotes after processing the voting data

After calculating the total votes received by each candidate, the three arrays are as shown in Figure 14-30.

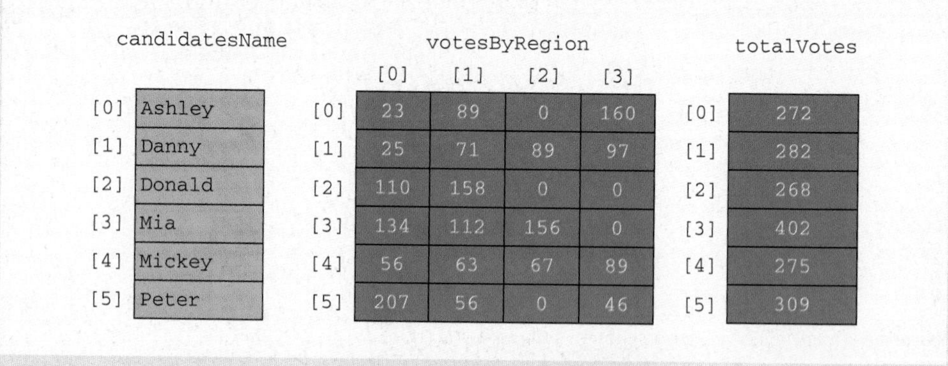

	candidatesName		votesByRegion					totalVotes
			[0]	[1]	[2]	[3]		
[0]	Ashley	[0]	23	89	0	160	[0]	272
[1]	Danny	[1]	25	71	89	97	[1]	282
[2]	Donald	[2]	110	158	0	0	[2]	268
[3]	Mia	[3]	134	112	156	0	[3]	402
[4]	Mickey	[4]	56	63	67	89	[4]	275
[5]	Peter	[5]	207	56	0	46	[5]	309

FIGURE 14-30 Arrays candidatesName, votesByRegion, and totalVotes after calculating the total votes received by each candidate

To calculate the total votes received by each candidate, we add the contents of each row in the **votesByRegion** array and store the sum in the corresponding row in the **totalVotes** array. This is accomplished by the method **addRegionsVote**, which is described next.

The method **addRegionsVote** calculates the total votes received by each candidate. This method must access the arrays **votesByRegion** and **totalVotes**. This method has two parameters: a parameter corresponding to the array **votesByRegion** and a parameter corresponding to the array **totalVotes**. The definition of this method is:

```
public static void addRegionsVote(int[][] vbRegion, int[] tVotes)
{
    for (int i = 0; i < tVotes.length; i++)
        for (int j = 0; j < vbRegion[0].length; j++)
            tVotes[i] = tVotes[i] + vbRegion[i][j];
}
```

The remaining methods to get the desired output are described next.

Method ntHeading

The method `printHeading` outputs the first four lines of the output, so it contains certain output statements. The definition of this method is:

```
public static void printHeading()
{
    System.out.println("   ---------------Election Results"
        + "--------------\n");
    System.out.println("Candidate                "
        + "         Votes");
    System.out.println("Name        Region1 Region2 "
        + "Region3 Region4   Total");
    System.out.println("----                 ------- ------- "
        + "------- -------   -----");
}
```

Method ntResults

The method `printResults` outputs the remaining lines of the output. Clearly, this method must have access to each of the three arrays. (Note that each array has the same number of rows.) Thus, this method has three parameters. Suppose that the parameter `cName` corresponds to `candidatesName`, the parameter `vbRegion` corresponds to `votesByRegion`, and the parameter `tVotes` corresponds to `totalVotes`.

Further suppose that the variable `sumVotes` holds the total votes polled for the election, the variable `largestVotes` holds the largest number of votes received by a candidate, and the variable `winLoc` holds the index of the winning candidate in the array `candidatesName`. The algorithm for this method is:

1. Initialize `sumVotes`, `largestVotes`, and `winLoc` to 0.
2. For each row in each array:
   a. `if(largestVotes < tVotes[i])`
      ```
      {
          largestVotes = tVotes[i];
          winLoc = i;
      }
      ```
   b. `sumVotes = sumVotes + tVotes[i];`
   c. Output the data from the corresponding rows of each array.
3. Output the final lines of the output.

1
4

The definition of this method is:

```java
public static void printResults(String[] cNames,
                                int[][] vbRegion, int[] tVotes)
{
    int largestVotes = 0;
    int winLoc = 0;
    int sumVotes = 0;

    for (int i = 0; i < tVotes.length; i++)
    {
        if (largestVotes < tVotes[i])
        {
            largestVotes = tVotes[i];
            winLoc = i;
        }

        sumVotes = sumVotes + tVotes[i];

        System.out.printf("%-11s ", cNames[i]);

        for (int j = 0; j < vbRegion[0].length; j++)
            System.out.printf("%6d  ", vbRegion[i][j]);

        System.out.printf("%5d%n", tVotes[i]);
    }

    System.out.println("\n\nWinner: " + cNames[winLoc]
                    + ",   Votes Received: "
                    + tVotes[winLoc]);
    System.out.println("Total votes polled: " + sumVotes);
}
```

Main Algorithm:
method `main`

Suppose that the variables in the method `main` are:

```java
String[] candidatesName = new String[NO_OF_CANDIDATES]; //array
                                    //to store candidates' names

int[][] votesByRegion =
            new int[NO_OF_CANDIDATES][NO_OF_REGIONS]; //array
                                //to hold voting data by region

int[] totalVotes = new int[NO_OF_CANDIDATES]; //array to hold
                                    //total votes received by
                                    //each candidate

Scanner inFile; //input file variable
```

Further suppose that the candidates' names are in the file candData.txt, and the voting data is in the file voteData.txt.

The algorithm for the method main is:

1. Declare and initialize the variables and the objects.

2. Open the input file candData.txt.

3. Read the data from the file candData.txt into the array candidatesName.

4. Sort the array candidatesName.

5. Open the input file voteData.txt.

6. Process the voting data and store the results in the array votesByRegion.

7. Calculate the total votes received by each candidate and store the results in the array totalVotes.

8. Print the heading.

9. Print the results.

PROGRAM LISTING

```
//****************************************************************
// Author: D.S. Malik
//
// Program: Election Results
// Given candidates' voting data, this program determines the
// winner of the election. The program outputs the votes
// received by each candidate and the winner.
//****************************************************************

import java.io.*;
import java.util.*;

public class ElectionResults
{
    final static int NO_OF_CANDIDATES = 6;
    final static int NO_OF_REGIONS = 4;

    public static void main (String[] args) throws
                                    FileNotFoundException
    {
            //Step 1
        String[] candidatesName = new String[NO_OF_CANDIDATES];

        int[][] votesByRegion =
                new int[NO_OF_CANDIDATES][NO_OF_REGIONS];

        int[] totalVotes = new int[NO_OF_CANDIDATES];

        Scanner inFile = new Scanner(new
                FileReader("candData.txt"));      //Step 2
```

1
4

```
        getCandidatesName(inFile, candidatesName);        //Step 3
        sortCandidatesName(candidatesName);               //Step 4

        inFile = null;
        inFile = new Scanner(new
                    FileReader("voteData.txt"));          //Step 5

        processVotes(inFile, candidatesName,
                    votesByRegion);                       //Step 6
        addRegionsVote(votesByRegion, totalVotes);        //Step 7

        printHeading();                                   //Step 8
        printResults(candidatesName, votesByRegion,
                    totalVotes);                          //Step 9
    }

    //Place the definitions of the methods getCandidatesName,
    //sortCandidatesName, binSearch, processVotes,
    //addRegionsVote, printHeading, and printResults,
    //as described in this section, here.

}
```

Sample Run: (After placing the definitions of all the methods as described and then executing the program, the output is as follows.)

```
---------------Election Results---------------

Candidate                      Votes
Name      Region1 Region2 Region3 Region4  Total
----      ------- ------- ------- -------  -----
Ashley        23      89       0     160    272
Danny         25      71      89      97    282
Donald       110     158       0       0    268
Mia          134     112     156       0    402
Mickey        56      63      67      89    275
Peter        207      56       0      46    309

Winner: Mia,  Votes Received: 402
Total votes polled: 1808
```

Input Files: The files candData.txt and voteData.txt are provided on the Web site, *www.course.com*, and the CD accompanying this book. Also, the Web site and the CD accompanying this book give the complete program listing of this program.

NOTE   The Web site and the CD accompanying this book contain the OOD version of this program. The name of the file containing the Programming Example is Chapter 14_ElectionResults_ OOD_Version.pdf.

QUICK REVIEW

1. A list is a set of elements of the same type.

2. The length of a list is the number of elements in the list.

3. A one-dimensional array is a convenient data structure for storing and processing lists.

4. A sequential search algorithm searches the list for a given item, starting with the first element in the list. It continues comparing this item with the elements in the list until either the item is found, or the list has no more elements left to compare with the search item.

5. On average, a sequential search searches half the list.

6. In a selection sort, a list is sorted by selecting elements in the list, one at a time, and moving them to their proper positions. This algorithm finds the location of the smallest element in the unsorted portion of the list and moves it to the top of the unsorted portion (i.e., the whole list) of the list.

7. For a list of length n, on average, a selection sort makes $\frac{n(n-1)}{2}$ key comparisons and $3(n-1)$ item assignments.

8. The insertion sort algorithm sorts the list by inserting each element in its proper place.

9. For a list of length n, on average, an insertion sort makes $\frac{n^2+3n-4}{4}$ key comparisons and about $\frac{n(n-1)}{4}$ item assignments.

10. In general, a binary search is much faster than a sequential search.

11. A binary search requires that the list elements be in order, that is, sorted.

EXERCISES

1. Mark the following statements as true or false.

   a. A sequential search of a list assumes that the list is in ascending order.

   b. A binary search of a list assumes that the list is in sorted order.

   c. A binary search is faster on ordered lists and slower on unordered lists.

2. Consider the following list: 63 45 32 98 46 57 28 100

   Using the sequential search (given in Chapter 9), how many comparisons are required to determine whether the following items are in the list? (Recall that comparisons mean item comparisons, not index comparisons.)

   a. 90   b. 57   c. 63   d. 120

3. Consider the following list: 5 12 17 35 46 65 78 85 93 110 115

   Using the binary search (given in this chapter), how many comparisons are required to determine whether the following items are in the list? (Recall that comparisons mean item comparisons, not index comparisons.)

   a. 35   b. 60   c. 78   d. 120

1
4

4. Consider the following list:

   2 10 17 45 49 55 68 85 92 98 110

   Using the binary search (given in this chapter), how many comparisons are required to determine whether the following items are in the list? Show the values of `first`, `last`, and `middle`, and the number of comparisons after each iteration of the loop.

   a. 15   b. 49   c. 98   d. 99

5. Sort the following list using the selection sort algorithm as discussed in this chapter. Show the list after each iteration of the outer `for` loop.

   26, 45, 17, 65, 33, 55, 12, 18

6. Sort the following list using the selection sort algorithm as discussed in this chapter. Show the list after each iteration of the outer `for` loop.

   36, 55, 17, 35, 63, 85, 12, 48, 3, 66

7. Assume the following list: 5, 18, 21, 10, 55, 20

   The first three keys are in order. To move 10 to its proper position, using the insertion sort as described in this chapter, exactly how many key comparisons are executed?

8. Assume the following list: 7, 28, 31, 40, 5, 20

   The first four keys are in order. To move 5 to its proper position, using the insertion sort as described in this chapter, exactly how many key comparisons are executed?

9. Assume the following list:

   28, 18, 21, 10, 25, 30, 12, 71, 32, 58, 15

   This list is to be sorted using the insertion sort algorithm as described in this chapter. Show the resulting list after six passes of the sorting phase—that is, after six iterations of the `for` loop.

10. Recall the insertion sort algorithm as discussed in this chapter. Assume the following list of keys:

    18, 8, 11, 9, 15, 20, 32, 61, 22, 48, 75, 83, 35, 3

    Exactly how many key comparisons are executed to sort this list using the insertion sort?

PROGRAMMING EXERCISES

1. Write a program to test the method `binarySearch`. Use either the method `insertionSort` or `selectionSort` to sort the list before the search.

2. Write a method, `remove`, that takes three parameters: an array of integers, the length of the array, and an integer, say, `removeItem`. The method

should find and delete the first occurrence of `removeItem` in the array. If the value does not exist or the array is empty, output an appropriate message. (Note that after deleting the element, the array size is reduced by 1.) You may assume that the array is unsorted.

3. Write a method, `removeAt`, that takes three parameters: an array of integers, the length of the array, and an integer, say, `index`. The method deletes the array element indicated by `index`. If `index` is out of range or the array is empty, output an appropriate message. (Note that after deleting the element, the array size is reduced by 1.) You may assume that the array is unsorted.

4. Write a method, `removeAll`, that takes three parameters: an array of integers, the length of the array, and an integer, say, `removeItem`. The method should find and delete all occurrences of `removeItem` from the array. If the value does not exist or the array is empty, output an appropriate message. (Note that after deleting the element, the array size will be reduced.) You may assume that the array is unsorted.

5. Redo Programming Exercises 2, 3, and 4 for a sorted array.

6. Write a method, `insertAt`, that takes four parameters: an array of integers; the length of the array; an integer, say, `insertItem`; and an integer, say, `index`. The method inserts `insertItem` in the array at the position specified by `index`. If `index` is out of range, output an appropriate message. (Note that `index` must be between 0 and `arraySize`, that is, $0 \leq index < arraySize$.) You may assume that the array is unsorted.

7. Write a version of a sequential search that can be used to search a string `Vector` object. Also, write a program to test your algorithm.

8. Write a version of a selection sort that can be used to sort a string `Vector` object. Also, write a program to test your algorithm.

9. Write a program to test the insertion sort algorithm as given in this chapter.

10. Write a version of the insertion sort algorithm that can be used to sort a string `Vector` object. Also, write a program to test your algorithm.

11. Write a version of a binary search that can be used to search a string `Vector` object. Also, write a program to test your algorithm. (Use the selection sort algorithm you developed in Programming Exercise 8 to sort the Vector.)

12. Redo the Programming Example Election Results so that the names of the candidates and the total votes are stored in `Vector` objects.

13. Write a program to keep track of a hardware store's inventory. The store sells various items. For each item in the store, the following information is kept: item ID, item name, number of pieces ordered, number of pieces currently in the store, number of pieces sold, manufacturer's price of the item, and the store's selling price. At the end of each week, the store manager would like to see a report in the following form:

1
4

```
                        Friendly Hardware Store

itemID itemName        pOrdered  pInStore pSold manufPrice sellingPrice
4444    Circular Saw        150       150    40      45.00       125.00
3333    Cooking Range        50        50    20     450.00       850.00
 .
 .
 .


Total Inventory: $#########.##
Total number of items in the store:  _____
```

The total inventory is the total selling value of all the items currently in the store. The total number of items is the sum of the number of pieces of all the items in the store.

Your program must be menu driven, giving the user various choices, such as: check whether an item is in the store, sell an item, and print the report. After inputting the data, sort it according to the items' names. Also, after an item is sold, update the appropriate counts.

Initially, the number of pieces (of an item) in the store is the same as the number of pieces ordered, and the number of pieces of an item sold is zero. Input to the program is a file consisting of data in the following form:

```
itemID
itemName
pOrdered manufPrice sellingPrice
```

Use seven parallel vectors to store the information. The program must contain at least the following methods—a method to input the data into the vectors, a method to display the menu, a method to sell an item, and a method to print the report for the manager. After inputting the data, sort it according to the items' names.

JAVA RESERVED WORDS

The following table lists Java reserved words in alphabetical order.

abstract	else	interface	switch
assert	enum	long	synchronized
boolean	extends	native	this
break	false	new	throw
byte	final	null	throws
case	finally	package	transient
catch	float	private	true
char	for	protected	try
class	goto	public	void
const	if	return	volatile
continue	implements	short	while
default	import	static	
do	instanceof	strictfp	
double	int	super	

The reserved words const and goto are *not* currently in use.

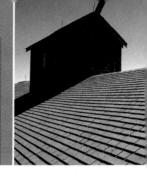

APPENDIX B
OPERATOR PRECEDENCE

The following table shows the precedence of operators in Java from highest to lowest, and their associativity.

Operator	Description	Precedence Level	Associativity
.	Object member access	1	Left to right
[ ]	Array subscripting	1	Left to right
(parameters)	Method call	1	Left to right
++	Postincrement	1	Left to right
--	Postdecrement	1	Left to right
++	Preincrement	2	Right to left
--	Predecrement	2	Right to left
+	Unary plus	2	Right to left
-	Unary minus	2	Right to left
!	Logical not	2	Right to left
~	Bitwise not	2	Right to left
new	Object instantiation	3	Right to left
(type)	Type conversion	3	Right to left
*	Multiplication	4	Left to right
/	Division	4	Left to right
%	Remainder (modulus)	4	Left to right
+	Addition	5	Left to right
-	Subtraction	5	Left to right
+	String concatenation	5	Left to right

Operator	Description	Precedence Level	Associativity
<<	Left shift	6	Left to right
>>	Right shift with sign extension	6	Left to right
>>>	Right shift with zero extension	6	Left to right
<	Less than	7	Left to right
<=	Less than or equal to	7	Left to right
>	Greater than	7	Left to right
>=	Greater than or equal to	7	Left to right
instanceof	Type comparison	7	Left to right
==	Equal to	8	Left to right
!=	Not equal to	8	Left to right
&	Bitwise AND	9	Left to right
&	Logical AND	9	Left to right
^	Bitwise XOR	10	Left to right
^	Logical XOR	10	Left to right
|	Bitwise OR	11	Left to right
|	Logical OR	11	Left to right
&&	Logical AND	12	Left to right
||	Logical OR	13	Left to right
? :	Conditional operator	14	Right to left

Operator	Description	Precedence Level	Associativity
=	Assignment	15	Right to left
Compound Operators			
+=	Addition, then assignment	15	Right to left
+=	String concatenation, then assignment	15	Right to left
-=	Subtraction, then assignment	15	Right to left
*=	Multiplication, then assignment	15	Right to left
/=	Division, then assignment	15	Right to left
%=	Remainder, then assignment	15	Right to left
<<=	Bitwise left shift, then assignment	15	Right to left
>>=	Bitwise right shift, then assignment	15	Right to left
>>>=	Bitwise unsigned-right shift, then assignment	15	Right to left
&=	Bitwise AND, then assignment	15	Right to left
&=	Logical AND, then assignment	15	Right to left
|=	Bitwise OR, then assignment	15	Right to left
|=	Logical OR, then assignment	15	Right to left
^=	Bitwise XOR, then assignment	15	Right to left
^=	Logical XOR, then assignment	15	Right to left

APPENDIX C
CHARACTER SETS

This appendix lists and describes the character sets for ASCII (American Standard Code for Information Interchange), which also comprises the first 128 characters of the Unicode character set, and EBCDIC (Extended Binary Coded Decimal Interchange Code).

ASCII (American Standard Code for Information Interchange), the First 128 Characters of the Unicode Character Set

The following table shows the first 128 characters of the Unicode (ASCII) character set.

ASCII										
	0	1	2	3	4	5	6	7	8	9
0	nul	soh	stx	etx	eot	enq	ack	bel	bs	ht
1	lf	vt	ff	cr	so	si	dle	dc1	dc2	dc3
2	dc4	nak	syn	etb	can	em	sub	esc	fs	gs
3	rs	us	b	!	"	#	$	%	&	'
4	(	)	*	+	,	-	.	/	0	1
5	2	3	4	5	6	7	8	9	:	;
6	<	=	>	?	@	A	B	C	D	E
7	F	G	H	I	J	K	L	M	N	O
8	P	Q	R	S	T	U	V	W	X	Y
9	Z	[	\	]	^	_	`	a	b	c
10	d	e	f	g	h	i	j	k	l	m
11	n	o	p	q	r	s	t	u	v	w
12	x	y	z	{			}	~	del		

> **NOTE** For more information on the Unicode/ASCII character set, visit the Web site at *http://www.unicode.org*.

Note that the character <u>b</u> at position 32 represents the space character. The first 32 characters, that is, the characters at positions 00–31 and at position 127 are nonprintable characters. The following table shows the abbreviations and meanings of these characters.

nul	null character	ff	form feed	can	cancel
soh	start of header	cr	carriage return	em	end of medium
stx	start of text	so	shift out	sub	substitute
etx	end of text	si	shift in	esc	escape
eot	end of transmission	dle	data link escape	fs	file separator
enq	enquiry	dc1	device control 1	gs	group separator
ack	acknowledge	dc2	device control 2	rs	record separator
bel	bell	dc3	device control 3	us	unit separator
bs	backspace	dc4	device control 4	<u>b</u>	space
ht	horizontal tab	nak	negative acknowledge	del	delete
lf	line feed	syn	synchronous idle		
vt	vertical tab	etb	end of transmitted block		

EBCDIC (Extended Binary Coded Decimal Interchange Code)

The following table shows some of the characters in the EBCDIC character set.

EBCDIC									
	0	1	2	3	4	5	6	7	8	9
6					<u>b</u>					
7					.		<	(	+	|
8	&									
9	!	$	*	)	;	¬	-	/		
10								,	%	_
11	>	?								
12		`	:	#	@	'	=	"		a

	0	1	2	3	4	5	6	7	8	9
						EBCDIC				
13	b	c	d	e	f	g	h	i		
14						j	k	l	m	n
15	o	p	q	r						
16		~	s	t	u	v	w	x	y	z
17										
18	[	]								
19			A	B	C	D	E	F	G	
20	H	I								J
21	K	L	M	N	O	P	Q	R		
22							S	T	U	V
23	W	X	Y	Z						
24	0	1	2	3	4	5	6	7	8	9

The numbers 6–24 in the first column specify the left digit(s) and the numbers 0–9 in the second row specify the right digits of the characters in the EBCDIC data set. For example, the character in the row marked 19 (the number in the first column) and the column marked 3 (the number in the second row) is A. Therefore, the character at position 193 (which is the 194th character) is A. Moreover, the character b̲ at position 64 represents the space character. This table does not show all the characters in the EBCDIC character set. In fact, the characters at positions 00–63 and 250–255 are nonprintable control characters.

Appendix D
Additional Java Topics

Binary (Base 2) Representation of a Nonnegative Integer

Converting a Base 10 Number to a Binary Number (Base 2)

Chapter 1 noted that A is the 66th character in the ASCII character set, but its position is 65 because the position of the first character is 0. Furthermore, the binary number 1000001 is the binary representation of 65. The number system that we use daily is called the **decimal number system** or **base 10 system**. The number system that the computer uses is called the **binary number system** or **base 2 system**. In this section, we describe how to find the binary representation of a nonnegative integer and vice versa.

Consider 65. Note that:

$$65 = 1 \times 2^6 + 0 \times 2^5 + 0 \times 2^4 + 0 \times 2^3 + 0 \times 2^2 + 0 \times 2^1 + 1 \times 2^0.$$

Similarly:

$$711 = 1 \times 2^9 + 0 \times 2^8 + 1 \times 2^7 + 1 \times 2^6 + 0 \times 2^5 + 0 \times 2^4 + 0 \times 2^3$$
$$+ 1 \times 2^2 + 1 \times 2^1 + 1 \times 2^0.$$

In general, if m is a nonnegative integer, then m can be written as:

$$m = a_k \times 2^k + a_{k-1} \times 2^{k-1} + a_{k-2} \times 2^{k-2} + \cdots + a_1 \times 2^1 + a_0 \times 2^0,$$

for some nonnegative integer k, and where $a_i = 0$ or 1, for each $i = 0, 1, 2, \ldots, k$. The binary number $a_k a_{k-1} a_{k-2} \ldots a_1 a_0$ is called the **binary** or **base 2 representation** of m. In this case, we usually write:

$$m_{10} = \left(a_k a_{k-1} a_{k-2} \cdots a_1 a_0 \right)_2$$

and say that m to the base 10 is $a_k a_{k-1} a_{k-2} \ldots a_1 a_0$ to the base 2.

For example, for the integer 65, $k = 6$, $a_6 = 1$, $a_5 = 0$, $a_4 = 0$, $a_3 = 0$, $a_2 = 0$, $a_1 = 0$, $a_0 = 1$. Thus, $a_6 a_5 a_4 a_3 a_2 a_1 a_0 = 1000001$, so the binary representation of 65 is 1000001, that is:

$65_{10} = (1000001)_2.$

If no confusion arises, then we write $(1000001)_2$ as 1000001_2.

Similarly, for the number 711, $k = 9$, $a_9 = 1$, $a_8 = 0$, $a_7 = 1$, $a_6 = 1$, $a_5 = 0$, $a_4 = 0$, $a_3 = 0$, $a_2 = 1$, $a_1 = 1$, $a_0 = 1$. Thus:

$711_{10} = 1011000111_2.$

It follows that to find the binary representation of a nonnegative integer, we need to find the coefficients, which are 0 or 1, of various powers of 2. However, there is an easy algorithm, described next, that can be used to find the binary representation of a nonnegative integer. First, note that:

$0_{10} = 0_2, 1_{10} = 1_2, 2_{10} = 10_2, 3_{10} = 11_2, 4_{10} = 100_2, 5_{10} = 101_2, 6_{10} = 110_2,$ and $7_{10} = 111_2.$

Let us consider the integer 65. Note that $65 / 2 = 32$ and $65 \% 2 = 1$, where % is the mod operator. Next, $32 / 2 = 16$, and $32 \% 2 = 0$, and so on. It can be shown that $a_0 = 65 \% 2 = 1$, $a_1 = 32 \% 2 = 0$, and so on. We can show this continuous division and obtain the remainder with the help of Figure D-1.

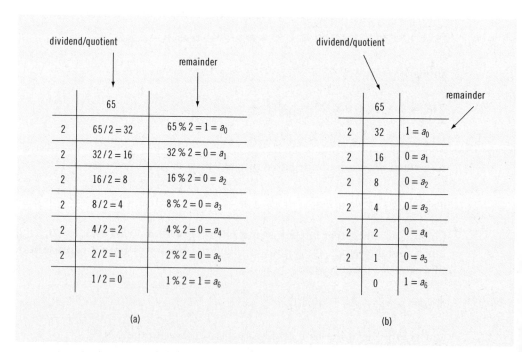

FIGURE D-1 Determining the binary representation of 65

Notice that in Figure D-1(a), starting at the second row, the second column contains the quotient when the number in the previous row is divided by 2, and the third column contains the remainder of that division. For example, in the second row, $65 / 2 = 32$, and $65 \% 2 = 1$. In the third row, $32 / 2 = 16$ and $32 \% 2 = 0$, and so on. For each row, the number in the second column is divided by 2, the quotient is written in the row below the current row, and the remainder appears in the third column. When using a figure such as D-1 to find the binary representation of a nonnegative integer, we typically show only the quotients and remainders, as shown in Figure D-1(b). You can write the binary representation of the number, starting with the last remainder in the third column, followed by the second to the last remainder, and so on. Thus:

$$65_{10} = 1000001_2.$$

Next, consider the number 711. Figure D-2 shows the quotients and the remainders.

FIGURE D-2 Determining the binary representation of 711

From Figure D-2, it follows that:

$$711_{10} = 1011000111_2.$$

Converting a Binary Number (Base 2) to Base 10

To convert a number from base 2 to base 10, we first find the weight of each bit in the binary number, which is assigned from right to left. The weight of the rightmost bit is 0.

The weight of the bit immediately to the left of the rightmost bit is 1, the weight of the bit immediately to the left of it is 2, and so on. Consider the binary number 1001101. The weight of each bit is as follows:

Weight   6   5   4   3   2   1   0

             1   0   0   1   1   0   1

We use the weight of each bit to find the equivalent decimal number. For each bit, we multiply the bit by 2 to the power of its weight and then we add all of the numbers. For the above binary number, the equivalent decimal number is:

$$1 \times 2^6 + 0 \times 2^5 + 0 \times 2^4 + 1 \times 2^3 + 1 \times 2^2 + 0 \times 2^1 + 1 \times 2^0$$

$$= 64 + 0 + 0 + 8 + 4 + 0 + 1$$

$$= 77.$$

Converting a Binary Number (Base 2) to Octal (Base 8) and Hexadecimal (Base 16)

The previous sections described how to convert a binary number to a decimal number (base 2). Even though the language of a computer is binary, if the binary number is too long, then it will be hard to manipulate it manually. To effectively deal with binary numbers, two more number systems, octal (base 8) and hexadecimal (base 16), are of interest to computer scientists.

The digits in the octal number system are 0, 1, 2, 3, 4, 5, 6, and 7. The digits in the hexadecimal number system are 0, 1, 2, 3, 4, 5, 6, 7, 8, 9, A, B, C, D, E, and F. So A in hexadecimal is 10 in decimal, B in hexadecimal is 11 in decimal, and so on.

The algorithm to convert a binary number into an equivalent number in octal (or hexadecimal) is quite simple. Before we describe the method to do so, let us review some notations. Suppose a_b represents the number a to the base b. For example, $2A0_{16}$ means 2A0 to the base 16, and 63_8 means 63 to the base 8.

First, we describe how to convert a binary number into an equivalent octal number and vice versa. Table D-1 describes the first 8 octal numbers.

TABLE D-1 Binary Representation of First 8 Octal Numbers

Binary	Octal		Binary	Octal
000	0		100	4
001	1		101	5
010	2		110	6
011	3		111	7

Consider the binary number 1101100010101. To find the equivalent octal number, starting from right to left, we consider three digits at a time and write their octal representation. Note that the binary number 1101100010101 has only 13 digits. So when we consider three digits at a time, at the end, we will be left with only one digit. In this case, we just add two 0s to the left of the binary number; the equivalent binary number is 001101100010101. Thus:

$$1101100010101_2 \; = \; 001101100010101_2$$

$$= \; 001 \; 101 \; 100 \; 010 \; 101$$

$$= \; 15425_8 \text{ because } 001_2 = 1_8, 101_2 = 5_8, 100_2 = 4_8, 010_2 = 2_8, \text{ and } 101_2 = 5_8.$$

Thus, $1101100010101_2 = 15425_8$.

To convert an octal number into an equivalent binary number, using Table D-1, write the binary representation of each octal digit in the number. For example:

$$3761_8 \; = \; 011 \; 111 \; 110 \; 001_2$$

$$= \; 011111110001_2$$

$$= \; 11111110001_2.$$

Thus, $3761_8 = 11111110001_2$.

Next, we discuss how to convert a binary number into an equivalent hexadecimal number and vice versa. The method to do so is similar to converting a number from binary to octal and vice versa, except that here we work with four binary digits. Table D-2 gives the binary representation of the first 16 hexadecimal numbers.

TABLE D-2 Binary Representation of First 16 Hexadecimal Numbers

Binary	Hexadecimal		Binary	Hexadecimal
0000	0		1000	8
0001	1		1001	9
0010	2		1010	A
0011	3		1011	B
0100	4		1100	C
0101	5		1101	D
0110	6		1110	E
0111	7		1111	F

Consider the binary number 1111101010001010101_2. Now:

$$1111101010001010101_2 \quad = \quad 111\ 1101\ 0100\ 0101\ 0101_2$$

$$= \quad 0111\ 1101\ 0100\ 0101\ 0101_2, \text{ add one zero to the left}$$

$$= \quad 7D455_{16}.$$

Hence, $1111101010001010101_2 = 7D455_{16}$.

Next, to convert a hexadecimal number into an equivalent binary number, write the four-digit binary representation of each hexadecimal digit into that number. For example:

$$A7F32_{16} \quad = \quad 1010\ 0111\ 1111\ 0011\ 0010_2$$

$$= \quad 10100111111100110010_2.$$

Thus, $A7F32_{16} = 10100111111100110010_2$.

Executing Java Programs Using the Command-Line Statements

When you install JDK 6.0 in the Windows XP environment, the system creates two main subdirectories: `Java\jdk1.6.0` and `Java\jre1.6.0`. These two subdirectories are, typically, created within the directory `c:\Program Files`. (Note that the names of these subdirectories depend on the version of Java you install. If you install Java 7.0, then the names of these subdirectories will be different. Check the exact names of these subdirectories on your computer.) The files necessary to compile and execute Java programs are placed within these subdirectories, along with other files. For example, the file `javac.exe` to compile a Java program and the file `java.exe` to execute a Java application program are placed within the subdirectory `Java\jdk1.6.0\bin`. You can set (or alter) the Windows system environment variable `Path` to add the path where the files `javac.exe` and `java.exe` are located. This will allow you to conveniently compile a Java program from within any subdirectory. In the Windows XP environment, you can also set the environment variable `CLASSPATH` so that when you execute a Java program, the system can find the compiled code of the program. Next, we describe how to set up the `Path`. Also, note that J2SE 6.0 or JDK 6.0 or JDK 1.6.0 refers to the same software to create Java programs.

Setting the `Path` in Windows (XP)

To set the `Path` so that you can compile a Java program from within any subdirectory, perform the following steps.

1. Click the `start` button (lower-left corner of the window).

2. Select `Control Panel`.

3. Select `System`. Double-click the `System` icon; a window similar to the window shown in Figure D-3 appears. (When you see the `Control Panel` window, it is

either in Category View or Classic View. If the window is in Classic View, you can see the System icon. If the window is in Category View, first select Performance and Maintenance and then System.)

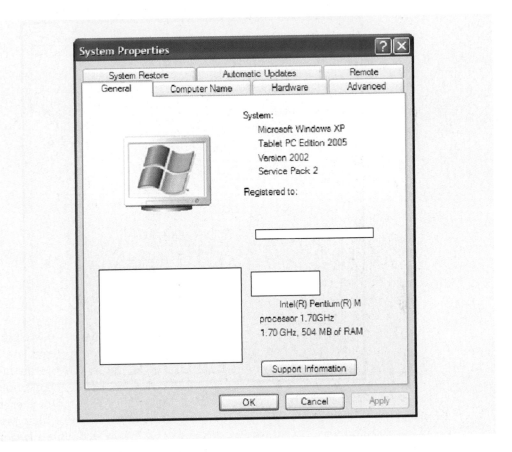

FIGURE D-3 System Properties window

4. In the **System Properties** window (see Figure D-4), select the **Advanced** tab.

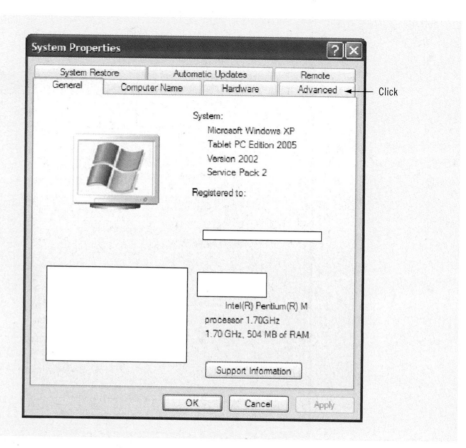

FIGURE D-4 Selecting the Advanced tab

5. After you select the **Advanced** tab, the window in Figure D-5 appears. In this window, click **Environment Variables**.

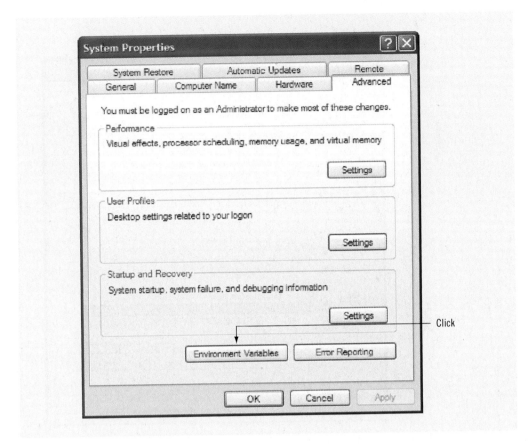

FIGURE D-5 Selecting Environment Variables

6. After selecting `Environment Variables`, a window similar to the one shown in Figure D-6 appears. In the window in the `System variables` section, scroll down, select `Path`, then click `Edit`.

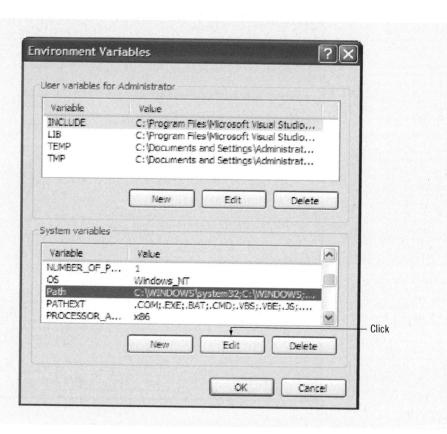

FIGURE D-6 Selecting Path in System variables

7. After you select `Edit`, the window in Figure D-7 appears. In the box following `Variable value:`, type the following at the end of the current Path value and then click `OK` three times.

`;C:\Program Files\Java\jdk1.6.0\bin`

The preceding steps should set the `Path`. To be absolutely certain about the `Path` and also to set the `CLASSPATH`, check your operating system's documentation.

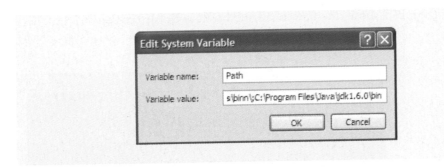

FIGURE D-7 Editing Path

 NOTE The steps for setting the path in Windows Vista are similar. Some of the Figures D-3 to D-7 will be different.

Executing Java Programs

The following discussion assumes that you have set the `Path` so that the files `javac.exe` and `java.exe` can be executed from within any subdirectory.

You can use an editor, such as Notepad, to create Java programs. The name of the class containing the Java program and the name of the file containing the program must be the same. Moreover, the file containing the Java program must have the extension `.java`.

Suppose that the file `Welcome.java` is in the subdirectory `c:\jpfpatpd` and contains the following Java application program:

```
public class Welcome
{
    public static void main(String[] args)
    {
        System.out.println("Welcome to Java Programming.");
    }
}
```

We assume that you have switched to the subdirectory `c:\jpfpatpd` (see Figure D-8).

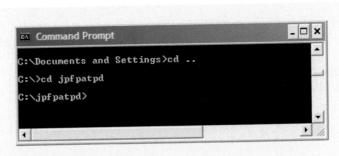

FIGURE D-8 Windows console environment

Figure D-9 shows the files in the subdirectory c:\jpfpatpd.

FIGURE D-9 Files in the subdirectory c:\jpfpatpd

To place the compiled code of the program Welcome.java in the subdirectory c:\jpfpatpd, you can execute the following command, as shown in Figure D-10:

javac Welcome.java

FIGURE D-10 Compile Welcome.java program

The preceding command creates the file Welcome.class, which contains the compiled code of the program Welcome and places it in the subdirectory c:\jpfpatpd (see Figure D-11).

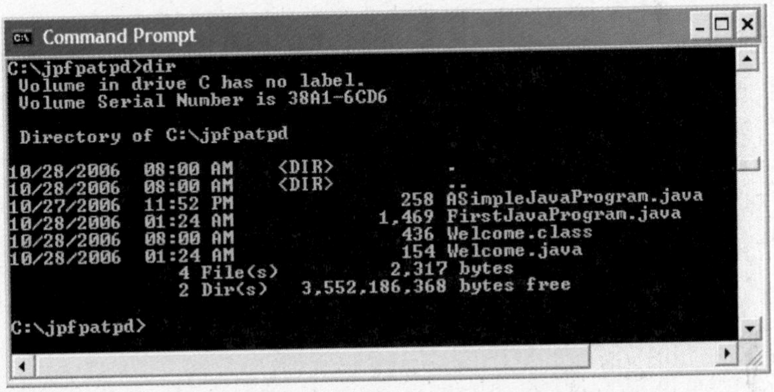

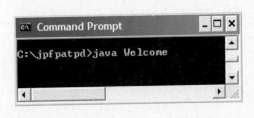

FIGURE D-11 The file `Welcome.class` program

You can now issue the following command to execute the `Welcome` program (see Figure D-12):

`java Welcome`

FIGURE D-12 Executing `Welcome` program

After this statement executes, the following line appears on the screen, as shown in Figure D-13:

`Welcome to Java Programming`

FIGURE D-13 Execution of the `Welcome` program

The preceding command, after compiling the program, places the compiled code in the same subdirectory as the program. However, when you compile a Java program using the command-line compiler, you can instruct the system to store the program's compiled code in any subdirectory you want. To place the compiled code in a specific directory, you include the option -d and the name of the subdirectory where you want the command code placed when you compile the program. For example, the command:

```
javac -d "c:\Program Files\Java\jre1.6.0\lib\classes" Welcome.java
```

places the compiled code of the program Welcome.java in the subdirectory:

```
c:\Program Files\Java\jre1.6.0\lib\classes
```

Note that the subdirectory c:\Program Files\Java\jre1.6.0\lib\classes must exist before you execute the command to compile the program. Also, note the double quotes in the javac command:

```
javac -d "c:\Program Files\Java\jre1.6.0\lib\classes" Welcome.java
```

The quotes are needed because there is a space in the name of the subdirectory Program Files. If the name of any subdirectory in the path does not contain any spaces, then in the javac command, the double quotes, as shown, are not needed.

Similarly, the following command places the compiled code of the program Welcome.java in the subdirectory c:\jpfpatpd:

```
javac -d c:\jpfpatpd Welcome.java
```

To be absolutely certain the directory path is correct, check your system's documentation.

Suppose that you have placed the file Welcome.class within the subdirectory c:\Program Files\Java\jre1.6.0\lib\classes. In addition, suppose that you have not set the CLASSPATH to allow the system to look for the compiled code on specific locations on your computer. In this case, you can use the option -classpath and the name of the subdirectory that contains the compiled code to execute the program. For example, the following command looks for the compiled code of the Welcome program in the subdirectory c:\Program Files\Java\jre1.6.0\lib\classes:

```
java -classpath "c:\Program Files\Java\jre1.6.0\lib\classes" Welcome
```

 NOTE If the compiled code of the classes is in the subdirectory, say, c:\jpfpatpd, you can set the system variable CLASSPATH to c:\jpfpatpd. If the system variable CLASSPATH already exists, you can add the path c:\jpfpatpd to it. To be absolutely certain how to set CLASSPATH in the Windows environment, check your operating system's documentation. Moreover, if you are using other operating systems, such as UNIX, check the documentation to set the variables so that you can conveniently compile and execute a Java program.

The subdirectory `c:\jpfpatpd` also contains the file `ASimpleJavaProgram.java`. Figure D-14 shows the compile command, execute command, and the output of the program.

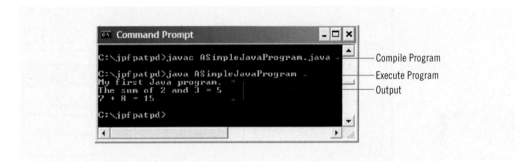

FIGURE D-14 Compiling and executing the program `ASimpleJavaProgram.java`

Note that the program `ASimpleJavaProgram` is the same as that discussed in Chapter 1.

The subdirectory `c:\jpfpatpd` also contains the file `FirstJavaProgram.java`. Figure D-15 shows the compile command, execute command, user input, and program output.

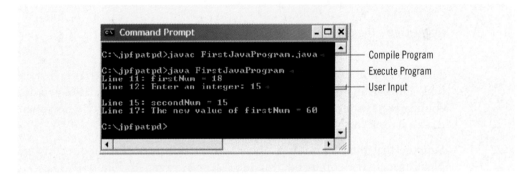

FIGURE D-15 Compiling and executing the program `FirstJavaProgram.java`

Note that the program `FirstJavaProgram` is the same as that discussed in Example 2-26 in Chapter 2.

Java Style Documentation

In this book, whenever we designed a class, among others, we provided an explanation of the methods. We also noted that Java provides a wealth of predefined classes. For example, if you visit the Web site *http://java.sun.com/javase/6/docs/api* or *http://download.java.net/jdk7/docs/api/* you can find a description of the **class** `String` as shown in Figure D-16.

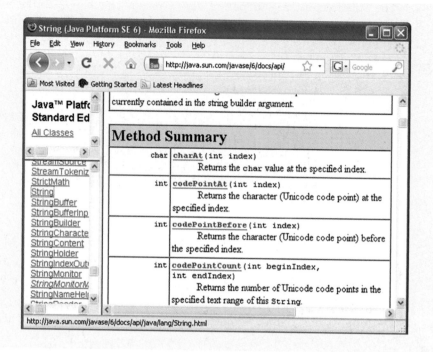

FIGURE D-16 The class String

This description of the **class String** as shown in Figure D-16 is Java style documentation. You can also produce this type of documentation for the classes you design using the command **javadoc**. We illustrate how to produce the Java style documentation of the **class Clock**, designed in Chapter 8.

Suppose that the definition of the **class Clock** is in the subdirectory **c:\jpfpatpd**. Next execute the command: **javadoc Clock.java**, see Figure D-17.

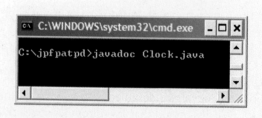

FIGURE D-17 Execute the command javadoc Clock.java

The preceding command creates a number of files as shown in Figure D-18.

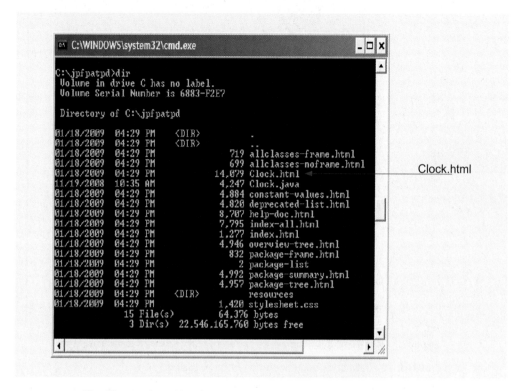

Clock.html

FIGURE D-18 The files produced by the command `javadoc Clock.java`

Next, if you switch to the Windows environment and double-click on the file Clock.html, it shows you the Java style documentation of the **class** Clock shown in Figure D-19.

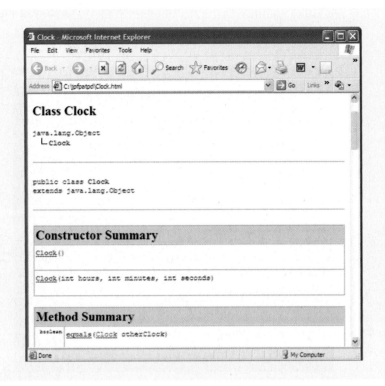

FIGURE D-19 Java style documentation of the **class** Clock

Creating Your Own Packages

Recall that a package is a collection of related classes. As you develop classes, you can create packages and categorize your classes. You can import your classes in the same way that you import classes from the packages provided by Java.

To create a package and add a class to the package so that the class can be used in a program, you do the following:

1. Define the class to be **public**. If the class is not **public**, it can be used only within the package.

2. Choose a name for the package. To organize your package, you can create subdirectories within the directory that contains the compiled code of the classes. For example, you could create a directory for the classes you create in this book. Because the title of this book is *Java Programming: From Problem Analysis to Program Design*, you could create a directory named **jpfpatpd**. You could then make subdirectories for the classes used in each chapter, such as the subdirectory **Appendix** within the directory **jpfpatpd**.

Suppose that you want to create a `package` to group the classes related to time. You could call this `package` `clockPackage`. To add the `class` `Clock` to this package and to place the package `clockPackage` within the subdirectory `Appendix` of the directory `jpfpatpd`, you include the following package statement with the file containing the `class` `Clock`:

```
package jpfpatpd.Appendix.clockPackage;
```

We put this statement before the definition of the `class`, like this:

```
package jpfpatpd.Appendix.clockPackage;

public class Clock
{
    //put instance variables and methods here
}
```

The name of the file containing the `package` statement and the definition of the `class` `Clock` is `Clock.java`. The next step is to compile the file `Clock.java` using the compile command in the IDE (integrated development environment) you are using.

The following discussion assumes that you have set the `Path` so that the files `javac.exe` and `java.exe` can be executed from within any subdirectory. Suppose that the file `Clock.java` is in the subdirectory `c:\jpfpatpd`. We assume that you have switched to the subdirectory `c:\jpfpatpd`.

If you are using Java 6.0, which contains a command-line compiler, you include the option `-d` to place the compiled code of the program `Clock.java` in a specific directory. For example, the command:

```
javac -d "c:\Program Files\Java\jre1.6.0\lib\classes" Clock.java
```

places the compiled code of the program `Clock.java` in the subdirectory:

```
c:\Program Files\Java\jre1.6.0\lib\classes\jpfpatpd\Appendix\
clockPackage
```

Similarly, the following command places the compiled code of the program `Clock.java` in the subdirectory `c:\jpfpatpd\Appendix\clockPackage`:

```
javac -d c:\ Clock.java
```

If the directories `jpfpatpd`, `Appendix`, and `clockPackage` do not exist, then the compiler automatically creates these directories. Note that for the earlier command to execute successfully, the subdirectory `c:\Program Files\Java\jre1.6.0\lib\classes` must exist. If this subdirectory does not exist, you must first create it. Also, to be absolutely sure about the correct directory path, check your system's documentation. Moreover, if you do not use the `-d` option with the path of the subdirectory to specify the subdirectory in which to store the compiled code, then the compiled code is, typically, stored in the current subdirectory.

Once the **package** is created, you can use the appropriate **import** command in your program to make use of the **class**. For example, to use the **class Clock**, as created in the preceding code, you use the following **import** statement in your program:

```
import jpfpatpd.Appendix.clockPackage.Clock;
```

In Java, **package** is a reserved word.

Example D-1 further explains how to use a package in a program. We assume that the **class Clock** has been compiled and placed in the subdirectory c:\jpfpatpd \Appendix\clockPackage.

EXAMPLE D-1

The following program uses the **class Clock**:

```
import jpfpatpd.Appendix.clockPackage.Clock;

public class TestClock
{
    public static void main(String[] args)
    {
        Clock myClock = new Clock(12,30,45);

        System.out.println("myClock: " + myClock);
    }
}
```

Because this program uses the **class Clock**, when you compile the program using the compiler command, you use the option **-classpath** to specify where to find the compiled code of the **class Clock**. Suppose that the file **TestClock.java** is in the subdirectory c:\jpfpatpd. Consider the following command:

```
javac -classpath c:\ TestClock.java
```

This command finds **Clock.class** in the subdirectory c:\jpfpatpd\Appendix \clockPackage. The compiled code **TestClock.class** of the program **TestClock.java** is placed in the current subdirectory. On the other hand, the following command places the compiled code, **TestClock.class**, in the subdirectory c:\jpfpatpd:

```
javac -d c:\jpfpatpd -classpath c:\ TestClock.java
```

Suppose the file **TestClock.class** is in the subdirectory c:\jpfpatpd. The following command executes the program **TestClock.class**:

```
java TestClass
```

If you are using an IDE to create Java programs, you need to be familiar with the commands to compile and execute them. Typically, an IDE automatically stores the compiled code of the classes in an appropriate subdirectory.

Multiple-File Programs

In the preceding section, you learned how to create a `package`. Creating a `package` to group related `class`(es) is very useful if the classes are to be used again and again. On the other hand, if a `class` is to be used in only one program, or if you have divided your program so that it uses more than one `class`, rather than create a `package`, you can directly add the file(s) containing the `class`(es) to the program.

The Java IDEs—J++ Builder and CodeWarrior—put the editor, compiler, and loader all into one program. With one command, a program is compiled. These SDKs also manage multiple-file programs in the form of a project. A **project** consists of several files, called the project files. These SDKs include a command that allows you to add several files to a project. Also, these SDKs usually have commands such as **build**, **rebuild**, or **make** (check your software's documentation) to automatically compile all the files required. When one or more files in the project change, you can use these commands to recompile the files.

Formatting the Output of Decimal Numbers Using the **class DecimalFormat**

Chapter 3 explained how to format the output of floating-point numbers, using the method format of the `class String`, to a specific number of decimal places. Chapter 3 also noted that another way to format the output of floating-point numbers is to use the `class DecimalFormat`.

Recall that the default output of decimal numbers of the type `float` is up to six decimal places. Similarly, the default output of decimal numbers of the type `double` is up to 15 decimal places. For example, consider the statements in Table D-3; the output is shown to the right.

TABLE D-3 Default Output of Floating-Point Numbers

Statement	Output
`System.out.println(22.0 / 7.0);`	3.142857142857143
`System.out.println(75.0 / 7.0);`	10.714285714285714
`System.out.println((float)(33.0 / 16.0));`	2.0625
`System.out.println((float)(22.0 / 7.0));`	3.142857

As discussed in Chapter 3, sometimes floating-point numbers must be output in a specific way. For example, a paycheck must be printed to two decimal places, whereas the results of a scientific experiment might require the output of floating-point numbers to six, seven, or perhaps even 10 decimal places.

You can use the Java **class** DecimalFormat to format decimal numbers in a specific manner. The method **format** of the **class** DecimalFormat is applied to the decimal value being formatted. The following steps explain how to use these features to format decimal numbers:

1. Create a `DecimalFormat` object and initialize it to the specific format. Consider the following statement:

   ```
   DecimalFormat twoDecimal = new DecimalFormat("0.00");
   ```

   This statement creates the `DecimalFormat` object `twoDecimal` and initializes it to the string "0.00". Each 0 in the string is a **format flag**. The string "0.00" specifies the formatting of the decimal number. This string indicates that the decimal number being formatted with the object `twoDecimal` will have at least one digit to the left of the decimal point and exactly two digits to the right of the decimal point. If the number being formatted does not meet the formatting requirement, that is, it does not have digits at the specified places, those places are automatically filled with 0. Moreover, suppose that you have the following statement:

   ```
   DecimalFormat twoDigits = new DecimalFormat("0.##");
   ```

   The object `twoDigits` can be used to format the number with two decimal places, but the `##` symbols indicate that trailing zeros will appear as spaces.

2. Next, use the method **format** of the **class** DecimalFormat. (Assume the first declaration of Step 1.) For example, the statement:

   ```
   twoDecimal.format(56.379);
   ```

   formats the decimal number 56.379 as 56.38 (the decimal number is rounded). The method format returns the string containing the digits of the formatted number.

3. The **class** DecimalFormat is included in the **package** java.text. You must import this **class** into your program.

Example D-2 illustrates how to format the output of decimal numbers.

EXAMPLE D-2

```
//Program: Formatting output of decimal numbers using
//the class DecimalFormat

import java.text.DecimalFormat;

public class FormattingDecimalNum
{
    public static void main(String[] args)
    {
        double x = 15.674;                          //Line 1
        double y = 235.73;                          //Line 2
        double z = 9525.9864;                       //Line 3
```

```
        DecimalFormat twoDecimal =
                    new DecimalFormat("0.00");       //Line 4
        DecimalFormat threeDecimal =
                    new DecimalFormat("0.000");     //Line 5

        System.out.println("Line 6: Outputting the "
                    + "values of x, y, and z \n"
                    + "         with two decimal "
                    + "places.");                    //Line 6
        System.out.println("Line 7: x = "
                    + twoDecimal.format(x));          //Line 7
        System.out.println("Line 8: y = "
                    + twoDecimal.format(y));          //Line 8
        System.out.println("Line 9: z = "
                    + twoDecimal.format(z));          //Line 9

        System.out.println("Line 10: Outputting the "
                    + "values of x, y, and z \n"
                    + "            with three "
                    + "decimal places.");             //Line 10
        System.out.println("Line 11: x = "
                    + threeDecimal.format(x));        //Line 11
        System.out.println("Line 12: y = "
                    + threeDecimal.format(y));        //Line 12
        System.out.println("Line 13: z = "
                    + threeDecimal.format(z));        //Line 13
    }
}
```

Sample Run:

```
Line 6: Outputting the values of x, y, and z
        with two decimal places.
Line 7: x = 15.67
Line 8: y = 235.73
Line 9: z = 9525.99
Line 10: Outputting the values of x, y, and z
        with three decimal places.
Line 11: x = 15.674
Line 12: y = 235.730
Line 13: z = 9525.986
```

The statements in Lines 1, 2, and 3 declare and initialize x, y, and z to 15.674, 235.73, and 9525.9864, respectively. The statement in Line 4 creates and initializes the DecimalFormat object twoDecimal to output decimal numbers to two decimal places. Similarly, the statement in Line 5 creates and initializes the DecimalFormat object threeDecimal to output decimal numbers with three decimal places.

The statements in Lines 7, 8, and 9 output the values of x, y, and z to two decimal places. Note that the printed values of x in Line 7 and z in Line 9 are rounded.

The statements in Lines 11, 12, and 13 output the values of x, y, and z, respectively, to three decimal places. Note that the value of y in Line 12 is output to three decimal places.

Because the number stored in `y` has only two decimal places, a `0` is printed as the third decimal place.

Packages and User-Defined Classes

Chapter 7 discusses user-defined methods, in particular methods with parameters. As explained in Chapter 3, there are two types of variables in Java—primitive and reference. The program in Example 7-8 illustrates that if a formal parameter is of the primitive type and the corresponding actual parameter is a variable, then the formal parameter cannot change the value of the actual parameter. Changing the value of a formal parameter of a primitive data type has no effect on the actual parameter. However, if a formal parameter is a reference variable, then both the actual and the formal parameter refer to the same object. That is, only formal parameters that are reference variables are capable of passing values outside the function.

Java provides classes corresponding to each primitive data type, so that values of primitive data types can be considered objects. For example, you can use the `class Integer` to treat `int` values as objects, `class Double` to treat `double` values as objects, and so on. These classes, called wrapper classes, were described in Chapter 6.

As noted in Chapter 7, Java does not provide any class that wraps primitive type values in objects and, when passed as parameters, change their values. If a method returns only one value of a primitive type, then you can write a value-returning method. However, if you encounter a situation that requires you to write a method that needs to pass more than one value of a primitive type, then you should design your own classes. In the next section, we introduce various classes to accomplish this. For example, we design the `class IntClass` so that values of the `int` type can be wrapped in an object. The `class IntClass` also provides methods to change the value of an `IntClass` object. We use reference variables of the `IntClass` type to pass `int` values outside a method.

Primitive Type Classes

This section presents the definitions of the `classes IntClass`, `LongClass`, `CharClass`, `FloatClass`, `DoubleClass`, and `BooleanClass`.

Class: IntClass

```
public class IntClass
{
    private int x;      //variable to store the number

        //default constructor
        //Postcondition: x = 0
    public IntClass()
    {
        x = 0;
    }
```

```java
    //constructor with parameter
    //Postcondition: x = num
public IntClass(int num)
{
    x = num;
}

    //Method to set the data member x
    //Postcondition: x = num
public void setNum(int num)
{
    x = num;
}

    //Method to return the value of x
    //Postcondition: The value of x is returned
public int getNum()
{
    return x;
}

    //Method to update the value of x by adding
    //the value of num
    //Postcondition: x = x + num;
public void addToNum(int num)
{
    x = x + num;
}
    //Method to update the value of x by multiplying
    //the value of x by num
    //Postcondition: x = x * num;
public void multiplyToNum(int num)
{
    x = x * num;
}

    //Method to compare the value of x with the value of num
    //Postcondition: Returns a value < 0 if x < num
    //              Returns 0 if x == num
    //              Returns a value > 0 if x > num
public int compareTo(int num)
{
    return (x - num);
}

    //Method to compare x with num for equality
    //Postcondition: Returns true if x == num;
    //              otherwise it returns false
public boolean equals(int num)
{
    if (x == num)
        return true;
    else
        return false;
}
```

```
    //Method to return the value of x as a string
    public String toString()
    {
        return (String.valueOf(x));
    }
}
```

Consider the following statements:

```
IntClass firstNum = new IntClass();        //Line 1
IntClass secondNum = new IntClass(5);       //Line 2
int num;                                    //Line 3
```

The statement in Line 1 creates the object `firstNum` and initializes it to 0. The statement in Line 2 creates the object `secondNum` and initializes it to 5. The statement in Line 3 declares `num` to be an `int` variable. Now consider the following statements:

```
firstNum.setNum(24);                        //Line 4
secondNum.addToNum(6);                      //Line 5
num = firstNum.getNum();                    //Line 6
```

The statement in Line 4 sets the value of `firstNum` (in fact, the value of the data member `x` of `firstNum`) to 24. The statement in Line 5 updates the value of `secondNum` to 11 (the previous value 5 is updated by adding 6 to it.) The statement in Line 6 retrieves the value of the object `firstNum` (the value of the data member `x`) and assigns it to `num`. After this statement executes, the value of `num` is 24.

The following statements output the values of `firstNum` and `secondNum` (in fact, the values of their data members):

```
System.out.println("firstNum = " + firstNum);
System.out.println("secondNum = " + secondNum);
```

Table D-4 shows how variables of `int` type and the corresponding reference variables of `IntClass` type work.

TABLE D-4 Variables of `int` Type and the Corresponding Reference Variables of `IntClass`

	int	IntClass

Declaration without or with initialization	int x, y = 5;	IntClass x, y;
		x = new IntClass();
		y = new IntClass(5);

Assignment	x = 24;	x.setNum(24);
	y = x;	y.setNum(x.getNum());
Addition	x = x + 10;	x.addToNum(10);
	x = x + y;	x.addToNum(y.getNum());

TABLE D-4 Variables of `int` Type and the Corresponding Reference Variables of `IntClass` (continued)

	int	IntClass
Multiplication	`x = x * 10;`	`x.multiplyToNum(10);`
	`x = x * y;`	`x.multiplyToNum(y.getNum());`
Comparison	`if (x < 10)`	`if (x.compareTo(10) < 0)`
	`if (x < y)`	`if (x.compareTo(y.getNum()) < 0)`
	`if (x <= 10)`	`if (x.compareTo(10) <= 0)`
	`if (x <= y)`	`if (x.compareTo(y.getNum()) <= 0)`

	`if (x == 10)`	`if (x.compareTo(10) == 0)`
		or
		`if (x.equals(10))`

	`if (x == y)`	`if (x.compareTo(y.getNum()) == 0)`
		or
		`if (x.equals(y.getNum()))`

	`if (x > 10)`	`if (x.compareTo(10) > 0)`
	`if (x > y)`	`if (x.compareTo(y.getNum()) > 0)`
	`if (x >= 10)`	`if (x.compareTo(10) >= 0)`
	`if (x >= y)`	`if (x.compareTo(y.getNum()) >= 0)`

	`if (x != 10)`	`if (x.compareTo(10) != 0)`
		or
		`if (!x.equals(10))`

	`if (x != y)`	`if (x.compareTo(y.getNum()) != 0)`
		or
		`if (!x.equals(y.getNum()))`

Output		`System.out.println(x);`
		`System.out.println(x);`

Class: LongClass

```java
public class LongClass
{
    private long x;

    public LongClass()
    {
        x = 0;
    }

    public LongClass(long num)
    {
        x = num;
    }

    public void setNum(long num)
    {
        x = num;
    }

    public long getNum()
    {
        return x;
    }

    public void addToNum(long num)
    {
        x = x + num;
    }

    public void multiplyToNum(long num)
    {
        x = x * num;
    }

    public long compareTo(long num)
    {
        return (x - num);
    }

    public boolean equals(long num)
    {
        if (x == num)
            return true;
        else
            return false;
    }

    public String toString()
    {
        return (String.valueOf(x));
    }
}
```

Class: `CharClass`

```
public class CharClass
{
    private char ch;

    public CharClass()
    {
        ch = ' ';
    }

    public CharClass(char c)
    {
        ch = c;
    }

    public void setChar(char c)
    {
        ch = c;
    }

    public int getChar()
    {
        return ch;
    }

    public char nextChar()
    {
        return (char)((int)ch + 1);
    }

    public char prevChar()
    {
        return (char)((int)ch - 1);
    }

    public String toString()
    {
        return (String.valueOf(ch));
    }
}
```

Class: `FloatClass`

```
public class FloatClass
{
    private float x;

    public FloatClass()
    {
        x = 0;
    }

    public FloatClass(float num)
    {
        x = num;
    }
```

```java
    public void setNum(float num)
    {
        x = num;
    }

    public float getNum()
    {
        return x;
    }

    public void addToNum(float num)
    {
        x = x + num;
    }

    public void multiplyToNum(float num)
    {
        x = x * num;
    }

    public float compareTo(float num)
    {
        return (x - num);
    }

    public boolean equals(float num)
    {
        if (x == num)
            return true;
        else
            return false;
    }

    public String toString()
    {
        return (String.valueOf(x));
    }
}
```

Class: DoubleClass

```java
public class DoubleClass
{
    private double x;

    public DoubleClass()
    {
        x = 0;
    }

    public DoubleClass(double num)
    {
        x = num;
    }
```

```java
    public void setNum(double num)
    {
        x = num;
    }

    public double getNum()
    {
        return x;
    }

    public void addToNum(double num)
    {
        x = x + num;
    }

    public void multiplyToNum(double num)
    {
        x = x * num;
    }

    public double compareTo(double num)
    {
        return (x - num);
    }

    public boolean equals(double num)
    {
        if (x == num)
            return true;
        else
            return false;
    }

    public String toString()
    {
        return (String.valueOf(x));
    }
}
```

Class: BooleanClass

```java
public class BooleanClass
{
    private boolean flag;

    public BooleanClass()
    {
        flag = false;
    }

    public BooleanClass(boolean f)
    {
        flag = f;
    }
```

```java
public boolean get()
{
    return flag;
}

public void set(boolean f)
{
    flag = f;
}

public String toString()
{
    return (String.valueOf(flag));
}

}
```

Using Primitive Type Classes in a Program

This section describes how to use the classes introduced in the previous section.

The class IntClass can be used in two ways. One way is to keep the file IntClass.java and the program in the same directory. First, compile the file IntClass.java, then compile the program.

The second way is to first create a package, and then put this class in that package. For example, you can create the package:

jpfpatpd.ch07.primitiveTypeClasses

and put the class in this package.

In this case, you place the statement:

package jpfpatpd.ch07.primitiveTypeClasses;

before the definition of the class IntClass.

The class IntClass definition is in the file IntClass.java. We need to compile this file and place the compiled code in the directory: jpfpatpd.ch07. primitiveTypeClasses. To do so, we execute the following command at the command line:

javac -d "c:\Program Files\Java\jre1.6.0\lib\classes" IntClass.java

The file IntClass.class is now placed in the subdirectory jpfpatpd\ch07 \primitiveTypeClasses of the directory c:\Program Files\Java\jre1.6.0 \lib\classes.

On the other hand, the command:

javac IntClass.java

places the file IntClass.class in the subdirectory jpfpatpd\ch07\primitive TypeClasses of the same directory. Note that the system automatically creates the subdirectory jpfpatpd\ch07\primitiveTypeClasses if it does not exist.

You can now import this class in a program using the import statement. For example, you can use either of the following statements to use the `class IntClass` in your program:

```
import jpfpatpd.ch07.primitiveTypeClasses.*;
```

or

```
import jpfpatpd.ch07.primitiveTypeClasses.IntClass;
```

USING A SOFTWARE DEVELOPMENT KIT (SDK)

If you are using an SDK, such as CodeWarrior or J++ Builder, you can place the file containing the definition of the class in the same directory that contains your program. You do not need to create a package. However, you can also create a package using the SDK. In this case, place the appropriate `package` statement before the definition of the class, and use the compile command provided by the SDK. (In most cases, you do not need to specify a subdirectory.) The compiled file will be placed in the appropriate directory. You can now import the class without adding it to the project.

 NOTE If you have created a package for your classes, to avoid compilation errors, do not add the file containing the definition of the class to the project.

Enumeration Types

Chapter 2 defined a data type as a set of values, combined with a set of operations on those values. It then introduced the primitive data types, `int`, `char`, `double`, and `float`. Using primitive data types, Chapter 8 discussed how to design classes to create your own data types. In other words, primitive data types are the building blocks of classes.

The values belonging to primitive data types are predefined. Java allows programmers to create their own data types by specifying the values of that data type. These are called **enumeration** or **enum** types and are defined using the keyword `enum`. *The values that you specify for the data types are identifiers.* For example, consider the following statement:

```
enum Grades {A, B, C, D, F};
```

This statement defines `Grades` to be an `enum` type; the values belonging to this type are A, B, C, D, and F. The values of an `enum` type are called **enumeration** or **enum** constants. Note that the values are enclosed in braces and separated by commas. Also, the `enum` constants within an `enum` type must be unique.

Similarly, the statement:

```
enum Sports {BASEBALL, BASKETBALL, FOOTBALL, GOLF,
             HOCKEY, SOCCER, TENNIS};
```

defines `Sports` to be an `enum` type and the values belonging to this type, that is, the `enum` constants, are BASEBALL, BASKETBALL, FOOTBALL, GOLF, HOCKEY, SOCCER, and TENNIS.

Each enum type is a *special type of class*, and the values belonging to the enum type are (special types of) objects of that class. For example, Grades is, in fact, a class and A, B, C, D, and F are public static reference variables to objects of the type Grades.

After an enum type is defined, you can declare reference variables of that type. For example, the following statement declares myGrade to be a reference variable of the Grades type:

```
Grades myGrade;
```

Because each of the variables A, B, C, D, and F is public and static, they can be accessed using the name of the class and the dot operator. Therefore, the following statement assigns the object B to myGrade:

```
myGrade = Grades.B;
```

The output of the statement:

```
System.out.println("myGrade: " + myGrade);
```

is:

```
myGrade: B
```

Similarly, the output of the statement:

```
System.out.println("Grades.B: " + Grades.B);
```

is:

```
Grades.B: B
```

Each enum constant in an enum type has a specific value, called the **ordinal value**. The ordinal value of the first enum constant is 0, the ordinal value of the second enum constant is 1, and so on. Therefore, in the enum type Grades, the ordinal value of A is 0 and the ordinal value of C is 2.

Associated with enum type is a set of methods that can be used to work with enum types. Table D–5 describes some of those methods.

TABLE D-5 Methods Associated with enum Types

Method	Description
ordinal()	Returns the ordinal value of an enum constant
name()	Returns the name of the enum value
values()	Returns the values of an enum type as a list

Example D–3 illustrates how these methods work.

EXAMPLE D-3

```java
public class EnumExample1
{
    enum Grades {A, B, C, D, F};                    //Line 1

    enum Sports {BASEBALL, BASKETBALL, FOOTBALL,
                 GOLF, HOCKEY, SOCCER, TENNIS};      //Line 2

    public static void main(String[] args)          //Line 3
    {
        Grades myGrade;                             //Line 4
        Sports mySport;                             //Line 5

        myGrade = Grades.A;                         //Line 6

        mySport = Sports.BASKETBALL;                //Line 7

        System.out.println("Line 8: My grade: "
                        + myGrade);                 //Line 8
        System.out.println("Line 9: The ordinal "
                        + "value of myGrade is "
                        + myGrade.ordinal());       //Line 9
        System.out.println("Line 10: myGrade name: "
                        + myGrade.name());          //Line 10

        System.out.println("Line 11: My sport: "
                        + mySport);                 //Line 11
        System.out.println("Line 12: The ordinal "
                        + "value of mySport is "
                        + mySport.ordinal());       //Line 12
        System.out.println("Line 13: mySport name: "
                        + mySport.name());          //Line 13

        System.out.println("Line 14: Sports: ");    //Line 14

        for (Sports sp : Sports.values())           //Line 15
            System.out.println(sp + "'s ordinal "
                            + "value is "
                            + sp.ordinal());        //Line 16

        System.out.println();                       //Line 17
    }
}
```

Sample Run:

```
Line 8: My grade: A
Line 9: The ordinal value of myGrade is 0
Line 10: myGrade name: A
Line 11: My sport: BASKETBALL
Line 12: The ordinal value of mySport is 1
```

```
Line 13: mySport name: BASKETBALL
Line 14: Sports:
BASEBALL's ordinal value is 0
BASKETBALL's ordinal value is 1
FOOTBALL's ordinal value is 2
GOLF's ordinal value is 3
HOCKEY's ordinal value is 4
SOCCER's ordinal value is 5
TENNIS's ordinal value is 6
```

The preceding program works as follows. The statements in Lines 1 and 2 define the enum type Grades and Sports, respectively. The statement in Line 4 declares myGrade to be a reference variable of the type Grades, and the statement in Line 5 declares mySport to be a reference variable of the type Sports. The statement in Line 6 assigns the object A to myGrade, and the statement in Line 7 assigns the object BASKETBALL to mySport.

The statement in Line 8 outputs myGrade, the statement in Line 9 uses the method ordinal to output the ordinal value of myGrade, and the statement in Line 10 uses the method name to output the name of myGrade.

The statement in Line 11 outputs mySport, the statement in Line 12 uses the method ordinal to output the ordinal value of mySport, and the statement in Line 13 uses the method name to output the name of mySport.

The foreach loop in Line 15 outputs the value of Sports and their ordinal values. Note that the method values, in the expression Sports.values(), returns the value of the enum type Sport as a list. The loop control variable sp ranges over those values one-by-one, starting at the first value.

The beginning of this section noted that an enum type is a special type of class, and the enum constants are reference variables to the objects of that enum type. Because each enum type is a class, in addition to the enum constants, it can also contain constructors, (private) data members, and methods. Before describing enumeration type or enum in more detail, let us note the following:

1. Enumeration types are defined using the keyword enum rather than class.
2. enum types are implicitly final because enum constants should not be modified.
3. enum constants are implicitly static.
4. Once an enum type is created, you can declare reference variables of that type, but you cannot instantiate objects using the operator new. In fact, an attempt to instantiate an object using the operator new will result in a compilation error.

(Because enum objects cannot be instantiated using the operator new, the constructor, if any, of an enumeration *cannot* be public. In fact, the constructors of an enum type are implicitly private.)

The enum type Grades was defined earlier in this section. Let us redefine this enum type by adding constructors, data members, and methods. Consider the following definition:

```java
public enum Grades
{
    A ("Range 90% to 100%"),
    B ("Range 80% to 89.99%"),
    C ("Range 70% to 79.99%"),
    D ("Range 60% to 69.99%"),
    F ("Range 0% to 59.99%");

    private final String range;

    private Grades()
    {
        range = "";
    }

    private Grades(String str)
    {
        range = str;
    }

    public String getRange()
    {
        return range;
    }
}
```

This enum type Grades contains the enum constants A, B, C, D, and F. It has a private named constant range of the type String, two constructors, and the method getRange. Note that each Grades object has the data member range. Let us consider the statement:

```java
A ("Range 90% to 100%")
```

This statement creates the Grades object, using the constructor with parameters, with the string "Range 90% to 100%", and assigns that object to the reference variable A. The method getRange is used to return the string contained in the object.

It is not necessary to specify the modifier private in the heading of the constructor. Each constructor is implicitly private. Therefore, the two constructors of the enum type Grades can be written as:

```java
Grades()
{
    range = "";
}

Grades(String str)
{
    range = str;
}
```

Example D-4 illustrates how the enum type Grades works.

EXAMPLE D-4

```
public class EnumExample2
{
    public static void main(String[] args)
    {
        System.out.println("Grade Ranges");      //Line 1

        for (Grades gr : Grades.values())        //Line 2
            System.out.println(gr + " "
                                + gr.getRange()); //Line 3

        System.out.println();                    //Line 4
    }
}
```

Sample Run:

```
Grade Ranges
A Range 90% to 100%
B Range 80% to 89.99%
C Range 70% to 79.99%
D Range 60% to 69.99%
F Range 0% to 59.99%
```

The foreach loop in Line 2 uses the method values to retrieve the enum constants as a list. The method getRange in Line 3 is used to retrieve the string contained in the Grades object.

The following programming example uses an enum type to create a program to play the game of rock, paper, and scissors.

PROGRAMMING EXAMPLE: The Rock, Paper, and Scissors Game

Everyone is familiar with the rock, paper, and scissors game. The game has two players, each of whom chooses one of the three objects: rock, paper, or scissors. If player 1 chooses rock and player 2 chooses paper, player 2 wins the game because paper covers the rock. The game is played according to the following rules:

- If both players choose the same object, this play is a tie.
- If one player chooses rock and the other chooses scissors, the player choosing the rock wins this play because the rock crushes the scissors.
- If one player chooses rock and the other chooses paper, the player choosing the paper wins this play because the paper covers the rock.
- If one player chooses scissors and the other chooses paper, the player choosing the scissors wins this play because the scissors cut the paper.

We write an interactive program that allows two players to play this game.

Input: This program has two types of input:

- The players' responses to play the game
- The players' choices

Output: The players' choices and the winner of each play. After the game is over, the total number of plays and the number of times that each player won should be output as well.

PROBLEM ANALYSIS AND ALGORITHM DESIGN

Two players play this game. Players enter their choices via the keyboard. Each player enters R or r for Rock, P or p for Paper, or S or s for Scissors. While the first player enters a choice, the second player looks away. Once both entries are in, if the entries are valid, the program outputs the players' choices and declares the winner of the play. The game continues until one of the players decides to quit. After the game ends, the program outputs the total number of plays and the number of times that each player won. This discussion translates into the following algorithm:

1. Provide a brief explanation of the game and how it is played.
2. Ask the users if they want to play the game.
3. Get plays for both players.
4. If the plays are valid, output the plays and the winner.
5. Update the total game count and winner count.
6. Repeat Steps 2–5 while the users continue to play the game.
7. Output the number of plays and times that each player won.

To describe the objects ROCK, PAPER, and SCISSORS, we define the following enum type:

```java
public enum RockPaperScissors
{
    ROCK ("Rock crushes scissors."),
    PAPER ("Paper covers rock."),
    SCISSORS ("Scissors cuts paper.");

    private String mgs;

    private RockPaperScissors()
    {
        mgs = "";
    }

    private RockPaperScissors(String str)
    {
        mgs = str;
    }

    public String getMessage()
    {
        return mgs;
    }
}
```

Variables (Method main) It is clear that you need the following variables in the method main:

```java
int gameCount;       //to count the number of
                     //games played
int winCount1;       //to count the number of
                     //games won by player 1
int winCount2;       //to count the number of
                     //games won by player 2
int gameWinner;
char response;       //to get the user's response
                     //to play the game
char selection1;
char selection2;

RockPaperScissors play1;  //player1's selection
RockPaperScissors play2;  //player2's selection
```

This program is divided into six methods, which the following sections describe in detail.

- **displayRules:** This method displays some brief information about the game and its rules.
- **validSelection:** This method checks whether a player's selection is valid. The only valid selections are R, r, P, p, S, and s.
- **retrievePlay:** This method uses the entered choice (R, r, P, p, S, or s) and returns the appropriate object.
- **gameResult:** This method outputs the players' choices and the winner of the game.
- **winningObject:** This method determines and returns the winning object.
- **displayResults:** After the game is over, this method displays the final results.

Method display Rules

This method has no parameters. It consists only of output statements to explain the game and rules of play. Essentially, this method's definition is:

```java
public static void displayRules()
{
    System.out.println("Welcome to the game of Rock, "
                    + "Paper, and Scissors.");
    System.out.println("This is a game for two players. "
                    + "For each game, each player \n"
                    + "selects one of the "
                    + "objects: Rock, Paper or "
                    + "Scissors.");
    System.out.println("The rules for winning the "
                    + "game are: ");
    System.out.println("1. If both players select the "
                    + "same object, it is a tie.");
    System.out.println("2. Rock crushes Scissors: The "
                    + "player who selects Rock wins.");
    System.out.println("3. Paper covers Rock: The "
                    + "player who selects Paper wins.");
    System.out.println("4. Scissors cuts Paper: The "
                    + "player who selects Scissors "
                    + "wins.");
    System.out.println("Enter R or r to select Rock, "
                    + "P or p to select Paper, \n"
                    + "and S or s to select Scissors.");
}
```

Method valid Selection

This method checks whether a player's selection is valid. Let's use a `switch` statement to check for the valid selection. The definition of this method is:

```
public static boolean validSelection(char selection)
{
    switch (selection)
    {
    case 'R':
    case 'r':
    case 'P':
    case 'p':
    case 'S':
    case 's':
        return true;

    default:
        return false;
    }
}
```

Method retrievePlay

This method uses the entered choice (R, r, P, p, S, or s) and returns the appropriate object. The method has one parameter of the type `char`. It is a value-returning method and returns a reference to a `RockPaperScissors` object.

The definition of the method `retrievePlay` is:

```
public static RockPaperScissors retrievePlay
                                (char selection)
{
    RockPaperScissors obj = RockPaperScissors.ROCK;

    switch (selection)
    {
    case 'R':
    case 'r':
        obj = RockPaperScissors.ROCK;
        break;

    case 'P':
    case 'p':
        obj = RockPaperScissors.PAPER;
        break;

    case 'S':
    case 's':
        obj = RockPaperScissors.SCISSORS;
    }

    return obj;
}
```

Method	This method decides whether a game is a tie or which player is the winner. It outputs
game	the players' selections and the winner of the game. This method has two parameters:
Result	player 1's choice and player 2's choice. It returns the number (1 or 2) of the winning
	player.

The definition of this method is:

```java
public static int gameResult(RockPaperScissors play1,
                             RockPaperScissors play2)
{
    int winner = 0;

    RockPaperScissors winnerObject;

    if (play1 == play2)
    {
        winner = 0;
        System.out.println("Both players selected "
                        + play1
                        + ". This game is a tie.");
    }
    else
    {
        winnerObject = winningObject(play1, play2);

            //Output each player's choice
        System.out.println("Player 1 selected " + play1
                        + " and player 2 selected "
                        + play2 + ".");

            //Decide the winner
        if (play1 == winnerObject)
            winner = 1;
        else if (play2 == winnerObject)
            winner = 2;

            //Output winning object's message
        System.out.println(winnerObject.getMessage());

            //Output the winner
        System.out.println("Player " + winner
                        + " wins this play.");
    }

    return winner;
}
```

Method winning Object

To decide the winner of the game, you look at the players' selections and then at the rules of the game. For example, if one player chooses ROCK and another chooses PAPER, the player who chose PAPER wins. In other words, the winning object is PAPER. The method winningObject, given two objects, decides and returns the winning object. Clearly, this method has two parameters of the type RockPaperScissors, and the value returned by this method is also of the type RockPaperScissors. The definition of this method is:

```java
public static RockPaperScissors winningObject
                        (RockPaperScissors play1,
                         RockPaperScissors play2)
{
    if ((play1 == RockPaperScissors.ROCK &&
        play2 == RockPaperScissors.SCISSORS)
      || (play2 == RockPaperScissors.ROCK &&
        play1 == RockPaperScissors.SCISSORS))
        return RockPaperScissors.ROCK;
    else if ((play1 == RockPaperScissors.ROCK &&
            play2 == RockPaperScissors.PAPER)
          || (play2 == RockPaperScissors.ROCK &&
            play1 == RockPaperScissors.PAPER))
        return RockPaperScissors.PAPER;
    else
        return RockPaperScissors.SCISSORS;
}
```

Method display Results

After the game is over, this method outputs the final results—that is, the total number of plays and the number of plays won by each player. The total number of plays is stored in the variable gameCount, the number of plays by player 1 is stored in the variable winCount1, and the number of plays won by player 2 is stored in the variable winCount2. This method has three parameters corresponding to these three variables. Essentially, the definition of this method is as follows:

```java
public static void displayResults(int gCount, int wCount1,
                                  int wCount2)
{
    System.out.println("The total number of plays: "
                    + gCount);
    System.out.println("The number of plays won by "
                    + "player 1: " + wCount1);
    System.out.println("The number of plays won by "
                    + "player 2: " + wCount2);
}
```

We are now ready to write the algorithm for the method main.

Main
Algorithm

1. Declare the variables.
2. Initialize the variables.
3. Display the rules.
4. Prompt the users to play the game.
5. Get the users' responses to play the game.
6. `while` (response is yes)

   {
   a. Prompt player 1 to make a selection.
   b. Get the play for player 1.
   c. Prompt player 2 to make a selection.
   d. Get the play for player 2.
   e. If both the plays are legal

      {
      i. Retrieve both plays.
      ii. Increment the total game count.
      iii. Declare the winner of the game.
      iv. Increment the winner's game win count by 1.
      }
   f. Prompt the users to determine whether they want to play again.
   g. Get the players' response.
   }
7. Output the game results.

PROGRAM LISTING

```java
import java.util.*;

public class GameRockPaperScissors
{
    static Scanner console = new Scanner(System.in);

    public static void main(String[] args)
    {
            //Step 1
        int gameCount;  //to count the number of
                        //games played
        int winCount1;  //to count the number of
                        //games won by player 1
        int winCount2;  //to count the number of
                        //games won by player 2
```

```java
    int gameWinner;
    char response;   //to get the user's response
                     //to play the game
    char selection1;
    char selection2;

    RockPaperScissors play1;   //player1's selection
    RockPaperScissors play2;   //player2's selection

        //Initialize the variables; Step 2
    gameCount = 0;
    winCount1 = 0;
    winCount2 = 0;

    displayRules();                                      //Step 3

    System.out.print("Enter Y/y to play "
                 + "the game: ");                        //Step 4
    response = console.nextLine().charAt(0);             //Step 5
    System.out.println();

    while (response == 'Y' || response == 'y')    //Step 6
    {
        System.out.print("Player 1 enter "
                     + "your choice: ");                 //Step 6a
        selection1 =
             console.nextLine().charAt(0);               //Step 6b
        System.out.println();

        System.out.print("Player 2 enter "
                     + "your choice: ");                 //Step 6c
        selection2 =
             console.nextLine().charAt(0);               //Step 6d
        System.out.println();

            //Step 6e
        if (validSelection(selection1) &&
            validSelection(selection2))
        {
            play1 = retrievePlay(selection1);
            play2 = retrievePlay(selection2);
            gameCount++;
            gameWinner = gameResult(play1, play2);

            if (gameWinner == 1)
                winCount1++;
            else if (gameWinner == 2)
                winCount2++;
        }//end if
```

```
            System.out.print("Enter Y/y to play "
                      + "the game: ");           //Step 6f
            response = console.nextLine().charAt(0); //Step 6g
            System.out.println();
        }//end while

        displayResults(gameCount, winCount1,
                      winCount2);                 //Step 7

    }//end main

    //Place the definitions of the methods displayRules,
    //validSelection, retrievePlay, winningObject,
    //gameResult, and displayResults here.

}
```

Sample Run: (In this sample run, the user input is shaded.)

```
Welcome to the game of Rock, Paper, and Scissors.
This is a game for two players. For each game, each player
selects one of the objects: Rock, Paper or Scissors.
The rules for winning the game are:
1. If both players select the same object, it is a tie.
2. Rock crushes Scissors: The player who selects Rock wins.
3. Paper covers Rock: The player who selects Paper wins.
4. Scissors cuts Paper: The player who selects Scissors wins.
Enter R or r to select Rock, P or p to select Paper,
and S or s to select Scissors.
Enter Y/y to play the game: y

Player 1 enter your choice: R

Player 2 enter your choice: S
Player 1 selected ROCK and player 2 selected SCISSORS.
Rock crushes scissors.
Player 1 wins this play.
Enter Y/y to play the game: Y

Player 1 enter your choice: S

Player 2 enter your choice: P
Player 1 selected SCISSORS and player 2 selected PAPER.
Scissors cuts paper.
Player 1 wins this play.
Enter Y/y to play the game: Y

Player 1 enter your choice: R
```

```
Player 2 enter your choice: P
Player 1 selected ROCK and player 2 selected PAPER.
Paper covers rock.
Player 2 wins this play.
Enter Y/y to play the game: n
The total number of plays: 3
The number of plays won by player 1: 2
The number of plays won by player 2: 1
```

Answers to Odd-Numbered Exercises

Chapter 1

1. a. True; b. False; c. True; d. True; e. False; f. False; g. True; h. True; i. True

3. Monitor and printer.

5. An operating system monitors the overall activity of the computer and provides services. Some of these services include memory management, input/output activities, and storage management.

7. Syntax errors.

9. Instructions in a high level language are closer to the natural language, such as English, and therefore, are easier to understand and learn than the machine language.

11. To find the weighted average of four test scores, first you need to know each test score and its weight. Next, you multiply each test score by its weight and then add these numbers to get the average. Therefore:

    1. Get `testScore1, weightTestScore1`
    2. Get `testScore2, weightTestScore2`
    3. Get `testScore3, weightTestScore3`
    4. Get `testScore4, weightTestScore4`
    5. ```
sum = testScore1 * weightTestScore1 +
          testScore2 * weightTestScore2 +
          testScore3 * weightTestScore3 +
          testScore4 * weightTestScore4;
```

13. To calculate the selling price of the item, we need to know the original price (the price the store pays) of the item. We can then use the following formula to find the selling price:

    ```
sellingPrice = originalPrice + originalPrice * .60
```

    The algorithm is as follows:

    a. Get `originalPrice`
    b. Calculate the `sellingPrice` using the formula:

    ```
sellingPrice = originalPrice + originalPrice * .60
```
    The information needed to calculate the selling price is the original price and the marked-up percentage.
```

15. Let r denote the radius of the circle. Given the lengths a, b, and c, such that $a + b$ + c is the circumference of the circle, we have $2\pi r = a + b + c$. This implies that $r = (a + b + c) / (2\pi)$. We can now write the algorithm as follows:

   a. Get the values of a, b, c

   b. Calculate r using the formula:

   ```
   r = (a + b + c) / (2π)
   ```

Chapter 2

1. a. False; b. False; c. False; d. False; e. True; f. True; g. True; h. False; i. True; j. False

3. a

5. a. 3; b. not possible; c. not possible; d. 38.5; e. 1; f. 2; g. 2; h. 420.0;

7. 7

9. a and c are valid

11. a. `10 * a`

   b. `'8'`

   c. `(b * b - 4 * a * c) / 2 * a`

   d. `(-b + (b * b - 4 * a * c)) / 2 * a`

13.
   ```
   x = 20
   y = 15
   z = 6
   w = 11.5
   t = 4.5
   ```

15. a. $x = 2$, $y = 5$, $z = 6$

   b. $x + y = 7$

   c. Sum of 2 and 6 is 8

   d. $z / x = 3$

   e. 2 times 2 = 4

17. `System.out.println();` or `System.out.print("\n");` or `System.out.print('\n');`

19. a. A correct answer is:

```
public class ProgWithErrorsA
{
    static final int   SECRET_NUM = 11213;
    static final double PAY_RATE = 18.35;

    public void main(String[] arg)
    {
        int one, two, three;
        double first, second;
```

```
        double paycheck, hoursWorked;

        one = 18;
        two = 11;
        three = 3;

        first = 25;
        second = first * three;

        second = 2 * SECRET_NUM;

        System.out.println(first + " " + second + " " + SECRET_NUM);

        hoursWorked = 35;

        paycheck = hoursWorked * PAY_RATE;

        System.out.println("Wages = " +  paycheck);
    }
}
```

b. A correct answer is:

```
public class ProgWithErrorsB
{
    static final char STAR = '*';
    static final int  PRIME = 71;

    public static void main(String[] arg)
    {
        int count = 1;
        int sum = count + PRIME;

        double x = 25.67;
        int newNum = count * PRIME + 2;

        sum = sum + count;
        x = x + sum * count;
        System.out.println(" count = " + count + ", sum = "
                        + sum + ", PRIME = " + PRIME);

    }
}
```

21. a. `x = x + 5 - z;`

b. `y = y * (2 * x + 5 - z);`

c. `w = w + 2 * z + 4;`

d. `x = x - (z + y - t);`

e. `sum = sum + num;`

f. `x = x / (y - 2);`

23.

	a	b	c	sum
`sum = a + b + (int)c;`	3	5	14.1	22
`c /= a;`	3	5	4.7	22
`b += (int)c - a;`	3	6	4.7	22
`a *= 2 * b + (int)c;`	48	6	4.7	22

25. (NOTE: The user input is shaded.)

```
Enter last name: Miller

Enter a two digit number: 34

Enter a positive integer less than 1000: 340

Name: Miller
Id: 3417
Mystery number: 3689
```

27. The program require three inputs. One possible form of input is:
```
number
string
number
```

Another possible form of input is:
```
number string
number
```

Chapter 3

1. a. False; b. True; c. True; d. True

3. An object is an instance of a specific class.

5. `str = new String("Java Programming");`

7. a. `Going`

b. `amusement`

c. `GOING TO THE AMUSEMENT PARK.`

d. going to the amusement park.

e. Going *o*he amusemen* park.

9. a. false

b. true

11. This statement causes the following input dialog box to appear allowing the user to enter the score.

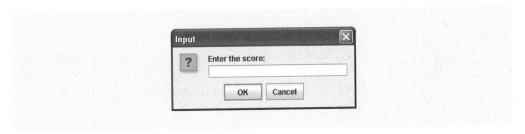

FIGURE E-1 Chapter 3 Exercise 11

13. JOptionPane.showMessageDialog(null,
                    "Current Temperature: 70 degrees",
                    "Temperature",
                    JOptionPane.QUESTION_MESSAGE);

15. x = console.nextInt();
    ch = console.next().charAt(0);
    y = console.nextInt();

17. a. Same as before.

b. The file contains the output produced by the program.

c. The file contains the output produced by the program. Old contents are erased.

d. The program would prepare the file and store the output in the file.

Chapter 4

1. a. True; b. False; c. False; d. False; e. False; f. False; g. False; h. False; i. True

3. 100 200 0

5. Omit the semicolon after else:

```
if (score >= 60)
    System.out.println("You pass.");
else
    System.out.println("You fail.");
```

7. a is invalid: The expression n <= 2 evaluates to a `boolean` value, which is not an integral type. The expression in the `switch` expression must evaluate to an integral value. b is invalid; A `case` value cannot appear more than once. c and d are valid.

9. 7

11. There is more than one answer. One possible answer is:

```java
import java.util.*;

public class Errors
{
    static Scanner console = new Scanner(System.in);

    public static void main(String[] args)
    {
        int a, b;
        int c;
        boolean found;

        System.out.print("Enter the first integer: ");
        a = console.nextInt();
        System.out.println();

        System.out.print("Enter the second integer: ");
        b = console.nextInt();

        if (a > a * b && 10 < b)
            found = 2 * a > b;
        else
        {
            found = 2 * a < b;
            if (found)
                a = 3;
            c = 15;
            if (b > 0)
            {
                b = 0;
                a = 1;
            }
        }
    }
}
```

Chapter 5

1. a. False; b. True; c. False; d. True; e. True; f. True; g. True; h. False

3. 5

5. When ch > 'Z'

7. Sum = 158

9. Sum = 158

11. 11 18 25

13. a. 18

    b. 14

    c. False

15. 2 7 17 37 77 157

17. a. *

    b. infinite loop

    c. infinite loop

    d. ****

    e. ******

    f. ***

19.
```
sum = 0;
for (i = 0; i <= 100; i = i + 5)
    sum = sum + i;
```

21.
```
0 - 24
25 - 49
50 - 74
75 - 99
100 - 124
125 - 149
150 - 174
175 - 200
```

23. a. Both; b. do...while; c. while; d. while

25. There is more than one answer to this problem. One solution is:

```
import java.util.*;

public class Strange
{
    static Scanner console = new Scanner(System.in);
```

```java
    public static void main(String[] args)
    {
        int total = 0;
        int number;

        do
        {
            number = console.nextInt();
            if (number != -1)
                total = total + number;
        }
        while (number != -1);

        System.out.println("The sum of the numbers entered is "
                            + total);
    }


}
```

27. a.
```java
    number = 1;
    while (number <= 10)
    {
        System.out.print(number + " ");
        number++;
    }

    System.out.println();
```
b.
```java
    number = 1;
    do
    {
        System.out.print(number + " ");
        number++;
    }
    while (number <= 10);

    System.out.println();
```
29. 11 18 25

Chapter 6

1. a. True; b. True; c. True; d. True; e. False; f. False; g. True; h. True; i. True; j. False; k. False; l. False

3. `JTextField`

5. To identify other GUI components such as a `JTextField`.

7. Through the process outlined, you have methodology which will allow you to critically think and plan your problem-solving approach. You may be able to identify the flaws involved in your thinking before you implement it. A well-analyzed problem leads to a well-designed algorithm. Also, a program that is well-analyzed is easier to modify and spot and fix errors. No one would build a house without a blueprint.

9.
```java
//Program: Determine the sum and product of two numbers.

import javax.swing.*;
import java.lang.*;
import java.awt.*;
import java.awt.event.*;

public class SumProduct extends JFrame
{
    private JLabel firstL, secondL, sumL, productL;

    private JTextField firstTF, secondTF, sumTF, productTF;

    private JButton calculateB, exitB;

    private CalculateButtonHandler cbHandler;
    private ExitButtonHandler ebHandler;

    private static final int WIDTH = 400;
    private static final int HEIGHT = 300;

    public SumProduct()
    {

            //Create four labels
        firstL = new JLabel("Enter the first number: ",
                        SwingConstants.RIGHT);
        secondL = new JLabel("Enter the second number: ",
                        SwingConstants.RIGHT);
        sumL = new JLabel("Sum: ", SwingConstants.RIGHT);
        productL = new JLabel("Product: ",
                        SwingConstants.RIGHT);
```

```java
        //Create four textfields
   firstTF = new JTextField(10);
   secondTF = new JTextField(10);
   sumTF = new JTextField(10);
   productTF = new JTextField(10);

        //Create Calculate Button
   calculateB = new JButton("Calculate");
   cbHandler = new CalculateButtonHandler();
   calculateB.addActionListener(cbHandler);

        //Create Exit Button
   exitB = new JButton("Exit");
   ebHandler = new ExitButtonHandler();
   exitB.addActionListener(ebHandler);

        //Set the title of the window
   setTitle("Sum and Product Calculation");

        //Get the container
   Container pane = getContentPane();

        //Set the layout
   pane.setLayout(new GridLayout(5, 2));

        //Place the components in the pane
   pane.add(firstL);
   pane.add(firstTF);
   pane.add(secondL);
   pane.add(secondTF);
   pane.add(sumL);
   pane.add(sumTF);
   pane.add(productL);
   pane.add(productTF);
   pane.add(calculateB);
   pane.add(exitB);

        //set the size of the window and display it
   setSize(WIDTH, HEIGHT);
   setVisible(true);
   setDefaultCloseOperation(EXIT_ON_CLOSE);
}
```

```
    private class CalculateButtonHandler
                        implements ActionListener
    {
        public void actionPerformed(ActionEvent e)
        {
            double second, first, sum, product;

            first = Double.parseDouble(firstTF.getText());
            second = Double.parseDouble(secondTF.getText());
            sum = first + second;
            product = first * second;

            sumTF.setText("" + sum);
            productTF.setText("" + product);
        }
    }

    private class ExitButtonHandler implements ActionListener
    {
        public void actionPerformed(ActionEvent e)
        {
            System.exit(0);
        }
    }

    public static void main(String[] args)
    {
        SumProduct sumProductObject = new SumProduct();
    }
}
```

11. a. `JLabel numOfCourses;`
       `numOfCourses = new JLabel("Enter the number of courses");`
   b. `JButton run;`
       `run = new JButton("Run");`
   c. `JTextField oneTextField ;`
       `oneTextField = new JTextField(15);`
   d. `setTitle("Welcome Home!");`
   e. `setSize(200, 400);`
   f. `JTextField oneTextField;`
       `oneTextField = new JTextField(15);`
       `oneTextField.setText("Apple tree");`

13. Lines with errors are in the comments. See the corrected lines.

```java
        //The following lines added.
import javax.swing.*;
import java.awt.*;

public class RTwo extends JFrame
{
    private JLabel length, width, area;
    static private final int WIDTH = 400;
    static private final int HEIGHT = 400;

    //public RTwoProgram()
    public RTwo()
    {
        //private JLabel length, width, area;
        setTitle("Good day area");

        //length = JLabel("Enter the length);
        length = new JLabel("Enter the length");

        //width = JLabel("Enter the width);
        width = new JLabel("Enter the width");

        area = new JLabel("Area: ");

        //containerPane = ContentPane();
        Container pane = getContentPane();

        //pane.setLayout(GridLayout(4, 1));
        pane.setLayout(new GridLayout(4, 1));

        setSize(WIDTH, HEIGHT);
        setVisible(true);
        setDefaultCloseOperation(EXIT_ON_CLOSE);
    }

    public static void main(String args[])
    {
        //RTwoProgram R2 = new RTwoProgram();
        RTwo R2 = new RTwo();
    }
}
```

15. `displayWelcome, getAcctNo, getPin, verifyAcct, deposit, withdraw, transfer, tenderCash, checkAcct,` and so on.

17. Customer: data members include `firstName, lastName, phone, email, address`; methods include `set` and `get` methods for data members.

   Account: `accountNumber, type, currentRate`; methods include `set` and `get` methods for data members.

   Loan: `loanNumber, type, currentRate`; methods include `set` and `get` methods for data member.

   Manager: data members include `firstName, lastName, phone, email, address`; methods include `set` and `get` methods for data members, `createAccount, approveLoan,` and so on.

   Teller: data members include `firstName, lastName, phone, email, address`; methods include `set` and `get` methods for data members, `processCheck, tenderCash, transferAmt,` and so on.

19. Company: data members include `accountNumber, name, phone, email, address, status, numOpenings`; methods include `set` and `get` methods for data members, `listOpenings, requestCandidate, cancelPosition,` and so on.

   Candidate: data members include `candidateID, firstName, lastName, phone, email, address, wage`; methods include `set` and `get` methods for data members, `listQualifications, calculateSalary, withholdIncomeTax,` and so on.

   Placement: data members include `candidateID, companyID, openingID, startDate, endDate`; methods include `set` and `get` methods for data members, `listQualifications, calculateSalary, informCompany, informCandidate,` and so on.

   Opening: data members include `openingID, companyID, startDate, endDate, qualificationID, salary`; methods include `set` and `get` methods for data members.

   Qualification: data members include `qualificationID, meanSalary, maximumSalary, minimumSalary, category`; methods include `set` and `get` methods for data members.

Chapter 7

1. a. True; b. True; c. True; d. True; e. False; f. True; g. False; h. False

3. a. Invalid; Method type is missing.

   b. Valid

   c. Invalid; Data type for the parameter b is missing.

   d. Invalid; Missing parentheses after the method name.

5. a. 4; b. 26; c. 10 4 0; d. 0

7. a. 14; b. 15; c. 30

9. 1
   2
   6
   24
   120

11. Method headings:

```
public static void main(String[] args)
public static void hello(int first, double second,
                                 char ch)
```

Method bodies:

   main: starts at Line 4 ends at Line 13

   hello: starts at Line 16 ends at Line 20

Method definitions:

   main: starts at Line 3 ends at Line 13

   hello: starts at Line 14 ends at Line 20

Formal parameters:

   main: args

   hello: first, second, ch

Actual parameters:

   x, y, z

   x + 2, y - 3.5, 'S'

Method calls: Statements in Lines 9 and 11

```
hello(x, y, z);              //Line 9
hello(x + 2, y - 3.5, 'S');  //Line 11
```

Local variables:

   main: x, y, z

   hello: num, y

13.   -14 20 126
     15 40 407
     15 80 1627
     70 160 6412

15. Line 3: In main: num1 = 10, num2 = 20
     Line 8: In funcOne: a = 10, b = 20, x = 20, and z = 30
     Line 10: In funcOne: a = 10, b = 20, x = 25, and z = 30
     Line 13: In funcOne: a = 18, b = 73, x = 25, and z = 30
     Line 5: In main after funcOne: num1 = 10, num2 = 73

Chapter 8

1. a. False; b. False; c. True; d. False; e. False

3. a.   i.   Constructor at Line 1.

      ii.   Constructor at Line 3.

      iii.   Constructor at Line 4.

   b.
```
public CC()
{
    u = 0;
    v = 0;
    w = 0.0;
}
```

   c.
```
public CC(int a)
{
    u = a;
    v = 0;
    w = 0.0;
}
```

   d.
```
public CC(int a, int b)
{
    u = a;
    v = b;
    w = 0.0;
}
```

   e.
```
public CC(int a, int b, double d)
{
    u = a;
    v = b;
    w = d;
}
```

5. `06:23:17`
   `06:23:17`

7. In shallow copying, two or more reference variables of the same type point to the same object.

9. Both **aa** and **bb** point to the object **bb**.

11. The purpose of the copy constructor is to initialize an object, when the object is instantiated, using an existing object of the same type.

13. No.

15.
```java
public class Secret
{
    private String name;
    private int age;
    private int weight;
    private double height;

    Secret()
    {
        name = "";
        age = 0;
        weight = 0;
        height = 0.0;
    }

    Secret(String n, int a, int w, double h)
    {
        name = n;
        age = a;
        weight = w;
        height = h;
    }

    public void setName(String n)
    {
        name = n;
    }

    public void setAge(int a)
    {
        age = a;
    }
```

```java
    public void setWeight(int w)
    {
        weight = w;
    }
    public void setHeight(double h)
    {
        height = h;
    }

    public String getName()
    {
        return name;
    }

    public int getAge()
    {
        return age;
    }

    public int getWeight()
    {
        return weight;
    }

    public int getHeight()
    {
        return height;
    }

    public void print()
    {
        System.out.println("Name: " + name + "\r\nAge: " + age +
                        "\r\nWeight: " + weight +
                        "\r\nHeight: " + height);
    }
}
```

Chapter 9

1. a. True; b. True; c. True; d. True; e. False; f. False; g. True

3. a. `funcOne(list, 50);`

   b. `System.out.print(funcSum(50, list[3]));`

    c. `System.out.print(funcSum(list[29], list[9]));`

    d. `funcTwo(list, Alist);`

5. The elements of `list` are: 5, 6, 9, 19, 23, 37

7. `One contains: 3 8 13 18 23`
    `Two contains: 5 15 25 35 45 28 33 38 43 48`

9. a. 30

    b. 5

    c. 6

    d. row

    e. column

11. a. `beta` is initialized to zero.

    b. First row of beta: 0 1 2
        Second row of beta: 1 2 3
        Third row of beta: 2 3 4

    c. First row of beta: 0 0 0
        Second row of beta: 0 1 2
        Third row of beta: 0 2 4

    d. First row of beta: 0 2 0
        Second row of beta: 2 0 2
        Third row of beta: 0 2 0

13. list = ["One", "Six", "Two", "Three", "Four", "Five"];

15. strList: [Hello, Happy, Sunny]
    intList: [10, 20, 30]
    strList: [Hello, Happy, Joy, Sunny]
    intList: [10, 30]

Chapter 10

1. a. False; b. False; c. False; d. True

3. Some of the data members that can be added to the `class` Employee are: `department`, `salary`, `employeeCategory` (such as supervisor and president), and `employeeID`. Some of the methods are: `setInfo`, `getSalary`, `getEmployeeCategory`, `setSalary`.

5. In overloading a method, two or more methods have the same name but have different formal parameter lists. In overriding, you are redefining a method of a superclass in a subclass. The two methods (the method in the superclass and its redefinition in the subclass) have the same name and formal parameter list.

7. a. The statement:

```
class BClass AClass
```

should be:

```
class BClass extends AClass
```

b. Variables u and v are private in `class AClass` and cannot be accessed directly in `class BClass`.

9. a.
```
public YClass()
{
    a = 0;
    b = 0;
}
```

b.
```
public XClass()
{
    super(0, 0);
    z = 0;
}
```

c.
```
public void two(int x, int y)
{
    a = x;
    b = y;
}
```

11. a.
```
public void setData(int a, int b, int c)
{
    super.setData(a, b);
    z = c;
}
```

b.
```
public void print()
{
    super.print();
    System.out.println(z);
}
```

13. The operator `instanceof` is used to determine if a reference variable points to an object of a particular class. For example, the statement:

```
rectRef instanceof BoxShape
```

returns `true` if the reference variable `rectRef` points to a `BoxShape` object.

15. An interface is a class that contains only abstract methods and/or named constants. It has no instance variables. An abstract class, on the other hand, can have instance variables. Further, an abstract class need not have any abstract methods.

Chapter 11

1. a. True; b. False; c. False; d. True; e. False; f. True; g. True; h. False; i. True; j. False

3. a. Entering the try block.
       Exception: Lower limit violation.
       After the catch block

   b. Entering the try block.
       Exception: / by zero
       After the catch block

   c. Entering the try block.
       Exiting the try block.
       After the catch block

   d. Entering the try block.
       Exception: / by zero
       After the catch block

5. There are two corrections in this program. The corrected program is as follows: (The lines in green indicate the corrections.)

```
import java.io.*;
import java.util.*;

public class SAverage
{
    public static void main(String[] args)
    {
        double test1, test2, test3, test4;
        double average;

        try
        {
            Scanner inFile = new
                    Scanner(new FileReader("test.txt"));
            PrintWriter outFile = new
                    PrintWriter("testavg.out");

            test1 = inFile.nextDouble();
            test2 = inFile.nextDouble();
            test3 = inFile.nextDouble();
            test4 = inFile.nextDouble();

            outFile.printf("Test scores: %.2f %.2f %.2f %.2f %n",
                    test1, test2, test3, test4);

            average = (test1 + test2 + test3 + test4) / 4.0;
```

```
           //outFile.println("Average test score: %.2f",
           //                      average);
           //Replace these lines with the following
           outFile.printf("Average test score: %.2f%n",
                              average);
           outFile.close();

       }
           //Change the order of the following two catch
           //blocks as follows
       catch (FileNotFoundException e)
       {
           System.out.println(e.toString());
       }
       catch (Exception e)
       {
           System.out.println(e.toString());
       }
   }
}


7.  public class Test
    {
        public static void main(String[] args)
        {
            int i = 8;

            try
            {
                if (i < 5)
                    throw new TornadoException();
                else
                    throw new TornadoException(i);
            }
            catch (TornadoException e)
            {
                System.out.println(e.getMessage());
            }
        }
    }
```

9. Any class can implement an interface. The three different options are to use an inner class, an anonymous inner class, or the application (the applet) program class itself to implement an interface.

Chapter 12

1. a. True; b. True; c. True; d. False; e. False; f. False; g. True; h. False; i. False

3. `JTextField` and `JTextArea`

5. Sometimes you want the user to select from a set of predefined values. In addition to freeing the user from typing in such values, to get a precise input, you want the user to select a value from a set of given values.

7. a.
```
private String[] fruitNames = {"orange",
                               "apple",
                               "banana",
                               "grape",
                               "pineapple"};

private JList fruitJList;
private JScrollPane selectionJS;

pictureJList = new JList(fruitNames);
fruitJList.setVisibleRowCount(3);
fruitJList.setSelectionMode
          (ListSelectionModel.SINGLE_SELECTION);
fruitJList.addListSelectionListener(this);
selectionJS = new JScrollPane(fruitJList);
```
b.
```
JCheckBox qualityCB;
qualityCB = new JCheckBox("draft");
```
c.
```
private JRadioButton homeRB, visitorRB, neutralRB;
private ButtonGroup ColorSelectBGroup;

homeRB = new JRadioButton("Home");
visitorRB = new JRadioButton("Visitor");
neutralRB = new JRadioButton("Neutral");

ColorSelectBGroup = new ButtonGroup();
ColorSelectBGroup.add(homeRB);
ColorSelectBGroup.add(visitorRB);
ColorSelectBGroup.add(neutralRB);
```
d. `private JMenuBar menuMB = new JMenuBar();`

e. `private Font myFont = new Font("Courier", Font.BOLD, 32);`

f. `private Color myColor = new Color(255, 200, 64);`

Chapter 13

1. a. True; b. True; c. False; d. False; e. False

3. The case in which the solution is defined in terms of smaller versions of itself.

5. A method that calls another method and eventually results in the original method call is said to be indirectly recursive.

7. a. The statements in Lines 2 and 3.

   b. The statements in Lines 4 and 5.

   c. Any nonnegative integer.

   d. It is a valid call. The value of mystery(0) is 0.

   e. It is a valid call. The value of mystery(5) is 15.

   f. It is an invalid call. It will result in the infinite recursion.

9. a. It does not produce any output.

   b. 5 6 7 8 9

   c. It does not produce any output.

   d. It does not produce any output.

11. a. 2

    b. 3

    c. 5

    d. 21

13. $multiply(m, n) = \begin{cases} 0 & if\ n = 0 \\ m & if\ n = 1 \\ m + multiply(m, n - 1) & otherwise \end{cases}$

Chapter 14

1. a. False; b. True; c. False;

3. a. 5; b. 8; c. 5; d. 8

5. List before the first iteration: 26, 45, 17, 65, 33, 55, 12, 18
   List after the first iteration: 12, 45, 17, 65, 33, 55, 26, 18
   List after the second iteration: 12, 17, 45, 65, 33, 55, 26, 18
   List after the third iteration: 12, 17, 18, 65, 33, 55, 26, 45
   List after the fourth iteration: 12, 17, 18, 26, 33, 55, 65, 45
   List after the fifth iteration: 12, 17, 18, 26, 33, 55, 65, 45
   List after the sixth iteration: 12, 17, 18, 26, 33, 45, 65, 55
   List after the seventh iteration: 12, 17, 18, 26, 33, 45, 55, 65

7. 3

9. 10, 12, 18, 21, 25, 28, 30, 71, 32, 58, 15

NDEX

Note: Boldface type indicates key terms.